GREEK GRAMMAR

BY

HERBERT WEIR SMYTH

LATE ELIOT PROFESSOR OF GREEK LITERATURE
IN HARVARD UNIVERSITY

REVISED BY

GORDON M. MESSING

HARVARD UNIVERSITY PRESS

LIBRARY OF CONGRESS CATALOG CARD NUMBER 57-2203

ISBN 0-674-36250-0

PRINTED IN THE UNITED STATES OF AMERICA

EDITOR'S PREFACE

WHEN the Department of Classics of Harvard University acquired the plates to *A Greek Grammar for Colleges* by Herbert Weir Smyth (1920), the decision was promptly reached that this excellent and detailed treatise should again appear in print. Its merits are obvious: Smyth's is by far the most complete reference grammar of ancient Greek to appear in English. It is for example the only English "school grammar" which E. Schwyzer sees fit to list in the voluminous bibliography of his own *Griechische Grammatik*. The non-specialist student of ancient Greek language and literature can count upon finding in Smyth a treatment of Greek morphology and syntax which will be more than adequate for his needs.

There is one strong advantage of Smyth's work which particularly commends it, despite the passage of time. This may be stated in the words of Smyth's original preface (1918): "it is a descriptive, not an historical, nor a comparative, grammar." Since Smyth's work is almost exclusively a description, on a scale unprecedented for a grammar of this kind in English, it has for the most part retained its accuracy and its usefulness. In particular, Smyth offered a treatment of Greek syntax which is exceptionally rich as well as subtle and well organized.

Nevertheless, it is only fair to the reader to point out certain features of the original work which called for revision. Smyth spoke in his preface of having "adopted many of the assured results of comparative linguistics"; inevitably, time has invalidated some of these supposedly assured results, and new discoveries have successively altered existing concepts or added to our fund of information. Since 1920, for example, scholars of Indo-European have had to reckon with the important new data contributed to their science by the newly deciphered Hittite and Tocharian texts. Unlikely as it might at first glance appear, some of these changes in the assumed structure of Proto-Indo-European, from which Greek is descended, are reflected even in a book like Smyth's which avowedly makes only limited use of such material. To take an example, at 253 b Smyth commented on the inflection of ὕδωρ 'water' (gen. ὕδατος) merely by saying that "the reason for this change is uncertain." We now have ample reason to believe that the *r/n* stem variation is extremely ancient and may be an important inherited feature of Indo-European (compare Hittite *watar* 'water,' gen. *wetenas*).

In a book of this sort there is perhaps no need to stress the still more far-reaching revisions which have been imposed on the Indo-European reconstructions of Smyth's day by the assumption of one or more laryngeal consonants in the parent tongue (Proto-Indo-European), still directly attested in Hittite. Nevertheless, the trace of such consonants has been more or less plausibly conjectured to explain e.g. cases of prothesis in Greek (Smyth, para 41) as well as numerous phenomena of vowel gradation.

Our knowledge of the ancient Greek language and its various dialects has vastly increased since Smyth wrote his grammar. Inscriptions drawn year after year from all parts of the ancient Greek-speaking world have contributed precious new information. Again a single example may serve to show that such material has a definite bearing even on the almost exclusively literary use of the Greek language as described by Smyth. In dealing with the endings of the optative mood, Smyth merely noted without comment at 464 that the first person singular ending except after *-ιη-* was *-μι*, despite his previous statement that the optative usually has the endings of the secondary tenses of the indicative. The anomaly of the usual ending *-μι* has now been resolved with the discovery of Arcadian present optative first singular *ἐξελαύνοια*, which shows the original secondary active ending (**oi-m̥*) previously assumed but hitherto unattested.

There is in fact scarcely any sector of Greek grammar which has not marked progress as a result of extensive research either derived from fresh data or else based upon ingenious combinations of existing data.

Nor has the science of language itself stood still. The linguistics implicit in Smyth is still that of the Neogrammarians of the late nineteenth century. In the intervening period, a new methodology has arisen, and questions of structure have assumed new prominence from Ferdinand de Saussure to Louis Hjelmslev. Techniques used in the study of living languages have also thrown some light upon the evolution of ancient Greek.

If a revision of Smyth was therefore from many points of view a desideratum, it was clear that a complete revision would be an extremely complex task, and also, because of the difficulty and expense of making alterations in the plates, a very costly one. Many of the texts cited by Smyth have since been re-edited; some of his citations would undoubtedly prove to be in conflict with the readings of our best current texts. Yet it would be a vast and perhaps profitless undertaking to verify all the citations, make alterations where necessary, and change the commentary to the extent required. Moreover, a thorough-going revision which might attempt to take into consideration all the multitudinous pertinent literature in the field of Greek grammar since Smyth's day would run the risk of turning Smyth into a completely different book.

As it turned out, even the much less ambitious revision of Smyth as originally conceived has not been possible, largely because of financial considerations. Accordingly, it is necessary to list here exactly in what respects the present revision of Smyth — which might more modestly be termed a corrected reprint — differs from its predecessor.

First of all, the present book has been re-christened simply *Greek*

Grammar instead of *A Greek Grammar for Colleges*. This is partly to differentiate this work conveniently from the earlier one, but also because there is now no longer any need to distinguish Smyth's *A Greek Grammar for Colleges* from his similar but more elementary work, *A Greek Grammar for Schools and Colleges*, now out of print.

Some changes have been made in the historical and comparative part of the work, particularly in Smyth's original introduction and here and there in his original Part I (Letters, Sounds, Syllables, Accent). A very few changes, again bearing on historical linguistics, have been introduced in Part II (Inflection). Prof. Sterling Dow has contributed a valuable revision of paragraphs 348 on the Greek system of notation and 350 d on dating.

In addition, lists of corrigenda have been supplied by several scholars, and these have been silently inserted wherever appropriate. Thanks are due to all who contributed such lists.

An unpretentious bibliography, of the sort most likely to be immediately useful to the reader, is added at the end of this preface. This includes only a few selected works which appeared subsequent to the publication of Smyth, with a very brief comment on each, to supplement Smyth's own list of "Advanced Works on Grammar and Dialects."

Perhaps one caveat is in order. The student unfamiliar with the reconstruction of assumed intermediary forms may sometimes be puzzled by Smyth's frequent use of such forms with no indication that they actually occurred or else are purely hypothetical. It would have been tempting to mark all the non-existent reconstructions with the now traditional asterisk as is customary in works on historical linguistics.

One important lacuna in Smyth must be pointed out since it has not been filled: there is no section on prosody.

This is a fitting place to thank the Smyth family, and above all the late Mrs. Smyth, for their interest and help in achieving this revision and new edition.

In concluding these remarks, I should like to express my satisfaction at being associated even to this limited extent with Smyth's great work and with Harvard University:

> *βουλαὶ δὲ πρεσβύτεραι*
> *ἀκίνδυνον ἐμοὶ ἔπος*
> *σὲ ποτὶ πάντα λόγον*
> *ἐπαινεῖν παρέχοντι*
>
> **Pind. Pyth. 2.65–7**

GORDON M. MESSING

ATHENS, GREECE
13 May 1956

SUPPLEMENTARY BIBLIOGRAPHY

Friedrich Blass, *Grammatik des neutestamentlichen Griechisch,* bearbeitet von A. Debrunner, Ninth Edition, Göttingen, 1954. Generally useful for New Testament and later Greek studies.

Carl D. Buck, *Comparative Grammar of Greek and Latin,* Chicago, 1933 (reprinted 1937 and corrected reprint 1948). The most convenient historical and comparative treatment in English.

Carl D. Buck, *The Greek Dialects,* Chicago, 1955. The most up-to-date and trustworthy study in concise form of the Greek dialects.

Pierre Chantraine, *Grammaire homérique:* I *Phonétique et morphologie,* Paris, 1942; II *Syntaxe,* Paris, 1953. Accurate and thorough survey of Homeric usage.

J. D. Denniston, *The Greek Particles,* Second Edition revised by K. J. Dover, Oxford, 1954. A model collection of material.

O. Hoffmann and A. Debrunner, *Geschichte der griechischen Sprache,* 2 volumes, Berlin, 1953–4. Meaty and useful despite the small format.

Antoine Meillet, *Aperçu d'une histoire de la langue grecque,* Sixth Edition, Paris, 1930. A stimulating picture of Greek in its evolution and structure.

Eduard Schwyzer, *Griechische Grammatik:* I, Munich, 1939; II, edited by A. Debrunner, Munich, 1950; III, Index Volume by Demetrius J. Georgacas, Munich, 1953. The most complete comparative Greek grammar in existence.

Edgar H. Sturtevant, *The Pronunciation of Greek and Latin,* Second Edition, Philadelphia, 1940. A reliable guide, solidly documented, with all pertinent evidence.

Albert Thumb, *Handbuch der griechischen Dialekte,* Second Edition, Volume I only, Heidelberg, 1932. A complement to Buck (see above).

Jakob Wackernagel, *Vorlesungen über Syntax,* Second Edition, 2 volumes, Basel, 1926–8 (reprint 1950). Only some of the material pertains to Greek syntax.

AUTHOR'S PREFACE

The present book, apart from its greater extent and certain differences of statement and arrangement, has, in general, the same plan as the author's *Greek Grammar for Schools and Colleges.* It is a descriptive, not an historical, nor a comparative, grammar. Though it has adopted many of the assured results of Comparative Linguistics, especially in the field of Analogy, it has excluded much of the more complicated matter that belongs to a purely scientific treatment of the problems of Morphology. It has been my purpose to set forth the essential forms of Attic speech, and of the other dialects, as far as they appear in literature; to devote greater attention to the Formation of Words and to the Particles than is usually given to these subjects except in much more extensive works; and to supplement the statement of the principles of Syntax with information that will prove of service to the student as his knowledge widens and deepens.

As to the extent of all amplification of the bare facts of Morphology and Syntax, probably no two makers of a book of this character, necessarily restricted by considerations of space, will be of the same mind. I can only hope that I have attained such a measure of success as will commend itself to the judgment of those who are engaged in teaching Greek in our colleges and universities. I trust, however, that the extent of the enlarged work may lead no one to the opinion that I advocate the study of formal grammar as an end in itself; though I would have every student come to know, and the sooner the better, that without an exact knowledge of the language there can be no thorough appreciation of the literature of Ancient Greece, or of any other land ancient or modern.

In addition to the authorities mentioned on page 5, I have consulted with profit Delbrück's *Syntaktische Forschungen*, Gildersleeve's numerous and illuminating papers in the American Journal of Philology and in the Transactions of the American Philological Association, Schanz's *Beiträge zur historischen Syntax der griechischen Sprache*, Riddell's *Digest of Platonic Idioms*, La Roche's *Grammatische Studien* in the Zeitschrift für oesterreichische Gymnasien for 1904, Forman's *Selections from Plato*, Schulze's *Quaestiones*

Epicae, Hale's *Extended and Remote Deliberatives in Greek* in the Transactions of the American Philological Association for 1893, Harry's two articles, *The Omission of the Article with Substantives after* οὗτος, ὅδε, ἐκεῖνος *in Prose* in the Transactions for 1898, and *The Perfect Subjunctive, Optative, and Imperative in Greek* in the Classical Review for 1905, Headlam's *Greek Prohibitions* in the Classical Review for 1905, Marchant's papers on *The Agent in the Attic Orators* in the same journal for 1889, Miss Meissner's dissertation on γάρ (University of Chicago), Stahl's *Kritisch-historische Syntax des griechischen Verbums*, and Wright's *Comparative Grammar of the Greek Language*. I have examined many school grammars of Greek in English, German, and French, among which I would particularize those of Hadley-Allen, Goodwin, Babbitt, Goodell, Sonnenschein, Kaegi, Koch, Croiset et Petitjean. I am much indebted also to Thompson's *Greek Syntax*.

I would finally express my thanks for helpful criticism from Professor Allen R. Benner of Andover Academy, Professor Haven D. Brackett of Clark College, Professor Hermann Collitz of the Johns Hopkins University, Professor Archibald L. Hodges of the Wadleigh High School, New York, Dr. Maurice W. Mather, formerly Instructor in Harvard University, Professor Hanns Oertel of Yale University, and Professor Frank E. Woodruff of Bowdoin College. Dr. J. W. H. Walden, formerly Instructor in Harvard, has lent me invaluable aid by placing at my service his knowledge and skill in the preparation of the Indices.

HERBERT WEIR SMYTH.

Cambridge,
Aug. 1, 1918.

CONTENTS

INTRODUCTION

PART I: LETTERS, SOUNDS, SYLLABLES, ACCENT

PART II: INFLECTION

PART III: FORMATION OF WORDS

PART IV: SYNTAX

SYNTAX OF THE SIMPLE SENTENCE

INTERROGATIVE SENTENCES

EXCLAMATORY SENTENCES

PAGE

NEGATIVE SENTENCES

PARTICLES

FIGURES

INTRODUCTION

THE GREEK LANGUAGE AND ITS DIALECTS

A. The Greek language has a continuous literary history which covers three millennia from the Homeric writings to the present day. There is reason to believe that the ancestors of the Greeks launched the first of a series of invasions of the Aegean world as early as 2000 B.C. A few centuries thereafter sufficed for them to displace or dominate the non-Indo-European peoples who had preceded them in what is now Greece, the Greek islands, and part of Asia Minor. It has been plausibly conjectured that the *Aḫḫiyawa* mentioned in Hittite letters of 1335–1325 B.C. are to be identified with the Achaeans of Homer. The various Greek communities referred to themselves (as the modern Greeks do) by the name *Hellenes* (Ἕλληνες); they called their country *Hellas* (ἡ Ἑλλάς) and their language the *Hellenic* language (ἡ Ἑλληνικὴ γλῶσσα). We call them *Greeks* from the Latin *Graeci*, the name given them by the Romans, who applied to the entire people a name properly restricted to the Γραῖοι, the first Hellenes of whom the Romans had knowledge.

N. 1. — *Graeci* (older *Graici*) contains a Latin suffix *-icus*; and the name Γραικοί, which occurs first in Aristotle, is borrowed from Latin. The Roman designation is derived either from the Γραῖοι, a Boeotian tribe that took part in the colonization of Cyme in Italy, or from the Γραῖοι, a larger tribe of the same stock that lived in Epirus.

N. 2. — No collective name for 'all Greece' appears in Homer, to whom the Hellenes are the inhabitants of Hellas, a district forming part of the kingdom of Peleus (B 683) and situated in the S.E. of the country later called Thessaly. Ἑλλάς for 'all Greece' occurs first in Hesiod. The Greeks in general are called by Homer Ἀχαιοί, Ἀργεῖοι, Δαναοί.

B. Greek constitutes one of a family of languages called Indo-European, all of which have evolved from a common original language (Proto-Indo-European), the nature of which may be reconstructed by comparison of known Indo-European languages. The main language groups apart from Greek within the Indo-European family are as follows: Hittite; Tocharian; Indic; Iranian; Armenian; Albanian; Slavic; Baltic; Germanic; Italic; Celtic. Other Indo-European languages are imperfectly or fragmentarily known (e.g. Venetic,

Messapic, Illyrian). The relationship of certain ones (particularly Hittite) to Proto-Indo-European is still a matter for scholarly controversy. It is possible that some Indo-European languages have vanished without leaving any trace, and it is equally possible that evidence for such languages may yet be unearthed, just as happened in the case of Tocharian or Hittite, both discovered or interpreted in comparatively recent times. Some of the groups mentioned above are closely related as shown through the presence of common linguistic traits. Indic and Iranian, for example, are particularly close. There is on the other hand no such close relationship as has often been postulated in the past to link Greek with Latin and the other Italic languages.

Naturally, the special linguistic changes which have occurred in all these groups of Indo-European languages, and still more the further specific changes which have occurred in the individual Indo-European languages derived from these groups, have greatly differentiated them. English, for example, even in its earliest attested form (Old English), shows a sound system very different from that which we reconstruct for Proto-Indo-European. The original stops have been systematically shifted in the Germanic languages. Thus for example the plain voiceless stops, *p*, *t*, *k* have (under certain well defined linguistic circumstances) regularly evolved to Germanic sounds which may be schematized as *f*, *θ*, *χ* (Grimm's Law). We may therefore directly compare the initial stops in such forms as:

Greek πούς, Lat. *pēs*, but German *Fuss*, Eng. *foot*;
Greek τρεῖς, Lat. *trēs*, but German *drei*, Eng. *three*;
Greek κολωνός 'hill,' Lat. *collis*, but OEng. *hyll*, Eng. *hill*.

In the above examples, the English words are said to be *cognate* with the Greek words. *Derived* words, such as *geography*, *theater*, are borrowed, directly or indirectly, from the Greek (γεωγραφία, θέᾱτρον) or are made up with Greek elements (*streptococcus*, *psychoanalysis*).

C. At the earliest known period of its history the Greek language was divided into dialects, even though the existence of a fairly unified Greek language may be presumed for a still earlier period. In this grammar, which is concerned chiefly with the literary language, the traditional differentiation of the dialects into Aeolic, Doric, and Ionic (of which Attic is a sister-dialect) has been retained, although it is no older than Strabo (8.333). Aeolic and Doric are more nearly related to each other than either is to Ionic. These groupings correspond to the principal Greek ethnic divisions of Aeolians, Dorians, and Ionians (a division unknown to Homer). The study of the Greek dialects in modern times, however, has been both enriched and complicated by the discovery of thousands of dialect inscriptions. These reveal a linguistic diversity which could scarcely be suspected from the literary monuments, since most of the dialects make no appearance in literature. Classification is fairly complex, although a basic division into East

Greek and West Greek is evident. East Greek consists of the Attic-Ionic group, the Arcado-Cyprian group, and the Aeolic group; West Greek consists of the Northwest Greek group and the Doric group. (For a detailed breakdown, see the introduction to C. D. Buck, *The Greek dialects.*)

Aeolic: spoken in Aeolis, Lesbos, and kindred with the dialect of Thessaly (except Phthiotis) and of Boeotia (though Boeotian has many Doric ingredients). In this book 'Aeolic' means Lesbian Aeolic.

N. 1. — Aeolic retains primitive ᾱ (30); changes τ before ι to σ (115); has recessive accent (162 D.), and many other peculiarities.

Doric: spoken in Peloponnesus (except Arcadia and Elis), in several of the islands of the Aegean (Crete, Melos, Thera, Rhodes, etc.), in parts of Sicily and in Southern Italy.

N. 2. — Doric retains primitive ᾱ (30), keeps τ before ι (115 D.). Almost all Doric dialects have -μες for -μεν (462 D.), the infinitive in -μεν for -ναι (469 D.), the future in -ξω from verbs in -ζω (516 D.), the future in -σῶ, -σοῦμαι (540 a).

N. 3. — The sub-dialects of Laconia, Crete, and Southern Italy, and of their several colonies, are often called Severer (or Old) Doric; the others are called Milder (or New) Doric. Severer Doric has η and ω where Milder Doric has ει and ου (59 D. 4, 5; 230 D.). There are also differences in verbal forms (654).

Ionic: spoken in Ionia, in most of the islands of the Aegean, in a few towns of Sicily, etc.

N. 4. — Ionic changes primitive ᾱ to η (30); changes τ before ι to σ (115); has lost digamma, which is still found in Aeolic and Doric; often refuses to contract vowels; keeps a mute smooth before the rough breathing (124 D.); has κ for π in pronominal forms (132 D.).

N. 5. — As explained above, some dialects are not accommodated into the traditional threefold division. Arcadian and Cyprian are closely related and probably represent the pre-Doric speech of most of the Peloponnesus. This group has gained in interest through the very recent partial decipherment of the tablets in Cretan script (so-called Linear B) from Pylos, Mycenae, and Cnossus dating from about 1400–1200 B.C. (Pylos) and earlier. Investigation to date tends to show that the dialect of these very early inscriptions may be an earlier stage of Arcado-Cyprian. Further research may throw considerable light upon the earliest history of the Greek language.

Northwest Greek (Phocian, Locrian, Elean, and the common dialect of Aetolia and other regions under the domination of the Aetolian League) forms another group apart although showing close affinities to Doric.

N. 6. — The dialects that retain ᾱ (30) are called Ᾱ dialects (Aeolic, Doric, etc.); Ionic and Attic are the only H dialects. The Eastern dialects (Aeolic, Ionic) change τι to σι (115).

N. 7. — The local dialects died out gradually and ceased to exist by 300 A.D., being everywhere replaced by the Koinè (see F below) with the single important exception of Tsakonian (still spoken in a small area of Laconia) which is largely derived from ancient Laconian.

D. The chief dialects that occur in literature are as follows (almost all poetry is composed in a mixture of dialects):

Aeolic: in the Lesbian lyric poets Alcaeus and Sappho (600 B.C.). Numerous Aeolisms appear in epic poetry, and some in tragedy. Theocritus' idylls 28–30 are in Aeolic.

Doric: in many lyric poets, notably in Pindar (born 522 B.C.); in the bucolic (pastoral) poetry of Theocritus (about 310–about 245 B.C.). Both of these poets adopt some epic and Aeolic forms. The choral parts of Attic tragedy also admit some Doric forms. There is no Doric, as there is no Aeolic, literary prose.

Ionic: (1) *Old Ionic or Epic*, the chief ingredient of the dialect of Homer and of Hesiod (before 700 B.C.). Almost all subsequent poetry admits epic words and forms. (2) *New Ionic* (500–400), the dialect of Herodotus (484–425) and of the medical writer Hippocrates (born 460). In the period between Old and New Ionic: Archilochus, the lyric poet (about 700–650 B.C.).

Attic: (kindred to Ionic) was used by the great writers of Athens in the fifth and fourth centuries B.C., the period of her political and literary supremacy. In it are composed the works of the tragic poets Aeschylus (525–456), Sophocles (496–406), Euripides (about 480–406), the comic poet Aristophanes (about 450–385), the historians Thucydides (died before 396) and Xenophon (about 434–about 355), the orators Lysias (born about 450), Isocrates (436–338), Aeschines (389–314), Demosthenes (383–322), and the philosopher Plato (427–347).

E. The Attic dialect was distinguished by its refinement, precision, and beauty; it occupied an intermediate position between the soft Ionic and the rough Doric, and avoided the pronounced extremes of other dialects. By reason of its cultivation at the hands of the greatest writers from 500 B.C. to 300 B.C., it became the standard literary dialect; though Old Ionic was still occasionally employed in later epic, and Doric in pastoral poetry.

N. 1. — The dialect of the tragic poets and Thucydides is often called *Old Attic* in contrast to *New Attic*, that used by most other Attic writers. Plato stands on the border-line. The dialect of tragedy contains some Homeric, Doric, and Aeolic forms; these are more frequent in the choral than in the dialogue parts. The choral parts take over forms used in the Aeolic-Doric lyric; the dialogue parts show the influence of the iambic poetry of the Ionians. But the tendency of Attic speech in literature was to free itself from the influence of the dialect used by the tribe originating any literary type; and by the fourth century pure Attic was generally used throughout. The normal language of the people ("Standard Attic") is best seen in Aristophanes and the orators. The native Attic speech as it appears in inscriptions shows no local differences; the speech of Attica was practically uniform. Only the lowest classes, among which were many foreigners, used forms that do not follow the ordinary phonetic laws. The language of the religious cults is sometimes archaic in character.

N. 2. — Old Attic writers use σσ for ττ (78), ρσ for ρρ (79), ξύν for σύν *with*, ἐς for εἰς *into*, ῃ for ει (λύῃ for λύει, *thou loosest*), -ῆς in the plural of substantives in -εύς (βασιλῆς, 277), and occasionally -αται and -ατο in the third plural of the perfect and pluperfect (465 f).

With the Macedonian conquest Athens ceased to produce great writers, but Attic culture and the Attic dialect were diffused far and wide. With this extension of its range, Attic lost its purity; which had indeed begun to decline in Aristotle (384–322 B.C.).

F. **Koinè** or **Common** dialect (ἡ κοινὴ διάλεκτος). The Koinè took its rise in the Alexandrian period, so called from the preëminence of Alexandria in Egypt as a centre of learning until the Roman conquest of the East; and lasted to the end of the ancient world (sixth century A.D.). It was the language used by persons speaking Greek from Gaul to Syria, and was marked by numerous varieties. In its spoken form the Koinè consisted of the spoken form of Attic intermingled with a considerable number of Ionic words and some loans from other dialects, but with Attic orthography. The literary form, a compromise between Attic literary usage and the spoken language, was an artificial and almost stationary idiom from which the living speech drew farther and farther apart.

In the Koinè are composed the writings of the historians Polybius (about 205–about 120 B.C.), Diodorus (under Augustus), Plutarch (about 46–about 120 A.D.), Arrian (about 95–175 A.D.), Cassius Dio (about 150–about 235 A.D.), the rhetoricians Dionysius of Halicarnassus (under Augustus), Lucian (about 120–about 180 A.D.), and the geographer Strabo (about 64 B.C.–19 A.D.). Josephus, the Jewish historian (37 A.D.–about 100), also used the Koinè.

N. 1. — The name *Atticist* is given to those reactionary writers in the Koinè dialect (*e.g.* Lucian) who aimed at reproducing the purity of the earlier Attic. The Atticists flourished chiefly in the second century A.D.

N. 2. — Some writers distinguish, as a form of the Koinè, the **Hellenistic**, a name restricted by them to the language of the New Testament and of the Septuagint (the partly literal, partly tolerably free, Greek translation of the Old Testament made by Grecized Jews at Alexandria and begun under Ptolemy Philadelphus 285–247 B.C.). The word *Hellenistic* is derived from Ἑλληνιστής (from ἑλληνίζω *speak Greek*), a term applied to persons not of Greek birth (especially Jews), who had learned Greek. The New Testament is composed in the popular language of the time, which in that work is more or less influenced by classical models. No accurate distinction can be drawn between the Koinè and Hellenistic.

G. The term Medieval Greek is sometimes applied to the form of Greek current from the middle of the sixth century A.D. to the fall of Constantinople in 1453. Modern Greek is a term applied loosely to a form of the language used as early as the eleventh century, when the literary tongue, which was still used by scholars and churchmen, was no longer in colloquial use by the common people. A contrast between learned and colloquial speech developed early. On the one hand, the eleventh to fourteenth centuries witnessed a strict revival of classical forms; on the other hand, the spoken idiom tended to diverge more and more. During the Middle Ages and until about the time of the Greek Revolution (1821–1831) the language was often called *Romaic* (*Ῥωμαϊκή*) because its speakers chose to call themselves *Ῥωμαῖοι*, i.e. *Romans*, since the capital of the Roman Empire had been transferred to Constantinople. The contrast between an idiom based on ancient models and one more in agreement with popular speech has given rise to a ceaseless conflict lasting into modern times. Greek speakers today must still learn two fairly distinct sets of linguistic patterns: the official language called *καθαρεύουσα* (the "purifying" language) is standard for virtually all written communication while it is spoken only for official purposes (in the Greek Orthodox Church, the Greek Parliament, and so on); the spoken language called *δημοτική* ("demotic") is the normal language for oral communication while it is written only in less formal literary contexts. The pronunciation of modern Greek (as far as this is not modified by the emergence of *modern* Greek dialects) is the same for both varieties and is considerably altered from that of the classical period.

ADVANCED WORKS ON GRAMMAR AND DIALECTS

AHRENS: De Graecae linguae dialectis (I. Aeolic 1839, II. Doric 1843). Göttingen. Still serviceable for Doric.

BLASS: Pronunciation of Ancient Greek. Translated from the third German edition by Purton. Cambridge, Eng., 1890.

BOISACQ: Les Dialectes doriens. Paris-Liége, 1891.

BRUGMANN: Griechische Grammatik. 4te Aufl. München, 1913. Purely comparative.

CHANDLER: Greek Accentuation. 2d ed. Oxford, 1881.

GILDERSLEEVE AND MILLER: Syntax of Classical Greek from Homer to Demosthenes. Part i. New York, 1900. Part ii, 1911.

GOODWIN: Syntax of the Moods and Tenses of the Greek Verb. Rewritten and enlarged. Boston, 1890.

HENRY: Précis de Grammaire comparée du Grec et du Latin. 5th ed. Paris, 1894. Translation (from the 2d ed.) by Elliott: A Short Comparative Grammar of Greek and Latin. London, 1890.

HIRT: Handbuch der Griechischen Laut- und Formenlehre. Heidelberg, 1902. Comparative.

HOFFMANN: Die griechischen Dialekte. Vol. i. Der süd-achäische Dialekt (Arcadian, Cyprian), Göttingen, 1891. Vol. ii. Der nord-achäische Dialekt (Thessalian, Aeolic, Boeotian), 1893. Vol. iii. Der ionische Dialekt (Quellen und Lautlehre), 1898.

KRÜGER: Griechische Sprachlehre. Part i, 5te Aufl., 1875. Part ii, 4te Aufl., 1862. Leipzig. Valuable for examples of syntax.

KÜHNER: Ausführliche Grammatik der griechischen Sprache. 3te Aufl. Part i by Blass. Part ii (Syntax) by Gerth. Hannover, 1890–1904. The only modern complete Greek Grammar. The part by Blass contains good collections, but is insufficient on the side of comparative grammar.

MEISTER: Die griechischen Dialekte. Vol. i. Asiatisch-äolisch, Böotisch, Thessalisch, Göttingen, 1882. Vol. ii. Eleisch, Arkadisch, Kyprisch, 1889.

MEISTERHANS: Grammatik der attischen Inschriften. 3te Aufl. Berlin, 1900.

MEYER: Griechische Grammatik. 3te Aufl. Leipzig, 1896. Comparative, with due attention to inscriptional forms. Deals only with sounds and forms.

MONRO: A Grammar of the Homeric Dialect. 2d ed. Oxford, 1891. Valuable, especially for its treatment of syntax.

RIEMANN AND GOELZER: Grammaire comparée du Grec et du Latin. Vol. i. Phonétique et Étude des Formes, Paris, 1901. Vol. ii. Syntaxe, 1897.

SMYTH: The Sounds and Inflections of the Greek Dialects. Ionic. Oxford, 1894.

VAN LEEUWEN: Enchiridium dictionis epicae. Lugd. Bat., 1892–94. Contains a full discussion of forms, and aims at reconstructing the primitive text of Homer.

VEITCH: Greek Verbs Irregular and Defective. New ed. Oxford, 1887.

ABBREVIATIONS

A. = Aeschylus.
- Ag. = Agamemnon.
- Ch. = Choephori.
- Eum. = Eumenides.
- Pers. = Persae.
- Pr. = Prometheus.
- Sept. = Septem.
- Supp. = Supplices.

Aes. = Aeschines.
And. = Andocides.
Ant. = Antiphon.
Antiph. = Antiphanes.
Ar. = Aristophanes.
- Ach. = Acharnenses.
- Av. = Aves.
- Eccl. = Ecclesiazusae.
- Eq. = Equites.
- Lys. = Lysistrata.
- Nub. = Nubes.
- P. = Pax.
- Plut. = Plutus.
- Ran. = Ranae.
- Thesm. = Thesmophoriazusae.
- Vesp. = Vespae.

C.I.A. = Corpus inscriptionum Atticarum.
Com. Fr. = Comic Fragments.
D. = Demosthenes.
Diog. Laert. = Diogenes Laertius.
E. = Euripides.
- Alc. = Alcestis.
- And. = Andromache.
- Bacch. = Bacchae.
- Cycl. = Cyclops.
- El. = Electra.
- Hec. = Hecuba.
- Hel. = Helena.
- Heracl. = Heraclidae.
- H. F. = Hercules furens.
- Hipp. = Hippolytus.
- I. A. = Iphigenia Aulidensis.
- I. T. = Iphigenia Taurica.
- Med. = Medea.
- Or. = Orestes.
- Phoen. = Phoenissae.
- Supp. = Supplices.
- Tro. = Troades.

Hdt. = Herodotus.
Hom. = Homer.

The books of the Iliad are designated by Greek capitals (Α, Β, Γ, etc.); those of the Odyssey by Greek small letters (α, β, γ, etc.).

I. = Isocrates.
I.G.A. = Inscriptiones Graecae antiquissimae.
Is. = Isaeus.
Lyc. = Lycurgus.
L. = Lysias.
Men. = Menander.
- Sent. = Sententiae.

Philem. = Philemon.
Pind. = Pindar.
P. = Plato.
- A. = Apologia.
- Alc. = Alcibiades.
- Charm. = Charmides.
- Cr. = Crito.
- Crat. = Cratylus.
- Criti. = Critias.
- Eu. = Euthydemus.
- Euth. = Euthyphro.
- G. = Gorgias.
- Hipp. M. = Hippias Major.
- Lach. = Laches.
- L. = Leges.
- Lys. = Lysis.
- Men. = Meno.
- Menex. = Menexenus.
- Par. = Parmenides.
- Ph. = Phaedo.
- Phae. = Phaedrus
- Phil. = Philebus.
- Pol. = Politicus.
- Pr. = Protagoras.
- R. = Respublica.
- Soph. = Sophistes.
- S. = Symposium.
- Th. = Theaetetus.
- Theag. = Theages.
- Tim. = Timaeus.

S. = Sophocles.
- Aj. = Ajax.
- Ant. = Antigone.
- El. = Electra.
- O. C. = Oedipus Coloneus.
- O. T. = Oedipus Tyrannus.
- Ph. = Philoctetes.
- Tr. = Trachiniae.

Stob. = Stobaeus.
- Flor. = Florilegium.

T. = Thucydides.
X. = Xenophon.
- A. = Anabasis.
- Ap. = Apologia.
- Ages. = Agesilaus.
- C. = Cyropaedia.
- Eq. = de re equestri.
- H. = Hellenica.
- Hi. = Hiero.
- Hipp. = Hipparchicus.
- M. = Memorabilia.
- O. = Oeconomicus.
- R. A. = Respublica Atheniensis.
- R. L. = Respublica Lacedaemonia.
- S. = Symposium.
- Vect. = de vectigalibus.
- Ven. = de venatione.

The dramatists are cited by Dindorf's lines. But Tragic fragments (Fr. or Frag.) are cited by Nauck's numbers, Comic fragments (except Menander's Sententiae) by Kock's volumes and pages. The Orators are cited by the numbers of the speeches and the sections in the Teubner editions.

Other abbreviations: — κ.τ.λ. = καὶ τὰ λοιπά (*et cetera*); *scil.* = *scilicet*; *i.e.* = *id est*; *ib.* = *ibidem*; *e.g.* = *exempli gratia*; I.E. = Indo-European;)(= *as contrasted with.*

PART I

LETTERS, SOUNDS, SYLLABLES, ACCENT

THE ALPHABET

1. The Greek alphabet has twenty-four letters. An approximate phonetic value is given in the last column. This is the pronunciation assumed for the classical period (see 25, 26) with some modifications.

Form		Name		Transliteration	Sound as in
Α	**α**	**ἄλφα**	*alpha*	*a*	*ă*: *a*ha; *ā*: f**a**ther
Β	**β**	**βῆτα**	*bēta*	*b*	beg
Γ	**γ**	γάμμα	*gamma*	*g*	go; also nasal (19 a)
Δ	**δ**	δέλτα	*delta*	*d*	dig
Ε	**ε**	**εἶ, ἒ** (ἐ ψῑλόν)	*ĕpsīlon*	*ĕ*	met
Ζ	**ζ**	ζῆτα	*zēta*	*z*	daze
Η	**η**	ἦτα	*ēta*	*ē*	Fr. fête
Θ	**θ, ϑ**	θῆτα	*thēta*	*th*	thin
Ι	**ι**	ἰῶτα	*iōta*	*i*	*ĭ*: meteor; *ī*: police
Κ	**κ**	κάππα	*kappa*	*c, k*	kin
Λ	**λ**	λάμβδα	*lambda*	*l*	let
Μ	**μ**	μῦ	*mu*	*m*	met
Ν	**ν**	νῦ	*nu*	*n*	net
Ξ	**ξ**	ξεῖ (ξῖ)	*xi*	*x*	lax
Ο	**ο**	**οὖ, ὂ** (ὀ μῑκρόν)	*ŏmīcron*	*ŏ*	obey
Π	**π**	**π**εῖ (πῖ)	*pi*	*p*	pet
Ρ	**ρ**	ῥῶ	*rho*	*r*	run
Σ	**σ, ς**	σίγμα	*sigma*	*s*	such
Τ	**τ**	ταῦ	*tau*	*t*	tar
Υ	**υ**	ὖ (ὖ ψῑλόν)	*ŭpsīlon*	(*u*) *y*	*ŭ*: Fr. tu; *ū*: Fr. sûr
Φ	**φ**	φεῖ (φῖ)	*phi*	*ph*	graphic
Χ	**χ**	χεῖ (χῖ)	*chi*	*ch*	Germ. machen, ich
Ψ	**ψ**	ψεῖ (ψῖ)	*psi*	*ps*	gypsum
Ω	**ω**	ὦ (ὦ μέγα)	*ōmĕga*	*ō*	note

a. Sigma (not capital) at the end of a word is written ς, elsewhere σ. Thus, σεισμός *earthquake*.

b. The names in parentheses, from which are derived those in current use, were given at a late period, some as late as the Middle Ages. Thus, *epsilon* means '*simple* e,' *upsilon* '*simple* u,' to distinguish these letters from αι, οι, which were sounded like ε and υ.

c. Labda is a better attested ancient name than lambda.

2. The Greek alphabet as given above originated in Ionia, and was adopted at Athens in 403 B.C. The letters from Α to Τ are derived from Phoenician and have Semitic names. The signs Υ to Ω were invented by the Greeks. From the Greek alphabet are derived the alphabets of most European countries. The ancients used only the large letters, called *majuscules* (capitals as Ε, uncials as Є); the small letters (*minuscules*), which were used as a literary hand in the ninth century, are cursive forms of the uncials.

a. Before 403 B.C. in the official Attic alphabet Ε stood for ε, η, spurious ει (6), Ο for ο, ω, spurious ου (6), Η for the rough breathing, ΧΣ for Ξ, ΦΣ for Ψ. Λ was written for γ, and Ⅴ for λ. Thus:

ΕΔΟΧΣΕΝΤΕΙΒΟⅤΕΙΚΑΙΤΟΙΔΕΜΟΙ	ἔδοξεν τῇ βουλῇ καὶ τῷ δήμῳ.
ΧΣΥΛΛΡΑΦΕΣΧΣΥΝΕΛΡΑΦΣΑΝ	ξυγγραφῆς ξυνέγραψαν.
ΕΠΙΤΕΔΕΙΟΝΕΝΑΙΑΠΟΤΟΑΡΛΥΡΙΟ	ἐπιτήδειον εἶναι ἀπὸ τοῦ ἀργυρίου.

3. In the older period there were two other letters: (1) Ϝ: ϝαῦ, *vau*, called digamma (*i.e. double-gamma*) from its shape. It stood after ε and was pronounced like *w*. ϝ was written in Boeotian as late as 200 B.C. (2) Ϙ: κόππα, *koppa*, which stood after π. Another *s*, called *san*, is found in the sign Ϡ, called *sampi*, *i.e. san + pi*. On these signs as numerals, see 348.

a. The Greek alphabet in later times served as a basis for other alphabets, notably, Coptic, Gothic, Armenian, and Cyrillic.

VOWELS AND DIPHTHONGS

4. There are seven vowels: α, ε, η, ι, ο, υ, ω. Of these ε and ο are always short, and take about half the time to pronounce as η and ω, which are always long; α, ι, υ are short in some syllables, long in others. In this Grammar, when α, ι, υ are not marked as long (ᾱ, ῑ, ῡ) they are understood to be short. All vowels with the circumflex (149) are long. On length by position, see 144.

a. Vowels are said to be *open* or *close* according as the mouth is more open

---

3 D. Vau was in use as a genuine sound at the time the Homeric poems were composed, though it is found in no Mss. of Homer. Many apparent irregularities of epic verse (such as *hiatus*, 47 D.) can be explained only by supposing that ϝ was actually sounded. Examples of words containing ϝ are: ἄστυ *town*, ἄναξ *lord*, ἀνδάνω *please*, εἴκω *give way* (cp. *weak*), εἴκοσι *twenty* (cp. *viginti*), ἕκαστος *each*, ἑκών *willing*, ἔλπομαι *hope* (cp. *voluptas*), ἔοικα *am like*, ἕο, οἷ, ἕ *him*, ἕξ *six*, ἔπος *word*, εἶπον *said*, ἔργον, ἔρδω *work*, ἕννῡμι *clothe*, fr. ϝεσ-νῡμι (cp. *vestis*), ἐρέω *will say* (cp. *verbum*), ἕσπερος *evening* (cp. *vesper*), ἴον *violet* (cp. *viola*), ἔτος *year* (cp. *vetus*), ἡδύς *sweet* (cp. *suavis*), ἰδεῖν (οἶδα) *know* (cp. *videre, wit*), ἴς *strength* (cp. *vis*), ἰτέα *willow* (cp. *vitis, withy*), οἶκος *house* (cp. *vicus*), οἶνος *wine* (cp. *vinum*), ὅς *his* (123), ὄχος *carriage* (cp. *veho, wain*). Vau was lost first before ο-sounds (ὁράω *see*, cp. be-*ware*). ϝ occurred also in the middle of words: κλέϝος *glory*, αἰϝεί *always*, ὄϝις *sheep* (cp. *ovis*), κληϝίς *key* (Dor. κλᾱΐς, cp. *clavis*), ξένϝος *stranger*, Διϝί *to Zeus*, καλϝός *beautiful*. Cp. 20, 31, 37 D., 122, 123.

or less open in pronouncing them, the tongue and lips assuming different positions in the case of each.

5. A diphthong (δίφθογγος *having two sounds*) combines two vowels in one syllable. The second vowel is ι or υ. The diphthongs are: αι, ει, οι, ᾱͅ, ῃ, ῳ; αυ, ευ, ου, ηυ, and υι. The ι of the so-called *improper* diphthongs, ᾱͅ, ῃ, ῳ, is written below the line and is called *iota subscript.* But with capital letters, ι is written on the line (*adscript*), as THI ΩΙΔΗΙ = τῇ ᾠδῇ or Ὠιδῇ *to the song.* All diphthongs are long.

a. In ᾳ, ῃ, ῳ the ι ceased to be written about 100 B.C. The custom of writing ι under the line is as late as about the eleventh century.

6. ει, ου are either *genuine* or *spurious* (apparent) diphthongs (25). Genuine ει, ου are a combination of ε + ι, ο + υ, as in λείπω *I leave* (cp. λέλοιπα *I have left,* 35 a), γένει *to a race* (49), ἀκόλουθος *follower* (cp. κέλευθος *way*). Spurious ει, ου arise from contraction (50) or compensatory lengthening (37). Thus, ἐφίλει *he loved,* from ἐφίλεε, θείς *placing* from θεντ-ς; ἐφίλουν *they loved* from ἐφίλεον, πλοῦς *voyage* from πλόος, δούς *giving* from δοντ-ς.

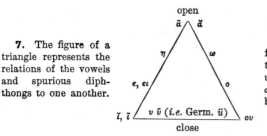

7. The figure of a triangle represents the relations of the vowels and spurious diphthongs to one another.

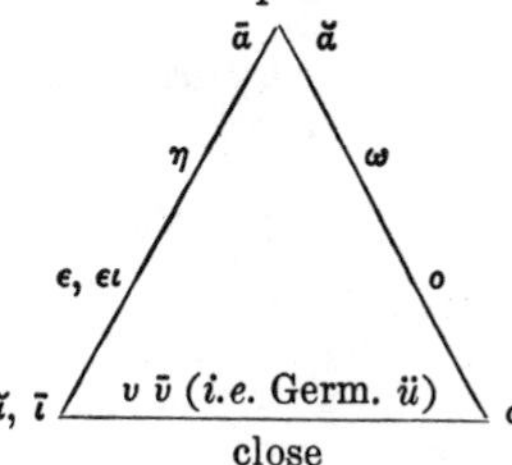

From ᾱ to ι and from ᾰ to ου the elevation of the tongue gradually increases. ω, ο, ου, υ are accompanied by rounding of the lips.

8. Diaeresis. — A double dot, the mark of diaeresis (διαίρεσις *separation*), may be written over ι or υ when these do not form a diphthong with the preceding vowel: προΐστημι *I set before,* νηΐ *to a ship.*

BREATHINGS

9. Every initial vowel or diphthong has either the rough (῾) or the smooth (᾿) breathing. The rough breathing (*spiritus asper*) is pronounced as *h,* which is sounded before the vowel; the smooth

---

5 D. A diphthong ωυ occurs in New Ionic (ὡυτός *the same* from ὁ αὐτός 68 D., ἐμωυτοῦ *of myself* = ἐμαυτοῦ 329 D., θωῦμα = θαῦμα *wonder*). Ionic has ηυ for Attic αυ in some words (Hom. νηῦς *ship*).

8 D. In poetry and in certain dialects vowels are often written apart which later formed diphthongs: πάις (or πάϊς) *boy* or *girl,* Πηλεΐδης *son of Peleus,* ἐύ (or ἐΰ) *well,* Ἀίδης (or Ἀΐδης) *Hades,* γένεϊ *to a race.*

9 D. The Ionic of Asia Minor lost the rough breathing at an early date. So also before ρ (13). Its occurrence in compounds (124 D.) is a relic of the period when

breathing (*spiritus lenis*) indicates absence of aspiration. Thus, ὅρος hóros *boundary*, ὄρος óros *mountain.*

10. Initial υ (ῠ and ῡ) always has the rough breathing.

11. Diphthongs take the breathing, as the accent (152), over the second vowel: αἱρέω hairéo *I seize*, αἴρω aíro *I lift*. But ᾳ, ῃ, ῳ take both the breathing and the accent on the first vowel, even when ι is written in the line (5): ᾄδω = Ἄιδω *I sing*, ᾅδης = Ἅιδης *Hades*, but Αἰνείᾱς *Aeneas*. The writing ἀΐδηλος (Ἀΐδηλος) *destroying* shows that αι does not here form a diphthong; and hence is sometimes written αϊ (8).

12. In compound words (as in προορᾶν *to foresee*, from πρό + ὁρᾶν) the rough breathing is not written, though it must often have been pronounced: cp. ἐξέδρᾱ *a hall with seats*, Lat. *exhedra*, *exedra*, πολυΐστωρ *very learned*, Lat. *polyhistor*. On Attic inscriptions in the old alphabet (2 a) we find ΕΥΗΟΡΚΟΝ εὔορκον *faithful to one's oath*.

13. Every initial ρ has the rough breathing: ῥήτωρ *orator* (Lat. *rhetor*). Medial ρρ is written ῤῥ in some texts: Πύῤῥος *Pyrrhus*.

14. The sign for the rough breathing is derived from H, which in the Old Attic alphabet (2 a) was used to denote *h*. Thus, HO ὁ *the*. After H was used to denote η, one half (Ͱ) was used for *h* (about 300 B.C.), and, later, the other half (⊣) for the smooth breathing. From Ͱ and ⊣ come the forms ʽ and ʼ.

CONSONANTS

15. The seventeen consonants are divided into stops (or mutes), spirants, liquids, nasals, and double consonants. They may be arranged according to the degree of tension or slackness of the vocal chords in sounding them, as follows:

a. Voiced (sonant, *i.e.* sounding) consonants are produced when the vocal chords vibrate. The sounds are represented by the letters β, δ, γ (stops), λ, ρ (liquids), μ, ν, γ-nasal (19 a) (nasals), and ζ. (All the vowels are voiced.) ρ with the rough breathing is voiceless.

b. Voiceless (surd, *i.e.* hushed) consonants require no exertion of the vocal chords. These are π, τ, κ, φ, θ, χ (stops), σ (spirant or sibilant), and ψ and ξ.

c. Arranged according to the increasing degree of noise, nearest to the vowels are the nasals, in sounding which the air escapes without friction through the nose; next come the semivowels ῠ̯ and ῐ̯ (20 a), the liquids, and the spirant σ, in

---

it was still sounded in the simple word. Hom. sometimes has the smooth where Attic has the rough breathing in forms that are not Attic: Ἀΐδης (Ἅιδης), the god *Hades*, ἆλτο *sprang* (ἅλλομαι), ἄμυδις *together* (cp. ἅμα), ἠέλιος *sun* (ἥλιος), ἠώς *dawn* (ἕως), ἴρηξ *hawk* (ἱέρᾱξ), οὖρος *boundary* (ὅρος). But also in ἄμαξα *wagon* (Attic ἅμαξα). In Laconian medial σ became ʽ (*h*): ἐνίκāἑ = ἐνίκησε *he conquered.*

10 D. In Aeolic, υ, like all the other vowels (and the diphthongs), always has the smooth breathing. The epic forms ὔμμες *you*, ὔμμι, ὔμμε (325 D.) are Aeolic.

sounding which the air escapes with friction through the cavity of the mouth; next come the stops, which are produced by a removal of an obstruction; and finally the double consonants.

16. Stops (or mutes). Stopped consonants are so called because in sounding them the breath passage is for a moment completely closed. The stops are divided into three *classes* (according to the part of the mouth chiefly active in sounding them) and into three *orders* (according to the degree of force in the expiratory effort).

	Classes				Orders		
Labial (lip sounds)	π	β	φ	Smooth	π	τ	κ
Dental (teeth sounds)	τ	δ	θ	Middle	β	δ	γ
Palatal (palate sounds)	κ	γ	χ	Rough	φ	θ	χ

a. The dentals are sometimes called *linguals*. The rough stops are also called *aspirates* (lit. breathed sounds) because they were sounded with a strong emission of breath (26). The smooth stops are thus distinguished from the rough stops by the absence of breathing. ʽ (*h*) is also an aspirate. The middle stops owe their name to their position in the above grouping, which is that of the Greek grammarians (they are also called voiced stops).

17. Spirants. — There is one spirant: σ (also called a *sibilant*).

a. A spirant is heard when the breath passage of the oral cavity is so narrowed that a rubbing noise is produced by an expiration. In later Greek, the voiced and aspirated stops became spirants.

18. Liquids. — There are two liquids: λ and ρ. Initial ρ always has the rough breathing (13).

19. Nasals. — There are three nasals: μ (labial), ν (dental), and γ-nasal (palatal).

a. Gamma before κ, γ, χ, ξ is called γ-nasal. It had the sound of *n* in *think*, and was represented by *n* in Latin. Thus, ἄγκῡρα (Lat. *ancora*) *anchor*, ἄγγελος (Lat. *angelus*) *messenger*, σφίγξ *sphinx*.

b. The name *liquids* is often used to include both liquids and nasals.

20. Semivowels. — ι, υ are often called semi-vowels (consonantal ι and ϝ — equal to consonantal υ — function as spirants).

a. When ι and υ correspond to *y* and *w* (cp. *minion*, *persuade*) they are said to be unsyllabic; and, with a following vowel, make one syllable out of two. Semivocalic ι and υ are written ι̯ and υ̯. Initial ι̯ passed into ʽ (*h*), as in ἧπαρ *liver*, Lat. *jecur*; and into ζ in ζυγόν *yoke*, Lat. *jugum* (here it is often called the spirant *yod*). Initial υ̯ was written ϝ (3). Medial ι̯, υ̯ before vowels were often lost, as in τῑμά-(ι̯)ω *I honour*, βο(υ̯)-ός, gen. of βοῦ-ς *ox*, *cow* (43).

b. The form of many words is due to the fact that the liquids, nasals, and σ may fulfil the office of a vowel to form syllables (cp. *bridle*, *even*, *pst*). This is expressed by λ̥, μ̥, ν̥, ρ̥, σ̥, to be read 'syllabic λ,' etc., or 'sonant λ' (see 35 b, c).

21. Double Consonants. —These are ζ, ξ, and ψ. ζ is a combination of σδ (or δς) or δι (26). ξ is written for κσ, γσ, χσ; ψ for πσ, βσ, φσ.

22. TABLE OF CONSONANT SOUNDS

Divisions	Physiological Differences	Labial	Dental	Palatal
Nasals	Voiced	μ	ν	γ-nasal (19 a)
Semivowels	Voiced	u̯(ϝ)		i̯(y)
Liquids	Voiced		λ ρ*	
Spirants	Voiced Voiceless		σ† σ, ς	
Stops	Voiced Voiceless Voiceless Aspirate	β (middle) π (smooth) φ (rough)	δ (middle) τ (smooth) θ (rough)	γ (middle) κ (smooth) χ (rough)
Double consonants	Voiced Voiceless	 ψ	ζ 	 ξ

* ῥ is voiceless. † σ was voiced only when it had the ζ sound (26).

ANCIENT GREEK PRONUNCIATION

23. The pronunciation of Ancient Greek varied much according to time and place, and differed in many important respects from that of the modern language. While in general Greek of the classical period was a phonetic language, *i.e.* its letters represented the sounds, and no heard sound was unexpressed in writing (but see 108), in course of time many words were retained in their old form though their pronunciation had changed. The tendency of the language was thus to become more and more unphonetic. Our current pronunciation of Ancient Greek is only in part even approximately correct for the period from the death of Pericles (429 B.C.) to that of Demosthenes (322); and in the case of several sounds, *e.g.* ζ, φ, χ, θ, it is certainly erroneous for that period. But ignorance of the exact pronunciation, as well as long-established usage, must render any reform pedantical, if not impossible. In addition to, and in further qualification of, the list of sound equivalents in 1 we may note the following:

24. Vowels. — Short α, ι, υ differed in sound from the corresponding long vowels only in being less prolonged; ε and ο probably differed from η and ω also in being less open, a difference that is impossible to parallel in English as our short vowels are more open than the long vowels. **ᾰ**: as *a* in Germ. *hat.* There is no true *ă* in accented syllables in English; the *a* of *idea*, *aha* is a neutral vowel. **ε**: as *é* in *bonté;* somewhat similar is *a* in *bakery.* **η**: as *ê* in *fête*, or

24 D. In Lesbos, Boeotia, Laconia, possibly in Ionia, and in some other places, υ was still sounded *oo* after it became like Germ. *ü* in Attic.

nearly as *e* in *where*. **ι**: nearly as the first *e* in *meteor*, *eternal*. **ο**: as *o* in Fr. *mot*, somewhat like unaccented *ŏ* in *obey* or *phonetic* (as often sounded). **ω**: as *o* in Fr. *encore*. Eng. *ō* is prevailingly diphthongal (o^u). **υ** was originally sounded as *u* in *prune*, but by the fifth century had become like that of Fr. *tu*, Germ. *thür*. It never had in Attic the sound of *u* in *mute*. After *υ* had become like Germ. *ü*, the only means to represent the sound of the old *υ* (*oo* in *moon*) was *ου* (25). Observe, however, that, in diphthongs, final *υ* retained the old *υ* sound.

25. Diphthongs. — The diphthongs were sounded nearly as follows:

αι as in *Cairo*	*αυ* as *ou* in *out*	*ηυ* as *ēh′-oo*
ει as in *vein*	*ευ* as *e* (met) + *oo* (moon)	*ωυ* as *ōh′-oo*
οι as in *soil*	*ου* as in *ourang*	*υι* as in Fr. *huit*

In **ᾳ, ῃ, ῳ** the long open vowels had completely overpowered the *ι* by 100 B.C., so that *ι* ceased to be written (5 a). The *ι* is now generally neglected in pronunciation though it may have still been sounded to some extent in the fourth century B.C. — The genuine diphthongs **ει** and **ου** (6) were originally distinct double sounds (*ĕh′-i*, *ŏh′-oo*), and as such were written ΕΙ, ΟΥ in the Old Attic alphabet (2 a): ΕΠΕΙΔΕ *ἐπειδή*, ΤΟΥΤΟΝ *τούτων*. The spurious diphthongs **ει** and **ου** (6) are digraphs representing the long sounds of simple *ε* (French *é*) and original *υ*. By 400 B.C. genuine *ει* and *ου* had become simple single sounds pronounced as *ei* in *vein* and *ou* in *ourang;* and spurious *ει* and *ου*, which had been written Ε and Ο (2 a), were now often written ΕΙ and ΟΥ. After 300 B.C. *ει* gradually acquired the sound of *ei* in *seize*. **ευ** was sounded like *eh′-oo*, **ηυ** and **ωυ** like *ēh′-oo*, *ōh′-oo*, pronounced rapidly but smoothly. **υι** is now commonly sounded as *ui* in *quit*. It occurred only before vowels, and the loss of the *ι* in *ὑός* *son* (43) shows that the diphthongal sound was unstable.

26. Consonants. — Most of the consonants were sounded as in English (1). Before **ι, κ, γ, τ, σ** never had a *sh* (or *zh*) sound heard in *Lycia* (Λυκίᾱ), *Asia* (Ἀσίᾱ). **σ** was usually like our sharp *s*; but before voiced consonants (15 a) it probably was soft, like *z*; thus we find both *κόζμος* and *κόσμος* on inscriptions. — **ζ** was probably = *zd*, whether it arose from an original *σδ* (as in Ἀθήναζε, from Ἀθηνα(ν)ς-δε *Athens-wards*), or from *dz*, developed from *dy* (as in *ζυγόν*, from (*d*)*yυγόν*, cp. *jugum*). The *z* in *zd* gradually extinguished the *d*, until in the Hellenistic period (p. 4) *ζ* sank to *z* (as in *zeal*), which is the sound in Modern Greek. — The aspirates **φ, θ, χ** were voiceless stops (15 b, 16 a) followed by a strong expiration: π^h, τ^h, κ^h as in *upheaval*, *hothouse*, *backhand* (though here *h* is in a different syllable from the stop). Thus, *φεύγω* was *π‛εύγω*, *θέλω* was *τ‛έλω*, *ἔχω* was *ἔ-κ‛ω*. Cp. *ἐφ' ᾧ* for *ἐπ*(*ί*) *‛ᾧ*, etc. Probably only one *h* was heard when two aspirates came together, as in *ἐχθρός* (*ἐκτ‛ρός*). After 300 A.D. (probably) *φ*, *θ*, and *χ* became spirants, *φ* being sounded as *f* (as in Φίλιππος *Philip*), *θ* as *th* in *theatre*, *χ* as *ch* in German *ich* or *loch*. The stage between aspirates and spirants is sometimes represented by the writing *πφ* (= *pf*), *τθ*, *κχ*,

---

26 D. Aeolic has *σδ* for *ζ* in *ὕσδος* (*ὄζος* *branch*). In late Laconian *θ* passed into *σ* (*σηρίον* = *θηρίον* *wild beast*). In Laconian and some other dialects *β* became a spirant and was written for *ϝ*. *δ* became a spirant in Attic after Christ.

which are affricata. — The neglect of the *h* in Latin representations of *φ, θ, χ* possibly shows that these sounds consisted of a stop + *h*. Thus, *Pilipus* = Φίλιππος, *tus* = θύος, *Aciles* = Ἀχιλλεύς. Modern Greek has the spirantic sounds, and these, though at variance with classical pronunciation, are now usually adopted. See also 108.

VOWEL CHANGE

27. Quantitative Vowel Gradation. — In the formation and inflection of words a short vowel often interchanges with its corresponding long vowel. Thus

SHORT	α	ε	ι	ο	υ
LONG	η (ᾱ after ε, ι, ρ, 31)	η	ῑ	ω	ῡ
τῑμά-ω	ἐά-ω	φιλέ-ω	ἱκάνω	δηλό-ω	φύ-σις
I honour	*I permit*	*I love*	*I come*	*I show*	*nature*
τῑμή-σω	ἐά-σω	φιλή-σω	ῑ̔κᾱνον	δηλώ-σω	φῦ-μα
future	future	future	imperf.	future	*growth*

28. Difference in quantity between Attic and Epic words is due chiefly either to (1) metrical lengthening, or to (2) different phonetic treatment, as καλϝός, τινϝω become Epic κᾱλός *fair*, τίνω *I pay* (37 D. 1), Attic κᾰλός, τῑνω.

29. The initial short vowel of a word forming the second part of a compound is often lengthened: στρατηγός *general* (στρατός *army* + ἄγειν *to lead* 887 d).

30. Attic η, ᾱ. — Attic has η for original ᾱ of the earlier period, as φήμη *report* (Lat. *fāma*). Ionic also has η for original ᾱ. Doric and Aeolic retain original ᾱ (φᾱ́μᾱ).

---

28 D. Metrical lengthening. — Many words, which would otherwise not fit into the verse, show in the Epic ει for ε, ου (rarely οι) for ο, and ᾱ, ῑ, ῡ for α, ι, υ. Thus, εἰνάλιος *in the sea* for ἐνάλιος, εἰαρινός *vernal* for ἐαρινός, ὑπείροχος *eminent* for ὑπέροχος, εἰλήλουθα *have come* for ἐλήλουθα, οὐλόμενος *destructive, accursed* for ὀλόμενος, οὔρεα *mountains* from ὄρος, Οὐλύμποιο *of Olympus* from Ὄλυμπος. ο before a vowel appears as οι in πνοιή *breath*. Similarly, ἠγάθεος *very holy* for ἀγάθεος; but ἠνεμόεις *windy* (from ἄνεμος) has the η of ὑπήνεμος *under the wind* (29), and τιθήμενος *placing* (for τιθέμενος) borrows η from τίθημι.

A short syllable under the rhythmic accent ('ictus') is lengthened metrically: (1) in words having three or more short syllables: the first of three shorts (οὐλόμενος), the second of four shorts (ὑπείροχος), the third of five shorts (ἀπερείσια *boundless*); (2) in words in which the short ictus syllable is followed by two longs and a short (Οὐλύμποιο). A short syllable not under the rhythmic accent is lengthened when it is preceded and followed by a long; thus, any vowel preceded by ϝ (πνείω *breathe* = πνεϝω), ι or υ before a vowel (προθῡμίῃσι *zeal*).

30 D. 1. Doric and Aeolic retain original ᾱ, as in μᾶλον *apple* (cp. Lat. *mālum*, Att. μῆλον), κᾶρυξ *herald* (Att. κῆρυξ). But Doric and Aeolic have original η when η interchanges with ε, as in τίθημι *I place*, τίθεμεν *we place*, μάτηρ μᾱτέρα *mother*, ποιμήν ποιμένι *shepherd*.

2. Ionic has η after ε, ι, and ρ. Thus, γενεή, σκιή, ἡμέρη.

a. This is true also of the ᾱ which is the result of early compensative lengthening, by which -ανσ-, -ασλ-, -ασμ-, and -ασν- changed to -ᾱσ-, -ᾱλ-, -ᾱμ-, and -ᾱν-. (See 37 b.) But in a few cases like τᾱ́ς for τάνς, and in πᾶσα for πάνσα (113) where the combination ανσ arose at a later period, ᾱ was not changed to η. ὑφᾶναι for ὑφῆναι *to weave* follows τετρᾶναι *to pierce*.

b. Original ᾱ became η after υ, as φυή *growth*. In some words, however, we find ᾱ.

31. In Attic alone ᾱ did not become η:

1. When preceded by a ρ; as ἡμέρᾱ *day*, χώρᾱ *country*. This appears to have held good even though an ο intervened: as ἀκρόᾱμα *a musical piece*, ἀθρόᾱ *collected*.

   Exceptions: (a) But ρϝη was changed to ρη: as κόρη for κορϝη *maiden*. (b) Likewise ρη, when the result of contraction of ρεα, remained: as ὄρη from ὄρεα *mountains*. (c) And ρση was changed to ρρη: as κόρρη for κόρση (79) *one of the temples*.

2. When preceded by ε or ι: as γενεᾱ́ *generation*, σκιᾱ́ *shadow*.

   This was the case even when the η would normally have resulted from the contraction of εα: as ὑγιᾶ *healthy*, ἐνδεᾶ *lacking*, for ὑγιῆ from ὑγιε(σ)α, ἐνδεῆ from ἐνδεε(σ)α; also, if originally a ϝ intervened, as νέᾱ for νεϝᾱ *young* (Lat. *nova*).

   Exceptions: Some exceptions are due to analogy: ὑγιῆ *healthy*, εὐφυῆ *shapely* (292 d) follow σαφῆ *clear*.

32. In the choruses of tragedy Doric ᾱ is often used for η. Thus, μᾱ́τηρ *mother*, ψῡχᾱ́ *soul*, γᾶ *earth*, δύστᾱνος *wretched*, ἔβᾱν *went*.

33. The dialects frequently show vowel sounds that do not occur in the corresponding Attic words.

34. Transfer of Quantity. — ηο, ηα often exchange quantities, becoming εω, εᾱ. Thus, ληός (Epic λᾱός *folk*) becomes λεώς, as πόληος becomes πόλεως *of a city*; τεθνηότος τεθνεῶτος *dead*; βασιλῆα βασιλέᾱ *king*.

35. Qualitative Vowel Gradation. — In the same root or suffix we find an interchange among different vowels (and diphthongs) similar to the interchange in *sing*, *sang*, *sung*.

---

33 D. **α** for **ε**: ἰαρός *sacred*, Ἄρταμις (for Ἄρτεμις), τράπω *turn* Dor.; **ε** for **α**: θέρσος *courage* Aeol., ἔρσην *male*, ὀρέω *see*, τέσσερες *four* (= τέτταρες) Ion.; **α** for **ο**: διᾱκάτιοι (for διᾱκόσιοι) 200 Dor., ὑπά *under* Aeol.; **ο** for **α**: στρότος (στρατός) *army*, ὄν (ἀνά) *up* Aeol., τέτορες (τέτταρες) *four* Dor.; **ε** for **η**: ἔσσων *inferior* (ἥττων) Ion.; **ε** for **ο**: Ἀπέλλων Dor. (also Ἀπόλλων); **ε** for **ει**: μέζων *greater* Ion.; **ε** for **ι**: κέρνᾱν *mix* (= κιρνάναι for κεραννύναι) Aeol.; **ι** for **ε**: ἰστίη *hearth* Ion., ἰστίᾱ Dor. (for ἑστίᾱ), χρῡ́σιος (χρῡ́σεος) *golden* Aeol., θιός *god* Boeot., κοσμίω *arrange* Dor.; **υ** for **α**: πίσυρες *four* (τέτταρες) Hom.; **υ** for **ο**: ὄνυμα *name* Dor., Aeol., ἀπύ *from* Aeol.; **ω** for **ου**: ὦν *accordingly* Ion., Dor.

34 D. Often in Ionic: Ἀτρεΐδεω from earlier Ἀτρεΐδᾱο *son of Atreus*, ἱκέτεω from ἱκέτᾱο *suppliant*. This εω generally makes a single syllable in poetry (60). The ηο intermediate between ᾱο and εω is rarely found.

a. This variation appears in *strong* grades and in a *weak* grade (including actual expulsion of a vowel — in diphthongs, of the first vowel). Thus, *φέρ-ω I carry*, *φόρ-ο-ς tribute*, *φώρ thief*, *φαρ-έ-τρᾱ quiver*, *δί-φ ρ-ο-ς chariot* (*two-carrier*), *λείπ-ω I leave*, *λέ-λοιπ-α I have left*, *λιπ-εῖν to leave*. The interchange is quantitative in *φόρ-ο-ς φώρ* (cp. 27).

b. When, by the expulsion of a vowel in the weak grade, an unpronounceable combination of consonants resulted, a vowel sound was developed to render pronunciation possible. Thus, *ρα* or *αρ* was developed from *ρ* between consonants, as in *πα-τρά-σι* from *πατρ̥-σι* (262); and *α* from *ν*, as in *αὐτό-μα-το-ν* for *αὐτο-μν̥-τον automaton* (*acting of its own will*), cp. *μέν-ο-ς rage*, *μέ-μον-α I yearn*. So in *ὀνομαίνω name* for *ὀνομν̥-ι̯ω*; cp. *ὄνομα*.

c. A vowel may also take the place of an original liquid or nasal after a consonant; as *ἔλῡσα* for *ἐλῡσμ̥*. This *ρ*, *λ*, *μ*, *ν* in **b** and **c** is called *sonant liquid* or *sonant nasal*.

d. Historically, these variations are of two types. The first is an *e/o* alternation often important in Greek word-formation (831). The second is the alternation of long vowel and *α* (or in some cases *ε*, *ο*) as seen for example in the conjugation of *-μι* verbs (738).

36. TABLE OF THE CHIEF VOWEL GRADES

	Strong Grades 1. 2.	Weak Grade		Strong Grades 1. 2.	Weak Grade
a.	ε : ο	— or α	d.	ᾱ : ω	α
b.	ει : οι	ι	e.	η : ω	ε or α
c.	ευ : ου	υ	f.	ω	ο

a.	*ἐ-γεν-ό-μην I became*	: *γέ-γον-α I am born*	*γί-γ ν-ο-μαι I become*
	τρέπω I turn	: *τροπ-ή rout*	*ἐ-τράπ-ην I was put to flight*
b.	*πείθ-ω I persuade*	: *πέ-ποιθ-α I trust* (568)	*πιθ-ανός persuasive*
c.	*ἐλεύ(θ)σ-ο-μαι I shall go*	: *ἐλ-ήλουθ-α I have gone*	*ἤλυθ-ο-ν I went* (Epic)
d.	*φᾱ-μί* (Dor., 30) *I say*	: *φω-νή speech*	*φα-μέν we speak*
e.	*τί-θη-μι I place*	: *θω-μό-ς heap*	*θε-τό-ς placed, adopted*
	ῥήγ-νῡ-μι I break	: *ἔ-ρρωγ-α I have broken*	*ἐ-ρράγ-η it was broken*
f.	——	*δί-δω-μι I give*	*δί-δο-μεν we give*

N. 1. — Relatively few words show examples of all the above series of grades. Some have five grades, as *πα-τήρ*, *πα-τέρ-α*, *εὐ-πά-τωρ*, *εὐ-πά-τορ-α*, *πα-τ ρ-ός*.

N. 2. — *ε* and *ι* vary in *πετάννῡμι πίτνημι spread out*.

COMPENSATORY LENGTHENING

37. Compensatory lengthening is the lengthening of a short vowel to make up for the omission of a consonant.

---

37 D. 1. Ionic agrees with Attic except where the omitted consonant was ϝ, which in Attic disappeared after a consonant without causing lengthening. Thus, *ξεῖνος* for *ξένος stranger*, *εἵνεκα on account of* (also in Dem.) for *ἕνεκα*, *οὖρος boundary* for *ὅρος*, *κοῦρος boy* for *κόρος*, *μοῦνος alone* for *μόνος*. These forms are also used generally in poetry.

The short vowels	α	ε	ι	ο	υ
are lengthened to	ᾱ	ει	ῑ	ου	ῡ
Thus the forms	τάν-ς	ἐ-μεν-σα	ἐκλιν-σα	τόνς	δεικνυντ-ς
become	τᾱ́ς	ἔμεινα	ἔκλῑνα	τούς	δεικνῡ́ς
	the	*I remained*	*I leaned*	*the*	*showing*

a. Thus are formed κτείνω *I kill* for κτεν-ι̯ω, φθείρω *I destroy* for φθερ-ι̯ω, δότειρα *giver* for δοτερ-ι̯α, κλῑ́νω *I lean* for κλιν-ι̯ω, ὀλοφύρω *I lament* for ὀλοφυρ-ι̯ω.

b. α becomes η in the σ-aorist of verbs whose stems end in λ, ρ, or ν, when not preceded by ι or ρ. Thus, ἐφαν-σα becomes ἔ-φηνα *I showed*, but ἐπεραν-σα becomes ἐπέρᾱνα *I finished.* So σελήνη *moon* for σελασ-νη (σέλας *gleam*).

c. The diphthongs ει and ου due to this lengthening are *spurious* (6).

38. ᾱ arises from αι upon the loss of its ι (43) in ᾱ̓εί *always* (from αἰεί), ᾱ̓ετός *eagle* (αἰετός), κλᾱ́ει *weeps* (κλαίει), ἐλᾱ́ᾱ *olive-tree* (ἐλαίᾱ, cp. Lat. *oliva*).

a. This change took place only when αι was followed by ϝ (αἰϝεί, αἰϝετός from ἀϝιετος, κλαιϝει from κλαϝιει, 111, 128) or ι (Θηβᾱΐς *the Thebaïd* from Θηβαιίς); and only when ϝ or ι was not followed by ο.

SHORTENING, ADDITION, AND OTHER VOWEL CHANGES

39. Shortening. — A long vowel may be shortened before another long vowel: βασιλέων from βασιλήων *of kings*, νεῶν from νηῶν *of ships*, τεθνεώς from τεθνηώς *dead.*

40. A long vowel before ι, υ, a nasal, or a liquid + a following consonant was regularly shortened: νᾰῦς from original νᾱυς *ship*, ἐμίγεν from ἐ-μιγη-ντ *were mixed.* The long vowel was often introduced again, as Ion. νηῦς *ship.*

41. Addition. — α, ε, ο are sometimes prefixed before λ, μ, ρ, ϝ (*prothetic vowels*). Thus, ἀ-λείφω *anoint with oil*, λίπος *fat;* ἐ-ρυθρός *red* (cp. Lat. *ruber*), ἐ-είκοσι from ἐ-(ϝ)είκοσι; ὀ-μόργνῡμι *wipe;* ἐ-χθές and χθές *yesterday*, ἴ-κτις *weasel* (κτιδέη *weasel-skin helmet*) are doubtful cases.

42. Development. — A medial vowel is sometimes developed from λ or ν between two consonants; thus αλ, λα; αρ, ρα; αν (35 b). Also (rarely) in forms like Ion. βάραγχος = Att. βράγχος *hoarseness.*

---

2. Doric generally lengthens ε and ο to η and ω: ξῆνος, ὧρος, κῶρος, μῶνος. So μῶσα *muse* from μονσα for μοντι̯α, τώς for τόνς *the*, ἠμί *am* for ἐσμι, χήλιοι 1000 for χεσλιοι, Ionic χείλιοι. (In some Doric dialects ϝ drops as in Attic (ξένος, ὅρος); and ανς, ονς may become ᾰ̔ς, ος: δεσπότᾰς *lords*, τός *the.*)

3. Aeolic has αις, εις (a *genuine* diphth.), οις from ανς, ενς, ονς. Thus, παῖσα *all* (Cretan πάνσα, Att. πᾶσα), λύοισι *they loose* from λύοντι. Elsewhere Aeol. prefers assimilated forms (ἔμεννα, ἔκλιννα, ξέννος, ἔννεκα, ὄρρος, ἔμμι, χέλλιοι). But single ν, ρ are also found, as in κόρᾱ, μόνος. Aeolic has φθέρρω, κλίννω, ὀλοφύρρω; cp. 37 a.

39 D. In the Ionic genitive of Ā stems (214 D. 8) -εων is from -ηων out of -ᾱων. So in Ionic βασιλέα from βασιλῆα *king.* So even before a short vowel in Hom. ἥρωος, ἥρωι *hero* (cp. 148 D. 3).

43. Disappearance. — The ι and υ of diphthongs often disappear before a following vowel. Thus, ὑός from υἱός *son*, βο-ός genitive of βοῦ-ς *ox, cow*. ι and υ here became semivowels (ι̯, υ̯), which are not written. Cp. 148 D. 3.

44. a. The disappearance of ε before a vowel is often called *hyphaeresis* (ὑφαίρεσις *omission*). Thus Ionic νοσσός *chick* for νεοσσός, ὀρτή for ἑορτή *festival*; ἀδεῶς *fearlessly* for ἀδεέως. Here ε was sounded nearly like *y* and was not written.

b. The disappearance of a short vowel between consonants is called *syncope* (συγκοπή *cutting up*). Thus πίπτω *fall* for πι-πετ-ω, πατρός *father* for πατέρος. Syncopated forms show the weak grade of vowel gradation (35, 36).

45. Assimilation. — A vowel may be assimilated to the vowel standing in the following syllable: βιβλίον *book* from βυβλίον (βύβλος *papyrus*).

a. On assimilation in distracted verbs (ὁράω *see*, etc.), see 643 ff., 652.

EUPHONY OF VOWELS

CONTACT OF VOWELS AND HIATUS

46. Attic more than any other dialect disliked the immediate succession of two vowel sounds in adjoining syllables. To avoid such succession, which often arose in the formation and inflection of words, various means were employed: *contraction* (48 ff.), when the vowels collided in the middle of a word; or, when the succession occurred between two words (*hiatus*), by *crasis* (62 ff.), *elision* (70 ff.), *aphaeresis* (76), or by affixing a movable consonant at the end of the former word (134).

47. Hiatus is usually avoided in prose writers by elision (70 ff.); but in cases where elision is not possible, hiatus is allowed to remain by different writers in different degrees, commonly after short words, such as ὦ, εἰ, ἤ, καί, μή, and the forms of the article.

---

43 D. So in Hdt. κέεται for κεῖται *lies*, βαθέα for βαθεῖα *deep*.

44 a. D. Cp. Hom. θεοί A 18 (one syllable). ι becomes ι̯ in Hom. πόλιος (two syllables) Φ 567. ι rarely disappears: δῆμον for δήμιον *belonging to the people* M 213.

47 D. Hiatus is allowed in certain cases.

1. *In epic poetry:* a. After ι and υ: ἄξονι ἀμφίς, σύ ἐσσι.

b. After a long final syllable having the rhythmic accent: μοι ἐθέλουσα (–́ ⏑ ⏑ –́ ⏑).

c. When a long final syllable is shortened before an initial vowel (*weak*, or *improper*, hiatus): ἀκτῇ ἐφ' ὑψηλῇ (–́ ⏑ ⏑ –́ – –́).

d. When the concurrent vowels are separated by the caesura; often after the fourth foot: ἀλλ' ἄγ' ἐμῶν ὀχέων ἐπιβήσεο, | ὄφρα ἴδηαι; very often between the short syllables of the third foot (the feminine caesura): as, ἀλλ' ἀκέουσα κάθησο, | ἐμῷ δ' ἐπιπείθεο μύθῳ; rarely after the first foot: αὐτὰρ ὁ ἔγνω A 333.

e. Where ϝ has been lost.

2. *In Attic poetry* hiatus is allowable, as in 1 c, and after τί *what?* εὖ *well*, interjections, πεοί *concerning*, and in οὐδὲ (μηδὲ) εἷς (for οὐδείς, μηδείς *no one*).

CONTRACTION

48. Contraction unites in a single long vowel or diphthong two vowels or a vowel and a diphthong standing next each other in successive syllables in the same word.

a. Occasion for contraction is made especially by the concurrence of vowel sounds which were once separated by σ, ͺ (ϝ), and ͺ (17, 20 a).

The following are the chief rules governing contraction:

49. (I) Two vowels which can form a diphthong (5) unite to form that diphthong: *γένεϊ = γένει, αἰδόϊ = αἰδοῖ, κλήϊθρον = κλῇθρον.*

50. (II) **Like Vowels.** — Like vowels, whether short or long, unite in the common long; εε, οο become ει, ου (6): *γέραα = γέρᾱ, φιλέητε = φιλῆτε; ἐφίλεε = ἐφίλει, δηλόομεν = δηλοῦμεν.*

a. ι is rarely contracted with ι (*ὄφι + ιδιον = ὀφίδιον small snake*) or υ with υ (*ῦς son* in inscriptions, from *ὑ(ι)ύς = υἱός*, 43).

51. (III) **Unlike Vowels.** — Unlike vowels are assimilated, either the second to the first (*progressive* assimilation) or the first to the second (*regressive* assimilation).

a. An *o* sound always prevails over an *a* or *e* sound: **ο** or **ω** before or after **α**, and before **η**, forms **ω**. **οε** and **εο** form **ου** (a spurious diphthong, 6). Thus, *τῑμάομεν = τῑμῶμεν, αἰδόα = αἰδῶ, ἥρωα = ἥρω, τῑμάω = τῑμῶ, δηλόητε = δηλῶτε*; but *φιλέομεν = φιλοῦμεν, δηλόετον = δηλοῦτον.*

b. When **α** and **ε** or **η** come together the vowel sound that precedes prevails, and we have **ᾱ** or **η**: *δραε = δρᾱ, τῑμάητε = τῑμᾶτε, δρεα = δρη.*

c. **υ** rarely contracts: **υ + ι = ῡ** in *ἰχθύδιον* from *ἰχθυίδιον small fish*; **υ + ε** strictly never becomes ῡ (273).

52. (IV) **Vowels and Diphthongs.** — A vowel disappears before a diphthong beginning with the same sound: *μνάαι = μναῖ, φιλέει = φιλεῖ, δηλόοι = δηλοῖ.*

53. A vowel before a diphthong not beginning with the same sound generally contracts with the first vowel of the diphthong; the last vowel, if ι, is *subscript* (5): *τῑμάει = τῑμᾷ, τῑμάοιμεν = τῑμῷμεν, λείπεαι = λείπῃ, μεμνηοίμην = μεμνῴμην.*

a. But **ε + οι** becomes **οι**: *φιλέοι = φιλοῖ*; **ο + ει, ο + η** become **οι**: *δηλόει = δηλοῖ, δηλόῃ = δηλοῖ.*

54. Spurious **ει** and **ου** are treated like **ε** and **ο**: *τῑμάειν = τῑμᾶν, δηλόειν = δηλοῦν, τῑμάουσι = τῑμῶσι* (but *τῑμάει = τῑμᾷ* and *δηλόει = δηλοῖ*, since **ει** is here genuine; 6).

---

50 D. ι + ι = ῑ occurs chiefly in the Ionic, Doric, and Aeolic dative singular of nouns in -ις (268 D.), as in *πόλιι = πόλῑ*; also in the optative, as in *φθι-ί-το = φθῖτο.*

55. (V) **Three Vowels.** — When three vowels come together, the last two unite first, and the resulting diphthong may be contracted with the first vowel: thus, *τῑμᾷ* is from *τῑμα-ῃ* out of *τῑμα-ε(σ)αι*; but Περικλέους from Περικλέεος.

56. **Irregularities.** — A short vowel preceding *α* or any long vowel or diphthong, in contracts of the first and second declensions, is apparently absorbed (235, 290): *χρύσεα* = *χρῡσᾶ* (not *χρῡσῆ*), *ἁπλόα* = *ἁπλᾶ* (not *ἁπλῶ*), by analogy to the *α* which marks the neuter plural, *χρῡσέαις* = *χρῡσαῖς*. (So *ἡμέας* = *ἡμᾶς* to show the *-ας* of the accus. pl.) Only in the singular of the first declension does *εᾱ* become *η* (or *ᾱ* after a vowel or *ρ*): *χρῡσέᾱς* = *χρῡσῆς*, *ἀργυρέᾳ* = *ἀργυρᾷ*. In the third declension *εεα* becomes *εᾱ* (265); *ιεα* or *υεα* becomes *ιᾱ* (*υᾱ*) or *ιη* (*υη*). See 292 d.

Various special cases will be considered under their appropriate sections.

57. The contraction of a long vowel with a short vowel sometimes does not occur by reason of analogy. Thus, *νηΐ* (two syllables) follows *νηός*, the older form of *νεώς* (275). Sometimes the long vowel was shortened (39) or transfer of quantity took place (34).

58. Vowels that were once separated by *σ* or *ι̯* (20) are often not contracted in dissyllabic forms, but contracted in polysyllabic forms. Thus, *θε(σ)ός* *god*, but Θουκῡδίδης *Thucydides* (*θεός* + *κῦδος* *glory*).

59. TABLE OF VOWEL CONTRACTIONS

[After *ει* or *ου*, *gen.* means *genuine*, *sp.* means *spurious*.]

α + α	= ᾱ	γέραα	= γέρᾱ	ε + αι	= ῃ	λύεαι	= λύῃ
ᾱ + α	= ᾱ	λᾶας	= λᾶς			whence λύει	
α + ᾱ	= ᾱ	βεβάᾱσι	= βεβᾶσι		= αι	χρῡσέαις	= χρῡσαῖς
α + αι	= αι	μνάαι	= μναῖ			(56)	
α + ᾳ	= ᾱͅ	μνάᾳ	= μνᾷ	ε + ε	= ει (sp.)	φιλέετε	= φιλεῖτε
α + ε	= ᾱ	τῑμάετε	= τιμᾶτε	ε + ει (gen.)	= ει (gen.)	φιλέει	= φιλεῖ
α + ει (gen.)	= ᾱͅ	τῑμάει	= τῑμᾷ	ε + ει (sp.)	= ει (sp.)	φιλέειν	= φιλεῖν
α + ει (sp.)	= ᾱ	τῑμάειν	= τῑμᾶν	ε + η	= η	φιλέητε	= φιλῆτε
α + η	= ᾱ	τῑμάητε	= τῑμᾶτε	ε + ῃ	= ῃ	φιλέῃ	= φιλῇ
α + ῃ	= ᾱͅ	τῑμάῃ	= τῑμᾷ	ε + ι	= ει (gen.)	γένεϊ	= γένει
α + ι	= αι	κέραϊ	= κέραι	ε + ο	= ου (sp.)	φιλέομεν	= φιλοῦμεν
ᾱ + ι	= ᾱͅ	ῥᾱΐτερος	= ῥᾴτερος	ε + οι	= οι	φιλέοιτε	= φιλοῖτε
α + ο	= ω	τῑμάομεν	= τῑμῶμεν	ε + ου (sp.)	= ου	φιλέουσι	= φιλοῦσι
α + οι	= ῳ	τῑμάοιμι	= τιμῷμι	ε + υ	= ευ	ἔϋ	= εὖ
α + ου (sp.)	= ω	ἐτῑμάε(σ)ο (55)		ε + ω	= ω	φιλέω	= φιλῶ
			= ἐτῑμῶ	ε + ῳ	= ῳ	χρῡσέῳ	= χρῡσῷ
α + ω	= ω	τῑμάω	= τῑμῶ	η + αι	= ῃ	λύη(σ)αι	= λύῃ
ε + α	= η	τείχεα	= τείχη	η + ε	= η	τῑμήεντος	= τῑμῆντος
	= ᾱ	ὀστέα	= ὀστᾶ (56)	η + ει (gen.)	= ῃ	ζήει	= ζῇ
ε + ᾱ	= η	ἁπλέᾱ	= ἁπλῆ	η + ει (sp.)	= η	τῑμήεις	= τῑμῆς

55 D. In Hom. *δεῖος* *of fear* from *δέε(σ)-ος* the *first* two vowels unite.

TABLE OF VOWEL CONTRACTIONS — Concluded

η + η	= η	φανήητε	= φανῆτε	ο + ῃ	= οι	δηλόῃ	= δηλοῖ
η + ῃ	= ῃ	ζήῃ	= ζῇ		= ῳ	δόῃς	= δῷς
η + οι	= ῳ	μεμνηοίμην =	μεμνῴμην	ο + ι	= οι	ἠχόϊ	= ἠχοῖ
				ο + ο	= ου (sp.)	πλόος	= πλοῦς
η + ι	= ῃ	κλῃΐς	= κλῇς	ο + οι	= οι	δηλόοιμεν	= δηλοῖμεν
ι + ι	= ῑ	Χίιος	= Χῖος	ο + ου (sp.)	= ου (sp.)	δηλόουσι	= δηλοῦσι
ο + α	= ω	αἰδόα	= αἰδῶ	ο + ω	= ω	δηλόω	= δηλῶ
	= ᾱ	ἁπλόα	= ἁπλᾶ	ο + ῳ	= ῳ	πλόῳ	= πλῷ
		(56)		υ + ι	= ῡ	ἰχθυΐδιον	= ἰχθῦδιον
ο + ε	= ου (sp.)	ἐδήλοε	= ἐδήλου	υ + υ	= ῡ	ὑύς (for υἱός)	= ὗς
ο + ει (gen.)	= οι	δηλόει	= δηλοῖ	ω + α	= ω	ἥρωα	= ἥρω
ο + ει (sp.)	= ου	δηλόειν	= δηλοῦν	ω + ι	= ῳ	ἥρωι	= ἥρῳ
ο + η	= ω	δηλόητε	= δηλῶτε	ω + ω	= ω	δώω (Hom.)	= δῶ

N. — The forms of ῥῑγόω *shiver* contract from the stem ῥῑγω- (yielding ω or ῳ).

SYNIZESIS

60. In poetry two vowels, or a vowel and a diphthong, belonging to successive syllables may unite to form a single syllable in pronunciation, but not in writing. Thus, βέλεα *missiles*, πόλεως *city*, Πηληϊάδεω *son of Peleus*, χρῡσέῳ *golden*. This is called *Synizēsis* (συνίζησις *settling together*).

61. Synizesis may occur between two words when the first ends in a long vowel or diphthong. This is especially the case with δή

---

59 D. Attic contracts more, Ionic less, than the other dialects. The laws of contraction often differ in the different dialects.

1. Ionic (Old and New) is distinguished by its absence of contraction. Thus, πλόος for πλοῦς *voyage*, τείχεα for τείχη *walls*, ὀστέα for ὀστᾶ *bones*, ἀοιδή for ᾠδή *song*, ἀεργός for ἀργός *idle*. The Mss. of Hdt. generally leave εε, εη uncontracted; but this is probably erroneous in most cases. Ionic rarely contracts where Attic does not: ὀγδώκοντα for ὀγδοήκοντα *eighty*.

2. εο, εω, εου generally remain open in all dialects except Attic. In Ionic εω is usually monosyllabic. Ionic (and less often Doric) may contract εο, εου to ευ: σεῦ from σέο *of thee*, φιλεῦσι from φιλέουσι *they love*.

3. αο, ᾱο, αω, ᾱω contract to ᾱ in Doric and Aeolic. Thus, Ἀτρείδᾱ from Ἀτρείδᾱο, Dor. γελᾶντι *they laugh* from γελάοντι, χωρᾶν from χωράων *of countries*. In Aeolic οᾱ = ᾱ in βᾱθόεντι (Ion. βωθόεντι) = Att. βοηθοῦντι *aiding* (dative).

4. Doric contracts αε to η; αη to η; αει, αῃ to ῃ. Thus, νίκη from νίκαε *conquer!* ὁρῇ from ὁράει and ὁράῃ; but ᾱε = ᾱ (ἅλιος from ἀέλιος, Hom. ἠέλιος *sun*).

5. The Severer (and earlier) Doric contracts εε to η, and οε, οο to ω. Thus, φιλήτω from φιλεέτω, δηλῶτε from δηλόετε, ἵππω from ἵππο-ο (230 D.); the Milder (and later) Doric and N. W. Greek contract to ει, and ου. Aeolic agrees with the Severer Doric.

now, ἤ *or*, ἦ (interrog.), μή *not*, ἐπεί *since*, ἐγώ *I*, ὦ *oh* ; as ἦ οὐ O 18.

a. The term synizesis is often restricted to cases where the first vowel is long. Where the first vowel is short, ε, ι were sounded nearly like *y*; υ nearly like *w*. Cp. 44 a. The single syllable produced by synizesis is almost always long.

CRASIS

62. Crasis (κρᾶσις *mingling*) is the contraction of a vowel or diphthong at the end of a word with a vowel or diphthong beginning the following word. Over the syllable resulting from contraction is placed a ᾿ called *corōnis* (κορωνίς *hook*), as τἆλλα from τὰ ἄλλα *the other things, the rest*.

a. The coronis is not written when the rough breathing stands on the first word: ὁ ἄνθρωπος = ἅνθρωπος.

b. Crasis does not occur when the first vowel may be elided. (Some editors write τἄλλα, etc.)

63. Crasis occurs in general only between words that belong together; and the first of the two words united by crasis is usually the less important; as the article, relative pronoun (ὅ, ἅ), πρό, καί, δή, ὦ. Crasis occurs chiefly in poetry.

a. It is rare in Hom., common in the dialogue parts of the drama (especially in comedy), and frequent in the orators.

64. π, τ, κ become φ, θ, χ when the next word begins with the rough breathing (124): τῇ ἡμέρᾳ = θἠμέρᾳ *the day*, καὶ οἱ *and the* = χοἰ (68 c).

65. Iota subscript (5) appears in the syllable resulting from crasis only when the first syllable of the second word contains an ι: ἐγὼ οἶδα = ἐγᾦδα *I know* (but τῷ ὀργάνῳ = τὠργάνῳ *the instrument*, 68 a).

66. The rules for crasis are in general the same as those for contraction (48 ff.). Thus, τὸ ὄνομα = τοὔνομα *the name*, ὁ ἐν = οὑν, ὦ ἄνερ = ὦνερ *oh man*, πρὸ ἔχων = προὔχων *excelling*, τὸ ἱμάτιον = θοἰμάτιον *the cloak* (64), ἃ ἐγώ = ἁγώ.
But the following exceptions are to be noted (67–69):

67. A diphthong may lose its final vowel: οἱ ἐμοί = οὑμοί, σοι ἐστί = σοὐστί, μου ἐστί = μοὐστί. Cp. 43, 68.

68. The final vowel or diphthong of the article, and of τοί, is dropped, and an initial α of the next word is lengthened unless it is the first vowel of a diphthong. The same rule applies in part to καί.

a. Article.—ὁ ἀνήρ = ἁνήρ, οἱ ἄνδρες = ἅνδρες, αἱ ἀγαθαί = ἁγαθαί, ἡ ἀλήθεια = ἀλήθεια, τοῦ ἀνδρός = τἀνδρός, τῷ ἀνδρί = τἀνδρί, ὁ αὐτός = αὑτός *the same*, τοῦ αὐτοῦ = ταὐτοῦ *of the same*.

b. τοί.—τοὶ ἄρα = τἆρα, μέντοι ἄν = μεντἄν.

c. καί.—(1) αι is dropped: καὶ αὐτός = καὐτός, καὶ οὐ = κοὐ, καὶ ἡ = χἠ, καὶ οἱ = χοἰ, καὶ ἱκετεύετε = χἰκετεύετε *and ye beseech* (64). (2) αι is contracted chiefly before ε and ει: καὶ ἐν = κἀν, καὶ ἐγώ = κἀγώ, καὶ ἐς = κἀς, καὶ εἶτα = κᾆτα (note however καὶ εἰ = κεἰ, καὶ εἰς = κεἰς); also before ο in καὶ ὅτε = χὤτε, καὶ ὅπως = χὤπως (64).

N. — The exceptions in 68 a–c to the laws of contraction are due to the desire to let the vowel of the more important word prevail: ἅνηρ, not ὡνηρ, because of ἀνήρ.

69. Most crasis forms of ἕτερος *other* are derived from ἅτερος, the earlier form: thus, ὁ ἕτερος = ἅτερος, οἱ ἕτεροι = ἅτεροι; but τοῦ ἑτέρου = θοὐτέρου (64).

ELISION

70. Elision is the expulsion of a short vowel at the end of a word before a word beginning with a vowel. An apostrophe (') marks the place where the vowel is elided.

ἀλλ' (ὰ) ἄγε, ἔδωκ' (α) ἐννέα, ἐφ' (= ἐπί) ἑαυτοῦ (64), ἔχοιμ' (ι) ἄν, γένοιτ' (ο) ἄν.

a. Elision is often not expressed to the eye except in poetry. Both inscriptions and the Mss. of prose writers are very inconsistent, but even where the elision is not expressed, it seems to have occurred in speaking; *i.e.* ὅδε εἶπε and ὅδ' εἶπε were spoken alike. The Mss. are of little value in such cases.

71. Elision affects only unimportant words or syllables, such as particles, adverbs, prepositions, and conjunctions of two syllables (except περί, ἄχρι, μέχρι, ὅτι 72 b, c), and the final syllables of nouns, pronouns, and verbs.

a. The final vowel of an emphatic personal pronoun is rarely elided.

72. Elision does not occur in

a. Monosyllables, except such as end in ε (τέ, δέ, γέ).

b. The conjunction ὅτι *that* (ὅτ' is ὅτε *when*).

c. The prepositions πρό *before*, ἄχρι, μέχρι *until*, and περί *concerning* (except before ι).

d. The dative singular ending ι of the third declension, and in σι, the ending of the dative plural.

e. Words with final υ.

73. Except ἐστί *is*, forms admitting movable ν (134 a) do not suffer elision in prose. (But some cases of ε in the perfect occur in Demosthenes.)

74. αι in the personal endings and the infinitive is elided in Aristophanes; scarcely ever, if at all, in tragedy; its elision in prose is doubtful. οι is elided in tragedy in οἴμοι *alas*.

---

68 D. Hom. has ὥριστος = ὁ ἄριστος, ωὐτός = ὁ αὐτός. Hdt. has οὕτερος = ὁ ἕτερος, ὡνήρ = ὁ ἀνήρ, ὡυτοί = οἱ αὐτοί, τὠυτό = τὸ αὐτό, τὠυτοῦ = τοῦ αὐτοῦ, ἑωυτοῦ = ἕο αὐτοῦ, ὦνδρες = οἱ ἄνδρες. Doric has κἠπί = καὶ ἐπί.

72 D. Absence of elision in Homer often proves the loss of ϝ (3), as in κατὰ ἄστυ X 1. Epic admits elision in σά *thy*, ῥά, in the dat. sing. of the third decl., in -σι and -αι in the personal endings, and in -ναι, -σθαι of the infinitive, and (rarely) in μοί, σοί, τοί. ἄνα *oh king*, and ἄνα = ἀνάστηθι *rise up*, elide only once, ἰδέ *and* never. Hdt. elides less often than Attic prose; but the Mss. are not a sure guide. περί sometimes appears as πέρ in Doric and Aeolic before words beginning with other vowels than ι. ὀξεῖ' ὀδύναι Λ 272. Cp. 148 D. 1.

73 D. In poetry a vowel capable of taking movable ν is often cut off.

75. Interior elision takes place in forming compound words. Here the apostrophe is not used. Thus, οὐδείς *no one* from οὐδὲ εἷς, καθοράω *look down upon* from κατὰ ὁράω, μεθίημι *let go* from μετὰ ἵημι (124).

a. ὁδί, τουτί *this* are derived from the demonstrative pronouns ὅδε, τοῦτο + the deictic ending ῑ (333 g) which is always accented.

b. Interior elision does not always occur in the formation of compounds. Thus, σκηπτοῦχος *sceptre-bearing* from σκηπτο + οχος (*i.e.* σοχος). Cp. 878.

c. On the accent in elision, see 174.

APHAERESIS (INVERSE ELISION)

76. Aphaeresis (ἀφαίρεσις *taking away*) is the elision of ε at the beginning of a word after a word ending in a long vowel or diphthong. This occurs only in poetry, and chiefly after μή *not*, ἤ *or*. Thus, μὴ 'νταῦθα, ἢ 'μέ, παρέξω 'μαυτόν, αὐτὴ 'ξῆλθεν. In some texts editors prefer to adopt crasis (62) or synizesis (60). α is rarely elided thus.

EUPHONY OF CONSONANTS

77. Assimilation. — A consonant is sometimes assimilated to another consonant in the same word. This assimilation may be either *partial*, as in ἐ-πέμφ-θην *I was sent* for ἐ-πεμπ-θην (82), or *complete*, as in ἐμμένω *I abide by* for ἐν-μενω (94).

a. A preceding consonant is generally assimilated to a following consonant. Assimilation to a preceding consonant, as in ὄλλῡμι *I destroy* for ὀλ-νῡ-μι, is rare.

DOUBLING OF CONSONANTS

78. Attic has ττ for σσ of Ionic and most other dialects: πράττω *do* for πράσσω, θάλαττα *sea* for θάλασσα, κρείττων *stronger* for κρείσσων.

a. Tragedy and Thucydides adopt σσ as an Ionism. On χαρίεσσα see 114 a.

b. ττ is used for that σσ which is regularly formed by κ or χ and ι (112), sometimes by τ, θ, and ι (114). On ττ in 'Αττικός see 83 a.

---

75 D. Apocope (ἀποκοπή *cutting off*) occurs when a final short vowel is cut off before an initial consonant. In literature apocope is confined to poetry, but in the prose inscriptions of the dialects it is frequent. Thus, in Hom., as separate words and in compounds, ἄν, κάτ, πάρ (ἀπ, ὑπ rarely) for ἀνά, κατά, παρά (ἀπό, ὑπό). Final τ is assimilated to a following consonant (but κατθανεῖν *to die*, not καθθανεῖν, cp. 83 a); so final ν by 91–95. Thus, ἀλλέξαι *to pick up*, ἂμ πόνον *into the strife*; κάββαλε *threw down*, κάλλιπε *left behind*, κακκείοντες lit. *lying down*, κανάξαις *break in pieces*, for καϝϝάξαις = κατ-ϝάξαις, κὰδ δέ, καδδῦσαι *entering into*, κὰπ πεδίον *through the plain*, κὰγ γόνυ *on the knee* (*kag* not *kang*), κὰρ ῥόον *in the stream*; ὑββάλλειν *interrupt*, ἀππέμψει *will send away*. When three consonants collide, the final consonant of the apocopate word is usually lost, as κάκτανε *slew*, from κάκκτανε out of κατ(έ)κτανε. Apocope occurs rarely in Attic poetry. πότ for ποτί (= πρός in meaning) is frequent in Doric and Boeotian.

N. — The shorter forms may have originated from elision.

79. Later Attic has ρρ for ρσ of older Attic: **θάρρος** *courage* = **θάρσος**, ἄρρην *male* = ἄρσην.

a. But ρσ does not become ρρ in the dative plural (ῥήτορ-σι *orators*) and in words containing the suffix -σις for -τις (ἄρ-σις *raising*).

b. Ionic and most other dialects have ρσ. ρσ in Attic tragedy and Thucydides is probably an Ionism. Xenophon has ρσ and ρρ.

80. An initial ρ is doubled when a simple vowel is placed before it in inflection or composition. Thus, after the syllabic augment (429), ἔ-ρρει *was flowing* from ῥέω; and in καλλί-ρροος *fair flowing.* After a diphthong ρ is not doubled: **εὔ-ροος** *fair flowing.*

a. This ρρ, due to assimilation of σρ (ἔ-ρρει, καλλί-ρροος), or ϝρ (ἐρρήθη *was spoken*), is strictly *retained* in the interior of a word; but simplified to single ρ when standing at the beginning, *i.e.* ῥέω is for ρρέω. In composition (εὔ-ροος) single ρ is due to the influence of the simplified initial sound.

b. A different ρρ arises from assimilation of ρσ (79), ρε (sounded like ρy, 44, 117), and νρ (95).

81. β, γ, δ are not doubled in Attic (cp. 75 D.). In γγ the first γ is nasal (19 a). φ, χ, θ are not doubled in Attic; instead, we have πφ, κχ, τθ as in Σαπφώ *Sappho*, Βάκχος *Bacchus*, Ἀτθίς (*Atthis*) *Attic*. Cp. 83 a.

CONSONANTS WITH CONSONANTS

STOPS BEFORE STOPS

82. A labial or a palatal stop (16) before a dental stop (τ, δ, θ) must be of the same order (16).

a. **βτ, φτ** become **ππ**: (τετρῖβ-ται) τέτρῖπται *has been rubbed* from τρίβ-ω *rub;* (γεγραφ-ται) γέγραπται *has been written* from γράφ-ω *write.* **γτ, χτ** become **κτ**: (λελεγ-ται) λέλεκται *has been said* from λέγ-ω *say;* (βεβρεχ-ται) βέβρεκται *has been moistened* from βρέχ-ω *moisten.*

---

80 D. In Hom. and even in prose ρ may remain single after a vowel: ἔ-ρεξε *did* from ῥέζω, καλλί-ροος. So ἰσό-ρροπος and ἰσό-ροπος (by analogy to ῥόπος) *equally balanced.* ἐκ χειρῶν βέλεᾱ ῥέον M 159 represents βέλεα ρρέον. Cp. 146 D.

81 D. 1. Hom. has many cases of doubled **liquids** and **nasals**: ἔλλαβε *took*, ἄλληκτος *unceasing*, ἄμμορος *without lot in*, φιλομμειδής *fond of smiles*, ἀγάννιφος *very snowy*, ἀργεννός *white*, ἔννεπε *relate.* These forms are due to the assimilation of σ and λ, μ, or ν. Thus, ἀγά-ννιφος is from ἀγα-σνιφος, cp. *sn* in *snow.*

2. Doubled **stops**: ὅττι *that* (σϝοδ-τι), ὁππότε *as* (σϝοδ-ποτε), ἔδδεισε *feared* (ἐδϝεισε).

3. **σσ** in μέσσος *middle* (for μεθιος *medius*, 114), ὀπίσσω *backward*, in the datives of σ-stems, as ἔπεσσι (250 D. 2), and in verbs with stems in σ (τρέσσε).

4. One of these doubled consonants may be dropped without lengthening the preceding vowel: Ὀδυσεύς from Ὀδυσσεύς, μέσος, ὀπίσω. So in Ἀχιλεύς from Ἀχιλλεύς. On δδ, ββ, see 75 D. Aeolic has many doubled consonants due to assimilation (37 D. 3).

b. **πδ, φδ** become **βδ**: (κλεπ-δην) κλέβδην *by stealth* from κλέπ-τ-ω *steal*; (γραφδην) γράβδην *scraping* from γράφ-ω *write* (originally *scratch, scrape*). **κδ** becomes **γδ**: (πλεκ-δην) πλέγδην *entwined* from πλέκ-ω *plait*.

c. **πθ, βθ** become **φθ**: (ἐπεμπ-θην) ἐπέμφθην *I was sent* from πέμπ-ω *send*; (ἐτρῑβ-θη) ἐτρίφθη *it was rubbed* (τρίβ-ω *rub*). **κθ, γθ** become **χθ**: (ἐπλεκ-θη) ἐπλέχθη *it was plaited* (πλέκ-ω *plait*); (ἐλεγ-θη) ἐλέχθη *it was said* (λέγ-ω *say*).

N. 1.—Cp. ἑπτά *seven*, ἕβδομος *seventh*, ἑφθήμερος *lasting seven days*.

N. 2.—But ἐκ *out of* remains unchanged: ἐκδίδωμι *surrender*, ἐκθέω *run out* (104).

83. A dental stop before another dental stop becomes σ.

ἀνυστός *practicable* for ἀνυτ-τος from ἀνύτω *complete*, ἴστε *you know* for ἰδ-τε, οἶσθα *thou knowest* for οἰδ-θα, πέπεισται *has been persuaded* for πεπειθ-ται, ἐπείσθην *I was persuaded* for ἐπειθ-θην.

a. ττ, τθ remain unchanged in Ἀττικός, Ἀτθίς *Attic*, and in κατθανεῖν *die* (75 D., 81). So ττ for σσ (78).

84. Any stop standing before a stop other than τ, δ, θ, or in other combination than πφ, κχ, τθ (81) is dropped, as in κεκόμι(δ)-κα *I have brought*. γ before κ, γ, or χ is gamma-nasal (19 a), not a stop.

STOPS BEFORE M

85. Before μ, the labial stops (π, β, φ) become μ; the palatal stops κ, χ become γ; γ before μ remains unchanged.

ὄμμα *eye* for ὀπ-μα (cp. ὄπωπα), λέλειμμαι *I have been left* for λελειπ-μαι from λείπ-ω *leave*, τέτρῑμμαι for τετρῑβ-μαι from τρίβ-ω *rub*, γέγραμμαι for γεγραφ-μαι from γράφ-ω *write*, πέπλεγμαι for πεπλεκ-μαι from πλέκ-ω *plait*, τέτευγμαι for τετευχ-μαι from τεύχ-ω *build*.

a. κ and χ may remain unchanged before μ in a noun-suffix: ἀκ-μή *edge*, δραχ-μή *drachma*. κμ remains when brought together by phonetic change (128 a), as in κέ-κμη-κα *am wearied* (κάμ-νω).

b. γγμ and μμμ become γμ and μμ. Thus, ἐλήλεγμαι for ἐληλεγγ-μαι from ἐληλεγχ-μαι (ἐλέγχ-ω *convict*), πέπεμμαι for πεπεμμ-μαι from πεπεμπ-μαι (πέμπ-ω *send*).

86. A dental stop (τ, δ, θ) before μ often appears to become σ. Thus, ἤνυσμαι for ἠνυτ-μαι (ἀνύτ-ω *complete*), πέφρασμαι for πεφραδ-μαι (φράζω *declare*), πέπεισμαι for πεπειθ-μαι (πείθ-ω *persuade*).

87. On the other hand, since these stops are actually retained in many words, such as ἐρετμόν *oar*, πότμος *fate*, ἀριθμός *number*, σ must be explained as due to analogy. Thus, ἤνυσμαι, πέφρασμαι, πέπεισμαι have taken on the ending -σμαι by analogy to -σται where σ is in place (πέφρασται for πεφραδ-ται). So ἴσμεν *we know* (Hom. ἴδμεν) follows ἴστε *you know* (for ἰδ-τε). ὀσμή *odor* stands for ὀδ-σμη.

---

85 a. D. So in Hom. ἴκμενος *favoring* (ἱκάνω), ἀκαχμένος *sharpened*.

CONSONANTS BEFORE N

88. *β* regularly and *φ* usually become *μ* before *ν*. Thus, **σεμνός** *revered* for *σεβ-νος* (*σέβ-ομαι*), *στυμνός firm* for *στυφ-νος* (*στῡ́φω contract*).

89. *γίγνομαι become*, *γιγνώσκω know* become *γίνομαι*, *γῑνώσκω* in Attic after 300 B.C., in New Ionic, late Doric, etc.

90. *λν* becomes *λλ* in *ὄλλῡμι destroy* for *ὀλ-νῡμι*.

λν is kept in *πίλναμαι approach*. On sigma before *ν* see 105.

N BEFORE CONSONANTS

91. *ν* before *π*, *β*, *φ*, *ψ* becomes *μ*: *ἐμπίπτω fall into* for *ἐν-πῑπτω*, *ἐμβάλλω throw in* for *ἐν-βαλλω*, *ἐμφαίνω exhibit* for *ἐν-φαινω*, *ἔμψῡχος alive* for *ἐν-ψῡχος*.

92. *ν* before *κ*, *γ*, *χ*, *ξ* becomes *γ*-nasal (19 a): *ἐγκαλέω bring a charge* for *ἐν-καλεω*, *ἐγγράφω inscribe* for *ἐν-γραφω*, *συγχέω pour together* for *συν-χεω*, *συγξῡ́ω grind up* for *συν-ξῑω*.

93. *ν* before *τ*, *δ*, *θ* remains unchanged. Here *ν* may represent *μ*: *βρον-τή thunder* (*βρέμ-ω roar*).

94. *ν* before *μ* becomes *μ*: *ἔμμετρος moderate* for *ἐν-μετρος*, *ἐμμένω abide by* for *ἐν-μενω*.

a. Verbs in *-νω* may form the perfect middle in *-σμαι* (489 h); as in *πέφασμαι* (from *φαίνω show*) for *πεφαν-μαι* (cp. *πέφαγ-κα*, *πέφαν-ται*).

b. Here *ν* does not *become σ*; but the ending *-σμαι* is borrowed from verbs with stems in a dental (as *πέφρασμαι*, on which see 87).

95. *ν* before *λ*, *ρ* is assimilated (*λλ*, *ρρ*): *σύλλογος concourse* for *συν-λογος*, *συρρέω flow together* for *συν-ρεω*.

96. *ν* before *σ* is dropped and the preceding vowel is lengthened (*ε* to *ει*, *ο* to *ου*, 37): *μέλᾱς black* for *μελαν-ς*, *εἷς one* for *ἑν-ς*, *τιθείς placing* for *τιθεν(τ)-ς*, *τούς* for *τόν-ς*.

a. But in the dative plural *ν* before *-σι* appears to be dropped without compensatory lengthening: *μέλασι* for *μελαν-σι*, *δαίμοσι* for *δαιμον-σι divinities*, *φρεσί* for *φρεν-σι mind*. But see 250 N.

CONSONANTS BEFORE Σ

97. With *σ* a labial stop forms *ψ*, a palatal stop forms *ξ*.

λείψω	*shall leave*	for *λειπ-σω*		*κῆρυξ*	*herald*	for *κηρυκ-ς*
τρίψω	*shall rub*	" *τρῑβ-σω*		*ἄξω*	*shall lead*	" *ἀγ-σω*
γράψω	*shall write*	" *γραφ-σω*		*βήξ*	*cough*	" *βηχ-ς*

---

90 D. Aeolic *βόλλα council*, Attic *βουλή* and Doric *βωλά* (with compensatory lengthening), probably for *βολνᾱ*.

a. The only stop that can stand before σ is π or κ, hence β, φ become π, and γ, χ become κ. Thus, γραφ-σω, ἀγ-σω become γραπ-σω, ἀκ-σω.

98. A dental stop before σ is assimilated (σσ) and one σ is dropped.

σώμασι *bodies* for σωμασσι out of σωματ-σι, ποσί *feet* for ποσσί out of ποδ-σι, ὄρνῑσι *birds* for ὀρνῑσσι out of ὀρνῑθ-σι. So πάσχω *suffer* for πασσχω out of παθ-σκω (cp. παθ-εῖν and 126).

a. δ and θ first become τ before σ: ποδ-σι, ὀρνῑθ-σι become ποτ-σι, ὀρνῑτ-σι.

99. κ is dropped before σκ in διδα(κ)-σκω *teach* (διδακ-τός *taught*).
π is dropped before σφ in βλα(π)σ-φημίᾱ *evil-speaking*.

100. ντ, νδ, νθ before σ form νσσ (98), then νσ, finally ν is dropped and the preceding vowel is lengthened (37).

πᾶσι *all* for πανσ-σι out of παντ-σι, τιθεῖσι *placing* for τιθενσ-σι out of τιθεντ-σι. So γίγᾱς *giant* for γιγαντ-ς, λύουσι *loosing* for λῡοντ-σι, σπείσω *shall make libation* for σπενδ-σω, πείσομαι *shall suffer* for πενθ-σομαι (πένθος *grief*).

101. a ἐν *in*, σύν *with* in composition are treated as follows:

ἐν before ρ, σ, or ζ keeps its ν: ἔν-ρυθμος *in rhythm*, ἐν-σκευάζω *prepare*, ἐν-ζεύγνῡμι *yoke in*.

σύν before σ and a vowel becomes συσ-: συσ-σῴζω *help to save*.
before σ and a consonant or ζ, becomes συ-: συ-σκευάζω *pack up*, σύ-ζυγος *yoked together*.

b. πᾶν, πάλιν before σ either keep ν or assimilate ν to σ: πάν-σοφος *all-wise*, παν-σέληνος or πασσέληνος *the full moon*, παλίν-σκιος *thick-shaded*, παλίσ-συτος *rushing back*.

102. On ρσ see 79 a. λσ is retained in ἄλσος *precinct*. ρσ, λσ may become ρ, λ with lengthening of the preceding vowel: ἤγειρα *I collected*, ἤγγειλα *I announced* for ἠγερ-σα, ἠγγελ-σα.

Σ BEFORE CONSONANTS

103. Sigma between consonants is dropped: ἤγγελ(σ)θε *you have announced*, γεγράφ(σ)θαι *to have written*, ἕκ(σ)μηνος *of six months* (ἕξ *six*, μήν *month*).

a. But in compounds σ is retained when the second part begins with σ: ἔν-σπονδος *included in a truce*. Compounds in δυσ- *ill* omit σ before a word beginning with σ: δύσχιστος *hard to cleave* for δυσ-σχιστος (σχίζω).

104. ἐξ *out of* (= ἐκς) drops σ in composition before another consonant, but usually retains its κ unaltered: ἐκτείνω *stretch out*, ἐκδίδωμι *surrender*,

---

98 D. Hom. often retains σσ: ποσσί, δάσσασθαι for δατ-σασθαι (δατέομαι *divide*).

102 D. Hom. has ὦρσε *incited*, κέρσε *cut*, ἔλσαι *to coop up*, κέλσαι *to put to shore*.

ἐκφέρω carry out, *ἐκθύω sacrifice*, *ἐκσῴζω preserve from danger* (not ἐξσῴζω), *ἐκμανθάνω learn thoroughly*. Cp. 82 N. 2, 136.

105. σ before μ or ν usually disappears with compensatory lengthening (37) as in εἰμί for ἐσ-μι. But σμ stays if μ belongs to a suffix and in compounds of δυσ- *ill*: δυσ-μενής *hostile*.

a. Assimilation takes place in Πελοπόννησος for Πέλοπος νῆσος *island of Pelops*, ἕννυμι *clothe* for ἑσ-νυμι (Ionic εἵνυμι), ἔρρει *was flowing* for ἐ-σρει, 80 a.

106. σδ becomes ζ in some adverbs denoting *motion towards*. Thus, Ἀθήναζε for Ἀθήνας-δε *Athens-wards* (26, 342 a).

107. Two sigmas brought together by inflection become σ: βέλεσι for βέλεσ-σι *missiles*, ἔπεσι for ἔπεσ-σι *words* (98), τελέσαι for τελέσ-σαι (from τελέω *accomplish*, stem τελεσ-).

a. σσ when = ττ (78) never becomes σ.

108. Many of the rules for the euphony of consonants were not established in the classical period. Inscriptions show a much freer practice, either marking the etymology, as σύνμαχος for σύμμαχος *ally* (94), ἐνκαλεῖν for ἐγκαλεῖν *to bring a charge* (92), or showing the actual pronunciation (phonetic spelling), as τὸγ (= τὸν) κακόν (92), τὴμ (= τὴν) βουλήν (91), τὸλ (= τὸν) λόγον, ἔγδοσις for ἔκδοσις *surrendering* (104), ἐχφέρω, ἐχθύω for ἐκφέρω, ἐκθύω (104).

CONSONANTS WITH VOWELS

CONSONANTS BEFORE I AND E

109. Numerous changes occur before the semivowel ι̯ (= *y*, 20) before a vowel. This *y* is often indicated by the sign ι̯. In 110–117 (except in 115) ι̯ is = *y*.

110. λι̯ becomes λλ: ἄλλος for ἀλι̯ος Lat. *alius*, ἄλλομαι for ἀλι̯ομαι Lat. *salio*, φύλλον for φυλι̯ον Lat. *folium*.

111. After αν, ον, αρ, ορ, ι̯ is shifted to the preceding syllable, forming αιν, οιν, αιρ, οιρ. This is called *Epenthesis* (ἐπένθεσις *insertion*) and is more exactly a partial assimilation of the preceding vowel sound to the following consonantal ι.

φαίνω *show* for φαν-ι̯ω, μέλαινα *black* for μελαν-ι̯α, σπαίρω *gasp* for σπαρ-ι̯ω, μοῖρα *fate* for μορ-ι̯α. (So κλαίω *weep* for κλαϝ-ι̯ω 38 a.) On ι after εν, ερ, ιν, ιρ, υν, υρ, see 37 a.

112. κι̯, χι̯ become ττ (= σσ 78): φυλάττω *guard* for φυλακ-ι̯ω (cp. φυλακή *guard*), ταράττω *disturb* for ταραχ-ι̯ω (cp. ταραχή *disorder*).

---

105 D. σ is assimilated in Aeol. and Hom. ἔμμεναι *to be* for ἐσ-μεναι (εἶναι), ἀργεννός *white* for ἀργεσ-νος, ἐρεβεννός *dark* (ἐρεβεσ-νος, cp. Ἔρεβος), ἄμμε *we*, ὔμμες *you* (ἀσμε, ὐσμες). Cp. 81 D.

106 D. Aeolic has σδ for medial ζ in ὔσδος *branch* (ὄζος), μελίσδω *make melody* (μελίζω). Cf. 26 D.

107 D. Homer often retains σσ: βέλεσσι, ἔπεσσι, τελέσσαι.

113. (I) τι̯, θι̯ after long vowels, diphthongs, and consonants become σ; after short vowels τι̯, θι̯ become σσ (not = ττ 78), which is simplified to σ.

αἶσα *fate* from αἰτ-ι̯α, πᾶσα *all* from παντ-ι̯α, μέσος *middle* (Hom. μέσσος) from μεθ-ι̯ος (cp. Lat. *med-ius*), τόσος *so great* (Hom. τόσσος) from τοτ-ι̯ος (cp. Lat. *toti-dem*).

a. In the above cases τι̯ passed into τσ. Thus παντ-ι̯α, παντσα, πανσσα, πάνσα (Cretan, Thessalian), πᾶσα (37 D. 3).

114. (II) τι̯, θι̯ become ττ (= σσ 78): μέλιττα *bee* from μελιτ-ι̯α (cp. μέλι, -ιτος *honey*), κορύττω *equip* from κορυθ-ι̯ω (cp. κόρυς, -υθος *helmet*).

a. χαρίεσσα *graceful* and other feminine adjectives in -εσσα are poetical, and therefore do not assume the native Attic prose form in ττ. But see 299 c.

b. ττ from τι̯, θι̯ is due to analogy, chiefly of ττ from κι̯.

115. τ before final ι often becomes σ. Thus, τίθησι *places* for τίθητι; also in πλούσιος *rich* for πλουτ-ιος (cp. πλοῦτος *wealth*).

a. ντ before final ι becomes νσ, which drops ν: ἔχουσι *they have* for ἔχοντι (37).

116. δι̯ between vowels and γι̯ after a vowel form ζ: thus, ἐλπίζω *hope* for ἐλπιδ-ι̯ω, πεζός *on foot* for πεδ-ι̯ος (cp. πεδ-ίο-ν *ground*), ἁρπάζω *seize* for ἁρπαγ-ι̯ω (cp. ἅρπαξ *rapacious*). After a consonant γι̯ forms δ: ἔρδω *work* from ἐργ-ι̯ω.

117. πι̯ becomes πτ, as in χαλέπτω *oppress* from χαλεπ-ι̯ω. ρε̯ becomes ρρ in Βορρᾶς from Βορέᾱς *Boreas*. Here ε was sounded nearly like *y* (44, 61 a).

DISAPPEARANCE OF Σ AND F

118. The spirant σ with a vowel before or after it is often lost. Its former presence is known by earlier Greek forms or from the cognate languages.

119. Initial σ before a vowel becomes the rough breathing.

ἑπτά *seven*, Lat. *septem*; ἥμισυς *half*, Lat. *semi-*; ἵστημι *put* for σι-στη-μι, Lat. *si-st-o*; εἱπόμην *I followed* from ἐ-σεπ-ο-μην, Lat. *sequor*.

a. When retained, this σ is due to phonetic change (as σύν for ξύν, σῑγή *silence* for σϝῑγη Germ. *schweigen*), or to analogy. On the loss of ʽ see 125 e.

120. Between vowels σ is dropped.

γένους *of a race* from γενε(σ)-ος, Lat. *gener-is*, λύει *thou loosest* from λύῃ for λῡε-(σ)αι, ἐλύου from ἐλῡε-(σ)ο *thou didst loose for thyself*, τιθεῖο for τιθεῖσο, εἴην from ἐσ-ιη-ν Old Lat. *siem*, ἀλήθε-ια *truth* from ἀληθεσ-ια.

---

115 D. Doric often retains τ (τίθητι, ἔχοντι). σέ is not from (Dor.) τέ (cp. Lat. *te*), nor is σοί from τοί.

a. Yet σ appears in some -μι forms (*τίθεσαι, ἵστασο*), and in *θρασύς* = *θαρσύς* 128. σ between vowels is due to phonetic change (as σ for σσ 107, *πλούσιος* for *πλουτιος* 115) or to analogy (as *ἔλῡσα* for *ἔλῡα*, modelled on *ἔδεικ-σ-α*), cp. 35 c.

121. σ usually disappears in the aorist of liquid verbs (active and middle) with lengthening of the preceding vowel (37): *ἔστειλα* *I sent* for *ἐστελ-σα*, *ἔφηνα* *I showed* for *ἐφαν-σα*, *ἐφήνατο* for *ἐφαν-σατο*. Cp. 102.

122. Digamma (3) has disappeared in Attic.

The following special cases are to be noted:

a. In nouns of the third declension with a stem in αυ, ευ, or ου (43). Thus, *ναῦς* *ship*, gen. *νεώς* from *νηϝ-ός*, *βασιλεύς* *king*, gen. *βασιλέως* from *βασιλῆϝ-ος* (34).

b. In the augment and reduplication of verbs beginning with ϝ: *εἰργαζόμην* *I worked* from *ἐ-ϝεργαζομην*, *ἔοικα* *am like* from *ϝεϝοικα*. Cp. 431, 443.

c. In verbs in εω for εϝω: *ῥέω* *I flow*, fut. *ῥεύ-σομαι*.

123. Some words have lost initial σϝ: *ἡδύς* *sweet* (Lat. *sua(d)vis*), *οὗ, οἷ, ἕ* *him*, *ὅς* *his* (Lat. *suus*), *ἔθος* *custom*, *ἦθος* *character* (Lat. *con-suetus*).

ASPIRATION

124. A smooth stop (π, τ, κ), brought before the rough breathing by elision, crasis, or in forming compounds, is made rough, becoming an aspirate (φ, θ, χ). Cp. 16 a.

ἀφ' οὗ for *ἀπ(ὸ) οὗ*, *νύχθ' ὅλην* for *νύκτ(α) ὅλην* (82); *θἅτερον* *the other* (69), *θοἰμάτιον* for *τὸ ἱμάτιον* *the cloak* (66); *μεθίημι* *let go* for *μετ(ὰ) ἵημι*, *αὐθάδης* *self-willed* from *αὐτός* *self* and *ἁδεῖν* *please*.

a. A medial rough breathing, passing over ρ, roughens a preceding smooth stop: *φρουρός* *watchman* from *προ-όρος*, *φροῦδος* *gone* from *πρό* and *ὁδός*, *τέθριππον* *four-horse chariot* (*τετρ* + *ἵππος*).

125. Two rough stops beginning successive syllables of the same word are avoided in Greek. A rough stop is changed into a smooth stop when the following syllable contains a rough stop.

a. In reduplication (441) initial φ, θ, χ are changed to π, τ, κ. Thus, *πέφευγα* for *φε-φευ-γα* perfect of *φεύγω* *flee*, *τί-θη-μι* *place* for *θι-θη-μι*, *κέ-χη-να* for *χε-χη-να* perf. of *χάσκω* *gape*.

b. In the first aorist passive imperative -θι becomes -τι after -θη-, as in *λύ-θη-τι* for *λυ-θη-θι*; elsewhere -θι is retained (*γνῶθι*).

c. In the aorist passive, θε- and θυ- are changed to τε- and τυ- in *ἐ-τέ-θην* *was placed* (*τίθημι*) and *ἐ-τύ-θην* *was sacrificed* (*θύω*).

d. From the same objection to a succession of rough stops are due *ἀμπέχω* *ἀμπίσχω* *clothe* for *ἀμφ-*, *ἐκε-χειρίᾱ* *truce* for *ἐχε-χειριᾱ* (from *ἔχω* and *χείρ*).

---

123 D. Hom. *εὔαδε* *pleased* stands for *ἐϝϝαδε* from *ἐσϝαδε*.

124 D. New Ionic generally leaves π, τ, κ before the rough breathing: *ἀπ' οὗ*, *μετίημι*, *τοὔτερον*. But in compounds (9 D.) φ, θ, χ may appear: *μέθοδος* *method* (*μετά* *after* + *ὁδός* *way*).

e. The rough breathing, as an aspirate (16 a), often disappeared when either of the two following syllables contains φ, θ, or χ. ἔχω *have* stands for ἕχω = σεχω (119, cp. ἔ-σχον), the rough changing to the smooth breathing before a rough stop. The rough breathing reappears in the future ἕξω. Cp. ἴσχω *restrain* for ἱσχω from σι-σχ-ω, ἔδεθλον *foundation*, but ἕδος *seat*, Lat. *sedes*.

f. In θρίξ *hair*, gen. sing. τριχ-ός for θριχος, dat. pl. θριξί; ταχύς *swift*, comparative ταχίων (rare) or θάττων (θάσσων) from θαχῑων (112).

g. In ταφ- (τάφος *tomb*), pres. θάπ-τ-ω *bury*, fut. θάψω, perf. τέθαμ-μαι (85); τρέφω *nourish*, fut. θρέψω, perf. τέ-θραμ-μαι; τρέχω *run*, fut. θρέξομαι; τρυφ- (τρυφή *delicacy*), pres. θρύπτω *enfeeble*, fut. θρύψω; τύφω *smoke*, perf. τέ-θῡμ-μαι.

N. — The two rough stops remain unchanged in the aorist passive ἐθρέφθην *was nourished*, ἐθρύφθην *was enfeebled*, ἐφάνθην *was shown forth*, ὠρθώθην *was set upright*, ἐθέλχθην *was charmed*, ἐκαθάρθην *was purified;* in the perfect inf. πεφάνθαι, κεκαθάρθαι, τεθάφθαι; in the imperatives γράφηθι *be written*, στράφηθι *turn about*, φάθι *say*.

126. **Transfer of Aspiration.** — Aspiration may be transferred to a following syllable: πάσχω for παθ-σκω (cp. 98).

127. Some roots show variation between a final smooth and a rough stop; δέχομαι *receive*, δωροδόκος *bribe-taker;* ἀλείφω *anoint*, λίπος *fat;* πλέκω *weave*, πλοχμός *braid of hair;* and in the perfect, as ἦχα from ἄγω *lead*.

VARIOUS CONSONANT CHANGES

128. **Metathesis** (*transposition*). — A vowel and a consonant often exchange places: Πνύξ *the Pnyx*, gen. Πυκνός, τίκτω *bear* for τι-τκ-ω (cp. τεκ-εῖν).

a. Transposition proper does not occur where we have to do with αρ, ρα = ρ̣ (20, 35 b) as in θάρσος and θράσος *courage;* or with syncope (44 b) due to early shifting of accent, as in πέτ-ομαι *fly*, πτε-ρόν *wing;* or where a long vowel follows the syncopated root, as in τέμ-νω τέ-τμη-κα *I have cut*.

In βέβληκα *I have thrown* (βάλλω *throw*), βλη is formed from βελε found in βέλε-μνον *missile*.

129. **Dissimilation.** — **a.** λ sometimes becomes ρ when λ appears in the same word: ἀργαλέος *painful* for ἀλγαλεος (ἄλγος *pain*).

b. A consonant (usually ρ) sometimes disappears when it occurs also in the adjoining syllable: δρύφακτος *railing* for δρυ-φρακτος (lit. *fenced by wood*).

c. Syllabic dissimilation or syncope occurs when the same or two similar syllables containing the same consonant succeed each other: ἀμφορεύς *a jar* for ἀμφι-φορευς, θάρσυνος *bold* for θαρσο-συνος. This is often called *haplology*.

d. See also under 99, 125 a, b.

---

126 D. Hdt. has ἐνθαῦτα *there* (ἐνταῦθα), ἐνθεῦτεν *thence* (ἐντεῦθεν), κιθών *tunic* (χιτών). This last was a Semitic loan, perhaps variously adapted.

127 D. Hom. and Hdt. have αὖτις *again* (αὖθις), οὐκί *not* (οὐχί). All the dialects except Attic have δέκομαι.

128 D. Hom. κραδίη, καρδίη *heart*, κάρτιστος *best* (κράτιστος), βάρδιστος *slowest* (βραδύς), δρατός and -δαρτος from δέρω *flay*, ἔ-δρακον *saw* from δέρκομαι *see*.

130. Development. — δ is developed between ν and ρ, as in ἀνδρός *of a man* for ἀνρος from ἀνήρ (cp. *cinder* with Lat. *cineris*); β is developed between μ and ρ (or λ), as in μεσημβρίᾱ *midday, south* from μεσ-ημριᾱ for μεσ-ημεριᾱ from μέσος *middle* and ἡμέρᾱ *day* (cp. *chamber* with Lat. *camera*).

131. Labials and dentals often correspond: ποινή and τίσις *retribution; φόνος murder*, θείνω *strike*. π and κ: αἰπόλος *goat-herd*, βουκόλος *ox-herd*. πτ for τ is found in πτόλεμος *war*, πτόλις *city* for πόλεμος, πόλις. Cp. *Neoptolemus* and *Ptolemy*. So χθ and χ in χθών *ground*, χαμαί *on the ground*. (These phenomena are commented upon at length in the various Greek comparative grammars.)

132. The dialects often show consonants different from Attic in the same or kindred words.

FINAL CONSONANTS

133. No consonant except ν, ρ, or σ (including ξ and ψ) can stand at the end of a Greek word. All other consonants are dropped.

a. Exceptions are the proclitics (179) ἐκ *out of*, derived from ἐξ (cp. 104, 136), and οὐκ *not*, of which οὐ is another form (137).

b. Examples of dropped final consonants: σῶμα *body* for σωματ (gen. σώματ-ος); παῖ *oh boy* for παιδ (gen. παιδ-ός); γάλα *milk* for γαλακτ (gen. γάλακτ-ος); φέρον *bearing* for φεροντ (gen. φέροντ-ος); κῆρ *heart* for κηρδ, cp. καρδ-ίᾱ; ἄλλο for ἀλιοδ (110), cp. Lat. *aliud*; ἔφερε-(τ) *was carrying*, ἔφερο-ν(τ) *were carrying* (464 c, e).

c. An original final *m* preceded by a vowel becomes ν, cp. ἵππον with Lat. *equum*. So ἕν *one* from ἐμ (349 a), Lat. *sem-el*, ἅμα *once*.

---

130 D. So in Hom. μέ-μβλω-κα *have gone* from μλω from μολ- in ἔ-μολ-ο-ν (128 a). At the beginning of words this μ is dropped; thus, βλώσκω *go*, βροτός *mortal* for μβρο-τος (root μρο-, μορ-, as in *mor-tuus*). In composition μ remains, as in ἄ-μβροτος *immortal*; but ἄ-βροτος *immortal* is formed from βροτός.

132 D. **τ** for σ: Doric τύ, τοί, τέ, διᾱκατίοι (διᾱκόσιοι), ϝίκατι (εἴκοσι), Ποτειδᾶν (Ποσειδῶν).
σ " τ: Doric σάμερον *to-day* (τήμερον Attic, σήμερον Ionic).
κ " π: Ionic (not Hom.) κότε *when*, κότερος *which of two?* ὅκως, κόσος, κῇ.
κ " τ: Doric πόκα (πότε), ὅκα (ὅτε).
γ " β: Doric γλέφαρον *eyelid*, γλάχων (Ion. γλήχων) *pennyroyal*.
δ " β: Doric ὀδελός (ὀβολός) *a spit*.
π " τ: Hom. πίσυρες, Aeol. πέσσυρες *four* (τέτταρες); Aeol. πήλυι *far off* (cp. τηλόσε), πέμπε *five* (πέντε).
θ " τ: see 126 D.
φ " θ: Hom. φήρ *centaur* (θήρ *beast*).
ρ " σ: (*rhotacism*): late Laconian, Elean τίρ *who*, Thessal. Θεόρδοτος *god-given*.
σ " θ: late Laconian σιός for θεός *god* (26 D.).
ν " λ: Doric ἐνθεῖν *come*.

MOVABLE CONSONANTS

134. Movable N may be added at the end of a word when the next word begins with a vowel. Movable ν may be annexed to words ending in -σι; to the third person singular in -ε; and to ἐστί *is.*

Thus, πᾶσιν ἔλεγεν ἐκεῖνα *he said that to everybody* (but πᾶσι λέγουσι ταῦτα), λέγουσιν ἐμοί *they speak to me* (but λέγουσί μοι), ἔστιν ἄλλος *there is another* (187 b), Ἀθήνησιν ἦσαν *they were at Athens.*

a. Except ἐστί, words that add ν do not elide their final vowel (73).

b. Verbs in -εω never (in Attic) add -ν to the 3 sing. of the *contracted* form: εὖ ἐποίει αὐτόν *he treated him well.* But ᾔει *went* and pluperfects (as ᾔδει *knew*) may add ν.

N. — Movable ν is called ν ἐφελκυστικόν (*dragging after*).

135. Movable ν is usually written at the end of clauses, and at the end of a verse in poetry. To make a syllable long by position (144) the poets add ν before words beginning with a consonant. Prose inscriptions frequently use ν before a consonant.

136. Movable Σ appears in οὕτως *thus,* ἐξ *out of,* before vowels, οὕτω, ἐκ before consonants. Thus, οὕτως ἐποίει *he acted thus* but οὕτω ποιεῖ *he acts thus;* ἐξ ἀγορᾶς but ἐκ τῆς ἀγορᾶς *out of the market-place.*

a. εὐθύς means *straightway,* εὐθύ *straight towards.*

137. οὐκ *not* is used before the smooth breathing, οὐχ (cp. 124) before the rough breathing: οὐκ ὀλίγοι, οὐχ ἡδύς. Before all consonants οὐ is written: οὐ πολλοί, οὐ ῥᾴδιος. Standing alone or at the end of its clause οὐ is written οὔ (rarely οὔκ), as πῶς γὰρ οὔ; *for how not?* Cp. 180 a.

a. A longer form is οὐχί (Ion. οὐκί) used before vowels and consonants.

b. μηκέτι *no longer* derives its κ from the analogy of οὐκέτι *no longer.*

SYLLABLES

138. There are as many syllables in a Greek word as there are separate vowels or diphthongs: thus, ἀ-λή-θει-α *truth.*

139. The last syllable is called the *ultima;* the next to the last syllable is called the *penult* (paen-ultima *almost last*); the one before the penult is called the *antepenult* (ante-paen-ultima).

---

134 D. Hom. has ἐγώ(ν) *I,* ἄμμι(ν) *to us,* ὔμμι(ν) *to you,* σφί(ν) *to them.* The suffixes -φι and -θε vary with -φιν and -θεν: θεόφι(ν), πρόσθε(ν). Also κέ(ν) = Attic ἄν, νύ(ν) *now.* The Mss. of Hdt. avoid movable ν, but it occurs in Ionic inscriptions. Hdt. often has -θε for -θεν (πρόσθε *before,* ὄπισθε *behind*).

136 D. Several adverbs often omit ς without much regard to the following word: ἀμφί *about,* ἀμφίς (poet.), μέχρι, ἄχρι *until* (rarely μέχρις, ἄχρις), ἀτρέμας and ἀτρέμα *quietly,* πολλάκις *often* (πολλάκι Hom., Hdt.).

140. In pronouncing Greek words and in writing (at the end of the line) the rules commonly observed are these:

a. A single consonant standing between two vowels in one word belongs with the second vowel: ἄ-γω, σο-φί-ζω.

b. Any group of consonants that can begin a word, and a group formed by a stop with μ or ν, and by μν, belongs with the second vowel: τύ-πτω, ὄ-γδοος, ἄ-στρον, ἔ-χθος; πρᾶ-γμα, ἔ-θνος, λί-μνη.

c. A group of consonants that cannot begin a word is divided between two syllables: ἄν-θος, ἐλ-πίς, ἔρ-γμα. Doubled consonants are divided: θάλατ-τα.

d. Compounds divide at the point of union: εἰσ-φέρω, προσ-φέρω; ἀν-άγω, εἰσ-άγω, συν-έχω. (But the ancients often wrote ἀ-νάγω, εἰ-σάγω, προ-σελθεῖν, ἐ-ξάγω, δυ-σάρεστος.)

e. σ, when followed by one or more consonants, is either attached to the preceding vowel (ἄ-ρισ-τος), or, with the consonant, begins the following syllable (ἄ-ρι-στος). (The ancients were not consistent, and there is evidence for the pronunciation ἄ-ρισ-στος.)

f. The ancients divided ἐκ τούτου as ἐ-κ τού-του. This practice is now abandoned.

141. A syllable ending in a vowel is said to be open; one ending in a consonant is closed. Thus, in μή-τηρ *mother* the first syllable is open, the second closed.

QUANTITY OF SYLLABLES

142. A syllable is short when it contains a short vowel followed by a vowel or a single consonant: θε-ός *god*, ἐ-νό-μι-σα *I thought*.

143. A syllable is long by *nature* when it contains a long vowel or a diphthong: χώ-ρᾱ *country*, δοῦ-λος *slave*.

144. A syllable is long by *position* when its vowel precedes two consonants or a double consonant: ἵππος *horse*, ἐξ *out of*.

a. One or both of the two consonants lengthening a final syllable by position may belong to the next word: ἄλλο̄ς πολίτης, ἄλλο̄ κτῆμα.

b. Length by position does not affect the natural quantity of a vowel. Thus, both λέ-ξω *I shall say* and λή-ξω *I shall cease* have the first *syllable* long by position; but the first *vowel* is short in λέξω, long in λήξω.

145. A stop with a liquid after a short vowel need not make the preceding syllable long by position. A syllable containing a short vowel before a stop and a liquid is *common* (either short or long). When short, such syllables are said to have *weak* position.

Thus, in δάκρυ, πατρός, ὅπλον, τέκνον, τί δρᾷ the first syllable is either long or short as the verse requires. In Homer the syllable before a stop with a liquid is usually long; in Attic it is usually short.

---

144 D. ϝ may be one of the two consonants: πρὸς (ϝ)οἶκον (— — ◡).

a. The stop and the liquid making weak position must stand in the same word or in the same part of a compound. Thus, in ἐκ-λύω *I release* the first syllable is always long, but in ἔ-κλυε *he heard* it is common.

b. β, γ, δ before μ, or ν, and usually before λ, make the preceding syllable long by position. Thus, ἁγνός (_ ◡) *pure*, βιβλίον (⏒ ◡ ◡) *book*.

N. — 'Common' quantity has been explained as due to a difference in syllabic division. Thus, in τέκνον, the first syllable is closed (τέκ-νον); while in τέκνον the first syllable is open (τέ-κνον). Cp. 141.

146. The quantity of most syllables is usually apparent. Thus, syllables

a. with η, ω, or a diphthong, are long.

b. with ε, ο, before a vowel or a single consonant, are short.

c. with ε, ο, before two consonants, or a double consonant, are long.

d. with α, ι, υ, before two consonants, or a double consonant, are long.

N. — But syllables with ε, ο, or α, ι, υ before a stop and a liquid may be short (145). Cp. also 147 c.

147. The quantity of syllables containing α, ι, υ before a vowel or a single consonant must be learned by observation, especially in poetry. Note, however, that α, ι, υ are always long

a. when they have the circumflex accent: πᾶς, ὑμῖν.

b. when they arise from contraction (59) or crasis (62): γέρᾱ from γέραα, ἀργός *idle* from ἀ-εργος (but ἀργός *bright*), κἀγώ from καὶ ἐγώ.

c. ι and υ are generally short before ξ (except as initial sounds in augmented forms, 435) and α, ι, υ before ζ. Thus, κῆρυξ, ἐκήρυξα, πνίξω, ἁρπάζω, ἐλπίζω.

d. ας, ις, and υς are long when ν or ντ has dropped out before ς (96, 100).

e. The accent often shows the quantity (163, 164, 170).

148. A vowel standing before another vowel in a Greek word is not necessarily short (as it usually is in classical Latin).

---

146 D. In Hom. an initial liquid, nasal, and digamma (3) was probably doubled in pronunciation when it followed a short syllable carrying the rhythmic accent. Here a final short vowel appears in a long syllable: ἐνὶ μεγάροισι (◡ ⏑́ ◡ ◡ ⏑́ ◡), cp. 28 D. The lengthening is sometimes due to the former presence of σ or ϝ before the liquid or nasal: ὅτε λήξειεν ◡ ⏑́ _ ⏑́ ◡ (cp. ἄλληκτος *unceasing* for ἀ-σληκτος), τε ῥήξειν ⏑́ _ ⏑́ (cp. ἄρρηκτος *unbroken* for ἀ-ϝρηκτος). (Cp. 80 a, 80 D., 81 D.)

147 D. α, ι, υ in Hom. sometimes show a different quantity than in Attic. Thus, Att. κᾰλός, τῑνω, φθᾰνω, λύω, ἵημι, Hom. κᾱλός, τίνω, φθάνω (28), and λῡω and ῑ̆ημι usually.

148 D. 1. In Hom., and sometimes in the lyric parts of the drama, a syllable ending in a long vowel or diphthong is shortened before an initial vowel: ἄξω ἑλών (⏑́ ◡ ◡ ⏑́), εὔχεται εἶναι (⏑́ ◡ ◡ ⏑́ _), κλῦθί μευ ἀργυρότοξ' (⏑́ ◡ ◡ ⏑́ ◡ ◡ ⏑́). Here ι and υ have become semivowels (20, 43); thus, εὔχετα | yεἶναι, cp. 67. -ᾳ, -ῃ, -ῳ were shortened like ᾱ, η, ω. Thus, ἀσπέτῳ ὄμβρῳ (⏑́ ◡ ◡ ⏑́ _).

2. This shortening does not occur when the rhythmic accent falls upon the final syllable: ἀντιθέῳ Ὀδυσῆι (⏑́ ◡ ◡ ⏑́ ◡ ◡ ⏑́ ◡), ᾧ ἔνι (⏑́ ◡ ◡).

ACCENT

149. There are three accents in Greek. No Greek accent can stand farther back than the antepenult.

1. **Acute** (´): over short or long vowels and diphthongs. It may stand on ultima, penult, or antepenult: καλός, δαίμων, ἄνθρωπος.

2. **Circumflex** (῀): over vowels long by nature and diphthongs. It may stand on ultima or penult: γῆ, θεοῦ, δῶρον, τοῦτο.

3. **Grave** (`): over short or long vowels and diphthongs. It stands on the ultima only: τὸν ἄνδρα, τὴν τύχην, οἱ θεοὶ τῆς Ἑλλάδος.

150. The acute marks syllables pronounced in a raised tone. The grave is a low-pitched tone as contrasted with the acute. The circumflex combines acute and grave.

151. Accented syllables in Ancient Greek had a higher *pitch* (τόνος) than unaccented syllables, and it was the rising and falling of the pitch that made Ancient Greek a musical language. The Greek word for *accent* is προσῳδίᾱ (Lat. *accentus:* from *ad-cano*), *i.e.* 'song accompanying words.' Musical accent (elevation and depression of tone) is to be distinguished from quantity (duration of tone), and from rhythmic accent (stress of voice at fixed intervals when there is a regular sequence of long and short syllables).

N. — The accent heard in Modern Greek and English is a *stress-accent.* Stress is produced by strong and weak expiration, and takes account of accented syllables to the neglect of the quantity of unaccented syllables. Thus, shortly after Christ, ἄνθρωπος was often pronounced like a dactyl, φίλος like a trochee; and πρόσωπον, ἐννέα, were even written πρόσοπον, ἐννήα.

152. The marks of accent are placed over the vowel of the accented syllable. A diphthong has the accent over its second vowel (τοῦτο), except in the case of capital ᾳ, ῃ, ῳ (as ῞Αιδης, 5), where the accent stands before the first vowel.

153. A breathing is written before the acute and grave (οἵ, ἥ), but under the circumflex (ὦ, οὗτος). Accents and breathings are placed before capitals: Ὅμηρος, Ὧραι. The accent stands over a mark of diaeresis (8): κληῗδι.

154. The grave is written in place of a final acute on a word that is followed immediately by another word in the sentence. Thus, μετὰ τὴν μάχην *after the battle* (for μετά τήν μάχην). It is also sometimes placed on τὶς, τὶ (334), to distinguish these indefinite pronouns from the interrogatives τίς, τί.

a. An oxytone (157) changes its acute to the grave when followed by another word, except: (1) when the oxytone is followed by an enclitic (183 a); (2) in τίς, τί interrogative, as τίς οὗτος; *who's this?* (3) when an elided syllable follows

---

3. The shortening rarely occurs in the interior of a word. Thus, Hom. ἥρωος (— ◡ ◡), υἱόν (◡ ◡), in the Attic drama αὐτηΐ (— ◡ —), τοιοῦτος (◡ — ◡), ποιῶ (◡ —), often written ποῶ in inscriptions (cp. 43).

the accented syllable: νύχθ' ὅλην (124), not νὺχθ' ὅλην (174 a); (4) when a colon or period follows. (Usage varies before a comma.)

155. The ancients regarded the grave originally as belonging to every syllable not accented with the acute or circumflex; and some Mss. show this in practice, *e.g.* πὰγκρὰτής. Later it was restricted to its use as a substitute for a final acute.

156. The circumflex is formed from the union of the acute and the grave (ʹ‵ = ˆ), never from ‵ʹ. Thus, παῖς = πάὶς, εὖ = ἔὐ. Similarly, since every long vowel may be resolved into two short units (*morae*), τῶν may be regarded as = τόὸν. The circumflex was thus spoken with a rising tone followed by one of lower pitch. μοῦσα, δῆμος are thus = μόὺσα, δέὲμος; μούσης, δήμου are = μὸύσης, δὲέμου. In διδοῦσα (*i.e.* διδόὺσα) compared with διδούς the accent has receded (159) one *mora*.

a. The whole vowel receives the acute when the second short unit of a vowel long by nature is accented: Διί = Διί.

157. Words are named according to their accent as follows:

Oxytone (acute on the ultima): θήρ, καλός, λελυκώς.
Paroxytone (acute on the penult): λύω, λείπω, λελυκότος.
Proparoxytone (acute on the antepenult): ἄνθρωπος, παιδεύομεν.
Perispomenon (circumflex on the ultima): γῆ, θεοῦ.
Properispomenon (circumflex on the penult): πρᾶξις, μοῦσα.
Barytone (when the ultima is unaccented, 158): μοῦσα, μήτηρ, πόλεμος.

158. A word is called *barytone* (βαρύ-τονος *deep-toned, low-toned*) when it has no accent on the ultima. All paroxytones, proparoxytones, and properispomena are also barytones.

159. An accent is called *recessive* when it moves back as far from the end of the word as the quantity of the ultima permits (166). The quantity of the *penult* is here disregarded (τρέπωμεν). Cp. 178.

160. *Oxytone* (ὀξύς, *sharp* + τόνος) means 'sharp-toned,' *perispomenon* (περισπώμενος) 'turned-around' (*circumflectus*, 156). *Paroxytone* and *proparoxytone* are derived from ὀξύτονος with the prepositions παρά and πρό respectively. *Acute* corresponds to Lat. *acutus* (ὀξεῖα, *scil.* προσῳδίā).

161. The invention of the marks of accent is attributed to Aristophanes of Byzantium, librarian at Alexandria about 200 B.C. The use of signs served to fix the correct accentuation, which was becoming uncertain in the third century B.C.; marked the variation of dialect usage; and rendered the acquisition of Greek easier for foreigners. The signs for the accents (and the breathings) were not regularly employed in Mss. till after 600 A.D.

162. The position of the accent has to be learned by observation. But the kind of accent is determined by the following rules.

---

162 D. 1. Aeolic has recessive (159) accent in all words except prepositions and conjunctions. Thus, σόφος, Ζεῦς, *i.e.* Ζέὺς, αὖτος, λίπειν (= λιπεῖν), λίποντος (= λιπόντος), ἄμμες (= ἡμεῖς).

163. The antepenult, if accented, can have the acute only (ἄνθρωπος, βασίλεια *queen*, οἰκοφύλακος *of a house-guard*). If the ultima is long, either by nature or by position (144), the antepenult cannot take an accent: hence ἀνθρώπου (176 a), βασιλείᾱ *kingdom*, οἰκοφύλαξ.

a. Some nouns in -εως and -εων admit the acute on the antepenult. Thus, the genitive of nouns in -ις and -υς (πόλεως, πόλεων, ἄστεως), the forms of the *Attic* declension, as ἵλεως (289). So the Ionic genitive in -εω (πολίτεω); also some compound adjectives in -ως, as δύσερως *unhappy in love*, ὑψίκερως *lofty antlered*. On ὥντινων see 186.

164. The penult, if accented and long, takes the circumflex when the ultima is short by nature (νῆσος, ταῦτα). In all other cases it has the acute (φόβος, λελυκότος, τούτου).

a. Apparent exceptions are ὥστε, οὔτις, ἥδε (properly ἦδε). See 186.

b. A final syllable containing a vowel short by nature followed by ξ or ψ does not permit the acute to stand on the antepenult (οἰκοφύλαξ); but the circumflex may stand on the penult (κῆρυξ).

165. The ultima, if accented and short, has the acute (ποταμός); if accented and long, has either the acute (λελυκώς), or the circumflex (Περικλῆς).

166. When the ultima is long, the acute cannot stand on the antepenult, nor the circumflex on the penult. Thus, ἄνθρωπου and δῶρου are impossible.

167. When the ultima is short, a word, if accented

- **a.** on the ultima, has the acute: σοφός.
- **b.** on a short penult, has the acute: νόμος.
- **c.** on a long penult, has the circumflex: δῶρον.
- **d.** on the antepenult, has the acute: ἄνθρωπος.

168. When the ultima is long, a word, if accented

- **a.** on the ultima, has the acute or the circumflex: ἐγώ, σοφῶς.
- **b.** on the penult, has the acute: λέων, δαίμων.

169. Final -αι and -οι are regarded as short: μοῦσαι, βούλομαι, πρόπαλαι, ἄνθρωποι. But in the optative -αι and -οι are long (λύσαι, βουλεύοι), as in contracted syllables. So also in the locative οἴκοι *at home* (but οἶκοι *houses*).

a. The difference in the quantitative treatment of -αι and -οι depends on an original difference of accentuation that may have vanished in Greek. -αι and

---

2. Doric regarded final -οι (169) as long (ἀνθρώποι), and probably -αι in nouns (χώραι); made paroxytones the 3 pl. act. of the past tenses (ἐφέρον, ἐλύσαν) and such words as παίδες, γυναίκες, πτώκας; made perispomena the gen. masc. pl. of pronouns (τουτῶν, ἀλλῶν) and the gen. fem. pl. of adj. in -ος (ἀμφοτερᾶν). The substitution, in the accus. pl., of -ᾰς and -ος for -ᾱς and -ους, caused no change in the accent (πάσᾰς, ἀμπέλος).

-οι, when short, were pronounced with a clipped, or simple, tone; when long, with a drawled, or compound, tone.

170. The quantity of α, ι, υ (147) may often be learned from the accent. Thus, in θάλαττα, ἥμισυς, πῆχυς, δύναμις, μῆνις, the vowel of the last syllable must be short; in φίλος the ι must be short (otherwise φῖλος). Cp. 163.

ACCENT AS AFFECTED BY CONTRACTION, CRASIS, AND ELISION

171. **Contraction.** — If either of the syllables to be contracted had an accent, the contracted syllable has an accent. Thus:

a. A contracted antepenult has the acute: φιλεόμενος = φιλούμενος.

b. A contracted penult has the circumflex when the ultima is short; the acute, when the ultima is long: φιλέουσι = φιλοῦσι, φιλεόντων = φιλούντων.

c. A contracted ultima has the acute when the uncontracted form was oxytone: ἑσταώς = ἑστώς; otherwise, the circumflex: φιλέω = φιλῶ.

N. 1. — A contracted syllable has the circumflex only when, in the uncontracted form, an acute was *followed* by the (unwritten) grave (155, 156). Thus, Περικλέὴς = Περικλῆς, τῑμάὼ = τῑμῶ. In all other cases we have the acute: φιλὲόντων = φιλούντων, βεβὰώς = βεβώς.

N. 2. — Exceptions to 171 are often due to the analogy of other forms (236 a, 264 e, 279 a, 290 c, 309 a).

172. If neither of the syllables to be contracted had an accent, the contracted syllable has no accent: φίλεε = φίλει, γένεϊ = γένει, περίπλοος = περίπλους. For exceptions, see 236 b.

173. **Crasis.** — In crasis, the first word (as less important) loses its accent: τἀγαθά for τὰ ἀγαθά, τἄν for τὰ ἐν, κἀγώ for καὶ ἐγώ.

a. If the second word is a dissyllabic paroxytone with short ultima, it is uncertain whether, in crasis, the paroxytone remains or changes to properispomenon. In this book τοὔργον, τἄλλα are written for τὸ ἔργον, τὰ ἄλλα; but many scholars write τοὖργον, τἆλλα.

174. **Elision.** — In elision, oxytone prepositions and conjunctions lose their accent: παρ' (for παρὰ) ἐμοῦ, ἀλλ' (for ἀλλὰ) ἐγώ. In other oxytones the accent is thrown back to the penult: πόλλ' (for πολλὰ) ἔπαθον.

a. Observe that in πόλλ' ἔπαθον the acute is not changed to the grave (154 a, 3). A circumflex does not result from the recession of the accent. Thus, φήμ' (not φῆμ') ἐγώ for φημὶ ἐγώ. τινά and ποτέ, after a word which cannot receive their accent (183 d), drop their accent: οὕτω ποτ' ἦν.

ANASTROPHE

175. Anastrophe (ἀναστροφή *turning-back*) occurs in the case of oxytone prepositions of two syllables, which throw the accent back on the first syllable.

a. When the preposition follows its case: τούτων πέρι (for περὶ τούτων) *about these things.* No other preposition than περί follows its case in prose.

N. 1. — In poetry anastrophe occurs with the other dissyllabic prepositions (except ἀντί, ἀμφί, διά). In Homer a preposition following its verb and separated from it by tmesis (1650) also admits anastrophe (λούσῃ ἄπο for ἀπολούσῃ).

N. 2. — When the final vowel of the preposition is elided, the accent is dropped if no mark of punctuation intervenes: χερσὶν ὑφ' ἡμετέρῃσιν B 374.

b. When a preposition stands for a compound formed of the preposition and ἐστί. Thus, πάρα for πάρεστι *it is permitted*, ἔνι for ἔνεστι *it is possible* (ἐνί is a poetic form of ἐν).

N. — In poetry, πάρα may stand for πάρεισι or πάρειμι; and ἄνα *arise! up!* is used for ἀνάστηθι. Hom. has ἔνι = ἔνεισι.

CHANGE OF ACCENT IN DECLENSION, INFLECTION, AND COMPOSITION

176. When a short ultima of the nominative is lengthened in an oblique case

a. a proparoxytone becomes paroxytone: θάλαττα θαλάττης, ἄνθρωπος ἀνθρώπου.

b. a properispomenon becomes paroxytone: μοῦσα μούσης, δῶρον δώρου.

c. an oxytone becomes perispomenon in the genitive and dative of the second declension: θεός θεοῦ θεῷ θεῶν θεοῖς.

177. When, for a long ultima, a short ultima is substituted in inflection

a. a dissyllabic paroxytone (with penult long by nature) becomes properispomenon: λύω λῦε.

b. a polysyllabic paroxytone (with penult either long or short) becomes proparoxytone: παιδεύω παίδευε, πλέκω πλέκομεν.

178. In composition the accent is usually recessive (159) in the case of substantives and adjectives, regularly in the case of verbs: βάσις ἀνάβασις, θεός ἄθεος, λῦε ἀπόλῡε.

a. Proper names having the form of a substantive, adjective, or participle, usually change the accent: Ἔλπις (ἐλπίς), Γλαῦκος (γλαυκός), Γέλων (γελῶν).

b. Special cases will be considered under Declension and Inflection.

PROCLITICS

179. Ten monosyllabic words have no accent and are closely connected with the following word. They are called *proclitics* (from προκλίνω *lean forward*). They are:

The forms of the article beginning with a vowel (ὁ, ἡ, οἱ, αἱ); the prepositions ἐν, εἰς (ἐς), ἐξ (ἐκ); the conjunction εἰ *if*; ὡς *as, that* (also a preposition *to*); the negative adverb οὐ (οὐκ, οὐχ, 137).

180. A proclitic sometimes takes an accent, thus:

a. οὐ at the end of a sentence: φῄς, ἢ οὔ; *do you say so or not?* πῶς γὰρ οὔ; *for why not?* Also οὔ *no* standing alone.

b. ἔξ, ἔν, and εἴς receive an acute in poetry when they follow the word to which they belong and stand at the end of the verse: κακῶν ἔξ *out of evils* Ξ 472.

c. ὡς *as* becomes ὥς in poetry when it follows its noun: θεὸς ὥς *as a god.* ὡς standing for οὕτως is written ὥς even in prose (οὐδ' ὥς *not even thus*).

d. When the proclitic precedes an enclitic (183 e): ἔν τισι.

N.—ὁ used as a relative (for ὅς, 1105) is written ὅ. On ὅ demonstrative see 1114.

ENCLITICS

181. Enclitics (from ἐγκλίνω *lean on, upon*) are words attaching themselves closely to the preceding word, after which they are pronounced rapidly. Enclitics usually lose their accent. They are:

a. The personal pronouns μοῦ, μοί, μέ; σοῦ, σοί, σέ; οὗ, οἷ, ἕ, and (in poetry) σφίσι.

b. The indefinite pronoun τὶς, τὶ in all cases (including τοῦ, τῷ for τινός, τινί, but excluding ἄττα = τινά); the indefinite adverbs πού (or ποθί), πῄ, ποί, ποθέν, ποτέ, πώ, πώς. When used as interrogatives these words are not enclitic (τίς, τί, ποῦ (or πόθι), πῇ, ποῖ, πόθεν, πότε, πῶ, πῶς).

c. All dissyllabic forms of the present indicative of εἰμί *am* and φημί *say* (*i.e.* all except εἶ and φῄς).

d. The particles γέ, τέ, τοί, πέρ; the inseparable -δε in ὅδε, τοσόσδε, etc.

N.—Enclitics, when they retain their accent, are called *orthotone.* See 187.

182. The accent of an enclitic, when it is thrown back upon the preceding word, always appears as an acute: θήρ τε (not θῆρ τε) from θήρ + τέ.

183. The word preceding an enclitic is treated as follows:

a. An oxytone keeps its accent, and does not change an acute to a grave (154 a): δός μοι, καλόν ἐστι.

b. A perispomenon keeps its accent: φιλῶ σε, τῑμῶν τινων.

c. A proparoxytone or properispomenon receives, as an additional accent, the acute on the ultima: ἄνθρωπός τις, ἄνθρωποί τινες, ἤκουσά τινων; σῶσόν με, παῖδές τινες.

d. A paroxytone receives no additional accent: a monosyllabic enclitic loses its accent (χώρᾱ τις, φίλος μου), a dissyllabic enclitic retains its accent (χώρᾱς τινός, φίλοι τινές) except when its final vowel is elided (174 a).

---

181 D. Also enclitic are the dialectic and poetical forms μεῦ, σέο, σεῦ, τοί, τέ, and τύ (accus. = σέ), ἕο, εὗ, ἕθεν, μίν, νίν, σφί, σφίν, σφέ, σφωέ, σφωΐν, σφέων, σφέας, σφᾶς and σφᾶς, σφέα; also the particles νύ or νύν (not νῦν), Epic κέ (κέν), θήν, ῥά; and Epic ἐσσί, Ion. εἶς, *thou art.*

N. — Like paroxytones are treated properispomena ending in ξ or ψ when followed by a dissyllabic enclitic: κῆρυξ ἐστί; and so probably κῆρυξ τις.

e. A proclitic (179) takes an acute: ἔν τινι, εἴ τινες.

184. Since an enclitic, on losing its accent, forms a part of the preceding word, the writing ἄνθρωπος τις would violate the rule (149) that no word can be accented on a syllable before the antepenult. A paroxytone receives no additional accent in order that two successive syllables may not have the acute (not φίλός ἐστιν).

185. When several enclitics occur in succession, each receives an accent from the following, only the last having no accent: εἴ πού τίς τινα ἴδοι ἐχθρόν *if ever any one saw an enemy anywhere* T. 4. 47.

186. Sometimes an enclitic unites with a preceding word to form a compound (cp. Lat. *-que*, *-ve*), which is accented as if the enclitic were still a separate word. Thus, οὔτε (not οὖτε), ὥστε, εἴτε, καίτοι, οὗτινος, ᾧτινι, ὧντινων; usually περ (ὥσπερ); and the inseparable -δε in ὅδε, τούσδε, οἴκαδε; and -θε and -χι in εἴθε (poetic αἴθε), ναίχι. οὔτε, ᾧτινι, etc., are not real exceptions to the rules of accent (163, 164).

a. οἷός τε *able* is sometimes written οἷόστε. οὐκ οὖν is usually written οὔκουν *not therefore*, and *not therefore?* in distinction from οὐκοῦν *therefore*. ἐγώ γε and ἐμοί γε may become ἔγωγε, ἔμοιγε.

187. An enclitic retains its accent (is orthotone, cp. 181 N.):

a. When it is emphatic, as in contrasts: ἢ σοὶ ἢ τῷ πατρί σου *either to you or to your father* (ἐμοῦ, ἐμοί, ἐμέ are emphatic: εἰπὲ καὶ ἐμοί *tell me too*), and at the beginning of a sentence or clause: φημὶ γάρ *I say in fact*.

b. ἐστί is written ἔστι at the beginning of a sentence; when it expresses existence or possibility; when it follows οὐκ, μή, εἰ, ὡς, καί, ἀλλά (or ἀλλ'), τοῦτο (or τοῦτ'); and in ἔστιν οἵ *some*, ἔστιν ὅτε *sometimes*. Thus, εἰ ἔστιν οὕτως *if it is so*, τοῦτο ὅ ἔστι *that which exists*.

c. In the phrases ποτὲ μὲν . . . ποτὲ δέ, τινὲς μὲν . . . τινὲς δέ.

d. After a word suffering elision: πολλοὶ δ' εἰσίν (for δέ εἰσιν), ταῦτ' ἐστί.

e. When a dissyllabic enclitic follows a paroxytone (183 d).

N. 1. — When they are used as indirect reflexives in Attic prose (1228), the pronouns of the third person οὗ and σφίσι are orthotone, οἷ is generally enclitic, while ἕ is generally orthotone.

N. 2. — After oxytone prepositions and ἕνεκα enclitic pronouns (except τὶς) usually keep their accent (ἐπὶ σοί, not ἐπί σοι; ἕνεκα σοῦ, not ἕνεκά σου; ἕνεκά του, not ἕνεκα τοῦ). ἐμοῦ, ἐμοί, ἐμέ are used after prepositions (except πρός με; and in the drama ἀμφί μοι).

MARKS OF PUNCTUATION

188. Greek has four marks of punctuation. The *comma* and *period* have the same forms as in English For the *colon* and *semicolon* Greek has only one sign, a point above the line (·): οἱ δὲ ἡδέως ἐπείθοντο· ἐπίστευον γὰρ αὐτῷ *and they gladly obeyed; for they trusted him* X. A. 1. 2. 2. The *mark of interrogation* (;) is the same as our semicolon: πῶς γὰρ οὔ; *for why not?* During the classical period words were usually run together in writing; the symbols : or ⁝ often represented a stop (colon, period).

PART II

INFLECTION

189. Parts of Speech. — Greek has the following parts of speech: substantives, adjectives, pronouns, verbs, adverbs, prepositions, conjunctions, and particles. In this Grammar *noun* is used to include both the substantive and the adjective.

190. Inflection is the change in the form of nouns, pronouns, and verbs which indicates their relation to other words in the sentence. *Declension* is the inflection of substantives, adjectives (including participles), and pronouns; *conjugation* is the inflection of verbs.

191. Stems. — Inflection is shown by the addition of endings to the *stem*, which is that part of a word which sets forth the *idea;* the endings fit the word to stand in various relations to other words in the sentence. The endings originally had distinct meanings, which are now seldom apparent. In verbs they represent the force of the personal pronouns in English; in nouns they often correspond to the ideas expressed by *of*, *to*, *for*, etc. Thus, the stem λογο- becomes λόγο-ς *word*, the stem λεγο- becomes λέγο-μεν *we say*. Whether a stem is used as a noun or a verb depends solely on its signification; many stems are used both for nouns and for verbs, as τῑμᾱ- in τῑμή *honour*, τῑμα- in τῑμά-ω *I honour;* ἐλπιδ- in ἐλπί(δ)-ς *hope*, ἐλπίζω *I hope* (ἐλπιδ-ι̯ω). The pure stem, that is, the stem without any ending, may serve as a word; as χώρᾱ *land*, λέγε *speak!* λόγε *O word!*

192. The stem often changes in form, but not in meaning, in nouns and verbs. Thus, the stem of λόγο-ς *word* is λογο- or λογε-, of πατήρ *father* is πατερ- (strong stem) or πατρ- (weak stem); of λείπο-μεν *we leave* is λειπο-, of ἔ-λίπο-μεν *we left* is λιπο-. The verbal stem is also modified to indicate change in time: τῑμή-σο-μεν *we shall honour*.

193. Roots. — The fundamental part of a word, which remains after the word has been analyzed into all its component parts, is called a *root*. When a stem agrees in form with a root (as in ποδ-ός, gen. of πούς *foot*) it is called a *root-stem*. A root contains the mere idea of a word in the vaguest and most abstract form possible. Thus, the root λεγ, and in another form λογ, contains the idea of *saying* simply. By the addition of a formative element ο we arrive at the stems λεγο- and λογο- in λέγο-μεν *we say*, λόγο-ς *word* (*i.e.* what is said).

Words are built by adding to the root certain formative suffixes by which the stem and then the word, ready for use, is constructed. Thus, from the root λυ are formed λύ-σι-ς *loosing*, λύ-τρο-ν *ransom*, λυ-τι-κό-ς *able to loose*, λυ-θῆ-ναι *to have been loosed*. The formation of the stem by the addition of suffixes to the root is treated in Part III. The root itself may assume various forms without change of meaning, as λεγ in λέγ-ο-μεν *we say*, λογ in λόγ-ο-ς *word*.

N. — Since Greek is connected with the other Indo-European languages, the roots which we establish in Greek by analysis of a word into its simplest form often reappear in the connected languages (p. 1, A). Thus, the root φερ of φέρω *I bear* is seen in Sanskrit *bhárāmi*, Lat. *fero*, Germ. *ge-bären*. The assumption of roots is merely a grammatical convenience in the analysis of word-forms, and their determination is part of comparative grammar. Roots and suffixes as such never existed as independent words in Greek, or indeed in any known period of the parent language from which Greek and the other Indo-European tongues are derived. The theory that all roots are monosyllables is ill supported. As far back as we can follow the history of the Indo-European languages we find only complete words; hence their analysis into component morphological elements is merely a scientific device for purposes of arrangement and classification.

DECLENSION

194. Declension deals with variations of number, gender, and case.

195. Number. — There are three numbers: singular, dual, and plural. The dual speaks of *two* or *a pair*, as τὼ ὀφθαλμώ *the two eyes;* but it is not often used, and the plural (which denotes *more than one*) is frequently substituted for it (οἱ ὀφθαλμοί *the eyes*).

196. Gender. — There are three genders: masculine, feminine, and neuter.

a. Gender strictly marks sex-distinction. But in Greek, as in German and French, many inanimate objects are regarded as masculine or feminine. Such words are said to have 'grammatical' gender, which is determined only by their *form*. Words denoting objects without natural gender usually show their grammatical gender by the form of the adjective, as μακρὸς λόγος *a long speech*, μακρᾶ νῆσος *a long island*, μακρὸν τεῖχος *a long wall*.

b. The gender of Greek words is usually indicated by means of the article: ὁ for masculine, ἡ for feminine, τό for neuter.

197. Rule of Natural Gender. — Nouns denoting male persons are masculine, nouns denoting female persons are feminine. Thus, ὁ ναύτης *seaman*, ὁ στρατιώτης *soldier*, ἡ γυνή *woman*, ἡ κόρη *maiden*.

a. A whole class is designated by the masculine: οἱ ἄνθρωποι *men*, i.e. *men and women*.

b. Exceptions to the Rule of Natural Gender. — Diminutives in -ιον are neuter (199 d), as τὸ ἀνθρώπιον *manikin* (ὁ ἄνθρωπος *man*), τὸ παιδίον *little child* (male or female, ὁ or ἡ παῖς *child*), τὸ γύναιον *little woman* (ἡ γυνή *woman*). Also the words τέκνον, τέκος *child* (strictly 'thing born'), ἀνδράποδον *captive*.

198. Common Gender. — Many nouns denoting persons are either masculine or feminine. Thus, ὁ παῖς *boy*, ἡ παῖς *girl*, ὁ θεός *god*, ἡ θεός (ἡ θεά poet.) *goddess*. So with names of animals: ὁ βοῦς *ox*, ἡ βοῦς *cow*, ὁ ἵππος *horse*, ἡ ἵππος *mare*.

a. Some names of animals have only one grammatical gender without regard to sex, as ὁ λαγώς *he-hare* or *she-hare*, ἡ ἀλώπηξ *he-fox* or *she-fox*.

199. Gender of Sexless Objects. — The gender of most nouns denoting sexless objects has to be learned by the endings (211, 228, 255) and by observation. The following general rules should be noted.

a. Masculine are the names of *winds*, *months*, and most *rivers*. Thus, ὁ Βορέᾱς *the North Wind*, ὁ Ἑκατομβαιών *Hecatombaeon*, ὁ Κηφισσός *Cephissus*.

N. — The gender of these proper names is made to correspond to ὁ ἄνεμος *wind*, ὁ μήν *month*, ὁ ποταμός *river*. In the case of winds and rivers the gender may be due in part to personification.

b. Feminine are the names of almost all *countries*, *islands*, *cities*, *trees*, and *plants*. Thus, ἡ Ἀττική *Attica*, ἡ Δῆλος *Delos*, ἡ Κόρινθος *Corinth*, ἡ πίτυς *pine*, ἡ ἄμπελος *vine*. The gender here follows that of ἡ γῆ or ἡ χώρᾱ *land*, *country*, ἡ νῆσος *island*, ἡ πόλις *city*, ἡ δρῦς, originally *tree* in general, but later *oak* (τὸ δένδρον is the ordinary word for *tree*).

c. Feminine are most abstract words, that is, words denoting a *quality* or a *condition*. Thus, ἡ ἀρετή *virtue*, ἡ εὔνοια *good-will*, ἡ ταχύτης *swiftness*, ἡ ἐλπίς *hope*.

d. Neuter are diminutives (197 b), words and expressions quoted, letters of the alphabet, infinitives, and indeclinable nouns. Thus, τὸ ὑμεῖς *the word* '*you*,' τὸ γνῶθι σεαυτόν *the saying* '*learn to know thyself*,' τὸ ἄλφα *alpha*, τὸ παιδεύειν *to educate*, τὸ χρεών *necessity*.

N. — But some names of women end in -ιον (197 b): ἡ Γλυκέριον *Glycerium*.

200. Remarks. — **a.** Most of the exceptions to 199 a–b are due to the endings; *e.g.* ἡ Λήθη *Lethe*, ἡ Στύξ *Styx* (rivers of the Lower World), τὸ Ἄργος *Argos*, ὁ Καλυδών *Calydon*, τὸ Ἴλιον *Ilium*, οἱ Δελφοί *Delphi*, ὁ λωτός *lotus*.

b. Change in gender is often associated with change in form: ὁ λύκος *he-wolf*, ἡ λύκαινα *she-wolf*, ὁ ποιητής *poet*, ἡ ποιήτρια *poetess*, ὁ βίοτος and ἡ βιοτή *life*, ὁ τρόπος *manner*, ἡ τροπή *rout*.

c. The gender of one word may influence that of another word of like meaning. Thus ἡ νῆσος *island* and ἡ λίθος *stone* are feminine probably because of ἡ γῆ *land* and ἡ πέτρᾱ *rock*.

201. Cases. — There are five cases: nominative, genitive, dative, accusative, and vocative. The genitive denotes *from* as well as *of*, the dative denotes *to* or *for* and also *by*, *with*, *on*, *in*, *at*, etc. The other cases are used as in Latin.

a. The genitive, dative, and accusative are called *oblique* cases to distinguish them from the nominative and vocative.

202. The vocative is often like the nominative in the singular; in the plural it is always the same. Nominative, vocative, and accusative have the same form in neuter words, and always have α in the plural. In the dual there are two forms, one for nominative, accusative, and vocative, the other for genitive and dative.

203. Lost Cases. — Greek has generally lost the *forms* of the instrumental and locative cases (which have become fused with the dative) and of the ablative. The Greek dative is used to express *by*, as in βίᾳ, Lat. *vī; with*, as in λίθοις *with stones;* and *in*, *on*, as in γῇ *on the earth*. *From* may be expressed by the genitive: πόρρω Σπάρτης *far from Sparta*. When the genitive and dative do duty for the ablative, prepositions are often used. Instances of the forms of the lost cases are given in 341.

204. Declensions. — There are three declensions, which are named from the stems to which the case endings are attached.

1. First or Â-declension, with stems in **ᾱ** } Vowel Declension.
2. Second or O-declension, with stems in **ο** }
3. Third or Consonant declension, with stems in a consonant or in **ι** and **υ**.

The nominative and accusative are alike in the singular and plural of all neuter nouns. The nominative and vocative are alike in the plural.

GENERAL RULES FOR THE ACCENT OF NOUNS

205. Substantives and adjectives accent, in the oblique cases, the same syllable as is accented in the nominative, provided the ultima permits (163); otherwise the following syllable receives the accent.

1 decl. θάλαττα, θαλάττης, θαλάττῃ, θάλατταν, θάλατται (169), θαλάτταις, θαλάττᾱς.

2 decl. ἄνθρωπος, ἀνθρώπου, ἀνθρώπῳ, ἄνθρωπον, ἄνθρωποι (169), ἀνθρώπων, ἀνθρώποις, ἀνθρώπους.

3 decl. λέων, λέοντος, λέοντι, λέοντα, λέοντες, λεόντων.

Adj.: ἄξιος (287), ἀξίᾱ, ἄξιον, ἀξίου, ἀξίᾱς, ἀξίῳ, ἀξίᾳ, ἀξίων, ἀξίοις.
χαρίεις (299), χαρίεντος, χαρίεντι, χαρίεντα, χαριέντων.

206. The character of the accent depends on the general laws (167, 168, 176). Thus, νίκη, νῖκαι (169); δῶρον, δώρου, δῶρα; σῶμα, σώματος, σωμάτων, σώματα.

207. Oxytones of the first and second declensions are perispomena in the genitive and dative of all numbers: σκιά, σκιᾶς, σκιᾷ, σκιῶν, σκιαῖς; θεός, θεοῦ, θεῷ, θεῶν, θεοῖς; φανερός, φανεροῦ, φανερῷ, φανερῶν, φανεροῖς.

208. The genitive plural of all substantives of the first declension has the circumflex on the ω of **-ων**. Thus, νίκη νῑκῶν; θάλαττα θαλαττῶν; πολίτης πολῑτῶν; νεᾱνίᾱς νεᾱνιῶν.

209. The fem. gen. plural of adjectives and participles in **-ος** has the same accent and form as the masculine and neuter. Thus, δίκαιος, gen. pl. δικαίων (in all genders); λυόμενος, gen. pl. λυομένων (in all genders).

210. CASE ENDINGS OF NOUNS

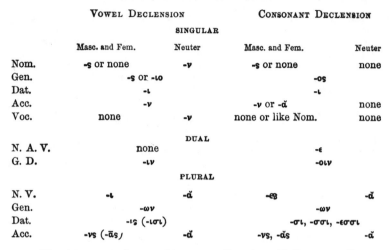

	Vowel Declension		Consonant Declension	
	Singular			
	Masc. and Fem.	Neuter	Masc. and Fem.	Neuter
Nom.	-ς or none	-ν	-ς or none	none
Gen.	-ς or -ιο		-ος	
Dat.	-ι		-ι	
Acc.	-ν		-ν or -ᾰ	none
Voc.	none	-ν	none or like Nom.	none
	Dual			
N. A. V.	none		-ε	
G. D.	-ιν		-οιν	
	Plural			
N. V.	-ι	-ᾰ	-ες	-ᾰ
Gen.	-ων		-ων	
Dat.	-ις (-ισι)		-σι, -σσι, -εσσι	
Acc.	-νς (-ᾱς)	-ᾰ	-νς, -ᾰς	-ᾰ

a. The stem may undergo a change upon its union with the case ending, as in the genitive plural of the first declension (213). Cp. 258, 264, 268, etc.

b. In the vowel declension, -ι of the nominative plural is borrowed from the inflection of pronouns (ἐκεῖνο-ι).

SUBSTANTIVES

FIRST DECLENSION (STEMS IN ᾱ)

211. Stems in ᾱ are masculine or feminine. The feminine nominative singular ends in -ᾱ, -ᾰ, or -η; the masculine nominative singular adds -ς to the stem, and thus ends in -ᾱς or -ης.

212. Table of the union of the case endings (when there are any) with the final vowel of the stem.

	Fem. Sing.		Masc. Sing.		Masc. Fem. Pl.	Masc. Fem. Dual	
Nom.	ᾱ or ᾰ	η	ᾱ-ς	η-ς	α-ι	N. A. V.	ᾱ
Gen.	ᾱ-ς or η-ς	η-ς	ᾱ-ιο (Hom. ᾱ-ο)		ῶν (for έ-ων, ά́-ων)	G. D.	α-ιν
Dat.	ᾱ-ι or η-ι	η-ι	ᾱ-ι	η-ι	α-ις or α-ισι(ν)		
Acc.	ᾱ-ν or ᾰ-ν	η-ν	ᾱ-ν	η-ν	ᾱς (for α-νς)		
Voc.	ᾱ or ᾰ	η	ᾱ	ᾰ or η	α-ι		

Observe the shortening of the stem in vocative singular and plural, in nominative and dative plural, and genitive and dative dual.

213. Accent. — For special rule of accent in the genitive plural, see 208. The genitive plural is always perispomenon since -ῶν is contracted from -έ-ων derived from original (and Hom.) -ά-ων (51). Final -αι is treated as short (169).

a. The form of the gen. pl. is taken from the pronominal adjective, *i.e.* (Hom.) θεάων *goddesses* follows the analogy of (Hom.) τάων (332 D.) for τᾱ-(σ)ων, cf. Lat. *istā-rum deā-rum.*

214. The dialects show various forms.

215. Dative Plural. — The ending -αισι(ν) occurs in Attic poetry (δίκαισι from δίκη *right*, δεσπόταισι from δεσπότης *lord*).

a. Attic inscriptions to 420 B.C. have -ῃσι (written -ηισι), -ησι, and (after ε, ι, ρ) -ᾳσι (written -αισι) and -ᾱσι. Thus, δραχμῇσι and δραχμῆσι *drachmas*, ταμίᾳσι and ταμίᾱσι *stewards.* -ησι and -ᾱσι are properly endings of the locative case (341).

---

214 D. 1. For η, Doric and Aeolic have original ᾱ; thus, νίκᾱ, νίκᾱς, νίκᾳ, νίκᾱν; πολίτᾱς, κριτᾱ́ς, Ἀτρείδᾱς.

2. Ionic has η for the ᾱ of Attic even after ε, ι, and ρ; thus, γενεή, οἰκίη, ἀγορή, μοίρης, μοίρῃ (nom. μοῖρᾰ), νεηνίης. Thus, ἀγορή, -ῆς, -ῇ, -ήν; νεηνίης, -ου, -ῃ, -ην. But Hom. has θεά *goddess*, Ἑρμείᾱς *Hermes.*

3. The dialects admit -ᾰ in the nom. sing. less often than does Attic. Thus, Ionic πρύμνη *stern*, κνίση *savour* (Att. πρύμνα, κνῖσα), Dor. τόλμᾱ *daring.* Ionic has η for ᾰ in the abstracts in -είη, -οίη (ἀληθείη *truth*, εὐνοίη *good-will*). Hom. has νύμφᾰ *oh maiden* from νύμφη.

4. **Nom. sing. masc.** — Hom. has -τα for -της in ἱππότα *horseman*, ἱππηλάτα *driver of horses*, νεφεληγερέτα *cloud-collector*, κυανοχαῖτα *dark-haired;* and, with recessive accent, μητίετα *counsellor.* So in the adj. εὐρύοπα *far-sounding.* Cp. Lat. *poeta, scriba.*

5. **Gen. sing. masc.** — (a) **-ᾱο**, the original form from ᾱ-(ι)ο, is used by Hom. (Ἀτρείδᾱο). It contracts in Aeolic and Doric to **-ᾱ** (Ἀτρείδᾱ).

(b) **-εω**, from ηο (= ᾱο) by 34, is also used by Hom., who makes it a single syllable by synizesis (60), as in Ἀτρείδεω͡. Hdt. has -εω, as πολίτεω (163 a).

(c) **-ω** in Hom. after a vowel, Βορέω (nom. Βορέης).

6. **Accus. sing. masc.** — In proper names Hdt. often has -εα borrowed from *s* stems (264), as Μιλτιάδεα for Μιλτιάδη-ν.

7. **Dual.** — Hom. has the nom. dual of masculines only. In the gen. and dat. Hom. has -αιν and also -αιιν.

8. **Gen. plur.** — (a) **-ᾱ́ων**, the original form, occurs in Hom. (μουσάων, ἀγοράων). In Aeolic and Doric -ᾱ́ων contracts to (b) **-ᾶν** (ἀγορᾶν). The Doric -ᾶν is found also in the choral songs of the drama (πετρᾶν *rocks*). (c) **-έων**, the Ionic form, appears in Homer, who usually makes it a single syllable by synizesis (60) as in βουλέω͡ν, from βουλή *plan.* -έων is from -ήων, Ionic for **-ᾱ́ων.** (d) **-ῶν** in Hom. generally after vowels (κλισιῶν, from κλισίη *hut*).

9. **Dat. plur.**: -ῃσι(ν), -ῃς, generally before vowels, and (rarely) **-αις** in Hom. Ionic has -ῃσι, Aeolic -αισι(ν), -αις, Doric -αις.

10. **Accus. plur.**: -ανς, -ᾰς, ᾱς in various Doric dialects, **-αις** in Aeolic.

216. I. FEMININES

SINGULAR

	ἡ χώρᾱ (χωρᾱ-) *land*	ἡ νίκη (νῑκᾱ-) *victory*	ἡ φυγή (φυγᾱ-) *flight*	ἡ μοῖρα (μοιρᾱ-) *fate*	ἡ γλῶττα (γλωττᾱ-) *tongue*	ἡ θάλαττα (θαλαττᾱ-) *sea*
Nom.	χώρᾱ	νίκη	φυγή	μοῖρα	γλῶττα	θάλαττα
Gen.	χώρᾱς	νίκης	φυγῆς	μοίρᾱς	γλώττης	θαλάττης
Dat.	χώρᾳ	νίκῃ	φυγῇ	μοίρᾳ	γλώττῃ	θαλάττῃ
Acc.	χώρᾱ-ν	νίκη-ν	φυγή-ν	μοῖρα-ν	γλῶττα-ν	θάλαττα-ν
Voc.	χώρᾱ	νίκη	φυγή	μοῖρα	γλῶττα	θάλαττα
			DUAL			
N. A. V.	χώρᾱ	νίκᾱ	φυγᾱ́	μοίρᾱ	γλώττᾱ	θαλάττᾱ
G. D.	χώραιν	νίκαιν	φυγαῖν	μοίραιν	γλώτταιν	θαλάτταιν
			PLURAL			
N. V.	χῶραι	νῖκαι	φυγαί	μοῖραι	γλῶτται	θάλατται
Gen.	χωρῶν	νῑκῶν	φυγῶν	μοιρῶν	γλωττῶν	θαλαττῶν
Dat.	χώραις	νίκαις	φυγαῖς	μοίραις	γλώτταις	θαλάτταις
Acc.	χώρᾱς	νίκᾱς	φυγᾱ́ς	μοίρᾱς	γλώττᾱς	θαλάττᾱς

ὥρᾱ *season*, ἡμέρᾱ *day*, σκιᾱ́ *shadow*, μάχη *battle*, τέχνη *art*, γνώμη *judgment*, τῑμή *honor*, ἀρετή *virtue*, μοῦσα *muse*, πρῷρα *prow*, ἅμαξα *wagon*, δόξα *opinion*.

217. Rules.—**a.** If the nominative singular ends in *alpha* preceded by a vowel (σκιᾱ́ *shadow*) or ρ (μοῖρα), *alpha* is kept throughout the singular.

b. If the nominative singular ends in *alpha* preceded by a consonant not ρ, *alpha* is changed to η in the genitive and dative singular.

c. If the nominative singular ends in η, η is kept in all the cases of the singular.

d. When the genitive singular has -ης, final α of the nominative singular is *always* short; when the genitive singular has -ᾱς, the final α is *generally* long.

Feminines fall into two classes:

218. (I) Feminines with ᾱ or η in all the cases of the singular.

After ε, ι, or ρ, ᾱ appears in all the cases of the singular, as in γενεᾱ́ *race*, οἰκίᾱ *house*, χώρᾱ *land*. Otherwise, η throughout the singular, as νίκη *victory*.

a. After ο, we find both ᾱ and η, as στοᾱ́ *porch*, βοή *shout*, ἀκοή *hearing*, ῥοή *current*, ῥόᾱ *pomegranate*. After ρ we have η in κόρη *girl*, δέρη *neck* (31).

219. (II) Feminines with ᾰ in the nominative, accusative, and vocative singular. The quantity of the vowel is generally shown by the accent (163, 164).

In this class are included:

1. **Substantives having σ (ξ, ψ, ττ, or σσ), ζ, λλ, or αιν before the final α show ᾰ in nom., accus., and voc. sing., and η in gen. and dat. sing. Thus,**

μοῦσα muse, *μούσης*, *μούσῃ*, *ἅμαξα wagon*, *τράπεζα table*, *γλῶττα tongue*, *ῥίζα root*, *ἅμιλλα contest*, *λέαινα lioness*. Others are *τόλμα daring*, *δίαιτα mode of life*, *ἄκανθα thorn*, *μυῖα fly*.

2. Substantives in ᾰ in nom., accus., and voc. sing., and ᾱ in gen. and dat. sing.
   a. Substantives in -εια and -τρια denoting females, as *βασίλεια queen* (but *βασιλείᾱ kingdom*), *ψάλτρια female harper*; so the fem. of adj. in -υς, as *γλυκύς*, *γλυκεῖα sweet*.
   b. Abstracts in -εια and -οια from adjectives in -ης and -οος, as *ἀλήθεια truth* (from *ἀληθής true*), *εὔνοια good will* (from *εὔνους*, *εὔνοος kind*, 290).
   c. Most substantives in -ρα after a diphthong or ῡ, as *μοῖρα fate*, *γέφῡρα bridge*.

220. Exceptions to 219, 1: *κόρση temple* (later *κόρρη*), *ἕρση dew*; to 2 b: in Attic poetry, *ἀληθείᾱ*, *εὐνοίᾱ*, *ἀγνοίᾱ ignorance*, which owe their ᾱ to the influence of the genitive and dative *ἀληθείᾱς*, *ἀληθείᾳ*, etc.

221. Most, if not all, of the substantives in ᾰ are formed by the addition of the suffix ι̯α or ια (20); thus, *γλῶττα* from *γλωχ-ι̯α* (cp. *γλωχῖν-ες points*), *γέφῡρα* from *γεφυρ-ι̯α*, *δότειρα giver* from *δοτερ-ι̯α* (and so *φέρουσα bearing* from *φεροντ-ι̯α*), *μοῖρα* from *μορ-ι̯α*, *ψάλτρ-ια*.

222. II. MASCULINES

SINGULAR

	ὁ νεᾱνίᾱς (νεᾱνιᾱ-) young man	ὁ πολίτης (πολῑτᾱ-) citizen	ὁ κριτής (κριτᾱ-) judge	Ἀτρείδης (Ἀτρειδᾱ-) son of Atreus
Nom.	νεᾱνίᾱ-ς	πολίτη-ς	κριτή-ς	Ἀτρείδη-ς
Gen.	νεᾱνίου	πολίτου	κριτοῦ	Ἀτρείδου
Dat.	νεᾱνίᾳ	πολίτῃ	κριτῇ	Ἀτρείδῃ
Acc.	νεᾱνίᾱ-ν	πολίτη-ν	κριτή-ν	Ἀτρείδη-ν
Voc.	νεᾱνίᾱ	πολῖτα	κριτά	Ἀτρείδη
	DUAL			
N. A. V.	νεᾱνίᾱ	πολίτᾱ	κριτᾱ́	Ἀτρείδᾱ
G. D.	νεᾱνίαιν	πολίταιν	κριταῖν	Ἀτρείδαιν
	PLURAL			
N. V.	νεᾱνίαι	πολῖται	κριταί	Ἀτρεῖδαι
Gen.	νεᾱνιῶν	πολῑτῶν	κριτῶν	Ἀτρειδῶν
Dat.	νεᾱνίαις	πολίταις	κριταῖς	Ἀτρείδαις
Acc.	νεᾱνίᾱς	πολίτᾱς	κριτᾱ́ς	Ἀτρείδᾱς

ταμίᾱς steward, *Αἰνείᾱς Aeneas*, — *ναύτης sailor*, *τοξότης bowman*, *στρατιώτης soldier*, *δεσπότης ruler*, — *μαθητής pupil*, *ποιητής poet* — *Πέρσης Persian*.

223. **Accent.** — The vocative of *δεσπότης lord* is *δέσποτα*.

224. ᾱ and η. — In the final syllable of the singular ᾱ appears after ε, ι, and ρ; otherwise we find η. Cp. 218.

a. Exceptions are compounds in -μέτρης: γεω-μέτρης *measurer of land.*

225. Genitive singular. — The form in -ου is borrowed from the genitive singular of the second declension. A few words in -ᾱς, generally names of persons not Greeks, have -ᾱ, the Doric genitive (214 D. 5): Ἀννίβᾱς *Hannibal*, gen. Ἀννίβᾱ.

226. Vocative singular. — Masculines in -ᾱς have the vocative in -ᾱ (νεᾱνίᾱ); those in -της have -ᾰ (πολῖτα), all others in -ης have -η (Ἀτρείδη, Κρονίδη *son of Kronos*) except names of nations and compounds: Πέρσᾰ *Persian*, Σκύθᾰ *Scythian*, γεω-μέτρᾰ (nom. γεω-μέτρης *measurer of land*), παιδο-τρίβᾰ *gymnastic master.*

CONTRACTS (FEMININES AND MASCULINES)

227. Contracts in ᾱ or η from εᾱ or αᾱ have the circumflex in all the cases: nominative feminine -ᾶ, -ῆ, masculine -ᾶς, -ῆς.

	ἡ μνᾶ *mina* (μνᾱ- for μναᾱ-)	ἡ σῦκῆ *fig tree* (σῡκη- for σῡκεᾱ-)	ὁ Βορρᾶς *Boreas* (Βορρᾱ- for Βορεᾱ- 117)	ὁ Ἑρμῆς *Hermes* (Ἑρμη- for Ἑρμεᾱ-)
	SINGULAR			
Nom.	μνᾶ	σῡκῆ	Βορρᾶ-ς	Ἑρμῆ-ς
Gen.	μνᾶς	σῡκῆς	Βορροῦ	Ἑρμοῦ
Dat.	μνᾷ	σῡκῇ	Βορρᾷ	Ἑρμῇ
Acc.	μνᾶ-ν	σῡκῆ-ν	Βορρᾶ-ν	Ἑρμῆ-ν
Voc.	μνᾶ	σῡκῆ	Βορρᾶ	Ἑρμῆ
	DUAL			
N. A. V.	μνᾶ	σῡκᾶ		Ἑρμᾶ
G. D.	μναῖν	σῡκαῖν		Ἑρμαῖν
	PLURAL			
N. V.	μναῖ	σῡκαῖ		Ἑρμαῖ
Gen.	μνῶν	σῡκῶν		Ἑρμῶν
Dat.	μναῖς	σῡκαῖς		Ἑρμαῖς
Acc.	μνᾶς	σῡκᾶς		Ἑρμᾶς

The dual and plural of Ἑρμῆς mean *statues of Hermes.*

Other examples: ἡ Ἀθηνᾶ *Athena* (from Ἀθηνα(ι)ᾱ-), γῆ *earth* (γεᾱ- or γαᾱ-) with no plural in Attic, ἡ γαλῆ *weasel* (γαλεᾱ-), ἡ ἀδελφιδῆ *niece* (ἀδελφιδεᾱ-), ὁ Ἀπελλῆς *Apelles* (Ἀπελλεᾱ-).

---

227 D. Hdt. has μνέαι, μνεῶν, μνέᾱς, γῆ and γεῶν, Ἑρμῆς, Βορῆς. Hom. has Ἀθηναίη, γῆ (and γαῖα), σῡκέη, Ἑρμείᾱς 214 D. 2, Βορέης.

SECOND DECLENSION (STEMS IN o)

228. O stems in the nominative add -ς to the stem in masculines and feminines; -ν in neuters. The feminines, of which there are few, are declined like the masculines. In the neuters, nominative, vocative, and accusative singular have the same form (in -ο-ν); in the plural these cases end in -α.

229. TABLE OF THE UNION OF THE CASE ENDINGS WITH THE STEM VOWEL

SINGULAR			DUAL		PLURAL		
	Masc. and Fem.	Neuter	Masc., Fem., and Neuter			Masc. and Fem.	Neuter
Nom.	ο-ς	ο-ν	N. A. V.	ω	Nom.	ο-ι	ᾰ
Gen.	ου (for ο-(ι)ο)		G. D.	ο-ιν	Gen.	ων	
Dat.	ῳ (for ο-ι)				Dat.	ο-ις or ο-ισι(ν)	
Acc.	ο-ν				Acc.	ους (for ο-νς)	ᾰ
Voc.	ε	ο-ν			Voc.	ο-ι	ᾰ

a. Final -οι is treated as short (169).

b. The dat. sing. in -ῳ represents fusion of the stem vowel -ο and -ει or -*ai*, the original case ending in the I. E. languages. Forms in -οι, as οἴκοι *at home*, may be locatives (-ο + *i*, the locative ending). — The stem vowel ο varies with ε, which appears in the vocative sing., and in πανδημεί (locative) *in full force.* — N. A. V. dual -ω is for I. E. *ōu*. — The genitive pl. -ων is due to the union of -ο + ων, which contracted to -ων in the earliest period of the language. — The neuter plural is probably the relic of a feminine collective ending in -ᾱ, which was shortened to -ᾰ.

230. The dialects show various forms.

231. SINGULAR

	ὁ ἵππος *horse* (ἱππο-)	ὁ ἄνθρωπος *man* (ἀνθρωπο-)	ἡ ὁδός *way* (ὁδο-)	τὸ δῶρον *gift* (δωρο-)
Nom.	ἵππο-ς	ἄνθρωπο-ς	ὁδό-ς	δῶρο-ν
Gen.	ἵππου	ἀνθρώπου	ὁδοῦ	δώρου
Dat.	ἵππῳ	ἀνθρώπῳ	ὁδῷ	δώρῳ
Acc.	ἵππο-ν	ἄνθρωπο-ν	ὁδό-ν	δῶρο-ν
Voc.	ἵππε	ἄνθρωπε	ὁδέ	δῶρο-ν

230 D. 1. Gen. sing. — -οιο, the original form, appears in Hom. πολέμοιο. By loss of ι (43) comes -οο, which is sometimes read in Hom. (Αἰόλοο for Αἰόλου κ 36). By contraction of οο comes -ου found in Hom., Ionic, Milder Doric. οο yields ω in Aeolic and Severer Doric (ἵππω).

2. **Dual.** — -οιιν in Hom. (ἵπποιιν).

3. **Dat. pl.** — -οισι(ν) Hom., Aeolic, Ionic.

4. **Acc. pl.** — -ους is from -ον-ς (found in Cretan), and variously treated: From -ονς comes -ως Severer Doric, -οις Aeolic, -ος Cretan and in Dor. poetry. -ους is Hom., Ionic, and Milder Doric.

DUAL

	ὁ ἵππος *horse* (ἱππο-)	**ὁ ἄνθρωπος** *man* (ἀνθρωπο-)	**ἡ ὁδός** *way* (ὁδο-)	**τὸ δῶρον** *gift* (δωρο-)
N. A. V.	**ἵππω**	**ἀνθρώπω**	**ὁδώ**	**δώρω**
G. D.	**ἵπποιν**	**ἀνθρώποιν**	**ὁδοῖν**	**δώροιν**

PLURAL

N. V.	**ἵπποι**	**ἄνθρωποι**	**ὁδοί**	**δῶρα**
Gen.	**ἵππων**	**ἀνθρώπων**	**ὁδῶν**	**δώρων**
Dat.	**ἵπποις**	**ἀνθρώποις**	**ὁδοῖς**	**δώροις**
Acc.	**ἵππους**	**ἀνθρώπους**	**ὁδούς**	**δῶρα**

Masculine: λόγος *word*, δῆμος *people*, δοῦλος *slave*, κίνδῡνος *danger*, πόλεμος *war*; ἀγρός *field*, ποταμός *river*, ἀριθμός *number*. Feminine: νῆσος *island*, ἤπειρος *mainland*; ὁ(ἡ) τροφός *nurse*. Neuter: ἔργον *work*, πτερόν *wing*, δεῖπνον *dinner*.

232. **Feminines.**—**a.** See 197 for νυός *daughter-in-law*; see 199 for νῆσος *island* (cp. 200 c), Δῆλος (the island of) *Delos*, Κόρινθος *Corinth*, φηγός (acorn-bearing) *oak*, ἄμπελος *vine*.

b. Some are properly adjectives used substantively: διάλεκτος (*scil.* γλῶττα *speech*) *dialect*, διάμετρος (*scil.* γραμμή *line*) *diameter*, αὔλειος (*scil.* θύρᾱ *door*) *house-door*, σύγκλητος (*scil.* βουλή *council*) *legislative body*, ἔρημος and ἤπειρος (*scil.* χώρᾱ *country*) *desert* and *mainland*.

c. Words for *way*: ὁδός and κέλευθος *way*; and ἁμαξιτός *carriage-road*, ἀτραπός *foot-path*, which may be adjectival (b) with ὁδός omitted.

d. Various other words: βάσανος *touch-stone*, βίβλος *book*, γέρανος *crane*, γνάθος *jaw*, γύψος *chalk*, δέλτος *writing-tablet*, δοκός *beam*, δρόσος *dew*, κάμῑνος *oven*, κάρδοπος *kneading-trough*, κῑβωτός *chest*, κόπρος *dung*, ληνός *wine-press*, λίθος *stone* (200 c), νόσος *disease*, πλίνθος *brick*, ῥάβδος *rod*, σορός *coffin*, σποδός *ashes*, τάφρος *trench*, χηλός *coffer*, ψάμμος *sand*, ψῆφος *pebble*.

233. **Vocative.**—The nominative θεός is used instead of the vocative. ἀδελφός *brother* retracts the accent (ἄδελφε).

234. **Dative Plural.**—The ending -οισι(ν) often appears in poetry, rarely in Attic prose (Plato).

a. In Old Attic inscriptions -οις displaces -οισι(ν) about 444 B.C.

CONTRACTED SUBSTANTIVES

235. Stems in εο and οο are contracted according to 50, 51. εα in the neuter becomes ᾱ (56).

---

235 D. Homeric and Ionic generally have the open forms. οἰνοχόος *wine-pourer* does not contract in Attic since it stands for οἰνοχοϝος.

	SINGULAR					
	ὁ νοῦς *mind* (νοο-)		ὁ περίπλους *sailing around* (περιπλοο-)		τὸ ὀστοῦν *bone* (ὀστεο-)	
Nom.	(νόο-ς)	νοῦ-ς	(περίπλοος)	περίπλου-ς	(ὀστέο-ν)	ὀστοῦ-ν
Gen.	(νόου)	νοῦ	(περιπλόου)	περίπλου	(ὀστέου)	ὀστοῦ
Dat.	(νόῳ)	νῷ	(περιπλόῳ)	περίπλῳ	(ὀστέῳ)	ὀστῷ
Acc.	(νόο-ν)	νοῦ-ν	(περίπλοο-ν)	περίπλου-ν	(ὀστέο-ν)	ὀστοῦ-ν
Voc.	(νόε)	νοῦ	(περίπλοε)	περίπλου	(ὀστέο-ν)	ὀστοῦ-ν
	DUAL					
N. A. V.	(νόω)	νώ	(περιπλόω)	περίπλω	(ὀστέω)	ὀστώ
G. D.	(νόοιν)	νοῖν	(περιπλόοιν)	περίπλοιν	(ὀστέοιν)	ὀστοῖν
	PLURAL					
N. V.	(νόοι)	νοῖ	(περίπλοοι)	περίπλοι	(ὀστέα)	ὀστᾶ
Gen.	(νόων)	νῶν	(περιπλόων)	περίπλων	(ὀστέων)	ὀστῶν
Dat.	(νόοις)	νοῖς	(περιπλόοις)	περίπλοις	(ὀστέοις)	ὀστοῖς
Acc.	(νόους)	νοῦς	(περιπλόους)	περίπλους	(ὀστέα)	ὀστᾶ

ὁ πλοῦς (πλόος) *voyage*, ὁ ῥοῦς (ῥόος) *stream*, τὸ κανοῦν (κάνεον) *basket*.

236. Accent.—a. The nominative dual is irregularly oxytone: νώ, ὀστώ, not νῶ, ὀστῶ according to 171, N. 2.

b. κανοῦν (κάνεον) *basket* receives its accent (not κάνουν) from that of the genitive and dative κανοῦ, κανῷ. Cp. 290 c.

c. Compounds retain the accent on the syllable that has it in the nominative singular: ἔκπλους from ἔκπλοος; ἔκπλου (not ἐκπλοῦ) from ἐκπλόου; ἔκπλων (not ἐκπλῶν) from ἐκπλόων.

ATTIC DECLENSION

237. Some substantives ending in -εως are placed under the Second Declension because they are derived from earlier o stems preceded by a long vowel (-εως from -ηος, 34). A few others have a consonant before -ως. The vocative has no special form.

N.—This declension is called "Attic" because the words in question generally show -ως in Attic and -ος in the Koinè dialect (p. 3, F).

238. ὁ νεώς *temple*

SINGULAR			DUAL			PLURAL		
Nom.	νεώ-ς	(Ionic νηό-ς)	N. A.	νεώ	(Ionic νηώ)	Nom.	νεῴ	(Ionic νηοί)
Gen.	νεώ	(" νηοῦ)	G. D.	νεῴν	(" νηοῖν)	Gen.	νεών	(" νηῶν)
Dat.	νεῴ	(" νηῷ)				Dat.	νεῴς	(" νηοῖς)
Acc.	νεών	(" νηό-ν)				Acc.	νεώς	(" νηούς)

238 D. Hom. has νηός *temple*, λᾱός *people*, κάλος *cable*, λαγωός *hare*, γάλοως *sister-in-law*, Ἄθόως, Κόως; Hdt. has λεώς, λαγός, Κέος. Hom. and Hdt. have

a. So ὁ λεώς *people*, ὁ Μενέλεως *Menelaus*, ὁ λαγώς *hare*. Observe that ω is found in every form, and that it takes ι *subscript* in the dative of all numbers where an ordinary ο stem has ι.

b. There are no neuter substantives belonging to the Attic declension in standard classical literature; but neuter adjectives (289) end in -ων.

c. νεώς and most words of this declension owe their forms to transfer of quantity (34) or to shortening (39). Thus, νεώς is from νηός (= Doric νᾱός), νεών from νηόν; νεῴ is from νηῷ. λαγώς is contracted from λαγωός.

d. In the accusative singular some words end in -ω or -ων, as λαγώ or λαγών *hare*. So ὁ Ἄθως, ἡ Κέως, ἡ Τέως, ἡ Κῶς, ὁ Μίνως. ἡ ἕως *dawn* always has ἕω.

239. **Accent.** — **a.** The accent of the nominative is kept in all cases. Μενέλεως (163 a) retains the accent of the earlier Μενέλᾱος.

b. The genitive and dative are oxytone when the final syllable is accented.

N. — The accentuation of the words of this declension is doubtful. Some of the ancients accented λαγώς, λαγών, others λαγῶς, λαγῶν, etc.

THIRD DECLENSION

240. This declension includes stems ending in a consonant, in ι, υ, or a diphthong, and some in ω and ο, representing ωϝ and οι.

N. — To determine whether a noun belongs to the third declension it is necessary in most cases to know the *stem*, which is usually found by dropping -ος of the genitive singular. Stems in ι and υ are classed under the consonant declension because neither of these vowels admits contraction with the case endings beginning with a vowel, herein being like a consonant.

FORMATION OF CASES: NOMINATIVE SINGULAR

241. Masculine and feminine stems *not ending in* ν, ρ, ς *and* οντ, add ς.

a. A labial (π, β, φ) + ς becomes ψ (97).

b. A dental (τ, δ, θ) + ς becomes σσ (98), which is reduced to ς (107).

c. A palatal (κ, γ, χ) or κτ + ς becomes ξ (97).

(The same changes occur in the dative plural.)

γύψ *vulture* γῡπ-ός, Ἄραψ *Arab* Ἄραβ-ος; κακότης *baseness* κακότητ-ος, ἐλπίς *hope* ἐλπίδ-ος, ὄρνῑς *bird* ὄρνῑθ-ος; φύλαξ *guard* φύλακ-ος, μάστῑξ *scourge* μάστῑγ-ος, σάλπιγξ *trumpet* σάλπιγγ-ος, ὄνυξ *nail* ὄνυχ-ος, νύξ *night* νυκτ-ός; ἅλ-ς *salt* ἁλ-ός, ἰχθῦς *fish* ἰχθύ-ος; ἐλέφᾱς *elephant* ἐλέφαντ-ος.

242. Masculine and feminine stems ending in ν, ρ, and ς reject ς and lengthen a preceding vowel if short (ε to η, ο to ω).

δαίμων *divinity* δαίμον-ος, χειμών *winter* χειμῶν-ος, λιμήν *harbour* λιμέν-ος, Ἕλλην *Greek* Ἕλλην-ος; ῥήτωρ *orator* ῥήτορ-ος, ἀήρ *air* ἀέρ-ος, φώρ *thief* φωρ-ός,

---

ἠώς, gen. ἠοῦς, *dawn*, whence Att. ἕως by 39. Hom. has Πετεῶ-ο, the original form of the genitive, from Πετεώς. νεώ is from νεωο out of νηοο.

τριήρης trireme (stem *τριηρεσ-*, 263 b), *αἰδώς shame* (stem *αἰδοσ-*, 266). On *μήν* see 259 end. For stems in *ες*, nominative *-ος*, see 263 c.

243. Masculine stems in *οντ* drop *τ* (133) and lengthen *ο* to *ω*: *γέρων old man γέροντ-ος*, *λέων lion λέοντ-ος*.

244. Neuters show the pure stem, from which final *τ* and other consonants not standing at the end of a word (133) are dropped: *ἅρμα chariot ἅρματ-ος*, *πρᾶγμα thing πράγματ-ος*, *γάλα milk γάλακτ-ος* (133 b).

245. **Summary.** — *ς* is added to stems ending in a labial, dental, palatal, and in *αντ*, *εντ*, *υντ*; to some stems in *ν* (as *εἷς one ἑν-ός*, *μέλᾱς black μέλαν-ος*); to stems in *ευ*, *αυ*, *ου*; and to masc. and fem. stems in *ι* and *υ*. *ς* is not added to most stems ending in *ν*, nor to those in *οντ*, *ρ*, *ες*, *ας*, *ος*, *υ* (neut.), *ω(ϝ)*, *ο(ι)*.

ACCUSATIVE SINGULAR

246. Masculines and feminines usually add *α* to stems ending in a consonant; *ν* to stems ending in *ι* or *υ*.

γῦπ-α, *ὄνυχ-α*, *ἐλέφαντ-α*, *λιμέν-α*, *ῥήτορ-α*, *λέοντ-α*; *πόλι-ν*, *ἰχθύ-ν*, *βοῦ-ν* from *πόλι-ς city*, *ἰχθύ-ς fish*, *βοῦ-ς ox, cow*. Stems in *ευ* take *α* (275).

247. Barytone stems of two syllables ending in *ιτ*, *ιδ*, *ῑθ* usually drop the dental and add *ν*.

χάρις grace (stem *χαριτ-*) *χάριν*, *ἔρις strife* (*ἐριδ-*) *ἔριν*, *ὄρνῑς bird* (*ὀρνῑθ-*) *ὄρνῑν*. So *εὔελπις hopeful* (*εὐελπιδ-*) *εὔελπιν* (292). Oxytones end in *α*: *ἐλπίδ-α*, *σφρᾱγῖδα* (*σφρᾱγίς seal*).

a. *κλεῖς key* (*κλειδ-*), Old Att. *κλῄς*, has *κλεῖν* (late *κλεῖδα*), acc. pl. *κλεῖς* (late *κλεῖδας*).

VOCATIVE SINGULAR

248. The vocative of masculines and feminines is usually the pure stem.

πόλι (*πόλι-ς city*), *βοῦ* (*βοῦ-ς ox, cow*), *Σώκρατες* (*Σωκράτης*). Stems in *ιδ* and *ντ* cannot retain final *δ* and *τ* (133), hence *Ἄρτεμι* from *Ἄρτεμις* (*Ἀρτεμιδ-*), *παῖ* from *παῖς boy, girl* (*παιδ-*), *νεᾶνι* from *νεᾶνις maiden* (*νεᾱνιδ-*); *γέρον* from *γέρων old man* (*γεροντ-*), *γίγαν* from *γίγᾱς giant* (*γιγαντ-*).

249. The vocative is the same as the nominative:

a. In stems ending in a stop (16) consonant (except those in *ιτ*, *ιδ*, *ῑθ*; *ντ* in nouns): *ὦ φύλαξ watchman.* (*Αἴᾱς Ajax* (*Αἰαντ-*) is nom. and voc.)

---

243 D. Hdt. has *ὀδών tooth ὀδόντ-ος.* Attic *ὀδούς* has the inflection of a participle in *-ους* (307).

247 D. The acc. in *α* (*χάριτα*, *ἔριδα*, *ὄρνῑθα*) occurs in Hom., Hdt., and in Attic poetry. So *κόρυθα* and *κόρυν* (*κόρυς helmet*) in Hom.

249 D. Hom. has *ἄνα oh king* as well as *ἄναξ* (*ἀνακτ-*); *Αἶαν* from *Αἰαντ-*. *Πουλυδάμᾱ*, *Λᾱοδάμᾱ* (from stems in *αντ*) are later forms due to analogy.

b. In oxytone stems ending in a liquid and not taking *ς* to form their nominative (242): ὦ ποιμήν *shepherd* (ποιμεν-); but ἀνήρ *man*, πατήρ *father* have ἄνερ, πάτερ (262). Barytones use the stem as the vocative: δαῖμον, ῥῆτορ from δαίμων *divinity*, ῥήτωρ *orator*.

c. In all participles.

DATIVE DUAL AND PLURAL

250. The dative plural adds -σι to the stem.

Ἄραψ (Ἀραβ-) Ἄραψι, μάστῑξ (μαστῑγ-) μάστιξι, φύλαξ (φυλακ-) φύλαξι, σῶμα (σωματ-) σώμασι (98), ἐλπίς (ἐλπιδ-) ἐλπίσι (98), ὄρνῑς (ὀρνῑθ-) ὄρνῑσι (98), ἐλέφᾱς (ἐλεφαντ-) ἐλέφᾱσι, θήρ (θηρ-) θηρσί.

a. Stems in ντ drop ντ and lengthen the preceding vowel (100): λέων (λεοντ-) λέουσι, γίγᾱς (γιγαντ-) γίγᾱσι.

b. Stems in ν drop ν without lengthening the preceding vowel (if short): δαίμων (δαιμον-) δαίμοσι, ποιμήν (ποιμεν-) ποιμέσι, φρήν *mind* (φρεν-) φρεσί.

N. — Strictly ν is not dropped, but since the stem of the dat. pl. is weak in form (253 a) the ν stood originally between two consonants and should become α (35 b). Thus, φρασί in Pindar is for φρν̥σι. Attic φρεσί borrows its ε from φρένες, φρενῶν, etc. So ποιμέσι, for ποιμασι from ποιμν̥σι, because of ποιμένες, etc.

c. ρσ is not changed to ρρ (79 a).

ACCUSATIVE PLURAL

251. **a.** The ending -ας is produced by adding ν̥ς to the stem (ν becoming α between two consonants by 35 b). Thus φύλακ-ας is from φυλακ-ν̥ς. This -ας may be added even to ι and υ stems: Hom. πόλι-ας, ἰχθύ-ας, Hdt. πήχε-ας. Hom. πόλῑς is from πόλι-νς (Cretan).

b. The nominative pl. masc. or fem. is sometimes used instead of the accusative pl.: τριήρεις 264, πόλεις and πήχεις 268.

ACCENT, STEM FORMATION, QUANTITY, GENDER

252. **Accent.** — Stems of one syllable accent the case ending in the genitive and dative of all numbers; and -ων and -οιν take the circumflex accent. Thus, φλέψ *vein*, φλεβ-ός, φλεβ-ῶν; θήρ *wild beast*, θηρ-ός, θηρ-οῖν, θηρ-ῶν; θρίξ *hair*, τριχ-ός, τριχ-ῶν.

a. Exceptions. The ending of the gen. dual and pl. is not accented in the case of ὁ, ἡ παῖς *boy*, *girl*, ὁ δμώς *slave*, ὁ θώς *jackal*, ὁ Τρώς *Trojan*, ἡ δᾴς *torch*,

---

250 D. 1. Hom. has only -οιιν in the gen. and dat. dual.

2. In the dat. pl. Hom. has -σι (βέλεσ-σι, δέπασ-σι), and in a few cases -εσι, reduced from -εσσι (ἀνάκτ-εσι); -σσι occurs after vowels (γένυ-σσι; for γένῡσι?). -εσσι was added both to stems not ending in σ (πόδ-εσσι, βό-εσσι, ἄνδρ-εσσι, οἴ-εσσι, 274 D.), and even to stems in σ (ἐπέ-εσσι). Hom. has also ποσσί, ποσί; Pind. χαρίτεσσι, θέμισσι. Tragedy has this -εσσι (κορύθ-εσσι), and so Aeolic, and the Doric of Corinth.

τὸ φῶς *light*, τὸ οὖς *ear*. Thus, παίδων (but παισί), Τρώων, ὤτων, etc. So ὤν *being*, ὄντων (305).

b. A trisyllabic form, if contracted, does not show the accent on the case ending: ἦρ-ος for ἔαρ-ος, ἦρ-ι for ἔαρ-ι, from τὸ ἔαρ *spring*.

253. Variation of Stem Formation. — Many words of the third declension show traces of an original variation of stem that is due to the influence of a shifting accent which is seen in some of the cognate languages. In Greek this variation has often been obscured by the analogy of other forms. Thus πατέρων, in comparison with Hom. πατρῶν, Lat. *patrum*, gets its ε from πατέρες.

a. Variation of stem is seen in ων, ον (259); ηρ, ερ, ρα (262); ης, εσ- (264); in stems in ι, ει (270); υ, ευ (270); ευ, ηυ (278); οι, ω (279), etc. Words in ων, ην show a middle form ον, εν, and a weak form in ν (250 N.).

b. Several words ending in ρ show a parallel stem in τ; thus, ὕδωρ *water* ὕδατ-ος, ἧπαρ *liver* ἥπατ-ος, φρέᾱρ *tank* φρέᾱτ-ος (but poet. δάμᾱρ *wife* δάμαρτ-ος). This variation between parallel *r* and *n* stems is inherited. Here -ατ represents -ṇτ after a consonant (35 b): ὑδṇτος, ἡπṇτος, cp. Lat. *jecinoris*, nom. *jecur*. ἧπαρ is probably derived from ἡπαρτ (133).

c. -ατος was transferred from such genitives as ὀνόματος, ἥπατος to other neuter words: γόνατος from γόνυ *knee*, instead of γονϝ-ος, whence Hom. γουνός. φῶς *light*, for φάος (stem φαεσ-), has taken on the τ inflection (φωτ-ός, etc.).

d. Neuter stems in -ες show -ος in the nominative. Cp. ἔτος *year* (stem ἐτεσ-) with Lat. *vetus*, *veter-is* (for *vetes-is*).

254. Variation of Quantity. — a. In poetry the quantity of ι in words in -ις may differ from that of prose; as in tragedy ὄρνῑς *bird*, κόνῑς *dust*, ὄφῑς *serpent* (in prose ὄρνῐς, κόνῐς, ὄφῐς); so in Pind. ἰχθῦς (prose ἰχθῦς) *fish*.

b. κῆρυξ *herald*, Φοῖνιξ *Phoenician*, μάστιξ *whip* have long υ and ι in the oblique cases except the dat. pl. (κήρῡκος, Φοίνῑκι, μάστῑγα, etc.). ἀλώπηξ *fox* has ε in the gen. ἀλώπεκος, etc., by analogy to such words as ποιμήν, ποιμένος (ἀλωπήκων occurs in Ionic). πῦρ *fire* has πῠρός, πῠρί, etc. (285, 25).

255. Gender. — The gender of substantives of the third declension is frequently known by the last letters of the stem.

1. Masculine are stems ending in

a. ντ: ὀδούς *tooth* (ὀδοντ-), δράκων *serpent* (δρακοντ-).

b. ητ, ωτ: πένης *day-labourer* (πενητ-), γέλως *laughter* (γελωτ-).
Exceptions. Stems in -τητ (2, b): ἡ ἐσθής *dress* (ἐσθητ-), τὸ φῶς *light* (φωτ-).

c. ν: λειμών *meadow* (λειμον-).
Exceptions. Fem.: stems in γον, δον (2, a), and φρήν *mind* (φρεν-), ἴς *strength* (ἰν-), ῥίς *nose* (ῥῑν-), ἀκτίς *ray* (ἀκτῑν-), γλωχίς *arrow-point* (γλωχῑν-), ὠδίς *birth-pang* (ὠδῑν-), εἰκών *image* (εἰκον-), ἠϊών *shore* (ἠϊον-), χθών *earth* (χθον-), χιών *snow* (χιον-), ἀλκυών *halcyon* (ἀλκυον-), etc., ὁ, ἡ χήν *goose* (χην-).

d. ρ: θήρ *wild beast* (θηρ-), φώρ *thief* (φωρ-).
Exceptions. Fem.: χείρ *hand* (χερ-), κήρ *fate* (κηρ-), γαστήρ *belly* (γαστερ-); neut.: stems in αρ (3, a), πῦρ *fire* (πυρ-), and the indeclinable πέλωρ *monster*, τέκμωρ (Hom.) *token*, etc.

e. ευ: γονεύς *parent*, φονεύς *murderer*.

2. Feminine are stems ending in

a. **γον, δον**: *σταγών drop* (σταγον-), *χελῑδών swallow* (χελῑδον-).
b. **τητ, δ, θ**: *κακότης baseness* (κακοτητ-), *ἔρις strife* (ἐριδ-), *ἐλπίς hope* (ἐλπιδ-).
Exceptions. Masc.: *πούς foot* (ποδ-), ὁ, ἡ *ὄρνῑς bird* (ὀρνῑθ-).
c. **ι, υ** with nom. in -ις, -υς: *πόλι-ς city*, *ἰσχύ-ς strength*.
Exceptions. Masc.: *ὄφι-ς serpent*, *ἔχι-ς viper*, *ὄρχι-ς testicle; βότρυ-ς cluster of grapes*, *ἰχθύ-ς fish*, *μῦ-ς mouse*, *νέκυ-ς corpse*, *στάχυ-ς ear of corn*, *πέλεκυ-ς axe*, *πῆχυ-ς fore-arm;* and ὁ, ἡ *σῦ-ς* or *ὗ-ς swine*.
d. **οι**: *ἠχώ echo*, *πειθώ persuasion*.

3. Neuter are stems ending in

a. **ατ, αρ**: *πρᾶγμα thing* (πρᾱγματ-), *νέκταρ nectar* (νεκταρ-). But ὁ *ψάρ starling*.
b. **ας, ες** (with nom. in -ος): *κρέας flesh* (κρεασ-), *γένος race* (γενεσ-).
c. **ι, υ** with nom. in -ι,-υ: *σίνᾱπι mustard*, *ἄστυ city*.

N.—No stem ending in π, β, φ or κ, γ, χ is neuter.

256. STEMS IN A LABIAL (π, β, φ) OR IN A PALATAL (κ, γ, χ)

SINGULAR

	ὁ Αἰθίοψ (Αἰθιοπ-) *Ethiopian*	ἡ φλέψ (φλεβ-) *vein*	ὁ φύλαξ (φυλακ-) *watchman*	ἡ φάλαγξ (φαλαγγ-) *phalanx*	ὁ ἡ αἴξ (αἰγ-) *goat*	ἡ θρίξ (τριχ-, 125 f) *hair*
Nom.	Αἰθίοψ	φλέψ	φύλαξ	φάλαγξ	αἴξ	θρίξ
Gen.	Αἰθίοπ-ος	φλεβ-ός	φύλακ-ος	φάλαγγ-ος	αἰγ-ός	τριχ-ός
Dat.	Αἰθίοπ-ι	φλεβ-ί	φύλακ-ι	φάλαγγ-ι	αἰγ-ί	τριχ-ί
Acc.	Αἰθίοπ-α	φλέβ-α	φύλακ-α	φάλαγγ-α	αἶγ-α	τρίχ-α
Voc.	Αἰθίοψ	φλέψ	φύλαξ	φάλαγξ	αἴξ	θρίξ
DUAL						
N. A. V.	Αἰθίοπ-ε	φλέβ-ε	φύλακ-ε	φάλαγγ-ε	αἶγ-ε	τρίχ-ε
G. D.	Αἰθιόπ-οιν	φλεβ-οῖν	φυλάκ-οιν	φαλάγγ-οιν	αἰγ-οῖν	τριχ-οῖν
PLURAL						
N. V.	Αἰθίοπ-ες	φλέβ-ες	φύλακ-ες	φάλαγγ-ες	αἶγ-ες	τρίχ-ες
Gen.	Αἰθιόπ-ων	φλεβ-ῶν	φυλάκ-ων	φαλάγγ-ων	αἰγ-ῶν	τριχ-ῶν
Dat.	Αἰθίοψι(ν)	φλεψί(ν)	φύλαξι(ν)	φάλαγξι(ν)	αἰξί(ν)	θριξί(ν)
Acc.	Αἰθίοπ-ας	φλέβ-ας	φύλακ-ας	φάλαγγ-ας	αἶγ-ας	τρίχ-ας

Masculine: *κλώψ thief* (κλωπ-), *γύψ vulture* (γῡπ-), *Ἄραψ Arab* (Ἀραβ-), *θώρᾱξ breastplate* (θωρᾱκ-), *ὄνυξ nail* (ὀνυχ-). Feminine: *κλῖμαξ ladder* (κλῑμακ-), *μάστῑξ whip* (μαστῑγ-, 254 b), *σάλπιγξ trumpet* (σαλπιγγ-), *κατῆλιψ upper story* (κατηλιφ-).

STEMS IN A DENTAL (τ, δ, θ)

257. A. MASCULINES AND FEMININES

	SINGULAR					
	ὁ θής (θητ-) *serf*	ἡ ἐλπίς (ἐλπιδ-) *hope*	ἡ χάρις (χαριτ-) *grace*	ὁ ἡ ὄρνῑς (ὀρνῑθ-) *bird*	ὁ γίγᾱς (γιγαντ-) *giant*	ὁ γέρων (γεροντ-) *old man*
Nom.	θής	ἐλπίς	χάρις	ὄρνῑς	γίγᾱς	γέρων
Gen.	θητ-ός	ἐλπίδ-ος	χάριτ-ος	ὄρνῑθ-ος	γίγαντ-ος	γέροντ-ος
Dat.	θητ-ί	ἐλπίδ-ι	χάριτ-ι	ὄρνῑθ-ι	γίγαντ-ι	γέροντ-ι
Acc.	θῆτ-α	ἐλπίδ-α	χάριν	ὄρνῑν	γίγαντ-α	γέροντ-α
Voc.	θής	ἐλπί	χάρι	ὄρνῑ	γίγαν	γέρον
	DUAL					
N. A. V.	θῆτ-ε	ἐλπίδ-ε	χάριτ-ε	ὄρνῑθ-ε	γίγαντ-ε	γέροντ-ε
G. D.	θητ-οῖν	ἐλπίδ-οιν	χαρίτ-οιν	ὀρνί̄θ-οιν	γιγάντ-οιν	γερόντ-οιν
	PLURAL					
N. V.	θῆτ-ες	ἐλπίδ-ες	χάριτ-ες	ὄρνῑθ-ες	γίγαντ-ες	γέροντ-ες
Gen.	θητ-ῶν	ἐλπίδ-ων	χαρίτ-ων	ὀρνί̄θ-ων	γιγάντ-ων	γερόντ-ων
Dat.	θησί(ν)	ἐλπίσι(ν)	χάρισι(ν)	ὄρνῑσι(ν)	γίγᾱσι(ν)	γέρουσι(ν)
Acc.	θῆτ-ας	ἐλπίδ-ας	χάριτ-ας	ὄρνῑθ-ας	γίγαντ-ας	γέροντ-ας

Masculine: γέλως *laughter* (γελωτ-), ἐλέφᾱς *elephant* (ἐλεφαντ-), λέων *lion* (λεοντ-), ὀδούς *tooth* (ὀδοντ-), voc. ὀδούς. Feminine: ἐσθής *clothing* (ἐσθητ-), ἔρις *strife* (ἐριδ-), ἀσπίς *shield* (ἀσπιδ-), πατρίς *fatherland* (πατριδ-), κόρυς *helmet* (κορυθ-).

a. In πούς *foot*, Doric πώς (stem ποδ-) ου is irregular.

258. B. NEUTERS WITH STEMS IN τ AND IN ᾰτ VARYING WITH ας

	SINGULAR				
	σῶμα *body* (σωματ-)	ἧπαρ *liver* (ἡπατ-)	τέρας *portent* (τερατ-)	κέρας *horn* (κερᾰτ-, κερασ-)		
N. A. V.	σῶμα	ἧπαρ	τέρας	κέρας		
Gen.	σώματ-ος	ἥπατ-ος	τέρατ-ος	κέρᾰτ-ος	(κέρα-ος)	κέρως
Dat.	σώματ-ι	ἥπατ-ι	τέρατ-ι	κέρᾰτ-ι	(κέρα-ϊ)	κέραι

257 D. χρώς *skin* (χρωτ-) and some other words often show a stem with no τ. Thus, Hom. χροός, χροΐ (also Hdt.), χρόα, and also, but rarely, χρωτός, χρῶτα. Hom. has ἱδρῷ, γέλῳ, ἔρῳ for Att. ἱδρῶτι (ἱδρώς *sweat*), γέλωτι (γέλως *laughter*), ἔρωτι (ἔρως *love*). Hom. has also acc. ἱδρῶ, γέλω (or γέλων), ἔρον (from ἔρος). Some stems in -ιδ are generally ι stems in Ionic, Doric, and Aeolic: Θέτις, Θέτιος (but Θέτιδος Θ 370), Πάρις, Πάριος.

258 D. The other dialects rarely show the τ forms. Hom. has τέρας, τέραα (τείρεα), τεράων, τεράεσσι, κέρας, κέραος, κέραι, κέρα, κεράων, κέρασι and κεράεσσι.

B. NEUTERS WITH STEMS IN τ AND IN ᾰτ VARYING WITH ας — Concluded

DUAL

	σῶμα *body* (σωματ-)	ἧπαρ *liver* (ἡπατ-)	τέρας *portent* (τερατ-)	κέρας *horn* (κερᾰτ-, κερασ-)		
N. A. V.	σώματ-ε	ἥπατ-ε	τέρατ-ε	κέρᾱτ-ε	(κέρα-ε)	κέρᾱ
G. D.	σωμάτ-οιν	ἡπάτ-οιν	τεράτ-οιν	κεράτ-οιν	(κερά-οιν)	κερῷν

PLURAL

N. V.	σώματ-α	ἥπατ-α	τέρατ-α	κέρᾱτ-α	(κέρα-α)	κέρᾱ
Gen.	σωμάτ-ων	ἡπάτ-ων	τεράτ-ων	κεράτ-ων	(κερά-ων)	κερῶν
Dat.	σώμασι(ν)	ἥπασι(ν)	τέρασι(ν)	κέρᾱσι(ν)		
Acc.	σώματ-α	ἥπατ-α	τέρατ-α	κέρᾱτ-α	(κέρα-α)	κέρᾱ

ὄνομα *name* (ὀνοματ-), στόμα *mouth* (στοματ), μέλι *honey* (μελιτ-), γάλα *milk* (γαλακτ-, 133 b), φῶς *light* (φωτ-), κῆρ *heart* (for κηρδ-, 133 b).

a. Stems in ας (264) drop σ before the endings and contract αο, αω to ω, and αα to ᾱ.

b. κέρας, meaning *wing of an army*, is declined from the stem κερασ- (ἐπὶ κέρως *in single file*); in the meaning *horn*, from the stem κερᾱτ-.

c. For the inflection ἧπαρ, ἥπατ-ος, see 253 b. Of like inflection are ἄλειφαρ *fat*, φρέᾱρ *cistern*, δέλεαρ *bait*, and poetic ἦμαρ *day*, εἶδαρ *food*, πεῖραρ *end*.

d. τέρας, κέρας form their nominative from a stem in ς. So, too, πέρας *end* πέρατ-ος, φῶς *light* (contracted from φάος) φωτ-ός (253 c).

259. STEMS IN A LIQUID (λ, ρ) OR A NASAL (ν).

SINGULAR

	ὁ θήρ (θηρ-) *wild beast*	ὁ ῥήτωρ (ῥητορ-) *orator*	ἡ ῥῑ́ς (ῥῑν-) *nose*	ἡγεμών (ἡγεμον-) *leader*	ἀγών (ἀγων-) *contest*	ποιμήν (ποιμεν-) *shepherd*
Nom.	θήρ	ῥήτωρ	ῥῑ́ς	ἡγεμών	ἀγών	ποιμήν
Gen.	θηρ-ός	ῥήτορ-ος	ῥῑν-ός	ἡγεμόν-ος	ἀγῶν-ος	ποιμέν-ος
Dat.	θηρ-ί	ῥήτορ-ι	ῥῑν-ί	ἡγεμόν-ι	ἀγῶν-ι	ποιμέν-ι
Acc.	θῆρ-α	ῥήτορ-α	ῥῖν-α	ἡγεμόν-α	ἀγῶν-α	ποιμέν-α
Voc.	θήρ	ῥῆτορ	ῥῑ́ς	ἡγεμών	ἀγών	ποιμήν

Hdt. has ε for α before a vowel (cp. 264 D. 3) in τέρεος, τέρεα (also τέρατος, τέρατα), κέρεος, κέρει, κέρεα, κερέων. Hom. has πεῖρας πείρατος for πέρας πέρατος. From φάος (φόως), whence φῶς, he has dat. φάει, pl. φάεα. φάος is used in tragedy.

259 D. Late Greek shows δελφίν, ῥίν, θίν *shore* (Hom. θίς). ἕλμινς *worm* in Hippocrates has its ν from the oblique cases. Hom. has ἠέρι, ἠέρα from ἀήρ *air*; from Κρονίων Hom. has Κρονίωνος and Κρονίονος. μάκαρς is Doric for μάκᾱρ *happy*. Pind. has φρασί (250 N.). Ionic μείς, Doric μής are from μενς for μηνς (40, 37 D. 1, 2). Aeolic gen. μῆννος is from μηνσ-ος.

STEMS IN A LIQUID (λ, ρ) OR A NASAL (ν) — *Concluded*

DUAL

	ὁ θήρ	ὁ ῥήτωρ	ἡ ῥῖς	ἡγεμών	ἀγών	ποιμήν
	(θηρ-)	(ῥητορ-)	(ῥῑν-)	(ἡγεμον-)	(ἀγων-)	(ποιμεν-)
	wild beast	*orator*	*nose*	*leader*	*contest*	*shepherd*
N. A. V.	θῆρ-ε	ῥήτορ-ε	ῥῖν-ε	ἡγεμόν-ε	ἀγῶν-ε	ποιμέν-ε
G. D.	θηρ-οῖν	ῥητόρ-οιν	ῥῑν-οῖν	ἡγεμόν-οιν	ἀγών-οιν	ποιμέν-οιν

PLURAL

N. V.	θῆρ-ες	ῥήτορ-ες	ῥῖν-ες	ἡγεμόν-ες	ἀγῶν-ες	ποιμέν-ες
Gen.	θηρ-ῶν	ῥητόρ-ων	ῥῑν-ῶν	ἡγεμόν-ων	ἀγών-ων	ποιμέν-ων
Dat.	θηρ-σί(ν)	ῥήτορ-σι(ν)	ῥῑσί(ν)	ἡγεμόσι(ν)	ἀγῶσι(ν)	ποιμέσι(ν)
Acc.	θῆρ-ας	ῥήτορ-ας	ῥῖν-ας	ἡγεμόν-ας	ἀγῶν-ας	ποιμέν-ας

ὁ αἰθήρ *upper air* (αἰθερ-), ὁ κρᾱτήρ *mixing bowl* (κρᾱτηρ-), ὁ φώρ *thief* (φωρ-), τὸ νέκταρ *nectar* (νεκταρ-), ὁ δελφίς *dolphin* (δελφιν-), ὁ Ἕλλην *Greek* (Ἑλλην-), ὁ δαίμων *divinity* (δαιμον-), voc. δαῖμον, 249 b. The only λ stem is ὁ ἅλς *salt* (pl. *grains of salt*); ἡ ἅλς (poetic) means *sea*. ὁ μήν *month* was originally a sigma stem (μηνσ-, cp. *mensis*).

260. Accusative Sing. — Ἀπόλλω and Ποσειδῶ are found as well as Ἀπόλλωνα, Ποσειδῶνα. The shorter forms are regular in inscriptions, and occur especially in expressions of swearing after νὴ τόν, μὰ τόν (1596 b).

261. Vocative. — σωτήρ *preserver*, Ἀπόλλων, Ποσειδῶν (from Ποσειδέων, -άων, -ᾱϝων) have voc. σῶτερ, Ἄπολλον, Πόσειδον with recessive accent. Recessive accent also occurs in compound proper names in -ων; as Ἀγαμέμνων, Ἀγάμεμνον; Αὐτομέδων, Αὐτόμεδον; but not in those in -φρων (Εὐθύφρον). Λακεδαίμων has Λακεδαῖμον, Φιλήμων, Φιλῆμον.

STEMS IN ερ VARYING WITH ρ

262. Several words in -τηρ show three forms of stem gradation: -τηρ strong, -τερ middle, -τρ weak. ρ between consonants becomes ρα (35 b). The vocative has recessive accent. ἀνήρ *man* has the weak form in ρ even before vowels; between ν and ρ, δ is inserted by 130.

---

260 D. κυκεών *potion* usually has κυκεῶ for κυκεῶνα.

262 D. Poetry often has πατέρος, πατέρι, μητέρος, μητέρι, etc. Poetical are πατρῶν; θυγατέρι, θύγατρα, θύγατρες, θυγατρῶν, θυγατέρεσσι, θύγατρας, γαστέρος, etc.; and ἀνέρος, ἀνέρι, ἀνέρα, ἀνέρες, ἀνέρων, ἀνέρας all with long α-. Hom. has ἄνδρεσσι and ἀνδράσι (with -ασι only in this word), Δήμητρος and Δημήτερος.

SINGULAR

	ὁ πατήρ (πατερ-) *father*	ἡ μήτηρ (μητερ-) *mother*	ἡ θυγάτηρ (θυγατερ-) *daughter*	ὁ ἀνήρ (ἀνερ- or ἀν(δ)ρ-) *man*
Nom.	**πατήρ**	**μήτηρ**	**θυγάτηρ**	**ἀνήρ**
Gen.	**πατρ-ός**	**μητρ-ός**	**θυγατρ-ός**	**ἀνδρ-ός**
Dat.	**πατρ-ί**	**μητρ-ί**	**θυγατρ-ί**	**ἀνδρ-ί**
Acc.	**πατέρ-α**	**μητέρ-α**	**θυγατέρ-α**	**ἄνδρ-α**
Voc.	**πάτερ**	**μῆτερ**	**θύγατερ**	**ἄνερ**
		DUAL		
N. A. V.	**πατέρ-ε**	**μητέρ-ε**	**θυγατέρ-ε**	**ἄνδρ-ε**
G. D.	**πατέρ-οιν**	**μητέρ-οιν**	**θυγατέρ-οιν**	**ἀνδρ-οῖν**
		PLURAL		
N. V.	**πατέρ-ες**	**μητέρ-ες**	**θυγατέρ-ες**	**ἄνδρ-ες**
Gen.	**πατέρ-ων**	**μητέρ-ων**	**θυγατέρ-ων**	**ἀνδρ-ῶν**
Dat.	**πατρά-σι(ν)**	**μητρά-σι(ν)**	**θυγατρά-σι(ν)**	**ἀνδρά-σι(ν)**
Acc.	**πατέρ-ας**	**μητέρ-ας**	**θυγατέρ-ας**	**ἄνδρ-ας**

a. The accent in the weak forms of μήτηρ, θυγάτηρ in the gen. and dat. sing. follows that of πατρός, πατρί.

b. γαστήρ *belly*, has γαστρός, etc. Δημήτηρ is inflected Δήμητρος, Δήμητρι, Δήμητρα, Δήμητερ.

c. ἀστήρ *star* has gen. ἀστέρος, dat. ἀστέρι, dat. pl. ἀστράσι.

STEMS IN SIGMA (ες, ας, ος)

263. Stems in sigma are contracted where σ falls out between the vowel of the stem and the vowel of the ending (120). Thus, γένος *race*, gen. γενε(σ)-ος γένους, dat. γενε(σ)-ι γένει, cp. Lat. *genus gener-is* (for *genes-is*), *gener-i*.

a. The masculine and feminine accusative plural, when it is contracted, borrows the form of the contracted nominative plural. -εις is not derived from -εας. In the dative plural the union of σ of the stem and σ of the ending produces σσ, which is reduced to σ without lengthening the preceding vowel (107).

b. Masculine stems in ες with the nominative in -ης are proper names; the feminine τριήρης *trireme* is an adjective used substantively (properly, *triply fitted; ἡ τριήρης* (ναῦς) 'ship with three banks of oars').

c. Neuters with stems in ες have -ος in the nominative, accusative, and vocative singular; neuters with stems in ας have -ας in these cases.

d. Some stems in ας have also a stem in ατ or ᾰτ (258).

264.

	ὁ Σωκράτης *Socrates* (Σωκρατεσ-)		ὁ Δημοσθένης *Demosthenes* (Δημοσθενεσ-)	
Nom.		**Σωκράτης**		**Δημοσθένης**
Gen.	(Σωκράτε-ος)	**Σωκράτους**	(Δημοσθένε-ος)	**Δημοσθένους**
Dat.	(Σωκράτε-ι)	**Σωκράτει**	(Δημοσθένε-ι)	**Δημοσθένει**
Acc.	(Σωκράτε-α)	**Σωκράτη**	(Δημοσθένε-α)	**Δημοσθένη**
Voc.		**Σώκρατες**		**Δημόσθενες**

SINGULAR

	ἡ τριήρης (τριηρεσ-) *trireme*		τὸ γένος (γενεσ-) *race*		τὸ γέρας (γερασ-) *prize*	
Nom.		**τριήρης**		**γένος**		**γέρας**
Gen.	(τριήρε-ος)	**τριήρους**	(γένε-ος)	**γένους**	(γέρα-ος)	**γέρως**
Dat.	(τριήρε-ι)	**τριήρει**	(γένε-ι)	**γένει**	(γέρα-ι)	**γέραι**
Acc.	(τριήρε-α)	**τριήρη**		**γένος**		**γέρας**
Voc.		**τριῆρες**		**γένος**		**γέρας**

DUAL

N. A. V.	(τριήρε-ε)	**τριήρει**	(γένε-ε)	**γένει**	(γέρα-ε)	**γέρᾱ**
G. D.	(τριηρέ-οιν)	**τριήροιν**	(γενέ-οιν)	**γενοῖν**	(γερά-οιν)	**γερῷν**

PLURAL

N. V.	(τριήρε-ες)	**τριήρεις**	(γένε-α)	**γένη**	(γέρα-α)	**γέρᾱ**
Gen.	(τριηρέ-ων)	**τριήρων**	(γενέ-ων)	**γενῶν**	(γερά-ων)	**γερῶν**
Dat.	(τριήρεσ-σι)	**τριήρεσι(ν)**	(γένεσ-σι)	**γένεσι(ν)**	(γέρασ-σι)	**γέρασι(ν)**
Acc.		**τριήρεις**	(γένε-α)	**γένη**	(γέρα-α)	**γέρᾱ**

Διογένης *Diogenes*, Ἱπποκράτης *Hippocrates*. Neuters: ἔτος *year*, εὖρος *width*, ξίφος *sword*, τεῖχος *wall*, γῆρας *old age*, κρέας *flesh* (for κέρας *horn* see 258).

a. Proper names in -ης have recessive accent in the vocative.

b. Proper names in -γένης, -κράτης, -μένης, -φάνης, etc., may have an accus. in -ην derived from the first declension. Thus, Σωκράτην, Ἀριστοφάνην, like Ἀτρείδην (222, 282 N.). But names in -κλῆς (265) have only -εᾱ.

c. Proper names in -ης often show -εος, -εα in the lyric parts of tragedy.

d. Neuters in -ος often show open forms (especially -εων) in Attic poetry. -εων is frequent in Xenophon.

e. τριήροιν and τριήρων have irregular accent by analogy to the other forms.

f. A preceding ρ does not prevent the contraction of εα to η, as ὄρη from τὸ ὄρος *mountain* (cp. 31. 1).

g. The dat. sing. of ας stems is properly -ᾰι; but -ᾳ is often written on the authority of the ancient grammarians. This ᾳ may possibly be due to the analogy of ᾳ in ᾱ stems.

---

264 D. 1. Hom. uses the open or the closed forms according to convenience. -ευς occurs in the gen. of a few words in -ος (βέλευς); -εων is often a monosyl-

265. When -εσ- of the stem is preceded by ε, the forms are inflected as follows: τὸ δέος *fear* (δεεσ-), Περικλῆς from Περικλέης *Pericles* (Περικλεεσ-):

Nom.		**δέος**	(Περικλέης)	**Περικλῆς**
Gen.	(δέε-ος)	**δέους**	(Περικλέε-ος)	**Περικλέους**
Dat.	(δέε-ι)	**δέει**	(Περικλέε-ι)	**Περικλεῖ**
Acc.		**δέος**	(Περικλέε-α)	**Περικλέᾱ**
Voc.		**δέος**	(Περίκλεες)	**Περίκλεις**

So Ἡρακλῆς *Heracles*, Σοφοκλῆς *Sophocles*.

a. After ε, εα contracts to ᾱ (56). On the contraction of -εεος, see **55.**

b. δέος is uncontracted because the form was originally δεϳος (58).

STEMS IN ος

266. ἡ αἰδώς *shame* is the only ος stem in Attic. It is inflected in the singular only. Nom. **αἰδώς**, Gen. **αἰδοῦς** (αἰδό-ος), Dat. **αἰδοῖ** (αἰδό-ι), Acc. **αἰδῶ** (αἰδό-α), Voc. **αἰδώς.**

STEMS IN ω(ϝ)

267. Stems in ωϝ have lost *vau* and appear as ω stems. This ω contracts with the case endings in the dative and accusative singular and in the nominative and accusative plural. Stems in ωϝ are masculine.

---

lable (60), as is the accus. sing. and pl. -εα from nom. -ης or -ος. Hdt. has open -εος, -εα, -εες (?), -εα. In the dat. pl. Hom. has βέλεσσι, βέλεσι, and βελέεσσι (250 D. 2) from βέλος *missile.*

2. Stems in ας are generally uncontracted in Hom. (γήραος, γήραϊ), but we find -αι in the dat. sing., κρεῶν and κρειῶν in the gen. pl. In the nom. and acc. pl. α is short (γέρᾰ), and this is sometimes the case even in Attic poetry (κρέᾰ). The explanation is obscure (γέρᾰ does not stand for γέρα'). Hom. has δέπασσι and δεπάεσσι (δέπας *cup*).

3. In Hom. and Hdt. several words in -ας show ε for α before a vowel (cp. ὁρέω in Hdt. for ὁράω). Hom.: οὖδας *ground*, οὔδεος, οὔδεϊ and οὔδει; κῶας *fleece*, κώεα, κώεσι; Hdt.: γέρας, γέρεος, but κρέας, κρέως, κρεῶν. In Attic poetry: βρέτας *image*, βρέτεος, βρέτει, etc. Cp. 258 D.

265 D. Hom. has κλέα (for κλέα' ?), and from -κλῆς: -ῆος, -ῆι; Hdt.: -έος (for -έεος), -έϊ, -εᾰ. For -ῆος, -ῆα the open -έεος, -έεα may be read. Attic poetry often has the open forms -έης (also in prose inscrip.), -έει, -εες.

266 D. Hom. and Ion. ἠώς *dawn* (ἠοσ-) is inflected like αἰδώς. For αἰδοῦς, ἠῶ we may read αἰδόος, ἠόα and some other open forms in Hom. The Attic form ἕως is declined according to 238; but the accus. is ἕω (238 d). Hom. has ἱδρόα from ἱδρώς *sweat* (usually a τ stem). Cp. 257 D.

267 D. Hom. has ἥρωϊ (for ἥρῳ read ἡρῷϊ), ἥρωα (or ἥρω'), ἥρωες ἥρωας, Μίνωα and Μίνω. Hdt. has the gen. Μίνω and Μίνωος, the acc. πάτρων, ἥρων, but μήτρωα.

	SINGULAR		DUAL		PLURAL
Nom.	ἥρως *hero*	N. A. V.	ἥρω-ε	N. V.	ἥρω-ες (rarely ἥρως)
Gen.	ἥρω-ος	G. D.	ἡρώ-οιν	Gen.	ἡρώ-ων
Dat.	ἥρω-ι (usually ἥρῳ)			Dat.	ἥρω-σι(ν)
Acc.	ἥρω-α (usually ἥρω)			Acc.	ἥρω-ας (rarely ἥρως)
Voc.	ἥρως				

Τρώς *Trojan* (252 a), πάτρως *father's brother*, μήτρως *mother's brother*, δμώς *slave* (poetic, cp. 252 a).

a. Forms of the Attic second declension (237) are gen. ἥρω, Μίνω, acc. ἥρων; dual ἥρῳν (on an inscription).

STEMS IN ι AND υ

268. Most stems in ι and some stems in υ show the pure stem vowel only in the nominative, accusative, and vocative singular. In the other cases they show an ε in place of ι and υ, and -ως instead of -ος in the genitive singular. Contraction takes place when this ε stands before ε, ι, or α of the case ending.

		ἡ πόλις *city* (πολι-)		ὁ πῆχυς *forearm* (πηχυ-)		τὸ ἄστυ *town* (ἀστυ-)	ἡ σῦς *sow* (συ-)	ὁ ἰχθῦς *fish* (ἰχθυ-)
				SINGULAR				
Nom.		πόλι-ς		πῆχυ-ς		ἄστυ	σῦ-ς	ἰχθῦ-ς
Gen.		πόλε-ως		πήχε-ως		ἄστε-ως	συ-ός	ἰχθύ-ος
Dat.	(πόλε-ι)	πόλει	(πήχε-ι)	πήχει	(ἄστε-ι)	ἄστει	συ-ΐ	ἰχθύ-ϊ
Acc.		πόλι-ν		πῆχυ-ν		ἄστυ	σῦ-ν	ἰχθῦ-ν
Voc.		πόλι		πῆχυ		ἄστυ	σῦ	ἰχθῦ
				DUAL				
N.A.V.	(πόλε-ε)	πόλει	(πήχε-ε)	πήχει	(ἄστε-ε)	ἄστει	σύ-ε	ἰχθύ-ε
G. D.		πολέ-οιν		πηχέ-οιν		ἀστέ-οιν	συ-οῖν	ἰχθύ-οιν
				PLURAL				
N. V.	(πόλε-ες)	πόλεις	(πήχε-ες)	πήχεις	(ἄστε-α)	ἄστη	σύ-ες	ἰχθύ-ες
Gen.		πόλε-ων		πήχε-ων		ἄστε-ων	συ-ῶν	ἰχθύ-ων
Dat.		πόλε-σι(ν)		πήχε-σι(ν)		ἄστε-σι(ν)	συ-σί(ν)	ἰχθύ-σι(ν)
Acc.		πόλεις		πήχεις	(ἄστε-α)	ἄστη	σῦς	ἰχθῦς

---

268 D. 1. ι stems. a. Doric, Aeolic, and New Ionic retain the ι stem without variation in all cases: πόλις, πόλιος, πόλῑ (from πολι-ι) and rarely πόλει in Hdt., πόλιν, πόλι, πόλιες, πολίων, πόλισι, πόλῑς from πόλινς (Cretan), and πόλιας.

269. Stems in ι and υ are of two kinds:—

1. **a.** Stems in ι, with genitive in -εως, as (masc.) μάντις *seer*, ἔχις *viper*; (fem.) πόλις *city*, ποίησις *poetry*, δύναμις *power*, στάσις *faction*, ὕβρις *outrage*. Neuter nominatives in -ι are not used in classical prose.

   b. Stems in ι, with genitive in -ιος, as ὁ κίς *weevil*, gen. κῑ-ός, dat. κῑ-ί; and so in proper names in -ις, as Λύγδαμις *Lygdamis*, gen. Λυγδάμιος.

2. **a.** Stems in υ, with genitive in -υος; as (masc.) μῦς *mouse*, βότρυς *cluster of grapes*, ἰχθύς *fish*; (fem.) δρῦς *oak*, ὀφρύς *eyebrow*, ἰσχύς *force*.

   b. Stems in υ, with genitive in -εως: (masc.) πῆχυς *forearm*, πέλεκυς *axe*; (neut.) ἄστυ *town*.

N. 1.—In the nom., acc., and voc. sing. barytone stems in υ have short υ; oxytone substantives (usually) and monosyllables have ῡ; and monosyllables circumflex the ῡ (σῦς, σῦν, σῦ).

N. 2.—ἡ ἔγχελυς *eel* follows ἰχθύς in the singular (ἐγχέλυ-ος, etc.), but πῆχυς in the plural (ἐγχέλεις, etc.). But this does not hold for Aristotle.

270. Stems in ι and υ vary with stronger stems, of which ε in the cases other than nom., acc., and voc. sing. is a survival. Thus:

a. ι, υ, as in πόλι-ς, πῆχυ-ς.

b. ει, ευ, which before vowels lost their ι and υ (43), as in πολε(ι̯)-ι, πολε(ι̯)-ες, πηχε(υ̯)-ες; which contract to πόλει, πόλεις, πήχεις.

c. There is also a stem in η, as in Hom. πόλη-ος (268 D. 1, c), whence πόλε-ως.

N. 1.—πόλε-ος in Attic poetry for the sake of the metre is due to the analogy of υ stems with gen. in -ε-ος (ἡδέ-ος, 297). Hom. πήχε-ος is the regular form (from πηχε(υ̯)-ος). Attic πήχε-ως follows πόλεως. πόλε-σι and πήχε-σι for πόλι-σι and πήχυ-σι are due to the analogy of forms from stems in ει, ευ (πόλε-ων, πήχε-ων, etc.).

N. 2.—The dual πόλεε occurs in some Mss.

271. Accent.—Final -ως of the genitive singular does not prevent the acute from standing on the antepenult (163 a). Thus πόλε-ως, πήχε-ως, ἄστε-ως. πόλε-ως retains the accent of the earlier πόλη-ος, which, by transference of quantity (34), became πόλε-ως. The accent of the gen. pl. follows that of the gen. sing.

272. Accusative plural.—πόλεις, πήχεις are borrowed from the nominative. ἰχθῦς is from ἰχθυν-ς. ἰχθύας occurs in late Greek. Cp. 251 a.

---

b. Hom. has πόλις, πόλιος, πόλῑ, πόλει or -ϊ (for which some read πόλῑ, as κόνῑ; πόσεϊ is correct) and πτόλεϊ, πόλιν, πόλι; pl. πόλιες, πολίων, πόλεσι (some read instead πόλισι) or πολίεσσι (250 D. 2) ἐπάλξεσιν, πόλῑς or πόλιας (πόλεις appears in some texts).

c. Hom. has also forms with η: πόληος, πόληι, πόληες, πόληας.

2. **υ** stems. **a.** Ionic, Doric, and Aeolic have the open forms πήχεες, ἄστεϊ, ἄστεα; in the gen. sing. -ος, never -ως (πήχεος, ἄστεος). In the dat. sing. of words of more than one syllable Hom. has -υϊ or -υι, as νέκυι (νέκυς *corpse*), but Hdt. does not show -υι.

b. The gen. pl. has the regular accent (πηχέων, ἀστέων). On the dat. πελέκεσσι, νέκυσσι, πίτυσσι (some would read νέκῡσι, πίτῡσι), νεκύεσσι, see 250 D. 2. Hom. has accus. ἰχθῦς and ἰχθύας, Hdt. has ἰχθύας very rarely.

273. Contraction. — ἰχθῦ (once) for ἰχθύε and ἰχθῦς for ἰχθύες occur in comedy. ἰχθῦ is not a legitimate contraction, as υ cannot contract with ε (51 c). ἰχθῦς (for ἰχθύες) is the accus. form used as the nom. (251 b).

274. οἶς *sheep* is declined as follows: οἶς, οἰ-ός, οἰ-ί, οἶ-ν, οἶ; dual, οἶ-ε, οἰ-οῖν; pl. οἶ-ες, οἰ-ῶν, οἰ-σί, οἶ-ς. Here the stem is οἰ, representing ὀϝι, which is properly an ι stem: ὀϝι-ς, Lat. *ovi-s*.

275. STEMS IN ευ, αυ, ου

		SINGULAR		
	ὁ βασιλεύ-ς *king*	ἡ γραῦ-ς *old woman*	ἡ ναῦ-ς *ship*	ὁ, ἡ βοῦ-ς *ox, cow*
Nom.	βασιλεύ-ς	γραῦ-ς	ναῦ-ς	βοῦ-ς
Gen.	βασιλέ-ως	γρᾱ-ός	νε-ώς	βο-ός
Dat. (βασιλέ-ι)	βασιλεῖ	γρᾱ-ΐ	νη-ΐ	βο-ΐ
Acc.	βασιλέ-ᾱ	γραῦ-ν	ναῦ-ν	βοῦ-ν
Voc.	βασιλεῦ	γραῦ	ναῦ	βοῦ
		DUAL		
N. A. V.	βασιλῆ	γρᾶ-ε	νῆ-ε	βό-ε
G. D.	βασιλέ-οιν	γρᾱ-οῖν	νε-οῖν	βο-οῖν
		PLURAL		
N. V.	βασιλῆς, later βασιλεῖς	γρᾶ-ες	νῆ-ες	βό-ες
Gen.	βασιλέ-ων	γρᾱ-ῶν	νε-ῶν	βο-ῶν
Dat.	βασιλεῦ-σι(ν)	γραυ-σί(ν)	ναυ-σί(ν)	βου-σί(ν)
Acc.	βασιλέ-ᾱς	γραῦ-ς	ναῦ-ς	βοῦ-ς

Like βασιλεύς are declined the masculine oxytones ὁ ἱππεύς *horseman*, ὁ ἱερεύς *priest*, ὁ γονεύς *parent*, ὁ φονεύς *murderer*; like βοῦς is declined ὁ χοῦς *three-quart measure* (but acc. χόᾱ and χόας).

---

274 D. Hom. has ὄϊς, ὄϊος and οἰός, ὄϊν, ὄϊες, ὀΐων and οἰῶν, ὀΐεσσι (οἴεσσι ο 386) and ὄεσσι, ὄϊς (ῑ).

275 D. 1. Hom. has βασιλῆος, -ῆι, -ῆα, -εῦ, -ῆες, -εῦσι (and -ήεσσι), -ῆας. Also -έος, -έϊ, -έᾰ, from the stem εϝ = εῠ. -εῦς and -εῖ for -έος and -έϊ are not common. Ἀτρεύς, Τῡδεύς have -έ(ϝ)-ος etc. regularly (Τῡδῆ from Τῡδέα). Hdt. has -έος, -έϊ or -εῖ, -έᾰ, -εῦ, -έες, -έων, -εῦσι, -έᾰς.

2. Hom. has γρηῦς or γρηΰς, γρηΐ, γρηῦ and γρηΰ; the unattic βόεσσι (and βουσί), βόας (and βοῦς), βῶν acc. sing. H 238. The Doric nom. sing. is βῶς, acc. pl. βῶς.

3. The declension of ναῦς in Doric, Homer, and Herodotus is as follows:

276. Substantives in -εύς preceded by a vowel may contract in the gen. and acc. sing. and pl. Thus, ἁλιεύς *fisherman* has gen. ἁλιέως or ἁλιῶς, acc. ἁλιέᾶ or ἁλιᾶ, gen. pl. ἁλιέων or ἁλιῶν, acc. pl. ἁλιέᾱς or ἁλιᾶς. All other forms are regular. The contracted forms were in use in the fifth century, but in the fourth (especially after 350 B.C.) the open forms are common. So are declined Εὐβοεύς *Euboean* from Εὐβοιεύς, Πειραιεύς *Peiraeus*, Πλαταιεύς *Plataean*.

277. Other Forms.—**a.** In the drama from words in -εύς we find rarely -έᾰ in acc. sing., -έᾱς in acc. pl. -έος and -ῆος, -ῆες, -ῆας are occasionally found.

b. The nom. pl. in older Attic ended in -ῆς (βασιλῆς), derived either from -ῆες by contraction or from -έης (once on an inscription) by 34. -ῆς occurs on inscriptions till about 350 B.C., and is the form to be adopted in the texts of authors of the fifth century and in Plato. -έες occurs rarely, but is suspected. βασιλεῖς (regular on inscriptions after 329 B.C.) is from analogy to ἡδεῖς.

c. The acc. pl. βασιλεῖς was not used till the end of the fourth century. -ῆς (the nom. form) is used for the acc. in a few passages (251 b).

278. Stem Variation.—Stems ending in ευ, αυ, ου lose υ before case endings beginning with a vowel, υ̯ passing into ϝ (43). Stems in ευ show the pure form only in the vocative; other forms are derived from the stronger stem ηυ. ηυ and ᾱυ before a consonant become ευ, ᾰυ (40) as in βασιλεύς, βασιλεῦσι, ναῦς, ναυσί from βασιληυς, νᾱυς, etc. From βασιλῆ(ϝ)-ος, -ῆ(ϝ)-ι, -ῆ(ϝ)-α, -ῆ(ϝ)-ας come, by transfer of quantity (34), the Attic forms. So νεώς is derived from νη(ϝ)-ός. In βασιλέων, νεῶν, ε is shortened from the η of βασιλήων, νηῶν by 39. βο-ός, etc. are from the stem βου- βοϝ-, cp. Lat. *bovis*.

STEMS IN οι

279. Stems in οι, with nominative in -ώ, turn ι into unwritten ι̯ (*y*) (43) before the endings beginning with a vowel. ἡ πειθώ *persuasion* is thus declined:

N. **πειθώ**. G. **πειθοῦς** (πειθό-ος). D. **πειθοῖ** (πειθό-ι). A. **πειθώ** (πειθό-α). V. **πειθοῖ**. Dual and plural are wanting.

	SINGULAR			PLURAL		
	Doric	Homer	Hdt.	Doric	Homer	Hdt.
Nom.	**ναῦ-ς**	**νηῦ-ς**	**νηῦ-ς**	**νᾶ-ες**	**νῆ-ες, νέ-ες**	**νέ-ες**
Gen.	**νᾱ-ός**	**νη-ός, νε-ός**	**νε-ός** (and **νη-ός**?)	**νᾱ-ῶν**	**νη-ῶν, νε-ῶν**	**νε-ῶν**
Dat.	**νᾱ-ΐ**	**νη-ΐ**	**νη-ΐ**	**ναυ-σί(ν), νᾱ́-εσσι(ν)**	**νηυ-σί(ν)** **νή-εσσι(ν), νέ-εσσι(ν)**	**νηυ-σί**
Acc.	**ναῦ-ν**	**νῆ-α, νέ-α**	**νέ-α**	**νᾶ-ας**	**νῆ-ας, νέ-ας**	**νέ-ας**

Hom. has ναυσί in ναυσικλυτός.

279 D. In Ionic the forms are contracted (πειθοῦς, etc.). Hdt. has acc. Ἰοῦν from Ἰώ, Λητοῦν, but also πειθώ.

So ἠχώ *echo*, εὐεστώ *well-being*, φειδώ *sparing*, Σαπφώ, Λητώ, Καλυψώ. οι stems are chiefly used for women's names.

a. A stronger form of the stem is ωι, seen in the earlier form of the nominative (Σαπφῴ, Λητῴ). The accusative has the accent of the nominative.

b. When dual and plural occur, they are of the second declension: nom. λεχοί (late) from λεχώ *woman in child-bed*, acc. γοργούς from γοργώ *gorgon*.

c. ἡ εἰκών *image*, ἡ ἀηδών *nightingale*, properly from stems in ον, have certain forms from this declension (εἰκοῦς, εἰκώ, voc. ἀηδοῖ).

CASES IN -φι(ν)

280. Cases in -φι(ν).—-φι(ν) is often added to noun stems in Hom. to express the relations of the lost instrumental, locative, and ablative, both singular and (more commonly) plural; rarely to express the relations of the genitive and dative cases. From ā stems are made singulars, from ο stems singulars or plurals, from consonant stems almost always plurals. Except in θεό-φιν *with the gods* -φι(ν) is not added to a stem denoting a person. (*a*) Instrumental: βίη-φι *by might*, ἑτέρη-φι *with the other* (*hand*), δακρυό-φιν *with tears*; (*b*) Locative: θύρη-φι *at the door*, ὄρεσ-φι *on the mountains*; (*c*) Ablative: κεφαλῆ-φιν *from off the head*; especially with prepositions, as ἐκποντό-φιν *from off the sea*, ἀπὸ ναῦ-φιν *from the ships*.

IRREGULAR DECLENSION

281. The gender in the singular and in the plural may not be the same: ὁ σῖτος *grain*, τὰ σῖτα; ὁ δεσμός *chain*, τὰ δεσμά *chains* (οἱ δεσμοί *cases of imprisonment*); τὸ στάδιον *stade*, *race-course*, pl. τὰ στάδια and οἱ στάδιοι.

282. Usually the irregularity consists in a word having two different stems.

a. Both stems have a common nominative singular: σκότος *darkness*, σκότου σκότῳ, etc. (like ἵππου ἵππῳ) or σκότους σκότει (like γένους γένει). So τὸν Ἄθω, and τὸν Ἄθων from Ἄθως (238 d), τὸν Σωκράτη and τὸν Σωκράτην (264 b). These are called *heteroclites* (ἑτερόκλιτα *differently declined*).

N. Many compound proper names in -ης (especially names of foreigners) have forms of the 1 and 3 decl., as Τισσαφέρνης, -νους, -νῃ and -νει. So Θεοκρίνη (voc.) in Demosth., Λεωνίδην and Λεωνίδεα in Hdt.

b. Certain cases are formed from another stem than that of the nom. singular: ὁ ὄνειρο-ς *dream*, gen. ὀνείρατ-ος (as if from τὸ ὄνειραρ), or (less freq.) ὀνείρου; so τὸν Ἀπόλλωνα and τὸν Ἀπόλλω (260), τοῦ υἱέος and τοῦ υἱοῦ (285, 27). These are called *metaplastic* forms (μεταπλασμός *change of formation*).

283. Defectives are substantives having, by reason of their meaning or use, only one number or only certain cases. Thus, sing. only: ὁ ἀήρ *air*, ὁ αἰθήρ *upper air*; plur. only: τὰ Διονύσια, τὰ Ὀλύμπια *the Dionysiac* (*Olympic*) *festival*, οἱ ἐτησίαι *annual winds*; in some cases only: ὦ μέλε *my good sir* or *madam*; ὄναρ *dream*; ὄφελος *use* only in nom.; λιβός λίβα from *λίψ *stream, libation*.

284. Indeclinables are substantives having one form for all cases: τὸ χρεών, τοῦ χρεών, etc. *fatality*, τὸ ἄλφα *alpha*, τὸ λέγειν *to speak*, most cardinal numbers (τὸ δέκα *ten*), several foreign words, as Ἰακώβ *Jacob*, Δαβίδ *David*.

285. LIST OF THE PRINCIPAL IRREGULAR SUBSTANTIVES

1. **Ἄρης** (ὁ) *Ares*, stems Ἀρεσ-, Ἀρευ- from Ἀρεσϝ-. G. Ἄρεως (poet. Ἄρεος), D. Ἄρει, A. Ἄρη (poet. Ἄρεα), Ἄρην. Epic G. Ἄρηος, Ἄρεος, D. Ἄρηι, Ἄρεϊ, A. Ἄρηα, Ἄρην. Hdt. Ἄρεος, Ἄρει, Ἄρεα. Aeolic Ἄρευς, Ἄρευος, etc.
2. **ἀρήν** (ὁ, ἡ) *lamb, sheep*, stems ἀρεν-, ἀρν-, ἀρνα-. Thus, ἀρν-ός, ἀρν-ί, ἄρν-α, ἄρν-ες, ἀρν-ῶν, ἀρνά-σι (Hom. ἄρν-εσσι), ἄρν-ας (declined like a subst. in -ηρ). Nom. ἀρήν occurs on inscript. but ἀμνός (2 decl.) is commonly used.
3. **γάλα** (τό) *milk* (133), γάλακτ-ος, γάλακτ-ι, etc.
4. **γέλως** (ὁ) *laughter*, γέλωτ-ος, etc. Attic poets A. γέλωτα or γέλων. Hom. has D. γέλῳ, A. γέλω, γέλων or γέλοι(?) from Aeol. γέλος. Cp. 257 D.
5. **γόνυ** (τό) *knee*, γόνατ-ος, etc. Ionic and poetic γούνατ-ος, γούνατ-ι, etc. Epic also γουν-ός, γουν-ί, γοῦν-α, pl. γούν-ων, γούν-εσσι (250 D. 2). The forms in ου are from γονϝ- (37 D. 1, 253 c); cf. Lat. *genu*.
6. **γυνή** (ἡ) *woman*, γυναικ-ός, γυναικ-ί, γυναῖκ-α, γύναι (133); dual γυναῖκ-ε, γυναικ-οῖν; pl. γυναῖκ-ες, γυναικ-ῶν, γυναιξί, γυναῖκ-ας. The gen. and dat. of all numbers accent the last syllable (cp. ἀνήρ). Comic poets have A. γυνήν, γυνάς, N. pl. γυναί.
7. **δάκρυον** (τό) *tear*, δακρύου, etc., in prose and poetry. δάκρυ (τό) is usually poetic, D. pl. δάκρυσι.
8. **δένδρον** (τό) *tree*, δένδρου, etc. Also D. sing. δένδρει, pl. δένδρη, δένδρεσι. Hdt. has δένδρον, δένδρεον and δένδρος.
9. **δέος** (τό) *fear* (δεεσ-), δέους, δέει. Hom. δείους, 55 D. Cp. 265.
10. **δόρυ** (τό) *spear*, δόρατ-ος, δόρατ-ι, pl. δόρατ-α, etc. Poetic δορ-ός, δορ-ί (also in prose) and δόρ-ει (like ἄστει). Ionic and poetic δούρατ-ος, etc., Epic also δουρ-ός δουρ-ί, dual δοῦρ-ε, pl. δοῦρ-α, δούρ-ων, δούρ-εσσι (250 D. 2). The forms with ου are from δορϝ- (37 D. 1).
11. **ἔρως** (ὁ) *love*, ἔρωτ-ος, etc. Poetical ἔρος, ἔρῳ, ἔρον. Cp. 257 D.
12. **Ζεύς** (ὁ) *Zeus*, Δι-ός, Δι-ί, Δί-α, Ζεῦ. Ζεύς is from Διευς, Δι-ός, etc., from Διϝ-. Ionic and poetic Ζηνός, Ζηνί, Ζῆνα.
13. **θέμις** (ἡ) *justice* and the goddess *Themis* (θεμιδ-), θέμιδ-ος, θέμιδ-ι, θέμι-ν. Hom. has θέμιστ-ος, etc. Pind. θέμιτ-ος, θέμι-ν, θέμιτ-ες. Hdt. θέμι-ος. In the phrase θέμις εἶναι *fas esse* (indic. θέμις ἐστί), θέμις is indeclinable.
14. **κάρᾱ** (τό) *head* (poetic) used in Attic only in N. A. V. sing., but dat. κάρᾳ. Other cases are from the stem κρᾱτ-, G. κρᾱτ-ός, D. κρᾱ-τί; also τὸ κρᾶτ-α N. A. sing., κρᾶτ-ας A. pl.

    Epic shows the stems κρᾱατ-, κρᾱτ-, καρηατ-, καρητ-. N. κάρη, G. κράατος, κρᾱτός, καρήατος, κάρητος, D. κράατι, κρᾱτί, καρήατι, κάρητι, A. κάρ. N. pl. κάρᾱ, κράατα, καρήατα, and κάρηνα, G. κράτων, καρήνων, D. κρᾱσί, A. κρᾶτα.
15. **κύων** (ὁ, ἡ) *dog*, κυν-ός, κυν-ί, κύν-α, κύον; κύν-ε, κυν-οῖν; κύν-ες, κυν-ῶν, κυσί, κύν-ας.
16. **λᾶας** (ὁ) *stone*, poetic also λᾶς, G. λᾶος (or λάου), D. λᾶϊ, A. λᾶαν, λᾶα; dual λᾶε; pl. λᾶ-ες, λά-ων, λά-εσσι, λά-εσι.
17. **μάρτυς** (ὁ, ἡ) *witness*, μάρτυρ-ος, etc., but D. pl. μάρτυ-σι. Hom. has N. μάρτυρος, pl. μάρτυροι.
18. **Οἰδίπους** (ὁ) *Oedipus*, G. Οἰδίποδος, Οἰδίπου, Οἰδιπόδᾱ (Dor.), D. Οἰδίποδι, A. Οἰδίπουν, Οἰδιπόδᾱν, V. Οἰδίπους, Οἰδίπου.

19. **ὄνειρος** (ὁ) and ὄνειρον (τό, Ionic and poetic) *dream*, ὀνείρου, etc., but also ὀνείρατ-ος, etc. τὸ ὄναρ only in N. A.
20. **ὄρνῖς** (ὁ, ἡ) *bird* (257). A. ὄρνῖθα and ὄρνῖν (247). Poetic ὄρνῖς, A. ὄρνῖν; pl. N. ὄρνεις, G. ὄρνεων, A. ὄρνεις or ὄρνῖς. Dor. G. ὄρνῖχ-ος, etc.
21. **ὄσσε** dual, *two eyes*, pl. G. ὄσσων, D. ὄσσοις (-οισι).
22. **οὖς** (τό) *ear*, ὠτ-ός, ὠτ-ί, pl. ὦτ-α, ὤτ-ων (252 a), ὠσί; from the stem ὠτ- contracted from οὔ(σ)ατ-, whence ὀ(ϝ)ατ-. οὖς is from ὄος, whence also the Doric nom. ὦς. Hom. G. οὔατ-ος, pl. οὔατ-α, οὔασι and ὠσί.
23. **Πνύξ** (ἡ) *Pnyx* (128), Πυκν-ός, Πυκν-ί, Πύκν-α, and also Πνυκ-ός, Πνυκ-ί, Πνύκ-α.
24. **πρεσβευτής** (ὁ) *envoy* has in the pl. usually the forms of the poetic πρέσβυς *old man*, properly an adj., *old*. Thus, N. sing. πρεσβευτής, G. πρεσβευτοῦ, etc., N. pl. πρέσβεις, G. πρέσβεων, D. πρέσβεσι, A. πρέσβεις (rarely πρεσβευταί, etc.). πρέσβυς meaning *old man* is poetic in the sing. (A. πρέσβυν, V. πρέσβυ) and pl. (πρέσβεις); meaning *envoy* πρέσβυς is poetic and rare in the sing. (dual πρεσβῆ from πρεσβεύς). πρεσβύτης *old man* is used in prose and poetry in all numbers.
25 **πῦρ** (τό) *fire* (πὔρ-, 254 b), πυρ-ός, πυρ-ί, pl. τὰ πυρά *watch-fires*, 2nd decl.
26. **ὕδωρ** (τό) *water*, ὕδατ-ος, ὕδατ-ι, pl. ὕδατ-α, ὑδάτ-ων, etc. Cp. 253 b.
27. **υἱός** (ὁ) *son* has three stems: 1. υἱο-, whence υἱοῦ, etc., according to the 2nd decl. 2. υἱυ-, whence υἱέος, υἱεῖ, dual υἱεῖ, υἱέοιν, pl. υἱεῖς, υἱέων, υἱέσι, υἱεῖς. The stems υἱο- and υἱυ-, usually lose their ι (43): ὑοῦ, ὑέος, etc. 3. υἱ- in Hom. G. υἷος, D. υἷι, A. υἷα, dual υἷε, pl. υἷες, υἱάσι, υἷας.
28. **χείρ** (ἡ) *hand*, χειρ-ός, χειρ-ί, χεῖρ-α; dual χεῖρ-ε, χερ-οῖν; pl. χεῖρ-ες, χειρ-ῶν, χερ-σί, χεῖρ-ας. Poetic also χερ-ός, χερ-ί, etc.; dual, χειρ-οῖν. Att. inscr. have χειροῖν, χειρσί. Hom. agrees with Att. prose and Hdt. except that he has also χερ-ί, χείρ-εσσι χείρ-εσι.
29. **χρώς** (ὁ) *skin*, χρωτ-ός, χρωτ-ί (but χρῴ in the phrase ἐν χρῴ), χρῶτα. Poetic χρο-ός, χρο-ΐ, χρό-α, like αἰδώς, 266.

ADJECTIVES

ADJECTIVES OF THE FIRST AND SECOND DECLENSIONS

286. Adjectives of Three Endings. — Most adjectives of the vowel declension have three endings: -ος, -η (or -ᾱ), -ον. The masculine and neuter are declined according to the second declension, the feminine according to the first.

a. When ε, ι, or ρ (30, 218) precedes -ος the feminine ends in -ᾱ, not in -η. But adjectives in -οος (not preceded by ρ) have η. Thus, ὄγδοος, ὀγδόη, ὄγδοον *eighth*, ἀθρόος, ἀθρόᾱ, ἀθρόον *crowded*. See 290 e.

287. ἀγαθός *good*, ἄξιος *worthy*, μακρός *long* are thus declined:

---

285 D. 27. Hom. has also υἱός, υἱοῦ, υἱόν, υἱέ, υἱῶν, υἱοῖσι; υἱέος, υἱέϊ, υἱέα, υἱέες and υἱεῖ˘, υἱέας. υι sometimes makes a short syllable in υἱός, υἱόν, υἱέ (148 D. 3).

287 D. In the fem. nom. sing. Ionic has -η, never -ᾱ; in the fem. gen. pl. Hom. has -άων (less often -έων); Hdt. has -έων in oxytone adjectives and participles, and so probably in barytones.

SINGULAR

Nom.	ἀγαθός	ἀγαθή	ἀγαθόν	ἄξιος	ἀξίᾱ	ἄξιον	μακρός	μακρᾱ́	μακρόν
Gen.	ἀγαθοῦ	ἀγαθῆς	ἀγαθοῦ	ἀξίου	ἀξίᾱς	ἀξίου	μακροῦ	μακρᾶς	μακροῦ
Dat.	ἀγαθῷ	ἀγαθῇ	ἀγαθῷ	ἀξίῳ	ἀξίᾳ	ἀξίῳ	μακρῷ	μακρᾷ	μακρῷ
Acc.	ἀγαθόν	ἀγαθήν	ἀγαθόν	ἄξιον	ἀξίᾱν	ἄξιον	μακρόν	μακρᾱ́ν	μακρόν
Voc.	ἀγαθέ	ἀγαθή	ἀγαθόν	ἄξιε	ἀξίᾱ	ἄξιον	μακρέ	μακρᾱ́	μακρόν

DUAL

N. A. V.	ἀγαθώ	ἀγαθᾱ́	ἀγαθώ	ἀξίω	ἀξίᾱ	ἀξίω	μακρώ	μακρᾱ́	μακρώ
G. D.	ἀγαθοῖν	ἀγαθαῖν	ἀγαθοῖν	ἀξίοιν	ἀξίαιν	ἀξίοιν	μακροῖν	μακραῖν	μακροῖν

PLURAL

N. V.	ἀγαθοί	ἀγαθαί	ἀγαθά	ἄξιοι	ἄξιαι	ἄξια	μακροί	μακραί	μακρά
Gen.	ἀγαθῶν	ἀγαθῶν	ἀγαθῶν	ἀξίων	ἀξίων	ἀξίων	μακρῶν	μακρῶν	μακρῶν
Dat.	ἀγαθοῖς	ἀγαθαῖς	ἀγαθοῖς	ἀξίοις	ἀξίαις	ἀξίοις	μακροῖς	μακραῖς	μακροῖς
Acc.	ἀγαθούς	ἀγαθᾱ́ς	ἀγαθά	ἀξίους	ἀξίᾱς	ἄξια	μακρούς	μακρᾱ́ς	μακρά

ἐσθλός *good*, κακός *bad*, σοφός *wise*, κοῦφος, κούφη, κοῦφον *light*, δῆλος *clear*; ἀνδρεῖος, ἀνδρείᾱ, ἀνδρεῖον *courageous*, δίκαιος *just*, ὅμοιος *like*, αἰσχρός, αἰσχρᾱ́, αἰσχρόν *base*, ἐλεύθερος *free*; all participles in -ος and all superlatives.

a. The accent in the feminine nominative and genitive plural follows that of the masculine: ἄξιαι, ἀξίων, not ἀξίαι, ἀξιῶν, as would be expected according to the rule for substantives (205), *e.g.* as in αἰτίᾱ *cause*, αἰτίαι, αἰτιῶν.

b. All adjectives and participles may use the masculine instead of the feminine dual forms: τὼ ἀγαθὼ μητέρε *the two good mothers.*

288. Adjectives of Two Endings. — Adjectives using the masculine for the feminine are called adjectives of two endings. Most such adjectives are compounds.

289. ἄδικος *unjust* (ἀ- *without*, δίκη *justice*), φρόνιμος *prudent*, and ἵλεως *propitious* are declined thus:

SINGULAR

	Masc. and Fem.	Neut.	Masc. and Fem.	Neut.	Masc. and Fem.	Neut.
Nom.	ἄδικος	ἄδικον	φρόνιμος	φρόνιμον	ἵλεως	ἵλεων
Gen.	ἀδίκου	ἀδίκου	φρονίμου	φρονίμου	ἵλεω	ἵλεω
Dat.	ἀδίκῳ	ἀδίκῳ	φρονίμῳ	φρονίμῳ	ἵλεῳ	ἵλεῳ
Acc.	ἄδικον	ἄδικον	φρόνιμον	φρόνιμον	ἵλεων	ἵλεων
Voc.	ἄδικε	ἄδικον	φρόνιμε	φρόνιμον	ἵλεως	ἵλεων

289 D. Hom. has ἵλᾱος or ἵλἄος; πλεῖος, πλείη, πλεῖον (Hdt. πλέος, πλέη, πλέον); σῶς (only in this form), and σόος, σόη, σόον. Hom. has N. ζώς, A. ζών *living*, and ζωός, ζωή, ζωόν *living*.

DUAL

	Masc. and Fem.	Neut.	Masc. and Fem.	Neut.	Masc. and Fem.	Neut
N. A. V.	ἀδίκω	ἀδίκω	φρονίμω	φρονίμω	ἵλεω	ἵλεω
G. D.	ἀδίκοιν	ἀδίκοιν	φρονίμοιν	φρονίμοιν	ἵλεων	ἵλεων

PLURAL

N. V.	ἄδικοι	ἄδικα	φρόνιμοι	φρόνιμα	ἵλεῳ	ἵλεα
Gen.	ἀδίκων	ἀδίκων	φρονίμων	φρονίμων	ἵλεων	ἵλεων
Dat.	ἀδίκοις	ἀδίκοις	φρονίμοις	φρονίμοις	ἵλεῳς	ἵλεῳς
Acc.	ἀδίκους	ἄδικα	φρονίμους	φρόνιμα	ἵλεως	ἵλεα

a. Like ἄδικος are declined the compounded ἄ-λογος *irrational*, ἄ-τῑμος *dishonoured*, ἀ-χρεῖος *useless*, ἔμ-πειρος *experienced*, ἐπί-φθονος *envious*, εὔ-ξενος *hospitable*, ὑπ-ήκοος *obedient*. Like φρόνιμος are declined the uncompounded βάρβαρος *barbarian*, ἥσυχος *quiet*, ἥμερος *tame*, λάλος *talkative*.

b. Like ἵλεως are declined other adjectives of the Attic declension (237), as ἄκερως *without horns*, ἀξιόχρεως *serviceable*. For the accent, see 163 a. Adjectives in -ως, -ων have -α in the neut. pl., but ἔκπλεω occurs in Xenophon.

c. **πλέως** *full* has three endings: πλέως, πλέᾱ, πλέων, pl. πλέῳ, πλέαι, πλέα, but most compounds, such as ἔμπλεως *quite full*, have the fem. like the masc. **σῶς** *safe* has usually sing. N. σῶς masc., fem. (rarely σᾶ), σῶν neut., A. σῶν; plur. N. σῷ masc., fem., σᾶ neut., A. σῶς masc., fem., σᾶ neut. Other cases are supplied by σῶος, σώᾱ, σῶον. σῶον also occurs in the accusative.

d. In poetry, and sometimes in prose, adjectives commonly of two endings have a feminine form, as πάτριος *paternal*, βίαιος *violent*; and those commonly of three endings have no feminine, as ἀναγκαῖος *necessary*, φίλιος *friendly*.

290. Contracted Adjectives. — Most adjectives in -εος and -οος are contracted. Examples: χρῡ́σεος *golden*, ἀργύρεος *of silver*, ἁπλόος *simple* (feminine ἁπλέᾱ).

SINGULAR

N. V.	(χρῡ́σεος)	χρῡσοῦς	(χρῡσέᾱ)	χρῡσῆ	(χρῡ́σεον)	χρῡσοῦν
Gen.	(χρῡσέου)	χρῡσοῦ	(χρῡσέᾱς)	χρῡσῆς	(χρῡσέου)	χρῡσοῦ
Dat.	(χρῡσέῳ)	χρῡσῷ	(χρῡσέᾳ)	χρῡσῇ	(χρῡσέῳ)	χρῡσῷ
Acc.	(χρῡ́σεον)	χρῡσοῦν	(χρῡσέᾱν)	χρῡσῆν	(χρῡ́σεον)	χρῡσοῦν

DUAL

N. A. V.	(χρῡσέω)	χρῡσώ	(χρῡσέᾱ)	χρῡσᾶ	(χρῡσέω)	χρῡσώ
G. D.	(χρῡσέοιν)	χρῡσοῖν	(χρῡσέαιν)	χρῡσαῖν	(χρῡσέοιν)	χρῡσοῖν

PLURAL

N. V.	(χρῡ́σεοι)	χρῡσοῖ	(χρῡ́σεαι)	χρῡσαῖ	(χρῡ́σεα)	χρῡσᾶ
Gen.	(χρῡσέων)	χρῡσῶν	(χρῡσέων)	χρῡσῶν	(χρῡσέων)	χρῡσῶν
Dat.	(χρῡσέοις)	χρῡσοῖς	(χρῡσέαις)	χρῡσαῖς	(χρῡσέοις)	χρῡσοῖς
Acc.	(χρῡσέους)	χρῡσοῦς	(χρῡσέᾱς)	χρῡσᾶς	(χρῡ́σεα)	χρῡσᾶ

			SINGULAR			
N. V.	(ἀργύρεος)	**ἀργυροῦς**	(ἀργυρέᾱ)	**ἀργυρᾶ**	(ἀργύρεον)	**ἀργυροῦν**
Gen.	(ἀργυρέου)	**ἀργυροῦ**	(ἀργυρέᾱς)	**ἀργυρᾶς**	(ἀργυρέου)	**ἀργυροῦ**
Dat.	(ἀργυρέῳ)	**ἀργυρῷ**	(ἀργυρέᾳ)	**ἀργυρᾷ**	(ἀργυρέῳ)	**ἀργυρῷ**
Acc.	(ἀργύρεον)	**ἀργυροῦν**	(ἀργυρέᾱν)	**ἀργυρᾶν**	(ἀργύρεον)	**ἀργυροῦν**
			DUAL			
N. A. V.	(ἀργυρέω)	**ἀργυρώ**	(ἀργυρέᾱ)	**ἀργυρᾶ**	(ἀργυρέω)	**ἀργυρώ**
G. D.	(ἀργυρέοιν)	**ἀργυροῖν**	(ἀργυρέαιν)	**ἀργυραῖν**	(ἀργυρέοιν)	**ἀργυροῖν**
			PLURAL			
N. V.	(ἀργύρεοι)	**ἀργυροῖ**	(ἀργύρεαι)	**ἀργυραῖ**	(ἀργύρεα)	**ἀργυρᾶ**
Gen.	(ἀργυρέων)	**ἀργυρῶν**	(ἀργυρέων)	**ἀργυρῶν**	(ἀργυρέων)	**ἀργυρῶν**
Dat.	(ἀργυρέοις)	**ἀργυροῖς**	(ἀργυρέαις)	**ἀργυραῖς**	(ἀργυρέοις)	**ἀργυροῖς**
Acc.	(ἀργυρέους)	**ἀργυροῦς**	(ἀργυρέᾱς)	**ἀργυρᾶς**	(ἀργύρεα)	**ἀργυρᾶ**

			SINGULAR			
N. V.	(ἁπλόος)	**ἁπλοῦς**	(ἁπλέᾱ)	**ἁπλῆ**	(ἁπλόον)	**ἁπλοῦν**
Gen.	(ἁπλόου)	**ἁπλοῦ**	(ἁπλέᾱς)	**ἁπλῆς**	(ἁπλόου)	**ἁπλοῦ**
Dat.	(ἁπλόῳ)	**ἁπλῷ**	(ἁπλέᾳ)	**ἁπλῇ**	(ἁπλόῳ)	**ἁπλῷ**
Acc.	(ἁπλόον)	**ἁπλοῦν**	(ἁπλέᾱν)	**ἁπλῆν**	(ἁπλόον)	**ἁπλοῦν**
			DUAL			
N. A. V.	(ἁπλόω)	**ἁπλώ**	(ἁπλέᾱ)	**ἁπλᾶ**	(ἁπλόω)	**ἁπλώ**
G. D.	(ἁπλόοιν)	**ἁπλοῖν**	(ἁπλέαιν)	**ἁπλαῖν**	(ἁπλόοιν)	**ἁπλοῖν**
			PLURAL			
N. V.	(ἁπλόοι)	**ἁπλοῖ**	(ἁπλέαι)	**ἁπλαῖ**	(ἁπλόα)	**ἁπλᾶ**
Gen.	(ἁπλόων)	**ἁπλῶν**	(ἁπλέων)	**ἁπλῶν**	(ἁπλόων)	**ἁπλῶν**
Dat.	(ἁπλόοις)	**ἁπλοῖς**	(ἁπλέαις)	**ἁπλαῖς**	(ἁπλόοις)	**ἁπλοῖς**
Acc.	(ἁπλόους)	**ἁπλοῦς**	(ἁπλέᾱς)	**ἁπλᾶς**	(ἁπλόα)	**ἁπλᾶ**

a. So χαλκοῦς, -ῆ, -οῦν *brazen*, φοινῑκοῦς, -ῆ, -οῦν *crimson*, πορφυροῦς, -ᾶ, -οῦν *dark red*, σιδηροῦς, -ᾶ, -οῦν *of iron*, διπλοῦς, -ῆ, -οῦν *twofold*, and other multiplicatives in -πλοῦς (354 b). Compounds of two endings (288): **εὔνους, -ουν** (εὔνοος) *well disposed*, **ἄπλους, -ουν** (ἄπλοος) *not navigable*, **εὔρους, -ουν** (εὔροος) *fair-flowing*. These have open **οα** in the neuter plural.

b. The vocative and dual of contracted adjectives are very rare.

c. Adjectives whose uncontracted form in the nom. sing. has the accent on the antepenult (χρύσεος, πορφύρεος) take in the contracted form a circumflex on their last syllable (χρῡσοῦς, πορφυροῦς) by analogy to the gen. and dat. sing. The accent of the nom. dual masculine and neuter is also irregular (χρῡσώ, not χρῡσῶ).

d. For peculiarities of contraction see 56. ἁπλῇ is from ἁπλέᾱ, not from ἁπλόη.

e. Some adjectives are not contracted: ἀργαλέος *difficult*, κερδαλέος *crafty*, νέος *young*, ὄγδοος *eighth*, ἀθρόος *crowded* (usually). (Here εο and οο were probably separated originally by ϝ, 3.)

ADJECTIVES OF THE CONSONANT DECLENSION

291. Such adjectives as belong only to the consonant declension have two endings. Most such adjectives have stems in ες (nominative -ης and -ες) and ον (nominative -ων and -ον). Under ον stems fall comparative adjectives, as βελτίων, βέλτῑον *better*.

a. There are some compounds with other stems: M. F. ἀπάτωρ, N. ἄπατορ *fatherless*, G. ἀπάτορος; ἄπολις ἄπολι *without a country*, ἀπόλιδος; αὐτοκράτωρ αὐτοκράτορ *independent*, αὐτοκράτορος; ἄρρην (older ἄρσην) ἄρρεν *male*, ἄρρενος; εὔχαρις εὔχαρι *agreeable*, εὐχάριτος; εὔελπις εὔελπι *hopeful*, εὐέλπιδος. For the acc. of stems in ιτ and ιδ see 247. Neut. εὔχαρι and εὔελπι for εὐχαριτ, εὐελπιδ (133).

292. ἀληθής (ἀληθεσ-) *true*, εὔ-ελπις (εὐελπιδ-) *hopeful* are thus declined:

	Masc. and Fem.		Neut.	Masc. and Fem.	Neut.
		SINGULAR			
Nom.	**ἀληθής**		**ἀληθές**	**εὔελπις**	**εὔελπι**
Gen.	(ἀληθέ-ος)	**ἀληθοῦς**		**εὐέλπιδ-ος**	
Dat.	(ἀληθέ-ι)	**ἀληθεῖ**		**εὐέλπιδ-ι**	
Acc.	(ἀληθέ-α) **ἀληθῆ**		**ἀληθές**	**εὔελπιν**	**εὔελπι**
Voc.	**ἀληθές**		**ἀληθές**	**εὔελπι**	
		DUAL			
N. A. V.	(ἀληθέ-ε)	**ἀληθεῖ**		**εὐέλπιδ-ε**	
G. D.	(ἀληθέ-οιν)	**ἀληθοῖν**		**εὐελπίδ-οιν**	
		PLURAL			
N. V.	(ἀληθέ-ες) **ἀληθεῖς**		(ἀληθέ-α) **ἀληθῆ**	**εὐέλπιδ-ες**	**εὐέλπιδ-α**
Gen.	(ἀληθέ-ων)	**ἀληθῶν**		**εὐελπίδ-ων**	
Dat.	(ἀληθέσ-σι 107)	**ἀληθέσι(ν)**		**εὐέλπισι(ν)**	
Acc.	**ἀληθεῖς**		(ἀληθέ-α) **ἀληθῆ**	**εὐέλπιδ-ας**	**εὐέλπιδ-α**

a. ἄληθες means *indeed!* Like ἀληθής are declined σαφής *clear*, εὐτυχής *lucky*, εὐγενής *high-born*, ἀσθενής *weak*, ἐγκρατής *self-restrained*, πλήρης *full*.

---

292 D. The uncontracted forms of ες stems appear in Hom. and Hdt. -εϊ and -εες are, however, sometimes contracted in Hom., and properly should be written -ει and -εις in Hdt. The acc. pl. masc. and fem. is -εας in Hom. and Hdt. From adj. in -εής Hdt. has ἐνδέᾰ for ἐνδεέα, Hom. ἐυκλεῖας for ἐυκλεέας, ἐυρρεῖος for ἐυρρεέος.

b. The accusative pl. ἀληθεῖς has the form of the nominative.

c. Compound adjectives in -ης not accented on the last syllable show recessive accent even in the contracted forms. Thus, φιλαλήθης *lover of truth*, neut. φιλάληθες, αὐτάρκης *self-sufficient*, neut. αὔταρκες, gen. pl. αὐτάρκων, not αὐταρκῶν.

N. — Except in neuter words in -ῶδες, -ῶλες, -ῶρες, and -ῆρες, as εὐῶδες *sweet-smelling*, ποδῆρες *reaching to the feet*. But τριήρων, not τριηρῶν, from τριήρης, 264.

d. εε(σ)α becomes εᾱ, not εη (56): εὐκλεᾶ, ἐνδεᾶ for εὐκλεέα, ἐνδεέα from εὐκλεής *glorious*, ἐνδεής *needy* (G. εὐκλεοῦς, ἐνδεοῦς). But ιε(σ)α and υε(σ)α yield ιᾱ or ιη, υᾱ or υη. Thus, ὑγιᾶ or ὑγιῆ (ὑγιής *healthy*), εὐφυᾶ or εὐφυῆ (εὐφυής *comely*), cp. 56, 31, 2. The forms in -ῆ are due to the analogy of such forms as ἐμφερῆ (ἐμφερής *resembling*),

293. Stems in ον: εὐδαίμων *happy*, βελτίων *better*:

	Masc. and Fem.	Neut.	Masc. and Fem.	Neut.
	SINGULAR			
Nom.	**εὐδαίμων**	**εὔδαιμον**	**βελτίων**	**βέλτῑον**
Gen.	**εὐδαίμον-ος**		**βελτίον-ος**	
Dat.	**εὐδαίμον-ι**		**βελτίον-ι**	
Acc.	**εὐδαίμον-α**	**εὔδαιμον**	**βελτίον-α** or **βελτίω**	**βέλτῑον**
Voc.	**εὔδαιμον**	**εὔδαιμον**	**βέλτῑον**	**βέλτῑον**
	DUAL			
N. A. V.	**εὐδαίμον-ε**		**βελτίον-ε**	
G. D.	**εὐδαιμόν-οιν**		**βελτῑόν-οιν**	
	PLURAL			
N. V.	**εὐδαίμον-ες**	**εὐδαίμον-α**	**βελτίον-ες** / **βελτίους**	**βελτίον-α** / **βελτίω**
Gen.	**εὐδαιμόν-ων**		**βελτῑόν-ων**	
Dat.	**εὐδαίμοσι(ν)**		**βελτίοσι(ν)**	
Acc.	**εὐδαίμον-ας**	**εὐδαίμον-α**	**βελτίον-ας** / **βελτίους**	**βελτίον-α** / **βελτίω**

a. Like εὐδαίμων are declined μνήμων μνῆμον *mindful*, ἀγνώμων ἄγνωμον *unfeeling*, ἄφρων ἄφρον *senseless*, πέπων πέπον *ripe*, σώφρων σῶφρον *prudent*.

b. Like βελτίων are declined μείζων μεῖζον *greater*, κακίων κάκῑον *baser*, ἐλάττων ἔλᾱττον *less*.

c. The neuter nominative and accusative have recessive accent.

d. Comparatives are formed from stems in ον and in ος; cp. Lat. *meliōris* for *meliōs-is*. ος appears in βελτίω for βελτῑο(σ)-α, acc. sing. masc. fem. and nom. acc. neut. pl., and in βελτίους for βελτῑο(σ)-ες, nom. pl. masc. fem. The accusative plural borrows the nominative form. Cp. 251 b. The shorter forms were more frequent in everyday speech than in literature.

CONSONANT AND VOWEL DECLENSION COMBINED

294. Adjectives of the consonant declension having a separate form for the feminine inflect the feminine like a substantive of the first declension ending in -ᾰ (216).

295. The feminine is made from the stem of the masculine (and neuter) by adding the suffix -ια (*ya*), which is combined with the preceding syllable in different ways. The genitive plural feminine is always perispomenon (cp. 208). For the feminine dual, see 287 b.

296. Stems in υ (-υς, -εια, -υ). — The masculine and neuter have the inflection of *πῆχυς* and *ἄστυ*, except that the genitive singular masculine and neuter ends in -ος (not -ως) and -εα in the neuter plural remains uncontracted.

297. *ἡδύς* *sweet* is thus declined:

		Masc.	Fem.		Neut.
		SINGULAR			
Nom.		ἡδύ-ς	ἡδεῖα		ἡδύ
Gen.		ἡδέ-ος	ἡδείᾱς		ἡδέ-ος
Dat.	(*ἡδέϊ*)	ἡδεῖ	ἡδείᾳ	(*ἡδέϊ*)	ἡδεῖ
Acc.		ἡδύ-ν	ἡδεῖα-ν		ἡδύ
Voc.		ἡδύ	ἡδεῖα		ἡδύ
		DUAL			
N. A. V.		ἡδέ-ε	ἡδείᾱ		ἡδέ-ε
G. D.		ἡδέ-οιν	ἡδεί-αιν		ἡδέ-οιν
		PLURAL			
N. V.	(*ἡδέες*)	ἡδεῖς	ἡδεῖαι		ἡδέ-α
Gen.		ἡδέ-ων	ἡδειῶν		ἡδέ-ων
Dat.		ἡδέ-σι(ν)	ἡδείαις		ἡδέ-σι(ν)
Acc.		ἡδεῖς	ἡδείᾱς		ἡδέ-α

So *βαθύς* *deep*, *γλυκύς* *sweet*, *εὐρύς* *broad*, *ὀξύς* *sharp*, *ταχύς* *swift*.

a. In *ἡδεῖα* -ια has been added to *ἡδεϝ-* = *ἡδευ-*, a stronger form of the stem *ἡδυ-* (cp. 270). The nominative masculine *ἡδεῖς* is used for the accusative.

b. The adjectives of this declension are oxytone, except *ἥμισυς* *half*, *θῆλυς* *female*, and some compounds, as *δίπηχυς* *of two cubits*.

298. Stems in ν (-ᾱς, -αινα, -αν; -ην, -εινα, -εν). *μέλᾱς* *black*, *τέρην* *tender* are declined as follows:

---

296 D. Hom. has usually -εῖα, -είης, -είῃ, etc.; sometimes -έα, -έης, -έῃ, etc. The forms without ι (43) are regular in Hdt. For -ύν Hom. has -έα in *εὐρέα πόντον* *the wide sea*. *ἡδύς* and *θῆλυς* are sometimes feminine in Hom.

		SINGULAR				
Nom.	μέλᾱς	μέλαινα	μέλαν	τέρην	τέρεινα	τέρεν
Gen.	μέλαν-ος	μελαίνης	μέλαν-ος	τέρεν-ος	τερείνης	τέρεν-ος
Dat.	μέλαν-ι	μελαίνῃ	μέλαν-ι	τέρεν-ι	τερείνῃ	τέρεν-ι
Acc.	μέλαν-α	μέλαινα-ν	μέλαν	τέρεν-α	τέρεινα-ν	τέρεν
Voc.	μέλαν	μέλαινα	μέλαν	τέρεν	τέρεινα	τέρεν
		DUAL				
N. A. V.	μέλαν-ε	μελαίνᾱ	μέλαν-ε	τέρεν-ε	τερείνᾱ	τέρεν-ε
G. D.	μελάν-οιν	μελαίναιν	μελάν-οιν	τερέν-οιν	τερείναιν	τερέν-οιν
		PLURAL				
N. V.	μέλαν-ες	μέλαιναι	μέλαν-α	τέρεν-ες	τέρειναι	τέρεν-α
Gen.	μελάν-ων	μελαινῶν	μελάν-ων	τερέν-ων	τερεινῶν	τερέν-ων
Dat.	μέλασι(ν)	μελαίναις	μέλασι(ν)	τέρεσι(ν)	τερείναις	τέρεσι(ν)
Acc.	μέλαν-ας	μελαίνᾱς	μέλαν-α	τέρεν-ας	τερείνᾱς	τέρεν-α

Like *μέλᾱς* is declined one adjective: *τάλᾱς, τάλαινα, τάλαν* *wretched.*

a. *μέλᾱς* is for *μελαν-ς* by 37, 96. With the exception of *μέλᾱς* and *τάλᾱς*, adjective stems in *ν* reject *ς* in the nom. sing. *μέλασι* for *μελαν-σι* 96 a, 250 N. The feminine forms *μέλαινα* and *τέρεινα* come from *μελαν-ι̯α, τερεν-ι̯α* by 111. The vocatives *μέλαν* and *τέρεν* are rare, the nominative being used instead.

299. Stems in *ντ* occur in a few adjectives and in many participles (301). *χαρίεις* *graceful* and *πᾶς* *all* are declined thus:

		SINGULAR				
Nom.	χαρίεις	χαρίεσσα	χαρίεν	πᾶς	πᾶσα	πᾶν
Gen.	χαρίεντ-ος	χαριέσσης	χαρίεντ-ος	παντ-ός	πᾱ́σης	παντ-ός
Dat.	χαρίεντ-ι	χαριέσσῃ	χαρίεντ-ι	παντ-ί	πᾱ́σῃ	παντ-ί
Acc.	χαρίεντ-α	χαρίεσσα-ν	χαρίεν	πάντ-α	πᾶσα-ν	πᾶν
Voc.	χαρίεν	χαρίεσσα	χαρίεν	πᾶς	πᾶσα	πᾶν
		DUAL				
N. A. V.	χαρίεντ-ε	χαριέσσᾱ	χαρίεντ-ε			
G. D.	χαριέντ-οιν	χαριέσσαιν	χαριέντ-οιν			
		PLURAL				
N. V.	χαρίεντ-ες	χαρίεσσαι	χαρίεντ-α	πάντ-ες	πᾶσαι	πάντ-α
Gen.	χαριέντ-ων	χαριεσσῶν	χαριέντ-ων	πάντ-ων	πᾱσῶν	πάντ-ων
Dat.	χαρίεσι(ν)	χαριέσσαις	χαρίεσι(ν)	πᾶσι(ν)	πᾱ́σαις	πᾶσι(ν)
Acc.	χαρίεντ-ας	χαριέσσᾱς	χαρίεντ-α	πάντ-ας	πᾱ́σᾱς	πάντ-α

299 D. Hom. has *αἱματόεσσα* *bloody*, *σκιόεντα* *shadowy*, but *τῑμῆς* and *τῑμήεις* *valuable*, *τῑμῆντα* and *τῑμήεντα*. Doric has sometimes *-ᾶς, -ᾶντος* for *-όεις, -όεντος*, as *φωνᾶντα*. Attic poetry often has the open forms *-όεις, -όεσσα*.

Like χαρίεις are inflected πτερόεις *winged*, φωνήεις *voiced*, δακρυόεις *tearful*. Adjectives in -όεις and -ήεις are generally poetical or Ionic. φωνήεντα meaning *vowels* is always open.

a. χαρίεις, πᾶς are derived from χαριεντ-ς, παντ-ς by 100; χαρίεν from χαριεντ- by 133. The ᾱ of πᾶν (for πᾰν(τ)-) is irregular and borrowed from πᾶς. Compounds have ᾰ: ἅπαν, σύμπαν.

b. From χαριετ- is derived χαρίεσσα with σσ, not ττ, by 114 a. χαριετ- is a weak form of the stem χαριεντ-; it appears also in χαρίεσι for χαριετ-σι (98). Participles in -εις (307) form the feminine from the strong stem -εντ + ῑα. πᾶσα stands for παντσα out of παντ-ῑα (113 a). πάντων, πᾶσι are accented contrary to 252; but παντός, παντί, πᾱσῶν are regular.

c. Adjectives in -όεις contract, as μελιτοῦς, μελιτοῦττα, μελιτοῦν, G. μελιτοῦντος, μελιτούττης, etc. (μελιτόεις *honied*). πτερόεις has πτεροῦντα, πτεροῦσσα. So in names of places: Ἀργεννοῦσσαι *Argennusae* for -όεσσαι; Ῥαμνοῦς, -οῦντος, for Ῥαμνόεις, -όεντος.

DECLENSION OF PARTICIPLES

300. Like ἀγαθός, -ή, -όν are inflected all the participles of the middle, and the future passive participle.

301. Participles of the active voice (except the perfect, 309), and the aorist passive participle have stems in ντ. The masculine and neuter follow the third declension, the feminine follows the first declension.

a. Most stems in οντ make the nom. sing. masc. without ς, like γέρων (243). But stems in οντ in the present and second aorist of μι-verbs (διδούς, δούς), and all stems in αντ, εντ, υντ, add ς, lose ντ (100), and lengthen the preceding vowel (-ους, -ᾱς, -εις, -ῡς, 37). In like manner the dat. pl. is formed: -οντ-σι = -ουσι, etc.

N. — The stem of participles in -ων, -οντος was originally ωντ. γέρων was orignally a participle.

b. The nominative neuter of all participles drops final τ of the stem (133).

c. The perfect active participle (stem οτ) has -ως in the masculine, -ος in the neuter. -ως and -ος are for -ϝωτ-ς, -ϝοτ-ς.

d. The feminine singular is made by adding ῑα to the stem. Thus, λύουσα (λῡοντ-ῑα), οὖσα (ὀντ-ῑα), ἱστᾶσα (ἱσταντ-ῑα), τιθεῖσα (τιθεντ-ῑα). The perfect adds -υ(σ)-ῑα, as in εἰδ-υῖα.

302. The vocative of all participles is the same as the nominative.

303. Participles in -ων, -ᾱς, -εις, -ους, -ῡς frequently use the masculine for the feminine in the dual.

304. The accent of monosyllabic participles is an exception to 252: ὤν, ὄντος (not ὀντός), στάς, στάντος.

305. Participles in **-ων, -ουσα, -ον** (ω-verbs): λύων *loosing* (stem λῡοντ-), ὤν *being* (stem ὀντ-).

---

305 D. In the feminine of participles from stems in οντ, αντ (306), Aeolic has -οισα, -αισα (λύοισα, λύσαισα), and -αις in the masculine (λύσαις).

	SINGULAR					
	Masc.	Fem.	Neut.	Masc.	Fem.	Neut.
N. V.	λύ͞ων	λύ͞ουσα	λῦον	ὤν	οὖσα	ὄν
Gen.	λύ͞οντ-ος	λῡούσης	λύ͞οντ-ος	ὄντ-ος	οὔσης	ὄντ-ος
Dat.	λύ͞οντ-ι	λῡούσῃ	λύ͞οντ-ι	ὄντ-ι	οὔσῃ	ὄντ-ι
Acc.	λύ͞οντ-α	λύ͞ουσα-ν	λῦον	ὄντ-α	οὖσα-ν	ὄν
	DUAL					
N. A. V.	λύ͞οντ-ε	λῡούσᾱ	λύ͞οντ-ε	ὄντ-ε	οὔσᾱ	ὄντ-ε
G. D.	λῡόντ-οιν	λῡούσαιν	λῡόντ-οιν	ὄντ-οιν	οὔσαιν	ὄντ-οιν
	PLURAL					
N. V.	λύ͞οντ-ες	λύ͞ουσαι	λύ͞οντ-α	ὄντ-ες	οὖσαι	ὄντ-α
Gen.	λῡόντ-ων	λῡουσῶν	λῡόντ-ων	ὄντ-ων	οὐσῶν	ὄντ-ων
Dat.	λύ͞ουσι(ν)	λῡούσαις	λύ͞ουσι(ν)	οὖσι(ν)	οὔσαις	οὖσι(ν)
Acc.	λύ͞οντ-ας	λῡούσᾱς	λύ͞οντ-α	ὄντ-ας	οὔσᾱς	ὄντ-α

So are inflected *παιδεύων educating*, *γράφων writing*, *φέρων bearing*.

a. All participles in -ων are inflected like λύων, those in -ών having the accent of ὤν, ὄντος, etc.; as λιπών, λιποῦσα, λιπόν *having left*. Such participles are from ω-verbs, in which ο is a part of the tense suffix.

b. Like participles are declined the adjectives ἑκών, ἑκοῦσα, ἑκόν *willing*, ἄκων, ἄκουσα, ἆκον *unwilling* (for ἀέκων, etc.), G. ἄκοντος, ἀκούσης, ἄκοντος.

306. Participles in -ᾱς, -ᾱσα, -αν: λύ͞σᾱς *having loosed*, ἱστάς *setting*.

	SINGULAR					
N. V.	λύ͞σᾱς	λύ͞σᾱσα	λῦσαν	ἱστάς	ἱστᾶσα	ἱστάν
Gen.	λύ͞σαντ-ος	λῡσά͞σης	λύ͞σαντ-ος	ἱστάντ-ος	ἱστά͞σης	ἱστάντ-ος
Dat.	λύ͞σαντ-ι	λῡσά͞σῃ	λύ͞σαντ-ι	ἱστάντ-ι	ἱστά͞σῃ	ἱστάντ-ι
Acc.	λύ͞σαντ-α	λύ͞σᾱσα-ν	λῦσαν	ἱστάντ-α	ἱστᾶσα-ν	ἱστάν
	DUAL					
N. A. V.	λύ͞σαντ-ε	λῡσά͞σᾱ	λύ͞σαντ-ε	ἱστάντ-ε	ἱστά͞σᾱ	ἱστάντ-ε
G. D.	λῡσάντ-οιν	λῡσά͞σαιν	λῡσάντ-οιν	ἱστάντ-οιν	ἱστά͞σαιν	ἱστάντ-οιν
	PLURAL					
N. V.	λύ͞σαντ-ες	λύ͞σᾱσαι	λύ͞σαντ-α	ἱστάντ-ες	ἱστᾶσαι	ἱστάντ-α
Gen.	λῡσάντ-ων	λῡσᾱσῶν	λῡσάντ-ων	ἱστάντ-ων	ἱστᾱσῶν	ἱστάντ-ων
Dat.	λύ͞σᾱσι(ν)	λῡσά͞σαις	λύ͞σᾱσι(ν)	ἱστᾶσι(ν)	ἱστά͞σαις	ἱστᾶσι(ν)
Acc.	λύ͞σαντ-ας	λῡσά͞σας	λύ͞σαντ-α	ἱστάντ-ας	ἱστά͞σᾱς	ἱστάντ-α

So are declined *παιδεύσᾱς having educated*, *στήσᾱς having set*.

307. Participles in **-εις, -εισα, -εν; -ους, -ουσα, -ον** (*μι*-verbs): **τιθείς** *placing*, **διδούς** *giving*.

SINGULAR

N. V.	τιθείς	τιθεῖσα	τιθέν	διδούς	διδοῦσα	διδόν
Gen.	τιθέντ-ος	τιθείσης	τιθέντ-ος	διδόντ-ος	διδούσης	διδόντ-ος
Dat.	τιθέντ-ι	τιθείσῃ	τιθέντ-ι	διδόντ-ι	διδούσῃ	διδόντ-ι
Acc.	τιθέντ-α	τιθεῖσα-ν	τιθέν	διδόντ-α	διδοῦσα-ν	διδόν

DUAL

N. A. V.	τιθέντ-ε	τιθείσᾱ	τιθέντ-ε	διδόντ-ε	διδούσᾱ	διδόντ-ε
G. D.	τιθέντ-οιν	τιθείσαιν	τιθέντ-οιν	διδόντ-οιν	διδούσαιν	διδόντ-οιν

PLURAL

N. V.	τιθέντ-ες	τιθεῖσαι	τιθέντ-α	διδόν-τες	διδοῦσαι	διδόντ-α
Gen.	τιθέντ-ων	τιθεισῶν	τιθέντ-ων	διδόντ-ων	διδουσῶν	διδόντ-ων
Dat.	τιθεῖσι(ν)	τιθείσαις	τιθεῖσι(ν)	διδοῦσι(ν)	διδούσαις	διδοῦσι(ν)
Acc.	τιθέντ-ας	τιθείσᾱς	τιθέντ-α	διδόντ-ας	διδούσᾱς	διδόντ-α

So are inflected θείς *having placed*, παιδευθείς *having been educated*, λυθείς *having been loosed*, δούς *having given*.

a. In participles with stems in οντ of *μι*-verbs the ο belongs to the verb-stem.

308. Participles in **-ῡς, -ῡσα, -υν**: δεικνύς *showing*, φύς *born*.

SINGULAR

N. V.	δεικνύς	δεικνῦσα	δεικνύν	φύς	φῦσα	φύν
Gen.	δεικνύντ-ος	δεικνύσης	δεικνύντ-ος	φύντ-ος	φύσης	φύντ-ος
Dat.	δεικνύντ-ι	δεικνύσῃ	δεικνύντ-ι	φύντ-ι	φύσῃ	φύντ-ι
Acc.	δεικνύντ-α	δεικνῦσα-ν	δεικνύν	φύντ-α	φῦσα-ν	φύν

DUAL

N. A. V.	δεικνύντ-ε	δεικνύσᾱ	δεικνύντ-ε	φύντ-ε	φύσᾱ	φύντ-ε
G. D.	δεικνύντ-οιν	δεικνύσαιν	δεικνύντ-οιν	φύντ-οιν	φύσαιν	φύντ-οιν

PLURAL

N. V.	δεικνύντ-ες	δεικνῦσαι	δεικνύντ-α	φύντες	φῦσαι	φύντ-α
Gen.	δεικνύντ-ων	δεικνῡσῶν	δεικνύντ-ων	φύντων	φῡσῶν	φύντ-ων
Dat.	δεικνῦσι(ν)	δεικνύσαις	δεικνῦσι(ν)	φῦσι(ν)	φύσαις	φῦσι(ν)
Acc.	δεικνύντ-ας	δεικνύσᾱς	δεικνύντ-α	φύντ-ας	φύσᾱς	φύντ-α

309. Perfect active participles in **-ως, -υια, -ος**: λελυκώς *having loosed*, εἰδώς *knowing*.

---

309 a. D. Hom. has ἑσταώς, ἑσταῶσα, ἑσταός, G. ἑσταότος, etc., Hdt. ἑστεώς, ἑστεῶσα, ἑστεός, G. ἑστεῶτος, etc. Some editions have ἑστεῶτα in Hom.

SINGULAR

N. V.	**λελυκώς**	**λελυκυῖα**	**λελυκός**	**εἰδώς**	**εἰδυῖα**	**εἰδός**
Gen.	**λελυκότ-ος**	**λελυκυίᾱς**	**λελυκότ-ος**	**εἰδότ-ος**	**εἰδυίᾱς**	**εἰδότ-ος**
Dat.	**λελυκότ-ι**	**λελυκυίᾳ**	**λελυκότ-ι**	**εἰδότ-ι**	**εἰδυίᾳ**	**εἰδότ-ι**
Acc.	**λελυκότ-α**	**λελυκυῖα-ν**	**λελυκός**	**εἰδότ-α**	**εἰδυῖα-ν**	**εἰδός**

DUAL

N.A.V.	**λελυκότ-ε**	**λελυκυίᾱ**	**λελυκότ-ε**	**εἰδότ-ε**	**εἰδυίᾱ**	**εἰδότ-ε**
G. D.	**λελυκότ-οιν**	**λελυκυίαιν**	**λελυκότ-οιν**	**εἰδότ-οιν**	**εἰδυίαιν**	**εἰδότ-οιν**

PLURAL

N. V.	**λελυκότ-ες**	**λελυκυῖαι**	**λελυκότ-α**	**εἰδότ-ες**	**εἰδυῖαι**	**εἰδότ-α**
Gen.	**λελυκότ-ων**	**λελυκυιῶν**	**λελυκότ-ων**	**εἰδότ-ων**	**εἰδυιῶν**	**εἰδότ-ων**
Dat.	**λελυκόσι(ν)**	**λελυκυίαις**	**λελυκόσι(ν)**	**εἰδόσι(ν)**	**εἰδυίαις**	**εἰδόσι(ν)**
Acc.	**λελυκότ-ας**	**λελυκυίᾱς**	**λελυκότ-α**	**εἰδότ-ας**	**εἰδυίᾱς**	**εἰδότ-α**

So are inflected πεπαιδευκώς, πεπαιδευκυῖα, πεπαιδευκός *having educated*; γεγονώς, γεγονυῖα, γεγονός *born*.

a. ἑστώς *standing* (contracted from ἑσταώς) is inflected ἑστώς, ἑστῶσα, ἑστός, G. ἑστῶτος (with irregular accent, from ἑσταότος), ἑστώσης, ἑστῶτος; pl. N. ἑστῶτες, ἑστῶσαι, ἑστῶτα, G. ἑστώτων, ἑστωσῶν. So τεθνεώς, τεθνεῶσα, τεθνεός *dead*.

N. — ἑστός (the usual spelling in the neut. nom.) has -ός (not -ώς) in imitation of εἰδός and of forms in -κός, thus distinguishing the neuter from the masculine.

310. Contracted Participles. — The present participle of verbs in -αω, -εω, -οω, and the future participle of liquid verbs (401) and of Attic futures (538) are contracted. τῑμῶν *honouring*, ποιῶν *making*, are thus declined:

SINGULAR

N. V.	(τῑμάων)	**τῑμῶν**	(τῑμάουσα)	**τῑμῶσα**	(τῑμάον)	**τῑμῶν**
Gen.	(τῑμάοντος)	**τῑμῶντ-ος**	(τῑμαούσης)	**τῑμώσης**	(τῑμάοντος)	**τῑμῶντ-ος**
Dat.	(τῑμάοντι)	**τῑμῶντ-ι**	(τῑμαούσῃ)	**τῑμώσῃ**	(τῑμάοντι)	**τῑμῶντ-ι**
Acc.	(τῑμάοντα)	**τῑμῶντ-α**	(τῑμάουσαν)	**τῑμῶσα-ν**	(τῑμάον)	**τῑμῶν**

DUAL

N. A.V.	(τῑμάοντε)	**τῑμῶντ-ε**	(τῑμαούσᾱ)	**τῑμώσᾱ**	(τῑμάοντε)	**τῑμῶντ-ε**
G. D.	(τῑμαόντοιν)	**τῑμώντ-οιν**	(τῑμαούσαιν)	**τῑμώσαιν**	(τῑμαόντοιν)	**τῑμώντ-οιν**

PLURAL

N. V.	(τῑμάοντες)	**τῑμῶντ-ες**	(τῑμάουσαι)	**τῑμῶσαι**	(τῑμάοντα)	**τῑμῶντ-α**
Gen.	(τῑμαόντων)	**τῑμώντ-ων**	(τῑμαουσῶν)	**τῑμωσῶν**	(τῑμαόντων)	**τῑμώντ-ων**
Dat.	(τῑμάουσι)	**τῑμῶσι(ν)**	(τῑμαούσαις)	**τῑμώσαις**	(τῑμάουσι)	**τῑμῶσι(ν)**
Acc.	(τῑμάοντας)	**τῑμῶντ-ας**	(τῑμαούσᾱς)	**τῑμώσᾱς**	(τῑμάοντα)	**τῑμῶντ-α**

310 D. Aeolic has also τίμαις, ποίεις, δήλοις from τίμᾱμι, ποίημι, δήλωμι.

	SINGULAR					
N. V.	(ποιέων)	ποιῶν	(ποιέουσα)	ποιοῦσα	(ποιέον)	ποιοῦν
Gen.	(ποιέοντος)	ποιοῦντ-ος	(ποιεούσης)	ποιούσης	(ποιέοντος)	ποιοῦντ-ος
Dat.	(ποιέοντι)	ποιοῦντ-ι	(ποιεούσῃ)	ποιούσῃ	(ποιέοντι)	ποιοῦντ-ι
Acc.	(ποιέοντα)	ποιοῦντ-α	(ποιέουσαν)	ποιοῦσα-ν	(ποιέον)	ποιοῦν
	DUAL					
N. A. V.	(ποιέοντε)	ποιοῦντ-ε	(ποιεούσᾱ)	ποιούσᾱ	(ποιέοντε)	ποιοῦντ-ε
G. D.	(ποιεόντοιν)	ποιούντ-οιν	(ποιεούσαιν)	ποιούσαιν	(ποιεόντοιν)	ποιούντ-οιν
	PLURAL					
N. V.	(ποιέοντες)	ποιοῦντ-ες	(ποιέουσαι)	ποιοῦσαι	(ποιέοντα)	ποιοῦντ-α
Gen.	(ποιεόντων)	ποιούντ-ων	(ποιεουσῶν)	ποιουσῶν	(ποιεόντων)	ποιούντ-ων
Dat.	(ποιέουσι)	ποιοῦσι(ν)	(ποιεούσαις)	ποιούσαις	(ποιέουσι)	ποιοῦσι(ν)
Acc.	(ποιέοντας)	ποιοῦντ-ας	(ποιεούσᾱς)	ποιούσᾱς	(ποιέοντα)	ποιοῦντ-α

a. The present participle of δηλῶ (δηλόω) *manifest* is inflected like ποιῶν: thus, δηλῶν, δηλοῦσα, δηλοῦν, G. δηλοῦντος, δηλούσης, δηλοῦντος, etc.

ADJECTIVES OF IRREGULAR DECLENSION

311. The irregular adjectives μέγας *great* (stems μεγα- and μεγαλο-) and πολύς *much* (stems πολυ- and πολλο-) are thus declined:

	SINGULAR					
Nom.	μέγας	μεγάλη	μέγα	πολύς	πολλή	πολύ
Gen.	μεγάλου	μεγάλης	μεγάλου	πολλοῦ	πολλῆς	πολλοῦ
Dat.	μεγάλῳ	μεγάλῃ	μεγάλῳ	πολλῷ	πολλῇ	πολλῷ
Acc.	μέγαν	μεγάλην	μέγα	πολύν	πολλήν	πολύ
Voc.	μεγάλε	μεγάλη	μέγα			
	DUAL					
N. A. V.	μεγάλω	μεγάλᾱ	μεγάλω			
G. D.	μεγάλοιν	μεγάλαιν	μεγάλοιν			
	PLURAL					
N. V.	μεγάλοι	μεγάλαι	μεγάλα	πολλοί	πολλαί	πολλά
Gen.	μεγάλων	μεγάλων	μεγάλων	πολλῶν	πολλῶν	πολλῶν
Dat.	μεγάλοις	μεγάλαις	μεγάλοις	πολλοῖς	πολλαῖς	πολλοῖς
Acc.	μεγάλους	μεγάλᾱς	μεγάλα	πολλούς	πολλᾱ́ς	πολλά

---

311 D. Hom. has some forms from the stem πολυ- (πουλυ-) which are not Attic: G. πολέος, N. pl. πολέες, G. πολέων, D. πολέεσσι (250 D. 2), πολέσσι and πολέσι,

a. Except in the forms μέγας, μέγαν, μέγα, the adjective μέγας is inflected as if the nominative sing. masc. were μεγάλος. μέγας is sometimes found in the voc. sing. Except in πολύς, πολύν, πολύ, the adjective πολύς is inflected as if the nominative sing. masc. were πολλός.

b. The stem πολλο- is from πολυ̯ο-, *i.e.* πολϝο-, λϝ being assimilated to λλ.

c. πρᾶος *mild* forms its masc. and neuter sing. and dual from the stem πρᾳο-; its fem. in all numbers from the stem πρᾱϋ-, as nom. πρᾱεῖα for πρᾱευ̯-ια formed like ἡδεῖα (297 a). Thus πρᾶος, πρᾱεῖα, πρᾶον, G. πρᾴου, πρᾱείᾱς, πρᾴου, etc. In the plural we have

N. V.	πρᾶοι or πρᾱεῖς	πρᾱεῖαι	πρᾶα or πρᾱέα
Gen.	πρᾴων or πρᾱέων	πρᾱειῶν	πρᾴων or πρᾱέων
Dat.	πρᾴοις or πρᾱέσι(ν)	πρᾱείαις	πρᾴοις or πρᾱέσι(ν)
Acc.	πρᾴους	πρᾱείᾱς	πρᾶα or πρᾱέα

d. Some compounds of πούς *foot* (ποδ-) have -ουν in the nom. sing. neut. and sometimes in the acc. sing. masc. by analogy to ἁπλοῦς (290). Thus, τρίπους *three-footed*, τρίπουν (but acc. τρίποδα *tripod*).

ADJECTIVES OF ONE ENDING

312. Adjectives of one ending have the same termination for masculine and feminine. The neuter (like masc. and fem.) sometimes occurs in oblique cases. Examples: ἀγνώς ἀγνῶτ-ος *unknown* or *unknowing*, ἄπαις ἄπαιδ-ος *childless*, ἀργής ἀργῆτ-ος *white*, ἅρπαξ ἅρπαγ-ος *rapacious*, μάκαρ μάκαρ-ος *blessed*, ἀκάμᾱς ἀκάμαντ-ος *unwearied*. Here belong also certain other adjectives commonly used as substantives, as γυμνής γυμνῆτ-ος *light armed*, πένης πένητ-ος *poor*, φυγάς φυγάδ-ος *fugitive*, ἧλιξ ἥλικ-ος *comrade*, ἀλαζών ἀλαζόν-ος *flatterer*. Some are masculine only, as ἐθελοντής (-οῦ) *volunteer*. Adj. in -ις -ιδος are feminine only: Ἑλληνίς *Greek*, πατρίς (*scil.* γῆ) *fatherland*, συμμαχίς (πόλις) *an allied state*.

COMPARISON OF ADJECTIVES

313. Comparison by -τερος, -τατος. — The usual endings are:

For the comparative: -τερος m. -τερᾱ f. -τερον n.
For the superlative: -τατος m. -τατη f. -τατον n.

The endings are added to the masculine stem of the positive. Comparatives are declined like ἄξιος, superlatives like ἀγαθός (287).

δῆλος (δηλο-) *clear*, **δηλό-τερος, δηλό-τατος**; **ἰσχῡρός** (ἰσχῡρο-) *strong*, **ἰσχῡρό-τερος, ἰσχῡρό-τατος**; **μέλᾱς** (μελαν-) *black*, **μελάν-τερος, μελάν-τατος**; **βαρύς** (βαρυ-) *heavy*, **βαρύ-τερος, βαρύ-τατος**; **ἀληθής** (ἀληθεσ-) *true*, **ἀληθέσ-τερος, ἀληθέσ-τατος**; **εὐκλεής** (εὐκλεεσ-) *famous*, **εὐκλεέσ-τερος, εὐκλεέσ-τατος**.

A. πολέας. Hom. has also πολλός, πολλή, πολλόν (like ἀγαθός), and these forms are commonly used by Hdt. πουλύς (for πολύς) is sometimes fem. in Hom.

a. χαριέστερος, -έστατος are from χαριετ-τερος, -τατος (83, 299 b), from χαρίεις *graceful*. Compounds of χάρις *grace* add ο to the stem (χαριτ-ο-), whence ἐπιχαριτώτερος *more pleasing*. πένης *poor* has πενέσ-τερος from πενετ-τερος, with ε for η.

b. Originally -τερος had no other force than to contrast one idea with another, and this function is retained in δεξίτερος *right*)(ἀρίστερος *left*, ἡμέτερος *our*)(ὑμέτερος *your*. Hom. has several such words: ἀγρότερος *wild*)(*tame*, θηλύτεραι γυναῖκες)(*men*, cp. Arcadian ἀρρέντερος from ἄρρην *male*. Cp. 1082 b.

314. Adjectives in -ος with a short penult lengthen ο to ω: νέο-ς *new*, νεώ-τερος, νεώ-τατος, χαλεπό-ς *difficult*, χαλεπώ-τερος, χαλεπώ-τατος. An undue succession of short syllables is thus avoided.

a. If the penult is long either by nature or by position (144), ο is not lengthened: λεπτός *lean*, λεπτότερος, λεπτότατος. A stop and a liquid almost always make position here (cp. 145); as πικρός *bitter*, πικρότερος, πικρότατος. κενός *empty* and στενός *narrow* were originally κενϝος, στενϝος (Ionic κεινός, στεινός, 37 D. 1), hence κενότερος, στενότερος.

315. The following drop the stem vowel ο: γεραιό-ς *aged*, γεραί-τερος, γεραί-τατος; παλαιό-ς *ancient*, παλαί-τερος, παλαί-τατος; σχολαῖο-ς *slow*, σχολαί-τερος, σχολαί-τατος; φίλο-ς *dear*, φίλ-τερος (poetic), φίλ-τατος (319, 11).

a. Some other adjectives reject the stem vowel ο and end in -αιτερος, -αιτατος, as ἥσυχος *quiet*, ἴσος *equal*, ὄρθριος *early*. These, like σχολαίτερος and γεραίτερος, imitate παλαίτερος, which is properly derived from the adverb πάλαι *long ago*. So μεσαίτερος, -αίτατος imitate μεσαι- in Hom. μεσαι-πόλιος *middle-aged*.

316. -εστερος, -εστατος. — By imitation of words like ἀληθέσ-τερος, ἀληθέσ-τατος (313), -εστερος, -εστατος are added to stems in ον and to some in οο (contracted to ου). Thus, εὐδαίμων *happy*, εὐδαιμον-έστερος, -έστατος; ἁπλοῦς *simple*, ἁπλούστερος (for ἁπλο-εστερος), ἁπλούστατος; εὔνους *well-disposed*, εὐνούστερος, -ούστατος, and so in all others in -νους from νοῦς *mind*. (Others in -οος have -οωτερος: ἀθροώτερος *more crowded* from ἀθρόος.)

a. Some stems in ον substitute ο for ον; as (from ἐπιλήσμων *forgetful*, ἐπιλησμονέσ-τερος) ἐπιλησμό-τατος; πίων *fat*, πῑότερος, πῑότατος; πέπων *ripe* has πεπαίτερος, πεπαίτατος. Cp. 315 a.

b. Other cases: (with loss of ο) ἐρρωμένο-ς *strong*, ἐρρωμενέστερος, -έστατος, ἄκρᾱτο-ς *unmixed*, ἀκρᾱτέστατος, ἄσμενο-ς *glad*, ἄφθονο-ς *abundant*.

317. -ιστερος, -ιστατος. — By imitation of words like ἀχαρίστερος for ἀχαριτ-τερος (83) from ἄχαρις *disagreeable*, -ιστερος, -ιστατος are used especially with adjectives of a bad meaning, as κλεπτ-ίστατος (κλέπτης *thief*, 321), κακηγορίστερος (κακήγορος *abusive*), λαλ-ίστερος (λάλος *talkative*).

318. Comparison by -ῑων, -ιστος. — Some adjectives add to the *root* of the positive the endings -ῑων for the masculine and feminine, -ῑον

---

314 a. D. Hom. ὀιζῡρώτατος (but cp. Att. οἰζῡρός), λᾱρώτατος (λᾰερώτατος ?).

318 D. Hom. and Doric poetry have also -ῐων, which is as old as -ῑων. Forms in -ῑων, -ιστος are much commoner in poetry than in prose. Hom. has βάθιστος (βαθύς *deep*), βράσσων (βραχύς *short*), βάρδιστος (βραδύς *slow*), κύδιστος (κῡδρός *glorious*), ὤκιστος (ὠκύς *quick*).

for the neuter to form the comparative, and -ιστος -η -ον to form the superlative. The vowel (or the syllable ρο) standing before ς of the nominative is thus lost.

Positive	Comparative	Superlative
ἡδ-ύ-ς *sweet* (ἡ ἡδ-ονή *pleasure*)	**ἡδ-ίων**	**ἥδ-ιστος**
ταχ-ύ-ς *swift* (τὸ τάχ-ος *swiftness*)	**θάττων** (112, 125 f)	**τάχ-ιστος**
μέγ-α-ς *great* (τὸ μέγ-εθος *greatness*)	**μείζων** (116)	**μέγ-ιστος**
ἀλγεινός *painful* (τὸ ἄλγ-ος *pain*)	**ἀλγ-ίων**	**ἄλγ-ιστος**
αἰσχ-ρό-ς *shameful* (τὸ αἶσχ-ος *shame*)	**αἰσχ-ίων**	**αἴσχ-ιστος**
ἐχθ-ρό-ς *hateful, hostile* (τὸ ἔχθ-ος *hate*)	**ἐχθ-ίων**	**ἔχθ-ιστος**

Forms in -ίων are declined like βελτίων (293), those in -ιστος like ἀγαθός (287).

319. Irregular Comparison. — The commonest adjectives forming irregular degrees of comparison by reason of the sound changes or because several words are grouped under one positive, are the following. Poetic or Ionic forms are in ( ).

1. **ἀγαθός** *good*	**ἀμείνων** (from ἀμεν-ῑων) (ἀρείων)	**ἄριστος** (ἀρ-ετή *virtue*)
	βελτίων (βέλτερος, not in Hom.)	**βέλτιστος** (βέλτατος, not in Hom.)
(κρατύς *powerful*) (cp. κράτος *strength*)	**κρείττων, κρείσσων** (κρέσσων) (φέρτερος)	**κράτιστος** (κάρτιστος) (φέρτατος, φέριστος)
	λῴων (λωίων, λωίτερος)	**λῷστος**
2. **κακός** *bad*	**κακίων** (κακώτερος) *peior*	**κάκιστος**
	χείρων (χερείων) *meaner, deterior* (χειρότερος, χερειότερος)	**χείριστος**
	ἥττων, ἥσσων (for ἡκ-ῑων) *weaker, inferior* (ἕσσων)	(ἥκιστος, rare), adv. ἥκιστα *least of all*
3. **καλός** *beautiful*	**καλλίων**	**κάλλιστος** (κάλλ-ος *beauty*)
4. **μακρός** *long*	**μακρότερος** (μάσσων)	**μακρότατος** (μήκιστος)
5. **μέγας** *great*	**μείζων** 318 (μέζων)	**μέγιστος**

319 D. Hom. has also κερδαλέος *gainful, crafty*, **κερδίων, κέρδιστος**; **ῥῑγίων**, ῥίγιστος *more, most dreadful* (cp. ῥῖγος *cold*, ῥῑγηλός *chilling*), κήδιστος (κηδεῖος *dear*, κῆδος *care*).

6. **μῑκρός** *small*	**μῑκρότερος**	**μῑκρότατος**
(ἐλάχεια, f. of ἐλαχύς)	**ἐλᾱ́ττων, ἐλᾱ́σσων** (for ἐλαχῑ́ων)	**ἐλάχιστος**
	μείων	(μεῖστος, rare)
7. **ὀλίγος** *little*, pl. *few*	**ὀλείζων** (inscriptions)	**ὀλίγιστος**
	(ὑπ-ολίζων Hom. *rather less*)	
8. **πολύς** *much*, pl. *many*	**πλείων, πλέων**, neut. **πλέον, πλεῖν**	**πλεῖστος**
9. **ῥᾴδιος** *easy*	**ῥᾴων** (Ion. ῥηίων)	**ῥᾷστος**
(ῥηίδιος)	(ῥηίτερος)	(ῥηίτατος, ῥήιστος)
10. **ταχύς** *quick*	**θᾱ́ττων, θᾱ́σσων**	**τάχιστος**
	(ταχύτερος)	(ταχύτατος)
11. **φίλος** *dear*	(φίλτερος)	**φίλτατος**
	φιλαίτερος (Xenoph.)	**φιλαίτατος** (Xenoph.)
	(φιλίων, rare in Hom.)	

a. ἀμείνων, ἄριστος express *aptitude, capacity* or *worth* (*able, brave, excellent*); βελτῑ́ων, βέλτιστος, *a moral idea* (*virtuous*); κρείττων, κράτιστος, *force* and *superiority* (*strong*) (ἥττων is the opposite of κρείττων); λῴων means *more desirable, more agreeable* (ὦ λῷστε *my good friend*); κακίων, κάκιστος express *moral perversity, cowardice*; χείρων, χείριστος, *insufficiency, lack* of a quality (*less good*) (*worthless, good for nothing* is φαῦλος).

b. ἐλάττων, ἔλᾱττον, ἐλάχιστος refer to size: *smaller* (opposed to μείζων); or to multitude: *fewer* (opp. to πλείων). μείων, μεῖον, ἧττον, ἥκιστα also belong both to μῑκρός and to ὀλίγος.

c. The orators prefer the longer form of πλείων, especially the contracted πλείω, πλείους, but the neut. πλέον. πλεῖν is not contracted from πλέον.

320. Defectives. — Some comparatives and superlatives are derived from prepositions or adverbs:

(πρό *before*)	πρότερος *former*	πρῶτος *first*
(ὑπέρ *over, beyond*)	ὑπέρτερος (poetic) *higher, superior.*	ὑπέρτατος (poetic) *highest, supreme.*
(πλησίον *near*)	πλησιαίτερος	πλησιαίτατος
(προὔργου *serviceable*)	προυργιαίτερος	
	ὕστερος *later, latter*	ὕστατος *latest, last*

a. -ατος appears in ὕπατος *highest*, ἔσχατος *farthest, extreme* (from ἐξ).

321. In poetry and sometimes in prose comparatives and superlatives are formed from substantives and pronouns. Hom. has βασιλεύτερος *more kingly*,

---

320 D. Hom. has ὁπλότερος *younger*, ὁπλότατος. Several defectives denote *place*; ἐπασσύτερος (ἆσσον *nearer*), παροίτερος (πάροιθεν *before*), μυχοίτατος (μυχοῖ *in a recess*). -ατος in μέσατος, μέσσατος (μέσος *middle*), πύματος *last*, νέατος *lowest*. For ὕστατος Hom. has ὑστάτιος; and δεύτατος *last* from δεύτερος *second*.

-τατος (βασιλεύς *king*), ἑταιρότατος *a closest companion* (ἑταῖρος *comrade*), κύντερος *more doglike*, -τατος (κύων *dog*), κουρότερος *more youthful* (κοῦρος *a youth*). Aristophanes has κλεπτίστατος *most thievish* (κλέπτης *thief*, 317), and αὐτότατος *his very self, ipsissimus*.

322. Double Comparison. — A double comparative occurs sometimes to produce a comic effect, as κυντερώτερος (321). A double superlative is πρώτιστος.

323. Comparison by μᾶλλον, μάλιστα. — Instead of the forms in -τερος, -τατος or -ῑων, -ιστος the adverbs μᾶλλον *more*, μάλιστα *most*, may be used with the positive; as μᾶλλον φίλος *more dear, dearer*, μάλιστα φίλος *most dear, dearest*. This is the only way of comparing participles and words that do not take the comparative and superlative endings (μᾶλλον ἑκών *more willing*).

a. Comparison by μᾶλλον, μάλιστα is common in the case of compound adjectives, adjectives with a prepositional prefix, verbal adjectives in -τός, and adjectives in -ιος.

324. To express *equality* or *inferiority* οὕτω *as* (often in correlation with ὥσπερ), ἧττον *less*, may be placed before the positive. Thus, *as good as handsome* may be expressed by οὕτως ἀγαθὸς ὥσπερ καὶ καλός, ὥσπερ ἀγαθὸς οὕτω καὶ καλός, οὐχ ἧττον καλὸς ἢ καὶ ἀγαθός.

PRONOUNS

325. The Personal Pronouns. — The pronouns of the first, second, and third person are declined as follows:

		SINGULAR	
Nom.	ἐγώ *I*	σύ *thou*	—— *he, she, it* (325 d)
Gen.	ἐμοῦ; μου enclitic	σοῦ; σου enclitic	οὗ; οὑ enclitic
Dat.	ἐμοί; μοι enclitic	σοί; σοι enclitic	οἷ; οἱ enclitic
Acc.	ἐμέ; με enclitic	σέ; σε enclitic	ἕ; ἑ enclitic
		DUAL	
N. A.	νώ *we two*	σφώ *you two*	
G. D.	νῷν	σφῷν	
		PLURAL	
Nom.	ἡμεῖς *we*	ὑμεῖς *you*	σφεῖς *they*
Gen.	ἡμῶν	ὑμῶν	σφῶν
Dat.	ἡμῖν	ὑμῖν	σφίσι(ν)
Acc.	ἡμᾶς	ὑμᾶς	σφᾶς

---

325 D. 1. Homer inflects the personal pronouns as follows. (The forms ἀμμ-, ὑμμ- are Aeolic).

a. The enclitic forms μου, μοι, με; σου, σοι, σε are used when the pronoun is unemphatic, the longer forms ἐμοῦ, ἐμοί, ἐμέ and the accented σοῦ, σοί, σέ are

SINGULAR

Nom.	ἐγώ, ἐγών	σύ, τύνη	
Gen.	ἐμεῖο, ἐμέο, ἐμεῦ, μευ (encl.), ἐμέθεν	σεῖο, σέο, σεο (encl. A 396), σεῦ, σευ (encl.), σέθεν	εἷο, ἕο, ἑο (encl.), εὗ, εὑ (encl.), ἕθεν, ἑθεν (encl.)
Dat.	ἐμοί, μοι (encl.)	σοί, τοι (encl.), τεΐν	ἑοῖ, οἷ, οἱ (encl.)
Acc.	ἐμέ, με (encl.)	σέ, σε (encl.)	ἑέ, ἕ, ἑ (encl.), μιν (encl.)

DUAL

N. A.	νῶϊ, νώ	σφῶϊ, σφώ	σφωε (encl.)
G. D.	νῶϊν	σφῶϊν, σφῷν (δ 62)	σφωϊν (encl.)

PLURAL

Nom.	ἡμεῖς, ἄμμες	ὑμεῖς, ὔμμες (and voc.)	
Gen.	ἡμείων, ἡμέων	ὑμείων, ὑμέων	σφείων, σφέων, σφεων (encl.), σφῶν
Dat.	ἡμῖν, ἄμμι(ν)	ὑμῖν, ὔμμι(ν)	σφίσι(ν), σφισι(ν) (encl.), σφιν (encl.)
Acc.	ἡμέας, ἄμμε	ὑμέας, ὔμμε	σφέας, σφεας (encl.), σφε (encl.)

σφε (encl.) is used as accus. of all genders and numbers.

2. Herodotus inflects the personal pronouns as follows:

SINGULAR

Nom.	ἐγώ	σύ	
Gen.	ἐμέο, ἐμεῦ, μευ (encl.)	σέο, σεῦ, σευ (encl.)	εὑ (encl.)
Dat.	ἐμοί, μοι (encl.)	σοί, τοι (encl.)	οἱ (encl.)
Acc.	ἐμέ, με (encl.)	σέ, σε (encl.)	ἑ (encl.), μιν (encl.)

PLURAL

Nom.	ἡμεῖς	ὑμεῖς	σφεῖς
Gen.	ἡμέων	ὑμέων	σφέων, σφεων (encl.)
Dat.	ἡμῖν	ὑμῖν	σφίσι, σφισι (encl.)
Acc.	ἡμέας	ὑμέας	σφέας, σφεας (encl.), neut. σφεα (encl.)

σφίσι is used for ἑαυτοῖς, -αῖς; σφι (encl.) for αὐτοῖς, -αῖς; σφεα (encl.) for αὐτά.

3. Ionic μιν (encl.) is used in all genders (*eum*, *eam*, *id*), but not in the plural. ἄμμι, ὔμμε occur a few times, σέθεν often, in tragedy.

4. The chief forms peculiar to Doric are: I. ἐγών also before consonants; G. ἐμέος, ἐμοῦς, ἐμεῦς; D. ἐμίν; Pl. N. ἁμές; G. ἁμέων, ἁμῶν; D. ἁμίν(ῐ), ἆμιν; A. ἁμέ. II. τύ, τύνη; G. τέος, τεοῦς, τεῦς, τέο, τεῦ, τεοῦ; D. τίν, τίνη; A. τέ, τίν, τύ; Pl. N. ὑμές; G. ὑμέων; D. ὑμίν, ὗμιν; A. ὑμέ. III. G. ἑοῦς, ἑοῦ; D. ϝίν; A. νίν; Pl. G. σφείων, ψέων; D. φίν, ψίν; A. σφέ, ψέ.

used when the pronoun is emphatic. Thus, *δός μοι τὸ βιβλίον give me the book*, *οὐκ ἐμοί, ἀλλὰ σοὶ ἐπιβουλεύουσι they are plotting not against* me, *but against* you. See 187 a. On the use after prepositions see 187 N. 2.

b. For *ἐγώ, ἐμοί, σύ* the emphatic *ἔγωγε, ἔμοιγε* (186 a), *σύγε* occur. Also *ἐμοῦγε, ἐμέγε.*

c. The use of the plural *you* for *thou* is unknown in Ancient Greek; hence *ὑμεῖς* is used only in addressing more than one person.

d. Of the forms of the third personal pronoun only the datives *οἷ* and *σφίσι(ν)* are commonly used in Attic prose, and then only as indirect reflexives (1228). To express the personal pronouns of the third person we find usually: *ἐκεῖνος, οὗτος,* etc., in the nominative (1194), and the oblique forms of *αὐτός* in all other cases.

e. For the accus. of *οὗ* the tragic poets use *νιν* (encl.) and *σφε* (encl.) for masc. and fem., both sing. and pl. (= *eum, eam; eos, eas*). Doric so uses *νιν. σφίν* is rarely singular (*ei*) in tragedy.

f. *ἡμῶν, ἡμῖν, ἡμᾶς, ὑμῶν, ὑμῖν, ὑμᾶς*, when unemphatic, are sometimes accented in poetry on the penult, and *-ῑν* and *-ᾱς* are usually shortened. Thus, *ἥμων, ἧμιν, ἧμας, ὕμων, ὗμιν, ὗμας* *-ῑν* and *-ᾱς* are sometimes shortened even if the pronouns are emphatic, and we have *ἡμίν, ἡμάς, ὑμίν, ὑμάς. σφάς* occurs for *σφᾶς.*

326. *Stems.*—I. *(ἐ)με-* (cp. Lat. *me*), *νω-* (cp. Lat. *nō-s*), *(ἐ)μο-, ἡμε-. ἐμοῦ* is from *ἐμέο*; *ἡμεῖς* from *ἀμμε-ες* (37) with the rough breathing in imitation of *ὑμεῖς*; *ἡμῶν* from *ἡμέων, ἡμᾶς* from *ἡμέας* with *ᾱ* not *η* by 56. *ἐγώ* is not connected with these stems. II. *συ-* and *σε-* from *τϝε*; *το-*; *σφω-*; *ὑμε-* from *ὑμμε-* (37). III. *ἕ* for *σϝε* (cp. Lat. *se*), *ἑέ* for *σεϝε*, *οἷ* for *σϝο-ι*, and *σφε-*. The form of the stems and formation of the cases is often obscure.

327. The Intensive Pronoun αὐτός.—*αὐτός self* is declined thus:

SINGULAR	Masc.	Fem.	Neut.	DUAL	Masc.	Fem.	Neut.	PLURAL	Masc.	Fem.	Neut.
Nom.	**αὐτός**	**αὐτή**	**αὐτό**	N. A.	**αὐτώ**	**αὐτᾱ́**	**αὐτώ**	Nom.	**αὐτοί**	**αὐταί**	**αὐτά**
Gen.	**αὐτοῦ**	**αὐτῆς**	**αὐτοῦ**	G. D.	**αὐτοῖν**	**αὐταῖν**	**αὐτοῖν**	Gen.	**αὐτῶν**	**αὐτῶν**	**αὐτῶν**
Dat.	**αὐτῷ**	**αὐτῇ**	**αὐτῷ**					Dat.	**αὐτοῖς**	**αὐταῖς**	**αὐτοῖς**
Acc.	**αὐτόν**	**αὐτήν**	**αὐτό**					Acc.	**αὐτούς**	**αὐτᾱ́ς**	**αὐτά**

αὐτός is declined like *ἀγαθός* (287), but there is no vocative and the neuter nominative and accusative have no *-ν*. But *ταὐτόν the same* is common (328 N.).

328. *αὐτός* is a definite adjective and a pronoun. It has three meanings:

a. *self:* standing by itself in the nominative, *αὐτὸς ὁ ἀνήρ* or *ὁ ἀνὴρ αὐτός the man himself*, or (without the article) in agreement with a substantive or pronoun; as *ἀνδρὸς αὐτοῦ of the man himself.*

---

327 D. Hdt. has *αὐτέων* in the genitive plural. For the crasis *ωὑτός* (Hom.), *ωὑτός, τωὐτό* (Hdt.), see 68 D.

b. *him, her, it, them,* etc.: standing by itself in an oblique case (never in the nominative). The oblique cases of *αὐτός* are generally used instead of *οὗ, οἷ, ἕ,* etc., as *ὁ πατὴρ αὐτοῦ his father, οἱ παῖδες αὐτῶν their children.*

c. *same:* when it is preceded by the article in any case: *ὁ αὐτὸς ἀνήρ the same man, τοῦ αὐτοῦ ἀνδρός of the same man.*

N.—The article and *αὐτός* may unite by crasis (68 a): *αὑτός, αὑτή, ταὐτό* or *ταὐτόν; ταὐτοῦ, ταὐτῆς; ταὐτῷ, ταὐτῇ,* etc. Distinguish *αὑτή the same* f. from *αὕτη this* f.; *ταὐτά the same* n. from *ταῦτα these things* n.; *ταὐτῇ* from *ταύτῃ.*

329. Reflexive Pronouns.—The reflexive pronouns (referring back to the subject of the sentence) are formed by compounding the stems of the personal pronouns with the oblique cases of *αὐτός*. In the plural both pronouns are declined separately, but the third person has also the compounded form. The nominative is excluded by the meaning. There is no dual.

	myself	*thyself*	*himself, herself, itself*
Gen.	**ἐμαυτοῦ, -ῆς**	**σεαυτοῦ, -ῆς (σαυτοῦ, -ῆς)**	**ἑαυτοῦ, -ῆς, -οῦ (αὑτοῦ, -ῆς, -οῦ)**
Dat.	**ἐμαυτῷ, -ῇ**	**σεαυτῷ, -ῇ (σαυτῷ, -ῇ)**	**ἑαυτῷ, -ῇ, -ῷ (αὑτῷ, -ῇ, -ῷ)**
Acc.	**ἐμαυτόν, -ήν**	**σεαυτόν, -ήν (σαυτόν, -ήν)**	**ἑαυτόν, -ήν, -ό (αὑτόν, -ήν, -ό)**

	ourselves	*yourselves*	*themselves*
Gen.	**ἡμῶν αὐτῶν**	**ὑμῶν αὐτῶν**	**ἑαυτῶν** or **σφῶν αὐτῶν**
Dat.	**ἡμῖν αὐτοῖς, -αῖς**	**ὑμῖν αὐτοῖς, -αῖς**	**ἑαυτοῖς, -αῖς, -οῖς** or **σφίσιν αὐτοῖς, -αῖς**
Acc.	**ἡμᾶς αὐτούς, -ᾱ́ς**	**ὑμᾶς αὐτούς, -ᾱ́ς**	**ἑαυτούς, -ᾱ́ς, -ά** or **σφᾶς αὐτούς, -ᾱ́ς**

a. For *ἑαυτῶν,* etc., we find *αὑτῶν, αὑτοῖς, -αῖς, αὑτούς, -άς.* Distinguish *αὑτοῦ of himself* from *αὐτοῦ* (328).

330. Possessive Pronouns.—Possessive pronouns, formed from the stems of the personal pronouns, are declined like *ἀγαθός, ἄξιος* (287).

ἐμός ἐμή ἐμόν	*my, my own; mine*	**ἡμέτερος -ᾱ -ον**	*our, our own; ours*
σός σή σόν	*thy, thine own; thine*	**ὑμέτερος -ᾱ -ον**	*your, your own; yours*
[**ὅς ἥ ὅν**	*his (her, its) own*]	**σφέτερος -ᾱ -ον**	*their own*

---

329 D. Hom. never compounds the two pronouns: thus, *ἐμέθεν αὐτῆς, σοὶ αὐτῷ, οἷ αὐτῷ, ἓε αὐτόν, ἓ αὐτήν.* Hdt. has a few cases of the uncompounded forms; usually *ἐμεωυτοῦ, -τῷ, -τόν, σεωυτοῦ, ἑωυτοῦ, ἑωυτῶν, -οῖσι, -ούς,* and *σφέων αὐτῶν,* etc. The forms with *εωυ* started with *ἑωυτῷ* in the dative from *ἑο(ῖ) αὐτῷ,* and spread thence to the other cases.

330 D. 1. Hom. has also *τεός thy, ἑός* for *ὅς his, her own, ἁμός our, ὑμός your, σφός their* (rarely of the singular), *νωΐτερος of us two, σφωΐτερος of you two.* For *ἐμός* Attic poetry may use *ἁμός* (sometimes printed *ἀμός*) *our.*

2. *ὅς, ἑός* in Hom. may mean *my own, your own* (1230 a).

a. Distinguish the adjectival from the pronominal use: ὁ ἐμὸς φίλος or ὁ φίλος ὁ ἐμός *my friend* (adj.) from φίλος ἐμός *a friend of mine* (pron.). See 1196 a.

b. ὅς is not used in Attic prose. For *his, her, its,* αὐτοῦ, -ῆς, -οῦ are used.

331. Reciprocal Pronoun. — The reciprocal pronoun, meaning *one another, each other,* is made by doubling the stem of ἄλλος (ἀλλ-αλλο-). It is used only in the oblique cases of the dual and plural. (Cp. *alii aliorum, alter alterius*).

	DUAL			PLURAL		
Gen.	ἀλλήλοιν	ἀλλήλαιν	ἀλλήλοιν	ἀλλήλων	ἀλλήλων	ἀλλήλων
Dat.	ἀλλήλοιν	ἀλλήλαιν	ἀλλήλοιν	ἀλλήλοις	ἀλλήλαις	ἀλλήλοις
Acc.	ἀλλήλω	ἀλλήλᾱ	ἀλλήλω	ἀλλήλους	ἀλλήλᾱς	ἄλληλα

332. The Definite Article. — The definite article ὁ, ἡ, τό (stems ὁ-, ἁ-, το-) is thus declined:

	SINGULAR				DUAL				PLURAL		
Nom.	ὁ	ἡ	τό	N. A.	τώ	τώ	τώ	Nom.	οἱ	αἱ	τά
Gen.	τοῦ	τῆς	τοῦ	G. D.	τοῖν	τοῖν	τοῖν	Gen.	τῶν	τῶν	τῶν
Dat.	τῷ	τῇ	τῷ					Dat.	τοῖς	ταῖς	τοῖς
Acc.	τόν	τήν	τό					Acc.	τούς	τᾱ́ς	τά

a. The definite article is a weakened demonstrative pronoun, and is still used as a demonstrative in Homer (1100).

b. τά (especially) and ταῖν, the feminine forms in the dual, are very rare in the authors, and are unknown on Attic prose inscriptions of the classical period.

333. Demonstrative Pronouns. — The chief demonstrative pronouns are ὅδε *this (here),* οὗτος *this, that,* ἐκεῖνος *that (there, yonder).*

	SINGULAR								
Nom.	ὅδε	ἥδε	τόδε	οὗτος	αὕτη	τοῦτο	ἐκεῖνος	ἐκείνη	ἐκεῖνο
Gen.	τοῦδε	τῆσδε	τοῦδε	τούτου	ταύτης	τούτου	ἐκείνου	ἐκείνης	ἐκείνου
Dat.	τῷδε	τῇδε	τῷδε	τούτῳ	ταύτῃ	τούτῳ	ἐκείνῳ	ἐκείνῃ	ἐκείνῳ
Acc.	τόνδε	τήνδε	τόδε	τοῦτον	ταύτην	τοῦτο	ἐκεῖνον	ἐκείνην	ἐκεῖνο

---

332 D. Hom. has also gen. τοῖο, gen. dat. dual τοῖιν; nom. pl. τοί, ταί; gen. pl. fem. τάων; dat. pl. masc. τοῖσι, fem. τῇσι, τῇς (Hdt. τοῖσι, τῇσι). Doric are τῶ, τᾶς, etc.; pl. also N. τοί, ταί; G. fem. τᾶν. Generally poetic are τοῖσι, ταῖσι. τοὶ μέν, τοὶ δέ occur rarely in tragedy for οἱ μέν, οἱ δέ.

333 D. For τοῖσδε Hom. has also τοῖσδεσσι or τοῖσδεσι. Doric has n. pl. τούτοι, ταύται, gen. pl. fem. ταυτᾶν (Aeol. ταύτᾱν). κεῖνος occurs in Hdt. (together with ἐκεῖνος). Doric and Aeolic have κῆνος.

DUAL

N. A.	τώδε	τώδε	τώδε	τούτω	τούτω	τούτω	ἐκείνω	ἐκείνω	ἐκείνω
G. D.	τοῖνδε	τοῖνδε	τοῖνδε	τούτοιν	τούτοιν	τούτοιν	ἐκείνοιν	ἐκείνοιν	ἐκείνοιν

PLURAL

Nom.	οἵδε	αἵδε	τάδε	οὗτοι	αὗται	ταῦτα	ἐκεῖνοι	ἐκεῖναι	ἐκεῖνα
Gen.	τῶνδε	τῶνδε	τῶνδε	τούτων	τούτων	τούτων	ἐκείνων	ἐκείνων	ἐκείνων
Dat.	τοῖσδε	ταῖσδε	τοῖσδε	τούτοις	ταύταις	τούτοις	ἐκείνοις	ἐκείναις	ἐκείνοις
Acc.	τούσδε	τᾱ́σδε	τάδε	τούτους	ταύτᾱς	ταῦτα	ἐκείνους	ἐκείνᾱς	ἐκεῖνα

a. ὅδε is formed from the old demonstrative ὁ, ἡ, τό *this* or *that*, with the indeclinable demonstrative (and enclitic) ending -δε *here* (cp. *hī-c* from *hī-ce*, Fr. *ce-ci*). For the accent of ἥδε, οἵδε, αἵδε see 186.

b. οὗτος has the rough breathing and τ in the same places as the article. ου corresponds to the ο, αυ to the α, of the article. For οὗτος as a vocative, see 1288 a. (οὗτος is from ὁ + the particle *υ + the demonstrative suffix το + ς).

c. ἐκεῖνος has a variant form κεῖνος in poetry, and sometimes in prose (Demosthenes). (ἐκεῖνος stands for ἐκε(ι)-ενος from ἐκεῖ *there* + suffix -ενος.)

d. Other demonstrative pronouns are

τοσόσδε	τοσήδε	τοσόνδε	*so much, so many*	pointing forward (to what follows).
τοιόσδε	τοιάδε	τοιόνδε	*such* (in *quality*)	
τηλικόσδε	τηλικήδε	τηλικόνδε	*so old, so great*	

These are formed from -δε and the (usually) poetic τόσος, τοῖος, τηλίκος with the same meanings.

e. Combinations of the above words and οὗτος are

τοσοῦτος	τοσαύτη	τοσοῦτο(ν)	*so much, so many*	pointing backward (to what precedes).
τοιοῦτος	τοιαύτη	τοιοῦτο(ν)	*such* (in *quality*)	
τηλικοῦτος	τηλικαύτη	τηλικοῦτο(ν)	*so old, so great*	

The forms in -ν are more common than those in -ο. Attic prose inscriptions have only -ον.

f. The dual rarely has separate feminine forms.

g. The deictic suffix -ῑ may be added to demonstratives for emphasis. Before it α, ε, ο are dropped. Thus, ὁδί *this man here*, ἡδί, τοδί, G. τουδί, τησδί, etc.; οὑτοσί, αὑτηί, τουτί, οὑτοιί, τουτωνί. So with other demonstratives and with adverbs: τοσουτοσί, οὑτωσί, ὡδί. For -ῑ we have, in comedy, -γῑ or (rarely) -δῑ formed from γ(ε), δ(ε) + ῑ. Thus, αὑτηγί, τουτογί, τουτοδί.

334. Interrogative and Indefinite Pronouns. — The interrogative pronoun τίς, τί *who, which, what?* never changes its accent to the grave (154). The indefinite pronoun τὶς, τὶ *any one, some one, anything, something* is enclitic (181 b).

---

333 e, D. Hom. always, Hdt. rarely, has the final ν.

334 D. Hom. and Hdt. have G. τέο, τεῦ, D. τέῳ (τῷ Hom.), G. τέων, D. τέοισι. These forms are also indefinite and enclitic (gen. τεῶν Hdt.). Hom. has ἀσσα for the indefinite τινά.

SINGULAR

	Interrogative			Indefinite		
Nom.	τίς		τί	τὶς		τὶ
Gen.		τίν-ος, τοῦ			τιν-ός, τοῦ	
Dat.		τίν-ι, τῷ			τιν-ί, τῷ	
Acc.	τίν-α		τί	τινά		τὶ
			DUAL			
N. A. V		τίν-ε			τιν-έ	
G. D.		τίν-οιν			τιν-οῖν	
			PLURAL			
Nom.	τίν-ες		τίν-α	τιν-ές		τιν-ά
Gen.		τίν-ων			τιν-ῶν	
Dat.		τί-σι(ν)			τι-σί(ν)	
Acc.	τίν-ας		τίν-α	τιν-άς		τιν-ά

a. ἄττα (not enclitic) is sometimes used for the indefinite τινά. ἄττα is derived from such locutions as πολλάττα, properly πολλά + ττα (for τ̯α).

335. ἄλλος. — The indefinite pronoun ἄλλος *another* (Lat. *alius*, cp. 110) is declined like αὐτός: ἄλλος, ἄλλη, ἄλλο (never ἄλλον).

336. Δεῖνα. — The indefinite pronoun δεῖνα, always used with the article, means *such a one*. It is declined thus: sing. ὁ, ἡ, τὸ δεῖνα; τοῦ, τῆς, τοῦ δεῖνος; τῷ, τῇ, τῷ δεῖνι; τόν, τήν, τὸ δεῖνα; plur. (masc.) οἱ δεῖνες, τῶν δείνων, τοὺς δεῖνας. Example: ὁ δεῖνα τοῦ δεῖνος τὸν δεῖνα εἰσήγγειλεν *such a one son of such a one impeached such a one* [D.] 13. 5. δεῖνα is rarely indeclinable. Its use is colloquial and it occurs (in poetry) only in comedy.

337. Other indefinite pronominal adjectives are: **ἕτερος, -ᾱ, -ον**: with article, *the other, one of two, the one* (Lat. *alter, alteruter*); without article, *other, another, a second* (*alius*). By crasis (69) ἅτερος, θάτερον, etc. **ἑκάτερος, -ᾱ, -ον**: *each* (of two) *uterque;* pl. *either party, both parties,* as *utrique.* **ἕκαστος, -η, -ον**: *each, each one, every, every one,* used of more than one (*quisque*). **μόνος, -η, -ον**: *alone, only, sole.* **πᾶς** (299): *all, entire, every.* The negatives **οὐδείς, μηδείς** (349 b) *no one* (poetical οὔτις, μήτις, in prose only οὔτι, μήτι, declined like τὶς; accent 186), Lat. *nemo, nullus.* **οὐδέτερος, μηδέτερος** *neither of two* (Lat. *neuter*).

338. Relative Pronouns. — The relative pronoun ὅς, ἥ, ὅ *who, which, that* is declined thus:

---

338 D. 1. Hom. uses the demonstrative forms ὁ, ἡ, τό (332) as relatives (1105). In this case the nom. pl. has τοί, ταί (332 D.).

2. Besides the forms in 338, Hom. has gen. ὅο (miswritten ὅου) and ἕης.

3. Hdt. has ὅς, ἥ, τό, οἵ, αἵ, τά. In the oblique cases he uses τοῦ, τῆς, etc.; though, especially after prepositions capable of elision, he has the relative forms, as δι' οὗ, παρ' ᾧ, κατ' ἥν, ὑπ' ὧν; also ἐς ὅ.

SINGULAR				DUAL				PLURAL			
Nom.	ὅς	ἥ	ὅ	N. A.	ὥ	ὥ	ὥ	Nom.	οἵ	αἵ	ἅ
Gen.	οὗ	ἧς	οὗ	G. D.	οἷν	οἷν	οἷν	Gen.	ὧν	ὧν	ὧν
Dat.	ᾧ	ᾗ	ᾧ					Dat.	οἷς	αἷς	οἷς
Acc.	ὅν	ἥν	ὅ					Acc.	οὕς	ἅς	ἅ

a. The feminine dual forms ἅ and αἷν are seldom, if ever, used in Attic.

b. ὅς is used as a demonstrative in Homer and sometimes in prose (1113).

c. The enclitic particle -περ may be added to a relative pronoun (or adverb) to emphasize the connection between the relative and its antecedent. Thus, ὅσ-περ, ἥ-περ, ὅ-περ *the very person who, the very thing which;* so ὥσπερ *just as.* ὅσπερ is declined like ὅς.

d. Enclitic τε is added in ἐφ᾽ ᾧτε *on condition that,* οἷός τε (186 a) *able to,* ἅτε *inasmuch as.*

339. The indefinite or general relative pronoun ὅστις, ἥτις, ὅ τι *whoever* (*any-who, any-which*), *any one who, whatever, anything which,* inflects each part (ὅς and τὶς) separately. For the accent, see 186.

	SINGULAR		
Nom.	ὅστις	ἥτις	ὅ τι
Gen.	οὗτινος, ὅτου	ἧστινος	οὗτινος, ὅτου
Dat.	ᾧτινι, ὅτῳ	ᾗτινι	ᾧτινι, ὅτῳ
Acc.	ὅντινα	ἥντινα	ὅ τι
	DUAL		
N. A.	ὥτινε	ὥτινε	ὥτινε
G. D.	οἷντινοιν	οἷντινοιν	οἷντινοιν
	PLURAL		
Nom.	οἵτινες	αἵτινες	ἅτινα, ἅττα
Gen.	ὧντινων, ὅτων	ὧντινων	ὧντινων, ὅτων
Dat.	οἷστισι(ν), ὅτοις	αἷστισι(ν)	οἷστισι(ν), ὅτοις
Acc.	οὕστινας	ἅστινας	ἅτινα, ἅττα

a. The neuter ὅ τι is sometimes printed ὅ,τι to avoid confusion with the conjunction ὅτι *that, because.*

b. The shorter forms are rare in prose, but almost universal in poetry (especially ὅτου, ὅτῳ). Inscriptions have almost always ὅτου, ὅτῳ, ἅττα.

c. The plural ἅττα is to be distinguished from ἄττα (334 a).

---

339 D. Hom. has the following special forms. The forms not in ( ) are used also by Hdt. In the nom. and acc. Hdt has the usual forms.

	SINGULAR		PLURAL	
Nom.	(ὅτις)	(ὅ ττι)		ἅσσα
Gen.	(ὅττεο), (ὅττευ) ὅτευ		ὅτεων	
Dat.	ὅτεῳ		ὁτέοισι	
Acc.	(ὅτινα)	(ὅ ττι)	(ὅτινας)	ἅσσα

d. τὶς may be added to ὁπότερος, ὅσος, οἷος (340) to make them more indefinite as ὁποῖός τις *of whatsoever kind.*

e. οὖν, δή, or δήποτε may be added to the indefinite pronouns to make them as general as possible, as ὁστισοῦν (or ὅστις οὖν), ἡτισοῦν, ὁτιοῦν *any one whatever*, *any thing whatever*, and so ὁποιουσ-τινας-οὖν, ὁστισ-δή-ποτε, or ὁστισ-δη-ποτ-οῦν. In these combinations all relative or interrogative force is lost.

f. The uncompounded relatives are often used in an exclamatory sense, and sometimes as indirect interrogatives. Indefinite relatives may be used as indirect interrogatives.

340. Correlative Pronouns. — Many pronominal adjectives correspond to each other in form and meaning. In the following list poetic or rare forms are placed in ( ).

Interrogative: Direct or Indirect	Indefinite (Enclitic)	Demonstrative	Relative (Specific) or Exclamatory	Indefinite Relative or Indirect Interrogative
τίς *who? which? what? qui?*	τὶς *some one, any one, aliquis, quidam*	(ὁ, ὅς) ὅδε *this* (here), *hic* οὗτος *this, that is, ille* ἐκεῖνος *ille*	ὅς *who, which qui*	ὅστις *whoever, any one who quisquis, quicunque*
πότερος *which of two? uter?*	πότερος or ποτερός *one of two* (rare)	ἕτερος *the one* or *the other of two alter*	ὁπότερος *whichever of the two*	ὁπότερος *whichever of the two utercumque*
πόσος *how much? how many? quantus? quot?*	ποσός *of some quantity* or *number*	(τόσος) τοσόσδε τοσοῦτος *so much, so many* *tantus, tot*	ὅσος *as much as, as many as quantus, quot*	ὁπόσος *of whatever size, number quantuscumque, quotquot*
ποῖος *of what sort? qualis?*	ποιός *of some sort*	(τοῖος) τοιόσδε τοιοῦτος *such talis*	οἷος *of which sort, (such) as qualis*	ὁποῖος *of whatever sort qualiscumque*
πηλίκος *how old? how large?*	πηλίκος *of some age, size*	(τηλίκος) τηλικόσδε τηλικοῦτος *so old, so young, so large, so great*	ἡλίκος *of which age, size, (as old, large) as*	ὁπηλίκος *of whatever age* or *size*

340 D. Hom. has (Aeolic) ππ in ὁππότερος, ὁπποῖος, and σσ in ὅσσος, τόσσος, etc Hdt. has κ for π in (ὁ)κότερος, (ὁ)κόσος, (ὁ)κοῖος.

ADVERBS

341. Origin. — Adverbs, like prepositions and conjunctions, were originally case forms, made from the stems of nouns and pronouns. Some of these nominal and pronominal stems have gone out of common use, so that only petrified forms are left in the adverbs. Some of these words were still felt to be live cases; in others no consciousness of their origin survived. Many adverbs show old suffixes joined to the stem or to a case form (342). It is sometimes uncertain whether we should speak of *adverbs* or of *nouns with local endings.*

Nominative (rare): πύξ *with clenched fist*, ἅπαξ *once*, ἀναμίξ *pell-mell.*

Genitive: ἔνης *day after to-morrow*, ἑξῆς *next*, ποῦ, οὗ *where*, αὐτοῦ *in the very place*, ἐκποδών *out of the way* (ἐκ + ποδῶν); by analogy, ἐμποδών *in one's way.*

Dative: δημοσίᾳ *at public cost*, λάθρᾳ *in secret*, κοινῇ *in common*, etc. (1527 b), ἄλλῃ *otherwise*, πῇ *how.*

Accusative: very common, especially such adverbs as have the form of the accusative of neuter adjectives, as πολύ *much*, μῑκρόν *a little*, πρῶτον *at first*, τήμερον *to-day*, πολλά *often*. See 1606–1611.

Locative: οἴκο-ι *at home* (οἶκο-ς *house*), Ἰσθμο-ῖ *at the Isthmus*, ποῖ *whither*, and all adverbs in -οι. The -ι of the consonantal declension is properly the ending of the locative, as in Μαραθῶν-ι *at Marathon;* -οισι (234) in O stems, in contrast to -οις; -ᾱσι (-ησι) in Ᾱ stems (215): θύρᾱσι *at the doors*, Πλαταιᾶσι *at Plataea*, Ἀθήνησι *at Athens;* further in πάλαι *long ago*, ἐκεῖ *there*, πανδημεί *in full force.*

Instrumental: ἄνω *above*, κάτω *below*, οὔπω *not yet*, ὥ-δε *thus* (but the forms in -ω may be ablatives); κρυφῇ and λάθρᾱ *in secret.*

Ablative: all adverbs in -ως, as ὡς *as*, οὕτως *thus*, ἑτέρως *otherwise*. Here, *e.g.* original ἑτερωδ (cp. Old Lat. *altōd*, abl. of *altus*) became ἑτερω (133), which took on -ς from the analogy of such words as ἀμφίς parallel to ἀμφί.

342. Place. — To denote place the common endings are: —

-ι, -θι, -σι *at, in* to denote place *where* (locative). -ου, the sign of the genitive, is also common.

-θεν *from* to denote the place *whence* (ablative).

-δε (-ζε), -σε *to, toward* to denote place *whither.*

In the following examples poetical words are bracketed.

οἴκο-ι (**οἴκο-θι**) *at home*	**οἴκο-θεν** *from home*	**οἴκαδε** (**οἰκόνδε**) *homeward* (οἰκα- is an old accusative form.)
ἄλλο-θι *elsewhere* or **ἀλλ-αχ-οῦ**	**ἄλλο-θεν** *from elsewhere* **ἀλλ-αχ-ό-θεν**	**ἄλλο-σε** *elsewhither* **ἀλλ-αχ-ό-σε**

---

342 D. Hom. has many cases of the local endings, *e.g.* οὐρανό-θι *in heaven*, ἀγορῆ-θεν *from the assembly;* also after prepositions as a genitive case: ἐξ ἁλό-θεν *out of the sea*, Ἰλιό-θι πρό *before Ilium*. Cp. ἐμέθεν, σέθεν, ἕθεν, 325 D. 1. -δε in ἅλα-δε *to the sea*, πόλιν-δε *to the city*, πεδίον-δε *to the plain*. Ἀιδόσ-δε *to* (the house of) *Hades*, ὅν-δε δόμον-δε *to his house.*

ἀμφοτέρω-θι *on both sides*	**ἀμφοτέρω-θεν** *from both sides*	(**ἀμφοτέρω-σε** *to both sides*)
παντ-αχ-οῦ *in every direction*	**παντ-αχ-ό-θεν** *from every side*	**παντ-αχ-ό-σε** *in all directions*
	πάντ-ο-θεν (rare)	**πάντ-ο-σε**
αὐτοῦ *in the very place*	**αὐτό-θεν** *from the very place*	**αὐτό-σε** *to the very place*
ὁμοῦ *at the same place*	**ὁμό-θεν** *from the same place*	**ὁμό-σε** *to the same place*
Ἀθήνη-σι *at Athens*	**Ἀθήνη-θεν** *from Athens*	**Ἀθήναζε** *to Athens*
Ὀλυμπίᾱ-σι *at Olympia*	**Ὀλυμπίᾱ-θεν** *from Olympia*	**Ὀλυμπίαζε** *to Olympia*

a. In -αζε, -δε is added to the accusative (1589), and stands for -α(ν)ς, the old acc. pl., + -δε (Eng. TO). Cp. 26, 106. The other endings are added to the stem. -σε is usually added only to pronominal stems. -σι forms a locative plural. ο sometimes takes the place of ᾱ of the first declension (ῥίζοθεν *from the root*, stem ῥιζᾱ-), or is added to consonant stems. Words in -τερο- lengthen ο to ω. Between stem and ending αχ is often inserted.

b. -θεν may take the form -θε in poetry, and especially when the idea of *whence* is lost, as πρόσθε *in front* (134 D.). -θα is found in ἔνθα in all dialects. -θα for -θεν occurs in Aeolic and Doric.

c. Some local adverbs are made from prepositions, as ἄνω *above*, ἔξω *outside*, ἔσω *within*, κάτω *below*, πρόσθεν *in front*.

343. **Manner.** — Adverbs of manner ending in -ως have the accent and form of the genitive plural masculine with -ς in place of -ν.

δίκαιος	*just*	genitive plural	**δικαίων**	**δικαίως**	*justly*
κακός	*bad*	" "	**κακῶν**	**κακῶς**	*ill*
ἁπλοῦς	*simple*	" "	**ἁπλῶν**	**ἁπλῶς**	*simply*
σαφής	*plain*	" "	**σαφῶν**	**σαφῶς**	*plainly*
ἡδύς	*pleasant*	" "	**ἡδέων**	**ἡδέως**	*pleasantly*
σώφρων	*prudent*	" "	**σωφρόνων**	**σωφρόνως**	*prudently*
ἄλλος	*other*	" "	**ἄλλων**	**ἄλλως**	*otherwise*
πᾶς	*all*	" "	**πάντων**	**πάντως**	*in every way*
ὤν	*being*	" "	**ὄντων**	**ὄντως**	*really*

a. Adverbs in -ως are not *formed from* the genitive plural, but are originally old ablatives from ο stems (341), and thence transferred to other stems. The analogy of the genitive plural assisted the transference.

344. **Various Other Endings.** — Adverbs have many other endings, *e.g.* : — **-α** : ἅμα *at the same time*, μάλα *very*, τάχα *quickly* (in Attic prose *perhaps*). **-ακις** : πολλάκις *many times, often*, ἑκαστάκις *each time*, τοσαυτάκις *so often*, ὁσάκις *as often as*, πλειστάκις *very often*, ὀλιγάκις *seldom*, πλεονάκις *more times*. The forms without -ς (ὁσάκι, πολλάκι) are earlier, and -ς has been added by imitation of δίς, τρίς. **-δην** : συλλήβδην *in short*. **-δον** : ἔνδον *within*, σχεδόν *almost*. **-ει** :

πανδημεί *in full levy* (341, locative). **-τε**: ὅτε *when* (Aeolic ὅτα, Dor. ὅκα). **-τι, -στι**: ἐθελοντί *voluntarily*, Ἑλληνιστί *in Greek (fashion)*.

345. Comparison of Adverbs. — In adverbs derived from adjectives the comparative is the same as the neuter singular of the comparative of the adjective; the superlative is the same as the neuter plural of the superlative adjective.

σοφῶς	*wisely*	**σοφώτερον**	**σοφώτατα**
χαριέντως	*gracefully*	**χαριέστερον**	**χαριέστατα**
εὐδαιμόνως	*happily*	**εὐδαιμονέστερον**	**εὐδαιμονέστατα**
καλῶς	*well*	**κάλλῑον**	**κάλλιστα**
ἡδέως	*pleasantly*	**ἥδῑον**	**ἥδιστα**
		ἧττον *less* (319, 2)	**ἥκιστα**
εὖ (adv. of **ἀγαθός** *good*)	*well*	**ἄμεινον**	**ἄριστα**
μάλα	*very*	**μᾶλλον**	**μάλιστα**

a. Adverbs of place ending in ω, and some others, retain ω in the comparative and superlative.

ἄνω	*above*	**ἀνωτέρω**	**ἀνωτάτω**
πόρρω	*afar*	**πορρωτέρω**	**πορρωτάτω**

b. ἐγγύς *near* has ἐγγύτερον (-τέρω), ἐγγυτάτω (-τατα rare). πρῴ *early* has πρωϊαίτερον, πρωϊαίτατα.

c. There are some forms in -ως from comparatives: ἀσφαλεστέρως (ἀσφαλέστερον) *more securely*, βελτῑόνως (βέλτῑον) *better*. Superlatives in -ον are usually poetic; as μέγιστον.

346. Correlative Adverbs. — Adverbs from pronominal stems often correspond in form and meaning. In the list on p. 102 poetic or rare words are in ( ).

a. The demonstratives in ( ) are foreign to Attic prose except in certain phrases, as καὶ ὥς *even thus*, οὐδ' (μηδ') ὥς *not even thus* (cp. 180 c); ἔνθα μὲν . . . ἔνθα δέ *here . . . there*, ἔνθεν (μέν) καὶ ἔνθεν (δέ) *from this side and that*. ἔνθα and ἔνθεν are usually relatives, ἔνθα taking the place of οὗ *where* and οἷ *whither*, and ἔνθεν of ὅθεν *whence*.

b. τοτὲ μὲν . . . τοτὲ δέ is synonymous with ποτὲ μὲν . . . ποτὲ δέ.

c. οὖν (339 e) may be added for indefiniteness: ὁπωσοῦν *in any way whatever*, ὁποθενοῦν *from what place soever*. ποτέ is often used after interrogatives to give an intensive force, as in τίς ποτε *who in the world* (as *qui tandem*); also with negatives, as in οὔποτε *never*, οὐπώποτε *never yet*. Other negatives are οὐδαμοῦ *nowhere*, οὐδαμῇ *in no way*, οὐδαμῶς *in no manner*.

---

346 D. 1. Hom. has (Aeolic) ππ in ὅππως, ὁππότε; Hdt. has κ for the π-forms, *e.g.* κοῦ, κού, ὅκου, κότε, etc. Hdt. has ἐνθαῦτα, ἐνθεῦτεν for ἐνταῦθα, ἐντεῦθεν (126 D.).
2. Poetic are πόθι for ποῦ, ὅθι for οὗ, ἦμος *when*, ᾗ *which way*, *where*, etc.

	Interrogative: Direct and Indirect	Indefinite (Enclitic)	Demonstrative	Relative Specific	Indefinite Relative or Indirect Interrogative
Place	ποῦ *where?*	πού *somewhere*	(ἔνθα) ἐνθάδε, ἐνταῦθα *there* ἐκεῖ *yonder*	οὗ *where* (ἔνθα *where*)	ὅπου *where-(ever)*
	πόθεν *whence?*	ποθέν *from some place*	(ἔνθεν) ἐνθένδε, ἐντεῦθεν *thence* ἐκεῖθεν *from yonder*	ὅθεν *whence* (ἔνθεν *whence*)	ὁπόθεν *whence-(soever)*
	ποῖ *whither?*	ποί *to some place*	(ἔνθα) ἐνθάδε, ἐνταῦθα *thither* ἐκεῖσε *thither*	οἷ *whither* (ἔνθα *whither*)	ὅποι *whither-(soever)*
Time	πότε *when?*	ποτέ *some time, ever*	τότε *then*	ὅτε *when*	ὁπότε *when-(ever)*
	πηνίκα *at what time?*		(τηνίκα) τηνικάδε τηνικαῦτα } *at that time*	ἡνίκα *at which time*	ὁπηνίκα *at which time*
Way	πῇ *which way? how?*	πῄ *some way, somehow*	(τῇ) τῇδε, ταύτῃ *this way, thus*	ᾗ *in which way, as*	ὅπῃ *in which way, as*
Manner	πῶς *how?*	πώς *somehow*	(τώς), (ὥς) ὧδε, οὕτω(ς) *thus, so, in this way* ἐκείνως *in that way*	ὡς *as, how*	ὅπως *how*

NUMERALS

347. The numeral adjectives and corresponding adverbs are as follows:

347 D. 1. For the cardinals 1–4, see 349 D. Hom. has, for 12, δώδεκα (for δϝώδεκα), δυώδεκα, and δυοκαίδεκα (also generally poetic); 20, εἴκοσι and ἐείκοσι; 30, τριήκοντα; 80, ὀγδώκοντα; 90, ἐνενήκοντα and ἐννήκοντα; 200 and 300, διηκόσιοι, τριηκόσιοι; 9000 and 10,000, ἐννεάχῑλοι, δεκάχῑλοι (-χειλοι?). He has also the ordinals 3d, τρίτατος; 4th, τέτρατος; 7th, ἑβδόματος; 8th, ὀγδόατος; 9th,

Sign		Cardinal	Ordinal	Adverb
1	α′	εἷς, μία, ἕν *one*	πρῶτος *first*	ἅπαξ *once*
2	β′	δύο *two*	δεύτερος *second*	δίς *twice*
3	γ′	τρεῖς, τρία *three*	τρίτος *third*	τρίς *thrice*
4	δ′	τέτταρες, τέτταρα (τέσσαρες, τέσσαρα)	τέταρτος, -η, -ον	τετράκις
5	ε′	πέντε	πέμπτος	πεντάκις
6	ϛ′	ἕξ	ἕκτος	ἑξάκις
7	ζ′	ἑπτά	ἕβδομος	ἑπτάκις
8	η′	ὀκτώ	ὄγδοος	ὀκτάκις
9	θ′	ἐννέα	ἔνατος	ἐνάκις
10	ι′	δέκα	δέκατος, -η, -ον	δεκάκις
11	ια′	ἕνδεκα	ἑνδέκατος	ἑνδεκάκις
12	ιβ′	δώδεκα	δωδέκατος	δωδεκάκις
13	ιγ′	τρεῖς (τρία) καὶ δέκα (or τρεισκαίδεκα)	τρίτος καὶ δέκατος	τρεισκαιδεκάκις
14	ιδ′	τέτταρες (τέτταρα) καὶ δέκα	τέταρτος καὶ δέκατος	τετταρεσκαιδεκάκις
15	ιε′	πεντεκαίδεκα	πέμπτος καὶ δέκατος	πεντεκαιδεκάκις
16	ιϛ′	ἑκκαίδεκα (for ἑξκαίδεκα 103)	ἕκτος καὶ δέκατος	ἑκκαιδεκάκις
17	ιζ′	ἑπτακαίδεκα	ἕβδομος καὶ δέκατος	ἑπτακαιδεκάκις
18	ιη′	ὀκτωκαίδεκα	ὄγδοος καὶ δέκατος	ὀκτωκαιδεκάκις
19	ιθ′	ἐννεακαίδεκα	ἔνατος καὶ δέκατος	ἐννεακαιδεκάκις
20	κ′	εἴκοσι(ν)	εἰκοστός, -ή, -όν	εἰκοσάκις
21	κα′	εἷς καὶ εἴκοσι(ν) or εἴκοσι (καὶ) εἷς	πρῶτος καὶ εἰκοστός	εἰκοσάκις ἅπαξ
30	λ′	τριᾱ́κοντα	τριᾱκοστός	τριᾱκοντάκις
40	μ′	τετταράκοντα	τετταρακοστός	τετταρακοντάκις
50	ν′	πεντήκοντα	πεντηκοστός	πεντηκοντάκις
60	ξ′	ἑξήκοντα	ἑξηκοστός	ἑξηκοντάκις
70	ο′	ἑβδομήκοντα	ἑβδομηκοστός	ἑβδομηκοντάκις
80	π′	ὀγδοήκοντα	ὀγδοηκοστός	ὀγδοηκοντάκις

εἴνατος; 12th, δυωδέκατος; 13th, τρῖσ(τρεισ-?)καιδέκατος; 20th, ἐεικοστός; and the Attic form of each.

2. Hdt. has δυώδεκα (δυωδέκατος), τεσσερεσκαίδεκα indeclinable (τεσσερεσκαιδέκατος), τριήκοντα (τριηκοστός), τεσσεράκοντα, ὀγδώκοντα, διηκόσιοι (διηκοσιοστός), τριηκόσιοι: for ἔνατος he has εἴνατος, and so εἰνάκις, εἰνακόσιοι, εἰνακισχῑ́λιοι.

3. Aeolic has πέμπε for 5 (cp. Hom. πεμπώβολον *five-pronged fork*), gen. plur. πέμπων inflected, as also δέκων, τεσσερακόντων, etc.; for 1000, χέλλιοι. Doric has, for 1, ἦς (37 D. 2); 4, τέτορες; 6, ϝέξ; 7th, ἕβδεμος; 12, δυώδεκα; 20, ϝῑ́κατι, ϝείκατι; 40, τετρώκοντα (τετρωκοστός); 200, etc., διᾱκατίοι, etc.; 1000, χηλίοι and χειλίοι (37 D. 2); for 1st, πρᾶτος.

	Sign	Cardinal	Ordinal	Adverb
90	ϙʹ	ἐνενήκοντα	ἐνενηκοστός	ἐνενηκοντάκις
100	ρʹ	ἑκατόν	ἑκατοστός, -ή, -όν	ἑκατοντάκις
200	σʹ	διᾱκόσιοι, -αι, -α	διᾱκοσιοστός	διᾱκοσιάκις
300	τʹ	τριᾱκόσιοι	τριᾱκοσιοστός	τριᾱκοσιάκις
400	υʹ	τετρακόσιοι	τετρακοσιοστός	τετρακοσιάκις
500	φʹ	πεντακόσιοι	πεντακοσιοστός	πεντακοσιάκις
600	χʹ	ἑξακόσιοι	ἑξακοσιοστός	ἑξακοσιάκις
700	ψʹ	ἑπτακόσιοι	ἑπτακοσιοστός	ἑπτακοσιάκις
800	ωʹ	ὀκτακόσιοι	ὀκτακοσιοστός	ὀκτακοσιάκις
900	ϡʹ	ἐνακόσιοι	ἐνακοσιοστός	ἐνακοσιάκις
1,000	͵α	χῑ́λιοι, -αι, -α	χῑλιοστός, -ή, -όν	χῑλιάκις
2,000	͵β	δισχῑ́λιοι	δισχῑλιοστός	δισχῑλιάκις
3,000	͵γ	τρισχῑ́λιοι	τρισχῑλιοστός	τρισχῑλιάκις
10,000	͵ι	μῡ́ριοι, -αι, -α	μῡριοστός	μῡριάκις
20,000	͵κ	δισμῡ́ριοι	δισμῡριοστός	δισμῡριάκις
100,000	͵ρ	δεκακισμῡ́ριοι	δεκακισμῡριοστός	δεκακισμῡριάκις

N. — Above 10,000 : *δύο μῡριάδες* 20,000, etc., *μῡριάκις μύριοι*, *i.e.* 10,000 × 10,000.

348. Greek Abbreviations. — The Greeks did not use abbreviations commonly; they had no instinct for abbreviating (cf. *infra*, on Numerals). When they did abbreviate, it was by simple suspension (or curtailment), usually self-intelligible, as e.g. in an inscribed list of officials: ΑΡΧ(*ων*) name, ΒΑΣ(*ιλευς*) name, ΠΟΛ(*εμαρχος*) name. Most Greek abbreviations are of three letters or more, rarely two. The purpose was often to save numerous repetitions in one document. In a long Athenian list, e.g., ΜΑΡ may stand for ΜΑΡ(*αθωνιος*), but on gravestones such demotics are almost invariably written out. Greek abbreviations are not standardized, but depended on the whim of the scribe. Contrast the habitual formulaic standardized Roman acrophonic (i.e. initial-letter) abbreviations, which require previous knowledge of what is abbreviated; and many modern abbreviations by compression, e.g. Me. for Maine, jr. for junior. A few Greek abbreviations are of this type.

348A. Numeral Notation. — **a.** In the system first used by Greeks, the unit stood apart: as for the Minoans, Romans, Arabs, and others, a single vertical mark, Ι, merely because it was *one* stroke, represented a unit. Most of the rest of the earliest Greek system was acrophonic, i.e. they used the initial letters of the word-designations, as Γ for five (ΓΕΝΤΕ). The complete system of the Athenian acrophonic numerals is as follows: Ι = 1, Γ = 5, Δ (*δέκα*) = 10, Η (*ἑκατόν*) = 100, Χ (*χίλιοι*) = 1000, Μ (*μύριοι*) = 10,000. Compound signs: 𐅄 or 𐅄 or 𐅄 = 50; 𐅅 = 500; 𐅆 = 5000; 𐅇 = 50,000. Example: 1959 = Χ𐅅ΗΗΗΗ𐅄ΓΙΙΙΙ.

In a context indicating money, the same (acrophonic) numerals mean drachmas, except that I = 1 obol, 𐅂 = 1 drachma, T = 1 talent (*τάλαντον*, 6000 drachmas; also a weight, ca. 57 lbs.), 𐅈 = 5 talents, 𐅉 = 10 talents, 𐅋 = 100 talents, 𐅍 = 1000 talents. Thus e.g. 𐅋𐅉𐅉𐅈TTT𐅆HHH𐅄𐅃𐅂𐅂𐅂IIIII = 128 talents, 5358 drachmas, 5 obols.

Besides these, Σ = *στατήρ* or *στάδιον*, and M = *μνᾶ* also occur, and are treated like the T = talent.

Apparently in Attica non-monetary fractions were not represented in any notation, acrophonic or alphabetic: but for fractional amounts of the drachma, along with I = one obol, II = two obols, etc., up to IIIII = five obols, we have C = ½ obol; Ɔ or T (*τεταρτημόριον*) = ¼ obol; X (*χαλκοῦς*) = ⅛ obol.

Known chiefly from inscriptions, acrophonic numerals were used all over Greece, but varied, sometimes to a surprising extent, from city to city. They were retained by conservative Athens, for official use, down to ca. 100 B.C., and were used there sporadically later still.

Until the Roman Empire, the Athenians and most other Greeks wrote out all ordinal numbers and most cardinal numbers. If they did use notation, Athenian authors of the fifth and earlier fourth centuries would use the acrophonic system, especially (to judge by inscriptions) for units of value, weight, or measure. Numerals in dates, numbers of prytanies, etc. are written out in all Athenian inscriptions down to the Empire.

b. Besides adopting most of the Phoenician letters, the Greeks had also adopted the Phoenician order of the letters, placing their own new letters fixedly in that order. Thus the 24 letters could be used as labels to distinguish non-verbal items (such as dedications in a temple) for purposes of records, and to give them a fixed order. The alphabet may have been so used in Athens in the fifth century; it certainly was in some inventories from at latest ca. 371/0 B.C. on. The alphabet could serve also to label items in an order already given, such as that of the books of the *Iliad* and *Odyssey*, as delimited by Alexandrian scholarship. In this system, viz. that of alphabetic letter-labels, Π, for instance, would designate the sixteenth item, or rather the item between O and P. Beyond 24 items, a plural number of letters was normally used: AA for the 25th, BB the 26th . . . AAA the 49th, etc., up to AAAAA . . . This was a system of numbers only in the sense of symbols designating a fixed order.

To a curiously limited extent, the fixed order of the alphabet was also used in antiquity to order lists of names and other words.

c. The acrophonic notation involved some complex characters, was limited in use, and varied from city to city. Hence this system was partially replaced, from the later fourth century B.C. on, but in Athens not largely until the Roman Empire, by the more uniform "alphabetic" system, which was invented apparently in the fifth century, became dominant in the Hellenistic period, and has lasted till now. The alphabetic numerals are given *supra* (**347**): A = 1, B = 2, etc., somewhat as in letter-labels; but the awkwardness e.g. of AA = 49 etc. was overcome by shifting to a quasi-decimal system. This required 27 letters: nine letters for the units (1, 2, . . . 9), nine for the tens (10, 20, . . . 90), and nine for the hundreds (100, 200, . . . 900). To obtain the 27 letters, three disused letters were pressed into service, one in each group: various forms (shown in *BSA* 45 [1950] 135; *supra*, **3**) of ϝ for 6, since its place was sixth in the Phoenician alphabet — the form later was ϛ, an abbreviation of *στ* (for *στίγμα*); Ϙ (koppa), which was put in the same place as in the Phoenician alphabetic order, which is the same place, again, as that of its derivative, Lat. q, for 90; epigraphical ϡ, printed ϡ (sampi), of uncertain origin, for 900. In the alphabetic system, therefore, Π had a value (80) different from its value in the acrophonic system (5) or as a letter-label (16).

In inscriptions, and doubtless in all fifth–fourth century writing, numerals were often marked off, or indicated, by blank spaces or by interpuncts; later, by various signs; but modern print uses, for 1–999, a stroke above and to the right of the letter; for 1000 and higher a stroke below and to the left. Thus: ρνϛʹ = 156, υαʹ = 401, ͵αϡιʹ = 1910. For 10,000, literary sources sometimes have α̈, for 20,000 β̈, etc. Inscriptions (and ante-Byzantine writings?) never have ͵Ι, ͵Κ, etc., but use the acrophonic Μ (υριάς or μύριοι); since Μ also = 40, they use a monogram of ΜΥ = 10,000, but $\overset{\mathrm{A}}{\mathrm{M}}$ = 10,000 also occurs; then $\overset{\mathrm{B}}{\mathrm{M}}$ = 20,000; $\overset{\Gamma}{\mathrm{M}}$ = 30,000; . . . $\overset{\mathrm{P}}{\mathrm{M}}$ = 1,000,000.

The alphabetic system was given wider use than the acrophonic had had: it was used for ordinal as well as cardinal numerals, for dates and for money, etc.

For all details about numerals, see M. N. Tod, in *Annual of the British School at Athens:* acrophonic, 18 (1911/12) 98–132, 28 (1926/7) 141–157, 37 (1936/7, pub. 1940) 236–258 (index 258); letter-labels, 49 (1954) 1–8; alphabetic, 45 (1950) 126–139.

d. In contrast with our Arabic decimal-place numeral system, the Greek acrophonic system, like Roman numerals, is a non-place-value system, and accordingly lacks the place-filler 0 (naught or zero), and the decimal point (incidentally this prevented designating fractions decimally). Thus eight places, our tens of millions, are needed for 88: 𐅅ΔΔΔΓΙΙΙ (cf. Roman LXXXVIII); whereas one place can give 10,000: Μ. The alphabetic system, similarly, has only an occasional superficial approximation to place value: ͵αϡνεʹ = 1955, yet the order could be reversed in numbers under 1000, or even mixed: τθιʹ = 319. Arithmetical computation in such systems, formerly considered impossible, has been proved to be feasible. Actually the abacus and finger-counting were used extensively.

349. The cardinals from 1 to 4 are declined as follows:

	one				*two*	*three*		*four*	
Nom.	**εἷς**	**μία**	**ἕν**	N. A.	**δύο**	**τρεῖς**	**τρία**	**τέτταρες**	**τέτταρα**
Gen.	**ἑνός**	**μιᾶς**	**ἑνός**	G. D.	**δυοῖν**	**τριῶν**		**τεττάρων**	
Dat.	**ἑνί**	**μιᾷ**	**ἑνί**			**τρισί(ν)**		**τέτταρσι(ν)**	
Acc.	**ἕνα**	**μίαν**	**ἕν**			**τρεῖς**	**τρία**	**τέτταρας**	**τέτταρα**

349 D. Hom. has, for *μία*, *ἴα* (*ἰῆς*, *ἰῇ*, *ἴαν*); for *ἑνί*, *ἰῷ*; *δύο*, *δύω* (undeclined); the adj. forms *δοιώ* and pl. *δοιοί* regularly declined. For 4, *τέσσαρες*, (Aeolic) *πίσυρες*; Pind. has *τέτρασιν*. Hdt. has *δύο* sometimes undeclined, also *δυῶν*, *δυοῖσι*; *τέσσερες*, *-α*, *τεσσέρων*, *τέσσερσι*; *τεσσερεσκαίδεκα* 14 undeclined. Aeolic *δύεσιν* 2; *πέσσυρες*, *πέσυρα* for 4.

a. εἷς is for ἐν-ς (cp. 245). The stem ἐν was originally σεμ (Lat. *semel, simplex, singuli*), weak forms of which are ἅ-παξ, ἁ-πλοῦς, from σμ-π- (35 b). μία stands for σμ-ια.

b. οὐδὲ εἷς, μηδὲ εἷς *not even one* unite (with change in accent) to form the compounds οὐδείς, μηδείς *no one*. These words are declined like εἷς: thus, οὐδείς, οὐδεμία, οὐδέν, οὐδενός, οὐδεμιᾶς, οὐδενός, etc., and sometimes in the plural (*no men, none* or *nobodies*) οὐδένες, οὐδένων, οὐδέσι, οὐδένας. For emphasis the compounds may be divided, as οὐδὲ εἷς *not* ONE. A preposition or ἄν may separate the two parts, as οὐδ' ἀπὸ μιᾶς *from not a single one*, οὐδ' ἂν ἑνί *ne uni quidem*.

c. πρῶτος (*primus*) means the first among more than two, πρότερος (*prior*) the first of two.

d. δύο may be used with the gen. and dat. pl., as δύο μηνῶν *of two months*. δυοῖν occurs rarely with plurals: παισὶν . . . δυοῖν D. 39. 32. δυεῖν for δυοῖν does not appear till about 300 B.C.

e. ἄμφω *both*, N. A. ἄμφω, G. D. ἀμφοῖν (Lat. *ambo*). But *both* is more commonly ἀμφότεροι, -αι, -α.

f. For τέτταρες, -ράκοντα, etc., early Attic prose and tragedy have τέσσαρες, etc.

g. The first numeral is inflected in τρεῖς καὶ δέκα 13, τέτταρες καὶ δέκα 14. τρεισκαίδεκα and Ionic τεσσερεσκαίδεκα (very rare in Attic) are indeclinable.

350. The cardinals from 5 to 199 are indeclinable; from 200 the cardinals, and all the ordinals from *first* on, are declined like ἀγαθός.

a. Compound numbers above 20 are expressed by placing the smaller number first (with καί) or the larger number first (with or without καί).

δύο καὶ εἴκοσι(ν) *two and twenty* — δεύτερος καὶ εἰκοστός

εἴκοσι καὶ δύο *twenty and two*, or εἴκοσι δύο *twenty-two* — εἰκοστὸς καὶ δεύτερος

555 = πέντε καὶ πεντήκοντα καὶ πεντακόσιοι or πεντακόσιοι (καὶ) πεντήκοντα (καὶ) πέντε.

b. For 21st, 31st, etc., εἷς (for πρῶτος) καὶ εἰκοστός (τριᾱκοστός) is permissible, but otherwise the cardinal is rarely thus joined with the ordinal.

c. Compounds of 10, 20, etc., with 8 and 9 are usually expressed by subtraction with the participle of δέω *lack*, as 18, 19, δυοῖν (ἑνός) δέοντες εἴκοσι. So ναυσὶ μιᾶς δεούσαις τετταράκοντα *with 39 ships*, δυοῖν δέοντα πεντήκοντα ἔτη *48 years;* and with ordinals ἑνὸς δέον εἰκοστὸν ἔτος *the 19th year*. The same method may be employed in other numbers than 8's or 9's: ἑπτὰ ἀποδέοντες τριᾱκόσιοι, *i.e.* 293.

d. For the system used in official documents to refer to the successive days of the Athenian civil month, see Note, page 722.

351. With the collective words (996) ἡ ἵππος *cavalry*, ἡ ἀσπὶς *men with shields*, numerals in -ιοι may appear even in the singular: διᾱκοσίᾱ ἵππος 200 *horse* T. 1. 62, ἀσπὶς μῡρίᾱ καὶ τετρακοσίᾱ 10,400 *men with shields* X. A. 1. 7. 10.

352. μύριοι, the greatest number expressed by a single word, means 10,000; μῡρίοι, *countless, infinite*. In the latter sense the singular may be used, as μῡρίᾱ ἐρημίᾱ *infinite solitude* P. L. 677 E.

353. Fractions are expressed in several ways: ἥμισυς ½, ὁ ἥμισυς τοῦ ἀριθμοῦ *half the number*, αἱ ἡμίσειαι τῶν νεῶν *half of the ships*, τὸ ἥμισυ τοῦ στρατοῦ *half the army*, ἡμιτάλαντον *half a talent*; τρία ἡμιτάλαντα 1½ *talents*, τρίτον ἡμίμναιον 2½ *minae*; τριτημόριον ⅓, πεμπτημόριον ⅕, ἐπίτριτος 1⅓, ἐπίπεμπτος 1⅕, τῶν πέντε αἱ δύο μοῖραι ⅖. But when the numerator is less by *one* than the denominator, the genitive is omitted and only the article and μέρη are used: as τὰ τρία μέρη ¾, *i.e. the three parts* (scil. *of four*).

354. Other classes of numeral words.

a. *Distributives* proper, answering the question *how many each?* are wanting in Greek. Instead, ἀνά, εἰς, and κατά, with the accus., and compounds of σύν *with*, are used: κατὰ δύο or σύνδυο *two by two, two each* (Lat. *bini*). The cardinals are often used alone, as ἀνδρὶ ἑκάστῳ δώσω πέντε ἀργυρίου μνᾶς *singulis militibus dabo quinas argenti minas* X. A. 1. 4. 13.

b. *Multiplicatives* in -πλοῦς *-fold* (from -πλοος, Lat. *-plex*), ἁπλοῦς *simple*, διπλοῦς *twofold*, τριπλοῦς *threefold*, πολλαπλοῦς *manifold*.

c. *Proportionals* in -πλασιος: διπλάσιος *twice as great* or (plur.) *as many*, πολλαπλάσιος *many times as great* (*many*).

d. διττός means *double*, τριττός *treble* (from διχ-ιος, τριχ-ιος 112).

N. — *Multiplication.* — Adverbs answering the question *how many times?* are used in multiplication: τὰ δὶς πέντε δέκα ἐστίν *twice five are ten*. See also 347 N.

e. *Abstract and Collective Numbers* in -άς (gen. -άδ-ος), all feminine: ἑνάς or μονάς *the number one, unity, monad*, δυάς *the number two, duality*, τριάς *trinity, triad*, δεκάς *decad, decade*, εἰκάς, ἑκατοντάς, χῑλιάς, μῡριάς *myriad*, ἑκατὸν μῡριάδες *a million*. Also in -ύς: τριττύς (-ύος) *the third of a tribe* (properly *the number three*), τετρακύς.

f. Adjectives in -αῖος, answering the question *on what day?* δευτεραῖος (or τῇ δευτεραίᾳ) ἀπῆλθε *he departed on the second day*.

g. *Adverbs of Division.* — μοναχῇ *singly, in one way only*, δίχα, διχῇ *in two parts, doubly*, τριχῇ, τέτραχα, etc., πολλαχῇ *in many ways*, πανταχῇ *in every way*.

VERBS

INFLECTION: PRELIMINARY REMARKS (355–380)

355. The Greek verb shows distinctions of voice, mood, verbal noun, tense, number, and person.

---

354 D. Hdt. has διξός (from διχθ-ιος), τριξός for διττός, τριττός; also -πλησιος and -φασιος. Hom. has δίχα and διχθά, τρίχα and τριχθά; τριπλῇ, τετραπλῇ.

356. Voices. — There are three voices: active, middle, and passive.

a. The middle usually denotes that the subject acts *on himself* or *for himself*, as λούομαι *wash myself*, ἀμύνομαι *defend myself* (lit. *ward off for myself*).

b. The passive borrows all its forms, except the future and aorist, from the middle.

c. Deponent verbs have an active *meaning* but only middle (or middle and passive) *forms*. If its aorist has the middle form, a deponent is called a middle deponent (χαρίζομαι *gratify*, ἐχαρισάμην); if its aorist has the passive form, a deponent is called a passive deponent (ἐνθυμέομαι *reflect on*, ἐνεθυμήθην). Deponents usually prefer the passive to the middle forms of the aorist.

357. Moods. — Four moods, the indicative, subjunctive, optative, imperative, are called *finite*, because the person is defined by the ending (366). The infinitive, strictly a verbal noun (358), is sometimes classed as a mood.

358. Verbal Nouns. — Verbal forms that share certain properties of nouns are called *verbal nouns*. There are two kinds of verbal nouns.

1. Substantival: the infinitive.

N. — The infinitive is properly a case form (chiefly dative, rarely locative), herein being like a substantive.

2. Adjectival (inflected like adjectives):
   a. Participles: active, middle, and passive.
   b. Verbal adjectives:
      In -τός, denoting possibility, as φιλητός *lovable*, or with the force of a perfect passive participle, as γραπτός *written*.
      In -τέος, denoting necessity, as γραπτέος *that must be written*.

359. Tenses. — There are seven tenses in the indicative: present, imperfect, future, aorist, perfect, pluperfect, and future perfect. The future perfect commonly has a passive force, but it may be active or middle in meaning (see 581).

The subjunctive has three tenses: present, aorist, and perfect.

The optative and infinitive have five tenses: present, future, aorist, perfect, and future perfect.

The imperative has three tenses: present, aorist, and perfect.

a. Greek also makes extensive use of *aspect* distinctions to qualify the type (rather than the time) of an action.

360. Primary and Secondary Tenses. — There are two classes of tenses in the indicative: (1) *Primary* (or *Principal*) tenses, the present and perfect expressing present time, the future and future perfect expressing future time; (2) *Secondary* (or *Historical*) tenses, the imperfect, pluperfect, and aorist expressing past time. The secondary tenses have an augment (428) prefixed.

---

359 D. Hom. does not use the future or future perfect in the optative.

361. Second Aorists, etc.—Some verbs have tenses called *second* aorists (active, middle, and passive), *second* perfects and pluperfects (active only), and *second* futures (passive). The meaning of these tenses ordinarily corresponds to that of the *first* aorist, etc.; but when a verb has both forms in any tense (which is rarely the case), the two forms usually differ in meaning. Sometimes one form is poetical, the other used in prose. (See 554 e.)

362. No single Greek verb shows all the tenses mentioned in 359 and 361; and the paradigms are therefore taken from different verbs.

363. Number.—There are three numbers: the singular, dual, and plural.

364. Person.—There are three persons (first, second, and third) in the indicative, subjunctive, and optative. The imperative has only the second and third persons.

a. Except in a few cases in poetry (465 c) the first person plural is used for the first person dual.

365. Inflection.—The inflection of a verb consists in the addition of certain endings to the different stems.

366. Endings.—The endings in the finite moods (357) show whether the subject is first, second, or third person; and indicate number and voice. See 462 ff.

a. The middle has a different set of endings from the active. The passive has the endings of the middle except in the aorist, which has the active endings.

b. The indicative has two sets of endings in the active and in the middle: one for primary tenses, the other for secondary tenses.

c. The subjunctive uses the same endings as the primary tenses of the indicative; the optative uses the same as those of the secondary tenses.

STEMS

367. A Greek verb has two kinds of stems: (1) the *tense-stem*, to which the endings are attached, and (2) a common *verb-stem* (also called *theme*) from which all the tense-stems are derived. The tense-stem is usually made from the verb-stem by prefixing a *reduplication-syllable* (439), and by affixing signs for *mood* (457, 459) and *tense* (455). A tense-stem may be identical with a verb-stem.

368. The Tense-stems.—The tenses fall into nine classes called *tense-systems*. Each tense-system has its own separate tense-stem.

SYSTEMS.		TENSES.
I. *Present,*	including	*present* and *imperfect.*
II. *Future,*	"	*future active* and *middle.*
III. *First aorist,*	"	*first aorist active* and *middle.*
IV. *Second aorist,*	"	*second aorist active* and *middle.*
V. *First perfect,*	"	*first perfect, first pluperfect,* and *fut. perf., active.*
VI. *Second perfect,*	"	*second perfect* and *second pluperfect active.*
VII. *Perfect middle,*	"	*perfect* and *pluperfect middle (pass.), future perfect.*
VIII. *First passive,*	"	*first aorist* and *first future passive.*
IX. *Second passive,*	"	*second aorist* and *second future passive.*

The tense-stems are explained in detail in 497–597.

a. Since few verbs have both the *first* and *second* form of the same tense (361), most verbs have only six of these nine systems; many verbs do not even have six. Scarcely any verb shows all nine systems.

b. There are also secondary tense-stems for the future passive, the pluperfect, and the future perfect.

c. The tense-stems assume separate forms in the different moods.

369. The *principal parts* of a verb are the first person singular indicative of the tense-systems occurring in it. These are generally six: the present, future, first aorist, first (or second) perfect active, the perfect middle, and the first (or second) aorist passive. The future middle is given if there is no future active. The second aorist (active or middle) is added if it occurs. Thus:

λῡ́ω *loose,* λῡ́σω, ἔλῡσα, λέλυκα, λέλυμαι, ἐλύθην.
λείπω *leave,* λείψω, λέλοιπα, λέλειμμαι, ἐλείφθην, 2 aor. ἔλιπον.
γράφω *write,* γράψω, ἔγραψα, γέγραφα, γέγραμμαι, 2 aor. pass. ἐγράφην.
σκώπτω *jeer,* σκώψομαι, ἔσκωψα, ἐσκώφθην.

370. The principal parts of deponent verbs (356 c) are the present, future, perfect, and aorist indicative. Both first and second aorists are given if they occur.

βούλομαι *wish,* βουλήσομαι, βεβούλημαι, ἐβουλήθην (passive deponent).
γίγνομαι *become,* γενήσομαι, γεγένημαι, 2 aor. ἐγενόμην (middle deponent).
ἐργάζομαι *work,* ἐργάσομαι, εἰργασάμην, εἴργασμαι, εἰργάσθην.

371. Verb-stem (or Theme). — The tense-stems are made from one fundamental stem called the verb-stem (or theme).

This verb-stem may be a root (193) as in τῑ́-ω *honour,* or a root to which a derivative suffix has been appended, as in τῑ-μά-ω *honour.*

372. A verb forming its tense-stems directly from a root is called a *primitive* verb. A *denominative* verb forms its tense-stems from a longer verb-stem, originally a noun-stem; as δουλόω *enslave* from δοῦλος *slave.* Verbs in μι (379), and verbs in ω of two syllables (in the present indicative active, as λέγ-ω *speak*) or of three syllables (in the middle, as δέχομαι *receive*) are *generally* primitive. Others are denominative.

373. The verb-stem may show numerous modifications in form.

Thus, corresponding to the gradations in *sing, sang, sung* (35), the verb λείπ-ω *leave* shows the stems λειπ-, λοιπ- (2 perf. λέ-λοιπ-α), λιπ- (2 aor. ἔ-λιπ-ο-ν); the verb φεύγ-ω *flee* shows φευγ- and φυγ- (2 aor. ἔ-φυγ-ο-ν). In ῥήγνῡμι *break* we find the three stems ῥηγ, ῥωγ (2 perf. ἔρρωγα), ῥαγ (2 aor. pass. ἐρράγην). στέλλ-ω *send* has the stems στελ- and σταλ- (perf. ἔ-σταλ-κα, 2 fut. pass. σταλ-ήσομαι).

a. When the fundamental stem shows modifications, it is customary for convenience to call its shorter (or shortest) form the verb-stem, and to derive the other forms from it. The student must, however, beware of assuming that the short forms are *older* than the other forms.

374. The verb-stem may also show modifications in quantity, as present λῡ́-ω *loose*, perfect λέ-λῠ-κα.

N. — Various causes produce this variation. λύω has ῡ from analogy to λύ-σω, ἔ-λῡ-σα where the verb-stem λῠ has been regularly lengthened (534, 543). For Attic φθάνω *anticipate* Hom. has φθάνω for φθανϝω (28, 147 D.).

375. ω Inflection and μι Inflection. — There are two slightly different methods of inflecting verbs, the first according to the *common*, the second according to the μι system. The names *ω-verbs* and *μι-verbs* (a small class) refer to the ending of the first person singular active of the present tense indicative only: λῡ́-ω *loose*, τίθη-μι *place*.

a. In the ω inflection the tense-stem ends in the thematic vowel. To this form belong all futures, and the presents, imperfects, and second aorists *showing the thematic vowel*.

376. According to the ending of the verb-stem, ω-verbs are termed:

1. Vowel (or pure) verbs:
   a. Not contracted: those that end in υ or ι, as λῡ́-ω *loose*, παιδεύ-ω *educate*, χρί-ω *anoint*. Such verbs retain the final vowel of the stem unchanged in all their forms.
   b. Contracted: those that end in α, ε, ο, as τῑμῶ *honour* from τῑμά-ω, ποιῶ *make* from ποιέ-ω, δηλῶ *manifest* from δηλό-ω.
2. Consonant verbs, as:
   Liquid or nasal verbs: δέρ-ω *flay*, μέν-ω *remain*.
   Verbs ending in a stop (or mute), as ἄγ-ω *lead*, πείθ-ω *persuade*.

N. — Verbs ending in a stop consonant are called labial, dental, or palatal verbs. Consonant verbs do not retain the final consonant of the stem unchanged in all their forms. The final consonant may be assimilated to a following consonant, or may form with it a double consonant.

377. Thematic Vowel. — Some tense-stems end in a vowel which varies between ο and ε (or ω and η) in certain forms. This is called the *thematic* (or *variable*) vowel. Thus λύο-μεν λύε-τε, λύω-μεν λύη-τε, λύσο-μεν λύσε-τε. The thematic vowel is written $^{o}/_{\epsilon}$ or $^{\omega}/_{\eta}$, as λῡ$^{o}/_{\epsilon}$-, γραφ$^{\omega}/_{\eta}$-. See 456.

378. ο is used before μ or ν in the indicative, and in the optative, ω before μ or ν in the subjunctive, elsewhere ε is used in the indicative (η in the subjunctive).

379. In the μι inflection no thematic vowel is employed, and the endings are attached directly to the tense-stem. The μι form is used only in the present, imperfect, and second aorist. In the other tenses, verbs in μι generally show the same inflection as ω-verbs. For further explanation of the ω and the μι inflection see 602 ff., 717 ff.

380. Meanings of the Tenses and Moods. — In the synopsis (382) meanings are given wherever these are not dependent on the use of the various forms in the sentence. The meanings of the subjunctive and optative forms and the difference between the tenses can be learned satisfactorily only from the syntax. Some of these meanings may here be given:

a. Subjunctive: λύωμεν or λύσωμεν *let us loose*, (ἐὰν) λύω or λύσω (if) *I loose*, (ἵνα) γράφω (that) *I may write*.

b. Optative: (εἴθε) λύοιμι or λύσαιμι (would) *that I may loose!* (εἰ) λύοιμεν or λύσαιμεν (if) *we should loose*.

381. CONJUGATION: LIST OF PARADIGMS

I. **Verbs in ω:**
- A. Vowel verbs not contracted:
  - Synopsis and conjugation of λύω (pp. 112–118).
  - Second aorist (active and middle) of λείπω (p. 119).
  - Second perfect and pluperfect (active) of λείπω.
- B. Vowel verbs contracted:
  - Present and imperfect of τῑμάω, ποιέω, δηλόω (pp. 120–123).
- C. Consonant verbs:
  - Liquid and nasal verbs: future and first aorist (active and middle), second aorist and second future passive of φαίνω (pp. 128–129).
  - Labial, dental, and palatal verbs: perfect and pluperfect, middle (passive) of λείπω, γράφω, πείθω, πράττω, ἐλέγχω (p. 130). Perfect of the liquid verbs ἀγγέλλω, φαίνω; and perfect of τελέω (p. 131).

II. **Verbs in μι.**
- A. Present, imperfect, and 2 aorist of τίθημι, ἵστημι, δίδωμι (pp. 135 ff.).
  - Second aorist middle of ἐπριάμην (p. 138).
- B. Present and imperfect of δείκνῡμι (p. 140).
  - Second aorist: ἔδῡν (p. 140).

CONJUGATION

I. (A) VOWEL VERBS:

382. SYNOPSIS OF

	I. PRESENT SYSTEM	II. FUTURE SYSTEM	III. FIRST AORIST SYSTEM
ACTIVE:	Present and Imperfect	Future	1 Aorist
Indic.	**λῡ́ω** *I loose* or *am loosing*	**λῡ́σω** *I shall loose*	
	ἔλῡον *I was loosing*		**ἔλῡσα** *I loosed*
Subj.	**λῡ́ω**		**λῡ́σω**
Opt.	**λῡ́οιμι**	**λῡ́σοιμι**	**λῡ́σαιμι**
Imper.	**λῦε** *loose*		**λῦσον** *loose*
Infin.	**λῡ́ειν** *to loose*	**λῡ́σειν** *to be about to loose*	**λῦσαι** *to loose* or *to have loosed*
Part.	**λῡ́ων** *loosing*	**λῡ́σων** *about to loose*	**λῡ́σᾱς** *having loosed*
MIDDLE:			
Indic.	**λῡ́ομαι** *I loose (for myself)*	**λῡ́σομαι** *I shall loose (for myself)*	
	ἐλῡόμην *I was loosing (for myself)*		**ἐλῡσάμην** *I loosed (for myself)*
Subj.	**λῡ́ωμαι**		**λῡ́σωμαι**
Opt.	**λῡοίμην**	**λῡσοίμην**	**λῡσαίμην**
Imper.	**λῡ́ου** *loose (for thyself)*		**λῦσαι** *loose (for thyself)*
Infin.	**λῡ́εσθαι** *to loose (for one's self)*	**λῡ́σεσθαι** *to be about to loose (for one's self)*	**λῡ́σασθαι** *to loose* or *to have loosed (for one's self)*
Part.	**λῡόμενος** *loosing (for one's self)*	**λῡσόμενος** *about to loose (for one's self)*	**λῡσάμενος** *having loosed (for one's self)*
		VIII FIRST PASSIVE SYSTEM	
PASSIVE:		1 Future	1 Aorist
Indic.	**λῡ́ομαι** *I am* / **ἐλῡόμην** *I was* } *(being) loosed*	**λυθήσομαι** *I shall be loosed*	**ἐλύθην** *I was loosed*
Subj.	Like Middle		**λυθῶ** (for *λυθέω*)
Opt.	" "	**λυθησοίμην**	**λυθείην**
Imper.	" "		**λύθητι** *be loosed*
Infin.	" "	**λυθήσεσθαι** *to be about to be loosed*	**λυθῆναι** *to be loosed* or *to have been loosed*
Part.	" "	**λυθησόμενος** *about to be loosed*	**λυθείς** *having been loosed*

Verbal adjectives: { **λυτός** *that may be loosed, loosed*
{ **λυτέος** *that must be loosed,* (requiring) *to be loosed*

OF Ω-VERBS:

NOT CONTRACTED

λύω (λῠ, λῡ) *loose*

V. FIRST PERFECT SYSTEM

1 Perfect and Pluperfect Active

λέλυκα *I have loosed*

ἐλελύκη *I had loosed*

λελυκὼς ὦ or **λελύκω**
λελυκὼς εἴην or **λελύκοιμι**
λελυκὼς ἴσθι or [**λέλυκε**][1]
λελυκέναι *to have loosed*

λελυκώς *having loosed*

VII. PERFECT MIDDLE SYSTEM

Perfect and Pluperfect Middle

λέλυμαι *I have loosed (for myself)*

ἐλελύμην *I had loosed (for myself)*

λελυμένος ὦ
λελυμένος εἴην
λέλυσο (712, 714)

λελύσθαι *to have loosed (for one's self)*

λελυμένος *having loosed (for one's self)*

Perfect and Pluperfect Passive	Future Perfect Passive
λέλυμαι *I have* { *been* / **ἐλελύμην** *I had* { *loosed*	**λελύσομαι** *I shall have been loosed*
Like Middle	
" "	**λελῡσοίμην**
" "	
" "	**λελύσεσθαι**
" "	**λελῡσόμενος**

[1] The simple forms of the perfect imperative active of λύω probably never occur in classical Greek (697), but are included to show the inflection.

I. (A) VOWEL VERBS:

383. 1. Active

		Present	Imperfect	Future
Indicative.	S. 1.	λύω	ἔλῡον	λύσω
	2.	λύεις	ἔλῡες	λύσεις
	3.	λύει	ἔλῡε	λύσει
	D. 2.	λύετον	ἐλύετον	λύσετον
	3.	λύετον	ἐλῡέτην	λύσετον
	P. 1.	λύομεν	ἐλύομεν	λύσομεν
	2.	λύετε	ἐλύετε	λύσετε
	3.	λύουσι	ἔλῡον	λύσουσι
Subjunctive.	S. 1.	λύω		
	2.	λύῃς		
	3.	λύῃ		
	D. 2.	λύητον		
	3.	λύητον		
	P. 1.	λύωμεν		
	2.	λύητε		
	3.	λύωσι		
Optative.	S. 1.	λύοιμι		λύσοιμι
	2.	λύοις		λύσοις
	3.	λύοι		λύσοι
	D. 2.	λύοιτον		λύσοιτον
	3.	λῡοίτην		λῡσοίτην
	P. 1.	λύοιμεν		λύσοιμεν
	2.	λύοιτε		λύσοιτε
	3.	λύοιεν		λύσοιεν
Imperative.	S. 2.	λῦε		
	3.	λῡέτω		
	D. 2.	λύετον		
	3.	λῡέτων		
	P. 2.	λύετε		
	3.	λῡόντων		
Infinitive.		λύειν		λύσειν
Participle.		λύων, λύουσα, λῦον (305)		λύσων, λύσουσα λῦσον (305)

NOT CONTRACTED

VOICE OF λύω

			1 Aorist	1 Perfect	1 Pluperfect
IND.	S.	1.	ἔλυσα	λέλυκα	ἐλελύκη
		2.	ἔλυσας	λέλυκας	ἐλελύκης
		3.	ἔλυσε	λέλυκε	ἐλελύκει(ν)
	D.	2.	ἐλύσατον	λελύκατον	ἐλελύκετον
		3.	ἐλυσάτην	λελύκατον	ἐλελυκέτην
	P.	1.	ἐλύσαμεν	λελύκαμεν	ἐλελύκεμεν
		2.	ἐλύσατε	λελύκατε	ἐλελύκετε
		3.	ἔλυσαν	λελύκᾱσι	ἐλελύκεσαν
SUBJ.	S.	1.	λύσω	λελυκὼς ὦ (691) or	λελύκω (692)
		2.	λύσῃς	λελυκὼς ᾖς	λελύκῃς
		3.	λύσῃ	λελυκὼς ᾖ	λελύκῃ
	D.	2.	λύσητον	λελυκότε ἦτον	λελύκητον
		3.	λύσητον	λελυκότε ἦτον	λελύκητον
	P.	1.	λύσωμεν	λελυκότες ὦμεν	λελύκωμεν
		2.	λύσητε	λελυκότες ἦτε	λελύκητε
		3.	λύσωσι	λελυκότες ὦσι	λελύκωσι
OPT.	S.	1.	λύσαιμι	λελυκὼς εἴην (694) or	λελύκοιμι, -οίην
		2.	λύσαις, λύσειας (668)	λελυκὼς εἴης	λελύκοις, -οίης
		3.	λύσαι, λύσειε (668)	λελυκὼς εἴη	λελύκοι, -οίη
	D.	2.	λύσαιτον	λελυκότε εἴητον, εἶτον	λελύκοιτον
		3.	λυσαίτην	λελυκότε εἰήτην, εἴτην	λελυκοίτην
	P.	1.	λύσαιμεν	λελυκότες εἴημεν, εἶμεν	λελύκοιμεν
		2.	λύσαιτε	λελυκότες εἴητε, εἶτε	λελύκοιτε
		3.	λύσαιεν, λύσειαν (668)	λελυκότες εἴησαν, εἶεν	λελύκοιεν
IMP.	S.	2.	λῦσον	λελυκὼς ἴσθι (697) or	[λέλυκε (697)
		3.	λυσάτω	λελυκὼς ἔστω	λελυκέτω
	D.	2.	λύσατον	λελυκότε ἔστον	λελύκετον
		3.	λυσάτων	λελυκότε ἔστων	λελυκέτων
	P.	2.	λύσατε	λελυκότες ἔστε	λελύκετε]
		3.	λυσάντων	λελυκότες ὄντων	
INF.			λῦσαι	λελυκέναι	
PART.			λύσᾱς, λύσᾱσα, λῦσαν (306)	λελυκώς, λελυκυῖα, λελυκός (309)	

2. Middle[1]

			Present	Imperfect	Future
Indicative.	S.	1.	λύομαι	ἐλῡόμην	λύσομαι
		2.	λύῃ, λύει (628)	ἐλύου	λύσῃ, λύσει (628)
		3.	λύεται	ἐλύετο	λύσεται
	D.	2.	λύεσθον	ἐλύεσθον	λύσεσθον
		3.	λύεσθον	ἐλῡέσθην	λύσεσθον
	P.	1.	λῡόμεθα	ἐλῡόμεθα	λῡσόμεθα
		2.	λύεσθε	ἐλύεσθε	λύσεσθε
		3.	λύονται	ἐλύοντο	λύσονται
Subjunctive.	S.	1.	λύωμαι		
		2.	λύῃ		
		3.	λύηται		
	D.	2.	λύησθον		
		3.	λύησθον		
	P.	1.	λῡώμεθα		
		2.	λύησθε		
		3.	λύωνται		
Optative.	S.	1.	λῡοίμην		λῡσοίμην
		2.	λύοιο		λύσοιο
		3.	λύοιτο		λύσοιτο
	D.	2.	λύοισθον		λύσοισθον
		3.	λῡοίσθην		λῡσοίσθην
	P.	1.	λῡοίμεθα		λῡσοίμεθα
		2.	λύοισθε		λύσοισθε
		3	λύοιντο		λύσοιντο
Imperative.	S.	2.	λύου		
		3.	λῡέσθω		
	D.	2.	λύεσθον		
		3.	λῡέσθων		
	P.	2.	λύεσθε		
		3.	λῡέσθων		
Infinitive.			λύεσθαι		λύσεσθαι
Participle.			λῡόμενος, λῡομένη, λῡόμενον (287)		λῡσόμενος, -η, -ον (287)

[1] λύω in the middle usually means *to release for one's self, get some one set free*, hence *to ransom, redeem, deliver*.

Voice of λῡ́ω

		1 Aorist	Perfect	Pluperfect
Indicative.	S. 1.	ἐλῡσάμην	λέλυμαι	ἐλελύμην
	2.	ἐλῡ́σω	λέλυσαι	ἐλέλυσο
	3.	ἐλῡ́σατο	λέλυται	ἐλέλυτο
	D. 2.	ἐλῡ́σασθον	λέλυσθον	ἐλέλυσθον
	3.	ἐλῡσάσθην	λέλυσθον	ἐλελύσθην
	P. 1.	ἐλῡσάμεθα	λελύμεθα	ἐλελύμεθα
	2.	ἐλῡ́σασθε	λέλυσθε	ἐλέλυσθε
	3.	ἐλῡ́σαντο	λέλυνται	ἐλέλυντο
Subjunctive.	S. 1.	λῡ́σωμαι	λελυμένος ὦ (599 f)	
	2.	λῡ́σῃ	λελυμένος ᾖς	
	3.	λῡ́σηται	λελυμένος ᾖ	
	D. 2.	λῡ́σησθον	λελυμένω ἦτον	
	3.	λῡ́σησθον	λελυμένω ἦτον	
	P. 1.	λῡσώμεθα	λελυμένοι ὦμεν	
	2.	λῡ́σησθε	λελυμένοι ἦτε	
	3.	λῡ́σωνται	λελυμένοι ὦσι	
Optative.	S. 1.	λῡσαίμην	λελυμένος εἴην (599 f)	
	2.	λῡ́σαιο	λελυμένος εἴης	
	3.	λῡ́σαιτο	λελυμένος εἴη	
	D. 2.	λῡ́σαισθον	λελυμένω εἴητον or εἶτον	
	3.	λῡσαίσθην	λελυμένω εἰήτην or εἴτην	
	P. 1.	λῡσαίμεθα	λελυμένοι εἴημεν or εἶμεν	
	2.	λῡ́σαισθε	λελυμένοι εἴητε or εἶτε	
	3.	λῡ́σαιντο	λελυμένοι εἴησαν or εἶεν	
Imperative.	S. 2.	λῦσαι	λέλυσο (599 g)	
	3.	λῡσάσθω	λελύσθω (712)	
	D. 2.	λῡ́σασθον	λέλυσθον	
	3.	λῡσάσθων	λελύσθων	
	P. 2.	λῡ́σασθε	λέλυσθε	
	3.	λῡσάσθων	λελύσθων	
Infinitive.		λῡ́σασθαι	λελύσθαι	
Participle.		λῡσάμενος, -η, -ον (287)	λελυμένος, -η, -ον (287)	

3. Passive Voice of λῡ́ω

			Future Perfect	1 Aorist	1 Future
Indicative.	S.	1.	λελῡ́σομαι	ἐλύθην	λυθήσομαι
		2.	λελῡ́σῃ, λελῡ́σει	ἐλύθης	λυθήσῃ, λυθήσει
		3.	λελῡ́σεται	ἐλύθη	λυθήσεται
	D.	2.	λελῡ́σεσθον	ἐλύθητον	λυθήσεσθον
		3.	λελῡ́σεσθον	ἐλυθήτην	λυθήσεσθον
	P.	1.	λελῡσόμεθα	ἐλύθημεν	λυθησόμεθα
		2.	λελῡ́σεσθε	ἐλύθητε	λυθήσεσθε
		3.	λελῡ́σονται	ἐλύθησαν	λυθήσονται
Subjunctive.	S.	1.		λυθῶ	
		2.		λυθῇς	
		3.		λυθῇ	
	D.	2.		λυθῆτον	
		3.		λυθῆτον	
	P.	1.		λυθῶμεν	
		2.		λυθῆτε	
		3.		λυθῶσι	
Optative.	S.	1.	λελῡσοίμην	λυθείην	λυθησοίμην
		2.	λελῡ́σοιο	λυθείης	λυθήσοιο
		3.	λελῡ́σοιτο	λυθείη	λυθήσοιτο
	D.	2.	λελῡ́σοισθον	λυθεῖτον or λυθείητον	λυθήσοισθον
		3.	λελῡσοίσθην	λυθείτην or λυθειήτην	λυθησοίσθην
	P.	1.	λελῡσοίμεθα	λυθεῖμεν or λυθείημεν	λυθησοίμεθα
		2.	λελῡ́σοισθε	λυθεῖτε or λυθείητε	λυθήσοισθε
		3.	λελῡ́σοιντο	λυθεῖεν or λυθείησαν	λυθήσοιντο
Imperative.	S.	2.		λύθητι	
		3.		λυθήτω	
	D.	2.		λύθητον	
		3.		λυθήτων	
	P.	2.		λύθητε	
		3.		λυθέντων	
Infinitive.			λελῡ́σεσθαι	λυθῆναι	λυθήσεσθαι
Participle.			λελῡσόμενος, -η, -ον (287)	λυθείς, λυθεῖσα, λυθέν (307)	λυθησόμενος, -η, -ον (287)

384. As examples of the second aorist and second perfect systems (368), the second aorist active and middle and the second perfect and pluperfect active of λείπω *leave* are here given.

			2 Aorist Active	2 Aorist Middle	2 Perfect	2 Pluperfect
IND.	S.	1.	ἔλιπον	ἐλιπόμην	λέλοιπα	ἐλελοίπη
		2.	ἔλιπες	ἐλίπου	λέλοιπας	ἐλελοίπης
		3.	ἔλιπε	ἐλίπετο	λέλοιπε	ἐλελοίπει(ν)
	D.	2.	ἐλίπετον	ἐλίπεσθον	λελοίπατον	ἐλελοίπετον
		3.	ἐλιπέτην	ἐλιπέσθην	λελοίπατον	ἐλελοιπέτην
	P.	1.	ἐλίπομεν	ἐλιπόμεθα	λελοίπαμεν	ἐλελοίπεμεν
		2.	ἐλίπετε	ἐλίπεσθε	λελοίπατε	ἐλελοίπετε
		3.	ἔλιπον	ἐλίποντο	λελοίπᾱσι	ἐλελοίπεσαν
SUBJ.	S.	1.	λίπω	λίπωμαι	λελοιπὼς ὦ (599 c) or	λελοίπω (692)
		2.	λίπῃς	λίπῃ	λελοιπὼς ᾖς	λελοίπῃς
		3.	λίπῃ	λίπηται	λελοιπὼς ᾖ	λελοίπῃ
	D.	2.	λίπητον	λίπησθον	λελοιπότε ἦτον	λελοίπητον
		3.	λίπητον	λίπησθον	λελοιπότε ἦτον	λελοίπητον
	P.	1.	λίπωμεν	λιπώμεθα	λελοιπότες ὦμεν	λελοίπωμεν
		2.	λίπητε	λίπησθε	λελοιπότες ἦτε	λελοίπητε
		3.	λίπωσι	λίπωνται	λελοιπότες ὦσι	λελοίπωσι
OPT.	S.	1.	λίποιμι	λιποίμην	λελοιπὼς εἴην (599 c) or	λελοίποιμι (695)
		2.	λίποις	λίποιο	λελοιπὼς εἴης	λελοίποις
		3.	λίποι	λίποιτο	λελοιπὼς εἴη	λελοίποι
	D.	2.	λίποιτον	λίποισθον	λελοιπότε εἴητον, εἶτον	λελοίποιτον
		3.	λιποίτην	λιποίσθην	λελοιπότε εἰήτην, εἴτην	λελοιποίτην
	P.	1.	λίποιμεν	λιποίμεθα	λελοιπότες εἴημεν, εἶμεν	λελοίποιμεν
		2.	λίποιτε	λίποισθε	λελοιπότες εἴητε, εἶτε	λελοίποιτε
		3.	λίποιεν	λίποιντο	λελοιπότες εἴησαν, εἶεν	λελοίποιεν
IMP.	S.	2.	λίπε	λιποῦ		
		3.	λιπέτω	λιπέσθω		
	D.	2.	λίπετον	λίπεσθον		
		3.	λιπέτων	λιπέσθων		
	P.	2.	λίπετε	λίπεσθε		
		3.	λιπόντων	λιπέσθων		
INF.			λιπεῖν	λιπέσθαι	λελοιπέναι	
PART.			λιπών, λιποῦσα, λιπόν (305 a)	λιπόμενος, -η, -ον (287)	λελοιπώς, -υῖα, -ός (309)	

I. (B) VOWEL VERBS: CONTRACTED VERBS

385. Verbs in -αω, -εω, -οω are contracted only in the present and imperfect. The principles of contraction are explained in 49–55. τῑμάω (τῑμα-) *honour*, ποιέω (ποιε-) *make*, and δηλόω (δηλο-) *manifest* are thus inflected in the present and imperfect of the active, middle and passive.

Active

PRESENT INDICATIVE

S. 1.	(τῑμάω)	**τῑμῶ**	(ποιέω)	**ποιῶ**	(δηλόω)	**δηλῶ**
2.	(τῑμάεις)	**τῑμᾷς**	(ποιέεις)	**ποιεῖς**	(δηλόεις)	**δηλοῖς**
3.	(τῑμάει)	**τῑμᾷ**	(ποιέει)	**ποιεῖ**	(δηλόει)	**δηλοῖ**
D. 2.	(τῑμάετον)	**τῑμᾶτον**	(ποιέετον)	**ποιεῖτον**	(δηλόετον)	**δηλοῦτον**
3.	(τῑμάετον)	**τῑμᾶτον**	(ποιέετον)	**ποιεῖτον**	(δηλόετον)	**δηλοῦτον**
P. 1.	(τῑμάομεν)	**τῑμῶμεν**	(ποιέομεν)	**ποιοῦμεν**	(δηλόομεν)	**δηλοῦμεν**
2.	(τῑμάετε)	**τῑμᾶτε**	(ποιέετε)	**ποιεῖτε**	(δηλόετε)	**δηλοῦτε**
3.	(τῑμάουσι)	**τῑμῶσι**	(ποιέουσι)	**ποιοῦσι**	(δηλόουσι)	**δηλοῦσι**

IMPERFECT

S. 1.	(ἐτίμαον)	**ἐτίμων**	(ἐποίεον)	**ἐποίουν**	(ἐδήλοον)	**ἐδήλουν**
2.	(ἐτίμαες)	**ἐτίμᾱς**	(ἐποίεες)	**ἐποίεις**	(ἐδήλοες)	**ἐδήλους**
3.	(ἐτίμαε)	**ἐτίμᾱ**	(ἐποίεε)	**ἐποίει**	(ἐδήλοε)	**ἐδήλου**
D. 2.	(ἐτῑμάετον)	**ἐτῑμᾶτον**	(ἐποιέετον)	**ἐποιεῖτον**	(ἐδηλόετον)	**ἐδηλοῦτον**
3.	(ἐτῑμαέτην)	**ἐτῑμᾱ́την**	(ἐποιεέτην)	**ἐποιείτην**	(ἐδηλοέτην)	**ἐδηλούτην**
P. 1.	(ἐτῑμάομεν)	**ἐτῑμῶμεν**	(ἐποιέομεν)	**ἐποιοῦμεν**	(ἐδηλόομεν)	**ἐδηλοῦμεν**
2.	(ἐτῑμάετε)	**ἐτῑμᾶτε**	(ἐποιέετε)	**ἐποιεῖτε**	(ἐδηλόετε)	**ἐδηλοῦτε**
3.	(ἐτίμαον)	**ἐτίμων**	(ἐποίεον)	**ἐποίουν**	(ἐδήλοον)	**ἐδήλουν**

PRESENT SUBJUNCTIVE

S. 1.	(τῑμάω)	**τῑμῶ**	(ποιέω)	**ποιῶ**	(δηλόω)	**δηλῶ**
2.	(τῑμάῃς)	**τῑμᾷς**	(ποιέῃς)	**ποιῇς**	(δηλόῃς)	**δηλοῖς**
3.	(τῑμάῃ)	**τῑμᾷ**	(ποιέῃ)	**ποιῇ**	(δηλόῃ)	**δηλοῖ**
D. 2.	(τῑμάητον)	**τῑμᾶτον**	(ποιέητον)	**ποιῆτον**	(δηλόητον)	**δηλῶτον**
3.	(τῑμάητον)	**τῑμᾶτον**	(ποιέητον)	**ποιῆτον**	(δηλόητον)	**δηλῶτον**
P. 1.	(τῑμάωμεν)	**τῑμῶμεν**	(ποιέωμεν)	**ποιῶμεν**	(δηλόωμεν)	**δηλῶμεν**
2.	(τῑμάητε)	**τῑμᾶτε**	(ποιέητε)	**ποιῆτε**	(δηλόητε)	**δηλῶτε**
3.	(τῑμάωσι)	**τῑμῶσι**	(ποιέωσι)	**ποιῶσι**	(δηλόωσι)	**δηλῶσι**

ACTIVE — *Concluded*

PRESENT OPTATIVE (see 393)

S. 1.	(τῑμαοίην)	τῑμῴην	(ποιεοίην)	ποιοίην	(δηλοοίην)	δηλοίην
2.	(τῑμαοίης)	τῑμῴης	(ποιεοίης)	ποιοίης	(δηλοοίης)	δηλοίης
3.	(τῑμαοίη)	τῑμῴη	(ποιεοίη)	ποιοίη	(δηλοοίη)	δηλοίη
D. 2.	(τῑμαοίητον)	τῑμῴητον	(ποιεοίητον)	ποιοίητον	(δηλοοίητον)	δηλοίητον
3.	(τῑμαοιήτην)	τῑμῳήτην	(ποιεοιήτην)	ποιοιήτην	(δηλοοιήτην)	δηλοιήτην
P. 1.	(τῑμαοίημεν)	τῑμῴημεν	(ποιεοίημεν)	ποιοίημεν	(δηλοοίημεν)	δηλοίημεν
2.	(τῑμαοίητε)	τῑμῴητε	(ποιεοίητε)	ποιοίητε	(δηλοοίητε)	δηλοίητε
3.	(τῑμαοίησαν)	τῑμῴησαν	(ποιεοίησαν)	ποιοίησαν	(δηλοοίησαν)	δηλοίησαν
	or		or		or	
S. 1.	(τῑμάοιμι)	τῑμῷμι	(ποιέοιμι)	ποιοῖμι	(δηλόοιμι)	δηλοῖμι
2.	(τῑμάοις)	τῑμῷς	(ποιέοις)	ποιοῖς	(δηλόοις)	δηλοῖς
3.	(τῑμάοι)	τῑμῷ	(ποιέοι)	ποιοῖ	(δηλόοι)	δηλοῖ
D. 2.	(τῑμάοιτον)	τῑμῷτον	(ποιέοιτον)	ποιοῖτον	(δηλόοιτον)	δηλοῖτον
3.	(τῑμαοίτην)	τῑμῴτην	(ποιεοίτην)	ποιοίτην	(δηλοοίτην)	δηλοίτην
P. 1.	(τῑμάοιμεν)	τῑμῷμεν	(ποιέοιμεν)	ποιοῖμεν	(δηλόοιμεν)	δηλοῖμεν
2.	(τῑμάοιτε)	τῑμῷτε	(ποιέοιτε)	ποιοῖτε	(δηλόοιτε)	δηλοῖτε
3.	(τῑμάοιεν)	τῑμῷεν	(ποιέοιεν)	ποιοῖεν	(δηλόοιεν)	δηλοῖεν

PRESENT IMPERATIVE

S. 2.	(τίμαε)	τίμᾱ	(ποίεε)	ποίει	(δήλοε)	δήλου
3.	(τῑμαέτω)	τῑμᾱ́τω	(ποιεέτω)	ποιείτω	(δηλοέτω)	δηλούτω
D. 2.	(τῑμάετον)	τῑμᾶτον	(ποιέετον)	ποιεῖτον	(δηλόετον)	δηλοῦτον
3.	(τῑμαέτων)	τῑμᾱ́των	(ποιεέτων)	ποιείτων	(δηλοέτων)	δηλούτων
P. 2.	(τῑμάετε)	τῑμᾶτε	(ποιέετε)	ποιεῖτε	(δηλόετε)	δηλοῦτε
3.	(τιμαόντων)	τῑμώντων	(ποιεόντων)	ποιούντων	(δηλοόντων)	δηλούντων

PRESENT INFINITIVE

(τῑμάειν)	τῑμᾶν	(ποιέειν)	ποιεῖν	(δηλόειν)	δηλοῦν

PRESENT PARTICIPLE

(τῑμάων)	τῑμῶν	(ποιέων)	ποιῶν	(δηλόων)	δηλῶν

For the inflection of contracted participles, see 310. For the infinitive, see 469 a.

Attic prose always, and Attic poetry usually, use the contracted forms.

N. 1. — The open forms of verbs in -αω are sometimes found in Homer. Verbs in -εω often show the uncontracted forms in Homer; in Herodotus contraction properly takes place except before ο and ω. Verbs in -οω never appear in their uncontracted forms in any author.

N. 2. — ποιέω sometimes loses its ι (43) except before ο sounds.

Middle and Passive

PRESENT INDICATIVE

S.	1.	(*τῑμάομαι*)	**τῑμῶμαι**	(*ποιέομαι*)	**ποιοῦμαι**	(*δηλόομαι*)	**δηλοῦμαι**
	2.	(*τῑμάῃ, τῑμάει*)	**τῑμᾷ**	(*ποιέῃ, ποιέει*)	**ποιῇ, ποιεῖ**	(*δηλόῃ, δηλόει*)	**δηλοῖ**
	3.	(*τῑμάεται*)	**τῑμᾶται**	(*ποιέεται*)	**ποιεῖται**	(*δηλόεται*)	**δηλοῦται**
D.	2.	(*τῑμάεσθον*)	**τῑμᾶσθον**	(*ποιέεσθον*)	**ποιεῖσθον**	(*δηλόεσθον*)	**δηλοῦσθον**
	3.	(*τῑμάεσθον*)	**τῑμᾶσθον**	(*ποιέεσθον*)	**ποιεῖσθον**	(*δηλόεσθον*)	**δηλοῦσθον**
P.	1.	(*τῑμαόμεθα*)	**τῑμώμεθα**	(*ποιεόμεθα*)	**ποιούμεθα**	(*δηλοόμεθα*)	**δηλούμεθα**
	2.	(*τῑμάεσθε*)	**τῑμᾶσθε**	(*ποιέεσθε*)	**ποιεῖσθε**	(*δηλόεσθε*)	**δηλοῦσθε**
	3.	(*τῑμάονται*)	**τῑμῶνται**	(*ποιέονται*)	**ποιοῦνται**	(*δηλόονται*)	**δηλοῦνται**

IMPERFECT

S.	1.	(*ἐτῑμαόμην*)	**ἐτῑμώμην**	(*ἐποιεόμην*)	**ἐποιούμην**	(*ἐδηλοόμην*)	**ἐδηλούμην**
	2.	(*ἐτῑμάου*)	**ἐτῑμῶ**	(*ἐποιέου*)	**ἐποιοῦ**	(*ἐδηλόου*)	**ἐδηλοῦ**
	3.	(*ἐτῑμάετο*)	**ἐτῑμᾶτο**	(*ἐποιέετο*)	**ἐποιεῖτο**	(*ἐδηλόετο*)	**ἐδηλοῦτο**
D.	2.	(*ἐτῑμάεσθον*)	**ἐτῑμᾶσθον**	(*ἐποιέεσθον*)	**ἐποιεῖσθον**	(*ἐδηλόεσθον*)	**ἐδηλοῦσθον**
	3.	(*ἐτῑμαέσθην*)	**ἐτῑμᾱ́σθην**	(*ἐποιεέσθην*)	**ἐποιείσθην**	(*ἐδηλοέσθην*)	**ἐδηλούσθην**
P.	1.	(*ἐτῑμαόμεθα*)	**ἐτῑμώμεθα**	(*ἐποιεόμεθα*)	**ἐποιούμεθα**	(*ἐδηλοόμεθα*)	**ἐδηλούμεθα**
	2.	(*ἐτῑμάεσθε*)	**ἐτῑμᾶσθε**	(*ἐποιέεσθε*)	**ἐποιεῖσθε**	(*ἐδηλόεσθε*)	**ἐδηλοῦσθε**
	3.	(*ἐτῑμάοντο*)	**ἐτῑμῶντο**	(*ἐποιέοντο*)	**ἐποιοῦντο**	(*ἐδηλόοντο*)	**ἐδηλοῦντο**

PRESENT SUBJUNCTIVE

S.	1.	(*τῑμάωμαι*)	**τῑμῶμαι**	(*ποιέωμαι*)	**ποιῶμαι**	(*δηλόωμαι*)	**δηλῶμαι**
	2.	(*τῑμάῃ*)	**τῑμᾷ**	(*ποιέῃ*)	**ποιῇ**	(*δηλόῃ*)	**δηλοῖ**
	3.	(*τῑμάηται*)	**τῑμᾶται**	(*ποιέηται*)	**ποιῆται**	(*δηλόηται*)	**δηλῶται**
D.	2.	(*τῑμάησθον*)	**τῑμᾶσθον**	(*ποιέησθον*)	**ποιῆσθον**	(*δηλόησθον*)	**δηλῶσθον**
	3.	(*τῑμάησθον*)	**τῑμᾶσθον**	(*ποιέησθον*)	**ποιῆσθον**	(*δηλόησθον*)	**δηλῶσθον**
P.	1.	(*τῑμαώμεθα*)	**τιμώμεθα**	(*ποιεώμεθα*)	**ποιώμεθα**	(*δηλοώμεθα*)	**δηλώμεθα**
	2.	(*τῑμάησθε*)	**τῑμᾶσθε**	(*ποιέησθε*)	**ποιῆσθε**	(*δηλόησθε*)	**δηλῶσθε**
	3.	(*τῑμάωνται*)	**τῑμῶνται**	(*ποιέωνται*)	**ποιῶνται**	(*δηλόωνται*)	**δηλῶνται**

PRESENT OPTATIVE

S.	1.	(*τῑμαοίμην*)	**τῑμῴμην**	(*ποιεοίμην*)	**ποιοίμην**	(*δηλοοίμην*)	**δηλοίμην**
	2.	(*τῑμάοιο*)	**τῑμῷο**	(*ποιέοιο*)	**ποιοῖο**	(*δηλόοιο*)	**δηλοῖο**
	3.	(*τῑμάοιτο*)	**τῑμῷτο**	(*ποιέοιτο*)	**ποιοῖτο**	(*δηλόοιτο*)	**δηλοῖτο**
D.	2.	(*τῑμάοισθον*)	**τῑμῷσθον**	(*ποιέοισθον*)	**ποιοῖσθον**	(*δηλόοισθον*)	**δηλοῖσθον**
	3.	(*τῑμαοίσθην*)	**τῑμῴσθην**	(*ποιεοίσθην*)	**ποιοίσθην**	(*δηλοοίσθην*)	**δηλοίσθην**
P.	1.	(*τῑμαοίμεθα*)	**τῑμῴμεθα**	(*ποιεοίμεθα*)	**ποιοίμεθα**	(*δηλοοίμεθα*)	**δηλοίμεθα**
	2.	(*τῑμάοισθε*)	**τῑμῷσθε**	(*ποιέοισθε*)	**ποιοῖσθε**	(*δηλόοισθε*)	**δηλοῖσθε**
	3.	(*τῑμάοιντο*)	**τῑμῷντο**	(*ποιέοιντο*)	**ποιοῖντο**	(*δηλόοιντο*)	**δηλοῖντο**

MIDDLE AND PASSIVE — *Concluded*

PRESENT IMPERATIVE

S. 2.	(τῑμάου)	**τῑμῶ**	(ποιέου)	**ποιοῦ**	(δηλόου)	**δηλοῦ**
3.	(τῑμαέσθω)	**τῑμάσθω**	(ποιεέσθω)	**ποιείσθω**	(δηλοέσθω)	**δηλούσθω**
D. 2.	(τῑμάεσθον)	**τῑμᾶσθον**	(ποιέεσθον)	**ποιεῖσθον**	(δηλόεσθον)	**δηλοῦσθον**
3.	(τῑμαέσθων)	**τῑμάσθων**	(ποιεέσθων)	**ποιείσθων**	(δηλοέσθων)	**δηλούσθων**
P. 2.	(τῑμάεσθε)	**τῑμᾶσθε**	(ποιέεσθε)	**ποιεῖσθε**	(δηλόεσθε)	**δηλοῦσθε**
3.	(τῑμαέσθων)	**τῑμάσθων**	(ποιεέσθων)	**ποιείσθων**	(δηλοέσθων)	**δηλούσθων**

PRESENT INFINITIVE

(τῑμάεσθαι) **τῑμᾶσθαι** (ποιέεσθαι) **ποιεῖσθαι** (δηλόεσθαι) **δηλοῦσθαι**

PRESENT PARTICIPLE

(τῑμαόμενος) **τῑμώμενος** (ποιεόμενος) **ποιούμενος** (δηλοόμενος) **δηλούμενος**

386. Examples of Contracted Verbs.

1. Verbs in -αω:

ἀπατάω *deceive* (ἀπάτη *deceit*)
βοάω *shout* (βοή *shout*)
μελετάω *practise* (μελέτη *practice*)
νῑκάω *conquer* (νίκη *victory*)
ὁρμάω *set in motion* (ὁρμή *impulse*)
πειράομαι *attempt* (πεῖρα *trial*)
τελευτάω *finish* (τελευτή *end*)
τολμάω *dare* (τόλμα *daring*)

2. Verbs in -εω:

ἀδικέω *do wrong* (ἄδικος *unjust*)
βοηθέω *assist* (βοηθός *assisting*)
κοσμέω *order* (κόσμος *order*)
μῑσέω *hate* (μῖσος *hate*)
οἰκέω *inhabit* (οἶκος *house*, poetic)
πολεμέω *make war* (πόλεμος *war*)
φθονέω *envy* (φθόνος *envy*)
φιλέω *love* (φίλος *friend*)

3. Verbs in -οω:

ἀξιόω *think worthy* (ἄξιος *worthy*)
δουλόω *enslave* (δοῦλος *slave*)
ἐλευθερόω *set free* (ἐλεύθερος *free*)
ζυγόω *put under the yoke* (ζυγόν *yoke*)
κῡρόω *make valid* (κῦρος *authority*)
πολεμόω *make an enemy of* (πόλεμος *war*)
στεφανόω *crown* (στέφανος *crown*)
ταπεινόω *humiliate* (ταπεινός *humbled*)

387. Principal parts of Contracted Verbs.

τῑμάω	**τῑμήσω**	**ἐτίμησα**	**τετίμηκα**	**τετίμημαι**	**ἐτῑμήθην**
θηράω	**θηράσω**	**ἐθήρᾱσα**	**τεθήρᾱκα**	**τεθήρᾱμαι**	**ἐθηράθην**
ποιέω	**ποιήσω**	**ἐποίησα**	**πεποίηκα**	**πεποίημαι**	**ἐποιήθην**
δηλόω	**δηλώσω**	**ἐδήλωσα**	**δεδήλωκα**	**δεδήλωμαι**	**ἐδηλώθην**

388. SYNOPSIS OF τῑμά-ω *honour*

	Pres. Act.	Impf. Act.	Fut. Act.	Aor. Act.	Perf. Act.	Plup. Act.
Ind.	τῑμῶ	ἐτίμων	τῑμήσω	ἐτίμησα	τετίμηκα	ἐτετῑμήκη
Sub.	τῑμῶ			τῑμήσω	τετῑμηκὼς ὦ	
Opt.	τῑμῴην, -ῷμι		τῑμήσοιμι	τῑμήσαιμι	τετῑμηκὼς εἴην	
Imp.	τίμᾱ			τίμησον		
Inf.	τῑμᾶν		τῑμήσειν	τῑμῆσαι	τετῑμηκέναι	
Par.	τῑμῶν		τῑμήσων	τῑμήσᾱς	τετῑμηκώς	
	Mid. Pass.		Middle	Middle	Mid. Pass.	
Ind.	τῑμῶμαι	ἐτῑμώμην	τῑμήσομαι	ἐτῑμησάμην	τετίμημαι	ἐτετῑμήμην
Sub.	τῑμῶμαι			τῑμήσωμαι	τετῑμημένος ὦ	
Opt.	τῑμῴμην		τῑμησοίμην	τῑμησαίμην	τετῑμημένος εἴην	
Imp.	τῑμῶ			τίμησαι	τετίμησο	
Inf.	τῑμᾶσθαι		τῑμήσεσθαι	τῑμήσασθαι	τετῑμῆσθαι	
Par.	τῑμώμενος		τῑμησόμενος	τῑμησάμενος	τετῑμημένος	
			Passive	Passive	Fut. Perf. Pass.	
Ind.			τῑμηθήσομαι	ἐτῑμήθην	τετῑμήσομαι	
Sub.				τῑμηθῶ		
Opt.			τῑμηθησοίμην	τῑμηθείην	τετῑμησοίμην	
Imp.				τῑμήθητι		
Inf.			τῑμηθήσεσθαι	τῑμηθῆναι	τετῑμήσεσθαι	
Par.			τῑμηθησόμενος	τῑμηθείς	τετῑμησόμενος	

Verbal adjectives: τῑμητός, τῑμητέος

389. SYNOPSIS OF θηρά-ω *hunt*

	Pres. Act.	Impf. Act.	Fut. Act.	Aor. Act.	Perf. Act.	Plup. Act.
Ind.	θηρῶ	ἐθήρων	θηρᾱ́σω	ἐθήρᾱσα	τεθήρᾱκα	ἐτεθηρᾱ́κη
Sub.	θηρῶ			θηρᾱ́σω	τεθηρᾱκὼς ὦ	
Opt.	θηρῴην, -ῷμι		θηρᾱ́σοιμι	θηρᾱ́σαιμι	τεθηρᾱκὼς εἴην	
Imp.	θήρᾱ			θήρᾱσον		
Inf.	θηρᾶν		θηρᾱ́σειν	θηρᾶσαι	τεθηρᾱκέναι	
Par.	θηρῶν		θηρᾱ́σων	θηρᾱ́σᾱς	τεθηρᾱκώς	
	Mid. Pass.		Middle	Middle	Mid. Pass.	
Ind.	θηρῶμαι	ἐθηρώμην	θηρᾱ́σομαι	ἐθηρᾱσάμην	τεθήρᾱμαι	ἐτεθηρᾱ́μην
Sub.	θηρῶμαι			θηρᾱ́σωμαι	τεθηρᾱμένος ὦ	
Opt.	θηρῴμην		θηρᾱσοίμην	θηρᾱσαίμην	τεθηρᾱμένος εἴην	
Imp.	θηρῶ			θήρᾱσαι	τεθήρᾱσο	
Inf.	θηρᾶσθαι		θηρᾱ́σεσθαι	θηρᾱ́σασθαι	τεθηρᾶσθαι	
Par.	θηρώμενος		θηρᾱσόμενος	θηρᾱσάμενος	τεθηρᾱμένος	
			Passive (late)	Passive		
Ind.			[θηρᾱθήσομαι]	ἐθηρᾱ́θην	Verbal adjectives:	
Sub.				θηρᾱθῶ	θηρᾱτός	
Opt.			[θηρᾱθησοίμην]	θηρᾱθείην	θηρᾱτέος	
Imp.				θηρᾱ́θητι		
Inf.			[θηρᾱθήσεσθαι]	θηρᾱθῆναι		
Par.			[θηρᾱθησόμενος]	θηρᾱθείς		

390. Synopsis of ποιέ-ω *make*

	Pres. Act.	Impf. Act.	Fut. Act.	Aor. Act.	Perf. Act.	Plup. Act.
Ind.	ποιῶ	ἐποίουν	ποιήσω	ἐποίησα	πεποίηκα	ἐπεποιήκη
Sub.	ποιῶ			ποιήσω	πεποιηκὼς ὦ	
Opt.	ποιοίην, -οῖμι		ποιήσοιμι	ποιήσαιμι	πεποιηκὼς εἴην	
Imp.	ποίει			ποίησον		
Inf.	ποιεῖν		ποιήσειν	ποιῆσαι	πεποιηκέναι	
Par.	ποιῶν		ποιήσων	ποιήσᾱς	πεποιηκώς	
	Mid. Pass.		Middle	Middle	Mid. Pass.	
Ind.	ποιοῦμαι	ἐποιούμην	ποιήσομαι	ἐποιησάμην	πεποίημαι	ἐπεποιήμην
Sub.	ποιῶμαι			ποιήσωμαι	πεποιημένος ὦ	
Opt.	ποιοίμην		ποιησοίμην	ποιησαίμην	πεποιημένος εἴην	
Imp.	ποιοῦ			ποίησαι	πεποίησο	
Inf.	ποιεῖσθαι		ποιήσεσθαι	ποιήσασθαι	πεποιῆσθαι	
Par.	ποιούμενος		ποιησόμενος	ποιησάμενος	πεποιημένος	
			Passive	Passive	Fut. Perf. Pass.	
Ind.			ποιηθήσομαι	ἐποιήθην	πεποιήσομαι	
Sub.				ποιηθῶ		
Opt.			ποιηθησοίμην	ποιηθείην	πεποιησοίμην	
Imp.				ποιήθητι		
Inf.			ποιηθήσεσθαι	ποιηθῆναι	πεποιήσεσθαι	
Par.			ποιηθησόμενος	ποιηθείς	πεποιησόμενος	

Verbal adjectives: ποιητός, ποιητέος

391. Synopsis of τελέ-ω *complete*

	Pres. Act.	Impf. Act.	Fut. Act.	Aor. Act.	Perf. Act.	Plup. Act.
Ind.	τελῶ	ἐτέλουν	τελῶ (τελέσω, 488)	ἐτέλεσα	τετέλεκα	ἐτετελέκη
Sub.	τελῶ			τελέσω	τετελεκὼς ὦ	
Opt.	τελοίην, -οῖμι		τελοίην, -οῖμι	τελέσαιμι	τετελεκὼς εἴην	
Imp.	τέλει			τέλεσον		
Inf.	τελεῖν		τελεῖν	τελέσαι	τετελεκέναι	
Par.	τελῶν		τελῶν	τελέσᾱς	τετελεκώς	
	Mid. Pass.		Middle	Middle	Mid. Pass.	
Ind.	τελοῦμαι	ἐτελούμην	τελοῦμαι	ἐτελεσάμην	τετέλεσμαι	ἐτετελέσμην
Sub.	τελῶμαι			τελέσωμαι	τετελεσμένος ὦ	
Opt.	τελοίμην		τελοίμην	τελεσαίμην	τετελεσμένος εἴην	
Imp.	τελοῦ			τέλεσαι	τετέλεσο	
Inf.	τελεῖσθαι		τελεῖσθαι	τελέσασθαι	τετελέσθαι	
Par.	τελούμενος		τελούμενος	τελεσάμενος	τετελεσμένος	
			Passive	Passive	Verbal adjectives	
Ind.			τελεσθήσομαι	ἐτελέσθην		
Sub.				τελεσθῶ	τελεστός	
Opt.			τελεσθησοίμην	τελεσθείην	τελεστέος	
Imp.				τελέσθητι		
Inf.			τελεσθήσεσθαι	τελεσθῆναι		
Par.			τελεσθησόμενος	τελεσθείς		

392. Synopsis of **δηλό-ω** *manifest*

	Pres. Act.	Impf. Act.	Fut. Act.	Aor. Act.	Perf. Act.	Plup. Act.
Ind.	**δηλῶ**	**ἐδήλουν**	**δηλώσω**	**ἐδήλωσα**	**δεδήλωκα**	**ἐδεδηλώκη**
Sub.	**δηλῶ**			**δηλώσω**	**δεδηλωκὼς ὦ**	
Opt.	**δηλοίην, -οῖμι**		**δηλώσοιμι**	**δηλώσαιμι**	**δεδηλωκὼς εἴην**	
Imp.	**δήλου**			**δήλωσον**		
Inf.	**δηλοῦν**		**δηλώσειν**	**δηλῶσαι**	**δεδηλωκέναι**	
Par.	**δηλῶν**		**δηλώσων**	**δηλώσᾱς**	**δεδηλωκώς**	

	Mid. Pass.		Middle	Middle	Mid. Pass.	
Ind.	**δηλοῦμαι**	**ἐδηλούμην**	**δηλώσομαι** (as pass., 809)		**δεδήλωμαι**	**ἐδεδηλώμην**
Sub.	**δηλῶμαι**				**δεδηλωμένος ὦ**	
Opt.	**δηλοίμην**		**δηλωσοίμην**		**δεδηλωμένος εἴην**	
Imp.	**δηλοῦ**				**δεδήλωσο**	
Inf.	**δηλοῦσθαι**		**δηλώσεσθαι**		**δεδηλῶσθαι**	
Par.	**δηλούμενος**		**δηλωσόμενος**		**δεδηλωμένος**	

	Passive	Passive	Fut. Perf. Pass.
Ind.	**δηλωθήσομαι**	**ἐδηλώθην**	**δεδηλώσομαι**
Sub.		**δηλωθῶ**	
Opt.	**δηλωθησοίμην**	**δηλωθείην**	**δεδηλωσοίμην**
Imp.		**δηλώθητι**	
Inf.	**δηλωθήσεσθαι**	**δηλωθῆναι**	**δεδηλώσεσθαι**
Par.	**δηλωθησόμενος**	**δηλωθείς**	**δεδηλωσόμενος**

Verbal adjectives: **δηλωτός, δηλωτέος**

REMARKS ON THE CONTRACTED VERBS

393. In the present optative active there are two forms: (1) that with the modal sign *-ιη-*, having *-ν* in the 1 sing., and *-σαν* in the 3 pl.; (2) that with the modal sign *-ῑ-*, having *-μι* in the 1 sing., and *-εν* in the 3 pl. The first form is more common in the singular, the second in the dual and plural.

τῑμῴην (rarely *τῑμῷμι*), **τῑμῷτον** (rarely *τῑμῴητον*), **τῑμῷμεν** (rarely *τῑμῴημεν*), **ποιοίην** (rarely *ποιοῖμι*), **ποιοῖτον** (rarely *ποιοίητον*), **ποιοῖμεν** (rarely *ποιοίημεν*), **δηλοίην** (rarely *δηλοῖμι*), **δηλοῖτον** (rarely *δηλοίητον*), **δηλοῖμεν** (rarely *δηλοίημεν*).

394. Ten verbs in *-αω* show **η** where we expect *ᾱ*. These are **διψῶ** *thirst*, **ζῶ** *live*, **πεινῶ** *hunger*, **κνῶ** *scrape*, **νῶ** *spin* (rare), **σμῶ** *wash*, **χρῶ** *give oracles*, **χρῶ** *am eager for* (rare), **χρῶμαι** *use*, and **ψῶ** *rub*. See 641.

395. *ζῶ live* and *χρῶμαι use* are inflected as follows in the present indicative, subjunctive and imperative and in the imperfect.

	Indic. and Subj.		Imperative		Imperfect	
S. 1.	ζῶ	χρῶμαι			ἔζων	ἐχρώμην
2.	ζῇς	χρῇ	ζῆ	χρῶ	ἔζης	ἐχρῶ
3.	ζῇ	χρῆται	ζήτω	χρήσθω	ἔζη	ἐχρῆτο
D. 2.	ζῆτον	χρῆσθον	ζῆτον	χρῆσθον	ἐζῆτον	ἐχρῆσθον
3.	ζῆτον	χρῆσθον	ζήτων	χρήσθων	ἐζήτην	ἐχρήσθην
P. 1.	ζῶμεν	χρώμεθα			ἐζῶμεν	ἐχρώμεθα
2.	ζῆτε	χρῆσθε	ζῆτε	χρῆσθε	ἐζῆτε	ἐχρῆσθε
3.	ζῶσι	χρῶνται	ζώντων	χρήσθων	ἔζων	ἐχρῶντο

Infinitive: ζῆν, χρῆσθαι Participle: ζῶν, χρώμενος

396. *καίω burn*, *κλαίω weep*, do not contract the forms in which ι has disappeared (38). Thus, *κάω, κάεις, κάει, κάομεν, κάετε, κάουσι.*

397. Verbs in -εω of two syllables do not contract ε with ο or ω. The present and imperfect indicative cf *πλέω sail* are inflected as follows.

πλέω		πλέομεν	ἔπλεον		ἐπλέομεν
πλεῖς	πλεῖτον	πλεῖτε	ἔπλεις	ἐπλεῖτον	ἐπλεῖτε
πλεῖ	πλεῖτον	πλέουσι	ἔπλει	ἐπλείτην	ἔπλεον

and so **πλέω, πλέοιμι, πλεῖ, πλεῖν, πλέων, πλέουσα, πλέον.** In like manner **θέω** *run*, **πνέω** *breathe*.

a. *δέω need* has *δεῖς, δεῖ it is necessary, δέῃ, δέοι, δεῖν, τὸ δέον what is necessary; δέομαι want, request*, has *δέει, δεῖται, δεόμεθα, δέωμαι.* But *δέω bind* is usually an exception, making *δεῖς, δεῖ, δοῦμεν, ἔδουν bound, τὸ δοῦν that which binds, δοῦμαι, δοῦνται*, but *δεόμενον, δέον* appear in some writers.

b. *ξέω scrape* contracts. *βδέω, ξέω* and *τρέω* have lost σ; *πλέω, θέω, πνέω* have lost ῠ(ϝ); *δέω need* is for *δευσω*; *δέω bind* is for *δεῐω.*

398. Two verbs in -οω, *ἱδρόω sweat, ῥῑγόω shiver*, may have ω and ῳ instead of ου and οι. See 641.

Thus, indic. *ῥῑγῶ, ῥῑγῷς, ῥῑγῷ* (or *ῥῑγοῖ*), opt. *ῥῑγῴην*, inf. *ῥῑγῶν* (or *ῥῑγοῦν*), part. *ῥῑγῶν.* So *ἱδρῶσι*, opt. *ἱδρῴη* (or *ἱδροῖ*), part. *ἱδρῶν* (or *ἱδροῦν*).

a. **λούω** *wash*, when it drops its υ (43), contracts like *δηλόω.* Thus, **λούω, λούεις, λούει**, but **λοῦμεν** (for λο(ῠ)ο-μεν), **λοῦτε, λοῦσι**; and so in other forms, as **ἔλου, λοῦται, λοῦσθαι, λούμενος.**

b. *οἴομαι think* (imperfect *ᾠόμην*) has the parallel forms *οἶμαι* (*ᾤμην*).

399. Movable ν is never (in Attic) added to the contracted 3 sing. imperfect (*ἐποίει*, not *ἐποίειν*).

I. (C) CONSONANT VERBS

400. Verbs whose stems end in a consonant are in general inflected like non-contracting ω-verbs in all tenses. The future active and middle of liquid and nasal verbs are inflected like contracted εω-verbs.

401. Liquid and Nasal Verbs: future active and middle of φαίνω *show.*

			Future Active		Future Middle	
INDICATIVE.	S.	1.	(φανέω)	**φανῶ**	(φανέομαι)	**φανοῦμαι**
		2.	(φανέεις)	**φανεῖς**	(φανέῃ or -έει)	**φανῇ** or **-εῖ**
		3.	(φανέει)	**φανεῖ**	(φανέεται)	**φανεῖται**
	D.	2.	(φανέετον)	**φανεῖτον**	(φανέεσθον)	**φανεῖσθον**
		3.	(φανέετον)	**φανεῖτον**	(φανέεσθον)	**φανεῖσθον**
	P.	1.	(φανέομεν)	**φανοῦμεν**	(φανεόμεθα)	**φανούμεθα**
		2.	(φανέετε)	**φανεῖτε**	(φανέεσθε)	**φανεῖσθε**
		3.	(φανέουσι)	**φανοῦσι**	(φανέονται)	**φανοῦνται**
OPTATIVE.	S.	1.	(φανεοίην)	**φανοίην**	(φανεοίμην)	**φανοίμην**
		2.	(φανεοίης)	**φανοίης**	(φανέοιο)	**φανοῖο**
		3.	(φανεοίη)	**φανοίη**	(φανέοιτο)	**φανοῖτο**
	D.	2.	(φανέοιτον)	**φανοῖτον**	(φανέοισθον)	**φανοῖσθον**
		3.	(φανεοίτην)	**φανοίτην**	(φανεοίσθην)	**φανοίσθην**
	P.	1.	(φανέοιμεν)	**φανοῖμεν**	(φανεοίμεθα)	**φανοίμεθα**
		2.	(φανέοιτε)	**φανοῖτε**	(φανέοισθε)	**φανοῖσθε**
		3.	(φανέοιεν)	**φανοῖεν**	(φανέοιντο)	**φανοῖντο**
			or			
	S.	1.	(φανέοιμι)	**φανοῖμι**		
		2.	(φανέοις)	**φανοῖς**		
		3.	(φανέοι)	**φανοῖ**		
	D.	2.	(φανέοιτον)	**φανοῖτον**		
		3.	(φανεοίτην)	**φανοιτην**		
	P.	1.	(φανέοιμεν)	**φανοῖμεν**		
		2.	(φανέοιτε)	**φανοῖτε**		
		3.	(φανέοιεν)	**φανοῖεν**		
INFINITIVE.			(φανέειν)	**φανεῖν**	(φανέεσθαι)	**φανεῖσθαι**
PARTICIPLE.			(φανέων, φανέουσα, φανέον)	**φανῶν, φανοῦσα, φανοῦν** (310)	(φανεόμενος, -η, -ον)	**φανούμενος, -η, -ον** (287)

402. Liquid and Nasal Verbs: first aorist active and middle, second aorist and second future passive of *φαίνω show.*

			1 Aorist Active	1 Aorist Middle	2 Aorist Passive	2 Future Passive
IND.	S.	1.	ἔφηνα	ἐφηνάμην	ἐφάνην	φανήσομαι
		2.	ἔφηνας	ἐφήνω	ἐφάνης	φανήσῃ, φανήσει
		3.	ἔφηνε	ἐφήνατο	ἐφάνη	φανήσεται
	D.	2.	ἐφήνατον	ἐφήνασθον	ἐφάνητον	φανήσεσθον
		3.	ἐφηνάτην	ἐφηνάσθην	ἐφανήτην	φανήσεσθον
	P.	1.	ἐφήναμεν	ἐφηνάμεθα	ἐφάνημεν	φανησόμεθα
		2.	ἐφήνατε	ἐφήνασθε	ἐφάνητε	φανήσεσθε
		3.	ἔφηναν	ἐφήναντο	ἐφάνησαν	φανήσονται
SUBJ.	S.	1.	φήνω	φήνωμαι	φανῶ	
		2.	φήνῃς	φήνῃ	φανῇς	
		3.	φήνῃ	φήνηται	φανῇ	
	D.	2.	φήνητον	φήνησθον	φανῆτον	
		3.	φήνητον	φήνησθον	φανῆτον	
	P.	1.	φήνωμεν	φηνώμεθα	φανῶμεν	
		2.	φήνητε	φήνησθε	φανῆτε	
		3.	φήνωσι	φήνωνται	φανῶσι	
OPT.	S.	1.	φήναιμι	φηναίμην	φανείην	φανησοίμην
		2.	φήναις or φήνειας (668)	φήναιο	φανείης	φανήσοιο
		3.	φήναι or φήνειε (668)	φήναιτο	φανείη	φανήσοιτο
	D.	2.	φήναιτον	φήναισθον	φανεῖτον or φανείητον	φανήσοισθον
		3.	φηναίτην	φηναίσθην	φανείτην or φανειήτην	φανησοίσθην
	P.	1.	φήναιμεν	φηναίμεθα	φανεῖμεν or φανείημεν	φανησοίμεθα
		2.	φήναιτε	φήναισθε	φανεῖτε or φανείητε	φανήσοισθε
		3.	φήναιεν or φήνειαν (668)	φήναιντο	φανεῖεν or φανείησαν	φανήσοιντο
IMP.	S.	2.	φῆνον	φῆναι	φάνηθι	
		3.	φηνάτω	φηνάσθω	φανήτω	
	D.	2.	φήνατον	φήνασθον	φάνητον	
		3.	φηνάτων	φηνάσθων	φανήτων	
	P.	2.	φήνατε	φήνασθε	φάνητε	
		3.	φηνάντων	φηνάσθων	φανέντων	
INF.			φῆναι	φήνασθαι	φανῆναι	φανήσεσθαι
PART.			φήνᾱς, -ᾱσα, φῆναν (306)	φηνάμενος, -η, -ον (287)	φανείς, φανεῖσα, φανέν (307)	φανησόμενος, -η, -ον (287)

PERFECT AND PLUPERFECT MIDDLE (AND PASSIVE)

403. In the perfect and pluperfect middle (and passive) of stems ending in a consonant certain euphonic changes (409) occur upon the addition of the personal endings.

404. Several verbs with stems ending in a short vowel retain that vowel in the perfect (and in other tenses); such stems originally ended in σ; as τελέ-ω *finish*, from τέλος *end* (τελεσ-). This σ appears in the perfect middle stem (τετέλε-σ-μαι, τετέλε-σ-ται). In the second person singular and plural but one σ is found: τετέλε-σαι, τετέλε-σθε. By analogy some other verbs have a σ at the end of the verbal stem.

405. In the perfect and pluperfect middle the third person plural of stems ending in a consonant or of stems adding σ consists of the perfect middle participle with εἰσί *are* (in the perfect) and ἦσαν *were* (in the pluperfect).

406. Perfect and pluperfect middle and passive of λείπω (λειπ-) *leave*, γράφω (γραφ-) *write*, πείθω (πειθ-) *persuade*, πρᾱ́ττω (πρᾱγ-) *do*.

Perfect Indicative

S. 1.	λέλειμμαι	γέγραμμαι	πέπεισμαι	πέπρᾱγμαι
2.	λέλειψαι	γέγραψαι	πέπεισαι	πέπρᾱξαι
3.	λέλειπται	γέγραπται	πέπεισται	πέπρᾱκται
D. 2.	λέλειφθον	γέγραφθον	πέπεισθον	πέπρᾱχθον
3.	λέλειφθον	γέγραφθον	πέπεισθον	πέπρᾱχθον
P. 1.	λελείμμεθα	γεγράμμεθα	πεπείσμεθα	πεπρᾱ́γμεθα
2.	λέλειφθε	γέγραφθε	πέπεισθε	πέπρᾱχθε
3.	λελειμμένοι εἰσί	γεγραμμένοι εἰσί	πεπεισμένοι εἰσί	πεπρᾱγμένοι εἰσί

Pluperfect

S. 1.	ἐλελείμμην	ἐγεγράμμην	ἐπεπείσμην	ἐπεπρᾱ́γμην
2.	ἐλέλειψο	ἐγέγραψο	ἐπέπεισο	ἐπέπρᾱξο
3.	ἐλέλειπτο	ἐγέγραπτο	ἐπέπειστο	ἐπέπρᾱκτο
D. 2.	ἐλέλειφθον	ἐγέγραφθον	ἐπέπεισθον	ἐπέπρᾱχθον
3.	ἐλελείφθην	ἐγεγράφθην	ἐπεπείσθην	ἐπεπρᾱ́χθην
P. 1.	ἐλελείμμεθα	ἐγεγράμμεθα	ἐπεπείσμεθα	ἐπεπρᾱ́γμεθα
2.	ἐλέλειφθε	ἐγέγραφθε	ἐπέπεισθε	ἐπέπρᾱχθε
3.	λελειμμένοι ἦσαν	γεγραμμένοι ἦσαν	πεπεισμένοι ἦσαν	πεπρᾱγμένοι ἦσαν

Perfect Subjunctive and Optative

λελειμμένος ὦ	γεγραμμένος ὦ	πεπεισμένος ὦ	πεπρᾱγμένος ὦ
λελειμμένος εἴην	γεγραμμένος εἴην	πεπεισμένος εἴην	πεπρᾱγμένος εἴην

Perfect Imperative

S. 2.	λέλειψο	γέγραψο	πέπεισο	πέπρᾱξο
3.	λελείφθω	γεγράφθω	πεπείσθω	πεπρᾱ́χθω
D. 2.	λέλειφθον	γέγραφθον	πέπεισθον	πέπρᾱχθον
3.	λελείφθων	γεγράφθων	πεπείσθων	πεπρᾱ́χθων
P. 2.	λέλειφθε	γέγραφθε	πέπεισθε	πέπρᾱχθε
3.	λελείφθων	γεγράφθων	πεπείσθων	πεπρᾱ́χθων

Perfect Infinitive and Participle

λελεῖφθαι	γεγράφθαι	πεπεῖσθαι	πεπρᾶχθαι
λελειμμένος, -η, -ον	γεγραμμένος, -η, -ον	πεπεισμένος, -η, -ον	πεπρᾱγμένος, -η, -ον

407. Perfect and pluperfect middle and passive of ἐλέγχω (ἐλεγχ-) *confute*, ἀγγέλλω (ἀγγελ-) *announce*, φαίνω (φαν-) *show*, τελέω (τελε-) *finish*.

Perfect Indicative

S. 1.	ἐλήλεγμαι	ἤγγελμαι	πέφασμαι	τετέλε-σ-μαι
2.	ἐλήλεγξαι	ἤγγελσαι	(πέφανσαι, 707 a)	τετέλε-σαι
3.	ἐλήλεγκται	ἤγγελται	πέφανται	τετέλε-σ-ται
D. 2.	ἐλήλεγχθον	ἤγγελθον	πέφανθον	τετέλε-σθον
3.	ἐλήλεγχθον	ἤγγελθον	πέφανθον	τετέλε-σθον
P. 1.	ἐληλέγμεθα	ἠγγέλμεθα	πεφάσμεθα	τετελέ-σ-μεθα
2.	ἐλήλεγχθε	ἤγγελθε	πέφανθε	τετέλε-σθε
3.	ἐληλεγμένοι εἰσί	ἠγγελμένοι εἰσί	πεφασμένοι εἰσί	τετελε-σ-μένοι εἰσί

Pluperfect Indicative

S. 1.	ἐληλέγμην	ἠγγέλμην	ἐπεφάσμην	ἐ-τετελέ-σ-μην
2.	ἐλήλεγξο	ἤγγελσο	(ἐπέφανσο, 707 a)	ἐ-τετέλε-σο
3.	ἐλήλεγκτο	ἤγγελτο	ἐπέφαντο	ἐ-τετέλε-σ-το
D. 2.	ἐλήλεγχθον	ἤγγελθον	ἐπέφανθον	ἐ-τετέλε-σθον
3.	ἐληλέγχθην	ἠγγέλθην	ἐπεφάνθην	ἐ-τετελέ-σθην
P. 1.	ἐληλέγμεθα	ἠγγέλμεθα	ἐπεφάσμεθα	ἐ-τετελέ-σ-μεθα
2.	ἐλήλεγχθε	ἤγγελθε	ἐπέφανθε	ἐ-τετέλε-σθε
3.	ἐληλεγμένοι ἦσαν	ἠγγελμένοι ἦσαν	πεφασμένοι ἦσαν	τετελε-σ-μένοι ἦσαν

Perfect Subjunctive and Optative

ἐληλεγμένος ὦ	ἠγγελμένος ὦ	πεφασμένος ὦ	τετελεσμένος ὦ
ἐληλεγμένος εἴην	ἠγγελμένος εἴην	πεφασμένος εἴην	τετελεσμένος εἴην

Perfect Imperative

S. 2.	ἐλήλεγξο	ἤγγελσο	(πέφανσο, 712 a)	τετέλε-σο
3.	ἐληλέγχθω	ἠγγέλθω	πεφάνθω	τετελέ-σθω
D. 2.	ἐλήλεγχθον	ἤγγελθον	πέφανθον	τετέλε-σθον
3.	ἐληλέγχθων	ἠγγέλθων	πεφάνθων	τετελέ-σθων
P. 2.	ἐλήλεγχθε	ἤγγελθε	πέφανθε	τετέλε-σθε
3.	ἐληλέγχθων	ἠγγέλθων	πεφάνθων	τετελέ-σθων

Perfect Infinitive and Participle

ἐληλέγχθαι	ἠγγέλθαι	πεφάνθαι	τετελέ-σθαι
ἐληλεγμένος, -η, -ον	ἠγγελμένος, -η, -ον	πεφασμένος, -η, -ον	τετελε-σ-μένος, -η, -ον

EXPLANATION OF THE PERFECT AND PLUPERFECT FORMS

408. The periphrastic third plural is used instead of the forms derived directly from the union of the stem with the ending.

Thus, γεγραμμένοι εἰσί is used for γεγραφ-νται which would become γεγράφαται by 35 b, ν between consonants passing into α. The periphrastic form is also used in verbs adding σ to their stems, as τετελε-σ-μένοι εἰσί for τετελε-σ-νται. Stems in ν that drop ν in the perfect system form their perfect and pluperfect regularly; thus, κρίνω (κριν-) *judge* has κέκρινται, ἐκέκριντο.

N. — On the retention of -αται, -ατο see 465 f.

409. Euphonic Changes. — For the euphonic changes in these forms see 82–87, 103.

a. Labial Stems. — λέλειμ-μαι is for λελειπ-μαι, λέλειφ-θον is for λελειπ-σθον, λέλειφθε is for λελειπ-σθε (103). In the same manner are inflected other labial stems, as τρίβω (τρῑβ-) *rub*, ῥίπτω (ῥῑπ-) *throw*: τέτρῑμ-μαι for τετρῑβ-μαι, τέτρῑψαι for τετρῑβ-σαι, etc. Stems ending in μπ drop π before μ, but retain it before other consonants. Thus,

πεπεμπ-μαι	becomes	πέπεμμαι	πεπεμπ-μεθα	becomes	πεπέμμεθα
πεπεμπ-σαι	"	πέπεμψαι	πεπεμπ-σθε	"	πέπεμφθε (103)
πεπεμπ-ται	"	πέπεμπται			

b. Dental Stems. — πέπεισ-ται is for πεπειθ-ται (83), πέπεισ-θον is for πεπειθ-θον (83), πέπεισθε is for πεπειθ-(σ)θε (83, 103). The σ thus produced was trans-

---

409 b. D. Hom. has the original forms πεφραδμένος, κεκορυθμένος.

ferred to the first persons πέπεισμαι, πεπείσμεθα (86, 87). Like πέπεισμαι, etc., are formed and inflected ἔψευσμαι from ψεύδω (ψευδ-) *deceive*, πέφρασμαι from φράζω (φραδ-) *declare*, ἔσπεισμαι (100) from σπένδω (σπενδ-) *pour a libation*.

c. **Palatal Stems.** — πέπρᾱξαι is for πεπρᾱγ-σαι (97), πέπρᾱκται is for πεπρᾱγ-ται (82 a), πέπρᾱχθε is for πεπρᾱγ-σθε (103). Like πέπρᾱγμαι are inflected πλέκω (πλεκ-) *weave* πέπλεγ-μαι, ἄγω (ἀγ-) *lead* ἦγμαι, ἀλλάττω (ἀλλαγ-) *exchange* ἤλλαγμαι, ταράττω (ταραχ-) *confuse* τετάραγμαι. Stems in -γχ change χ before μ to γ and drop one γ (as in ἐλήλεγ-μαι for ἐληλεγγ-μαι, 85 and 85 b), but keep the second palatal before other consonants (as in ἐλήλεγξαι for ἐληλεγχ-σαι, 97; ἐλήλεγκ-ται for ἐληλεγχ-ται, 82). On the reduplication see 446.

d. **Liquid and Nasal Stems.** — Stems in λ or ρ are inflected like ἤγγελμαι, as στέλλω (στελ-, σταλ-) *send* ἔσταλμαι, αἴρω (ἀρ-) *raise* ἦρμαι, ἐγείρω (ἐγερ-) *wake* ἐγήγερμαι (446). Stems in ν retaining the nasal are inflected like πέφασμαι, as σημαίνω (σημαν-) *signify* σεσήμασμαι. (For -σμαι see 94 a and b.) Stems in ν dropping the nasal (559 a) are inflected like λέλυμαι, as κρίνω (κριν-) *judge* κέκριμαι.

e. **Vowel Stems adding σ.** — Here the stem ends in a vowel except before μ and τ; thus, τετέλε-σαι, τετέλε-σθον, τετέλε-σθε: but τετέλε-σ-μαι, τετελέ-σ-μεθα, τετέλε-σ-ται.

N. — Since the stem of τελέω is properly τελεσ- (τελεσ-ι̯ω, 624), the original inflection is τετελεσ-σαι, whence τετέλε-σαι (107); τετέλεσ-ται; τετελεσ-σθον, τετελεσ-σθε, whence τετέλεσθον, τετέλεσθε (103). τετέλεσμαι and τετελέσμεθα are due to the analogy of the other forms.

410. The forms πέφανσαι, ἐπέφανσο, and πέφανσο are not attested. Cp. 707 a.

411. The principal parts of the verbs in 406–407 are as follows:

ἀγγέλλω *announce* (ἀγγελ-), **ἀγγελῶ, ἤγγειλα, ἤγγελκα, ἤγγελμαι, ἠγγέλθην.**

γράφω *write* (γραφ-), **γράψω, ἔγραψα, γέγραφα, γέγραμμαι,** 2 aor. pass. **ἐγράφην.**

ἐλέγχω *confute* (ἐλεγχ-), **ἐλέγξω, ἤλεγξα, ἐλήλεγμαι, ἠλέγχθην.**

λείπω *leave* (λιπ-, λειπ-, λοιπ-), **λείψω,** 2 perf. **λέλοιπα, λέλειμμαι, ἐλείφθην,** 2 a. **ἔλιπον.**

πείθω *persuade* (πιθ-, πειθ-, ποιθ-), **πείσω, ἔπεισα,** 1 perf. **πέπεικα** *I have persuaded*, 2 perf. **πέποιθα** *I trust*, **πέπεισμαι, ἐπείσθην.**

πρᾱ́ττω *do* (πρᾱγ-), **πρᾱ́ξω, ἔπρᾱξα,** 2 perf. **πέπρᾱγα** *I have fared* and *I have done*, **πέπρᾱγμαι, ἐπρᾱ́χθην.**

τελέω *finish* (τελε-σ-), **τελῶ, ἐτέλεσα, τετέλεκα, τετέλεσμαι, ἐτελέσθην.**

φαίνω *show* (φαν-), **φανῶ, ἔφηνα,** 1 perf. **πέφαγκα** *I have shown*, 2 perf. **πέφηνα** *I have appeared*, **πέφασμαι, ἐφάνθην** *I was shown*, 2 aor. pass. **ἐφάνην** *I appeared.*

CONJUGATION OF μι-VERBS

412. The conjugation of *μι*-verbs differs from that of *ω*-verbs only in the present, imperfect, and second aorist active and middle; and (rarely) in the second perfect. The *μι* forms are made by adding the endings *directly* to the tense-stem without any thematic vowel, except in the subjunctive of all verbs, and in the optative of verbs ending in *-νῡμι*.

413. Verbs having second aorists and second perfects of the *μι* form are, as a rule, *ω*-verbs, not *μι*-verbs, in the present. Thus, the second aorists: *ἔβην* (*βαίνω* *go*), *ἔγνων* (*γιγνώσκω* *know*); the second perfect: *τέθναμεν* (*θνῄσκω* *die*).

414. There are two main classes of *μι*-verbs.

A. The root class. This class commonly ends in *-η-μι* or *-ω-μι* (from stems in *ε*, *α*, or *ο*). The present stem is usually reduplicated, but may be the same as the verb-stem, which is a root.

Verb-stem	Present Stem	Present
θε-, *θη-*	*τιθε-*, *τιθη-* (for *θιθε*, *θιθη*, 125 a)	*τίθημι* *place*
ἑ-, *ἡ-*	*ἱε-*, *ἱη-* (for *σισε*, *σιση* or *ι̯ι̯ε*, *ι̯ι̯η*)	*ἵημι* *send*
στα-, *στη-*	*ἱστα-*, *ἱστη-* (for *σιστα*, *σιστη*, 119)	*ἵστημι* *set*
δο-, *δω-*	*διδο-*, *διδω-*	*δίδωμι* *give*
φα-, *φη-*	*φα-*, *φη-*	*φημί* *say*

B. The *-νῡμι* class. This class adds *νυ* (*νῡ*), after a vowel *ννυ* (*ννῡ*), to the verb-stem. In the subjunctive and optative regularly, and sometimes in the indicative, verbs in *-νῡμι* are inflected like verbs in *-ω*.

Verb-stem	Present Stem	Present
δεικ-	*δεικνυ-*, *δεικνῡ-*	*δείκνῡμι* *show*
ζευγ-	*ζευγνυ-*, *ζευγνῡ-*	*ζεύγνῡμι* *yoke*
κερα-	*κεραννυ-*, *κεραννῡ-*	*κεράννῡμι* *mix*
ῥηγ-	*ῥηγνυ-*, *ῥηγνῡ-*	*ῥήγνῡμι* *break*
σβε-	*σβεννυ-*, *σβεννῡ-*	*σβέννῡμι* *extinguish*

C. There are some (mostly poetic) verbs in *-νημι*, which add *να-*, *νη-* to form the present stem; as *δάμ-νη-μι* *I subdue*, *δάμ-να-μεν* *we subdue*.

415. All the possible *μι* forms do not occur in any single verb. *τίθημι* and *δίδωμι* are incomplete and irregular in the second aorist active; and *ἔσβην* *went out* from *σβέννῡμι* is the only second aorist formed from *νῡμι*-verbs. *ἐπριάμην* *I bought*, second aorist middle (from the stem *πρια-* with no present), is given in the paradigms in place of the missing form of *ἵστημι*; and *ἔδῡν* *I entered* from *δύω* (but formed as if from *δῦμι*) in place of a second aorist of the *νῡμι*-verbs.

416. (A) **Root Class.** — Inflection of *τίθημι place, ἵστημι set, δίδωμι give*, in the present, imperfect, and second aorist tenses; and of *ἐπριάμην I bought.*

ACTIVE

Present Indicative

S. 1.	τί-θη-μι	ἵ-στη-μι	δί-δω-μι
2.	τί-θη-ς	ἵ-στη-ς	δί-δω-ς
3.	τί-θη-σι	ἵ-στη-σι	δί-δω-σι
D. 2.	τί-θε-τον	ἵ-στα-τον	δί-δο-τον
3.	τί-θε-τον	ἵ-στα-τον	δί-δο-τον
P. 1.	τί-θε-μεν	ἵ-στα-μεν	δί-δο-μεν
2.	τί-θε-τε	ἵ-στα-τε	δί-δο-τε
3.	τι-θέ-ᾱσι	ἱ-στᾶσι	δι-δό-ᾱσι

Imperfect

S. 1.	ἐ-τί-θη-ν	ἵ-στη-ν	ἐ-δί-δουν (746 b)
2.	ἐ-τί-θεις (746 b)	ἵ-στη-ς	ἐ-δί-δους
3.	ἐ-τί-θει	ἵ-στη	ἐ-δί-δου
D. 2.	ἐ-τί-θε-τον	ἵ-στα-τον	ἐ-δί-δο-τον
3.	ἐ-τι-θέ-την	ἱ-στά-την	ἐ-δι-δό-την
P. 1.	ἐ-τί-θε-μεν	ἵ-στα-μεν	ἐ-δί-δο-μεν
2.	ἐ-τί-θε-τε	ἵ-στα-τε	ἐ-δί-δο-τε
3.	ἐ-τί-θε-σαν	ἵ-στα-σαν	ἐ-δί-δο-σαν

Present Subjunctive

S. 1.	τι-θῶ	ἱ-στῶ	δι-δῶ
2.	τι-θῇ-ς	ἱ-στῇ-ς	δι-δῷ-ς
3.	τι-θῇ	ἱ-στῇ	δι-δῷ
D. 2.	τι-θῆ-τον	ἱ-στῆ-τον	δι-δῶ-τον
3.	τι-θῆ-τον	ἱ-στῆ-τον	δι-δῶ-τον
P. 1.	τι-θῶ-μεν	ἱ-στῶ-μεν	δι-δῶ-μεν
2.	τι-θῆ-τε	ἱ-στῆ-τε	δι-δῶ-τε
3.	τι-θῶ-σι	ἱ-στῶ-σι	δι-δῶ-σ

Present Optative

S. 1.	τι-θείη-ν	ἱ-σταίη-ν	δι-δοίη-ν
2.	τι-θείη-ς	ἱ-σταίη-ς	δι-δοίη-ς
3.	τι-θείη	ἱ-σταίη	δι-δοίη
D. 2.	τι-θεῖ-τον	ἱ-σταῖ-τον	δι-δοῖ-τον
3.	τι-θεί-την	ἱ-σταί-την	δι-δοί-την
P. 1.	τι-θεῖ-μεν	ἱ-σταῖ-μεν	δι-δοῖ-μεν
2.	τι-θεῖ-τε	ἱ-σταῖ-τε	δι-δοῖ-τε
3.	τι-θεῖε-ν	ἱ-σταῖε-ν	δι-δοῖε-ν

Active — *Concluded*

Present Optative

	or (750)	or (750)	or (750)
D. 2.	τι-θείη-τον	ἱ-σταίη-τον	δι-δοίη-τον
3.	τι-θειή-την	ἱ-σταιή-την	δι-δοιή-την
P. 1.	τι-θείη-μεν	ἱ-σταίη-μεν	δι-δοίη-μεν
2.	τι-θείη-τε	ἱ-σταίη-τε	δι-δοίη-τε
3.	τι-θείη-σαν	ἱ-σταίη-σαν	δι-δοίη-σαν

Present Imperative

S. 2.	τί-θει (746 b)	ἵ-στη	δί-δου
3.	τι-θέ-τω	ἱ-στά-τω	δι-δό-τω
D. 2.	τί-θε-τον	ἵ-στα-τον	δί-δο-τον
3.	τι-θέ-των	ἱ-στά-των	δι-δό-των
P. 2.	τί-θε-τε	ἵ-στα-τε	δί-δο-τε
3.	τι-θέ-ντων	ἱ-στά-ντων	δι-δό-ντων

Present Infinitive

τι-θέ-ναι	ἱ-στά-ναι	δι-δό-ναι

Present Participle

τι-θείς, -εῖσα, -έν (307)	ἱ-στᾱ́ς, -ᾶσα, -άν (306)	δι-δούς, -οῦσα, -όν (307)

Middle and Passive

Present Indicative

S. 1.	τί-θε-μαι	ἵ-στα-μαι	δί-δο-μαι (747 f)
2.	τί-θε-σαι	ἵ-στα-σαι	δί-δο-σαι
3.	τί-θε-ται	ἵ-στα-ται	δί-δο-ται
D. 2.	τί-θε-σθον	ἵ-στα-σθον	δί-δο-σθον
3.	τί-θε-σθον	ἵ-στα-σθον	δί-δο-σθον
P. 1.	τι-θέ-μεθα	ἱ-στά-μεθα	δι-δό-μεθα
2.	τί-θε-σθε	ἵ-στα-σθε	δί-δο-σθε
3.	τί-θε-νται	ἵ-στα-νται	δί-δο-νται

Imperfect

S. 1.	ἐ-τι-θέ-μην	ῑ̔-στά-μην	ἐ-δι-δό-μην (747 f)
2.	ἐ-τί-θε-σο	ῑ̔́-στα-σο	ἐ-δί-δο-σο
3.	ἐ-τί-θε-το	ῑ̔́-στα-το	ἐ-δί-δο-το
D. 2.	ἐ-τί-θε-σθον	ῑ̔́-στα-σθον	ἐ-δί-δο-σθον
3.	ἐ-τι-θέ-σθην	ῑ̔-στά-σθην	ἐ-δι-δό-σθην
P. 1.	ἐ-τι-θέ-μεθα	ῑ̔-στά-μεθα	ἐ-δι-δό-μεθα
2.	ἐ-τί-θε-σθε	ῑ̔́-στα-σθε	ἐ-δί-δο-σθε
3.	ἐ-τί-θε-ντο	ῑ̔́-στα-ντο	ἐ-δί-δο-ντο

MIDDLE AND PASSIVE — *Concluded*

Present Subjunctive

S.	1.	τι-θῶ-μαι	ἱ-στῶ-μαι	δι-δῶ-μαι
	2.	τι-θῇ	ἱ-στῇ	δι-δῷ
	3.	τι-θῆ-ται	ἱ-στῆ-ται	δι-δῶ-ται
D.	2.	τι-θῆ-σθον	ἱ-στῆ-σθον	δι-δῶ-σθον
	3.	τι-θῆ-σθον	ἱ-στῆ-σθον	δι-δῶ-σθον
P.	1.	τι-θώ-μεθα	ἱ-στώ-μεθα	δι-δώ-μεθα
	2.	τι-θῆ-σθε	ἱ-στῆ-σθε	δι-δῶ-σθε
	3.	τι-θῶ-νται	ἱ-στῶ-νται	δι-δῶ-νται

Present Optative

S.	1.	τι-θεί-μην	ἱ-σταί-μην	δι-δοί-μην
	2.	τι-θεῖ-ο	ἱ-σταῖ-ο	δι-δοῖ-ο
	3.	τι-θεῖ-το	ἱ-σταῖ-το	δι-δοῖ-το
D.	2.	τι-θεῖ-σθον	ἱ-σταῖ-σθον	δι-δοῖ-σθον
	3.	τι-θεί-σθην	ἱ-σταί-σθην	δι-δοί-σθην
P.	1.	τι-θεί-μεθα	ἱ-σταί-μεθα	δι-δοί-μεθα
	2.	τι-θεῖ-σθε	ἱ-σταῖ-σθε	δι-δοῖ-σθε
	3.	τι-θεῖ-ντο	ἱ-σταῖ-ντο	δι-δοῖ-ντο

or

S.	1.	τι-θεί-μην
	2.	τι-θεῖ-ο
	3.	τι-θοῖ-το (746 c)
D.	2.	τι-θοῖ-σθον
	3.	τι-θοί-σθην
P.	1.	τι-θοί-μεθα
	2.	τι-θοῖ-σθε
	3.	τι-θοῖ-ντο

Present Imperative

S.	2.	τί-θε-σο	ἵ-στα-σο	δί-δο-σο
	3.	τι-θέ-σθω	ἱ-στά-σθω	δι-δό-σθω
D.	2.	τί-θε-σθον	ἵ-στα-σθον	δί-δο-σθον
	3.	τι-θέ-σθων	ἱ-στά-σθων	δι-δό-σθων
P.	2.	τί-θε-σθε	ἵ-στα-σθε	δί-δο-σθε
	3.	τι-θέ-σθων	ἱ-στά-σθων	δι-δό-σθων

Present Infinitive

τί-θε-σθαι	ἵ-στα-σθαι	δί-δο-σθαι

Present Participle

τι-θέ-μενος	ἱ-στά-μενος	δι-δό-μενος

Second Aorist

Indicative

	Active	Middle	Active	Middle	Active	Middle
S. 1.	(ἔθηκα, 755)	ἐ-θέ-μην	ἔ-στη-ν *stood*	ἐπριάμην (415)	(ἔδωκα, 755)	ἐ-δό-μην (756 b)
2.	(ἔθηκας)	ἔ-θου	ἔ-στη-ς	ἐπρίω	(ἔδωκας)	ἔ-δου
3.	(ἔθηκε)	ἔ-θε-το	ἔ-στη	ἐπρίατο	(ἔδωκε)	ἔ-δο-το
D. 2.	ἔ-θε-τον	ἔ-θε-σθον	ἔ-στη-τον	ἐ-πρία-σθον	ἔ-δο-τον	ἔ-δο-σθον
3.	ἐ-θέ-την	ἐ-θέ-σθην	ἐ-στή-την	ἐ-πριά-σθην	ἐ-δό-την	ἐ-δό-σθην
P. 1.	ἔ-θε-μεν	ἐ-θέ-μεθα	ἔ-στη-μεν	ἐ-πριά-μεθα	ἔ-δο-μεν	ἐ-δό-μεθα
2.	ἔ-θε-τε	ἔ-θε-σθε	ἔ-στη-τε	ἐ-πρία-σθε	ἔ-δο-τε	ἔ-δο-σθε
3.	ἔ-θε-σαν	ἔ-θε-ντο	ἔ-στη-σαν	ἐ-πρία-ντο	ἔ-δο-σαν	ἔ-δο-ντο

Subjunctive

S. 1.	θῶ	θῶ-μαι	στῶ	πρίω-μαι (424, N. 2)	δῶ	δῶ-μαι
2.	θῇ-ς	θῇ	στῇ-ς	πρίῃ	δῷ-ς	δῷ
3.	θῇ	θῆ-ται	στῇ	πρίη-ται	δῷ	δῶ-ται
D. 2.	θῆ-τον	θῆ-σθον	στῆ-τον	πρίη-σθον	δῶ-τον	δῶ-σθον
3.	θῆ-τον	θῆ-σθον	στῆ-τον	πρίη-σθον	δῶ-τον	δῶ-σθον
P. 1.	θῶ-μεν	θώ-μεθα	στῶ-μεν	πριώ-μεθα	δῶ-μεν	δώ-μεθα
2.	θῆ-τε	θῆ-σθε	στῆ-τε	πρίη-σθε	δῶ-τε	δῶ-σθε
3.	θῶ-σι	θῶ-νται	στῶ-σι	πρίω-νται	δῶ-σι	δῶ-νται

Optative

S. 1.	θείη-ν	θεί-μην	σταίη-ν	πριαί-μην	δοίη-ν	δοί-μην
2.	θείη-ς	θεῖ-ο	σταίη-ς	πρίαι-ο (424, N. 2)	δοίη-ς	δοῖ-ο
3.	θείη	θεῖ-το, θοῖ-το	σταίη	πρίαι-το	δοίη	δοῖ-το
D. 2.	θεῖ-τον	θεῖ-σθον	σταῖ-τον	πρίαι-σθον	δοῖ-τον	δοῖ-σθον
3.	θεί-την	θεί-σθην	σταί-την	πριαί-σθην	δοί-την	δοί-σθην
P. 1.	θεῖ-μεν	θεί-μεθα	σταῖ-μεν	πριαί-μεθα	δοῖ-μεν	δοί-μεθα
2.	θεῖ-τε	θεῖ-σθε	σταῖ-τε	πρίαι-σθε	δοῖ-τε	δοῖ-σθε
3.	θεῖε-ν	θεῖ-ντο	σταῖε-ν	πρίαι-ντο	δοῖε-ν	δοῖ-ντο
	or (758)	or (746 c)	or (758)		or (758)	
D. 2.	θείη-τον		σταίη-τον		δοίη-τον	
3.	θειή-την		σταιή-την		δοιή-την	
P. 1.	θείη-μεν	θοίμεθα	σταίη-μεν		δοίη-μεν	
2.	θείη-τε	θοῖσθε	σταίη-τε		δοίη-τε	
3.	θείη-σαν	θοῖντο	σταίη-σαν		δοίη-σαν	

Second Aorist — *Concluded*

Imperative

S. 2.	θέ-ς	θοῦ	στῆ-θι	πρίω	δό-ς	δοῦ
3.	θέ-τω	θέ-σθω	στή-τω	πριά-σθω	δό-τω	δό-σθω
D. 2.	θέ-τον	θέ-σθον	στῆ-τον	πρία-σθον	δό-τον	δό-σθον
3.	θέ-των	θέ-σθων	στή-των	πριά-σθων	δό-των	δό-σθων
P. 2.	θέ-τε	θέ-σθε	στῆ-τε	πρία-σθε	δό-τε	δό-σθε
3.	θέ-ντων	θέ-σθων	στά-ντων	πριά-σθων	δό-ντων	δό-σθων

Infinitive

θεῖ-ναι	θέ-σθαι	στῆ-ναι	πρία-σθαι	δοῦ-ναι	δό-σθαι

Participle

θείς, θεῖσα, θέ-μενος, -η, στᾱ́ς, στᾶσα, πριά-μενος, -η, δούς, δοῦσα, δό-μενος,
θέ-ν (307) -ον στά-ν (306) -ον (287) δό-ν (307) -η, -ον

SECOND PERFECT OF μι-VERBS

417. A few verbs of the μι class have a second perfect and pluperfect. Only the dual and plural occur; for the singular, the first perfect and pluperfect are used. The second perfect and pluperfect of ἵστημι are inflected as follows:

Second Perfect

	Indicative	Subjunctive	Optative	Imperative
S. 1.	(ἕστηκα) *stand*	ἑ-στῶ	ἑ-σταίη-ν (poetic)	
2.	(ἕστηκας)	ἑ-στῇ-ς	ἑ-σταίη-ς	ἕ-στα-θι (poetic)
3.	(ἕστηκε)	ἑ-στῇ	ἑ-σταίη	ἑ-στά-τω
D. 2.	ἕ-στα-τον	ἑ-στῆ-τον	ἑ-σταῖ-τον or -αίητον (461 b)	ἕ-στα-τον
3.	ἕ-στα-τον	ἑ-στῆ-τον	ἑ-σταί-την or -αιήτην	ἑ-στά-των
P. 1.	ἕ-στα-μεν	ἑ-στῶ-μεν	ἑ-σταῖ-μεν or -αίημεν	
2.	ἕ-στα-τε	ἑ-στῆ-τε	ἑ-σταῖ-τε or -αίητε	ἕ-στα-τε
3.	ἑ-στᾶσι	ἑ-στῶ-σι	ἑ-σταῖε-ν or -αίησαν	ἑ-στά-ντων

Infinitive ἑ-στά-ναι Participle ἑ-στώ-ς, ἑ-στῶσα, ἑ-στός (309 a)

Second Pluperfect

S. 1. (εἱστήκη) *stood*	D. 2. ἕ-στα-τον	P. 1. ἕ-στα-μεν
2. (εἱστήκης)	3. ἑ-στά-την	2. ἕ-στα-τε
3. (εἱστήκει)		3. ἕ-στα-σαν

For a list of second perfects of the μι form, see 704–705.

418. (B) **-νῡμι Class.** — Inflection of the present system of **δείκνῡμι** *show* and of the second aorist **ἔδῡν** *entered.*

Indicative

	Active		Middle and Passive		Active
	Present	Imperfect	Present	Imperfect	2 Aorist
S. 1.	δείκ-νῡ-μι (746 a)	ἐ-δείκ-νῡ-ν (746 a)	δείκ-νυ-μαι	ἐ-δεικ-νύ-μην	ἔ-δῡ-ν (415)
2.	δείκ-νῡ-ς	ἐ-δείκ-νῡ-ς	δείκ-νυ-σαι	ἐ-δείκ-νυ-σο	ἔ-δῡ-ς
3.	δείκ-νῡ-σι	ἐ-δείκ-νῡ	δείκ-νυ-ται	ἐ-δείκ-νυ-το	ἔ-δῡ
D. 2.	δείκ-νυ-τον	ἐ-δείκ-νυ-τον	δείκ-νυ-σθον	ἐ-δείκ-νυ-σθον	ἔ-δῡ-τον
3.	δείκ-νυ-τον	ἐ-δεικ-νύ-την	δείκ-νυ-σθον	ἐ-δεικ-νύ-σθην	ἐ-δῡ́-την
P. 1.	δείκ-νυ-μεν	ἐ-δείκ-νυ-μεν	δεικ-νύ-μεθα	ἐ-δεικ-νύ-μεθα	ἔ-δῡ-μεν
2.	δείκ-νυ-τε	ἐ-δείκ-νυ-τε	δείκ-νυ-σθε	ἐ-δείκ-νυ-σθε	ἔ-δῡ-τε
3.	δεικ-νύ-ᾱσι	ἐ-δείκ-νυ-σαν	δείκ-νυ-νται	ἐ-δείκ-νυ-ντο	ἔ-δῡ-σαν

Subjunctive

S. 1.	δεικνύω	δεικνύωμαι	δύω
2.	δεικνύῃς	δεικνύῃ	δύῃς
3.	δεικνύῃ	δεικνύηται	δύῃ
D. 2.	δεικνύητον	δεικνύησθον	δύητον
3.	δεικνύητον	δεικνύησθον	δύητον
P. 1.	δεικνύωμεν	δεικνυώμεθα	δύωμεν
2.	δεικνύητε	δεικνύησθε	δύητε
3.	δεικνύωσι	δεικνύωνται	δύωσι

Optative

S. 1.	δεικνύοιμι	δεικνυοίμην
2.	δεικνύοις	δεικνύοιο
3.	δεικνύοι	δεικνύοιτο
D. 2.	δεικνύοιτον	δεικνύοισθον
3.	δεικνυοίτην	δεικνυοίσθην
P. 1.	δεικνύοιμεν	δεικνυοίμεθα
2.	δεικνύοιτε	δεικνύοισθε
3.	δεικνύοιεν	δεικνύοιντο

Imperative

S. 2.	δείκ-νῡ (746 a)	δείκ-νυ-σο	δῦ-θι
3.	δεικ-νύ-τω	δεικ-νύ-σθω	δῡ́-τω
D. 2.	δείκ-νυ-τον	δείκ-νυ-σθον	δῦ-τον
3.	δεικ-νύ-των	δεικ-νύ-σθων	δῡ́-των
P. 2.	δείκ-νυ-τε	δείκ-νυ-σθε	δῦ-τε
3.	δεικ-νύ-ντων	δεικ-νύ-σθων	δῡ́-ντων

Infinitive

δεικ-νύ-ναι (746 a)	δείκ-νυ-σθαι	δῦ-ναι

Participle

δεικ-νύς -ῦσα, -ύν (308, 746 a)	δεικ-νύ-μενος, -η, -ον	δῡ́ς, δῦσα, δύν (308)

419. Synopsis of **τίθημι** (*θε-, θη-*) *place*

	Pres. Act.	Impf. Act.	Fut. Act.	Aor. Act.	1 Perf. Act.	1 Plup. Act.
Ind.	**τίθημι**	**ἐτίθην**	**θήσω**	**ἔθηκα**	**τέθηκα**	**ἐτεθήκη**
Sub.	**τιθῶ**			**θῶ**	**τεθηκὼς ὦ**	
Opt.	**τιθείην**		**θήσοιμι**	**θείην**	**τεθηκὼς εἴην**	
Imp.	**τίθει**			**θές**		
Inf.	**τιθέναι**		**θήσειν**	**θεῖναι**	**τεθηκέναι**	
Par.	**τιθείς**		**θήσων**	**θείς**	**τεθηκώς**	
	Pres. M. P.	Impf. M. P.	Fut. Mid.	2 Aor. Mid.	Perf. M. P.	Plup. M. P.
Ind.	**τίθεμαι**	**ἐτιθέμην**	**θήσομαι**	**ἐθέμην**	**τέθειμαι**	**ἐτεθείμην**
Sub.	**τιθῶμαι**			**θῶμαι**	**τεθειμένος ὦ**	
Opt.	**τιθείμην**		**θησοίμην**	**θείμην**	**τεθειμένος εἴην**	
Imp.	**τίθεσο**			**θοῦ**	**τέθεισο**	
Inf.	**τίθεσθαι**		**θήσεσθαι**	**θέσθαι**	**τεθεῖσθαι**	
Par.	**τιθέμενος**		**θησόμενος**	**θέμενος**	**τεθειμένος**	
			1 Fut. Pass.	1 Aor. Pass.		
Ind.			**τεθήσομαι**	**ἐτέθην**		
Sub.				**τεθῶ**		
Opt.			**τεθησοίμην**	**τεθείην**		
Imp.				**τέθητι**		
Inf.			**τεθήσεσθαι**	**τεθῆναι**		
Par.			**τεθησόμενος**	**τεθείς**		

Verbal adjectives: **θετός, θετέος.**

420. Synopsis of **ἵστημι** (*στα-, στη-*) *set* (in perf. and 2 aor. *stand*)

	Pres. Impf. Act.	Fut. Act.	1 Aor. Act.	2 Aor. Act.	Perf. Plup. Act.
Ind.	**ἵστημι** *set*	**στήσω** *shall set*			**ἕστηκα** *stand*
	ἵστην		**ἔστησα** *set*	**ἔστην** *stood*	**εἱστήκη** *stood*
Sub.	**ἱστῶ**		**στήσω**	**στῶ**	**ἑστήκω, ἑστῶ**
Opt.	**ἱσταίην**	**στήσοιμι**	**στήσαιμι**	**σταίην**	**ἑστήκοιμι, ἑσταίην**
Imp.	**ἵστη**		**στῆσον**	**στῆθι**	**ἕσταθι**
Inf.	**ἱστάναι**	**στήσειν**	**στῆσαι**	**στῆναι**	**ἑστηκέναι, ἑστάναι**
Par.	**ἱστᾱ́ς**	**στήσων**	**στήσᾱς**	**στᾱ́ς**	**ἑστηκώς, ἑστώς**
	Pres. Impf. M. P.	Fut. Mid.	1 Aor. Mid.		Fut. Perf. Act.
Ind.	**ἵσταμαι** *stand*	**στήσομαι** (intrans.)			**ἑστήξω** *shall stand*
	ἱστάμην		**ἐστησάμην** (trans.)		
Sub.	**ἱστῶμαι**		**στήσωμαι**		
Opt.	**ἱσταίμην**	**στησοίμην**	**στησαίμην**		**ἑστήξοιμι**
Imp.	**ἵστασο**		**στῆσαι**		
Inf.	**ἵστασθαι**	**στήσεσθαι**	**στήσασθαι**		**ἑστήξειν**
Par.	**ἱστάμενος**	**στησόμενος**	**στησάμενος**		**ἑστήξων**
		1 Fut. Pass.	1 Aor. Pass.		
Ind.		**σταθήσομαι** *shall be set up*	**ἐστάθην** *was set*		
Sub.			**σταθῶ**		
Opt.		**σταθησοίμην**	**σταθείην**		
Imp.			**στάθητι**		
Inf.		**σταθήσεσθαι**	**σταθῆναι**		
Par.		**σταθησόμενος**	**σταθείς**		

Verbal adjectives: **στατός, στατέος.**

421. Synopsis of **δίδωμι** (*δο-, δω-*) *give*

	Pres. Act.	Impf. Act.	Fut. Act.	Aor. Act.	1 Perf. Act.	1 Plup. Act.
Ind.	δίδωμι	ἐδίδουν	δώσω	ἔδωκα	δέδωκα	ἐδεδώκη
Sub.	διδῶ			δῶ	δεδωκὼς ὦ	
Opt.	διδοίην		δώσοιμι	δοίην	δεδωκὼς εἴην	
Imp.	δίδου			δός		
Inf.	διδόναι		δώσειν	δοῦναι	δεδωκέναι	
Par.	διδούς		δώσων	δούς	δεδωκώς	
	Pres. M. P.	Impf. M. P.	Fut. Mid.	2 Aor. Mid.	Perf. M. P.	Plup. M. P.
Ind.	δίδομαι	ἐδιδόμην	δώσομαι	ἐδόμην	δέδομαι	ἐδεδόμην
Sub.	διδῶμαι			δῶμαι	δεδομένος ὦ	
Opt.	διδοίμην		δωσοίμην	δοίμην	δεδομένος εἴην	
Imp.	δίδοσο			δοῦ	δέδοσο	
Inf.	δίδοσθαι		δώσεσθαι	δόσθαι	δεδόσθαι	
Par.	διδόμενος		δωσόμενος	δόμενος	δεδομένος	
			1 Fut. Pass.	1 Aor. Pass.		
Ind.			δοθήσομαι	ἐδόθην		
Sub.				δοθῶ		
Opt.				δοθείην		
Imp.			δοθησοίμην	δόθητι		
Inf.			δοθήσεσθαι	δοθῆναι		
Par.			δοθησόμενος	δοθείς		

Verbal adjectives: **δοτός, δοτέος**

422. Synopsis of **δείκνῡμι** (*δεικ-*) *show*

	Pres. Act.	Impf. Act.	Fut. Act.	1 Aor. Act.	1 Perf. Act.	1 Plup. Act.
Ind.	δείκνῡμι	ἐδείκνῡν	δείξω	ἔδειξα	δέδειχα	ἐδεδείχη
Sub.	δεικνύω			δείξω	δεδειχὼς ὦ	
Opt.	δεικνύοιμι		δείξοιμι	δείξαιμι	δεδειχὼς εἴην	
Imp.	δείκνῡ			δεῖξον		
Inf.	δεικνύναι		δείξειν	δεῖξαι	δεδειχέναι	
Par.	δεικνῡ́ς		δείξων	δείξᾱς	δεδειχώς	
	Pres. M. P.	Impf. M. P.	Fut. Mid.	1 Aor. Mid.	Perf. Mid.	Plup. Mid.
Ind.	δείκνυμαι	ἐδεικνύμην	δείξομαι	ἐδειξάμην	δέδειγμαι	ἐδεδείγμην
Sub.	δεικνύωμαι			δείξωμαι	δεδειγμένος ὦ	
Opt.	δεικνυοίμην		δειξοίμην	δειξαίμην	δεδειγμένος εἴην	
Imp.	δείκνυσο			δεῖξαι	δέδειξο	
Inf.	δείκνυσθαι		δείξεσθαι	δείξασθαι	δεδεῖχθαι	
Par.	δεικνύμενος		δειξόμενος	δειξάμενος	δεδειγμένος	
			Fut. Pass.	1 Aor. Pass.		
Ind.			δειχθήσομαι	ἐδείχθην		
Sub.				δειχθῶ		
Opt.			δειχθησοίμην	δειχθείην		
Imp.				δείχθητι		
Inf.			δειχθήσεσθαι	δειχθῆναι		
Par.			δειχθησόμενος	δειχθείς		

Verbal adjectives: **δεικτός, δεικτέος**

ACCENT

423. Simple or compound verbs usually throw the accent as far back as the quantity of the last syllable permits (recessive accent, 159).

λύω, λύομεν, ἐλῡόμην; παιδεύω, παιδεύουσι, ἐπαιδευέτην; ἀποβάλλω, ἀπόβαλλε; ἀπολύω, ἀπέλῡον; ἄπειμι, σύνεσμεν, σύμφημι, πάρεστι.

424. To this general rule there are exceptions.

a. Enclitics. — All the forms of φημί *say*, and εἰμί *am*, except φῄς and εἶ.

b. Imperatives. — (1) The second person sing. of the second aorist active imperative of five verbs is oxytone: εἰπέ *say*, ἐλθέ *come*, εὑρέ *find*, ἰδέ *see*, λαβέ *take*. Their plurals are accented εἰπέτε, ἐλθέτε, etc.; compounds have recessive accent: κάτειπε, ἄπελθε, ἔφευρε, παράλαβε.

(2) The second aorist middle (2 sing.) is perispomenon, as λαβοῦ, παραβαλοῦ, καθελοῦ.

c. Contracted verbs are only apparent exceptions: thus, *e.g.*, τῑμᾷ for τῑμάει, δηλοῦσι for δηλόουσι, φιλεῖν for φιλέειν. So the subjunctive of the first and second aorist passive λυθῶ for λυθέω, φανῶ for φανέω; the optatives λυθεῖμεν from λυθέ-ῑ-μεν, διδοῖμεν from διδό-ῑ-μεν; the futures φανῶ for φανέω, φανοῖμι for φανέοιμι, φανεῖν for φανέειν, φανῶν for φανέων; λιπεῖν for λιπέεν; and the present and second aorist active and middle subjunctive of most μι-verbs, as τιθῶ for τιθέω, ἱστῶμαι, θῶμαι, perf. κεκτῶμαι. On διδοῦσι, τιθεῖσι, see 463 d.

N. 1. — In athematic optatives the accent does not recede beyond the diphthong containing -ῑ-, the sign of the optative mood: ἱσταῖο, ἱσταῖμεν, ἱσταῖτο, διδοῖτο; and so in λυθεῖμεν, λυθεῖεν.

N. 2. — δύναμαι *am able*, ἐπίσταμαι *understand*, κρέμαμαι *hang*, ὀνίνημι *profit*, and ἐπριάμην *bought* (749 b, 750 b, 757 a) have recessive accent in the subjunctive and optative (δύνωμαι, ἐπίστωμαι, δύναιτο, κρέμαιτο).

d. Poetic forms sometimes fail to follow the rule, as ἐών *being*.

425. Infinitives, participles, and verbal adjectives are verbal nouns (358), and hence do not regularly show recessive accent.

a. Infinitives. — The following infinitives accent the penult: all infinitives in -ναι, as λελυκέναι, λυθῆναι, ἱστάναι, στῆναι (except Epic -μεναι, as στήμεναι); in verbs in ω the first aorist active, as λῦσαι, παιδεῦσαι, the second aorist middle, as λιπέσθαι, the perfect (middle) passive, as λελύσθαι, πεπαιδεῦσθαι, πεποιῆσθαι.

N. — The present inf. of contracted verbs and the second aorist active inf. of ω-verbs have the perispomenon by 424 c.

b. Participles. — (1) Oxytone: the masculine and neuter sing. of the second aorist active, as λιπών, λιπόν; and of all participles of the third declension ending in -ς in the masculine (except the first aorist active), as λυθείς λυθέν, λελυκώς λελυκός, ἑστώς ἑστός, τιθείς τιθέν, διδούς διδόν, ἱστάς ἱστάν, δεικνύς δεικνύν (but λύσᾱς, ποιήσᾱς). Also ἰών *going* from εἶμι.

---

425 a. D. The 2. aor. mid. inf. in Hom. is recessive in ἀγέρεσθαι (ἀγείρω *assemble*); so the perf. ἀλάλησθαι (ἀλάομαι *wander*), ἀκάχησθαι (ἄχνυμαι *am distressed*).

(2) Paroxytone: the perfect middle (passive): λελυμένος.

N. — Participles are accented like adjectives, not like verbs. The fem. and neuter nom. accent the same syllable as the masc. nom. if the quantity of the ultima permits, thus παιδεύων, παιδεύουσα, παιδεῦον (not παίδευον); ποιήσᾱς, ποιήσᾱσα, ποιῆσαν (not ποίησαν); φιλῶν, φιλοῦσα, φιλοῦν (from φιλέον).

c. **Verbal Adjectives.** — The verbal adjective in -τος is accented on the ultima (λυτός); that in -τεος on the penult (λυτέος).

N. — Prepositional compounds in -τος denoting possibility generally accent the last syllable and have three endings (286), as διαλυτός *dissoluble*, ἐξαιρετός *removable*. Such compounds as have the force of a perfect passive participle accent the antepenult and have two endings, as διάλυτος *dissolved*, ἐξαίρετος *chosen*. All other compounds in -τος accent the antepenult and have two endings, as ἄβατος *impassable*, χειροποίητος *artificial*.

426. Exceptions to the recessive accent of compound verbs. — a. The accent cannot precede the augment or reduplication: ἄπειμι *am absent*, ἀπῆν *was absent*, εἰσ-ῆλθον *they entered*, ἀπ-ῆσαν *they were absent*; ἀφ-ῖκται *arrived* (cp. ἶκται).

N. — A long vowel or diphthong not changed by the augment receives the accent: ὑπ-εῖκε *was yielding* (indic. ὑπ-είκω, imper. ὕπ-εικε).

b. The accent cannot precede the last syllable of the preposition before the simple verb nor move back to the first of two prepositions: περίθες *put around*, συνέκδος *give up together* (not σύνεκδος), συγκάθες *put down together* (not σύγκαθες). Compounds of the second aorist active imperatives δός, ἕς, θές, and σχές are thus paroxytone: ἐπίθες *set on*, περίθες *put around*, ἐπίσχες *hold on*.

c. When compounded with a monosyllabic preposition, monosyllabic second aorist middle imperatives in -οῦ from μι-verbs retain the circumflex: προδοῦ *betray*, ἐνθοῦ *put in*. But the accent recedes when these imperatives prefix a dissyllabic preposition: ἀπόδου *sell*, κατάθου *put down*. The open forms always have recessive accent, as ἔνθεο, κατάθεο.

d. The accent of uncompounded infinitives, participles, aorist passive, perfect passive, and of the second aorist middle imperative (2. p. sing., but see 426 c) is retained in composition.

e. ἀπέσται *will be far from*, ἐπέσται *will be upon* do not have recessive accent.

f. Compound subjunctives are differently accentuated in the Mss.: ἀποδῶμαι and ἀπόδωμαι, ἐπιθῆται and ἐπίθηται; the aorist of ἵημι has προῶμαι and πρόωμαι. ἀπέχω has ἀπόσχωμαι. Compound optatives retain the accent of the primitives: ἀποδοῖτο, as δοῖτο. For συνθοῖτο, προσθοῖσθε (746 c) the Mss. occasionally have σύνθοιτο, πρόσθοισθε; and so πρόοιτο.

427. Final -αι (and -οι) are regarded as long in the optative (169), elsewhere as short. Hence distinguish the forms of the first aorist.

	3. Sing. Opt. Act.	Infin. Act.	2. Sing. Imper. Mid.
λύ́ω	λύ́σαι	λῦσαι	λῦσαι
ἀπολύ́ω	ἀπολύ́σαι	ἀπολῦσαι	ἀπόλῡσαι
παιδεύω	παιδεύσαι	παιδεῦσαι	παίδευσαι

---

425 b (2) D. But Hom. has ἀλαλήμενος (ἀλάομαι *wander*), ἀκαχήμενος or ἀκηχέμενος (ἄχνυμαι *am distressed*), ἐσσύμενος (σεύω *drive*).

AUGMENT

428. The augment (*increase*) denotes past time. It appears only in the secondary or past tenses of the indicative mood, namely, imperfect, aorist, and pluperfect. The augment has two forms, the syllabic and the temporal.

429. Syllabic Augment. — Verbs beginning with a consonant prefix ε as the augment, which thus increases the word by one syllable. In the pluperfect ε is prefixed to the reduplication.

λύω	*loose*	ἔ-λῡον	ἔ-λῡσα	ἐ-λελύκη
παιδεύω	*educate*	ἐ-παίδευον	ἐ-παίδευσα	ἐ-πεπαιδεύκη

a. Verbs beginning with ρ double the ρ after the augment. ῥίπτω *throw*, ἔ-ρρῑπτον, ἔ-ρρῑψα, ἐ-ρρίφθην; ῥήγνῡμι *break*, ἔ-ρρηξα, ἐ-ρράγην.

N. — ρρ is here due to assimilation of ϝρ, as in Hom. ἔρρεξα *did* (and ἔρεξα); of σρ in ἔρρεον *flowed*. Cp. 80 a.

430. βούλομαι *wish*, δύναμαι *am able*, μέλλω *intend* augment with ε or with η (especially in later Attic); thus, ἐβουλόμην and ἠβουλόμην, ἐδυνάμην and ἠδυνάμην, ἐδυνήθην and ἠδυνήθην.

a. These forms seem to be due to parallelism with ἤθελον (from ἐθέλω *wish*) and ἔθελον (from θέλω).

431. Some verbs beginning with a vowel take the syllabic augment because they formerly began with a consonant. Thus,

ἄγνῡμι *break* (**ϝάγνῡμι**), **ἔᾱξα**, aor. pass. **ἐάγην**.
ἁλίσκομαι *am captured* (**ϝαλίσκομαι**), imperf. **ἡλισκόμην**, aor. **ἑάλων** (with temporal augment) or **ἥλων**.
ἁνδάνω *please* (**ϝανδάνω**), aor. **ἕαδον** (Ionic).
ἀν-οίγω *open* (**ϝοίγνῡμι**), imperf. **ἀν-έῳγον**.
ἐάω *permit* (**σεϝαω**), **εἴων**, **εἴᾱσα**, **εἰάθην**.
ἕζομαι *sit* (for **σεδι̯ομαι**), **εἱσάμην**.
ἐθίζω *accustom* (**σϝεθίζω**, cp. 123), **εἴθιζον**, **εἴθισα**, **εἰθίσθην**.
ἑλίττω *roll* (**ϝελίττω**), **εἵλιττον**, **εἵλιξα**, **εἱλίχθην**.
ἕλκω or ἑλκύω *draw* (**σελκω**), **εἷλκον**, **εἵλκυσα**, **εἱλκύσθην**.
ἕπομαι *follow* (**σεπομαι**), **εἱπόμην**.
ἐργάζομαι *work* (**ϝεργάζομαι**), **εἰργασάμην**.
ἕρπω *creep* (**σερπω**), **εἷρπον**.
ἑστιάω *entertain* (**ϝεστίαω**), **εἱστίων**, **εἱστίᾱσα**, **εἱστιάθην**.

---

429 a. D. Hom. has ἔλλαβε *took* (for ἐ-σλαβε), ἔννεον *swam* (for ἐ-σνεον), ἐσσείοντο *shook* (for ἐ-τϝειοντο), ἔδδεισε *feared* (for ἐ-δϝεισε). ἔμμαθε *learned* is due to analogy.

431 D. Syllabic augment in Homer before a vowel is a sure proof of initial ϝ in ἔειπον and some other verbs. Similar Ionic and poetic forms occur from εἶδον, εἴλω, εἴρω, ἔλπω, ἕννῡμι, ἔρδω, οἰνοχοέω, etc.

ἔχω *hold* (σεχω), εἶχον.
ἵημι *send* (σισημι), aor. du. εἷτον for ἑ-ἑ-τον, εἵθην for ἑ-ἑ-θην.
ἵστημι *put* (σιστημι), plup. εἱστήκη for ἑ-σε-στηκη.
ὁράω *see* (ϝοράω), ἑώρων, ἑώρᾱκα or ἑόρᾱκα.
ὠθέω *push* (ϝωθέω), ἐώθουν, ἔωσα, ἐώσθην.
ὠνέομαι *buy* (ϝωνέομαι), ἐωνούμην, ἐωνήθην.
εἶδον *saw*, 2 aor. of ὁράω (for ἑ-ϝιδον).
εἷλον *took*, 2 aor. of αἱρέω (for ἑ-ἑλον).

432. Some forms of some verbs in 431 are augmented as if no consonant had preceded the first vowel, as ἠργαζόμην (and εἰργαζόμην).

433. Since ϝ disappeared early, many augmented forms show no trace of its existence, as, ᾤκουν from οἰκέω *dwell* (ϝοῖκος). Besides ε, η was also used as the syllabic augment. This appears in Hom. ἠ-είδεις (-ης ?), Attic ᾔδεις *you knew*.

434. The verbs ἄγνῡμι, ἁλίσκομαι, (ἀν)οίγνῡμι, ὁράω, which began originally with ϝ, show forms that appear to have a double augment; as ἐάγην, ἑάλων, (ἀν)έῳγον (rarely ἤνοιγον), ἑώρων, ἑώρᾱκα (and ἑόρᾱκα). These forms appear to be due to transference of quantity (34) from ἠ-ϝάγην, ἠ-ϝοιγον, ἠ-ϝορων (cp. 433).

435. Temporal Augment. — Verbs beginning with a vowel take the temporal augment by lengthening the initial vowel. The temporal augment is so called because it usually increases the *time* required to pronounce the initial syllable. Diphthongs lengthen their first vowel.

α becomes η:	ἄγω *lead*	ἦγον		ἦχα	ἤχη
ε " η:	ἐλπίζω *hope*	ἤλπιζον	ἤλπισα	ἤλπικα	ἠλπίκη
ι " ῑ:	ἱκετεύω *supplicate*	ῑ̔κέτευον	ῑ̔κέτευσα	ῑ̔κέτευκα	ῑ̔κετεύκη
ο " ω:	ὁρίζω *mark off*	ὥριζον	ὥρισα	ὥρικα	ὡρίκη
υ " ῡ:	ὑβρίζω *insult*	ὕβριζον	ὕβρισα	ὕβρικα	ὑβρίκη
αι " ῃ:	αἱρέω *seize*	ᾕρουν		ᾕρηκα	ᾑρήκη
αυ " ηυ:	αὐλέω *play the flute*	ηὔλουν	ηὔλησα	ηὔληκα	ηὐλήκη
ει " ῃ:	εἰκάζω *liken*	ᾔκαζον	ᾔκασα		
ευ " ηυ:	εὔχομαι *pray*	ηὐχόμην	ηὐξάμην	ηὖγμαι	ηὔγμην
οι " ῳ:	οἰκέω *dwell*	ᾤκουν	ᾤκησα	ᾤκηκα	ᾠκήκη

436. Initial ᾳ becomes ῃ: ᾄδω *sing*, ᾖδον. Initial η, ῑ, ῡ, ω remain unchanged. Initial ᾱ usually becomes η: ἀριστάω *breakfast*, ἠρίστησα. ἀνᾱλίσκω and ἀνᾱλόω *expend* form ἀνάλωσα and ἀνήλωσα, ἀνᾱλώθην and ἀνηλώθην.

437. Initial diphthongs are sometimes unaugmented: **αυ** in αὐαίνομαι *dry*; **ει**: εἴκαζον, ᾔκαζον; **ευ**: εὑρέθην and ηὑρέθην from εὑρίσκω *find*, εὐξάμην and ηὐξάμην from εὔχομαι *pray*; **ου** is never augmented, since it is never a pure diphthong when standing at the beginning of a verb-form.

---

435 D. Initial α becomes ᾱ in Doric and Aeolic; initial αι and αυ remain.

438. Omission of the Augment. — **a.** In Attic tragedy the augment is sometimes omitted in choral passages, rarely in the dialogue parts (messengers' speeches), which are nearer akin to prose.

b. In χρῆν (from χρή + ἦν) the augment is strictly unnecessary, but is often added (ἐχρῆν) since the composition of χρῆν was forgotten.

c. In Homer and the lyric poets either the syllabic or the temporal augment is often absent; as φάτο and ἔφατο, βῆν and ἔβην, ἔχον and εἶχον. Iteratives (495) in Hom. usually have no augment (ἔχεσκον).

N. — In Homer the absence of the augment represents the usage of the parent language, in which the augment was not necessarily added to mark past time. It is therefore erroneous, historically, to speak of the *omission* of the augment in Homer.

d. In Herodotus the syllabic augment is omitted only in the case of pluperfects and iteratives in σκον; the temporal augment is generally preserved, but it is always omitted in verbs beginning with αι, αυ, ει, ευ, οι, and in ἀγῑνέω, ἀεθλέω, ἀνώγω, ἔρδω, ἐάω, ὁρμέω, etc.; in others it is omitted only in some forms (as ἀγορεύω, ἄγω, ἕλκω, ὁρμάω), and in others it is variable (ἀγγέλλω, ἅπτω, ἄρχω, ἐπίσταμαι, ἀνέχομαι); in cases of Attic reduplication the augment is never added. Hdt. omits the augment for the reduplication in the above verbs.

REDUPLICATION

439. Reduplication is the doubling of the sound standing at the beginning of a word. It is used in the perfect, pluperfect, and future perfect tenses in all the moods, to denote completed action. It is sometimes found also in the present and second aorist.

440. Verbs beginning with a simple consonant (except ρ) or with a stop and a liquid (λ, μ, ν, ρ) place the initial consonant with ε before the stem. λύω *loose*, λέ-λυκα, λε-λυκέναι, λέ-λυμαι, λε-λύσομαι; γράφω *write*, γέ-γραφα; κλίνω *incline*, κέ-κλικα; βλάπτω *injure*, βέ-βλαφα; πρίω *saw*, πέ-πρῑσμαι.

a. Exceptions: verbs beginning with γν, most of those with γλ, and some with βλ. Thus, γνωρίζω *recognize*, ἐ-γνώρικα; γι-γνώσκω *know*, ἔ-γνωκα; γλύφω *carve*, ἔ-γλυφα; βλαστάνω *sprout*, ἐ-βλάστηκα (usu. βεβλάστηκα).

441. An initial aspirate is reduplicated by the corresponding smooth stop: φονεύω *murder*, πε-φόνευκα; θύω *sacrifice*, τέ-θυκα; χορεύω *dance*, κε-χόρευκα.

442. In all other cases the reduplication is formed like the augment.

a. Verbs beginning with a short vowel lengthen the vowel, as ἄγω *lead*, ἦχα; ὀρθόω *set upright*, ὤρθωκα; ἀγγέλλω *announce*, ἤγγελκα.

b. Verbs beginning with two or more consonants (except a stop with a liquid), a double consonant, and ρ simply prefix ε. ρ is here doubled (cp. 429 a).

---

439 D. Reduplication (or the augment for the reduplication) is generally retained in Hom. Exceptions are ἔρχαται and ἔρχατο from ἔργω *shut*, ἄνωγα *order*, ἕσται from ἕννῡμι *clothe*. On δέχαται *await*, ἐδέγμην *was expecting* cp. 634.

442. b. D. Hom. has ῥε-ρυπωμένος (ῥυπόω *soil*), ἔμμορε (μείρομαι *obtain*) for ἐ-σμορε 445 a, ἔσσυμαι (σεύω *urge*) for ἐ-κι̯υ-μαι; Ionic has ἔκτημαι.

Thus, **κτίζω** *found*, **ἔ-κτικα**; **σπείρω** *sow*, **ἔ-σπαρμαι**; **στρατηγέω** *am general*, **ἐ-στρατήγηκα**; **ζητέω** *seek*, **ἐ-ζήτηκα**; **ψαύω** *touch*, **ἔ-ψαυκα**; **ῥίπτω** *throw*, **ἔρρῖφα**.

N. — **μιμνήσκω** *remind* and **κτάομαι** *acquire* are exceptions: **μέ-μνημαι**, **ἐ-με-μνήμην**; **κέ-κτημαι**, **ἐ-κε-κτήμην**.

443. The verbs mentioned in 431 which originally began with a consonant now lost, reduplicate regularly. Since the reduplicated consonant has disappeared only **ε** is left, and this often contracts with the initial vowel of the theme. Thus, **ἔᾱγα** for **ϝε-ϝᾱγα** from **ϝάγνῡμι** *break*; **ἔωσμαι** for **ϝε-ϝωσμαι** from **ϝωθέω** *push*; **ἕστηκα** for **σεστηκα** from **ἵστημι** *set*; **εἷκα** for **σεσεκα** from **ἵημι** (**σι-σημι**) *send*.

444. Pluperfect. — The pluperfect prefixes the syllabic augment **ε** to the reduplicated perfect beginning with a consonant; when the perfect stem begins with a vowel the pluperfect retains the prefix of the perfect.

Thus perf. **λέλυκα**, **λέλυμαι**, plup. **ἐ-λελύκη**, **ἐ-λελύμην**; perf. **ἔ-σταλκα**, **ἔ-σταλμαι**, plup. **ἐ-στάλκη**, **ἐ-στάλμην** from **στέλλω** *send*; perf. **ἠγόρευκα**, plup. **ἠγορεύκη** from **ἀγορεύω** *harangue*; perf. **ᾕρηκα**, plup. **ᾑρήκη** from **αἱρέω** *seize*.

a. Verbs showing 'Attic' reduplication (446), in almost all cases augment the pluperfect.

b. The verbs of 431 follow the perfects of 443; as **ἐάγη** (**ἄγνῡμι**), **ἐώσμην** (**ὠθέω**), **εἵμην** (**ἵημι**), **ἐρρώγη** from (**ϝ**)**ρήγνῡμι**. **ἵστημι** forms **εἱστήκη** (= **ἐ-(σ)εστηκη**), Ion. and poet. **ἑστήκη** (rare in Att. prose). **ἔοικα** *am like* forms **ἐῴκη**.

445. Some verbs beginning with a liquid or **μ** take **ει** instead of the reduplication: **λαμβάνω** (**λαβ-**) *take*, **εἴ-ληφα**, **εἴ-λημμαι**, **εἰ-λήφη**; **λαγχάνω** (**λαχ-**) *obtain by lot*, **εἴ-ληχα**, **εἰ-λήχη**; **λέγω** *collect* (in composition) **-εἴ-λοχα**, **-ει-λόχη**, **-εἴ-λεγμαι** (rarely **λέ-λεγμαι**); **μείρομαι** *receive a share*, **εἴ-μαρται** *it is fated*, **εἵ-μαρτο** with rough breathing; also the stems **ερ**, **ρη** *say*, **εἴ-ρηκα**, **εἰ-ρήκη**.

a. **εἴληφα** is from **σε-σληφα** by 37 (cp. Hom. **ἔλλαβον** for **ἐ-σλαβον**), **εἵμαρται** is from **σε-σμαρται** (cp. Hom. **ἔμμορε**). The other forms are probably analogues of **εἴληφα**.

446. Attic Reduplication. — Some verbs whose themes begin with **α**, **ε**, or **ο**, followed by a single consonant, reduplicate by repeating the initial vowel and the consonant and by lengthening **α** and **ε** to **η**, **ο** to **ω**. Thus ἀγείρω *collect*, ἀγ-ήγερκα, ἀγ-ήγερμαι; ἐγείρω *awaken*,

---

444 b. D. Hdt. has **οἶκα** (for **ἔοικα**), **ἔωθα**, **ἐώθεα**; Hom. has **ἔωθεν** and **εἰώθε**.

445 D. Hom. **δείδω** *fear* stands for **δε-δϝω** from **δε-δϝο(ι̯)α** (cp. **δϝέος**). So **δείδοικα** for **δε-δϝοικα**. For **δείδεκτο** *greeted* we should read **δήδεκτο** with **η**-reduplication. Hdt. has **λελάβηκα** and **-λελαμμένος**. **λέλημμαι** occurs in tragedy.

446 D. — In Hom. 'Attic' reduplication is even more frequent than in Attic; thus, **ἐδηδώς** from **ἔδω** *eat*, **ἐρήριπα** *have fallen*, **ἐρέριπτο** (without lengthening) from **ἐρείπω** *overthrow*, **ὀρωρέχαται** from **ὀρέγω** *reach*. For other poetical forms see in the List of Verbs **ἀγείρω**, **αἱρέω**, **ἀλάομαι**, **ἀραρίσκω**, **ἐρείδω**, **ἐρίζω**, **ἔχω**, **ὄζω**, **ὀράω**, **ὄρνῡμι**.

ἐγ-ήγερμαι; ἐλέγχω *confute*, ἐλ-ήλεγμαι; ὀρύττω *dig*, ὀρ-ώρυχα, ὀρ-ώρυγμαι; ὄμ-νῡμι *swear*, ὀμ-ώμοκα; ὄλ-λῡμι *destroy*, ὀλ-ώλεκα. So also φέρω *bear*, ἐν-ήνοχα, ἐν-ήνεγμαι.

a. The name 'Attic' was given by the Greek grammarians to this form of reduplication though it occurs in Homer and in the other dialects.

b. ἀκούω *hear* has ἀκ-ήκοα for ἀκ-ήκο(ϝ)α; ἄγω has ἀγ-ήοχα for ἀγ-ή(γ)οχα. The pluperfect augments except in the case of verbs with initial ε: ἠκ-ηκόη, ὠμ-ωμόκη, ἀπωλώλη; but ἐλ-ηλύθη, ἐν-ηνέγμην.

447. Reduplication in the Present. — A few verbs reduplicate in the present by prefixing the initial consonant and ι, as γί-γνομαι, γι-γνώσκω, μι-μνῄσκω, τί-κτω for τι-τ(ε)κω, πί-πτω for πι-π(ε)τω, ἵ-στημι for σι-στημι, τί-θημι for θι-θημι (125 a), δί-δωμι. πίμ-πλη-μι *fill* (πλα-, πλη-) and πίμπρημι *burn* (πρα-, πρη-) insert μ.

a. In some verbs the reduplication belongs to the verbal stem: βιβάζω *make go* ἐβίβασα, διδάσκω *teach* ἐδίδαξα.

448. Reduplication in the Second Aorist. — ἄγω *lead* forms the second aorist ἤγ-αγον, ἀγ-άγω, ἀγ-άγοιμι, ἀγ-αγεῖν, middle ἠγ-αγόμην. So also ἤν-εγκα and ἤν-εγκον from φέρω.

POSITION OF AUGMENT AND REDUPLICATION IN COMPOUND VERBS

449. In verbs compounded with a preposition, augment and reduplication stand between the preposition and the verb.

Thus, ὑπερβαίνω *pass over*, ὑπερέβαινον, ὑπερβέβηκα; εἰσβάλλω *throw into*, εἰσέβαλλον, εἰσβέβληκα.

a. Before ε of the augment ἐκ regains its fuller form ἐξ (133 a), and ἐν and σύν reappear in their proper forms which were modified in the present. Thus ἐκβάλλω *throw out*, ἐξέβαλλον, ἐκβέβληκα; ἐμβάλλω *throw into*, ἐνέβαλλον; συλλέγω *collect*, συνέλεγον, συνείλοχα; συρρίπτω *throw together*, συνέρρῑψα, συνέρρῑφα; συσκευάζω *pack together*, συνεσκεύαζον, συνεσκευάσθην.

b. Prepositions (except περί and πρό) drop their final vowel: ἀποβάλλω *throw away*, ἀπ-έβαλλον; but περιβάλλω *throw around*, περιέβαλλον, προβαίνω *step forward*, προέβην. But πρό may contract with the augment (προὔβην).

450. But some verbs, which are not often used except as compounds, are treated like uncompound verbs and take the augment before the preposition, as ἐκαθήμην *sat* from κάθημαι, ἐκάθιζον *set*, *sat* from καθίζω, ἠμφίεσα *clothed* from ἀμφιέννῡμι, ἐκάθευδον (and καθηῦδον) *slept* from καθεύδω, ἠπιστάμην, ἠπιστήθην from ἐπίσταμαι *understand*. ἵημι forms ἀφίει and ἠφίει. The simple verbs occur mostly in poetry. But ἀπολαύω *enjoy* makes ἀπολέλαυκα, ἐξετάζω *review* ἐξήτακα.

---

448 D. Hom. has many reduplicated second aorists, as πέ-πιθον from πείθω (πιθ-) *persuade*, κεκλόμην, κε-κλόμενος from κέλομαι *command*, λε-λαθέσθαι from λανθάνω (λαθ-) *escape the notice of*, πε-φιδέσθαι from φείδομαι (φιδ-) *spare*, ἤρ-αρον from ἀραρίσκω (ἀρ-) *join*, ὤρ-ορον from ὄρνῡμι *arouse*. The indicative forms may take the syllabic augment, as in ἐ-πέ-φραδον from φράζω (φραδ-) *tell*. From ἐνίπτω *chide* and ἐρύκω *check* come ἠνίπαπον and ἐνένῑπον, and ἠρύκακον.

451. Double Augment. — Some verbs take two augments, one before and the other after the preposition, as ἠν-ειχόμην, ἠν-εσχόμην from ἀν-έχομαι *endure*, ἠν-ώχλουν from ἐνοχλέω *annoy*, ἐπηνώρθωμαι from ἐπανορθόω *set upright*. So also, by analogy to the foregoing, a few verbs derived from compound words: ἠμφεσβήτουν from ἀμφισβητέω *dispute*, ἠντεδίκει from ἀντιδικέω *go to law* (ἀντίδικος).

452. Compounds of **δυσ-** *ill* and **εὖ** *well*. (1) δυστυχέω *am unhappy*, ἐ-δυσ-τύχουν, δε-δυσ-τύχηκα. δυσ-ηρέστουν, δυσ-ηρέστηκα from δυσ-αρεστέω do not occur. (2) εὐεργετέω *do good*, εὐεργέτησαν, εὐεργέτηκα (inscrip.), εὐηργέτηκα (texts).

453. Verbs derived from compound nouns take the augment and the reduplication at the beginning; as ἐμυθολόγουν, μεμυθολόγηκα from μυθολογέω *tell legends* (μυθολόγος *teller of legends*); ᾠκοδόμουν, ᾠκοδόμηκα from οἰκοδομέω *build* (οἰκοδόμος *house-builder*); ἠμπόλων, ἠμπόληκα from ἐμπολάω *traffic in* (ἐμπολή *traffic*).

a. ἐκκλησιάζω *hold an assembly* (ἐκκλησίᾱ) makes ἠκ-κλησίαζον or ἐξ-ε-κλησίαζον. ἐγγυάω *pledge* makes ἐνεγύων, ἐνεγύησα and (better) ἠγγύων, ἠγγύησα.

454. Verbs derived from compound nouns whose first part is a preposition are commonly treated as if compounded of a preposition and a simple verb; as κατηγορέω *accuse* (κατήγορος), κατηγόρουν, κατηγόρηκα; ἐνθυμέομαι *ponder* (ἔνθυμος) ἐνεθυμήθην, ἐντεθυμῆσθαι; ἐπιορκέω *swear falsely* (ἐπίορκος), ἐπιώρκηκα; ἐγχειρίζω *entrust* (ἐν χειρί), ἐνεχείρισα.

a. But several verbs are not treated as compounds, such as ἀπατάω *deceive*, ἀπιστέω *distrust*, ἀπορέω *am in difficulty*, παρρησιάζομαι *speak freely*.

TENSE-SUFFIXES, THEMATIC VOWEL, MOOD-SUFFIXES

455. Tense-Suffixes. — The tense-suffixes, which are added to the verb-stem to form the tense-stems, consist of the thematic vowel and certain other letters. No tense-suffixes are added to the verb-stem (1) in the second aorist active and middle, and second perfect and pluperfect, of μι-verbs; (2) in the perfect and pluperfect middle of verbs in -ω and -μι. The tense-suffixes are as follows: —

1. Present system, -%ε-, -τ%ε-, -ι̯%ε-, -ν%ε-, -αν%ε-, -νε%ε-, -να-, -νυ-, -(ι)σκ%ε; or none, as in φα-μέν.
2. Future system, -σ%ε-.
3. First aorist sytem, -σα-.
4. Second aorist system, -%ε-; or none, as in ἔ-στη-ν.
5. First perfect system, -κα- (plupf. -κη- from -κεα-; -κει- from -κεε-; -κε-).
6. Second perfect system, -α- (plupf. -η-, -ει-, or -ε-); or none, as in ἕ-στα-τε.
7. Perfect middle system, none (future perfect -σ%ε-).
8. First passive system, θη-, -θε- (future passive -θησ%ε-).
9. Second passive system, η, -ε- (future passive -ησ%ε-).

N. — -α in the aorist is properly a relic of the personal ending (666).

456. Thematic Vowel. — The thematic, or variable, vowel appears at the end of the tense-stems in the present, imperfect, and second aorist active and

---

455. D. For the Doric future -σε%ε-, see 540. — For the Epic first aorist -σ%ε-, see 542 D. — For the doubling of σ in the future and first aorist, see 534 b. D., 544 b. D.

middle of ω-verbs, and in all futures and future perfects. The thematic vowel in the indicative is ο before μ or ν (and in the optative of the tenses mentioned); elsewhere it is ε. Thus, λῡ°/ε-, λιπ°/ε-, λῡσ°/ε-, λυθησ°/ε-, λελῡσ°/ε-; λύο-ῑ-μι. In the subjunctive it is ω/η.

a. Attic inscriptions have both -εσθων and -οσθων in the imperative.

457. Subjunctive. — In the subjunctive of all verbs the thematic vowel is ω/η-. Thus, λύω-μεν, λύη-τε, λύσω-μεν, στείλη-τε.

a. Verbs in -νῡμι form their subjunctive like ω-verbs.

458. In the present and second aorist of μι-verbs, and in the aorist passive, ω/η is added to the tense stem. Thus τιθῶμεν from τιθέ-ω-μεν, θῶ from θέ-ω, τιθῆτε from τιθέ-η-τε, λυθῶ from λυθέ-ω.

459. Suffix of the Optative. — The optative adds the mood suffix -ῑ-, or -ιη- which contracts with the final vowel of the tense-stem: λύοιμι for λύο-ῑ-μι, φιλοίην for φιλεο-ίη-ν, τιθείην for τιθε-ίη-ν. -ιη- occurs only before active endings. When the suffix is -ιη-, the 1 pers. sing. ends in -ν; as τῑμαο-ίη-ν = τῑμῴην; when it is -ῑ-, the 1 pers. sing. ends in -μι, as τῑμάο-ῑ-μι = τῑμῷμι.

460. ιη is used as follows (in all other cases -ῑ-): —

a. In contracted verbs in the singular, rarely in the dual and plural. -ῑ- appears in the dual and plural, rarely in the singular.

b. In liquid verbs in the future active singular: φανοίη-ν for φανεο-ίη-ν. In the dual and plural -ῑ-: φανοῖτον, φανοῖμεν for φανεό-ῑ-τον, φανεό-ῑ-μεν.

c. In the singular of μι-verbs: τιθείην for τιθε-ίη-ν, διδοίην for διδο-ίη-ν, θείην for θε-ίη-ν. Here the modal sign is added to the tense-stem without any thematic vowel. -ῑ- is more common in the dual and plural: τιθεῖμεν for τιθέ-ῑ-μεν, διδοῖμεν for διδό-ῑ-μεν, θεῖτε for θέ-ῑ-τε. Verbs in -νῡμι make their optatives like λύω.

d. In the aorist passive: λυθείην for λυθε-ίη-ν, φανείην for φανε-ίη-ν. In the dual and plural -ῑ- is more common: λυθεῖμεν for λυθέ-ῑ-μεν, φανεῖτε for φανέ-ῑ-τε.

e. In some second perfects, as προεληλυθοίης, and in the second aorist σχοίην from ἔχω (but -σχοῖμι in composition).

N. — In the 3 pl. -ιε- is regular before -ν: λύο-ιε-ν, τιθε-ῖε-ν, λυθε-ῖε-ν.

461. a. In the 1 aor. opt. act. of ω-verbs the endings -ειας, -ειε, and -ειαν are more common than -αις, -αι, -αιεν.

b. In the aor. opt. passive of all verbs and in the opt. of μι-verbs and of contract verbs -ιτον, -ιτην, -ιμεν, -ιτε, -ιεν are commoner than -ιητον, -ιητην, -ιημεν, -ιητε, -ιησαν. Prose writers use either the shorter or the longer forms; poets use only the shorter forms. Except in contract verbs -ιητε is very common in the 2 pl. and is sometimes the only form in the Mss., as δοίητε, θείητε, γνοίητε, -βαίητε, λυθείητε, φανείητε; but the forms in question occur in prose writers and their genuineness is therefore unsupported by metrical evidence.

---

457 D. Hom. has -°/ε- instead of -ω/η-, especially in the 1 aor., 2 aor. of μι-verbs, and 2 aor. pass. (ἐρύσσομεν, δώομεν, τραπείομεν; also in ἴομεν, εἴδομεν). These forms do not occur in the sing. or 3 pl. active. Verbs in ω rarely show this °/ε in the present. (Other examples 532, 667 D., 682 D.)

460 D. -ιη- is very rare in Hom. in the dual and plural.

ENDINGS OF THE VERB: PERSONAL ENDINGS

462. To make the complete verbal forms, to the tense-stems in the various moods are attached the personal endings in the finite moods and other endings in the infinitives, participles, and verbal adjectives. See 366. The personal endings of the four finite moods are given below. In many forms only the *μι*-verbs preserve distinct endings. Some of the endings are due to analogy of others and many are still unexplained. The first person dual, when it is used, has the form of the first person plural.

	Active		Middle	
	INDICATIVE (primary tenses) AND SUBJUNCTIVE	INDICATIVE (secondary tenses) AND OPTATIVE	INDICATIVE (primary tenses) AND SUBJUNCTIVE	INDICATIVE (secondary tenses) AND OPTATIVE
Sing. 1.	— or **-μι**	**-ν**	**-μαι**	**-μην**
2.	**-ς** (for *-σι*), **-θα** (*-σθα*)	**-ς, -σθα**	**-σαι**	**-σο**
3.	**-σι** (for *-τι*)	—	**-ται**	**-το**
Dual 2.	**-τον**	**-τον**	**-σθον**	**-σθον**
3.	**-τον**	**-την**	**-σθον**	**-σθην**
Plur. 1.	**-μεν**	**-μεν**	**-μεθα**	**-μεθα**
2.	**-τε**	**-τε**	**-σθε**	**-σθε**
3.	**-νσι** (for *-ντι*)	**-ν, -σαν,**	**-νται**	**-ντο**

IMPERATIVE	Active	Middle
Sing. 2.	—, **-θι, -ς**	**-σο**
3.	**-τω**	**-σθω**
Dual 2.	**-τον**	**-σθον**
3.	**-των**	**-σθων**
Plur. 2.	**-τε**	**-σθε**
3.	**-ντων** (*-τωσαν*)	**-σθων** (*-σθωσαν*)

---

462 D. Doric has *-τι* for *-σι*, *-μες* for *-μεν*, *-ντι* in 3 pl., and *-τᾱν*, *-σθᾱν*, *-μᾱν* for *-την*, *-σθην*, *-μην*. *-τᾱν*, *-σθᾱν*, *-μᾱν* are also Aeolic.

The close agreement between Greek and Sanskrit may be illustrated by the inflection of Old Greek and Doric *φᾱμί* *say*, Skt. bhā́mi *shine*, *ἔφερον*, Skt. ábharam *bore*.

φᾱ-μί	bhā́-mi	*φᾰ-τόν*	bhā-tás	*ἔφερο-ν*	ábhara-m	*ἐφερέ-την*	ábhara-tām
φᾴ-ς	bhā́-si	*φᾰ-μές*	bhā-más	*ἔφερε-ς*	ábhara-s	*ἐφέρο-μεν*	ábharā-ma
φᾱ-τί	bhā́-ti	*φᾰ-τέ*	bhā-thá	*ἔφερε-(τ)*	ábhara-t	*ἐφέρε-τε*	ábhara-ta
φᾰ-τόν	bhā-thás	*φᾰ-ντί*	bhā́-nti	*ἐφέρε-τον*	ábhara-tam	*ἔφερο-ν(τ)*	ábhara-n(t)

463. PRIMARY ENDINGS OF THE ACTIVE (IND. AND SUBJ.)

a. 1 Sing. — -μι is found only in μι-verbs. Verbs in -ω have no ending and simply lengthen the thematic vowel (λύω, λείπω). The perfect has no personal ending, -α taking the place of a thematic vowel.

b. 2 Sing. — (1) -σι is found in Hom. ἐσσί *thou art* from the μι-verb εἰμί *I am;* possibly also in φῄς *thou sayest.* Attic εἶ *thou art* is derived from ἐ-σι. τίθη-ς is obscure. λύεις is probably for λῡε-σι, λῡεϊ, λῡει, to which ς has been added. Subj. λύῃ-ς follows the analogy of the indicative, but with long thematic vowel. τιθῇς for τιθέ-ῃς. In the perfect -ς (*not* for -σι) has been added.

(2) -θα is a perfect ending, as in οἶσθα *knowest* for οἰδ + θα (83). From the perfect it spread to the imperfects ἦσθα *wast,* ᾔεισθα *wentst,* ἔφησθα *saidst,* and to ᾔδησθα or ᾔδεισθα *knewest.* The perfect has commonly -α-ς. οἶσθας and ἦσθας are late.

c. 3 Sing. — -τι is found in μι-verbs: ἐσ-τί, τίθησι for τίθη-τι (Doric) by 115. λύει is obscure, but it cannot be derived from λῡε-σι for λῡε-τι. λύῃ, τιθῇ (for τιθέῃ) follow λύει, but with long thematic vowel. In the perfect, -ε with no personal ending.

d. 3 Pl. — Original -ντι is retained in Doric λύοντι, whence Attic λύουσι (115 a); ἐντί, Attic εἰσί. Subj. λύωσι from λύω-ντι, τιθῶσι from τιθέω-ντι, ποιῶσι from ποιῶντι (Dor.). Many μι forms are derived from -αντι, as τιθέᾱσι (τιθέ-αντι), διδόᾱσι (διδό-αντι), ἑστᾶσι (ἑστά-αντι), ἱστᾶσι (from ἱστά-αντι), the accent of which has been transferred to τιθεῖσι (747 D. 1), διδοῦσι from (Dor.) τίθε-ντι, δίδο-ντι. -ᾰτι from -ν̥τι (35 b), properly the ending of the perfect after a consonant, appears as -ᾰσι in Hom. πεφύκᾰσι; but it has been replaced by -ᾱσι out of -αντι, as in τετράφ-ᾱσι.

464. SECONDARY ENDINGS OF THE ACTIVE (IND. AND OPT.)

The optative usually has the endings of the secondary tenses of the indicative.

---

463 a. D. The Hom. subj. ἐθέλωμι, τύχωμι, ἀγάγωμι, are new formations. Aeolic has φίλημι, δοκίμωμι (indic.).

b. (1) εἶς or εἷς in Hom. and Hdt. is derived from εἶ + ς. For this form ἐσσ(ί) may be read in Hom. Theocr. has -ες for -εις (ἀμέλγες, etc.) and perf. πεπόνθεις (557. 2. D.).

b. (2) -σθα in Hom. indic. φῆσθα, τίθησθα, ᾔδησθα; subj. ἐθέλῃσθα also written ἐθέλησθα; opt. (rarely) κλαίοισθα, βάλοισθα. -σθα occurs also occasionally in Doric (ποθορῆσθα) and Aeolic (ἔχεισθα, φίλησθα).

c. Aeolic has τίθη, ποίη, στεφάνοι, but ἦσι *says.* Subj.: Hom. ἐθέλῃσι (also written ἐθέλησι; cp. Arcad. ἔχη), φορέῃσι, θέῃσι.

d. Hom. has -ᾱσι in ἴᾱσι *they go,* ἔᾱσι *they are,* and in βεβάᾱσι, γεγάᾱσι. Aeolic has λύοισι, φίλεισι, τίμαισι.

464 a. D. -ν for -μι is very rare (τρέφοιν in Eur., ἁμάρτοιν in Cratinus).

c. Doric ἦς *was* for ἦσ(τ).

e. -ν is regular in Doric and common in Hom. and later poetry; as ἔστᾰ-ν

a. 1 Sing. — -ν stands for μ (133 c), cp. ἔφερο-ν, Skt. ábhara-m. After a consonant μ (sonant nasal, 20 b, 35 c) became α: ἔλῡσα for ἐλῡσμ̥, Epic ἦα *was* for ἠ(σ)α from ἠσμ̥. In the pluperfect -η is from ε-α (467). -ν is found in the optative when the mood suffix is -ιη-; elsewhere the optative has -μι.

b. 2 Sing. — On -σθα see 463 b (2).

c. 3 Sing. — -τ dropped (133 b) in ἔλῡε, ἐτίθη, and in the opt. λύοι, εἴη (cp. Old Lat. *sied*). ἔλῡσε has its -ε from the perfect (cp. οἶδε) and shows no personal ending.

d. Dual. — -την is rarely found for -τον in the 2 dual (εὑρέτην in Plato). Hom. has ἐτεύχετον as 3 dual.

e. 3 Pl. — -ν for -ντ by 133 b. -σαν (taken from the 1 aorist) is used (1) in the imperf. and 2 aor. of μι-verbs, as ἐτίθε-σαν, ἔθε-σαν; (2) in the aor. pass. ἐλύθη-σαν, ἐφάνη-σαν (here -ν preceded by a short vowel occurs in poetry, 585 a. D.); (3) in the pluperf. ἐλελύκε-σαν; (4) in the opt. when -ιη- is the modal suffix (460). In the opt. -σαν is rare.

465. ENDINGS OF THE MIDDLE (INDIC., SUBJ., OPT.)

a. 2 Sing. — Primary -σαι retains its σ in the perfect of all verbs (λέλυ-σαι), and in the pres. of μι-verbs (τίθε-σαι). Elsewhere σ drops between vowels, as in λύῃ or λύει from λύε-σαι, λυθήσῃ or -ει, φανῇ from φανέε-σαι, τῑμᾷ from τῑμάε-σαι; subj. λύῃ from λύη-σαι, φήνῃ from φήνη-σαι, θῇ from θήε-σαι, δῷ from δώη-σαι, ᾖ from ἔη-σαι, φιλῇ from φιλέη-σαι, δηλοῖ from δηλόῃ = δηλόη-σαι.

N. 1. — The forms -ῃ and -ει are found in the present, future, and future perfect. See 628.

N. 2. — δύνᾳ and δύνῃ for δύνασαι, ἐπίστᾳ and ἐπίστῃ for ἐπίστασαι, ἐφίει for ἐφίεσαι, are poetic and dialectic or late.

b. 2 Sing. — -σο stays in all plups. and in the imperf. of μι-verbs. Elsewhere it loses its σ, as in ἐλύου from ἐλύε-σο, ἐλύσω from ἐλύσα-σο, ἐφήνω from ἐφήνα-σο, ἐλίπου from ἐλίπε-σο, ἔθου from ἔθε-σο, ἐπρίω from ἐπρία-σο, ἐτῑμῶ from ἐτῑμάε-σο, ἐφιλοῦ from ἐφιλέε-σο. In the optative, λύοιο, λίποιο, τιθεῖο, εἷο, λύσαιο, from λύοι-σο, etc.; τῑμῷο from τῑμάοι-σο.

N. 1. — ἐδύνω or ἠδύνω and ἠπίστω are commoner than ἐδύνασο and ἠπίστασο from δύναμαι *am able* and ἐπίσταμαι *understand*.

N. 2. — After a diphthong or a long vowel in the 2 aor. indic. mid. -σο is retained, as εἷσο (ἵημι *send*), ὤνησο (ὀνίνημι *benefit*).

(ἔστη-σαν), ἔδιδο-ν (ἐδίδο-σαν), φίληθεν (ἐφιλήθη-σαν), τράφεν (ἐτράφη-σαν). The short vowel before ν(τ) is explained by 40. Hom. ἦε-ν *were* became ἦν, used in Dor. as 3 pl.; in Attic it was used as 3 sing.

465 a. D. Hom. has βούλεαι, perf. μέμνηαι, but pres. δύνασαι, παρίστασαι; ὄψει is unique (for ὄψεαι); subj. δύνηαι. Doric often contracts, as οἴῃ for οἴε-αι. Aeolic generally leaves εαι open (κείσε-αι). Hdt. has open -εαι, -ηαι.

b. Hom., Doric, and Aeolic have generally open forms, as Hom. βάλλε-ο (rarely βάλλευ), ὠδύσα-ο. ἔρειο, σπεῖο are from -εεο. Hom. has ἐμάρναο for Attic ἐμάρνασο, and may drop σ even in the pluperfect (ἔσσυο). When Doric contracts αο we have ᾱ. In Hdt. αο, εο are open, but the writing ευ for εο is found.

c. **Dual.**—The 1 pl. is used for the 1 dual except in the three poetic forms περιδώμεθον, λελείμμεθον, ὁρμώμεθον. Hom. has -σθον for -σθην in θωρήσσεσθον.

d. 1 **Pl.**—In epic and dramatic poetry -μεσθα is often used for -μεθα for metrical reasons (βουλόμεσθα, ἐπιστάμεσθα).

e. 2 **Pl.**—On the loss of σ in σθε (ἔσταλθε), see 103.

f. 3 **Pl.**—After vowel stems -νται, -ντο are preserved. After stems ending in a consonant -νται, -ντο became -αται, -ατο by 35 b. These forms were retained in prose till about 400 B.C. (*e.g.* τετάχαται, ἐτετάχατο).

466. ENDINGS OF THE IMPERATIVE

1. Active.

a. 2 **Sing.**—λῦε, λίπε, τίθει (for τίθε-ε) have not lost -θι. -θι is found in 2 aor. pass. φάνη-θι; in στῆ-θι and ἕστα-θι; in some 2 aorists, like γνῶ-θι, τλῆ-θι, πῖ-θι, which are μι forms though they have presents of the ω form (687). Also in ἴσ-θι *be* or *know*, ἴθι *go*, φάθι or φαθί *say*. λύθητι is for λυθηθι by 125 b.

b. -ς occurs in θές, ἕς, δός, σχές (and in the rare θίγες, πίεις). This -ς is *not* derived from -θι.

c. λῦσ-ον aor. act. and λῦσ-αι aor. mid. are obscure in origin.

2. Middle.

a. 2 **Sing.**—-σο retains its σ in the (rare) perf. of all verbs and in the pres. of μι-verbs (λέλυσο, τίθεσο, ἵστασο). Elsewhere σ is dropped, as in λύου from λύε-σο, λιποῦ from λιπέ-σο, θοῦ from θέ-σο, οὗ from ἕ-σο, πρίω from πρία-σο, τῑμῶ from τῑμάε-σο.

N.—τίθου, ἵστω, δίδου are poetic or late.

3. 3 **Pl.**—For -ντων and -σθων we find -τωσαν and -σθωσαν in prose after Thucydides, in Euripides, and in inscriptions after 300 B.C. Thus, λῡέτωσαν, λῡσάτωσαν, λῡέσθωσαν, λῡσάσθωσαν, λυθήτωσαν, λιπέτωσαν, λιπέσθωσαν, φηνάσθωσαν, φανήτωσαν, τῑμάσθωσαν, φιλείσθωσαν, γεγράφθωσαν, πεπείσθωσαν, τιθέτωσαν, διδότωσαν, θέτωσαν, τιθέσθωσαν, θέσθωσαν, -ἕτωσαν, -ἕσθωσαν.

N.—ἔστων for ὄντων is rare. Attic inscriptions have (very rarely) -ντωσαν.

---

f. -αται, -ατο occur in Hom. regularly in the perfect and pluperfect of consonant stems, as τετράφαται, ἕαται for ἑσ-νται, ἥατο for ἡσ-ντο from ἧμαι (ἡσμαι); also in stems ending in -ι, as ἐφθίατο. -αται, -ατο were transferred to vocalic stems, as βεβλήαται, βεβλήατο, Hdt. δυνέαται. Hom. has -δ-αται in ἐληλάδαται from ἐλαύνω *drive*. In the opt. -ατο always (γενοίατο for γένοιντο). In Hdt. η before -αται, -ατο is shortened, as perf. ἡγέαται for ἡγή-αται = ἥγηνται, ἐβεβλέατο for -ηατο. For κεῖνται, Hom. κείαται and κέαται, Hdt. has κέαται. In the opt. Hdt. has -ατο: βουλοίατο, δεξαίατο. In Hdt. -αται, -ατο occur even in the present system, τιθέαται, δυνέαται, ἱστέατο.

466 a. D. -θι is not rare in Hom., pres. δίδωθι = δίδου, ὄρνυθι, aor. κλῦθι, perf. τέτλαθι. Aeolic has ἴστᾱ, φίλη. πίει, δέχοι, δίδοι (Pindar) are very rare.

3. Doric has also -ντω, as in παρεχόντω; Aeolic -ντον, as φέροντον. Doric has -σθω (pl.) and -σθων.

ENDINGS OF THE PLUPERFECT, ENDINGS IN σθ

467. Endings of the Pluperfect Active.—-η, -ης, -ει(ν) are derived from -ε(σ)α, -ε(σ)ας, -ε(σ)ε. In later Greek the endings are -ειν, -εις, -ει(ν), -ειτον, -ειτην, -ειμεν, -ειτε, and very late -εισαν.

468. The Endings -σθε, etc.—The σ of the endings -σθε, -σθω, -σθον, -σθων, -σθαι (409 N.) has no exact parallel in cognate languages, and seems to have spread in Greek from forms like τετέλεσ-θε, ἔζωσ-θε, etc., where a sigma-stem was followed by original -θε.

ENDINGS OF THE INFINITIVE, PARTICIPLE, AND VERBAL ADJECTIVE

469. Infinitive.—The following are the endings added to the tense-stem to make the infinitive.

a. **-εν**: in present and 2 aorist active of ω-verbs, all futures active. Thus, λύειν, τῑμᾶν, λιπεῖν, λύσειν, φανεῖν from λύε-εν, τῑμάε-εν, λιπέ-εν, λύσε-εν, φανέε-εν.

b. **-αι**: in 1 aor. active, as λῦσαι, παιδεῦσαι, δεῖξαι.

c. **-ναι**: (1) present, 2 perf. of μι-verbs, the two passive aorists, as τιθέ-ναι, ἑστά-ναι, λυθῆ-ναι, φανῆ-ναι; (2) perfect active, λελυκέ-ναι, and εἰδέ-ναι from εἰδ-ε (οἶδα).

N. 1.—The ending εναι appears in the 2 aor. of μι-verbs, as δοῦναι from δό-εναι, θεῖναι from θέ-εναι.

d. **-σθαι**: in other cases.

N. 2.—The infinitives are old cases of substantives, those in -αι being datives, the others locatives.

470. Participles.—The stem of the participle is formed by adding the following endings to the tense stem.

a. **-ντ-**: in all active tenses except the perfect, and in 1 and 2 aor. passive (301).

b. **-οτ-**: in the perfect active (for -ϝοτ-); masc. -ώς, fem. -υῖα, neut. -ός (301 c).

c. **-μενο-**: in the middle, and in the passive except in the aorist.

471. Verbal Adjectives.—Most of the verbals in -τός and -τέος are formed by adding these suffixes to the verbal stem of the aorist passive (first or second). Thus, φιλητός, -τέος (ἐ-φιλή-θην); πειστός, -τέος (ἐ-πείσ-θην); τελεστός, -τέος (ἐ-τελέσ-θην); σταλτός, -τέος (ἐ-στάλ-ην); βλητός, -τέος (ἐ-βλή-θην). On the accent of compound verbals, see 425 c.

---

467 D. Hom. has -εα, -ης, -ει or ει-ν (-εε only in ᾔδεε), -εσαν, and rarely -ον, -ες, -ε; Hdt. has -εα, -εας, -εε (-ει?), -εατε, -εσαν.

469 D. -εν appears also in Hom. ἰδέεν (miswritten ἰδέειν). Hom. has no case of -εναι (for ἰέναι write ἴμεναι). For -εν or -ναι Hom. often uses **-μεναι** (also Aeolic) and **-μεν** (which is also Doric); both endings show the accent on the preceding syllable, as ζευγνύμεναι, ἔμμεναι (= εἶναι), φιλήμεναι, στήμεναι, ἑστάμεναι, ἀξέμεναι, ὁμοιωθήμεναι, δαήμεναι; τιθέμεν, ἔμμεν, ἴμεν, θέμεν, ἐλθέμεν, ἀξέμεν. Doric has -μεν in the aorist passive, as αἰσχυνθῆμεν. -μεν is preceded by a short syllable and generally stands before a vowel. -ναι always follows a long vowel. Doric has -ην and -εν in the present. Aeolic has -ην in the present and 2 aorist.

a. Some are derived from other stem forms (pres. and fut.), as φερ-τός, ἰ-τέον, δυνα-τός; μενετός (cp. μενέ-ω = μενῶ fut.).

472. Verbals in -τός, -τή, -τόν either (1) have the meaning of a perfect passive participle, as κρυπτός *hidden*, παιδευτός *educated*, or (2) express *possibility*, as νοητός *thinkable*, ὁρᾱτός *visible*. Many have either signification, but some are passive only, as ποιητός *done*. See 425 c. N.

a. Usually passive in meaning are verbals from deponent verbs, as μῑμητός *imitated*.

b. Usually active in meaning are compounds derived from transitive active verbs; but some intransitive verbs make active verbals, as ῥυτός *flowing*.

c. Many are active or passive, others only active: μεμπτός *blamed, blamable, blaming*, πιστός *trusting in* (rare), *trusted*, ἄπρᾱκτος *doing nothing, not done*, φθεγκτός *sounding*.

473. Verbals in -τέος, -τέᾱ, -τέον express *necessity* (cp. the Lat. gerundive in *-ndus*), as δοτέος *that must be given*, παιδευτέος *educandus*.

FORMATION OF THE TENSE-SYSTEMS (Ω AND MI-VERBS)

CHANGES IN THE VERB-STEM

474. From the verb-stem (or theme) each tense-stem is formed by the addition of a tense-suffix (455) or of a prefix, or of both. In 475–495 certain modifications of the verb-stem are considered.

475. Variation in Quantity. — Many verbs of the first class (498 ff.) show variation in the quantity of the vowel of the verb-stem, which is commonly long in the present but fluctuates in other tenses, as λῡ́-ω, λῡ́-σω, ἔλῡ-σα, but λέλῠ-κα, λέλῠ-μαι, ἐλῠ́-θην. (Other examples, 500.)

a. Some verbs of the Fourth Class (523 c) lengthen a short vowel of the present in some other tenses. Thus, λαμβάνω (λαβ-) *take*, λήψομαι, εἴληφα, εἴλημμαι, ἐλήφθην, but 2 aor. ἔλαβον.

476. Vowel Gradation (35, 36). — Verbs of the first class show a variation between a strong grade (or two strong grades) and a weak grade. The weak grades, ῐ, ῠ, ᾰ, appear especially in the second aorist and second passive systems; the corresponding strong grades, ει (οι), ευ (ου), η (ω), appear usually in the other systems (οι, ου, ω, in the second perfect).

a. Expulsion of a short vowel between consonants (so-called syncope 493) produces a weak form of the stem of the same grade as ι, υ, α (36). Cp. γί-γν-ο-μαι *become* (aor. ἐ-γεν-ό-μην), ἐ-πτ-ό-μην (pres. πέτ-ο-μαι *fly*) with ἔ-λιπ-ο-ν, ἔ-φυγ-ο-ν, ἐ-τάκ-η-ν (477 c). So ἔ-σχ-ο-ν *got* from ἔχ-ω *have*.

b. α is the weak form of η (ᾱ), as in τήκω ἐτάκην; and of ε, when ε has λ, μ, ν, ρ before or after it, as in τρέπω, ἐτράπην (479).

477. The following examples illustrate the principles of 476.

a. ει οι ι: λείπω *leave*, λείψω, 2 perf. λέλοιπα, λέλειμμαι, ἐλείφθην, 2 aor. ἔλιπον.

N. — The weak form appears when the verb undergoes Attic reduplication (446); as in ἀλείφω *anoint*, 2 perf. ἀλήλιφα, ἀλήλιμμαι; ἐρείκω *tear* (Ionic and poetic), 2 perf. ἐρήριγμαι, 2 aor. ἤρικον; ἐρείπω *overthrow*, Epic ἐρήριπα; but ἐρείδω *prop*, ἐρήρεισμαι.

b. **ευ ου υ**: ἐλεύ(θ)σομαι *I shall go*, 2 perf. ἐλήλυθα (Epic ἐλήλουθα), 2 aor. (Epic ἤλυθον); φεύγω *flee*, φεύξομαι or φευξοῦμαι, 2 perf. πέφευγα, 2 aor. ἔφυγον; ῥέω *flow* (for ῥευ-ω, 43), ῥεύσομαι, ἐρρύηκα (ῥυε-), 2 aor. pass. ἐρρύην.

N. — χέω *pour* (for χευ-ω, 43), ἔχεα (for ἔχευα), has υ in κέχυκα, κέχυμαι, ἐχύθην; σεύω (poetic) *urge*, ἔσσευα, ἔσσυμαι, ἐσσύθην or ἐσύθην *rushed*. See also τεύχω in the List of Verbs.

c. **η ω ᾰ**: ῥήγ-νῡμι *break*, ῥήξω, ἔρρηξα, 2 perf. ἔρρωγα, 2 aor. pass. ἐρράγην; τήκ-ω *melt*, τήξω, ἔτηξα, τέτηκα, ἐτήχθην, 2 aor. pass. ἐτάκην.

N. — Verbs of class c usually have ᾰ in the 2 aorist, ω in the 2 perfect (if there is one), elsewhere η. ω occurs in the present in τρώγω *gnaw*, 2 aor. ἔτραγον.

478. Change of ε to ο in the Second Perfect. — In the second perfect ε of the verb-stem is changed to ο.

κλέπ-τ-ω *steal* κέκλοφα, (ἀπο-)κτείνω *kill* (κτεν-, 519) -έκτονα, λέγ-ω *collect* εἴλοχα, πάσχω, fut. πείσομαι (from πενθσομαι, 100) πέπονθα, πέμπ-ω *send* πέπομφα, στέργ-ω *love* ἔστοργα, τίκτω *beget* τέτοκα, τρέπ-ω *turn* τέτροφα, τρέφ-ω *nourish* τέτροφα, φθείρ-ω *corrupt* ἔφθορα. So in γίγ(ε)νομαι *become* ἐγενόμην, γέγονα; ἐγείρω *awaken* ἐγρήγορα (446). This change corresponds to that of ει to οι (477 a).

479. Change of ε to α. — In verb-stems containing λ, μ, ν, ρ, an ε is usually changed to α in the first perfect, perfect middle, and second passive systems.

τρέπ-ω *turn*, τέτραμμαι, ἐτράπην (1 aor. ἐτρέφθην); τρέφ-ω *feed*, τέθραμμαι, ἐτράφην (1 aor. ἐθρέφθην); σπείρω (σπερ-) *sow*, ἔσπαρμαι, ἐσπάρην; φθείρω (φθερ-) *destroy*, ἔφθαρμαι, ἐφθάρην; στέλλω (στελ-) *send*, ἔσταλκα, ἔσταλμαι, ἐστάλην; τείνω (τεν-) *stretch*, τέτακα, τέταμαι, ἐτάθην (1 aor.).

a. Also in the 2 aor. pass. of κλέπτω *steal* (ἐκλάπην), πλέκω *weave* (ἐπλάκην), τέρπω *gladden* (Epic ἐτάρπην). Many of these verbs also show ο in the second perfect (478).

480. This ᾰ is also found in the second aorist active and middle of κτείνω *kill* (ἔκτανον poetic), τέμνω *cut* (dialectal ἔταμον), τρέπω *turn* (ἔτραπον poetic), τέρπω *gladden* (ἐταρπόμην poetic), poetic δέρκομαι *see* (ἔδρακον). Also πέρθω, πτήσσω.

481. ε in the perfect middle in κέκλεμμαι (κλέπτω *steal*), πέπλεγμαι (πλέκω *weave*) is introduced from the present.

482. The ᾰ in 479, 480 is developed from a liquid or nasal brought between two consonants (35 b). Thus, ἔσταλμαι, τέταμαι from ἐστλ̥μαι, τετν̥μαι, ἐτάθην from ἐτν̥θην (20 b). Here στλ, τν represent weak grades of the stem.

483. a. The variations ε, ο, α, ω appear in τρέπω *turn*, τρέψω, ἔτρεψα, 2 perf. τέτροφα, τέτραμμαι, ἐτρέφθην, 2 aor. pass. ἐτράπην; frequentative τρωπάω (867).

b. The variations ε, ο, ω appear in πέτομαι *fly*, ποτέομαι (poet.) and frequentative πωτάομαι (poet., 867) *fly about*.

484. η, α in the Second Perfect. — In the second perfect ᾰ of the verb-stem is lengthened to η (ᾱ): θάλλω (θαλ-) *bloom*, τέθηλα; φαίνω (φαν-) *show*, πέφηνα; μαίνω (μαν-) *madden*, μέμηνα; κρᾱ́ζω (κραγ-) *cry out*, κέκρᾱγα.

485. Addition of ε. — a. To the verb-stem ε is added to make the present stem in δοκέω *seem*, fut. δόξω, aor. ἔδοξα (δοκ-); so in γαμέω *marry*, ὠθέω *push*. Usually ε is added in some stem other than the present.

b. In many verbs ε is added to the verb-stem to form the tense-stems other than present, second aorist, and second perfect, *e.g.* μάχομαι (μαχ-) *fight*, μαχοῦμαι (= μαχε(σ)ομαι), ἐμαχεσάμην, μεμάχημαι. So ἄχθομαι *am grieved*, βούλομαι *wish*, γίγνομαι *become*, δέω *want*, (ἐ)θέλω *wish*, μέλλω *intend*, μέλει *is a care*, οἴομαι *think*.

c. In some verbs ε is added to form one or more tense-stems, as μένω (μεν-) *remain*, μεμένηκα (μενε-) to avoid -ν-κα in the perfect. So, νέμω *distribute*, ἔχω *have*, οἴχομαι *am gone*. So also δαρθάνω, ὀσφαίνομαι, ῥέω, στείβω (poetic), τυγχάνω.

d. Some verbs have alternative presents with or without ε. Here sometimes one is used in prose, the other in poetry, sometimes both are poetic or both used in prose. Thus, ἕλκω *draw* (Hom. also ἑλκέω), ἰάχω ἰαχέω *sound* (both poetic), μέδω μεδέω (both poetic), ῥίπτω and ῥῑπτέω *throw* (both in prose).

486. Addition of α and ο. — α or ο is added to the verb-stem in some verbs. Thus, μῡκάομαι *bellow* (Epic 2 aor. μύκον), ἐμῡκησάμην; ἁλίσκομαι (ἁλ-) *be captured*, ἁλώσομαι from ἁλο-; ὄμνῡ-μι *swear* (ὀμ-) ὤμοσα, ὀμώμοκα etc. (ὀμο-); οἴχομαι *am gone*, Epic οἴχωκα or ᾤχωκα.

487. Lengthening of Short Final Vowel. — Verb-stems ending in a short vowel generally lengthen that vowel before the tense-suffix in all tenses (except the present and imperfect) formed from them. Here α (except after ε, ι, and ρ) and ε become η, ο becomes ω.

τῑμά-ω (τῑμα-) *honour*, τῑμή-σω, ἐτίμη-σα, τετίμη-κα, τετίμη-μαι, ἐτῑμή-θην; θηρά-ω (θηρα-) *hunt*, θηρᾱ́-σω, ἐθήρᾱ-σα, etc. (389); ποιέω (ποιε-) *make*, ποιή-σω, ἐποίη-σα, πεποίη-κα, πεποίη-μαι, ἐποιή-θην; δηλόω (δηλο-) *manifest*, δηλώ-σω, ἐδήλω-σα, etc.; ἐάω *permit*, ἐάσω, etc.

a. Note ἀκροᾱ́σομαι, ἠκροᾱσάμην, etc., from ἀκροάομαι *hear*; χρήσω, ἔχρησα from χράω *give oracles*; χρήσομαι, ἐχρησάμην from χράομαι *use*; τρήσω and ἔτρησα from τετραίνω *bore* are from τρε-.

b. Verb-stems adding ε or ο (486), and stems apparently receiving a short final vowel by metathesis (128), lengthen the short final vowel, as βούλομαι (βουλ-) *wish*, βουλή-σομαι (βουλε-, 485), κάμνω (καμ-) *am weary*, κέκμη-κα (κμα-).

---

485 D. Some Ionic and poetic verbs adding ε are ἀλέξω, ἄλθομαι, γεγωνέω, γηθέω, δουπέω, εἴρομαι, εἰλέω, ἐπαυρέω, κελαδέω, κέλομαι, κεντέω, κήδω, κτυπέω, κυρέω, λάσκω, μέδομαι, μύζω, πατέομαι, ῥῑγέω, στυγέω, τορέω, χάζω, φιλέω (poetic forms), χραισμέω; ἀμπλακίσκω, ἀπαφίσκω; Epic ἐδιδάσκησα (διδάσκω), πιθήσω, πεπιθήσω, πιθήσᾱς (πείθω), πεφιδήσομαι (φείδομαι).

486 D. α is added also in βρῡχάομαι, γοάω, δηριάομαι, λιχμάω, μηκάομαι, μητιάω. All these are mainly poetic.

488. Retention of Short Final Vowel. — Many verb-stems ending apparently in a short vowel retain the short vowel, contrary to 487, in some or all the tenses.

γελᾰ́-ω laugh, γελᾰ́σομαι, ἐγέλᾰσα, ἐγελᾰ́σθην; τελέω *finish*, τελῶ from τελέ-ω, ἐτέλεσα, τετέλεκα, τετέλεσμαι, ἐτελέσθην; ἀνύω *accomplish*, ἀνῠ́σω, ἤνῠσα, ἤνῠσμαι.

a. The following verbs retain the final short vowel of the verb-stem in all tenses: ἄγα-μαι, αἰδέ-ομαι, ἀκέ-ομαι, ἀλέ-ω, ἀνύ-ω, ἀρέσκω (ἀρε-), ἀρκέ-ω, ἀρό-ω, ἀρύ-ω, γελά-ω, ἐλαύνω (ἐλα-), ἑλκύ-ω, and ἕλκ-ω (ἑλκ-ε-), ἐμέ-ω, ἐρά-ω, ἔρα-μαι (poet.), ἐσθίω (ἐσθι-, ἐδ-ε-, ἐδο-), ζέ-ω, θλά-ω, ἱλάσκομαι (ἱλα-), κλά-ω *break*, μεθύσκω (μεθυ-), ξέ-ω, πτό-ω (πτῡ-, πτῠ-), σπά-ω, τελέ-ω, τρέ-ω, φθίνω (φθι-), φλά-ω, χαλά-ω, χέ-ω (χυ-). Also all verbs in -αννῡμι and -εννῡμι (except ἔσβηκα from σβέννῡμι *extinguish*), and ὄλλῡμι (ὀλ-ε-), ὄμνῡμι (ὀμ-, ὀμε-, ὀμο-), στόρνῡμι (στορ-ε).

b. The following verbs keep short the final vowel in the future, but lengthen it in one or more other tense-systems, or have double future forms, one with the short vowel, the other with the long vowel: αἰνέω (αἰνέσω, ᾔνεσα, ᾔνεκα, ᾐνέθην, ᾔνημαι), ἄχθομαι (ἀχθ-, ἀχθε-), καλέ-ω, μάχομαι (μαχ-ε-), μύω, πίνω (πι-, πο-), ποθέ-ω, πονέ-ω, ἐρύ-ω (Epic), φθάνω (φθα-).

c. In some verbs the final short vowel of the verb-stem remains short in one or more tense-stems, but is lengthened in the future, as δέ-ω *bind*, δήσω, ἔδησα, δέδεκα, δέδεμαι, ἐδέθην. So αἱρέω, βαίνω (βα-), βῡνέω (βυ-), δίδωμι (δο-, δω-), δύνα-μαι, δύω (δῠ-, δῡ-), εὑρίσκω (εὑρ-ε-), ἔχω (σεχ-, σχε-), θύω (θῠ-, θῡ-), ἵημι (ἑ-, ἡ-), ἵστημι (στᾰ-, στη-), λύω (λῠ-, λῡ-), τίθημι (θε-, θη-), τίνω (τι-), φύω (φῠ-, φῡ-), and the root ἐρ-, ῥε- (εἶπον).

d. Most of the verbs refusing to lengthen a final short vowel have verb-stems originally ending in σ (624); as τελέω from τελεσ-ι̯ω (cp. τὸ τέλος). By analogy to these, other verbs retain their short final vowel.

489. Insertion of σ. — In the perfect middle and first aorist passive systems, verbs which retain a short final vowel and some others usually insert σ before the personal ending.

Thus, τελέω (488 d), τετέλεσμαι, ἐτελέσθην; σπάω *draw*, ἔσπασμαι, ἐσπάσθην; κελεύω *order*, κεκέλευσμαι, ἐκελεύσθην; γιγνώσκω *know*, ἔγνωσμαι, ἐγνώσθην.

a. If the aorist passive ends in -θην and not in -σθην, the perfect middle does not insert σ. Thus -θην, not -σθην, occurs in all verbs in -ευω except λεύω *stone to death*, in all verbs in -εω which have -θην preceded by η, in all verbs in -οω except χόω *heap up*, and in all verbs in -αω except those that retain ᾰ. Stems originally ending in σ (624) properly show σ.

b. If the aorist passive ends in -σθην, the perfect middle may or may not insert σ. Verbs in -αζω and -ιζω (stems -αδ, -ιδ) regularly have σ by 83, 587. In the case of other verbs some always show σ, some never show σ, and some are doubtful. In many cases the later usage with σ has crept into the Mss. of

---

488 D. Here belong Epic ἀκηδέω, κοτέω, λοέω, νεικέω, and the forms ἄασα, -άμην, ἄεσα. ἐρύω shows ἐρῡ- and ἐρῠ-.

489 D. Hom. has original forms in πεφραδμένος (φράζω), κεκορυθμένος (κορύττω), ἐπέπιθμεν (πείθω).

the classical authors (so with the perfect of ἀλέω, βαίνω, δράω, ζώννῡμι, κλείω (κλῄω), σῴζω, χρίω, and with the aorist of παύω).

c. The following verbs show an inserted σ both in the perfect middle and the aorist passive in classical Greek: αἰδέομαι, γιγνώσκω, ἑλκύω, θλάω, θραύω, κελεύω, κλάω, κνα(ί)ω, κορέννῡμι, κυλίω, ξύω, πίμπλημι, πρίω, πτίττω, σβέννῡμι, σείω, σκεδάννῡμι, σπάω, τανύω, τελέω, τίνω, ὕω, φλάω, χόω, χρῴζω.

d. The following form only the perfect middle with σ in classical Greek: βῡνέω, ἕννῡμι (εἷμαι, but ἕστο Hom.), ἐρύω, ζώννῡμι, ξέω, *ὀδύσσομαι, πλέω, φλεύω (Hdt.).

e. The following form only the aorist passive with σ in classical Greek: ἄγαμαι, ἀκούω, ἀνύω, ἀρέσκω, ἄχθομαι, γελάω, δαίνῡμι, δράω, ἐλύω, ἔραμαι, ἐράω, ἱλάσκομαι, κλείω (κλῄω), λεύω, μεθύσκω, μιμνῄσκω, οἴω, ὄνομαι (Hdt.), παίω, παλαίω, πετάννῡμι, πίμπρημι, ῥαίω, ῥώννῡμι, στόρνῡμι, χαλάω, χράομαι, χράω, χρίω.

f. Only in post-classical Greek is σ attested both in the perfect middle and aorist passive in ἀρκέω, ζέω, κλαίω, (ἀπο) λαύω, λόω, ὄλλῡμι, πνέω, πταίω, σάω, ψαύω. — Only in the **perfect middle**: ἄγαμαι, ἀκούω, ἀνύω, γελάω, δράω, ἐμέω, ἔραμαι, κεράννῡμι, κολούω, μεθύσκω, ναίω, νάω *spin*, ὀπυίω, παίω, παλαίω, πετάννῡμι (and in Ionic), πίμπρημι (Aristotle; earlier perf. πέπρημαι), στόρνῡμι, χαλάω, ψαύω. When the perfect middle is not attested in classical Greek some at least of the σ forms from the above verbs may represent classical usage, provided the aorist passive has -σθην. — Only in the **aorist passive**: ἀκέομαι, ἀλέω, ἀρύω, βαίνω, βῡνέω, γεύω, εἰλύω, ἐλαύνω, ἔρυμαι, ἐρύω, ζώννῡμι, καίω, ξέω, μάχομαι, νέω *heap up*, *ὀδύσσομαι, πλέω, πτύω, σῴζω, φθάνω.

g. Some verbs have double forms (one of which may be disputed) in the classical period: **δύναμαι**: ἐδυνήθην and ἐδυνάσθην (chiefly Ionic and poetic); **κεράννῡμι**: ἐκράθην and ἐκεράσθην; **κρούω**: κέκρουμαι better than κέκρουσμαι; **νέω**: νένημαι and νένησμαι; **ὄμνῡμι**: ὀμώμομαι (and ὀμώμοσται), ὠμόθην and ὠμόσθην. — Dialectal or dialectal and late are ἐβώσθην for ἐβοήθην (βοάω), ἐλήλασμαι ἠλάσθην (ἐλαύνω), κεκόρημαι for κεκόρεσμαι (κορέννῡμι), πεπέτασμαι (πετάννῡμι).

h. Some verb-stems ending in ν show -σ-μαι in the perfect middle: ἡδύνω, μιαίνω, παχύνω, περαίνω, ὑφαίνω, φαίνω. Thus πέφασμαι, ἥδυσμαι, μεμίασμαι. Dialectal or late: θηλύνω, κοιλαίνω, λεπτύνω, λῡμαίνομαι, ξαίνω, ξηραίνω, σημαίνω. On -μμαι see 579.

i. Observe that some vowel verbs inserting σ do not lengthen the final vowel of the verb-stem in any tense (γελάω, τελέω); and that some not inserting σ (δέω, θύω, λύω) do not lengthen the final vowel in some tenses. ἐπ-αινέω *commend* and παρ-αινέω *exhort* do not insert σ and have the short vowel in *all* tenses.

j. The insertion of σ in the perfect middle started in the 3 sing. and 2 pl. Before the endings -ται and -σθε, σ was retained in the case of verbs with stems originally ending in σ (as τελέω), or where σ developed from τ, δ, θ (98) before -ται, -σθε (πέπεισται from πεπειθται). See 409 b, 624. In all cases where the verb-stem did not originally end in σ, the sigma forms are due to analogy; as in κεκέλευσμαι (κελεύω), πέπλησμαι (πίμπλημι), ἔγνωσμαι (γιγνώσκω).

490. Addition of θ. — The present stems of some poetical verbs are made by the addition of θ; as νή-θ-ω *spin*, πλή-θ-ω *am full* (πίμ-πλη-μι). Cp. 832.

---

490 D. A few verbs make poetic forms by adding -θ%ε- to the present or the 2 aorist tense-stem, in which α or ε (υ once) takes the place of the thematic

a. Most of the indicative forms seem to be imperfects, but since some have the force of aorists (*e.g.*, Soph. *O. C.* 862, 1334, *O. T.* 650), in certain editions they are regarded as second aorists, and the infinitives and participles are accented (against the Mss.) on the ultima (διωκαθεῖν, εἰκαθών).

491. Omission of ν. — Some verbs in -νω drop the ν of the verbal stem in the first perfect, perfect middle, and first passive systems.

κρίνω (κριν-), *judge*, κέκρι-κα, κέκρι-μαι, ἐκρί-θην. So also κλίνω *incline*, πλύνω *wash*.

492. Metathesis. — The verbal stem may suffer metathesis (128).

a. In the present: θνῄσκω *die*, 2 aor. ἔθανον, perf. τέθνηκα.

b. In other tenses: βάλλω *throw* (βαλ-), perf. βέβληκα, ἐβλήθην (βλη-); τέμνω *cut* (τεμ-ν-), 2 aor. ἔτεμον, perf. τέτμηκα; δέρκομαι (δερκ-) *see*, 2 aor. ἔδρακον; τέρπω *delight*, 2 aor. pass. ἐτάρπην and ἐτράπην (both poetical).

493. Syncope. — Some verbs suffer syncope (44 b).

a. In the present: πίπτω *fall* for πι-π(ε)τ-ω, ἴσχω *hold* for (σ)ι-σ(ε)χ-ω (125 e), μίμνω for μι-μεν-ω.

b. In the future: πτήσομαι from πέτομαι *fly*.

c. In the second aorist: ἔσχον for ἐ-σεχ-ον from ἔχω (ἐχ- for σεχ-, 125 e).

d. In the perfect: πέ-πτα-μαι *have expanded* from πετά-ννῡμι.

N. — Syncopated forms are properly *weak* stems (476 a).

494. Reduplication. — The verb-stem may be reduplicated.

a. In the present with ι: γι-γνώ-σκω (γνω-) *know*, τί-θη-μι *place*, ἵ-στη-μι *set*, δί-δω-μι *give*. The present reduplication may be carried over to other tenses: διδά(κ)σκω *teach* (99), διδάξω. With ε: τε-τραίνω *bore*.

b. In the second aorist: ἄγω (ἀγ-) *lead*, ἤγ-αγ-ον; ἕπομαι *follow*, ἑσπόμην (for σε-σπ-ομην).

c. Regularly with ε in the perfect.

495. Iterative Imperfects and Aorists in -σκ%ε-. — Homer and Herodotus have iterative imperfects and aorists in -σκον and -σκομην denoting a customary or repeated past action. Homer has iterative forms in the imperfect and 1 and 2 aorist active and middle. Herodotus has no iteratives in the 1 aorist and few

---

vowel of the simple verb. Such forms are chiefly Homeric, but occur sometimes in Attic poetry, very rarely in prose. Thus, φλεγέθω (φλέγω *burn*), ἐδιώκαθον (διώκω *pursue*), ἔσχεθον (ἔχω *have*). θ-forms are found in moods other than the indicative (εἰκάθω, εἰκάθοιμι, ἀμῡνάθατε, διωκάθειν, εἰκάθων).

492 D. See the List of Verbs for poetical forms of ἁμαρτάνω, δαρθάνω, θράττω, βλώσκω, δαμάζω, δέμω, πορ-.

493 D. See the List of Verbs for poetical forms of πέλω, πελάζω, μέλω, μέλομαι; also ἔτετμον *found*, ἔπεφνον *slew*.

494 D. Poetic ἀραρίσκω (ἀρ) *fit*, and the intensives (867) μαρ-μαίρω (μαρ-) *flash*, πορ-φύρω (φυρ-) *grow red*, παμ-φαίνω (φαν-) *shine brightly*, ποι-πνύω (πνυ-) *puff*. Also with η in δη-δέκ-το *greeted* (Mss. δείδεκτο).

in the 2 aorist; and only from ω-verbs. Herodotus regularly and Homer usually omit the augment. -αω verbs have -αα-σκον or -α-σκον; -εω verbs -εε-σκον, in Hom. also -ε-σκον. -α-σκον is rare in other verbs than those in -αω. The vowel preceding the suffix is always short.

a. The suffix -σκ%ε- is added to the tense-stem. *Imperf.*: φεύγε-σκε (φεύγω *flee*), ἔχε-σκον (ἔχω *have*), νῑκά-σκομεν (νῑκάω *conquer*), γοάα-σκε (γοάω *bewail*), κρύπτα-σκε (κρύπτω *hide*), καλέε-σκον (καλέω *call*), ζωννύσκετο (ζώννῡμι *gird*); *1 aor.*: ἀπο-τρέψα-σκε (ἀποτρέπω *turn away*); *2 aor.*: φύγε-σκε, στά-σκε *stood*.

VERB-STEM AND PRESENT STEM

496. From the verb-stem (or theme) the present stem is formed in several ways. All verbs are arranged in the present system according to the method of forming the present stem from the verb-stem. Verbs are named according to the last letter of the verb-stem (376): 1. Vowel Verbs, 2. Liquid Verbs (including liquids and nasals), 3. Stop Verbs.

I. PRESENT SYSTEM

(PRESENT AND IMPERFECT ACTIVE AND MIDDLE)

497. The present stem is formed from the verb-stem in five different ways. There are, therefore, five classes of present stems. The verb-stem is sometimes the present stem, but usually it is strengthened in different ways. A sixth class consists of irregular verbs, the present stem of which is not connected with the stem or stems of other tenses.

FIRST OR SIMPLE CLASS

498. Presents of the Simple Class are formed from the verb-stem with or without the thematic vowel.

499. (I) Presents with the thematic vowel (ω-verbs). The present stem is made by adding the thematic vowel %ε- to the verb-stem, as λύ-ω, παιδεύ-ω, παύ-ω, μέν-ω, πείθ-ω, φεύγ-ω, and the denominative verbs τῑμά-ω, φιλέ-ω, βασιλεύ-ω. For the personal endings, see 463 ff. For the derivation of many of these verbs, see 522.

500. The final vowel of the verb-stem is long in the present indicative, but either long or short in the other tense-stems, of the following verbs in -υω or -ιω.

1. a. Verbs in -υω generally have ῡ in Attic in the present; as λύω *loose*, δύω *go under*, θύω *sacrifice* (almost always), φύω *make grow* (usually). Also in ἀλύω, ἀρτύω, βρενθύομαι, γηρύομαι, δακρύω (once ῠ), ἱδρύω, ἰσχύω, καττύω, κνύω,

---

500. 1. D. Homer has short υ in ἀλύω, ἀνύω, βρύω, δύω, ἐρύω, ἠμύω, τανύω, φύω, and in all denominative verbs except ἐρητύοντο and ἐπῑθύουσι, where ῡ is metrically necessary; long υ in ξύω, πτύω, ὕω; anceps in θύω *sacrifice* (ῡ doubt-

κωκύω, κωλύω (usually), μηνύω, ὀπύω (ὀπυίω), πτύω, ῥύομαι, στύομαι, τρύω, ὕει, possibly in εἰλύομαι, ἠμύω, μύω, ξύω, φλύω; ἐλινύω, μηρύομαι, πληθύω (once ῠ), φῑτύω. ὠρύω (ῡ̆) is doubtful.

b. -υω has υ short in ἀνύω, ἀρύω, βρύω, κλύω (but κλῦθι), μεθύω, and in all verbs in -νυω.

2. Attic has ῑ in primitive verbs in -ιω, as πρίω, χρίω, χλίω, but ῐ in τίω. Denominative verbs have ῑ; but ἐσθίω.

501. Several verbs with medial ῑ, ῡ in the present, show ῐ or ῑ, ῠ or ῡ in some other tense or tenses. Thus, θλίβω *press* τέθλιφα, πνίγω *choke* ἐπνίγην, τρίβω *rub* τέτριφα ἐτρίβην, τύφω *raise smoke* ἐτύφην, ψύχω *cool* ἐψύχην.

502. Verb-stems having the weak grades α, ι, υ, show the strong grades η, ει, ευ in the present; as τήκ-ω (τᾰκ-) *melt*, λείπω (λιπ-) *leave*, φεύγω (φυγ-) *flee*.

a. To this class belong also λήθω, σήπω, τέθηπα *am astonished*, 2 aor. ἔταφον, ἀλείφω, (δέδοικα, 703), εἴκω (ἔοικα), (εἴωθα, 563 a), ἐρείκω, ἐρείπω, πείθω, στείβω, στείχω, φείδομαι; ἐρεύγομαι, κεύθω, πεύθομαι, τεύχω.

503. **Present Stems in -ε%- for ευ%-.** — The strong form ευ before the thematic vowel became εϝ (ευ̯) and then ε (20 a, 43) in the verbs θέω *run* θεύσομαι, νέω *swim* ἔνευσα, πλέω *sail* ἔπλευσα, πνέω *breathe* ἔπνευσα, ῥέω *flow* ῥεύσομαι, χέω *pour* κέχυκα, κέχυμαι, ἐχύθην.

504. (II) Presents without the thematic vowel (μι-verbs). The personal ending is added directly to the verb-stem, which is often reduplicated. The verb-stem shows different vowel grades, strong forms η, ω in the singular, weak forms ε (α), ο in the dual and plural. Thus τί-θη-μι, τί-θε-μεν; ἵ-στη-μι for σι-στη-μι (= σι-στᾱ-μι), ἵ-στα-μεν; δί-δω-μι, δί-δο-μεν.

a. All verbs in μι (enumerated 723 ff) belong to this class except those in -νῡμι (523 f) and -νημι (523 g).

SECOND OR T CLASS (VERBS IN -πτω)

505. The present stem is formed by adding -τ%- to the verb-stem, which ends in π, β, or φ. The verb-stem is ascertained from the second aorist (if there is one) or from a word from the same root.

---

ful), θύω *rush on*, *rage*, λῡ́ω (rarely λύω), ποιπνύω, ῥύομαι. Pindar has υ short in θύω *sacrifice*, ἰσχύω, λύω, μανύω, ῥύω, ῥύομαι, in presents in -νυω, and in denominative verbs.

2. Hom. has ῑ in the primitives πίομαι and χρίω; but τίω and τίω (τείω?); -ῐω in denominatives (except μήνῑε B 769). κονίω, ὀίομαι are from κονι(σ)-ι̯ω, ὀι(σ)-ι̯ομαι.

3. Where Attic has ῡ, ῑ in the present, and Epic ῠ, ῐ, the former are due to the influence of ῡ, ῑ in the future and aorist.

503 D. These verbs end in -ευω in Aeolic (πνεύω etc.). Epic πλείω, πνείω have ει by metrical lengthening (28 D.).

κόπτω *cut*,	verb-stem κοπ-	in 2 aor. pass.	ἐ-κόπ-ην.
βλάπτω *injure*,	" " βλαβ-	" " "	ἐ-βλάβ-ην.
καλύπτω *cover*,	" " καλυβ-	"	καλύβ-η *hut*.
ῥίπτω *throw*,	" " ῥιφ-, ῥῑφ-	" 2 aor. pass.	ἐ-ρρίφ-ην.

a. ἀστράπτω *lighten*, χαλέπτω *oppress* may be from -πι̯ω (117, 507).

506. Some of the verbs of this class add ε in the present or other tenses, as ῥῑπτέω *throw*, πεκτέω *comb*, τύπτω *strike* τυπτήσω.

THIRD OR IOTA CLASS

507. The present stem is formed by adding -ι̯%ε- to the verb-stem and by making the necessary euphonic changes (109–116).

I. PRESENTS IN -ζω

508. Dental Verb-stems. — Verb-stems in δ unite with ι̯ to form presents in -ζω (116), as φράζω *tell* (φραδ-ι̯ω), ἐλπίζω *hope* (ἐλπιδ-), κομίζω *carry* (κομιδ-ή *a carrying*), ὄζω *smell* (ὀδ-μή *odour*), καθέζομαι *seat myself* (ἕδ-ος *seat*).

a. σῴζω *save* (for σω-ιζω) forms its tenses partly from the verb-stem σω-, partly from the verb-stem σωι-.

509. Stems in γ. — Some verbs in -ζω are derived from stems in γ preceded by a vowel; as ἁρπάζω *seize* for ἁρπαγ-ι̯ω (cp. ἁρπαγ-ή *seizure*), κρᾱ́ζω *cry out* (2 aor. ἔκραγον). See 116, other examples 623 γ III.

a. νίζω *wash* makes its other tenses from the verb-stem νιβ- (fut. νίψω, cp. Hom. νίπτομαι).

510. A few verbs with stems in γγ lose one γ and have presents in -ζω; as κλάζω *scream* (κλαγγ-ή), fut. κλάγξω; σαλπίζω *sound the trumpet* ἐσάλπιγξα (also λύζω *sob*, πλάζω *cause to wander*).

511. ῥεγι̯ω, ἐργι̯ω yield ῥέζω *do* (poetic) and ἔρδω (Ionic and poetic). See 116.

512. Most verbs in -ζω are not formed from stems in δ or γ, but are due to analogy. See 516, 623 γ III, 866. 6.

II. PRESENTS IN -ττω (IONIC AND LATER ATTIC -σσω, 78)

513. Palatal Verb-stems. — Stems ending in κ or χ unite with ι̯ to form presents in -ττω (-σσω).

φυλάττω *guard* from φυλακ-ι̯ω (φυλακ-ή *guard* (112)); κηρύττω *proclaim* from κηρῡκ-ι̯ω (κῆρυξ, κήρῡκ-ος); ταράττω *disturb* from ταραχ-ι̯ω (ταραχ-ή *confusion*).

a. πέττω *cook* is for πεκ-ι̯ω; all other tenses are made from πεπ-.

---

508 D. Aeolic has -σδω for -ζω.

514. Several verbs showing forms in γ seem to unite γ with ι̯ to form presents in -ττω (-σσω.) Thus ἀλλάττω *change*, μάττω *knead*, πλήττω *strike* (with the 2 aorists passive ἠλλάγ-ην, ἐμάγ-ην, ἐπλήγ-ην), πράττω *do* (2 perf. πέπρᾱγα, 571), τάττω *arrange* (τᾱγ-ός *commander*).

a. So δράττομαι *grasp*, νάττω *compress* (515 b), νύττω *push*, πτύσσω *fold*, σάττω *load*, σῡρίττω *pipe*, σφάττω *kill*, φράττω *fence*. πράττω has the late perf. πέπρᾱχα.

515. Some presents in -ττω (-σσω) are formed from stems in τ, θ like those from κ, χ.

Poet. ἐρέσσω *row* (ἐρέτ-ης *rower*) aor. ἤρεσα; poet. κορύσσω *arm* (κόρυς κόρυθ-ος *helmet*), imperf. ἐκόρυσσε.

a. So also βλίττω *take honey*, πάττω *sprinkle*, πτίττω *pound*, and perhaps πλάττω *form*; also ἀφάσσω Hdt., and poetic ἱμάσσω, λαφύσσω, λίσσομαι.

b. νάττω *compress* (ναγ-, ναδ-) ἔναξα, νένασμαι and νέναγμαι. Cp. 514 a.

516. Formations by Analogy. — a. As γ + ι̯ and δ + ι̯ unite to form ζ, none of the verbs in -ττω can be derived from -γι̯ω or -δι̯ω. Since the future and aorist of verbs in -ζω might often seem to be derived from stems in κ, χ, or τ, θ, uncertainty arose as to these tenses: thus the future σφάξω (σφαγ-σω) from Epic σφάζω *slay* (σφαγ-ι̯ω) was confused in formation with φυλάξω (φυλακ-σω), and a present σφάττω was constructed like φυλάττω. Similarly, Attic ἁρπάσω (-ομαι) for Epic ἁρπάξω; and so in place of (poetic) ἁρμόζω *fit* (ἁρμοδ-) the form ἁρμόττω was constructed.

III. LIQUID AND NASAL STEMS

517. (I) Presents in -λλω are formed from verb-stems in λ, to which ι̯ is assimilated (110). Thus, ἀγγέλλω *announce* (ἀγγελ-ι̯ω), στέλλω *send* (στελ-ι̯ω).

518. (II) Presents in -αινω and -αιρω are formed from verb-stems in -αν and -αρ, the ι̯ being thrown back to unite with the vowel of the verb-stem (111). Thus, φαίνω *show* (φαν-ι̯ω), ὀνομαίνω *name* (ὀνομαν-ι̯ω), χαίρω *rejoice* (χαρ-ι̯ω).

a. Many verbs add -ι̯ω to the weak form of the stem, as ὀνομαίν-ω for ὀνομαν-ι̯ω from ὀνομν̥-ι̯ω, cp. *nomen* (35 b).

b. Hom. has κῡδαίνω and κῡδάνω *honour*, μελαίνω *blacken* and μελάνω *grow black*. ὀλισθαίνω *slip* is late for ὀλισθάνω.

c. The ending -αινω has been attached, by analogy, in θερμαίνω *make hot*, etc. (620 III, 866.7). Likewise -ῡνω (519) in poetic ἀρτΰνω *prepare*, parallel to ἀρτύω (in composition), by analogy to βαρύνω *weigh down*, ἡδύνω *sweeten*.

---

516 D. Homer has many cases of this confusion; as πολεμίζω (πολεμιδ-) but πολεμίξω. In Doric the ξ forms from -ζω verbs are especially common, as χωρίζω *separate*, χωριξῶ, ἐχώριξα. παίζω *sport* has (late) ἔπαιξα.

519. (III) Presents in -εινω, -ειρω, -ῑνω, -ῑρω, -ῡνω, and -ῡρω are formed from stems in εν, ερ, ἴν, ἴρ, ὔν, ὔρ with ι̯%ε- added. Here ι̯ disappears and the vowel preceding ν or ρ is lengthened by compensation (ε to ει; ι to ῑ; υ to ῡ). See 37 a, 111.

τείνω *stretch* (τεν-ι̯ω), φθείρω *destroy* (φθερ-), κρίνω (κριν-), οἰκτίρω *pity* (οἰκτιρ-) generally written οἰκτείρω, ἀμύνω *ward off* (ἀμυν-), μαρτύρομαι *call to witness* (μαρτυρ-).

a. ὀφείλω (ὀφελ-) *owe, am obliged* is formed like τείνω, φθείρω in order to distinguish it from ὀφέλλω (ὀφελ-) *increase* formed regularly. Hom. has usually Aeolic ὀφέλλω in the sense of ὀφείλω. δείρω *flay* (δερ-ι̯ω) is parallel to δέρ-ω (499).

520. Verb-stems in -αυ- for (αυ̯, -αϝ-). — Two verbs with verb-stems in -αυ have presents in -αιω from -αιϝω out of -αϝ-ι̯ω (38 a): **καίω** *burn* (καυ-, καϝ-), fut. καύ-σω; and **κλαίω** *weep* (κλαυ-, κλαϝ-), fut. κλαύ-σομαι. Others 624 b.

a. Attic prose often has κάω and κλάω, derived from αιϝ before ει (κάεις, and, with ᾱ extended to the 1 person, κάω). Cp. 396.

521. Addition of ε. — The following verbs add ε in one or more tense-stems other than the present: βάλλω *throw*, καθίζω *sit*, κλαίω *weep*, ὄζω *smell*, ὀφείλω *owe, am obliged*, χαίρω *rejoice*.

522. Contracted Verbs and Some Verbs in -ιω, -υω. — **a.** Verbs in -αω, -εω, -οω, which for convenience have been treated under the first class, properly belong here, ι̯ (*y*) having been lost between vowels. Thus, τῑμάω from τῑμα-ι̯ω (τῑμᾱ-), οἰκέω *dwell* from οἰκε-ι̯ω (οἰκε- alternate stem to οἰκο-, 229 b), δηλόω from δηλο-ι̯ω. So in denominatives, as poetic μηνίω *am wroth* (μηνι-ι̯ω), φῑτύω *sow* (φῑτυ-ι̯ω). Primitives in -ῑω, -ῡω are of uncertain origin. Cp. 608, 624.

N. — The rare spellings ἀλυίω, θυίω, μεθυίω, φυίω indicate their origin from -ι̯ω.

b. So with stems in long vowels: δρῶ *do* from δρᾱ-ι̯ω, ζῶ *live* from ζη-ι̯ω (cp. ζῆθι), χρῶ *give oracles* from χρη-ι̯ω (2 pers. χρῇς, 394).

FOURTH OR N CLASS

523. The present stem of the N class is formed from the verb-stem by the addition of a suffix containing ν.

a. -ν%ε- is added: δάκ-νω *bite*, τέμ-νω *cut*.

So δύνω, κάμνω, πίνω, πίτνω poet., τίνω, φθάνω, φθίνω.

b. -αν%ε- is added: αἰσθ-άν-ομαι *perceive*, ἁμαρτ-άν-ω *err*.

So αὐξάνω, βλαστάνω, δαρθάνω, ἀπεχθάνομαι, οἰδάνω, ὀλισθάνω, ὀφλισκάνω (526).

c. -αν%ε- is added and a nasal (μ, ν, or γ nasal) inserted in the verb-stem: λα-μ-β-άν-ω (λαβ-) *take*, λα-ν-θ-άν-ω *escape notice* (λαθ-), τυ-γ-χ-άν-ω *happen* (τυχ-).

So ἁνδάνω *please* (ἁδ-), θιγγάνω *touch* (θιγ-), κιγχάνω *find* (κιχ-), λαγχάνω *obtain by lot* (λαχ-), μανθάνω *learn* (μαθ-), πυνθάνομαι *inquire* (πυθ-).

d. -νε%ε- is added: βῡ-νέ-ω *stop up* (also βύω), ἱκ-νέ-ο-μαι *come* (also ἵκω),

---

519 D. Aeolic has here -εννω, -ερρω, -ιννω, -ιρρω, -υννω, -υρρω (37 D. 3); for κτείνω, it has κταίνω; cp. Doric φθαίρω for φθείρω.

κυ-νέ-ω *kiss*, ἀμπ-ισχ-νέ-ο-μαι *have on*, ὑπ-ισχ-νέ-ο-μαι *promise* (cp. ἴ-σχ-ω for σι-σχ-ω, 493 a).

e. -υν%- is added: ἐλαύνω *drive* for ἐλα-νυ-ω.

f. -νυ (-ννυ after a short vowel) is added (second class of μι-verbs, 414): δείκ-νῡ-μι *show* (δεικ-, present stem δεικνῡ-), ζεύγ-νῡ-μι *yoke* (ζευγ-), ὄλλῡμι *destroy* (for ὀλ-νῡμι, 77 a); κερά-ννῡ-μι *mix* (κερα-), σκεδά-ννῡ-μι *scatter* (σκεδα-). Others 729 ff. Some of these verbs have presents in -νω (746).

N. 1. — The forms in -ννῡμι spread from ἕννῡμι, σβέννῡμι, which are derived from ἐσ-νῡμι, σβεσ-νῡμι.

N. 2. — Some verbs in -νω are formed from -νϝ%- for -νυ̯%-; as Hom. τίνω, φθίνω, φθάνω, ἄνομαι from τι-νϝ-ω, etc., (37 D. 1). Attic τίνω, etc. dropped the ϝ.

g. -να, -νη are added (third class of μι-verbs 412); as in (poetic) δάμ-νη-μι *I conquer*, δάμ-να-μεν *we conquer* (δαμ-), and in σκίδ-νη-μι (rare in prose for σκεδάννῡμι) *scatter*. The verbs of this class are chiefly poetic (Epic), and most have alternative forms in -αω. See 737.

In two further divisions there is a transition to the Iota Class.

h. -ιν%- for -ν-ι̯% is added: βαίνω *go* (βα-ν-ι̯ω), κερδαίνω *gain* (κερδα-ν-ι̯ω), τετραίνω *bore* (τετρα-ν-ιω). So poetic ῥαίνω *sprinkle*. For the added ν, cp. δάκ-ν-ω (523 a). See 518 a.

i. -αιν%- for αν-ι̯% is added: ὀσφραίνομαι *smell* (ὀσφραν-ι̯ομαι), Hom. ἀλιταίνομαι *sin* (also ἀλιτραίνω). See 518 a.

524. A short vowel of the verb-stem is lengthened in the case of some verbs to form one or more of the tense-stems other than the present. Thus, λαμβάνω (λαβ-) *take* λήψομαι (ληβ-); δάκνω (δακ-) *bite* δήξω (δηκ-). So λαγχάνω, λανθάνω, τυγχάνω, πυνθάνομαι (πυθ-) *inquire*, fut. πεύσομαι (πευθ-).

a. ζεύγνῡμι *yoke*, πήγνῡμι *fasten*, ῥήγνῡμι *break* have the strong grade in all tenses except the 2 pass. system. μείγνῡμι *mix* (commonly written μίγνῡμι) has μἴγ- only in the 2 perf. and 2 pass. systems.

525. Addition of ε and ο. — **a.** Many verbs add ε to the verb-stem to form all the tenses except present, 2 aorist, and 2 perfect; as αἰσθάνομαι, ἁμαρτάνω, ἁνδάνω, αὐξάνω, ἀπεχθάνομαι, βλαστάνω, δαρθάνω, κιγχάνω, μανθάνω, ὀλισθάνω, ὀφλισκάνω. One or more tenses with ε added are formed by κερδαίνω, ὄλλῡμι, ὀσφραίνομαι, στόρνῡμι, τυγχάνω.

b. ὄμνῡμι *swear* has ὀμο- in all systems except the present and future, as ὤμοσα, ὀμώμοκα, but fut. ὀμοῦμαι from ὀμεομαι.

FIFTH OR INCEPTIVE CLASS (VERBS IN -σκω)

526. The present stem is formed by adding the suffix -σκ%- to the verb-stem if it ends in a vowel; -ισκ%- if it ends in a consonant. Thus, ἀρέ-σκω *please*, εὑρ-ίσκω *find*.

a. This class is called *inceptive* (or *inchoative*) because some of the verbs belonging to it have the sense of *beginning* or *becoming* (cp. Lat. *-sco*); as γηράσκω *grow old*. But very few verbs have this meaning.

b. In θνῄσκω *die*, μιμνῄσκω *remind*, -ισκω was later added to verb-stems ending in a vowel. The older forms are θνήσκω, μιμνήσκω.

c. The verb-stem is often reduplicated in the present; as γι-γνώ-σκω *know*, βι-βρώ-σκω *eat*, δι-δρά-σκω *run away*. Poetic ἀρ-αρ-ίσκω *fit*, poetic ἀπ-αφ-ίσκω *deceive*, have the form of Attic reduplication. μίσγω may stand for μι-(μ)σγω.

d. A stop consonant is dropped before -σκω (99); as δι-δά(κ)-σκω *teach* (cp. δι-δακ-τός), ἀλύ(κ)-σκω *avoid*, λά(κ)-σκω *speak*. πάσχω *suffer* is for πα(θ)-σκω (126).

e. The present stem often shows the strong grades ω (weak ο) and ᾱ or η (weak α). See b, c. Weak grades appear in φάσκω *say*, βόσκω *feed*.

f. On the iteratives in -σκω see 495.

527. The following verbs belong to this class (poetic and Ionic forms are starred):

a. Vowel stems: ἀλδήσκω* (ἀλδη-), ἀναβιώσκομαι* (βιο-), ἀρέσκω (ἀρε-), βάσκω* (βα- for βυ̯-, 35 b), βιβρώσκω (βρο-), βλώσκω* (μολ-, μλο-, βλο-, 130 D.), βόσκω (βο-), γενειάσκω (cp. γενειάω), γηράσκω (γηρα-), γιγνώσκω (γνο-), δεδίσκομαι *frighten*, διδράσκω (δρα-), ἡβάσκω (ἡβα-), ἡλάσκω* (ἡλα-), θνῄσκω (θαν-, θνα-), θρῴσκω* (θορ-, θρο-), ἱλάσκομαι (ἱλα-), κικλήσκω* (καλε-, κλη-), κυΐσκομαι* (κυ-), μεθύσκω (μεθυ-), μιμνῄσκω (μνα-), πιπίσκω* (πι-), πιπράσκω (πρα-), πινύσκω* (πινυ-), πιφαύσκω* (φαυ-), τιτρώσκω (τρο-), φάσκω (φα-), χάσκω* (χα-).

b. Consonant stems: ἁλίσκομαι (ἁλ-ο-), ἀλύσκω* (ἀλυκ-), ἀμβλίσκω (ἀμβλ- ἀμβλο-), ἀμπλακίσκω* (ἀμπλακ-), ἀνᾱλίσκω (ἀν-ᾱλ-ο-), ἀπαφίσκω* (ἀπ-αφ-), ἀραρίσκω* (ἀρ-), δεδίσκομαι* *welcome* (δε-δικ-) and δηδίσκομαι (usually written δειδ-) *welcome*, διδάσκω (διδαχ-), ἐΐσκω (ἐϊκ-), ἐπαυρίσκω* (αὐρ-), εὑρίσκω (εὑρ-ε-), λάσκω* (λακ-), μίσγω* (μιγ-), ὀφλισκάνω (ὀφλ-ε-), πάσχω (παθ-), στερίσκω (στερ-ε-), τιτύσκομαι* (τι-τυκ-), ὑλάσκω* (ὑλακ-), χρηΐσκομαι* (χρη-).

528. Addition of ε and ο.—στερίσκω *deprive* (cp. στέρομαι) makes all the other tense-stems from στερε-; εὑρίσκω has εὑρε- except in the present and 2 aorist. —ἁλίσκομαι *am captured* (ἁλ-) adds ο in other tense-stems.

SIXTH OR MIXED CLASS

529. This class includes some irregular verbs, one or more of whose tense-stems are quite different from others, as Eng. *am*, *was*, *be*, Lat. *sum*, *fui*. For the full list of forms see the List of Verbs.

1. αἱρέω (αἱρε-, ἑλ-) *take*, fut. αἱρήσω, ᾕρηκα, etc., 2 aor. εἷλον.
2. εἶδον (ϝιδ-, ἰδ-) *saw*, *vidi*, 2 aorist (with no present act.); 2 pf. οἶδα *know* (794). Middle εἴδομαι (poetic). εἶδον is used as 2 aor. of ὁράω (see below).
3. εἶπον (εἰπ-, ἐρ-, ῥε-) *spoke*, 2 aor. (no pres.); fut. (ἐρέω) ἐρῶ, perf. εἴ-ρη-κα, εἴρημαι, aor. pass. ἐρρήθην. The stem ἐρ- is for ϝερ-, seen in Lat. *ver-bum*. (Cp. 492.) ῥε- is for ϝρε, hence εἴρημαι for ϝε-ϝρη-μαι.
4. ἔρχομαι (ἐρχ-, ἐλευθ-, ἐλυθ-, ἐλθ-), *go*. Fut. ἐλεύσομαι (usually poet.), 2 perf. ἐλήλυθα, 2 aor. ἦλθον. The Attic future is εἶμι *shall go* (774). The imperf. and the moods of the pres. other than the indic. use the forms of εἶμι.

---

526 c. D. Hom. has ἐΐσκω *liken* for ϝεϝί(κ)-σκω, also ἴσκω from ϝί(κ)-σκω, τιτύ(κ)-σκομαι *prepare*, δε-δί(κ)-σκομαι *welcome*.

5. ἐσθίω (ἐσθ-, ἐδ-, φαγ-) *eat*, fut. ἔδομαι (541), pf. ἐδήδοκα, -ἐδήδεσμαι, ἠδέσθην, 2 aor. ἔφαγον.
6. ὁράω (ὁρα-, ὀπ-, ϝιδ-) *see*, fut. ὄψομαι, perf. ἑώρᾱκα or ἑόρᾱκα, perf. mid. ἑώρᾱμαι or ὦμμαι (ὠπ-μαι), ὤφθην, 2 aor. εἶδον (see 2 above).
7. πάσχω (παθ-, πενθ-) *suffer*, fut. πείσομαι for πενθ-σομαι (100), 2 pf. πέπονθα, 2 aor. ἔπαθον. (See 526 d.)
8. πίνω (πι-, πο-) *drink*, from πί-ν-ω (523 a), fut. πίομαι (541), pf. πέπωκα, 2 aor. ἔπιον, imp. πῖθι (466. 1, a, 687).
9. τρέχω (τρεχ- for θρεχ- (125 g), δραμ-, δραμε-) *run*, fut. δραμοῦμαι, pf. δεδράμηκα, 2 aor. ἔδραμον.
10. φέρω (φερ-, οἰ-, ἐνεκ-, by reduplication and syncope ἐν-ενεκ and ἐνεγκ-) *bear*; fut. οἴσω, aor. ἤνεγκα, perf. ἐν-ήνοχ-α (446, 478), ἐν-ήνεγ-μαι, aor. pass. ἠνέχθην.
11. ὠνέομαι (ὠνε-, πρια-) *buy*, fut. ὠνήσομαι, perf. ἐώνημαι, ἐωνήθην. For ἐωνησάμην the form ἐπριάμην is used.

530. Apart from the irregularities of Class VI, some verbs may, by the formation of the verb-stem, belong to more than one class, as βαίνω (III, IV), ὀσφραίνομαι (III, IV), ὀφλισκάνω (IV, V).

531. Many verbs have alternative forms, often of different classes, as κῡδάνω κῡδαίνω *honour*, ἵκω ἱκάνω *come*, μελάν-ω *grow black*, μελαίνω (μελαν-ι̯ω) *blacken*, κλάζω (κλαγγ-) κλαγγ-άν-ω *scream*, σφάζω σφάττω *slay* (516). Cp. also ἀνύω ἀνύτω *accomplish*, ἀρύω ἀρύτω *draw water*, Hom. ἐρύκω, ἐρῡκάνω, ἐρῡκανάω *restrain*. Cp. 866. 10.

II. FUTURE SYSTEM

(FUTURE ACTIVE AND MIDDLE)

532. Many, if not all, future forms in σ are in reality subjunctives of the first aorist. λύσω, παιδεύσω, λείψω, στήσω are alike future indicative and aorist subjunctive in form. In poetry and in some dialects there is no external difference between the future indicative and the aorist subjunctive when the latter has (as often in Hom.) a short mood-sign (457 D.); *e.g.*, Hom. βήσομεν, ἀμείψεται, Ionic inscriptions ποιήσει.

533. The future stem is formed by adding the tense-suffix -σ%- (-εσ%- in liquid stems, 535) to the verb-stem: λῡ́-σω, *I shall* (or *will*) *loose*, λῡ́σομαι; θή-σω from τί-θη-μι *place*; δείξω from δείκ-νῡ-μι *show*.

a. In verbs showing strong and weak grades (476) the ending is added to the strong stem: λείπω λείψω, τήκω τήξω, πνέω πνεύσομαι (503), δίδωμι δώσω.

534. Vowel Verbs. — Verb-stems ending in a short vowel lengthen the vowel before the tense suffix (α to η except after ε, ι, ρ). Thus, τῑμάω, τῑμήσω; ἐάω, ἐάσω; φιλέω, φιλήσω.

a. On χράω *give oracles*, χράομαι *use*, ἀκροάομαι *hear*, see 487 a.

b. For verbs retaining a short final vowel, see 488.

---

534 D. Doric and Aeolic always lengthen α to ᾱ (τῑμᾱ́σω).

b. In verbs with stems originally ending in -σ Hom. often has σσ in the future: ἀνύω ἀνύσσεσθαι, τελέω τελέσσω; by analogy ὄλλῡμι ὀλέσσω (and ὀλέσω, ὀλεῖται).

535. Liquid Verbs. — Verb-stems ending in λ, μ, ν, ρ, add -εσ%-; then σ drops and ε contracts with the following vowel.

φαίνω (φαν-) *show*, φανῶ, φανεῖς from φαν-έ(σ)ω, φαν-έ(σ)εις; στέλλω (στελ-) *send*, στελοῦμεν, στελεῖτε from στελ-έ(σ)ομεν, στελ-έ(σ)ετε. See p. 128.

536. σ is retained in the poetic forms κέλσω (κέλλω *land*, κελ-), κύρσω (κύρω *meet*, κυρ-), θέρσομαι (θέρομαι *warm myself*, θερ-), ὄρσω (ὄρνῡμι *rouse*, ὀρ-). So also in the aorist. See ἀραρίσκω, εἴλω, κείρω, φθείρω, φύρω in the List of Verbs.

537. Stop Verbs. — Labial (π, β, φ) and palatal (κ, γ, χ) stops at the end of the verb-stem unite with σ to form ψ or ξ. Dentals (τ, δ, θ) are lost before σ (98).

κόπ-τ-ω (κοπ-) *cut*, κόψω, κόψομαι; βλάπ-τ-ω (βλαβ-) *injure*, βλάψω, βλάψομαι; γράφ-ω *write*, γράψω, γράψομαι; πλέκ-ω *weave*, πλέξω, πλέξομαι; λέγ-ω *say*, λέξω, λέξομαι; ταράττω (ταραχ-) *disturb*, ταράξω, ταράξομαι; φράζω (φραδ-) *say*, φράσω; πείθω (πιθ-, πειθ-) *persuade*, πείσω, πείσομαι.

a. When ε or ο is added to the verb-stem, it is lengthened to η or ω: as βούλομαι (βουλ-ε-) *wish* βουλήσομαι, ἁλίσκομαι (ἁλ-ο-) *am captured* ἁλώσομαι. So also in the first aorist and in other tenses where lengthening is regular.

538. Attic Future. — Certain formations of the future are called *Attic* because they occur especially in that dialect in contrast to the later language; they occur also in Homer, Herodotus, and in other dialects.

539. These futures usually occur when σ is preceded by ᾰ or ε and these vowels are not preceded by a syllable long by nature or position. Here σ is dropped and -άω and -έω are contracted to -ῶ. When ι precedes σ, the ending is ι-(σ)έω which contracts to -ιῶ.

a. καλέω *call*, τελέω *finish* drop the σ of καλέσω καλέσομαι, τελέσω τελέσομαι and the resulting Attic forms are καλῶ καλοῦμαι, τελῶ (τελοῦμαι poetic).

b. ἐλαύνω (ἐλα-) *drive* has Hom. ἐλάω, Attic ἐλῶ. — καθέζομαι (καθεδ-) *sit* has Attic καθεδοῦμαι. — μάχομαι (μαχ-ε-) *fight* has Hom. μαχέσομαι (and μαχήσομαι), Attic μαχοῦμαι. — ὄλλῡμι (ὀλ-ε-) *destroy* has Hom. ὀλέσω, Attic ὀλῶ.

c. All verbs in -αννῡμι have futures in -ά(σ)ω, -ῶ. Thus, σκεδάννῡμι (σκεδα-) *scatter*, poet. σκεδάσω, Attic σκεδῶ. Similarly some verbs in -εννῡμι: ἀμφιέννῡμι (ἀμφιε-) *clothe*, Epic ἀμφιέσω, Attic ἀμφιῶ; στόρνῡμι (στορ-ε-) *spread*, late στορέσω, Attic στορῶ.

d. A very few verbs in -αζω have the contracted form. βιβάζω (βιβαδ-) *cause to go* usually has Attic βιβῶ from βιβάσω. So ἐξετῶμεν = ἐξετάσομεν from ἐξετάζω *examine*.

e. Verbs in -ιζω of more than two syllables drop σ and insert ε, thus making -ι(σ)έω, -ι(σ)έομαι, which contract to -ιῶ and -ιοῦμαι, as in the Doric future (540).

---

535 D. These futures are often uncontracted in Homer (βαλέω, κτενέεις, ἀγγελέουσιν); regularly in Aeolic; in Hdt. properly only when ε comes before ο or ω.

537 D. Doric has -ξω from most verbs in -ζω (516 D.).

539. b. D. For Hom. -οω for -αω, see 645.

So νομίζω (νομιδ-) *consider* makes νομισεω, νομι-εω, νομιῶ and in like manner νομιοῦμαι, both inflected like ποιῶ, ποιοῦμαι. So ἐθιοῦσι, οἰκιοῦντες from ἐθίζω *accustom*, οἰκίζω *colonize*. But σχίζω (σχιδ-) *split* makes σχίσω. νομιῶ etc. are due to the analogy of the liquid verbs.

N. — Such forms in Attic texts as ἐλάσω, τελέσω, νομίσω, βιβάσω are erroneous.

540. Doric Future. — Some verbs, which have a future middle with an active meaning, form the stem of the future middle by adding -σε%-, and contracting -σέομαι to -σοῦμαι. Such verbs (except νέω, πίπτω) have also the regular future in -σομαι.

κλαίω (κλαυ-, 520) *weep* κλαυσοῦμαι, νέω (νυ-, νευ-) *swim* νευσοῦμαι (doubtful), πλέω (πλυ-, πλευ-) *sail* πλευσοῦμαι, πνέω (πνυ-, πνευ-) *breathe* πνευσοῦμαι, πίπτω (πετ-) *fall* πεσοῦμαι, πυνθάνομαι (πυθ-, πευθ-) πευσοῦμαι (once), φεύγω (φυγ-, φευγ-) φευξοῦμαι, χέζω (χεδ-) χεσοῦμαι.

a. The inflection of the Doric future is as follows: —

λῡσῶ, -σοῦμαι	λῡσοῦμες, -σούμεθα	λῡσῶν, -σούμενος
λῡσεῖς, -σῇ	λῡσεῖτε, -σεῖσθε	λῡσεῖν, -σεῖσθαι
λῡσεῖ, -σεῖται	λῡσοῦντι, -σοῦνται	

b. These are called *Doric* futures because Doric usually makes all futures (active and middle) in -σέω -σῶ, -σέομαι -σοῦμαι.

c. Attic πεσοῦμαι (Hom. πεσέομαι) from πίπτω *fall* comes from πετεομαι. Attic ἔπεσον is derived from 2 aor. ἔπετον (Dor. and Aeol.) under the influence of πεσοῦμαι.

541. Futures with Present Forms. — The following verbs have no future suffix, the future thus having the form of a present: ἔδομαι (ἐδ-) *eat*, πίομαι (πι-) *drink*, χέω (χυ-) and χέομαι, *pour*. See 529. 5, 8.

a. These are probably old subjunctives which have retained their future meaning. In ἔδομαι and πίομαι the mood-sign is short (457 D.). Hom. has βέομαι or βείομαι *live*, δήω *find*, κήω (written κείω) *lie*, ἐξανύω *achieve*, ἐρύω *draw*, τανύω *stretch*, and ἀλεύεται *avoid*. νέομαι *go* is for νεσομαι.

III. FIRST (SIGMATIC) AORIST SYSTEM

(FIRST AORIST ACTIVE AND MIDDLE)

542. The first aorist stem is formed by adding the tense suffix -σα to the verb-stem: ἔ-λῡ-σα *I loosed*, λῡ́σω, λῡ́σαιμι; ἔ-δειξα *I showed*, from δείκ-νῡ-μι. See 666.

---

539 D. Hom. has ἀεικιῶ, κομιῶ, κτεριῶ; and also τελέω, καλέω, ἐλάω, ἀντιόω, δαμόωσι (645), ἀνύω, ἐρύουσι, τανύουσι. Hdt. always uses the -ιῶ and -ιοῦμαι forms. Homeric futures in -εω have a liquid before ε, and are analogous to the futures of liquid verbs.

540 D. Hom. ἐσσεῖται (and ἔσσεται, ἔσεται, ἔσται). In Doric there are three forms: (1) -σέω (and -σῶ), -σέομαι (and -σοῦμαι); and often with ευ from εο as -εῦντι, -εῦμες; (2) -σίω with ι from ε before ο and ω; (3) the Attic forms.

542 D. Mixed Aorists. — Hom. has some forms of the first aorist with the thematic vowel (%ε) of the second aorist; as ἄξετε, ἄξεσθε (ἄγω *lead*), ἐβήσετο,

a. In verbs showing strong and weak grades (476), the tense-suffix is added to the strong stem: πείθω ἔπεισα, τήκω ἔτηξα, πνέω ἔπνευσα, ἵστημι (στα-, στη-) ἔστησα, ἐστησάμην.

N.—τίθημι (θε-, θη-) *place*, δίδωμι (δο-, δω-) *give*, ἵημι (ἑ-, ἡ-) *send* have aorists in -κα (ἔθηκα, ἔδωκα, ἧκα in the singular: with κ rarely in the plural). See 755.

543. Vowel Verbs.—Verb-stems ending in a vowel lengthen a short final vowel before the tense-suffix (α to η except after ε, ι, ρ). Thus, τῑμάω ἐτί̄μησα, ἐάω εἴᾱσα (431), φιλέω ἐφίλησα.

a. χέω (χυ-, χευ-, χεϝ-) *pour* has the aorists ἔχεα, ἐχεάμην (Epic ἔχευα, ἐχευάμην) from ἐχευσα, ἐχευσαμην.

b. For verbs retaining a short final vowel see 488.

544. Liquid Verbs.—Verb-stems ending in λ, μ, ν, ρ lose σ and lengthen their vowel in compensation (37): α to η (after ι or ρ to ᾱ), ε to ει, ῐ to ῑ, ῠ to ῡ.

φαίνω (φαν-) *show*, ἔφηνα for ἐφανσα; περαίνω (περαν-) *finish*, ἐπέρᾱνα for ἐπερανσα; στέλλω (στελ-) *send*, ἔστειλα for ἐστελσα; κρίνω (κριν-) *judge*, ἔκρῑνα for ἐκρινσα; ἅλλομαι (ἁλ-) *leap*, ἡλάμην for ἡλσαμην.

a. Some verbs in -αινω (-αν-) have -ᾱνα instead of -ηνα; as γλυκαίνω *sweeten* ἐγλύκᾱνα. So ἰσχναίνω *make thin*, κερδαίνω *gain*, κοιλαίνω *hollow out*, λιπαίνω *fatten*, ὀργαίνω *be angry*, πεπαίνω *make ripe*. Cp. 30 a.

b. The poetic verbs retaining σ in the future (536) retain it also in the aorist.

c. αἴρω (ἀρ-) *raise* is treated as if its verb-stem were ἀρ- (contracted from ἀερ- in ἀείρω): aor. ἦρα, ἄρω, ἄραιμι, ἆρον, ἆραι, ἄρας, and ἠράμην, ἄρωμαι, ἀραίμην, ἄρασθαι, ἀράμενος.

d. ἤνεγκα is used as the first aorist of φέρω *bear*. εἶπα is rare for εἶπον (549).

545. Stop Verbs.—Labial (π, β, φ) and palatal (κ, γ, χ) stops at the end of the verb-stem unite with σ to form ψ or ξ. Dentals (τ, δ, θ) are lost before σ (cp. 98).

πέμπ-ω *send* ἔπεμψα, ἐπεμψάμην; βλάπτω (βλαβ-) *injure* ἔβλαψα; γράφ-ω *write* ἔγραψα, ἐγραψάμην; πλέκ-ω *weave* ἔπλεξα, ἐπλεξάμην; λέγ-ω *say* ἔλεξα; ταράττω (ταραχ-) *disturb* ἐτάραξα, ἐταραξάμην; poetic ἐρέσσω (ἐρετ-) *row* ἤρεσα; φράζω (φραδ-) *tell* ἔφρασα, ἐφρασάμην; πείθ-ω (πιθ-, πειθ-, ποιθ-) *persuade* ἔπεισα.

a. On forms in σ from stems in γ see 516.

---

imper. βήσεο (βαίνω *go*), ἐδύσετο (δύω *set*), ἶξον (ἵκω *come*), οἶσε, οἴσετε, οἰσέμεν, οἰσέμεναι (φέρω *bring*), imper. ὄρσεο *rise* (ὄρνῡμι *rouse*).

543 a. D. Homeric ἠλευάμην and ἠλεάμην *avoided*, ἔκηα *burned* (Att. ἔκαυσα), ἔσσευα *drove*, also have lost σ.

543 b. D. Hom. often has original σσ, as γελάω ἐγέλασσα, τελέω ἐτέλεσσα; in others by analogy, as ὄλλῡμι ὄλεσσα, ὄμνῡμι ὄμοσσα, καλέω κάλεσσα.

544 D. Hom. has Ionic -ηνα for -ᾱνα after ι or ρ. Aeolic assimilates σ to a liquid; as ἔκριννα, ἀπέστελλα, ἐνέμματο, συνέρραισα (= συνείρᾱσα). Cp. Hom. ὤφελλε (ὀφέλλω *increase*).

545 D. Hom. often has σσ from dental stems, as ἐκόμισσα ἐκομισσάμην (κομίζω). Doric has -ξα from most verbs in -ζω; Hom. also has ξ (ἥρπαξε). See 516 D.

IV. SECOND AORIST SYSTEM

(SECOND AORIST ACTIVE AND MIDDLE)

546. The second aorist is formed without any tense-suffix and only from the simple verb-stem. Only primitive verbs (372) have second aorists.

547. (I) **Ω-Verbs.** — Ω-verbs make the second aorist by adding %- to the verb-stem, which regularly ends in a consonant. Verbs showing vowel gradations (476) use the weak stem (otherwise there would be confusion with the imperfect).

λείπω (λιπ-, λειπ-) *leave* ἔλιπον, -ἐλιπόμην; φεύγω (φυγ-, φευγ-) *flee* ἔφυγον; πέτομαι *fly* ἐπτόμην (476 a); λαμβάνω (λαβ-) *take* ἔλαβον.

548. **a.** Vowel verbs rarely form second aorists, as the irregular αἱρέω *seize* (εἷλον, 529. 1), ἐσθίω *eat* (ἔφαγον), ὁράω (εἶδον). ἔπιον *drank* (πίνω) is the only second aorist in prose from a vowel stem and having thematic inflection.

b. Many ω-verbs with stems ending in a vowel have second aorists formed like those of μι-verbs. These are enumerated in 687.

549. Verbs of the First Class (499) adding a thematic vowel to the verb-stem form the second aorist (1) by reduplication (494), as ἄγω *lead* ἤγαγον, and εἶπον probably for ἐ-ϝε-ϝεπ-ον; (2) by syncope (493), as πέτομαι *fly* ἐπτόμην, ἐγείρω (ἐγερ-) *rouse* ἠγρόμην, ἕπομαι (σεπ-) *follow* ἑσπόμην, imperf. εἱπόμην from ἐ-σεπομην, ἔχω (σεχ-) *have* ἔσχον; (3) by using α for ε (476 b) in poetic forms (480), as τρέπω *turn* ἔτραπον; (4) by metathesis (492), as poet. δέρκομαι *see* ἔδρακον.

550. (II) **Μι-Verbs.** — The stem of the second aorist of μι-verbs is the verb-stem without any thematic vowel. In the indicative active the strong form of the stem, which ends in a vowel, is regularly employed. The middle uses the weak stem form.

---

546 D. Hom. has more second aorists than Attic, which favoured the first aorist. Some derivative verbs have Homeric second aorists classed under them for convenience only, as κτυπέω *sound* ἔκτυπον; μῡκάομαι *roar* ἔμυκον; στυγέω *hate* ἔστυγον. These forms are derived from the pure verb-stem (485 d, 553).

547 D. Hom. often has no thematic vowel in the middle voice of ω-verbs (ἐδέγμην from δέχομαι *receive*). See 634, 688.

549 D. (1) Hom. has (ἐ)κέκλετο (κέλο-μαι *command*), λέλαθον (λήθ-ω *lie hid*), ἐπέφραδε (φράζω *tell*), πεπιθεῖν (πείθ-ω *persuade*). ἠρύκακον (ἐρύκ-ω *check*), ἠνίπαπον and ἐνένῑπον (ἐνίπτω *chide*, ἐνιπ-) have unusual formation. (2) ἔ-πλ-όμην (πέλο-μαι *am, come*, πελ-). (3) ἔπραθον (πέρθ-ω *sack*), ἔταμον (τέμ-ν-ω *cut*). (4) βλῆτο (βάλλω *hit*, 128 a).

ἵ-στη-μι (*στα-*, *στη-*) *set*, second aorist ἔστην, ἔστης, ἔστη, ἔστητον, ἐστήτην, ἔστημεν, ἔστητε, ἔστησαν; middle ἐ-θέ-μην from τίθημι (θε-, θη-) *place*, ἐ-δό-μην from δίδωμι (δο-, δω-) *give*.

551. Originally only the dual and plural showed the weak forms, which are retained in the second aorists of τίθημι, δίδωμι, and ἵημι: ἔθεμεν, ἔδομεν, εἷμεν (ἐ-έ-μεν), and in Hom. βάτην (also βήτην) from ἔβην *went*. Elsewhere the weak grades have been displaced by the strong grades, which forced their way in from the singular. Thus, ἔγνον, ἔφῠν in Pindar (= ἔγνω-σαν, ἔφῡ-σαν), which come from ἔγνων(τ), ἔφῡν(τ) by 40. So Hom. ἔτλᾰν, ἔβᾰν. Such 3 pl. forms are rare in the dramatic poets.

a. For the singular of τίθημι, δίδωμι, ἵημι, see 755; for the imperatives, 759; for the infinitives, 760.

552. No verb in -ῡμι has a second aorist in Attic from the stem in υ.

553. The difference between an imperfect and an aorist depends *formally* on the character of the present. Thus ἔ-φη-ν *said* is called an 'imperfect' of φη-μί: but ἔ-στη-ν *stood* is a 'second aorist' because it shows a different tense-stem than that of ἵστημι. Similarly ἔ-φερ-ον is 'imperfect' to φέρω, but ἔ-τεκ-ον 'second aorist' to τίκτω because there is no present τεκω. ἔστιχον is imperfect to στίχω, but second aorist to στείχω. Cp. 546 D.

NOTE ON THE SECOND AORIST AND SECOND PERFECT

554. **a**. The second aorist and the second perfect are usually formed only from primitive verbs (372). These tenses are formed by adding the personal endings (inclusive of the thematic or tense vowel) to the verb-stem without any consonant tense-suffix. Cp. ἔλιπο-ν with ἔλῡ-σ-α, ἐτράπ-ην with ἐτρέφ-θ-ην (τρέπω *turn*), γέ-γραφ-α with λέλυ-κ-α.

b. The second perfect and second aorist passive are historically older than the corresponding first perfect and first aorist.

c. τρέπω *turn* is the only verb that has three first aorists and three second aorists (596).

d. Very few verbs have both the second aorist active and the second aorist passive. In cases where both occur, one form is rare, as ἔτυπον (once in poetry), ἐτύπην (τύπτω *strike*).

e. In the same voice both the first and the second aorist (or perfect) are rare, as ἔφθασα, ἔφθην (φθάνω *anticipate*). When both occur, the first aorist (or perfect) is often transitive, the second aorist (or perfect) is intransitive (819); as ἔστησα *I erected*, i.e. *made stand*, ἔστην *I stood*. In other cases one aorist is used in prose, the other in poetry: ἔπεισα, poet. ἔπιθον (πείθω *persuade*); or they occur in different dialects, as Attic ἐτάφην, Ionic ἐθάφθην (θάπτω *bury*); or one is much later than the other, as ἔλειψα, late for ἔλιπον.

---

551 D. Hom. has ἔκτᾰν *I slew* (κτείνω, κτεν-) with ᾰ taken from ἔκτᾰμεν, and οὖτα *he wounded* (οὐτάω).

V. FIRST (K) PERFECT SYSTEM

(FIRST PERFECT AND PLUPERFECT ACTIVE)

555. The stem of the first perfect is formed by adding -κα to the reduplicated verb-stem. λέ-λυ-κα *I have loosed*, ἐ-λε-λύκη *I had loosed*.

a. The κ-perfect is later in origin than the second perfect and seems to have started from verb-stems in -κ, as ἔ-οικ-α (= ϝέ-ϝοικ-α) from εἴκω *resemble*.

b. Verbs showing the gradations ει, ευ : οι, ου : ι, υ (476) have ει, ευ ; as πείθω (πιθ-, πειθ-) *persuade* πέπεικα (560). But δέδοικα *fear* has οι (cp. 564).

556. The first perfect is formed from verb-stems ending in a vowel, a liquid, or a dental stop (τ, δ, θ).

557. Vowel Verbs. — Vowel verbs lengthen the final vowel (if short) before -κα, as τῑμά-ω *honour* τε-τί̄μη-κα, ἐά-ω *permit* εἴᾱ-κα, ποιέ-ω *make* πε-ποίη-κα, τίθημι (θε-, θη-) *place* τέ-θη-κα, δίδωμι (δο-, δω-) *give* δέ-δω-κα.

558. This applies to verbs that add ε (485). For verbs that retain a short final vowel, see 488. (Except σβέννῡμι (σβε-) *extinguish*, which has ἔσβηκα.)

559. Liquid Verbs. — Many liquid verbs have no perfect or employ the second perfect. Examples of the regular formation are φαίνω (φαν-) *show*, πέφαγκα, ἀγγέλλω (ἀγγελ-) *announce*, ἤγγελκα.

a. Some liquid verbs drop ν ; as κέκρικα, κέκλικα from κρί̄νω (κριν-) *judge*, κλί̄νω (κλιν-) *incline*. τείνω (τεν-) *stretch* has τέτακα from τετ̥κα.

b. Monosyllabic stems change ε to α ; as ἔσταλκα, ἔφθαρκα from στέλλω (στελ-) *send*, φθείρω (φθερ-) *corrupt*.

N. For α we expect ο ; α is derived from the middle (ἔσταλμαι, ἔφθαρμαι).

c. All stems in μ and many others add ε (485) ; as νέμω (νεμ-ε-), *distribute* νενέμηκα, μέλω (μελ-ε-) *care for* μεμέληκα, τυγχάνω(τυχ-ε) *happen* τετύχηκα.

d. Many liquid verbs suffer metathesis (492) and thus get the form of vowel verbs ; as βάλλω (βαλ-) *throw* βέβληκα ; θνῄσκω (θαν-) *die* τέθνηκα ; καλέω (καλε-, κλη-) *call* κέκληκα ; κάμνω (καμ-) *am weary* κέκμηκα ; τέμνω (τεμ-) *cut* τέτμηκα. Also πί̄πτω (πετ-, πτο-) *fall* πέπτωκα. See 128 a.

---

555 b. D. Hom. δείδω (used as a present) is for δε-δϝο(ι̯)-α. δειδ- was written on account of the metre when ϝ was lost. Hom. δέδια is for δε-δ(ϝ)ι-α with the weak root that is used in δέδιμεν. See 703 D.

557 D. 1. Hom. has the κ-perfect only in verbs with vowel verb-stems. Of these some have the second perfect in -α, particularly in participles. Thus κεκμηώς, Attic κεκμηκώς (κάμ-ν-ω *am weary*); κεκορηώς (κορέ-ννῡμι *satiate*) ; πεφύκᾱσι and πεφύᾱσι (φύω *produce*).

2. In some dialects a present was derived from the perfect stem ; as Hom. ἀνώγω, Theocr. δεδοίκω, πεφύκει (in the 2 perf.: Theocr. πεπόνθω). Inf. τεθνάκην (Aeol.), part. κεκλήγοντες (Hom.), πεφρίκων (Pind.).

3. From μέμηκα (μηκάομαι *bleat*) Hom. has the plup. ἐμέμηκον.

560. Stop Verbs. — Dental stems drop τ, δ, θ before -κα; as πείθω (πιθ-, πειθ-, ποιθ-) *persuade* πέπεικα, κομίζω (κομιδ-) *carry* κεκόμικα.

VI. SECOND PERFECT SYSTEM

(SECOND PERFECT AND PLUPERFECT ACTIVE)

561. The stem of the second perfect is formed by adding α to the reduplicated verb-stem: γέ-γραφ-α *I have written* (γράφ-ω).

562. The second perfect is almost always formed from stems ending in a liquid or a stop consonant, and not from vowel stems.

a. ἀκήκοα (ἀκούω *hear*) is for ἀκηκο(ϝ)-α (ἀκοϝ- = ἀκου̯-, 43).

563. Verb-stems showing variation between short and long vowels (476) have long vowels in the second perfect (ᾰ is thus regularly lengthened). Thus, τήκω (τακ-, τηκ-) *melt* τέτηκα, κράζω (κραγ-) *cry out* κέκρᾱγα, φαίνω (φαν-) *show* πέφηνα *have appeared* (but πέφαγκα *have shown*), ῥήγνῡμι (ῥαγ-, ῥηγ-, ῥωγ-, 477 c) *break* ἔρρωγα.

a. εἴωθα *am accustomed* (= σε-σϝωθ-α) has the strong form ω (cp. ἦθος *custom*, 123); Hom. ἔθω (Attic ἐθίζω *accustom*).

564. The second perfect has ο, οι when the verb-stem varies between α, ε, ο (478, 479) or ι, ει, οι (477 a): τρέφ-ω (τρεφ-, τροφ-, τραφ-) *nourish* τέτροφα, λείπω (λιπ-, λειπ-, λοιπ-) *leave* λέλοιπα, πείθω (πιθ-, πειθ-, ποιθ-) *persuade* πέποιθα *trust*.

565. Similarly verbs with the variation υ, ευ, ου (476) should have ου; but this occurs only in Epic εἰλήλουθα (= Att. ἐλήλυθα); cp. ἐλεύ(θ)-σομαι. Other verbs have ευ, as φεύγω *flee* πέφευγα.

566. After Attic reduplication (446) the stem of the second perfect has the weak form; ἀλείφω (ἀλειφ-, ἀλιφ-) *anoint* ἀλήλιφα.

567. Apart from the variations in 563–566 the vowel of the verb-stem remains unchanged: as γέγραφα (γράφω *write*), κέκῡφα (κύπτω *stoop*, κῡφ-).

568. The meaning of the second perfect may differ from that of the present; as ἐγρήγορα *am awake* from ἐγείρω *wake up*, σέσηρα *grin* from σαίρω *sweep*. The second perfect often has the force of a present; as πέποιθα *trust* (πέπεικα *have persuaded*). See 819.

569. Aspirated Second Perfects. — In many stems a final π or β changes to φ: a final κ or γ changes to χ. (φ and χ here imitate verb-stems in φ and χ, as τρέφω, ὀρύττω.)

---

561 D. Hom. has several forms unknown to Attic: δέδουπα (δουπ-έ-ω *sound*), ἔολπα (ἔλπ-ω *hope*), ἔοργα (ῥέζω *work*), προ-βέβουλα (βούλομαι *wish*), μέμηλα (μέλω *care for*).

562 D. But δέδια *fear* from δϝι-. See 555 b. D., 703.

569 D. Hom. never aspirates π, β, κ, γ. Thus κεκοπώς = Att. κεκοφώς (κόπ-τ-ω *cut*). The aspirated perfect occurs once in Hdt. (ἐπεπόμφει 1. 85); but is unknown in Attic until the fifth century B.C. Soph. *Tr.* 1009 (ἀνατέτροφας) is the only example in tragedy.

κόπτω (κοπ-) *cut* κέκοφα, πέμπ-ω *send* πέπομφα, βλάπτω (βλαβ-) *injure* βέβλαφα, τρίβω (τρῑβ-) *rub* τέτριφα, φυλάττω (φυλακ-) *guard* -πεφύλαχα; τρέφ-ω (τρεφ-) *nourish* τέτροφα; ὀρύττω (ὀρυχ-) *dig* ὀρώρυχα.

570. Most such stems have a short vowel immediately before the final consonant; a long vowel precedes *e.g.* in δείκ-νῡ-μι δέδειχα, κηρύττω (κηρῡκ-) -κεκήρῡχα, πτήσσω (πτηκ-) ἔπτηχα. τέτριφα and τέθλιφα show ῐ in contrast to ῑ in the present (τρίβω, θλίβω). στέργω, λάμπω do not aspirate (ἔστοργα, poet. λέλαμπα).

571. The following verbs have aspirated second perfects: ἄγω, ἀλλάττω, ἀνοίγω, βλάπτω, δείκνῡμι, διώκω (rare), θλίβω, κηρύττω, κλέπτω, κόπτω, λαγχάνω, λαμβάνω, λάπτω, λέγω *collect*, μάττω, μείγνῡμι, πέμπω, πλέκω, πράττω, πτήσσω, τάττω, τρέπω, τρίβω, φέρω (ἐνήνοχα), φυλάττω. ἀνοίγω or ἀνοίγνῡμι has two perfects: ἀνέῳχα and ἀνέῳγα. πράττω *do* has πέπρᾱγα *have done* and *fare* (*well* or *ill*), and (generally later) πέπρᾱχα *have done*.

572. Second Perfects of the μι-form. — Some verbs add the endings directly to the reduplicated verb-stem. Such second perfects lack the singular of the indicative.

ἵστημι (στα-, στη-) *set*, 2 perf. stem ἑστα-: ἕστα-μεν, ἕστα-τε, ἑστᾶ-σι, inf. ἑστά-ναι; 2 plup. ἕστα-σαν (417). The singular is supplied by the forms in -κα; as ἕστηκα. These second perfects are enumerated in 704.

573. Stem Gradation. — Originally the second perfect was inflected throughout without any thematic vowel (cp. the perfect middle), but with stem-gradation: strong forms in the singular, weak forms elsewhere. -α (1 singular) was introduced in part from the aorist and spread to the other persons. Corresponding to the inflection of οἶδα (794) we expect πέποιθα, πέποισθα, πέποιθε, πέπιστον, πέπιθμεν, πέπιστε, πεπίθατι (from πεπιθn̥τι). Traces of this mode of inflection appear in Hom. γεγάτην (from γεγn̥την, 35 b) γέγαμεν from γέγονα; ἔϊκτον, ἐΐκτην, εἰκώς from ἔοικα; ἐπέπιθμεν; μέμαμεν from μέμονα; πέπασθε (for πεπαθτε = πεπn̥θτε) from πέπονθα (other examples 704, 705). So the masc. and neut. participles have the strong forms, the feminine has the weak forms (μεμηκώς, μεμακυῖα as εἰδώς, ἰδυῖα).

VII. PERFECT MIDDLE SYSTEM

(PERFECT AND PLUPERFECT MIDDLE AND PASSIVE, FUTURE PERFECT PASSIVE)

574. The stem of the perfect and pluperfect middle and passive is the reduplicated verb-stem, to which the personal endings are directly attached. λέλυ-μαι *I have loosed myself* or *have been loosed*, ἐ-λελύ-μην; δέδο-μαι (δί-δω-μι *give*), δέδειγ-μαι (δείκ-νῡ-μι *show*). On the euphonic changes of consonants, see 409.

---

574 D. A thematic vowel precedes the ending in Hom. μέμβλεται (μέλω *care for*), ὀρώρεται (ὄρνῡμι *rouse*).

575. The stem of the perfect middle is in general the same as that of the first perfect active as regards its vowel (557), the retention or expulsion of ν (559 a), and metathesis (559 d).

τῑμά-ω *honour* τετίμη-μαι ἐτετῑμήμην; ποιέ-ω *make* πεποίη-μαι ἐπεποιήμην; γράφ-ω *write* γέγραμ-μαι; κρίνω (κριν-) *judge* κέκρι-μαι; τείνω (τεν-) *stretch* τέτα-μαι; φθείρω (φθερ-) *corrupt* ἔφθαρ-μαι; βάλλω (βαλ-) *throw* βέβλη-μαι ἐβεβλήμην; πείθω (πιθ-, πειθ-, ποιθ-) *persuade* πέπεισμαι ἐπεπείσμην.

576. The vowel of the perfect middle stem should show the weak form when there is variation between ε (ει, ευ) : ο (οι, ου) : α (ι, υ). The weak form in α appears regularly in verbs containing a liquid (479): that in υ, in πέπυσμαι from πυνθάνομαι (πυθ-, πευθ-) *learn*, poet. ἔσσυμαι *hasten* from σεύω (συ-, σευ-) *urge*.

577. The vowel of the present has often displaced the weak form, as in πέπλεγμαι (πλέκ-ω *weave*), λέλειμμαι (λείπ-ω *leave*), πέπεισμαι (πείθ-ω *persuade*), ἔζευγμαι (ζεύγ-νῡ-μι *yoke*).

578. A final short vowel of the verb-stem is not lengthened in the verbs given in 488 a. ε is added (485) in many verbs. For metathesis see 492; for Attic reduplication see 446.

579. ν is retained in endings not beginning with μ, as φαίνω (φαν-) *show*, πέφανται, πέφανθε. Before -μαι, we have μ in ὤξυμμαι from ὀξύνω (ὀξυν-) *sharpen*, but usually ν is replaced by σ. On the insertion of σ, see 489.

580. Future Perfect. — The stem of the future perfect is formed by adding -σ%- to the stem of the perfect middle. A vowel immediately preceding -σ%- is always long, though it may have been short in the perfect middle.

λύ-ω *loose*, λελύ-σομαι *I shall have been loosed* (perf. mid. λέλῠ-μαι), δέ-ω *bind* δεδή-σομαι (perf. mid. δέδε-μαι), γράφ-ω *write* γεγράψ-ομαι, καλέω *call* κε-κλήσομαι.

581. The future perfect usually has a passive force. The *active* meaning is found where the perfect middle or active has an active meaning (1946, 1947).

κεκτήσομαι *shall possess* (κέκτημαι *possess*), κεκράξομαι *shall cry out* (κέκρᾱγα *cry out*), κεκλάγξομαι *shall scream* (κέκλαγγα *scream*), μεμνήσομαι *shall remember* (μέμνημαι *remember*), πεπαύσομαι *shall have ceased* (πέπαυμαι *have ceased*).

582. Not all verbs can form a future perfect; and few forms of this tense occur outside of the indicative: διαπεπολεμησόμενον Thuc. 7. 25 is the only sure example of the participle in classical Greek. The infinitive μεμνήσεσθαι occurs in Hom. and Attic prose.

583. The periphrastic construction (601) of the perfect middle (passive) participle with ἔσομαι may be used for the future perfect, as ἐψευσμένος ἔσομαι *I shall have been deceived.*

---

580 D. Hom. has δεδέξομαι, μεμνήσομαι, κεκλήσῃ, κεχολώσεται; κεκαδήσομαι, πεφιδήσεται are from reduplicated aorists.

584. Future Perfect Active. — The future perfect active of most verbs is formed periphrastically (600). Two perfects with a present meaning, ἕστηκα *I stand* (ἵστημι *set*) and τέθνηκα *I am dead* (θνῄσκω), form the future perfects ἑστήξω *I shall stand*, τεθνήξω *I shall be dead.*

VIII. FIRST PASSIVE SYSTEM (ΘΗ PASSIVE)

(FIRST AORIST AND FIRST FUTURE PASSIVE)

FIRST AORIST PASSIVE

585. The stem of the first aorist passive is formed by adding -θη- (or -θε-) directly to the verb-stem: ἐ-λύ-θη-ν *I was loosed*, ἐ-φάν-θη-ν *I was shown* (φαίνω, φαν-), ἐ-δό-θη-ν *I was given* (δίδωμι, δο-, δω-).

a. -θη- appears in the indicative, imperative (except the third plural), and infinitive; -θε- appears in the other moods. -θη- is found before a single consonant, -θε- before two consonants or a vowel except in the nom. neuter of the participle.

586. The verb-stem agrees with that of the perfect middle herein:

a. Vowel verbs lengthen the final vowel of the verb-stem, as τε-τίμη-μαι, ἐ-τῑμή-θην. On verbs which do not lengthen their final vowel, see 488.

b. Liquid stems of one syllable change ε to α, as τέ-τα-μαι, ἐ-τά-θην (τείνω *stretch*, τεν-). But στρέφω *turn*, τρέπω *turn*, τρέφω *nourish* have ἐστρέφθην, ἐτρέφθην, ἐθρέφθην (rare), though the perfect middles are ἔστραμμαι, τέτραμμαι, τέθραμμαι.

c. Primitive verbs showing in their stems the gradations ε (ει, ευ) : ο (οι, ου) : α (ι, υ) have a strong form, as ἐτρέφθην from τρέπω (τρεπ-, τροπ-, τραπ-) *turn*, ἐλείφθην from λείπω (λιπ-, λειπ-, λοιπ-) *leave*, ἐπλεύσθην from πλέω (πλυ-, πλευ-) *sail.*

d. Primitive verbs showing in their stems a variation between ε : η and ο : ω have, in the first aorist passive, the short vowel. Thus, τίθημι (θε-, θη-) ἐτέθην, δίδωμι (δο-, δω-) ἐδόθην.

e. Final ν is dropped in some verbs: κέ-κρι-μαι, ἐκρίθην. See 491.

f. The verb-stem may suffer metathesis: βέ-βλη-μαι, ἐ-βλή-θην. See 492.

g. Sigma is often added: κε-κέλευσ-μαι, ἐ-κελεύσ-θην. See 489.

587. Before θ of the suffix, π and β become φ; κ and γ become χ (82 c); τ, δ, θ become σ (83). φ and χ remain unaltered.

λείπ-ω ἐλείφ-θην, βλάπτω (βλαβ-) ἐβλάφ-θην; φυλάττω (φυλακ-) ἐφυλάχ-θην, ἄγ-ω ἤχ-θην; κομίζω (κομιδ-) ἐκομίσ-θην, πείθ-ω ἐπείσ-θην; γράφ-ω ἐγράφ-θην, ταράττω (ταραχ-) ἐταράχ-θην.

---

584 D. Hom. has κεχαρήσω and κεχαρήσομαι from χαίρω (χαρ-) *rejoice.*

585 a. D. For -θησαν we find -θεν in Hom., as διέκριθεν.

586 b. D. ἐστράφθην is Ionic and Doric; Hom. and Hdt. have ἐτράφθην from τρέπω. Hom. has ἐτάρφθην and ἐτέρφθην from τέρπω *gladden.*

586 e. D. Hom. has ἐκλίνθην and ἐκλίθην, ἐκρίνθην and ἐκρίθην; ἱδρύνθην = Att. ἱδρύθην (ἱδρύω *erect*), ἀμπνύνθην (ἀναπνέω *revive*).

588. θ of the verb-stem becomes τ in ἐ-τέ-θην for ἐ-θε-θην, and in ἐ-τύ-θην for ἐ-θυ-θην from τίθημι (θε-, θη-) *place* and θύω (θυ-, θῡ-) *sacrifice*. See 125 c.

FIRST FUTURE PASSIVE

589. The stem of the first future passive is formed by adding -σ%- to the stem of the first aorist passive. It ends in -θησομαι. Thus, παιδευθή-σομαι *I shall be educated*, λυθή-σομαι *I shall be loosed*.

τῑμάω, ἐτῑμήθην τῑμηθήσομαι; ἐάω, εἰάθην ἐᾱθήσομαι; λείπω, ἐλείφθην λειφθήσομαι; πείθω, ἐπείσθην πεισθήσομαι; τείνω, ἐτάθην ταθήσομαι; τάττω, ἐτάχθην ταχθήσομαι; τίθημι, ἐτέθην τεθήσομαι; δίδωμι, ἐδόθην δοθήσομαι; δείκνῡμι, ἐδείχθην δειχθήσομαι.

IX. SECOND PASSIVE SYSTEM (H PASSIVE)

(SECOND AORIST AND SECOND FUTURE PASSIVE)

SECOND AORIST PASSIVE

590. The stem of the second aorist passive is formed by adding -η- (or -ε-) directly to the verb-stem. Thus, ἐβλάβην *I was injured* from βλάπτω (βλαβ-).

a. -η- appears in the indicative, imperative (except the third plural), and infinitive; -ε- appears in the other moods. -η- is found before a single consonant, -ε- before two consonants or a vowel except in the nom. neut. of the participle.

591. The second aorist passive agrees in form with the second aorist active of μι-verbs; cp. intransitive ἐχάρην *rejoiced* with ἔστην *stood*. The passive use was developed from the intransitive use.

592. Primitive verbs showing in their stems the grades ε : ο : α have α. Thus an ε of a monosyllabic verb-stem becomes α, as in πλέκ-ω *weave* ἐπλάκην, κλέπ-τ-ω *steal* ἐκλάπην, φθείρω (φθερ-) *corrupt* ἐφθάρην, στέλλω (στελ-) *send* ἐστάλην. But λέγω *collect* has ἐλέγην.

593. Primitive verbs showing in their stems a variation between a short and long vowel have, in the second aorist passive, the short vowel. Thus τήκω (τακ-, τηκ-) *melt* ἐτάκην, ῥήγνῡμι (ῥαγ-, ῥηγ-, ῥωγ-) *break* ἐρράγην.

a. But πλήττω (πλαγ-, πληγ-) *strike* has ἐπλάγην only in composition, as ἐξεπλάγην; otherwise ἐπλήγην.

594. The second aorist passive is the only aorist passive formed in Attic prose by ἄγνῡμι (ἐάγην), γράφω (ἐγράφην), δέρω (ἐδάρην), θάπτω (ἐτάφην), κόπτω (ἐκόπην), μαίνω (ἐμάνην), πνῑ́γω (ἐπνῑ́γην), ῥάπτω (ἐρράφην), ῥέω (ἐρρύην active), ῥήγνῡμι (ἐρράγην), σήπω (ἐσάπην), σκάπτω (ἐσκάφην), σπείρω (ἐσπάρην), στέλλω (ἐστάλην), σφάζω or σφάττω (ἐσφάγην), σφάλλω (ἐσφάλην), τύφω (ἐτύφην), φθείρω (ἐφθάρην pass. and intr.), φύω (in subj. φυῶ), χαίρω (ἐχάρην active).

---

589 D. Hom. has no example of the first future passive. To express the idea of the passive future the future middle is used. See 802. Doric shows the active endings in both futures passive: δειχθησοῦντι, ἀναγραφησεῖ.

590 a. D. For -ησαν we generally find -εν (from -ηντ, 40) in Hom.; also in Doric.

595. Both the first aorist passive and the second aorist passive are formed by ἀλείφω (ἠλείφθην), ἀλλάττω (-ηλλάχθην, ἠλλάγην), βάπτω (ἐβάφην), βλάπτω (ἐβλάφθην, ἐβλάβην), βρέχω (ἐβρέχθην), ζεύγνῡμι (ἐζύγην), θλῑ́βω (ἐθλῑ́φθην), κλέπτω (ἐκλάπην), κλῑ́νω (-εκλίνην), κρύπτω (ἐκρύφθην), λέγω *collect* (διελέχθην, but συνελέγην), μάττω (ἐμάγην), μείγνῡμι (ἐμίγην), πήγνῡμι (ἐπάγην), πλέκω (ἐπλάκην), πλήττω (ἐπλήγην and -επλάγην), ῥῑ́πτω (ἐρρῑ́φθην, ἐρρίφην), στερίσκω (ἐστερήθην), στρέφω (ἐστράφην), τάττω (ἐτάχθην), τήκω (ἐτάκην), τρέπω (ἐτράπην pass. and intr.), τρέφω (ἐτράφην pass. and intr.), τρῑ́βω (ἐτρίβην, ἐτρίφθην), φαίνω (ἐφάνθην *was shown*, ἐφάνην *appeared*), φράγνῡμι (ἐφράχθην), ψῡ́χω (ἐψύχην). Most of these verbs use either the one in prose and the other in poetry, the dialects, or late Greek. Only the forms in common prose use are inserted in brackets.

596. Only those verbs which have no second aorist active show the second aorist passive; except τρέπω, which has all the aorists: active ἔτρεψα and ἔτραπον *turned;* middle ἐτρεψάμην *put to flight*, ἐτραπόμην *turned myself, took to flight;* passive ἐτρέφθην *was turned*, ἐτράπην *was turned* and *turned myself.*

SECOND FUTURE PASSIVE

597. The stem of the second future passive is formed by adding -σ%ε- to the stem of the second aorist passive. It ends in -ησομαι. Thus, βλαβήσομαι *I shall be injured* from βλάπτω (βλαβ-) ἐ-βλάβη-ν.

κόπ-τ-ω, ἐκόπην κοπήσομαι; γράφω, ἐγράφην γραφήσομαι; φαίνω, ἐφάνην *appeared*, φανήσομαι; φθείρω, ἐφθάρην φθαρήσομαι; πήγνῡμι *fix*, ἐπάγην παγήσομαι.

598. Most of the verbs in 594, 595 form second futures passive except ἄγνῡμι, ἀλείφω, βάπτω, βρέχω, ζεύγνῡμι, θλῑ́βω, κλέπτω, μαίνω, μάττω, ῥάπτω. But many of the second futures appear only in poetry or in late Greek, and some are found only in composition.

PERIPHRASTIC FORMS

599. Perfect. — For the simple perfect and pluperfect periphrastic forms are often used.

a. For the perfect or pluperfect active indicative the forms of the perfect active participle and εἰμί or ἦν may be used: as λελυκώς εἰμι for λέλυκα, λελυκὼς ἦν for ἐλελύκη. So βεβοηθηκότες ἦσαν for ἐβεβοηθήκεσαν (βοηθέω *come to aid*); εἰμὶ τεθηκὼς for τέθηκα *I have placed;* γεγραφὼς ἦν for ἐγεγράφη *I had written;* πεπονθὼς ἦν *I had suffered.* Such forms are more common in the pluperfect and in general denote *state* rather than *action.*

b. For the perfect active a periphrasis of the aorist participle and ἔχω is sometimes used, especially when a perfect active form with transitive meaning is lacking; as στήσᾱς ἔχω *I have placed* (ἕστηκα, intransitive, *stand*), ἐρασθεὶς ἔχω *I have loved.* So often because the aspirated perfect is not used, as ἔχεις ταράξᾱς *thou hast stirred up.* Cp. *habeo* with the perfect participle.

---

597 D. Hom. has only δαήσεαι (ἐδάην *learned*), μιγήσεσθαι (μείγνῡμι *mix*).

c. In the perfect active subjunctive and optative the forms in -κω and -κοιμι are very rare. In their place the perfect active participle with ὦ and εἴην is usually employed: λελυκὼς (λελοιπὼς) ὦ, εἴην. Other forms than 3 sing. and 3 pl. are rare. Cp. 691, 694.

d. The perfect or pluperfect passive is often paraphrased by the perfect participle and ἐστί or ἦν; as γεγραμμένον ἐστί *it stands written*, ἐστὶ δεδογμένον *it stands resolved*, παρηγγελμένον ἦν = παρήγγελτο (παραγγέλλω *give orders*).

e. In the third plural of the perfect and pluperfect middle (passive) the perfect middle participle with εἰσί (ἦσαν) is used when a stem ending in a consonant would come in direct contact with the endings -νται, -ντο. See 408.

f. The perfect subjunctive and optative middle are formed by the perfect middle participle with ὦ or εἴην: λελυμένος ὦ, εἴην.

g. The perfect imperative of all voices may be expressed by combining the perfect participle with ἴσθι, ἔστω (697). λελυκὼς ἴσθι *loose*, etc., εἰρημένον ἔστω *let it have been said*, γεγονὼς ἔστω P. L. 951 c, γεγονότες ἔστωσαν P. L. 779 d.

h. Periphrasis of the infinitive is rare: τεθνηκότα εἶναι *to be dead* X. C. 1. 4. 11.

600. Future Perfect Active. — The future perfect active of most verbs is formed by combining the perfect active participle with ἔσομαι *shall be*. Thus γεγραφὼς ἔσομαι *I shall have written*, cp. Lat. *nactus ero I shall have got*. For the two verbs which do not use this periphrasis, see 584.

a. The perfect middle participle is used in the case of deponent verbs: ἀπολελογημένος ἔσομαι And. 1. 72.

601. Future Perfect Passive. — The future perfect passive may be expressed by using the perfect middle (passive) participle with ἔσομαι *shall be*. Thus, ἐψευσμένοι ἔσεσθε *you will have been deceived*.

FIRST CONJUGATION OR VERBS IN Ω

602. Verbs in -ω have the thematic vowel -$^{o}/_{\epsilon}$ (-$^{\omega}/_{\eta}$-) between the tense-stem and the personal endings in the present system. The name "ω-conjugation," or "thematic conjugation," is applied to all verbs which form the present and imperfect with the thematic vowel.

603. Inflected according to the ω-conjugation are all thematic presents and imperfects; those second aorists active and middle in which the tense-stem ends with the thematic vowel; all futures, all first aorists active and middle; and most perfects and pluperfects active.

604. Certain tenses of verbs ending in -ω in the first person present indicative active, or of deponent verbs in which the personal endings are preceded by the thematic vowel, are inflected without the thematic vowel, herein agreeing with μι-verbs. These tenses are: all aorists passive; all perfects and pluperfects middle and passive; a few second perfects and pluperfects active; and those second aorists active and middle in which the tense-stem does not end with the thematic vowel. But all subjunctives are thematic.

605. Verbs in -ω fall into two main classes, distinguished by the last letter of the verb-stem:

1. Vowel verbs: a. Uncontracted verbs. b. Contracted verbs.
2. Consonant verbs: a. Liquid verbs. b. Stop (or mute) verbs.

N. Under 2 fall also (c) those verbs whose stems ended in σ or ϝ (624).

606. Vowel Verbs. — Vowel verbs usually do not form second aorists, second perfects, and second futures in the passive. A vowel short in the present is commonly lengthened in the other tenses. Vowel verbs belong to the first class of present stems (498–504; but see 612).

607. Vowel Verbs not contracted. — Vowel verbs not contracted have verb-stems ending in ῐ̄, ῠ̄, or in a diphthong (αι, ει, αυ, ευ, ου).

(ι) ἐσθίω *eat*, πρίω *saw*, χρίω *anoint*, poet. δίω *fear*, τίω *honour* (500. 2); (υ) ἀνύω *accomplish*, μεθύω *am intoxicated*, λύω *loose*, θύω *sacrifice*, φύω *produce*, κωλύω *hinder* (and many others, 500. 1 a); (αι) κναίω *scratch*, παίω *strike*, πταίω *stumble*, παλαίω *wrestle*, ἀγαίομαι *am indignant*, δαίω *kindle*, δαίομαι *divide*, λιλαίομαι *desire eagerly*, poet. μαίομαι *desire*, ναίω *dwell*, ῥαίω *strike*; (ει) κλῄω (later κλείω) *shut*, σείω *shake*, Epic κείω *split* and *rest*; (αυ) αὔω *kindle*, θραύω *break*, ἀπολαύω *enjoy*, παύω *make cease* (παύομαι *cease*), poet. ἰαύω *rest*; (ευ) βασιλεύω *am king*, βουλεύω *consult* (βουλεύομαι *deliberate*), θηρεύω *hunt*, κελεύω *order*, λεύω *stone*, παιδεύω *educate*, χορεύω *dance*, φονεύω *slay*. Most verbs in -ευω are either denominatives, as βασιλεύω from βασιλεύς; or are due to the analogy of such denominatives, as παιδεύω. γεύομαι *taste* is a primitive. θέω *run*, νέω *swim*, πλέω *sail*, πνέω *breathe*, ῥέω *flow*, χέω *pour* have forms in ευ, υ; cp. poet. σεύω *urge*, ἀλεύω *avert*, ἀχεύω *am grieved*; (ου) ἀκούω *hear*, κολούω *dock*, κρούω *beat*, λούω *wash*.

608. Some primitive vowel verbs in -ιω, -υω (522) formed their present stem by the aid of the suffix ῐ̯(*y*), which has been lost. Denominatives in -ιω, -υω, -ευω regularly added the suffix, as poet. μηνί-ω *am wroth* from μηνι-ῐ̯ω (μῆνι-ς *wrath*), poet. δακρύω *weep* (δάκρυ *tear*), poet. φῑτύ-ω *beget* from φῑτυ-ῐ̯ω, μεθύω *am drunk*, βασιλεύω *am king*. Poet. δηρίομαι, μαστίω, μητίομαι, κηκίω, ἀχλύω, γηρύω, ἰθύω.

609. The stem of some of the uncontracted vowel verbs originally ended in σ or ϝ (624).

610. Some verbs with verb-stems in vowels form presents in -νω (523), as πίνω *drink*, φθίνω *perish*; and in -σκω (526).

611. Vowel Verbs contracted. — Vowel verbs that contract have verb-stems ending in α, ε, ο, with some in ᾱ, η, ω.

612. All contracted verbs form their present stem by the help of the suffix ῐ̯(*y*), and properly belong to the Third Class (522).

613. Some contracted verbs have verb-stems which originally ended in σ or ϝ (624).

614. Liquid Verbs. — Liquid verbs have verb-stems in λ, μ, ν, ρ.

The present is rarely formed from the simple verb-stem, as in *μέν-ω remain;* ordinarily the suffix ι̯ (*y*) is added, as in *στέλλω* (*στελ-ι̯ω*) *send*, *κρίνω* (*κρῐν-ι̯ω*) *judge*, *κτείνω* (*κτεν-ι̯ω*) *slay*, *φαίνω* (*φαν-ι̯ω*) *show*.

615. A short vowel of the verb-stem remains short in the future but is lengthened in the first aorist (544). Thus:

a. α in the future, η in the aorist: *φαίνω* (*φαν-*) *show*, *φανῶ*, *ἔφηνα*. In this class fall all verbs in *-αινω*, *-αιρω*, *-αλλω*.

b. ε in the future, ει in the aorist: *μέν-ω remain*, *μενῶ*, *ἔμεινα*; *στέλλω* (*στελ-*) *send*, *στελῶ*, *ἔστειλα*. Here belong verbs in *-ελλω*, *-εμω*, *-εμνω*, *-ερω*, *-ειρω*, *-ενω*, *-εινω*.

c. ῐ in the future, ῑ in the aorist: *κλίνω* (*κλιν-*) *incline*, *κλῐνῶ*, *ἔκλῑνα*. Here belong verbs in *-ιλλω*, *-ῑνω*, *-ῑρω*.

d. ῠ in the future, ῡ in the aorist: *σύρω* (*συρ-*) *drag*, *σῠρῶ*, *ἔσῡρα*. Here belong verbs in *-ῡρω*, *-ῡνω*.

For the formation of the future stem see 535, of the aorist stem see 544.

616. For the perfect stem see 559. Few liquid verbs make second perfects. On the change of ε, α of the verb-stem to ο, η in the second perfect, see 478, 484. Liquid verbs with futures in *-ῶ* do not form future perfects.

617. Monosyllabic verb-stems containing ε have α in the first perfect active, perfect middle, first aorist and future passive and in all second aorists, but ο in the second perfect. Thus, *φθείρω* (*φθερ-*) *corrupt*, *ἔφθαρκα*, *ἔφθαρμαι*, *ἐφθάρην*, but *δι-έφθορα have destroyed* (819).

618. A few monosyllabic stems do not change ε to α in the 2 aor., as *τέμνω cut* *ἔτεμον* (but *ἔταμον* in Hom., Hdt. etc.), *γίγνομαι* (*γεν-*) *become* *ἐγενόμην*. See also *θείνω*, *θέρομαι*, *κέλομαι*, root *φεν-*. Few liquid verbs form second aorists.

619. Stems of more than one syllable do not change the vowel of the verb-stem.

620. List of Liquid Verbs. — The arrangement is according to the classes of the present stem. Words poetic or mainly poetic or poetic and Ionic are starred.

I. *βούλομαι* (*βουλ-ε-*), *ἐθέλω* (*ἐθελ-ε-*), *εἰλέω** (*εἰλ-ε-*), *ἴλλω**, *μέλλω*, *μέλω*, *πέλομαι**, *φιλέω* (Epic *φιλ-*). — *βρέμω**, *γέμω*, *δέμω**, *θέρμω**, *νέμω*, *τρέμω*, and *γαμέω* (*γαμ-ε-*). — *γίγνομαι* (*γεν-ε-*), *μένω*, *μίμνω** (*μεν-*), *πένομαι*, *σθένω**, *στένω*, and *γεγωνέω** (*γεγων-ε-*). — Verbs in *-εμω* and *-ενω* have only pres. and imperf., or form their tenses in part from other stems. — *δέρω*, *ἔρομαι* (*ἐρ-ε-*), *ἔρρω* (*ἐρρ-ε-*), *θέρομαι**, *στέρομαι*, *φέρω*, *ἐπαυρέω**, (*ἐπαυρ-ε-*), and *κυρέω** (*κυρ-ε-*), *τορέω** (*τορ-ε*).

III. *ἀγάλλομαι*, *ἀγγέλλω*, *αἰόλλω**, *ἅλλομαι*, *ἀτιτάλλω**, *βάλλω*, *δαιδάλλω**, *θάλλω*, *ἰάλλω**, *ἰνδάλλομαι**, *ὀκέλλω*, *ὀφείλω* (*ὀφελ-*, *ὀφειλε-*), *ὀφέλλω**, *πάλλω*, *ποικίλλω*, *σκέλλω**, *στέλλω*, *-τέλλω*, *τίλλω**, *σφάλλω*, *ψάλλω*. — *-αινω* verbs (the following list includes primitives, and most of the denominatives in classical Greek from extant ν-stems, or from stems which once contained ν; 518 a): *αἴνω**, *ἀσθμαίνω**, *ἀφραίνω**, *δειμαίνω**, *δραίνω**, *εὐφραίνω*,

---

614 D. *πεφύρσεσθαι* in Pindar is made from *φύρσω* (*φύρω knead*).

θαυμαίνω, ἰαίνω*, καίνω*, κραίνω*, κῡμαίνω*, κωμαίνω*, λῡμαίνομαι, μελαίνομαι, ξαίνω, ὀνομαίνω*, πημαίνω*, πιαίνω*, ποιμαίνω, ῥαίνω, σαίνω, σημαίνω, σπερμαίνω*, τεκταίνομαι, φαίνω, φλεγμαίνω, χειμαίνω*, χραίνω. All other denominatives in -αινω are due to analogy; as ἀγριαίνω, αὐαίνω, γλυκαίνω, δυσχεραίνω, ἐχθραίνω, θερμαίνω, ἰσχναίνω, κερδαίνω, κοιλαίνω, κῡδαίνω*, λεαίνω, λευκαίνω*, μαραίνω, μαργαίνω*, μιαίνω, μωραίνω, ξηραίνω, ὀρμαίνω*, ὀσφραίνομαι, πεπαίνω, περαίνω, πικραίνω, ῥυπαίνω, τετραίνω, ὑγιαίνω, ὑδραίνω*, ὑφαίνω, χαλεπαίνω. — **ἀλεείνω***, γείνομαι*, ἐρεείνω*, θείνω*, κτείνω, πειρείνω*, στείνω*, τείνω, φαείνω*. — **κλίνω** (κλι-ν-), κρίνω (κρι-ν-), ὀρίνω*, σίνομαι (Xenoph.), ὠδίνω. — **αἰσχύνω**, ἀλγύνω, ἀρτύνω*, βαθύνω, βαρύνω, βραδύνω*, ἡδύνω, θαρσύνω, ἰθύνω*, λεπτύνω, ὀξύνω, ὀρτύνω*, πλύνω. — **αἴρω**, ἀσπαίρω, γεραίρω*, ἐναίρω*, ἐχθαίρω*, καθαίρω, μαρμαίρω*, μεγαίρω*, σαίρω*, σκαίρω, τεκμαίρομαι, χαίρω (χαρ-ε-), ψαίρω. — **ἀγείρω**, ἀμείρω*, δείρω, ἐγείρω, εἴρομαι*, -εἴρω *join*, εἴρω* *say*, ἱμείρω*, κείρω, μείρομαι, πείρω*, σπείρω, τείρω*, φθείρω. — **οἰκτίρω** (miswritten οἰκτείρω). — **κινύρομαι***, μαρτύρομαι, μινύρομαι*, μορμύρω*, μύρω*, ὀδύρομαι, ὀλοφύρομαι, πορφύρω*, σύρω, φύρω*.

IV. a. κάμνω, τέμνω; b. ὀφλισκάνω (ὀφλ-ε-); h. βαίνω, κερδαίνω, τετραίνω (also Class III); i. ὀσφραίνομαι (ὀσφρ-ε-), also Class III. V. See 527.

621. Stop Verbs. — Many verb stems end in a stop (or mute) consonant.

The present is formed either from the simple verb-stem, as in πλέκ-ω *weave*, or by the addition of τ or ι̯ (*y*) to the verb-stem, as in βλάπτω (βλαβ-) *injure*, φυλάττω (φυλακ-ι̯ω) *guard*. All tenses except the present and imperfect are formed without the addition of τ or ι̯ to the verb-stem; thus, βλάψω from βλαβ-σ-ω, φυλάξω from φυλακ-σ-ω.

622. Some monosyllabic stems show a variation in the quantity of the stem vowel ι or υ, as τρίβω *rub* perf. τέτρῐφα, ψύχω *cool* 2 aor. pass. ἐψῠ́χην, τήκω *melt* (Doric τάκω) 2 aor. pass. ἐτᾰ́κην. Cp. 475, 477 c, 500. Many monosyllabic stems show qualitative vowel gradation: **ι ει οι; υ ευ ου; α η ω; α ε ο.** For examples see 477–484.

623. List of Stop Verbs. — The arrangement of the examples is by classes of the present stem. Words poetic or mainly poetic or poetic and Ionic are starred. The determination of the final consonant of the verb-stem of verbs in -ζω, -ττω (poetic, Ionic, and later Attic -σσω) is often impossible (516).

π — I. βλέπω, δρέπω, ἔλπω*, ἐνέπω*, ἕπομαι, ἐρείπω*, ἕρπω, λάμπω, λείπω, λέπω, μέλπω*, πέμπω, πρέπει, ῥέπω, τέρπω, τρέπω.

II. ἀστράπτω, γνάμπτω*, δάπτω*, ἐνίπτω*, ἐρέπτομαι*, ἰάπτω*, κάμπτω, κλέπτω, κόπτω, μάρπτω*, σκέπτομαι, σκήπτω, σκηρίπτομαι*, σκώπτω, χαλέπτω, and δουπέω* (δουπ-ε-), κτυπέω* (κτυπ-ε-), τύπτω (τυπ-ε-).

β — I. ἀμείβομαι, θλίβω, λείβω*, σέβομαι, στείβω*, τρίβω, φέβομαι*.

II. βλάπτω, καλύπτω. — IV. c. λαμβάνω (λαβ-).

φ — I. ἀλείφω, γλύφω, γράφω, ἐρέφω, μέμφομαι, νείφει (νίφει), νήφω, στέφω, στρέφω, τρέφω, τύφω*.

II. ἅπτω, βάπτω, δρύπτω*, θάπτω (125 g), θρύπτω (125 g), κρύπτω (κρυφ-, κρυβ-), κόπτω, λάπτω, ῥάπτω, ῥίπτω (ἐρρίφ-ην, but ῥῑπ-ή), σκάπτω.

IV. a. πίτνω* = πίπτω. — ἀλφάνω* (ἀλφ-). — V. ἀπαφίσκω* (ἀφ-ε-).

τ— I. *δατέομαι* (δατ-ε-), κεντέω* (κεντ-ε-), πατέομαι (πατ-ε-), πέτομαι (πετ-, πτε-).*

III. *ἀγρώσσω*, αἱμάσσω*, βλίττω (βλιτ-* from *μλιτ-*, 130), *βράττω, ἐρέσσω*, λίσσομαι*, πυρέττω (πυρετ-, πυρεγ-).*

IV. b. *ἁμαρτάνω (ἁμαρτ-ε-), βλαστάνω (βλαστ-ε-).*

δ— I. *ᾄδω, ἀλίνδω* (ἀλινδ-ε-), ἀμέρδω*, ἄρδω, ἕδω*, εἴδομαι*, ἐπείγω, ἐρείδω*, (καθ)εύδω (εὐδ-ε-), ἥδομαι, κήδω* (κηδ-ε-), κυλίνδω*, μέδομαι* (μεδ-ε-), μήδομαι*, πέρδομαι, σπένδω, σπεύδω, φείδομαι* (also Epic *φειδε-*), *ψεύδομαι*, and *κελαδέω* (κελαδ-ε-).*

III. Examples of denominatives from actual δ-stems. *γυμνάζω, δεκάζω, διχάζω, μιγάζομαι*, ὀπίζομαι*, παίζω, πεμπάζω, ψακάζω. — αὐλίζομαι, δωρίζω, ἐλπίζω, ἐρίζω, κερκίζω, ληΐζομαι, στολίζω, φροντίζω, ψηφίζω.*

IV. *ἁνδάνω* (ἁδ-ε-), κερδαίνω (κερδαν-, κερδ-ε-), οἰδάνω* (οἰδ-ε-), χανδάνω (χαδ-, χανδ-, χενδ-).*

θ— I. *αἴθω*, ἄλθομαι* (ἀλθ-ε-), ἄχθομαι, βρώθω*, εἴωθα (ἐθ-,* 563 a), *ἐρεύθω*, ἔχθω*, κεύθω*, κλώθω*, λήθω*, πείθω, πέρθω*, πεύθομαι*, πῡθω*, and *γηθέω (γηθ-ε-), ὠθέω (ὠθ-ε-).*

III. *κορύσσω*.*

IV. b. *αἰσθάνομαι (αἰσθ-ε-), ἀπεχθάνομαι (ἐχθ-ε-), δαρθάνω (δαρθ-ε-), ὀλισθάνω (ὀλισθ-ε-), λανθάνω (λαθ-), μανθάνω (μαθ-ε-), πυνθάνομαι (πυθ-).*

V. *πάσχω* for *παθ-σκω* (98, 126).

κ— I. *βρύκω, δέρκομαι*, διώκω, εἴκω* yield, *εἴκω** resemble, *ἕλκω, ἐρείκω*, ἐρύκω*, ἥκω, ἵκω*, πείκω*, πλέκω, ῥέγκω*, τήκω, τίκτω (τεκ-)* and *δοκέω (δοκ-ε-), μηκάομαι (μηκ-α-), μῡκάομαι (μῡκ-α-).*

III. *αἰνίττομαι, ᾴττω, δεδίττομαι, ἑλίττω, ἐνίσσω*, θωρήσσω*, κηρῡττω, μαλάττω, μύττω, πέττω* (and *πέπτω*), *πλίσσομαι*, φρίττω, πτήσσω, φυλάττω.*

IV. a. *δάκνω*; d. *ἱκνέομαι (ἱκ-).* — V. See 527 b.

γ— I. *ἄγω, ἀμέλγω, ἀρήγω*, ἐπείγω, εἴργω, ἐρεύγομαι*, θέλγω*, θήγω, λέγω, λήγω, ὀρέγω*, πνίγω, στέγω, στέργω, σφίγγω, τέγγω, τμήγω*, τρώγω, φεύγω, φθέγγομαι, φλέγω, φρῡγω, ψέγω*, and *ῥιγέω (ῥῑγ-ε-), στυγέω (στυγ-ε-).*

III. *ἔρδω** and *ῥέζω** (511). — *ἅζομαι*, ἀλαλάζω*, ἀλαπάζω*, ἁρπάζω, αὐδάζω, βαστάζω, κράζω, πλάζω*, στάζω, στενάζω, σφάζω* (σφάττω). — δαΐζω*, θωμίζω*, κρίζω, μαστίζω, σαλπίζω, στηρίζω, στίζω, στροφαλίζω*, σῡρίζω, τρίζω*, φορμίζω*. — ἀτύζομαι*, γρύζω, μύζω, ὀλολύζω, σφύζω. — οἰμώζω.*

IV. c. *θιγγάνω (θιγ-).* — V. *μίσγω* (526 c).

χ— I. *ἄγχω, ἄρχω, βραχ-* in *ἔβραχε*, βρέχω, γλίχομαι, δέχομαι, ἐλέγχω, ἔρχομαι, εὔχομαι, ἔχω (σεχ-), ἰάχω*, ἴσχω (σισχ-ω), λείχω*, μάχομαι (μαχ-ε-), νήχω*, οἴχομαι (οἰχ-ε-, οἰχ-ο-), σμῡχω*, σπέρχω*, στείχω*, τεύχω*, τρέχω, τρῡχω (τρῡχ-ο-), ψήχω, ψῡχω*, and *βρῡχάομαι* (βρῡχ-α-).*

III. *ἀμύσσω*, βήττω, θράττω, ὀρύττω, πτύσσω, πτώσσω*, ταράττω.*

IV. c. *κιγχάνω* (κιχ-ε-), λαγχάνω (λαχ-), τυγχάνω (τυχ-ε, τευχ-).* — d. *ἀμπισχνέομαι (ἀμπεχ-), ὑπισχνέομαι (ὑπεχ-).* — V. *διδάσκω (διδαχ-).*

ξ, ψ— I. *ἀλέξω* (ἀλεξ-ε-, ἀλεκ-), αὔξω.* — IV. b. *αὐξάνω (αὐξ-ε-).* — I. *ἕψω (ἑψ-ε-).*

624. Verbs in σ or ϝ(υ̯). — Some verb-stems ended originally in σ or ϝ.

a. **Sigma-stems** (cp. 488 d) with presents either from *-σ-ω* or *-σ-ι̯ω*. Thus (1) from *-σ-ω*: ἀκούω, αὔω *burn*, γεύω, εὔω, ζέω, θραύω, κρούω, νίσομαι* (νι-νσ-ομαι, cp. νόσ-τος), ξέω, σείω, τρέω*; (2) from *-σ-ι̯ω* (488 d): ἀγαίομαι*, αἰδέομαι, ἀκέομαι (Hom. ἀκείομαι), ἀρκέω, γελάω, κείω* *split*, κλείω* (*i.e.* κλεέω) *celebrate*, κονίω*, λιλαίομαι*, μαίομαι*, ναίω* *dwell*, νεικέω (Hom. νεικείω), οἰνοβαρείω*, οἴομαι (from ὀΐομαι), πενθέω (Hom. πενθείω), πτίττω (πτινσ-ι̯ω), τελέω (Hom. τελείω), and some others that do not lengthen the vowel of the verb-stem (488).

Also others, such as ἀρέσκω (ἀρεσ-), ἕννυμι, ζώννυμι, σβέννυμι (732). — σ is retained in τέρσομαι*.

b. ϝ-stems (from *-υ̯-ι̯ω*): γαίω*, δαίω* *kindle*, καίω (520), κλαίω (520), ναίω* *swim, flow* ι 222. — For the loss of ϝ in θέω, etc., see 43, 503.

INFLECTION OF Ω-VERBS

625. Verbs which end in ω in the first person present indicative active, and deponent verbs in which the personal endings are preceded by the thematic vowel, have the following peculiarities of inflection:

a. The thematic vowel usually appears in all tenses except the perfect and pluperfect middle (passive) and the aorist passive (except in the subjunctive). These three tenses are inflected like μι-verbs.

b. The present and future singular active end in *-ω*, *-εις*, *-ει* (463). The ending *-μι* appears only in the optative.

c. The thematic vowel ο unites in the indicative with the ending *-ντι*, and forms *-ουσι* (463 d).

d. The third plural active of past tenses ends in *-ν*.

e. The imperative active has no personal ending in the second person singular except *-ο-ν* in the first aorist.

f. Except in the perfect and pluperfect the middle endings *-σαι* and *-σο* lose σ and contract with the final vowel of the tense-stem (465 a, b). In the optative contraction cannot take place (λύοι-(σ)ο, λύσαι-(σ)ο).

g. The infinitive active has *-ειν* (for *-ε-εν*) in the present, future, and second aorist; *-ε-ναι* in the perfect; and *-αι* in the aorist.

h. Active participles with stems in *-οντ-* have the nominative masculine in *-ων*.

626. In 627–716 the method of inflection of all ω-verbs, both vowel and consonant, is described. The examples are generally taken from vowel verbs, but the statements hold true of consonant verbs.

Forms of ω-verbs which are inflected according to the non-thematic conjugation are included under the ω-verbs.

PRESENT AND IMPERFECT ACTIVE AND MIDDLE (PASSIVE)

For the formation of the present stem see 497–531.

627. **Indicative.** — Vowel and consonant verbs in *-ω* inflect the present by attaching the primary endings (when there are any) to the present stem in *-ο/ε*

(-ω/η-). λύω, τῑμῶ (τῑμά-ω), φαίνω, λείπω. The imperfect attaches the secondary endings to the present stem with the augment. See the paradigms, pp. 114, 120. For the active forms -ω, -εις, -ει, see 463.

628. -ῃ and -ει are found in the pres. fut. mid. and pass., fut. perf. pass. ε-(σ)αι yields ῃ (written EI in the Old Attic alphabet, 2 a), which is usually given as the proper spelling in the texts of the tragic poets, whereas ει is printed in the texts of prose and comedy. ει was often written for ηι (ῃ) after 400 B.C., as in ἀγαθεῖ τύχει, since both had the sound of a close long *e*. It is often impossible to settle the spelling; but βούλει *wishest*, οἴει *thinkest*, and ὄψει *shalt see* (from ὁράω) have only the -ει forms. -ει is sometimes called Attic and Ionic in contrast to -ῃ of the other dialects, including the Koiné.

629. Subjunctive. — The present subjunctive adds the primary endings to the tense-stem with the long thematic vowel. For the endings -ῃς, -ῃ see 463. Thus, λύω, -ῃς, -ῃ, τῑμᾷς (= τῑμά-ῃς), τῑμᾷ (= τῑμά-ῃ), φαίνωμεν, -ητε, -ωσι (from -ωντι). Middle λύω-μαι, λύῃ (= λύη-σαι), λύη-ται; τῑμᾶ-σθον (= τῑμάη-σθον); φαινώ-μεθα, φαίνη-σθε, φαίνω-νται.

630. Optative. — To the tense-stem ending in the thematic vowel (always ο) are added the mood-sign -ῑ- (-ιε-) or -ιη- (459, 460) and the secondary personal endings (except -μι for -ν, where the mood sign is -ῑ-, 459). In the 3 pl. we have -ιε-ν.

a. The final vowel of the tense-stem (ο) contracts with the mood suffix (ῑ), ο-ῑ becoming οι. Thus λύοιμι (λύο-ῑ-μι), λύοις (λύο-ῑ-ς), λύοιεν (λύο-ιε-ν), λῡοίμην (λῡο-ί-μην), λύοιο (λύο-ῑ-σο).

631. Imperative. — The present imperative endings are added to the tense-stem with the thematic vowel ε (ο before -ντων). The 2 pers. sing. active has no ending, but uses the tense-stem instead (παίδευε, φαῖνε). In the middle -σο loses its σ (466, 2 a); λύου from λύε-σο, φαίνου from φαίνε-σο. On the forms in -ετωσαν and -εσθωσαν for -οντων and -εσθων, see 466, 2 b.

632. Infinitive. — The present stem unites with -εν: λύε-εν = λύειν, λείπε-εν = λείπειν. In the middle (passive) -σθαι is added: λύε-σθαι, λείπε-σθαι.

633. Participle. — The present participle adds -ντ- to the present stem ending in the thematic vowel ο. Stems in -ο-ντ have the nominative singular in -ων. Thus masc. λύων from λῡοντ-ς, fem. λύουσα from λῡοντ-ϳα, neut. λῦον from λῡον(τ). See 301 a and N.

634. A few ω-verbs in the present and imperfect show forms of the μι-conjugation. These are usually Epic.

δέχομαι, 3 pl. δέχαται *await* for δεχχται, part. δέγμενος, imperf. ἐδέγμην. But these are often regarded as perfect and pluperfect without reduplication. ἐδέγμην

632 D. Severer Doric has ἔχην and ἔχεν; Milder Doric has ἔχειν; Aeolic has ἔχην. Hom. has ἀμύνειν, ἀμῡνέμεναι, ἀμῡνέμεν.

633 D. Aeolic has fem. -οισα in the present and second aorist (37 D. 3), λύοισα, λίποισα.

in some passages is a second aorist (688).—ἔδω *eat* (529. 5), inf. ἔδμεναι.—ἐρύω (or εἰρύω) in εἰρύαται.—λοῦται *wash* is from λόεται, not from λούω (cp. 398 a).—οἶμαι *think* is probably a perfect to οἴομαι (οἰ-ο-).—οὐτάω *wound* in οὖτα, οὐτάμεναι is 2 aor.—φέρω *bear*, imper. φέρτε.

CONTRACT VERBS

635. Verbs in -αω, -εω, -οω contract the final α, ε, ο of the verb-stem with the thematic vowel -ο/ε (-ω/η) in the present and imperfect tenses. Thus, τῑμάω τῑμῶ, ποιέω ποιῶ, δηλόω δηλῶ; ἐτί̄μαον ἐτί̄μων, ἐποίεον ἐποίουν, ἐδήλοον ἐδήλουν. The rules of contraction are given in 49–55; the paradigms, p. 120.

a. Open forms of -εω verbs occur in the lyric parts of tragedy.

636. Subjunctive.—The subjunctive adds the primary endings. For the contractions see 59.

637. Optative.—άοι becomes ῴ, έοι and όοι become οῖ. Thus, -άο-ῑ-μι = -ῷμι, -αο-ίη-ν = -ῴην, -αο-ί̄-μην = -ῴμην; -έο-ῑ-μι = -οῖμι, -εο-ίη-ν = -οίην, -εο-ί̄-μην = -οίμην; -όο-ῑ-μι = -οῖμι, -ο-ίη-ν = -οίην, -οο-ί̄-μην = -οίμην. Thus, τῑμῴην (τῑμαο-ίη-ν), τῑμῴης (τῑμαο-ίη-ς), τῑμῴη (τῑμαο-ίη), τῑμῴμην (τῑμαο-ί̄-μην), ποιοῖο (ποιέο-ῑ-σο), ποιοῖτο (ποιέο-ῑ-το).

638. In the *singular* -αω verbs usually end in -ῴην, -ῴης, -ῴη, rarely in -ῷμι, -ῷς, -ῷ. -εω verbs usually end in -οίην, -οίης, -οίη, rarely in -οῖμι, -οῖς, -οῖ (-οῖ chiefly in Plato).

639. In the *dual* and *plural* -αω verbs usually end in -ῷτον, -ῴτην, -ῷμεν, -ῷτε, -ῷεν, rarely in -ῴητον, -ῳήτην, -ῴημεν, -ῴητε, -ῴησαν. -εω verbs usually end in -οῖτον, -οίτην, -οῖμεν, -οῖτε, -οῖεν, rarely in -οίητον, -οιήτην, -οίημεν, -οίητε, -οίησαν.

640. Few cases of the optative of -οω verbs occur. In the sing. both -οίην and -οῖμι are found; in the plur. -οῖμεν, -οῖτε, -οῖεν. For ῥῑγῴην from ῥῑγόω *shiver* see 641.

641. Several contract verbs have stems in -ᾱ, -η, -ω.

These are the verbs of 394, 398 with apparently irregular contraction, and δρῶ *do*; with presents made from -ᾱ-ι̯ω, -η-ι̯ω, -ω-ι̯ω. Thus, from ζήω, ζήεις, ζήει and χρήομαι, χρήε(σ)αι, χρήεται come ζῶ, ζῇς, ζῇ and χρῶμαι, χρῇ, χρῆται; so διψῆν, πεινῆν from διψή-εν, πεινή-εν. ἱδρόω, ῥῑγόω (398) derive the forms in ω and ῳ from ἱδρω-, ῥῑγω- (ἱδρώω, ῥῑγώω from ἱδρωσ-ι̯ω, ῥῑγωσ-ι̯ω). The forms in -οω are from the weaker stems ἱδροσ-, ῥῑγοσ-.

---

641 D. Hom. has διψάων, πεινάων, πεινήμεναι, μνάομαι, χρήων (Mss. χρείων) *uttering oracles*, γελώω, ἱδρώω. The verbs in 394, except διψῶ and πεινῶ, have stems in η and ᾰ (36 e); thus, in Hdt., χρᾶται from χράεται, but χρέω imper., χρεώμενος from χρῆο, χρηόμενος by 34. Hom. and Ion. ζώω has the stem ζω (ζω-ι̯ω). Hdt. has ζῆν, διψῆν, but κνᾶν, σμᾶν.

CONTRACT VERBS IN THE DIALECTS

642. -αω Verbs in Homer. — Hom. leaves -αω verbs open 64 times, as ναιετάω, -άουσι, ὑλάει, ἀοιδιάουσα, γοάοιμεν, τηλεθάοντας. When contracted, -αω verbs have the Attic forms, as ὁρῶ, ὁρᾷς, ὁρᾷ; as πειρᾷ *makest trial* from πειράε-(σ)αι from πειράομαι; ἠρῶ *didst pray* from ἠράε-(σ)ο from ἀράομαι.

643. When uncontracted, verbs in -αω often show in the Mss. of Hom., not the original open forms, but "assimilated" forms of the concurrent vowels, αε, αει, αη giving a double *a* sound by α prevailing over the *e* sound; αο, αω, αοι, αου giving a double *o* sound by the *o* sound prevailing over the α. One of the vowels is commonly lengthened, rarely both.

αε = (1) **αα**: ὁράεσθαι = ὁράασθαι, ἀγάεσθε = ἀγάασθε.
= (2) **ᾱα**: μνάεσθαι = μνάασθαι, ἠγάεσθε = ἠγάασθε.
αει = (1) **αᾳ**: ὁράεις = ὁράᾳς, ἑάει = ἑάᾳ.
= (2) **ᾱᾳ**: μενοινάει = μενοινάᾳ.
αη = (1) **αᾳ**: ἑάῃς = ἑάᾳς.
= (2) **ᾱᾳ**: μνάῃ *wooest* 2 sing. mid. = μνάᾳ.
αο = (1) **οω**: ὁράοντες = ὁρόωντες.
= (2) **ωο**: ἡβάοντες = ἡβώοντες, μνάοντο = μνώοντο.
αω = (1) **οω**: ὁράω = ὁρόω, βοάων = βοόων.
= (2) **ωω**: μενοινάω = μενοινώω.
αοι = (1) **οῳ**: ὁράοιτε = ὁρόῳτε.
= (2) **ωοι**: ἡβάοιμι = ἡβώοιμι.
αου = (1) **οω**: ὁράουσα = ὁρόωσα, ὁράουσι = ὁρόωσι, ἀλάου (from ἀλάεο imper. of ἀλάομαι) = ἀλόω.
= (2) **ωω**: ἡβάουσα = ἡβώωσα, δράουσι = δρώωσι. ου here is a spurious diphthong (6) derived from -οντ-: ὁραοντ-ι̯α, ἡβαοντ-ι̯α, δράοντι; or by contraction in ἀλάου from ἀλάεο.

N. — ἀλόω from ἀλάεο *wander* is unique. γελώοντες is from γελώω (641).

644. The assimilated forms are used only when the second vowel (in the unchanged form) stood in a syllable long by nature or position. Hence ὁροωμεν, ὁρααττε, ὁρaατο, do not occur for ὁράομεν, etc. (μνωόμενος for μνᾱόμενος is an exception.) The first vowel is lengthened only when the metre requires it, as in ἡβώοντες for ἡβάοντες — ⏑ — ⏑. Thus two long vowels do not occur in succession except to fit the form to the verse, as μενοινώω for μενοινάω; but ἡβώοιμι, not ἡβώῳμι. When the first vowel is metrically lengthened, the second vowel is not lengthened, though it may be long either in a final syllable (as in μενοινάᾳ) or when it represents the spurious diphthong ου from -οντ- (as in ἡβώωσα, δρώωσι for ἡβάουσα, δράουσι from -οντι̯α, -οντι).

645. The assimilated forms include the "Attic" future in -αω from -ασω (539); as ἐλόωσι (= ἐλάουσι), κρεμόω, δαμάᾳ, δαμόωσι.

646. The assimilated forms are found only in the artificial language of Homer, Hesiod, and their imitators, and nowhere in the living speech. They are commonly explained as derived from the contracted forms by a process of 'distraction,' and as inserted in the text for the sake of the metre. Thus ὁρᾷς, βοῶντες, the spoken forms which had taken the place of original ὁράεις, βοάοντες, in the text, were expanded into ὁράᾳς, βοόωντες, by repetition of the α and ο. While the restoration of the original uncontracted forms is generally possible, and is adopted in several modern editions, a phonetic origin of many of the forms in question is still sought by some scholars who regard ὁρόω as an intermediate stage between ὁράω and ὁρῶ. It will be observed, however, that the forms in 648 can be derived only from the unassimilated forms.

647. In the imperfect contraction generally occurs, and assimilation is rare.

648. Some verbs show εο for αο, as ἤντεον, τρόπεον, μενοίνεον, ποτέονται. Cp. 649, 653.

649. -αω verbs in Herodotus. — Hdt. contracts -αω verbs as they are contracted in Attic. In many cases before an ο sound the Mss. substitute ε for α (τολμέω, ὁρέων, ἐφοίτεον). This ε is never found in *all* the forms of the same verb, and the Mss. generally disagree on each occurrence of any form. — Hdt. always has -ῴην, -ῴμην, in the optative.

650. -εω verbs in Homer. — **a.** Hom. rarely contracts εω and εο (except in the participle). In a few cases ευ appears for εο, as ποιεύμην; rarely for εου, as τελεῦσι. When the metre allows either -εε and -εει, or -ει, the open forms are slightly more common. ει is often necessary to admit a word into the verse (as ἡγεῖσθαι, ἐφίλει), and is often found at the verse-end. -έ-ε-αι, -έ-ε-ο, in the 2 sing. mid. may become -εῖαι, -εῖο, or -έαι, -έο, by the expulsion of one ε; as μῡθεῖαι or μῡθέαι *sayest*, αἰδεῖο *show regard*.

b. νεικείω, τελείω, from -εσ-ιω (νεικεσ-, τελεσ-) are older forms than νεικέω, τελέω. See 488 d, 624. θείω, πλείω, πνείω show metrical lengthening (28 D.).

c. On -ημεναι in Hom. see 657.

651. -εω verbs in Herodotus. — **a.** Hdt. generally leaves εο, εω, εου, open, except when a vowel precedes the ε, in which case we find ευ for εο (ἀγνοεῦντες). In the 3 plur. -έουσι is kept except in ποιεῦσι. For -έ-εο in the 2 sing. mid. we find έ-ο in αἰτέο. εε, εει, in stems of more than one syllable, are usually uncontracted in the Mss., but this is probably an error. δεῖ *it is necessary* and δεῖν are never written otherwise. — The Ion. ευ for εο, εου, occurs rarely in tragedy.

b. In the optative Hdt. has -έοι after a consonant, as καλέοι, but -οῖ after a vowel, as ποιοῖμι, ποιοῖ.

652. Verbs in -οω. — **a.** Hom. always uses the contracted forms except in the case of such as show assimilation like that in -αω verbs.

οο = (1) οω : δηϊόοντο = δηϊόωντο.	οοι = οῳ : δηιόοιεν = δηιόῳεν.
(2) ωο : ὑπνόοντας = ὑπνώοντας.	οου = οω : ἀρόουσι = ἀρόωσι.

b. Hdt. contracts -οω verbs as in Attic. Forms with ευ for ου, as δικαιεῦσι, ἐδικαίευν, are incorrect.

653. Doric. — Doric (59 D.) contracts αε and αη to η; αει and αῃ to ῃ; αο, αω, to ᾱ except in final syllables: τῑμῶ, τῑμῇς, τῑμῇ, τῑμᾶμες, τῑμῆτε, τῑμᾶντι, τίμη, τῑμῆν. Monosyllabic stems have ω from α + ο or α + ω. Some verbs in -αω have alternative forms in -εω (648), as ὁρέω, τῑμέω.

654. The contractions of -εω verbs in Doric may be illustrated thus:

Severer Doric	Milder Doric
φιλέω, φιλῶ, φιλίω	φιλέω, φιλῶ
φιλεῖς, φιλές(?)	φιλεῖς, φιλές(?)
φιλεῖ	φιλεῖ
φιλέομες, φιλίομες, φιλίωμες, φιλῶμες	φιλέομες, φιλοῦμες, φιλεῦμες
φιλῆτε	φιλεῖτε
φιλέοντι, φιλίοντι, φιλόντι	φιλέοντι, φιλοῦντι, φιλεῦντι

a. ιω for εο is a diphthong. ευ for εο is common in Theocritus. In Cretan ι (= y) for ε is often expelled (κοσμόντες = κοσμέοντες).

655. Verbs in -οω contract οο and οε to ω in Severer Doric and to ου in Milder Doric.

656. Aeolic. — In Aeolic contract verbs commonly pass into the μι-conjugation: τίμαιμι, -αις, -αι, τίμᾱμεν, τίμᾱτε, τίμαισι, imperfect, ἐτίμᾱν, ἐτίμᾱς, ἐτίμᾱ, etc. inf. τίμᾱν, part. τίμαις, -αντος, mid. τίμᾱμαι, inf. τῑμάμεναι. So φίλημι, φίλημεν, φίλητε, φίλεισι, ἐφίλην, inf. φίλην, part. φίλεις, -εντος. Thus ὄρημι from ὁρέω = Att. ὁράω, κάλημι, αἴνημι. So also δήλωμι, 3 pl. δήλοισι, inf. δήλων. Besides these forms we find a few examples of the earlier inflection in -αω, -εω, -οω, but these forms usually contract except in a few cases where ε is followed by an ο sound (ποτέονται). From other tenses, *e.g.* the fut. in -ησω, η has been transferred to the present in ἀδικήω, ποθήω.

657. Hom. has several cases of contract verbs inflected according to the μι-conjugation in the 3 dual: σῡλή-την (σῡλάω *spoil*), προσαυδή-την (προσαυδάω *speak to*), ἀπειλή-την (ἀπειλέω *threaten*), ὁμαρτή-την (ὁμαρτέω *meet*); also σάω 3 sing. imperf. (σαόω *keep safe*). In the infinitive -ημεναι, as γοήμεναι (γοάω), πεινήμεναι (πεινάω, 641), φιλήμεναι (φιλέω), φορήμεναι and φορῆναι (φορέω). But ἀγῑνέω has ἀγῑνέμεναι.

FUTURE ACTIVE AND MIDDLE (532 ff.). FUTURE PERFECT (580 ff.)

658. All vowel and consonant verbs in -ω inflect the future alike.

659. Indicative. — The future active and middle add the primary endings, and are inflected like the present; as λύσω, λύσομαι. On the two endings of the second singular middle, see 628. Liquid verbs, Attic futures (538), Doric futures (540) are inflected like contract verbs in -εω; thus φανῶ φανοῦμαι, καλῶ καλοῦμαι, and πεσοῦμαι, follow ποιῶ ποιοῦμαι (385).

a. The only future perfect active from an ω-verb is τεθνήξω *shall be dead* (584), which is inflected like a future active. Ordinarily the periphrastic formation is used: λελυκὼς ἔσομαι *shall have loosed*. The future perfect passive (λελύσομαι *shall have been loosed*) is inflected like the future middle. The periphrastic forms and the future perfect passive rarely occur outside of the indicative.

660. Optative. — The inflection is like the present: λύσο-ι-μι, λῡσο-ί-μην. In the optative singular of liquid verbs, -ιη-ν, -ιη-ς, -ιη, in the dual and plural -ῑ-τον,

-ῑ-την, -ῑ-μεν, -ῑ-τε, -ιε-ν, are added to the stem ending in the thematic vowel ο; thus φανεο-ίην = φανοίην, φανέο-ῑ-μεν = φανοῖμεν. So in Attic futures in -άζω, as βιβάζω (539 d) *cause to go*: βιβῴην, -ῴης, -ῴη, pl. βιβῷμεν.

661. Infinitive. — The future infinitive active adds -εν, as λύσειν from λύσε-εν, φανεῖν from φανέ(σ)ε-εν. The infinitive middle adds -σθαι, as λύσε-σθαι, φανεῖσθαι, from φανέ(σ)ε-σθαι.

662. Participle. — The future participle has the same endings as the present: λύσων λύσουσα λῦσον, φανῶν φανοῦσα φανοῦν; middle, λῡσόμενος, φανούμενος.

FIRST AND SECOND FUTURE PASSIVE (589, 597)

663. All verbs inflect the first and second future passive alike, that is, like the future middle.

664. The indicative adds -μαι to the stem ending in -θησο- or -ησο-, as λυθή-σο-μαι, φανή-σο-μαι. For the two forms of the second person singular see 628. The optative adds -ῑ-μην, as λυθησο-ί-μην, φανησο-ί-μην. The infinitive adds -σθαι, as λυθή-σε-σθαι, φανή-σε-σθαι. The participle adds -μενος, as λυθησό-μενος, φανη-σό-μενος.

FIRST AORIST ACTIVE AND MIDDLE (542)

665. All vowel and consonant ω-verbs inflect the first aorist alike.

666. Indicative. — The secondary endings of the first aorist active were originally added to the stem ending in -σ-; thus, ἔλῡσμ̥, ἔλῡσ-ς, ἔλῡσ-τ, ἔλῡσ-μεν, ἔλῡσ-τε, ἔλῡσ-ντ. From ἔλῡσμ̥ came ἔλῡσα (by 35 c), the α of which spread to the other forms except in the 3 sing., where ε was borrowed from the perfect.

a. In the middle the secondary endings are added to the stem ending in -σα-. For the loss of σ in -σο, see 465 b.

667. Subjunctive. — In the subjunctive the long thematic vowel -ω/η- is substituted for the α of the indicative, and these forms are inflected like the present subjunctive: λύσω λύσωμαι, φήνω φήνωμαι. For the loss of σ in -σαι see 465 a.

668. Optative. — To the stem ending in α the mood-suffix ῑ is added, making αι, to which the same endings are affixed as in the present: λύσα-ῑ-μι = λύσαιμι, λῡσα-ί-μην = λῡσαίμην, φηνα-ῑ-μι = φήναιμι. The inflection in the middle is like that of the present. For the loss of σ in -σο see 465 b. — In the active -ειας, -ειε, -ειαν are more common than -αις, -αι, -αιεν.

---

661 D. Hom. has ἀξέμεναι, ἀξέμεν, ἄξειν. Doric has -ην, -ειν; Aeolic has -ην.

667 D. Hom. has forms with the short thematic vowel, as ἐρύσσομεν, ἀλγή-σετε, νεμεσήσετε; μῡθήσομαι, ἐφάψεαι, ἱλασόμεσθα, δηλήσεται. In such forms aorist subjunctive and future indicative are alike (532). Pindar has βάσομεν, αὐδάσομεν (457 D.).

668 D. Hom. has both sets of endings, but that in αι is rarer. In the drama -ειας is very much commoner than -αις. -αις is most frequent in Plato and Xeno-

669. Imperative. — The regular endings (462) are added to the stem in -σα (or -α in liquid verbs) except in the active and middle 2 sing., in which -ον and -αι take the place of -α: λῦσον λῡσάτω, λῦσαι λῡσάσθω, φῆνον φηνάτω, φῆναι φηνάσθω.

670. Infinitive. — The aorist active infinitive ends in -αι, which is an old dative: the middle ends in -σθαι: λῦσαι λύσα-σθαι, φῆναι φήνα-σθαι, πλέξαι πλέξα-σθαι.

671. Participle. — The active participle adds -ντ like the present: masc. λύσᾱς from λῡσαντ-ς, fem. λύσᾱσα from λυσᾱντ-ι̯α, neut. λῦσαν from λῡσαν(τ). See 301. The middle ends in -μενος: λῡσά-μενος, φηνά-μενος.

FIRST AND SECOND AORIST PASSIVE (585, 590)

672. All vowel and consonant verbs in -ω inflect the aorists passive alike, that is, according to the μι-conjugation, except in the subjunctive.

a. Vowel verbs rarely form second aorists that are passive in form, as ῥέω *flow*, ἐρρύην (803). But ῥέω is properly not a vowel verb (see 503).

673. Indicative. — The indicative adds the active secondary endings directly to the tense stem ending in -θη- (first aorist) or -η- (second aorist). The inflection is thus like that of the imperfect of a verb in -μι.

ἐλύθη-ν	ἐτίθη-ν			ἐλύθη-μεν	ἐτίθε-μεν
ἐλύθη-ς	ἐτίθη-ς	ἐλύθη-τον	ἐτίθε-τον	ἐλύθη-τε	ἐτίθε-τε
ἐλύθη	ἐτίθη	ἐλυθή-την	ἐτιθέ-την	ἐλύθη-σαν	ἐτίθε-σαν

a. For -σαν we find -ν from -ν(τ) in poetical and dialectic forms before which η has been shortened to ε (40), thus ὤρμηθεν for ὡρμήθησαν from ὁρμάω *urge*.

674. Subjunctive. — The subjunctive adds -ω/η- to the tense stem ending in -θε- or -ε- and contracts: λυθῶ, -ῇς, -ῇ, etc., from λυθέω, -έῃς, -έῃ, etc.; φανῶ, -ῇς, -ῇ from φανέω, -έῃς, -έῃ, etc.

675. Optative. — The optative adds -ῑ- or -ιη- to the tense-stem ending in -θε- or -ε-, and contracts. In the singular -ιη- is regular; in the dual and plural -ῑ- is generally preferred. Thus λυθείην from λυθε-ίη-ν, φανείην from φανε-ίη-ν,

---

phon, less common in poetry, and very rare in the orators. Neither Thuc. nor Hdt. has -αις. -αι is rare in prose, most examples being in Plato and Demosthenes. Hdt. has no case. In Aristotle -αι is as common as -ειε. -αῖεν is very rare in poetry, in Thuc. and Hdt., but slightly better represented in Xenophon and the orators. -ειαν is probably the regular form in the drama. — The forms in -ειας, -ειε, -ειαν are called "Aeolic," but do not occur in the remains of that dialect.

671 D. Aeolic has -αις, -αισα, -αν (37 D. 3).

674 D. Hdt. leaves εω open (αἱρεθέω, φανέωσι) but contracts εη, εῃ (φανῇ). Hom. has some forms like the 2 aor. subj. of μι-verbs. Thus, from δαμνάω (δάμνημι) *subdue*: δαμήω, -ήῃς, -ήῃ, -ήετε. So also δαήω (δα- *learn*), σαπήῃ (σήπω *cause to rot*), φανήῃ (φαίνω *show*), τραπήομεν (τέρπω *amuse*). The spellings with ει (*e.g.* δαμείω, δαείω) are probably incorrect.

λυθεῖτον from λυθέ-ῑ-τον, φανεῖτον from φανέ-ῑ-τον, λυθεῖμεν from λυθέ-ῑ-μεν, φανεῖεν from φανέ-ιε-ν. The inflection is like that of the present optative of a μι-verb.

λυθε-ίη-ν	τιθε-ίη-ν			λυθε-ῖ-μεν	τιθε-ῖ-μεν
λυθε-ίη-ς	τιθε-ίη-ς	λυθε-ῖ-τον	τιθε-ῖ-τον	λυθε-ῖ-τε	τιθε-ῖ-τε
λυθε-ίη	τιθε-ίη	λυθε-ί-την	τιθε-ί-την	λυθε-ῖε-ν	τιθε-ῖε-ν

a. -είημεν is used only in prose (but Plato and Isocrates have also -εῖμεν). -είητε is almost always found in the Mss. of prose writers; -εῖτε occurs only in poetry (except from μι-verbs). -εῖεν is more common in prose than -είησαν.

676. Imperative. — The endings of the imperative are added to the tense-stem ending in -θη- or -η-. Before -ντων, -θη- and -η- become -θε- and -ε- (λυθέντων, φανέντων). For -τι instead of -θι in the first aorist (λύθητι) see 125 b.

677. Infinitive. — -ναι is added to the tense-stem in -θη- or -η-: λυθῆ-ναι, φανῆ-ναι.

678. Participle. — The participle adds -ντ, as masc. λυθείς from λυθεντ-ς, fem. λυθεῖσα from λυθεντ-ια, neut. λυθέν from λυθεν(τ). See 301. So φανείς, etc.

SECOND AORIST ACTIVE AND MIDDLE (546)

679. Most verbs in -ω inflect the second aorist according to the ω-conjugation; some inflect it according to the μι-conjugation.

680. The inflection of most second aorists of ω-verbs is like that of an imperfect of ω-verbs in the indicative, and like that of a present in the other moods.

ἔ-λιπο-ν	ἔ-λῡο-ν	λίπε	λῦε
ἐ-λιπό-μην	ἐ-λῡό-μην	λιποῦ (424 b. 2)	λῡ́ου
λίπω	λῡ́ω	λιπεῖν (λιπέ-εν, 424 c)	λῡ́ειν (λῡ́ε-εν)
λίπω-μαι	λῡ́ω-μαι	λιπέ-σθαι	λῡ́ε-σθαι
λιπο-ίμην	λῡο-ίμην	λιπών	λῡ́ων
		λιπό-μενος	λῡό-μενος

For the loss of σ in -σο in the second person singular see 465 b.

681. A number of ω-verbs form their second aorists without a thematic vowel, herein agreeing with the second aorists of μι-verbs. Cp. ἔδῡν p. 140. The second aorist of γι-γνώ-σκω *know* is inflected as follows.

---

677 D. Hom. has -μεναι, as ὁμοιωθήμεναι, δαήμεναι (and δαῆναι). Doric has -μεν, Aeolic -ν (μεθύσθην = μεθυσθῆναι).

680 D. Hom. has the infinitives εἰπέμεναι, εἰπέμεν, εἰπεῖν. For θανέειν (Attic θανεῖν) etc., θανέεν should be read. -έειν in Hdt. is erroneous. Doric has -ῆν, as μολῆν (βλώσκω *go*). Aeolic has -ην, as λάβην.

682. The indicative is inflected like ἔστην (p. 138); the subjunctive, like δῶ (p. 138).

ἔ-γνω-ν		ἔ-γνω-μεν	γνῶ		γνῶ-μεν
ἔ-γνω-ς	ἔ-γνω-τον	ἔ-γνω-τε	γνῷ-ς	γνῶ-τον	γνῶ-τε
ἔ-γνω	ἐ-γνώ-την	ἔ-γνω-σαν	γνῷ	γνῶ-τον	γνῶ-σι

a. We expect ἔγνοτον, ἔγνομεν, etc. (551), but the strong stem γνω- has been transferred to the dual and plural. So also in ἔβην, ἔφθην, ἑάλων.—Subjunctive βῶ, βῇς, βῇ, βῆτον, βῶμεν, βῆτε, βῶσι. On the formation of the subjunctive see 757 D.

683. The optative is inflected like δοίην (p. 138).

γνοίην		γνοῖμεν or γνοίημεν
γνοίης	γνοῖτον or γνοίητον	γνοῖτε or γνοίητε
γνοίη	γνοίτην or γνοιήτην	γνοῖεν or γνοίησαν

a. So βαίην, βαῖτον or βαίητον, βαῖμεν or βαίημεν. In the 2 plur. the Mss. of prose writers have only -ιητε (γνοίητε, -βαίητε); but -ιητε is not attested by the evidence of verse.

684. The imperative is inflected like στῆθι (p. 139).

γνῶθι, γνώτω	γνῶτον, γνώτων	γνῶτε, γνόντων

a. In composition διάγνωθι, ἀνάβηθι (423). For βῆθι (from βαίνω) -βᾱ in composition occurs in poetry, as ἀνάβᾱ.

685. The infinitive adds -εναι, as γνῶναι from γνώ-εναι (like στῆναι from στή-εναι). In composition διαγνῶναι (426 d).

686. The participle adds -ντ-, as masc. γνούς from γνοντ-ς, fem. γνοῦσα from γνοντ-ιa, neut. γνόν from γνον(τ). See 301. In composition διαγνούς (426 d).

a. Before ντ the long vowel ω is regularly shortened to ο by 40.

687. The following ω-verbs have second aorists of the μι form.

ἁλίσκομαι (ἁλ-ο-) *am captured*, ἑάλων or ἥλων (ἁλῶ, ἁλοίην, ἁλῶναι, ἁλούς).
βαίνω (βα-) *go*, ἔβην (βῶ, βαίην, βῆθι and also -βᾱ in composition, βῆναι, βάς).
βιόω (βιο-) *live*, ἐβίων (βιῶ, βιῴην, βιῶναι, βιούς). Hom. βιώτω imper.
γηράσκω (γηρα-) *grow old*, γηρᾶναι poet., γηράς Hom.
γιγνώσκω (γνο-, γνω-) *know*, ἔγνων (γνῶ, γνοίην, γνῶθι, γνῶναι, γνούς).
-διδράσκω (δρᾱ-) *run*, only in composition, -έδρᾱν (-δρῶ, -δραίην, -δρᾶναι, -δράς). Hdt. has ἔδρην, δρῆναι, δράς in composition.
δύω (δῡ-) *enter* ἔδῡν *entered* inflected p. 140 (δύω, opt. Hom. δύη and ἐκδῦμεν for δυ-ίη, ἐκδύ-ῑ-μεν; δῦθι, δῦναι, δύς).
ἔχω (σχε-) *have*, σχές imper.

---

682 D. ἔγνον, from ἔγνων(τ) by 40, is found in Pind. Hom. has ἔδυν, ἔτλαν, ἔκταν; Pind. ἔφυν.—Hom. has βάτην and βήτην.—Hom. has βλήεται, ἄλεται.—Subj.: Hom. has γνώω ἁλώω, γνώῃς γνῷς, γνώῃ γνῷ, ἐμβήῃ ἀναβῇ, γνῶτον, γνώομεν γνῶμεν, -βήομεν φθέωμεν, γνώωσι γνῶσιν βῶσιν φθέωσιν.

685 D. Hom. has γνώμεναι, δύμεναι, κτάμεναι, and -κτάμεν.

κτείνω (κτεν-, κτα-) *kill*, ἔκτᾰν, ἔκτᾰς, ἔκτᾰ, ἔκτᾰμεν, 3 pl. ἔκτᾰν 551 D, subj. κτέωμεν, inf. κτάμεναι κτάμεν, part. κτάς; ἐκτάμην *was killed* (κτάσθαι, κτάμενος); all poetic forms.
πέτομαι (πετ-, πτε-, πτα-) *fly*, poet. ἔπτην (πταίην, πτάς), middle ἐπτάμην (πτάσθαι, πτάμενος). πτῶ, πτῆθι, πτῆναι are late.
πίνω (πι-) *drink*, πῖθι imper.
σκέλλω in ἀποσκέλλω (σκελ-, σκλε-) *dry up*, ἀποσκλῆναι.
τλα- *endure*, fut. τλήσομαι, poetic ἔτλην (τλῶ, τλαίην, τλῆθι, τλῆναι, τλάς).
φθάνω (φθα-) *anticipate*, ἔφθην (φθῶ, φθαίην, φθῆναι, φθάς).
φύω (φῡ-) *produce*, ἔφῡν *was produced*, *am* (φύω subj., φῦναι, φύς 308).

688. The following ω-verbs have in poetry (especially in Homer) second aorists of the μι form: ἄλλομαι (ἆλσο, ἆλτο), ἀπαυράω (ἀπούρᾱς), ἀραρίσκω (ἄρμενος), ἄω (ἄμεναι), βάλλω (ξυμβλήτην, ἔβλητο), βιβρώσκω (ἔβρων), root γεν- (γέντο *grasped*), δέχομαι (δέκτο), Epic κιχάνω (ἐκίχην, κιχήω, κιχείη, κιχῆναι and κιχήμεναι, κιχείς and κιχήμενος; properly from κίχημι), κλάω (ἀπόκλᾱς), κλύω (κλῦθι, κέκλυθι), κτίζω (κτίμενος), root λεχ- (ἔλεκτο *laid himself to rest*), λύω (λύτο), οὐτάω (οὖτα, οὐτάμενος), πάλλω (πάλτο), πελάζω (ἐπλήμην), πέρθω (πέρθαι = περθ-σθαι), πλώω (ἔπλων), πνῡ- (ἄμπνῡτο *revived*), πτήσσω (καταπτήτην), σεύω (ἐσσύμην, ἔσυτο, σύμενος), φθίνω (ἐφθίμην), χέω (ἐχύμην, χύμενος).
ἔλεκτο, πάλτο are properly first aorists (for ἐλεκ-σ-το, παλ-σ-το), σ being lost between two consonants (103).

FIRST AND SECOND PERFECT AND PLUPERFECT ACTIVE (555, 561)

689. All vowel and consonant verbs in -ω inflect the first perfect alike. Some verbs in -ω inflect the second perfect according to the ω-conjugation, others inflect it according to the μι-conjugation.

690. Indicative. — Originally the endings were added to the stem without any thematic vowel. Of this unthematic formation a few traces survive (573). In the 2 p. sing. the ending is -ς, but originally -θα; in the 3 pl. -κᾱσι stands for κα-νσι out of κα-ντι (100). Thus λέλυκα, -ας, -ε, πέπομφα, -ας, -ε, etc. The periphrastic combination occurs in the indicative (599 a).

691. Subjunctive. — The perfect subjunctive is commonly formed periphrastically by the perfect active participle and ὦ, ᾖς, ᾖ, etc. Thus λελυκὼς (γεγραφὼς) ὦ, etc., λελυκότες (γεγραφότες) ὦμεν, etc. Of the periphrastic forms only the 1 and 3 sing., 2 and 3 plur. are attested.

692. Instances of the simple perfect subjunctive (λελύκω, γεγράφω) are very rare. The simple form is made by substituting the thematic vowel ω/η for α in the tense-stem. Only the sing. and the 3 plur. are attested from ω-verbs.

693. Besides εἰδῶ (οἶδα) and ἑστήκῃ, etc., Attic prose has only about 16 occurrences of the simple perf. subj., and from the following verbs only: βαίνω, δέδια, ἐγείρω, ἔοικα, θνῄσκω, λαμβάνω, λανθάνω, πάσχω, ποιῶ, φύω. Hippocr. has forms from βιβρώσκω, πονῶ, τεύχω. There are about 30 occurrences in the poetry. Attic prose writers show about 25 cases of the periphrasis from all ω-verbs.

694. Optative. — The perfect optative is commonly formed periphrastically by the perfect active participle and εἴην, εἴης, εἴη, etc. Thus λελυκὼς (γεγραφὼς) εἴην, etc., λελυκότες (γεγραφότες) εἶμεν, etc. The dual is exceedingly rare.

695. Occasionally the simple forms are used (λελύκοιμι, γεγράφοιμι). These are formed by adding the mood-sign ῑ, and the endings, to the tense-stem with the thematic vowel (ο). All the -ιη-forms are attested; of the -ῑ-forms only the 3 sing. and 1 and 3 plur.

696. Of the simple optative there are about 25 occurrences in Attic prose, and from the following verbs only: ἀποχωρῶ, ἐξαπατῶ, εἰσβάλλω, παραδίδωμι, ἔοικα, -εστήκοι, ὑπηρετῶ, θνῄσκω, λανθάνω, καταλείπω, ποιῶ, πάσχω, προέρχομαι, ἐμπίπτω, φύω. In the poets there are about 16 occurrences. Prose writers show about 106 occurrences of the periphrastic forms.

697. Imperative. — The usual form of the first perfect imperative is periphrastic: λελυκὼς ἴσθι, ἔστω, etc. No classical Attic writer uses the simple forms.

698. The second perfect is rare, and occurs only in the case of verbs which have a present meaning. From active verbs inflected according to the ω- conjugation there occur κεχήνετε *gape*, Ar. *Ach.* 133 (χάσκω, χαν-), and κεκράγετε *screech*, *Vesp.* 415 (κράζω). Most second perfects show the μι form and have present meaning, as τέθναθι (Hom.) τεθνάτω from θνῄσκω *die*, δέδιθι from δέδια *fear*, and κέκρᾱχθι from κράζω in Aristophanes. Most such second perfects are poetical.

699. Infinitive. — The perfect infinitive adds -έ-ναι, as λελυκέναι, λελοιπέναι.

700. Participle. — The suffixes of the perfect participle in the nominative are -(ϝ)ώς, -υῖα, -(ϝ)ός, as λελυκώς, λελοιπώς. See 301 c, d, 309.

701. Pluperfect Active. — The pluperfect is formed by adding -εα, -εας, -εε, -ετον, -ετην, -εμεν, -ετε, -εσαν to the reduplicated stem. By contraction from ἐλελύκεα, -εας, -εε come the forms ἐλελύκη, -ης -ει(ν). In the later language ει spread from the 3 sing. and was used throughout, as ἐλελύκειν, -εις, -ει, -ειτον, -είτην, -ειμεν, -ειτε, and very late -εισαν. The best Mss. of Demosthenes have -ειν in 1 sing. Instead of the simple pluperfect we find periphrastic forms, 599 a.

SECOND PERFECTS OF THE μι-FORM

702. A few ω-verbs form their second perfects in the dual and plural without α by adding the endings directly to the stem. Herein these forms agree with the second perfect of μι-verbs (417). In the singular α is used.

---

699 D. Doric has -ην and -ειν, as δεδύκην = δεδυκέναι, γεγάκειν = γεγονέναι. Aeolic has -ην, as τεθνάκην.

700 D. In the 2 perf. Hom. sometimes has -ῶτ-ος for -ότ-ος, as κεκμηώς, -ῶτος (κάμνω *am weary*). In the 2 perf. Hom. sometimes has α for Attic η in the feminine, as ἀρηρώς ἀραρυῖα from ἄρηρα (ἀραρίσκω *fit*). See 573. Aeolic inflects the perfect participle as a present in -ων, -οντος. Thus Hom. κεκλήγοντας for κεκληγότας (κλάζω *scream*), Pind. πεφρίκοντας (φρίττω *shudder*).

703. The second perfect δέδια *I fear* usually has the forms of the first perfect δέδοικα in the singular, less frequently in the plural.

Perfect	Pluperfect	
δέδοικα or δέδια	ἐδεδοίκη or ἐδεδίη	Subjunctive: δεδίω (rare)
δέδοικας or δέδιας	ἐδεδοίκης or ἐδεδίης	Optative: δεδιείην (rare)
δέδοικε or δέδιε	ἐδεδοίκει or ἐδεδίει	
δέδιτον	ἐδέδιτον	Imperative: δέδιθι (poet.)
δέδιτον	ἐδεδίτην	
δέδιμεν or δεδοίκαμεν	ἐδέδιμεν	Infinitive: δεδιέναι or δεδοικέναι
δέδιτε or δεδοίκατε	ἐδέδιτε	
δεδίᾱσι or δεδοίκᾱσι	ἐδέδισαν or ἐδεδοίκεσαν	Participle: δεδιώς, -υῖα, -ός or δεδοικώς, -υῖα, -ός.

704. Other second perfects inflected like δέδια are the following:

a. βαίνω (βα-) *go*, 1 perf. βέβηκα *have gone, stand fast* regular; 2 perf. 3 pl. βεβᾶσι (poet.), subj. 3 pl. βεβῶσι, inf. βεβάναι (poet. and Ion.), part. βεβώς (contracted from βεβαώς) βεβῶσα, gen. βεβῶτος.

b. γίγνομαι (γεν-, γα-) *become*, 2 perf. γέγονα *am* regular; 2 perf. part. poet. γεγώς (contracted from γεγαώς), γεγῶσα, gen. γεγῶτος.

c. θνῄσκω (θαν-, θνα-) *die*, 1 perf. τέθνηκα *am dead* regular; 2 perf. du. τέθνατον, pl. τέθναμεν, τέθνατε, τεθνᾶσι, 2 plup. 3 pl. ἐτέθνασαν, 2 perf. opt. τεθναίην, imper. τεθνάτω, inf. τεθνάναι, part. τεθνεώς, -εῶσα, -εός, gen. -εῶτος.

d. ἔοικα (ϝε-ϝοικ-α) *am like, appear* (ἰκ-, εἰκ-) has the μι forms ἔοιγμεν (poet.), εἴξᾱσι for ἐοικ-σ-ᾱσι (poet. and in Plato). ἔοικα (ἐῴκη plup.) has also the foll. forms: ἐοίκω, ἐοίκοιμι, ἐοικέναι (εἰκέναι poet.), ἐοικώς (εἰκώς also in Plato).

e. κράζω (κραγ-) *cry out*, 2 perf. κέκρᾱγα as present, imper. κέκρᾱχθι and κεκράγετε, a thematic form (both in Aristoph.).

705. Other verbs with second perfects of the μι-form (chiefly Homeric) are: ἄνωγα (ἄνωχθι), βιβρώσκω (βεβρῶτες), ἐγείρω (ἐγρήγορα), ἔρχομαι (εἰλήλυθμεν),

---

703 D. The root of δέδια is δϝι-, strong forms δϝει-, δϝοι-. Hom. has δίε, δίον *feared, fled;* for δέδοικα, δέδια he has δείδοικα, δείδια, etc. (once δεδίᾱσι). Here ει is due to metrical lengthening. δείδω, a present in form, is really a perfect for δε-δϝο(ι̯)-α.

704 a. D. Hom. has 3 pl. βεβάᾱσι, inf. βεβάμεν, part. βεβαώς, βεβαυῖα, gen. βεβαῶτος; 2 plup. βέβασαν.

b. Hom. has γεγάᾱτε and γεγάᾱσι, inf. γεγάμεν, part. γεγαώς, γεγαυῖα; 2 plup. ἐκγεγάτην.

c. Hom. τέθναθι, τεθνάμεναι and τεθνάμεν, τεθνηώς -ηῶτος and -ηότος, fem. τεθνηυίης.

d. Hom. imperf. εἶκε, 2 perf. 3 du. ἔϊκτον, 2 plup. ἐῴκει ἐΐκτην, ἐοίκεσαν, part. ἐοικώς (εἰκώς Φ 254), εἰκυῖα and ἐϊκυῖα (εἰοικυῖαι Σ 418); mid. ἤϊκτο, ἔϊκτο. Hdt. has οἶκα, οἰκώς.

μέμονα (μεμαώς), πάσχω (πέποσθε), πείθω (ἐπέπιθμεν), πίπτω (πεπτώς), root δα- *learn* (δεδαώς), root τλα- (τέτλαμεν, τετλαίην, τέτλαθι, τετλάμεναι and τετλάμεν, τετληώς).

PERFECT AND PLUPERFECT MIDDLE AND PASSIVE (574)

706. All vowel and consonant verbs in -ω inflect the perfect middle according to the μι-conjugation.

707. Indicative. — The perfect middle is inflected by adding the primary middle endings directly to the tense-stem, herein agreeing with the μι-conjugation. The pluperfect adds the secondary middle endings. In vowel verbs the formation is simple, as in λέλυ-μαι, ἐλελύ-μην. But in consonant verbs, the consonant at the end of the stem comes into collision with the consonant at the beginning of the ending; hence certain euphonic changes described in 409. The periphrastic form occurs in the 3 pl. and sometimes in the 3 sing. (599 d, e).

a. Stems in ν avoid the forms -ν-σαι, -ν-σο; thus, from φαίνω, instead of πέφανσαι, ἐπέφανσο the periphrastic πεφασμένος εἶ, ἦσθα were probably used.

708. Subjunctive. — The perfect middle subjunctive is commonly formed by periphrasis of the perfect middle participle and ὦ, ᾖς, ᾖ, etc. Thus λελυμένος ὦ.

709. From two verbs, whose perfect stem ends in η-(α), the simple forms are constructed. **κτάομαι** (κτα-) *acquire*, perf. κέκτημαι *possess* (1946), forms its subjunctive by adding the thematic vowel -ω/η- to κε-κτα; thus κε-κτά-ω-μαι = κεκτῶμαι, κε-κτά-η-σαι = κεκτῇ, κε-κτά-η-ται = κεκτῆται, etc. — **μιμνῄσκω** (μνα-) *remind*, perf. μέμνημαι *remember* (1946): με-μνά-ω-μαι = μεμνῶμαι, μεμνη-ώ-μεθα = μεμνώμεθα. With κεκτῶμαι, μεμνῶμαι, cp. ἱστῶμαι, p. 137. The periphrastic κεκτημένος ὦ, μεμνημένος ὦ occur.

710. Optative. — The perfect middle optative is commonly formed by the periphrasis of the perfect middle participle and εἴην, εἴης, εἴη, etc. Thus λελυμένος εἴην, etc.

711. Some verbs add -ῑ-μην, -ο-ῑ-μην to the tense-stem (709). — **a.** κτάομαι (κτα-) *acquire*, perf. κέκτημαι *possess* (1946): opt. κεκτη-ῑ-μην = κεκτῄμην, κεκτή-ῑ-σο = κεκτῇο, κεκτή-ῑ-το = κεκτῇτο. Less frequent and doubtful are κεκτῴμην, -ῷο, -ῷτο, -ῴμεθα from κεκτη-ο-ῑ-μην, etc.

b. μιμνῄσκω (μνα-) *remind*, perf. μέμνημαι *remember*; opt. μεμνη-ῑ-μην = μεμνῄμην, μεμνή-ῑ-σο = μεμνῇο, μεμνή-ῑ-το = μεμνῇτο, etc. The forms μεμνῴμην, -ῷο, -ῷτο, etc., from μεμνη-ο-ῑ-μην, etc., are uncommon and suspected.

c. καλέω (καλε-, κλη-) *call*, perf. κέκλημαι *am called* (1946); opt. κεκλη-ῑ-μην, etc. = κεκλῄμην, κεκλῇο, κεκλῇτο, κεκλῄμεθα.

d. βάλλω (βαλ-, βλη-) *throw*, perf. διαβέβλημαι, opt. διαβεβλῇσθε.

N. — The forms in -ῄμην, etc., have the μι-form; the doubtful -ῴμην, etc., belong to the ω-conjugation.

---

708 D. Hdt. has μεμνεώμεθα, and this form may be read in ξ 168.

711 D. Hom. has λελῦτο σ 238 = λελύ-ῑ-το (cp. δαινῦτο). Pind. has μεμναίατο. μέμνοιο in Xen. is from μέμνομαι.

712. Imperative. — In the third person singular the perfect meaning is regularly retained, as εἰρήσθω *let it have been said.* The 2 sing. and pl. are generally found only in the case of perfects with a present meaning, as μέμνησθε *remember!* μὴ πεφόβησθε *do not be afraid!* πέπαυσο *stop!* See 698.

a. The dual and 3 pl. are apparently wanting. The 2 sing. in -νσο from stems in -ν does not occur. For πέφανσο, πεφασμένος ἴσθι was probably used.

713. Attic prose writers have ἀναβεβλήσθω, ἀποκεκρίσθω, εἰρήσθω, ἐκτήσθω, ἐψεύσθω, κεῖσο, -κείσθω, κέκτησο, μέμνησθε, πεπαίσθω, πεπεράνθω, πεποίησο, πεπράσθω, πεφάσθω, πεφόβησθε, τετάχθω, τετολμήσθω.

714. Instead of the simple forms of the imperative we find the periphrastic use of the perfect participle and ἴσθι, ἔστω, etc. (599 g). Thus εἰρημένον ἔστω = εἰρήσθω.

715. Infinitive. — The perfect infinitive adds -σθαι, as λελύ-σθαι. Consonant stems lose the σ by 103, as λελεῖφθαι, πεπρᾶχθαι (406), ἐληλέγχθαι, πεφάνθαι (407).

716. Participle. — The perfect participle adds -μένος, as λελυμένος, λελειμμένος, πεπρᾱγμένος (406, 407). On the σ of πεφασμένος see 409 d.

SECOND CONJUGATION OR VERBS IN MI

717. Verbs in -μι usually have no thematic vowel between the tense-stem and the personal endings in the present system (except in the subjunctive). The name "μι-conjugation," or "non-thematic" conjugation," is applied to all verbs which form the present and imperfect without the thematic vowel.

718. Of verbs ending in -μι the following tenses are inflected according to the μι-conjugation (except in the subjunctive): all non-thematic presents and imperfects; all aorists passive; all perfects and pluperfects middle; those second aorists active and middle in which the tense-stem does not end with the thematic vowel; one verb (ἵστημι) in the second perfect and pluperfect active.

719. Certain tenses of verbs ending in -μι in the first person present indicative active, or in -μαι in the present middle (and passive) when not preceded by the thematic vowel, are inflected according to the ω-conjugation. These tenses are: all futures, all first aorists active and middle, most perfects and pluperfects active, and all subjunctives. Verbs in -νῡμι regularly inflect the subjunctive and the optative according to the ω-conjugation. Furthermore, the 2 sing. in the present and 2 and 3 sing. in the imperfect active of certain verbs, and some other forms, follow the ω-conjugation (746).

720. Verbs in -μι add the endings directly either to the verb-stem (here a root) or after the suffixes νυ or νη. Hence three classes are to be distinguished.

A. Root class; as φη-μί *say*, verb-stem (and root) φα-, φη-. This class often shows reduplication in the present and imperfect, as δί-δω-μι *give*.

N. — Two verbs have verb-stems ending in a consonant: εἰμί *am* (ἐσ-μι) and ἧμαι *sit* (ἡσ-μαι).

B. -νυ- class; as δείκ-νῡ-μι *show*, verb-stem δεικ-, present stem δεικνῡ-.

C. A few verbs, mainly poetical, add να-, νη-; as σκίδ-νη-μι σκίδ-να-μεν *scatter*, δάμ-νη-μι δάμ-να-μεν, *subdue*.

721. Deponent verbs without the thematic vowel are inflected according to the μι-conjugation.

PRESENT SYSTEM

722. Verbs in -μι belong to the first or simple class (504) or to the fourth class (523).

FIRST OR SIMPLE CLASS

723. The present is made by adding the personal endings directly to the verb-stem, which is a root. This verb-stem may be used in its pure form or it may be reduplicated.

a. Some verbs of this class with no active have a verb-stem of more than one syllable (usually two syllables).

724. Unreduplicated Presents: εἰμί (ἐσ-) *am*, εἶμι (ἰ-, εἰ-) *go*, ἧμαι (ἡσ-) *sit*, ἠμί *say* (ἦ *said*, 3 sing.), κεῖμαι (κει-) *lie*, φημί (φα-, φη-) *say*, χρή *it is necessary* (793); and poet. ἄημι (ἀη-) *blow*.

725. Deponents. — ἄγα-μαι (and ἀγάομαι) *admire*, δέα-μαι *appear*, δίε-μαι *flee, make flee* (cp. δίω), δύνα-μαι *am able* (737 a), ἐπί-στα-μαι *understand*, ἔρα-μαι *love* (poet. for ἐράω), ἵπταμαι *fly* (late, see 726 a), κρέμα-μαι *hang* (intrans.), ὄνο-μαι *insult*, πέτα-μαι (poet. by-form of πέτομαι) *fly*, ἐπριάμην *bought* a second aorist, στεῦμαι *affirm*.

a. Other such forms are Hom. ἵεμαι (ϝίεμαι) *strive*, εἴρυμαι and ἔρυμαι *rescue*, Ion. λάζυμαι *take*. ἐπίστηται Π 243 owes its η to such non-present forms as ἐπιστήσομαι.

726. Reduplicated Presents. — δίδημι *bind* (rare for δέω), δίδωμι (δο-, δω-) *give*, ἵημι (ἑ-, ἡ-) *send*, ἵστημι (στα-, στη-) *set*, κίχρημι (χρα-, χρη-) *lend*, ὀνίνημι (ὀνα-, ὀνη-) *benefit*, πίμπλημι (πλα-, πλη-) *fill*, πίμπρημι (πρα-, πρη-) *burn*, τίθημι (θε-, θη-) *place*.

a. Also poetic βίβημι (βα-, βη-) *go*, in Hom. βιβάς *striding*, δί-ζημαι (also Ion.) *seek*, for δι-δ̯ιη-μαι by 116 (cp. ζητέω *seek*), ἵλημι (ἱλα-, ἱλη- for σισλα-, σισλη-) *am propitious*. ἵπταμαι (late) for πέτομαι *fly* is an analogue of ἵσταμαι and is not properly reduplicated. τίτρημι *bore* is late.

727. Verbs in -μι reduplicate with ι in the present. See 414, 447. πί-μ-πλημι and πί-μ-πρημι may lose the inserted nasal in compounds of ἐν, but only when ἐν- takes the form ἐμ-; as ἐμπίπλημι, but ἐνεπίμπλασαν. Doric has κίγχημι. In ὀ-νί-νη-μι the reduplication takes place after a vowel (verb-stem ὀνα-, ὀνη-).

a. Reduplication is in place only in present and imperfect; but Hom. has *διδώσομεν*.

FOURTH CLASS

728. Most *μι*-verbs of the fourth class add *-νυ-* (after a vowel, *-ννυ-*) to the verb-stem.

729. Verb-stems in *-α*: *κερά-ννῡμι* *mix*, *κρεμά-ννῡμι* *hang* (intrans.), *πετά-ννῡμι* *spread*, *σκεδά-ννῡμι* *scatter*.

730. Verb-stems in *ε* (for *εσ*): *ἕ-ννῡμι* (in prose *ἀμφιέ-ννῡμι*) *clothe*, *κορέ-ννῡμι* *satiate*, *σβέ-ννῡμι* *extinguish*.

731. Verb-stems in *ω*: *ζώ-ννῡμι* *gird*, *ῥώ-ννῡμι* *strengthen*, *στρώ-ννῡμι* *spread*.

732. All the forms in *-ννῡμι* started from verb-stems ending in *σ*: *ἕννῡμι* from *ἑσ-νῡ-μι*, *σβέννῡμι* from *σβεσ-νῡ-μι*, *ζώννῡμι* from *ζωσ-νῡ-μι*. All the other verbs are analogues of these.

733. Verb-stems in a consonant: *ἄγ-νῡμι* *break*, *ἄρ-νυμαι* *earn*, *δείκ-νῡμι* *show*, *εἴργ-νῡμι* (= *εἴργω*) *shut in*, *ζεύγ-νῡμι* *yoke* (*ἀπο*)*κτει-νῡμι* often written *-κτίννῡμι* (= *κτείνω*) *kill*, *μείγ-νῡμι* (miswritten *μίγ-νῡμι*) *mix*, *-οίγ-νῡμι* (= *-οίγω*) *open*, *ὄλλῡμι* (*ὀλ-ε*) *destroy*, *ὄμ-νῡμι* (*ὀμ-ε-*, *ὀμ-ο*) *swear*, *ὀμόργ-νῡμι* *wipe off*, *ὄρ-νῡμι* *rouse*, *πήγ-νῡμι* (*παγ-*, *πηγ-*) *fix*, *πλήγ-νῡμι* (once, in *ἐκπλήγνυσθαι* Thuc. 4. 125; cp. *πλήττω*), *πτάρ-νυμαι* *sneeze*, *ῥήγ-νῡμι* (*ῥαγ-*, *ῥηγ-*, *ῥωγ-*) *break*, *στόρ-νῡμι* *spread*, *φράγ-νῡμι* (= *φράττω*) *inclose*.

734. Poetic verbs: *αἴ-νυμαι* *take*, *ἄ-νῡμι* *complete* (*ἀνύω*), *ἄχ-νυμαι* *am troubled*, *γά-νυμαι* *rejoice*, *δαί-νῡμι* *entertain*, *καί-νυμαι* *excel*, *κί-νυμαι* *move myself* (cp. *κῑνέω*), *ὀρέγ-νῡμι* *reach*, *τά-νυμαι* *stretch*, with *νυ* carried into other tenses (*τανύω*), *τί-νυμαι* (cp. Epic *τίνω* from *τι-νϝ-ω*) better *τείνυμαι*, *chastise*.

735. The verbs whose verb-stem ends in a liquid or nasal often form the tenses other than the present by adding *ε* or *ο*, as *ὄλλῡμι* (from *ὀλνῡμι*) *ὤλεσα*, *ὀλώλεκα* (*ὀλ-ε-*), *ὄμνῡμι* *ὤμοσα* (*ὀμ-ο-*).

736. *νῡμι*-verbs form only the present and imperfect according to the *μι*-conjugation; with the exception of *σβέ-ννῡμι*, which has 2 aor. *ἔσβην*. The 2 aorist passive and 2 future passive are rare, as *ῥήγνῡμι* *ἐρράγην* *ἐκραγήσομαι*, *ζεύγνῡμι* *ἐζύγην*.

737. *-νημι* class. A few verbs add *νη-* in the singular, *να-* in the plural, to the verb-stem. These verbs are almost entirely poetical or dialectical; and show by-forms in *-ναω*. They are:

δάμνημι (*δαμνάω*) *subdue*, *κίρνημι* (*κιρνάω* also Epic) *mix*, *κρίμνημι* (miswritten *κρήμνημι*) *suspend*, *πέρνημι* *sell*, *πίτνημι* (*πετνάω*) *spread*, *σκίδνημι* (and *κίδνημι*) *scatter*.

---

736 D. From verbs in *-νῡμι* second aorists middle are formed in Hom. by only three verbs: *μείγνῡμι* (commonly written *μίγνῡμι*) *mix* *ἔμικτο*, *ὄρνῡμι* *rouse* *ὦρτο*, *πήγνῡμι* *fix* *κατέπηκτο*.

a. Only in the middle: *μάρναμαι fight*, *πίλναμαι* (*πιλνάω*) *approach*. In *δύναμαι am able*, *να* has grown fast (cp. *δυνατός*).

738. Stem Gradation. — Verbs of the root class show in the stem vowel a variation between strong and weak grades in the present and imperfect indicative active. The singular has the strong grade, the dual and plural have the weak grade. The optative active and most middle forms have the weak grade.

a. η strong (original and Dor. ᾱ), α weak; φημί φαμέν, ἔφην ἔφαμεν; ἵστημι ἵσταμεν, ἵστην ἵσταμεν; δάμνημι δάμναμεν.

b. η strong, ε weak: τίθημι τίθεμεν, ἐτίθην ἐτίθεμεν; ἵημι ἵεμεν.

c. ω strong, ο weak: δίδωμι δίδομεν.

d. ει strong, ι weak (cp. λείπω ἔλιπον): εἶμι *will go*, ἴμεν. The grades ει, οι, ι appear in εἰδῶ, subjunctive of οἶδα *know*, pl. ἴσμεν for ἴδμεν (799).

739. In the second aorist ἔστην *I stood* the strong form has been carried from the singular through the dual and plural of the indicative. The strong stem occurs also in the imperative (στῆθι, στῆτε) and infinitive (στῆναι).

740. The second aorist infinitive shows the weak stem: θεῖναι from θέ-εναι, δοῦναι from δό-εναι. Cp. 469 N. στῆναι is, however, from στή-εναι (469 c. N.).

741. A few root verbs retain the strong grade η throughout. Thus, poet. ἄημι *blow* ἄημεν; ἀέντες is from ἀηντες by 40; δίζημαι *seek* (poet. δίζεσθαι is from δίζομαι); πίμπλημι *fill* 2 aor. ἐνεπλήμην, opt. ἐμπλήμην.

742. Verbs adding νυ show the strong form of the verb-stem in the present. ῥήγ-νῡ-μι *break* 2 aor. pass. ἐρράγην, μείγ-νῡ-μι (miswritten μίγνῡμι) *mix* 2 aor. pass. ἐμίγην, ζεύγ-νῡ-μι *yoke* 2 aor. pass. ἐζύγην.

743. The ending νυ varies between strong νῡ and weak νῠ. Thus δείκνῡμι δείκνῠμεν, ἐδείκνῡν ἐδείκνῠμεν.

INFLECTION OF MI-VERBS

744. Verbs in -μι differ in inflection from verbs in -ω in the present and second aorist systems and (rarely) in the second perfect system. Verbs in -μι have the following peculiarities of inflection:

a. The endings -μι and -σι (for original -τι) occur in the present indicative active: τίθη-μι, τίθη-σι; φη-μί φη-σί.

b. The 3 plural present indicative active has generally the ending -ᾱσι, from α-αντι, as τιθέᾱσι, ἱστᾶσι. So in the 2 perf. active ἑστᾶσι.

c. The 3 plural of active past tenses has -σαν: ἐτίθε-σαν.

d. The imperative ending -θι is sometimes retained: φα-θί, στῆ-θι; some forms never had it: τίθει, ἵστη.

e. The middle endings -σαι and -σο regularly retain σ: τίθε-σαι, ἐτίθε-σο.

N. — But not in the subjunctive or optative; and usually not in the second aorist; as τιθῇ for τιθέη-σαι, τιθεῖο for τιθέ-ῑ-σο, ἔθου for ἔθε-σο.

f. The infinitive active has -ναι: τιθέ-ναι, διδό-ναι; the 2 aorist active has -εναι rarely: θεῖναι for θέ-εναι, δοῦναι for δό-εναι.

g. Active participles with stems in -οντ- have the nominative sing. masc. in -ούς (301 a, 307 a): διδούς, διδό-ντ-ος.

745. Forms of -μι verbs which are inflected according to the thematic conjugation are included under the Second Conjugation.

746. μι-verbs may pass into the ω inflection elsewhere than in the subjunctive. **a.** Verbs in -νῡμι often inflect the present and imperfect active (not the middle) from a present in -νύω; as δεικνύω (but usually δείκνῡμι), δεικνύεις, δεικνύει, imperf. ἐδείκνυον, -ες, -ε, etc.; imper. δείκνυε, inf. δεικνύειν, part. δεικνύων.

b. τίθημι, ἵστημι, δίδωμι, ἵημι, etc., show some ω-forms in pres. (and imperf.) indic. opt. imper. and infin.; but the forms τιθέω, ἱστέω, διδόω, ἱέω, do not occur in the 1 sing.

c. In the present and second aorist optative of τίθημι and ἵημι there is a transition to the ω-conjugation but not in the 1 and 2 singular. The accent is differently reported: (1) as if the presents were τιθέω, ἱέω; (2) as if the presents were τίθω, ἵω. Thus:

Active: ἀφίοιτε for ἀφῑεῖτε, ἀφίοιεν for ἀφῑεῖεν. — Middle: τιθοῖτο, ἐπιθοίμεθα, συνθοῖτο, ἐπιθοῖντο (also accented τίθοιτο, ἐπίθοιντο); προοῖτο, προοῖσθε, προοῖντο (also accented πρόοιτο, πρόοιντο). Hdt. has -θέοιτο and -θεῖτο. The form in -οῖτο for -εῖτο occurs especially in Plato.

d. The Mss. vary between τιθῶμαι and τίθωμαι, ἀποθῶμαι and ἀπόθωμαι (426 f).

e. Some other μι-verbs show alternative ω-forms, as πιμπλάω, -εω (πίμπλημι), πιπράω (πίμπρημι), Hom. ἀγάομαι (ἄγαμαι), and ἱλάομαι (ἵλημι). So often with -νημι verbs (737), as δαμνᾷ and δάμνησι, ἐκίρνᾱ and κιρνᾱ́ς.

PRESENT AND IMPERFECT ACTIVE AND MIDDLE (PASSIVE)

747. Present Indicative. — **a.** The primary personal endings are added to the stem with the strong form in the singular and the weak form in the dual and plural.

b. In the 2 sing. τίθης, ἵης, ἵστης, δείκνῡς, etc., σ has been added to the stem. This σ is obscure in origin, but cannot be derived from -σι. τιθεῖς is rare.

c. 3 sing. τίθησι, ἵστησι, etc., with -σι for -τι (463 c).

d. 3 plur. τιθέᾱσι, ἱστᾶσι, etc., from τιθέ-αντι, ἱστά-αντι (463 d).

e. For the retention of σ in τίθε-σαι, etc., see 465 a, b, and N. 2.

f. δίδομαι in the middle present and imperfect is used only in composition, as ἀποδίδομαι. But the simple form occurs in the passive.

---

746 D. The tragic poets never have the ω-forms; the poets of the Old Comedy seldom; those of the New Comedy often have the ω-forms. — Plato usually has -νύᾱσι. Hom. has ζεύγνυον (and ζεύγνυσαν, ὤρνυον, ὤμνυε, ὀμνυέτω, etc.). Hdt. usually keeps the μι-forms, but has some ω-forms in 2, 3 sing. 3 pl. present indic. and part., and 1 sing., 3 pl. imperfect. Doric usually has the ω-forms; Aeolic has ζεύγνῡ, and ὄμνῡν infin.

747 D. 1. Hom. has τίθησθα, τίθησι and τιθεῖ, τιθεῖσι; διδοῖς and διδοῖσθα, δίδωσι (usually) and διδοῖ, διδοῦσι, ῥηγνῦσι from ῥηγνυ-ντι, ἴᾱσι *they go* and ἔᾱσι *they are*. On ἵστασκε see 495. Mid. ἐμάρναο from μάρναμαι.

748. Imperfect. — ἐτίθεις ἐτίθει, ἐδίδουν ἐδίδους ἐδίδου (for ἐδιδων, -ως, -ω) are thematic forms (746 b). For the imperfect of δύναμαι and ἐπίσταμαι see 465 b, N. 1. For the retention of σ in ἐτίθεσο see 465 b.

749. Subjunctive. — Attic τιθῶ, etc., are derived by contraction from the forms of the weak stem to which the thematic vowel ω/η has been added. Thus τιθέω, -έῃς, -έῃ, τιθέωμεν, -έητε, -έωσι; διδόω, -όῃς, -όῃ, διδόωμεν, -όητε, -όωσι. ἱστῶ is derived from ἱστέω. See 746 b. Verbs in -νῡμι regularly inflect the subjunctive like ω-verbs: δεικνύω, -ύῃς, -ύῃ.

a. Similarly the middle (passive) forms are derived from τιθέω-μαι τιθέη-(σ)αι, etc., διδόω-μαι διδόη-(σ)αι, ἱστέω-μαι ἱστέη-(σ)αι, etc. For the loss of σ in -σαι see 465 a. -νῡμι verbs inflect the mid. subj. like λύωμαι.

b. δύναμαι *am able*, ἐπίσταμαι *understand*, κρέμαμαι *hang*, and ἄγαμαι *admire* put ω/η in place of the stem-vowel so that there is no contraction: δύνωμαι, δύνῃ, δύνηται, δυνώμεθα, etc. So, too, ἐπριάμην, πρίωμαι (757 a).

c. Traces of -ῡται in -νῡμι verbs are very rare: ῥήγνῡται Hipponax 19; cp. διασκεδάννῡται P. Ph. 77 b.

750. Present Optative. — The optative active has the secondary endings and the mood sign -ιη- in the singular, -ῑ- (-ιε- 3 pl.) in the dual and plural. In the dual and plural the longer (-ιη-) forms are rare. Thus τιθείην (τιθε-ίη-ν), τιθεῖμεν (τιθέ-ῑ-μεν), ἱσταίην (ἱστα-ίη-ν) ἱσταῖεν (ἱστά-ιε-ν). The shorter forms in dual and plural occur in poetry and prose, the longer forms only in prose.

a. The middle (passive) has the secondary endings and the mood sign -ῑ- throughout: τιθείμην (τιθε-ί-μην), ἱσταίμην (ἱστα-ί-μην), ἱσταίμεθα (ἱστα-ί-μεθα), διδοῖντο (διδό-ῑ-ντο). On τιθοῖτο, etc., see 746 c.

b. The accent follows 424 c, N. 1 (τιθεῖτο not τίθειτο). But the verbs of 749 b are exceptional: δύναιο δύναιτο; and so ὄναιο ὄναιτο from ὀνίνημι *benefit* (424 c, N. 2).

751. Present Imperative. — τίθει and δίδου are formed (cp. ποίει and δήλου) from τίθε-ε, δίδο-ε. ἵστη and δείκνῡ show the stronger stem forms.

For the middle endings and the retention of σ, see 466. 2. a. — On the forms τιθέτωσαν for τιθέντων, τιθέσθωσαν for τιθέσθων, see 466. 2. b.

---

2. Hdt. has τιθεῖ τιθεῖσι; ἱστᾷ is doubtful; διδοῖς, διδοῖ, διδοῦσι, ἱᾶσι ἑᾶσι, -νῦσι and -νύουσι. Middle: -αται and -ατο (imperf.) for -νται, -ντο in τιθέαται ἐτιθέατο, ἱστέαται ἱστέατο, δυνέαται ἐδυνέατο. -αται, -ατο have been transferred from the perfect and pluperfect of consonant stems, such as γεγράφαται, ἐγεγράφατο (465 f).

3. Doric has ἵστᾱμι, and ᾱ for η in all tenses (στάσω, ἔστᾱσα, ἔστᾱν); -τι in 3 sing. τίθητι; -ντι in 3 pl. τίθεντι, δίδοντι.

4. Aeolic has τίθης, τίθη, τίθεισι; ἴστᾱς, ἴστᾱ; δίδως, δίδω; δάμνᾱς.

748 D. Hom. has ἐτίθει, ἐδίδους, ἐδίδου. — Hdt. has ὑπερετίθεα 1 sing., ἐδίδουν, ἐδίδου, ἵστᾱ and ἀνίστη (both in Mss.). — In poetry -ν occurs for -σαν as τίθεν, ἵστᾰν, δίδον (464 e. D.).

749 D. Dor. has τιθέω, -έωμεν, but contracts ε + η to η; pl. διδῶντι (and τίθηντι). Dor. has δύνᾱμαι, ἵστᾱται; Hdt. ἐνίστηται, ἐπιστέωνται, δυνέωνται.

750 D. Hom. has the μι-forms δαινῦτο and δαινύατο, Plato has πηγνῦτο.

751 D. Hom. has ἵστη and καθίστᾱ, δίδωθι, ἐμπίπληθι, ὄμνυθι, ὄρνυθι, ἵστασο and ἵσταο. τίθου, ἵστω occur in the drama. Pind. has δίδοι (active).

752. Present Infinitive. — The active adds -ναι, the middle -σθαι. δείκνῡμι admits the form δεικνύειν.

753. Present Participle. — The active adds -ντ-, the middle -μενος. Thus τιθείς (τιθε-ντ-ς), τιθεῖσα (τιθε-ντ-ιa) ; τιθέ-μενος. For δεικνύς we find δεικνύων.

THE FUTURES

754. The futures of verbs in -μι do not differ in formation and inflection from those of verbs in -ω.

τίθημι: θήσω, θήσομαι, τεθήσομαι ; ἵστημι: στήσω, στήσομαι, σταθήσομαι, ἑστήξω ; ἵημι: ἥσω, -ἥσομαι, -ἑθήσομαι ; δίδωμι: δώσω, -δώσομαι, δοθήσομαι ; δείκνῡμι: δείξω, δείξομαι, δειχθήσομαι, δεδείξομαι (late) or δεδειγμένος ἔσομαι ; μείγνῡμι: μείξω, -μιχθήσομαι, μιγήσομαι (poet.), μεμείξομαι (poet.) ; πήγνῡμι: πήξω, παγήσομαι.

a. ἑστήξω is the only future perfect from a μι-verb (584).

FIRST AORIST ACTIVE AND MIDDLE

755. The verbs τίθημι, ἵημι, δίδωμι form the singular active of the first aorist in -κ-α, thus, ἔθηκα, ἔδωκα, ἧκα. The forms of the second aorist (756) are generally used in the dual and plural and in the other moods.

a. The form in κ rarely appears outside of the singular, chiefly in the 3 pl., as ἔδωκαν (= ἔδοσαν), less frequently in the 1 and 2 pl., as ἐδώκαμεν, -ατε.

b. That κ was not a suffix but a part of an alternative root appears from a comparison of θηκ- in ἔθηκα and perf. τέθηκα with *fēc-* in *fēci*.

c. ἵστημι has ἔστησα *I set, placed* (mid. ἐστησάμην), to be distinguished from 2 aor. ἔστην *I stood*.

d. ἐθηκάμην is un-Attic ; ἡκάμην (in comp.) is rare and probably found only in the indic. ; ἐδωκάμην is very late.

SECOND AORIST ACTIVE AND MIDDLE

756. Indicative. — τίθημι, ἵημι, δίδωμι use the short grade forms in dual and plural active: ἔ-θε-τον, ἔ-θε-μεν, ἔθε-σαν ; εἶ-τον, εἷ-μεν, εἶ-σαν (for ἑ-ἑ-τον, etc.) ; ἔ-δο-μεν, ἔ-δο-σαν. In the singular the κ-forms, ἔθηκα, ἧκα, ἔδωκα, are used. ἵστημι has ἔστην, ἔστης, ἔστη (for ἐστητ, 464 c), ἔστημεν, etc. (p. 138).

a. σβέννῡμι *extinguish* is the only verb in -νῡμι forming a second aorist (ἔσβην, σβῶ, σβείην, σβῆθι, σβῆναι, σβείς).

---

752 D. Hom. has -μεναι or -ναι preceded by η in ἀήμεναι ἀῆναι from ἄημι *blow*, τιθήμεναι, κιχήμεναι and κιχῆναι as from κίχημι. Also ἱστάμεναι (and ἱστάμεν), ζευγνύμεναι (and ζευγνύμεν, once ζευγνῦμεν). -μεν after a short vowel, as τιθέμεν, διδόμεν (once διδοῦναι). Doric has τιθέμεν, διδόμεν. Theognis has τιθεῖν, συνιεῖν.

753 D. Hom. has τιθήμενος Κ 34.

755 D. Hom. has ἔθηκαν, ἔδωκαν, ἐνήκαμεν, θήκατο ; Hdt. συνθήκαντο ; Pind. θηκάμενος.

756 D. Hom. has older -ν for -σαν in ἔστᾰν (he uses ἔστησαν also), Dor. has ἔθεν, ἔστᾰν, ἔδον. For the iterative στά-σκε, δό-σκον see 495.

b. The middle uses the weak stems -θε-, -ἑ-, -δο- in ἐ-θέ-μην, -εἵμην (for ἑ-ἑ-μην), ἐ-δό-μην (only in composition). For the loss of σ in -σο (ἔθου, ἔδου) see 465 b.

c. In prose the only uncompounded second aorists middle are ἐπριάμην *bought* (pres. ὠνέομαι) and ὠνήμην *derived benefit* (ὀνίνημι). ὠνήμην keeps η (poet. ὄνησο, ὀνήμενος). ἵστημι does not make the form ἐσταμην.

757. Second Aorist Subjunctive. — All the forms of the 2 aor. subj. are due to contraction of the thematic vowel with the weak stem-vowel. Thus θῶ, etc., from θέω, θέῃς, θέῃ, θέωμεν, etc.; ὧ, etc., from ἕω, ἕῃς, ἕωσι; δῶ, etc., from δόω, δόῃς, δόῃ; στῶ, etc., from στέω, στέῃς, etc., with ε from η before a vowel. Cp. 682.

a. ἐπριάμην has πρίωμαι with ω/η in place of the final vowel of the stem (749 b).

758. Second Aorist Optative. — The forms of the optative of the second aorist are made and inflected like those of the present except for the reduplication. Thus, in the active: θείην (θε-ίη-ν), σταίην (στα-ίη-ν), δοῖμεν (δό-ῑ-μεν), δοῖεν (δό-ιε-ν). The shorter forms are preferred in the dual and plural, and poetry has only these; prose admits either the longer or the shorter forms.

a. In the 2 pl. cases of -ιη-τε (δοίητε) are more numerous than -ι-τε; but they usually lack metrical warrant.

b. Second aorists of stems in υ lack the optative in Attic.

c. In the middle: θείμην (θε-ί-μην), δοίμην (δο-ί-μην), -εἵμην (ἑ-ί-μην). For θοίμεθα see 746 c. For the accent of πρίαιο see 424 c, N. 2.

759. Second Aorist Imperative. — On θέ-ς, δό-ς, ἕ-ς, see 466. 1. b. These verbs show the weak form of the stem (θέ-τω, θέ-ντων). ἵστημι and σβέννῡμι have -θι in στῆ-θι, σβῆ-θι. For στῆ-θι the poets may use -στᾱ in composition, as ἀπόστᾱ *stand off*.

a. The middle adds -σο, which loses its σ after a short vowel, as in θοῦ for θέ-σο, δοῦ for δό-σο, πρίω (and poet. πρία-σο). σ is not dropped after a long vowel (ὄνησο). Cp. 465 b, N. 2.

---

c. D. In poetry: ἐπτάμην (prose -ἐπτόμην) from πέταμαι *fly*; Hom. πλῆτο *approached*, ἔβλητο *was hit* (others, 688).

757 D. The subjunctive shows traces of an earlier double form of inflection:

1. With short thematic vowel: θήεις, θήει, θήετον, θήομεν, θήετε, θήουσι. Homer: θήομεν, στήομεν, -στήετον, κιχήομεν, δώομεν, ἀποθήομαι.

2. With long thematic vowel: θήω, θήῃς, θήῃ, θήητον, θήωμεν, θήητε, θήωσι Hom. θήω, θήῃς, θήῃ, στήῃς, στήῃ, ἀνήῃ, δώῃ or δώῃσι, περιστήωσι, δώωσι.

By shortening of the long vowel of the stem we obtain a third form:

3. θέω, θέῃς, θέῃ, θέητον, θέωμεν, θέητε, θέωσι. Hom. ἀφέῃ, θέωμεν, στέωμεν, Hdt. θέω, θέωμεν, θέωσι, θέωμαι, στέωμεν, ἀποστέωσι, Aeolic θέω.

4. From 3 are derived the contracted forms θῶ, θῇς, θῇ, etc. Hom. ἀναστῇ, δῷς, δῷ or δῷσι, δῶμεν; Dor. δῶντι; Hdt. -θῇ, -θῆται; δῶμεν, -δῶτε, δῶσι.

N. — In Hom. the Mss. often have ει for η of the stem, as θείω, βείω, θείομεν, κιχείομεν.

758 D. Hom. has σταίησαν P 733, the only case of -ιη- outside of the singular; δύη (for δυ-ίη), ἐκδῦμεν (for -δύ-ῑ-μεν), and φθῖτο (for φθί-ῑ-το) from φθίνω *perish*.

759 D. Hom. has θέο and ἔνθεο.

b. In composition περίθες, ἀπόδος, παράστηθι, ἐνθοῦ, προδοῦ; but κατάθου, περίδου, περίδοσθε (426 b–c).

c. For the 3 pl. θέτωσαν, δότωσαν, ἔσθωσαν, see 466. 2. b.

760. Second Aorist Infinitive. — The active adds -εναι in θεῖναι (θέ-εναι), στῆναι (στή-εναι), δοῦναι (δό-εναι), εἶναι (ἕ-εναι). The middle adds -σθαι, as θέ-σθαι.

761. Second Aorist Participle. — The active adds -ντ- like the present: θείς (θε-ντ-ς), θεῖσα (θε-ντ-ι̯α), θέν (θε-ντ); στάς (στα-ντ-ς), στᾶσα (στα-ντ-ι̯α), στάν (στα-ντ). The middle adds -μενος, as θέ-μενος.

FIRST AND SECOND PERFECT (AND PLUPERFECT) ACTIVE

762. Indicative. — The perfect of τίθημι is τέθηκα. A later form τέθεικα, not found on Attic inscriptions till after 200 B.C. and due to the analogy of εἷκα, still appears in some texts. τέθεκα is Doric. For καθέστακα Attic used καταστήσᾱς ἔχω (cp. 599 b).

a. The dual and plural of the second perfect and pluperfect of ἵστημι (417) are formed without κ: ἕστατον, ἕσταμεν (without augment in the pluperf.), ἑστᾶσι from ἑ-στα-αντι, pluperf. ἕστα-σαν. The singular is supplied by the 1 perf. ἕστηκα *I stand*.

763. Subjunctive. — ἑστήκω and ἑστῶ appear in prose and poetry, ἑστηκὼς ὦ in prose.

764. Optative. — ἑστήκοιμι occurs in comp. in prose, ἀφεστῶτες εἶεν in Plato, τεθηκὼς εἴης and δεδωκότες εἶεν in Demosthenes. ἑσταίην is poetical.

765. Imperative. — ἕσταθι is poetical.

766. Infinitive and Participle. — ἑστάναι and ἑστώς are much more common than ἑστηκέναι and ἑστηκώς.

PERFECT MIDDLE (PASSIVE)

767. τέθειμαι even in composition is rare and is unknown on Attic inscriptions. For the pass. perf. κεῖμαι (791) was used. Doric has τέθεμαι.

IRREGULAR MI-VERBS

768. εἰμί (ἐσ-, cp. Lat. *es-se*) *am* has only the present and future systems.

---

760 D. Hom. has θέμεναι, θέμεν; στήμεναι; δόμεναι, δόμεν; and θεῖναι, στῆναι, δοῦναι. Dor. has θέμεν, δόμεν, στᾶμεν.

766 D. Hom. has ἑστάμεναι and ἑστάμεν, ἑσταώς, -αότος. Hdt. has ἑστεώς, -εῶτος. Doric has -εῖα for -υῖα (ἑστᾱκεῖα).

768 D. 1. Homer has the following forms:

Pres. ind. 2 sing. ἐσσί and εἷς, 1 pl. εἰμέν, 3 pl. (εἰσί, and) ἔᾱσι not enclitic.

Imperf. ἦα, ἔα, ἔον, 2 sing. ἦσθα, ἔησθα, 3 sing. ἦεν, ἔην, ἤην, ἦν (rare), 3 pl. ἦσαν, ἔσαν; iterative (495) ἔσκον (for ἐσ-σκον).

		Present				Imperfect
		Indicative	Subjunctive	Optative	Imperative	Indicative
Sing.	1	**εἰμί**	**ὦ**	**εἴην**		**ἦ** or **ἦν**
	2	**εἶ**	**ᾖς**	**εἴης**	**ἴσθι**	**ἦσθα**
	3	**ἐστί**	**ᾖ**	**εἴη**	**ἔστω**	**ἦν**
Dual	2	**ἐστόν**	**ἦτον**	**εἴητον** or **εἶτον**	**ἔστον**	**ἦστον**
	3	**ἐστόν**	**ἦτον**	**εἰήτην** or **εἴτην**	**ἔστων**	**ἤστην**
Plur.	1	**ἐσμέν**	**ὦμεν**	**εἴημεν** or **εἶμεν**		**ἦμεν**
	2	**ἐστέ**	**ἦτε**	**εἴητε** or **εἶτε**	**ἔστε**	**ἦτε** or **ἦστε** (rare)
	3	**εἰσί**	**ὦσι**	**εἴησαν** or **εἶεν**	**ἔστων**	**ἦσαν**

Infin. **εἶναι** Participle **ὤν, οὖσα, ὄν**, gen. **ὄντος, οὔσης, ὄντος**, etc. (305)

Future (with middle forms)

ἔσομαι, ἔσῃ (or **ἔσει**), **ἔσται, ἔσεσθον, ἔσεσθον, ἐσόμεθα, ἔσεσθε, ἔσονται**, opt. **ἐσοίμην**, inf. **ἔσεσθαι**, part. **ἐσόμενος, -η, -ον**.

a. The imperative 3 pl. *ἔστωσαν* occurs in Plato and Demosthenes; *ὄντων* in Plato and on inscriptions.

b. In composition *ὤν* retains its accent, as *ἀπών, ἀποῦσα, ἀπόντος*, etc.; and so *ἔσται*, as *ἀπέσται* (426 e).

769. The optative forms *εἴημεν, εἴητε, εἴησαν* are found only in prose writers. *εἶμεν* occurs in poetry and Plato, *εἶτε* only in poetry, *εἶεν* in poetry and prose and more frequently than *εἴησαν*.

770. The indicative *εἰμί* is for **ἐσ-μι* (37); *εἶ* is for **ἐσι* (originally *ἐσ-σί*, 463 b); *ἐσ-τί* retains the original ending *τι*; *εἰσί* is for (*σ-*)*εντι*, cp. Lat. *sunt*; *ἐσμέν*, with *σ* before *μ* despite 105; the *σ* is due to the influence of *ἐστέ*. The subjunctive *ὦ* is for *ἔω*, from *ἐσ-ω*; the optative *εἴην* is for *ἐσ-ιη-ν*; *εἶμεν* for *ἐσ-ῑ-μεν*, cp. Lat. *sīmus*. The infinitive *εἶναι* is for *ἐσ-ναι*; the participle *ὤν* is for *ἐών*, from *ἐσ-ων*.

Subj. *ἔω, ἔῃς*, 3 sing. *ἔῃ, ἔῃσι, ᾖσι*, 3 pl. *ἔωσι* (twice *ὦσι*); *μέτειμι* has 1 sing. *μετέω*, and *μετείω* (with metrical lengthening).

Opt. *εἴην*, etc., also *ἔοις, ἔοι*; Imper. 2 sing. *ἔσ-σο* (middle form), *ἔστω*, 3 pl. *ἔστων*.

Inf. *εἶναι* and *ἔμμεναι* (for *ἐσ-μεναι*), *ἔμμεν*, also *ἔμεναι, ἔμεν*.

Part. *ἐών, ἐοῦσα, ἐόν*, etc., rarely the Attic forms.

Fut. often with *σσ*: *ἔσσομαι* and *ἔσομαι*; 3 sing. *ἔσεται, ἔσται, ἔσσεται*, also *ἐσσεῖται* (as in Dor.), *ἔσσεσθαι, ἐσσόμενος*.

2. Herodotus has pres. ind. 2 sing. *εἶς*, 1 pl. *εἰμέν*; imperf., the Attic forms and **ἔα**, 2 sing. *ἔας*, 2 pl. *ἔατε*; iterative *ἔσκον*; subj. *ἔω, ἔωσι*; opt. once *ἐν-έοι, εἴησαν*, less freq. *εἶεν*; part. *ἐών*.

3. Dor. pres. ind. 1 sing. *ἠμί* and *εἰμί*, 2 sing. *ἐσσί*, 1 pl. *ἠμές* and *εἰμές* (Pind. *εἰμέν*), 3 pl. *ἐντί*; imperf. 3 sing. *ἦς* (for *ἠσ-τ*), 1 pl. *ἦμες*, 3 pl. *ἦσαν* and *ἦν*; inf. *ἦμεν, εἶμεν*; part. *ἐών* and fem. *ἔασσα*, pl. *ἔντες*. Fut. *ἐσσεῦμαι, -ῇ, -ῆται* or *-εῖται*, *ἐσσοῦνται* (540 D.).

4. Aeolic *ἔμμι* out of *ἐσμι*; imper. *ἔσσο*, part. *ἔων, ἔσσα* (Sappho); imperf. *ἔον*.

771. Old Attic ᾖ is from ᾖα (Hom.) = ἠσμ̥, *i.e.* ἐσ- augmented + the secondary ending μ, which becomes α by 35 c. ᾖς for ᾖσθα is rare. The 3 pl. was originally ἦν, contracted from ἦεν (Hom.); this ἦν came to be used as 3 sing. By analogy to ἦμεν ἦστε the 1 sing. ἦν was formed.

772. Inflected according to the ω-conjugation are the subjunctive, the participle ὤν, and several dialect forms.

773. **εἶμι** (ἰ-, εἰ-; cp. Lat. ī-*re*) *go* has only the present system.

		Present				Imperfect
		Indicative	Subjunctive	Optative	Imperative	Indicative
Sing.	1	**εἶμι**	**ἴω**	**ἴοιμι** or **ἰοίην**		**ᾖα** or **ᾔειν**
	2	**εἶ**	**ἴῃς**	**ἴοις**	**ἴθι**	**ᾔεισθα** or **ᾔεις**
	3	**εἶσι**	**ἴῃ**	**ἴοι**	**ἴτω**	**ᾔειν** or **ᾔει**
Dual	2	**ἴτον**	**ἴητον**	**ἴοιτον**	**ἴτον**	**ᾖτον**
	3	**ἴτον**	**ἴητον**	**ἰοίτην**	**ἴτων**	**ᾔτην**
Plur.	1	**ἴμεν**	**ἴωμεν**	**ἴοιμεν**		**ᾖμεν**
	2	**ἴτε**	**ἴητε**	**ἴοιτε**	**ἴτε**	**ᾖτε**
	3	**ἴᾱσι**	**ἴωσι**	**ἴοιεν**	**ἰόντων**	**ᾖσαν** or **ᾔεσαν**

Infinitive: **ἰέναι.** Participle: **ἰών, ἰοῦσα, ἰόν**, gen. **ἰόντος, ἰούσης, ἰόντος**, etc.

Verbal Adjectives: **ἰτός** (poet.), **ἰτέος, ἰτητέος.**

a. The imperative 3 pl. ἴτωσαν occurs rarely in Xenophon and Plato.

b. The participle ἰών is accented like a second aorist. The accent of the simple form of participle and infinitive is kept in composition, as παριών, παριοῦσα, ἀπιέναι. Otherwise the compounds have recessive accent so far as the rules allow: πάρειμι, ἄπεισι, but ἀπῇα, προσῇμεν.

774. εἶμι in the indicative present means *I shall go, I am going.* See 1880. For *I go* ἔρχομαι is used in the present indicative, but not (in prose) in the imperfect, or in the other moods. The scheme of moods and tenses is as follows: **Present**: indic. ἔρχομαι, subj. ἴω, opt. ἴοιμι or ἰοίην, imper. ἴθι, inf. ἰέναι, part. ἰών. **Imperfect**: ᾖα. **Future**: εἶμι, ἐλευσοίμην, ἐλεύσεσθαι, ἐλευσόμενος.

775. In the imperfect the older prose writers usually have ᾖα, ᾔεισθα, ᾔει-ν, the later have ᾔειν, ᾔεις, ᾔει. The plural forms ᾔειμεν and ᾔειτε are not classical. Prose writers seem to prefer ᾔεσαν to ᾖσαν. The η here is the stem ει augmented.

776. The part., the subjv., and the opt. are inflected with the thematic vowel; and so also some of the dialectical forms.

---

773 D. Hom. has 2 sing. εἶσθα (Hesiod εἶς); subj. ἴῃσθα and ἴῃς, ἴῃσιν and ἴῃ, ἴομεν and ἴομεν; opt. ἰείη and ἴοι; infin. ἴμεναι, ἴμεν, and ἰέναι (twice). *Imperf.*: 1 sing. ἤϊα, ἀνήϊον, 3 sing. ἤϊε, ᾖε, ᾔει (at the verse-end, ᾖε?), ἴε; dual ἴτην, pl. ᾔομεν, ἤϊσαν, ἐπῇσαν, ἴσαν, ἤϊον. For ἤϊα, ἤϊε, ἤϊσαν some write ᾔεα, ᾔεε, ᾔεσαν. *Future*: εἴσομαι Ω 462, ο 213. ϝείσομαι Ξ 8 and ϝείσατο, ἐϝείσατο probably come from ϝίεμαι *strive* (778).

Hdt.: ἤϊα, ἤϊε, ἤϊσαν (Mss.), but η for ηι is correct.

777. **ἵημι** (ἑ-, ἡ-) *send* is inflected nearly like *τίθημι* (p. 135). The inflection of the present and second aorist systems is as follows:

		ACTIVE			MIDDLE (PASSIVE)		MIDDLE
		INDICATIVE			INDICATIVE		
		Pres.	Imperf.	Second Aor.	Pres.	Imperf.	Second Aor.
S.	1	ἵημι	ἵην	(ἧκα)	ἵεμαι	ἱέμην	— εἵμην
	2	ἵης, ἱεῖς (746 b)	ἵεις (746 b)	(ἧκας)	ἵεσαι (465 a)	ἵεσο	— εἷσο
	3	ἵησι	ἵει	(ἧκε)	ἵεται	ἵετο	— εἷτο
D.	2	ἵετον	ἵετον	— εἷτον	ἵεσθον	ἵεσθον	— εἷσθον
	3	ἵετον	ἱέτην	— εἵτην	ἵεσθον	ἱέσθην	— εἵσθην
P.	1	ἵεμεν	ἵεμεν	— εἷμεν	ἱέμεθα	ἱέμεθα	— εἵμεθα
	2	ἵετε	ἵετε	— εἷτε	ἵεσθε	ἵεσθε	— εἷσθε
	3	ἱᾶσι (463 d)	ἵεσαν	— εἷσαν	ἵενται	ἵεντο	— εἷντο
				SUBJUNCTIVE			
S.	1	ἱῶ		— ὧ	ἱῶμαι		— ὧμαι
	2	ἱῇς		— ᾗς	ἱῇ		— ᾗ
	3	ἱῇ		— ᾗ	ἱῆται		— ἧται
D.	2	ἱῆτον		— ἧτον	ἱῆσθον		— ἧσθον
	3	ἱῆτον		— ἧτον	ἱῆσθον		— ἧσθον
P.	1	ἱῶμεν		— ὧμεν	ἱώμεθα		— ὥμεθα
	2	ἱῆτε		— ἧτε	ἱῆσθε		— ἧσθε
	3	ἱῶσι		— ὧσι	ἱῶνται		— ὧνται
				OPTATIVE			
S.	1	ἱείην		— εἵην	ἱείμην		— εἵμην (758 c)
	2	ἱείης		— εἵης	ἱεῖο		— εἷο
	3	ἱείη		— εἵη	ἱεῖτο		— εἷτο (— οἷτο)
D.	2	ἱεῖτον or ἱείητον		— εἷτον or — εἵητον	ἱεῖσθον		— εἷσθον
	3	ἱείτην or ἱειήτην		— εἵτην or — εἱήτην	ἱείσθην		— εἵσθην

777 D. 1. In Hom. *ἵημι* usually has the initial *ι* short. *Present:* -*ιεῖς*, *ἵησι* and -*ιεῖ*, *ἱεῖσι* from *ἱε-ντι*, inf. *ἱέμεναι* and -*ιέμεν*. *Imperf.:* -*ἵειν*, -*ἵεις*, -*ἵει*, 3 pl. *ἵεν*. *Future:* *ἥσω*, once *ἀν-έσει*. *First Aorist:* *ἧκα* and *ἕηκα*, *ἐνήκαμεν* once, *ἧκαν* once. *Second Aorist:* for the augmented *ει*-forms Hom. has usually the unaugmented *ἑ*-; as *ἕσαν*, *ἕντο*. In the subjunctive *μεθείω*, *μεθήῃ*, *ἀφέῃ*, *μεθῶμεν*.

2. Hdt. has -*ιεῖ* (accented -*ἷει*), *ἱεῖσι*, imperf. -*ἵει*, perf. *ἀνέωνται* for *ἀνεῖνται*, part. *με-μετ-ι-μένος* for *μεθειμένος*.

3. Dor. has perf. *ἕωκα*, *ἕωμαι*.

P. 1	ἱεῖμεν or ἱείημεν	— εἷμεν or — εἵημεν	ἱείμεθα	— εἵμεθα (— οἵμεθα)
2	ἱεῖτε or ἱείητε	— εἷτε or — εἵητε	ἱεῖσθε	— εἷσθε (— οἷσθε)
3	ἱεῖεν or ἱείησαν	— εἷεν or — εἵησαν	ἱεῖντο	— εἷντο (— οἷντο)
		IMPERATIVE		
S. 2	ἵει (746 b)	— ἕς	ἵεσο	— οὗ
3	ἱέτω	— ἕτω	ἱέσθω	— ἕσθω
D. 2	ἵετον	— ἕτον	ἵεσθον	— ἕσθον
3	ἱέτων	— ἕτων	ἱέσθων	— ἕσθων
P. 2	ἵετε	— ἕτε	ἵεσθε	— ἕσθε
3	ἱέντων (466. 2, b)	— ἕντων	ἱέσθων (466. 2, b)	— ἕσθων
		INFINITIVE		
	ἱέναι	— εἷναι	ἵεσθαι	— ἕσθαι
		PARTICIPLE		
	ἱείς, ἱεῖσα, ἱέν	— εἵς, — εἷσα, — ἕν	ἱέμενος	— ἕμενος

Future: — ἥσω in prose only in composition; — ἥσομαι only in composition.
First Aorist: ἧκα in prose usually in comp., — ἡκάμην; both only in the indic.
Perfect Active: — εἷκα only in composition.
Perfect Middle (Passive): — εἷμαι (plup. — εἵμην), — εἵσθω, — εἷσθαι, — εἱμένος, only in composition.
Aorist Passive: — εἵθην, — ἑθῶ, — ἑθῆναι, — ἑθείς, only in composition.
Future Passive: — ἑθήσομαι, only in composition.
Verbal Adjectives: — ἑτός, — ἑτέος, only in composition.

778. Since ἵημι is reduplicated (probably for σι-ση-μι) the initial ι should be short, as it is in Hom. (rarely in Attic poetry). ῑ is probably due to confusion with the ῑ of Hom. ἵεμαι (ϝίεμαι) *strive*, a meaning that ἵεμαι occasionally shows in Attic. ἵεμαι meaning *hasten* occurs only in the present and imperfect.

779. ει is for ε + ε in the second aorist active (ἑ-έ-μεν = εἷμεν), perfect active (ἑ-έ-κα = εἷκα), perfect middle (ἑ-έ-μαι = εἷμαι), second aorist passive (ἑ + ἑ-θην = εἵθην). In the aorists ἑ is the augment, in the perfects the first ἑ is the reduplication of the weak stem ἑ-. The first aorist ἡ-κα has the strong stem form. Present subj. ἱῶ, ἱῇς, etc., are for ἱέω, ἱέῃς, etc.; aor. subj. -ὧ, -ᾗς, etc., are for -ἕ-ω, -ἕ-ῃς, etc.

780. Much confusion exists in the Mss. as regards the accentuation. Thus for ἱεῖς we find ἵεις, and in Hom. προΐει (present), as if from ἱω. See 746 c.

781. For ἀφίοιτε, ἀφίοιεν and προοῖτο, προοῖσθε, προοῖντο (also accented πρόοιτο, etc.) see 746 c.

782. The imperfect of ἀφίημι is either ἀφίην or ἠφίην (450).

783. **φημί** (φα-, φη-, cp. Lat. *fā-ri*) *say, say yes,* or *assent* is inflected in the present as follows:

		PRESENT				IMPERFECT
		Indic.	Subj.	Opt.	Imper.	
Sing.	1	**φημί**	**φῶ**	**φαίην**		**ἔφην**
	2	**φῄς**	**φῇς**	**φαίης**	**φαθί** or **φάθι**	**ἔφησθα** or **ἔφης**
	3	**φησί**	**φῇ**	**φαίη**	**φάτω**	**ἔφη**
Dual	2	**φατόν**	**φῆτον**	not found	**φάτον**	**ἔφατον**
	3	**φατόν**	**φῆτον**	not found	**φάτων**	**ἐφάτην**
Plur.	1	**φαμέν**	**φῶμεν**	**φαῖμεν** or **φαίημεν**		**ἔφαμεν**
	2	**φατέ**	**φῆτε**	**φαίητε**	**φάτε**	**ἔφατε**
	3	**φᾱσί**	**φῶσι**	**φαῖεν** or **φαίησαν**	**φάντων**	**ἔφασαν**

Infin.: **φάναι**; Partic.: poet. **φᾱ́ς**, **φᾶσα**, **φάν** (Attic prose **φάσκων**); Verbal Adj.: **φατός** (poet.), **φατέος**.

Future: **φήσω**, **φήσειν**, **φήσων**.

First Aorist: **ἔφησα**, **φήσω**, **φήσαιμι**, ——, **φῆσαι**, **φήσᾱς**.

Perf. Pass. Imper.: **πεφάσθω** *let it be said.*

784. All the forms of the present indicative except φῄς are enclitic (181 c). — In composition σύμφημι, σύμφης (but the Mss. often have συμφῄς and συμφῇς), συμφῶ, σύμφαθι. Instead of φῄς, the spelling φής is infrequently found.

785. In the optative φαῖτε does not occur, perhaps by chance (461, 683 a). φαῖμεν, φαῖεν are ordinary Attic; φαίημεν, φαίησαν are rare.

786. Middle forms in present, imperfect, and future are dialectic.

787. οὔ φημι means *refuse* (Lat. *nego*). In the meaning *assert*, φάσκω is commonly used outside of the indicative. In the meaning *say often*, φάσκω is used. ἔφησα and φήσω are aor. and fut. in the meanings *say yes* and *assent.* ἔφην, ἔφη (and φάναι) often correspond to Lat. *inquam, inquit.*

788. ἔφην and φῶ, φαίην may have an aoristic force. ἔφην and poet. ἐφάμην are both imperfect and second aorist.

---

783 D. 1. Hom. has φῇσθα for φῄς; subj. φήῃ and φῇσι (463 c. D) for φῇ; imperf. ἔφην, φῆν, ἔφησθα, φῆσθα, ἔφης, φῆς, 3 s. ἔφην, rarely φῆ, 1 pl. φαμέν, 3 pl. ἔφασαν, φάσαν, ἔφαν, φάν.

2. Doric φᾱμί, φᾱτί, φαντί; imperf. ἔφᾱ, φᾶ; inf. φάμεν; fut. φᾱ́σω, φᾱ́σομαι; aor. ἔφᾱσα.

3. Aeolic φᾶμι or φαῖμι, φαῖσθα, 3 s. φαῖσι, 3 pl. φαῖσι.

786 D. Middle forms of φημί are rare or unknown in Attic (Plato has perf. imper. πεφάσθω), but common in other dialects; yet the pres. indicative middle is rare. Hom. has imperf. ἐφάμην, ἔφατο or φάτο, etc., imper. φάο, φάσθω, etc., inf. φάσθαι (and in choral poetry), part. φάμενος (also in Hdt.). These middle forms are active in meaning.

789. **ἧμαι** (ἡσ-) *sit* is inflected only in the present system. The σ of the verb-stem appears only before -ται, -το.

Present			Imperative	Imperfect		
ἧμαι		ἥμεθα		ἥμην		ἥμεθα
ἧσαι	ἧσθον	ἧσθε	ἧσο	ἧσο	ἧσθον	ἧσθε
ἧσται	ἧσθον	ἧνται	ἥσθω, etc.	ἧστο	ἥσθην	ἧντο

The subjunctive and optative are wanting; present infinitive ἧσθαι; participle ἥμενος.

a. Uncompounded ἧμαι occurs only in Epic, tragedy, and Herodotus. The missing tenses are supplied by ἕζομαι, ἵζω and ἵζομαι.

790. In place of ἧμαι we find usually κάθ-ημαι in Attic prose and comedy. κάθημαι sometimes is perfect in meaning (*I have sat, I have been seated*). The σ of the verb-stem does not appear except before -το.

	Present				Imperfect	
	Indicative	Subjunctive	Optative	Imperative	Indicative	
S. 1	κάθημαι	καθῶμαι	καθοίμην		ἐκαθήμην (450) or	καθήμην
2	κάθησαι	καθῇ	καθοῖο	κάθησο	ἐκάθησο	καθῆσο
3	κάθηται	καθῆται	καθοῖτο	καθήσθω	ἐκάθητο	καθῆστο or καθῆτο
D. 2	κάθησθον	καθῆσθον	καθοῖσθον	κάθησθον	ἐκάθησθον	καθῆσθον
3	κάθησθον	καθῆσθον	καθοίσθην	καθήσθων	ἐκαθήσθην	καθήσθην
P. 1	καθήμεθα	καθώμεθα	καθοίμεθα		ἐκαθήμεθα	καθήμεθα
2	κάθησθε	καθῆσθε	καθοῖσθε	κάθησθε	ἐκάθησθε	καθῆσθε
3	κάθηνται	καθῶνται	καθοῖντο	καθήσθων	ἐκάθηντο	καθῆντο

Infinitive: καθῆσθαι; Participle: καθήμενος.

a. The imperative has κάθου in comedy for κάθησο. In the imperfect ἐκαθήμην is used about as often as καθήμην.

b. The missing tenses are supplied by καθέζομαι, καθίζω, καθίζομαι.

791. **κεῖμαι** (κει-) *lie, am laid*, regularly used in the present and imperfect instead of the perfect and pluperfect passive of τίθημι *place*.

---

789 D. Hom. has εἵαται, and ἕαται (twice), εἵατο, and ἕατο once (once ἧντο). ἡ- is probably the correct spelling for εἱ-.

790 D. Hom. has 3 pl. καθείατο (καθήατο ?). Hdt. has κατέαται, κατέατο; καθῆστο not καθῆτο.

791 D. Hom. has 3 pl. pres. κείαται, κέαται, κέονται; imperf. κεῖντο, κείατο, κέατο, iter. κέσκετο; subj. κῆται, and κεῖται for κε(ι̯)-ε-ται; fut. κείσομαι.

Hdt. has 3 sing. pres. κέεται and κεῖται, 3 pl. κέαται; imperf. ἔκειτο, pl. ἐκέατο.

	Present				Imperfect
	Indic.	Subj.	Opt.	Imper.	Indic.
Sing. 1	κεῖμαι				ἐκείμην
2	κεῖσαι			κεῖσο	ἔκεισο
3	κεῖται	κέηται	κέοιτο	κείσθω	ἔκειτο
Dual 2	κεῖσθον			κεῖσθον	ἔκεισθον
3	κεῖσθον			κείσθων	ἐκείσθην
Plur. 1	κείμεθα				ἐκείμεθα
2	κεῖσθε	(δια)κέησθε		κεῖσθε	ἔκεισθε
3	κεῖνται	(κατα)κέωνται	(προσ)κέοιντο	κείσθων	ἔκειντο

Infinitive: κεῖσθαι; Participle: κείμενος.

Future: κείσομαι, κείσῃ or κείσει, κείσεται, etc.

a. In the subjunctive and optative *κει-* becomes *κε-* before a vowel (43).

b. Compounds have recessive accent in the present indicative and imperative: *παράκειμαι, παράκεισο*, but *παρακεῖσθαι*.

792. ἠ-μί (cp. Lat. *a-io*) *say* occurs only in the present and imperfect 1 and 3 sing., and is used in parentheses (as Lat. *inquam, inquit*).

Forms: *ἠμί, ἠσί; ἦν, ἦ.* Examples: *παῖ, ἠμί, παῖ boy, I say, boy!* (emphatic repetition). *ἦν δ' ἐγώ said I, ἦ δ' ὅς said he* (1113).

793. χρή *it is necessary* is really an indeclinable substantive meaning *necessity* with the verb understood. In the present indicative *ἐστί* is to be supplied. Elsewhere *χρή* unites with the form of the verb to be supplied; as subj. *χρῇ* (*χρὴ + ᾖ*), opt. *χρείη* (*χρὴ + εἴη*), inf. *χρῆναι* (*χρὴ + εἶναι*), part. indeclinable *χρεών* (*χρὴ + ὄν*); imperf. *χρῆν* (*χρὴ + ἦν*), and less commonly *ἐχρῆν* with an augment because the composite character of *χρῆν* was forgotten, fut. *χρῆσται* (*χρὴ + ἔσται*).

a. ἀπόχρη *it suffices* has pl. *ἀποχρῶσι*, part. *ἀποχρῶν, -χρῶσα, -χρῶν*, imperf. *ἀπέχρη*, fut. *ἀποχρήσει*, aor. *ἀπέχρησε*.

794. οἶδα (*ἰδ, εἰδ-ε, οἰδ-* originally with *ϝ*; cp. Lat. *video*) *know* is a second perfect with the meaning of a present, and formed without reduplication. The second perfect and second pluperfect are inflected as follows:

---

792 D. Hom has *ἦ*, Doric *ἠτί*, Aeolic *ἦσι*.

793 D. Hdt. has *χρή, χρῆν, χρῆναι*, but *ἀπροχρᾷ, ἀποχρᾶν*.

794 D. 1. Hom. has *οἶδας* α 337, *ἴδμεν, ἴσᾱσι* (*ἴσσᾱσι* for *ἴσᾱσι* I 36); subj. *εἰδέω* π 236 and *ἰδέω* (? Ξ 235), *εἴδομεν* and *εἴδετε* with short thematic vowels; inf. *ἴδμεναι, ἴδμεν*; part. *εἰδυῖα* and *ἰδυῖα*. Pluperf. *ᾔδεα, ᾔδησθα* τ 93, *ἠείδεις*(*-ης*?) Χ 280 with *η* as augment (433), *ᾔδη, ᾔδεε, ἠείδει* ι 206, 3 pl. *ἴσαν* for *ἴδ-σαν*. Fut. *εἴσομαι*, inf. *εἰδησέμεν* and *-σειν*.

2. Hdt. has *οἶδας, ἴδμεν* and *οἴδαμεν* (rarely), *οἴδᾱσι*, subj. *εἰδέω*, plup. *ᾔδεα, ᾔδεε* (*ᾔδει*?), *-ῃδέατε, ᾔδεσαν*, fut. *εἰδήσω*.

3. Dor. has *ἴσᾱμι* (pl. *ἴσαμεν, ἴσαντι*) and *οἶδα*. Boeotian has *ἴττω* for *ἴστω*. Aeolic has *ϝοίδημι* and *οἶδα*.

		Second Perfect				Second Pluperfect
	Indic.	Subj.	Opt.	Imper.	Indic.	
Sing. 1	**οἶδα**	**εἰδῶ**	**εἰδείην**		**ᾔδη** or **ᾔδειν**	
2	**οἶσθα**	**εἰδῇς**	**εἰδείης**	**ἴσθι**	**ᾔδησθα** or **ᾔδεις**	
3	**οἶδε**	**εἰδῇ**	**εἰδείη**	**ἴστω**	**ᾔδει(ν)**	
Dual 2	**ἴστον**	**εἰδῆτον**	**εἰδεῖτον**	**ἴστον**	**ᾖστον**	
3	**ἴστον**	**εἰδῆτον**	**εἰδείτην**	**ἴστων**	**ᾔστην**	
Plur. 1	**ἴσμεν**	**εἰδῶμεν**	**εἰδεῖμεν** or **εἰδείημεν**		**ᾖσμεν** or **ᾔδεμεν**	
2	**ἴστε**	**εἰδῆτε**	**εἰδεῖτε** **εἰδείητε**	**ἴστε**	**ᾖστε** **ᾔδετε**	
3	**ἴσᾱσι**	**εἰδῶσι**	**εἰδεῖεν** **εἰδείησαν**	**ἴστων**	**ᾖσαν** **ᾔδεσαν**	

Infinitive **εἰδέναι**; Participle **εἰδώς, εἰδυῖα, εἰδός** (309); Verbal Adj. **ἰστέος**; Future **εἴσομαι**. Compound **σύνοιδα** *am conscious of.*

795. The verb-stem has the meaning *find out;* hence the perfect *οἶδα* means *I have found out* and hence *I know.*

796. In Ionic and late Greek we find *οἶδας, οἴδαμεν*, etc. These forms are rare in Attic. *οἶσθας* occurs in comedy.

797. In the optative dual and plural prose writers have either the shorter or the longer forms; the poets only the shorter forms.

798. Pluperfect *ᾔδειν, ᾔδεις* occur in later Attic (Demosthenes), but are suspicious in earlier writers. *ᾔδεισθα* occurs in the best Mss. of Plato and elsewhere, but it is less correct Attic. *ᾔδης* is incorrect. *ᾔδει* is rare. *ᾖστον, ᾔστην* are almost entirely poetic. In the plural *ᾔδειμεν, ᾔδειτε, ᾔδεισαν* are post-classical. *ᾔδεμεν, ᾔδετε* occur rarely in the Attic poets.

799. *οἶσθα* is from *οἰδ* + *θα*; *ἴστε* from *ἰδ* + *τε*; *ἴσθι* from *ἰδ* + *θι* (83). *ἴσμεν* (older *ἴδμεν*) gets its *σ* from *ἴστε* (87). *ἴσᾱσι* is from *ἰδ* + *σαντι*, with *σ* from (Hom.) *ἴσαν* = *ἰδ-σαν* with the ending *-σαν* (cp. *εἴξᾱσι* 704 d). *ᾔδη* is for *ἠ-είδη* with *η* as augment (433).

PECULIARITIES IN THE USE OF THE VOICE-FORMS, ETC.

800. Some verbs in the present appear in classical Greek in the active voice only, as *βαίνω go, ἕρπω creep, τρέω tremble;* others in the middle only, as *ἅλλομαι leap, βούλομαι wish, κάθημαι sit, κεῖμαι lie.*

801. Outside of the present some active verbs show middle forms especially in the future, as *βήσομαι shall go, ἀκούσομαι shall hear* (805); and some verbs exclusively or chiefly deponent show active forms especially in the perfect, as *γίγνομαι become γέγονα, μαίνομαι rage μέμηνα, δέρκομαι* poet., 2 aor. *ἔδρακον*, perf. *δέδορκα*.

802. For the passive voice the middle forms sufficed in most cases; many middle futures are still used passively (807), as *ἀδικήσο-*

802 D. Hom. has *ἐκτάμην was killed, ἐσχόμην was stayed.* Cp. also *ᾐδεσάμην* and *αἴδεσθεν* (*αἰδέομαι respect*), *ὀΐσατο* and *ὠΐσθην* (*οἴομαι think*), *ἐχολωσάμην* and *ἐχολώθην* (*χολόω enrage*).

μαι shall be wronged; and traces of the passive use of the aorist middle appear in Hom., as ἔβλητο *was hit.* This use was largely abandoned when -ην and -θην came to be used as special marks of the passive. Originally neither -ην nor -θην was passive in meaning.

803. The second aorist in -ην is primarily intransitive and shows active inflection (as ἔστην *stood*). Many so-called passive forms are in fact merely intransitive aorists of active verbs, as ἐρρύην from ῥέω *flow*, κατεκλίνην from κατακλίνω *lie down*, and do not differ in meaning from the aorists of deponent verbs, as ἐμάνην from μαίνομαι *rage*.

804. The aorists in -θην that are called passive are often active or middle in meaning, as ἥσθην *took pleasure in* from ἥδομαι, ᾐσχύνθην *felt ashamed* from αἰσχύνω *disgrace*, αἰσχύνομαι *am ashamed;* ὠργίσθην *became angry* from ὀργίζω *anger.*

FORMS OF ONE VOICE IN THE SENSE OF ANOTHER

805. Future Middle with Active Meaning. — Many verbs have no active future, but use instead the future middle in an active sense: λαμβάνω *take* λήψομαι, γιγνώσκω *know* γνώσομαι.

a. Most such verbs denote a physical action, as the action of the vocal organs; the action of the organs of sight, hearing, smell, touch; the action of throat, mouth, lips; bodily activity in general, voluntary or involuntary; and other aspects of the physical side of human organism.

806. In the following list of active verbs with middle futures those marked * have also an active future; those marked † sometimes have an active future in late Greek. All verbs adding -αν- to form the present stem (523, b, c) have a middle future except αὐξάνω, λανθάνω, ὀφλισκάνω. Verbs denoting praise or blame usually have both an active and a middle future.

*ᾄδω	†βοάω	εἰμί	*κλάζω	οἶδα	πίπτω	*τίκτω
†ἀκούω	†γελάω	*ἐμέω	*κλαίω	†οἰμώζω	πλέω	†τλάω (ἔτλην)
ἀλαλάζω	*γηράσκω	*ἐπαινέω	κρᾱ́ζω	ὀλολύζω	πνέω	τρέχω
†ἁμαρτάνω	γηρύω	ἐρυγγάνω	†κύπτω	†ὄμνῡμι	*ποθέω	τρώγω
†ἀπαντάω	γιγνώσκω	ἐσθίω	†κωκύω	ὁράω	ῥέω	τυγχάνω
†ἀπολαύω	*γρύζω	θαυμάζω	λαγχάνω	ὀτοτύζω	*ῥοφέω	τωθάζω
*ἁρπάζω	δάκνω	*θέω	λαμβάνω	οὐρέω	†σῑγάω	φεύγω
βαδίζω	δείδω	*θιγγάνω	λάσκω	παίζω	†σιωπάω	*φθάνω
βαίνω		(see 703) -θνῄσκω	μανθάνω	πάσχω	σκώπτω	χάσκω
†βιόω	-διδρᾱ́σκω	θρῴσκω	*νεύω	†πηδάω	†σπουδάζω	χέζω
*βλέπω	*διώκω	κάμνω	νέω *swim*	πίνω	(late)	*χωρέω
βλώσκω	*ἐγκωμιάζω	κι(γ)χάνω				

a. Compounds of χωρέω with ἀπο-, συγ-, παρα-, προσ- have both active and middle futures; other compounds have only the active futures.

807. Future Middle with Passive Meaning. — In many verbs the future middle has the meaning of the future passive, as ἀδικέω *wrong*, ἀδικήσομαι *shall be wronged.*

808. The following verbs commonly use the future middle in a passive sense. (All of these have the future passive in late Greek, except ἀμφισβητέω, ἐάω, εἴργω, ἐνεδρεύω, οἰκέω, παιδαγωγέω, προαγορεύω, στρεβλόω, στυγέω.)

ἀγνοέω *not to know*
ἀγωνίζομαι *contend*
ἀδικέω *wrong*
ἀμφισβητέω *dispute*
ἀνοίγνῡμι *open*, C.I.A. 2. 1054 (not found in literature)
ἄρχω *rule*
διδάσκω *teach*
ἐάω *permit*
εἴργω *shut*
ἐκπλύνω *wash out*
ἐνεδρεύω *lie in wait for*
ἐπιβουλεύω *plot against*
ἐχθαίρω *hate*
ἔχω *have*
θεραπεύω *tend*
κωλύω *prevent*
μαστῑγόω *whip*
οἰκέω *inhabit*
ὁμολογέω *agree*
ὀνειδίζω *reproach*
παιδαγωγέω *educate*
πολεμέω *wage war*
προαγορεύω *foretell*
σταθμάω *measure*
στρεβλόω *rack*
στυγέω *hate* (poet.)
ταράττω *disturb*
τηρέω *guard*
τρέφω *nourish*
τρίβω *rub*
ὕω *rain*
φιλέω *love*
φυλάττω *guard*

809. Some verbs use in a passive sense both a future middle form and a future passive form; on the difference in meaning see 1738.

ἄγω *lead*, ἄξομαι, ἀχθήσομαι.
ἀπατάω *deceive*, ἀπατήσομαι, ἐξαπατηθήσομαι.
αὐξάνω *increase*, αὐξήσομαι, αὐξηθήσομαι.
βλάπτω *hurt*, βλάψομαι, βλαβήσομαι.
δηλόω *manifest*, δηλώσομαι, δηλωθήσομαι.
ζημιόω *fine*, ζημιώσομαι, ζημιωθήσομαι.
καλέω *call*, καλοῦμαι (rare), κληθήσομαι.
κηρύττω *proclaim*, κηρύξομαι (rare), κηρυχθήσομαι.
κρίνω *judge*, κρινοῦμαι, κριθήσομαι.
λέγω *say*, λέξομαι (tragic), λεχθήσομαι.
λείπω *leave*, ἀπολείψομαι, ἀπολειφθήσομαι.
μαρτυρέω *bear witness*, μαρτυρήσομαι, μαρτυρηθήσομαι.
πολιορκέω *besiege*, πολιορκήσομαι, πολιορκηθήσομαι.
πράττω *do*, πρᾱ́ξομαι (rare), πρᾱχθήσομαι.
στερέω *deprive*, ἀποστερήσομαι, ἀποστερηθήσομαι.
τῑμάω *honour*, τῑμήσομαι, τῑμηθήσομαι.
ὑβρίζω *insult*, ὑβριοῦμαι, ὑβρισθήσομαι.
φέρω *bear*, οἴσομαι, οἰσθήσομαι, κατενεχθήσομαι.
φρονέω: καταφρονήσομαι *despise*, καταφρονηθήσομαι.
ὠφελέω *aid*, ὠφελήσομαι, ὠφεληθήσομαι.

810. Middle Deponents. — Deponent verbs whose aorists have an active or middle meaning with middle forms are called *middle deponents.* The aorist passive of such verbs, when it occurs, has a passive force. Thus αἰτιάομαι *accuse*, ᾐτιᾱσάμην *accused*, ᾐτιάθην *was accused.* Others 813 c.

811. Passive Deponents. — Deponent verbs whose aorists have the passive form but the active or middle meaning are called *passive deponents;* as βούλομαι *wish*, aor. ἐβουλήθην. The future is usually middle in form. Most passive deponents express mental action of some sort.

812. In the following list verbs marked * have a future passive form and also a future middle form; as διαλέγομαι *converse*, aor. διελέχθην *conversed*, fut. διαλέξομαι and διαλεχθήσομαι *shall converse.* But ἥδομαι *take pleasure in* has only ἡσθήσομαι, and ἡττάομαι *yield to, am worsted* has only ἡττηθήσομαι. Verbs with † have also an aorist middle, but it is less common, or poetic, or late Greek.

†ἄγαμαι *admire*, ἠγάσθην
*†αἰδέομαι *feel shame*, ᾐδέσθην
ἀλάομαι (usu. poet.) *wander*, ἠλήθην
†ἁμιλλάομαι *contend*, ἡμιλλήθην
†ἀρνέομαι *deny*, ἠρνήθην
*ἄχθομαι *am grieved*, ἠχθέσθην
βούλομαι *wish*, ἐβουλήθην (430)
δέομαι *want*, ἐδεήθην
δέρκομαι (poet.) *see*, ἐδέρχθην
δύναμαι *am able*, ἐδυνήθην (430)
ἐναντιόομαι *oppose*, ἠναντιώθην
ἐπίσταμαι *understand*, ἠπιστήθην
ἔραμαι ἐράω *love*, ἠράσθην
εὐλαβέομαι *am cautious*, ηὐλαβήθην
†ἥδομαι *take pleasure in*, ἥσθην
*ἡττάομαι *yield to*, ἡττήθην
(ἐν-)θῡμέομαι *consider*, ἐνεθῡμήθην
(προ-)θῡμέομαι *am eager*, προεθῡμήθην
*†(δια-)λέγομαι *converse*, διελέχθην
(ἐπι-)μέλομαι *care for*, ἐπεμελήθην
(μετα-)μέλομαι *regret*, μετεμελήθην
(ἀπο-)νοέομαι *despair*, ἀπενοήθην
*(δια-)νοέομαι *reflect*, διενοήθην
(ἐν-)νοέομαι *think of*, ἐνενοήθην
†(ἐπι-)νοέομαι *think on*, ἐπενοήθην
†(προ-)νοέομαι *foresee, provide*, προενοήθην
οἴομαι *think*, ᾠήθην
φιλοτῑμέομαι *am ambitious*, ἐφιλοτῑμήθην

a. Some verbs use either the aorist middle or aorist passive without distinction, as ἐναυλίζομαι *bivouac*, πρᾱγματεύομαι *am engaged in.*

b. Some verbs use both, but prefer the aorist middle, as ἀποκρίνομαι *answer*, ἀπολογέομαι *speak in defence*, μέμφομαι *blame.*

c. Some verbs use the aorist passive in an active or middle sense, as ἀπορέομαι *doubt*, pass. *be disputed*, aor. ἠπορήθην; πειράω *prove*, πειράομαι *try*, aor. ἐπειράθην (less often ἐπειρᾱσάμην), fut. πειράσομαι and πειρᾱθήσομαι. ἐράω (poet. ἔραμαι) *love* has ἠράσθην *fell in love with*, fut. ἐρασθήσομαι.

813. Deponents with Passive Meaning. — Some deponent verbs have a passive meaning. This is avoided by good writers in the present and imperfect or future passive, is not frequent in the aorist, but is common in the perfect and pluperfect passive. Thus ἀπεκρίνεται (ἀπεκρίθη) ταῦτα *this answer is* (*was*) *made* is not good Greek. Few verbs show the passive meaning in most of these tenses; as ὠνέομαι *buy, am bought*, ἐωνήθην *was bought*, ἐώνημαι *have bought, have been bought.*

a. Present and Imperfect: ἀγωνίζομαι *contend, am contended for*, βιάζομαι *force, am forced*, λῡμαίνομαι *maltreat, am maltreated*, ὠνέομαι *buy, am bought.*

b. Future Passive: ἀπαρνέομαι *deny*, ἀπαρνηθήσομαι, ἐργάζομαι *work, do*, ἐργασθήσομαι.

c. Aorist Passive: These verbs (*middle deponents*, 810) have also an aorist middle; the aorist passive is used in a passive sense: ἀγωνίζομαι *contend*, αἰκίζομαι *harass*, αἰνίττομαι *speak darkly*, αἰτιάομαι *accuse*, ἀκέομαι *heal*, βιάζομαι *force*, δέχομαι *receive*, δωρέομαι *present*, ἐργάζομαι *work, do*, ἡγέομαι *lead*, θεάομαι *behold*, ἰάομαι *heal*, κτάομαι *acquire*, λῡμαίνομαι *maltreat*, λωβάομαι *abuse*, μῑμέομαι *imitate*, ὀλοφύρομαι *lament*, προφασίζομαι *feign an excuse*, χράομαι *use*, ὠνέομαι *buy*. ἀποκρίνομαι has ἀπεκρίνατο *answered*, ἀπεκρίθην usu. means *was separated.*

d. Perfect and Pluperfect: These verbs use the perfect middle in the middle or the passive sense: ἀγωνίζομαι *contend*, αἰνίττομαι *speak darkly*, αἰτιάομαι *accuse*, ἀποκρίνομαι *answer*, ἀπολογέομαι *make a defence*, βιάζομαι *force*, ἐνθῡμέομαι *consider*, ἐργάζομαι *work, do*, εὔχομαι *pray*, ἡγέομαι *lead*, κτάομαι *acquire*, λωβάομαι *abuse*, μηχανάομαι *devise*, μῑμέομαι *imitate*, παρρησιάζομαι *speak boldly*, πολῑτεύομαι *act as (discharge the duties of) a citizen*, πρᾶγματεύομαι *am engaged in*, σκέπτομαι *view*, χράομαι *use*, ὠνέομαι *buy*.

814. Active Verbs with Aorist Passive in a Middle Sense. — The aorist passive of some active verbs has a reflexive or middle sense, either sometimes or always. Thus εὐφραίνω *gladden*, ηὐφράνθην *rejoiced*, κῑνέω *move*, ἐκῑνήθην *was moved* or *moved myself*, φαίνω *show*, ἐφάνην *showed myself, appeared* (ἐφάνθην usually *was shown*).

a. These verbs are often called *middle passives*.

b. The middle and the passive form of the future of such verbs is often found, the middle being frequently preferred.

815. Aorist Passive and Future Middle forms:

αἰσχύνω *disgrace*, ᾐσχύνθην *felt ashamed*, αἰσχυνοῦμαι
ἀνιάω *vex*, ἠνιάθην *felt vexed*, ἀνιάσομαι
ἐπείγω *urge*, ἠπείχθην *urged*, ἐπείξομαι
εὐφραίνω *gladden*, ηὐφράνθην *rejoiced*, εὐφρανοῦμαι
κῑνέω *move*, ἐκῑνήθην *moved (bestirred) myself*, κῑνήσομαι
κοιμάω *put to sleep*, ἐκοιμήθην *lay down to sleep*, κοιμήσομαι
λῡπέω *vex*, ἐλῡπήθην *grieved*, λῡπήσομαι
ὀργίζω *anger*, ὠργίσθην *became angry*, ὀργιοῦμαι
ὁρμάω *incite*, ὡρμήθην *set out*, ὁρμήσομαι
πείθω *persuade*, ἐπείσθην *obeyed*, πείσομαι
πλανάω *cause to wander*, ἐπλανήθην *wandered*, πλανήσομαι
πορεύω *convey*, ἐπορεύθην *marched*, πορεύσομαι
φοβέω *terrify*, ἐφοβήθην *was afraid*, φοβήσομαι

a. ἀνάγομαι *set sail*, κατάγομαι *land*, ὁπλίζομαι *arm myself*, ὁρμίζομαι *lie at anchor*, generally have an aorist middle.

816. Aorist Passive and Future Passive forms:

μιμνῄσκω *remind*, ἐμνήσθην *remembered*, μνησθήσομαι
στρέφω *turn*, ἐστράφην *turned*, στραφήσομαι
σφάλλω *trip up, deceive*, ἐσφάλην *erred, failed*, σφαλήσομαι
τήκω *cause to melt*, ἐτάκην *dissolved, languished*, τακήσομαι

817. Passive Aorist and Middle and Passive Future forms:

ἀπαλλάττω *release*, ἀπηλλάγην *departed*, ἀπαλλάξομαι, ἀπαλλαγήσομαι.
φαίνω *show*, ἐφάνην *appeared*, φανοῦμαι, φανήσομαι (819).

818. Some verbs have a passive aorist rarely in a middle sense; with the middle aorist in a different meaning.

κομίζω *bring*, ἐκομίσθην *betook myself*, ἐκομισάμην *carried off*.
σῴζω *save*, ἐσώθην *saved myself (was saved)*, ἐσωσάμην *saved for myself*.
ψεύδω *deceive*, ἐψεύσθην *deceived myself (was deceived)*, ἐψευσάμην *lied*.

819. In some verbs showing 1st and 2nd aorist, or 1st and 2nd perfect, the first tenses are generally transitive, the second tenses generally intransitive. The future active of these verbs is transitive. In some transitive verbs the perfect (usually the 2nd perf.) is intransitive.

ἄγνῡμι: trans. κατάγνῡμι *break*, -έᾱξα; intrans. κατάγνυμαι *break*, 2 aor. -εάγην; 2 perf. -έᾱγα *am broken*.

βαίνω *go*: trans. βήσω *shall cause to go*, 1 aor. ἔβησα, Ion. and poet.; intrans. 2 aor. ἔβην *went*, pf. βέβηκα *have gone, stand fast*.

δύω: trans. *cause to enter, sink, put on*, δύσω, ἔδῡσα, δέδῠκα; intrans. *enter, pass under*, δύομαι, δύνω, 2 aor. ἔδῡν *dived, went down*, δέδῡκα *have entered, gone down*. In prose usually καταδύω *make sink*, κατέδῡσα, καταδύσω; καταδύομαι *sink*, καταδύσομαι, κατέδῡν. — Of *another's* clothes, ἐνδύω (ἐνέδῡσα) means *put on*, ἀποδύω ἐκδύω (ἀπέδῡσα ἐξέδῡσα) mean *take off*; of *one's own* clothes, ἐνδύομαι and ἐνέδῡν mean *put on*, ἀποδύομαι ἐκδύομαι (ἀπέδῡν ἐξέδῡν) mean *take off*.

ἐγείρω: trans. *rouse, wake up*, ἐγερῶ, ἤγειρα, etc.; intrans. ἐγείρομαι *wake, am awake*, ἐγερθήσομαι, ἠγέρθην, 2 aor. ἠγρόμην *awoke*, 2 perf. ἐγρήγορα *am awake*.

ἵστημι *set*: trans. στήσω *shall set*, 1 aor. ἔστησα *set*, ἐστάθην *was set*, ἵσταμαι *set for myself*, στήσομαι, ἐστησάμην. Four active tenses are intrans.: 2 aor. ἔστην (set myself) *stood*, pf. ἕστηκα (have set myself) *stand, am standing*, εἱστήκη *stood, was standing*, 2 perf. ἕστατον *stand*, fut. pf. ἑστήξω *shall stand*. So also ἵσταμαι *set myself, stand*, στήσομαι.

N. — The same distinction prevails in the compounds: ἀνίστημι *raise up*, ἀνέστην *stood up*, ἀφίστημι *set off, cause to revolt*, ἀπέστην *stood off, revolted*, ἀφέστηκα *am distant, am in revolt*; ἐφίστημι *set over*, ἐπέστην *set myself over*, ἐφέστηκα *am set over*; καθίστημι *set down, establish*, κατέστην *established myself, became established*, καθέστηκα *am established*. The aorist middle has a different meaning: κατεστήσατο *established for himself*; συνίστημι *introduce, unite*, συνέστημεν *banded together*.

λείπω *leave*: trans. λείψω, ἔλιπον, λέλοιπα *have left, have failed, am wanting*. λείπομαι mid. = *remain* (*leave myself*), pass. = *am left, am left behind, am inferior*; 2 aor. mid. ἐλιπόμην *left for myself* (in Hom. *was left, am inferior*), λείψομαι *will leave for myself, will remain, be left*.

μαίνω: trans. *madden*, ἐκμαίνω, -μανῶ, -έμηνα; intrans. *rage*, μαίνομαι, μανοῦμαι, ἐμάνην, 2 perf. μέμηνα *am raging*.

ὄλλῡμι: trans. *destroy* (*perdo*), ἀπόλλῡμι, -ολῶ, -ώλεσα, -ολώλεκα *have ruined* (*perdidi*); intrans. *perish* (*pereo*), ἀπόλλυμαι, -ολοῦμαι, 2 aor. -ωλόμην, 2 perf. -όλωλα *am ruined* (*perii*).

πείθω: trans. *persuade*, πείσω, ἔπεισα, πέπεικα *have persuaded*, ἐπείσθην, πεισθήσομαι; intrans. (*persuade myself*) *obey, believe*, πείθομαι, πείσομαι, ἐπείσθην, πέπεισμαι *am convinced*; 2 perf. πέποιθα *I trust* (= πιστεύω) is rare in prose.

πήγνῡμι: trans. *fix, make fast*, πήξω, ἔπηξα, ἐπήχθην; intrans. *am fixed, freeze*, πήγνυμαι, παγήσομαι, ἐπάγην, 2 perf. πέπηγα *am fixed, frozen*.

πίνω *drink*: 2 aor. ἔπιον *drank*, 1 aor. ἔπῑσα *caused to drink*.

πλήττω: trans. *terrify*, ἐκπλήττω, καταπλήττω, -έπληξα; intrans. *am affrighted*, ἐκπλήττομαι, -επλάγην.

πρᾱ́ττω *do*: πέπρᾱχα (probably late) *have done*, πέπρᾱγα *have fared* (*well* or *ill*) and *have done*.

ῥήγνῡμι: trans. *break*, -ῥήξω, ἔρρηξα; intrans. *break, burst*, ῥήγνυμαι, -ῥαγήσομαι, ἐρράγην, 2 perf. ἔρρωγα *am broken*.

σβέννῡμι: trans. *extinguish, put out*, ἀποσβέννῡμι, ἀπέσβεσα, ἀπεσβέσθην; intrans.

be extinguished, go out, ἀποσβέννυμαι, ἀποσβήσομαι, ἀπέσβην *went out*, ἀπέσβηκα *am extinguished.*

σήπω: trans. *make rot;* intrans. *rot*, σήπομαι, ἐσάπην *rotted*, 2 perf. σέσηπα *am rotten.*

τήκω: trans. *cause to melt;* intrans. *melt*, τήκομαι, ἐτάκην, 2 perf. τέτηκα *am melted.*

φαίνω: trans. *show*, φανῶ, ἔφηνα, πέφαγκα *have shown*, πέφασμαι, ἐφάνθην *was shown, made known;* trans. also *show, declare*, φαίνομαι, φανοῦμαι, ἐφηνάμην *showed* (rare and poetic in the simple form; ἀπεφηνάμην *declared* is common); intrans. *show oneself, appear*, φαίνομαι, φανήσομαι and φανοῦμαι, ἐφάνην *appeared*, 2 perf. πέφηνα *have shown myself, appeared.* The middle means *show oneself, appear;* the passive, *am shown, am made evident.* φανήσομαι means *shall appear* or *shall be shown*, and is not very different in sense from φανοῦμαι (but see 1738, 1911).

φθείρω: trans. *destroy*, διαφθείρω, -φθερῶ, -έφθειρα, -έφθαρκα; intrans. *am ruined*, διαφθείρομαι, -εφθάρην, -φθαρήσομαι, 2 perf. διέφθορα *am ruined* in Hom., *have destroyed* in Attic poetry.

φύω: trans. *bring forth, produce*, φύσω, ἔφῡσα; intrans. *am produced, come into being*, φύομαι, φύσομαι, ἔφῡν, 2 perf. πέφῡκα *am by nature.*

820. Poetic forms: ἀραρίσκω (ἀρ-) *fit*, 2 aor. ἤραρον trans. and intrans. — γείνομαι *am born*, ἐγεινάμην *begat.* — ἐρείκω *rend*, 2 aor. ἤρικον trans. *rent* and intrans. *shivered.* — ἐρείπω *throw down*, ἤριπον trans. *threw down* and intrans. *fell.* — ὄρνῡμι *rouse*, 2 aor. ὤρορον trans. *roused* and intrans. *have risen.* — ἀναγιγνώσκω *read*, ἀνέγνωσα *persuaded* in Hdt., 2 aor. ἀνέγνων *read, recited.*

821. The following are poetic intransitive second perfects: ἄρᾱρα *fit* (ἀραρίσκω *fit*, trans.). — ἔολπα *hope* (Epic ἔλπω *cause to hope*). — κέκηδα *sorrow* (κήδω *trouble*). — ὄρωρα *have arisen* (ὄρνῡμι *rouse*).

PART III

FORMATION OF WORDS

822. Inflected words generally consist of two distinct parts: a stem and an inflectional ending (191):

δῶρο-ν	*gift,*	stem δωρο-,	inflectional ending ν;
λῡ́ο-μεν	*we loose,*	stem λῡο-,	inflectional ending μεν.

a. The inflectional endings of nouns and verbs, and the formation of verbal stems, have been treated under Inflection. The formation of words, as discussed here, deals primarily with the formation of noun-stems, of verbal stems derived from nouns, and of compound words. Uninflected words (adverbs, prepositions, conjunctions, and particles) are mostly of pronominal origin and obscure; such adverbs as show case forms are mentioned in 341 ff.

823. Some stems are identical with roots (*root-stems,* 193) to which only an inflectional ending, or no ending at all, has been added.

βοῦ-ς *ox, cow*	μῦ-ς *mouse*	ὗ-ς *hog, sow*
εἷς *one* (stem ἑν-)	ναῦ-ς *ship*	φλόξ *flame* (φλέγ-ω *burn*)
θήρ *wild beast* (gen. θηρ-ός)	ὄψ *voice* (stem ὀπ-)	χείρ *hand* (gen. χειρ-ός)
κλώψ *thief* (κλέπ-τ-ω *steal*)	πούς *foot* (stem ποδ-)	χθών *earth* (stem χθον-)

824. Most stems are derived from roots by the addition of one or more formative suffixes.

δῶ-ρο-ν	*gift,*	stem δωρο-,	root δω (δί-δω-μι *give*),	suffix ρο-.
γραμ-ματ-εύ-ς	*scribe,*	stem γραμματευ-,	root γραφ,	suffixes ματ and ευ.

a. Most words are therefore built up from root, suffix, and inflectional ending by a process of composition analogous to that seen in compounds (869 ff.), in which the union of the various elements yields an idea different from that seen in each of the parts.

825. A stem is *primary* if only one suffix is added to the root (δῶ-ρο-ν); *secondary,* when more than one suffix is added to the root (γραμ-ματ-εύ-ς).

826. There are two kinds of stems: noun-stems (substantive and adjective) and verb-stems.

827. Words containing a single stem are called *simple* words, as λόγο-ς *speech;* words containing two or more stems are called *compound* words, as λογο-γράφο-ς *speech-writer.*

828. According to the character of the suffix words are called:

a. **Primitive** (or **Primary**): formed by the addition of a suffix either to a root or to a verb-stem to which a vowel, usually ε, has been added (485, 486).

Root γραφ: γράφ-ω *write*, γραφ-ή *writing*, γραφ-εύ-ς *writer*, γράμ-μα *something written*, γραμ-μή *line*.

Verb-stem γεν-ε in γενέ-σθαι *become* (ἐγενόμην, γί-γν-ομαι): γένε-σι-ς *genesis, origin*; τερ-ε (τέρω *bore*): τέρε-τρο-ν *gimlet, instrument for boring.*

b. **Denominative** (or **Secondary**): formed from a noun-stem (substantive or adjective) or adverb.

γραμ-ματ-εύς *writer* (stem γραμματ-, nom. γράμμα); εὐδαιμον-ίᾱ *happiness* (stem εὐδαιμον-, nom. εὐδαίμων); δικαιο-σύνη *justice*, δίκα-ιο-ς *just* (δίκη *right*); φίλ-ιο-ς *friendly* (φίλο-ς *dear*); δουλό-ω *enslave* (δοῦλο-ς *slave*); παλαι-ό-ς *ancient, of old date*, from the adverb πάλαι *long ago*.

829. Suffixes forming primitive words are called *primary* suffixes; suffixes forming denominative words are called *secondary* suffixes.

a. The distinction between primary and secondary suffixes is not original and is often neglected. Thus, in δεινός *terrible* (δει- *fear*), νο is a primary suffix; in σκοτεινός *dark* (σκότος, 858. 11), it is secondary. So English *-able* is both primary (*readable*) and secondary (*companionable*).

b. It is often difficult to determine whether a suffix is added to a verb-stem or to a noun-stem: ἰσχῡ-ρός *strong* (ἰσχύ-ς *strength*, ἰσχύ-ω *am strong*).

c. A primitive word may be formed from a verb-stem which is itself denominative: τοξευ-τής *bowman* from τοξεύ-ω *shoot with the bow*, derived from τόξο-ν *bow*. A primitive may be formed with a suffix derived from a denominative: φλεγ-υρό-ς *burning* (φλέγ-ω *burn*) with υρο from λιγυ-ρό-ς (λιγύ-ς) *shrill*.

d. A denominative often has no corresponding primitive; sometimes the latter has been lost, sometimes it was presumed for the purpose of word-formation by the imitative process always at work in the making of language. Thus, δέμ-ν-ιο-ν *bed*, from δεμ-νο-ν (δέμ-ω *build, construct*).

830. To determine the root all suffixes must be removed from the stem until only that part remains which contains the fundamental idea.

a. Most roots are noun-roots or verb-roots; but originally a root was neither noun or verb (193). Some roots are pronominal, and express direction or position. Greek has many words whose roots cannot be discovered. The form of a root in Greek is not necessarily that which Comparative Grammar shows was common to the cognate languages.

b. Since the origin of many words, even with the help of the cognate languages, is uncertain, we are often at a loss where to make the dividing line between root and suffix. Suffixes are often preceded by a vowel which may be regarded as a part of the suffix or as an expansion of the root (by some scholars regarded as a part of the root itself).

831. Changes of the root-vowel. — a. The root-vowel is sometimes strong, sometimes weak: **ει, οι** (weak **ι**); **ευ, ου** (weak **υ**); **η** or **ω** (weak **α** or **ε**). λεῖμ-μα *remnant*, λοιπ-ό-ς *remaining*, cp. λείπ-ω, ἔ-λιπ-ον; ζεῦγ-ος *team*, cp. ζεύγ-νῡ-μι, ζυγ-όν *yoke*; σπουδ-ή *zeal*, σπεύδ-ω *hasten*; λήθ-η *forgetfulness*, λανθάνω (λαθ-) *forget*; ἦθ-ος *disposition*, ἔθ-ος *custom, habit*; ῥωχ-μός *cleft*, ῥήγ-νῡ-μι *break* (ῥαγ-, ῥηγ-, ῥωγ-). Cp. 36.

b. **ε** often varies with **ο**, sometimes with **α**; **η** sometimes varies with **ω**. γόν-ο-ς *offspring*, γί-γν-ομαι (γεν-); τόν-ο-ς *tone*, τείνω (τεν-) *stretch*; τραφ-ερός *well-fed*, τροφ-ή *nourishment*, τρέφ-ω *nourish*; ἀρωγ-ό-ς *helping*, ἀρήγ-ω *help*. Cp. 36.

832. Root-determinatives. — A consonant standing between root and suffix (or ending), and not modifying the meaning of the root, is called a *root-determinative*.

βά-θ-ρο-ν *pedestal*, from βαίνω *go* (βα-); ἔσ-θ-ω (poetical for ἐσθίω) *eat*, for ἔδ-θ-ω, cp. Ionic ἔδ-ω; πλή-θ-ω (poet.) *am full*, πλῆ-θ-ος *crowd*, πλη-θ-ώρη *satiety*, cp. πίμ-πλη-μι; στα-θ-μός *day's journey*, στά-θ-μη *a rule*, from ἵστημι (στα-); σμή-χ-ω *wipe*, cp. σμάω *wipe*. — On the insertion of σ, see 836.

a. The origin of root-determinatives is obscure. In part they may be relics of roots, in part due to the analogy of words containing the consonants in question.

833. Suffixes. — A suffix is a formative element added to a root (or to a stem) and standing between the root and the ending. Suffixes limit or particularize the general meaning of the root; but only in a few cases is the distinct meaning of the suffix known to us.

a. The origin of the Greek suffixes is often obscure; of those inherited from the parent language only some were employed to make new words; others were formed by Greek itself (productive suffixes). From the analogy of the modern languages we infer that some suffixes were once independent words, which, on becoming a part of a compound, lost their signification. Thus *-hood*, *-head* in *childhood*, *godhead* are derived from Old Eng. 'hād,' Gothic 'haidus' *character, nature*; *-ship* in *ownership*, *courtship*, comes from a lost word meaning 'shape'; *-ly* in *friendly* from Old Eng. 'līc' *body*. So -ώδης meaning *smelling* (ὄζω), as in εὐώδης *fragrant*, acquired a range of meaning originally inappropriate to it by passing into the general idea of 'full of,' 'like,' as in ποιώδης *grassy* (ποίᾱ), λοιμώδης *pestilential* (λοιμός), σφηκώδης *wasp-like* (σφήξ). This suffix is distinct from -ειδής *having the form of, like* (898 a).

Conversely, many suffixes, themselves insignificant, acquired a definite meaning by reason of the root with which they were associated. — Irrespective of its meaning, one word may serve as a model for the creation of another word; as *starvation*, *constellation*, etc., are modelled on *contemplation*, etc.

b. Many dissyllabic suffixes, due to a combination of the final letter or letters of the stem and an original monosyllabic suffix, adapt themselves to independent use. Cp. *ego-tism* for *ego-ism* because of *patriot-ism*, *-able* in *laughable* and *probable* (from *proba-bilis*). Thus, patronymics in -άδης, -ιάδης 845. 2, 3; words in -αινα 843 b, 5; -αῖος 858. 2 a; -εῖον 851. 1; -έστερος 316; -έτης 843 a, N.; -ήεις 858. 3; -ήϊος 858. 2 b; -εῖος 858. 2 a; -όεις 858. 3; -ίδιον 852. 2; -ίτης 843 a, N., 844. 2 a; -σιμος 858. 9; -ώτης 843 a, N., 844. 2 a; and many others.

c. Simple suffixes are often added to case forms or adverbs, thus producing, by contamination, dissyllabic suffixes; as ἀρχαῖ-ο-ς *ancient* 858. 2 a; παλαι-ό-ς *of old date* 828 b, ἐαρι-νό-ς *vernal* 858. 12; φυσι-κό-ς *natural* 858. 6 b; cp. ἐν-άλι-ο-ς *marine* (ἅλς).

d. Many compound suffixes are formed by the union of two suffixes, new stems being created by the addition of a suffix to a stem, as: τηρ-ιο 851. 2, ισκ-ιο 852. 6, ισκ-ιδιο 854. See 854.

e. Suffixes often show gradations: **τηρ, τωρ, τερ, τρ** (36 N. 1) as in δο-τήρ, δώ-τωρ, δότειρα (out of δοτερ-ι̯α) *giver*; ψάλ-τρ-ια *harp-player*; **μην μν**: λι-μήν *harbour*, λί-μν-η *lake*; **μωρ μαρ**: τέκ-μωρ, τέκ-μαρ *goal*; **ωρ ρ**: ὕδ-ωρ *water*, ὕδ-ρᾱ *hydra*; **ων αν**: τέκτ-ων *carpenter*, fem. τέκταινα, from τεκταν-ι̯α; and in λέων *lion*, fem. λέαινα (843 b. 5).

834. Changes in stems. — Various changes occur when a suffix is added to a stem.

a. The final vowel of a stem is contracted with the initial vowel of a suffix: ὀφίδιον *small snake* (ὀφι- + ιδιον from ὄφι-ς). So when a consonant is dropped at the end of a stem: αἰδο-ῖο-ς *venerable* (αἰδώς *reverence*, stem αἰδοσ-), βασιλε-ίᾱ *kingdom* (βασιλεύ-ς *king*, stem βασιλεϝ- for βασιλευ̯-, 43), ἀστε-ῖο-ς *refined* (ἄστυ *city*, stem ἀστεϝ- for ἀστευ̯-, 43). Cp. 858. 2.

b. A long final vowel of a stem may be shortened before the initial vowel of a suffix: δίκᾰ-ιο-ς *just*, δίκη *right*, stem δικᾱ-. (Properly δίκαι is an old case form, 833 c, to which -ο-ς is added.)

c. A final vowel or diphthong may be dropped before the initial vowel of a suffix: σοφ-ίᾱ *wisdom* (σοφό-ς *wise*), τίμ-ιο-ς *honoured, costly* (τῑμή *honour*, stem τῑμᾱ-), βασιλ-ικό-ς *royal* (βασιλεύ-ς *king*), πολῑτ-ικό-ς *civic* (πολίτης *citizen*, stem πολῑτᾱ-).

d. The final letter or letters of a consonant stem may be dropped: σωφρο-σύνη *temperance, moderation* (σώφρων *temperate*, stem σωφρον-), μελ-ύδριον *little song* (μέλ-ος *song*, μελεσ-), ἀληθ-ινό-ς *genuine* (ἀληθής -ές *true*). So apparently in the case of a vowel stem in δεσπό-συνος *belonging to the master* (δεσπότης).

e. The final consonant of a stem undergoes regular euphonic change before the initial consonant of a suffix: βλέμ-μα *glance* (βλέπ-ω *look*), δικασ-τής *a judge* (δικαδ-της, from δικάζω *judge*, stem δικαδ-), πίσ-τι-ς *faith* (= πιθ-τι-ς, from πείθ-ω *persuade*, stem πιθ-), λέξις *style* (= λεγ-σι-ς, from λέγ-ω *speak*).

f. Stems in ο have an alternative in ε (cp. ἵππο-ς, voc. ἵππε; 229 b). This ε often appears in denominatives: οἰκέ-ω *dwell*, οἰκέ-της *house-servant*, οἰκε-ῖο-ς *domestic* (οἶκο-ς *house*).

g. Derivatives of ᾱ stems may apparently show ω in place of ᾱ; as στρατιώ-της *soldier* (στρατιά *army*), Ἰταλιώ-της *an Italiote*, Greek inhabitant of Italy (Ἰταλίᾱ *Italy*). See 843 a, N. Stems in ᾱ have η in τῑμή-εις *honoured* (τῑμή, stem τῑμᾱ-).

h. Vowel stems, especially those derived from verbs, often lengthen a final short vowel before a suffix beginning with a consonant: ποίη-μα *poem*, ποίη-σι-ς *poetry*, ποιη-τή-ς *poet*, ποιη-τι-κό-ς *creative, poetical* (ποιέ-ω *make*); δεσμώ-τη-ς *prisoner* (δεσμό-ς, δεσμά *fetters*). Verbs with stems in α, ε, ο usually show in derivatives the stem vowel as found in the tenses other than the present; as δηλό-ω *manifest*, fut. δηλώ-σω, δήλω-σι-ς *manifestation*; ἀρόω *plough*, fut. ἀρό-σω, ἄρο-σι-ς *arable land*, ἀρο-τήρ *ploughman*; εὑρ-ίσκ-ω *find out*, fut. εὑρ-ή-σω, εὕρ-η-μα *discovery*, but εὕρ-ε-σις *discovery*, εὑρ-ε-τής *discoverer*.

i. Vowel stems sometimes insert a vowel before a suffix beginning with a consonant: πολι-ή-τη-ς, Ionic for πολί-τη-ς *citizen*, πτολί-ε-θρο-ν (poetic) *city*.

j. Consonant stems, and vowel stems not ending in ο, often show ο before a suffix in denominatives; a stem in -ον is thus replaced by one in -ο: σωφρο-σύνη *temperance* (σώφρων *temperate*, σωφρον-); αἱματ-ό-εις *bloody* (αἷμα, -ατος *blood*) and σκι-ό-εις *shadowy* (σκιά *shadow*) by analogy to δολό-εις *wily*, 858. 3. Cp. 873–875.

835. Several substantives are formed by reduplication: ἀγ-ωγ-ή *training* (ἄγ-ω *lead*), ἐδ-ωδ-ή *food* (Ionic ἔδ-ω *eat*), γί-γᾱς, -αντος *giant*. Some, by metathesis (128 a): τμῆ-σι-ς *cutting* (τέμ-ν-ω *cut*).

836. Insertion of sigma. — Between root (or stem) and suffix σ is often found, and in some cases it has become attached to the suffix. This parasitic letter spread from the perfect middle, where it is properly in place only in stems in τ, δ, θ, or σ; as in σχι-σ-μό-ς *cleaving* with σ from ἔ-σχι-σ-μαι by analogy to ἔ-σχισ-ται for ἐ-σχιδ-ται (σχίζω *cleave*). In -σ-της the transference was made easier by words like σχισ-τός *cloven* for σχιδ-τος. This σ appears before many suffixes, and usually where the perfect middle has acquired it (489).

μα: σπά-σ-μα *spasm* (σπάω *rend*, ἔσπασμαι), κέλευ-σ-μα *command* (κελεύ-ω *command*, κεκέλευσμαι), μία-σ-μα *stain* (μιαίνω *stain*, μεμίασμαι). — **μο**: σπα-σ-μός = σπά-σ-μα, κελευ-σ-μός *command*. — **μη**: δύ-σ-μη *setting* (δύω *set*). — **της**: κελευ-σ-τής *signal-man*, ὀρχη-σ-τής *dancer* (ὀρχ-έ-ομαι *dance*), δυνά-σ-της *lord* (δύνα-μαι *am able*). Also in δρα-σ-τήριος *efficacious* (δρά-ω *do*), ὀρχή-σ-τρᾱ *dancing-place*, πλη-σ-μόνη *fulness*. -σ-μ has displaced δμ, -θ-μ (832) in ὀσμή *odour* (earlier ὀδμή), ῥυ-σ-μός (and ῥυ-θ-μός) *rhythm*.

837. Insertion of tau. — In a few words τ is inserted before the suffixes μο, μα, μη, μην. Thus, ἐφ-ε-τ-μή *command* (ἐφίημι, root ἑ, ἡ), λαῖ-τ-μα *depth of the sea*, ἀϋ-τ-μή and ἀϋ-τ-μήν *breath* (ἄημι *blow*). In ἐρετ-μό-ν *oar* the τ may be part of the verb-stem (ἐρέσσω, 515), and have spread thence to the other words.

FORMATION OF SUBSTANTIVES

838. Some suffixes have a special significance; of these the most important are given in 839–856. But suffixes commonly used with a special function (such as to denote *agency, action, instrument*, etc.) are not restricted to this function. Only a few have one function, as τερο to denote comparison.

a. The instrument may be viewed as the agent, as in ῥαι-σ-τήρ *hammer*, lit. *smasher*, from ῥαί-ω *smash*. τρο (863. 16) may express the agent, instrument, or place. Suffixes used to denote actions or abstract ideas often make concrete words, as τροφ-ή *nurture* and *nourishment*, ἀγγελ-ίᾱ *message* (cp. Eng. *dwelling*, *clothing*). πορθμεῖον means *ferry*, *ferry-boat*, *ferryman's fee*. Words originally denoting an agent have lost that meaning, as πα-τήρ *father* (perh. *protector*), and in many cases the original force is changed.

839. AGENCY

a. The primary suffixes τᾱ, τηρ, τορ, τρο, ευ, denoting the *agent* or *doer of an action*, are masculine.

1. **τᾱ** (nom. -τή-ς): κρι-τή-ς *judge* (κρίνω *decide*, κρι-), κλέπ-τη-ς *thief* (κλέπ-τ-ω *steal*), ποιη-τή-ς *poet*, i.e. *maker* (ποιέ-ω *make*), αὐλη-τή-ς *flute-player* (αὐλέ-ω *play the flute*), μαθ-η-τή-ς *pupil* (μανθάνω *learn*, μαθ-ε-), ἱκ-έ-τη-ς *suppliant* (ἱκ-νέ-ομαι *come*, ἱκ-).
2. **τηρ** (nom. -τήρ): δο-τήρ *giver* (δί-δω-μι *give*, δο-, δω-), σω-τήρ *saviour* (σῴ-ζω *save*).
3. **τορ** (nom. -τωρ): ῥή-τωρ *orator* (ἐρέω *shall say*, ἐρ-, ῥε-), εἴ-ρη-κα *have spoken*, κτίσ-τωρ *founder* (κτίζω *found*, κτιδ-), σημάντωρ *commander*, poet. (σημαίνω *give a signal*, σημαν-).
4. **τρο** (nom. -τρό-ς): ἰᾱ-τρό-ς *physician* (ἰά-ομαι *heal*).
5. **ευ** (nom. -εύ-ς): γραφ-εύ-ς *writer* (γράφ-ω *write*), τοκ-εύ-ς *father* (τίκτω *beget*, τεκ-).

b. The primary suffixes τριδ, τριᾱ, τειρᾱ, τιδ are feminine.

1. **τριδ** (nom. -τρίς): αὐλη-τρίς *female flute-player.*
2. **τριᾱ** (nom. -τρια): ποιή-τρια *poetess* (late), ψάλ-τρια *female harper* (ψάλλω *play the harp*, ψαλ-).
3. **τειρᾱ** (nom. -τειρα from τερ-ι̯α): σώ-τειρα fem. of σω-τήρ, δό-τειρα fem. of δο-τήρ.
4. **τιδ** (nom. -τις): ἱκ-έ-τις *female suppliant* fem. of ἱκ-έ-της.

c. The same root or verb-stem may have different suffixes denoting the agent: γεν-έ-της, γεν-ε-τήρ, γεν-έ-τωρ *begetter;* μαθ-η-τρίς, or μαθ-ή-τρια *female pupil*, fem. of μαθ-η-τής.

d. Words in -τηρ, -τρις, -ευς are oxytone. Words in -τωρ, -τειρα, -τρια have recessive accent. Words in -της are oxytone or paroxytone.

e. See also ον (nom. -ων) 861. 18.

840. NAMES OF ACTIONS AND ABSTRACT SUBSTANTIVES

a. Substantives denoting actions often express abstract ideas, and names of actions and verbal abstracts are often used concretely. The following suffixes (except μο, nominative -μό-ς, and εσ, nominative -ος) form feminines; all are primary except ιᾱ in some words.

1. **τι** (nom. -τι-ς): πίσ-τι-ς *faith* (πείθ-ω *persuade*, πιθ-), φά-τι-ς *rumour* (φημί *say*, φα-).
2. **σι** (nom. -σι-ς): λέξις *style* (λέγ-ω *speak*), ποίη-σι-ς *poetry* (ποιέ-ω *make*), φθί-σι-ς *decay* (φθί-ν-ω *decay*), δό-σι-ς *act of giving* or *gift* (δί-δω-μι *give*, δο-, δω-), θέ-σι-ς *placing* (τί-θη-μι *place*, θε-, θη-), τά-σι-ς *tension* (for τν̥-σι-ς 35 b, from τείνω *stretch*, τεν-). σι is derived from τι after a vowel (115).
3. **σιᾱ** (nom. -σίᾱ): in substantives from verbs in -αζω out of -αδ-ι̯ω; as δοκιμασίᾱ *examination* (δοκιμάζω *examine*, δοκ μαδ-).
4. **τυ** (nom. -τύ-ς 863 a. 17): rare, poetic and dialectic, ἐδ-η-τύς *eating* (poet. ἔδ-ω *eat*), βοη-τύ-ς *shouting* (βοά-ω *shout*).
5. **μο** (nom. -μό-ς, masc.): διωγ-μό-ς *pursuit* (διώκ-ω *pursue*), πταρ-μό-ς *sneezing* (πτάρ-νυ-μαι *sneeze*). On θ-μο see 832, σ-μο 836, τ-μο 837. Cp. 861. 1.

6. **μᾱ** (nom. -μη): γνώ-μη *knowledge* (γι-γνώ-σκω *know*), φή-μη *report, omen* (φη-μί *say*), τῑ-μή *honour* (poet. τί-ω *honour*), μνή-μη *memory* (μι-μνῄ-σκω *remind*). See also 861. 1.
7. **μᾰ** (nom. -μᾰ): τόλ-μα *daring* (τλῆ-ναι *dare*).
8. **εσ** (nom. -ος, neut.): δέ-ος *fear*, ῥῖγ-ος *cold*.
9. **ιᾱ** (nom. -ίᾱ): primitive, from verb-stems, as μαν-ίᾱ *madness* (μαίνομαι *rage*, μαν-). Denominative: ἡγεμον-ίᾱ *sovereignty* (ἡγεμών *leader*), εὐεργεσία *kind service* (εὐεργετ-ια from εὐεργέτης *doer of good deeds*). Without any noun-stem: πολιορκίᾱ *siege* (πολιορκέω *besiege*). Verbs in -ευω derived from substantives, as παιδεύ-ω *educate* (παῖς *child*), show abstracts in -είᾱ for ε(υ̯)-ιᾱ (43): παιδείᾱ *education*, στρατείᾱ *campaign* (στρατεύομαι *take the field*), βασιλείᾱ *reign, kingdom* (βασιλεύ-ω *am king*).
10. **ο, α**: see 859. 1, 2.

b. Many feminine substantives expressing the abstract notion of the adjective are derived from adjective stems (a few from substantive or verb stems). Many of these denominatives express *quality*, cp. Eng. *-ness, -hood*.

1. **ιᾰ** (nom. -ιᾰ): from adjectives in -ης and -οος, -ους, as ἀλήθεια *truth* for ἀληθεσ-ια from ἀληθής *true*; ἔνδεια *want* for ἐνδε(ε)σ-ια from ἐνδεής *needy*, 44 a, 292 d; εὔνοια *kindness* for εὐνο(ο)-ια from εὔνοο-ς εὔνους *kind*.
2. **ιᾱ** (nom. -ίᾱ): εὐδαιμον-ίᾱ *happiness* (εὐδαίμων *happy*), συμμαχίᾱ *alliance* (σύμμαχος *fighting along with*), σοφ-ίᾱ *wisdom* (σοφό-ς *wise*). Since τ becomes σ before ιᾱ we have ἀθανασίᾱ *immortality* (ἀθάνατο-ς *immortal*). Cp. 859. 6.
3. **συνᾱ** (nom. -σύνη): δικαιο-σύνη *justice* (δίκαιο-ς *just*). Abstracts in -συνη are properly fem. of adj. in -συνος, as γηθο-σύνη *joy* (γηθό-συνος *joyful*). -οσύνη by analogy in μαντ-οσύνη *art of divination* (μάντι-ς *seer*). See 865. 7.
4. **τητ** (nom. -της): φιλό-της, -τητος *friendship* (φίλο-ς *friend*), ἰσό-της, -τητος *equality* (ἴσο-ς *equal*), νεό-της *youth* (νέο-ς *young*), παχύ-της *thickness* (παχύ-ς *thick*).
5. **αδ** (nom. -άς): abstract substantives of number, as τρι-άς, -άδος *triad* (τρεῖς). μον-άς, -άδος *unit* (μόνο-ς *alone, single*). See also 863 b. 8.

c. Some neuter abstracts express quality: τάχ-ος *speed* (ταχ-ύ-ς *swift*), εὖρ-ος *width* (εὐρ-ύ-ς *broad*). See 840 a. 8.

d. A feminine adjective is used substantively in poet. πινυτή *wisdom* from πινυτό-ς *wise*; with recessive accent in ἔχθρᾱ *enmity* from ἐχθρό-ς *hostile*, θέρμη *warmth* from θερμό-ς *warm*.

e. Some compound adjectives in -ής yield (by analogy) abstracts in -ιᾱ not in -ειᾰ; as ἀτυχίᾱ *misfortune* from ἀ-τυχ-ής *unfortunate*. Fluctuation often occurs, as in κακοήθεια κακοηθίᾱ *malignity* from κακο-ήθης *ill-disposed*; Old Attic ἀληθείᾱ (= Ion. ἀληθείη) for ἀλήθεια.

841. RESULT OF ACTION

The result or effect of an action is expressed by the primary suffixes

1. **ες** (nom. -ος, neut.): γέν-ος *race, family*, stem γεν-εσ- (γί-γν-ομαι *am born*, ἐ-γεν-όμην, γεν-), τέκ-ος *child*, stem τεκ-εσ- (τίκτω *bring forth*, τεκ-), ψεῦδ-ος *lie*, stem ψευδ-εσ- (ψεύδ-ω *deceive*).
2. **ματ** (nom. -μα, neut.): γράμ-μα *thing written* (γράφ-ω *write*), νόη-μα *thought* (νοέω *think*), ποίη-μα *poem* (ποιέ-ω *make*), δέρ-μα *hide* (δέρ-ω *flay*), τμῆ-μα *section* (τέμ-νω *cut*, τεμ-, τμη-, 128 a).

842. INSTRUMENT OR MEANS OF ACTION

The instrument or means of an action is expressed by the primary suffixes

1. **τρο** (nom. -τρο-ν, neut.): ἄρο-τρο-ν *plough* (ἀρό-ω *plough*), λύ-τρο-ν *ransom* (λύ-ω *release*, λῡ-), σεῖ-σ-τρο-ν *rattle* (σεί-ω *shake*, 624 a), δί-δακ-τρο-ν *teacher's pay* (διδάσκω *teach*, διδαχ-), λου-τρό-ν *bath* (bathing-water; λού-ω *wash*).
2. **θ-ρο** (nom. -θρο-ν, neut.): κλεῖ-θρο-ν *bar* for closing a door (κλεί-ω *shut*, 832).
3. **τρᾱ** (nom. -τρᾱ, fem.): μάκ-τρᾱ *kneading-trough* (μάττω *knead*, μαγ-), ῥή-τρᾱ *compact* (ἐρέω ἐρῶ *shall say*, ἐρ-, ῥε-), χύ-τρᾱ *pot* (χέω *pour*, χυ-).
4. **τηρ-ιο-** (nom. -τηρ-ιο-ν, neut.): in a few words, as πο-τήρ-ιο-ν *cup* (πίνω *drink*, πο- 529); θελκ-τήρ-ιο-ν *spell, charm* (θέλγ-ω *charm*). See 858. 14.
5. **ειο** (rare; nom. -εῖον, neut.): τροφεῖα *pay for rearing*. See 863 a. 8.
6. **ρο** (nom. -ρό-ν, neut.): πτ-ε-ρό-ν *wing* (πέτ-ομαι *fly*).

843. THE PERSON CONCERNED

a. The person concerned or occupied with anything is denoted by a denominative formed by one of the following secondary suffixes:

1. **ευ** (nom. -εύ-ς, masc.): γραμ-ματ-εύ-ς *secretary* (γράμμα, -ατος *anything written*), ἱερ-εύ-ς *priest* (ἱερό-ς *sacred*), ἱππ-εύ-ς *horseman* (ἵππο-ς *horse*), χαλκ-εύ-ς *coppersmith* (χαλκό-ς *copper*).
2. **τᾱ** (nom. -τη-ς, masc.): ναύ-τη-ς *sailor* (ναῦ-ς *ship*), τοξό-της *bowman* (τόξο-ν *bow*), οἰκέ-της *house-servant* (οἶκο-ς *house*, 834 f), δεσμώ-τη-ς *prisoner* (834 h).

N.—By analogy are formed: εὐν-έτη-ς *bed-fellow* (εὐνή *bed*), following οἰκέ-τη-ς; ὁπλ-ίτη-ς *heavy-armed soldier* (ὅπλο-ν, ὅπλα *armour*) following πολί-τη-ς from older πόλῑ-ς; στρατι-ώτη-ς *soldier* (στρατιά *army*) following δεσμώ-τη-ς. See 834 g.

b. The following secondary suffixes form feminine substantives:

1. **ιᾰ** (nom. -ιᾰ): corresponding to masculines in -εύ-ς, as ἱέρεια *priestess* for ἱερ-ευ̯-ια (ἱερ-εύ-ς *priest*), βασίλεια *queen* (βασιλ-εύ-ς *king*). See -αινα below.
2. **ιδ** (nom. -ίς): φαρμακ-ίς *sorceress* (φάρμακο-ν *charm, poison*, φαρμακ-εύ-ς *sorcerer*), καπηλ-ίς *female huckster* (κάπηλο-ς *huckster*), φυλακ-ίς *female guard* (φύλαξ).
3. **τιδ** (nom. -τις): corresponding to masculines in -τη-ς: οἰκέ-τις *house-maid* (οἰκέ-της), πολῖ-τις *female citizen* (πολί-της).
4. **ιττᾱ, ισσᾱ** (nom. -ιττα, -ισσα): from ι̯α added to stems in τ or κ (112, 114), as θῆττα *female serf* from θητ-ι̯α (θής, θητ-ός *serf*), Κίλισσα *Cilician woman* from Κιλικ-ι̯α (Κίλιξ *Cilician*); later, by analogy, βασίλισσα *queen*.
5. **αινᾱ** (nom. -αινα) corresponding to masculines in -ων: λέ-αινα *lioness* (λέ-ων

lion), θεράπ-αινα *handmaid* (θεράπ-ων *attendant*), Λάκ-αινα *woman of Laconia* (Λάκ-ων *a Laconian*). By analogy, in ο stems: λύκ-αινα *she-wolf* (λύκο-ς). -αινα stands for -αν-ι̯α, -αν being a weak form of -ων (833 e, 35 b).

N. — Names of *dealers* in anything usually end in -πώλης, -ου; fem. -πωλις, -ιδος (πωλέω *sell*), as βιβλιο-πώλης *bookseller* (βιβλίο-ν *book*), σῖτο-πώλης *grain-dealer* (σῖτο-ς *grain*), ἀρτό-πωλις *bread-woman* (ἄρτο-ς *bread*). Cp. also καπηλίς under ιδ.

844. GENTILES OR PLACE NAMES

Gentiles are denominative nouns denoting belonging to or coming from a particular *country, nation,* or *city.* Gentiles are formed from proper nouns by secondary suffixes.

1. **ευ** (nom. -εύς, gen. -έως, masc.), **ιδ** (nom. -ίς, gen. ίδ-ος, fem.):
   Πλαταιεύς -έως, Πλαταΐς -ίδος *a Plataean* (ἡ Πλάταια); Ἐρετριεύς *an Eretrian* (ἡ Ἐρέτρια); Μεγαρεύς, Μεγαρίς *a Megarian* (τὰ Μέγαρα); Αἰολεύς *Aeolian* (Αἴολος, mythical ancestor of the Aeolians).
   a. -ίς (-ίδος) may denote a *land* or a *dialect:* ἡ Δωρίς (γῆ) *Doris;* ἡ Αἰολίς (γλῶττα) *the Aeolic dialect.*
2. **τᾱ** (nom. -τη-ς, masc.), **τιδ** (nom. -τις, fem.): Τεγεά-της, Τεγεᾶ-τις *of Tegea* (ἡ Τεγέᾱ); Σπαρτ-ιά-της, Σπαρτ-ιᾶ-τις *of Sparta* (ἡ Σπάρτᾱ); Αἰγῑνή-της, Αἰγῑνῆ-τις *of Aegina* (ἡ Αἴγῑνα); Συβαρ-ί-της, Συβαρ-ῖ-τις *Sybarite* (ἡ Σύβαρις); Σικελι-ώ-της, Σικελι-ῶ-τις *Siciliote* (ἡ Σικελίᾱ).
   a. The endings -ῑτης, -ωτης are due to analogy; see 843 a. N.
3. Other gentiles, properly adjectives, end in **-ιος**, **-ιᾱ**, as Ἀθηναῖο-ς, -αίᾱ *of Athens* (αἱ Ἀθῆναι), Μῑλήσ-ιο-ς for Μῑλητ-ιο-ς *of Miletus* (Μίλητος), Ὀπούντ-ιο-ς *of Opus* (Ὀποῦς); (ι)**κός**, (ι)**κά**, as Ἰων-ικός *Ionic* (Ἴων-ες *Ionians*); **νό-ς**, **νή** preceded by ᾱ(η), ῑ, as Σαρδι-ᾱνό-ς *of Sardis* (Σάρδεις), Λαμψακ-ηνό-ς *of Lampsacus* (Λάμψακος), Βυζαντ-ῖνο-ς *Byzantine* (Βυζάντιον). See 863 b. 12.

845. PATRONYMICS

Patronymics, or denominative proper names denoting descent from a father or ancestor, are formed from proper names of persons by means of the following suffixes:

1. **δᾱ** (nom. -δη-ς, masc.), **δ** (nom. -ς, fem.):

Βορεᾱ́-δη-ς	*son of Boreas*	fem. Βορεᾱ́-ς, -δος	from Βορέᾱ-ς

   Stems in ᾱ shorten ᾱ to α; from such forms arose

2. **αδᾱ** (nom. -άδη-ς, masc.), **αδ** (nom. -άς, fem.):

Θεστι-άδη-ς	*son of Thestius*	fem. Θεστι-άς, -άδος	from Θέστιο-ς

   From this type arose a new formation:

3. **ιαδᾱ** (nom. -ιάδη-ς, masc.), **ιαδ** (nom. -ιάς, fem.):

Φερητ-ιάδη-ς	*son of Pheres*	fem. Φερητ-ιάς, -ιάδ-ος	from Φέρης (-ητος)
Περση-ϊάδη-ς	*son of Perseus*	(fem. Περση-ΐς, -ΐδ-ος)	from Περσεύ-ς
Τελαμων-ιάδη-ς	*son of Telamon*		from Τελαμών (-ῶνος)

4. **ιδᾱ** (nom. -ίδη-ς, masc.), **ιδ** (nom. -ίς, fem.):

Ταντα-λίδη-ς	*son of Tantalus*	fem. Ταντα-λίς, -ίδ-ος	from Τάνταλο-ς
Κεκροπ-ίδη-ς	*son of Cecrops*	fem. Κεκροπ-ίς, -ίδ-ος	from Κέκροψ (-οπος)
Οἰνε-ίδη-ς	*son of Oeneus*	fem. Οἰνη-ΐς, -ίδ-ος	from Οἰνεύ-ς
Λητο-ΐδη-ς	*son of Leto*	fem. Λητω-ΐς, -ίδ-ος	from Λητώ (279)

Stems in ο drop ο; stems in ευ (ηυ) drop υ; stems in οι (ωι) drop ι.

5. **ῑον** or **ῑων** (poetic and rare; nom. -ίων, masc.):

Κρον-ίων *son of Cronus* (also Κρον-ίδη-ς), gen. Κρον-ίον-ος or Κρον-ίων-ος according to the metre, from Κρόνο-ς.

6. **ιωνᾱ** or **ῑνᾱ** (poetic and rare; nom. -ιώνη or ΐνη, fem.):

Ἀκρισ-ιώνη *daughter of* Ἀκρίσιο-ς — Ἀδρηστ-ΐνη *daughter of* Ἄδρηστο-ς

846. Variations occur especially in poetry: **a.** Hom. Πηλε-ίδη-ς, Πηλε-ΐδη-ς, Πηλη-ϊάδη-ς, and Πηλε-ΐων, *son of* Πηλεύ-ς; Ἀτρε-ίδη-ς, Ἀτρε-ΐδη-ς, and Ἀτρε-ΐων, *son of* Ἀτρεύ-ς.

b. Two patronymic endings: Ταλα-ϊον-ίδη-ς *son of* Ταλαό-ς.

c. The stem drops or adds a syllable: Δευκαλ-ίδη-ς *son of* Δευκαλίων, -ίων-ος; Λαμπ-ετ-ίδη-ς *son of* Λάμπο-ς.

d. -ιδης is used in comic formations: κλεπτ-ίδη-ς *son of a thief.*

e. -νδᾱς occurs in the dialects, as Ἐπαμεινώνδᾱ-ς *Epaminondas.*

f. -ιος, -ειος, may indicate descent, as Τελαμώνιε παῖ *oh son of Telamon*, Τυνδαρεία θυγάτηρ *daughter of Tyndareus*; cp. Tennyson's "Niobean daughter."

847. A patronymic may include the father, as Πεισιστρατίδαι *the Peisistratidae* (Peisistratus and his sons).

848. Most genuine patronymics are poetical and belong to the older language. In the classical period patronymics rarely indicate descent in the case of historical persons; as Εὐρῑπίδης, Ἀριστείδης.

849. Metronymics denote descent from the mother, as Δᾱνα-ΐδη-ς *son of* Δανάη, Φιλυρ-ίδη-ς *son of* Φιλύρᾱ.

850. Relationship is sometimes denoted by the suffixes **ιδεο** (nom. -ιδοῦ-ς *son of*) and **ιδεᾱ** (nom. -ιδῆ *daughter of*); as ἀδελφ-ιδοῦ-ς *nephew*, ἀδελφ-ιδῆ *niece* (ἀδελφό-ς *brother*).

PLACE

851. Place may be expressed by the secondary suffixes

1. **ιο** (nom. -ιο-ν, neut.): Διονύσιον (scil. ἱερόν) *temple of Dionysus*, Ἥραιον *Heraeum.*

   Also **-ε-ιο** (nom. -εῖο-ν, neut.): from substantives in -εύ-ς and by extension in others; as χαλκε-ῖο-ν *forge* (χαλκ-εύ-ς *coppersmith*), Θησε-ῖον *Theseum* (Θησεύ-ς), λογ-εῖο-ν *place for speaking* (λόγο-ς *speech*), μουσ-εῖο-ν *seat of the Muses* (μοῦσα *muse*), Ὀλυμπι-εῖο-ν *Olympieum* (Ὀλύμπιο-ς *Olympian Zeus*).

2. **τηρ-ιο** (nom. -τήρ-ιο-ν, neut.): derived from substantives in -τήρ (or -τής); as ἀκροᾱτήρ-ιο-ν *auditorium* (ἀκροᾱτήρ or ἀκροᾱτής *hearer*), ἐργαστήρ-ιο-ν *workshop* (ἐργαστήρ *workman*), βουλευτήριον *senate house* (βουλευτήρ or βουλευτής *councillor, senator*). See 863 a. 8.

3. **ων** (nom. -ών, gen. -ῶν-ος, masc.) : ἀνδρ-ών *apartment for men* (ἀνήρ, ἀνδρ-ός *man*), ἱππ-ών *stable* (ἵππο-ς *horse*), παρθεν-ών *maiden's apartment, Parthenon*, temple of Pallas (παρθένο-ς *maiden*), οἰν-ών *wine-cellar* (οἶνο-ς *wine*), ἀμπελ-ών *vineyard* (ἄμπελο-ς *vine*). Forms in **-εών** occur, as περιστερ-εών *dove-cote* (περιστερά *dove*), οἰνεών.
4. **ῑτιδ** (nom. -ῖτις, fem.) : added to ων, ἀνδρων-ῖτις *apartment for men*, γυναικων-ῖτις *apartment for women*.
5. **ωνιᾱ** (nom. -ωνιά, fem.) : ῥοδ-ωνιά *rose-bed* (ῥόδο-ν *rose*).
6. **τρᾱ** (rare ; nom. -τρᾱ, fem.) : ὀρχή-σ-τρᾱ *dancing-place* (ὀρχέ-ομαι *dance*), παλαί-σ-τρᾱ *wrestling-ground* (παλαί-ω *wrestle*). Cp. 836.

DIMINUTIVES

852. Diminutives are denominatives formed from the stems of substantives by various secondary suffixes.

1. **ιο** (nom. -ιο-ν, neut.) : παιδ-ίο-ν *little child* (παῖς, παιδ-ός), ὀρνίθ-ιο-ν *small bird* (ὄρνῑς, ὄρνῑθος), ἀσπίδ-ιο-ν *small shield* (ἀσπίς, ἀσπίδ-ος).

N. — Trisyllabic words are paroxytone if the first syllable is long by nature or position.

2. **ιδ-ιο** (nom. -ίδιο-ν, neut.) : derived from such words as ἀσπίδ-ιο-ν ; as ξιφ-ίδιο-ν *dagger* (ξίφος *sword*, stem ξιφεσ-), βο-ίδιο-ν *small cow* (βοῦ-ς), οἰκίδιο-ν *small house*, οἰκι + ιδιον (οἰκίᾱ), ἰχθύδιο-ν *small fish* (ἰχθύς). See 833 b.
3. **αρ-ιο** (nom. -άριον, neut.) : παιδ-άριο-ν *little child*.
4. **υδ-ριο** (nom. -ύδριον, neut.) : μελ-ύδριο-ν *little song* (μέλος).
5. **υλλιο** (nom. -ύλλιον, neut.) : ἐπ-ύλλιο-ν *little epic* or *versicle* (ἔπος).
6. **ισκο, ισκᾱ** (nom. -ίσκος, masc., -ίσκη, fem.): ἀνθρωπ-ίσκο-ς *manikin*, παιδ-ίσκο-ς *young boy*, παιδ-ίσκη *young girl*. From this comes -ισκ-ιο in ἀσπιδ-ίσκιο-ν *small shield*.

853. Many other diminutives occur, as **ακνᾱ** : in πιθάκνη *wine-jar* (πίθος) ; **ιδ, ῑδ** : in ἁμαξίς, -ίδος *small wagon* (ἅμαξα), νησίς, -ῖδος *islet* (νῆσο-ς) ; **ιδ-ευ** : of the young of animals, as λυκ-ιδεύς *wolf's whelp* (λύκο-ς), also ὑϊδεύς *son's son, grandson* (υἱός) ; **ιχο**: ὀρτάλιχος *young bird* (ὀρταλίς) *chick ;* **ιχνᾱ**: κυλίχνη (and κυλίχνιον, κυλιχνίς) *small cup* (κύλιξ). Rare or late are -ᾱκίδιον, -άσιον, -άφιον, -ιδάριον, -ισκάριον, ιον, 861. 19, -ύλος, and over 25 others. See λο, 860. 1.

854. Diminutives are often combined: παιδ-ισκ-άριον *stripling*, μειράκ-ιον, μειρακ-ίσκος, μειρακ-ύλλ-ιον, μειρακ-υλλ-ίδιον *stripling* (μεῖραξ *lass*), χλαν-ισκ-ίδιον *cloaklet* (χλανίς), ζῳδάριον *insect* (ζῷον *animal*).

855. Some words, especially such as denote parts of the body, are diminutive in form, but not in meaning; as κρᾱνίον *skull*, θηρίον *beast* (= θήρ), πεδίον *plain* (πέδον *ground*), all in Homer, who has no diminutives. Diminutives often employed tend to lose their diminutive value.

856. Diminutives may express affection, familiarity, daintiness, and sometimes pity or contempt (cp. *dar-ling, lord-ling*). See the examples under 852, and also πατρ-ίδιον *daddy* (πατήρ), ἀδελφ-ίδιο-ν *dear little brother*, Σωκρατ-ίδιον *dear Socky*, ἀνθρώπ-ιον *manikin*. Some endings often have an ironical force, as πλούτ-ᾱξ *rich churl*, γάστρ-ων *fat-belly*.

FORMATION OF ADJECTIVES

857. Adjectives are formed by the same suffixes as are used in substantives, the same formation producing in one case a substantive, in another an adjective. Many words formed with certain suffixes (ιο, μο, νο, ρο, το) are used as adjectives or as abstract substantives (usually feminine or neuter). Thus φιλίᾱ *friendly* or *friendship;* so στέφ-ανο-ς *crown* (στέφ-ω *encircle*) was originally an adjective. Many suffixes have no characteristic signification.

Adjectives are either primitive (from roots or verb-stems) or denominative (from substantives or other adjectives). But this distinction is often obliterated and difficult to determine.

858. The following are the chief adjectival suffixes:

1. **ο, ᾱ** (nom. -ο-ς, -η or -ᾱ, -ο-ν): primary: λοιπ-ό-ς *remaining* (λείπ-ω *leave*, λιπ-, λειπ-, λοιπ-), λευκ-ό-ς *bright* (λεύσσω *shine*, λευκ-ι̯ω).

2. **ιο, ιᾱ**: a common suffix expressing that which *pertains* or *belongs* in any way to a person or thing. By union with a preceding stem vowel we have αιο, ειο, οιο, ῳο, υιο.

   Primary (rare): ἅγ-ιο-ς *sacred* (ἄγος expiation); with a comparative force: ἄλλος *other* (ἀλ-ι̯ο-ς *alius*), μέσος *middle* (μεθ-ι̯ο-ς *medius*, 113).

   Secondary in τίμ-ιο-ς *worthy, costly* (τῑμή *honour*); φίλ-ιο-ς *friendly* (φίλο-ς *dear*); ὄρθ-ιο-ς *steep* (ὀρθό-ς *straight*); πλούσ-ιο-ς *rich* (πλοῦτο-ς *riches*, 115); δίκα-ιο-ς *just* (δίκ-η *right*, 834 b); οἰκε-ῖο-ς *domestic* (οἶκο-ς *house*, 834 f); πάτρ-ιο-ς *hereditary* (πατήρ *father*, πατρ-, 262); βασίλε-ιο-ς *royal* (βασιλεύ-ς *king*); θέρε-ιο-ς *of summer* (θέρος, stem θερεσ-); αἰδο-ῖο-ς *venerable* (αἰδώς *shame*, stem αἰδοσ-, 266); ἡρῷος *heroic* (ἥρως *hero*, ἡρωϝ-, 267); πήχυ-ιο-ς *a cubit long* (πῆχυ-ς, 268). The feminines are often abstract substantives, as φιλ-ίᾱ *friendship*.

   a. The ending -αῖος has been transferred from ᾱ stems, as in χερσ-αῖο-ς *of* or *from dry land* (χέρσ-ος). The form ι-αῖος occurs: δραχμ-ιαῖο-ς *worth a drachma* (δραχμή). -εῖος has become independent in ἀνδρ-εῖος *manly* (ἀνήρ). On gentiles in -ιος, see 844. 3.

   b. Ionic **η-ϊο** (nom. -ήϊος), properly from stems in ευ (ηυ), as Hom. χαλκή-ϊο-ς *brazen* (pertaining to a χαλκεύ-ς *brazier;* Attic χάλκεος, -οῦς, see 858. 4), βασιλή-ϊο-ς *royal;* and transferred in Ionic to other stems, as in πολεμή-ϊο-ς *warlike*, ἀνθρωπ-ήϊο-ς *human* (Attic ἀνθρώπειο-ς), ἀνδρ-ήϊο-ς *manly.*

3. **εντ** for ϝεντ (nom. -εις) forms denominative adjectives denoting *fulness* or *abundance* (mostly poetic).

   τῑμή-εις (τῑμῆς) *honoured*, and by analogy δενδρ-ήεις *woody* (δένδρο-ν *tree*); χαρί-εις *graceful* (χάρι-ς), δολό-εις *wily* (δόλο-ς), and by analogy αἱματ-ό-εις *bloody* (αἷμα, -ατ-ος *blood*, 834 j), ἰχθυ-ό-εις *full of fish*, κρυ-ό-εις *chilling* (κρύ-ος *chill*). Also in εὐρώ-εις *mouldy* (εὐρώς, -ῶτος).

4. **εο** (nom. -εο-ς, -οῦς, 290) forms denominative adjectives denoting *material:* χρύσεος, χρῡσοῦς *golden* (χρῡσό-ς *gold*).

a. *εο* is derived from *ε-ϳο*, seen in *χρύσειος* (poetic). Here *ε* is part of the stem (834 f). On -*ηϊος* see 858. 2 b.

5. **εσ** (nom. -*ής*, -*ές*): primitive: *ψευδ-ής false* (*ψεύδ-ω deceive*), *σαφ-ής clear*, *πρην-ής prone*, *ὑγι-ής healthy*. Very common in compounds, as *ἀ-σφαλ-ής unharmed, secure* (*ἀ*-priv. + *σφαλ*- in *σφάλλω trip*).

6. **κο, ακο, ικο** (nom. -*κος*, very common, cp. 864. 1): many denominatives formed by these suffixes denote *relation*, many others *fitness* or *ability*.

a. Denominatives: *μαντι-κό-ς prophetic* (*μάντι-ς prophet*); *φυσι-κό-ς natural* (*φύσι-ς nature*); *θηλυ-κό-ς feminine* (*θῆλυ-ς female*); *Δᾱρει-κό-ς Daric* (*Δᾱρεῖο-ς Darius*).

b. From *φυσι-κό-ς*, etc., *ικο* was taken as an independent suffix in *μουσ-ικό-ς musical* (*μοῦσα muse*); *βαρβαρ-ικό-ς barbaric* (*βάρβαρο-ς barbarian, foreigner*); *διδασκαλ-ικό-ς able to teach* (*διδάσκαλο-ς teacher*); *μαθηματ-ικό-ς fond of learning* (*μάθημα, -ματος thing learnt*); *Κεραμε-ικό-ς Potters' quarter, Ceramīcus* (*κεραμεύ-ς potter*); *βασιλ-ικό-ς royal* (*βασιλεύ-ς king*); *ἡρω-ϊκό-ς heroic*, from *ἥρω(ϝ),-ος hero*; *Ἀχαι-ικό-ς* or *Ἀχᾱ-ικό-ς* (38) *Achaean* (*Ἀχαιό-ς Achaean*).

N. — *ἀρχ-ικό-ς able to rule* (*ἀρχ-ή*), *γραφ-ικό-ς able to write* or *draw* (*γραφ-ή*), need not be derived directly from the root.

c. *Κορινθι-ακό-ς Corinthian* (*Κορίνθ-ιο-ς Corinthian*); *σπονδει-ακό-ς consisting of spondees* (*σπονδ-εῖο-ς spondee*).

d. **τ-ικό** represents *ικό* added to the verbal in *τό*- (cp. also *μαθηματ-ικό-ς*). Thus, *λεκ-τικό-ς suited to speaking* (*λέγ-ω speak*); *αἰσθη-τικό-ς capable of feeling* (*αἰσθ-άνομαι feel*); *ἀριθμη-τικό-ς skilled in numbering* (*ἀριθ-μέω to number*); *πρᾱκ-τικό-ς practical, able to do* (*πράττω do*); *σκεπ-τικό-ς reflective* (*σκέπ-τ-ομαι look carefully, consider*). Added to a noun-stem: *ναυ-τικό-ς nautical* (*ναῦ-ς ship*).

7. **λο** (nom. -*λο-ς*): primary (usually active) and secondary. Cp. 860. 1. Primary in *δει-λό-ς cowardly* (*δέδοι-κα fear, δι-, δει-, δοι-*); *στρεβ-λό-ς twisted* (*στρέφ-ω turn*); *τυφ-λό-ς blind* (*τύφ-ω raise a smoke*); *κοῖλος hollow* (= *κοϝ-ιλο-ς*, Lat. *cav-us*); *τροχ-αλό-ς running* (*τρέχ-ω run*); *εἴκ-ελο-ς like* (*ἔοικα am like, εικ-*); *καμπ-ύλο-ς bent* (*κάμπ-τ-ω bend*); *φειδ-ωλό-ς sparing* (*φείδ-ομαι spare*). *ἀπατ-η-λός deceitful* (*ἀπάτη deceit, ἀπατά-ω deceive*) may be a primitive or a denominative. Cp. 860. 1.

α-λεο denoting *quality* in *ἁρπ-αλέο-ς attractive, ravishing* (*ἁρπάζω seize*), *θαρσ-αλέο-ς bold* (*θάρσ-ος boldness*).

8. **μο** (nom. -*μο-ς*, 861. 1): primary: *θερ-μό-ς warm* (*θέρ-ω warm*); secondary in *ἕβδ-ο-μο-ς seventh*.

9. **ι-μο, σ-ιμο** (nom. -*ιμο-ς*, -*σιμο-ς*): often denoting *able to* or *fit to*. Adjectives in *ιμο* are primitive or denominative, and are derived from *ι*-stems; those in -*σιμο* are denominative and come mostly from stems in *σι* + *μο* (as *χρή-σι-μο-ς useful*, from *χρῆ-σι-ς use*); but *σιμο* has thence been abstracted as an independent suffix.

δόκ-ιμο-ς approved (*δοκ-έ-ω seem good*); *μάχ-ιμο-ς warlike* (*μάχη battle*); *νόμ-ιμο-ς conformable to law* (*νόμο-ς*); *ἐδ-ώδ-ιμο-ς eatable* (*ἐδ-ωδ-ή food*, poet. *ἔδ-ω eat*); *καύσι-μο-ς combustible* (*κάω burn, καῦ-σι-ς burn-*

ing); λύσι-μο-ς *able to loose* (λύ-σι-ς *loosing*); ἱππά-σιμο-ς *fit for riding* (ἱππάζομαι *ride*); ἁλώ-σιμο-ς *easy to take* (ἁλίσκομαι, ἑάλων).

10. **μον** (nom. -μων, -μον): primary in μνή-μων *mindful* (μι-μνῄ-σκομαι *remember*), τλή-μων *enduring, wretched* (ἔ-τλη-ν *endured*). Cp. 861. 8.

11. **νο** (nom. -νο-ς, 861. 11): primary (usually passive) and secondary (829 a). Sometimes denoting that which *may*, *can*, or *must be done*.

Primary in δει-νό-ς *fearful* (δέ-δοι-κα *fear*, δι-, δει-, δοι-); σεμ-νό-ς *to be revered* (σέβ-ομαι *revere*); πιθ-ανό-ς *persuasive* (πείθ-ω *persuade*, πιθ-, πειθ-, ποιθ-); πίσ-υνο-ς *trusting* (πείθ-ω). Secondary in σκοτει-νό-ς *dark* (= σκοτεσ-νο-ς from σκότ-ος *darkness*).

12. **ινο** (nom. -ινο-ς, 861. 11): forms denominative adjectives of *material*, as λίθ-ινο-ς *of stone* (λίθο-ς), ξύλ-ινο-ς *wooden* (ξύλο-ν); to denote *time*, and derived from such forms as ἐαρι-νό-ς *vernal* (ἔαρ *spring*), as in ἡμερ-ινό-ς *by day* (ἡμέρᾱ), χθεσ-ινό-ς *of yesterday* (χθές); other uses: ἀνθρώπ-ινο-ς *human* (ἄνθρωπο-ς *man*), ἀληθ-ινό-ς *genuine* (ἀληθής *true*).

ινεο in λα-ΐνεο-ς = λά-ϊνο-ς *stony* (λᾶς *stone*). On -ηνος, -ῑνος in gentiles, see 844. 3.

13. **ρο, ρᾱ** (nom. -ρό-ς, -ρά): primary, and secondary. Primary, in ἐχθ-ρό-ς *hated, hostile* (ἔχθ-ω *hate*), λαμπ-ρό-ς *shining* (λάμπ-ω *shine*), χαλα-ρό-ς *slack* (χαλά-ω *slacken*). Secondary, in φοβε-ρό-ς *fearful* (φόβο-ς *fear*, φοβ%ε-, 834 f), κρατ-ερό-ς *mighty* (κράτ-ος *might*); primary or secondary in ἀνιᾱ-ρό-ς *grievous* (ἀνίᾱ *grief*, ἀνιά-ω *grieve*). See 860. 3.

14. **τηρ-ιο** (nom. -τήριο-ς): in denominatives, derived from substantives in -τηρ (or -της) by the suffix ιο; but the substantive is not always found.

σω-τήρ-ιο-ς *preserving* (σω-τήρ *saviour*), whence the abstract σωτηρίᾱ (858. 2) *safety*; θελκ-τήρ-ιο-ς *enchanting* (θελκ-τήρ *charmer*, θέλγ-ω *enchant*), whence θελκτήριον (842. 4), λυ-τήρ-ιο-ς *delivering* (λυ-τήρ), ὁρμητήριον *starting-place* (ὁρμάω, ὁρμῶμαι *start*).

15. **υ** (nom. -ύ-ς, -εῖα, -ύ): primitives are ἡδύ-ς *sweet* (ἥδ-ομαι *am pleased*), ταχ-ύ-ς *swift* (τάχ-ος *swiftness*), βαθ-ύ-ς *deep* (βάθ-ος *depth*). Cp. 859. 8.

16. **ωδεσ** (nom. -ώδης, -ῶδες): in primitives (rare), as πρεπ-ώδης *proper* (πρέπ-ω *beseem*); usually in denominatives denoting *fulness* or *similarity*: ποι-ώδης *grassy* (ποίᾱ), αἱματ-ώδης *looking like blood* (αἷμα). See 833 a.

17. Suffixes of Degree: **ῑον** and **ιστο** (318) usually form primitives; **τερο** and **τατο** (313 ff.), denominatives. τερο occurs also in πό-τερο-ς *which of two?* πρό-τερο-ς *earlier*, ὕσ-τερο-ς *later*, ἑκά-τερο-ς *each*. On the suffix τερο apparently without comparative force, see 1066, 1082 b. ἔν-τερο-ν is substantivized (*bowel*); from ἐν *in*.

18 Suffixes of Participles and Verbal Adjectives (primary): active ντ, οτ, 301 a, c; middle and passive μενο. Verbal adjectives denoting completion (usually passive) το; possibility and necessity το, τεο (471–473).

On the formation of Adverbs, see 341 ff.

LIST OF NOUN SUFFIXES

The list includes the chief suffixes used in substantives and adjectives. Separation of a suffix from the root is often arbitrary and uncertain.

859. **VOWEL SUFFIXES**

1. **ο**: nom. -ο-ς masc., fem., -ο-ν neut. A common suffix in primitives denoting persons (usually male agents) or things (often abstracts).

   ἀρχ-ό-ς *leader* from ἄρχ-ω *lead;* ζυγ-ό-ν *yoke* from ζεύγ-νῡ-μι *yoke* (ζυγ-, ζευγ-); λόγ-ο-ς *speech* from λέγ-ω *speak;* νόμ-ο-ς *custom, law* from νέμ-ω *distribute;* στόλ-ο-ς *expedition* from στέλλω (στελ-) *send;* τροφ-ό-ς (ὁ, ἡ) *nurse* from τρέφ-ω *nourish;* φόρ-ο-ς *tribute* from φέρ-ω *bear, bring.*

   a. The roots of some words appear only in other languages: οἶκ-ο-ς *house*, Lat. *vīc-u-s.*

   b. The suffix has the accent when the agent is denoted. ε of the root varies with ο (831 b).

2. **ᾱ**: nom. -ᾱ or -η fem. A common suffix in primitives, usually to denote things, often abstracts (*action*).

   ἀρχ-ή *beginning* from ἄρχ-ω *begin;* λοιβ-ή *pouring* from λείβ-ω *pour;* μάχ-η *fight* from μάχ-ομαι *fight;* σπουδ-ή *haste* from σπεύδ-ω *hasten;* στέγ-η *roof* from στέγ-ω *shelter;* τροφ-ή *nourishment* from τρέφ-ω *nourish;* τύχ-η *chance* from τυγχάνω *happen* (τυχ-); φορ-ά *crop* from φέρ-ω *bear;* φυγ-ή *flight* from φεύγω *flee* (φυγ-, φευγ-).

   a. The roots of some words appear only in other languages: γυν-ή *woman* (Eng. *queen*).

   b. Most substantives accent the suffix; but many accent the penult.

3. **ᾱ**: nom. -ᾱς, -ης, in a few masculines, usually compounds: παιδο-τρίβ-η-ς *trainer of boys in gymnastics* (τρίβω *rub*).

4. **ῐ, ῑ**: primary, in ὄφ-ι-ς *snake*, poet. τρόχ-ι-ς *runner* (τρέχ-ω *run*), πόλ-ι-ς *city* (originally πόλ-ῑ-ς), ἦν-ῑ-ς *yearling.* Many words with the ι-suffix have taken on δ or τ; as ἐλπ-ί-ς *hope* ἐλπί-δ-ος (ἔλπ-ομαι *hope*), χάρ-ι-ς *grace* χάρι-τ-ος (χαίρω *rejoice*, χαρ-).

5. **ιο**: in a few primitive verbal adjectives (ἅγ-ιο-ς 858. 2), but common in denominate adjectives (858. 2), rare in substantives: νυμφ-ίο-ς *bridegroom* (νύμφη *bride*); in names of things more concrete than those ending in -ιᾱ: μαρτύρ-ιο-ν *a testimony* (cp. μαρτύρ-ιᾱ *testimony*); in gentiles (844. 3); in diminutives (852. 1), often in combination with other diminutive suffixes (αριο, ιδιο, υλλιο, etc. 852); often in combination with a final stem vowel (851. 1, 858. 2).

6. **ιᾰ, ιᾱ**: rarely primary, in φύζα *flight* (φεύγ-ω *flee*); in verbal abstracts: μανίᾱ *madness* (840 a. 9); usually secondary in the fem. of adj. in -ύς: βαρεῖα = βαρεῡ-ια, πίττα *pitch* (= πικ-ι̯α, cp. Lat. *pic-us*), γλῶττα *tongue* = γλωχ-ι̯α (cp. γλωχ-ί-ς *point*, γλῶχ-ες *beards of corn*), θῆττα *serf* (843 b. 4); in the nom. fem. of participles in ντ, οτ (λύουσα from λῡοντ-ι̯α, λελυκυ-ῖα); in denominative abstracts expressing quality (840 b. 1, 2); in names of persons: ταμ-ίᾱ-ς *steward* (τέμ-ν-ω *cut*, ἔ-ταμ-ον), Νῑκ-ίᾱ-ς *Nicias* (νίκη *victory*). — Often in combination with other suffixes: αινα 843 b. 5; -ε-ια 840 a. 9; ισσα 843 b. 4; τρια, τειρᾱ 839 b. 2, 3.

7. **ϝο, ϝᾱ**: primary, in ὅρος for ὅρ(ϝ)ος *boundary*, κεν(ϝ)ός *empty*, λαι(ϝ)ός *left* (Lat. *laevus*), καλ(ϝ)ός *beautiful;* (probably) secondary in verbals in -τέος (λυτέος *that must be loosed*) and in adj. in -αλέος (860. 1).

8. **υ (ευ)** : primary, in adjectives (858. 15), in substantives : *γέν-υ-ς chin*, *πῆχ-υ-ς fore-arm.* — 9. **ῡ** : primary, in feminines : *ἰσχ-ύ-ς strength*, *ὀφρ-ῦ-ς eye-brow*, *νέκ-ῡ-ς* (Hom.) *corpse*, cf. Lat. *nec-are.* — 10. **ευ (ηυ)** : primary of the agent (839 a. 5) ; rarely of things : *κοπ-εύ-ς chisel* (*κόπ-τ-ω cut*) ; secondary, of the person concerned (843 a. 1), in gentiles (844. 1), rarely of things : *δονακ-εύ-ς reed-thicket* (*δόναξ reed*) ; in diminutives in *-ιδεύς* (853). — 11. **οι** (nom. *-ώ*): primary in *πειθ-ώ πειθοῦς persuasion* (279). — 12. **ωϝ** (nom. *-ως*) : primary in *ἥρ-ως ἥρω-ος hero* (267).

860. SUFFIXES WITH LIQUIDS (λ, ρ)

1. **λο, λᾱ** : primary, in *φῦ-λο-ν race*, *φῡ-λή clan* (*φύ-ω produce*), *πῖ-λο-ς felt* (Lat. *pi-lu-s*), *ζεύγ-λη loop of a yoke* (*ζεύγ-νῡ-μι yoke*); *ἆθ-λο-ς contest*, *ἆθ-λο-ν prize*, *τυφ-λό-ς blind* (*τύφ-ω raise a smoke*), *στρεβ-λό-ς twisted* (*στρέφ-ω turn*). Cp. 858. 7. Secondary, in *παχυ-λό-ς thickish* (dimin.). **αλο, αλᾱ** : primary, in *ὀμφ-αλό-ς navel*, *κρότ-αλο-ν clapper* (*κρότ-ο-ς noise*), *κεφ-αλή head*, *τροχ-αλό-ς running* (*τρέχ-ω*), *πῖ-αλο-ς fat* (*πῑαίνω fatten*) ; secondary, in *ὁμ-αλό-ς level* (*ὁμό-ς one and the same*). Developed from this are **αλεο, αλεᾱ** : *πῑ-αλέο-ς fat*, *κερδ-αλέο-ς wily* (*κέρδ-ος gain*), see 858. 7. **ελο, ελᾱ** : primary (prob.), in *εἴκ-ελο-ς like* (*ἔοικα am like*, *εικ-*), *νεφ-έλη cloud* (Lat. *nebula*) ; secondary, in *θυ-μέ-λη altar.* **ηλο, ηλᾱ** : *κάπ-ηλο-ς huckster* (agency), *θυ-ηλή sacrifice* (*θύ-ω*), *ὑψ-ηλό-ς lofty* (*ὕψ-ος height*); primary or secondary : *ἀπατ-η-λό-ς guileful* (*ἀπάτη guile*, *ἀπατά-ω cheat*), *σῑγ-ηλό-ς mute* (*σῑγή silence*, *σῑγά-ω am mute*). **ιλο, ιλᾱ** : primary, in *τροχ-ίλο-ς sandpiper* (*τρέχ-ω run*) ; secondary, in *ὀργ-ίλο-ς passionate* (*ὀργή*). **ῑλο, ῑλα** : primary, in *στρόβ-ῑλο-ς top* (*στρέφ-ω turn*) ; secondary, in *πέδ-ῑλο-ν sandal* (*πέδ-η fetter*, *πούς foot*). **υλο, υλᾱ** : primary, in *δάκτ-υλο-ς finger*, *σταφ-υλή bunch of grapes.* Secondary, in *μῑκκ-ύλο-ς small* (*μῑκκ-ό-ς*). **ῡλο, ῡλᾱ** : *σφονδ-ύλη beetle.* **ωλο, ωλᾱ** : primary, in *εἴδ-ωλο-ν image* (*εἴδ-ομαι resemble*), *εὐχ-ωλή prayer* (*εὔχ-ομαι*). Rare forms : **αλιο, αλιμο, ελιο, ηλιο.**
2. **λυ** : primary, in *θῆ-λυ-ς female* (root *θη give suck*).
3. **ρο, ρᾱ**: primary, in substantives : *ἀγ-ρό-ς field*, Lat. *ager* (*ἄγ-ω*), *νεκ-ρό-ς corpse* (cp. *νέκ-ῡ-ς*), *γαμ-β-ρό-ς son-in-law* (*γαμ-έ-ω marry*, for *β* see 130), *ἐχθ-ρό-ς enemy*, *ἔχθ-ρᾱ hatred* (*ἔχθ-ω hate*), *ἄργυ-ρο-ς silver*, *ὕδ-ρᾱ hydra* (*ὕδ-ωρ water*); rarely, of instrument 842. 6 ; of place, in *ἕδ-ρᾱ seat* ; primary, in adjectives (858. 13). **αρο, αρᾱ** : primary, in *βλέφ-αρο-ν eye-lid* (*βλέπ-ω look*), *τάλ-αρο-ς basket* (*τλάω*, *τλῆναι bear*), *λιπ-αρό-ς shiny* (cp. *λίπ-ος fat*). **ᾱρο (ηρο), ᾱρᾱ (ηρᾱ)** : primary or secondary, in *ἀνι-ᾱ-ρό-ς grievous* (*ἀνίᾱ grief*, *ἀνιά-ω grieve*), *λῡπ-η-ρό-ς painful* (*λύπη pain*, *λῡπέ-ω grieve*); secondary, in *ἀνθ-ηρό-ς flowery* (*ἄνθ-ος*), and perhaps in *πον-ηρό-ς toilsome* (*πόνο-ς*, *πονέ-ομαι toil*). **ερο, ερᾱ** : secondary, in *φοβε-ρό-ς terrible* (*φόβο-ς terror*), whence *σκι-ερό-ς shady* (*σκιά shade*); also in *πενθ-ερό-ς father-in-law* = lit. one who binds (cp. *πεῖσμα* = *πενθ-σμα cable*), *ἕν-εροι those below the earth* (*ἐν*). **υρο, υρᾱ** : secondary, in *λιγυ-ρό-ς* (*λιγύ-ς*) *shrill*, whence primary *ἄχ-υρο-ν chaff*, *φλεγ-υρό-ς burning* (*φλέγ-ω burn*). **ῡρο, ῡρᾱ** : primary or secondary, in *ἰσχῡ-ρό-ς strong* (*ἰσχύ-ω am strong*, *ἰσχύ-ς strength*); primary, in *λέπ-ῡρο-ν rind* (*λέπ-ω peel*), *γέφ-ῡρα bridge.* **ωρο, ωρᾱ** : primary, in *ὀπ-ώρᾱ late summer* (*ὄπ-ισθεν at the rear, after*).

4. **ρι** (rare): primary, in ἄκ-ρι-ς *hill-top* (ἄκ-ρο-ς *highest*), ἴδ-ρι-ς *knowing* (εἶδον, ἰδεῖν).
5. **ρυ** (rare): primary, in δάκ-ρυ *tear;* cp. Old Lat. *dacruma* for *lacrima.*
6. **αρ**: primary, in ἧπ-αρ, ἥπατ-ος *liver* (253 b), πῖ-αρ *fat*, ἔ-αρ *spring.* — 7. **ερ, ηρ**: primary, in ἀήρ ἀέρ-ος *air* (ἄημι *blow*, of the wind), αἰθ-ήρ, -έρ-ος *upper air* (αἴθ-ω *kindle*). — 8. **ωρ**: primary: gen. -ατ-ος: ὕδ-ωρ *water;* gen. -ωρος: ἰχώρ *ichor, serum;* gen. -ορος: by analogy in αὐτο-κράτ-ωρ *possessing full powers* (κράτ-ος *power*). — 9. **ωρᾱ**: primary, in πλη-θ-ώρη (Ionic) *satiety*, cp. 832.

861. SUFFIXES WITH NASALS (μ, ν)

1. **μο, μᾱ** (nom. μο-ς; -μᾰ and -μη): primary, in substantives denoting actions or abstract ideas (840 a. 5–7), and in some concretes: χῡ-μό-ς *juice* (χέω *pour*, χυ-), γραμ-μή *line* (γράφ-ω *write, draw*); in adjectives (858. 8, 9). On -τ-μο -τ-μα, -θ-μο -θ-μα, -σ-μο -σ-μα see 837, 832, 836; secondary, rarely in substantives: δρῡ-μό-ς *coppice* (δρῦ-ς *tree, oak*), or adjectives: ἔτυ-μο-ς *true* (ἐτεϝός *real*). — **ι-μο**: secondary, derived from ι stems (858. 9). — 2. **ματ** (nom. -μα): primary, denoting result (841. 2). Here to μα from μ̥ (cp. ὄνομα *name*, Lat. *nomen;* τέρμα *goal*, Lat. *termen*) τ has been added; cp. *cognomentum.* — 3. **μεν** (nom. -μην): primary, in ποι-μήν *shepherd*, λι-μήν *harbour.* — 4. **μενο**: primary, in participles: λῡό-μενο-ς. — 5. **μι** (rare): primary, in φῆ-μι-ς *speech* (poet. for φή-μη). — 6. **μιν** (nom. -μῖς): prim., ῥηγ-μῖ-ς *surf* (ῥήγ-νῡ-μι *break*). — 7. **μνο, μνᾱ**: prim., in στά-μνο-ς *jar* (ἵ-στη-μι *set, stand*, στα-), βέλε-μνο-ν *dart* (βάλλω *throw*), ποί-μνη *flock*, λί-μνη *lake.* — 8. **μον** (nom. -μων): primary, in ἡγε-μών *leader* (ἡγέ-ομαι *lead*); adjectives 858. 10. — 9. **μονᾱ**: primary, in πλη-σ-μονή *fulness* (πίμ-πλη-μι *fill*). — 10. **μων** (nom. -μων): primary, in χει-μών *winter*, λει-μών *meadow.*

11. **νο, νᾱ**: primary, in ὕπ-νο-ς *sleep*, καπ-νό-ς *smoke*, ποι-νή *punishment*, φερ-νή *dower* (φέρ-ω *bring*), τέκ-νο-ν *child* (τίκτω *bear*, τεκ-), in adjectives (858. 11); secondary, in adjectives (858. 11), in σελή-νη *moon* (= σελασ-νη, σέλας *gleam*). — **ανο, ανᾱ**: primary, in στέφ-ανο-ς *crown*, στεφ-άνη *diadem* (στέφ-ω *encircle*), δρέπ-ανο-ν, δρεπ-άνη *sickle* (δρέπ-ω *pluck*), ὄργ-ανο-ν *instrument* (ἔργον *work*), θηγ-άνη *whetstone* (θήγ-ω *whet*); in adjectives: στεγ-ανό-ς (cp. στεγ-νός) *water-tight* (στέγ-ω *shelter*); secondary, in βο-τ-άνη *fodder* (βο-τό-ς, βό-σκω *graze*), ἕδρ-ανο-ν *seat* (ἕδ-ρᾱ *seat*). **ᾱνο** (**ηνο**), **ᾱνᾱ** (**ηνᾱ**): secondary, in gentiles (844. 3). **ενο, ενᾱ**: primary, in παρθ-ένο-ς *maiden*, ὠλ-ένη *elbow.* **ηνο, ηνᾱ**: primary, in τι-θή-νη *nurse* (θῆσθαι *give suck*). **ινο, ινᾱ**: secondary, in adjectives of material and time (858. 12), and in ῥαδ-ινό-ς *slender*, μελ-ίνη *millet.* **ινεο, ινεᾱ**: secondary, in adjectives of material (858. 12). **ῑνο, ῑνα**: primary, in χαλ-ῑνό-ς *bridle*, σέλ-ῑνο-ν *parsley;* secondary, in gentiles (844. 3); in patronymics (845. 6); in ἐρυθρ-ῖνο-ς *red mullet* (ἐρυθρό-ς *red*); βολβ-ίνη a kind of βολβ-ός (a *bulb-root*). **ονο, ονᾱ**: primary, in κλ-όνο-ς *battle-rout* (κέλ-ομαι *urge on*); in abstracts, as ἡδ-ονή *pleasure* (ἥδ-ομαι *am pleased*). **υνο, υνᾱ**: primary, in κορ-ύνη *club*, πίσ-υνο-ς *relying on* (πείθ-ω *persuade*). **ῡνο, ῡνᾱ**: primary, in κίνδ-ῡνο-ς *danger*, αἰσχ-ύνη *disgrace.* **ωνο, ωνᾱ**: primary, in κολ-ωνό-ς *hill*, κορ-ώνη *crow.* — 12. **νυ** (rare): primary, in λιγ-νύ-ς *smoky fire.*

13. **αινα**: secondary, of the person concerned (843 b. 5). — 14. **αν**: primary, in μέλᾱς μέλαν-ος *black*. — 15. **εν** (nom. -ην): primary, in τέρ-ην *tender*, ἄρρ-ην *male*. — 16. **ην**: primary, in πευθ-ήν *inquirer* (πεύθ-ομαι, πυνθάνομαι *inquire*). — 17. **ῑν** (nom. -ῑς): primary, in δελφίς *dolphin*, ὠδίς *travail*. — 18. **ον** (nom. -ων): primary, in words of agency: τέκτ-ων *carpenter*, τρῡγ-ών *turtle-dove* (τρύζω *murmur*, τρυγ-), κλύδ-ων *wave* (κλύζω *dash*, κλυδ-); and in others, as εἰκ-ών *image* (ἔοικα *am like*, εἰκ-), χι-ών *snow*. — 19. **ιον**: secondary, in μαλακ-ίων *darling*, diminutive of μαλακό-ς *soft*. — **ῑον**: primary, in comparatives; ἡδ-ίων *sweeter* (ἡδ-ύ-ς); secondary, in patronymics (845. 5). — **ϝον**: primary, in πίων *fat*. — 20. **ων**: secondary, in words denoting persons possessing some physical or mental quality, as γάστρ-ων *glutton* (γαστήρ *belly*); to denote place (851. 3); in names of months: Ἀνθεστηριών. — 21. **ϝων**: primary, in αἰ(ϝ)ών *age*, gen. αἰῶν-ος. — 22. **ιων**: secondary, in patronymics (845. 5). — 23. **ιωνᾱ**: secondary, in patronymics (845. 6).

862. SUFFIXES WITH LABIALS (π, φ)

1. **οπ**: primary, in σκόλ-οψ *stake, pale* (σκάλλω *stir up; split ?*). — 2. **ωπ**: primary, in κών-ωψ *gnat*. — 3. **φο, φᾱ** (rare): primary, in κρότ-αφοι *the temples*, κορυ-φή *head* (κόρυς *helmet*); usually in names of animals, as ἔρ-ιφο-ς *kid*, ἔλαφος *deer*; secondary, in late diminutives: θηρ-άφιο-ν *insect* (θήρ *beast*), κερδ-ύφιο-ν *petty gain* (κέρδ-ος *gain*).

863. SUFFIXES WITH DENTALS (τ, δ, θ)

a. Suffixes with τ.

1. **τ**: primary, at the end of stems, as ἀ-γνώς, ἀ-γνῶ-τ-ος *unknown* (γι-γνώ-σκω *know*).

2. **το, τᾱ**: primary, in verbal adjectives in -τό-ς (471) with the force of a perfect participle, as γνω-τό-ς *known* (γι-γνώ-σκω *know*), στα-τό-ς *placed, standing* (ἵ-στη-μι *set, place*), or with the idea of possibility, as λυ-τό-ς *able to be loosed*; in verbal abstracts, which sometimes become concrete: κοῖ-το-ς, κοί-τη *bed* (κεῖ-μαι *lie*), βρον-τή *thunder* (βρέμ-ω *roar*), φυ-τό-ν *plant* (φύω *produce*), πο-τό-ν *drink* (πίνω *drink*, πο- 529), βιο-τός, βιο-τή *life, means of living* (βίο-ς *life*); in numerals, τρί-το-ς *third*, ἕκ-το-ς *sex-tu-s*. — In superlatives, **ισ-το** primary, as ἥδ-ιστο-ς *sweetest* (ἡδ-ύ-ς); **τατο**, secondary, as ἀληθέσ-τατο-ς *most true* (ἀληθής). — **τᾱ** (nom. -τη-ς): primary, to denote the agent (839 a. 1); secondary, to denote the person concerned (843 a. 2). — **ατο, ατᾱ**: primary, in θάν-ατο-ς *death* (θνῄ-σκω, θαν-εῖν *die*), κάμ-ατο-ς *weariness* (κάμ-νω, καμ-εῖν *am weary*). **ετο, ετᾱ**: primary, in παγ-ετό-ς *frost* (πήγ-νῡ-μι *make hard*); secondary, in εὐν-έτη-ς *bed-fellow* (εὐνή *bed*, 843 a. N.). **ᾱτᾱ ᾱτιδ, ητᾱ ητιδ, ῑτᾱ ῑτιδ, ωτᾱ ωτιδ**, in gentiles (844. 2).

3. **τᾱτ (τητ)**: secondary, in substs. denoting quality (840 b. 4). — 4. **τεϝο**: primary, in verbal adjectives (473). — 5. **τειρᾱ**: primary, of the agent (839 b. 3). — 6. **τερο**: secondary, in comparatives (313); substantivized in ἔν-τερο-ν *bowel*. — 7. **τηρ**: primary, to denote the agent (839 a. 2), often regarded as the instrument: ῥαιστήρ *hammer* (838 a), ἀρυ-τήρ

ladle. — 8. **τηρ-ιο**: compound suffix, of place (851. 2), of means (842. 4), of wages (842. 5): *θρεπ-τήρια reward for rearing* (*τρέφ-ω*); in adjectives, 858. 14. — 9. **τι**: primary, to denote action or an abstract idea (840 a. 1); rarely, of persons: *μάν-τι-ς seer* (*μαίν-ομαι rage, am inspired, μαν-*). — 10. **τιδ**: primary, of the agent (839 b. 4). — 11. **τορ**: primary, of the agent (839 a. 3). — 12. **τρᾱ**: primary, of instrument or means (842. 3); of place (851. 6). — 13. **τριᾱ** (nom. *-τρια*): primary, of the agent (839 b. 2). — 14. **τριδ** (nom. *-τρίς*): primary, of the agent (839 b. 1). — 15. **τριο**: secondary, in *ἀλλό-τρ-ιο-ς belonging to another.* — 16. **τρο** (*-τρο-ς, -τρο-ν*): primary, to denote the agent (839 a. 4), instrument (842. 1), place, as *θέᾱ-τρο-ν theatre* (*place for seeing*), *λέκ-τρο-ν bed.* — 17. **τυ**: primary, of actions or abstract ideas (840 a. 4); in *ἄσ-τυ city*, *φῖ-τυ sprout* (*φύ-ω produce*); secondary, denoting connection with a numeral: *τριτ-τύ-ς third of a tribe* (*τρί-το-ς third*).

18. **ᾰτ**: primary, in *κέρᾱς, κέρᾱτ-ος* (and *κέρως*, 258) *horn.* — 19. **ητ**: primary, in *πένης, -ητ-ος serf* (*πέν-ομαι toil*), *πλάν-ητ-ες planets* (*πλανά-ω wander*). — 20. **ιτ**: primary, in *μέλι, -ιτ-ος honey* (Lat. *mel*), *χάρ-ις grace* (*χαίρω rejoice, χαρ-*). See 859. 4. — 21. **ῑτιδ** (nom. *-ῖτις*, fem.): secondary in words denoting place (851. 4). — 22. **ωτ**: primary, in *γέλως, -ωτος laughter* (*γελά-ω* laugh). — 23. **ντ**: primary, in active participles (except the perfect), as *λύο-ντ-ος*; in some adjectives inflected like participles (*ἑκών willing*), and in participial substantives: *δράκ-ων serpent* (*δέρκ-ομαι gleam, δρακ-εῖν*), also in *λέων lion*, *ἀδάμᾱς adamant.* — 24. **ϝεντ** (nom. *-εις*): secondary, in adjectives denoting *fulness* (858. 3), and in some proper names of places: *Ὀποῦς Opus* from *Ὀπο-ϝεντ-ς* (844. 3).

b. Suffixes with **δ**.

1. **δ**: secondary, in patronymics (845. 1). — 2. **δ-ανο**: secondary, in *οὐτι-δανό-ς a nobody* (*οὔτις nobody*), properly from *τιδ*, neuter of *τί*, + *ανό-ς*. — **ε-δανο**: primary, in *ῥῑγ-ε-δανό-ς chilling* (*ῥῑγ-έω shudder*). — 3. **δ-απο**: secondary, in *ἀλλοδαπός foreign*, properly = *ἀλλοδ*, neuter of *ἄλλος* (cp. *aliud*), + *από-ς*. — 4. **δ-ᾱ**: secondary, in patronymics (845. 1). — 5. **δ-ιο**: *στά-δ-ιο-ς standing* (*ἵ-στη-μι*), with *δ* prob. from a word containing the suffix *δ*, as *ἀμ-φάδιο-ς public* from *ἀμ-φαδό-ν publicly.* — 6. **δων**: primary, in *μελ-ε-δών care* (*μέλει is a care*), *ἀλγ-η-δών pain* (*ἀλγέ-ω suffer*); secondary, in *κοτυληδών a cup-shaped hollow* (*κοτύλη cup*); cp. *ἀχθ-η-δών distress* (*ἄχθ-ος burden*). — 7. **δωνᾱ**: primary, in *μελ-ε-δώνη care* (see *δων*).

8. **αδ**: primary, in *νιφ-άς, -άδ-ος snow-flake* (*νίφ-ω*, better *νείφ-ω, snow*), *φυγ-άς exile* (*φεύγ-ω flee, φυγ-*), *λαμπ-άς torch* (*λάμπ-ω shine*); secondary, in abstract feminines denoting number (840 b. 5). — 9. **ιαδ**, 10. **ιαδᾱ**: secondary, in patronymics (845. 3). — 11. **αδιο**: secondary, in *κατ-ωμ-άδιο-ς from the shoulder* (*ὦμο-ς*), derived from *διχθ-άδ-ιο-ς divided* (*διχθάς, -άδος divided*). — 12. **ιδ**: primary, in *ἀσπ-ίς, -ίδ-ος shield*, *ἐλπ-ίς hope* (*ἔλπομαι hope*); secondary, in adj. as *συμμαχίς allied* (*πόλις*) from *σύμμαχο-ς allied with;* in words denoting the person concerned (843 b. 2); in gentiles (844. 1), as *Περσίς Persian woman;* in feminine patronymics (845. 4). — 13. **ιδᾱ**: secondary, in patronymics

(845. 4).—14. **ιδεο**: secondary, in names of relationship (850).—15. **ιδευ**: secondary, in diminutives (853).—16. **ιδιο**: secondary, in diminutives (852. 2), and transferred in *μοιρ-ίδιο-ς doomed* (*μοῖρα doom*).—17. **ῑδ**: secondary, in *κνημίς greave* (*κνήμη leg, thigh*).—18. **νδᾱ**: secondary, in patronymics (846, e).—19. **ωδεσ**: secondary, in adjectives of *fulness* (858. 16).

c. Suffixes with **θ**.

1. **θ** appears in suffixes that are obscure in relation to root or stem (832): *ὄρνῑς ὄρνῑθ-ος bird, ψάμαθος sand, κύαθος cup, πέλεθος ordure*; several in *-νθ* (probably not Greek), as *ἐρέβ-ινθος chick-pea*.—2. **θλο, θλᾱ**: primary, in *γέν-ε-θλο-ν, γεν-έ-θλη race* (*γίγ-νομαι become, γεν-*).—3. **θλιο**: secondary, in *γεν-έ-θλιο-ς belonging to one's birth*.—4. **θρο, θρα**: primary, in *ἄρ-θρο-ν joint* (*ἀραρίσκω join, ἀρ-*), *ἐπι-βά-θρᾱ ladder* (*βαίνω go, βα-*).

864. SUFFIXES WITH PALATALS (κ, γ, χ)

1. **κο, κᾱ**: primary (rare), in *θή-κη box* (*τί-θη-μι place*); secondary, in adjectives (858. 6).—**ακο** (rare): primary, in *μαλ-ακό-ς soft* (cp. Lat. *mollis*); secondary in adjectives (858. 6. c).—**ιακο**: secondary, in *κῡρ-ιακό-ς of the Lord*.—**ικο, ικᾱ**: secondary, in adjectives (858. 6), in gentiles (844. 3).—2. **σκο, σκᾱ**: primary, in *δίσκος quoit* (= *δικ* + *σκο-ς* from *δικ-εῖν throw*), *βο-σκή food* (cp. *βό-σκω feed*).—**ισκο**: secondary, in diminutives (852. 6).

3. **ακ**: primary, in *μεῖραξ lass, μειράκ-ιο-ν lad* dimin. 854, *κόλαξ flatterer*.—4. **ᾱκ**: primary, in *θώρᾱξ breast-plate*.—5. **ικ**: primary, in *κύλιξ cup, ἧλιξ comrade*.—6. **ῑκ**: primary, in *πέρδιξ, -ῑκος partridge*.—7. **ῡκ**: primary, in *κῆρυξ, -ῡκος herald*.

8. **αγ**: primary, in *ἅρπαξ rapacious, ἁρπαγ-ή seizure* (cp. *ἁρπάζω seize*).—9. **ῑγ**: primary, in *μάστιξ, -ῑγ-ος whip*.—10. **υγ**: primary, in *ἄντυξ, -υγος rim*.—11. **γγ**: primary, denoting something hollow, in *φάλαγξ phalanx, σάλπιγξ trumpet, λάρυγξ larynx*.

12. **ιχο**: secondary, in *ὀρτάλ-ιχο-ς chick*, dimin. (*ὀρταλί-ς chicken*).

865. SUFFIXES WITH SIGMA

1. **σι** (= *τι*): primary, denoting actions or abstract ideas (840 a. 2); rarely of persons: *πό-σι-ς husband*.—2. **σιᾱ**: primary, denoting actions or abstract ideas (840 a. 3).—3. **σιο**: primary, in *μετ-άρ-σιο-ς raised from the ground* (*μετ-αίρω lift up, ἀρ-*).—4. **σιμο**: in adj. (858. 9).—5. **στηνο**: in *δύ(σ)-στηνο-ς unhappy*.—6. **στο**: secondary, in *τριᾱκοστό-ς thirtieth* from *τριᾱ-κοντ* + *το-ς*.—7. **συνο, συνᾱ**: secondary, in adjectives: *δουλό-συνος enslaved* (*δοῦλο-ς*), *θάρσυνος bold* = *θαρσο-συνος* (*θάρσ-ος courage*, 129 c), and in the feminine, to make abstract substantives (840 b. 3).

8. **ασ**: primary, in *γέρ-ας prize*; varying with *ατ*, as in *τέρ-ας τέρατ-ος portent* (258), or with *εσ* (264 D. 3).—9. **εσ**: primary, denoting quality (840 a. 8) or result (841. 1) in adjectives (858. 5.)—10. **ισ**: primary, in *κόνις dust*, found in *κονίω* (= *κονισ-ιω*, 500. 2, D).—11. **ισσᾱ**: secondary, in words denoting the person concerned (843 b. 4).—12. **οσ**: primary, in *αἰδώς shame* (*αἰδοῦς* from *αἰδο(σ)-ος*, 266).—13. **ῑοσ**: primary, in comparatives (293 d, 318).

DENOMINATIVE VERBS

The formation of primitive verbs (372) is treated in **496–529, 607–624,** 722–743.

866. Denominative verbs are formed from the stems of nouns (substantives or adjectives). Verbs lacking such a noun-stem are made on the model of the ordinary denominative verb. The principal terminations are as follows:

1. -αω : derived chiefly from words with ᾱ stems (a few from words of the second declension). Verbs in -αω denote *to do*, *to be*, or *to have*, that which is expressed by the stem.

τῑμά-ω *honour* (τῑμή, stem τῑμᾱ-), ἀριστά-ω *breakfast* (ἄριστο-ν *breakfast*), τολμά-ω *dare* (τόλμα *daring*, stem τολμᾱ-), κομά-ω *wear long hair* (κόμη *hair*). κοιμά-ω, *lull to sleep*, has no primitive noun.

On -ιαω and -αω denoting a desire or a bodily condition, see 868 b.

2. -εω : derived chiefly from %ε- stems (834 f), and thence extended to all kinds of stems. Verbs in -εω denote a *condition* or an *activity*, and are often intransitive.

οἰκέ-ω *dwell* (οἶκο-ς *house*, οἰκ%ε-), φιλέ-ω *love* (φίλο-ς *dear*, φιλ%ε-), ὑπηρετέω *serve* (ὑπηρέτης *servant*, ὑπηρετᾱ-), εὐτυχ-έ-ω *am fortunate* (εὐτυχής *fortunate*, εὐτυχεσ-), μῑσ-έ-ω *hate* (μῖσος *hate*, μῑσεσ-), σωφρον-έ-ω *am temperate* (σώφρων), μαρτυρ-έ-ω *bear witness* (μάρτυς, -υρ-ος).

a. Some εω-verbs from εσ-stems have older forms in -είω (624 a).

3. -οω : chiefly derived from ο-stems. Verbs in -οω are usually factitive, denoting *to cause* or *to make*.

δηλό-ω *manifest, make clear* (δῆλο-ς), δουλό-ω *enslave* (δοῦλο-ς), ζηλό-ω *emulate* (ζῆλο-ς *emulation*), ζημιό-ω *punish* (ζημίᾱ *damage*), μαστῑγό-ω *whip* (μάστιξ, -ῑγος *whip*). ἀρόω *plough* has no primitive.

On the formation of the present stem of verbs in -αω, -εω, -οω, see 522.

4. -ευω : derived from substantives from ευ-stems (607) and thence extended to other stems. ευω-verbs usually denote a *condition*, sometimes an *activity*.

βασιλεύ-ω *am king, rule* (βασιλεύ-ς), βουλεύ-ω *counsel* (βουλή), κινδῡνεύ-ω *venture, incur danger* (κίνδῡνο-ς), παιδεύ-ω *educate* (παῖς *boy, girl*), θεραπεύ-ω *attend* (θεράπων *attendant*).

5. -ῡω (rare): from υ-stems, as δακρύ-ω *weep* (δάκρυ *tear*). Cp. 608.

6. -αζω, -ιζω : derived originally from stems in δ or γ (as ἐλπίζω *hope* = ἐλπιδ-ι̯ω, ἁρπάζω *seize* = ἁρπαγ-ι̯ω), and thence widely extended to other stems (cp. 623 δ, γ). Such verbs denote *action*.

γυμνάζω *exercise* (γυμνάς, -άδ-ος *stripped, naked*); ἀναγκάζω *compel* (ἀνάγκη *necessity*); ἀτῑμάζω *dishonour* (ἄτῑμος); βιάζομαι *use force* (βίᾱ *force*); θαυμάζω *wonder* (θαῦμα); φροντίζω *take care* (φροντίς); ὑβρίζω *insult* (ὕβρι-ς *outrage*); νομίζω *consider* (νόμο-ς *custom, law*); τειχίζω *fortify* (τεῖχ-ος *wall*, stem τειχεσ-); χαρίζομαι *do a favour* (χάρις, -ιτος *favour*).

a. Verbs in -ιζω **and** -ιαζω **derived from proper names express an adoption of** *language, manners, opinions,* or *politics:*

ἑλληνίζω *speak Greek* (Ἕλλην), βακχιάζω *act like a bacchante* (βακχιάς), λακωνίζω *imitate Laconian manners* (Λάκων), μηδίζω *side with the Medes* (Μῆδος).

b. Verbs in -εζω, -οζω, and -υζω are rare (πιέζω *press*, poet. δεσπόζω *am lord*, κοκκύζω *cry cuckoo*).

7. **-αινω**: originally from stems in -αν + ̯ιω (518), but usually extended to other stems. See 620, III.

μελαίνω *blacken* (μέλᾱς *black*, μελαν-), εὐφραίνω *gladden* (εὔφρων *glad*, εὐφρον-), σημαίνω *signify* (σῆμα, σήματ-ος *sign*), χαλεπαίνω *am angry* (χαλεπό-ς *hard, angry*).

8. **-ῡνω**: from stems in υν + ̯ιω (519). The primitive words often show stems in υ. See 620, III.

βαθύνω *deepen* (βαθύ-ς *deep*), ταχύνω *hasten* (ταχύ-ς *swift*), αἰσχύνω *disgrace* (αἶσχ-ος *shame*), θαρρύνω *encourage* (θάρρ-ος *courage*).

9. On other denominatives in λω, νω, ρω, see 620, III; on inceptives see 526–528.

10. Parallel formations are frequent, often with different meanings.

ἀριστάω *take a midday meal*, ἀριστίζω *give a midday meal;* ἀτιμάω, (poet.) ἀτῑμόω, ἀτῑμάζω *dishonour;* δουλόω *enslave*, δουλεύω *am a slave;* εὐδαιμονέω *am happy*, εὐδαιμονίζω *account happy, congratulate;* θαρρέω *am courageous*, θαρρύνω *encourage;* ὁρκόω, ὁρκίζω *make one swear an oath;* ὁρμάω *urge on*, ὁρμαίνω (poet.) *ponder;* ὁρμέω *lie at anchor*, ὁρμίζω *anchor* trans. (ὅρμος *anchorage*); πολεμέω (πολεμίζω Epic) *wage war*, πολεμόω *make hostile;* σκηνάω *put in shelter*, mid. *take up one's abode*, σκηνέω *am in camp*, σκηνόω *encamp, go into quarters;* σωφρονέω *am temperate*, σωφρονίζω *chasten;* τυραννέω, τυραννεύω *am absolute ruler*, τυραννίζω *take the part of absolute ruler*, τυραννιάω (late) *smack of tyranny*. Cp. 531.

867. Frequentatives and Intensives. — These are mostly poetical. **-αω** in στρωφάω *turn constantly* (στρέφω *turn*), τρωχάω *gallop* (τρέχω *run*), ποτάομαι, πωτάομαι, and ποτέομαι, *fly about* (πέτομαι *fly*). **-στρεω** in ἐλαστρέω *drive* (ἐλάω, ἐλαύνω). **-ταω** in σκιρτάω *spring* (σκαίρω *skip*). **-ταζω** in ἑλκυστάζω *drag about* (ἕλκω *drag*). With reduplication, often with change of the stem-vowel, in ποιπνύω *puff* (πνέω *breathe*, πνυ-), πορφύρω *gleam darkly* (φύρω *mix*), παμφαίνω *shine brightly* (φαίνω *bring to light, make appear*).

868. Desideratives express *desire*. Such verbs end in **-σειω, -ιαω,** and rarely in **-αω**. Thus, πολεμησείω *desire to wage war* (πολεμέω), ἀπαλλαξείω *wish to get rid of* (ἀλλάττω *exchange*), γελασείω *wish to laugh* (γελάω); στρατηγιάω *wish to be general* (στρατηγός); φονάω *wish to shed blood* (φόνος *murder*).

a. Verbs in -ιαω and -αω are formed from substantives. Those in -σειω may come from the future stem.

b. -ιαω and -αω may denote a bodily affection: ὀφθαλμιάω *suffer from ophthalmia* (ὀφθαλμίᾱ), βραγχάω *am hoarse* (βραγχός *hoarse*). Some verbs in -ωττω (-ωσσω) have a similar meaning: τυφλώττω *am blind* (τυφλός), and even λῑμώσσω *am hungry* (λῑμός *hunger*).

COMPOUND WORDS

869. A compound word is formed by the union of two or more parts; as λογο-γράφο-ς *speech-writer,* δι-έξ-οδο-ς *outlet* (lit. *way out through*).

a. Compounds of three or more parts usually fall into two separate units; as βατραχο-μῡο—μαχίᾱ *battle of the frogs-and-mice.* Such compounds are common in comedy; as στρεψο-δικο—παν-ουργίᾱ *rascally perversion of justice.*

b. In a compound word two or more members are united under one accent; as in *bláckberry* contrasted with *black berry.* Most compounds in Greek, an inflected language, are genuine compounds, not mere word-groups such as are common in English, which is for the most part devoid of inflections.

c. Every compound contains a defining part and a defined part. The defining part usually precedes: εὐ-τυχής *fortunate,* as opposed to δυσ-τυχής *unfortunate.* The parts of a compound stand in various syntactical relations to each other, as that of adjective or attributive genitive to a substantive, or that of adverb or object to a verb, etc. Compounds may thus be regarded as abbreviated forms of syntax. Cp. 895 a, 897 N. 1.

FIRST PART OF A COMPOUND

870. The first part of a compound may be a noun-stem, a verb-stem, a numeral, a preposition or adverb, or an inseparable prefix.

a. The use of stems in composition is a survival of a period in the history of language in which inflections were not fully developed.

FIRST PART A NOUN-STEM

871. First Declension (ᾱ-stems). — The first part may

a. end in ᾱ or η (rarely): ἀγορᾱ-νόμο-ς *clerk of the market* (ἀγορά), νῑκη-φόρο-ς *bringing victory* (νίκη).

b. end in ο: δικο-γράφο-ς *writer of law-speeches* (δίκη *justice*). Here ο is substituted for ᾱ of the stem by analogy to ο-stems.

N. — Compounds of γῆ *earth* have γεω- (for γηο- by 34); as γεω-μέτρης *surveyor* (*land-measurer;* μετρέω *measure*). Doric has γᾱ-μέτρης. Cp. 224 a.

c. lose its vowel before a vowel: κεφαλ-αλγής *causing head-ache* (κεφαλή *head,* ἄλγ-ος *pain*).

872. Second Declension (ο-stems). — The first part may

a. end in ο: λογο-γράφο-ς *speech-writer.*

b. end in ᾱ or η (rarely): ἐλαφη-βόλο-ς *deer-shooting* (ἔλαφος, βάλλω). Here η is due to the analogy of ᾱ-stems.

c. lose ο before a vowel: μόν-αρχο-ς *monarch* (*sole ruler:* μόνο-ς *alone,* ἄρχ-ω *rule*).

N. — Words of the 'Attic' declension may end in ω, as νεω-κόρο-ς *custodian of a temple* (νεώς).

873. Third Declension (consonant stems). — The first part may

a. show the stem (ι, υ, αυ, ου): μαντι-πόλο-ς *inspired* (μάντι-ς *seer*, πέλ-ω, cp. -κολος), ἰχθυ-βόλο-ς *catching-fish* (ἰχθύς, βάλλω), βου-κόλο-ς *ox-herd* (βοῦ-ς, -κολο-ς, cp. Lat. *colo*, and 131).

N. — A few consonant stems retain the consonant: μελάγ-χολος *dipped in black bile* (μέλᾱς, χολή). See also 876.

b. add ο to the stem: σωματ-ο-φύλαξ *body-guard* (σῶμα *body*, φυλάττω *guard*), μητρ-ό-πολις *mother-city, metropolis* (μήτηρ, πόλις), φυσι-ο-λόγος *natural philosopher* (φύσι-ς *nature*), ἰχθυ-ο-πώλης *fishmonger* (ἰχθύς, πωλέω *sell*).

c. add ᾰ (rarely η): ποδ-ά-νιπτρο-ν *water for washing the feet* (πούς, νίπτω), λαμπαδ-η-δρομίᾱ *torch-race.*

874. Compounds of πᾶς *all* usually show πᾰν-, as πάν-σοφο-ς (and πάσ-σοφος 101 b) *all-wise*, παρ-ρησίᾱ *frankness* ('all-speaking'); but also παντ- in πάντ-αρχος *all-ruling;* and παντ-ο- in παντ-ο-πώλιο-ν *bazaar* (πωλέω *sell*).

875. Neuter stems in ματ usually show ματ-ο, as ἀγαλματ-ο-ποιό-ς *sculptor* (ἄγαλμα *statue*, ποιέω *make*). Some have μα, as ὀνομα-κλυτό-ς *of famous name;* some show μο for ματο, as αἱμο-ρραγίᾱ *hemorrhage* (αἷμα, -ατος *blood*, ῥήγνῡμι *break*, 80).

876. Stems in εσ (nom. -ης or -ος) usually drop εσ and add ο; as ψευδ-ο-μαρτυρίᾱ *false testimony* (ψευδ-ής); and so stems in ασ, as κρεο-φάγο-ς *flesh-eating* (κρέας, φαγεῖν 529. 5). Some stems in εσ and ασ retain εσ and ασ (in poetry), as σακεσ-πάλο-ς *wielding a shield* (σάκος, πάλλω), σελασ-φόρο-ς *light-bringing* (σέλας, φέρω); some add ι (for sake of the metre), as ὀρεσ-ί-τροφος *mountain-bred* (ὄρος, τρέφω); these may belong to 879.

877. Other abbreviations: γαλα-θηνό-ς *nurse* (γαλακτ- *milk*, θῆ-σθαι *give suck*), μελι-ηδής *honey-sweet* (μελιτ-), κελαι-νεφής *black with clouds* from κελαινό-ς *black* (cp. 129 c) and νέφος *cloud*.

878. Words once beginning with ϝ or σ. — When the second part consists of a word beginning with digamma, a preceding vowel is often not elided: κακο-εργός (Epic) *doing ill* (later κακοῦργος) from ϝέργο-ν *work;* μηνο-ειδής *crescent-shaped* (μήνη *moon*, ϝεῖδος *shape*); τῑμά-ορος (later τῑμωρός) *avenging* (τῑμή *honour*, ϝοράω *observe, defend*). — Compounds of -οχος, from ἔχω *have* (orig. σέχω, -σοχος) contract: κληροῦχος *holding an allotment* of land (κλῆρο-ς *lot*), πολι-οῦχος *protecting a city* (for πολι-ο-οχος).

879. Flectional Compounds. — A compound whose first part is a case form, not a stem, is called a flectional compound (cp. *sportsman, kinsfolk*): (1) nominative: τρεισ-καί-δεκα *thirteen;* (2) genitive: Διόσ-κουροι *Dioscuri* (*sons of Zeus*), Ἑλλήσ-ποντος *Helle's sea*, Πελοπόν-νησος (for Πελοποσ-νησος, 105 a) *Pelops' island;* (3) dative: δορί-ληπτος *won by the spear;* (4) locative: ὁδοι-πόρος *wayfarer*, Πυλοι-γενής *born in Pylus.* — From such compounds derivatives may be formed, as Ἑλλησπόντιος *of the Hellespont*, θεοισεχθρίᾱ *hatred of the gods.*

FIRST PART A VERB-STEM

880. Some compounds have as their first part a verb-stem (cp. *break-water, pick-pocket, catch-penny*). Such compounds are usually poetic adjectives. The verb-stem is usually transitive and has the form that appears in the present or aorist.

881. Before a vowel the verb-stem remains unchanged or drops a final vowel; before a consonant it adds ε, ο, or ι: φέρ-ασπις *shield-bearing*, μῑσ-άνθρωπος *man-hating* (μῑσέ-ω), ἐκ-ε-χειρίᾱ (125 d) *holding of hands, truce*, λιπ-ο-στρατίᾱ *desertion of the army*, νῑκ-ό-βουλος *prevailing in the Senate*, ἀρχ-ι-τέκτων *master-builder*.

882. The verb-stem adds σι (before a vowel, σ). Some insert ε before σι (σ): σω-σί-πολις *saving the state* (σῴζω), ῥίψ-ασπις *craven*, lit. throwing away a shield (ῥίπ-τ-ω), δηξί-θῡμος (and δακ-έ-θῡμος) *heart-eating* (δάκ-ν-ω), ἑλκ-ε-σίπεπλος *with long train*, lit. trailing the robe (cp. ἑλκ-ε-χίτων)

a. This ε is the vowel added in many verb-stems (485).

FIRST PART A NUMERAL

883. The first part of a compound is often a numeral: δί-πους *biped*, τρί-πους *tripod* (having *three feet*), τέθρ-ιππον *four-horse chariot*, πέντ-ᾱθλον *contest in five events*.

FIRST PART A PREPOSITION OR ADVERB

884. A preposition or adverb is often the first part of a compound: εἴσ-οδος *entrance*, ἀπο-φεύγω *flee from*, εὐ-τυχής *happy*, ἀείμνηστος *ever to be remembered*.

a. Except when the substantive is treated as a verbal (as in εἴσ-οδος *entrance*, cp. εἰσ-ιέναι *enter*), prepositions are rarely compounded with substantives. Thus, σύν-δουλος *fellow-slave*, ὑπο-διδάσκαλος (= ὁ ὑπό τινι δ.) *under-teacher*; also ὑπό-λευκος *whitish*.

b. The ordinary euphonic changes occur. Observe that πρό *before* may contract with ο or ε to ου: προέχω or προὔχω *hold before* (cp. 449 b). See 124 a.

c. η sometimes is inserted after a preposition or takes the place of a final vowel: ὑπερ-ή-φανος *conspicuous*, ἐπ-ή-βολος *having achieved*.

d. Akin to adverbial compounds are some in φιλ-ο, as φιλο-μαθής *one who gladly learns*.

FIRST PART AN INSEPARABLE PREFIX

885. Several prefixes occur only in composition:

1. ἀ(ν)- (ἀν- before a vowel, ἀ- before a consonant; *alpha privative*) with a negative force like Lat. *in-*, Eng. *un-* (or *-less*): ἀν-άξιος *unworthy* (= οὐκ ἄξιος), ἀν-όμοιος *unlike*, ἀν-ώδυνος *anodyne* (ὀδύνη *pain*, cp. 887), ἄ-νους *silly*, ἄ-τῑμος *unhonoured*, ἄ-θεος *godless*, γάμος ἄγαμος *marriage that is no marriage*. ἀ- is also found before words once beginning with digamma or sigma: ἀ-ηδής *unpleasant* (ϝηδύς), ἀ-όρᾱτος *unseen* (ϝοράω), ἄ-οπλος *without shields* (σοπλον), and, by contraction with the following vowel, ἄκων (ἀ-ϝέκων *unwilling*). But ἀν- often appears: ἀν-έλπιστος (and ἄ-ελπτος) *unhoped for* (ϝελπίς), ἄν-οπλος *without shield*.

a. ἀ-, ἀν- (for $\underset{\circ}{\nu}$, 35 b) represent weak forms of I. E. *ne* 'not.'

2. **ἡμι-** *half* (Lat. *sēmi-*): ἡμι-κύκλιος *semi-circular* (κύκλος), ἡμι-όλιος *half as much again* (ὅλος *whole*), ἡμι-θνής *half-dead*.
3. **δυσ-** (opposed to εὖ *well*) *ill*, *un-*, *mis-*, denoting something *difficult*, *bad*, or *unfortunate*, as δυσ-τυχής *unfortunate*, δυσ-χερής *hard to manage*, δυσ-δαίμων *of ill fortune* (contrast εὐ-τυχής, εὐ-χερής, εὐ-δαίμων), δυσ-άρεστος *ill-pleased*, Δύσ-παρις *ill-starred Paris*.
4. **ἀ-** (or ἁ-) *copulative* denotes *union*, *likeness* (cp. Lat. *con-*); ἀ-κόλουθος *attendant*, *agreeing with* (κέλευθος *path*: *i.e.* going on the same road), ἁ-τάλαντος *of the same weight*, ἅ-πᾱς *all together*. A variation of ἁ-copulative is ἀ-*intensive*: ἀ-τενής *stretched* (τείνω *stretch*), ἄ-πεδος *level* (πέδον *ground*).
   a. ἁ-*copulative* stands for σα- (from σm̥ 20, 35 c), and is connected with ἅμα, ὁμοῦ, and ὁμο- *together*.
5. **νη-** (poetic) with the force of a negative (cp. Lat. *nē*): νή-ποινος *unavenged* (ποινή *punishment*), νη-πενθής *freeing from pain and sorrow* (πένθος). In some cases νη- may be derived from ν (*not*) and the η of the second part, as ν-ῆστις *not eating* (poetic ἔδ-ω, cp. 887).
6. **ἀρι-**, **ἐρι-** (poetic) with intensive force (cp. ἄρι-στος *best*), ἀρι-πρεπής *very distinguished* (πρέπω), ἐρί-τῑμος *precious*.
7. **ἀγα-** (poetic) intensive (cp. ἄγαν *very*): ἀγά-στονος *loud wailing* (στένω *groan*).
8. **ζα-**, **δα-** (poetic) intensive (for δι̯α = δια- *very*, 116): ζα-μενής *very courageous* (μένος *courage*), δά-σκιος *thick-shaded* (σκιά).

LAST PART OF A COMPOUND

886. Compound Substantives and Adjectives. — The last part of a noun-compound consists of a noun-stem or of a verb-stem with a noun-suffix.

887. Nouns beginning with ᾰ, ε, ο lengthen these vowels (ᾰ and ε to η, ο to ω) unless they are long by position. στρατ-ηγός *army-leading*, *general* (στρατός, ἄγω), εὐ-ήνεμος *with fair wind* (εὖ *well*, ἄνεμος), ξεν-ηλασίᾱ *driving out of foreigners* (ξένος, ἐλαύνω), ἀν-ώνυμος *nameless* (ἀν-, ὄνομα), ἀν-ώμαλος *uneven* (ἀν-, ὁμαλός).

a. Some compounds of ἄγω *lead* show ᾱ: λοχ-ᾱγός *captain* (λόχος *company*).

b. By analogy to the compound the simple form sometimes assumes a long vowel: ἠνεμόεσσα *windy*. Cp. 28 D.

c. Lengthening rarely occurs when a preposition or πᾶς precedes: συν-ωμοσίᾱ *conspiracy* (ὄμνῡμι *swear*), παν-ήγυρις *general assembly* (ἄγυρις = ἀγορά).

d. The lengthening in 887 is properly the result of early contraction (στρατο + αγος). On the pattern of such contracted forms irrational lengthening occurs when the first part of the compound ends in a consonant, as δυσ-ηλεγής (for δυσ-αλεγής) *cruel* from ἀλέγω *care for*.

888. A noun forming the last part of a compound often changes its final syllable.

N. Masculine or feminine nouns of the second or third declensions usually remain unaltered: ἔν-θεος *inspired*, ἄ-παις *childless*.

a. **-ος, -η, -ον**: form compound adjectives from nouns of the first declension, neuters of the second declension, nouns of the third declension, and from many verb-stems. ἄ-τῑμος *dishonoured* (τῑμή), σύν-δειπνος *companion at table* (δεῖπνο-ν *meal*), ἄν-αιμος *bloodless* (αἷμα, 875), ἑκατόγ-χειρος *hundred-handed* (χείρ), δασμο-φόρος *bringing tribute* (φέρ-ω), γεω-γράφος *geographer* 871 b. N. (γράφ-ω), ἰχθυ-ο-φάγος *fish-eating* (φαγεῖν 529. 5).

b. **-ης, -ες**: form compound adjectives from nouns of the first and third declensions, and from many verb-stems: ἀ-τυχής *unfortunate* (τύχη), δεκα-ετής *of ten years* (ϝέτος), εὐ-ειδής *beautiful in form* (εἶδος), εὐ-μαθής *quick at learning* (μανθάνω, μαθ-), ἀ-φανής *invisible* (φαίνω, φαν-).

c. Other endings are **-ης** (gen. -ου), **-της, -τηρ**: γεω-μέτρης *surveyor* (871 b. N.), νομο-θέτης *law-giver* (νόμος, τίθημι, θε-), μηλο-βοτήρ *shepherd* (μῆλον, βό-σκω *feed*).

d. Neuters in **-μα** make adjectives in -μων: πρᾶγμα *thing*, ἀ-πράγμων *inactive*. φρήν *mind* becomes **-φρων**: εὔ-φρων *well-minded, cheerful*.—πατήρ *father* becomes **-πάτωρ**: ἀ-πάτωρ *fatherless*, φιλο-πάτωρ *loving his father*.

e. Compounds of γῆ *land* end in -γειος, -γεως: κατά-γειος *subterranean*, λεπτό-γεως *of thin soil*.—Compounds of ναῦς *ship*, κέρας *horn*, γῆρας *old age* end in -ως, as περί-νεως *supercargo*, ὑψί-κερως *lofty-antlered* (163 a), ἀ-γήρως *free from old age*.

889. The last member of a compound is often a verbal element that is not used separately: ἀγαλματ-ο-ποιός *statue-maker, sculptor*, ὑπ-ήκοος *subject* (ἀκούω *hear*, ἀκήκοα), λογο-γράφος *speech-writer*. -φορος *bringing*, -δομος *building*, -δρομος *running* are used separately in the meanings *tribute, building, race*.

890. An abstract word can enter into composition only by taking a derivative ending (usually -ιᾱ) formed from a real or assumed compound adjective: ναῦ-ς *ship*, μάχη *fight* = ναύ-μαχος, whence ναυ-μαχίᾱ *naval battle*; εὖ *well*, βουλή *counsel* = εὔ-βουλος, whence εὐ-βουλίᾱ *good counsel*; ἀν-neg., ἀρχή *rule* = ἄν-αρχος, whence ἀν-αρχίᾱ *anarchy*; εὖ *well*, πρᾶξις *doing* = *εὐπρᾱξος, whence εὐ-πρᾱξίᾱ *well-doing*. Contrast εὐ-βουλίᾱ with προ-βουλή *forethought*, εὐ-λογίᾱ *eulogy* with πρό-λογος *prologue*.

a. Only after a preposition does an abstract word remain unchanged: προ-βουλή *forethought*. Exceptions are rare: μισθο-φορά *receipt of wages* (μισθός, φορά).

891. Compound Verbs.—Verbs can be compounded *directly* only by prefixing a preposition, as συμ-μάχομαι *fight along with*.

a. A preposition (πρό-θεσις) derived its name from this use as a prefix. Originally all prepositions were adverbs modifying the verb, and in Homer are partly so used. See 1638, 1639. Cp. *upheave* and *heave up*.

892. All compound verbs not compounded with prepositions are denominatives (ending in -εω) and formed from real or assumed compound nouns. From ναῦς *ship* and μάχη *fight* comes ναύμαχος *fighting in ships*, whence ναυμαχέω *fight in ships*; so οἰκοδομέω *build a house* from οἰκο-δόμος *house-builder* (οἶκος, δέμω). Contrast ἀνα-πείθω *bring over, convince* with ἀ-πιστέω *disbelieve* (ἄ-πιστος); ἀντι-λέγω *speak against* with ὁμο-λογέω *agree* (ὁμόλογος *agreeing*).—εὖ ἀγγέλλω *announce good news* cannot form a verb εὐαγγελλω.

a. ἀτῑμάω (ἀτίω) *dishonour*, δακρυχέω *shed tears* are exceptions. ἀν-ομοιόω *make unlike* is not from ἀν- and ὁμοιόω but from ἀν-όμοιος *unlike*.

ACCENT OF COMPOUNDS

893. Compounds generally have recessive accent, as φιλό-τῑμος *loving-honour* (τῑμή). But there are many exceptions, *e.g.*—

a. Primitives in -ά, -ή, -ής, -εύς, -μός, and -έος usually keep their accent when compounded; except dissyllabic words in -ά, -ή, -ής whose first part is not a preposition. Thus, κριτής *judge*, ὑποκριτής *actor*, ὀνειροκρίτης *interpreter of dreams*.

b. Compound adjectives in -ης, -ες are usually oxytone: εὐ-γενής *well-born*.

894. Compounds in -ος (not -τος or -κος) formed by the union of a noun or adverb and the stem of a transitive verb are:

a. *oxytone*, when they have a long penult and an active meaning: στρατ-ηγός *general*.

b. *paroxytone*, when they have short penult and an active meaning: πατρο-κτόνος *parricide*, λιθο-βόλος *throwing-stones*, λαιμο-τόμος *throat-cutting*, ὑδρο-φόρος *water-carrier*.

c. *proparoxytone*, when they have a short penult and passive meaning: πατρό-κτονος *slain by a father*, λιθό-βολος *pelted with stones*, λαιμό-τομος *with throat cut*, αὐτό-γραφος *written with one's own hand*.

N.—Active compounds of -οχος (ἔχ-ω, 878), -αρχος (ἄρχ-ω), -σῦλος (σῡλά-ω *rob*), -πορθος (πέρθ-ω *destroy*) are proparoxytone; ἡνί-οχος (*rein-holder*) *charioteer*, ἵππ-αρχος *commander of horses*, ἱερό-σῡλος *temple-robber*, πτολί-πορθος *sacking cities*. ῥαβδοῦχος *staff-bearer* (ῥαβδός) is contracted from ῥαβδό-οχος.

MEANING OF COMPOUNDS

895. Compound nouns (substantives and adjectives) are divided, according to their meaning, into three main classes: *determinative*, *possessive*, and *prepositional-phrase*, compounds.

a. The logical relation of the parts of compounds varies so greatly that boundary-lines between the different classes are difficult to set up, and a complete formal division is impossible. The poets show a much wider range of usage than the prose-writers.

896. Determinative Compounds.—In most determinative compounds the first part modifies or *determines* the second part: the modifier stands first, the principal word second.

Thus by *hand-work* a particular kind of work is meant, as contrasted with *machine-work;* cp. *speech-writer* and *letter-writer*, *race-horse* and *horse-race*.

a. The first part may be an adjective, an adverb, a preposition, an inseparable prefix, or, in a few cases, a substantive.

897. There are two kinds of determinative compounds.

(1) **Descriptive determinative compounds.**—The first part defines or explains the second part in the sense of an adjective or adverb. (This class is less numerous than the second class.)

ἀκρό-πολις *upper city*, *citadel* (ἄκρᾱ πόλις), ὁμό-δουλος *fellow-slave* (ὁμοῦ δουλεύων, cp. 885. 4 a), ὀψί-γονος *late-born* (ὀψὲ γενόμενος), προ-βουλή *forethought*, ἀμφι-θέᾱτρον *amphitheatre* (a place-for-seeing round about), ἄ-γραφος *not written* (οὐ γεγραμμένος).

a. *Copulative compounds* are formed by the coördination of two substantives or adjectives: ἰᾱτρό-μαντις *physician and seer*, γλυκύ-πικρος *sweetly-bitter*. Similar is *deaf-mute*. So also in numerals: δώ-δεκα *two (and) ten* = 12.

b. *Comparative compounds* (generally poetic) are μελι-ηδής *honey-sweet* (μέλι, ἡδύς), ποδ-ήνεμος Ἶρις *Iris, with feet swift as the wind*. Cp. *eagle-eyed, goldfish, blockhead*. Such compounds are often possessive (898), as ῥοδο-δάκτυλος *rosy-fingered*, χρῡσο-κόμης *golden-haired*.

(2) **Dependent determinative compounds.** — A substantive forming either the first or the second part stands in the sense of an oblique case (with or without a preposition) to the other part.

Accusative: λογο-γράφος *speech-writer* (λόγους γράφων), στρατ-ηγός *army-leading, general* (στρατὸν ἄγων), φιλ-άνθρωπος *loving mankind* (φιλῶν ἀνθρώπους), δεισι-δαίμων *superstitious* (δεδιὼς τοὺς δαίμονας); cp. *pickpocket, sightseer, painstaking, soothsayer, laughter-loving*.

Genitive: στρατό-πεδον *camp* (στρατοῦ πέδον *ground on which an army is encamped*). In ἀξιό-λογος *worthy of mention* (ἄξιος λόγου) the defining part stands second (869 c) and is governed by the adjective part like a preposition (cp. 899). Cp. *ringmaster, law-officer, jest-book*.

(Ablative): ἀνεμο-σκεπής *sheltering from the wind*; cp. *land-breeze, sea-breeze*.

Dative: ἰσό-θεος *godlike* (ἴσος θεῷ); cp. *churchgoer, blood-thirsty*.

(Instrumental): χειρ-ο-ποίητος *made by hand* (χερσὶ ποιητός), χρῡσό-δετος *bound with gold* (χρῡσῷ δετός); cp. *thunder-struck, storm-swept, star-sown*.

(Locative): οἰκο-γενής *born in the house* (ἐν οἴκῳ γενόμενος), ὁδοι-πόρος *wayfarer* (879); cp. *heart-sick*.

N. 1. — The Greeks did not think of any actual case relation as existing in these compounds, and the case relation that exists is purely logical. The same form may be analysed in different ways, as φιλάνθρωπος = φιλῶν ἀνθρώπους or = φίλος ἀνθρώπων.

N. 2. — Such compounds may often be analysed by a preposition and a dependent noun: θεό-δμητος *god-built* (ὑπὸ τῶν θεῶν δμητός).

898. Possessive Compounds. — In possessive compounds the first part defines the second as in determinatives; but the whole compound is an adjective expressing a quality, with the idea of possession understood. In most possessive compounds the idea of *having* (ἔχων) is to be supplied.

So, in English, *redbreast* is a bird *having* a red breast, the first part being an attribute of the second.

ἀργυρό-τοξος *having a silver bow*; μακρό-χειρ *having long arms, long-armed*; θεο-ειδής *having the appearance* (εἶδος) *of a god, godlike*; σώ-φρων *having sound mind, temperate*; τέθρ-ιππος *having four horses*; ὁμό-τροπος *of like character* (ὁμο- occurs only in compounds, but note ὅμοιος *like*); πολυ-κέφαλος *many-headed*; εὐ-τυχής *having good fortune, fortunate*; δεκα-ετής *lasting ten years* (cp. *a two-year-old*); ἀμφι-κίων *having pillars round about*; ἔν-θεος *inspired* (*having a god within*: ἐν ἑαυτῷ θεὸν ἔχων).

a. Adjectives in -ειδής from εἶδος *form* (ἀστερ-ο-ειδής *star-like*, ἰχθυ-ο-ειδής *fish-like*, μηνο-ειδής *crescent*, πολυ-ειδής *of many kinds*, σφαιρ-ο-ειδής *spherical*) are to be distinguished from those in -ώδης derived from ὄζω *smell* (833 a).

b. English possessive compounds in *-ed* apply that ending only to the compound as a whole and not to either member. In Milton: *deep-throated, white-handed, open-hearted;* in Keats: *subtle-cadenced.* Besides those in *-ed* there are others such as *Bluebeard.*

c. Many possessive compounds begin with ἀ(ν)- negative or δυσ- *ill;* as ἄ-παις *childless* (*having no children* or *not having children*, παῖδας οὐκ ἔχων), ἄ-τῑμος *dishonoured* (*having no honour*), δύσ-βουλος *ill advised* (*having evil counsels*).

899. Prepositional-phrase Compounds. — Many phrases made of a preposition and its object unite to form a compound and take on adjectival inflection. Such compounds are equivalent to the phrases in question with the idea of *being* or the like added.

ἄπ-οικος *colonist* (*away from home:* ἀπ' οἴκου); ἐγχειρίδιος *in the hand, dagger* (ἐν χειρί); ἐγχώριος *native* (*in the country:* ἐν χώρᾳ); ἐπιθαλάττιος *dwelling on the coast* (ἐπὶ θαλάττῃ); ἐφέστιος *on the hearth* (ἐφ' ἑστίᾳ); κατάγειος *underground*, cp. *subterranean* (κατὰ γῆς); παρά-δοξος *contrary to opinion* (παρὰ δόξαν); παρά-φρων *out of one's mind*, Lat. *de-mens* (παρὰ τὴν φρένα); ὑπ-εύθῡνος *under liability to give account* (ὑπ' εὐθύναις); so φροῦδος *gone* (= πρὸ ὁδοῦ γενόμενος, cp. 124 a).

a. From such phrases are derived verbs and substantives: ἐγχειρίζω *put into one's hands, entrust*, διαχειρίζω *have in hand, manage* (διὰ χειρῶν), διαπᾱσῶν *octave-scale* (ἡ διὰ πᾱσῶν χορδῶν συμφωνίᾱ *the concord through all the notes*). By analogy to ἐκποδών *out of the way* (ἐκ ποδῶν) come ἐμποδών *in the way* and ἐμπόδιος *impeding*, ἐμποδίζω *impede.*

b. The compounds of 899 represent bits of syntax used so frequently together that they have become adherent.

PART IV

SYNTAX

DEFINITIONS

900. A sentence expresses a thought. Syntax (σύνταξις *arranging together*) shows how the different parts of speech and their different inflectional forms are employed to form sentences.

901. Sentences are either *complete* or *incomplete* (904).

902. Every complete sentence must contain two members:
1. The Subject: the person or thing about which something is said.
2. The Predicate: what is said about the subject.

Thus, τὸ θέρος (subj.) ἐτελεύτᾱ (pred.) *the summer* | *came to an end* T. 3. 102, ἦλθε (pred.) κῆρυξ (subj.) *a herald* | *came* 3. 113.

903. Complete sentences are *simple, compound,* or *complex.* In the *simple* sentence subject and predicate occur only once. A *compound* sentence (2162) consists of two or more simple sentences coördinated: τῇ δ' ὑστεραίᾳ ἐπορεύοντο διὰ τοῦ πεδίου, καὶ Τισσαφέρνης εἵπετο *but on the next day they marched through the plain and Tissaphernes kept following them* X. A. 3. 4. 18. A *complex* sentence (2173) consists of a main sentence and one or more subordinate sentences: ὁπότε δέοι γέφῡραν διαβαίνειν, ἔσπευδεν ἕκαστος *whenever it was necessary to cross a bridge, every one made haste* 3. 4. 20.

904. Incomplete sentences consist of a single member only. Such sentences stand outside the structure of the sentence. The chief classes of incomplete sentences are

a. Interjections, such as ὦ, φεῦ, αἰαῖ, οἴμοι.

b. Asseverations which serve as a predicate to a sentence spoken by another: ναί *yes, surely,* οὔ *no,* μάλιστα *certainly,* καλῶς *very well!*

c. Headings, titles: Κύρου Ἀνάβασις *the Expedition of Cyrus,* Ἀντιγόνη *the Antigone,* συμμαχίᾱ Ἀθηναίων καὶ Θετταλῶν *the Alliance of the Athenians and Thessalians* C. I. A. 4. 2. 59 b.

d. Vocatives (1283), and nominatives used in exclamation (1288).

e. Exclamations without a verb: δεῦρο *hither!*

N.—Examples of such incomplete sentences in English are *oh, assuredly, no wonder, right about face, away, fire!*

905. True impersonal verbs (932) have a grammatical subject in the personal ending; but the real subject is properly an idea more or less vague that is present to the mind of the speaker. Similar in nature are infinitives used in commands (2013).

SYNTAX OF THE SIMPLE SENTENCE

906. The most simple form of sentence is the finite verb: ἐσ-τί *he-is*, λέγο-μεν *we-say*, ἕπε-σθε *you-follow*.

Here the subject is in the personal ending, the predicate in the verbal stem. No other single word than a verb can of itself form a complete sentence.

907. The subject of a sentence is a substantive or one of its equivalents.

908. Equivalents of the Substantive. — The function of the substantive may be assumed by a pronoun, adjective (in masculine and feminine more frequently with the article), numeral, participle, relative clause (οἳ ἐλήφθησαν τῶν πολεμίων ταὐτὰ ἤγγελλον *those of the enemy who were captured made the same report* X. A. 1. 7. 13); by the article with an adverb (οἱ τότε *the men of that day*), or with the genitive (τὰ τῆς τύχης *the incidents of fortune, fortune* (1299)); by a prepositional phrase (οἱ ἀμφὶ τὸν Σωκράτη *Socrates and his followers*; ἐπὶ μέγα *a great part*), a preposition with a numeral (ἔφυγον περὶ ὀκτακοσίους *about eight hundred took to flight* X. H. 6. 5. 10); by an infinitive with or without the article (1984, 2025); and by any word or phrase viewed merely as a thing (τὸ ὑμεῖς ὅταν λέγω, τὴν πόλιν λέγω *when I say You, I mean the State* D. 18. 88). Cp. 1153 g. (Furthermore, by a clause in a complex sentence, 2189. 1.)

909. The predicate of a sentence is always a verb. The verb may either stand alone, as in Περικλῆς ἀπῆλθε *Pericles departed*; or it may have certain modifiers, called *complements to the predicate* (nouns, participles, adverbs), as Περικλῆς ἀπῆλθε πρῶτος *first* (ὀργιζόμενος *in anger*; τότε *then*). Cp. 924.

910. Predicate Nouns. — Nouns (substantival or adjectival) are often used as complements to the predicate. Thus,

a. A *predicate substantive* is a substantive forming part of the predicate and asserting something of its substantive: Περικλῆς ᾑρέθη στρατηγός *Pericles was elected general*, εἵλεσθε ἐκεῖνον πρεσβευτήν *you elected him envoy* L. 13. 10.

b. A *predicate adjective* is an adjective forming part of the predicate and asserting something of its substantive: ὁ ἀνὴρ δίκαιός ἐστι *the man is just*, ἐνόμισαν Περικλέᾱ εὐτυχῆ *they thought Pericles fortunate*.

911. A predicate substantive or adjective may often be distinguished from an *attributive* (912) in that the former implies some form of εἶναι *be*. Thus, πρεσβευτήν and εὐτυχῆ in 910. After verbs signifying *to name* or *call*, εἶναι is sometimes expressed (1615).

912. Attributive Adjective. — An attributive adjective is an adjective simply added to a noun to describe it, and not forming any part of an assertion made about it: ὁ δίκαιος ἀνήρ *the just-man*.

913. All adjectives that are not attributive are predicate. So πρῶτοι ἀφίκοντο *they were the first to arrive* (1042 b), τούτῳ φίλῳ χρῶμαι *I treat this man as a friend* (= οὗτος, ᾧ χρῶμαι, φίλος ἐστί).

914. Under adjectives are included participles: ὁ μέλλων (attrib.) πόλεμος *the future war*, ταῦτα εἰπὼν (pred.) ἀπῄειν *saying this he went off*, ὁρῶ σε κρύπτοντα (pred.) *I see you hiding.*

915. Predicate substantives, adjectives, and participles, in agreement either with subject or object, are more common in Greek than in English, and often call for special shifts in translation: μετεώρους ἐξεκόμισαν τὰς ἁμάξᾱς *they lifted the wagons and carried them out* X. A. 1. 5. 8. Cp. 1579.

916. Appositive. — An appositive is a noun added to another noun or to a pronoun to describe or define it: Μιλτιάδης ὁ στρατηγός *Miltiades, the general*, ὑμεῖς οἱ ἱερεῖς *you, the priests*, τοῦτο, ὃ σὺ εἶπες, ἀεὶ πάρεστι, σχολή *this, which you mentioned, is always present*, (I mean) *leisure* P. Th. 172 d.

917. Copula. — An indeterminate verb that serves simply to couple a predicate substantive or adjective to the subject is called a *copula:* Ξενοφῶν ἦν Ἀθηναῖος *Xenophon was an Athenian.*

a. The most common copulative verbs are εἶναι *be* and γίγνεσθαι *become.* Many other verbs serve as copulas: καθίστασθαι *become*, πεφῡκέναι, ὑπάρχειν, πέλειν (poetical) *be*, δοκεῖν *seem*, φαίνεσθαι *appear*, καλεῖσθαι, ὀνομάζεσθαι, ἀκούειν, κλύειν (poetical) *be called*, τυγχάνειν, κυρεῖν (poet.) *happen, turn out*, αἱρεῖσθαι *be chosen*, νομίζεσθαι *be regarded*, κρίνεσθαι *be judged*, and the like.

918. a. The copula is strictly the predicate or is a part of the predicate with its supplements.

b. The above verbs may also be complete predicates: ἔστι θεός *there is a god.*

c. For the omission of the copula, see 944.

d. A predicate substantive or adjective stands in the same case as the subject when coupled to it by a copulative verb (939).

e. For εἶναι added to a copulative verb, see 1615.

919. Object. — A verb may have an object on which its action is exerted. The object is a substantive (or its equivalent, 908) in an oblique case. An object may be *direct* (in the accusative) or *indirect* (in the genitive or dative): Κῦρος δώσει ἓξ μνᾶς (direct) τῷ δούλῳ (indirect) *Cyrus will give six minae to the slave*, ἔλαβον τῆς ζώνης (indirect) τὸν Ὀρόντᾱν (direct) *they took hold of Orontas by the girdle* X. A. 1. 6. 10.

920. Transitive and Intransitive Verbs. — Verbs capable of taking a direct object are called *transitive* because their action *passes over* to an object. Other verbs are called *intransitive.*

a. But many intransitive verbs, as in English, are used transitively (1558, 1559), and verbs usually transitive often take an indirect object (1341 ff., 1460 ff., 1471 ff.).

KINDS OF SIMPLE SENTENCES

921. Simple sentences have six forms: Statements; Assumptions, Commands, Wishes; Questions; and Exclamations. Of these, Assumptions, Commands, and Wishes express *will*. See 2153 ff.

EXPANSION OF THE SIMPLE SENTENCE

922. The subject and the predicate may be expanded by amplification or qualification:

923. Expansion of the Subject. — The subject may be expanded: A. By *amplification:* Ξενίᾱς καὶ Πᾱσίων ἀπέπλευσαν *Xenias and Pasion sailed away.* B. By *qualification:* 1. By an attributive adjective, ὁ ἀγαθὸς ἀνήρ *the good man*, an attributive substantive denoting *occupation*, *condition*, or *age*, ἀνὴρ στρατηγός *a general* (986), an adjective pronoun or numeral: ἡμέτερος φίλος *a friend of ours*, δύο παῖδες *two children*. 2. By the genitive of a noun or substantive pronoun (adnominal or attributive genitive): στέφανος χρῡσοῦ *a crown of gold*, ὁ πατὴρ ἡμῶν *our father*. 3. By a prepositional phrase: ὁδὸς κατὰ τοῦ γηλόφου *a way down the hill*. 4. By an adverb: οἱ νῦν ἄνθρωποι *the men of the present day*. 5. By an appositive (916). A substantive in any case may be qualified like the subject.

924. Expansion of the Predicate. — The predicate may be expanded: A. By *amplification:* οἱ λοχᾱγοὶ ἀπῆλθον καὶ ἐποίουν οὕτω *the captains departed and did so*. B. By *qualification:* 1. By the oblique case of a noun, a substantive pronoun, or a numeral. This is called the object (919, 920). Thus: ὁρῶ τὸν ἄνδρα *I see the man*, φωνῆς ἀκούω *I hear a voice*, εἵπετο τῷ ἡγεμόνι *he followed the guide*, ἀγαπᾷ ἡμᾶς *he loves us*, ἐνίκησε τὴν μάχην *he won the battle* (cognate accusative, 1567), ἔδωκα δέκα *I gave ten*. The oblique case may be followed by an adnominal genitive or a dative: ὁρῶ πολλοὺς τῶν πολῑτῶν *I see many of the citizens*. 2. By a preposition with its appropriate case: ἦλθον ἐπὶ τὰς σκηνάς *they went to their tents*. 3. By an infinitive: ἐθέλει ἀπελθεῖν *he wishes to depart*. 4. By a participle: ἄρξομαι λέγων *I will begin my speech*. 5. By an adverb or adverbial expression: εὖ ἴστω *let him know well*, τῆς νυκτὸς ἦλθε *he came during the night*, ἀπῆλθε τριταῖος *he departed on the third day* (1042). On complements to the predicate, see 909.

AGREEMENT: THE CONCORDS

925. There are three concords in simple sentences:

1. A finite verb agrees with its subject in number and person (949).

2. A word in apposition with another word agrees with it in case (976).

3. An adjective agrees with its substantive in gender, number, and case (1020).

(For the concord of relative pronouns, see 2501.)

926. Apparent violation of the concords is to be explained either by

a. *Construction according to sense*, where the agreement is with the real gender or number (*e.g.* 949 a, 950–953, 958, 996, 997, 1013, 1044, 1050, 1055 a, 1058 b); or by

b. *Attraction*, when a word does not have its natural construction because of the influence of some other word or words in its clause (*e.g.* 1060 ff., 1239, 1978, 2465, 2502, 2522 ff.). This principle extends to moods and tenses (2183 ff.).

THE SUBJECT

927. The subject of a finite verb is in the nominative: **Κῦρος ἐβόᾱ** *Cyrus called out.*

928. The subject nominative may be replaced

a. By a prepositional phrase in the accusative: *ἐνθῡμεῖσθε καθ' ἑκάστους τε καὶ ξύμπαντες consider individually and all together* T. 7. 64.

b. By a genitive of the divided whole (1318): *Πελληνεῖς δὲ κατὰ Θεσπιέᾱς γενόμενοι ἐμάχοντό τε καὶ ἐν χώρᾳ ἔπῑπτον ἑκατέρων the Pellenians who were opposed to the Thespians kept up the contest and several on both sides fell on the spot* X. H. 4. 2. 20.

OMISSION OF THE SUBJECT

929. An unemphatic pronoun of the first or second person is generally omitted: *λέγε τὸν νόμον read the law* (spoken to the clerk of the court) D. 21. 8.

930. An emphatic pronoun is generally expressed, as in contrasts: *σὺ μὲν κεῖνον ἐκδέχου, ἐγὼ δ' ἄπειμι do thou wait for him, but I will depart* S. Ph. 123. But often in poetry and sometimes in prose the pronoun is expressed when no contrast is intended. The first of two contrasted pronouns is sometimes omitted: *ἀλλά, εἰ βούλει, μέν' ἐπὶ τῷ στρατεύματι, ἐγὼ δ' ἐθέλω πορεύεσθαι but, if you prefer, remain with your division, I am willing to go* X. A. 3. 4. 41. Cp. 1190, 1191.

931. The nominative subject of the third person may be omitted

a. When it is expressed or implied in the context: *ὁ σὸς πατὴρ φοβεῖται μὴ τὰ ἔσχατα πάθῃ your father is afraid lest he suffer death* X. C. 3. 1. 22.

b. When the subject is indefinite, especially when it is the same person or thing as the omitted subject of a preceding infinitive (937 a): *ἡ τοῦ οἴεσθαι εἰδέναι (ἀμαθίᾱ), ἃ οὐκ οἶδεν the ignorance of thinking* one *knows what* one *does not know* P. A. 29 b. Often in legal language: *ὁ νόμος, ὃς κελεύει τὰ ἑαυτοῦ ἐξεῖναι διαθέσθαι ὅπως ἂν ἐθέλῃ the law, which enjoins that* a man *has the right to dispose of his property as he wishes* Is. 2. 13.

c. When a particular person is meant, who is easily understood from the situation: *τοὺς νόμους ἀναγνώσεται he* (the clerk) *will read the laws* Aes. 3. 15.

d. When it is a general idea of person, and usually in the third person plural of verbs of *saying* and *thinking*: *ὡς λέγουσιν as they say* D. 5. 18. So *φᾱσί they say*, *οἴονται people think*; cp. *aiunt*, *ferunt*, *tradunt*.

e. In descriptions of locality: ἦν δὲ κρημνῶδες *for it* (the place) *was steep* T. 7. 84.

f. In impersonal verbs (932, 934).

932. Impersonal Verbs (905). — The subject of a true impersonal verb is a vague notion that cannot be supplied from the context: ὀψὲ ἦν *it was late*, καλῶς ἔχει *it is well*, ἤδη ἦν ἀμφὶ ἀγορὰν πλήθουσαν *it was already about the time when the market-place is full* X. A. 1. 8. 1, αὐτῷ οὐ προυχώρει *it* (the course of events) *did not go well with him* T. 1. 109.

933. An impersonal verb the subject of which may be derived from the context is called *quasi-impersonal.*

a. When the indefinite *it* anticipates an infinitive or subordinate proposition which forms the logical subject (1985). So with δοκεῖ *it seems*, συμβαίνει *it happens*, ἔξεστι *it is permitted*, πρέπει, προσήκει *it is fitting*, φαίνεται *it appears*, ἐγένετο *it happened*, εἰσῄει με *venit me in mentem*, δηλοῖ *it is evident*, etc. Thus, ὑμᾶς προσήκει προθυμοτέρους εἶναι *it behooves you to be more zealous* X. A. 3. 2. 15, εἰσῄει αὐτοὺς ὅπως ἂν οἴκαδε ἀφίκωνται *it came into their thoughts how they should reach home* 6. 1. 17.

b. So also with χρή, δεῖ *it is necessary*; as, δεῖ σ' ἐλθεῖν *you ought to go* (lit. *to go binds you*). The impersonal construction with -τέον is equivalent to δεῖ (2152 a): βοηθητέον ἐστὶ τοῖς πράγμασιν ὑμῖν *you must rescue the interests at stake* D. 1. 17.

934. In some so-called impersonal verbs the person is left unexpressed because the actor is understood or implied in the action. So

a. In expressions of natural phenomena originally viewed as produced by a divine agent: βροντᾷ *tonat*, ὕει *pluit*, νείφει *ningit*, χειμάζει *it is stormy*, ἔσεισε *it shook, there was an earthquake.* The agent (Ζεύς, ὁ θεός) is often (in Hom. always) expressed, as Ζεὺς ἀστράπτει *Iuppiter fulget.*

b. When the agent is known from the action, which is viewed as alone of importance: σαλπίζει *the trumpet sounds* (*i.e.* ὁ σαλπιγκτὴς σαλπίζει *the trumpeter sounds the trumpet*), ἐκήρυξε *proclamation was made* (*scil.* ὁ κῆρυξ), σημαίνει *the signal is given* (*scil.* ὁ κῆρυξ or ὁ σαλπιγκτής).

935. In impersonal passives the subject is merely indicated in the verbal ending: λέγεταί τε καὶ γράφεται *speeches* (λόγοι) *and writings* (γράμματα) *are composed* P. Phae. 261 b. This construction is relatively rare, but commonest in the perfect and pluperfect: οὐκ ἄλλως αὐτοῖς πεπόνηται *their labour has not been lost* P. Phae. 232 a, ἐπεὶ αὐτοῖς παρεσκεύαστο *when their preparations were completed* X. H. 1. 3. 20.

936. Subject of the Infinitive. — The subject of the infinitive is in the accusative: ἐκέλευον αὐτοὺς πορεύεσθαι *they ordered that they should proceed* X. A. 4. 2. 1.

a. See 1975. On the nominative subject of the infinitive, see 1973.

937. Omission of the Subject of the Infinitive. — The subject of the infinitive is usually not expressed when it is the same as the subject or object (direct or indirect) of the principal verb: ἔφη ἐθέλειν *he said he was willing* X. A. 4. 1. 27 (contrast *dixit se velle*), πάντες αἰτοῦνται τοὺς θεοὺς τὰ φαῦλα ἀπο-

τρέπειν everybody prays the gods to avert evil X. S. 4. 47, δός μοι τρεῖς ἡμέρᾱς ἄρξαι αὐτοῦ *grant me the control of him for three days* X. C. 1. 3. 11. Cp. 1060, 1973.

a. An indefinite subject of the infinitive (τινά, ἀνθρώπους) is usually omitted. Cp. 931 b, 1980.

CASE OF THE SUBJECT: THE NOMINATIVE

938. The nominative is the case of the subject; the oblique cases, with the exception of the adnominal genitive (1290 ff.) and adnominal dative (1502), are complements of the predicate.

939. The nominative is the case of the subject of a finite verb and of a predicate noun in agreement with the subject. Πρόξενος παρῆν *Proxenus was present* X. A. 1. 2. 3, Κλέαρχος φυγὰς ἦν *Clearchus was an exile* 1. 1. 9.

a. On the nominative subject of the infinitive, see 1973; in exclamations, 1288.

940. Independent Nominative. — The nominative may be used independently in citing the names of persons and things: προσείληφε τὴν τῶν πονηρῶν κοινὴν ἐπωνυμίᾱν σῡκοφάντης *he received the common appellation of the vile, i.e. 'informer'* Aes. 2. 99, τὸ δ' ὑμεῖς ὅταν λέγω, λέγω τὴν πόλιν *when I say You, I mean the State* D. 18. 88. Cp. 908. (The accus. is also possible.) So in lists (cp. 904 c): τίθημι δύο ποιητικῆς εἴδη· θείᾱ μὲν καὶ ἀνθρωπίνη *I assume two kinds of poetry: the divine and the human* P. Soph. 266 d.

941. A sentence may begin with the nominative as the subject of the thought in place of an oblique case: οἱ δὲ φίλοι, ἄν τις ἐπίστηται αὐτοῖς χρῆσθαι, τί φήσομεν αὐτοὺς εἶναι; *but as for friends, if one knows how to treat them, what shall we call them?* X. O. 1. 14 (for τοὺς δὲ φίλους . . . τί φήσομεν εἶναι).

a. On the nominative in suspense see under Anacoluthon (Index).

942. In referring to himself in letters a man may use his own name in the nominative, either in apposition to the first person contained in the verb (976), or as subject of a verb in the third person: Θεμιστοκλῆς ἥκω παρὰ σέ *I, Themistocles, have come to you* T. 1. 137, Ἀρταξέρξης νομίζει *Artaxerxes thinks* X. H. 5. 1. 31.

a. A speaker referring to himself in the third person usually soon reverts to the first person (D. 18. 79).

943. When there is no danger of obscurity, the subject may shift without warning: μίαν μὲν ναῦν λαμβάνουσιν, τὰς δ' ἄλλᾱς οὐκ ἐδυνήθησαν, ἀλλ' ἀποφεύγουσιν *they captured one ship; the rest they were unable to capture; but they* (the ships) *escaped* T. 7. 25, τῶν νόμων αὐτῶν ἀκούετε τί κελεύουσι καὶ τί παραβεβήκᾱσιν *hear what the laws themselves command and what transgressions they* (my opponents) *have committed* D. 59. 115.

THE PREDICATE

Omission of the Verb

944. Ellipsis of the Copula. — The copulative verb εἶναι is often omitted, especially the forms ἐστί and εἰσί. This occurs chiefly

a. In general or proverbial statements: κοινὴ ἡ τύχη καὶ τὸ μέλλον ἀόρᾱτον *chance is common to all and the future cannot be scanned* I. 1. 29; **b.** in expressions of necessity, duty, etc.: ἀνάγκη φυλάττεσθαι *it is necessary to be on our guard* D. 9. 6. So with ὥρᾱ, καιρός, εἰκός, χρεών, δέον, verbals in -τέον (2152), as θεραπευτέον τοὺς θεούς *we must serve the gods* X. M. 2. 1. 28; c. with various adjectives: ἄξιος, δυνατός, πρόθῡμος, δίκαιος, οἷος, φροῦδος, ἕτοιμος; thus, ἡ ψῡχὴ δουλεύειν ἑτοίμη *the soul is ready to be a servant* P. Phae. 252 a, εἴ τις ἐπερωτῴη πότερον κρεῖττον *if anybody should ask whether it is better* X. M. 1. 1. 9.

945. Other forms of εἶναι are less commonly omitted: κοινωνεῖν ἕτοιμος (*scil.* εἰμί), οἶμαι δὲ καὶ Λάχητα τόνδε (*scil.* ἕτοιμον εἶναι) *I am ready to assist you and I think that Laches here is also ready* P. Lach. 180 a, οὐ σὺ λογογράφος (*scil.* εἶ); *are you not a speech-writer?* D. 19. 250, νὺξ ἐν μέσῳ (*scil.* ἦν) *the night was half gone* Aes. 3. 71, ἄτοπα λέγεις καὶ οὐδαμῶς πρὸς σοῦ (*scil.* ὄντα) *you are talking absurdly and not at all like yourself* X. M. 2. 3. 15, τοῖς θεοῖς μεγίστη χάρις (*scil.* ἔστω) *to the gods let our heartiest thanks be given* X. C. 7. 5. 72. Cp. 1041.

946. In lively discourse the form of a verb signifying *to do, speak, come, go,* etc., may be omitted for brevity. The ellipsis is often unconscious and it is frequently uncertain what is to be supplied to complete the thought. Thus, τί ἄλλο (*scil.* ἐποίησαν) ἢ ἐπεβούλευσαν; *what else* did they do *except plot against* us? T. 3. 39, οὐδὲν ἄλλο (*scil.* ποιῶν) ἢ πόλιν τὴν αὑτοῦ ἀπολείπων doing *nothing else except leaving his native city* 2. 16, ἵνα τί (*scil.* γένηται); *to what purpose?* D. 19. 257, περὶ μὲν τούτου κατὰ σχολήν (*scil.* λέξω) *about this by and by* 24. 187, μή μοί γε μύθους (*scil.* λέξητε) *none of your legends for me!* Ar. Vesp. 1179, ἀλλ' (σκέψασθε) ἕτερον *but* consider *another point* L. 13. 79, ὦ φίλε Φαῖδρε, ποῖ δὴ (*scil.* εἶ) καὶ πόθεν (*scil.* ἥκεις); *my dear Phaedrus whither, I beg of you,* are you going *and whence* do you come? P. Phae. 227 a, οὐκ ἐς κόρακας (*scil.* ἐρρήσεις); *will you not* be off *to the crows?* Ar. Nub. 871, πρός σε (*scil.* ἱκετεύω) γονάτων I entreat *thee by thy knees* E. Med. 324. Cp. 1599.

947. Καὶ ταῦτα *and that too* takes up a preceding expression: ἀγριωτέρους αὐτοὺς ἀπέφηνε . . . καὶ ταῦτ' εἰς αὑτόν *he made them more savage and that too towards himself* P. G. 516 c; often with concessive participles (2083): Μένωνα δ' οὐκ ἐζήτει, καὶ ταῦτα παρ' Ἀριαίου ὢν τοῦ Μένωνος ξένου *he did not ask for Menon and that too although he came from Ariaeus, Menon's guest-friend* X. A. 2. 4. 15. Cp. 1246, 2083.

948. A verb that may easily be supplied from the context is often omitted. Thus, ἐὰν μάθω, παύσομαι (*scil.* ποιῶν) ὅ γε ἄκων ποιῶ *if I learn* better, *I shall leave off* doing *what I do unintentionally* P. A. 26 a, ἀμελήσᾱς ὧνπερ οἱ πολλοί (*scil.* ἐπιμελοῦνται) *not caring for what most men* care for 36 b, ἐὰν αὖθις ζητήσετε ταῦτα, οὕτως (*scil.* ἔχοντα) εὑρήσετε *if you inquire about this later, you will find that it is so* 24 b. See under Brachylogy (Index).

CONCORD OF SUBJECT AND PREDICATE

949. A finite verb agrees with its subject in number and person.

Thus, τοῦτο τὸ ψήφισμα ἐγένετο *this bill was passed* L. 13. 56, ὃ δέδοικ' ἐγὼ μὴ πάθηθ' ὑμεῖς *which I fear lest you may suffer* D. 9. 65, ἣν δ' ἀποψηφίσωνται οἱ ἄλλοι, ἄπιμεν ἅπαντες τοὔμπαλιν *but if the rest vote against* (following), *we shall all return back again* X. A. 1. 4. 15, τὼ ξένω τώδε φίλω ἐστὸν ἐμώ *these two strangers are friends of mine* P. G. 487 a.

a. The verbal predicate, when a copulative verb (917), may be attracted to the number of a predicate noun, which often stands between subject and verb: τὸ χωρίον τοῦτο, ὅπερ πρότερον Ἐννέα ὁδοὶ ἐκαλοῦντο *this place which was formerly called Nine Ways* T. 4. 102, ἅπᾱν τὸ μέσον τῶν τειχῶν ἦσαν στάδιοι τρεῖς *the entire space between the walls was three stades* X. A. 1. 4. 4. So with the participles of such copulative verbs: τὴν ἡδονὴν διώκετε ὡς ἀγαθὸν ὄν (for οὖσαν) *you chase after pleasure as if it were a good* P. Pr. 354 c.

WITH ONE SUBJECT

Subject in the Singular, Verb in the Plural

950. With singular collective substantives (996) denoting persons and with like words implying a plural, the verb may stand in the plural.

Thus, τὸ στρατόπεδον ἐν αἰτίᾳ ἔχοντες τὸν Ἆγιν ἀνεχώρουν *the army returned holding Agis at fault* T. 5. 60, τοιαῦτα ἀκούσᾱσα ἡ πόλις Ἀγησίλᾱον εἵλοντο βασιλέᾱ *the city, after hearing such arguments, chose Agesilaus king* X. H. 3. 3. 4. So with βουλή *senate*, μέρος *part*, πλῆθος *multitude*, δῆμος *people*, ὄχλος *throng*.

951. So with ἕκαστος: τῶν ἑαυτοῦ ἕκαστος καὶ παίδων καὶ χρημάτων ἄρχουσι *every man is master of his own children and property* X. R. L. 6. 1.

952. If ἕκαστος, ἑκάτερος, ἄλλος are added in apposition to a plural subject, the verb generally remains plural: ἐγώ τε καὶ σὺ μακρὸν λόγον ἑκάτερος ἀπετείναμεν *both you and I have carried on a long controversy* P. Pr. 361 a. If the verb follows the apposition, it may be singular: οὗτοι μὲν ἄλλος ἄλλα λέγει *these say, some one thing, some another* X. A. 2. 1. 15. Cp. 982.

953. A subject in the singular, followed by a clause containing the preposition μετά *with*, rarely takes a plural verb: Ἀλκιβιάδης μετὰ Μαντιθέου ἵππων εὐπορήσαντες ἀπέδρᾱσαν *Alcibiades and Mantitheus escaped because they were well provided with horses* X. H. 1. 1. 10.

Subject in the Dual, Verb in the Plural

954. The first person dual agrees in form with the first person plural (462).

955. A dual subject may take a plural verb: Ξενοφῶντι προσέτρεχον δύο νεᾱνίσκω *two youths ran up to Xenophon* X. A. 4. 3. 10. In the orators the dual verb is almost always used.

956. The dual and plural verb may alternate: αἵρεσιν εἱλέτην τε καὶ διεπρᾱ́ξαντο *the* two souls *have made their choice and put it into effect* P. Phae. 256 c.

957. The neuter dual may be followed by the dual, the plural, or the singular verb (A 104, 200, M 466).

Subject in the Plural, Verb in the Singular

958. A neuter plural subject is regarded as a collective (996), and has its verb in the singular: καλὰ ἦν τὰ σφάγια *the sacrifices were propitious* X. A. 4. 3. 19.

N. — The neuter plural seems to have been originally in part identical in form with the feminine singular in ᾱ, and to have had a collective meaning.

959. A plural verb may be used when stress is laid on the fact that the neuter plural subject is composed of persons or of several parts: τὰ τέλη τῶν Λακεδαιμονίων αὐτὸν ἐξέπεμψαν *the Lacedaemonian magistrates despatched him* T. 4. 88, φανερὰ ἦσαν καὶ ἵππων καὶ ἀνθρώπων ἴχνη πολλά *many traces both of horses and of men were plain* X. A. 1. 7. 17.

a. With the above exception Attic regularly uses the singular verb. Homer uses the singular three times as often as the plural, and the plural less frequently with neuter adjectives and pronouns than with substantives. In some cases (B 135) the metre decides the choice.

960. Following the construction of δοκεῖ ταῦτα, we find δόξαν ταῦτα *when it had been thus decided* X. A. 4. 1. 13, and also δόξαντα ταῦτα X. H. 3. 2. 19. See 2078 a.

961. *Pindaric Construction.* A masculine or feminine plural subject occasionally is used with ἔστι, ἦν, γίγνεται, as: ἔστι καὶ ἐν ταῖς ἄλλαις πόλεσιν ἄρχοντές τε καὶ δῆμος *there are in the other cities too rulers and populace* P. R. 462 e. The verb usually precedes, and the subject is still undetermined; hence the plural is added as an afterthought. (Cp. Shakesp. "far behind his worth | Comes all the praises.") In Greek poetry this construction is rarely used with other verbs. On ἔστιν οἵ, see 2513.

a. ἦν was originally plural (464 e. D), and seems to survive in that use.

Subject in the Plural, Verb in the Dual

962. A plural subject may take a dual verb when the subject is a pair or two pairs: αἱ ἵπποι δραμέτην *the span of mares ran* Ψ 392.

a. This is common when δύο, ἄμφω, ἀμφότεροι are used with a plural subject: δύο ἄνδρες προσελθόντε Ἄγιδι διελεγέσθην μὴ ποιεῖν μάχην *two men coming to Agis urged him not to fight* T. 5. 59. But even with these words the plural is preferred. The neuter plural with δύο rarely takes the dual verb (P. Tim. 56 e).

WITH TWO OR MORE SUBJECTS

963. (I) When the subjects are different individuals or things and stand in the *third* person

964. With two subjects in the singular, the verb may be dual or plural: Κριτίᾱς καὶ Ἀλκιβιάδης ἐδυνάσθην ἐκείνῳ χρωμένω συμμάχῳ τῶν ἐπιθῡμιῶν κρατεῖν *Critias and Alcibiades were able to keep control of their appetites by the help*

of his example X. M. 1. 2. 24, Εὐρυμέδων καὶ Σοφοκλῆς ἀφικόμενοι ἐς Κέρκῡραν ἐστράτευσαν *on their arrival in Corcyra Eurymedon and Sophocles proceeded to make an attack* T. 4. 46.

965. In Homer the verb may intervene between the subjects (*Alcmanic Construction*): εἰς Ἀχέροντα Πυριφλεγέθων τε ῥέουσιν Κώκῡτός τε *Pyriphlegethon and Cocytus flow into Acheron* κ 513.

966. The verb may agree with the nearest or most important of two or more subjects. The verb may be placed

a. Before both subjects: ἧκε μὲν ὁ Θερσαγόρᾱς καὶ ὁ Ἐξήκεστος εἰς Λέσβον καὶ ᾤκουν ἐκεῖ *Thersagoras and Execestus came to Lesbos and settled there* D. 23. 143.

b. After the first subject: ὅ τε Πολέμαρχος ἧκε καὶ Ἀδείμαντος καὶ Νικήρατος καὶ ἄλλοι τινές *Polemarchus came and Adimantus and Niceratus and certain others* P. R. 327 b, Φαλῖνος ᾤχετο καὶ οἱ σὺν αὐτῷ *Phalinus and his companions departed* X. A. 2. 2. 1.

c. After both subjects: τὸ βουλευτήριον καὶ ὁ δῆμος παροράται *the senate and the people are disregarded* Aes. 3. 250. (Cp. Shakesp. "my mistress and her sister stays.")

967. (II) With several subjects referring to different persons the verb is in the plural; in the *first* person, if one of the subjects is first person; in the *second* person, if the subjects are second and third person: ὑμεῖς δὲ καὶ ἐγὼ τάδε λέγομεν *but you and I say this* P. L. 661 b, ἡμεῖς καὶ οἵδε οὐκ ἄλλην ἂν τινα δυναίμεθα ᾠδὴν ᾄδειν *we and these men could not sing any other song* 666 d, οὐ σὺ μόνος οὐδὲ οἱ σοὶ φίλοι πρῶτοι ταύτην δόξαν ἔσχετε *not you alone nor your friends are the first who have held this opinion* 888 b.

968. But the verb may be singular if it refers to the nearer or more important or more emphatic subject: πάρειμι καὶ ἐγὼ καὶ οὗτος Φρῡνίσκος καὶ Πολυκράτης *I am present and so are Phryniscus here and Polycrates* X. A. 7. 2. 29.

969. The verb may agree in person with the nearer or more important subject: σύ τε γὰρ Ἕλλην εἶ καὶ ἡμεῖς *for you are a Greek and so are we* X. A. 2. 1. 16.

970. With subjects connected by the disjunctives ἤ *or*, ἤ — ἤ *either — or*, οὔτε — οὔτε *neither — nor*, the verb agrees in number with the nearer subject when each subject is taken by itself: οὔτε σὺ οὔτ' ἂν ἄλλος οὐδεὶς δύναιτ' ἀντειπεῖν *neither you nor anybody else could reply* X. M. 4. 4. 7.

971. When the subjects are taken together, the plural occurs: ἃ Δημοφῶν ἢ Θηριππίδης ἔχουσι τῶν ἐμῶν *what Demophon or Therippides have of my property* D. 27. 12. This is unusual.

972. When ἤ *than* unites two subjects, if the verb follows ἤ, it agrees with the second subject: τύχη ἀεὶ βέλτῑον ἢ ἡμεῖς ἡμῶν αὐτῶν ἐπιμελούμεθα *fortune always takes better care of us than we do of ourselves* D. 4. 12.

CONCORD OF PREDICATE SUBSTANTIVES

973. A predicate substantive agrees with its subject in case: Μιλτιάδης ἦν στρατηγός *Miltiades was a general.*

974. A predicate substantive may agree in gender and number with its subject; but this is often impossible: τύχη τὰ θνητῶν πρᾶγματα *the affairs of mortals are chance* Trag. frag. p. 782, πάντ' ἦν Ἀλέξανδρος *Alexander was everything* D. 23. 120.

975. A predicate substantive or adjective agrees with the subject of the governing verb when the subject of the infinitive is omitted because it is the same as that of the governing verb (937): οὐχ ὁμολογήσω ἄκλητος ἥκειν *I shall not admit that I have come uninvited* P. S. 174 d, εἴπερ ἀξιοῦμεν ἐλεύθεροι εἶναι *if indeed we claim to be free* X. C. 8. 1. 4.

On the agreement of demonstrative and relative pronouns with a predicate substantive, see 1239, 2502 e.

APPOSITION

976. Concord. — An appositive (916) agrees in case with the word it describes: κόλακι, δεινῷ θηρίῳ καὶ μεγίστῃ βλάβῃ *to a flatterer, a terrible beast and a very great source of injury* P. Phae. 240 b. An appositive also agrees in case with the pronoun contained in a verb: Ταλθύβιος, ἥκω, Δαναϊδῶν ὑπηρέτης *I, Talthybius, have come, the servant of the Danaids* E. Hec. 503. Cp. 942.

977. An appositive to a possessive pronoun stands in the genitive, in agreement with the personal pronoun implied in the possessive: τὸν ἐμὸν (= ἐμοῦ) τοῦ ταλαιπώρου βίον *the life of me, wretched one* Ar. Plut. 33, τὰ ὑμέτερ' (= ὑμῶν) αὐτῶν κομιεῖσθε *you will regain your own* D. 4. 7. Cp. 1200. 2. b, 1202. 2. b.

978. An appositive in the genitive may follow an adjective equivalent to a genitive: Ἀθηναῖος (= Ἀθηνῶν) ὤν, πόλεως τῆς μεγίστης *being an Athenian, a citizen of the greatest city* P. A. 29 d.

979. Agreement in *number* between the appositive and its noun is unnecessary and often impossible: Θῆβαι, πόλις ἀστυγείτων *Thebes, a neighbouring city* Aes. 3. 133. So with δῶρα in poetry: γάμος, χρυσῆς Ἀφροδίτης δῶρα, *marriage, gift of golden Aphrodite* Theognis 1293.

980. An appositive to two substantives is dual or plural: θάρρος καὶ φόβος, ἄφρονε ξυμβούλω *daring and fear, two unintelligent counsellors* P. Tim. 69 d, ὕπνος πόνος τε, κύριοι συνωμόται *sleep and toil, supreme conspirators* A. Eum. 127.

981. Partitive Apposition (σχῆμα καθ' ὅλον καὶ μέρος, *construction of the whole and part*). The parts are represented by the appositives, which stand in the same case as the whole, which is placed first to show the subject or object of the sentence: τὼ ὁδώ, ἡ μὲν εἰς μακάρων νήσους, ἡ δ' εἰς τάρταρον *two roads, the one to the Islands of the Blest, the other to Tartarus* P. G. 524 a (*distributive* apposition). The appositives are generally in the nominative (ὁ μέν, ἡ δέ; οἱ μέν, οἱ δέ), rarely in the accusative.

a. The whole may stand in the singular: *λέγεται ψῡχὴ ἡ μὲν νοῦν ἔχειν, ἡ δὲ ἄνοιαν; with regard to the soul, is one said to have intelligence, the other folly?* P. Ph. 93 b.

982. To the word denoting the whole the appositive may be a collective singular (*adjunctive* apposition): *οὗτοι μὲν ἄλλος ἄλλα λέγει these say, some one thing, some another* X. A. 2. 1. 15 (cp. *ἠρώτων δὲ ἄλλος ἄλλο* P. Charm. 153 c), *οἱ στρατηγοὶ βραχέως ἕκαστος ἀπελογήσατο each of the generals defended himself briefly* X. H. 1. 7. 5. Cp. 952.

983. The apposition may be limited to one or more parts: *Πελοποννήσιοι καὶ οἱ ξύμμαχοι τὰ δύο μέρη two-thirds of the Peloponnesians and the allies* T. 2. 47. Often with participles: (*οἱ Ἀθηναῖοι*) *ἀνεμνήσθησαν καὶ τοῦδε τοῦ ἔπους, φάσκοντες οἱ πρεσβύτεροι πάλαι ᾄδεσθαι the Athenians bethought themselves of this verse too, the old men saying that it had been uttered long before* T. 2. 54.

984. In partitive apposition emphasis is laid on the *whole*, which is stated at once as the subject or object of the sentence. In the genitive of the divided whole (1306) emphasis is laid on the *parts*; thus, *τῶν πόλεων αἱ μὲν τυραννοῦνται, αἱ δὲ δημοκρατοῦνται, αἱ δὲ ἀριστοκρατοῦνται of states some are despotic, others democratic, others aristocratic* P. R. 338 d.

985. Construction of the Whole and Part in Poetry. — In Homer and later poets a verb may take two objects, one denoting the person, the other the part especially affected by the action: *τὸν δ' ἄορι πλῆξ' αὐχένα him he smote in the neck with his sword* Λ 240, *ἥ σε πόδας νίψει she will wash thy feet* τ 356. But the accusative of the part, often explained as an appositive, was an external object (1554 b) that became an accusative of respect (1601 a). In *Ἀχαιοῖσιν δὲ μέγα σθένος ἔμβαλ' ἑκάστῳ καρδίῃ and she set mighty strength in the heart of each of the Achaeans* Λ 11, *ἑκάστῳ* is a partitive appositive, *καρδίῃ* is local dative and grammatically independent of *Ἀχαιοῖσιν*. The construction is very rare in prose: *τοῖς υἱέσιν αὐτῶν ἀρετὴ παραγενομένη ταῖς ψῡχαῖς if virtue is imparted in the souls of their sons* P. Lach. 190 b.

986. Attributive Apposition. — A substantive may be used as an attributive to another substantive. This is common with substantives denoting *occupation*, *condition*, or *age* (usually with *ἀνήρ, ἄνθρωπος, γυνή*): *ἀνὴρ ῥήτωρ a public speaker, ἀνὴρ τύραννος a despot, πρεσβῦται ἄνθρωποι old men, γραῦς γυνή an old woman.* So also *πελτασταὶ Θρᾷκες Thracian targeteers* X. A. 1. 2. 9, *ὄλεθρος Μακεδών a scoundrel of a Macedonian* D. 9. 31, *Ἕλλην* (for *Ἑλληνικός*), as *οἱ Ἕλληνες πελτασταί the Greek targeteers* X. A. 6. 5. 26.

a. In standard prose *Ἕλλην* is used as an adjective only of persons (in poetry also of things).

b. The addition of *ἀνήρ* often implies respect: *ἄνδρες στρατιῶται fellow soldiers* X. A. 1. 3. 3, *ὦ ἄνδρες δικασταί jurymen, gentlemen of the jury* D. 27. 1. (Cp. *foemen.*) The addition of *ἄνθρωπος* often implies contempt: *ἄνθρωπος γόης a juggling fellow* Aes. 2. 153.

c. Many of the substantives thus qualified by an attributive substantive were originally participles, as *γέρων ἀνήρ an old man* P. Lys. 223 b.

987. Descriptive Apposition. — Here the appositive describes something definite that has just been mentioned: ἡ ἡμετέρᾱ πόλις, ἡ κοινὴ καταφυγὴ τῶν Ἑλλήνων *our city, the common refuge of the Greeks* Aes. 3. 134.

988. Explanatory Apposition. — Here the appositive explains a general or vague statement: τούτου τῑμῶμαι, ἐν πρυτανείῳ σῑτήσεως *I propose this as the penalty, maintenance in the Prytaneum* P. A. 37 a, μεγίστου κακοῦ ἀπαλλαγή, πονηρίᾱς *deliverance from the greatest of evils, vice* P. G. 478 d. So in geographical statements: Κύπρον ἵκᾱνε . . . ἐς Πάφον *she came to Cyprus, to Paphos* θ 362; cp. ἐς Δωριᾶς, Βοιόν *to the territory of the Dorians in which Boeum lies* T. 1. 107.

989. In Homer the substantival article at the beginning of a sentence may be followed by an appositive noun at or near the end: ἡ δ' ἀέκουσ' ἅμα τοῖσι γυνὴ κίεν *but she, the woman, went unwillingly with them* A 348.

990. τοῦτο, αὐτὸ τοῦτο, αὐτό, ἐκεῖνο often introduce emphatically a following substantive (or an equivalent, 908): ἐκεῖνο κερδαίνειν ἡγεῖται, τὴν ἡδονήν *this* (namely) *pleasure it regards as gain* P. R. 606 b. Cp. 1248.

991. Apposition to a Sentence. — A noun in the nominative or accusative may stand in apposition to the action expressed by a whole sentence or by some part of it.

a. The appositive is nominative when a nominative precedes: ἐμέθυον· ἱκανὴ πρόφασις *I was tipsy, a sufficient excuse* Philemon (Com. frag. 2. 531).

b. The appositive is accusative, and states a reason, result, intention, effect, or the like: ῥίψει ἀπὸ πύργου, λυγρὸν ὄλεθρον *will hurl thee from the battlement, a grievous death* Ω 735, Ἑλένην κτάνωμεν, Μενέλεῳ λύπην πικράν *let us slay Helen* and thus cause *a sore grief to Menelaus* E. Or. 1105, εὐδαιμονοίης, μισθὸν ἡδίστων λόγων *blest be thou — a return for thy most welcome tidings* E. El. 231.

N. — The appositive accusative is often cognate (1563 f.): ὁρᾷς Εὐρυσθέᾱ, ἄελπτον ὄψιν *thou beholdest Eurystheus, an unexpected sight* E. Heracl. 930.

992. An effect or result may be denoted by an appositive in other cases: ἐπῳδῶν προσδεῖσθαί μοι δοκεῖ μύθων ἔτι τινῶν *we need, it seems, some further words to act as a spell* P. L. 903 b.

993. From the construction in 991 b arose many adverbial accusatives (1606 ff.) such as χάριν *on account of*, πρόφασιν *in pretence*, δωρεάν *gratis*; as ὅς τις δὲ Τρώων ἐπὶ νηυσὶ φέροιτο . . . χάριν Ἕκτορος *whoever of the Trojans rushed at the ships as a favour to Hector* (*for Hector's sake*) O 744.

994. Many neuter words are used in apposition to a sentence or clause, which they usually precede. Such are ἀμφότερον, ἀμφότερα *both*, τὸ δεινότατον *the most dreadful thing*, δυοῖν θάτερον or θάτερα *one or the other*, τὸ ἐναντίον *the contrary*, τὸ κεφάλαιον *the chief point*, τὸ λεγόμενον *as the saying is*, οὐδέτερον *neither thing*, σημεῖον δέ *sign*, τεκμήριον δέ *evidence*, τὸ τελευταῖον *the last thing*, τὸ τῆς παροιμίᾱς *as the proverb* *runs,* αὐτὸ τοῦτο *this very thing,* ταὐτὸ τοῦτο *this same thing.* Thus, τοὺς ἀμφότερα ταῦτα, καὶ εὔνους τῇ πόλει καὶ πλουσίους *those who are both loyal to the State and rich* D. 18. 171, εἶπεν ὅτι δεῖ δυοῖν θάτερον, ἢ κείνους ἐν Ὀλύνθῳ μὴ οἰκεῖν ἢ αὑτὸν ἐν Μακεδονίᾳ *he said that one of two things was necessary — either that they should not live at Olynthus or he himself in Macedon* 9. 11, τὸ δὲ μέγιστον, πόλεμον ἀντ' εἰρήνης ἔχοντες *and what is worst of all, having war instead of peace* T. 2. 65, ἀλλ' ἦ, τὸ λεγόμενον, κατόπιν ἑορτῆς ἥκομεν; *but have we come 'after a feast' as the saying is?* P. G. 447 a, τοῦτο αὐτὸ τὸ τοῦ Ὁμήρου *in these very words of Homer* P. A. 34 d.

995. Very common are introductory relative clauses forming a nominative predicate of the sentence that follows: ὃ δὲ πάντων δεινότατον *but what is most terrible of all* L. 30. 29. ἐστί is regularly omitted (944). Such relative clauses are followed by an independent sentence, a clause with ὅτι, by ὅτε γάρ, ὅταν, ὅταν γάρ, εἰ. Similarly τὸ δ' ἔσχατον πάντων, ὅτι *but what is worst of all* P. Ph. 66 d, etc.

PECULIARITIES IN THE USE OF NUMBER

996. Collective Singular. — A noun in the singular may denote a number of persons or things: ὁ Μῆδος *the Medes* T. 1. 69, τὸ Ἑλληνικόν *the Greeks* 1. 1, τὸ βαρβαρικόν *the barbarians* 7. 29, ἡ πλίνθος *the bricks* 3. 20, ἵππον ἔχω εἰς χῑλίᾱν *I have about a thousand horse* X. C. 4. 6. 2, μῡρίᾱ ἀσπίς *ten thousand heavy armed* X. A. 1. 7. 10. On the plural verb with collectives, see 950. Cp. 1024, 1044.

a. So with the neuter participle: τὸ μαχόμενον almost = οἱ μαχόμενοι *the combatants* T. 4. 96.

b. The name of a nation with the article may denote one person as the representative (King, etc.) of a class: ὁ Μακεδών *the Macedonian* (Philip) D. 7. 6.

997. The inhabitants of a place may be implied in the name of the place: Λέσβος ἀπέστη βουληθέντες καὶ πρὸ τοῦ πολέμου *Lesbos revolted, having wished to do so even before the war* T. 3. 2.

998. Distributive Singular. — The singular of abstract nouns may be used distributively (rarely with concrete substantives): ὅσοι δίκαιοι ἐγένοντο ἐν τῷ ἑαυτῶν βίῳ *all who proved themselves just in their lives* P. A. 41 a, διάφοροι τὸν τρόπον *different in character* T. 8. 96. The distributive plural (1004) is more common than the distributive singular: cp. νεᾱνίαι τὰς ὄψεις *youths in appearance* L. 10. 29 with ἡδεῖς τὴν ὄψιν *pleasing in appearance* P. R. 452 b.

999. Dual. — The dual is chiefly employed of two persons or things which, by nature or association, form a pair: ὀφθαλμώ *the eyes (both eyes),* χεῖρε *the hands,* ἵππω *a span of horses.* The addition of ἄμφω *both* indicates that the two things belong together: δύο emphasizes the number. Both ἄμφω and δύο were early used with the plural. The dual died out in the living speech of Attica by 300 B.C. Aeolic has no dual, and Ionic lost it very early. In Hom. the dual is used freely, and often in conjunction with the plural.

1000. Plural. — The plural of proper names, of materials, and of abstracts is used to denote a class. (1) *of proper names:* Θησέες *men like Theseus* P. Th. 169 b. (2) *of materials:* here the plural denotes the parts, the different kinds of a thing, a mass, etc.: τόξα *bow* Hdt. 3. 78, πῡροί, κρῑθαί *wheat, barley* X. A. 4. 5. 26, οἶνοι *wines* 4. 4. 9, κρέᾱ *meat* Ar. Ran. 553 (κρέας *piece of meat*), ἥλιοι *hot days* T. 7. 87, ξύλα *timber* T. 7. 25. (3) *of abstracts:* here the plural refers to the single kinds, cases, occasions, manifestations of the idea expressed by the abstract substantive; or is referred to several persons: ἀγνωμοσύναι *misunderstandings* X. A. 2. 5. 6, θάλπη *degrees of heat* X. M. 1. 4. 13. Used in the plural, abstract nouns may become concrete, as ταφαί *funeral* T. 2. 34 (ταφή *sepulture*), εὐφροσύναι *good cheer* X. C. 7. 2. 28 (εὐφροσύνη *mirth*), χάριτες *proofs of good will, presents* D. 8. 53, εὖνοιαι *cases of benevolence, presents* D. 8. 25.

a. Many concrete substantives are commonly used only in the plural: πύλαι *gate*, θύραι *door*, τὰ Ὀλύμπια *the Olympic festival;* and in poetry δώματα *house*, κλίμακες *ladder*, λέκτρα *bed;* cp. 1006.

b. The plural, especially in poetry, may correspond to the English indefinite singular: ἐπὶ ναυσί *by ship.*

1001. In Homer the plural denotes the various forms in which a quality is manifested: τεκτοσύναι *the arts of the carpenter* ε 250. In poetry, often of feelings, emotions, etc.: μανίαι (attacks of) *madness* A. Pr. 879.

1002. οὐδένες (μηδένες) denotes classes of men, states, nations (D. 5. 15).

1003. The neuter plural is often used even in reference to a single idea or thought in order to represent it in its entirety or in its details, as τὰ ἀληθῆ *the truth.* This is very common with neuter pronouns: ἐχειρονόμουν δέ· ταῦτα γὰρ ἠπιστάμην *but I waved my arms, for I knew how to do this* X. S. 2. 19, διὰ ταχέων *quickly* P. A. 32 d.

a. Thucydides is fond of the neuter plural of verbal adjectives used impersonally: ἐψηφίσαντο πολεμητέα εἶναι *they voted that it was necessary to make war* T. 1. 88, ἀδύνατα ἦν *it was impossible* 4. 1. Cp. 1052.

1004. Distributive Plural. — Abstract substantives are often used distributively in the plural: σῑγαὶ τῶν νεωτέρων παρὰ πρεσβυτέροις *the silence of the younger men in the presence of their elders* P. R. 425 a.

1005. Names of towns and parts of the body are sometimes plural: Ἀθῆναι *Athens*, Θῆβαι *Thebes*, στήθη and στέρνα *breast* (chiefly poetic). The name of the inhabitants is often used for the name of a city: Δελφοί D. 5. 25.

1006. Plural of Majesty (poetic). — The plural may be used to lend dignity: θρόνοι *throne* S. Ant. 1041, σκῆπτρα *scepter* A. Ag. 1265, δώματα *dwelling* ε 6; παιδικά *favourite* in prose (only in the plural form).

1007. Here belongs the *allusive plural* by which one person is alluded to in the plural number: δεσποτῶν θανάτοισι *by the death of* *our lord* A. Ch. 52, παθοῦσα πρὸς τῶν φιλτάτων *I* (Clytaemnestra) *having suffered at the hands of my dearest ones* (Orestes) A. Eum. 100.

1008. Plural of Modesty.—A speaker in referring to himself may use the first person plural as a modest form of statement. In prose, of an author: ἔννοιά ποθ' ἡμῖν ἐγένετο *the reflection once occurred to me* X. C. 1. 1. 1. In tragedy, often with interchange of plural and singular: εἰ κωλῡόμεσθα μὴ μαθεῖν ἃ βούλομαι *if I* (Creusa) *am prevented from learning what I wish* E. Ion 391, ἱκετεύομεν ἀμφὶ σὰν γενειάδα . . . προσπίτνων *I entreat thee, as I grasp thy beard* E. H. F. 1206. See 1009.

1009. In tragedy, if a woman, speaking of herself, uses the plural verb (1008), an adjective or participle, in agreement with the subject, is feminine singular or masculine plural: ἥλιον μαρτῡρόμεσθα, δρῶσ' ἃ δρᾶν οὐ βούλομαι *I call the sun to witness, that I am acting against my will* E. H. F. 858, ἀρκοῦμεν ἡμεῖς οἱ προθνῄσκοντες σέθεν *it is enough that I* (Alcestis) *die in thy stead* E. Alc. 383.

1010. εἰπέ, φέρε, ἄγε may be used as stereotyped formulas, without regard to the number of persons addressed: εἰπέ μοι, ὦ Σώκρατές τε καὶ ὑμεῖς οἱ ἄλλοι *tell me, Socrates and the rest of you* P. Eu. 283 b.

1011. One person may be addressed as the representative of two or more who are present, or of his family: Ἀντίνο', οὔ πως ἔστιν . . . μεθ' ὑμῖν δαίνυσθαι *Antinous, it is in no wise possible to feast with you* β 310, ὦ τέκνον, ἦ πάρεστον; *my children, are ye here?* S. O. C. 1102. So in dramatic poetry, the coryphaeus may be regarded as the representative of the whole chorus, as ὦ ξένοι, μή μ' ἀνέρῃ τίς εἰμι *strangers* (addressed to the whole chorus) *do not ask* (the singular of the coryphaeus) *me who I am* S. O. C. 207.

1012. Greek writers often shift from a particular to a general statement and *vice versa*, thus permitting a free transition from singular to plural, and from plural to singular: οὐδὲ τότε συγχαίρει ὁ τύραννος· ἐνδεεστέροις γὰρ οὖσι ταπεινοτέροις αὐτοῖς οἴονται χρῆσθαι *not even then does the despot rejoice with the rest; for the more they are in want, the more submissive he thinks to find them* X. Hi. 5. 4.

PECULIARITIES IN THE USE OF GENDER

1013. Construction according to the Sense (926 a).—The real, not the grammatical, gender often determines the agreement: ὦ φίλτατ', ὦ περισσὰ τῑμηθεὶς τέκνον *O dearest, O greatly honoured child* E. Tro. 735 (this use of the attributive adjective is poetical), τὰ μειράκια πρὸς ἀλλήλους διαλεγόμενοι *the youths conversing with one another* P. Lach. 180 e, ταῦτ' ἔλεγεν ἡ ἀναιδὴς αὕτη κεφαλή, ἐξεληλυθώς *this shameless fellow spoke thus when he came out* D. 21. 117.

1014. So in periphrases: ἲς Τηλεμάχοιο ἐς πατέρα ἰδών *mighty Telemachus, gazing at his father* π 476, τὸ δὲ τῶν πρεσβυτέρων ἡμῶν . . . χαίροντες τῇ ἐκείνων παιδιᾷ *we the elders delighting in their sport* P. L. 657 d.

1015. The masculine is used for person in general: οὐκ ἀνέξεται τίκτοντας ἄλλους, οὐκ ἔχουσ' αὐτὴ τέκνα *unfruitful herself, she will not endure that others* *bear children* E. And. 712, ὁπότερος ἂν ᾖ βελτίων, εἴθ' ὁ ἀνὴρ εἴθ' ἡ γυνή *which ever of the two is superior, whether the man or the woman* X.O. 7.27. So οἱ γονεῖς *parents*, οἱ παῖδες *children*. See 1055.

See also 1009, 1050.

PECULIARITIES IN THE USE OF PERSON

1016. τὶς or πᾶς may be used in the drama with the second person of the imperative: ἴτω τις, εἰσάγγελλε *go, one of you, announce* E. Bacch. 173.

1017. The second person singular is used to designate an imaginary person, as in proverbs: ψυχῆς ἐπιμελοῦ τῆς σεαυτοῦ *care for thy own soul* Men. Sent. 551, and in such phrases as εἶδες ἂν *you would have seen* (1784 a), ἡγήσαιο ἂν *you might think*, as *crederis* (1824).

a. Hdt. uses the second person in directions to travellers (2.30).

See also 942.

ADJECTIVES

1018. Adjectives modify substantives (including words used substantively, 908), and substantive pronouns. Adjectives are either *attributive* (912) or *predicate* (910).

1019. The equivalents of an adjective are: a participle (οἱ παρόντες πολῖται *the citizens who are present*); a noun in apposition (Δημοσθένης ὁ ῥήτωρ *Demosthenes the orator*, *i.e.* not Δημοσθένης ὁ στρατηγός, ὑμεῖς οἱ Ἀθηναῖοι *you Athenians*); an oblique case (στέφανος χρυσοῦ *a crown of gold*, τῆς αὐτῆς γνώμης ἐγώ *I am likeminded*); an oblique case with a preposition (αἱ ἐν τῇ Ἀσίᾳ πόλεις *the cities in Asia*); an adverb (οἱ πάλαι *the ancients*). (Furthermore, a clause in a complex sentence: τὸ τείχισμα, ὃ ἦν αὐτόθι, αἱροῦσι *they captured the fortress which was there*; cp. 2542.)

1020. Concord. — An adjective agrees with its substantive in gender, number, and case. This holds true also of the article, adjective pronouns, and participles: thus, A. *Attributive:* ὁ δίκαιος ἀνήρ *the just man*, τοῦ δικαίου ἀνδρός, τὼ δικαίω ἄνδρε, οἱ δίκαιοι ἄνδρες, etc., οὗτος ὁ ἀνήρ *this man*, τούτου τοῦ ἀνδρός, etc., ἡ φιλοῦσα θυγάτηρ *the loving daughter*. B. *Predicate:* καλὸς ὁ ἀγών *the prize is glorious*, ταῦτ' ἐστὶν ἀληθῆ *these things are true*, αἱ ἄρισται δοκοῦσαι εἶναι φύσεις *the natures which seem to be best* X. M. 4. 1. 3.

On the agreement of demonstrative pronouns used adjectively with a predicate substantive, see 1239. For relative pronouns, see 2501.

ATTRIBUTIVE ADJECTIVES

ADJECTIVES USED SUBSTANTIVELY

1021. An attributive adjective (or participle) generally with the article, often dispenses with its substantive, and thus itself acquires the value of a substantive.

a. This occurs when the substantive may be supplied from the context; when it is a general notion; or when it is omitted in common expressions of a definite character, when the ellipsis is conscious.

1022. Masculine or feminine, when the substantive is a person: ὁ δίκαιος *the just man*, δίκαιος *a just man*, οἱ Ἀθηναῖοι *the Athenians*, οἱ πολλοί *the many, the rabble*, οἱ ὀλίγοι *the oligarchical party*, οἱ βουλόμενοι *all who will*, ἡ καλή *the beautiful woman*, ἡ τεκοῦσα *the mother* (poet., E. Alc. 167), ἐκκλησιάζουσαι *women in assembly*.

1023. Neuter, when the substantive idea is *thing* in general: τὸ ἀγαθόν *the* (highest) *good* P. R. 506 b (but τὰ ἀγαθά *good things* L. 12. 33), τὸ ἀληθές *truth* P. G. 473 b, τὸ κοινόν *the commonwealth* Ant. 3. β. 3, τὸ ἐσόμενον *the future* Aes. 3. 165, τὸ λεγόμενον *as the saying is* T. 7. 68, ἀμφὶ μέσον ἡμέρᾱς *about mid-day* X. A. 4. 4. 1, ἐπὶ πολύ *over a wide space* T. 1. 18.

1024. In words denoting a collection (996) of persons or facts: τὸ ὑπήκοον *the subjects* T. 6. 69, τὸ βαρβαρικόν *the barbarian force* X. A. 1. 2. 1, τὸ ξυμμαχικόν *the allied forces* T. 4. 77 (and many words in -ικόν), τὰ Ἑλληνικά *Greek history* T. 1. 97; and in words denoting *festivals* (τὰ Ὀλύμπια *the Olympian games* X. H. 7. 4. 28).

1025. With participles, especially in Thucydides: τὸ ὀργιζόμενον τῆς ὀργῆς *their angry feelings* T. 2. 59, τῆς πόλεως τὸ τῑμώμενον *the dignity of the State* 2. 63. The action of the verb is here represented as taking place under particular circumstances or at a particular time. These participles are not dead abstractions, but abstract qualities in action.

1026. A substantivized adjective may appear in the neuter plural as well as in the neuter singular: τὰ δεξιὰ τοῦ κέρᾱτος *the right of the wing* X. A. 1. 8. 4, τῆς Σαλαμῖνος τὰ πολλά *the greater part of Salamis* T. 2. 94, ἐπὶ πλεῖστον ἀνθρώπων *to the greatest part of mankind* 1. 1, ἐς τοῦτο δυστυχίᾱς *to this degree of misfortune* 7. 86 (cp. 1325).

a. On the construction of τῆς γῆς ἡ πολλή *the greater part of the land* T. 2. 56, see 1313.

1027. In common expressions a definite noun is often implied (such as ἡμέρᾱ *day*, ὁδός *way*, χείρ *hand*).

a. Masculine: **κόλπος** *gulf*, ὁ Ἰόνιος *the Ionian* gulf T. 6. 34, **στρατός** *force*, ὁ πεζός *the land* force 1. 47.

b. Feminine: **γῆ** *land* (**χώρᾱ** *country*) — ἀπὸ τῆς ἑαυτῶν *from their own* country T. 1. 15; οὔθ' ἡ Ἑλλὰς οὔθ' ἡ βάρβαρος *neither Greece nor barbaric* land D. 9. 27; **γνώμη** *judgment*: κατὰ τὴν ἐμήν *according to my* opinion Ar. Eccl. 153, ἐκ τῆς νῑκώσης *according to the prevailing* opinion X. A. 6. 1. 18; **δίκη** *suit*: ἐρήμην κατηγοροῦντες *bringing an accusation in a case where there is no defence* P. A. 18 c; **ἡμέρᾱ** *day*: τὴν ὑστεραίᾱν *the next day* X. C. 1. 2. 11, τῇ προτεραίᾳ *the day before* L. 19. 22; **κέρας** *wing*: τὸ εὐώνυμον *the left* wing T. 4. 96; **μερίς** *part*: εἰκοστή *a twentieth* 6. 54; **μοῖρα** *portion*: ἡ πεπρωμένη (I. 10. 61) or ἡ εἱμαρμένη (D. 18. 205) *the allotted portion, destiny*; **ναῦς** *ship*: ἡ τριήρης the ship *with three banks of oars*; **ὁδός** *way*: εὐθείᾳ *by the straight* road P. L. 716 a, τὴν ταχίστην *by the* *shortest* way X. A. 1. 3. 14; **τέχνη** *art*: *μουσική* the art of *music* P. L. 668 a; **χείρ** *hand*: *ἐν δεξιᾷ on the right* hand X. A. 1. 5. 1, *ἐξ ἀριστερᾶς on the left* 4. 8. 2; **ψῆφος** *vote*: *τὴν ἐναντίᾱν* Νικίᾳ *ἔθετο he voted in opposition to Nicias* P. Lach. 184 d.

1028. The context often determines the substantive to be supplied: *τοῦτον ἀνέκραγον ὡς ὀλίγᾱς* (*πληγὰς*) *παίσειεν they shouted that he had dealt him* (too, 1063) *few* blows X. A. 5. 8. 12, *τρία τάλαντα καὶ χῑλίᾱς* (*δραχμάς*) *three talents and a thousand* drachmas D. 27. 34; cp. *a dollar and twenty* (cents). Cp. 1572.

1029. From such substantivized adjectives arose many prepositional and adverbial expressions of whose source the Greeks themselves had probably lost sight. Many of these seem to be analogues of phrases once containing ὁδός: *τὴν ἄλλως ψηφίζεσθε you vote to no purpose* D. 19. 181 (*i.e. the way* leading *elsewhere* than the goal), *ἀπὸ τῆς πρώτης at the very beginning* T. 7. 43, *ἀπὸ τῆς ἴσης on an equality* 1. 15, *ἐξ ἐναντίᾱς from an opposite direction, facing* 7. 44.

AGREEMENT OF ATTRIBUTIVE ADJECTIVES

1030. An attributive adjective belonging to more than one substantive agrees with the nearest: *τὸν καλὸν κἀγαθὸν ἄνδρα καὶ γυναῖκα εὐδαίμονα εἶναί φημι the perfect man and woman are happy I maintain* P. G. 470 e. In some cases it is repeated with each substantive (often for emphasis): *ἓν σῶμ' ἔχων καὶ ψῡχὴν μίαν having one body and one soul* D. 19. 227.

1031. But occasionally the adjective agrees with the more important substantive: *ὁ σίγλος δύναται ἑπτὰ ὀβολοὺς καὶ ἡμιωβόλιον Ἀττικούς the siglus is worth seven and a half Attic obols* X. A. 1. 5. 6.

1032. Of two adjectives with one substantive, one may stand in closer relation to the substantive, while the other qualifies the expression thus formed: *πόλις ἐρήμη μεγάλη a large deserted-city* X. A. 1. 5. 4.

1033. If one substantive has several attributive adjectives, these are sometimes added without a conjunction (by *Asyndeton*): *κρέᾱ ἄρνεια, ἐρίφεια, χοίρεια flesh of lambs, kids, swine* X. A. 4. 5. 31. This is commoner in poetry, especially when the adjectives are descriptive: *ἔγχος βρῑθὺ μέγα στιβαρόν a spear heavy, huge, stout* Π 141.

1034. Two adjectives joined by *καί* may form one combined notion in English, which omits the conjunction. So often with *πολύς* to emphasize the idea of plurality: *πολλὰ κἀγαθά many blessings* X. A. 5. 6. 4, *πολλὰ καὶ δεινά many dreadful sufferings* D. 37. 57.

a. *καλὸς κἀγαθός* means *an aristocrat* (in the political sense), or is used of *a perfect quality* or *action* (in the moral sense) as T. 4. 40, P. A. 21 d.

1035. An attributive adjective is often used in poetry instead of the attributive genitive: βίη Ἡϝᾱκληείη B 658 *the might of Heracles* (cp. "a Niobean daughter" Tennyson); rarely in prose: ποταμός, εὖρος πλεθριαῖος *a river, a plethron in width* X. A. 4. 6. 4.

1036. An attributive adjective belonging logically to a dependent genitive is often used in poetry with a governing substantive: νεῖκος ἀνδρῶν ξύναιμον *kindred strife of men* S. A. 793 (for *strife of kindred men*). Rarely in prose in the case of the possessive pronoun: ἐν τῷ ὑμετέρῳ ἀσθενεῖ τῆς γνώμης *in the weakness of your purpose* T. 2. 61.

1037. An attributive adjective may dispense with its substantive when that substantive is expressed in the context: μετέχει τῆς καλλίστης (τέχνης) τῶν τεχνῶν *he shares in the fairest of the arts* P. G. 448 c.

1038. A substantivized participle may take the genitive rather than the case proper to the verb whence it is derived: βασιλέως προσήκοντες *relations of the king* T. 1. 128; contrast Περικλῆς ὁ ἐμοὶ προσήκων *Pericles my relation* X. H. 1. 7. 21.

1039. Adjectives used substantively may take an attributive: οἱ ὑμέτεροι δυσμενεῖς *your enemies* X. H. 5. 2. 33.

PREDICATE ADJECTIVES

1040. The predicate adjective is employed

a. With intransitive verbs signifying *to be, become*, and the like (917): ἡ δὲ χάρις ἄδηλος γεγένηται *the favour has been concealed* Aes. 3. 233. So with active verbs which take a preposition: νόμους ἔθεσθε ἐπ' ἀδήλοις τοῖς ἀδικήσουσι *you have enacted laws with regard to offenders who are unknown* D. 21. 30.

b. With transitive verbs: (1) to qualify the object of the verb directly and immediately: τοὺς κακοὺς χρηστοὺς νομίζειν *to judge bad men good* S. O. T. 609, (2) to express the result of the action (the proleptic use, 1579). So with αὔξειν *grow*, αἴρειν *raise* with μέγας *great*, μετέωρος *on high*, ὑψηλός *high*, μακρός *large*.

1041. With verbs of *saying* and *thinking* the predicate adjective is usually connected with its noun by εἶναι, with verbs of *perceiving, showing*, by ὤν (2106): οὐδένα γὰρ οἶμαι δαιμόνων εἶναι κακόν *for I think no one of the gods is base* E. I. T. 391, δηλοῖ ψευδῆ τὴν διαθήκην οὖσαν *it shows that the will is false* D. 45. 34. But εἶναι is sometimes omitted (945), as τὰς γὰρ καλὰς πρᾱ́ξεις ἁπᾱ́σᾱς ἀγαθὰς ὡμολογήσαμεν *for we have agreed that all honourable actions are good* P. Pr. 359 e. On the omission of ὤν, see 2117. For εἶναι with verbs of *naming* and *calling*, see 1615.

1042. Several adjectives of *time, place, order of succession*, etc., are used as predicates where English employs an adverb or a preposition with its case: ἀφικνοῦνται τριταῖοι *they arrive on the third day* X. A. 5. 3. 2, κατέβαινον σκοταῖοι *they descended in the dark* 4. 1. 10. In such cases the adjective is regarded as a *quality* of the subject; whereas an adverb would regard the *manner* of the action.

a. *Time, place:* χρόνιος *late*, ὄρθριος *in the morning*, δευτεραῖος *on the second day*, ποσταῖος *how many days?* ὑπαίθριος *in the open air*.

b. *Order of succession:* πρῶτος, πρότερος *first*, ὕστερος *later*, μέσος *in the midst*, τελευταῖος *last*, ὕστατος *last*.

N. — When one action is opposed to another in order of sequence, the adverbs πρῶτον, πρότερον, ὕστατον, etc., not the adjectives πρῶτος, etc., must be used: πρῶτον μὲν ἐδάκρῡε πολὺν χρόνον . . . εἶτα δὲ ἔλεξε τοιάδε *first he wept for a long time, then he spoke as follows* X. A. 1. 3. 2. Hence distinguish

πρῶτος τῇ πόλει προσέβαλε	*he was the first to attack the city.*
πρώτῃ τῇ πόλει προσέβαλε	*the city was the first place he attacked.*
πρῶτον τῇ πόλει προσέβαλε	*his first act was to attack the city.*

The same rule applies in the case of μόνος, μόνον, as μόνην τὴν ἐπιστολὴν ἔγραψα *this is the only letter I wrote*, μόνον ἔγραψα τὴν ἐπιστολήν *I only wrote* (but did not send) *the letter*. But this distinction is not always observed (Aes. 3. 69).

1043. So also with adjectives of *degree*, *mental attitude*, *manner*, etc.: φέρονται οἱ λίθοι πολλοί *the stones are thrown in great numbers* X. A. 4. 7. 7, τοὺς νεκροὺς ὑποσπόνδους ἀπέδοσαν *they restored the dead under a truce* T. 1. 63, οἱ θεοὶ εὐμενεῖς πέμπουσί σε *the gods send you forth favourably* X. C. 1. 6. 2. So with μέγας *high*, ἄσμενος *gladly*, ἑκούσιος, ἑκών *willingly*, ὅρκιος *under oath*, αἰφνίδιος *suddenly*. On ἄλλος, see 1272.

AGREEMENT OF PREDICATE ADJECTIVES (AND PARTICIPLES)

WITH ONE SUBJECT

1044. A circumstantial participle (2054) referring to a collective noun (996) may be plural: τὸ στράτευμα ἐπορίζετο σῖτον κόπτοντες τοὺς βοῦς *the army provided itself with provisions by killing the cattle* X. A. 2. 1. 6. So after οὐδείς, as οὐδεὶς ἐκοιμήθη (= πάντες ἐν ἀγρυπνίᾳ ἦσαν) τοὺς ἀπολωλότας πενθοῦντες *no one slept because they were all bewailing the dead* X. H. 2. 2. 3. Cp. 950.

1045. A plural participle may be used with a dual verb: ἐγελασάτην ἄμφω βλέψαντες εἰς ἀλλήλους *both looked at each other and burst out laughing* P. Eu. 273 d. A dual participle may be used with a plural verb: ποῦ ποτ' ὄνθ' ηὑρήμεθα; *where in the world are we?* E. I. T. 777.

1046. A dual subject may be followed by a plural predicate adjective or participle: εἰ γάρ τις φαίη τὼ πόλει τούτω πλείστων ἀγαθῶν αἰτίᾱς γεγενῆσθαι *if any one should assert that these two cities have been the cause of very many blessings* I. 12. 156.

1047. A predicate adjective is neuter singular when the subject is an infinitive, a sentence, or a general thought: ἡδὺ πολλοὺς ἐχθροὺς ἔχειν; *is it pleasant to have many enemies?* D. 19. 221, δῆλον δ' ὅτι ταῦτ' ἐστὶν ἀληθῆ *it is clear that these things are true* 2. 19.

1048. A predicate adjective referring to a masculine or feminine singular subject is often neuter singular and equivalent to a substantive. This occurs chiefly in statements of a general truth, where the subject refers to a whole class, not to an individual thing. Thus, καλὸν εἰρήνη *peace is a fine thing* D. 19. 336, ἄπιστον ταῖς πολῑτείαις ἡ τυραννίς *despotism is an object of mistrust to free states* 1. 5, μεῖζον πόλις ἑνὸς ἀνδρός *the state is larger than the individual* P. R. 368 e. So also in the plural (1056).

1049. So with names of places: ἔστι δὲ ἡ Χαιρώνεια ἔσχατον τῆς Βοιωτίᾶς *Chaeronea is on the frontier of Boeotia* T. 4. 76.

1050. A predicate superlative agrees in gender either with the subject or (usually) with a dependent genitive: νόσων χαλεπώτατος φθόνος *envy* is *the most fell of diseases* Men. fr. 535, σύμβουλος ἀγαθὸς χρησιμώτατον ἁπάντων τῶν κτημάτων *a good counsellor* is *the most useful of all possessions* I. 2. 53.

1051. For a predicate adjective used where English has an adverb, cp. 1042.

1052. A predicate adjective is often used in the neuter plural (especially with verbal adjectives in -τός and -τέος in Thucydides and the poets): ἐπειδὴ ἑτοῖμα ἦν, ἀνήγετο *when* (all) *was ready, he put out to sea* T. 2. 56, ἀδύνατα ἦν τοὺς Λοκροὺς ἀμύνεσθαι *it was impossible to resist the Locrians* 4. 1, ἐδόκει ἐπιχειρητέα εἶναι *they decided to make the attempt* 2. 3. Cp. 1003 a.

WITH TWO OR MORE SUBJECTS

1053. With two or more substantives a predicate adjective is plural, except when it agrees with the nearer subject: φόβος καὶ νόμος ἱκανὸς ἔρωτα κωλῡ́ειν *fear and the law are capable of restraining love* X. C. 5. 1. 10, πολλῶν δὲ λόγων καὶ θορύβου γιγνομένου *there arising much discussion and confusion* D. 3. 4. See 968.

1054. With substantives denoting persons of like gender, a predicate adjective is of the same gender: Ἀγάθων καὶ Σωκράτης λοιποί *Agathon and Socrates* are *left* P. S. 193 c.

1055. When the persons are of different gender, the masculine prevails: ὡς εἶδε πατέρα τε καὶ μητέρα καὶ ἀδελφοὺς καὶ τὴν ἑαυτοῦ γυναῖκα αἰχμαλώτους γεγενημένους, ἐδάκρῡσε *when he saw that his father and mother and brothers and wife had been made prisoners of war, he burst into tears* X. C. 3. 1. 7.

a. But persons are sometimes regarded as things: ἔχω αὐτῶν καὶ τέκνα καὶ γυναῖκας φρουρούμενα *I have their children and wives under guard* X. A. 1. 4. 8.

1056. With substantives denoting things of like gender a predicate adjective is of the same gender and plural. A neuter plural with the singular verb is often preferred: εὐγένειαί τε καὶ δυνάμεις καὶ τῑμαὶ δῆλά ἐστιν ἀγαθὰ ὄντα *noble birth and power and honour are clearly good things* P. Eu. 279 b.

1057. When the things are of different gender, a predicate adjective is neuter plural with singular verb: λίθοι τε καὶ πλίνθοι καὶ ξύλα καὶ κέραμος ἀτάκτως ἐρρῑμμένα οὐδὲν χρήσιμά ἐστιν *stones and bricks and pieces of wood and tiles thrown together at random are useless* X. M. 3. 1. 7.

1058. When the substantives denote both persons and things, a predicate adjective is—**a.** plural, and follows the gender of the person, if the person is more important, or if the thing is treated as a person: γρᾴδια καὶ γερόντια καὶ *πρόβατα ὀλίγα καὶ βοῦς καταλελειμμένους old women and old men and a few sheep and oxen that had been left behind* X. A. 6. 3. 22, *ἡ τύχη καὶ Φίλιππος ἦσαν τῶν ἔργων κύριοι Fortune and Philip were masters of the situation* Aes. 2. 118,

b. or is neuter plural if the person is treated like a thing: *ἡ καλλίστη πολῑτείᾱ τε καὶ ὁ κάλλιστος ἀνὴρ λοιπὰ ἂν ἡμῖν εἴη διελθεῖν we should still have to treat of the noblest polity and the noblest man* P. R. 562 a.

1059. The verbal and the adjective predicate may agree with the first of two subjects as the more important: *Βρᾱσίδᾱς καὶ τὸ πλῆθος ἐπὶ τὰ μετέωρα τῆς πόλεως ἐτράπετο βουλόμενος κατ᾽ ἄκρᾱς ἑλεῖν αὐτήν Brasidas with the bulk of his troops turned to the upper part of the city wishing to capture it completely* T. 4. 112.

For further uses of predicate adjectives, see 1150 ff., 1168 ff., 2647.

ATTRACTION OF PREDICATE NOUNS WITH THE INFINITIVE TO THE CASE OF THE OBJECT OF THE GOVERNING VERB

1060. When the subject of the infinitive is the same as a genitive or dative depending on the governing verb, it is often omitted.

1061. A predicate adjective referring to a *genitive* regularly stands in the genitive, but a predicate substantive or participle generally stands in the accusative in agreement with the unexpressed subject of the infinitive: *Κύρου ἐδέοντο ὡς προθῡμοτάτου γενέσθαι they entreated Cyrus to show himself as zealous as possible* X. H. 1. 5. 2, *ὑπὸ τῶν δεομένων μου προστάτην γενέσθαι by those who begged me to become their chief* X. C. 7. 2. 23, *δέομαι ὑμῶν ἐθελῆσαί μου ἀκοῦσαι, ὑπολογιζομένους τὸ πλῆθος τῶν αἰτιῶν I beg of you that you be willing to listen to me, paying heed to the number of charges* Aes. 2. 1.

1062. A predicate substantive, adjective, or participle referring to a *dative* stands in the dative or in the accusative in agreement with the unexpressed subject of the infinitive: *νῦν σοι ἔξεστιν ἀνδρὶ γενέσθαι now it is in your power to prove yourself a man* X. A. 7. 1. 21, *Λακεδαιμονίοις ἔξεστιν ὑμῖν φίλους γενέσθαι it is in your power to become friends to the Lacedaemonians* T. 4. 29, *ἔδοξεν αὐτοῖς . . . ἐξοπλισαμένοις προϊέναι they decided to arm themselves fully and to advance* X. A. 2. 1. 2, *ἔδοξεν αὐτοῖς προφυλακᾶς καταστήσαντας συγκαλεῖν τοὺς στρατιώτᾱς they decided to station pickets and to assemble the soldiers* 3. 2. 1, *συμφέρει αὐτοῖς φίλους εἶναι μᾶλλον ἢ πολεμίους it is for their interest to be friends rather than enemies* X. O. 11. 23.

For predicate nouns in the nominative or accusative in agreement with omitted *subject* of the infinitive, see 1973–1975.

COMPARISON OF ADJECTIVES (AND ADVERBS)

POSITIVE

1063. The positive, used to imply that something is not suited or inadequate for the purpose in question, is especially common before an infinitive with or without ὥστε (ὡς): (τὸ ὕδωρ) ψῡχρόν ἐστιν ὥστε λούσασθαι *the water is* too *cold for bathing* X. M. 3. 13. 3, νῆες ὀλίγαι ἀμύνειν *ships* too *few to defend* T. 1. 50, μακρὸν ἂν εἴη μοι λέγειν *it would take* too *long for me to state* And. 2. 15.

1064. A positive adjective followed by the genitive of the same adjective has, in poetry, the force of a superlative: κακὰ κακῶν *woe of woe* S. O. C. 1238.

1065. μᾶλλον ἤ *rather than, more ... than* may be used after a positive: προθύμως μᾶλλον ἢ φίλως *more prompt than kindly* A. Ag. 1591.

COMPARATIVE

1066. The comparative expresses contrast or comparison. Thus, δεξίτερος is *right* in contrast to its opposite, ἀριστερός *left.* Cp. 1082 b. Usually comparison is expressed, as εὖ τε καὶ χεῖρον *well or ill* T. 2. 35.

a. When the positive precedes, μᾶλλον alone may stand for the comparative; as in ἐκεῖνοί τε ἄξιοι ἐπαίνου καὶ ἔτι μᾶλλον (*i.e.* ἀξιώτεροι) οἱ πατέρες *they are worthy of praise and still more worthy are our fathers* T. 2. 36.

b. The persons or things with which comparison is made may include *all* others of the same class: ἡμῶν ὁ γεραίτερος *the elder* (= eldest) *of us* X. C. 5. 1. 6.

1067. The comparative is sometimes used merely as an intensive and does not differ essentially from the positive: τούτων καταδεέστερος *at a disadvantage with* (inferior to) *these men* D. 27. 2.

1068. For the use of μᾶλλον instead of the comparative, and μάλιστα instead of the superlative, see 323. When either form can be used, that with μᾶλλον or μάλιστα is more emphatic. Thucydides sometimes uses πλέον (τι), τὸ πλέον instead of μᾶλλον.

1069. The comparative degree may be followed by the genitive (1431) or by ἤ *than:* σοφώτερος ἐμοῦ or σοφώτερος ἢ ἐγώ *wiser than I.* The genitive may precede or follow the comparative. With ἤ, the persons or things compared usually stand in the same case, and always so when they are connected by the same verb: φιλῶ γὰρ οὐ σὲ μᾶλλον ἢ δόμους ἐμούς *for I do not love thee more than my own house* E. Med. 327.

a. The genitive is usual if two subjects would have the same verb in common; as οἱ Κρῆτες βραχύτερα τῶν Περσῶν ἐτόξευον *the Cretans shot a shorter distance than the Persians* (= ἢ οἱ Πέρσαι) X. A. 3. 3. 7.

b. When two objects have the same verb in common: if the object stands (1) in the *accusative*, the genitive is preferred, as ἐμοὶ δοκεῖ Κῦρος, οὕστινας ἂν ὁρᾷ ἀγαθούς, φιλεῖν οὐδὲν ἧττον ἑαυτοῦ *Cyrus seems to me to love all whom he finds excellent quite as much as he loves himself* X. C. 2. 3. 12, but the accusative is not uncommon, as E. Med. 327 quoted above; (2) in the *dative*, the genitive is frequent, as προσήκει μοι μᾶλλον ἑτέρων . . . ἄρχειν *it behooves me rather than others to rule* T. 6. 16; (3) in the *genitive*, the genitive is very rare (X. M. 4. 3. 10). Here ἤ is preferred to the genitive for the sake of euphony: οἱ γὰρ πονηροὶ πολὺ πλειόνων εὐεργεσιῶν ἢ οἱ χρηστοὶ (not τῶν χρηστῶν) δέονται *for the wicked need more favours than the good* X. M. 2. 6. 27.

c. The genitive is often used where ἤ would be followed by some other case than nominative or accusative, or by a preposition: ταῦτα τοῖς ὁπλίταις οὐχ ἧσσον τῶν ναυτῶν (= ἢ τοῖς ναύταις) παρακελεύομαι *I address these exhortations to the hoplites not less than to the sailors* T. 7. 63, (δεῖ βλέπειν) εἰς τὴν ἐμπειρίᾱν μᾶλλον τῆς ἀρετῆς (= ἢ εἰς τὴν ἀρετήν) *we must look at skill more than* (at) *courage* Aristotle, Politics 1309 b 5.

d. ἐλάττων (χείρων, ἐνδεέστερος, ὕστερος, etc.) οὐδενός *inferior to none, greater than all*; here ἤ is not used). Thus, δουλεύειν δουλείᾱν οὐδεμιᾶς ἧττον αἰσχρᾱ́ν *to endure a most disgraceful slavery* X. M. 1. 5. 6.

1070. The word following ἤ may be the subject of a new verb (expressed or understood): ἡμεῖς ὑπὸ κρείττονος διδασκάλου πεπαιδεύμεθα ἢ οὗτοι *we have been educated by a better teacher than they* (have been) X. C. 2. 3. 13; but this word is more often attracted into the case of the preceding word: τινὲς καὶ ἐκ δεινοτέρων ἢ τοιῶνδε (= ἢ τοιάδε ἐστίν) ἐσώθησαν *some have been rescued from dangers even greater than these* T. 7. 77. The genitive is also common without ἤ: λέγων ὅτι οὔπω . . . τούτου ἡδίονι οἴνῳ ἐπιτύχοι *saying that he had never met with sweeter wine than this* X. A. 1. 9. 25.

1071. ὡς for ἤ is rare, and suspected by some. But cp. A. Pr. 629, P. A. 30 b, 36 d, R. 526 c.

1072. μᾶλλον ἤ may be used though a comparative precedes: αἱρετώτερόν ἐστι μαχομένους ἀποθνῄσκειν μᾶλλον ἢ φεύγοντας σῴζεσθαι *it is more desirable for men to die fighting* (rather) *than to save themselves by running away* X. C. 3. 3. 51. Here μᾶλλον ἤ is to be taken with the verb.

1073. Instead of the genitive or ἤ, the prepositions ἀντί, πρό (w. gen.) or πρός, παρά (w. accus.) are sometimes used with the comparative: κατεργάσασθαι αἱρετώτερον εἶναι τὸν καλὸν θάνατον ἀντὶ τοῦ αἰσχροῦ βίου *to make a noble death more desirable than* (instead of) *a shameful life* X. R. L. 9. 1, μὴ παῖδας περὶ πλείονος ποιοῦ πρὸ τοῦ δικαίου *do not consider children of more account than* (before) *justice* P. Cr. 54 b, χειμὼν μείζων παρὰ τὴν καθεστηκυῖαν ὥρᾱν *a cold too severe for* (in comparison with) *the actual time of year* T. 4. 6.

1074. In statements of number and measure ἤ may be omitted after the adverbial comparatives πλέον (πλεῖν) *more*, ἔλᾱττον (μεῖον) *less*, which do not alter their case and number: πέμπει οὐκ ἔλᾱττον δέκα φέροντας πῦρ *he sends not less* than *ten men carrying fire* X. H. 4. 5. 4, πόλις πλέον πεντακισχῑλίων ἀνδρῶν *a city of more* than *5000 men* 5. 3. 16. Even when ἤ is kept, πλέον (πλεῖν), etc., remains unchanged: ἐν πλεῖν (= πλείοσιν) ἢ διᾱκοσίοις ἔτεσιν *in more than 200 years* D. 24. 141, τοξότᾱς πλεῖν ἢ εἴκοσι μῡριάδας *more bowmen than 20 myriads* X. C. 2. 1. 6.

a. In place of the adverbial πλέον, etc., we find also the adjectival forms with or without ἤ or with the genitive: τοξότᾱς πλείους ἢ τετρακισχῑλίους *more bowmen than 4000* X. C. 2. 1. 5, ἔτη γεγονὼς πλείω ἑβδομήκοντα *more* than *70 years old* P. A. 17 d, ἱππέᾱς πλείους τριᾱκοσίων *more than 300 horse* X. H. 1. 3. 10.

1075. The genitive sometimes occurs together with ἤ, and either when the genitive has a separate construction, or is a pronoun to which the ἤ clause stands as an appositive, or of which it is explanatory. Thus, προῄει πλέον . . . ἢ δέκα σταδίων *he advanced more than ten stades* X. H. 4. 6. 5 (here πλέον is treated as a substantive), τίς γὰρ ἂν γένοιτο ταύτης μανίᾱ μείζων ἢ . . . ἡμᾶς κακῶς ποιεῖν; *for what madness could be greater than (this) . . . to use us ill?* Is. 1. 20. Cp. 1070.

1076. Compendious Comparison. — The possessor, rather than the object possessed, may be put in the genitive after a comparative: εἰ δ' ἡμεῖς ἱππικὸν κτησαίμεθα μὴ χεῖρον τούτων (= τοῦ τούτων ἱππικοῦ) *but if we should raise a cavalry-force not inferior to theirs* X. C. 4. 3. 7.

1077. Comparison with a Noun representing a clause. — When one person or thing is to be compared, not with another person or thing in regard to its quality, but with an entire idea expressed by a clause (*e.g.* ἢ ὥστε with the infinitive, ἢ ὡς with the potential optative, or ἢ and a finite verb), this clause may be abridged into a substantive or a participle. Thus, πρᾶγμα ἐλπίδος κρεῖσσον *an event beyond our expectations* (too great to be expected) T. 2. 64, προσωτέρω τοῦ καιροῦ προϊόντες *advancing further than the proper measure* (i.e. *further than they should have gone*) X. A. 4. 3. 34, ὡς τῶν γε παρόντων οὐκ ἂν πράξαντες χεῖρον *in the belief that they could not fare worse than at present* (ἢ τὰ παρόντα ἐστίν) T. 7. 67.

1078. Reflexive Comparison. — The comparative followed by the reflexive pronoun in the genitive is used to denote that an object displays a quality in a higher degree than usual. The degree of increase is measured by comparison with the subject itself. αὐτός is often added to the subject: αὐτοὶ αὑτῶν εὐμαθέστεροι γίγνονται *they learn more easily than before* I. 15. 267, πλουσιώτεροι ἑαυτῶν γιγνόμενοι *becoming richer than they were before* T. 1. 8. Cp. 1093.

1079. Proportional Comparison. — After a comparative, ἢ κατά with the accusative (1690. 2 c), or ἢ ὥστε, ἢ ὡς, rarely ἤ alone, with the infinitive (not with the indicative), denote too high or too low a degree: ὅπλα ἔτι πλείω ἢ κατὰ τοὺς νεκροὺς ἐλήφθη *more arms were taken than there were men slain* T. 7. 45, φοβοῦμαι μή τι μεῖζον ἢ ὥστε φέρειν δύνασθαι κακὸν τῇ πόλει συμβῇ *I fear lest there should befall the State an evil too great for it to be able to bear* X. M. 3. 5. 17 (2264).

1080. Double Comparison. — Two adjectives (or adverbs) referring to the same subject, when compared with each other, are both put in the comparative; ἤ is always used: ἡ εἰρήνη ἀναγκαιοτέρᾱ ἢ καλλίων *a peace inevitable rather than honourable* Aes. 3. 69, συντομώτερον ἢ σαφέστερον διαλεχθῆναι *to discourse briefly rather than clearly* I. 6. 24.

a. μᾶλλον may be used with the first adjective in the positive (cp. 1065), and ἢ before the second: πρόθῡμος μᾶλλον ἢ σοφωτέρᾱ *with more affection than prudence* E. Med. 485.

1081. A comparative may follow a positive to mark the contrast with it: καὶ μῑκρὰ καὶ μείζω *both small and great*(er) D. 21. 14.

1082. The comparative may stand alone, the second part being implied.

a. That which is exceeded is indicated by the sense only: οἱ σοφώτεροι *the wiser* (those wiser than the rest); ἐν εἰρήνῃ αἱ πόλεις ἀμείνους τας γνώμᾱς ἔχουσιν *in* *time of peace States are actuated by higher convictions* (than in time of war) T. 3. 82. So τι νεώτερον *something new* (more recent than that already known) P. Pr. 310 a (often = *a calamity* or *a revolutionary movement*); ὕστερον ἧκον *they came too late* T. 7. 27; and often where we supply *is usual* (*right*, *fitting*, etc.).

b. The Hom. θηλύτεραι γυναῖκες implies a comparison with men. In Κῦρος . . . ἐγεγόνει μητρὸς ἀμείνονος, πατρὸς δὲ ὑποδεεστέρου *Cyrus was born of a mother of superior, but of a father of inferior race* (Hdt. 1. 91) the comparison is between the qualities of mother and father respectively. Cp. 313 b.

c. The comparative denotes excess: μείζοσιν ἔργοις ἐπιχειροῦντες οὐ μῑκροῖς κακοῖς περιπίπτουσι *by entering upon undertakings too great they encounter no slight troubles* X. M. 4. 2. 35.

d. The comparative is used to soften an expression (*rather*, *somewhat*): ἀγροικότερον *somewhat boorishly* P. G. 486 c, ἀμελέστερον ἐπορεύετο *he proceeded rather carelessly* X. H. 4. 8. 36. Here the quality is compared with its absence or with its opposite.

1083. The comparative is often used where English requires the positive: οὐ γὰρ χεῖρον πολλάκις ἀκούειν *for 'tis not a bad thing to hear often* P. Ph. 105 a.

1084. Strengthened forms. — The comparative may be strengthened by ἔτι, πολλῷ, μακρῷ (1513), πολύ (1609), πολὺ ἔτι, etc. μᾶλλον is sometimes used with the comparative: αἰσχυντηροτέρω μᾶλλον τοῦ δέοντος *more bashful than they ought to be* P. G. 487 b. So the correlative ὅσῳ, ὅσον: ὅσῳ μείζους εἰσὶ τᾶς ὄψεις, τοσούτῳ μᾶλλον ὀργῆς ἄξιοί εἰσι *the braver they are to appearances, the more they deserve our anger* L. 10. 29.

SUPERLATIVE

1085. The superlative expresses either the highest degree of a quality (the *relative* superlative: ὁ σοφώτατος ἀνήρ *the wisest man*) or a very high degree of a quality (the *absolute* superlative, which does not take the article: ἀνὴρ σοφώτατος *a very wise man*). The relative superlative is followed by the genitive of the person or thing surpassed (1315, 1434). On the agreement, see 1050.

a. The class to which an individual, marked by the superlative, belongs, may be designated by a genitive of the divided whole (1315): ὁ σοφώτατος τῶν Ἑλλήνων *the wisest of the Greeks.* So often by πάντων: πάντων ἀνθρώπων ἀγνωμονέστατοι *the most senseless of all men* Lyc. 54. On the superlative with ἄλλων, see 1434.

b. With *two* the comparative exhausts all the degrees of comparison: hence πρότερος and πρῶτος, ὕστερος and ὕστατος, ἑκάτερος *each of two*, and ἕκαστος *each of several*, are carefully to be distinguished.

1086. Strengthened Forms. — The superlative may be strengthened by prefixing ὅτι or ὡς, rarely ᾗ (also ὅσον or ὅπως in poetry): ὅτι πλεῖστοι *as many men as possible*, ὅτι τάχιστα *as quickly as possible*, ᾗ ἄριστον *the very best way* X. C. 7. 5. 82 (ὅπως ἄριστα A. Ag. 600). ὅτι or ὡς is always added when a preposition precedes the superlative: ὡς εἰς στενώτατον *into as narrow compass as possible* X. O. 18. 8. ὡς and ὅτι may be used together: ὡς ὅτι βέλτιστον ἐμὲ γενέσθαι *for me to become as good as may be* P. S. 218 d.

a. With ὡς and ᾗ, rarely with ὅπῃ (not with ὅτι), a form of δύναμαι or οἷός τέ εἰμι, etc., may be employed: διηγήσομαι ὑμῖν ὡς ἂν δύνωμαι διὰ βραχυτάτων *I will relate to you in the briefest terms I can* I. 21. 2.

1087. οἷος may strengthen the superlative: ὁρῶντες τὰ πράγματα οὐχ οἷα βέλτιστα ἐν τῇ πόλει ὄντα *observing that affairs are not in the very best state in the city* L. 13. 23. If ὅσος or ὁπόσος take the place of οἷος, a form, or a synonym, of δύναμαι is usually added: ἤγαγον συμμάχους ὁπόσους πλείστους ἐδυνάμην *I brought the very largest number of allies I could* X. C. 4. 5. 29. ὁποῖος is rare (Thuc., Plato).

1088. εἷς ἀνήρ in apposition to the person designated may be added to strengthen the superlative: Ἀντιφῶν πλεῖστα εἷς ἀνὴρ δυνάμενος ὠφελεῖν *Antiphon being able to render* (most aid as one man) *aid beyond any other man* T. 8. 68.

1089. ἐν τοῖς is used before the superlative in all genders and numbers (esp. in Hdt., Thuc., Plato): ὠμὴ ἡ στάσις . . . ἔδοξε μᾶλλον, διότι ἐν τοῖς πρώτη ἐγένετο *the revolution seemed the more cruel since it was the first* T. 3. 81, ἐν τοῖς πλεῖσται δὴ νῆες ἅμ' αὐτοῖς ἐγένοντο *they had the very largest number of ships* 3. 17.

1090. μάλιστα, or πλεῖστον, μέγιστον, occurs with the superlative: οἱ μάλιστα ἀνοητότατοι *the very stupidest* P. Tim. 92 a. In poetry βαθυ- has the effect of a superlative: βαθύπλουτος *exceeding rich* A. Supp. 555.

1091. καί *even*, πολλῷ, μακρῷ (1513), πολύ (1609), παρὰ πολύ, πάντα (τὰ πάντα), the correlative ὅσῳ also strengthen the superlative.

1092. In poetry (rarely in prose) a superlative may be strengthened by the addition of the genitive of the same adjective in the positive: ὦ κακῶν κάκιστε *oh, vilest of the vile* S. O. T. 334.

1093. Reflexive comparison (cp. 1078) occurs with the superlative: ἀμβλύτατα αὐτὸς αὑτοῦ ὁρᾷ *his sight is at its dullest* P. L. 715 d.

ADVERBS

1094. Adverbs are of two kinds

a. Ordinary adverbs, denoting manner, degree, time, place, etc. Ordinary adverbs qualify verbs, adjectives, other adverbs, and (rarely) substantives: ὄπισθεν γενόμενος *getting behind* X. A. 1. 8. 24, εὐθὺς ἐβόᾱ *straightway he shouted* 1. 8. 1, φανερὸν ἤδη *already clear* L. 4. 6, πολὺ θᾶττον *much more quickly* X. A. 1. 5. 2, εὖ μάλα *very easily* 6. 1. 1, εἰκότως τρόπον τινά *in a way reasonably* D. 8. 41, μάλα συμφορᾱ́ *a great misfortune* X. C. 4. 2. 5, μάλα στρατηγός *an excellent general* X. H. 6. 2. 39.

b. Sentence adverbs (or *particles*) are adverbs that affect the sentence as a whole or give emphasis to particular words of any kind. Greek has many sentence adverbs, some of which are treated more fully under Particles.

Such are words of interrogation (ἦ, ἆρα, μῶν); of affirmation and confidence (δή *now, indeed*, δῆτα *surely*, γέ *at least, even*, ἦ *really*, μήν *in truth*, νή *surely*, *τοί surely*); of uncertainty (*ἴσως, πού, τάχα perhaps*); of negation (*οὐ, μή, οὔτοι, μήτοι*, etc.); of limitation (*ἄν* 1761 ff.).

1095. The equivalents of an ordinary adverb are: an oblique case (*ἐβασίλευεν εἴκοσιν ἔτη he reigned for twenty years*, 1581, 1582; *ἀκούειν σπουδῇ to listen attentively, τῇ ὑστεραίᾳ ἐπορεύοντο they proceeded on the next day*, and many other datives, 1527 b; *ἧκε τὴν ταχίστην he came in the quickest way*, and many other accusatives, 1606–1611); an oblique case with a preposition (*διὰ τάχους ἦλθε he came quickly = ταχέως, ἀπ' οἴκου ὁρμῶμαι I start from home = οἴκοθεν, ἐν τῷ ἐμφανεῖ clearly, ἐδίδου πρὸς τὴν ἀξίᾱν he gave according to merit = ἀξίως, πρὸς βίᾱν forcibly = βιαίως*); a participle (*γελῶν εἶπε he said with a laugh, laughingly*). (Furthermore, a clause in a complex sentence, as *εἰσπηδήσαντες . . . θᾶττον ἢ ὥς τις ἂν ᾤετο leaping in more quickly than one would have thought* X. A. 1. 5. 8; cp. 2189. 3.)

1096. In the attributive position an ordinary adverb may serve as an adjective: *ἐν τῷ πλησίον παραδείσῳ in the neighbouring park* X. A. 2. 4. 16, *ὁ ἐκεῖθεν ἄγγελος the messenger from that quarter* P. R. 619 b, *ταραχὴ ἡ τότε the confusion of that time* L. 6. 35. See 1153 e. N.

1097. **a.** An ordinary adverb qualifying a verb is often so used that it may be referred to the subject or object of the sentence where an adjective could stand. Thus, *ὥστε . . . ὑπολαμβάνεσθαι μειζόνως ἢ κατὰ τὴν ἀξίᾱν so as to be regarded as greater* (lit. *in a greater way*) *than* (*according to*) *their deserts* I. 11. 24.

b. *δίχα* and *χωρίς apart, ἑκάς far, ἐγγύς near* and some other ordinary adverbs supply, with *εἶναι* or *γίγνεσθαι*, the place of missing adjectives. Thus, *χωρὶς σοφίᾱ ἐστὶν ἀνδρείᾱς wisdom is different from courage* P. Lach. 195 a.

1098. For adjectives used adverbially, see 1042; for degrees of comparison, 345, 1068; for the genitive or dative after adverbs, 1437 ff., 1499 ff.; for adverbs used as prepositions, 1700 ff.; for a relative adverb used with names of things as an equivalent of a relative pronoun preceded by *ἐν, εἰς, ἐξ*, see 2499.

THE ARTICLE—ORIGIN AND DEVELOPMENT

1099. The article ὁ, ἡ, τό, was originally a demonstrative pronoun, and as such supplied the place of the personal pronoun of the third person. By gradual weakening it became the definite article. It also served as a relative pronoun (1105). (Cp. Germ. *der*, demonstrative article and relative; French *le* from *ille*.) ὁ as a demonstrative is still retained in part in Attic prose (1106), while the beginnings of its use as the article are seen even in Homer (1102).

ὁ, ἡ, τό IN HOMER

1100. In Homer ὁ, ἡ, τό is usually a demonstrative pronoun and is used substantively or adjectively; it also serves as the personal pronoun of the third person: *ἀλλὰ τὸ θαυμάζω but I marvel at this* δ 655, *τὸν λωβητῆρα ἐπεσβόλον this prating brawler* B 275, *τὴν δ' ἐγὼ οὐ λύσω but her I will not release* A 29.

1101. In its *substantival* use ὁ either marks a contrast or recalls the subject (the anaphoric use). But with ἀλλά, δέ, αὐτάρ the subject is generally changed. It often precedes an explanatory relative clause: τῶν οἳ νῦν βροτοί εἰσι *of those who are now mortal men* A 272.

1102. ὁ, ἡ, τό often approaches to its later use as the definite article or is actually so used: τὸν μέν . . . τὸν δ' ἕτερον E 145 (cp. 1107). **a.** The substantive often stands in apposition, and is added, as an afterthought, to the demonstrative (especially ὁ δέ) which is still an independent pronoun: αὐτὰρ ὁ τοῖσι γέρων ὁδὸν ἡγεμόνευεν *but he, the old man, was leading the way for them* ω 225. In some cases the appositive is needed to complete the sense: ἐπεὶ τό γε καλὸν ἀκουέμεν ἐστὶν ἀοιδοῦ *since this — to listen to a minstrel — is a good thing* α 370. **b.** Often with adjectives and participles used substantively, with pronouns, and adverbs; especially when a contrast or distinction is implied: οἱ ἄλλοι *the others* Φ 371, τὰ ἐσσόμενα *the things that are to be* A 70, τὸ πάρος *formerly* N 228. The attributive adj. before the noun: τοὺς σούς *thy* Ψ 572, τὰ μέγιστα ἄεθλα *the greatest prizes* Ψ 640; and in apposition: Ἶρον τὸν ἀλήτην *Irus, the beggar* σ 333. Hom. has πατὴρ οὑμός Θ 360 (but does not use ὁ πατὴρ ὁ ἐμός).

1103. In Hom. ὁ *contrasts* two objects, indicates a change of person, or a change of action on the part of the same person. Attic ὁ *defines*.

1104. The transition from the demonstrative to the article is so gradual that it is often impossible to distinguish between the two. Ordinarily Homer does not use the article where it is required in Attic prose. The Epic use is adopted in general by the lyric poets and in the lyric parts of tragedy. Even in tragic dialogue the article is less common than in prose. Hdt. has ὁ δέ *and he*, ὁ γάρ *for he*.

ὁ, ἡ, τό AS A RELATIVE

1105. The demonstrative ὅ, ἥ, τό is used as a relative pronoun in Homer only when the antecedent is definite (cp. *that*): τεύχεα δ' ἐξενάριξε, τά οἱ πόρε χάλκεος Ἄρης *he stripped off the arms that brazen Ares had given him* H 146. The tragic poets use only the forms in τ-, and chiefly to avoid hiatus or to produce position: κτείνουσα τοὺς οὐ χρὴ κτανεῖν *slaying those whom it is not right to slay* E. And. 810. (ὅ = ὅς E. Hipp. 525.) On the use in Herodotus, see 338 D. 3.

ὁ, ἡ, τό AS A DEMONSTRATIVE IN ATTIC PROSE

1106. The demonstrative force of ὁ, ἡ, τό survives chiefly in connection with particles (μέν, δέ, γέ, τοί; and with καί preceding ὁ).

1107. ὁ is a demonstrative commonly before μέν, δέ, and especially in contrasted expressions: ὁ μέν . . . ὁ δέ *the one, this . . . the other, that*, as in οἱ μὲν ἐπορεύοντο, οἱ δ' εἵποντο *the one party proceeded, the other followed* X. A. 3. 4. 16.

1108. The reference may be indefinite; in which case τὶς is often added: τοὺς μὲν ἀπέκτεινε, τοὺς δ' ἐξέβαλεν *some he put to death, and others he expelled* X. A. 1. 1. 7, οἱ μέν τινες ἀπέθνῃσκον, οἱ δ' ἔφευγον *some were killed, but others escaped* C. 3. 2. 10.

1109. With prepositions the order is usually inverted: *ἐκ μὲν τῶν, εἰς δὲ τά* (1663 a).

1110. In late writers (but in Demosthenes) the relative is used as in 1107: *πόλεις, ἃς μὲν ἀναιρῶν, εἰς ἃς δὲ τοὺς φυγάδας κατάγων destroying some cities, into others bringing back their exiles* D. 18. 71 (the first instance).

1111. Note the adverbial expressions: *τὸ (τὰ) μέν . . . τὸ (τὰ) δέ on the one hand . . . on the other hand, partly . . . partly* (so also *τοῦτο μέν . . . τοῦτο δέ* 1256); *τὸ δέ τι partly, τῇ μέν . . . τῇ δέ in this way . . . in that way, τὸ δέ whereas* (1112), *τῷ τοι therefore.*

1112. *ὁ δέ, ἡ δέ, τὸ δέ* (without a preceding *μέν* clause) often mean *but* (or *and*) *he, she, this.* In the nominative the person referred to is usually different from the subject of the main verb: *Κῦρος δίδωσιν αὐτῷ μῡρίους δᾱρεικούς· ὁ δὲ λαβὼν τὸ χρῡσίον κ.τ.λ. Cyrus gives him* (Clearchus) *10,000 darics; and he taking the money*, etc. X. A. 1. 1. 9, *ταῦτα ἀπαγγέλλουσι τοῖς στρατιώταις· τοῖς δὲ ὑποψίᾱ ἦν ὅτι ἄγοι πρὸς βασιλέᾱ they report this to the soldiers; and they had a suspicion that he was leading* (them) *against the king* X. A. 1. 3. 21, *τὸ δ' οὐκ ἔστι τοιοῦτον whereas this is not so* P. A. 37 a.

VARIOUS USES OF ὁ (ὅς), ἡ (ἥ), τό DEMONSTRATIVE

1113. As a personal pronoun, chiefly after *καί*, and in the nominative: *καὶ ὅς (ἥ) and he (she)*: *καὶ οἳ εἶπον and they said* X. A. 7. 6. 4. Also in *ἦ δ' ὅς and he said* P. R. 327 c (792). So *καὶ τόν (τήν)* used as the accusative of *καὶ ὅς*, as subject of a following infinitive in indirect discourse: *καὶ τὸν εἰπεῖν and* (he said that) *he said* P. S. 174 a.

1114. In the nominative *ὅς, ἥ*, are usually thus written. Some write *ὅ, ἥ, οἵ, αἵ* when these words are used as demonstratives; but *ὃ μέν . . . ὃ δέ* is rare.

a. The forms *ὅς, ἥ*, here apparently relatives with an older demonstrative force, may be in reality demonstratives, *ὅς* being the demonstrative (article) *ὁ* to which the nominative sign -*s* has been added. From this *ὅς* may be derived, by analogy, the demonstrative use of *ὅ*, and of *οἷς, οὕς* in fixed expressions (1110).

1115. Also in *τὸν καὶ τόν this one and that one* L. 1. 23, *τὸ καὶ τό this and that* D. 9. 68, *τὰ καὶ τά* D. 21. 141, *οὔτε τοῖς οὔτε τοῖς neither to these nor to those* P. L. 701 e. In the nom. *ὃς καὶ ὅς such and such an one* Hdt. 4. 68.

1116. In an oblique case before the relatives *ὅς, ὅσος, οἷος*: *τόν τε Εὐθύκριτον . . . καὶ τὸν ὃς ἔφη δεσπότης τούτου εἶναι, μάρτυρας παρέξομαι and as witness I will produce both Euthycritus and the man who said he was his master* L. 23. 8, *ὀρέγεται τοῦ ὅ ἔστιν ἴσον he aims at that which is equal* P. Ph. 75 b, and often in Plato in defining philosophical terms.

1117. Rarely with prepositions, except in *πρὸ τοῦ* (or *προτοῦ*) *before this time* T. 1. 118. On *ἐν τοῖς* with the superlative, see 1089.

ὁ, ἡ, τό AS AN ARTICLE (*the*) IN ATTIC (ESPECIALLY IN PROSE)

1118. The article *ὁ, ἡ, τό* marks objects as definite and known, whether individuals (the *particular* article) or classes (the *generic* article). The context must determine the presence of the generic article.

a. There is no indefinite article in Greek, but *a*, *an* is often represented by τὶς (1267).

THE PARTICULAR ARTICLE

1119. The particular article denotes individual persons or things as distinguished from others of the same kind. Thus, μαίνεται ἄνθρωπος *the man is mad* (a definite person, distinguished from other men) P. Phae. 268 c.

1120. Special uses of the particular article. The particular article defines

a. Objects well known: ὁ τῶν ἑπτὰ σοφώτατος Σόλων *Solon the wisest of the Seven* (*Sages*) P. Tim. 20 d.

b. Objects already mentioned or in the mind of the speaker or writer (the *anaphoric* article): εἶπον ὅτι τάλαντον ἀργυρίου ἕτοιμος εἴην δοῦναι . . . ὁ δὲ λαβὼν τὸ τάλαντον κ.τ.λ. *I said that I was ready to give him a talent of silver . . . and he taking the talent*, etc. L. 12. 9–10.

c. Objects specially present to the senses or mind (the *deictic* article): λαβὲ τὸ βιβλίον *take the book* P. Th. 143 c, βουλόμενος τὴν μάχην ποιῆσαι *wishing to fight the battle* T. 4. 91. Hence the article is regularly used with demonstrative pronouns (1176).

N.—The foregoing (a–c) uses recall the old demonstrative force of the article. Words that ordinarily have no article may receive the article when this older force is present.

d. Objects particularized by an attributive or by a following description: ὁ δῆμος ὁ Ἀθηναίων *the people of the Athenians* Aes. 3. 116, λέγε τὴν ἐπιστολήν, ἣν ἔπεμψεν *read the letter that he sent* D. 18. 39. Cp. 1178 d.

e. Objects marked as *usual* or *proper* under the circumstances: τὸ μέρος τῶν ψήφων ὁ διώκων οὐκ ἔλαβεν *the prosecutor did not get the* (requisite) *part of the votes* D. 18. 103.

f. Objects representative of their class (the *distributive* article, which resembles the generic use; often translated by *a*, *each*): ὑπισχνεῖται δώσειν τρία ἡμιδᾱρεικὰ τοῦ μηνὸς τῷ στρατιώτῃ *he promises to give each soldier three half-darics a month* X. A. 1. 3. 21. But the article may be omitted: καὶ εἵλοντο δέκα, ἕνα ἀπὸ φῡλῆς *and they chose ten, one from* (*each*) *tribe* X. H. 2. 4. 23.

1121. The article often takes the place of an unemphatic possessive pronoun when there is no doubt as to the possessor: Κῦρος καταπηδήσᾱς ἀπὸ τοῦ ἅρματος τὸν θώρᾱκα ἐνέδῡ *Cyrus leaped down from his chariot and put on his breastplate* X. A. 1. 8. 3.

THE GENERIC ARTICLE

1122. The generic article denotes an entire class as distinguished from other classes. Thus, ὁ ἄνθρωπος *man* (as distinguished from other beings), οἱ γέροντες *the aged*; δεῖ τὸν στρατιώτην φοβεῖσθαι μᾶλλον τὸν ἄρχοντα ἢ τοὺς πολεμίους *the* (*a*) *soldier should fear his commander* *rather than the enemy* X. A. 2. 6. 10, πονηρὸν ὁ σῡκοφάντης *the informer is a vile thing* D. 18. 242.

1123. In the singular the generic article makes a single object the representative of the entire class; in the plural it denotes all the objects belonging to a class. The generic article is especially common, in the plural, with adjectives used substantively: οὐκ ἄν τις εἴποι ὡς τοὺς κακούργους καὶ ἀδίκους εἴᾱ καταγελᾶν *no one could say that he permitted the malefactor and the wrongdoer to deride him* X. A. 1. 9. 13.

1124. The Article with Participles. — A participle with the article may denote an entire class: ὁ βουλόμενος *any one who wishes.* Cp. 2050, 2052.

ὁ τυχών *any chance comer*, ὁ ἡγησόμενος *a guide*, οὐκ ἀπορήσετε τῶν ἐθελησόντων ὑπὲρ ὑμῶν κινδῡνεύειν *you will not be in want of those who will be willing to encounter danger for you* D. 20. 166, οἱ λογοποιοῦντες *newsmongers* 4. 49. The same sense is expressed by πᾶς ὁ with a participle or adjective. On the article with a participle in the predicate, see 1152.

a. When the reference is to a particular occasion, the article may be particular (2052); as ὁ λέγων the speaker on a definite occasion.

THE ARTICLE WITH NUMERALS

1125. The article may be used with cardinal numerals

a. When the numeral states the definite part of a whole (expressed or understood): ἀπῆσαν τῶν λόχων δώδεκα ὄντων οἱ τρεῖς *of the companies, numbering twelve* (in all), *there were absent three* X. H. 7. 5. 10, εἷς παρὰ τοὺς δέκα *one man in* (comparison with) *ten* X. O. 20. 16, τῶν πέντε τὰς δύο μοίρᾱς *two fifths* T. 1. 10, δύο μέρη *two thirds* 3. 15. (The genitive is omitted when the denominator exceeds the numerator by *one.*)

b. When the numeral is *approximate:* ἔμειναν ἡμέρᾱς ἀμφὶ τὰς τριάκοντα *they remained about thirty days* X. A. 4. 8. 22, γεγονότες τὰ πεντήκοντα ἔτη *about fifty years of age* X. C. 1. 2. 13.

c. When the number is used abstractly (without reference to any definite object): ὅπως μὴ ἐρεῖς ὅτι ἔστιν τὰ δώδεκα δὶς ἕξ *beware of saying 12 is twice 6* P. R. 337 b.

N. Ordinals usually omit the article and regularly do so in statements of time in the dative (1540): δευτέρῳ μηνὶ τὴν πόλιν ἐτείχιζον *in the second month they fortified the city* T. 8. 64.

FLUCTUATION IN THE USE OF THE ARTICLE: OMISSION OF THE ARTICLE

1126. The article is often omitted (1) in words and phrases which have survived from the period when ὁ, ἡ, τό was a demonstrative pronoun; (2) when a word is sufficiently definite by itself; (3) when a word expresses a general conception without regard to its application to a definite person. The generic article is frequently omitted, especially with abstracts (1132), without appreciable difference in meaning. Its presence or absence is often determined by the need of distinguishing subject from predicate (1150), by the rhythm of the sentence, etc.

1127. The article is omitted in many adverbial designations of *time*, mostly with prepositions (except ἡμέρᾱς *by day*, νυκτός *by night*).

Thus, περὶ μέσᾱς νύκτας *about midnight*, ἅμα ἕῳ *just before daylight*, ὥρᾳ ἔτους *at the season of the year*. So with ὄρθρος *daybreak*, δείλη *afternoon*, ἑσπέρᾱ *evening*, ἔαρ *spring*; and ἐκ παίδων *from childhood*. Most of the above cases are survivals of the older period when the article had a demonstrative force.

1128. The article is very often omitted in phrases containing a preposition: ἐν ἀρχῇ τοῦ λόγου *in the beginning of the speech* D. 37. 23, ἔξω βελῶν *out of reach of the missiles* X. A. 3. 4. 15, Ἠιόνα τὴν ἐπὶ Στρῡμόνι *Eion on the Strymon* T. 1. 98.

1129. Words denoting persons, when they are used of a class, may omit the article. So ἄνθρωπος, στρατηγός, θεός *divinity*, *god* (ὁ θεός the particular god). Thus, πάντων μέτρον ἄνθρωπός ἐστιν *man is the measure of all things* P. Th. 178 b.

1130. Adjectives and participles used substantively have no article when the reference is general: μέσον ἡμέρᾱς *midday* X. A. 1. 8. 8, ψῡχρόν *cold*, θερμόν *heat* P. S. 186 d, πέμψαι προκαταληψομένους τὰ ἄκρα *to send* men *to preoccupy the heights* X. A. 1. 3. 14. Rarely when an adverb is used adjectively: τῶν ἐχθρῶν ἄρδην ὄλεθρος *the utter destruction of the enemy* D. 19. 141.

THE ARTICLE WITH ABSTRACT SUBSTANTIVES

1131. Abstract substantives generally have the article: ἡ ἀρετὴ μᾶλλον ἢ ἡ φυγὴ σῴζει τὰς ψῡχάς *valour rather than flight saves men's lives* X. C. 4. 1. 5.

1132. The names of the *virtues*, *vices*, *arts*, *sciences*, *occupations* often omit the article: τί σωφροσύνη, τί μανίᾱ; *what is temperance*, *what is madness?* X. M. 1. 1. 16, ἀρχὴ φιλίᾱς μὲν ἔπαινος, ἔχθρᾱς δὲ ψόγος *praise is the beginning of friendship, blame of enmity* I. 1. 33. Similarly μουσική *music*, γεωργίᾱ *agriculture*. So also with δόξα *opinion*, νοῦς *mind*, τέχνη *art*, νόμος *law*.

1133. The article must be used when reference is made to a definite person or thing or to an object well known: ἡ τῶν Ἑλλήνων εὔνοια *the goodwill of the Greeks* Aes. 3. 70, (ὑμῖν) ἡ σχολή *your usual idleness* D. 8. 53.

1134. The article may be omitted in designations of *space*; as βάθος *depth*, ὕψος *height*; also μέγεθος *size*, πλῆθος *size*, *amount*. γένος and ὄνομα, used as accusatives of respect (1600), may omit the article.

1135. The article may be omitted with some concrete words conveying a general idea, as ψῡχή *soul*, σῶμα *body* (but the parts of the body regularly have the article).

THE ARTICLE WITH PROPER NAMES

1136. Names of *persons* and *places* are individual and therefore omit the article unless previously mentioned (1120 b) or specially marked as well known: Θουκῡδίδης Ἀθηναῖος *Thucydides an Athenian* T. 1. 1, τοὺς στρατιώτᾱς αὐτῶν, τοὺς παρὰ Κλέαρχον ἀπελθόντας, εἴᾱ Κῦρος τὸν Κλέαρχον ἔχειν *their soldiers who seceded to Clearchus, Cyrus allowed Clearchus to retain* X. A. 1. 4. 7, ὁ Σόλων D. 20. 90, οἱ Ἡρᾱκλέες *the Heracleses* P. Th. 169 b.

1137. Names of **deities** omit the article, except when emphatic (*νὴ τὸν Δία by Zeus*) or when definite cults are referred to: *τὸ τῆς Ἀθηνᾶς ἕδος the sanctuary of Athena* (at Athens) I. 15. 2. Names of **festivals** vary in prose writers (no article in inscriptions): Παναθήναια *the Panathenaea* (but Παναθηναίοις τοῖς μῑκροῖς *at the Lesser Panathenaea* L. 21. 4). Names of **shrines** have the article.

1138. Names of **nations** may omit the article, but οἱ Ἕλληνες is usual when opposed to οἱ βάρβαροι *the barbarians.* When nations are opposed, the article is usually absent: ὁ πόλεμος Ἀθηναίων καὶ Πελοποννησίων T. 2. 1 (but ὁ πόλεμος τῶν Πελοποννησίων καὶ Ἀθηναίων 1. 1). The name of a nation without the article denotes the entire people. Names of **families** may omit the article: Ἀσκληπιάδαι P. R. 406 a.

1139. Continents: ἡ Εὐρώπη *Europe*, ἡ Ἀσίᾱ *Asia.* Other names of countries, except those originally adjectives (as ἡ Ἀττική *Attica*), omit the article (Λιβύη *Libya*). γῆ and χώρᾱ may be added only to such names as are treated as adjectives: ἡ Βοιωτίᾱ (γῆ) *Boeotia.* The names of countries standing in the genitive of the divided whole (1311) usually omit the article only when the genitive precedes the governing noun: Σικελίᾱς τὸ πλεῖστον *the most of Sicily* T. 1. 12. The article is generally used with names of **mountains** and **rivers**; but is often omitted with names of *islands*, *seas* (but ὁ Πόντος *the Pontus*), and *winds.* Names of **cities** usually omit the article. Names of cities, rivers, and mountains often add πόλις, ποταμός, ὄρος (1142 c). The article is omitted with proper names joined with αὐτός used predicatively (1206 b): αὐτοὺς Ἀθηναίους *the Athenians themselves* T. 4. 73.

1140. Several appellatives, treated like proper names, may omit the article: βασιλεύς the king of Persia (ὁ βασιλεύς is anaphoric (1120 b) or refers expressly to a definite person). **Titles of official persons**: πρυτάνεις *the Prytans*, στρατηγοί *the Generals.* **Names of relationship**, etc.: πατήρ *father*, ἀνήρ *husband*, γυνή *wife* (but the article is needed when a definite individual is spoken of). Thus: ἧκον δὲ τῷ μὲν μήτηρ, τῷ δὲ γυνὴ καὶ παῖδες *to one there came his mother, to another his wife and children* And. 1. 48. So also πατρίς *fatherland.*

1141. Similarly in the case of words forming a class by themselves, and some others used definitely: ἥλιος *sun*, οὐρανός *heaven*, ὧραι *seasons*, κεραυνός *thunder*, θάνατος *death*; ἄστυ, πόλις *city*, ἀκρόπολις *citadel*, ἀγορά *market-place*, τεῖχος *city-wall*, πρυτανεῖον *prytaneum*, νῆσος *island* (all used of definite places), θάλαττα *sea* as opposed to the mainland, but ἡ θάλαττα of a definite sea; similarly γῆ *earth, land.*

1142. When the name of a person or place is defined by an appositive (916) or attributive, the following distinctions are to be noted:

a. **Persons**: Περδίκκᾱς Ἀλεξάνδρου *Perdiccas, son of Alexander* T. 2. 99: the *official* designation merely stating the parentage. Δημοσθένης ὁ Ἀλκισθένους (the *popular* designation) distinguishes *Demosthenes, the son of Alcisthenes* (T. 3. 91) from other persons named Demosthenes. (Similarly with names of *nations.*)

b. **Deities**: the article is used with the name *and* with the epithet or (less often) with neither: τῷ Διὶ τῷ Ὀλυμπίῳ *to Olympian Zeus* T. 5. 31, Διὶ ἐλευθερίῳ *to Zeus guardian of freedom* 2. 71.

c. **Geographical Names** are usually treated as attributives, as ὁ Εὐφράτης ποταμός *the river Euphrates* X. A. 1. 4. 11, ἡ Βόλβη λίμνη *lake Bolbe* T. 4. 103. In a very few cases (six times in Thuc.) ὁ is omitted with the name of a river when ποταμός is inserted; but Hdt. often omits ὁ. With the names of **mountains** the order is τὸ Πήλιον ὄρος *Mt. Pelion* Hdt. 7. 129 when the gender agrees, but otherwise ἐς τὸ ὄρος τὴν Ἰστώνην *to Mt. Istone* T. 3. 85 (rarely as ὑπὸ τῇ Αἴτνῃ τῷ ὄρει *at the foot of Mt. Aetna* T. 3. 116). With names of **islands, towns**, etc., the order varies: τὸ Παρθένιον πόλισμα *the town of Parthenium* X. A. 7. 8. 21; ἡ Ψυττάλεια νῆσος *the island of Psyttalea* Hdt. 8. 95; Τραγίᾱ ἡ νῆσος *the island of Tragia* T. 1. 116; τοῦ Πειραιῶς τοῦ λιμένος *of the harbour of Peiraeus* T. 2. 93; τὸ φρούριον τὸ Λάβδαλον *fort Labdalon* 7. 3. *The city of Mende* would be Μένδη πόλις, ἡ Μένδη ἡ πόλις, Μένδη ἡ πόλις.

OTHER USES OF THE ARTICLE

1143. A single article, used with the first of two or more nouns connected by *and*, produces the effect of a single notion: οἱ στρατηγοὶ καὶ λοχᾱγοί *the generals and captains* (the commanding officers) X. A. 2. 2. 8, τᾱ̀ς μεγίστᾱς καὶ ἐλαχίστᾱς ναῦς *the largest and the smallest ships* (the whole fleet) T. 1. 10, ἡ τῶν πολλῶν διαβολή τε καὶ φθόνος *the calumniation and envy of the multitude* P. A. 28 a. Rarely when the substantives are of different genders: περὶ τᾱ̀ς ἑαυτῶν ψῡχᾱ̀ς καὶ σώματα *concerning their own lives and persons* X. A. 3. 2. 20.

1144. A repeated article lays stress on each word: ὁ Θρᾷξ καὶ ὁ βάρβαρος *the Thracian and the barbarian* D. 23. 132 (here the subject remains the same), οἱ στρατηγοὶ καὶ οἱ λοχᾱγοί *the generals and the captains* X. A. 7. 1. 13.

1145. Instead of repeating a noun with the article it may suffice to repeat the article: ὁ βίος ὁ τῶν ἰδιωτευόντων ἢ ὁ τῶν τυραννευόντων *the life of persons in a private station or that of princes* I. 2. 4.

1146. A substantive followed by an attributive genitive and forming with it a compound idea, usually omits the article: τελευτὴ τοῦ βίου (the) *end of his life* ('life-end' as *life-time*) X. A. 1. 1. 1. (Less commonly ἡ τελευτὴ τοῦ βίου X. A. 1. 9. 30.) Cp. 1295 a.

1147. When the genitive dependent on a substantive is a proper name: μετὰ Εὐβοίᾱς ἅλωσιν *after the capture of Euboea* T. 2. 2, and μετὰ τὴν Λέσβου ἅλωσιν *after the capture of Lesbos* 3. 51. A preceding genitive thus often takes the place of the article: διὰ χρόνου πλῆθος *by reason of the extent of time* T. 1. 1.

1148. Concrete coördinated words forming a copulative expression may omit the article: πρὸς οὖν παίδων καὶ γυναικῶν ἱκετεύω ὑ̄μᾶς *by your children and wives I beseech you* L. 4. 20, πόλιν καὶ οἰκίᾱς ἡμῖν παράδοτε *surrender to us your city and houses* T. 2. 72, ἱέρειαι καὶ ἱερεῖς *priestesses and priests* P. R. 461 a. Cp. *man and wife, horse and rider.*

1149. An appositive to the personal pronouns of the first and second persons has the article when the appositive would have it (as third person) with the pronoun omitted: ὑμεῖς οἱ ἡγεμόνες πρὸς ἐμὲ πάντες συμβάλλετε *do you, captains, all confer with me* (οἱ ἡγεμόνες συμβάλλουσι) X. C. 6. 2. 41, οὐ σφόδρα χρώμεθα οἱ Κρῆτες τοῖς ξενικοῖς ποιήμασιν *we Cretans do not make very much use of foreign* *poems* P. L. 680 c, χαίρω ἀκούων ὑμῶν τῶν σοφῶν *I delight in listening to you sages* P. Ion 532 d.

THE ARTICLE AND A PREDICATE NOUN

1150. A predicate noun has no article, and is thus distinguished from the subject: καλεῖται ἡ ἀκρόπολις ἔτι ὑπ' Ἀθηναίων πόλις *the acropolis is still called 'city' by the Athenians* T. 2. 15.

1151. Predicate comparatives and superlatives, possessive pronouns, and ordinals have no article: ᾤμην τὴν ἐμαυτοῦ γυναῖκα πασῶν σωφρονεστάτην εἶναι *I thought that my wife was* (the) *most virtuous of all* L. 1. 10, Χαιρεφῶν ἐμὸς ἑταῖρος ἦν *Chaerephon was a friend of mine* P. A. 21 a. Cp. 1125 d.

1152. Even in the predicate the article is used with a noun referring to a definite object (an *individual* or a *class*) that is well known, previously mentioned or hinted at, or identical with the subject: οἱ δ' ἄλλοι ἐπιχειροῦσι βάλλειν τὸν Δέξιππον ἀνακαλοῦντες τὸν προδότην *the rest try to strike Dexippus calling him 'the traitor'* X. A. 6. 6. 7, οὗτοι ἦσαν οἱ φεύγοντες τὸν ἔλεγχον *these men were those who* (*as I have said*) *avoided the inquiry* Ant. 6. 27. οἱ τιθέμενοι τοὺς νόμους οἱ ἀσθενεῖς ἄνθρωποί εἰσι καὶ οἱ πολλοί *the enactors of the laws are the weak men and the multitude* P. G. 483 b, ὑπώπτευε δὲ εἶναι τὸν διαβάλλοντα Μένωνα *he suspected that it was Menon who traduced him* X. A. 2. 5. 28 (here subject and predicate could change places). So also with ὁ αὐτός *the same* (1209 a), θἄτερον *one of two* (69), τοὐναντίον *the opposite*.

SUBSTANTIVE-MAKING POWER OF THE ARTICLE

1153. The article has the power to make substantival any word or words to which it is prefixed.

a. Adjectives: ὁ σοφός *the wise man*, τὸ δίκαιον *justice*.

b. Participles (with indefinite force): ὁ βουλόμενος *whoever wills, the first that offers*. Cp. 1124.

N. 1. — Such participial nouns appear in active, middle, and passive forms, and admit the distinctions of tense: οἱ ἐθελήσοντες μένειν *those who shall be willing to remain* X. H. 7. 5. 24.

N. 2. — Thucydides often substantivizes the neuter participle to form abstract expressions: τῆς πόλεως τὸ τῑμώμενον *the dignity of the State* 2. 63. Such participial nouns denote an action regulated by time and circumstance. Contrast τὸ δεδιός *fear* (in actual operation) 1. 36 with τὸ δέος (simply *fear* in the abstract).

c. Preposition and case: οἱ ἐπὶ τῶν πρᾱγμάτων *those in power, the government* D. 18. 247, οἱ ἐν τῇ ἡλικίᾳ *those in the prime of life* T. 6. 24.

d. With the genitive, forming a noun-phrase (1299): τὰ τῶν στρατιωτῶν *the condition of the soldiers* X. A. 3. 1. 20, τὰ τῆς ὀργῆς *the outbursts of wrath* T. 2. 60.

e. Adverbs: οἵ τ' ἔνδον συνελαμβάνοντο καὶ οἱ ἐκτὸς κατεκόπησαν *those who were inside were arrested and those outside were cut down* X. A. 2. 5. 32. Similarly οἱ τότε *the men of that time*, οἱ ἐκεῖ *the dead*, οἱ πάλαι *the ancients*.

N. — An adverb preceded by the article may be used like an adjective: ὁ ὀρθῶς κυβερνήτης *the good pilot* P. R. 341 c. The article is rarely omitted.

f. Infinitives: καλοῦσί γε ἀκολασίᾱν τὸ ὑπὸ τῶν ἡδονῶν ἄρχεσθαι *they call intemperance being ruled by one's pleasures* P. Ph. 68 e.

g. Any single word or clause: τὸ ὑμεῖς ὅταν λέγω, τὴν πόλιν λέγω *when I say You, I mean the State* D. 18. 88, ὑπερβὰς τὸ δικᾱς ὑπεχέτω τοῦ φόνου *omitting* (the words) '*let him submit to judgment for the murder*' D. 23. 220.

POSITION OF THE ARTICLE

Attributive Position of the Article

1154. A word or group of words standing between the article and its noun, or immediately after the article if the noun, with or without the article, precedes, is an *attributive*. Thus, ὁ σοφὸς ἀνήρ, ὁ ἀνὴρ ὁ σοφός, or ἀνὴρ ὁ σοφός (cp. 1168).

1155. This holds true except in the case of such post-positive words as μέν, δέ, γέ, τέ, γάρ, δή, οἶμαι, οὖν, τοίνυν; and τὶς in Hdt.: τῶν τις Περσέων *one of the Persians* 1. 85. In Attic, τὶς intervenes only when an attributive follows the article: τῶν βαρβάρων τινὲς ἱππέων *some of the barbarian cavalry* X. A. 2. 5. 32.

1156. Adjectives, participles, adverbs, and (generally) prepositions with their cases, if preceded by the article, have *attributive position.*

1157. (1) Commonly, as in English, the article and the attributive precede the noun: ὁ σοφὸς ἀνήρ *the wise man.* In this arrangement the emphasis is on the attributive. Thus, τῇ πρώτῃ ἡμέρᾳ *on the first day* T. 3. 96, ἐν τῷ πρὸ τοῦ χρόνῳ *in former times* D. 53. 12, τὸν ἐκ τῶν Ἑλλήνων εἰς τοὺς βαρβάρους φόβον ἰδών *seeing the terror inspired by the Greeks in the barbarians* X. A. 1. 2. 18.

1158. (2) Less often, the article and the attributive follow the noun preceded by the article: ὁ ἀνὴρ ὁ σοφός *the wise man.* Thus, τὸ στράτευμα τὸ τῶν Ἀθηναίων *the army of the Athenians* T. 8. 50, ἐν τῇ πορείᾳ τῇ μέχρι ἐπὶ θάλατταν *on the journey as far as the sea* X. A. 5. 1. 1. In this arrangement the emphasis is on the noun, as something definite or previously mentioned, and the attributive is added by way of explanation. So τοὺς κύνας τοὺς χαλεποὺς διδέᾱσι *they tie up the dogs, the savage ones* (I mean) X. A. 5. 8. 24.

1159. (3) Least often, the noun takes no article before it, when it would have none if the attributive were dropped: ἀνὴρ ὁ σοφός *the wise man* (lit. *a man*, I mean *the wise* one). Thus, μάχαις ταῖς πλείοσι *in the greater number of battles* T. 7. 11, σύνειμι μὲν θεοῖς, σύνειμι δὲ ἀνθρώποις τοῖς ἀγαθοῖς *I associate with gods, I associate with good men* X. M. 2. 1. 32. In this arrangement the attributive is added by way of explanation; as in the last example: *with men, the good* (I mean).

1160. A proper name, defining a preceding noun with the article, may itself have the article: ὁ ἀδελφὸς ὁ Ἀρεθούσιος (his) *brother Arethusius* D. 53. 10. Cp. 1142 c. An appositive to a proper name has the article when it designates a characteristic or something well known: ὁ Σόλων ὁ παλαιὸς ἦν φιλόδημος *Solon of ancient times was a lover of the people* Ar. Nub. 1187, Πᾱσίων ὁ Μεγαρεύς *Pasion, the Megarian* X. A. 1. 4. 7.

1161. The genitive of a substantive limiting the meaning of another substantive may take any one of four positions: —

a. τὸ τοῦ πατρὸς βιβλίον *the father's book* (very common). Thus, ἡ τῶν τεθνεώτων ἀρετή *the valour of the dead* L. 12. 36.

b. τὸ βιβλίον τὸ τοῦ πατρός (less common). Thus, ἡ οἰκίᾱ ἡ Σίμωνος *the house of Simon* L. 3. 32.

c. τοῦ πατρὸς τὸ βιβλίον (to emphasize the genitive or when a genitive has just preceded). Thus, τῆς νίκης τὸ μέγεθος *the greatness of the victory* X. H. 6. 4. 19.

d. τὸ βιβλίον τοῦ πατρός (very common). Thus, ἡ τόλμα τῶν λεγόντων *the effrontery of the speakers* L. 12. 41. The genitive of the divided whole (1306) is so placed or as in **c**.

N. 1. — A substantive with no article is sometimes followed by the article and the attributive genitive: ἐπὶ σκηνὴν ἰόντες τὴν Ξενοφῶντος *going to the tent* (namely, that) *of Xenophon* X. A. 6. 4. 19. Cp. 1159.

1162. The order bringing together the *same* forms of the article (περὶ τοῦ τοῦ πατρὸς βιβλίου) is avoided, but two or three articles of *different* form may stand together: τὸ τῆς τοῦ ξαίνοντος τέχνης ἔργον *the work of the art of the wool-carder* P. Pol. 281 a.

1163. The attributive position is employed with the possessive pronouns and the possessive genitives of the reflexive and demonstrative pronouns (1184), αὐτός meaning *same* (1173), and πᾶς expressing the *sum total* (1174).

1164. Two or more attributives of a substantive are variously placed: (1) εἰς τᾱ̀ς ἄλλᾱς Ἀρκαδικᾱ̀ς πόλεις *to the other Arcadian cities* X. H. 7. 4. 38. (2) τὸ ἐν Ἀρκαδίᾳ τὸ τοῦ Διὸς τοῦ Λυκαίου ἱερόν *the sanctuary of Lycean Zeus in Arcadia* P. R. 565 d. (3) ἐς τὸν ἐπὶ τῷ στόματι τοῦ λιμένος στενοῦ ὄντος τὸν ἕτερον πύργον *to the other tower at the mouth of the harbour which was narrow* T. 8. 90. (4) ἐν τῇ οἰκίᾳ τῇ Χαρμίδου τῇ παρὰ τὸ Ὀλυμπιεῖον *in the house of Charmides by the Olympieum* And. 1. 16. (5) ἀπὸ τῶν ἐν τῇ Ἀσίᾳ πόλεων Ἑλληνίδων *from the Greek cities in Asia* X. H. 4. 3. 15. (6) πρὸς τὴν ἐκ τῆς Σικελίᾱς τῶν Ἀθηναίων μεγάλην κακοπρᾱγίᾱν *with regard to the great failure of the Athenians in Sicily* T. 8. 2. (7) τὸ τεῖχος τὸ μακρὸν τὸ νότιον *the long southern wall* And. 3. 7.

1165. A relative or temporal clause may be treated as an attributive: Σόλων ἐμίσει τοὺς οἷος οὗτος ἀνθρώπους *Solon detested men like this man here* D. 19. 254.

1166. Position of an attributive participle with its modifiers (A = article, N = noun, P = participle, D = word or words dependent on P): (1) APND: τὸν ἐφεστηκότα κίνδῡνον τῇ πόλει *the danger impending over the State* D. 18. 176. (2) APDN: τοὺς περιεστηκότας τῇ πόλει κινδῡ́νους D. 18. 179. (3) ADPN: τὸν τότε τῇ πόλει περιστάντα κίνδῡνον D. 18. 188. (4) NADP: ἕτοιμον ἔχει δύναμιν τὴν . . . καταδουλωσομένην ἅπαντας *he has in readiness a force to enslave all* D. 8. 46.

1167 a. Especially after verbal substantives denoting an *action* or a *state* an attributive prepositional phrase is added without the article being repeated: τὴν μεγάλην στρατείᾱν Ἀθηναίων καὶ τῶν ξυμμάχων ἐς Αἴγυπτον *the great expedition of the Athenians and their allies to Egypt* T. 1. 110.

b. A word defining a substantivized participle, adjective, or infinitive may be placed before the article for emphasis: **καὶ ταῦτα τοὺς εἰδότας καλοῦμεν** *and we will summon those who have knowledge of this* D. 57. 65, **τούτων τοῖς ἐναντίοις** *with the opposite of these* T. 7. 75.

Predicate Position of Adjectives

1168. A predicate adjective either precedes or follows the article and its noun: σοφὸς ὁ ἀνήρ or ὁ ἀνὴρ σοφός *the man is wise.*

Thus, ἀτελεῖ τῇ νίκῃ ἀνέστησαν *they retired with their victory incomplete* T. 8. 27, ψῑλὴν ἔχων τὴν κεφαλήν *with his head bare* X. A. 1. 8. 6, τὰς τριήρεις ἀφείλκυσαν κενάς *they towed off the ships without their crews* T. 2. 93.

a. This is called the predicate position, which often lends emphasis.

1169. A predicate adjective or substantive may thus be the equivalent of a clause of a complex sentence: ἀθάνατον τὴν περὶ αὑτῶν μνήμην καταλείψουσιν *they will leave behind a remembrance of themselves that will never die* I. 9. 3, ἐπήρετο πόσον τι ἄγοι τὸ στράτευμα *he asked about how large the force was that he was leading* (= πόσον τι εἴη τὸ στράτευμα ὃ ἄγοι 2647) X. C. 2. 1. 2, παρ' ἑκόντων τῶν ξυμμάχων τὴν ἡγεμονίᾱν ἔλαβον *they received the leadership from their allies* (being willing) *who were willing to confer it* I. 1. 17.

1170. A predicate expression may stand inside an attributive phrase: ὁ δεινὸς (pred.) λεγόμενος γεωργός *he who is called a skilful agriculturist* X. O. 19. 14. This is common with participles of *naming* with the article.

1171. The predicate position is employed with the demonstratives οὗτος, ὅδε, ἐκεῖνος, and ἄμφω, ἀμφότερος, ἑκάτερος, and ἕκαστος; with the possessive genitives of personal and relative pronouns (1185, 1196) and of αὐτός (1201); with αὐτός meaning *self* (1206 b); with the genitive of the divided whole (1306), as τούτων οἱ πλεῖστοι *the most of these* X. A. 1. 5. 13, οἱ ἄριστοι τῶν περὶ αὐτόν *the bravest of his companions* 1. 8. 27; and with πᾶς meaning *all* (1174 b).

a. *This wise man* is οὗτος ὁ σοφὸς ἀνήρ, ὁ σοφὸς ἀνὴρ οὗτος (and also ὁ σοφὸς οὗτος ἀνήρ).

PECULIARITIES OF POSITION WITH THE ARTICLE

1172. Adjectives of Place. — When used in the predicate position (1168) **ἄκρος** (*high*) means *the top of*, **μέσος** (*middle*) means *the middle of*, **ἔσχατος** (*extreme*) means *the end of.* Cp. *summus, medius, extremus.*

Attributive Position	*Predicate Position*	
τὸ ἄκρον ὄρος *the lofty mountain*	ἄκρον τὸ ὄρος τὸ ὄρος ἄκρον	*the top of the mountain*
ἡ μέση ἀγορά *the central market*	μέση ἡ ἀγορά ἡ ἀγορὰ μέση	*the centre of the market*
ἡ ἐσχάτη νῆσος *the farthest island*	ἐσχάτη ἡ νῆσος ἡ νῆσος ἐσχάτη	*the verge of the island*

Thus, περὶ ἄκραις ταῖς χερσὶ χειρῖδες *gloves on the fingers (points of the hands)* X. C. 8. 8. 17, διὰ μέσου τοῦ παραδείσου ῥεῖ *flows through the middle of the park* X. A. 1. 2. 7. The meaning of the predicate position is also expressed by (τὸ) ἄκρον τοῦ ὄρους, (τὸ) μέσον τῆς ἀγορᾶς, etc.

1173. **μόνος, ἥμισυς.** — (1) Attributive: ὁ μόνος παῖς *the only son*, αἱ ἡμίσειαι χάριτες *half-favours.* (2) Predicate: μόνος ὁ παῖς (or ὁ παῖς μόνος) παίζει *the boy plays alone*, ἥμισυς ὁ βίος (or ὁ βίος ἥμισυς) *half of life*, τὰ ἅρματα τὰ ἡμίσεα *half of the chariots.*

αὐτός: (1) Attributive: ὁ αὐτὸς ἀνήρ *the same man.* (2) Predicate: αὐτὸς ὁ ἀνήρ or ὁ ἀνὴρ αὐτός *the man himself.*

1174. **πᾶς** (and in the strengthened forms ἅπᾱς, σύμπᾱς *all together*). **a.** In the attributive position πᾶς denotes the whole regarded as the sum of all its parts (the *sum total*, the *collective body*): οἱ πάντες πολῖται *the whole body of citizens*, ἡ πᾶσα Σικελίᾱ *the whole of Sicily*, ἀποκτεῖναι τοὺς ἅπαντας Μυτιληναίους *to put to death the entire Mitylenean population* T. 3. 36.

N. — Hence, with numbers, οἱ πάντες, τὰ σύμπαντα *in all*: ἑξακόσιοι καὶ χῑ́λιοι οἱ πάντες *1600 in all* T. 1. 60.

b. In the predicate (and usual) position πᾶς means *all*: πάντες οἱ πολῖται or (often emphatic) οἱ πολῖται πάντες *all the citizens* (individually), περὶ πάντας τοὺς θεοὺς ἠσεβήκᾱσι καὶ εἰς ἅπᾱσαν τὴν πόλιν ἡμαρτήκᾱσιν *they have committed impiety towards all the gods and have sinned against the whole State* L. 14. 42.

c. Without the article: πάντες πολῖται *all* (conceivable) *citizens*, μισθωσάμενοι πάντας ἀνθρώπους *hiring every conceivable person* L. 12. 60.

N. 1. — In the meaning *pure, nothing but*, πᾶς is strictly a predicate and has no article: κύκλῳ φρουρούμενος ὑπὸ πάντων πολεμίων *hemmed in by a ring of guards all of whom are his enemies* (= πάντες ὑφ᾽ ὧν φρουρεῖται πολέμιοί εἰσι) P. R. 579 b. So πᾶσα κακίᾱ *utter baseness.*

N. 2. — The article is not used with πᾶς if the noun, standing alone, would have no article.

N. 3. — In the singular, πᾶς often means *every*: σὺν σοὶ πᾶσα ὁδὸς εὔπορος *with you every road is easy to travel* X. A. 2. 5. 9, πᾶσα θάλασσα *every sea* T. 2. 41.

1175. **ὅλος**: (1) Attributive: τὸ ὅλον στράτευμα *the whole army*; (2) Predicate: ὅλον τὸ στράτευμα (or τὸ στράτευμα ὅλον) *the army as a whole*, τὴν νύκτα ὅλην *the entire night.* With no article: ὅλον στράτευμα *a whole army*, ὅλα στρατεύματα *whole armies.*

1176. The demonstrative pronouns οὗτος, ὅδε, ἐκεῖνος, and αὐτός *self*, in agreement with a noun, usually take the article, and stand in the predicate position (1168): οὗτος ὁ ἀνήρ or ὁ ἀνὴρ οὗτος (never ὁ οὗτος ἀνήρ) *this man*, αὐτὸς ὁ ἀνήρ or ὁ ἀνὴρ αὐτός *the man himself* (ὁ αὐτὸς ἀνήρ *the same man* 1173).

1177. One or more words may separate the demonstrative from its noun: ὁ τούτου ἔρως τοῦ ἀνθρώπου *the love of this man* P. S. 213 c. Note also τῶν οἰκείων τινὲς τῶν ἐκείνων *some of their slaves* (*some of the slaves of those men*) P. A. 33 d.

1178. οὗτος, ὅδε, ἐκεῖνος sometimes omit the article.

a. Regularly, when the noun is in the predicate: αὕτη ἔστω ἱκανὴ ἀπολογίᾱ *let this be a sufficient defence* P. A. 24 b, οἶμαι ἐμὴν ταύτην πατρίδα εἶναι *I think this is my native country* X. A. 4. 8. 4.

b. Usually, with proper names, except when anaphoric (1120 b): ἐκεῖνος Θουκῡδίδης *that* (well-known) *Thucydides* Ar. Ach. 708.

c. Usually, with definite numbers: ταύτᾱς τριάκοντα μνᾶς *these thirty minae* D. 27. 23.

d. Optionally, when a relative clause follows: ἐπὶ γῆν τήνδε ἤλθομεν, ἐν ᾗ οἱ πατέρες ἡμῶν Μήδων ἐκράτησαν *we have come against this land, in which our fathers conquered the Medes* T. 2. 74.

e. In the phrase (often contemptuous) οὗτος ἀνήρ P. G. 505 c; and in other expressions denoting some emotion: ἄνθρωπος οὑτοσί D. 18. 243.

f. Sometimes, when the demonstrative follows its noun: ἐπίγραμμα τόδε T. 6. 59. So often in Hdt.

g. Frequently, in poetry.

1179. ἄμφω, ἀμφότερος *both*, ἑκάτερος *each* (of two), ἕκαστος *each* (of several) have the predicate position. But with ἕκαστος the article is often omitted: κατὰ τὴν ἡμέρᾱν ἑκάστην *(day by day and) every day*, καθ' ἑκάστην ἡμέρᾱν *every day*.

1180. The demonstratives of *quality* and *quantity*, τοιοῦτος, τοιόσδε, τοσοῦτος, τοσόσδε, τηλικοῦτος, when they take the article, usually follow it: τῶν τοσούτων καὶ τοιούτων ἀγαθῶν *of so many and such blessings* D. 18. 305, τοῦτο τὸ τοιοῦτον ἔθος *such a practice as this* 21. 123. ὁ δεῖνα *such a one* (336) regularly takes the article.

a. But the predicate position occurs: τοσαύτη ἡ πρώτη παρασκευὴ πρὸς τὸν πόλεμον διέπλει *so great was the first armament which crossed over for the war* T. 6. 44.

1181. An attributive, following the article, may be separated from its noun by a pronoun: ἡ πάλαι ἡμῶν φύσις *our old nature* P. S. 189 d, ἡ στενὴ αὕτη ὁδός (for αὕτη ἡ στενὴ ὁδός) *this narrow road* X. A. 4. 2. 6.

1182. Possessive pronouns take the article only when a definite person or thing is meant, and stand between article and noun: τὸ ἐμὸν βιβλίον *my book*, τὰ ἡμέτερα βιβλία *our books*.

a. But names of relationship, πόλις, πατρίς, etc., do not require the article (1140).

1183. The article is not used with possessive pronouns or the genitive of personal and reflexive pronouns (cp. 1184, 1185):

a. When no particular object is meant: ἐμὸν βιβλίον or βιβλίον μου *a book of mine*.

b. When these pronouns belong to the predicate: μαθητὴς γέγονα σός *I have become a pupil of yours* P. Euth. 5 a, οὐ λόγους ἐμαυτοῦ λέγων *not speaking words of my own* D. 9. 41.

POSITION OF THE GENITIVE OF PRONOUNS AND THE ARTICLE

1184. In the attributive position (1154) stands the genitive of the demonstrative, reflexive, and reciprocal pronouns. τὸ τούτου βιβλίον or τὸ βιβλίον τὸ τούτου *his book*, τὸ ἐμαυτοῦ βιβλίον or τὸ βιβλίον τὸ ἐμαυτοῦ *my own book*; μετεπέμψατο τὴν ἑαυτοῦ θυγατέρα καὶ τὸν παῖδα αὐτῆς *he sent for his daughter and her child* X. C. 1. 3. 1.

a. The type τὸ βιβλίον τούτου is rare and suspected except when another attributive is added: τῇ νῦν ὕβρει τούτου D. 4. 3. The types τὸ βιβλίον ἐμαυτοῦ (Hdt. 6. 23) and τὸ αὑτοῦ βιβλίον (T. 6. 102) are rare.

1185. In the predicate position stands

a. The genitive of the personal pronouns (whether partitive or not): τὸ βιβλίον μου (σου, αὐτοῦ, etc.), or μου (σου, αὐτοῦ, etc.) τὸ βιβλίον when other words precede, as ὃς ἔχει σου τὴν ἀδελφήν *who has your sister to wife* And. 1. 50.

b. The genitive of the other pronouns used partitively.

N. 1. — Homer does not use the article in the above cases, and often employs the orthotone forms (σεῖο μέγα κλέος *thy great fame* π 241). Even in Attic ἐμοῦ for μου occurs (ἐμοῦ τὰ φορτία *my wares* Ar. Vesp. 1398).

N. 2. — The differences of position between 1184 and 1185 may be thus illustrated:

My book is pretty:	καλόν ἐστι τὸ βιβλίον μου.
	καλόν ἐστί μου τὸ βιβλίον.
My pretty book:	τὸ καλόν μου βιβλίον.
They read their books:	τὰ ἑαυτῶν βιβλία ἀναγιγνώσκουσι.

INTERROGATIVES, ἄλλος, πολύς, ὀλίγος WITH THE ARTICLE

1186. The interrogatives τίς, ποῖος may take the article when a question is asked about an object before mentioned: ΣΩ. νῦν δὴ ἐκεῖνα, ὦ Φαῖδρε, δυνάμεθα κρίνειν. ΦΑΙ. τὰ ποῖα; Socr. *Now at last we can decide those questions.* Ph. (*The*) *what questions?* P. Phae. 277 a.

1187. So even with a personal pronoun: A. δεῦρο δὴ εὐθὺ ἡμῶν . . . B. ποῖ λέγεις καὶ παρὰ τίνας τοὺς ὑμᾶς; A. *Come hither straight to us.* B. *Whither do you mean and who are you that I am to come to* (you being who)? P. Lys. 203 b.

1188. **ἄλλος** *other.* — ὁ ἄλλος in the singular usually means *the rest* (ἡ ἄλλη Ἑλλάς *the rest of Greece*); in the plural, *the others* (οἱ ἄλλοι Ἕλληνες *the other* (*ceteri*) *Greeks*, but ἄλλοι Ἕλληνες *other* (*alii*) *Greeks*). A substantivized adjective or participle usually has the article when it stands in apposition to οἱ ἄλλοι: τἆλλα τὰ πολῑτικά *the other civic affairs* X. Hi. 9. 5. On ἄλλος, ὁ ἄλλος (sometimes ἕτερος) *besides*, see 1272.

1189. **πολύς, ὀλίγος**: τὸ πολύ usually means *the great(er) part*, οἱ πολλοί *the multitude, the vulgar crowd; πλείονες several*, οἱ πλείονες *the majority, the mass;* πλεῖστοι *very many*, οἱ πλεῖστοι *the most;* ὀλίγοι *few*, οἱ ὀλίγοι *the oligarchs* (as opposed to οἱ πολλοί). Note πολύς predicative: ἐπεὶ ἑώρᾱ πολλὰ τὰ κρέᾱ *when he saw that there was abundance of meat* X. C. 1. 3. 6.

PRONOUNS

THE PERSONAL PRONOUNS

1190. The nominative of the personal pronoun is usually omitted except when emphatic, *e.g.* in contrasts, whether expressed or implied: ἐπεὶ ὑμεῖς ἐμοὶ οὐ θέλετε πείθεσθαι, ἐγὼ σὺν ὑμῖν ἕψομαι *since you are not willing to obey me, I will follow along with you* X. A. 1. 3. 6. In contrasts the first pronoun is sometimes omitted (930).

1191. Where there is no contrast the addition of the pronoun may strengthen the verb: εἰ μηδὲ τοῦτο βούλει ἀποκρίνασθαι, σὺ δὲ τοὐντεῦθεν λέγε *if you do not wish to reply even to this, tell me then* X. C. 5. 5. 21.

1192. The forms ἐμοῦ, ἐμοί, and ἐμέ and the accented forms of the pronoun of the second person (325 a) are used when emphatic and usually after prepositions: καὶ πείσᾱς ἐμὲ πιστὰ ἔδωκάς μοι καὶ ἔλαβες παρ' ἐμοῦ *and after prevailing on me you gave me pledges of faith and received them from me* X. A. 1. 6. 7. Cp. 187 N. 2. On the reflexive use of the personal pronouns of the first and second persons, see 1222–1224.

1193. ἐγώ, σύ (ἐμός, σός) are rarely used of an imaginary person ('anybody'): D. 9. 17, X. R. A. 1. 11.

1194. The nominative of the pronoun of the third person is replaced by ἐκεῖνος (of absent persons), ὅδε, οὗτος (of present persons), ὁ μέν . . . ὁ δέ (at the beginning of a sentence), and by αὐτός *in contrasts.* The oblique cases of the foregoing replace οὗ, etc., which in Attic prose are usually indirect reflexives (1228, 1229). οὗ and ἕ in Attic prose occur chiefly in poetical passages of Plato; in Attic poetry they are personal pronouns. The pronoun of the third person is very rare in the orators.

1195. Homer uses ἕο, οἷ, etc., as personal pronouns (= αὐτοῦ, αὐτῷ, etc., in Attic), in which case they are enclitic: διὰ μαντοσύνην, τήν οἱ πόρε Φοῖβος *by the art of divination, which Phoebus gave to him* A 72. Homer also uses ἕο, οἷ, etc., either as direct (= ἑαυτοῦ, etc., 1218) or as indirect reflexives (= αὐτοῦ, etc., 1225). In the former case they are orthotone; in the latter, either enclitic or orthotone. Thus, οἷ παῖδα ἐοικότα γείνατο *he begat a son like unto himself* E 800, οὔ τινά φησιν ὁμοῖον οἷ ἔμεναι Δαναῶν *he says there is no one of the Danaans like unto himself* I 306. Hdt. agrees with Hom. except that εὗ, οἷ are not direct reflexives and orthotone; σφίσι (not σφί) is reflexive.

THE POSSESSIVE PRONOUNS

For the article with a possessive pronoun see 1182–1183.

1196. The possessive pronouns (330) of the first and second persons are the equivalents of the possessive genitive of the personal pronouns: ἐμός = μου, σός = σου, ἡμέτερος = ἡμῶν, ὑμέτερος = ὑμῶν.

a. When the possessives refer to a definite, particular thing, they have the article, which always precedes (1182); the personal pronouns have the predicate position (1185). Distinguish ὁ ἐμὸς φίλος, ὁ φίλος ὁ ἐμός, ὁ φίλος μου *my friend* from φίλος ἐμός, φίλος μου *a friend of mine.*

b. A word may stand in the genitive in apposition to the personal pronoun implied in a possessive pronoun. See 977.

1197. A possessive pronoun may have the force of an objective genitive (cp. 1331) of the personal pronoun: φιλίᾳ τῇ ἐμῇ *out of friendship for me* X. C. 3. 1. 28. (φιλίᾱ ἡ ἐμή usually means *my friendship* (*for others*)).

1198. The possessive pronouns of the first and second persons are sometimes reflexive (when the subject of the sentence and the possessor are the same person), sometimes not reflexive.

1199. FIRST AND SECOND PERSONS SINGULAR

1. Not reflexive (adjective *my, thy* (*your*); pronoun *mine, thine* (*yours*)).

ἐμός, σός: ὁρᾷ τὸν ἐμὸν φίλον *he sees my friend*, ὁρᾷ τὸν σὸν πατέρα *she sees your father*, στέργει τὸν ἐμὸν πατέρα *he loves my father* (or τὸν πατέρα τὸν ἐμόν or πατέρα τὸν ἐμόν; or τὸν πατέρα μου or μου τὸν πατέρα), οἱ ἐμοὶ ὀφθαλμοὶ καλλίονες ἂν τῶν σῶν εἴησαν *my eyes will prove to be more beautiful than yours* X. S. 5. 5.

2. Reflexive (*my own, thine* (*your*) *own*).

a. **ἐμαυτοῦ, σεαυτοῦ**, in the attributive position (very common): ἔλαβον τὸν ἐμαυτοῦ μισθόν (or τὸν μισθὸν τὸν ἐμαυτοῦ) *I received my* (*own*) *pay*, τὸν ἀδελφὸν τὸν ἐμαυτοῦ ἔπεμψα *I sent my* (*own*) *brother* Aes. 2. 94, κἀπὶ τοῖς σαυτῆς κακοῖσι κἀπὶ τοῖς ἐμοῖς γελᾷς; *art thou laughing at thine own misery and at mine?* S. El. 879.

b. **ἐμός, σός** (less common): στέργω τὸν ἐμὸν πατέρα *I love my* (*own*) *father*, στέργεις τὴν σὴν μητέρα *you love your* (*own*) *mother*, ἡ ἐμὴ γυνή *my wife* X. C. 7. 2. 28, ἀδελφὸς τῆς μητρὸς τῆς ἐμῆς *brother of my mother* And. 1. 117.

c. **ἐμὸς αὐτοῦ, σὸς αὐτοῦ** (poetical): τὸν ἐμὸν αὐτοῦ πατέρα (β 45, S. O. T. 416).

d. **μου, σου** (rare): τὸν πατέρα μου Ant. 1. 23.

N. — When the possessor is not to be mistaken, the article alone is placed before the substantive and the possessive or reflexive pronoun is omitted (cp. 1121). Thus, στέργεις τὸν πατέρα *you love your* (own) *father*, στέργει τὸν πατέρα *he loves his* (own) *father*, στέργουσι τὸν πατέρα *they love their* (own) *father.*

1200. FIRST AND SECOND PERSONS PLURAL

1. Not reflexive (adjective *our, your;* pronoun *ours, yours*).

a. **ἡμέτερος, ὑμέτερος**: ὁ ἡμέτερος φίλος *our friend* (more common than ὁ φίλος ἡμῶν), ὁ ὑμέτερος φίλος *your friend* (more common than ὁ φίλος ὑμῶν), ζήτησιν ποιούμενοι ἢ ὑμῶν ἢ τῶν ὑμετέρων τινός *making a search for you or for anything of yours* L. 12. 30.

2. Reflexive (*our own, your own*).

a. **ἡμέτερος, ὑμέτερος** (common): στέργομεν τὸν ἡμέτερον φίλον *we love our own friend*, στέργετε τὸν ὑμέτερον φίλον *you love your own friend.*

b. Usually the intensive αὐτῶν is used with ἡμέτερος, ὑμέτερος in agreement with ἡμῶν (ὑμῶν) implied in the possessive forms. This gives a stronger form of reflexive. Thus:

ἡμέτερος αὐτῶν, ὑμέτερος αὐτῶν: στέργομεν τὸν ἡμέτερον αὐτῶν φίλον *we love our own friend*, οἰκοδόμημα ἢ τῶν φίλων τινὶ ἢ ἡμέτερον αὐτῶν *a house either for some one of our friends or our own* P. G. 514 b; στέργετε τὸν ὑμέτερον αὐτῶν φίλον *you love your own friend*, διδάσκετε τοὺς παῖδας τοὺς ὑμετέρους αὐτῶν *teach your own children* I. 3. 57.

c. **ἡμῶν, ὑμῶν** (rare): αἰτιώμεθα τοὺς πατέρας ἡμῶν *let us accuse our* (*own*) *fathers* P. Lach. 179 c.

d. **ἡμῶν αὐτῶν, ὑμῶν αὐτῶν** (very rare): δίκαιον ἡμᾶς . . . φαίνεσθαι μήτε ἡμῶν αὐτῶν τῆς δόξης ἐνδεεστέρους *it is not right for us to show ourselves inferior to our own fame* T. 2. 11, τὰ τῶν ἵππων καὶ τὰ ὑμῶν αὐτῶν ὅπλα *the equipments both of your horses and yourselves* X. C. 6. 3. 21.

1201. THIRD PERSON SINGULAR

1. Not reflexive (*his, her, its*).

a. **αὐτοῦ, αὐτῆς, αὐτοῦ** in the predicate position (very common): ὁρῶ τὸν φίλον αὐτοῦ (αὐτῆς) *I see his (her) friend*, γιγνώσκων αὐτοῦ τὴν ἀνδρείᾱν *knowing his courage* P. Pr. 310 d.

b. **ἐκείνου**, etc., or **τούτου**, etc. in the attributive position (very common): ὁρῶ τὸν ἐμὸν φίλον, οὐ τὸν ἐκείνου *I see my friend, not his*, ἀφικνοῦνται παρ' Ἀριαῖον καὶ τὴν ἐκείνου στρατιάν *they come up with Ariaeus and his army* X. A. 2. 2. 8, παρεκάλεσέ τινας τῶν τούτου ἐπιτηδείων *he summoned some of his friends* L. 3. 11.

c. **ὅς, ἥ, ὅν**, Hom. ἑός, ἑή, ἑόν (poetical): τὴν γῆμεν ἑὸν διὰ κάλλος *he married her because of her beauty* λ 282. Hom. has εὖ rarely for αὐτοῦ, αὐτῆς.

2. Reflexive (*his own, her own*).

a. **ἑαυτοῦ, ἑαυτῆς**, in the attributive position (very common): στέργει τὸν ἑαυτοῦ φίλον *he loves his own friend*, ὁρᾷ τὴν ἑαυτῆς μητέρα *she sees her own mother*, τὴν ἑαυτοῦ ἀδελφὴν δίδωσι Σεύθῃ *he gives his own sister in marriage to Seuthes* T. 2. 101, ὑβρίζει γυναῖκα τὴν ἑαυτοῦ *he misuses his own wife* And. 4. 15. This is the only way in prose to express *his own, her own*.

b. **ὅς (ἑός)**: poetical. Sometimes in Homer ὅς (ἑός) has the sense of *own* with no reference to the third person (1230 a).

c. **ὃς αὐτοῦ, αὐτῆς** (poetical): ὃν αὐτοῦ πατέρα (K 204).

1202. THIRD PERSON PLURAL

1. Not reflexive (*their*).

a. **αὐτῶν** in the predicate position (very common): ὁ φίλος αὐτῶν *their friend*.

b. **ἐκείνων, τούτων** in the attributive position (very common): ὁ τούτων (ἐκείνων) φίλος *their friend*, διὰ τὴν ἐκείνων ἀπιστίᾱν *because of distrust of them* And. 3. 2.

c. **σφέων** (Ionic): Hdt. 5. 58.

2. Reflexive (*their own*).

a. **ἑαυτῶν** (very common): στέργουσι τοὺς ἑαυτῶν φίλους *they love their own friends*, τῶν ἑαυτῶν συμμάχων κατεφρόνουν *they despised their own allies* X. H. 4. 4. 7.

b. **σφέτερος αὐτῶν**, the intensive αὐτῶν agreeing with σφῶν implied in σφέτερος (common): οἰκέτᾱς τοὺς σφετέρους αὐτῶν ἐπικαλοῦνται *they call their own slaves as witnesses* Ant. 1. 30.

c. **σφῶν αὐτῶν**, without the article (rare): τὰ ὀνόματα διαπράττονται σφῶν αὐτῶν προσγραφῆναι *they contrived that their own names were added* L. 13. 72. Cp. 1234. τὸν σφῶν αὐτῶν is not used.

d. **σφέτερος** (rare in prose): Βοιωτοὶ μέρος τὸ σφέτερον παρείχοντο *the Boeotians furnished their own contingent* T. 2. 12.

e. **σφῶν** in the predicate position, occasionally in Thucydides, as τοὺς ξυμμάχους ἐδέδισαν σφῶν *they were afraid of their own allies* 5. 14. Cp. 1228 N. 2.

1203. Summary of possessive forms (poetical forms in parenthesis).

a. Not reflexive

my	ἐμός	μου	*our*	ἡμέτερος	ἡμῶν
thy	σός	σου	*your*	ὑμέτερος	ὑμῶν
his, her	(ὅς Hom., rare)	αὐτοῦ, -ῆς (εὖ Hom., rare)	*their*		αὐτῶν (σφέων Ionic)

N. — ἡμέτερος and ὑμέτερος are more used than ἡμῶν and ὑμῶν.

b. Reflexive

my own	ἐμός (ἐμὸς αὐτοῦ, -ῆς)	ἐμαυτοῦ, -ῆς	*our own*	ἡμέτερος	ἡμέτερος αὐτῶν
thy own	σός (σὸς αὐτοῦ, -ῆς)	σεαυτοῦ, -ῆς	*your own*	ὑμέτερος	ὑμέτερος αὐτῶν
his, her own	(ὅς) (poet. and Ionic) (ὃς αὐτοῦ, -ῆς)	ἑαυτοῦ, -ῆς	*their own*	σφέτερος (rare)	σφέτερος αὐτῶν, ἑαυτῶν, σφῶν (rare), σφῶν αὐτῶν

N. — In the plural ἡμῶν αὐτῶν, ὑμῶν αὐτῶν are replaced by ἡμέτερος αὐτῶν, ὑμέτερος αὐτῶν, and these forms are commoner than ἡμέτερος, ὑμέτερος. σφέτερος αὐτῶν is less common than ἑαυτῶν. σφέτερος in poetry may mean *mine own, thine own, your own.*

THE PRONOUN αὐτός

1204. αὐτός is used as an adjective and as a pronoun. It has three distinct uses: (1) as an intensive adjective pronoun it means *self* (*ipse*). (2) As an adjective pronoun, when preceded by the article, it means *same* (*idem*). (3) In oblique cases as the personal pronoun of the third person, *him, her, it, them* (*eum, eam, id, eos, eas, ea*).

1205. Only the first two uses are Homeric. In Hom. αὐτός denotes the principal person or thing, in opposition to what is subordinate, and is intensive by contrast: αὐτὸν καὶ θεράποντα *the man himself and his attendant* Z 18 (cp. σώσᾱσ' αὐτὸν καὶ παῖδας P. G. 511 e and see 1208 d). On αὐτός as a reflexive, see 1228 a; on αὐτός emphatic with other pronouns, see 1233 ff.

1206. αὐτός is intensive (*self*)

a. In the *nominative* case, when standing alone: αὐτοὶ τὴν γῆν ἔσχον *they* (the Athenians) *seized the land themselves* T. 1. 114. Here αὐτός emphasizes the word understood and is not a personal pronoun.

b. In *any* case, when in the predicate position (1168) with a substantive, or in agreement with a pronoun: αὐτὸς ὁ ἀνήρ, ὁ ἀνὴρ αὐτός *the man himself*, αὐτοῦ τοῦ ἀνδρός, τοῦ ἀνδρὸς αὐτοῦ, etc.

1207. With a proper name or a word denoting an individual, the article is omitted: αὐτὸς Μένων *Menon himself* X. A. 2. 1. 5, πρὸ αὐτοῦ βασιλέως *in front of the Great King himself* 1. 7. 11.

1208. The word emphasized may be an oblique case which must be supplied: ἔλεγε δὲ καὶ αὐτὸς ὁ Βρᾱσίδᾱς τῇ Θεσσαλῶν γῇ καὶ αὐτοῖς (*scil.* τοῖς Θεσσαλοῖς) φίλος ὢν ἰέναι *and Brasidas himself also said that he came as a friend to the country* *of the Thessalians and to the Thessalians themselves* T. 4. 78, δεῖ τοίνυν τοῦτ' ἤδη σκοπεῖν (*scil.* ἡμᾶς) αὐτούς *we must forthwith consider this matter ourselves* D. 2. 2.

1209. Special renderings of the emphatic αὐτός:

a. *By itself, in itself, unaided, alone,* etc.: αὐτὴ ἡ ἀλήθεια *the naked truth* Aes. 3. 207, τὸ πλέον τοῦ χωρίου αὐτὸ καρτερὸν ὑπῆρχε *the greater part of the place was strong in itself* (without artificial fortification) T. 4. 4. On αὐτοῖς ἀνδράσι *men and all,* see 1525. αὐτό with a noun of any gender is used by Plato to denote the *abstract idea* of a thing: αὐτὸ τὸ καλόν *ideal beauty* R. 493 e, αὐτὸ δικαιοσύνη *ideal justice* 472 c.

b. *Just, merely:* αὐτὸ τὸ δέον *just what we want* X. A. 4. 7. 7, αὐτὰ τάδε *merely this* T. 1. 139.

c. *Voluntarily:* ἄνδρας οἳ καὶ τοῖς μὴ ἐπικαλουμένοις αὐτοὶ ἐπιστρατεύουσι *men who uninvited turn their arms even against those who do not ask their assistance* T. 4. 60.

d. *The Master* (said by a pupil or slave): Αὐτὸς ἔφα *the Master* (Pythagoras) *said it* (*ipse dixit*) Diog. Laert. 8. 1. 46, τίς οὗτος; Αὐτός. τίς Αὐτός; Σωκράτης *Who's this? The Master. Who's the Master? Socrates* Ar. Nub. 220.

e. With ordinals: ᾑρέθη πρεσβευτὴς δέκατος αὐτός *he was chosen envoy with nine others* (*i.e.* himself the tenth) X. H. 2. 2. 17.

1210. After the article, in the attributive position (1154), αὐτός in any case means *same.*

Thus ὁ αὐτὸς ἀνήρ, rarely (ὁ) ἀνὴρ ὁ αὐτός *the same man;* τοῦ αὐτοῦ θέρους *in the same summer* T. 4. 58, τὰ αὐτὰ ταῦτα *these same things* X. A. 1. 1. 7, οἱ τοὺς αὐτοὺς αἰεὶ περὶ τῶν αὐτῶν λόγους λέγοντες *the people who are continually making the same speeches about the same things* Ant. 5. 50.

a. So as a predicate: ἐγὼ μὲν ὁ αὐτός εἰμι, ὑμεῖς δὲ μεταβάλλετε *I am the same, it is you who change* T. 2. 61.

1211. In Hom. αὐτός, without the article, may mean *the same:* ἦρχε δὲ τῷ αὐτὴν ὁδόν, ἥνπερ οἱ ἄλλοι *and he guided him by the same way as the others had gone* θ 107.

1212. αὐτός when unemphatic and standing alone in the oblique cases means *him, her, it, them.* ἐκέλευον αὐτὴν ἀπιέναι *they ordered her to depart* L. 1. 12.

1213. Unemphatic αὐτοῦ, etc., do not stand at the beginning of a sentence.

1214. αὐτοῦ, etc., usually take up a preceding noun (the anaphoric use): καλέσας δὲ Δάμνιππον λέγω πρὸς αὐτὸν τάδε *summoning Damnippus, I speak to him as follows* L. 12. 14. But an oblique case of αὐτός is often suppressed where English employs the pronoun of the third person: ἐμπιπλὰς ἁπάντων τὴν γνώμην ἀπέπεμπε *having satisfied the minds of all he dismissed* them X. A. 1. 7. 8.

1215. αὐτοῦ, etc., may be added pleonastically; πειράσομαι τῷ πάππῳ, κράτιστος ὢν ἱππεύς, συμμαχεῖν αὐτῷ *I will try, since I am an excellent horseman, to be an ally to my grandfather* X. C. 1. 3. 15.

1216. αὐτοῦ, etc., are emphatic (= αὐτοῦ τούτου, etc.) in a main clause when followed by a relative clause referring to αὐτοῦ, etc.: εἴρηκας αὐτό, δι' ὅπερ ἔγωγε *τὰ ἐμὰ ἔργα πλείστου ἄξια νομίζω εἶναι you have mentioned the very quality for which I consider my work worth the highest price* X. M. 3. 10. 14. But when the relative clause precedes, *αὐτοῦ*, etc., are not emphatic: *οὓς δὲ μὴ εὕρισκον, κενοτάφιον αὐτοῖς ἐποίησαν they built a cenotaph for those whom they could not find* X. A. 6. 4. 9.

1217. *αὐτοῦ*, etc., are often used where, after a conjunction, we expect the oblique case of a relative pronoun: *ὃ μὴ οἶδε μηδ' ἔχει αὐτοῦ σφρᾶγῖδα which he does not know nor does he have the seal of it* P. Th. 192 a.

THE REFLEXIVE PRONOUNS

1218. Direct Reflexives. — The reflexive pronouns are used *directly* when they refer to the chief word (usually the subject) of the sentence or clause in which they stand.

γνῶθι σεαυτόν learn to know thyself P. Charm. 164 e, *σφάττει ἑαυτήν she kills herself* X. C. 7. 3. 14, *καθ' ἑαυτοὺς βουλευσάμενοι τὰ ὅπλα παρέδοσαν καὶ σφᾶς αὐτούς after deliberating apart by themselves they surrendered their arms and themselves* (their persons) T. 4. 38. Less commonly the reference is to the object, which often stands in a prominent place: *τοὺς δὲ περιοίκους ἀφῆκεν ἐπὶ τὰς ἑαυτῶν πόλεις but the perioeci he dismissed to their own cities* X. H. 6. 5. 21.

1219. The direct reflexives are regular in prose if, in the same clause, the pronoun refers emphatically to the subject and is the direct object of the main verb: *ἐμαυτὸν* (not *ἐμὲ*) *ἐπαινῶ I praise myself.* The usage of poetry is freer: *στένω σὲ μᾶλλον ἢ 'μέ I mourn thee rather than myself* E. Hipp. 1409.

1220. The reflexives may retain or abandon their differentiating force. Contrast the third example in 1218 with *παρέδοσαν σφᾶς αὐτούς they surrendered* (themselves) T. 7. 82.

1221. The reflexives of the first and second persons are not used in a subordinate clause to refer to the subject of the main clause.

1222. The personal pronouns are sometimes used in a reflexive sense: *θρηνοῦντός τέ μου καὶ λέγοντος πολλὰ καὶ ἀνάξια ἐμοῦ wailing and saying much unworthy of myself* P. A. 38 e (contrast *ἀκούσει πολλὰ καὶ ἀνάξια σαυτοῦ you will hear much unworthy of yourself* P. Cr. 53 e), *δοκῶ μοι ἀδύνατος εἶναι I* (*seem to myself to be*) *think I am unable* P. R. 368 b (less usually *δοκῶ ἐμαυτῷ*). So in Hom.: *ἐγὼν ἐμὲ λύσομαι I will ransom myself* K 378. Cp. 1195.

1223. *ἐμέ, σέ*, not *ἐμαυτόν, σεαυτόν*, are generally used as subject of the infinitive: *ἐγὼ οἶμαι καὶ ἐμὲ καὶ σὲ τὸ ἀδικεῖν τοῦ ἀδικεῖσθαι κάκῑον ἡγεῖσθαι I think that both you and I believe that it is worse to do wrong than to be wronged* P. G. 474 b.

1224. The use in 1222, 1223 generally occurs when there is a contrast between two persons, or when the speaker is not thinking of himself to the exclusion of others. Cp. 1974.

1225. Indirect Reflexives. — The reflexive pronouns are used *indirectly* when, in a dependent clause, they refer to the subject of the main clause.

Ὀρέστης ἔπεισεν Ἀθηναίους ἑαυτὸν κατάγειν *Orestes persuaded the Athenians to restore him(self)* T. 1. 111, ἐβούλετο ὁ Κλέαρχος ἅπαν τὸ στράτευμα πρὸς ἑαυτὸν ἔχειν τὴν γνώμην *Clearchus wished the entire army to be devoted to himself* X. A. 2. 5. 29. Cp. *sibi, se.*

1226. When the subject of the leading clause is not the same as the subject of the subordinate clause or of the accusative with the infinitive (1975), the context must decide to which subject the reflexive pronoun refers: (ὁ κατήγορος) ἔφη . . . ἀναπείθοντα τοὺς νέους αὐτὸν . . . οὕτω διατιθέναι τοὺς ἑαυτῷ συνόντας κ.τ.λ. the accuser *said that, by persuading the young, he* (Socrates) *so disposed his* (*i.e.* Socrates') *pupils*, etc. X. M. 1. 2. 52.

1227. ἑαυτοῦ, etc., are rarely used as indirect reflexives in adjectival clauses: τὰ ναυάγια, ὅσα πρὸς τῇ ἑαυτῶν (γῇ) ἦν, ἀνείλοντο *they took up the wrecks, as many as were close to their own land* T. 2. 92.

1228. Instead of the indirect ἑαυτοῦ, etc., there may be used

a. The oblique cases of αὐτός: ἐπειρᾶτο τοὺς Ἀθηναίους τῆς ἐς αὐτὸν ὀργῆς παραλύειν *he tried to divert the Athenians from their anger against himself* T. 2. 65. When ἑαυτοῦ, etc. precede, αὐτοῦ, etc. are usual instead of the direct reflexive: τὴν ἑαυτοῦ γνώμην ἀπεφαίνετο Σωκράτης πρὸς τοὺς ὁμιλοῦντας αὐτῷ *Socrates was wont to set forth his opinion to those who conversed with him* X. M. 4. 7. 1.

b. Of the forms of the third personal pronoun, οἷ and σφίσι (rarely οὗ, σφεῖς, σφῶν, and σφᾶς). Thus, ἠρώτᾱ αὐτὴν εἰ ἐθελήσοι διᾱκονῆσαί οἱ *he asked her if she would be willing to do him a service* Ant. 1. 16, τοὺς παῖδας ἐκέλευον τοῦ Κύρου δεῖσθαι διαπράξασθαι σφίσιν *they ordered their boys to ask Cyrus to get it done for them* X. C. 1. 4. 1, κελεύουσι γὰρ ἡμᾶς κοινῇ μετὰ σφῶν πολεμεῖν *for they urge us to make war in common with them* And. 3. 27, ἔφη δέ, ἐπειδὴ οὗ ἐκβῆναι τὴν ψῡχὴν . . . . . . ἀφικνεῖσθαι σφᾶς εἰς τόπον τινὰ δαιμόνιον *he said that when his soul had departed out of him, they* (he and others) *came to a mysterious place* P. R. 614 b. See 1195.

N. 1. — σφεῖς may be employed in a dependent sentence if the pronoun is itself the subject of a subordinate statement, and when the reference to the subject of the leading verb is demanded by way of contrast or emphasis: εἰσαγαγὼν τοὺς ἄλλους στρατηγοὺς . . . λέγειν ἐκέλευεν αὐτοὺς ὅτι οὐδὲν ἂν ἧττον σφεῖς ἀγάγοιεν τὴν στρατιὰν ἢ Ξενοφῶν *after bringing in the rest of the generals he urged them to say that they could lead the army just as well as Xenophon* X. A. 7. 5. 9. Here αὐτοί (*ipsi*) is possible. In the singular αὐτός is necessary.

N. 2. — Thucydides often uses the plural forms in reference to the *nearest* subject: τοὺς ξυμμάχους ἐδέδισαν σφῶν *they were afraid of their own allies* (= σφῶν αὐτῶν) 5. 14.

N. 3. — ἑαυτοῦ, etc., are either direct or indirect reflexives, οἷ and σφίσι are only indirect reflexives.

1229. οὗ, σφίσι, etc., and the oblique cases of αὐτός are used when the subordinate clause does not form a part of the thought of the principal subject. This is usual in subordinate indicative clauses, and very common in ὅτι and ὡς clauses, in indirect questions, and in general in subordinate clauses not directly dependent on the main verb: τῶν πρέσβεων, οἳ σφίσι (1481) περὶ τῶν σπονδῶν ἔτυχον ἀπόντες, ἠμέλουν *they thought no more about their envoys, who were absent* *on the subject of the truce* T. 5. 44, ἐφοβοῦντο μὴ ἐπιθοῖντο αὐτοῖς οἱ πολέμιοι *they were afraid lest the enemy should attack them(selves)* X. A. 3. 4. 1.

1230. The reflexive pronoun of the third person is sometimes used for that of the first or second: δεῖ ἡμᾶς ἀνερέσθαι ἑαυτούς *we must ask ourselves* P. Ph. 78 b, παράγγελλε τοῖς ἑαυτοῦ *give orders to your men* X. C. 6. 3. 27.

a. In Homer ὅς *his* is used for ἐμός or σός: οὔτοι ἔγωγε ἧς γαίης δύναμαι γλυκερώτερον ἄλλο ἰδέσθαι *I can look on nothing sweeter than my own land* ι 28.

1231. Reciprocal Reflexive. — The plural forms of the reflexive pronouns are often used for the reciprocal ἀλλήλων, ἀλλήλοις, etc.: ἡμῖν αὐτοῖς διαλεξόμεθα *we will converse with (ourselves) one another* D. 48. 6.

1232. But the reciprocal must be used when the idea 'each for or with himself' is expressed or implied: μᾶλλον χαίρουσιν ἐπὶ τοῖς ἀλλήλων κακοῖς ἢ τοῖς αὑτῶν ἰδίοις ἀγαθοῖς (= ἢ ἐπὶ τοῖς αὑτοῦ ἕκαστος ἀγαθοῖς) *they take greater pleasure in one another's troubles than each man in his own good fortune* I. 4. 168, οὔτε γὰρ ἑαυτοῖς οὔτε ἀλλήλοις ὁμολογοῦσιν *they are in agreement neither with themselves nor with one another* P. Phae. 237 c. Reciprocal and reflexive may occur in the same sentence without difference of meaning (D. 48. 9). The reflexive is regularly used when there is a contrast (expressed or implied) with ἄλλοι: φθονοῦσιν ἑαυτοῖς μᾶλλον ἢ τοῖς ἄλλοις ἀνθρώποις *they envy one another more than* (they envy) *the rest of mankind* X. M. 3. 5. 16.

αὐτός EMPHATIC OR REFLEXIVE WITH OTHER PRONOUNS

1233. Of the plural forms, ἡμῶν αὐτῶν, etc. may be either emphatic or reflexive; αὐτῶν ἡμῶν, etc. are emphatic only; but σφῶν αὐτῶν is only reflexive (αὐτῶν σφῶν is not used). In Hom. αὐτόν may mean *myself, thyself*, or *himself*, and ἓ αὐτόν, οἷ αὐτῷ, etc. are either emphatic or reflexive.

1234. ἡμῶν (ὑμῶν, σφῶν) αὐτῶν often mean 'their own men,' 'their own side': φυλακὴν σφῶν τε αὐτῶν καὶ τῶν ξυμμάχων καταλιπόντες *leaving a garrison* (consisting) *of their own men and of the allies* T. 5. 114.

1235. αὐτός, in agreement with the subject, may be used in conjunction with a reflexive pronoun for the sake of emphasis: αὐτοὶ ἐφ' ἑαυτῶν ἐχώρουν *they marched by themselves* X. A. 2. 4. 10, αὐτὸς . . . ἑαυτὸν ἐν μέσῳ κατετίθετο τοῦ στρατοπέδου *he located himself in the centre of the camp* X. C. 8. 5. 8.

1236. αὐτός may be added to a personal pronoun for emphasis. The forms ἐμὲ αὐτόν, αὐτόν με, etc. are not reflexive like ἐμαυτόν, etc. Thus, τοὺς παῖδας τοὺς ἐμοὺς ᾔσχυνε καὶ ἐμὲ αὐτὸν ὕβρισε *he disgraced my children and insulted me myself* L. 1. 4. Cp. αὐτῷ μοι ἐπέσσυτο *he sprang upon me myself* E 459. Cp. 329 D.

1237. The force of αὐτός thus added is to differentiate. Thus ἐμὲ αὐτόν means *myself and no other*, ἐμαυτόν means simply *myself* without reference to others. ὑμᾶς αὐτούς is the usual order in the reflexive combination; but the differentiating *you yourselves (and no others)* may be ὑμᾶς αὐτούς or αὐτοὺς ὑμᾶς.

THE DEMONSTRATIVE PRONOUNS

1238. The demonstrative pronouns are used substantively or adjectively: **οὗτος**, or **οὗτος ὁ ἀνήρ**, *this man.*

1239. A demonstrative pronoun may agree in gender with a substantive predicated of it, if connected with the substantive by a copulative verb (917) expressed or understood: **αὕτη** (for **τοῦτο**) **ἀρίστη διδασκαλίᾱ** *this is the best manner of learning* X. C. 8. 7. 24, εἰ δέ τις ταύτην (for τοῦτο) εἰρήνην ὑπολαμβάνει *but if any one regards this as peace* D. 9. 9.

a. But the unattracted neuter is common, especially in definitions where the pronoun is the predicate: τοῦτ' ἔστιν ἡ δικαιοσύνη *this is* (what we call) *justice* P. R. 432 b. So οὐχ ὕβρις ταῦτ' ἐστί; *is not this insolence?* Ar. Ran. 21.

1240. οὗτος and ὅδε *this* usually refer to something near in place, time, or thought; ἐκεῖνος *that* refers to something more remote. οὑτοσί and ὁδί are emphatic, deictic (333 g) forms (*this here*).

1241. Distinction between οὗτος and ὅδε. — ὅδε *hic* points with emphasis to an object in the immediate (actual or mental) vicinity of the speaker, or to something just noticed. In the drama it announces the approach of a new actor. ὅδε is even used of the speaker himself as the demonstrative of the first person (1242). **οὗτος** *iste* may refer to a person close at hand, but less vividly, as in statements in regard to a person concerning whom a question has been asked. When ὅδε and οὗτος are contrasted, ὅδε refers to the more important, οὗτος to the less important, object. Thus, ἀλλ' ὅδε βασιλεὺς χωρεῖ *but lo! here comes the king* S. Ant. 155, αὕτη πέλας σοῦ *here she* (the person you ask for) *is near thee* S. El. 1474, καὶ ταῦτ' ἀκούειν κἄτι τῶνδ' ἀλγίονα *so that we obey both in these things and in things yet more grievous* S. Ant. 64. See also 1245. οὗτος has a wider range of use than the other demonstratives.

1242. ὅδε is used in poetry for ἐγώ: τῆσδέ (= ἐμοῦ) γε ζώσης ἔτι *while I still live* S. Tr. 305. Also for the possessive pronoun of the first person: εἴ τις τούσδ' ἀκούσεται λόγους *if any one shall hear these my words* S. El. 1004.

1243. οὗτος is sometimes used of the second person: τίς οὑτοσί; *who's this here?* (= *who are you?*) Ar. Ach. 1048. So in exclamations: οὗτος, τί ποιεῖς; *you there! what are you doing?* Ar. Ran. 198.

1244. τάδε, τάδε πάντα (ταῦτα πάντα) are used of something close at hand: οὐκ Ἴωνες τάδε εἰσίν *the people here are not Ionians* T. 6. 77.

1245. οὗτος (τοιοῦτος, τοσοῦτος, and οὕτως) generally refers to what precedes, ὅδε (τοιόσδε, τοσόσδε, τηλικόσδε, and ὧδε) to what follows.

Thus, τοιάδε ἔλεξεν *he spoke as follows*, but τοιαῦτα (τοσαῦτα) εἰπών *after speaking thus.* Cp. ὁ Κῦρος ἀκούσᾱς τοῦ Γωβρύου τοιαῦτα τοιάδε πρὸς αὐτὸν ἔλεξε *Cyrus after hearing these words of Gobryas answered him as follows* X. C. 5. 2. 31.

1246. καὶ οὗτος meaning (1) *he too, likewise;* (2) *and in fact, and that too,* points back: Ἀγίᾱς καὶ Σωκράτης . . . καὶ τούτω ἀπεθανέτην *Agias and Socrates . . . they too were put to death* X. A. 2. 6. 30; ἀπόρων ἐστὶ . . . καὶ τούτων πονηρῶν *it is characteristic of men without resources and that too worthless* 2. 5. 21 (cp. 1320). On καὶ ταῦτα see 947.

1247. But οὗτος, etc. sometimes (especially in the neuter) refer to what follows, and ὅδε, etc. (though much less often) refer to what precedes: *μετὰ δὲ τοῦτον εἶπε τοσοῦτον* *but after him he spoke as follows* X. A. 1. 3. 14, *τοιούτους λόγους εἶπεν* *he spoke as follows* T. 4. 58, *τοιάδε παρακελευόμενος* *exhorting them thus* (as set forth before) 7. 78, *ὧδε θάπτουσιν* *they bury them thus* (as described before) 2. 34, *οὕτως ἔχει* *the case is as follows* (often in the orators).

1248. οὗτος (especially in the neuter τοῦτο) may refer forward to a word or sentence in apposition: *ὡς μὴ τοῦτο μόνον ἐννοῶνται, τί πείσονται* *that they may not consider this alone* (namely) *what they shall suffer* X. A. 3. 1. 41. So also οὕτως. ἐκεῖνος also may refer forward: *ἐκεῖνο κερδαίνειν ἡγεῖται τὴν ἡδονήν* *this* (namely) *pleasure, it regards as gain* P. R. 606 b. Cp. 990.

1249. οὗτος (τοιοῦτος, etc.) is regularly, ὅδε (τοιόσδε, etc.) rarely, used as the demonstrative antecedent of a relative: *ὅταν τοιαῦτα λέγῃς, ἃ οὐδεὶς ἂν φήσειεν ἀνθρώπων* *when you say such things as no one in the world would say* P. G. 473 e. οὗτος is often used without a conjunction at the beginning of a sentence.

1250. When ὅδε retains its full force the relative clause is to be regarded as a supplementary addition: *οὗ δὴ οὖν ἕνεκα λέγω ταῦτα πάντα τόδ᾽ ἐστί* *but here's the reason why I say all this!* P. Charm. 165 a.

1251. The demonstratives οὗτος, etc., when used as antecedents, have an emphatic force that does not reproduce the (unemphatic) English demonstrative *those*, *e.g.* in *you released those who were present.* Here Greek uses the participle (τοὺς παρόντας ἀπελύσατε L. 20. 20) or omits the antecedent.

1252. οὗτος (less often ἐκεῖνος) may take up and emphasize a preceding subject or object. In this use the pronoun generally comes first, but may be placed after an emphatic word: *ποιήσαντες στήλην ἐψηφίσαντο εἰς ταύτην ἀναγράφειν τοὺς ἀλιτηρίους* *having made a slab they voted to inscribe on it the* (names of the) *offenders* Lyc. 117, *ἃ ἂν εἴπῃς, ἔμμενε τούτοις* *whatever you say, hold to it* P. R. 345 b. The anaphoric αὐτός in its oblique cases is weaker (1214).

1253. τοῦτο, ταῦτα (and αὐτό) may take up a substantive idea not expressed by a preceding neuter word: *οἳ τὴν Ἑλλάδα ἠλευθέρωσαν· ἡμεῖς δὲ οὐδ᾽ ἡμῖν αὐτοῖς βεβαιοῦμεν αὐτό* (*i.e.* τὴν ἐλευθερίᾱν) *who freed Greece; whereas we cannot secure this* (liberty) *even for ourselves* T. 1. 122.

1254. οὗτος (less frequently ἐκεῖνος) is used of well known persons and things. Thus, Γοργίᾱς οὗτος *this* (famous) *Gorgias* P. Hipp. M. 282 b (cp. *ille*), τούτους τοὺς σῡκοφάντᾱς *these* (notorious) *informers* P. Cr. 45 a (cp. *iste*), τὸν Ἀριστείδην ἐκεῖνον *that* (famous) *Aristides* D. 3. 21, Καλλίᾱν ἐκεῖνον *that* (infamous) *Callias* 2. 19. ἐκεῖνος may be used of a deceased person (P. R. 368 a).

1255. When, in the same sentence, and referring to the same object, οὗτος (or ἐκεῖνος) is used more than once, the object thus designated is more or less emphatic: *ὁ θεὸς ἐξαιρούμενος τούτων τὸν νοῦν τούτοις χρῆται ὑπηρέταις* *the god deprives them of their senses and employs them as his ministers* P. Ion 534 c. For the repeated οὗτος (ἐκεῖνος) an oblique case of αὐτός is usual.

1256. τοῦτο μέν . . . τοῦτο δέ *first . . . secondly, partly . . . partly* has, especially in Hdt., nearly the sense of τὸ μέν . . . τὸ δέ (1111).

1257. ἐκεῖνος refers back (rarely forward, 1248), but implies remoteness in place, time, or thought.

Κῦρος καθορᾷ βασιλέᾱ καὶ τὸ ἀμφ' ἐκεῖνον στῖφος *Cyrus perceives the king and the band around him* X. A. 1. 8. 26, νῆες ἐκεῖναι ἐπιπλέουσιν *yonder are ships sailing up* to us T. 1. 51.

1258. ἐκεῖνος may refer to any person other than the speaker and the person addressed; and may be employed of a person not definitely described, but referred to in a supposed case. It is even used of the person already referred to by αὐτός in an oblique case: ἂν αὐτῷ διδῷς ἀργύριον καὶ πείθῃς ἐκεῖνον *if you give him money and persuade him* P. Pr. 310 d. ἐκεῖνος, when so used, usually stands in a different case than αὐτός. The order ἐκεῖνος . . . αὐτός is found: πρὸς μὲν ἐκείνους οὐκ εἶπεν ἣν ἔχοι γνώμην, ἀλλ' ἀπέπεμψεν αὐτούς *he did not tell them the plan he had, but dismissed them* X. H. 3. 2. 9.

1259. When used to set forth a contrast to another person, ἐκεῖνος may even refer to the subject of the leading verb (apparent reflexive use): ὅταν ἐν τῇ γῇ ὁρῶσιν ἡμᾶς δῃοῦντάς τε καὶ τἀκείνων φθείροντας *when they* (the Athenians) *see us* (the Dorians) *in their land plundering and destroying their property* (= τὰ ἑαυτῶν) T. 2. 11, ἔλεξε τοῖς Χαλδαίοις ὅτι ἥκοι οὔτε ἀπολέσαι ἐπιθῡμῶν ἐκείνους οὔτε πολεμεῖν δεόμενος *he said to the Chaldaeans that he had come neither with the desire to destroy them* (ἐκείνους is stronger than αὐτούς) *nor because he wanted to war with them* X. C. 3. 2. 12.

1260. In the phrase ὅδε ἐκεῖνος, ὅδε marks a person or thing as present, ἐκεῖνος a person or thing mentioned before or well known: ὅδ' ἐκεῖνος ἐγώ *lo! I am he* S. O. C. 138. Colloquial expressions are τοῦτ' ἐκεῖνο *there it is!* (lit. *this is that*) Ar. Ach. 41, and τόδ' ἐκεῖνο *I told you so* E. Med. 98.

1261. Distinction between οὗτος and ἐκεῖνος. — When reference is made to one of two contrasted objects, οὗτος refers to the object nearer to the speaker's thought, or to the more important object, or to the object last mentioned. Thus, ὥστε πολὺ ἂν δικαιότερον ἐκείνοις τοῖς γράμμασιν ἢ τούτοις πιστεύοιτε *so that you must with more justice put your trust in those lists* (not yet put in as evidence) *than in these muster-rolls* (already mentioned) L. 16. 7, εἰ δὲ τοῦτό σοι δοκεῖ μῑκρὸν εἶναι, ἐκεῖνο κατανόησον *but if this appear to you unimportant, consider the following* X. C. 5. 5. 29. ἐκεῖνος may refer to an object that has immediately preceded: καὶ (δεῖ) τὸ βέλτιστον ἀεί, μὴ τὸ ῥᾷστον, ἅπαντας λέγειν· ἐπ' ἐκεῖνο μὲν (*i.e.* τὸ ῥᾷστον) γὰρ ἡ φύσις αὐτὴ βαδιεῖται, ἐπὶ τοῦτο δὲ (τὸ βέλτιστον) τῷ λόγῳ δεῖ προάγεσθαι διδάσκοντα τὸν ἀγαθὸν πολῑτην *it is necessary that all should speak what is always most salutary, not what is most agreeable; for to the latter nature herself will incline; to the former a good citizen must direct by argument and instruction* D. 8. 72.

THE INTERROGATIVE PRONOUNS

1262. The interrogative pronouns are used substantively τίς; *who?* or adjectively τίς ἀνήρ; *what man?*

1263. The interrogatives (pronouns and adverbs, 340, 346) are used in direct and in indirect questions. In indirect questions the indefinite relatives ὅστις, etc., are generally used instead of the interrogatives.

τί βούλεται ἡμῖν χρῆσθαι; *for what purpose does he desire to employ us?* X. A. 1. 3. 18, οὐκ οἶδα ὅ τι ἂν τις χρήσαιτο αὐτοῖς *I do not know for what service any one could employ them* 3. 1. 40, A. πηνίκ' ἐστὶν ἄρα τῆς ἡμέρας; B. ὁπηνίκα; A. *What's the time of day?* B. (*You ask*), *what time of day it is?* Ar. Av. 1499.

N. — For peculiarities of Interrogative Sentences, see 2666, 2668.

1264. τί is used for τίνα as the predicate of a neuter plural subject when the general result is sought and the subject is considered as a unit: ταῦτα δὲ τί ἐστιν; *but these things, what are they?* Aes. 3. 167. τίνα emphasizes the details: τίν' οὖν ἐστι ταῦτα; D. 18. 246.

1265. τίς asks a question concerning the class, τί concerning the nature of a thing: εἰπὲ τίς ἡ τέχνη *say of what sort the art is* P. G. 449 a, τί σωφροσύνη, τί πολῑτικός; *what is temperance, what is a statesman?* X. M. 1. 1. 16, φθόνον δὲ σκοπῶν ὅ τι εἴη *considering what envy is* (*quid sit invidia*) X. M. 3. 9. 8.

THE INDEFINITE PRONOUNS

1266. The indefinite pronoun τὶς, τὶ is used both substantively (*some one*) and adjectively (*any, some*). τὶς, τὶ cannot stand at the beginning of a sentence (181 b).

1267. In the singular, τὶς is used in a collective sense: *everybody* (for *anybody*); cp. Germ. *man*, Fr. *on*: ἀλλὰ μισεῖ τις ἐκεῖνον *but everybody detests him* D. 4. 8. ἕκαστός τις, πᾶς τις *each one, every one* are generally used in this sense. τὶς may be a covert allusion to a known person: δώσει τις δίκην *some one* (i.e. *you*) *will pay the penalty* Ar. Ran. 554. It may also stand for *I* or *we*. Even when added to a noun with the article, τὶς denotes the indefiniteness of the person referred to: ὅταν δ' ὁ κύριος παρῇ τις, ὑμῶν ὅστις ἐστὶν ἡγεμὼν κτλ. *but whenever your master arrives, whoever he be that is your leader*, etc. S. O. C. 289. With a substantive, τὶς may often be rendered *a, an*, as in ἕτερός τις δυνάστης *another dignitary* X. A. 1. 2. 20; or, to express indefiniteness of nature, by *a sort of*, etc., as in εἰ μὲν θεοί τινές εἰσιν οἱ δαίμονες *if the 'daimones' are a sort of gods* P. A. 27 d.

1268. With adjectives, adverbs, and numerals, τὶς may strengthen or weaken an assertion, apologize for a comparison, and in general qualify a statement: δεινός τις ἀνήρ *a very terrible man* P. R. 596 c, μύωψ τις *a sort of gad-fly* P. A. 30 e, σχεδόν τι *pretty nearly* X. O. 4. 11, τριάκοντά τινες *about 30* T. 8. 73. But in παρεγένοντό τινες δύο νῆες the numeral is appositional to τινές (*certain, that is, two ships joined* them) T. 8. 100.

1269. τὶς, τὶ sometimes means *somebody*, or *something, of importance*: τὸ δοκεῖν τινὲς εἶναι *the seeming to be somebody* D. 21. 213, ἔδοξέ τι λέγειν *he seemed to say something of moment* X. C. 1. 4. 20.

1270. τὶ is not omitted in θαυμαστὸν λέγεις *what you say is wonderful* P. L. 657 a. ἤ τις ἢ οὐδείς means *few or none* X. C. 7. 5. 45, ἤ τι ἢ οὐδέν *little or nothing* P. A. 17 b.

THE ADJECTIVE PRONOUNS ἄλλος AND ἕτερος

1271. ἄλλος strictly means *other* (of several), ἕτερος *other* (of two). On ὁ ἄλλος, οἱ ἄλλοι see 1188.

a. ἕτερος is sometimes used loosely for ἄλλος, but always with a sense of *difference;* when so used it does not take the article.

1272. ἄλλος, and ἕτερος (rarely), may be used attributively with a substantive, which is to be regarded as an appositive. In this sense they may be rendered *besides, moreover, as well:* οἱ ἄλλοι Ἀθηναῖοι *the Athenians as well* (*the others,* i.e. *the Athenians*) T. 7. 70, τοὺς ὁπλίτᾱς καὶ τοὺς ἄλλους ἱππέᾱς *the hoplites and the cavalry besides* X. H. 2. 4. 9, γέρων χωρεῖ μεθ' ἑτέρου νεᾱνίου *an old man comes with* (*a second person, a young man*) *a young man besides* Ar. Eccl. 849. Cp. " And there were also two other malefactors led with him to be put to death " St. Luke 23. 32.

1273. ἄλλος *other, rest* often precedes the particular thing with which it is contrasted: τά τε ἄλλα ἐτῑ́μησε καὶ μῡρίους ἔδωκε δᾱρεικούς *he gave me ten thousand darics besides honouring me in other ways* (lit. *he both honoured me in other ways and* etc.) X. A. 1. 3. 3, τῷ μὲν ἄλλῳ στρατῷ ἡσύχαζεν, ἑκατὸν δὲ πελταστὰς προπέμπει *with the rest of the army he kept quiet, but sent forward a hundred peltasts* T. 4. 111.

1274. ἄλλος followed by another of its own cases or by an adverb derived from itself (cp. *alius aliud, one . . . one, another . . . another*) does not require the second half of the statement to be expressed: ἄλλος ἄλλα λέγει *one says one thing, another* (*says*) *another* X. A. 2. 1. 15 (lit. *another other things*). So ἄλλοι ἄλλως, ἄλλοι ἄλλοθεν.

a. Similarly ἕτερος, as συμφορᾱ̀ ἑτέρᾱ ἑτέρους πιέζει *one calamity oppresses one, another others* E. Alc. 893.

1275. After ὁ ἄλλος an adjective or a participle used substantively usually requires the article: τἆλλα τὰ μέγιστα *the other matters of the highest moment* P. A. 22 d. Here τὰ μέγιστα is in apposition to τἆλλα (1272). οἱ ἄλλοι πάντες οἱ, τἆλλα πάντα τά sometimes omit the final article.

1276. ὁ ἄλλος often means *usual, general:* παρὰ τὸν ἄλλον τρόπον *contrary to my usual disposition* Ant. 3. β. 1.

THE RECIPROCAL PRONOUN

1277. The pronoun ἀλλήλοιν expresses reciprocal relation: ὡς δ' εἰδέτην ἀλλήλους ἡ γυνὴ καὶ ὁ Ἀβραδάτᾱς, ἠσπάζοντο ἀλλήλους *when Abradatas and his wife saw each other, they mutually embraced* X. C. 6. 1. 47.

1278. To express reciprocal relation Greek uses also (1) the middle forms (1726); (2) the reflexive pronoun (1231); or (3) a substantive is repeated: ἀνὴρ ἕλεν ἄνδρα *man fell upon man* Ο 328.

On Relative Pronouns see under Complex Sentences (2493 ff.).

THE CASES

1279. Of the cases belonging to the Indo-European language, Greek has lost the free use of three: instrumental, locative, and ablative. A few of the *forms* of these cases have been preserved (341, 1449, 1535); the syntactical *functions* of the instrumental and locative were taken over by the dative; those of the ablative by the genitive. The genitive and dative cases are therefore *composite* or *mixed* cases.

N.—The reasons that led to the formation of *composite* cases are either (1) formal or (2) functional. Thus (1) χώρᾳ is both dat. and loc.; λόγοις represents the instr. λόγοις and the loc. λόγοισι; in consonantal stems both ablative and genitive ended in -ος; (2) verbs of *ruling* may take either the dat. or the loc., hence the latter case would be absorbed by the former; furthermore the use of prepositions especially with loc. and instr. was attendeu by a certain indifference as regards the form of the case.

1280. Through the influence of one construction upon another it often becomes impossible to mark off the later from the original use of the genitive and dative. It must be remembered that since language is a natural growth and Greek was spoken and written before formal categories were set up by Grammar, all the uses of the cases cannot be apportioned with definiteness.

1281. The cases fall into two main divisions. Cases of the Subject: nominative (and vocative). Cases of the Predicate: accusative, dative. The genitive may define either the subject (with nouns) or the predicate (with verbs). On the nominative, see 938 ff.

1282. The content of a thought may be expressed in different ways in different languages. Thus, πείθω σε, but *persuadeo tibi* (in classical Latin): and even in the same language, the same verb may have varying constructions to express different shades of meaning.

VOCATIVE

1283. The vocative is used in exclamations and in direct address: ὦ Ζεῦ καὶ θεοί *oh Zeus and ye gods* P. Pr. 310 d, ἄνθρωπε *my good fellow* X. C. 2. 2. 7. The vocative forms an incomplete sentence (904 d).

a. The vocative is never followed immediately by δέ or γάρ.

1284. In ordinary conversation and public speeches, the polite ὦ is usually added. Without ὦ the vocative may express astonishment, joy, contempt, a threat, or a warning, etc. Thus ἀκούεις Αἰσχίνη; *d'ye hear, Aeschines?* D. 18. 121. But this distinction is not always observed, though in general ὦ has a familiar tone which was unsuited to elevated poetry.

1285. The vocative is usually found in the interior of a sentence. At the beginning it is emphatic. In prose ἔφη, in poetry ὦ, may stand between the vocative and an attributive or between an attributive and the vocative; in poetry ὦ may be repeated for emphasis.

1286. In late poetry a predicate adjective may be attracted into the vocative: ὄλβιε κῶρε γένοιο *blessed, oh boy, mayest thou be* Theocr. 17. 66. Cp. *Matutine pater seu Iane libentius audis* Hor. S. 2. 6. 20.

1287. By the omission of σύ or ὑμεῖς the nominative with the article may stand in apposition to a vocative: ὦ ἄνδρες οἱ παρόντες *you, gentlemen, who are present* P. Pr. 337 c, ὦ Κῦρε καὶ οἱ ἄλλοι Πέρσαι *Cyrus and the rest of you Persians* X. C. 3. 3. 20; and in apposition to the pronoun in the verb: ὁ παῖς, ἀκολούθει *boy, attend me* Ar. Ran. 521.

1288. The nominative may be used in exclamations as a predicate with the subject unexpressed: ὦ πικρὸς θεοῖς *oh loathed of heaven* S. Ph. 254, φίλος ὦ Μενέλᾱε *ah dear Menelaus* Δ 189; and connected with the vocative by *and:* ὦ πόλις καὶ δῆμε *oh city and people* Ar. Eq. 273. In exclamations about a person: ὢ γενναῖος *oh the noble man* P. Phae. 227 c.

a. οὗτος is regular in address: οὗτος, τί πάσχεις, ὦ Ξανθίᾱ; *ho there, I say, Xanthias, what is the matter with you?* Ar. Vesp. 1; ὦ οὗτος, Αἶᾱς *ho there, I say, Ajax* S. Aj. 89.

GENITIVE

1289. The genitive most commonly limits the meaning of substantives, adjectives, and adverbs, less commonly that of verbs.

Since the genitive has absorbed the ablative it includes (1) the genitive proper, denoting the class to which a person or thing belongs, and (2) the ablatival genitive.

a. The name *genitive* is derived from *casus genitivus, the case of origin,* the inadequate Latin translation of γενικὴ πτῶσις *case denoting the class.*

THE GENITIVE PROPER WITH NOUNS

(ADNOMINAL GENITIVE)

1290. A substantive in the genitive limits the meaning of a substantive on which it depends.

1291. The genitive limits for the time being the scope of the substantive on which it depends by referring it to a particular class or description, or by regarding it as a part of a whole. The genitive is akin in meaning to the adjective and may often be translated by an epithet. Cp. στέφανος χρῡσίου with χρῡσοῦς στέφανος, φόβος πολεμίου with πολέμιος φόβος, τὸ εὖρος πλέθρου with τὸ εὖρος πλεθριαῖον (1035). But the use of the adjective is not everywhere parallel to that of the genitive.

1292. In poetry a genitive is often used with βίᾱ, μένος, σθένος *might*, etc., instead of the corresponding adjective: βίη Διομήδεος *mighty Diomede* E 781.

1293. In poetry δέμας *form*, κάρᾱ and κεφαλή *head*, etc., are used with a genitive to express majestic or loved persons or objects: Ἰσμήνης κάρᾱ S. Ant. 1.

1294. χρῆμα *thing* is used in prose with a genitive to express size, strength, etc.: σφενδονητῶν πάμπολύ τι χρῆμα *a very large mass of slingers* X. C. 2. 1. 5. Cp. 1322.

1295. The genitive with substantives denotes in general a connection or dependence between two words. This connection must often be determined (1) by the meaning of the words, (2) by the context, (3) by the facts presupposed as known (1301). The same construction may often be placed under more than one of the different classes mentioned below; and the connection between the two substantives is often so loose that it is difficult to include with precision all cases under specific grammatical classes.

a. The two substantives may be so closely connected as to be equivalent to a single compound idea: τελευτὴ τοῦ βίου 'life-end' (cp. *life-time*) X. A. 1. 1. 1. Cp. 1146.

b. The genitive with substantives has either the attributive (1154), or, in the case of the genitive of the divided whole (1306), and of personal pronouns (1185), the predicate, position (1168).

1296. Words denoting number, especially numerals or substantives with numerals, often agree in case with the limited word instead of standing in the genitive: φόρος τέσσαρα τάλαντα *a tribute of four talents* T. 4. 57 (cp. 1323), ἐς τὰς ναῦς, αἳ ἐφρούρουν δύο, καταφυγόντες *fleeing to the ships, two of which were keeping guard* 4. 113. So with οἱ μέν, οἱ δέ in apposition to the subject (981).

GENITIVE OF POSSESSION OR BELONGING

1297. The genitive denotes ownership, possession, or belonging: ἡ οἰκίᾱ ἡ Σίμωνος *the house of Simon* L. 3. 32, ὁ Κῡ́ρου στόλος *the expedition of Cyrus* X. A. 1. 2. 5. Cp. the dative of possession (1476).

1298. Here may be classed the genitive of origin: οἱ Σόλωνος νόμοι *the laws of Solon* D. 20. 103, ἡ ἐπιστολὴ τοῦ Φιλίππου *the letter of Philip* 18. 37, κύματα παντοίων ἀνέμων *waves caused by all kinds of winds* B 396.

1299. The possessive genitive is used with the neuter article (singular or plural) denoting affairs, conditions, power, and the like: τὸ τῶν ἐφόρων *the power of the ephors* P. L. 712 d, τὸ τῆς τέχνης *the function of the art* P. G. 450 c, τὸ τοῦ Σόλωνος *the maxim of Solon* P. Lach. 188 b, ἄδηλα τὰ τῶν πολέμων *the chances of war are uncertain* T. 2. 11, τὰ τῆς πόλεως *the interests of the State* P. A. 36 c, τὰ τοῦ δήμου φρονεῖ *is on the side of the people* Ar. Eq. 1216. Sometimes this is almost a mere periphrasis for the thing itself: τὸ τῆς τύχης *chance* D. 4. 12 τὰ τῆς σωτηρίᾱς *safety* 23. 163, τὸ τῆς ὁσίᾱς, ὁτιδήποτ' ἐστί *the quality of holiness, whatever it is* 21. 126, τὸ τῶν πρεσβυτέρων ἡμῶν *we elders* P. L. 657 d. So τὸ τούτου S. Aj. 124 is almost = οὗτος, as τοὐμόν is = ἐγώ or ἐμέ. Cp. L. 8. 19.

1300. The genitive of possession may be used after a demonstrative or relative pronoun: τοῦτό μου διαβάλλει *he attacks this action of mine* D. 18. 28.

1301. With persons the genitive may denote the relation of child to parent, wife to husband, and of inferior to superior: Θουκῡδίδης ὁ Ὀλόρου *Thucydides, the son of Olorus* T. 4. 104 (and so υἱός is regularly omitted in Attic official documents), Διὸς Ἄρτεμις *Artemis, daughter of Zeus* S. Aj. 172, ἡ Σμῑκυθίωνος Μελιστίχη *Melistiche wife of Smicythion* Ar. Eccl. 46, Λῡδὸς ὁ Φερεκλέους *Lydus, the slave of Pherecles* And. 1. 17, οἱ Μένωνος *the troops of Menon* X. A. 1. 5. 13 (οἱ τοῦ Μένωνος στρατιῶται 1. 5. 11).

a. In poetry we may have an attributive adjective: Τελαμώνιος Αἴᾱς (= Αἴᾱς ὁ Τελαμῶνος) B 528. Cp. 846 f.

1302. The word on which the possessive genitive depends may be represented by the article: ἀπὸ τῆς ἑαυτῶν *from their own* country (γῆς) T. 1. 15 (cp. 1027 b). A word for *dwelling* (οἰκίᾱ, δόμος, and also ἱερόν) is perhaps omitted after ἐν, εἰς, and sometimes after ἐξ. Thus, ἐν Ἀρίφρονος *at Ariphron's* P. Pr. 320 a, ἐν Διονύσου (*scil.* ἱερῷ) *at the shrine of Dionysus* D. 5. 7, εἰς διδασκάλου φοιτᾶν *to go to school* X. C. 2. 3. 9, ἐκ Πατροκλέους ἔρχομαι *I come from Patroclus's* Ar. Plut. 84. So, in Homer, εἰν(εἰς) Ἀΐδᾱο.

1303. Predicate Use. — The genitive may be connected with the noun it limits by means of a verb.

Ἱπποκράτης ἐστὶ οἰκίᾱς μεγάλης *Hippocrates is of an influential house* P. Pr. 316 b, Βοιωτῶν ἡ πόλις ἔσται *the city will belong to the Boeotians* L. 12. 58, ἡ Ζέλειά ἐστι τῆς Ἀσίᾱς *Zelea is in Asia* D. 9. 43, οὐδὲ τῆς αὐτῆς Θρᾴκης ἐγένοντο *nor did they belong to the same Thrace* T. 2. 29, ἃ διώκει τοῦ ψηφίσματος, ταῦτ' ἐστίν *the clauses in the bill which he attacks, are these* D. 18. 56.

1304. The genitive with εἰμί may denote the person whose *nature, duty, custom*, etc., it is to do that set forth in an infinitive subject of the verb: πενίᾱν φέρειν οὐ παντός, ἀλλ' ἀνδρὸς σοφοῦ *'tis the sage, not every one, who can bear poverty* Men. Sent. 463, δοκεῖ δικαίου τοῦτ' εἶναι πολῑ́του *this seems to be the duty of a just citizen* D. 8. 72, τῶν νῑκώντων ἐστὶ καὶ τὰ ἑαυτῶν σῴζειν καὶ τὰ τῶν ἡττωμένων λαμβάνειν *it is the custom of conquerors to keep what is their own and to take the possessions of the defeated* X. A. 3. 2. 39.

1305. With verbs signifying to refer or attribute, by thought, word, or action, anything to a person or class. Such verbs are *to think, regard, make, name, choose, appoint*, etc.

λογίζου . . . τὰ δ' ἄλλα τῆς τύχης *deem that the rest belongs to chance* E. Alc. 789, τῶν ἐλευθερωτάτων οἴκων νομισθεῖσα *deemed a daughter of a house most free* E. And. 12, ἐμὲ γράφε τῶν ἱππεύειν ὑπερεπιθῡμούντων *put me down as one of those who desire exceedingly to serve on horseback* X. C. 4. 3. 21, τῆς πρώτης τάξεως τεταγμένος *assigned to the first class* L. 14. 11, τῆς ἀγαθῆς τύχης τῆς πόλεως εἶναι τίθημι *I reckon as belonging to the good fortune of the State* D. 18. 254, εἰ δέ τινες τὴν Ἀσίᾱν ἑαυτῶν ποιοῦνται *but if some are claiming Asia as their own* X. Ages. 1. 33, νομίζει ὑμᾶς ἑαυτοῦ εἶναι *he thinks that you are in his power* X. A. 2. 1. 11.

GENITIVE OF THE DIVIDED WHOLE (PARTITIVE GENITIVE)

1306. The genitive may denote a whole, a part of which is denoted by the noun it limits. The genitive of the divided whole may be used with any word that expresses or implies a part.

1307. Position. — The genitive of the whole stands before or after the word denoting the part: τῶν Θρᾳκῶν πελτασταί *targeteers of the Thracians* T. 7. 27, οἱ ἄποροι τῶν πολῑτῶν *the needy among the citizens* D. 18. 104; rarely between the limited noun and its article: οἱ τῶν ἀδίκων ἀφικνούμενοι *those of the unrighteous who come here* P. G. 525 c. Cp. 1161 N. 1.

1308. When all are included there is no partition: so in οὗτοι πάντες *all of these, all these*, τέτταρες ἡμεῖς ἦμεν *there were four of us*, τὸ πᾶν πλῆθος τῶν ὁπλῑτῶν *the entire body of the hoplites* T. 8. 93, ὅσοι ἐστὲ τῶν ὁμοίων *as many of you as belong to the 'peers'* X. A. 4. 6. 14.

1309. The idea of division is often not explicitly stated. See third example in 1310.

1310. (I) The genitive of the divided whole is used with substantives.

μέρος τι τῶν βαρβάρων *some part of the barbarians* T. 1. 1, οἱ Δωριῆς ἡμῶν *those of us who are Dorians* 4. 61. The governing word may be omitted: Ἀρχίᾱς τῶν Ἡρᾱκλειδῶν *Archias* (one) *of the Heraclidae* T. 6. 3. To an indefinite substantive without the article may be added a genitive denoting the special sort: Φεραύλᾱς Πέρσης τῶν δημοτῶν *Pheraulas, a Persian, one of the common people* X. C. 2. 3. 7.

1311. Chorographic Genitive. — τῆς Ἀττικῆς ἐς Οἰνόην *to Oenoë in Attica* T. 2. 18 (or ἐς Οἰνόην τῆς Ἀττικῆς, *not* ἐς τῆς Ἀττικῆς Οἰνόην), τῆς Ἰταλίᾱς Λοκροί *the Locrians in Italy* 3. 86. The article, which is always used with the genitive of the country (as a place well known), is rarely added to the governing substantive (τὸ Κήναιον τῆς Εὐβοίᾱς *Cenaeum in Euboea* T. 3. 93).

1312. (II) With substantive adjectives and participles.

οἱ ἄδικοι τῶν ἀνθρώπων *the unjust among men* D. 27. 68 (but always οἱ θνητοὶ ἄνθρωποι), μόνος τῶν πρυτάνεων *alone of the prytans* P. A. 32 b, ὀλίγοι αὐτῶν *few of them* X. A. 3. 1. 3, τῶν ἄλλων Ἑλλήνων ὁ βουλόμενος *whoever of the rest of the Greeks so desires* T. 3. 92. So τὸ καταντικρὺ αὐτῶν τοῦ σπηλαίου *the part of the cavern facing them* P. R. 515 a. For *nihil novi* the Greek says οὐδὲν καινόν.

1313. Adjectives denoting magnitude, and some others, may conform in gender to the genitive, instead of appearing in the neuter: ἔτεμον τῆς γῆς τὴν πολλήν *they ravaged most of the land* T. 2. 56, τῆς γῆς ἡ ἀρίστη *the best of the land* 1. 2. This construction occurs more frequently in prose than in poetry.

1314. But such adjectives, especially when singular, may be used in the neuter: τῶν Ἀργείων λογάδων τὸ πολύ *the greater part of the picked Argives* T. 5. 73, ἐπὶ πολὺ τῆς χώρᾱς *over a great part of the land* 4. 3.

1315. (III) With comparatives and superlatives.

ἡμῶν ὁ γεραίτερος *the elder of us* X. C. 5. 1. 6 (1066 b), οἱ πρεσβύτατοι τῶν στρατηγῶν *the oldest of the generals* X. A. 3. 3. 11, σίτῳ πάντων ἀνθρώπων πλείστῳ χρώμεθ' ἐπεισάκτῳ *we make use of imported grain more than all other people* D. 18. 87. So with a superlative adverb: ἡ ναῦς ἄριστά μοι ἔπλει παντὸς τοῦ στρατοπέδου *my ship was the best sailer of the whole squadron* L. 21. 6.

1316. In poetry this use is extended to positive adjectives: ἀριδείκετος ἀνδρῶν *conspicuous among men* Λ 248, ὦ φίλᾱ γυναικῶν *oh dear among women* E. Alc. 460. In tragedy an adjective may be emphasized by the addition of the same adjective in the genitive: ἄρρητ' ἀρρήτων *horrors unspeakable* S. O. T. 465. Cp. 1064.

1317. (IV) With substantive pronouns and numerals.

οἱ μὲν αὐτῶν, οἱ δ' οὔ *some of them and not others* P. A. 24 e, οἱ ὕστερον ἐλήφθησαν τῶν πολεμίων *those of the enemy who were taken later* X. A. 1. 7. 13, οὐδεὶς ἀνθρώπων *no one in the world* P. S. 220 a, τὶ τοῦ τείχους *a part of the wall* T. 7. 4, τὶς θεῶν *one of the gods* E. Hec. 164 (τὶς θεός *a god* X. C. 5. 2. 12), ἓν τῶν πολλῶν *one of the many things* P. A. 17 a; rarely after demonstrative pronouns: τούτοις τῶν ἀνθρώπων *to these (of) men* T. 1. 71.

a. With ὀλίγοι and with numerals ἀπό and ἐξ are rarely added: ἐκ τριῶν ἕν *one of three* S. Tr. 734. ἐξ with superlatives is also rare. See also 1688. 1 c.

1318. The genitive of the divided whole may do duty as the subject of a finite verb (928 b) or of the infinitive: (ἔφασαν) ἐπιμειγνύναι σφῶν πρὸς ἐκείνους *they said that* some *of their number associated with them* X. A. 3. 5. 16.

1319. Predicate Use.—ἦν δ' αὐτῶν Φαλῖνος *and among them was Phalinus* X. A. 2. 1. 7, Σόλων τῶν ἑπτὰ σοφιστῶν ἐκλήθη *Solon was called* one *of the Seven Sages* I. 15. 235, τῶν ἀτοπωτάτων ἂν εἴη *it would be very strange* D. 1. 26; and often with verbs signifying *to be, become, think, say, name, choose.* With some of these verbs εἰς with the genitive may be used instead of the genitive alone.

GENITIVE OF QUALITY

1320. The genitive to denote quality occurs chiefly as a predicate.

ἐὼν τρόπου ἡσυχίου *being of a peaceful disposition* Hdt. 1. 107, οἱ δέ τινες τῆς αὐτῆς γνώμης ὀλίγοι κατέφυγον *but some few of the same opinion fled* T. 3. 70, ταῦτα παμπόλλων ἐστὶ λόγων *this calls for a thorough discussion* P. L. 642 a, θεωρήσατ' αὐτόν, μὴ ὁποτέρου τοῦ λόγου, ἀλλ' ὁποτέρου τοῦ βίου ἐστίν *consider, not the manner of his speech, but the manner of his life* Aes. 3. 168, εἰ δοκεῖ ταῦτα καὶ δαπάνης μεγάλης καὶ πόνων πολλῶν καὶ πρᾱγματείᾱς εἶναι *if these matters seem to involve great expense and much toil and trouble* D. 8. 48.

a. The attributive use occurs in poetry: χόρτων εὐδένδρων Εὐρώπᾱς *Europe with its pastures amid fair trees* E. I. T. 134, λευκῆς χιόνος πτέρυξ *a wing white as snow* (of white snow) S. Ant. 114.

1321. The use of the genitive to express quality, corresponding to the Latin genitive, occurs in the non-predicate position, only when *age* or *size* is exactly expressed by the addition of a numeral (genitive of measure, 1325). The Latin genitive of quality in *mulier mirae pulchritudinis* is expressed by γυνὴ θαυμασίᾱ κάλλος (or τοῦ κάλλους), γυνὴ θαυμασίᾱ ἰδεῖν, γυνὴ ἔχουσα θαυμάσιον σχῆμα, etc.

GENITIVE OF EXPLANATION (APPOSITIVE GENITIVE)

1322. The genitive of an explicit word may explain the meaning of a more general word.

Ἰλίου πόλις E 642, as *urbs Romae*, ἄελλαι παντοίων ἀνέμων *blasts formed of winds of every sort* ε 292. This construction is chiefly poetic, but in prose we find ὑὸς μέγα χρῆμα *a monster* (great affair, 1294) *of a boar* Hdt. 1. 36, τὸ ὄρος τῆς Ἰστώνης *Mt. Istone* T. 4. 46 (very rare, 1142 c). An articular infinitive in the genitive often defines the application of a substantive: ἀμαθίᾱ ἡ τοῦ οἴεσθαι εἰδέναι ἃ οὐκ οἶδεν *the ignorance of thinking one knows what one does not know* P. A. 29 b.

a. But with ὄνομα the person or thing named is usually in apposition to ὄνομα: τῷ δὲ νεωτάτῳ ἐθέμην ὄνομα Καλλίστρατον *I gave the youngest the name Callistratus* D. 43. 74.

GENITIVE OF MATERIAL OR CONTENTS

1323. The genitive expresses material or contents.

ἕρκος ὀδόντων *the fence* (consisting) *of the teeth* Δ 350, κρήνη ἡδέος ὕδατος *a spring of sweet water* X. A. 6. 4. 4, σωροὶ σίτου, ξύλων, λίθων *heaps of corn, wood, stones* X. H. 4. 4. 12, ἑξακόσια τάλαντα φόρου *six hundred talents in taxes* T. 2. 13 (cp. 1296).

1324. **Predicate Use**: στεφάνους ῥόδων ὄντας, ἀλλ' οὐ χρῡσίου *crowns that were of roses, not of gold* D. 22. 70, ἐστρωμένη ἐστὶ ὁδὸς λίθου *a road was paved with stone* Hdt. 2. 138, and often with verbs of *making*, which admit also the instrumental dative. Hdt. has ποιεῖσθαι ἀπό and ἐκ τινος.

GENITIVE OF MEASURE

1325. The genitive denotes measure of space, time, or degree.

ὀκτὼ σταδίων τεῖχος *a wall eight stades long* T. 7. 2, πέντε ἡμερῶν σῖτία *provisions for five days* 7. 43 (cp. *fossa pedum quindecim, exilium decem annorum*). Less commonly with a neuter adjective or pronoun: ἐπὶ μέγα ἐχώρησαν δυνάμεως *they advanced to a great pitch of power* T. 1. 118, τὶ δόξης *some honour* (*aliquid famae*) 1. 5, ἀμήχανον εὐδαιμονίᾱς (*something infinite in the way of happiness*) *infinite happiness* P. A. 41 c (with emphasis on the adj.). But the phrases εἰς τοῦτο, εἰς τοσοῦτο ἀφικέσθαι (ἥκειν, ἐλθεῖν, προσβαίνειν, usually with a personal subject) followed by the genitive of abstracts are common: εἰς τοῦτο θράσους ἀφίκετο *he reached such a pitch of boldness* D. 21. 194, ἐν παντὶ ἀθῡμίᾱς *in utter despondency* T. 7. 55, ἐν τούτῳ παρασκευῆς *in this stage of preparation* 2. 17, κατὰ τοῦτο καιροῦ *at that critical moment* 7. 2. The article with this genitive is unusual in classical Greek: εἰς τοῦτο τῆς ἡλικίᾱς *to this stage of life* L. 5. 3. Some of these genitives may also be explained by 1306.

1326. Under the head of *measure* belongs *amount*: δυοῖν μναῖν πρόσοδος *an income of two minae* X. Vect. 3. 10. Cp. 1296, 1323.

1327. **Predicate Use.**—ἐπειδὰν ἐτῶν ᾖ τις τριάκοντα *when a man is thirty years old* P. L. 721 a, τὰ τείχη ἦν σταδίων ὀκτώ *the walls were eight stades long* T. 4. 66.

SUBJECTIVE AND OBJECTIVE GENITIVE

1328. With a verbal noun the genitive may denote the subject or object of the action expressed in the noun.

a. Many of these genitives derive their construction from that of the kindred verbs: τοῦ ὕδατος ἐπιθῡμίᾱ *desire for water* T. 2. 52 (1349), χόλος υἱός *anger because of his son* O 138 (1405). But the verbal idea sometimes requires the accusative, or (less commonly) the dative.

1329. In poetry an adjective may take the place of the genitive: νόστος ὁ βασίλειος *the return of the king* A. Pers. 8. Cp. 1291.

1330. The **Subjective Genitive** is active in sense: τῶν βαρβάρων φόβος *the fear of the barbarians* (which they feel: οἱ βάρβαροι φοβοῦνται) X. A. 1. 2. 17, ἡ βασιλέως ἐπιορκίᾱ *the perjury of the king* (βασιλεὺς ἐπιορκεῖ) 3. 2. 4, τὸ ὀργιζόμενον τῆς γνώμης *their angry feelings* T. 2. 59 (such genitives with substantive participles are common in Thucydides; cp. 1153 b, N. 2).

1331. The **Objective Genitive** is passive in sense, and is very common with substantives denoting a frame of mind or an emotion: φόβος τῶν Εἱλώτων *the fear of the Helots* (felt towards them: φοβοῦνται τοὺς Εἵλωτας) T. 3. 54, ἡ τῶν Ἑλλήνων εὔνοια *good-will towards the Greeks* (εὐνοεῖ τοῖς Ἕλλησι) X. A. 4. 7. 20, ἡ τῶν καλῶν συνουσίᾱ *intercourse with the good* (σύνεισι τοῖς καλοῖς) P. L. 838 a.

a. The objective genitive often precedes another genitive on which it depends: μετὰ τῆς ξυμμαχίᾱς τῆς αἰτήσεως *with the request for an alliance* T. 1. 32.

1332. Various prepositions are used in translating the objective genitive: ὁ θεῶν πόλεμος *war with the gods* X. A. 2. 5. 7, ὅρκοι θεῶν *oaths by the gods* E. Hipp. 657, θεῶν εὐχαί *prayers to the gods* P. Phae. 244 e, ἀδικημάτων ὀργή *anger at injustice* L. 12. 20, ἐγκράτεια ἡδονῆς *moderation in pleasure* I. 1. 21, ἡ τῶν ἡδονῶν νίκη *victory over pleasures* P. L. 840 c, τρόπαια βαρβάρων *memorials of victory over barbarians* X. A. 7. 6. 36, παραινέσεις τῶν ξυναλλαγῶν *exhortations to reconciliation* T. 4. 59, μῦθος φίλων *tidings about friends* S. Ant. 11, σοῦ μῦθος *speech with thee* S. O. C. 1161. In θανάτου λύσις *release from death* ι 421, μεταπαυσωλὴ πολέμοιο *respite from war* T 201, it is uncertain whether the genitive is objective or ablatival (1392).

1333. The objective genitive is often used when a prepositional expression, giving greater precision, is more usual: τὸ Μεγαρέων ψήφισμα *the decree relating to* (περί) *the Megarians* T. 1. 140, ἀπόβασις τῆς γῆς *a descent upon the land* (ἐς τὴν γῆν) 1. 108, ἀπόστασις τῶν Ἀθηναίων *revolt from the Athenians* (ἀπὸ τῶν Ἀθηναίων) 8. 5.

1334. For the objective genitive a possessive pronoun is sometimes used: σὴν χάριν *for thy sake* P. Soph. 242 a, διαβολὴ ἡ ἐμή *calumniation of me* P. A. 20 e. ὁ ἐμὸς φόβος is usually objective: *the fear which I inspire*. (But σοῦ μῦθος *speech with thee* S. O. C. 1161.)

1335. Predicate Use. — οὐ τῶν κακούργων οἶκτος, ἀλλὰ τῆς δίκης *compassion is not for wrong-doers, but for justice* E. fr. 270.

GENITIVE OF VALUE

1336. The genitive expresses value.

ἱερὰ τριῶν ταλάντων *offerings worth three talents* L. 30. 20, χῑλίων δραχμῶν δίκην φεύγω *I am defendant in an action involving a thousand drachmas* D. 55. 25.

1337. Predicate Use: τοὺς αἰχμαλώτους τοσούτων χρημάτων λύεσθαι *to ransom the captives at so high a price* D. 19. 222, τριῶν δραχμῶν πονηρὸς ὤν *a threepenny rogue* 19. 200.

TWO GENITIVES WITH ONE NOUN

1338. Two genitives expressing different relations may be used with one noun.

οἱ ἄνθρωποι διὰ τὸ αὐτῶν δέος τοῦ θανάτου καταψεύδονται *by reason of their fear of death men tell lies* P. Ph. 85 a, Διονύσου πρεσβῡτῶν χορός *a chorus of old men in honour of Dionysus* P. L. 665 b, ἡ τοῦ Λάχητος τῶν νεῶν ἀρχή *Laches' command of the fleet* T. 3. 115, ἡ Φαιάκων προενοίκησις τῆς Κερκῡρᾱς *the former occupation of Corcyra by the Phaeacians* 1. 25.

GENITIVE WITH VERBS

1339. The genitive may serve as the immediate complement of a verb, or it may appear, as a secondary definition, along with an accusative which is the immediate object of the verb (920, 1392, 1405).

1340. The subject of an active verb governing the genitive may become the subject of the passive construction: Νῑκήρατος ἐρῶν τῆς γυναικὸς ἀντερᾶται *Niceratus, who is in love with his wife, is loved in return* X. S. 8. 3. Cp. 1745 a.

THE GENITIVE PROPER WITH VERBS

THE PARTITIVE GENITIVE

1341. A verb may be followed by the partitive genitive if the action affects the object only in part. If the *entire* object is affected, the verb in question takes the accusative.

Ἀδρήστοιο δ' ἔγημε θυγατρῶν *he married* one *of Adrastus' daughters* Ξ 121, τῶν πώλων λαμβάνει *he takes* some *of the colts* X. A. 4. 5. 35, λαβόντες τοῦ βαρβαρικοῦ στρατοῦ *taking* part *of the barbarian force* 1. 5. 7, κλέπτοντες τοῦ ὄρους *seizing* part of *the mountain secretly* 4. 6. 15 (cp. τοῦ ὄρους κλέψαι τι 4. 6. 11), τῆς γῆς ἔτεμον *they ravaged* part of *the land* T. 2. 56 (cp. τὴν γῆν πᾶσαν ἔτεμον 2. 57 and ἔτεμον τῆς γῆς τὴν πολλήν 2. 56), κατεάγη τῆς κεφαλῆς *he had a hole knocked* somewhere *in his head* Ar. Vesp. 1428 (τὴν κεφαλὴν κατεᾱγέναι *to have one's head broken* D. 54. 35).

1342. With impersonals a partitive genitive does duty as the subject: πολέμου οὐ μετῆν αὐτῇ *she had no share in war* X. C. 7. 2. 28, ἐμοὶ οὐδαμόθεν προσήκει τούτου τοῦ πράγματος *I have no part whatever in this affair* And. 4. 34. Cp. 1318.

1343. The genitive is used with verbs of *sharing*.

πάντες μετεῖχον τῆς ἑορτῆς *all took part in the festival* X. A. 5. 3. 9, μετεδίδοσαν ἀλλήλοις ὧν (= τούτων ἃ) εἶχον ἕκαστοι *they shared with each other what each had* 4. 5. 6, τὸ ἀνθρώπινον γένος μετείληφεν ἀθανασίᾱς *the human race has received a portion of immortality* P. L. 721 b, σίτου κοινωνεῖν *to take a share of food* X. M. 2. 6. 22, δικαιοσύνης οὐδὲν ὑμῖν προσήκει *you have no concern in righteous dealing* X. H. 2. 4. 40, πολῑτείᾱ, ἐν ᾗ πένησιν οὐ μέτεστιν ἀρχῆς *a form of government in which the poor have no part in the management of affairs* P. R. 550 c. So with μεταλαγχάνειν *get a share* (along with somebody else), συναίρεσθαι and κοινοῦσθαι *take part in*, μεταιτεῖν and μεταποιεῖσθαι *demand a share in.*

1344. The part received or taken, if expressed, stands in the accusative. οἱ τύραννοι τῶν μεγίστων ἀγαθῶν ἐλάχιστα μετέχουσι *tyrants have the smallest por-*

tion in the greatest blessings X. Hi. 2. 6, τούτων μεταιτεῖ τὸ μέρος *he demands his share of this* Ar. Vesp. 972.

a. With μέτεστι the part may be added in the nominative: μέτεστι χὐμῖν τῶν πεπρᾱγμένων μέρος *ye too have had a share in these doings* E. I. T. 1299.

1345. The genitive is used with verbs signifying *to touch, take hold of, make trial of.*

(ἡ νόσος) ἥψατο τῶν ἀνθρώπων *the plague laid hold of the men* T. 2. 48, τῆς γνώμης τῆς αὐτῆς ἔχομαι *I hold to the same opinion* 1. 140, ἐν τῇ ἐχομένῃ ἐμοῦ κλίνῃ *on the couch next to me* P. S. 217 d, ἀντιλάβεσθε τῶν πρᾱγμάτων *take our public policy in hand* D. 1. 20, ὅπως πειρῷντο τοῦ τείχους *to make an attempt on* (a part of) *the wall* T. 2. 81. So with ψαύειν *touch* (rare in prose), ἀντέχεσθαι *cling to*, ἐπιλαμβάνεσθαι and συλλαμβάνεσθαι *lay hold of.*

1346. The genitive of the *part*, with the accusative of the *person* (the whole) who has been touched, is chiefly poetical: τὸν δὲ πεσόντα ποδῶν ἔλαβε *but him as he fell, he seized by his feet* Δ 463, ἔλαβον τῆς ζώνης τὸν Ὀρόντᾱν *they took hold of Orontas by the girdle* X. A. 1. 6. 10 (but μοῦ λαβόμενος τῆς χειρός *taking me by the hand* P. Charm. 153 b), ἄγειν τῆς ἡνίᾱς τὸν ἵππον *to lead the horse by the bridle* X. Eq. 6. 9 (cp. βοῦν δ' ἀγέτην κεράων *they led the cow by the horns* γ 439).

1347. Verbs of *beseeching* take the genitive by analogy to verbs of *touching:* ἐμὲ λισσέσκετο γούνων *she besought me by (clasping) my knees* I 451 (cp. γενείου ἁψάμενος λίσσεσθαι *beseech by touching his chin* K 454).

1348. The genitive is used with verbs of *beginning.*

a. Partitive: ἔφη Κῦρον ἄρχειν τοῦ λόγου ὧδε *he said that Cyrus began the discussion as follows* X. A. 1. 6. 5, τοῦ λόγου ἤρχετο ὧδε *he began his speech as follows* 3. 2. 7. On ἄρχειν as distinguished from ἄρχεσθαι see 1734. 5.

b. Ablatival (1391) denoting the point of departure: σέο δ' ἄρξομαι *I will make a beginning with thee* I 97. In this sense ἀπό or ἐξ is usually added: ἀρξάμενοι ἀπὸ σοῦ D. 18. 297, ἄρξομαι ἀπὸ τῆς ἰᾱτρικῆς λέγων *I will make a beginning by speaking of medicine* P. S. 186 b.

1349. The genitive is used with verbs signifying *to aim at, strive after, desire* (genitive of the end desired).

ἀνθρώπων στοχάζεσθαι *to aim at men* X. C. 1. 6. 29, ἐφῑέμενοι τῶν κερδῶν *desiring gain* T. 1. 8, πάντες τῶν ἀγαθῶν ἐπιθῡμοῦσιν *all men desire what is good* P. R. 438 a, τὸ ἐρᾶν τῶν καλῶν *the passionate love of what is noble* Aes. 1. 137, πεινῶσι χρημάτων *they are hungry for wealth* X. S. 4. 36, πόλις ἐλευθερίᾱς διψήσᾱσα *a state thirsting for freedom* P. R. 562 c. So with ὀϊστεύειν *shoot at* (poet.), λιλαίεσθαι *desire* (poet.), γλίχεσθαι *desire.* φιλεῖν *love*, ποθεῖν *long for* take the accusative.

1350. The genitive is used with verbs signifying *to reach, obtain* (genitive of the end attained).

τῆς ἀρετῆς ἐφικέσθαι *to attain to virtue* I. 1. 5, οἱ ἀκοντισταὶ βραχύτερα ἠκόντιζον ἢ ὡς ἐξικνεῖσθαι τῶν σφενδονητῶν *the javelin-throwers did not hurl far enough to reach the slingers* X. A. 3. 3. 7, σπονδῶν ἔτυχε *he obtained a truce* 3. 1. 28.

So with κυρεῖν *obtain* (poet.), κληρονομεῖν *inherit*, ἀποτυγχάνειν *fail to hit*. τυγχάνειν, when compounded with ἐν, ἐπί, παρά, περί, and σύν, takes the dative. λαγχάνειν *obtain by lot* usually takes the accusative.

a. This genitive and that of 1349 form the *genitive of the goal.*

1351. The genitive of the thing obtained may be joined with an ablatival genitive (1410) of the person: οὗ δὲ δὴ πάντων οἰόμεθα τεύξεσθαι ἐπαίνου *in a case where we expect to win praise from all men* X. A. 5. 7. 33. But where the thing obtained is expressed by a neuter pronoun, the accusative is employed.

1352. It is uncertain whether verbs signifying *to miss* take a partitive or an ablatival genitive: οὐδεὶς ἡμάρτανεν ἀνδρός *no one missed his man* X. A. 3. 4. 15, σφαλέντες τῆς δόξης *disappointed in expectations* T. 4. 85.

1353. Verbs of *approaching* and *meeting* take the genitive according to 1343 or 1349. These verbs are poetical. Thus, ἀντιόων ταύρων *for the purpose of obtaining* (his share of) *bulls* α 25, ἀντήσω τοῦδ' ἀνέρος *I will encounter this man* Π 423, πελάσαι νεῶν *to approach the ships* S. Aj. 709. In the meaning *draw near to* verbs of *approaching* take the dative (1463).

1354. The genitive is used with verbs of *smelling.*

ὄζω μύρου *I smell of perfume* Ar. Eccl. 524. So πνεῖν μύρου *to breathe* (smell of) *perfume* S. fr. 140.

1355. The genitive is used with verbs signifying *to enjoy, taste, eat, drink.*

ἀπολαύομεν πάντων τῶν ἀγαθῶν *we enjoy all the good things* X. M. 4. 3. 11, εὐωχοῦ τοῦ λόγου *enjoy the discourse* P. R. 352 b, ὀλίγοι σίτου ἐγεύσαντο *few tasted food* X. A. 3. 1. 3. So (rarely) with ἥδεσθαι *take pleasure in.*

a. Here belong ἐσθίειν, πίνειν when they do not signify *to eat up* or *drink up*: ὠμῶν ἐσθίειν αὐτῶν *to eat them alive* X. H. 3. 3. 6, πίνειν οἴνοιο *drink some wine* χ 11, as *boire du vin* (but πίνειν οἶνον *drink wine* Ξ 5, as *boire le vin*). Words denoting *food* and *drink* are placed in the accusative when they are regarded as kinds of *nourishment.*

1356. The genitive is used with verbs signifying *to remember, remind, forget, care for,* and *neglect.*

τῶν ἀπόντων φίλων μέμνησο *remember your absent friends* I. 1. 26, βούλομαι δ' ὑμᾶς ἀναμνῆσαι τῶν ἐμοὶ πεπρᾱγμένων *I desire to remind you of my past actions* And. 4. 41, δέδοικα μὴ ἐπιλαθώμεθα τῆς οἴκαδε ὁδοῦ *I fear lest we may forget the way home* X. A. 3. 2. 25, ἐπιμελόμενοι οἱ μὲν ὑποζυγίων, οἱ δὲ σκευῶν *some taking care of the pack animals, others of the baggage* 4. 3. 30, τῆς τῶν πολλῶν δόξης δεῖ ἡμᾶς φροντίζειν *we must pay heed to the world's opinion* P. Cr. 48 a, τί ἡμῖν τῆς τῶν πολλῶν δόξης μέλει; *what do we care for the world's opinion?* 44 c, τοῖς σπουδαίοις οὐχ οἷόν τε τῆς ἀρετῆς ἀμελεῖν *the serious cannot disregard virtue* I. 1. 48, μηδενὸς ὀλιγωρεῖτε μηδὲ καταφρονεῖτε (cp. 1385) τῶν προστεταγμένων *neither neglect nor despise any command laid on you* 3. 48.

1357. So with μνημονεύειν *remember* (but usually with the accus., especially of things), ἀμνημονεῖν *not to speak of*, κήδεσθαι *care for*, ἐντρέπεσθαι *give heed to*, *ἐνθυμεῖσθαι* **think deeply of, προορᾶν make provision for** (in Hdt.), *μεταμέλει μοι* **it repents me, καταμελεῖν neglect.**

1358. Many of these verbs also take the accusative. With the accus. *μεμνῆσθαι* means *to remember something as a whole*, with the gen. *to remember something about a thing, bethink oneself.* The accus. is usually found with verbs of *remembering* and *forgetting* when they mean *to hold* or *not to hold in memory*, and when the object is a thing. Neuter pronouns must stand in the accus. *ἐπιλανθάνεσθαι forget* takes either the genitive or the accusative, *λανθάνεσθαι* (usually poetical) always takes the genitive. *μέλει it is a care, ἐπιμέλεσθαι care for, μεμνῆσθαι think about* may take *περί* with the genitive. *οἶδα* generally means *I remember* when it has a person as the object (in the accusative).

1359. Verbs of *reminding* may take two accusatives: *ταῦθ' ὑπέμνησ' ὑμᾶς I have reminded you of this* D. 19. 25 (1628).

1360. With *μέλει*, the subject, if a neuter pronoun, may sometimes stand in the nominative (the personal construction): *ταῦτα θεῷ μελήσει God will care for this* P. Phae. 238 d. Except in poetry the subject in the nominative is very rare with other words than neuter pronouns: *χοροὶ πᾶσι μέλουσι* P. L. 835 e.

1361. The genitive is used with verbs signifying *to hear* and *perceive: ἀκούειν, κλύειν* (poet.) *hear, ἀκροᾶσθαι listen to, αἰσθάνεσθαι perceive, πυνθάνεσθαι hear, learn of, συνιέναι understand, ὀσφραίνεσθαι scent.* The person or thing, whose words, sound, etc. are perceived by the senses, stands in the genitive; the words, sound, etc. generally stand in the accusative.

τινὸς ἤκουσ' εἰπόντος I heard somebody say D. 8. 4, *ἀκούσαντες τῆς σάλπιγγος hearing the sound of the trumpet* X. A. 4. 2. 8, *ἀκούσαντες τὸν θόρυβον hearing the noise* 4. 4. 21, *ἀκροώμενοι τοῦ ᾄδοντος listening to the singer* X. C. 1. 3. 10, *ὅσοι ἀλλήλων ξυνίεσαν all who understood each other* T. 1. 3, *ἐπειδὰν συνιῇ τις τὰ λεγόμενα when one understands what is said* P. Pr. 325 c (verbs of *understanding*, *συνιέναι* and *ἐπίστασθαι*, usually take the accus.), *κρομμύων ὀσφραίνομαι I smell onions* Ar. Ran. 654.

a. A supplementary participle is often used in agreement with the genitive of the person from whom something is heard: *λέγοντος ἐμοῦ ἀκροάσονται οἱ νέοι the young men will listen when I speak* P. A. 37 d.

b. The accusative is almost always used when the thing heard is expressed by a substantivized neuter adjective or participle, but the genitive plural in the case of *οὗτος, ὅδε, αὐτός*, and *ὅς* is frequent.

1362. A double genitive, of the person and of the thing, is rare with *ἀκούειν*: *τῶν ὑπὲρ τῆς γραφῆς δικαίων ἀκούειν μου to listen to my just pleas as regards the indictment* D. 18. 9.

1363. *ἀκούειν, αἰσθάνεσθαι, πυνθάνεσθαι*, meaning *to become aware of, learn*, take the accusative (with a participle in indirect discourse, 2112 b) of a personal or impersonal object: *οἱ δὲ Πλαταιῆς, ὡς ᾔσθοντο ἔνδον τε ὄντας τοὺς Θηβαίους καὶ κατειλημμένην τὴν πόλιν but the Plataeans, when they became aware that the Thebans were inside and that the city had been captured* T. 2. 3, *πυθόμενοι Ἀρταξέρξην τεθνηκότα having learned that Artaxerxes was dead* 4. 50.

a. *To hear a thing* is usually ἀκούειν τι when the thing heard is something definite and when the meaning is simply *hear*, not *listen to*.

1364. ἀκούειν, ἀκροᾶσθαι, πυνθάνεσθαι, meaning *to hear from*, *learn from*, take the genitive of the actual source (1411).

1365. ἀκούειν, κλύειν, πυνθάνεσθαί τινος may mean *to hear about*, *hear of*: εἰ δέ κε τεθνηῶτος ἀκούσῃς *but if you hear that he is dead* α 289, κλύων σοῦ *hearing about thee* S. O. C. 307, ὡς ἐπύθοντο τῆς Πύλου κατειλημμένης *when they heard of the capture of Pylos* T. 4. 6. For the participle (not in indirect discourse) see 2112 a. περί is often used with the genitive without the participle.

1366. In the meaning *heed*, *hearken*, *obey*, verbs of *hearing* generally take the genitive: ἄκουε πάντων, ἐκλέγου δ' ἃ συμφέρει *listen to everything, but choose that which is profitable* Men. Sent. 566, τῶν πολεμίων ἀκούειν *to submit to enemies* X. C. 8. 1. 4. πείθεσθαι takes the genitive, instead of the dative, by analogy to this use (Hdt. 6. 12, T. 7. 73). (On the dative with ἀκούειν *obey* see 1465.)

1367. αἰσθάνεσθαι takes the genitive, or (less frequently) the accusative, of the thing immediately perceived by the senses: τῆς κραυγῆς ᾔσθοντο *they heard the noise* X. H. 4. 4. 4, ᾔσθετο τὰ γιγνόμενα *he perceived what was happening* X. C. 3. 1. 4. The genitive is less common than the accusative when the perception is intellectual: ὡς ᾔσθοντο τειχιζόντων *when they heard that they were progressing with their fortification* T. 5. 83. Cp. 1363.

1368. Some verbs, ordinarily construed with the accusative, take the genitive by the analogy of αἰσθάνεσθαι, etc.: ἔγνω ἄτοπα ἐμοῦ ποιοῦντος *he knew that I was acting absurdly* X. C. 7. 2. 18, ἀγνοοῦντες ἀλλήλων ὅ τι λέγομεν *each of us mistaking what the other says* P. G. 517 c. This construction of verbs of *knowing* (and *showing*) occurs in Attic only when a participle accompanies the genitive.

1369. The genitive is used with verbs signifying *to fill, to be full of*. The thing filled is put in the accusative.

οὐκ ἐμπλήσετε τὴν θάλατταν τριήρων; *will you not cover the sea with your triremes?* D. 8. 74, ἀναπλῆσαι αἰτιῶν *to implicate in guilt* P. A. 32 c, τροφῆς εὐπορεῖν *to have plenty of provisions* X. Vect. 6. 1, τριήρης σεσαγμένη ἀνθρώπων *a trireme stowed with men* X. O. 8. 8, ὕβρεως μεστοῦσθαι *to be filled with pride* P. L. 713 c. So with πλήθειν, πληροῦν, γέμειν, πλουτεῖν, βρίθειν (poet.), βρύειν (poet.).

a. Here belong also χεὶρ στάζει θυηλῆς Ἄρεος *his hand drips with sacrifice to Ares* S. El. 1423, μεθυσθεὶς τοῦ νέκταρος *intoxicated with nectar* P. S. 203 b, ἡ πηγὴ ῥεῖ ψυχροῦ ὕδατος *the spring flows with cold water* P. Phae. 230 b. The instrumental dative is sometimes used.

1370. The genitive is used with verbs signifying *to rule, command, lead*.

θεῖον τὸ ἐθελόντων ἄρχειν *it is divine to rule over willing subjects* X. O. 21. 12, τῆς θαλάττης ἐκράτει *he was master of the sea* P. Menex. 239 e, Ἔρως τῶν θεῶν βασιλεύει *Love is king of the gods* P. S. 195 c, ἡγεῖτο τῆς ἐξόδου *he led the expedition* T. 2. 10, στρατηγεῖν τῶν ξένων *to be general of the mercenaries* X. A.

2. 6. 28. So with τυραννεῖν *be absolute master of*, ἀνάσσειν *be lord of* (poet.), ἡγεμονεύειν *be commander of*. This genitive is connected with that of 1402.

1371. Several verbs of *ruling* take the accusative when they mean *to conquer, overcome* (so κρατεῖν), or when they express the domain over which the rule extends; as τὴν Πελοπόννησον πειρᾶσθε μὴ ἐλάσσω ἐξηγεῖσθαι *try not to lessen your dominion over the Peloponnese* T. 1. 71. ἡγεῖσθαί τινι means *to be a guide to any one, show any one the way*. Cp. 1537.

GENITIVE OF PRICE AND VALUE

1372. The genitive is used with verbs signifying *to buy, sell, cost, value, exchange*. The price for which one gives or does anything stands in the genitive.

ἀργυρίου πρίασθαι ἢ ἀποδόσθαι ἵππον *to buy or sell a horse for money* P. R. 333 b, Θεμιστοκλέᾱ τῶν μεγίστων δωρεῶν ἠξίωσαν *they deemed Themistocles worthy of the greatest gifts* I. 4. 154, οὐκ ἀνταλλακτέον μοι τὴν φιλοτῑμίᾱν οὐδενὸς κέρδους *I must not barter my public spirit for any price* D. 19. 223. So with τάττειν *rate*, μισθοῦν *let*, μισθοῦσθαι *hire*, ἐργάζεσθαι *work*, and with any verb of doing anything for a wage, as οἱ τῆς παρ' ἡμέρᾱν χάριτος τὰ μέγιστα τῆς πόλεως ἀπολωλεκότες *those who have ruined the highest interests of the State to purchase ephemeral popularity* D. 8. 70, πόσου διδάσκει; πέντε μνῶν *for how much does he teach? for five minae* P. A. 20 b, οἱ Χαλδαῖοι μισθοῦ στρατεύονται *the Chaldaeans serve for pay* X. C. 3. 2. 7.

a. The instrumental dative is also used. With verbs of *exchanging*, ἀντί is usual (1683).

1373. *To value highly* and *lightly* is περὶ πολλοῦ (πλείονος, πλείστου) and περὶ ὀλίγου (ἐλάττονος, ἐλαχίστου) τῑμᾶσθαι or ποιεῖσθαι: τὰ πλείστου ἄξια περὶ ἐλαχίστου ποιεῖται, τὰ δὲ φαυλότερα περὶ πλείονος *he makes least account of what is most important, and sets higher what is less estimable* P. A. 30 a. The genitive of value, without περί, is rare: πολλοῦ ποιοῦμαι ἀκηκοέναι ἃ ἀκήκοα Πρωταγόρου *I esteem it greatly to have heard what I did from Protagoras* P. Pr. 328 d.

a. The genitive of cause is rarely used to express the thing bought or that for which pay is demanded: οὐδένα τῆς συνουσίᾱς ἀργύριον πράττει *you charge nobody anything for your teaching* X. M. 1. 6. 11, τρεῖς μναῖ διφρίσκου *three minae for a small chariot* Ar. Nub. 31.

1374. In legal language τῑμᾶν τινι θανάτου is *to fix the penalty at death* (said of the jury, which is not interested in the result), τῑμᾶσθαί τινι θανάτου *to propose death as the penalty* (said of the accuser, who is interested), and τιμᾶσθαί τινος *to propose a penalty against oneself* (said of the accused). Cp. τῑμᾶταί μοι ὁ ἀνὴρ θανάτου *the man proposes death as my penalty* P. A. 36 b, ἀλλὰ δὴ φυγῆς τῑμήσωμαι; ἴσως γὰρ ἄν μοι τούτου τῑμήσαιτε *but shall I propose exile as my penalty? for perhaps you* (the jury) *might fix it at this* 37 c. So θανάτου with κρίνειν, διώκειν, ὑπάγειν. Cp. 1379.

GENITIVE OF CRIME AND ACCOUNTABILITY

1375. With verbs of judicial action the genitive denotes the crime, the accusative denotes the person accused.

αἰτιᾶσθαι ἀλλήλους τοῦ γεγενημένου *to accuse one another of what had happened* X. Ages. 1. 33, διώκω μὲν κακηγορίᾱς, τῇ δ' αὐτῇ ψήφῳ φόνου φεύγω *I bring an accusation for defamation and at the same trial am prosecuted for murder* L. 11. 12, ἐμὲ ὁ Μέλητος ἀσεβείᾱς ἐγράψατο *Meletus prosecuted me for impiety* P. Euth. 5 c, δώρων ἐκρίθησαν *they were tried for bribery* L. 27. 3. On verbs of *accusing* and *condemning* compounded with κατά, see 1385.

1376. So with ἀμύνεσθαι and κολάζειν *punish*, εἰσάγειν and προσκαλεῖσθαι *summon into court*, αἱρεῖν *convict*, τῑμωρεῖσθαι *take vengeance on*. With τῑμωρεῖν *avenge* and λαγχάνειν *obtain leave to bring a suit*, the person avenged and the person against whom the suit is brought are put in the dative. So with δικάζεσθαί τινί τινος *to go to law with a man about something*.

1377. Verbs of judicial action may take a cognate accusative (δίκην, γραφήν), on which the genitive of the crime depends: γραφὴν ὕβρεως καὶ δίκην κακηγορίᾱς φεύξεται *he will be brought to trial on an indictment for outrage and on a civil action for slander* D. 21. 32. From this adnominal use arose the construction of the genitive with this class of verbs.

1378. ἁλίσκεσθαι (ἁλῶναι) *be convicted*, ὀφλισκάνειν *lose a suit*, φεύγειν *be prosecuted* are equivalent to passives: ἐάν τις ἁλῷ κλοπῆς . . . κἂν ἀστρατείᾱς τις ὄφλῃ *if any one be condemned for theft . . . and if any one be convicted of desertion* D. 24. 103, ἀσεβείᾱς φεύγοντα ὑπὸ Μελήτου *being tried for impiety on the indictment of Meletus* P. A. 35 d. ὀφλισκάνειν may take δίκην as a cognate accus. (ὠφληκέναι δίκην *to be cast in a suit* Ar. Av. 1457); the crime or the penalty may stand in the genitive (with or without δίκην), or in the accusative: ὁπόσοι κλοπῆς ἢ δώρων ὄφλοιεν *all who had been convicted of embezzlement or bribery* And. 1. 74, ὑφ' ὑμῶν θανάτου δίκην ὀφλών *having incurred through your verdict the penalty of death*, ὑπὸ τῆς ἀληθείᾱς ὠφληκότες μοχθηρίᾱν *condemned by the truth to suffer the penalty of wickedness* P. A. 39 b.

1379. With verbs of judicial action the genitive of the penalty may be regarded as a genitive of value: θανάτου κρίνουσι *they judge in matters of life and death* X. C. 1. 2. 14. So ὑπάγειν τινὰ θανάτου *to impeach a man on a capital charge* X. H. 2. 3. 12; cp. τῑμᾶν θανάτου 1374.

a. With many verbs of judicial action περί is used.

GENITIVE OF CONNECTION

1380. The genitive may express a more or less close connection or relation, where περί is sometimes added.

With verbs of *saying* or *thinking*: τί δὲ ἵππων οἴει; *but what do you think of horses?* P. R. 459 b. Often in poetry: εἰπὲ δέ μοι πατρός *but tell me about my father* λ 174, τοῦ κασιγνήτου τί φῄς; *what dost thou say of thy brother?* S. El. 317.

1381. The genitive is often used loosely, especially at the beginning of a construction, to state the subject of a remark: ἵππος ἢν κακουργῇ, τὸν ἱππέᾱ κακίζομεν· τῆς δὲ γυναικός, εἰ κακοποιεῖ κτλ. *if a horse is vicious, we lay the fault to the groom; but as regards a wife, if she conducts herself ill*, etc. X. O. 3. 11, ὡσαύτως δὲ καὶ τῶν ἄλλων τεχνῶν *and so in the case of the other arts too* P. Charm. 165 d, τί δὲ τῶν πολλῶν καλῶν; *what about the many beautiful things?* P. Ph. 78 d.

GENITIVE WITH COMPOUND VERBS

1382. The genitive depends on the meaning of a compound verb as a whole (1) if the simple verb takes the genitive without a preposition, as ὑπείκειν *withdraw*, παραλύειν *release*, παραχωρεῖν *surrender* (1392), ἐφίεσθαι *desire* (1349); or (2) if the compound has acquired through the preposition a signification different from that of the simple verb with the preposition: thus ἀπογνόντες τῆς ἐλευθερίᾶς *despairing of freedom* L. 2. 46 cannot be expressed by γνόντες ἀπὸ τῆς ἐλευθερίᾶς. But it is often difficult to determine whether the genitive depends on the compound verb as a whole or on the preposition contained in it.

1383. A verb compounded with a preposition taking the dative or accusative may take the genitive by analogy of another compound verb whose preposition requires the genitive: so ἐμβαίνειν ὅρων *to set foot on the boundaries* S. O. C. 400 by analogy to ἐπιβαίνειν τῶν ὅρων P. L. 778 e.

1384. Many verbs compounded with ἀπό, πρό, ὑπέρ, ἐπί, and κατά take the genitive when the compound may be resolved into the simple verb and the preposition without change in the sense: τοὺς συμμάχους ἀποτρέψαντες τῆς γνώμης *dissuading the allies from their purpose* And. 3. 21, προαπεστάλησαν τῆς ἀποστάσεως *they were despatched before the revolt* T. 3. 5, πολλοῖς ἡ γλῶττα προτρέχει τῆς διανοίᾶς *in many people the tongue outruns the thought* I. 1. 41, (οἱ πολέμιοι) ὑπερκάθηνται ἡμῶν *the enemy are stationed above us* X. A. 5. 1. 9, τῷ ἐπιβάντι πρώτῳ τοῦ τείχους *to the first one setting foot on the wall* T. 4. 116. This use is most frequent when the prepositions are used in their proper signification. Many compounds of ὑπέρ take the accusative.

a. This use is especially common with κατά *against* or *at*: μή μου κατείπῃς *don't speak against me* P. Th. 149 a, κατεψεύσατό μου *he spoke falsely against me* D. 18. 9, ψευδῆ κατεγλώττιζέ μου *he mouthed lies at me* Ar. Ach. 380. The construction in 1384 is post-Homeric.

1385. The verbs of *accusing* and *condemning* (cp. 1375) containing κατά in composition (καταγιγνώσκειν *decide against*, καταδικάζειν *adjudge against*, καταψηφίζεσθαι *vote against*, κατακρίνειν *give sentence against*) take a genitive of the *person*, and an accusative of the *penalty*. κατηγορεῖν *accuse*, καταγιγνώσκειν and καταψηφίζεσθαι take a genitive of the *person*, an accusative of the *crime*: καταγνῶναι δωροδοκίᾶν ἐμοῦ *to pronounce me guilty of bribery* L. 21. 21, τούτου δειλίᾶν καταψηφίζεσθαι *to vote him guilty of cowardice* 14. 11, τῶν διαφυγόντων θάνατον καταγνόντες *having condemned the fugitives to death* T. 6. 60; *person, crime*, and *penalty*: πολλῶν οἱ πατέρες μηδισμοῦ θάνατον κατέγνωσαν *our fathers passed sentence of death against many for favouring the Persians* I. 4. 157. The genitive is rarely used to express the *crime* or the *penalty*: παρανόμων αὐτοῦ κατηγορεῖν *to accuse him of proposing unconstitutional measures* D. 21. 5; cp. ἀνθρώπων καταψηφισθέντων θάνατον *men who have been condemned to death* P. R. 558 a.

1386. In general, prose, as distinguished from poetry, repeats the preposition contained in the compound; but κατά is not repeated.

1387. **Passive.** — θάνατος αὐτῶν κατεγνώσθη *sentence of death was passed on* *them* L. 13. 39 (so κατεψηφισμένος ἦν μου ὁ θάνατος X. Ap. 27), κατηγορεῖτο αὐτοῦ οὐχ ἥκιστα μηδισμός *he was especially accused of favouring the Persians* T. 1. 95.

FREE USES OF THE GENITIVE

1388. Many verbs ordinarily construed with the accusative are also followed by a genitive of a person, apparently dependent on the verb but in reality governed by an accusative, generally a neuter pronoun or a dependent clause. Thus, τάδ' αὐτοῦ ἄγαμαι *I admire this in him* X. Ages. 2. 7, τοῦτο ἐπαινῶ Ἀγησιλάου *I praise this in Agesilaus* 8. 4, αὐτῶν ἓν ἐθαύμασα *I was astonished at one thing in them* P. A. 17 a, Ἀθηναῖοι σφῶν ταῦτα οὐκ ἀποδέξονται *the Athenians will not be satisfied with them in this* T. 7. 48, ὃ μέμφονται μάλιστα ἡμῶν *which they most censure in us* 1. 84, εἰ ἄγασαι τοῦ πατρὸς ὅσα πέπρᾱχε *if you admire in my father what he has done* (the actions of my father) X. C. 3. 1. 15, διαθεώμενος αὐτῶν ὅσην χώρᾱν ἔχοιεν *contemplating how large a country they possess* X. A. 3. 1. 19, θαυμάζω τῶν στρατηγῶν ὅτι οὐ πειρῶνται ἡμῖν ἐκπορίζειν σῖτηρέσιον *I wonder that the generals do not try to supply us with money for provisions* 6. 2. 4, ἐνενόησε δὲ αὐτῶν καὶ ὡς ἐπηρώτων ἀλλήλους *he took note also how they asked each other questions* X. C. 5. 2. 18. So with θεωρεῖν *observe*, ὑπονοεῖν *feel suspicious of*, ἐνθῡμεῖσθαι *consider*, etc.

1389. From such constructions arose the use of the genitive in actual dependence on the verb without an accusative word or clause: ἄγασαι αὐτοῦ *you admire him* X. M. 2. 6. 33, θαυμάζω τῶν ὑπὲρ τῆς ἰδίᾱς δόξης ἀποθνῄσκειν ἐθελόντων *I wonder at those who are willing to die in defence of their personal opinions* I. 6. 93. The use in 1389 recalls that with αἰσθάνεσθαι (1367). On ἄγασθαι, θαυμάζειν with the genitive of cause, see 1405.

1390. A form of the genitive of possession appears in poetry with verbal adjectives and passive participles to denote the personal origin of an action (cp. 1298): κείνης διδακτά *taught of her* S. El. 344, ἐκδιδαχθεὶς τῶν κατ' οἶκον *informed by those in the house* S. Tr. 934, πληγεὶς θυγατρός *struck by a daughter* E. Or. 497. Cp. διόσδοτος *given of God;* and "beloved of the Lord."

On the genitive absolute, see 2070.

THE ABLATIVAL GENITIVE WITH VERBS

1391. The same verb may govern both a true genitive and an ablatival genitive. So ἄρχεσθαι *to begin* (1348 a) and *to start from*, ἔχεσθαι *to hold to* (1345) and *to keep oneself from*. In many cases it is difficult to decide whether the genitive in question was originally the true genitive or the ablatival genitive, or whether the two have been combined; *e.g.* in κυνέη ῥῑνοῦ ποιητή *a cap made of hide* K 262, κύπελλον ἐδέξατο ἧς ἀλόχοιο *he received a goblet from his wife* Ω 305. So with verbs *to hear from*, *know of* (1364, 1411), and verbs of emotion (1405), the partitive idea, cause, and source are hard to distinguish. Other cases open to doubt are verbs of *missing* (1352), *being deceived* (1392) and the exclamatory genitive (1407).

GENITIVE OF SEPARATION

1392. With verbs signifying *to cease, release, remove, restrain, give up, fail, be distant from,* etc., the genitive denotes separation.

λήγειν τῶν πόνων *to cease from toil* I. 1. 14, ἐπιστήμη χωριζομένη δικαιοσύνης *knowledge divorced from justice* P. Menex. 246 e, μεταστᾱ̀ς τῆς Ἀθηναίων ξυμμαχίᾱς *withdrawing from the alliance with the Athenians* T. 2. 67, παύσαντες αὐτὸν τῆς στρατηγίᾱς *removing him from his office of general* X. H. 6. 2. 13, εἴργεσθαι τῆς ἀγορᾶς *to be excluded from the forum* L. 6. 24, σῶσαι κακοῦ *to save from evil* S. Ph. 919, ἐκώλῡον τῆς πορείᾱς αὐτόν *they prevented him from passing* X. Ages. 2. 2, πᾶς ἀσκὸς δύο ἄνδρας ἕξει τοῦ μὴ καταδῦναι *each skin will keep two men from sinking* X. A. 3. 5. 11, λόγου τελευτᾶν *to end a speech* T. 3. 59, τῆς ἐλευθερίᾱς παραχωρῆσαι Φιλίππῳ *to surrender their freedom to Philip* D. 18. 68, οὐ πόνων ὑφίετο, οὐ κινδῡ́νων ἀφίστατο, οὐ χρημάτων ἐφείδετο *he did not relax his toil, stand aloof from dangers, or spare his money* X. Ages. 7. 1, ψευσθέντες τῶν ἐλπίδων *disappointed of their expectations* I. 4. 58 (but cp. 1352), ἡ νῆσος οὐ πολὺ διέχουσα τῆς ἠπείρου *the island being not far distant from the mainland* T. 3. 51.

1393. Several verbs of separation, such as ἐλευθεροῦν (especially with a personal subject), may take ἀπό or ἐξ when the local idea is prominent. Many take also the accusative.

1394. The genitive, instead of the accusative (1628), may be used with verbs of *depriving:* ἀποστερεῖ με τῶν χρημάτων *he deprives me of my property* I. 17. 35, τῶν ἄλλων ἀφαιρούμενοι χρήματα *taking away property from others* X. M. 1. 5. 3.

1395. The genitive of the place *whence* is employed in poetry where a compound verb would be used in prose: βάθρων ἵστασθε *rise from the steps* S. O. T. 142 (cp. ὑπανίστανται θᾱ́κων *they rise from their seats* X. S. 4. 31), χθονὸς ἀείρᾱς *raising from the ground* S. Ant. 417.

1396. The genitive with verbs signifying *to want, lack, empty*, etc. may be classed with the genitive of separation.

τῶν ἐπιτηδείων οὐκ ἀπορήσομεν *we shall not want provisions* X. A. 2. 2. 11, ἐπαίνου οὔποτε σπανίζετε *you never lack praise* X. Hi. 1. 14, ἀνδρῶν τάνδε πόλιν κενῶσαι *to empty this city of its men* A. Supp. 660. So with ἐλλείπειν and στέρεσθαι *lack*, ἐρημοῦν *deliver from.*

1397. δέω *I lack* (the personal construction) usually takes the genitive of quantity: πολλοῦ γε δέω *nothing of the sort* P. Phae. 228 a, μῑκροῦ ἔδεον ἐν χερσὶ τῶν ὁπλῑτῶν εἶναι *they were nearly at close quarters with the hoplites* X. H. 4. 6. 11, τοσούτου δέω ζηλοῦν *I am so far from admiring* D. 8. 70 (also τοσοῦτον δέω).

1398. δέομαι *I want, request* may take the genitive, or the accusative (regularly of neuter pronouns and adjectives), of the thing wanted; and the genitive of the person: ἐρωτώμενος ὅτου δέοιτο, Ἀσκῶν, ἔφη, δισχῑλίων δεήσομαι *being asked what he needed, he said 'I shall have need of two thousand skins'* X. A. 3. 5. 9, τοῦτο ὑμῶν δέομαι *I ask this of you* P. A. 17 c. The genitive of the thing and of the person is unusual: δεόμενοι Κύρου ἄλλος ἄλλης πράξεως *petitioning Cyrus about different matters* X. C. 8. 3. 19.

1399. δεῖ (impersonal) is frequently used with genitives of quantity: πολλοῦ δεῖ οὕτως ἔχειν *far from that being the case* P. A. 35 d, οὐδὲ πολλοῦ δεῖ D. 8. 42 (only in D.) and οὐδ' ὀλίγου δεῖ *no, far from it* D. 19. 184. δεῖν may be omitted (but not with πολλοῦ), leaving ὀλίγου and μῑκροῦ in the sense of *almost, all but:*

ὀλίγου πάντες *almost all* P. R. 552 d, ὀλίγου εἷλον τὴν πόλιν *they all but took the city* T. 8. 35. On δεῖν used absolutely, see 2012 d; on δέων with numerals, 350 c.

1400. δεῖ μοί τινος means *I have need of something.* In place of the dative (1467) an accusative of the person is rarely allowed in poetry on the analogy of δεῖ with the infinitive (1985): οὐ πόνου πολλοῦ με δεῖ *I have need of no great toil* E. Hipp. 23 (often in E.). The thing needed is rarely put in the accusative: εἴ τι δέοι τῷ χορῷ *if the chorus need anything* Ant. 6. 12 (here some regard τὶ as nominative). Cp. 1562.

GENITIVE OF DISTINCTION AND OF COMPARISON

1401. The genitive is used with verbs of *differing.*

ἄρχων ἀγαθὸς οὐδὲν διαφέρει πατρὸς ἀγαθοῦ *a good ruler differs in no respect from a good father* X. C. 8. 1. 1.

1402. With verbs signifying *to surpass, be inferior to,* the genitive denotes that with which anything is compared.

τῑμαῖς τούτων ἐπλεονεκτεῖτε *you had the advantage over them in honours* X. A. 3. 1. 37, ἡττῶντο τοῦ ὕδατος *they were overpowered by the water* X. H. 5. 2. 5, ὑστερεῖν τῶν ἔργων *to be too late for operations* D. 4. 38, ἡμῶν λειφθέντες *inferior to us* X. A. 7. 7. 31. So with πρεσβεύειν *hold the first place,* ἀριστεύειν *be best* (poet.), μειοῦσθαι *fall short of,* μειονεκτεῖν *be worse off,* ἐλαττοῦσθαι *be at a disadvantage.* νικᾶσθαί τινος is chiefly poetic. ἡττᾶσθαι often takes ὑπό. Akin to this genitive is that with verbs of *ruling* (1370), which are often derived from a substantive signifying *ruler.*

1403. Many verbs compounded with πρό, περί, ὑπέρ denoting superiority take the genitive, which may depend on the preposition (1384): τάχει περιεγένου αὐτοῦ *you excelled him in speed* X. C. 3. 1. 19, γνώμῃ προέχειν τῶν ἐναντίων *to excel the enemy in spirit* T. 2. 62, τοῖς ὅπλοις αὐτῶν ὑπερφέρομεν *we surpass them in our infantry* 1. 81. So with περιεῖναι, ὑπερέχειν. προτῑμᾶν, προκρΐνειν, and προαιρεῖσθαι *prefer,* προεστηκέναι *be at the head of* certainly take the genitive by reason of the preposition. ὑπερβάλλειν and ὑπερβαίνειν *surpass* take the accusative.

1404. The object compared may be expressed by πρό, ἀντί with the genitive, or by παρά, πρός with the accusative. See under Prepositions. That *in which* one thing is superior or inferior to another usually stands in the dative (1513, 1515).

GENITIVE OF CAUSE

1405. With verbs of emotion the genitive denotes the cause. Such verbs are *to wonder at, admire, envy, praise, blame. hate, pity, grieve for, be angry at, take vengeance on,* and the like.

ἐθαύμασα τῆς τόλμης τῶν λεγόντων *I wondered at the hardihood of the speakers* L. 12. 41, τοῦτον ἀγασθεὶς τῆς πρᾳότητος *admiring him for his mildness* X. C. 2. 3. 21, ζηλῶ σε τοῦ νοῦ, τῆς δὲ δειλίᾱς στυγῶ *I envy thee for thy prudence, I hate thee for thy cowardice* S. El. 1027, σὲ ηὐδαιμόνισα τοῦ τρόπου *I thought you happy because of your disposition* P. Cr. 43 b, συγχαίρω τῶν γεγενημένων *I share the joy at what has happened* D. 15. 15, ἀνέχεσθαι τῶν οἰκείων ἀμελουμένων *to put up with the neglect of my household affairs* P. A. 31 b, τὸν ξένον δίκαιον αἰνέσαι προθῡμίᾱς *it is right to praise the stranger for his zeal* E. I. A. 1371, οὔποτ' ἀνδρὶ τῷδε κηρῡκευμάτων μέμψῃ *never wilt thou blame me for my tidings* A. Sept. 651, τοῦ πάθους ᾤκτῑρεν αὐτόν *he pitied him for his misery* X. C. 5. 4. 32, οὐδ' εἰκὸς χαλεπῶς φέρειν αὐτῶν *nor is it reasonable to grieve about them* T. 2. 62, οὐκέτι ὧν οὗτοι κλέπτουσιν ὀργίζεσθε, ἀλλ' ὧν αὐτοὶ λαμβάνετε χάριν ἴστε *you are no longer angry at their thefts, but you are grateful for what you get yourselves* L. 27. 11, τῑμωρήσασθαι αὐτοὺς τῆς ἐπιθέσεως *to take revenge on them for their attack* X. A. 7. 4. 23. Here belongs, by analogy, συγγιγνώσκειν αὐτοῖς χρὴ τῆς ἐπιθῡμίᾱς *it is necessary to forgive them for their desire* P. Eu. 306 c (usually συγγιγνώσκειν τὴν ἐπιθῡμίᾱν τινί or τῇ ἐπιθῡμίᾳ τινός).

a. The genitive of cause is partly a true genitive, partly ablatival.

1406. With the above verbs the person stands in the accusative or dative. Some of these verbs take the dative or ἐπί and the dative (*e.g.* ἀλγεῖν, στένειν, ἄχθεσθαι, φθονεῖν) to express the cause of the emotion. See the Lexicon.

1407. The genitive of cause is used in exclamations and is often preceded by an interjection: φεῦ τοῦ ἀνδρός *alas for the man!* X. C. 3. 1. 39, τῆς τύχης *my ill luck!* 2. 2. 3. In tragedy, the genitive of a pronoun or adjective after οἴμοι or ὤμοι refers to the second or third person. For the first person the nominative is used (οἴμοι τάλαινα *ah me, miserable!* S. Ant. 554).

1408. Allied to the genitive of cause is the genitive of purpose in τοῦ with the infinitive (esp. with μή, 2032 e), and in expressions where ἕνεκα is usually employed, as ἡ πᾶσ' ἀπάτη συνεσκευάσθη τοῦ περὶ Φωκέᾱς ὀλέθρου *the whole fraud was contrived for the purpose of ruining the Phocians* D. 19. 76.

1409. Closely connected with the genitive of cause is the genitive with verbs of *disputing*: οὐ βασιλεῖ ἀντιποιούμεθα τῆς ἀρχῆς *we have no dispute with the king about his empire* X. A. 2. 1. 23, ἠμφισβήτησεν Ἐρεχθεῖ τῆς πόλεως *he disputed the possession of the city with Erechtheus* I. 12. 193, ἆρ' οὖν μὴ ἡμῖν ἐναντιώσεται τῆς ἀπαγωγῆς; *well then he will not oppose us about the removal* (of the army), *will he?* X. A. 7. 6. 5. ἀντιποιεῖσθαι *claim* may follow 1349 (τῆς πόλεως ἀντεποιοῦντο *they laid claim to the city* T. 4. 122). Verbs of *disputing* are sometimes referred to 1343 or 1349.

GENITIVE OF SOURCE

1410. The genitive may denote the source.

πίθων ἠφύσσετο οἶνος *wine was broached from the casks* ψ 305, Δᾱρείου καὶ Παρυσάτιδος γίγνονται παῖδες δύο *of Darius and Parysatis are born two sons* X. A. 1. 1. 1, ταῦτα δέ σου τυχόντες *obtaining this of you* 6. 6. 32, μάθε μου καὶ τάδε *learn this also from me* X. C. 1. 6. 44.

1411. With verbs of *hearing from* and the like the genitive is probably ablatival rather than partitive (1364): ἐμοῦ ἀκούσεσθε πᾶσαν τὴν ἀλήθειαν *from me you shall hear the whole truth* P. A. 17 b, τούτων πυνθάνομαι ὅτι οὐκ ἄβατόν ἐστι τὸ ὄρος *I learn from these men that the mountain is not impassable* X. A. 4. 6. 17, τοιαῦτά *του παρόντος ἔκλυον such a tale I heard from some one who was present* S. El. 424, *εἰδέναι δέ σου χρῄζω I desire to know of thee* S. El. 668.

a. Usually (except with πυνθάνεσθαι) we have παρά (ἀπό rarely), ἐξ or πρός (in poetry and Hdt.) with verbs of *hearing from*.

b. The genitive with εἶναι in πατρὸς δ' εἴμ' ἀγαθοῖο *I am of a good father* Φ 109, τοιούτων μέν ἐστε προγόνων *of such ancestors are you* X. A. 3. 2. 13 is often regarded as a genitive of source, but is probably possessive.

GENITIVE WITH ADJECTIVES

1412. The genitive is used with many adjectives corresponding in derivation or meaning to verbs taking the genitive.

1413. The adjective often borrows the construction with the genitive from that of the corresponding verb; but when the verb takes another case (especially the accusative), or when there is no verb corresponding to the adjective, the adjective may govern the genitive to express possession, connection more or less close, or by analogy. Many of the genitives in question may be classed as objective as well as partitive or ablatival. Rigid distinction between the undermentioned classes must not be insisted on.

1414. Possession and Belonging (1297). — ὁ ἔρως κοινὸς πάντων ἀνθρώπων *love common to all men* P. S. 205 a (cp. κοινωνεῖν 1343), ἱερὸς τοῦ αὐτοῦ θεοῦ *sacred to the same god* P. Ph. 85 b, οἱ κίνδῡνοι τῶν ἐφεστηκότων ἴδιοι *the dangers belong to the commanders* D. 2. 28. So with οἰκεῖος and ἐπιχώριος *peculiar to*. κοινός (usually), οἰκεῖος *inclined to, appropriate to*, and ἴδιος also take the dative (1499).

1415. Sharing (1343). — σοφίᾱς μέτοχος *partaking in wisdom* P. L. 689 d, ἰσόμοιροι πάντων *having an equal share in everything* X. C. 2. 1. 31, ὕβρεως ἄμοιρος *having no part in wantonness* P. S. 181 c. So ἄκληρος *without lot in*, ἀμέτοχος *not sharing in*.

1416. Touching, Desiring, Attaining, Tasting (1345, 1350, 1355). — ἄψαυστος ἔγχους *not touching a spear* S. O. T. 969, χάρις ὧν πρόθῡμοι γεγενήμεθα *gratitude for the objects of our zeal* T. 3. 67, παιδείᾱς ἐπήβολοι *having attained to* (possessed of) *culture* P. L. 724 b, ἐλευθερίᾱς ἄγευστος *not tasting freedom* P. R. 576 a. So δύσερως *passionately desirous of*.

1417. Connection. — ἀκόλουθα ἀλλήλων *dependent on one another* X. O. 11. 12, τὰ τούτων ἀδελφά *what is akin to this* X. Hi. 1. 22, τῶν προειρημένων ἑπόμεναι ἀποδείξεις *expositions agreeing with what had preceded* P. R. 504 b, φέγγος ὕπνου διάδοχον *light succeeding sleep* S. Ph. 867. All these adjectives take also the dative; as does συγγενής *akin*, which has become a substantive.

1418. Capacity and Fitness. — Adjectives in -ικός from active verbs, and some others: παρασκευαστικὸν τῶν εἰς τὸν πόλεμον τὸν στρατηγὸν εἶναι χρὴ καὶ ποριστικὸν τῶν ἐπιτηδείων τοῖς στρατιώταις *the general must be able to provide what is needed in war and to supply provisions for his men* X. M. 3. 1. 6. So διδασκαλικός *able to instruct*, πρᾱκτικός *able to effect*. Here may belong γάμου ὡραίᾱ *ripe for marriage* X. C. 4. 6. 9.

1419. Experience (1345). — ὁδῶν ἔμπειρος *acquainted with the roads* X. C. 5. 3. 35, τῆς θαλάσσης ἐπιστήμων *acquainted with the sea* T. 1. 142, ἰδιώτης τούτου τοῦ ἔργου *unskilled in this business* X. O. 3. 9. So with τρίβων *skilled in*, τυφλός *blind*, ἄπειρος *unacquainted*, ἀγύμναστος *unpractised*, ἀπαίδευτος *uneducated*, ἀήθης *unaccustomed*, ὀψιμαθής *late in learning*, φιλομαθής *fond of learning*.

1420. Remembering, Caring For (1356). — κακῶν μνήμονες *mindful of crime* A. Eum. 382, ἐπιμελὴς τῶν φίλων *attentive to friends* X. M. 2. 6. 35, ἀμνήμων τῶν κινδύνων *unmindful of dangers* Ant. 2. α. 7 ; and, by analogy, συγγνώμων τῶν ἀνθρωπίνων ἁμαρτημάτων *forgiving of human errors* X. C. 6. 1. 37. So ἀμελής *careless of*, ἐπιλήσμων *forgetful of*.

1421. Perception (1361). — Compounds in -ήκοος from ἀκούω : λόγων καλῶν ἐπήκοοι *hearers of noble words* P. R. 499 a, ὑπήκοοι Θεσσαλῶν *subjects of the Thessalians* T. 4. 78, ὑπήκοος τῶν γονέων *obedient to parents* P. R. 463 d, ἀνήκοοι παιδείᾱς *ignorant of culture* Aes. 1. 141. So συνήκοος *hearing together*, κατήκοος *obeying*. ἐπήκοος, κατήκοος, and ὑπήκοος also take the dative.

1422. Fulness (1369). — χαρᾶς ἡ πόλις ἦν μεστή *the city was full of rejoicing* D. 18. 217, παράδεισος ἀγρίων θηρίων πλήρης *a park full of wild beasts* X. A. 1. 2. 7, πλουσιώτερος φρονήσεως *richer in good sense* P. Pol. 261 e, φιλόδωρος εὐμενείᾱς *generous of good-will* P. S. 197 d, ἄπληστος χρημάτων *greedy of money* X. C. 8. 2. 20. So with ἔμπλεως, σύμπλεως. πλήρης may take the dative.

1423. Ruling (1370). — ταύτης κύριος τῆς χώρᾱς *master of this country* D. 3. 16, ἀκρατὴς ὀργῆς *unrestrained in passion* T. 3. 84. So with ἐγκρατής *master of*, αὐτοκράτωρ *complete master of*, ἀκράτωρ *intemperate in*.

1424. Value (1372). — τάπις ἀξίᾱ δέκα μνῶν *a rug worth ten minae* X. A. 7. 3. 27, δόξα χρημάτων οὐκ ὠνητή *reputation is not to be bought for money* I. 2. 32. So with ἀντάξιος *worth*, ἰσόρροπος *in equal poise with* (T. 2. 42), ἀξιόχρεως *sufficient*, ἀνάξιος *unworthy*. ἄξιόν τινι with the infinitive denotes *it is meet for a person to do something* or the like.

1425. Accountability (1375).—αἴτιος τούτων *accountable for this* P. G. 447 a, ἔνοχος λιποταξίου *liable to a charge of desertion* L. 14. 5, ἀσεβείᾱς ὑπόδικος *subject to a trial for impiety* P. L. 907 e, ὑποτελὴς φόρου *subject to tribute* T. 1. 19, τούτων ὑπεύθῡνος ὑμῖν *responsible to you for this* D. 8. 69, ἀθῷοι τῶν ἀδικημάτων *unpunished for offences* Lyc. 79. ἔνοχος usually takes the dative, and so ὑπεύθῡνος meaning *dependent on* or *exposed to*. The above compounds of ὑπό take the genitive by virtue of the substantive contained in them.

1426. Place. — ἐναντίος *opposite* and a few other adjectives denoting nearness or approach (1353) may take the genitive, chiefly in poetry : ἐναντίοι ἔσταν Ἀχαιῶν *they stood opposite the Achaeans* P 343. Cp. τοῦ Πόντου ἐπικάρσιαι *at an angle with the Pontus* Hdt. 7. 36. ἐναντίος usually takes the dative.

1427. Separation (1392). — φίλων ἀγαθῶν ἔρημοι *deprived of good friends* X. M. 4. 4. 24, ψῡχὴ ψῑλὴ σώματος *the soul separated from the body* P. L. 899 a, φειδωλοὶ χρημάτων *sparing of money* P. R. 548 b (or perhaps under 1356), ὕλης καθαρόν *clear of undergrowth* X. O. 16. 13, ἄπαυστος γόων *never ceasing lamentations* E. Supp. 82. So with ἐλεύθερος *free from*, ἁγνός *pure from*, *innocent of*, ὀρφανός *bereft of*, γυμνός *stripped of*, μόνος *alone*.

1428. Compounds of alpha privative. — In addition to the adjectives with *alpha privative* which take the genitive by reason of the notion expressed in the verb, or by analogy, there are many others, some of which take the genitive because of the idea of separation, especially when the genitive is of kindred meaning and an attributive adjective is added for the purpose of more exact definition. Thus, ἄτῑμος *deprived of*, ἀπαθής *not suffering*, ἀτελής *free from* (1392): as τῑμῆς ἄτῑμος *deprived of honour* P. L. 774 b, ἄπαις ἀρρένων παίδων *without male children* I. 12. 126, τοῦ ἡδίστου θεάματος ἀθέᾱτος *not seeing the most pleasant sight* X. M. 2. 1. 31, ἄφωνος τῆσδε τῆς ἀρᾶς *without uttering this curse* S. O. C. 865. This is more frequent in poetry than prose.

a. So when the adjectives are passive: φίλων ἄκλαυτος *unwept by friends* S. Ant. 847, cp. κακῶν δυσάλωτος οὐδείς *no one is hard for evil fortune to capture* S. O. C. 1722. The genitive with adjectives in *alpha privative* is sometimes called the genitive of *relation.*

1429. Want (1396). — ἅρματα κενὰ ἡνιόχων *chariots deprived of their drivers* X. A. 1. 8. 20, ἐνδεὴς ἀρετῆς *lacking virtue* P. R. 381 c. So with πένης *poor*, ἐλλιπής and ἐπιδεής *lacking.*

1430. Distinction (1401). — διάφορος τῶν ἄλλων *different from the rest* P. Par. 160 d, ἕτερον τὸ ἡδὺ τοῦ ἀγαθοῦ *pleasure is different from what is good* P. G. 500 d, ἄλλα τῶν δικαίων *at variance with justice* X. M. 4. 4. 25 (ἄλλος is almost a comparative). So with ἀλλοῖος and ἀλλότριος *alien from* (also with dat. *unfavourable to, disinclined to*). διάφορος with dative means *at variance with.*

1431. Comparison (1402). — Adjectives of the comparative degree or implying comparison take the genitive. The genitive denotes the standard or point of departure from which the comparison is made, and often expresses a condensed comparison when actions are compared. Thus, ἥττων ἀμαθὴς σοφοῦ, δειλὸς ἀνδρείου *an ignorant man is inferior to a wise man, a coward to a brave man* P. Phae. 239 a, κρεῖττόν ἐστι λόγου τὸ κάλλος τῆς γυναικός *the beauty of the woman is too great for description* X. M. 3. 11. 1, Ἐπύαξα προτέρᾱ Κύρου πέντε ἡμέραις ἀφίκετο *Epyaxa arrived five days before Cyrus* X. A. 1. 2. 25, καταδεεστέρᾱν τὴν δόξαν τῆς ἐλπίδος ἔλαβεν *the reputation he acquired fell short of his expectation* I. 2. 7. So with δεύτερος, ὑστεραῖος, περιττός. Comparatives with ἤ, 1069.

1432. So with *multiplicatives* in -πλοῦς and -πλάσιος: διπλάσια ἀπέδωκεν ὧν ἔλαβεν *it returned double what it received* X. C. 8. 3. 38. So with πολλοστός.

1433. The genitive with the comparative often takes the place of ἤ with another construction: ἀθλιώτερόν ἐστι μὴ ὑγιοῦς σώματος (= ἢ μὴ ὑγιεῖ σώματι) μὴ ὑγιεῖ ψῡχῇ συνοικεῖν *it is more wretched to dwell with a diseased soul than a diseased body* P. G. 479 b, πλείοσι ναυσὶ τῶν Ἀθηναίων (= ἢ οἱ Ἀθηναῖοι) παρῆσαν *they came with more ships than the Athenians* T. 8. 52.

1434. The superlative with the genitive is both partitive and ablatival; the latter, when a thing is compared with many things taken singly. Thus, σοφώτατος ἀνθρώπων P. A. 22 c means *wisest among men* (part.) and *wiser than any other single man.* The partitive idea is the stronger. The comparative and the superlative idea are both expressed in ἀνὴρ ἐπιεικὴς υἱὸν ἀπολέσᾱς οἴσει ῥᾷστα τῶν ἄλλων *a reasonable man will bear the loss of a son more easily than other men* (and *most easily of all men*) P. R. 603 e, στρατείᾱ μεγίστη τῶν πρὸ αὐτῆς *an expedition greater than any preceding it* T. 1. 10, τῶν ἄλλων ὕστατοι *the last among nations* D. 8. 72. Cp. μόνος τῶν ἄλλων = *alone of all* D. 21. 223.

1435. Cause (1405). — *εὐδαίμων τοῦ τρόπου happy because of his disposition* P. Ph. 58 e, *δείλαιος τῆς συμφορᾶς wretched because of thy lot* S. O. T. 1347, *βάλανοι θαυμάσιαι τοῦ μεγέθους dates wonderful for their size* X. A. 2. 3. 15, *περίφοβος τοῦ καταφρονηθῆναι fearful of becoming an object of contempt* P. Phae. 239 b. So with *τάλᾱς* and *τλήμων wretched.*

1436. Free Use. — **a.** Compound adjectives formed of a preposition and substantive may take a genitive dependent on the substantive: *σκηνῆς ὕπαυλος under the shelter of the tent* S. Aj. 796 (= *ὑπὸ αὐλῇ*). Frequent in poetry.

b. Some adjectives are freely used with the genitive in poetry, as *γάμοι Πάριδος ὀλέθριοι φίλων the marriage of Paris bringing ruin on his friends* A. Ag. 1156. This is rare in prose: *τὸ πῦρ ἐπίκουρον ψύχους fire that protects against cold* X. M. 4. 3. 7, *κακοῦργος μὲν τῶν ἄλλων, ἑαυτοῦ δὲ κακουργότερος doing evil to the others but more to himself* 1. 5. 3, *ὁ τῆς Ἑλλάδος ἀλιτήριος the curse and destroyer of Greece* Aes. 3. 157. These adjectives are practically equivalent to substantives. Cp. *amans patriae.*

GENITIVE WITH ADVERBS

1437. The genitive is used with adverbs derived from adjectives which take the genitive, and with adverbs akin to verbs followed by the genitive.

τὰ τούτου ἑξῆς what comes after this P. R. 390 a (1345), *ἐρωτικῶς ἔχουσι τοῦ κερδαίνειν they are in love with gain* X. O. 12. 15 (cp. 1349), *εὐθὺ Λυκείου straight for the Lyceum* P. Lys. 203 b (cp. *ἴθυσε νεός he made straight for the ship* O 693; 1353), *ἐναντίον ἁπάντων in the presence of all* T. 6. 25, *πλησίον Θηβῶν near Thebes* D. 9. 27, *Νείλου πέλας near the Nile* A. Supp. 308 (1353), *γονέων ἀμελέστερον ἔχειν be too neglectful of one's parents* P. L. 932 a (1356), *ἐκ πάντων τῶν ἐμπείρως αὐτοῦ ἐχόντων of all those acquainted with him* X. A. 2. 6. 1, *μηδενὸς ἀπείρως ἔχειν to be inexperienced in nothing* I. 1. 52 (1345), *ἀξίως ἀνδρὸς ἀγαθοῦ in a manner worthy of a good man* P. A. 32 e, *πρεπόντως τῶν πρᾱξάντων in a manner appropriate to the doers* P. Menex. 239 c (1372), *διαφερόντως τῶν ἄλλων ἀνθρώπων above the rest of men* X. Hi. 7. 4 (1401), *πονηρίᾱ θᾶττον θανάτου θεῖ 'wickedness flies faster than fate'* P. A. 39 a (1402), *πενθικῶς ἔχουσα τοῦ ἀδελφοῦ mourning for her brother* X. C. 5. 2. 7 (1405).

1438. An adverb with *ἔχειν* or *διακεῖσθαι* is often used as a periphrasis for an adjective with *εἶναι* or for a verb.

1439. The genitive is used with many adverbs (a) of place, (b) of time, (c) of quantity.

a. *ἐμβαλεῖν που τῆς ἐκείνων χώρᾱς to make an attack at some point of their country* X. C. 6. 1. 42, *αἰσθόμενος οὗ ἦν κακοῦ perceiving what a plight he was in* D. 23. 156, *οἷ προελήλυθ' ἀσελγείᾱς to what a pitch of wanton arrogance he has come* 4. 9, *ἐνταῦθα τῆς πολῑτείᾱς at that point of the administration* 18. 62, *εἰδέναι ὅπου γῆς ἐστιν to know where in the world he is* P. R. 403 e, *πόρρω ἤδη τοῦ βίου, θανάτου δὲ ἐγγύς already far advanced in life, near death* P. A. 38 c, *ἐπὶ τάδε Φασήλιδος on this side of Phaselis* I. 7. 80, *πρὸς βορέᾱν τοῦ Σκόμβρου north of Mt. Scombrus* T. 2. 96, *ἄλλοι ἄλλῃ τῆς πόλεως some in one part, others in another* *part of the city* 2. 4, ἀπαντικρὺ τῆς Ἀττικῆς *opposite Attica* D. 8. 36. So with ἐντός *inside*, εἴσω *within*, ἑκατέρωθεν *on both sides*, ὄπισθεν *behind*, πρόσθεν *before*.

b. πηνίκ' ἐστὶν ὥρα τῆς ἡμέρᾱς; *at what time of day?* Ar. Av. 1498, τῆς ἡμέρᾱς ὀψέ *late in the day* X. H. 2. 1. 23.

c. τῶν τοιούτων ἅδην *enough of such matters* P. Charm. 153 d, τούτων ἅλις *enough of this* X. C. 8. 7. 25.

1440. Most of the genitives in 1439 are partitive. Some of the adverbs falling under 1437 take also the dative (ἄγχι, ἐγγύς, πλησίον in the poets, ἑξῆς, ἐφεξῆς).

1441. The genitive is used with adverbs of manner, especially with the intransitive ἔχω, ἥκω (Hdt.). The genitive usually has no article: ὡς τάχους ἕκαστος εἶχεν *as fast as each could* (with what measure of speed he had) X. H. 4. 5. 15, ὡς ποδῶν εἶχον *as fast as my legs could carry me* Hdt. 6. 116, ἔχοντες εὖ φρενῶν *being in their right minds* E. Hipp. 462, εὖ σώματος ἔξειν *to be in good bodily condition* P. R. 404 d (cp. 407 c, τοὺς ὑγιεινῶς ἔχοντας τὰ σώματα *those who are sound in body:* with the article, 1121), χρημάτων εὖ ἥκοντες *well off* Hdt. 5. 62, τοῦ πολέμου καλῶς ἐδόκει ἡ πόλις καθίστασθαι . . . τῆς τε ἐπὶ Θρᾴκης παρόδου χρησίμως ἕξειν *they thought that the city was well situated for the war and would prove useful for the march along Thrace* T. 3. 92.

1442. This use is probably derived from that with adverbs of place: thus πῶς ἔχεις δόξης; *in what state of mind are you?* P. R. 456 d is due to the analogy of ποῦ δόξης; (cp. ὅποι γνώμης S. El. 922).

1443. The genitive is used with many adverbs denoting separation. Thus, ἔσται ἡ ψῡχὴ χωρὶς τοῦ σώματος *the soul will exist without the body* P. Ph. 66 e, δίχα τοῦ ὑμετέρου πλήθους *separate from your force* X. C. 6. 1. 8, πρόσω τῶν πηγῶν *far from the sources* X. A. 3. 2. 22, ἐμποδὼν ἀλλήλοις πολλῶν καὶ ἀγαθῶν ἔσεσθε *you will prevent one another from enjoying many blessings* X. C. 8. 5. 24, λάθρᾳ τῶν στρατιωτῶν *without the knowledge of the soldiers* X. A. 1. 3. 8. So with ἔξω *outside*, ἐκτός *without, outside*, πέρᾱν *across*, κρύφα *unbeknown to*.

GENITIVE OF TIME AND PLACE

1444. Time. — The genitive denotes the time *within which*, or at a certain point *of which*, an action takes place. As contrasted with the accusative of time (1582), the genitive denotes a portion of time. Hence the genitive of time is partitive. Cp. τὸν μὲν χειμῶνα ὕει ὁ θεός, τοῦ δὲ θέρεος χρηίσκονται τῷ ὕδατι *during the* (entire) *winter the god rains, but in* (a part of) *summer they need the water* Hdt. 3. 117.

ἡμέρᾱς *by day*, νυκτός *at* or *by night*, μεσημβρίᾱς *at midday*, δείλης *in the afternoon*, ἑσπέρᾱς *in the evening*, θέρους *in summer*, χειμῶνος *in winter*, ἦρος *in spring*, ὀπώρᾱς *in autumn*, τοῦ λοιποῦ *in the future*. The addition of article or attributive usually defines the time more exactly. Thus, οὐκοῦν ἡδὺ μὲν θέρους ψῡχεινὴν ἔχειν, ἡδὺ δὲ χειμῶνος ἀλεεινήν; *is it not pleasant to have (a house) cool in summer, and warm in winter?* X. M. 3. 8. 9, ᾤχετο τῆς νυκτός *he departed during the night* X. A. 7. 2. 17, καὶ ἡμέρᾱς καὶ νυκτὸς ἄγων ἐπὶ τοὺς πολεμίους *both by day and by night leading against the enemy* 2. 6. 7, ἔλεγον τοῦ λοιποῦ μηκέτι ἐξεῖναι ἀνομίᾱς ἄρξαι *they said that for the future* (at any time in the future) *it should no longer be permitted to set an example of lawlessness* 5. 7. 34. (Distinguish τὸ λοιπόν *for the* (entire) *future* 3. 2. 8.) ἐντός *within* is sometimes added to the genitive.

1445. The addition of the article may have a distributive sense: δραχμὴν ἐλάμβανε τῆς ἡμέρᾱς *he received a drachm a day* T. 3. 17.

1446. The genitive may denote the time *since* an action has happened or the time *until* an action will happen: οὐδείς μέ πω ἠρώτηκε καινὸν οὐδὲν πολλῶν ἐτῶν *for many years nobody has put a new question to me* P. G. 448 a, βασιλεὺς οὐ μαχεῖται δέκα ἡμερῶν *the king will not fight for ten days* X. A. 1. 7. 18.

1447. The genitive may or may not denote a definite part of the time during which anything takes place; the dative fixes the time explicitly either by specifying a definite point in a given period or by contracting the whole period to a definite point; the accusative expresses the whole extent of time from beginning to end: cp. τῇ δὲ ὑστεραίᾳ οἱ μὲν Ἀθηναῖοι τό τε προάστειον εἷλον καὶ τὴν ἡμέρᾱν ἅπᾱσαν ἐδῄουν τὴν γῆν, οἵ τε τριᾱκόσιοι τῶν Σκιωναίων τῆς ἐπιούσης νυκτὸς ἀπεχώρησαν *on the next day the Athenians captured the suburb and laid waste the land for that entire day, while the three hundred Scionaeans departed in the course of the following night* T. 4. 130; ἡμέρᾳ δὲ ἀρξάμενοι τρίτῃ ὡς οἴκοθεν ὥρμησαν, ταύτην τε εἰργάζοντο καὶ τὴν τετάρτην καὶ τῆς πέμπτης μέχρι ἀρίστου *beginning on the third day after their departure, they continued their work* (all) *this day and the fourth, and on the fifth until the mid-day meal* 4. 90.

a. The genitive of time is less common than the dative of time (1539) with ordinals, or with ὅδε, οὗτος, ἐκεῖνος; as ταύτης τῆς νυκτός T. 6. 97, P. Cr. 44 a, ἐκείνου τοῦ μηνός *in the course of that month* X. M. 4. 8. 2. For θέρους we find ἐν θέρει rarely and, in poetry, θέρει. T. 4. 133 has both τοῦ αὐτοῦ θέρους and ἐν τῷ αὐτῷ θέρει *in the course of the same summer*; cp. ἶσος ῥέει ἔν τε θέρεϊ καὶ χειμῶνι ὁ Ἴστρος Hdt. 4. 50 and Ἴστρος ἶσος ῥέει θέρεος καὶ χειμῶνος 4. 48 (*the Ister flows with the same volume in summer and winter*).

1448. Place. — The genitive denotes the place *within which* or *at which* an action happens. This is more frequent in poetry than in prose.

πεδίοιο διωκέμεν *to chase over the plain* E 222, ἷζεν τοίχου τοῦ ἑτέροιο *he was sitting by the other wall* (lit. in a place of the wall) I 219, λελουμένος Ὠκεανοῖο *having bathed in Oceanus* E 6, οὔτε Πύλου ἱερῆς οὔτ' Ἄργεος οὔτε Μυκήνης *neither in sacred Pylos nor in Argos nor in Mycenae* φ 108, τόνδ' εἰσεδέξω τειχέων *thou didst admit this man within the walls* E. Phoen. 451, ἰέναι τοῦ πρόσω *to go forward* X. A. 1. 3. 1, ἐπετάχῡνον τῆς ὁδοῦ τοὺς σχολαίτερον προσιόντας *they hastened on their way those who came up more slowly* T. 4. 47; λαιᾶς χειρὸς οἰκοῦσι *they dwell on the left hand* A. Pr. 714 (possibly ablatival).

1449. Many adverbs of place are genitives in form (αὐτοῦ *there*, ποῦ *where?* οὐδαμοῦ *nowhere*). Cp. 341.

DATIVE

1450. The Greek dative does duty for three cases: the dative proper, and two lost cases, the instrumental and the locative.

a. The dative derives its name (ἡ δοτικὴ πτῶσις, *casus dativus*) from the use with διδόναι (1469).

1451. The dative is a necessary complement of a verb when the information given by the verb is incomplete without the addition of the idea expressed by the dative. Thus, πείθεται *he obeys*, calls for the addition of an idea to complete the sense, as τοῖς νόμοις *the laws*.

1452. The dative as a voluntary complement of a verb adds something unessential to the completion of an idea. Thus, αὐτοῖς οἱ βάρβαροι ἀπῆλθον *the barbarians departed—for them* (to their advantage). Here belongs the dative of interest, 1474 ff.

1453. But the boundary line between the necessary and the voluntary complement is not always clearly marked. When the idea of the action, not the object of the action, is emphatic, a verb, usually requiring a dative to complete its meaning, may be used alone, as πείθεται *he is obedient.*

1454. With many intransitive verbs the dative is the sole complement. With transitive verbs it is the indirect complement (dative of the *indirect* or *remoter* object, usually a person); that is, it further defines the meaning of a verb already defined in part by the accusative.

1455. Many verbs so vary in meaning that they may take the dative either alone or along with the accusative (sometimes the genitive). No rules can be given, and English usage is not always the same as Greek usage.

1456. The voice often determines the construction. Thus, πείθειν τινά *to persuade some one*, πείθεσθαί τινι *to persuade oneself for some one* (*obey some one*), κελεύειν τινὰ ταῦτα ποιεῖν *to order some one to do this*, παρακελεύεσθαί τινι ταῦτα ποιεῖν *to exhort some one to do this.*

DATIVE PROPER

1457. The dative proper denotes that *to* or *for* which something is or is done.

1458. It is either (1) used with single words (verbs, adjectives, and sometimes with adverbs and substantives) or (2) it serves to define an entire sentence; herein unlike the genitive and accusative, which usually modify single members of a sentence. The connection between dative and verb is less intimate than that between genitive or accusative and verb.

1459. The dative proper is largely personal, and denotes the person who is interested in or affected by the action; and includes 1461–1473 as well as 1474 ff. The dative proper is not often used with things; when so used there is usually personification or semi-personification.

THE DATIVE DEPENDENT ON A SINGLE WORD

DATIVE AS DIRECT COMPLEMENT OF VERBS

1460. The dative may be used as the sole complement of many verbs that are usually transitive in English. Such are

1461. (I) *To benefit, help, injure, please, displease, be friendly* or *hostile, blame, be angry, threaten, envy.*

βοηθεῖν τοῖσιν ἠδικημένοις *to help the wronged* E. I. A. 79, οὐκ ἂν ἠνώχλει νῦν ἡμῖν *he would not now be troubling us* D. 3. 5, ἀντὶ τοῦ συνεργεῖν ἑαυτοῖς τὰ συμφέροντα ἐπηρεάζουσιν ἀλλήλοις *instead of coöperating for their mutual interests, they revile one another* X. M. 3. 5. 16, εἰ τοῖς πλέοσιν ἀρέσκοντές ἐσμεν, τοῖσδ' ἂν μόνοις οὐκ ὀρθῶς ἀπαρέσκοιμεν *if we are pleasing to the majority, it would not be right if we should displease them alone* T. 1. 38, εὐνοεῖν τοῖς κακόνοις *to be friendly to the ill-intentioned* X. C. 8. 2. 1, ἐμοὶ ὀργίζονται *they are angry at me* P. A. 23 c, τῷ Θηρᾱμένει ἠπείλουν *they threatened Theramenes* T. 8. 92, οὐ φθονῶν τοῖς πλουτοῦσιν *not cherishing envy against the rich* X. A. 1. 9. 19.

1462. Some verbs of *benefiting* and *injuring* take the accusative (ὠφελεῖν, βλάπτειν, 1591 a); μισεῖν τινα *hate some one.* λῡσιτελεῖν, συμφέρειν *be of advantage* take the dative.

1463. (II) *To meet, approach, yield.*

ἐπεὶ δὲ ἀπήντησαν αὐτοῖς οἱ στρατηγοί *but when the generals met them* X. A. 2. 3. 17, περιτυγχάνει Φιλοκράτει *he meets Philocrates* X. H. 4. 8. 24, ποίοις οὐ χρὴ θηρίοις πελάζειν *what wild beasts one must not approach* X. C. 1. 4. 7, σὺ δ' εἴκ' ἀνάγκῃ καὶ θεοῖσι μὴ μάχου *yield to necessity and war not with heaven* E. fr. 716. On the genitive with verbs of *approaching*, see 1353.

1464. (III) *To obey, serve, pardon, trust, advise, command,* etc.

τοῖς νόμοις πείθου *obey the laws* I. 1. 16, τῷ ὑμετέρῳ ξυμφόρῳ ὑπακούειν *to be subservient to your interests* T. 5. 98, ἂν μηδεμιᾷ δουλεύῃς τῶν ἡδονῶν *if you are the slave of no pleasure* I. 2. 29, ἐπίστευον αὐτῷ αἱ πόλεις *the cities trusted him* X. A. 1. 9. 8, στρατηγῷ στρατιώταις παραινοῦντι *a general advising his men* P. Ion 540 d, τῷ Μυσῷ ἐσήμηνε φεύγειν *he ordered the Mysian to flee* X. A. 5. 2. 30, τῷ Κλεάρχῳ ἐβόᾱ ἄγειν *he shouted to Clearchus to lead* X. A. 1. 8. 12.

1465. κελεύειν *command* (strictly *impel*) may be followed in Attic by the accusative and (usually) the infinitive; in Hom. by the dative either alone or with the infinitive. Many verbs of *commanding* (παραγγέλλειν, διακελεύεσθαι) take in Attic the accusative, not the dative, when used with the infinitive (1996 N.). ὑπακούειν (and ἀκούειν = *obey*) may take the genitive (1366).

1466. (IV) *To be like* or *unlike, compare, befit.*

ἐοικέναι τοῖς τοιούτοις *to be like such men* P. R. 349 d, τί οὖν πρέπει ἀνδρὶ πένητι; *what then befits a poor man?* P. A. 36 d.

1467. The dative of the person and the genitive of the thing are used with the impersonals δεῖ (1400), μέτεστι, μέλει, μεταμέλει, προσήκει. Thus, μισθοφόρων ἀνδρὶ τυράννῳ δεῖ *a tyrant needs mercenaries* X. Hi. 8. 10, ὡς οὐ μετὸν αὐτοῖς Ἐπιδάμνου *inasmuch as they had nothing to do with Epidamnus* T. 1. 28, οὐχ ὧν ἐβιάσατο μετέμελεν αὐτῷ *he did not repent of his acts of violence* And. 4. 17, τούτῳ τῆς Βοιωτίᾱς προσήκει οὐδέν *he has nothing to do with Boeotia* X. A. 3. 1. 31. ἔξεστί μοι *it is in my power* does not take the genitive. For the accusative instead of the dative, see 1400. Cp. 1344.

a. For δοκεῖ μοι *it seems to me* (*mihi videtur*), δοκῶ μοι (*mihi videor*) may be used. **b.** For other cases of the dative as direct complement see 1476, 1481.

1468. An intransitive verb taking the dative can form a personal passive, the dative becoming the nominative subject of the passive. Cp. 1745.

DATIVE AS INDIRECT COMPLEMENT OF VERBS

1469. Many verbs take the dative as the indirect object together with an accusative as the direct object. The indirect object is commonly introduced in English by *to*.

Κῦρος δίδωσιν αὐτῷ ἓξ μηνῶν μισθόν *Cyrus gives him pay for six months* X. A. 1. 1. 10, τῷ Ὑρκανίῳ ἵππον ἐδωρήσατο *he presented a horse to the Hyrcanian* X. C. 8. 4. 24, τὰ δὲ ἄλλα διανεῖμαι τοῖς στρατηγοῖς *to distribute the rest to the generals* X. A. 7. 5. 2, μῑκρὸν μεγάλῳ εἰκάσαι *to compare a small thing to a great thing* T. 4. 36, πέμπων αὐτῷ ἄγγελον *sending a messenger to him* X. A. 1. 3. 8, ὑπισχνοῦμαί σοι δέκα τάλαντα *I promise you ten talents* 1. 7. 18, τοῦτο σοὶ δ' ἐφίεμαι *I lay this charge upon thee* S. Aj. 116, παρῄνει τοῖς Ἀθηναίοις τοιάδε *he advised the Athenians as follows* T. 6. 8, ἐμοὶ ἐπιτρέψαι ταύτην τὴν ἀρχὴν *to entrust this command to me* X. A. 6. 1. 31, λέγειν ταῦτα τοῖς στρατιώταις *to say this to the soldiers* 1. 4. 11 (λέγειν πρός τινα lacks the personal touch of the dative, which indicates interest in the person addressed). A dependent clause often represents the accusative.

1470. **Passive.** — The accusative of the active becomes the subject of the passive, the dative remains: ἐκείνῳ αὕτη ἡ χώρᾱ ἐδόθη *this land was given to him* X. H. 3. 1. 6.

DATIVE AS DIRECT OR INDIRECT COMPLEMENT OF VERBS

1471. Many verbs may take the dative either alone or with the accusative.

οὐδενὶ μέμφομαι *I find fault with no one* D. 21. 190, τί ἄν μοι μέμφοιο; *what fault would you have to find with me?* X. O. 2. 15; ὑπηρετῶ τοῖς θεοῖς *I am a servant of the gods* X. C. 8. 2. 22, Ἔρωτι πᾶν ὑπηρετεῖ *he serves Eros in everything* P. S. 196 c; παρακελεύονται τοῖς περὶ νίκης ἁμιλλωμένοις *they exhort those who are striving for victory* I. 9. 79, ταῦτα τοῖς ὁπλίταις παρακελεύομαι *I address this exhortation to the hoplites* T. 7. 63; ὀνειδίζετε τοῖς ἀδικοῦσιν *you reproach the guilty* L. 27. 16 (also accus.), Θηβαίοις τὴν ἀμαθίᾱν ὀνειδίζουσι *they upbraid the Thebans with their ignorance* I. 15. 248; θεοῖς εὐξάμενοι *having prayed to the gods* T. 3. 58, εὐξάμενοι τοῖς θεοῖς τἀγαθά *having prayed to the gods for success* X. C. 2. 3. 1 (cp. αἰτεῖν τινά τι, 1628). So ἐπιτῑμᾶν (ἐγκαλεῖν) τινι *to censure* (*accuse*) *some one*, ἐπιτῑμᾶν (ἐγκαλεῖν) τί τινι *censure something in* (*bring an accusation against*) *some one*. So ἀπειλεῖν *threaten*; and ἀμύνειν, ἀλέξειν, ἀρήγειν *ward off* (τινί τι in poetry, 1483).

1472. τῑμωρεῖν (poet. τῑμωρεῖσθαί) τινι means *to avenge some one* (*take vengeance for some one*), as τῑμωρήσειν σοι τοῦ παιδὸς ὑπισχνοῦμαι *I promise to avenge you because of* (on the murderer of) *your son* X. C. 4. 6. 8, εἰ τῑμωρήσεις

Πατρόκλῳ τὸν φόνον *if you avenge the murder of Patroclus* P. A. 28 c. τιμωρεῖσθαί (rarely τῑμωρεῖν) τινα means *to avenge oneself upon some one* (*punish some one*).

1473. For the dative of purpose (*to what end?*), common in Latin with a second dative (*dono dare*), Greek uses a predicate noun: ἐκείνῳ ἡ χώρᾱ δῶρον ἐδόθη *the country was given to him as a gift* X. H. 3. 1. 6. The usage in Attic inscriptions (ἧλοι ταῖς θύραις *nails for the doors* C. I. A. 2, add. 834 b, 1, 38) is somewhat similar to the Latin usage. Cp. 1502.

a. The infinitive was originally, at least in part, a dative of an abstract substantive, and served to mark purpose: τίς τ' ἄρ σφωε θεῶν ἔριδι ξυνέηκε μάχεσθαι; *who then of the gods brought the twain together* (for) *to contend in strife?* A 8. Cp. "what went ye out for to see?" St. Matth. 11. 8.

DATIVE AS A MODIFIER OF THE SENTENCE

DATIVE OF INTEREST

1474. The person *for whom* something is or is done, or in reference to whose case an action is viewed, is put in the dative.

a. Many of the verbs in 1461 ff. take a dative of interest. 1476 ff. are special cases.

1475. After verbs of motion the dative (usually personal) is used, especially in poetry: χεῖρας ἐμοὶ ὀρέγοντας *reaching out their hands to me* μ 257, ψῡχὰς Ἄϊδι προΐαψεν *hurled their souls on to Hades* (a person) A 3; rarely, in prose, after verbs not compounded with a preposition: σχόντες (*scil.* τὰς ναῦς) Ῥηγίῳ *putting in at Rhegium* T. 7. 1. Cp. 1485.

1476. Dative of the Possessor. — The person for whom a thing exists is put in the dative with εἶναι, γίγνεσθαι, ὑπάρχειν, φῦναι (poet.), etc., when he is regarded as interested in its possession.

ἄλλοις μὲν χρήματά ἐστι, ἡμῖν δὲ ξύμμαχοι ἀγαθοί *others have riches, we have good allies* T. 1. 86, τῷ δικαίῳ παρὰ θεῶν δῶρα γίγνεται *gifts are bestowed upon the just man by the gods* P. R. 613 e, ὑπάρχει ἡμῖν οὐδὲν τῶν ἐπιτηδείων *we have no supply of provisions* X. A. 2. 2. 11, πᾶσι θνᾱτοῖς ἔφῡ μόρος *death is the natural lot of all men* S. El. 860.

1477. So with verbs of *thinking* and *perceiving*: τὸν ἀγαθὸν ἄρχοντα βλέποντα νόμον ἀνθρώποις ἐνόμισεν *Cyrus considered that a good ruler was a living law to man* X. C. 8. 1. 22, θαρροῦσι μάλιστα πολέμιοι, ὅταν τοῖς ἐναντίοις πράγματα πυνθάνωνται *the enemy are most courageous when they learn that the forces opposed to them are in trouble* X. Hipp. 5. 8.

1478. In the phrase ὄνομά (ἐστί) τινι the name is put in the same case as ὄνομα. Thus, ἔδοξα ἀκοῦσαι ὄνομα αὐτῷ εἶναι Ἀγάθωνα *I thought I heard his name was Agathon* P. Pr. 315 e. ὄνομά μοί ἐστι and ὄνομα (ἐπωνυμίᾱν) ἔχω are treated as the passives of ὀνομάζω. Cp. 1322 a.

1479. Here belong the phrases (1) τί (ἐστιν) ἐμοὶ καὶ σοί; *what have I to do with thee?*; cp. τί τῷ νόμῳ καὶ τῇ βασάνῳ; *what have the law and torture in common?* D. 29. 36. (2) τί ταῦτ' ἐμοί; *what have I to do with this?* D. 54. 17. (3) τί ἐμοὶ πλέον; *what gain have I?* X. C. 5. 5. 34.

1480. The dative of the possessor denotes that something is at the disposal of a person or has fallen to his share temporarily. The genitive of possession lays stress on the *person* who owns something. The dative answers the question *what is it that he has?*, the genitive answers the question *who is it that has something?* The uses of the two cases are often parallel, but not interchangeable. Thus, in Κῦρος, οὗ σὺ ἔσει τὸ ἀπὸ τοῦδε *Cyrus, to whom you will henceforth belong* X. C. 5. 1. 6, ᾧ would be inappropriate. With a noun in the genitive the dative of the possessor is used (τῶν ἑκατέροις ξυμμάχων T. 2. 1); with a noun in the dative, the genitive of the possessor (τοῖς ἑαυτῶν ξυμμάχοις 1. 18).

1481. Dative of Advantage or Disadvantage (*dativus commodi et incommodi*). — The person or thing for whose advantage or disadvantage, anything is or is done, is put in the dative. The dative often has to be translated as if the possessive genitive were used; but the meaning is different.

ἐπειδὴ αὐτοῖς οἱ βάρβαροι ἐκ τῆς χώρᾱς ἀπῆλθον *after the barbarians had departed* (for them, to their advantage) *from their country* T. 1. 89, ἄλλο στράτευμα αὐτῷ συνελέγετο *another army was being raised for him* X. A. 1. 1. 9, ἄλλῳ ὁ τοιοῦτος πλουτεῖ, καὶ οὐχ ἑαυτῷ *such a man is rich for another, and not for himself* P. Menex. 246 e, στεφανοῦσθαι τῷ θεῷ *to be crowned in honour of the god* X. H. 4. 3. 21, Φιλιστίδης ἔπρᾱττε Φιλίππῳ *Philistides was working in the interest of Philip* D. 9. 59, τὰ χρήματ᾽ αἴτι᾽ ἀνθρώποις κακῶν *money is a cause of misery to mankind* E. Fr. 632, οἱ Θρᾷκες οἱ τῷ Δημοσθένει ὑστερήσαντες *the Thracians who came too late* (for, *i.e.*) *to help Demosthenes* T. 7. 29, ἥδε ἡ ἡμέρᾱ τοῖς Ἕλλησι μεγάλων κακῶν ἄρξει *this day will be to the Greeks the beginning of great sorrows* 2. 12, ἄν τις σοι τῶν οἰκετῶν ἀποδρᾷ *if any of your slaves runs away* X. M. 2. 10. 1.

a. For the middle denoting to do something for oneself, see 1719.

b. In the last example in 1481, as elsewhere, the dative of a personal pronoun is used where a possessive pronoun would explicitly denote the owner.

1482. A dative, dependent on the sentence, may appear to depend on a substantive: σοὶ δὲ δώσω ἄνδρα τῇ θυγατρί *to you I will give a husband for your daughter* X. C. 8. 4. 24. Common in Hdt.

1483. With verbs of *depriving*, *warding off*, and the like, the dative of the person may be used: τὸ συστρατεύειν ἀφελεῖν σφίσιν ἐδεήθησαν *they asked him to relieve them* (lit. *take away for them*) *from serving in the war* X. C. 7. 1. 44, Δαναοῖσιν λοιγὸν ἄμῡνον *ward off ruin from* (for) *the Danai* A 456. So ἀλέξειν τινί τι (poet.). Cp. 1392, 1628.

1484. With verbs of *receiving* and *buying*, the person who *gives* or *sells* may stand in the dative. In δέχεσθαί τί τινι (chiefly poetic) the dative denotes the interest of the recipient in the donor: Θέμιστι δέκτο δέπας *she took the cup from* (for, *i.e.* to please) *Themis* O 87. So with πόσου πρίωμαί σοι τὰ χοιρίδια; *at what price am I to buy the pigs of you?* Ar. Ach. 812.

1485. With verbs of motion the dative of the person *to whom* is properly a dative of advantage or disadvantage: ἦλθε τοῖς Ἀθηναίοις ἡ ἀγγελίᾱ *the message came to* (for) *the Athenians* T. 1. 61. Cp. 1475.

1486. Dative of Feeling (Ethical Dative). — The personal pronouns of the first and second person are often used to denote the interest of the speaker, or to secure the interest of the person spoken to, in an action or statement.

μέμνησθέ μοι μὴ θορυβεῖν *pray remember not to make a disturbance* P. A. 27 b, ἀμουσότεροι γενήσονται ὑμῖν οἱ νέοι *your young men will grow less cultivated* P. R. 546 d, τοιοῦτο ὑμῖν ἐστι ἡ τυραννίς *such a thing, you know, is despotism* Hdt. 5. 92 η, Ἀρταφέρνης ὑμῖν Ὑστάσπεός ἐστι παῖς *Artaphernes, you know, is Hystaspes' son* 5. 30. The dative of feeling may denote surprise: ὦ μῆτερ, ὡς καλός μοι ὁ πάππος *oh mother, how handsome grandpa is* X. C. 1. 3. 2. With the dative of feeling cp. "knock me here" Shakesp. *T. of Sh.* 1. 2. 8, "study me how to please the eye" *L. L. L.* i. 1. 80. τοί *surely*, often used to introduce general statements or maxims, is a petrified dative of feeling (= σοί).

a. This dative in the third person is very rare (αὐτῇ in P. R. 343 a).

b. This construction reproduces the familiar style of conversation and may often be translated by *I beg you, please, you see, let me tell you*, etc. Sometimes the idea cannot be given in translation. This dative is a form of 1481.

1487. **ἐμοὶ βουλομένῳ ἐστί**, etc. — Instead of a sentence with a finite verb, a participle usually denoting *inclination* or *aversion* is added to the dative of the person interested, which depends on a form of εἶναι, γίγνεσθαι, etc.

τῷ πλήθει τῶν Πλαταιῶν οὐ βουλομένῳ ἦν τῶν Ἀθηναίων ἀφίστασθαι *the Plataean democracy did not wish to revolt from the Athenians* (= τὸ πλῆθος οὐκ ἐβούλετο ἀφίστασθαι) T. 2. 3 (lit. *it was not for them when wishing*), ἂν βουλομένοις ἀκούειν ᾖ τουτοισί, μνησθήσομαι *if these men* (the jury) *desire to hear it, I shall take the matter up later* (= ἂν οὗτοι ἀκούειν βούλωνται) D. 18. 11, ἐπανέλθωμεν, εἴ σοι ἡδομένῳ ἐστίν *let us go back if it is your pleasure to do so* P. Ph. 78 b, εἰ μὴ ἀσμένοις ὑμῖν ἀφῖγμαι *if I have come against your will* T. 4. 85, Νικίᾳ προσδεχομένῳ ἦν τὰ παρὰ τῶν Ἐγεσταίων *Nicias was prepared for the news from the Egestaeans* 6. 46, ἦν δὲ οὐ τῷ Ἀγησιλάῳ ἀχθομένῳ *this was not displeasing to Agesilaus* X. H. 5. 3. 13. Cp. *quibus bellum volentibus erat.*

1488. **Dative of the Agent.** — With passive verbs (usually in the perfect and pluperfect) and regularly with verbal adjectives in -τός and -τέος, the person in whose interest an action is done, is put in the dative. The notion of agency does not belong to the dative, but it is a natural inference that the person interested is the agent.

ἐμοὶ καὶ τούτοις πέπρᾱκται *has been done by* (for) *me and these men* D. 19. 205, ἐπειδὴ αὐτοῖς παρεσκεύαστο *when they had got their preparations ready* T. 1. 46, τοσαῦτά μοι εἰρήσθω *let so much have been said by me* L. 24. 4, ἐψηφίσθαι τῇ βουλῇ *let it have been decreed by the senate* C. I. A. 2. 55. 9.

a. With verbal adjectives in -τός and -τέος (2149): τοῖς οἴκοι ζηλωτός *envied by those at home* X. A. 1. 7. 4, ἡμῖν γ' ὑπὲρ τῆς ἐλευθερίᾱς ἀγωνιστέον *we at least must struggle to defend our freedom* D. 9. 70. For the accus. with -τέον, see 2152 a.

1489. The usual restriction of the dative to tenses of completed action seems to be due to the fact that the agent is represented as placed in the position of viewing an already completed action in the light of its relation to himself (interest, advantage, possession).

1490. The dative of the agent is rarely employed with other tenses than perfect and pluperfect: λέγεται ἡμῖν *is said by us* P. L. 715 b, τοῖς Κερκῡραίοις οὐχ ἑωρῶντο the ships *were not seen by* (were invisible to) *the Corcyraeans* T. 1. 51; present, T. 4. 64, 109; aorist T. 2. 7.

1491. The person *by whom* (not *for whom*) an action is explicitly said to be done, is put in the genitive with ὑπό (1698. 1. b).

1492. The dative of the personal agent is used (1) when the subject is impersonal, the verb being transitive or intransitive, (2) when the subject is personal and the person is treated as a thing in order to express scorn (twice only in the orators: D. 19. 247, 57. 10).

1493. ὑπό with the genitive of the personal agent is used (1) when the subject is a person, a city, a country, or is otherwise quasi-personal, (2) when the verb is intransitive even if the subject is a thing, as τῶν τειχῶν ὑπὸ τῶν βαρβάρων πεπτωκότων *the walls having been destroyed by the barbarians* Aes. 2. 172, (3) in a few cases with an impersonal subject, usually for the sake of emphasis, as ὡς ἑταίρᾱ ἦν . . . ὑπὸ τῶν ἄλλων οἰκείων καὶ ὑπὸ τῶν γειτόνων μεμαρτύρηται *that she was an hetaera has been testified by the rest of his relatives and by his neighbours* Is. 3. 13.

a. νῑκᾶσθαι, ἡττᾶσθαι *to be conquered* may be followed by the dative of a person, by ὑπό τινος, or by the genitive (1402).

1494. When the agent is a thing, not a person, the dative is commonly used whether the subject is personal or impersonal. If the subject is personal, ὑπό *may* be used; in which case the inanimate agent is personified (see 1698. 1. N. 1). ὑπό is rarely used when the subject is impersonal. ὑπό is never used with the impersonal perfect passive of an intransitive verb.

DATIVE OF RELATION

1495. The dative may be used of a person to whose case the statement of the predicate is limited.

φεύγειν αὐτοῖς ἀσφαλέστερόν ἐστιν ἢ ἡμῖν *it is safer for them to flee than for us* X. A. 3. 2. 19, τριήρει ἐστὶν εἰς Ἡράκλειαν ἡμέρᾱς μακρᾶς πλοῦς *for a trireme it is a long day's sail to Heraclea* 6. 4. 2. Such cases as δρόμος ἐγένετο τοῖς στρατιώταις *the soldiers began to run* X. A. 1. 2. 17 belong here rather than under 1476 or 1488.

a. ὡς restrictive is often added: μακρᾱ̀ ὡς γέροντι ὁδός *a long road* (at least) *for an old man* S. O. C. 20, σωφροσύνης δὲ ὡς πλήθει οὐ τὰ τοιάδε μέγιστα; *for the mass of men are not the chief points of temperance such as these?* P. R. 389 d.

1496. Dative of Reference. — The dative of a noun or pronoun often denotes the person in whose opinion a statement holds good.

γάμους τοὺς πρώτους ἐγάμει Πέρσῃσι ὁ Δᾱρεῖος *Darius contracted marriages most distinguished in the eyes of the Persians* Hdt. 3. 88, πᾶσι νῑκᾶν τοῖς κριταῖς *to be victorious in the judgment of all the judges* Ar. Av. 445, πολλοῖσιν οἰκτρός *pitiful in the eyes of many* S. Tr. 1071. παρά is often used, as in παρὰ Δᾱρείῳ κριτῇ *in the opinion of Darius* Hdt. 3. 160.

1497. The dative participle, without a noun or pronoun, is frequently used in the singular or plural to denote indefinitely the person judging or observing. This construction is most common with participles of verbs of *coming* or *going* and with participles of verbs of *considering*.

ἡ Θρᾴκη ἐστὶν ἐπὶ δεξιὰ εἰς τὸν Πόντον εἰσπλέοντι *Thrace is on the right as you sail into the Pontus* X. A. 6. 4. 1, ἔλεγον ὅτι ἡ ὁδὸς διαβάντι τὸν ποταμὸν ἐπὶ Λῡδίᾱν φέροι *they said that, when you had crossed the river, the road led to Lydia* 3. 5. 15, οὐκ οὖν ἄτοπον διαλογιζομένοις τᾱ̀ς δωρεᾱ̀ς νῡνὶ πλείους εἶναι; *is it not strange, when we reflect, that gifts are more frequent now?* Aes. 3. 179, τὸ μὲν ἔξωθεν ἁπτομένῳ σῶμα οὐκ ἄγᾱν θερμὸν ἦν *if you touched the surface the body was not very hot* T. 2. 49, πρὸς ὠφέλειαν σκοπουμένῳ ὁ ἐπαινέτης τοῦ δικαίου ἀληθεύει *if you look at the matter from the point of view of advantage, the panegyrist of justice speaks the truth* P. R. 589 c. So (ὡς) συνελόντι εἰπεῖν (X. A. 3. 1. 38) *to speak briefly* (lit. *for one having brought the matter into small compass*), συνελόντι D. 4. 7.

a. The participle of verbs of *coming* or *going* is commonly used in statements of geographical situation.

b. The present participle is more common than the aorist in the case of all verbs belonging under 1497.

1498. Dative of the Participle expressing Time. — In expressions of time a participle is often used with the dative of the person interested in the action of the subject, and especially to express the time that has passed *since* an action has occurred (cp. "and this is the sixth month with her, who was called barren" St. Luke i. 36).

ἀπορoῦντι δ' αὐτῷ ἔρχεται Προμηθεύς *Prometheus comes to him in his perplexity* P. Pr. 321 c, Ξενοφῶντι πορευομένῳ οἱ ἱππεῖς ἐντυγχάνουσι πρεσβύταις *while Xenophon was on the march, his horsemen fell in with some old men* X. A. 6. 3. 10. The idiom is often transferred from persons to things: ἡμέραι μάλιστα ἦσαν τῇ Μυτιλήνῃ ἑᾱλωκυίᾳ ἑπτά, ὅτ' ἐς τὸ Ἔμβατον κατέπλευσαν *about seven days had passed since the capture of Mytilene, when they sailed into Embatum* T. 3. 29. This construction is frequent in Hom. and Hdt. The participle is rarely omitted (T. 1. 13.).

a. A temporal clause may take the place of the participle: τῇ στρατιᾷ, ἀφ' οὗ ἐξέπλευσεν εἰς Σικελίᾱν, ἤδη ἐστὶ δύο καὶ πεντήκοντα ἔτη *it is already fifty-two years since the expedition sailed to Sicily* Is. 6. 14.

DATIVE WITH ADJECTIVES, ETC.

1499. Adjectives, adverbs, and substantives, of kindred meaning with the foregoing verbs, take the dative to define their meaning.

βασιλεῖ φίλοι *friendly to the king* X. A. 2. 1. 20, εὔνους τῷ δήμῳ *well disposed to the people* And. 4. 16, τοῖς νόμοις ἔνοχος *subject to the laws* D. 21. 35, ἐχθρὸν ἐλευθερίᾳ καὶ νόμοις ἐναντίον *hostile to liberty and opposed to law* 6. 25, ξυμμαχίᾳ πίσυνοι *relying on the alliance* T. 6. 2, φόρῳ ὑπήκοοι *subject to tribute* 7. 57, ἢν ποιῆτε ὅμοια τοῖς λόγοις *if you act in accordance with your words* 2. 72, στρατὸς ἴσος καὶ παραπλήσιος τῷ προτέρῳ *an army equal or nearly so to the former* 7. 42, ἀδελφὰ τὰ βουλεύματα τοῖς ἔργοις *plans like the deeds* L. 2. 64, ἀλλήλοις ἀνομοίως *in a way unlike to each other* P. Tim. 36 d. For substantives see 1502.

a. Some adjectives, as φίλος, ἐχθρός, may be treated as substantives and take the genitive. Some adjectives often differ slightly in meaning when they take the genitive.

1500. With ὁ αὐτός *the same.*—τὴν αὐτὴν γνώμην ἐμοὶ ἔχειν *to be of the same mind as I am* L. 3. 21, τοῦ αὐτοῦ ἐμοὶ πατρός *of the same father as I am* D. 40. 34, ταὐτὰ φρονῶν ἐμοί *agreeing with me* 18. 304.

1501. With adjectives and adverbs of similarity and dissimilarity the comparison is often condensed (*brachylogy*): ὁμοίᾱν ταῖς δούλαις εἶχε τὴν ἐσθῆτα *she had a dress on like* (that of) *her servants* X. C. 5. 1. 4 (the possessor for the thing possessed, = τῇ ἐσθῆτι τῶν δουλῶν), Ὀρφεῖ γλῶσσα ἡ ἐναντίᾱ *a tongue unlike* (that of) *Orpheus* A. Ag. 1629.

a. After adjectives and adverbs of likeness we also find καί, ὅσπερ (ὥσπερ). Thus, παθεῖν ταὐτὸν ὅπερ πολλάκις πρότερον πεπόνθατε *to suffer the same as you have often suffered before* D. 1. 8, οὐχ ὁμοίως πεποιήκᾱσι καὶ Ὅμηρος *they have not composed their poetry as Homer did* P. Ion 531 d.

1502. The dative after substantives is chiefly used when the substantive expresses the act denoted by the kindred verb requiring the dative: ἐπιβουλὴ ἐμοί *a plot against me* X. A. 5. 6. 29, διάδοχος Κλεάνδρῳ *a successor to Cleander* 7. 2. 5, ἡ ἐμὴ τῷ θεῷ ὑπηρεσίᾱ *my service to the god* P. A. 30 a. But also in other cases: φιλίᾱ τοῖς Ἀθηναίοις *friendship for the Athenians* T. 5. 5, ὕμνοι θεοῖς *hymns to the gods* P. R. 607 a, ἐφόδια τοῖς στρατευομένοις *supplies for the troops* D. 3. 20, ἧλοι ταῖς θύραις *nails for the doors* (1473).

a. Both a genitive and a dative may depend on the same substantive: ἡ τοῦ θεοῦ δόσις ὑμῖν *the god's gift to you* P. A. 30 d.

INSTRUMENTAL DATIVE

1503. The Greek dative, as the representative of the lost instrumental case, denotes that *by which* or *with which* an action is done or accompanied. It is of two kinds: (1) The instrumental dative proper; (2) The comitative dative.

1504. When the idea denoted by the noun in the dative is the *instrument* or *means*, it falls under (1); if it is a person (not regarded as the instrument or means) or any other living being, or a thing regarded as a person, it belongs under (2); if an action, under (2).

1505. Abstract substantives with or without an attributive often stand in the instrumental dative instead of the cognate accusative (1577).

INSTRUMENTAL DATIVE PROPER

1506. The dative denotes instrument or means, manner, and cause.

1507. **Instrument or Means.**—ἔβαλλέ με λίθοις *he hit me with stones* L. 3. 8. ἵησι τῇ ἀξίνῃ *he hurls his ax* at him (*hurls with his ax*) X. A. 1. 5. 12, ταῖς μαχαίραις κόπτοντες *hacking* them *with their swords* 4. 6. 26, οὐδὲν ἤνυε τούτοις *he accomplished nothing by this* D. 21. 104, ἐζημίωσαν χρήμασιν *they punished* him *by a fine* T. 2. 65, ὕοντος πολλῷ (ὕδατι) *during a heavy rain* X. H. 1. 1. 16 (934). So with δέχεσθαι: τῶν πόλεων οὐ δεχομένων αὐτοὺς ἀγορᾷ οὐδὲ ἄστει, ὕδατι δὲ καὶ ὅρμῳ *as the cities did not admit them to a market nor even into the town, but* (only) *to water and anchorage* T. 6. 44. Often with passives: ᾠκοδομημένον πλίνθοις *built of bricks* X. A. 2. 4. 12.

a. The instrumental dative is often akin to the comitative dative: ἀλώμενος νηΐ τε καὶ ἑτάροισι *wandering with his ship and companions* λ 161, νηυσὶν οἰχήσονται *they shall go with their ships* Ω 731, θυμῷ καὶ ῥώμῃ τὸ πλέον ἐναυμάχουν ἢ ἐπιστήμῃ *they fought with passionate violence and brute force rather than by a system of tactics* T. 1. 49.

b. Persons may be regarded as instruments: φυλαττόμενοι φύλαξι *defending themselves by pickets* X. A. 6. 4. 27. Often in poetry (S. Ant. 164).

c. Verbs of *raining* or *snowing* take the dative or accusative (1570 a).

1508. Under **Means** fall:

a. The dative of *price* (cp. 1372): μέρει τῶν ἀδικημάτων τὸν κίνδυνον ἐξεπρίαντο *they freed themselves from the danger at the price of a part of their unjust gains* L. 27. 6.

b. Rarely, the dative with verbs of *filling* (cp. 1369): δάκρυσι πᾶν τὸ στράτευμα πλησθέν *the entire army being filled with tears* T. 7. 75.

c. The dative of *material* and *constituent parts:* κατεσκευάσατο ἅρματα τροχοῖς ἰσχυροῖς *he made chariots with strong wheels* X. C. 6. 1. 29.

1509. χρῆσθαι *use* (strictly *employ oneself with, get something done with;* cp. *uti*), and sometimes νομίζειν, take the dative. Thus, οὔτε τούτοις (τοῖς νομίμοις) χρῆται οὔθ᾽ οἷς ἡ ἄλλη Ἑλλὰς νομίζει *neither acts according to these institutions nor observes those accepted by the rest of Greece* T. 1. 77. A predicate noun may be added to the dative: τούτοις χρῶνται δορυφόροις *they make use of them as a body-guard* X. Hi. 5. 3. The use to which an object is put may be expressed by a neuter pronoun in the accus. (1573); τί χρησόμεθα τούτῳ; *what use shall we make of it?* D. 3. 6.

1510. The instrumental dative occurs after substantives: μίμησις σχήμασι *imitation by means of gestures* P. R. 397 b.

1511. The instrumental dative of means is often, especially in poetry, reinforced by the prepositions ἐν, σύν, ὑπό: ἐν λόγοις πείθειν *to persuade by words* S. Ph. 1393, οἱ θεοὶ ἐν τοῖς ἱεροῖς ἐσήμηναν *the gods have shown by the victims* X. A. 6. 1. 31; σὺν γήρᾳ βαρεῖς *heavy with old age* S. O. T. 17; πόλις χερσὶν ὑφ᾽ ἡμετέρῃσιν ἁλοῦσα *a city captured by our hands* B 374.

1512. Dative of Standard of Judgment. — That by which anything is measured, or judged, is put in the dative: ξυνεμετρήσαντο ταῖς ἐπιβολαῖς τῶν πλίνθων *they measured* the ladders *by the layers of bricks* T. 3. 20, τῷδε δῆλον ἦν *it was plain from what followed* X. A. 2. 3. 1, οἷς πρὸς τοὺς ἄλλους πεποίηκε δεῖ τεκμαίρεσθαι *we must judge by what he has done to the rest* D. 9. 10, τίνι χρὴ κρίνεσθαι τὰ μέλλοντα καλῶς κριθήσεσθαι; ἆρ᾽ οὐκ ἐμπειρίᾳ τε καὶ φρονήσει καὶ λόγῳ; *by what standard must we judge that the judgment may be correct? Is it not by* *experience and wisdom and reasoning?* P. R. 582 a. With verbs of *judging* ἐκ and ἀπό are common.

1513. **Manner** (see also 1527). — The dative of manner is used with comparative adjectives and other expressions of comparison to mark the degree by which one thing differs from another (**Dative of Measure of Difference**).

κεφαλῇ ἐλάττων *a head shorter* (lit. *by the head*) P. Ph. 101 a, οὐ πολλαῖς ἡμέραις ὕστερον ἦλθεν *he arrived not many days later* X. H. 1. 1. 1, ἰόντες δέκα ἡμέραις πρὸ Παναθηναίων *coming ten days before the Panathenaic festival* T. 5. 47, τοσούτῳ ἥδιον ζῶ ὅσῳ πλείω κέκτημαι *the more I possess the more pleasant is my life* X. C. 8. 3. 40, πολλῷ μείζων ἐγίγνετο ἡ βοὴ ὅσῳ δὴ πλείους ἐγίγνοντο *the shouting became much louder as the men increased in number* X. A. 4. 7. 23. So with πολλῷ *by much*, ὀλίγῳ *by little*, τῷ παντί *in every respect* (by all odds).

a. With the superlative: μακρῷ ἄριστα *by far the best* P. L. 858 e.

1514. With comparatives the accusatives (1586) τί, τὶ, οὐδέν, μηδέν without a substantive are always used: οὐδὲν ἧττον *nihilo minus* X. A. 7. 5. 9. In Attic prose (except in Thuc.) πολύ and ὀλίγον are more common than πολλῷ and ὀλίγῳ with comparatives. Hom. has only πολὺ μείζων.

1515. Measure of difference may be expressed by ἔν τινι; εἴς τι, κατά τι; or by ἐπί τινι.

1516. The dative of manner may denote the particular point of view from which a statement is made. This occurs chiefly with intransitive adjectives but also with intransitive verbs (**Dative of Respect**). (Cp. 1600.)

ἀνὴρ ἡλικίᾳ ἔτι νέος *a man still young in years* T. 5. 43, τοῖς σώμασι τὸ πλέον ἰσχύουσα ἢ τοῖς χρήμασιν a power *stronger in men than in money* 1. 121, ἀσθενὴς τῷ σώματι *weak in body* D. 21. 165, τῇ φωνῇ τρᾱχύς *harsh of voice* X. A. 2. 6. 9, φρονήσει διαφέρων *distinguished in understanding* X. C. 2. 3. 5, τῶν τότε δυνάμει προύχων *superior in power to the men of that time* T. 1. 9, ὀνόματι σπονδαί *a truce so far as the name goes* 6. 10.

a. The accusative of respect (1600) is often nearly equivalent to the dative of respect.

1517. **Cause.** — The dative, especially with verbs of emotion, expresses the occasion (external cause) or the motive (internal cause).

Occasion: τῇ τύχῃ ἐλπίσᾱς *confident by reason of his good fortune* T. 3. 97, θαυμάζω τῇ ἀποκλήσει μου τῶν πυλῶν *I am astonished at being shut out of the gates* 4. 85, τούτοις ἥσθη *he was pleased at this* X. A. 1. 9. 26, ἠχθόμεθα τοῖς γεγενημένοις *we were troubled at what had occurred* 5. 7. 20, χαλεπῶς φέρω τοῖς παροῦσι πράγμασιν *I am troubled at the present occurrences* 1. 3. 3. Motive: φιλίᾳ καὶ εὐνοίᾳ ἑπόμενοι *following out of friendship and good will* X. A. 2. 6. 13. Occasion and motive: οἱ μὲν ἀπορίᾳ ἀκολούθων, οἱ δὲ ἀπιστίᾳ *some* (carried their own food) *because they lacked servants, others through distrust of them* T. 7. 75, ὕβρει καὶ οὐκ οἴνῳ τοῦτο ποιῶν *doing this out of insolence and not because he was drunk* D. 21. 74.

1518. Some verbs of emotion take ἐπί (with dat.) to denote the cause; so always μέγα φρονεῖν *to plume oneself*, and often χαίρειν *rejoice*, λῡπεῖσθαι *grieve*, ἀγανακτεῖν *be vexed*, αἰσχύνεσθαι *be ashamed*. Many verbs take the genitive (1405).

1519. The dative of cause sometimes approximates to a dative of purpose (1473): Ἀθηναῖοι ἐφ' ἡμᾶς ὥρμηνται Λεοντίνων κατοικίσει *the Athenians have set out against us (with a view to) to restore the Leontines* T. 6. 33. This construction is common with other verbal nouns in Thucydides.

1520. Cause is often expressed by διά with the accusative, ὑπό with the genitive, less frequently by ἀμφί or περί with the dative (poet.) or ὑπέρ with the genitive (poet.).

COMITATIVE DATIVE

1521. The comitative form of the instrumental dative denotes the persons or things which accompany or take part in an action.

1522. Prepositions of accompaniment (μετά with gen., σύν) are often used, especially when the verb does not denote accompaniment or union.

1523. Dative of Association. — The dative is used with words denoting friendly or hostile association or intercourse. This dative is especially common in the plural and after middle verbs.

a. κακοῖς ὁμῑλῶν καὐτὸς ἐκβήσῃ κακός *if thou associate with the evil, in the end thou too wilt become evil thyself* Men. Sent. 274, ἀλλήλοις διειλέγμεθα *we have conversed with each other* P. A. 37 a, τῷ πλήθει τὰ ῥηθέντα κοινώσαντες *communicating to the people what had been said* T. 2. 72, δεόμενοι τοὺς φεύγοντας ξυναλλάξαι σφίσι *asking that they reconcile their exiles with them* 1. 24, εἰς λόγους σοι ἐλθεῖν *to have an interview with you* X. A. 2. 5. 4, μετεσχήκαμεν ὑμῖν θυσιῶν *we have participated in your festivals* X. H. 2. 4. 20, ἀλλήλοις σπονδὰς ἐποιήσαντο *they made a truce with one another* 3. 2. 20, αὐτοῖς διὰ φιλίᾱς ἰέναι *to enter into friendship with them* X. A. 3. 2. 8. So with verbs of *meeting*: προσέρχεσθαι, προστυγχάνειν and ἐντυγχάνειν, ἀπαντᾶν.

b. πολλοῖς ὀλίγοι μαχόμενοι *few fighting with many* T. 4. 36, Κύρῳ πολεμοῦντες *waging war with Cyrus* 1. 13, ἀμφισβητοῦσι μὲν δι' εὔνοιαν οἱ φίλοι τοῖς φίλοις, ἐρίζουσι δὲ οἱ διάφοροι ἀλλήλοις *friends dispute with friends good-naturedly, but adversaries wrangle with one another* P. Pr. 337 b, δίκᾱς ἀλλήλοις δικάζονται *they bring lawsuits against one another* X. M. 3. 5. 16, διαφέρεσθαι τούτοις *to be at variance with these men* D. 18. 31 (and so many compounds of διά), οὐκ ἔφη τοὺς λόγους τοῖς ἔργοις ὁμολογεῖν *he said their words did not agree with their deeds* T. 5. 55. So also τινὶ διὰ πολέμου (διὰ μάχης, εἰς χεῖρας) ἰέναι, τινὶ ὁμόσε χωρεῖν, etc.

N. 1. — πολεμεῖν (μάχεσθαι) σύν τινι (μετά τινος) means *to wage war in conjunction with some one.*

N. 2. — Verbs of friendly or hostile association, and especially periphrases with ποιεῖσθαι (πόλεμον, σπονδάς), often take the accusative with πρός.

1524. Dative of Accompaniment. — The dative of accompaniment is used with verbs signifying *to accompany, follow*, etc.

ἀκολουθεῖν τῷ ἡγουμένῳ *to follow the leader* P. R. 474 c, ἕπεσθαι ὑμῖν βούλομαι

I am willing to follow you X. A. 3. 1. 25. μετά with the genitive is often used, as are σύν and ἅμα with the dative.

1525. With αὐτός.—The idea of accompaniment is often expressed by αὐτός joined to the dative. This use is common when the destruction of a person or thing is referred to. Thus, τῶν νεῶν μία αὐτοῖς ἀνδράσιν *one of the ships with its crew* T. 4. 14, εἶπεν ἥκειν εἰς τὰς τάξεις αὐτοῖς στεφάνοις *he bade them come to their posts, crowns and all* X. C. 3. 3. 40. The article after αὐτός is rare; and σύν is rarely added (X. C. 2. 2. 9). Hom. has this dative only with lifeless objects.

1526. Dative of Military Accompaniment.—The dative is used in the description of military movements to denote the accompaniment (troops, ships, etc.) of a leader: ἐξελαύνει τῷ στρατεύματι παντί *he marches out with all his army* X. A. 1. 7. 14. σύν is often used with words denoting troops (T. 6. 62).

a. An extension of this usage occurs when the persons in the dative are essentially the same as the persons forming the subject (distributive use): ἡμῖν ἐφείποντο οἱ πολέμιοι καὶ ἱππικῷ καὶ πελταστικῷ *the enemy pursued us with their cavalry and peltasts* X. A. 7. 6. 29.

b. The dative of military accompaniment is often equivalent to a dative of means when the verb does not denote the leadership of a general.

1527. Dative of Accompanying Circumstance.—The dative, usually of an abstract substantive, may denote accompanying circumstance and manner.

a. The substantive has an attribute: πολλῇ βοῇ προσέκειντο *they attacked with loud shouts* T. 4. 127, παντὶ σθένει *with all one's might* 5. 23, τύχῃ ἀγαθῇ *with good fortune* C. I. A. 2. 17. 7. So παντὶ (οὐδενί, ἄλλῳ, τούτῳ τῷ) τρόπῳ. Manner may be expressed by the adjective, as βιαίῳ θανάτῳ ἀποθνῄσκειν *to die (by) a violent death* X. Hi. 4. 3 (= βίᾳ).

b. Many particular substantives have no attribute and are used adverbially: θεῖν δρόμῳ *to run at full speed* X. A. 1. 8. 19, βίᾳ *by force*, δίκῃ *justly*, δόλῳ *by craft*, (τῷ) ἔργῳ *in fact*, ἡσυχῇ *quietly*, κομιδῇ (*with care*) *entirely*, κόσμῳ *in order, duly*, κύκλῳ *round about*, (τῷ) λόγῳ *in word*, προφάσει *ostensibly*, σιγῇ, σιωπῇ *in silence*, σπουδῇ *hastily, with difficulty*, τῇ ἀληθείᾳ *in truth*, τῷ ὄντι *in reality*, ὀργῇ *in anger*, φυγῇ *in hasty flight.*

N.—When no adjective is used, prepositional phrases or adverbs are generally employed: σὺν κραυγῇ, σὺν δίκῃ, μετὰ δίκης, πρὸς βίᾱν (or βιαίως).

c. Here belongs the dative of feminine adjectives with a substantive (ὁδῷ, etc.) omitted, as ταύτῃ *in this way, here*, ἄλλῃ *in another way, elsewhere*, πῇ, ᾗ *in what (which) way.* So δημοσίᾳ *at public expense*, ἰδίᾳ *privately*, κοινῇ *in common*, πεζῇ *on foot.*

N.—Some of these forms are instrumental rather than comitative, *e.g.* ταύτῃ.

1528. Space and Time.—The dative of space and time may sometimes be regarded as comitative.

a. Space: *the way by which* (*qua*), as ἐπορεύετο τῇ ὁδῷ ἣν πρότερον ἐποιήσατο *he marched by the road* (or *on the road?*) *which he had made before* T. 2. 98; **b.** Time: κατηγόρει ὡς ἐκείνῃ τῷ χρόνῳ πεισθείη *she charged that she had been* *persuaded in (by) the course of time* L. 1. 20. Some of these uses are instrumental rather than comitative.

WITH ADJECTIVES, ETC.

1529. Many adjectives and adverbs, and some substantives, take the instrumental dative by the same construction as the corresponding verbs.

σύμμαχος αὐτοῖς *their ally* D. 9. 58, χώρᾱ ὅμορος τῇ Λακεδαιμονίων *a country bordering on that of the Lacedaemonians* 15. 22, ἀκόλουθα τούτοις *conformable to this* 18. 257. So κοινός (cp. 1414), σύμφωνος, συγγενής, μεταίτιος, and διάφορος meaning *at variance with.*— ἑπομένως τῷ νόμῳ *conformably to the law* P. L. 844 e, ὁ ἑξῆς νόμος τούτῳ *the law next to this* D. 21. 10. Many of the adjectives belonging here also take the genitive when the idea of possession or connection is marked.— ἅμα chiefly in the meaning *at the same time.*— κοινωνίᾱ τοῖς ἀνδράσι *intercourse with men* P. R. 466 c, ἐπιδρομὴ τῷ τειχίσματι *attack on the fort* T. 4. 23.

LOCATIVE DATIVE

1530. The dative as the representative of the locative is used to express place and time.

a. On the instrumental dative of space and time, see 1528.

1531. Dative of Place.— In poetry the dative without a preposition is used to denote place.

a. *Where a person or thing is:* στὰς μέσῳ ἕρκεϊ *taking his stand in the middle of the court* Ω 306, γῇ ἔκειτο *she lay on the ground* S. O. T. 1266, ναίειν ὄρεσιν *to dwell among the mountains* O. T. 1451. Often of the parts of the body (Hom. θυμῷ, καρδίῃ, etc.). With persons (generally in the plural): ἀριπρεπὴς Τρώεσσιν *conspicuous among the Trojans* Z 477. τοῖσι δ' ἀνέστη A 68 may be *rose up among them* or a dative proper (*for them*).

b. *Place whither* (limit of motion): πεδίῳ πέσε *fell on the ground* E 82, κολεῷ ἄορ θέο *put thy sword into its sheath* κ 333.

1532. After verbs of motion the dative, as distinguished from the locative, denotes direction *towards* and is used of persons (1485), and is a form of the dative of interest.

1533. Many verbs capable of taking the locative dative in poetry, require, in prose, the aid of a preposition in composition. The limit of motion is usually (1589) expressed by the accusative with a preposition (*e.g.* εἰς, πρός).

1534. In prose the dative of place (chiefly *place where*) is used only of proper names: Πῡθοῖ *at Pytho*, Ἰσθμοῖ *at the Isthmus*, Σαλαμῖνι *at Salamis*, Ὀλυμπίᾱσι *at Olympia*, Ἀθήνησι *at Athens* (inscr.); especially with the names of Attic demes, as Φαληροῖ, Θορικοῖ, Μαραθῶνι. But ἐν Μαραθῶνι and ἐν Πλαταιαῖς occur. Some deme-names require ἐν, as ἐν Κοίλῃ.

1535. Many adverbs are genuine locatives, as οἴκοι, πάλαι, πανδημεί, Φαληροῖ; Ἀθήνησι, Πλαταιᾶσι; others are datives in form, as κύκλῳ, Πλαταιαῖς.

1536. With names of countries and places, ἐν is more common than the locative dative, and, with the above exceptions, the place *where* is expressed in Attic prose with ἐν.

1537. Verbs of *ruling* often take the dative, especially in Homer: Μυρμιδόνεσσιν ἄνασσε Α 180, Γιγάντεσσιν βασίλευεν η 59, ἦρχε δ' ἄρα σφιν Ἀγαμέμνων Ξ 134. Rarely in prose: ἡγεῖσθαί τινι *to serve as guide* (leader) *to some one*, ἐπιστατεῖν τινι *to be set over one*; ἄρχειν τινί means only = *to be archon* (Πυθοδώρου ἄρχοντος Ἀθηναίοις T. 2. 2). Cp. 1371.

a. Only when stress is not laid on the idea of supremacy is the dative, instead of the genitive (1370), used with verbs of *ruling*.

1538. It is not clear whether the dative with verbs of *ruling* is a dative proper (*for*), a locative (*among*; cp. ἐν Φαίηξιν ἄνασσε η 62), or an instrumental (*by*). ἄρχειν, ἡγεῖσθαι may take the dative proper, ἀνάσσειν, βασιλεύειν, κρατεῖν may take the locative dative.

1539. Dative of Time. — The dative without a preposition is commonly used to denote a definite point of time (chiefly *day, night, month, year, season*) *at which* an action occurred. The dative contrasts one point of time with another, and is usually accompanied by an attributive.

1540. The dative denotes the time *at which* an action takes place and the date of an event.

ταύτην μὲν τὴν ἡμέρᾱν αὐτοῦ ἔμειναν, τῇ δὲ ὑστεραίᾳ κτλ. *throughout that day they waited there, but on the day following*, etc. X. H. 1. 1. 14. So τῇ προτεραίᾳ *the day before*, τῇ δευτέρᾳ *the second day*, Ἐλαφηβολιῶνος μηνὸς ἕκτῃ (ἡμέρᾳ) φθίνοντος *on the sixth of waning Elaphebolion* Aes. 2. 90, ἕνῃ καὶ νέᾳ *on the last of the month* D. 18. 29; τρίτῳ μηνί *in the third month* L. 21. 1, περιιόντι τῷ θέρει *when summer was coming to an end* T. 1. 30, ἑξηκοστῷ ἔτει *in the sixtieth year* 1. 12; also with ὥρᾳ (χειμῶνος ὥρᾳ *in the winter season* And. 1. 137).

1541. The names of the regular recurring festivals which serve to date an occurrence stand in the dative: Παναθηναίοις *at the Panathenaea* D. 21. 156, τοῖς Διονυσίοις *at the Dionysia* 21. 1, ταῖς πομπαῖς *at the processions* 21. 171, τοῖς τραγῳδοῖς *at the representations of the tragedies* Aes. 3. 176. ἐν is rarely added.

1542. ἐν is added:

a. To words denoting time when there is no attributive: ἐν τῷ χειμῶνι *in winter* X. O. 17. 3; cp. 1444. **b.** When the attributive is a pronoun (sometimes): (ἐν) ἐκείνῃ τῇ ἡμέρᾳ. **c.** To statements of the time within the limits of which an event may take place (where ἐντός with the genitive is common); to statements of how much time anything takes; with numbers, ὀλίγος, πολύς, etc. Thus, ἐν τρισὶν ἡμέραις *for* (during) *three days* X. A. 4. 8. 8, οὐ ῥᾴδιον τὰ ἐν ἅπαντι τῷ χρόνῳ πρᾱχθέντα ἐν μιᾷ ἡμέρᾳ δηλωθῆναι *it is not easy to set forth in a single day the acts of all time* L. 2. 54, ἐξελέσθαι τὴν διαβολὴν ἐν οὕτως ὀλίγῳ χρόνῳ *to clear myself of calumny in so brief a time* P. A. 19 a. ἐν is rarely omitted in prose, and chiefly when there is an attributive: μιᾷ νυκτί T. 6. 27. **d.** Always with adjectives or adverbs used substantively: ἐν τῷ παρόντι, ἐν τῷ τότε. **e.** To words denoting the date of an event, not a point of time: ἐν τῇ προτέρᾳ πρεσβείᾳ *in the first embassy* Aes. 2. 123. Thuc. employs ἐν, as ἐν τῇ ὑστεραίᾳ ἐκκλησίᾳ *in* *the assembly held the day after* 1. 44, but usu. the simple dative, as μάχῃ *in the battle* 3. 54, ἐκείνῃ τῇ ἐσβολῇ *in that incursion* 2. 20, τῇ προτέρᾳ ἐκκλησίᾳ *in the first assembly* 1. 44.

1543. The dative and genitive of time are sometimes employed with only a slight difference (1447 a).

DATIVE WITH COMPOUND VERBS

1544. Many compound verbs take the dative because of their meaning as a whole. So ἀντέχειν *hold out against*, ἀμφισβητεῖν *dispute with* (1523 b).

1545. The dative is used with verbs compounded with σύν (regularly), with many compounded with ἐν, ἐπί, and with some compounded with παρά, περί, πρός, and ὑπό, because the preposition keeps a sense that requires the dative.

ἐμβλέψᾱς αὐτῷ *looking at him* P. Charm. 162 d, ἐλπίδας ἐμποιεῖν ἀνθρώποις *to create expectations in men* X. C. 1. 6. 19, αὐτοῖς ἐπέπεσε τὸ Ἑλληνικόν *the Greek force fell upon them* X. A. 4. 1. 10, ἐπέκειντο αὐτοῖς *they pressed hard upon them* 5. 2. 5, συναδικεῖν αὐτοῖς *to be their accomplice in wrong-doing* 2. 6. 27, ξυνίσᾱσι Μελήτῳ ψευδομένῳ *they are conscious that Meletus is speaking falsely* (*i.e.* they know it as well as he does) P. A. 34 b, οὗτοι οὐ παρεγένοντο βασιλεῖ *these did not join the king* X. A. 5. 6. 8, παρέστω ὑμῖν ὁ κῆρυξ *let the herald come with us* 3. 1. 46, Ξενοφῶντι προσέτρεχον δύο νεᾱνίσκω *two youths ran up to Xenophon* 4. 3. 10, ὑποκεῖσθαι τῷ ἄρχοντι *to be subject to the ruler* P. G. 510 c.

a. So especially with verbs of motion and rest formed from ἰέναι, πίπτειν, τιθέναι, τρέχειν, εἶναι, γίγνεσθαι, κεῖσθαι, etc.

1546. Some verbs of motion compounded with παρά, περί, ὑπό take the accusative (1559).

1547. Some verbs have an alternative construction, *e.g.* περιβάλλειν: τινί τι *invest a person with something*, τί τινι *surround something with something.*

1548. Compounds of σύν take the instrumental, compounds of ἐν take the locative dative.

1549. When the idea of place is emphatic, the preposition may be repeated: ἐμμείναντες ἐν τῇ Ἀττικῇ *remaining in Attica* T. 2. 23; but it is generally not repeated when the idea is figurative: τοῖς ὅρκοις ἐμμένων *abiding by one's oath* I. 1. 13. μετά may be used after compounds of σύν: μετ' ἐμοῦ συνέπλει *he sailed in company with me* L. 21. 8.

1550. The prepositions are more frequently repeated in prose than in poetry.

ACCUSATIVE

1551. The accusative is a form of defining or qualifying the verb.

a. The accusative derives its name from a mistranslation (*casus accusativus*) of the Greek (ἡ αἰτιᾱτικὴ πτῶσις, properly *casus effectivus*, 1554 a).

1552. A noun stands in the accusative when the idea it expresses is most immediately (in contrast to the dative) and most completely (in contrast to the genitive) under the influence of the verbal conception (in contrast to the nominative).

1553. The accusative is the case of the direct object (919). The accusative is used with all transitive verbs (and with some intransitive verbs used transitively), with some verbal nouns, and with adjectives.

1554. The direct object is of two kinds:

a. The internal object (object effected): ὁ ἀνὴρ τύπτει πολλὰς πληγᾱ́ς *the man strikes many blows.*

N. 1.—Here the object is already contained (or implied) in the verb, and its addition is optional. The accusative of the internal object is sometimes called the accusative of content. The object stands in apposition to the result of the verbal action. The effect produced by the verb is either (1) transient, when the object is a *nomen actionis*, and disappears with the operation of the verb, as in μάχην μάχεσθαι *to fight a battle*, or (2) permanent, and remains after the verbal action has ceased, as in τεῖχος τειχίζειν *to build a wall.* The latter form is the accusative of result (1578).

N. 2.—Almost any verb may take one of the varieties of the internal object.

b. The external object (object affected): ὁ ἀνὴρ τύπτει τὸν παῖδα *the man strikes the boy.*

N.—Here the object is not contained in the verb, but is necessary to explain or define the character of the action in question. The external object stands outside the verbal action.

1555. Many verbs may take an accusative either of the external or of the internal object: τέμνειν ὕλην *fell timber*, τέμνειν τὰς τρίχας *cut off the hair*, τέμνειν ὁδόν *open a road*, but σπονδὰς or ὅρκια τέμνειν, with a specialized verbal idea, *to make a treaty* by slaying a victim (pass. ὅρκια ἐτμήθη), τέμνειν ὁδόν *make one's way* (poet.), τειχίζειν χωρίον *fortify a place*, but τειχίζειν τεῖχος *build a wall.* Cp. E. Supp. 1060: A. νῑκῶσα νίκην τίνα; μαθεῖν χρῄζω σέθεν. B. πάσᾱς γυναῖκας, κτλ. A. *Victorious in what victory? This I would learn of thee.* B. *Over all women.* Here the construction shifts from the internal to the external object.

1556. The direct object of an active transitive verb becomes the subject of the passive: ὁ παῖς ὑπὸ τοῦ ἀνδρὸς τύπτεται *the boy is struck by the man.*

a. The object of a verb governing the genitive or dative as principal object may also become the subject of the passive (1340).

1557. In Greek many verbs are transitive the ordinary English equivalents of which are intransitive and require a preposition. So σιωπᾶν τι, σῑγᾶν τι *to keep silence about something.*

1558. Many verbs that are usually intransitive are also used transitively in Greek. Thus, ἀσεβεῖν *sin against*, δυσχεραίνειν *be disgusted at*, χαίρειν *rejoice at*, ἥδεσθαι *be pleased at*, δακρύειν *weep for.* Cp. 1595 b.

a. Poetical: ᾄσσειν *agitate*, περᾶν πόδα *pass on her way* E. Hec. 53, πλεῖν *sail*, κροταλίζειν *rattle along* (κροτεῖν *strike* Hdt. 6. 58), λάμπειν *make shine*, χορεύειν θεόν, ἑλίσσειν θεόν *celebrate the god by choruses, by dancing.*

1559. Many intransitive verbs are used transitively when compounded with a preposition, *e.g.* ἀναμάχεσθαι *fight over again.* — ἀπομάχεσθαι *drive off*, ἀποστρέφεσθαι *abandon*, ἀποχωρεῖν *leave.* — διαβαίνειν *pass over*, διαπλεῖν *sail across*, διεξέρχεσθαι *go through.* — εἰσιέναι *come into the mind*, εἰσπλεῖν *sail into.* — ἐκβαίνειν *pass*, ἐκτρέπεσθαι *get out of the way of*, ἐξαναχωρεῖν *shun*, ἐξίστασθαι *avoid.* — ἐπιστρατεύειν *march against.* — καταναυμαχεῖν *beat at sea*, καταπολεμεῖν *subdue completely*, καταπολῑτεύεσθαι *reduce by policy.* — μετέρχεσθαι *seek, pursue*, μετιέναι *go in quest of.* — παραβαίνειν *transgress.* — περιιέναι *go round*, περιίστασθαι *surround.* — προσοικεῖν *dwell in*, προσπαίζειν *sing in praise of.* — ὑπερβαίνειν *omit.* — ὑπεξέρχεσθαι *escape from.* — ὑπέρχεσθαι *fawn on*, ὑποδύεσθαι *withstand*, ὑποχωρεῖν *shun*, ὑφίστασθαι *withstand.*

1560. Conversely, many verbs that are usually transitive are used intransitively (with gen., dat., or with a preposition). Some of these are mentioned in 1591, 1592, 1595. Sometimes there is a difference in meaning, as ἀρέσκειν = *satisfy*, with accus., = *please*, with dat.

1561. The same verb may be used transitively or intransitively, often with little difference of signification. Cp. 1709. This is generally indicated in the treatment of the cases, *e.g.* αἰσθάνεσθαί τι or τινος *perceive something*, ἐνθῡμεῖσθαί τι or τινι *consider something*, μέμφεσθαί τινα or τινι *blame some one.*

1562. On δεῖ μοί τινος and δεῖ μέ τινος see 1400. With the inf. the accus. is usual (dat. and inf. X. A. 3. 4. 35). χρή μέ τινος is poetical; with the inf. χρή takes the accus. (except L. 28. 10, where some read δικαίους). (χρή is an old noun; cp. χρεώ, χρεία *need* and 793.)

INTERNAL OBJECT (OBJECT EFFECTED)

COGNATE ACCUSATIVE

1563. The cognate accusative is of two kinds, of which the second is an extension of the first.

1564. (I) The substantive in the accusative is of the *same origin* as the verb.

πολλὴν φλυᾱρίᾱν φλυᾱροῦντα *talking much nonsense* P. A. 19 c, ξυνέφυγε τὴν φυγὴν ταύτην *he shared in the recent exile* 21 a, τὴν ἐν Σαλαμῖνι ναυμαχίᾱν ναυμαχήσαντες *victorious in the sea-fight at Salamis* D. 59. 97, τὰς ὑποσχέσεις ἃς οὗτος ὑπισχνεῖτο *the promises which he made* 19. 47, ἡ αἰτίᾱ ἣν αἰτιῶνται *the charge they bring* Ant. 6. 27.

a. Sometimes the verb may be suppressed, as ἡμῖν μὲν εὐχὰς τάσδε (εὔχομαι) *for us these prayers* A. Ch. 142.

1565. The cognate accusative occurs even with adjectives of an intransitive character: μήτε τι σοφὸς ὢν τὴν ἐκείνων σοφίᾱν μήτε ἀμαθὴς τὴν ἀμαθίᾱν *being neither at all wise after the fashion of their wisdom nor ignorant after the fashion of their ignorance* P. A. 22 e, ἀτίμους ἐποίησαν ἀτῑμίᾱν τοιάνδε ὥστε κτλ.

they disfranchised them in such a way that, etc. T. 5. 34 (ἀτίμους ἐποίησαν = ἠτίμησαν, cp. 1598).

1566. **Passive**: πόλεμος ἐπολεμεῖτο *war was waged* X. H. 4. 8. 1.

1567. (II) The substantive in the accusative is of *kindred meaning* with the verb.

ἐξῆλθον ἄλλᾱς ὁδούς *they went forth on other expeditions* X. H. 1. 2. 17, τὸν ἱερὸν καλούμενον πόλεμον ἐστράτευσαν *they waged what is called the Sacred War* T. 1. 112, ἠσθένησε ταύτην τὴν νόσον *he fell ill of this disease* I. 19. 24, ἀνθρώπου φύσιν βλαστών *born to man's estate* S. Aj. 760.

1568. **Passive**: πόλεμος ἐταράχθη *war was stirred up* D. 18. 151.

1569. An extension of the cognate accusative appears in poetry with κεῖσθαι, στῆναι, καθίζειν and like verbs: τόπον, ὅντινα κεῖται *the place in which he is situated* S. Ph. 145, τί ἕστηκε πέτρᾱν; *why stands she on the rock?* E. Supp. 987, τρίποδα καθίζων *sitting on the tripod* E. Or. 956.

1570. An attributive word is usually necessary (but not in Hom.); otherwise the addition of the substantive to the verb would be tautologous. But the attribute is omitted:

a. When the nominal idea is specialized: φυλακὰς φυλάττειν *to stand sentry* X. A. 2. 6. 10, φόρον φέρειν *to pay tribute* 5. 5. 7.

b. When the substantive is restricted by the article: τὸν πόλεμον πολεμεῖν *to wage the present war* T. 8. 58, τὴν πομπὴν πέμπειν *to conduct the procession* 6. 56.

c. When a plural substantive denotes repeated occurrences: ἐτριηράρχησε τριηραρχίᾱς *he performed the duty of trierarch* D. 45. 85.

d. In various expressions: Ὀλύμπια νῑκᾶν *to win an Olympian victory* T. 1. 126, τὴν ναυμαχίᾱν νῑκῆσαι *to be victorious in the sea-fight* L. 19. 28, θύειν τὰ εὐαγγέλια *to offer a sacrifice in honour of good news* X. H. 1. 6. 37.

e. In poetry the use of a substantive to denote a special form of the action of the verb is much extended: στάζειν αἷμα *to drip* (drops of) *blood* S. Ph. 783, Ἄρη πνεῖν *to breathe war* A. Ag. 375, πῦρ δεδορκώς *looking* (a look of) *fire* τ 446. This use is common, especially in Aristophanes, with verbs signifying the *look* of another than the speaker: βλέπειν νᾶπυ *to look mustard* Eq. 631, βλέπειν ἀπιστίᾱν *to look unbelief* Com. fr. 1. 341 (No. 309); cp. "looked his faith": Holmes.

1571. The substantive without an attribute is (rarely) added to the verb as a more emphatic form of statement: λῆρον ληρεῖν *to talk sheer nonsense* Ar. Pl. 517, ὕβριν ὑβρίζειν *to insult grievously* E. H. F. 708. Often in Euripides.

1572. The substantive may be omitted, leaving only the adjectival attribute: παῖσον διπλῆν (*scil.* πληγήν) *strike twice* (a double blow) S. El. 1415, τοῦτον ἀνέκραγον ὡς ὀλίγᾱς (*scil.* πληγὰς) παίσειεν *they called out that he had dealt him* too (1063) *few* blows X. A. 5. 8. 12. Cp. 1028.

1573. Usually an adjective, pronoun, or pronominal adjective is treated as a neuter substantive. Cp. μεγάλ' ἁμαρτάνειν *to commit grave errors* D. 5. 5 with μέγιστα ἁμαρτήματα ἁμαρτάνουσι P. G. 525 d. The singular adjective is used in certain common phrases in prose, but is mainly poetical; the plural is ordinarily used in prose.

ἡδὺ γελᾶν poet. (= *ἡδὺν γέλωτα γελᾶν*) *to laugh sweetly*, *μέγα* (*ψεῦδος*) *ψεύδεται he is a great liar*, *μέγα φρονήσᾱς ἐπὶ τούτῳ highly elated at this* X. A. 3. 1. 27, *μεῖζον φρονεῖ he is too proud* 5. 6. 8, *τὰ τῶν Ἑλλήνων φρονεῖν to be on the side of the Greeks* D. 14. 34, *μέγιστον ἐδύναντο had the greatest influence* L. 30. 14, *δεινὰ ὑβρίζειν to maltreat terribly* X. A. 6. 4. 2, *ταὐτὰ ἐπρεσβεύομεν we fulfilled our mission as ambassadors in the same way* D. 19. 32, *τί βούλεται ἡμῖν χρῆσθαι; what use does he wish to make of us?* X. A. 1. 3. 18 (= *τίνα βούλεται χρείᾱν χρῆσθαι*, cp. *χρῆσθαί τινι χρείαν* P. L. 868 b).

1574. **Passive**: *τοῦτο οὐκ ἐψεύσθησαν they were not deceived in this* X. A. 2. 2. 13, *ταῦτα οὐδεὶς ἂν πεισθείη no one would be persuaded of this* P. L. 836 d.

1575. For a cognate accusative in conjunction with a second object, see 1620.

1576. Note the expressions *δικάζειν δίκην decide a case*, *δικάζεσθαι δίκην τινί go to law with somebody*, *διώκειν γραφήν τινα indict somebody*, *φεύγειν δίκην τινός be put on one's trial for something; γράφεσθαί τινα γραφήν indict one for a public offence*, *φεύγειν γραφήν be put on one's trial for a public offence.* Also *ἀγωνίζεσθαι στάδιον* (= *ἀγῶνα σταδίου*) *be a contestant in the race-course*, *νῑκᾶν στάδιον be victorious in the race-course*, *νῑκᾶν δίκην win a case*, *νῑκᾶν γνώμην carry a resolution* (pass. *γνώμην ἡττᾶσθαι*), *ὀφλεῖν δίκην lose a case.*

1577. The (rarer) dative (*φόβῳ ταρβεῖν*, *βιαίῳ θανάτῳ ἀποθνῄσκειν*, *φεύγειν φυγῇ*) expresses the cause (1517), manner (1513), or means (1507).

ACCUSATIVE OF RESULT

1578. The accusative of result denotes the effect enduring after the verbal action has ceased.

ἕλκος οὐτάσαι to smite (and thus *make*) *a wound* E 361 (so *οὐλὴν ἐλαύνειν* ψ 74), *πρεσβεύειν τὴν εἰρήνην to negotiate the peace* (go as ambassadors (*πρέσβεις*) to make the peace) D. 19. 134, but *πρεσβεύειν πρεσβείᾱν to go on an embassy* Dinarchus 1. 16, *νόμισμα κόπτειν to coin money* Hdt. 3. 56, *σπονδᾱ́ς*, or *ὅρκια*, *τέμνειν* (1555).

1579. Verbs signifying *to effect anything* (*αἴρειν raise*, *αὔξειν exalt*, *διδάσκειν teach*, *τρέφειν rear*, *παιδεύειν train*) show the result of their action upon a substantive or adjective predicate to the direct object: *σὲ Θῆβαί γ' οὐκ ἐπαίδευσαν κακόν Thebes did not train thee to be base* S. O. C. 919, *τοῦτον τρέφειν τε καὶ αὔξειν μέγαν to nurse and exalt him into greatness* P. R. 565 c, *ἐποικοδομήσαντες αὐτὸ ὑψηλότερον raising it higher* T. 7. 4. Such predicate nouns are called *proleptic.* Passive: *μέγας ἐκ μῑκροῦ Φίλιππος ηὔξηται Philip has grown from a mean to be a mighty person* D. 9. 21. Cp. 1613.

ACCUSATIVE OF EXTENT

1580. The accusative denotes extent in space and time.

1581. **Space.** — The accusative denotes the space or way *over which* an action is extended, and the measure of the space traversed.

ἄγειν (*στρατιᾱ́ν*) *στενὰς ὁδούς to lead an army over narrow roads* X. C. 1. 6. 43, *ἐξελαύνει σταθμοὺς τρεῖς, παρασάγγᾱς εἴκοσι καὶ δύο he advances three stages, twenty-*

two parasangs X. A. 1. 2. 5, ἀπέχει ἡ Πλάταια τῶν Θηβῶν σταδίους ἑβδομήκοντα *Plataea is seventy stades distant from Thebes* T. 2. 5.

a. This use is analogous to the cognate accusative after verbs of motion (ἐξόδους ἐξελθεῖν, πλεῖν θάλατταν).

1582. Time. — The accusative denotes extent of time.

ἔμεινεν ἡμέρᾱς ἑπτά *he remained seven days* X. A. 1. 2. 6, ξυμμαχίᾱν ἐποιήσαντο ἑκατὸν ἔτη *they made an alliance for a hundred years* T. 3. 114.

1583. The accusative of time implies that the action of the verb covers the *entire* period. When emphasis is laid on the uninterrupted duration of an action, παρά with the accusative (1692. 3. b) and διά with the genitive (1685. 1. b) are used. The accusative of time is rarely employed where the dative (1540) is properly in place: τήνδε τὴν ἡμέρᾱν Aes. 3. 7.

1584. Duration of life may be expressed by γεγονώς: ἔτη γεγονὼς ἑβδομήκοντα *seventy years old* P. A. 17 d. (Also by εἶναι and the genitive, 1327.)

1585. To mark (a) *how long* a situation has lasted or (b) how much time has elapsed since something happened, an ordinal is used without the article, but often with the addition of οὑτοσί. The current day or year is included. Thus (a) τὴν μητέρα τελευτήσᾱσαν τρίτον ἔτος τουτὶ *my mother who died two years ago* L. 24. 6, ἐπιδεδήμηκε τρίτην ἤδη ἡμέρᾱν *he has been in the city since day before yesterday* P. Pr. 309 d. (b) ἀπηγγέλθη Φίλιππος τρίτον ἢ τέταρτον ἔτος τουτὶ Ἡραῖον τεῖχος πολιορκῶν *this is the third or fourth year since it was announced that Philip was besieging fort Heraeum* D. 3. 4.

1586. On the accusative of extent in degree, see 1609. With a comparative we find πολύ and ὀλίγον as well as πολλῷ and ὀλίγῳ (1514); and always τί, τὶ, οὐδέν with the comparative.

1587. Time and degree are often expressed by prepositions with the accusative. See Prepositions under ἀμφί, ἀνά, διά, ἐπί, κατά, παρά, πρός, ὑπό.

TERMINAL ACCUSATIVE (IN POETRY)

1588. In poetry after verbs of motion the accusative may be used without a preposition to express the goal.

ἄστυ Καδμεῖον μολών *having come to the city of Cadmus* S. O. T. 35, πέμψομέν νιν Ἑλλάδα *we will convey her to Greece* E. Tro. 883. Of *persons* in Hom. (especially with ἱκνέομαι, ἵκω, ἱκάνω = *reach*) and in the lyric parts of the drama: μνηστῆρας ἀφίκετο *came unto the suitors* α 332. Cp. "arrived our coast": Shakesp. In Hdt. 9. 26 φαμὲν ἡμέας ἱκνέεσθαι means *we declare that it befits us.*

1589. The limit of motion is also expressed by -δε (ἄστυδε Hom., in prose, Ἀθήναζε = Ἀθήνᾱς + δε; χαμᾶζε or χαμάζε = χαμᾱς + δε, cp. χαμα-ί; οἴκαδε) and, regularly in prose, by εἰς, ἐπί, παρά, πρός, ὡς (with a person) with the accusative.

EXTERNAL OBJECT (OBJECT AFFECTED)

1590. Of the many transitive verbs taking this accusative the following deserve mention:

1591. (I) *To do anything to* or *say anything of* a person.

a. εὖ (καλῶς) ποιεῖν, δρᾶν (rarely with πράττειν), εὐεργετεῖν, ὀνινάναι, ὠφελεῖν (also with dat.), θεραπεύειν, κακῶς ποιεῖν, κακοῦν, κακουργεῖν, βλάπτειν, ἀδικεῖν, ὑβρίζειν, βιάζεσθαι, ἀμείβεσθαι *requite*, τῑμωρεῖσθαι *punish*, λῡμαίνεσθαι (also with dat.), λωβᾶσθαι (also with dat.).

b. εὖ (καλῶς) λέγειν, εὐλογεῖν, κολακεύειν, θωπεύειν, προσκυνεῖν, κακῶς λέγειν, κακολογεῖν, κακηγορεῖν, λοιδορεῖν.

1592. συμφέρειν and λῡσιτελεῖν *profit*, βοηθεῖν *help*, λοιδορεῖσθαι *rail at* take the dat., ἀδικεῖν *injure* and ὑβρίζειν *insult* also take εἴς τινα or πρός τινα.

1593. εὖ (κακῶς) ἀκούειν, πάσχειν are used as the passives of εὖ (κακῶς) λέγειν, ποιεῖν. Cp. 1752.

1594. Many of the above-mentioned verbs take a double accusative (1622).

1595. (II) Verbs expressing emotion and its manifestations.

a. φοβεῖσθαι, δεδιέναι, τρεῖν, ἐκπλήττεσθαι, καταπλήττεσθαι *fear*, πτήσσειν *crouch before*, εὐλαβεῖσθαι *beware of*, θαρρεῖν *have no fear of* (have confidence in), αἰδεῖσθαι *stand in awe of*, αἰσχύνεσθαι *feel shame before*, δυσχεραίνειν *be disgusted at*, ἐλεεῖν *pity*, πενθεῖν, θρηνεῖν, δακρύειν, κλάειν (κλαίειν) *lament*, *weep over*.

b. χαίρειν *rejoice at* and ἥδεσθαι *be pleased to hear* take the accus. of a person only in the poets and only with a predicate participle (2100). αἰσχύνεσθαι, χαίρειν, ἥδεσθαι, δυσχεραίνειν usually take the dat. in prose. θαρρεῖν may take the instr. dat. (Hdt. 3. 76).

1596. (III) Verbs of *swearing*.

ὀμνύναι *swear by* (τοὺς θεούς, pass. Ζεὺς ὀμώμοται) and *swear to* (τὸν ὅρκον, pass. ὁ ὅρκος ὀμώμοται). So ἐπιορκεῖν *swear falsely by*.

a. ὀμνύναι τοὺς θεούς may be an abbreviation of ὀμνύναι ὅρκον (internal object) τῶν θεῶν.

b. The accusative is used in asseverations with the adverbs of swearing μά, οὐ μά, ναὶ μά, νή.

Nay, by Zeus: μὰ (τὸν) Δία, οὐ μὰ (τὸν) Δία.
Yea, by Zeus: ναὶ μὰ (τὸν) Δία, νὴ (τὸν) Δία.

μά is negative, except when preceded by ναί. μά may stand alone when a negative precedes (often in a question) or when a negative follows in the next clause: μὰ τὸν Ἀπόλλω, οὔκ Ar. Thesm. 269. μά is sometimes omitted after οὐ, and after ναί: οὐ τὸν Ὄλυμπον S. O. T. 1088, ναὶ τὰν κόρᾱν Ar. Vesp. 1438.

c. The name of the deity may be omitted in Attic under the influence of sudden scrupulousness: μὰ τὸν — οὐ σύ γε *not you, by* — P. G. 466 e.

1597. (IV) Various other verbs.

φεύγειν *flee from*, ἀποδιδράσκειν *escape from*, ἐνεδρεύειν *lie in wait for*, φθάνειν *anticipate*, φυλάττεσθαι *guard oneself against*, ἀμύνεσθαι *defend oneself against*, λανθάνειν *escape the notice of*, μένειν *wait for*, ἐκλείπειν and ἐπιλείπειν *give out*, *fail* (τὸ στράτευμα ὁ σῖτος ἐπέλιπε *corn failed the army* X. A. 1. 5. 6).

1598. The accusative is rarely found after verbal nouns and adjectives, and in periphrastic expressions equivalent to a transitive verb. (This usage is post-Homeric and chiefly poetical.)

χοᾶς προπομπός (= προπέμπουσα) *escorting the libations* A. Ch. 23, τὰ μετέωρα φροντιστής *a speculator about things above the earth* P. A. 18 b, ἐπιστήμονες ἦσαν τὰ προσήκοντα *they were acquainted with their duties* X. C. 3. 3. 9, πόλεμος ἄπορα πόριμος *war providing difficulties* (things for which there is no provision) A. Pr. 904, πολλὰ συνίστωρ (a house) *full of guilty secrets* A. Ag. 1090, σὲ φύξιμος *able to escape thee* S. Ant. 787; ἔξαρνός εἰμι (= ἐξαρνοῦμαι) τὰ ἐρωτώμενα *say 'no' to the question* P. Charm. 158 c, τεθνᾶσι τῷ δέει τοὺς ἀποστόλους *they are in mortal fear of the envoys* D. 4. 45; other cases 1612.

1599. Elliptical Accusative. — The accusative is sometimes used elliptically.

οὗτος, ὦ σέ τοι (*scil.* καλῶ) *ho! you there, I am calling you!* Ar. Av. 274, μή, πρός σε θεῶν τλῇς με προδοῦναι (= μή, πρὸς θεῶν σε αἰτῶ) *do not, I implore thee by the gods, have the heart to leave me!* E. Alc. 275, μή μοι πρόφασιν (*scil.* πάρεχε) *no excuse!* Ar. Ach. 345. Cp. 946.

FREE USES OF THE ACCUSATIVE

ACCUSATIVE OF RESPECT

1600. To verbs denoting a state, and to adjectives, an accusative may be added to denote a thing *in respect to which* the verb or adjective is limited.

a. The accusative usually expresses a local relation or the instrument. The word restricted by the accusative usually denotes *like* or *similar to*, *good* or *better*, *bad* or *worse*, a physical or a mental quality, or an emotion.

1601. The accusative of respect is employed

a. Of the parts of the body: ὁ ἄνθρωπος τὸν δάκτυλον ἀλγεῖ *the man has a pain in his finger* P. R. 462 d, τυφλὸς τά τ' ὦτα τόν τε νοῦν τά τ' ὄμματ' εἶ *blind art thou in ears, and mind, and eyes* S. O. T. 371, πόδας ὠκὺς Ἀχιλλεύς Hom.

N. — The accusative of the *part* in apposition to the *whole* (985) belongs here, as is seen by the passive. Cp. τὸν πλῆξ' αὐχένα *him he smote on the neck* Λ 240 (βάλε θοῦρον Ἄρηα κατ' αὐχένα Φ 406) with βέβληαι κενεῶνα *thou art smitten in the abdomen* E 284.

b. Of qualities and attributes (nature, form, size, name, birth, number, etc.): διαφέρει γυνὴ ἀνδρὸς τὴν φύσιν *woman differs from man in nature* P. R. 453 b, οὐδὲ ἔοικεν θνητὰς ἀθανάτῃσι δέμας καὶ εἶδος ἐρίζειν *nor is it seemly that mortal women should rival the immortals in form and appearance* ε 213, ποταμός, Κύδνος ὄνομα, εὖρος δύο πλέθρων *a river, Cydnus by name, two plethra in width* X. A. 1. 2. 23 (so with ὕψος, βάθος, μέγεθος), πλῆθος ὡς δισχίλιοι *about two thousand in number* 4. 2. 2, λέξον ὅστις εἶ γένος *tell me of what race thou art* E. Bacch. 460.

c. Of the sphere in general: δεινοὶ μάχην *terrible in battle* A. Pers. 27, γένεσθε τὴν διάνοιαν *transfer yourselves in thought* Aes. 3. 153, τὸ μὲν ἐπ' ἐμοὶ οἴχομαι, τὸ δ' ἐπὶ σοὶ σέσωσμαι *so far as I myself was concerned I was lost, but through you am saved* X. C. 5. 4. 11. Often of indefinite relations: πάντα κακός *base in all things* S. O. T. 1421, ταῦτα ἀγαθὸς ἕκαστος ἡμῶν, ἅπερ σοφός, ἃ δὲ ἀμαθής, ταῦτα δὲ κακός *each one of us is good in matters in which he is skilled, but bad in those in which he is ignorant* P. Lach. 194 d.

1602. Very rarely after substantives: χεῖρας αἰχμητής *a warrior valiant with (thy) arm* π 242, νεᾶνίαι τὰς ὄψεις *youths by their appearance* L. 10. 29.

1603. For the acccusative of respect the instrumental dative (1516) is also employed, and also the prepositions εἰς, κατά, πρός, *e.g.* διαφέρειν ἀρετῇ or εἰς ἀρετήν.

1604. Not to be confused with the accusative of respect is the accusative after intransitive adjectives (1565) or after the passives of 1632.

1605. The accusative of respect is probably in its origin, at least in part, an accusative of the internal object.

ADVERBIAL ACCUSATIVE

1606. Many accusatives marking limitations of the verbal action serve the same function as adverbs.

1607. Most of these adverbial accusatives are accusatives of the internal object: thus, in τέλος δὲ εἶπε *but at last he said*, τέλος is to be regarded as standing in apposition to an unexpressed object of the verb — *words, which were the end.* Many adverbial accusatives are thus accusatives in apposition (991) and some are accusatives of respect (1600). It is impossible to apportion all cases among the varieties of the accusatives; many may be placed under different heads. The use of adjectives as adverbs (μέγα πλούσιος *very rich*) is often derived from the cognate accusative with verbs (μέγα πλουτεῖν).

1608. Manner. — τρόπον τινά *in some way*, τίνα τρόπον *in what way?* τόνδε (τοῦτον) τὸν τρόπον *in this way*, πάντα τρόπον *in every way* (also παντὶ τρόπῳ), τὴν ταχίστην (ὁδόν) *in the quickest way*, τὴν εὐθεῖαν (ὁδόν) *straightforward*, προῖκα, δωρεάν *gratis* (1616), δίκην *after the fashion of* (δίκην τοξότου *like an archer* P. L. 705 e), πρόφασιν *in pretence* (ἔπλεε πρόφασιν ἐπ᾽ Ἑλλησπόντου *he sailed professedly for the Hellespont* Hdt. 5. 33), χάριν *for the sake of* (lit. *favour*): οὐ τὴν Ἀθηναίων χάριν ἐστρατεύοντο *did not engage in the expedition out of good will to the Athenians* Hdt. 5. 99, τοῦ χάριν *for what reason?* Ar. Plut. 53, τὴν σὴν ἥκω χάριν *for thy sake I have come* S. Ph. 1413. Cp. 993.

1609. Measure and Degree. — μέγα, μεγάλα *greatly*, πολύ, πολλά *much*, τὸ πολύ, τὰ πολλά *for the most part*, ὅσον *as much as*, οὐδέν, μηδέν *not at all*, τοσοῦτον *so much*, τὶ *somewhat*, ἀρχήν or τὴν ἀρχήν *at all* with οὐ or μή (ἐν τῷ παραχρῆμα οὐκ ἔστιν ἀρχὴν ὀρθῶς βουλεύεσθαι *it is utterly impossible to deliberate correctly offhand* Ant. 5. 73).

1610. Motive. — τί *why?* τοῦτο, ταῦτα *for this reason* (cognate accus.): τί ἦλθες *quid (cur) venisti* = τίνα ἴξιν ἦλθες; τοῦτο χαίρω (= ταύτην τὴν χαρὰν χαίρω) *therefore I rejoice*, αὐτὰ ταῦτα ἥκω *for this very reason have I come* P. Pr. 310 e, τοῦτ᾽ ἄχθεσθε *for this reason you are vexed* X. A. 3. 2. 20.

1611. Time and Succession (1582): τὸ νῦν *now*, τὸ πάλαι *of old*, πρότερον *before*, τὸ πρότερον *the former time*, πρῶτον *first*, τὸ κατ᾽ ἀρχάς *in the beginning*, τὸ πρῶτον *in the first place*, τὸ τελευταῖον *in the last place* (for τὸ δεύτερον in a series use ἔπειτα or ἔπειτα δέ), τὸ λοιπόν *for the future*, ἀκμήν *at the point, just*, καιρόν *in season*.

TWO ACCUSATIVES WITH ONE VERB

1612. A compound expression, consisting of the accusative of an abstract substantive and ποιεῖσθαι, τίθεσθαι, ἔχειν, etc., is often treated as a simple verb; and, when transitive, governs the accusative: τὴν χώρᾱν καταδρομαῖς λείᾱν ἐποιεῖτο (= ἐλῄζετο) *he ravaged the country by his incursions* T. 8. 41, Ἰλίου φθορᾶς ψήφους ἔθεντο (= ἐψηφίσαντο) *they voted for the destruction of Ilium* A. Ag. 814, μομφὴν ἔχω ἓν μὲν πρῶτά σοι (= ἓν μέμφομαι) *I blame thee first for one thing* E. Or. 1069, τὰ δ' ἐν μέσῳ λῆστιν ἴσχεις (= ἐπιλανθάνει) *what lies between thou hast no memory of* S. O. C. 583. See 1598. So with other periphrases in poetry: τέκνα μηκύνω λόγον (= μακρότερον προσφωνῶ) *I speak at length to my children* S. O. C. 1120, εἰ δέ μ' ὧδ' ἀεὶ λόγους ἐξῆρχες (= ἦρχου λέγειν) *if thou didst always (begin to) address me thus* S. El. 556.

EXTERNAL OBJECT AND PREDICATE ACCUSATIVE

1613. Verbs meaning *to appoint, call, choose, consider, make, name, show*, and the like, may take a second accusative as a predicate to the direct object.

στρατηγὸν αὐτὸν ἀπέδειξε *he appointed him general* X. A. 1. 1. 2, πατέρα ἐμὲ ἐκαλεῖτε *you were wont to call me father* 7. 6. 38, αἱρεῖσθαι αὐτὸν τὸν Ἰνδῶν βασιλέᾱ δικαστήν *to choose the king of the Indians himself to be arbitrator* X. C. 2. 4. 8, οὐ γὰρ δίκαιον οὔτε τοὺς κακοὺς μάτην χρηστοὺς νομίζειν οὔτε τοὺς χρηστοὺς κακούς *for it is not just to consider bad men good at random, or good men bad* S. O. T. 609, Τῑμόθεον στρατηγὸν ἐχειροτόνησαν *they elected Timotheus general* X. H. 6. 2. 11, τὴν σῑγήν σου ξυγχώρησιν θήσω *I shall consider your silence as consent* P. Crat. 435 b, ἑαυτὸν δεσπότην πεποίηκεν *he has made himself master* X. C. 1. 3. 18, ἐὰν ἐμὲ σὸν θεράποντα ποιήσῃ *if you make me your servant* X. O. 7. 42, εἰς τοὺς Ἕλληνας σαυτὸν σοφιστὴν παρέχων *showing yourself a sophist before the Greeks* P. Pr. 312 a, εὐμαθῆ πάντα παρέχειν *to render everything easy to learn* X. O. 20. 14. Cp. 1579.

1614. The absence of the article generally distinguishes the predicate noun from the object: ἐπηγγέλλετο τοὺς κόλακας τοὺς αὑτοῦ πλουσιωτάτους τῶν πολῑτῶν ποιήσειν *he promised to make his flatterers the richest of the citizens* L. 28. 4.

1615. Especially in Plato and Herodotus, after verbs signifying *to name, to call*, the predicate noun may be connected with the external object by (a redundant) εἶναι (911); σοφιστὴν ὀνομάζουσι τὸν ἄνδρα εἶναι *they call the man a sophist* P. Pr. 311 e, ἐπωνυμίᾱν ἔχει σμῑκρός τε καὶ μέγας εἶναι *he is called both short and tall* P. Ph. 102 c. This is due to the analogy of verbs signifying *to think* or *say* (1041).

1616. A predicate accusative may stand in apposition to the object: ἔδωκα δωρειᾱ̀ν τὰ λύτρα *I gave* them *the price of their ransom as a free gift* D. 19. 170.

1617. This use is the source of many adverbial accusatives (993, 1606 ff.).

1618. **Passive**: both the object and the predicate accusative of the active construction become nominative (1743) in the passive construction: αὐτὸς στρατηγὸς ᾑρέθη *he himself was chosen general* L. 12. 65, αὐτοὶ νομοθέται κληθήσονται *they shall themselves be called lawgivers* P. L. 681 d.

INTERNAL AND EXTERNAL OBJECT WITH ONE VERB

1619. Many verbs take both an internal and an external object.

1620. The external object refers to a person, the internal object (cognate accusative, 1563 ff.) refers to a thing. Here the internal object stands in closer relation to the verb.

ὁ πόλεμος ἀείμνηστον παιδείᾱν αὐτοὺς ἐπαίδευσε *the war taught them a lesson they will hold in everlasting remembrance* Aes. 3. 148, τοσοῦτον ἔχθος ἐχθαίρω σε *I hate thee with such an hate* S. El. 1034, Μέλητός με ἐγράψατο τὴν γραφὴν ταύτην *Meletus brought this accusation against me* P. A. 19 b, ἕλκος, τό μιν βάλε *the wound that he dealt him* E 795 (1578), Μιλτιάδης ὁ τὴν ἐν Μαραθῶνι μάχην τοὺς βαρβάρους νῑκήσᾱς *Miltiades who won the battle at Marathon over the barbarians* Aes. 3. 181, τὸν ἄνδρα τύπτειν τὰς πληγάς *to strike the man the blows* Ant. 4. γ. 1, καλοῦσί με τοῦτο τὸ ὄνομα *they give me this appellation* X. O. 7. 3.

1621. Passive (1747): πᾶσαν θεραπείᾱν θεραπευόμενος *receiving every manner of service* P. Phae. 255 a, τύπτεσθαι πεντήκοντα πληγάς *to be struck fifty blows* Aes. 1. 139, ἡ κρίσις, ἣν ἐκρίθη *the sentence that was pronounced* upon him L. 13. 50, τὰς μάχᾱς, ὅσᾱς Πέρσαι ἡττήθησαν ἐῶ *I omit the battles in which the Persians were defeated* I. 4. 145, ὄνομα ἓν κεκλημένοι Σικελιῶται *called by the one name of Sicilians* T. 4. 64.

1622. So with verbs signifying *to do anything to* or *say anything of* a person (1591): πολλὰ ἀγαθὰ ὑμᾶς ἐποίησεν *he did you much good* L. 5. 3, ταυτί με ποιοῦσι *that's what they are doing to me* Ar. Vesp. 696, τὰ τοιαῦτα ἐπαινῶ Ἀγησίλᾱον *I praise Agesilaus for such merits* X. Ages. 10. 1, τοὺς Κορινθίους πολλά τε καὶ κακὰ ἔλεγε *he said many bad things about the Corinthians* Hdt. 8. 61. For the accusative of the thing, εὖ (καλῶς), κακῶς may be substituted; and εἰς and πρός with the accusative occur.

1623. The accusative of the person may depend on the idea expressed by the combination of verb and accusative of the thing (1612); as in τοὺς πολεμίους εἰργάσθαι κακά *to have done harm to the enemy* L. 21. 8 (here εἰργάσθαι of itself does not mean *to do anything to* a person).

1624. When the dative of the person is used, something is done *for* (1474), not *to* him: πάντα ἐποίησαν τοῖς ἀποθανοῦσιν *they rendered all honours to the dead* X. A. 4. 2. 23. εἰς or πρός with the accusative is also employed.

1625. Passive of 1622: ὅσα ἄλλα ἡ πόλις ἠδικεῖτο *all the other wrongs that the State has suffered* D. 18. 70.

1626. Verbs of *dividing* (νέμειν, κατανέμειν, διαιρεῖν, τέμνειν) may take two accusatives, one of the thing divided, the other of its parts (cognate accus.). Thus, Κῦρος τὸ στράτευμα κατένειμε δώδεκα μέρη *Cyrus divided the army into twelve divisions* X. C. 7. 5. 13. εἰς or κατά may be used with the accusative of the parts.

1627. Passive: διῄρηται ἡ ἀγορὰ τέτταρα μέρη *the Agora is divided into four parts* X. C. 1. 2. 4. εἰς and κατά may be used with the accusative of the parts.

DOUBLE OBJECT WITH VERBS SIGNIFYING TO ASK, DEMAND, ETC.

1628. Verbs signifying *to ask, clothe* or *unclothe, conceal, demand, deprive, persuade, remind, teach,* take two objects in the accusative, one of a person, the other of a thing.

οὐ τοῦτ' ἐρωτῶ σε *that's not the question I'm asking you* Ar. Nub. 641; χιτῶνα τὸν ἑαυτοῦ ἐκεῖνον ἠμφίεσε *he put his own tunic on him* X. C. 1. 3. 17, ἰδοὺ δ' Ἀπόλλων αὐτὸς ἐκδύων ἐμὲ χρηστηρίᾱν ἐσθῆτα *lo Apollo himself divests me of my oracular garb* A. Ag. 1269; τὴν θυγατέρα ἔκρυπτε τὸν θάνατον τοῦ ἀνδρός *he concealed from his daughter her husband's death* L. 32. 7; Κῦρον αἰτεῖν πλοῖα *to ask Cyrus for boats* X. A. 1. 3. 14, ὡς ἐγώ ποτέ τινα ἢ ἐπρᾱξάμην μισθὸν ἢ ᾔτησα *that I ever exacted or asked pay of any one* P. A. 31 c; τούτων τὴν τῑμὴν ἀποστερεῖ με *he deprives me of the value of these things* D. 28. 13; ὑμᾶς τοῦτο οὐ πείθω *I cannot persuade you of this* P. A. 37 a; ἀναμνήσω ὑμᾶς καὶ τοὺς κινδύνους *I will remind you of the dangers also* X. A. 3. 2. 11; οὐδείς ἐδίδαξέ με ταύτην τὴν τέχνην *nobody taught me this art* X. O. 19. 16.

1629. Both person and thing are equally governed by the verb. The accusative of the person is the external object; the accusative of the thing is sometimes a cognate accusative (internal accusative).

1630. Some of these verbs also take the genitive or dative, or employ prepositions. Thus ἐρωτᾶν τινα περί τινος, αἰτεῖν (αἰτεῖσθαί) τι παρά τινος, ἀποστερεῖν or ἀφαιρεῖσθαί τινά τινος (τινός τι) (1394), or τινί τι (1483); ἀναμιμνῄσκειν τινά τινος (1356); παιδεύειν τινά τινι or τινὰ εἰς (or πρός) with the accusative.

1631. The poets employ this construction with verbs of *cleansing* (a form of *depriving*): χρόα νίζετο ἅλμην *he was washing the brine from his skin* ζ 224, αἷμα κάθηρον Σαρπηδόνα *cleanse the blood from Sarpedon* Π 667. And with other verbs (in tragedy), *e.g.* τῑμωρεῖσθαι *avenge on,* μετελθεῖν *seek to avenge on,* μετιέναι *execute judgment on,* ἐπισκήπτειν *charge.*

1632. **Passive** (1747): ὑπὸ βασιλέως πεπρᾱγμένος τοὺς φόρους *having had the tribute demanded of him by the king* T. 8. 5, ὅσοι ἵππους ἀπεστέρηνται *all who have been deprived of their horses* X. C. 6. 1. 12, οὐκ ἐπείθοντο τὰ ἐσαγγελθέντα *they would not credit the news* Hdt. 8. 81, μουσικὴν παιδευθείς *having been instructed in music* P. Menex. 236 a (here μουσικῇ is possible), οὐδὲν ἄλλο διδάσκεται ἄνθρωπος ἢ ἐπιστήμην *man is taught nothing else except knowledge* P. Men. 87 c.

1633. The accusative of extent (1580) is freely used in the same sentence with other accusatives, as ὑπερενεγκόντες τὸν Λευκαδίων ἰσθμὸν τὰς ναῦς *having hauled the ships across the isthmus of Leucas* T. 3. 81.

On the accusative of the whole and part, see 985; on the accusative subject of the infinitive, see 1972 ff.; on the accusative absolute, see 2076. See also under *Anacoluthon.*

TWO VERBS WITH A COMMON OBJECT

1634. The case of an object common to two verbs is generally that demanded by the nearer: οὐ δεῖ τοῖς παιδοτρίβαις ἐγκαλεῖν οὐδ' ἐκβάλλειν ἐκ τῶν πόλεων *we must not accuse the trainer or banish him from the cities* P. G. 460 d.

a. The farther verb may contain the main idea: ἐπιτῑμᾷ καὶ ἀποδοκιμάζει τισί *he censures some and rejects them at the scrutiny* L. 6. 33.

1635. The construction is usually ruled by the participle, not by the finite verb, when they have a common object but different constructions, and especially when the object stands nearer the participle: τούτῳ δοὺς ἡγεμόνας πορεύεσθαι ἐκέλευσεν ἡσύχως *having given him guides he ordered him to proceed quietly* X. C. 5. 3. 53; and when the common object stands between, as προσπεσόντες τοῖς πρώτοις τρέπουσι *falling upon the foremost they put them to flight* T. 7. 53.

a. Sometimes the finite verb regulates the construction, as καλέσᾱς παρεκελεύετο τοῖς Ἕλλησι *he summoned the Greeks and exhorted them* X. A. 1. 8. 11.

PREPOSITIONS

1636. Prepositions define the relations of a substantival notion to the predicate.

a. All prepositions seem to have been adverbs originally and mostly adverbs of place; as adverbs they are case-forms. Several are locatives, as περί.

1637. The prepositions express primarily notions of space, then notions of time, and finally are used in figurative relations to denote cause, agency, means, manner, etc. Attic often differs from the Epic in using the prepositions to denote metaphorical relations. The prepositions define the character of the verbal action and set forth the relations of an oblique case to the predicate with greater precision than is possible for the cases without a preposition. Thus, μετὰ δὲ μνηστῆρσιν ἔειπε *he spake among the suitors* ρ 467 specifies the meaning with greater certainty than μνηστῆρσιν ἔειπε. So ὁ Ἑλλήνων φόβος may mean *the fear felt by the Greeks* or *the fear caused by the Greeks;* but with ἐξ or παρά (cp. X. A. 1. 2. 18, Lyc. 130) the latter meaning is stated unequivocally. The use of a preposition often serves to show how a construction with a composite case (1279) is to be regarded (genitive or ablative; dative, instrumental, or locative).

1638. Development of the Use of Prepositions. —

a. Originally the preposition was a free adverb limiting the meaning of the verb but not directly connected with it: κατ' ἄρ' ἕζετο *down he sate him* A 101. In this use the preposition may be called a 'preposition-adverb.'

b. The preposition-adverb was also often used in sentences in which an oblique case depended directly on the verb without regard to the preposition-adverb. Here the case is independent of the preposition-adverb, as in βλεφάρων ἄπο δάκρυα πίπτει *from her eyelids, away, tears fall* ξ 129. Here βλεφάρων is ablatival genitive and is not *governed* by ἀπό, which serves merely to define the relation between verb and noun.

c. Gradually the preposition-adverb was brought into closer connection either (1) with the verb, whence arose compounds such as ἀποπίπτειν, or (2) with the noun, the preposition-adverb having freed itself from its adverbial relation to the verb. In this stage, which is that of Attic prose, the noun was felt to depend on the preposition. Hence arose many syntactical changes, *e.g.*

the accusative of the limit of motion (1588) was abandoned in prose for the preposition with the accusative.

Prepositions have three uses.

1639. (I) Prepositions appear as adverbs defining the action of verbs.

1640. The preposition-adverb usually precedes the verb, from which it is often separated in Homer by nouns and other words: ἡμῖν ἀπὸ λοιγὸν ἀμῦναι *to ward off destruction from* (for) *us* A 67, πρὸ γὰρ ἧκε θεά *the goddess sent* her *forth* A 195, ἔχεν κάτα γαῖα *the earth held* him *fast* B 699.

1641. So, as links connecting sentences, πρὸς δὲ καί and καὶ πρός *and besides*, ἐπὶ δέ *and besides*, μετὰ δέ *and next, thereupon* (both in Hdt.), ἐν δέ *and among the number* (Hdt.).

1642. The verb (usually ἐστί or εἰσί, rarely εἰμί) may be omitted: οὐ γάρ τις μέτα τοῖος ἀνήρ *for no such man is among them* φ 93. Cp. 944.

1643. The preposition-adverb may do duty for the verb in parallel clauses: ἄνδρες ἀνέσταν, ἂν μὲν ἄρ' Ἀτρεΐδης . . . ἂν δ' ἄρα Μηριόνης *the men rose up, rose up Atreides, rose up Meriones* Ψ 886. So in Hdt.

1644. (II) Prepositions connect verbs and other words with the oblique cases of nouns and pronouns.

1645. It is often impossible to decide whether the preposition belongs to the verb or to the noun. Thus, ἐκ δὲ Χρυσηῒς νηὸς βῆ A 439 may be *Chryseïs went out of the ship* or *Chryseïs went-out-from* (ἐξέβη) *the ship.* When important words separate the prep.-adv. from the noun, the prep.-adv. is more properly regarded as belonging with the verb, which, together with the prep.-adv., governs the noun: ἀμφὶ δὲ χαῖται ὤμοις ἀΐσσονται *and his mane floats-about his shoulders* Z 509. The Mss. often vary: τοῖσιν ἐγὼ μεθ' ὁμίλεον (or μεθομίλεον) *with these I was wont to associate* A 269.

1646. (III) Prepositions unite with verbs (less frequently with nouns and other prepositions) to form compounds. Cp. 886 ff.

a. From this use as a prefix the name 'preposition' (πρόθεσις *praepositio*) is derived. The original meaning of some prepositions is best seen in compounds.

1647. Improper prepositions (1699) are adverbs used like prepositions, but incapable of forming compounds. The case (usually the genitive) following an improper preposition depends on the preposition alone without regard to the verb; whereas a true preposition was attached originally, as an adverb, to a case depending directly on the verb.

1648. The addition of a preposition (especially διά, κατά, σύν) to a verbal form may mark the completion of the action of the verbal idea (perfective action). The local force of the preposition is here often lost. So διαφεύγειν *succeed in escaping*, καταδιώκειν *succeed in pursuing*, συντελεῖν *accomplish, carry into effect* (τελεῖν *do, perform*).

1649. Two or more prepositions may be used with one verb, either separately, as adverbs, or in composition with the verb. Thus, στῆ δὲ παρέξ (or παρ' ἐξ) *he stood forth beside him* Λ 486. When two prepositions of like meaning are used in composition, that preposition precedes which has the narrower range: συμμετέχειν *take part in with*, ἀμφιπεριστέφεσθαι *to be put round about as a crown*. When two prepositions are used with one noun, the noun usually depends on the second, while the first defines the second adverbially; as ἀμφὶ περὶ κρήνην *round about a spring* B 305. It is often uncertain whether or not two prepositions should be written together.

a. Such compound prepositions are ἀμφιπερί, παρέξ, ὑπέκ, ἀπέκ, διέκ, ἀποπρό, διαπρό, περιπρό. Improper prepositions may be used with true prepositions, as μέχρι εἰς τὸ στρατόπεδον *as far as* (into) *the camp* X. A. 6. 4. 26.

1650. Tmesis (τμῆσις *cutting*) denotes the separation of a preposition from its verb, and is a term of late origin, properly descriptive only of the post-epic language, in which preposition and verb normally formed an indissoluble compound. The term 'tmesis' is incorrectly applied to the language of Homer, since in the Epic the prep.-adv. was still in process of joining with the verb.

1651. In Attic poetry tmesis occurs chiefly when the preposition is separated from the verb by unimportant words (particles, enclitics), and is employed for the sake of emphasis or (in Euripides) as a mere ornament. Aristophanes uses tmesis only to parody the style of tragic choruses.

1652. Hdt. uses tmesis frequently in imitation of the Epic; the intervening words are ὦν (= οὖν), enclitics, δέ, μὲν . . . δέ, etc.

1653. In Attic prose tmesis occurs only in special cases: ἀντ' εὖ ποιεῖν (πάσχειν) and σὺν εὖ (κακῶς) ποιεῖν (πάσχειν). Thus, ὅσους εὖ ποιήσαντας ἡ πόλις ἀντ' εὖ πεποίηκεν *all whom the city has requited with benefits for the service they rendered it* D. 20. 64. Here εὖ πεποίηκεν is almost equivalent to a single notion.

1654. The addition of a preposition to a verb may have no effect on the construction, as in ἐκβῆναι τῆς νεώς, whereas βῆναι τῆς νεώς originally, and still in poetry, can mean *go from-the-ship;* or it may determine the construction, as in περιγενέσθαι ἐμοῦ *to surpass me* D. 18. 236. Prose tends to repeat the prefixed preposition: ἐκβῆναι ἐκ τῆς νεώς T. 1. 137.

1655. A preposition usually assumes the force of an adjective when compounded with substantives which do not change their forms on entering into composition, as σύνοδος *a national meeting* (ὁδός). Otherwise the compound usually gets a new termination, generally -ον, -ιον neuter, or -ίς feminine, as ἐνύπνιον *dream* (ὕπνος), ἐπιγουνίς *thigh-muscle* (γόνυ).

1656. The use of prepositions is, in general, more common in prose than in poetry, which retained the more primitive form of expression.

1657. A noun joined by a preposition to its case without the help of a verb has a verbal meaning: ἀπὸ πᾱσῶν ἀρχῶν ἐλευθερίᾱ *freedom from all rule* P. L. 698 a (cp. ἐλευθεροῦν ἀπό τινος).

1658. In general, when depending on prepositions expressing relations of place, the accusative denotes the place (or person) *toward which* or the place *over which, along which* motion takes place, the dative denotes *rest in* or *at*, the genitive (ablative) *passing from*. Thus, ἥκω παρὰ σέ *I have come to you* T. 1. 137, οἱ παρ' ἑαυτῷ βάρβαροι *the barbarians in his own service* X. A. 1. 1. 5, παρὰ βασιλέως πολλοὶ πρὸς Κῦρον ἀπῆλθον *many came over from the king to Cyrus* 1. 9. 29. The true genitive denotes various forms of connection.

1659. Constructio Praegnans. — **a.** A verb of motion is often used with a preposition with the dative to anticipate the rest that follows the action of the verb: ἐν τῷ ποταμῷ ἔπεσον *they fell* (into and were) *in the river* X. Ages. 1. 32. This use is common with τιθέναι, ἱδρύειν, καθιστάναι, etc., and with tenses of completed action which imply rest; as οἱ ἐν τῇ νήσῳ ἄνδρες διαβεβηκότες *the men who had crossed to* (and were in) *the island* T. 7. 71.

b. A verb of rest is often followed by a preposition with the accusative to denote motion previous to or following upon the action of the verb: παρῆσαν εἰς Σάρδεις (they came to Sardis and were in the city) *they arrived at Sardis* X. A. 1. 2. 2, ἐς Κυρήνην ἐσώθησαν *they were saved by reaching Cyrene* T. 1. 110, ᾑρέθη πρεσβευτὴς εἰς Λακεδαίμονα *he was chosen ambassador* (to go) *to Lacedaemon* X. H. 2. 2. 17. Cp. 1692. 1. a.

1660. Stress is often laid on (a) the starting-point or (b) the goal of an action.

a. καταδήσᾱς ἀπὸ δένδρων τοὺς ἵππους *tying his horses to* (from) *trees* X. H. 4. 4. 10. By anticipation of the verbal action (attraction of the prep. with the article): τὴν ἀπὸ στρατοπέδου τάξιν ἔλιπεν *he deserted his post in the army* Aes. 3. 159, οἱ ἐκ τῆς ἀγορᾶς καταλιπόντες τὰ ὤνια ἔφυγον *the market-people* (οἱ ἐν τῇ ἀγορᾷ) *left their wares and fled* X. A. 1. 2. 18.

b. With verbs of *collecting* (ἀθροίζειν, συλλέγειν) and *enrolling* (ἐγγράφειν): εἰς πεδίον ἀθροίζονται *they are mustered in(to) the plain* X. A. 1. 1. 2, εἰς ἄνδρας ἐγγράψαι *to enrol in(to) the list of men* D. 19. 230.

1661. So with adverbs: ὅπου ἐληλύθαμεν *where* (= *whither*, ὅποι) *we have gone* X. C. 6. 1. 14, ὅθεν ἀπελίπομεν, ἐπανέλθωμεν *let us return to the point whence* (= *where*, ὅπου) *we left off* P. Ph. 78 b, ἀγνοεῖ τὸν ἐκεῖθεν πόλεμον δεῦρο ἥξοντα *he does not know that the war in that region will come hither* (= τὸν ἐκεῖ πόλεμον ἐκεῖθεν) D. 1. 15.

1662. Some adverbs and adverbial phrases meaning *from* are used with reference to the point of view of the observer: ἑκατέρωθεν *on either side*, ἔνθεν καὶ ἔνθεν *on this side and that*, ἐκ δεξιᾶς *on the right* (*a dextra*), οἱ ἀπὸ τῆς σκηνῆς *the actors*, τὸ ἐκ τοῦ ἰσθμοῦ τεῖχος, τὸ ἐς τὴν Παλλήνην τεῖχος *the wall* (seen) *from the isthmus, the wall toward* (looking to) *Pallene* T. 1. 64 (of the same wall).

1663. Position. — The preposition usually precedes its noun. It may be separated from it

a. By particles (μέν, δέ, γέ, τέ, γάρ, οὖν) and by οἶμαι *I think*: ἐν οὖν τῇ πόλει P. R. 456 d, εἰς δέ γε οἶμαι τὰς ἄλλᾱς πόλεις *to the other cities I think* 568 c.

Note that the order τὴν μὲν χώρᾱν (1155) usually becomes, *e.g.* πρὸς μὲν τὴν χώρᾱν or πρὸς τὴν χώρᾱν μέν. Demonstrative ὁ μέν and ὁ δέ, when dependent on a preposition, regularly follow the preposition, and usually with order reversed (1109): ἐν μὲν ἄρα τοῖς συμφωνοῦμεν, ἐν δὲ τοῖς οὔ *in some things then we agree, but not in others* P. Phae. 263 b.

b. By attributives: εἰς Καΰστρου πεδίον *to the plain of the Cayster* X. A. 1. 2. 11.

c. By the accusative in oaths and entreaties (with πρός): πρός σε τῆσδε μητρός *by my mother here* I implore *thee* E. Phoen. 1665; cp. *per te deos oro* and see 1599.

N. — A preposition is usually placed before a superlative and after ὡς or ὅτι qualifying the superlative: ὡς ἐπὶ πλεῖστον τοῦ ὁμίλου *over the very greatest part of the throng* T. 2. 34. πολύ, πάνυ, μάλα may precede the preposition and its case: πολὺ ἐν πλείονι αἰτίᾳ *with far better reason* T. 1. 35.

1664. In poetry a preposition is often placed between an adjective and its substantive; very rarely in prose (τοιᾷδε ἐν τάξει *in the following manner* P. Criti. 115 c).

1665. περί is the only true preposition that may be placed after its case in Attic prose: σοφίᾱς πέρι *about wisdom* P. Phil. 49 a, ὧν ἐγὼ οὐδὲν οὔτε μέγα οὔτε μῑκρὸν πέρι ἐπαΐω *about which I understand nothing either much or little* P. A. 19 c. When used with two substantives πέρι is placed between them: τοῦ ὁσίου τε πέρι καὶ τοῦ ἀνοσίου *concerning both that which is holy and that which is unholy* P. Euth. 4 e. πέρι occurs very often in Plato, only once in the orators and possibly twice in Xenophon. On anastrophe, see 175.

a. ἕνεκα and χάριν (usually) and ἄνευ (sometimes) are postpositive. The retention of the postpositive use of περί may be due to the influence of ἕνεκα. In poetry many prepositions are postpositive.

VARIATION OF PREPOSITIONS

1666. The preposition in the second of two closely connected clauses may be different from that used in the first clause either (1) when the relation is essentially the same or (2) when it is different. Thus (1) ἔκ τε τῆς Κερκύρᾱς καὶ ἀπὸ τῆς ἠπείρου *from Corcyra and the mainland* T. 7. 33, and (2) οὔτε κατὰ γῆν οὔτε διὰ θαλάσσης *neither by land nor by* (the help of the, the medium of the) *sea* 1. 2. Cp. 1668.

REPETITION AND OMISSION OF PREPOSITIONS, ETC.

1667. a. For the sake of emphasis or to mark opposition and difference, a preposition is repeated with each noun dependent on the preposition: κατά τε πόλεμον καὶ κατὰ τὴν ἄλλην δίαιταν *in the pursuit of war and in the other occupations of life* P. Tim. 18 c.

b. A preposition is used with the first noun and omitted with the second when the two nouns (whether similar or dissimilar in meaning) unite to form a complex: περὶ τοῦ δικαίου καὶ ἀρετῆς '*concerning the justice of our cause and the honesty of our intentions*' T. 3. 10.

c. In poetry a preposition may be used only with the second of two nouns dependent on it: Δελφῶν κἀπὸ Δαυλίᾱς *from Delphi and Daulia* S. O. T. 734.

1668. In contrasts or alternatives expressed by ἤ, ἢ . . . ἤ, καὶ . . . καί, etc., the preposition may be repeated or omitted with the second noun: καὶ κατὰ γῆν καὶ κατὰ θάλατταν *both by land and by sea* X. A. 1. 1. 7, πρὸς ἐχθρὸν ἢ φίλον *to foe or friend* D. 21. 114.

1669. When prepositions of different meaning are used with the same noun, the noun is repeated; thus *neither upon (the earth) nor under the earth* is οὔτ' ἐπὶ γῆς οὐθ' ὑπὸ γῆς P. Menex. 246 d.

1670. In explanatory appositional clauses (988) the preposition may be repeated for the sake of clearness or emphasis; as ἐκ τούτων οἱ ὀνομαστοὶ γίγνονται, ἐκ τῶν ἐπιτηδευσάντων ἕκαστα *the men of mark come from those who have practised each art* P. Lach. 183 c, and commonly after demonstratives. The preposition is not repeated when such an appositional clause is closely connected with what precedes: εἰκὸς μηδὲ νομίσαι περὶ ἑνὸς μόνου, δουλείᾱς ἀντ' ἐλευθερίᾱς, ἀγωνίζεσθαι *nor should you think that you are contending for a single issue alone:* to avert *slavery instead of* maintaining your *freedom* T. 2. 63. A preposition is usually not repeated before descriptive appositional clauses (987): περὶ χρημάτων λαλεῖς, ἀβεβαίου πράγματος *you are talking about wealth, an unstable thing* Com. frag. 3. 38 (No. 128).

1671. Before a relative in the same case as a noun or pronoun dependent on a preposition, the preposition is usually omitted: κατὰ ταύτην τὴν ἡλικίᾱν ἧν ἦν ἐγὼ νῦν *he was at that age at which I now am* D. 21. 155, φιλεῖται ὑπὸ ὧν (= τούτων ὧν) φιλεῖται *is loved by whom it is loved* P. Euth. 10 c. But the preposition is repeated if the relative precedes: πρὸς ὅ τις πέφῡκε, πρὸς τοῦτο ἕνα πρὸς ἓν ἕκαστον ἔργον δεῖ κομίζειν *it is necessary to set each individual to some one work to which he is adapted by nature* P. R. 423 d.

1672. In Plato a preposition is often omitted in replies: ἡττώμενος — ὑπὸ τίνος; φήσει. τοῦ ἀγαθοῦ, φήσομεν *overcome — by what? he will say. By the good, we shall say* Pr. 355 c.

1673. The preposition is usually omitted with the main noun or pronoun when it is used in a clause of comparison with ὡς (rarely ὥσπερ) *as:* δεῖ ὡς περὶ μητρὸς καὶ τροφοῦ τῆς χώρᾱς βουλεύεσθαι *they ought to take thought for their country as their mother and nurse* P. R. 414 e; so, usually, when the two members are closely united: ὡς πρὸς εἰδότ' ἐμὲ σὺ τἀληθῆ λέγε *speak the truth to me as to one who knows* Ar. Lys. 993. The preposition is often omitted in the clause with ὡς (ὥσπερ) *as*, ἤ *than:* οἳ παρ' οὐδὲν οὕτως ὡς τὸ τοιαῦτα ποιεῖν ἀπολώλᾱσιν *who owe their ruin to nothing so much as to such a course of action* D. 19. 263, περὶ τοῦ μέλλοντος μᾶλλον βουλεύεσθαι ἢ τοῦ παρόντος *to deliberate about the future rather than the present* T. 3. 44.

1674. A preposition with its case may have the function of the subject, or the object, of a sentence; or it may represent the protasis of a condition.

Subject: ἔφυγον περὶ ὀκτακοσίους *about eight hundred took to flight* X. H. 6. 5. 10; (gen. absol.) συνειλεγμένων περὶ ἑπτακοσίους, λαβὼν αὐτοὺς καταβαίνει *when about seven hundred had been collected he marched down with them* 2. 4. 5. Object: διέφθειραν ἐς ὀκτακοσίους *they killed about eight hundred* T. 7. 32. Protasis: ἐπεὶ διά γ' ὑμᾶς αὐτοὺς πάλαι ἂν ἀπωλώλειτε *for had it depended on your selves you would have perished long ago* D. 18. 49 (cp. 2344).

ORDINARY USES OF THE PREPOSITIONS

1675. Use of the Prepositions in Attic Prose. —

With the accusative only: ἀνά, εἰς.

With the dative only: ἐν, σύν.
With the genitive only: ἀντί, ἀπό, ἐξ, πρό.
With the accusative and genitive: ἀμφί, διά, κατά, μετά, ὑπέρ.
With accusative, genitive, and dative: ἐπί, παρά, περί, πρός, ὑπό.

a. With the dative are also used in poetry: ἀνά, ἀμφί (also in Hdt.), μετά. ἀπό (ἀπύ), ἐξ (ἐς) take the dative in Arcadian and Cyprian.

b. The genitive is either the genitive proper (of the goal, 1349, 1350, etc.) or the ablatival genitive.

c. The dative is usually the locative or the instrumental, rarely the dative proper (as with ἐπί and πρός of the goal).

1676. Ordinary Differences in Meaning. —

	Genitive	Accusative
ἀμφί, περί	*concerning*	*round about, near*
διά	*through*	*owing to*
κατά	*against*	*along, over, according to*
μετά	*with*	*after*
ὑπέρ	*above, in behalf of*	*over, beyond*

	Genitive	Dative	Accusative
ἐπί	*on*	*on*	*to, toward, for*
παρά	*from*	*with, near*	*to, contrary to*
πρός	*on the side of*	*at, besides*	*to, toward*
ὑπό	*by, under*	*under*	*under*

1677. Certain prepositions are parallel in many uses; *e.g.* ἀνά and κατά, ἀντί and πρό, ἀπό and ἐκ, ἀμφί and περί, ὑπέρ and περί, ἐπί and πρός, σύν and μετά.

1678. The *agent* is expressed by different prepositions with the genitive:

ὑπό of persons and things personified (1698. 1. N. 1): the normal usage in Attic prose.
παρά: here the agent is viewed as the source. The action is viewed as starting near a person, or *on the part of* a person.
διά *through:* the intermediate agent.
ἀπό: indirect agent and source (rare) to mark the point of departure of the action. Chiefly in Thuc.
ἐξ: chiefly in poetry and Hdt. In Attic prose of emanation from a source.
πρός: to mark the result as due to the *presence* (*before*) of a person; chiefly in poetry and Hdt.

1679. *Means* is expressed by διά with the genitive (the normal usage in Attic prose), ἀπό, ἐξ, ἐν, σύν. *Motive* is expressed by ὑπό (gen.), διά (accus.), ἕνεκα.

1680. Prepositions in composition (chiefly ἀπό, διά, κατά, σύν) may give an idea of completion to the action denoted by the verb (1648).

a. For the usage after compound verbs see 1382 ff., 1545 ff., 1559.

LIST OF PREPOSITIONS

1681. ἀμφί (cp. ἄμφω, ἀμφότερος, Lat. *ambi-*, *amb-*, *am-*) originally

on both sides (either externally only, or inside and outside), hence ***about***. Cp. the use of περί (1693) throughout. Chiefly poetic, Ionic, and Xenophontic. In Attic prose chiefly with the accusative.

1. **ἀμφί** *with the Genitive*

Local (very rare and doubtful): οἱ ἀμφὶ ταύτης οἰκέοντες τῆς πόλιος *dwellers round about this city* Hdt. 8. 104 (only here). Cause: *about, concerning:* ἀμφὶ σῆς λέγω παιδός *I speak about thy child* E. Hec. 580, ἀμφὶ ὧν εἶχον διαφερόμενοι *quarrelling about what they had* X. A. 4. 5. 17.

2. **ἀμφί** *with the Dative*

Local: ἀμφ' ὤμοισιν ἔχει σάκος *he has a shield about his shoulders* Λ 527. Cause: φοβηθεὶς ἀμφὶ τῇ γυναικί *afraid on account of his wife* Hdt. 6. 62, ἀμφὶ φόβῳ *by reason of* (encompassed by) *terror* E. Or. 825; Means: ἀμφὶ σοφίᾳ '*with the environment of poetic art*' Pind. P. 1. 12. Often in Pindar.

3. **ἀμφί** *with the Accusative*

Local: ἀμφὶ Μίλητον *about Miletus* X. A. 1. 2. 3, ἔδραμον ἀμφ' Ἀχιλῆα *they ran around Achilles* Σ 30; temporal: ἀμφὶ δείλην *towards evening* X. A. 2. 2. 14. Number: ἀμφὶ τοὺς δισχῑλίους *about two thousand* 1. 2. 9; of occupation with an object: ἀμφὶ δεῖπνον εἶχεν *he was busy about dinner* X. C. 5. 5. 44.

a. οἱ ἀμφί τινα the attendants, followers of a person, or the person himself with his attendants, etc.: ἀνὴρ τῶν ἀμφὶ Κῦρον πιστῶν *one of the trusty adherents of Cyrus* X. A. 1. 8. 1, οἱ ἀμφὶ Χειρίσοφον *Chirisophus and his men* 4. 3. 21, οἱ ἀμφὶ Πρωταγόρᾱν *the school of Protagoras* P. Th. 170 c. This last phrase contains the only use of ἀμφί in Attic prose outside of Xenophon.

4. **ἀμφί** *in Composition*

Around, about· ἀμφιβάλλειν *throw around* (*on both sides*), ἀμφιλέγειν *dispute* (*speak on both sides*).

1682. **ἀνά** (Lesb. ὀν, Lat. *an-* in *anhelare*, Eng. *on*): originally *up to, up* (opposed to κατά). Cp. ἄνω.

1. **ἀνά** *with the Dative*

Local only (Epic, Lyric, and in tragic choruses): ἀνὰ σκήπτρῳ *upon a staff* Α 15.

2. **ἀνά** *with the Accusative*

Up along; over, through, among (of horizontal motion). Usually avoided by Attic prose writers except Xenophon (three times in the orators).

a. Local: To a higher point: ἀνὰ τὸν ποταμόν *up stream* Hdt. 1. 194 (cp. κατὰ τὸν ποταμόν). Extension: ἀνὰ στρατόν *through the camp* Α 10, ἀνὰ πᾶσαν τὴν γῆν *over the whole earth* X. Ag. 11. 16, βασιλῆας ἀνὰ στόμ' ἔχων *having kings in thy mouth* Β 250 (cp. διὰ στόματος ἔχειν).

b. Extension in Time: ἀνὰ νύκτα *through the night* Ξ 80. See c.

c. Other relations: Distributively: ἀνὰ ἑκατὸν ἄνδρας *by hundreds* X. A. 3. 4. 21, ἀνὰ πᾶσαν ἡμέρᾱν *daily* X. C. 1. 2. 8. Manner: ἀνὰ κράτος *with all their might* (up to their strength) X. A. 1. 10. 15 (better Attic κατὰ κράτος), ἀνὰ λόγον *proportionately* P. Ph. 110 d.

3. ἀνά *in Composition*

Up (ἀνίστασθαι *stand up*, ἀναστρέφειν *turn upside down*), *back* (ἀναχωρεῖν *go back*, ἀναμιμνῄσκειν *remind*), *again* (ἀναπνεῖν *breathe again*, ἀναπειρᾶσθαι *practise constantly*), often with a reversing force force (ἀναλύειν *unloose*).

1683. ἀντί: originally *in the face of, opposite to;* cp. ἄντα, ἐναντίος, Lat. *ante* (with meaning influenced by *post*), Germ. *Antwort*, 'reply.'

1. ἀντί *with the Genitive only*

Local: ἀνθ' ὧν ἑστηκότες *standing opposite to* (from the point of view of the speaker, i.e. *behind*) *which* (pine-trees) X. A. 4. 7. 6. In other meanings: *Instead of, for, as an equivalent to:* ἀντὶ πολέμου εἰρήνη *peace instead of war* T. 4. 20, τὰ παρ' ἐμοὶ ἑλέσθαι ἀντὶ τῶν οἴκοι *to prefer what I have to offer you here instead of what you have left at home* X. A. 1. 7. 4, τὴν τελευτὴν ἀντὶ τῆς τῶν ζώντων σωτηρίᾱς ἠλλάξαντο *they exchanged death for the safety of the living* P. Menex. 237 a; *in return for*, hence ἀνθ' ὅτου *wherefore* S. El. 585; for πρός in entreaty: σ' ἀντὶ παίδων τῶνδε ἱκετεύομεν *we entreat thee by these children here* S. O. C. 1326.

2. ἀντί *in Composition*

Instead, in return (ἀντιδιδόναι *give in return*), *against, in opposition to* (ἀντιλέγειν *speak against*).

1684. ἀπό (Lesb. etc. ἀπύ) *from, off, away from;* originally of separation and departure. Cp. Lat. *ab*, Eng. *off, of.*

1. ἀπό *with the Genitive only*

a. Local: καταπηδήσᾱς ἀπὸ τοῦ ἵππου *leaping down from his horse* X. A. 1. 8. 28, ἐθήρευεν ἀπὸ ἵππου *he used to hunt* (from a horse) *on horseback* 1. 2. 7, ἀπὸ θαλάσσης *at a distance from the sea* T. 1. 7. Figuratively: ἀπὸ θεῶν ἀρχόμενοι *beginning with the gods* X. A. 6. 3. 18.

b. Temporal: ἀφ' ἑσπέρᾱς *after evening began* (after sundown) X. A. 6. 3. 23, ἀπὸ τοῦ αὐτοῦ σημείου *on the same signal* 2. 5. 32, ἀπὸ τῶν σίτων *after meals* X. R. L. 5. 8, ἀφ' οὗ *since*.

c. Other relations: (1) Origin, Source: in prose of more remote ancestry: τοὺς μὲν ἀπὸ θεῶν, τοὺς δ' ἐξ αὐτῶν τῶν θεῶν γεγονότας *some descended* (remotely) *from gods, others begotten* (directly) *of the gods themselves* I. 12. 81. (This distinction is not always observed.) Various other relations may be explained as source.

(2) Author: as agent with passives and intransitives, when an action is done indirectly, through the influence of the agent (ὑπό of the direct action of the agent himself). Not common, except in Thuc. (chiefly with πράττεσθαι, λέγεσθαι, and verbs of like meaning): ἐπράχθη ἀπ' αὐτῶν οὐδὲν ἔργον *nothing was done under their rule* T. 1. 17. The starting-point of an action is often emphasized rather than the agent: ἀπὸ πολλῶν καὶ πρὸς πολλοὺς λόγοι γιγνόμενοι *speeches made by many and to many* T. 8. 93.

(3) Cause (remote): ἀπὸ τούτου τοῦ τολμήματος ἐπῃνέθη *he was praised in consequence of this bold deed* T. 2. 25, ταῦτα οὐκ ἀπὸ τύχης ἐγίγνετο, ἀλλ' ἀπὸ παρασκευῆς τῆς ἐμῆς *this happened not from chance but by reason of the preparations I made* L. 21. 10.

(4) Means, Instrument: στράτευμα συνέλεξεν ἀπὸ χρημάτων *he raised an army by means of money* X. A. 1. 1. 9; rarely of persons: ἀπ' αὐτῶν βλάψαι *to do injury by means of them* T. 7. 29.

(5) Manner: ἀπὸ τοῦ προφανοῦς *openly* T. 1. 66.

(6) Conformity: ἀπὸ τοῦ ἴσου *on a basis of equality* T. 3. 10, ἀπὸ ξυμμαχίᾱς αὐτόνομοι *independent by virtue of (according to) an alliance* 7. 57.

N. — ἀπό with gen. is sometimes preferred to the simple gen., often for emphasis: οἱ λόγοι ἀφ' ὑμῶν *the words that proceed from you* T. 6. 40, ὀλίγοι ἀπὸ πολλῶν *a few of the many* 1. 110 (cp. 1317 a). Thuc. has many free uses of ἀπό.

2. **ἀπό** *in Composition*

From, away, off (ἀπιέναι *go away*, ἀποτειχίζειν *wall off*), *in return, back* (ἀποδιδόναι *give back* what is due, ἀπαιτεῖν *demand what is one's right*). Separation involves completion (hence ἀπανᾱλίσκειν *utterly consume*, ἀποθύειν *pay off a vow*), or privation and negation (ἀπαγορεύειν *forbid*, ἀποτυγχάνειν *miss*). Often almost equivalent to an intensive (ἀποφάναι *speak out*, ἀποδεικνύναι *point out*, ἀποτολμᾶν *dare without reserve*).

1685. **διά** (Lesb. ζά) *through*, originally *through and out of*, and *apart* (separation by cleavage), a force seen in comp. (cp. Lat. *dis-*, Germ. *zwi-schen*).

1. **διά** *with the Genitive*

a. Local: *through and out of* (cp. Hom. διέκ, διαπρό), as δι' ὤμου ἔγχος ἦλθεν *the spear went clear through his shoulder* Δ 481, ἀκοῦσαι διὰ τέλους *to listen from beginning to end* Lyc. 16. *Through*, but not *out of:* διὰ πολεμίᾱς (γῆς) πορεύεσθαι *to march through the enemy's country* X. Hi. 2. 8 and often in figurative expressions: διὰ χειρὸς ἔχειν *to control* T. 2. 13, διὰ στόματος ἔχειν *to have in one's mouth (be always talking of)* X. C. 1. 4. 25 (also ἀνὰ στόμα).

b. Temporal: of uninterrupted duration, as διὰ νυκτός *through the night* X. A. 4. 6. 22, διὰ παντός *constantly* T. 2. 49.

c. Intervals of Space or Time: διὰ δέκα ἐπάλξεων *at intervals of ten battlements* T. 3. 21, διὰ χρόνου *after an interval* L. 1. 12, *intermittently* Aes. 3. 220, διὰ πολλοῦ *at a long distance* T. 3. 94.

d. Other relations: Means, Mediation (*per*): αὐτὸς δι' ἑαυτοῦ *ipse per se* D. 48. 15, διὰ τούτου γράμματα πέμψᾱς *sending a letter by this man* Aes. 3. 162. State or feeling: with εἶναι, γίγνεσθαι, ἔχειν, of a property or quality: διὰ φόβου εἰσί *they are afraid* T. 6. 34, δι' ἡσυχίᾱς εἶχεν *he kept in quiet* 2. 22, ἐλθεῖν ἡμῖν διὰ μάχης *to meet us in battle* 2. 11, αὐτοῖς διὰ φιλίᾱς ἰέναι *to enter into friendship with them* X. A. 3. 2. 8. Manner: διὰ ταχέων *quickly* T. 4. 8.

2. **διά** *with the Accusative*

a. Local: of space traversed, *through, over* (Epic, Lyric, tragic choruses): διὰ δώματα *through the halls* A 600; διὰ νύκτα Θ 510 is quasi-temporal.

b. Cause: *owing to, thanks to, on account of, in consequence of* (cp. *propter, ob*): διὰ τοὺς θεοὺς ἐσῳζόμην *I was saved thanks to the gods* D. 18. 249, τῑμώμενος μὴ δι' ἑαυτόν, ἀλλὰ διὰ δόξαν προγόνων *honoured, not for himself, but on account of the renown of his ancestors* P. Menex. 247 b. So in εἰ μὴ διά τινα (τι) *had it not been for* in statements of an (unsurmounted) obstacle: φαίνονται κρατήσαντες ἂν τῶν βασιλέως πρᾱγμάτων, εἰ μὴ διὰ Κῦρον *it seems they would have got the better of the power of the king, had it not been for Cyrus* I. 5. 92.

c. διά is rarely used (in place of ἕνεκα) to denote a purpose or object: διὰ τὴν σφετέρᾱν δόξαν *for the sake of their honour* T. 2. 89, δι' ἐπήρειαν *for spite* D. 39. 32 (cp. διὰ νόσον ἕνεκα ὑγιείᾱς *on account of disease in order to gain health* P. Lys. 218 e).

d. διά with gen. is used of direct, διά with accus. of indirect, agency (fault, merit, of a person, thing, or situation). διά with gen. is used of an agent employed to bring about an intended result; διά with accus. is used of a person, thing, or state beyond our control (accidental agency). (1) Persons: ἔπρᾱξαν ταῦτα δι' Εὐρυμάχου *they effected this by the mediation of Eurymachus* T. 2. 2, τὰ διὰ τούτους ἀπολωλότα *what has been lost by* (*the fault of*) *these men* D. 6. 34. The accus. marks a person as an agent not as an instrument. (2) Things: νόμοι, δι' ὧν ἐλευθέριος ὁ βίος παρασκευασθήσεται *laws, by means of which a life of freedom will be provided* X. C. 3. 3. 52, διὰ τοὺς νόμους βελτίους γιγνόμενοι ἄνθρωποι *men become better thanks to the laws* 8. 1. 22. Sometimes there is little difference between the two cases: δι' ὧν ἅπαντ' ἀπώλετο D. 18. 33, δι' οὓς ἅπαντ' ἀπώλετο 18. 35.

N. — διά with gen. (= *through*) is distinguished from the simple dative (= *by*): δι' οὗ ὁρῶμεν καὶ ᾧ ἀκούομεν P. Th. 184 c.

e. For διά with accus. to express the reason for an action, the dative is sometimes used (1517): τοῖς πεπρᾱγμένοις φοβούμενος τοὺς Ἀθηναίους *fearing the Athenians by reason of what had happened* T. 3. 98. The dative specifies the reason less definitely than διά with the accusative.

f. When used in the same sentence, the dative may express the immediate, διά with the accus. the remoter, cause: ἀσθενείᾳ σωμάτων διὰ τὴν σῑτοδείᾱν ὑπεχώρουν *they gave ground from the fact that they were weak through lack of food* T. 4. 36.

g. διά with accus. contrasted with ὑπό with gen.: φήσομεν αὐτὸ δι' ἐκεῖνα ὑπὸ τῆς αὐτοῦ κακίᾱς ἀπολωλέναι *we shall say that it* (the body) *is destroyed on account of those* (remoter) *causes* (as badness of food) *by its own evil* (immediately) P. R. 609 e.

3. **διά** *in Composition*

Through, across, over (διαβαίνειν *cross*), *apart, asunder* (διακόπτειν *cut in two*, διακρίνειν *discernere*, διαφέρειν *differ*, διαζυγνύναι *disjoin*), *severally* (διαδιδόναι *distribute*).

δια- often denotes intensity, continuance, or fulfilment (διαμένειν *remain to the end*, διαφθείρειν *destroy completely*). δια- is common in the reciprocal middle (1726), as in διαλέγεσθαι *converse;* often of rivalry (οἱ διαπολῑτευόμενοι *rival statesmen*, διακοντίζεσθαι *contend in throwing the javelin*).

1686. **εἰς, ἐς** *into, to,* opposed to ἐξ; from ἐν + ς (cp. Lat. *abs* from *ab* + *s*). See on ἐν. On εἰς with the genitive by ellipsis, see 1302.

1. **εἰς** *with the Accusative only*

In the Old Attic alphabet (2 a), generally used in Attica in the fifth century, ΕΣ was written, and this may be either εἰς or ἐς. In the fourth century ΕΙΣ was generally written. In Thuc. ἐς is printed, but its correctness may be doubted; other Attic prose writers use εἰς, the poets εἰς or (less frequently) ἐς. It is not true that in poetry ἐς is used only before consonants, εἰς only before vowels.

a. Local: of the goal: Σικελοὶ ἐξ Ἰταλίᾱς διέβησαν ἐς Σικελίᾱν *the Sicels crossed over out of Italy into Sicily* T. 6. 2; with a personal object: ἦλθεν ἐκ τῆς Ἀσίᾱς ἐς ἀνθρώπους ἀπόρους *he came from Asia to* (a land of) *poor men* T. 1. 9, ἐσπέμπει γράμματα ἐς (*v. l.* πρὸς) βασιλέᾱ *he dispatches a letter to* (the palace of) *the king* 1. 137 (of sending, etc., to individuals ὡς or πρός is used); *against:* ἐστράτευσαν ἐς τὴν Ἀττικήν *they invaded Attica* T. 3. 1, πόλεμος τοῖς Κορινθίοις ἐς τοὺς Ἀθηναίους *war between the Corinthians and the Athenians* 1. 55; with verbs of rest, 1659 b. The idea of motion holds where Eng. uses *in* or *at:* τελευτᾶν εἴς τι *to end in* T. 2. 51. Extension: Πελοποννησίους διαβαλεῖν ἐς τοὺς Ἕλληνας *to raise a prejudice against the Peloponnesians among the Greeks* T. 3. 109; *in the presence of* (*coram*): ἐς τὸ κοινὸν λέγειν *to speak before the assembly* 4. 58.

b. Temporal: of the goal: *up to, until:* ἐς ἐμέ *up to my time* Hdt. 1. 52, ἐς τέλος *finally* 3. 40; *at* (*by*) *such a time* (of a fixed or expected time): προεῖπε εἰς τρίτην ἡμέρᾱν παρεῖναι *commanded* them *to be present on the third day* X. C. 3. 1. 42, ἥκετε εἰς τριᾱκοστὴν ἡμέρᾱν *come on the thirtieth day* 5. 3. 6. Limit of time attained: εἰς τοιοῦτον καιρὸν ἀφῑγμένοι *arriving at such a time* L. 16. 5. Extension (over future time): εἰς τὸν λοιπὸν χρόνον *in all future time* L. 16. 2.

c. Measure and Limit with numerals: εἰς χῑλίους *to the number of* (up to) *a thousand* X. A. 1. 8. 5, εἰς δύο *two abreast* 2. 4. 26, ἐς δραχμήν *to the amount of a drachma* T. 8. 29.

d. Other relations: Goal, Purpose, Intention: ἡ σὴ πατρὶς εἰς σὲ ἀποβλέπει *your country looks for help to you* X. H. 6. 1. 8, χρῆσθαι εἰς τὰς σφενδόνᾱς *to use for the slings* X. A. 3. 4. 17, παιδεύειν εἰς ἀρετήν *to train with a view to virtue* P. G. 519 e. Relation to: καλὸν εἰς στρατιάν *excellent for the army* X. C. 3. 3. 6, often in Thuc. (= πρός with accus.). Manner: εἰς καιρόν *in season* X. C. 3. 1. 8, εἰς δύναμιν *to the extent of one's powers* 4. 5. 52.

2. **εἰς** *in Composition*

Into, in, to (εἰσβαίνειν *enter,* εἰσπράττειν *get in,* exact a debt).

1687. **ἐν** *in* (poetic ἐνί, εἰν, εἰνί), Lat. *in* with the abl., *en-*; opposed to εἰς *into,* ἐξ *out of.* On ἐν with the genitive by ellipsis, see 1302.

1. **ἐν** *with the Dative* (*Locative*) *only*

a. Local: *in, at, near, by, on, among:* ἐν Σπάρτῃ *in Sparta* T. 1. 128, ἡ ἐν Κορίνθῳ μάχη *the battle at Corinth* X. Ages. 7. 5, πόλις οἰκουμένη ἐν τῷ Εὐξείνῳ πόντῳ *a city built on the Euxine* X. A. 4. 8. 22, ἐν τῇ κλίνῃ ἑστηκώς *standing upon the bed* L. 1. 24 (ἐν of superposition is rare), νόμοι ἐν πᾶσιν εὐδόκιμοι τοῖς Ἕλλησιν *laws famous among all the Greeks* P. L. 631 b, ἐν ὑμῖν ἐδημηγόρησεν *he made an harangue before* (*coram*) *you* D. 8. 74. With verbs of motion, see 1659 a. Of circumstance, occupation, as οἱ ἐν τοῖς πράγμασιν *the men at the head of affairs* D. 9. 56 (so ἐν εἰρήνῃ, ἔργῳ, ὠφελείᾳ, φιλοσοφίᾳ, φόβῳ εἶναι; ἐν αἰτίᾳ ἔχειν *to blame*, ἐν ὀργῇ ἔχειν *to be angry with*); *in the power of*: ἐν τῷ θεῷ τὸ τέλος ἦν, οὐκ ἐμοί *the issue rested with God, not with me* D. 18. 193, ἐν ἑαυτῷ ἐγένετο *he came to himself* X. A. 1. 5. 17.

b. Temporal: *in, within, during* (cp. 1542): ἐν πέντε ἔτεσιν *in five years* L. 19. 29, ἐν σπονδαῖς *during a truce* T. 1. 55, ἐν ᾧ *while*.

c. Instrument, Means, Cause, Manner (originally local): ἐν ὀφθαλμοῖσιν ἴδωμαι *see with the eyes* A 587, ἐν ἑνὶ κινδῡνεύεσθαι *to be endangered by* (i.e. *to depend on*) *a single person* T. 2. 35, ἐν τούτοις ἢ λῡπούμενοι ἢ χαίροντες *either grieving or rejoicing at this* P. R. 603 c, ἐν τούτῳ δηλῶσαι *to make clear by this* 392 e, ἐν τῷ φανερῷ *openly* X. A. 1. 3. 21. Conformity: ἐν τοῖς ὁμοίοις νόμοις ποιήσαντες τὰς κρίσεις *deciding according to equal laws* T. 1. 77, ἐν ἐμοί *in my opinion* E. Hipp. 1320.

N. — In many dialects, *e.g.* those north of the Corinthian Gulf (rarely in Pindar), ἐν retains its original meaning of *in* (with dat.) and *into* (with accus.). The latter use appears in ἐνδέξια *towards the right*.

2. ἐν *in Composition*

In, at, on, among (ἐμπίπτειν *fall in* or *on*, ἐντυγχάνειν *fall in with*, ἐγγελᾶν *laugh at*, ἐνάπτειν *bind on*).

1688. ἐξ, ἐκ *out, out of, from, from within*, opposed to ἐν, εἰς; cp. Lat. *ex, e.* As contrasted with ἀπό *away from*, ἐξ denotes *from within*.

1. ἐξ, ἐκ *with the* (*Ablatival*) *Genitive only*

In Arcadian and Cyprian ἐς (= ἐξ) takes the dative.

a. Local: ἐκ Φοινίκης ἐλαύνων *marching out of Phoenicia* X. A. 1. 7. 12; of transition: ἐκ πλείονος ἔφευγον *they fled when at* (from) *a greater distance* 1. 10. 11. On ἐξ in the *constructio praegnans*, see 1660 a.

b. Temporal: ἐκ τοῦ ἀρίστου *after breakfast* X. A. 4. 6. 21, ἐκ παίδων *from boyhood* 4. 6. 14.

c. Other relations: immediate succession or transition: ἄλλην ἐξ ἄλλης πόλεως ἀμειβόμενος *exchanging one city for another* P. A. 37 d, ἐκ πολέμου ποιούμενος εἰρήνην *making peace after* (a state of) *war* D. 19. 133, ἐκ πτωχῶν πλούσιοι γίγνονται *from beggars they become rich* 8. 66. Origin: immediate origin (whereas ἀπό is used of remote origin, 1684. 1. c): ἀγαθοὶ καὶ ἐξ ἀγαθῶν *noble and of noble breed* P. Phae. 246 a. Agent, regarded as the source: with pass. and intr. verbs instead of ὑπό (chiefly poetic and in Hdt.): πόλεις ἐκ βασιλέως δεδομέναι *cities a gift* (having been given) *of* (by) *the king* X. A. 1. 1. 6, ὡμολογεῖτο ἐκ πάντων *it was agreed by all* T. 2. 49; but ἐκ is often used with a different force, as ἐκ τῶν τυχόντων ἀνθρώπων συνοικισθῆναι *to have been settled by the vulgar* (as constituent parts of a whole) Lyc. 62. Consequence: ἐξ αὐτοῦ τοῦ ἔργου *in consequence of the fact itself* T. 1. 75. Cause or ground of judgment (where the dat. is more usual with inanimate objects): ἐξ οὗ διέβαλλεν αὐτόν *for which reason he accused him* X. A. 6. 6. 11. Material: τὸ ἄγκιστρον ἐξ ἀδάμαντος *the hook of adamant* P. R. 616 c. Instrument and means: ἐκ τῶν πόνων τὰς ἀρετᾶς κτᾶσθαι *to acquire by labour the fruits of virtue* T. 1. 123. Conformity: ἐκ τῶν νόμων *in accordance with the laws* D. 24. 28. Manner (rare): ἐκ τοῦ ἴσου *on equal terms* T. 2. 3. Partitive (cp. 1317 a): ἐκ τῶν δυναμένων εἰσί *they belong to the class that has power* P. G. 525 e.

2. ἐξ, ἐκ *in Composition*

Out, from, off, away (cp. ἐξελαύνειν *drive out* and *away*); often with an implication of fulfilment, completion, thoroughness, resolution (ἐκπέρθειν *sack utterly*, ἐκδιδάσκειν *teach thoroughly*). Cp. 1648.

1689. ἐπί (cp. Lat. *ob*) *upon, on, on the surface of;* opposed to ὑπό *under*, and to ὑπέρ when ὑπέρ means *above the surface of.*

1. ἐπί *with the Genitive*

a. Local: *upon:* οὔτ' ἐπὶ γῆς οὔθ' ὑπὸ γῆς *neither upon the earth nor under the earth* P. Menex. 246 d, ἐπὶ θρόνου ἐκαθέζετο *he seated himself on a throne* X. C. 6. 1. 6; of the vehicle (lit. or figur.) *upon which:* ἐπὶ τῶν ἵππων ὀχεῖσθαι *to ride on horseback* 4. 5. 58 (never ἐπί with dat.), ἐπὶ τῆς ἐμῆς νεώς *on my ship* L. 21. 6; *in the direction of:* ἐπὶ Σάρδεων ἔφευγε *he fled toward Sardis* X. C. 7. 2. 1; *in the presence of* (cp. παρά with dat.): ἐπὶ μαρτύρων *before witnesses* Ant. 2. γ. 8. ἐπί is rarely used of mere proximity in poetry or standard prose.

N. — In expressions of simple superposition ἐπί with the gen. denotes familiar relations and natural position; whereas ἐπί with the dat. gives clear and emphatic outlines to statements of the definite place of an object or action, is used in detailed pictures, and marks the object in the dative as distinct from the subject of the verbal action. ἐπί with the gen. is colourless and phraseological, and often makes, with the verb or the subject, a compound picture. Even in contrasting two objects ἐπί with gen. is used since no special point is made of position. With (unemphatic) pronouns of reference (αὐτοῦ) ἐπί with gen. is much more frequent than ἐπί with dat. The distinction between the two cases is often the result of feeling; and certain phrases become stereotyped, now with the gen., now with the dat.

b. Temporal, usually with personal gen.: *in the time of:* ἐπὶ τῶν προγόνων *in the time of our ancestors* Aes. 3. 178, ἐπ' ἐμοῦ *in my time* T. 7. 86, ἐπὶ τοῦ Δεκελεικοῦ πολέμου *in the Decelean war* D. 22. 15.

c. Other relations: μενεῖν ἐπὶ τῆς ἀνοίᾱς τῆς αὐτῆς *to persist in the same folly* D. 8. 14, ἃ ἐπὶ τῶν ἄλλων ὁρᾶτε, ταῦτ' ἐφ' ὑμῶν αὐτῶν ἀγνοεῖτε *what you see in the case of others, that you ignore in your own case* I. 8. 114, ἐφ' ἑαυτῶν ἐχώρουν *they proceeded by themselves* X. A. 2. 4. 10, ἐπὶ τεττάρων *four deep* 1. 2. 15, οἱ ἐπὶ τῶν πρᾱγμάτων *the men in power* D. 18. 247.

2. ἐπί *with the Dative*

a. Local: *on, by:* οἰκοῦσιν ἐπὶ τῷ ἰσθμῷ *they dwell on the isthmus* T. 1. 56, τὸ ἐπὶ θαλάσσῃ τεῖχος *the wall by the sea* 7. 4. The dat. with ἐπί denotes proximity much more frequently than the gen. with ἐπί; but denotes superposition less often than the gen. with ἐπί.

b. Temporal (rare in prose): ἦν ἥλιος ἐπὶ δυσμαῖς *the sun was near setting* X. A. 7. 3. 34.

c. Other relations: Succession, Addition: τὸ ἐπὶ τούτῳ γ' ἀποκρῖναι *answer the next question* P. A. 27 b, ἀνέστη ἐπ' αὐτῷ *he rose up after him* X. C. 2. 3. 7, ἐπὶ τῷ σίτῳ ὄψον *relish with bread* X. M. 3. 14. 2. Supervision: ἄρχων ἐπὶ τούτοις ἦν *there was a commander over them* X. C. 5. 3. 56. Dependence: καθ' ὅσον ἐστὶν ἐπ' ἐμοί *as far as is in my power* I. 6. 8. Condition: ἐφ' οἷς τὴν εἰρήνην ἐποιησάμεθα *on what terms we made the peace* D. 8. 5. Reason, motive, end, as with verbs of emotion (instead of the simple dative, 1517): πάντα ταῦτα θαυμάζω ἐπὶ τῷ κάλλει *I am astonished at all these* trees *because of their beauty* X. O. 4. 21, οὐκ ἐπὶ τέχνῃ ἔμαθες ἀλλ' ἐπὶ παιδείᾳ *you learned* this *not to make it a profession but to gain general culture* P. Pr. 312 b. Hostility (less common in prose than in poetry; usually with accus.): ἡ ἐπὶ τῷ Μήδῳ ξυμμαχίᾱ *the alliance against the Medes* T. 3. 63. Price: ἐπὶ πόσῳ; *for how much?* P. A. 41 a.

3. ἐπί *with the Accusative*

a. Local: of the goal: ἐξελαύνει ἐπὶ τὸν ποταμόν *he marches to the river* X. A. 1. 4. 11, ἀφίκοντο ἐπὶ τὸν ποταμόν *they arrived at the river* 4. 7. 18 (rarely the gen. with verbs of *arrival*), ἀνέβαινεν ἐπὶ τὸν ἵππον *he mounted his horse* X. C. 7. 1. 1. Extension: ἐπὶ πᾶσαν Ἀσίᾱν ἐλλόγιμοι *famous over all Asia* P. Criti. 112 e.

b. Temporal: extension: ἐπὶ πολλὰς ἡμέρᾱς *for many days* D. 21. 41.

c. Quantity, measure: ἐπὶ μῑκρόν *a little*, ἐπὶ πλέον *still more*, ἐπὶ πᾶν *in general*, πλάτος ἔχων πλεῖον ἢ ἐπὶ δύο στάδια *wider than* (up to) *two stades* X. C. 7. 5. 8.

d. Other relations: Purpose, object in view: πέμπειν ἐπὶ κατασκοπήν *to send for the purpose of reconnoitering* X. C. 6. 2. 9, ἀπέστειλαν ἐπὶ χρήματα *they sent for money* T. 6. 74. Hostility: ἔπλεον ἐπὶ τοὺς Ἀθηναίους *they sailed against the Athenians* 2. 90. Reference: τὸ ἐπ' ἐμέ (with or without εἶναι) *as far as I am concerned* (more commonly ἐπ' ἐμοί); τό γε ἐπ' ἐκεῖνον εἶναι L. 13. 58.

N. — To express purpose ἐπί with accus. is generally used when the purpose involves actual or implied motion to an object; ἐπί with dat. is used when the purpose may be attained by mental activity.

4. ἐπί *in Composition*

Upon (ἐπιγράφειν *write upon*), *over* (ἐπιπλεῖν *sail over*), *at*, of cause (ἐπιχαίρειν *rejoice over* or *at*), *to, toward* (ἐπιβοηθεῖν *send assistance to*), *in addition* (ἐπιδιδόναι *give in addition*), *against* (ἐπιβουλεύειν *plot against*), *after* (ἐπιγίγνεσθαι *be born after*, ἐπισκευάζειν *repair*); causative (ἐπαληθεύειν *verify*); intensity (ἐπικρύπτειν *hide*; ἐπιβουλεύεσθαι *further deliberate* = *reflect*); reciprocity (ἐπιμείγνυσθαι ἀλλήλοις *exchange friendly dealings*).

1690. **κατά** *down* (cp. κάτω), opposed to ἀνά. With the genitive (the genitive proper (of the goal) and the ablatival genitive) and the accusative. With the genitive, the motion is perpendicular; with the accusative, horizontal.

1. **κατά** *with the Genitive*

a. Local: *down from, down toward, under:* ἁλάμενοι κατὰ τῆς πέτρᾱς *having leapt down from the rock* X. A. 4. 2. 17, κατ' ἄκρᾱς *utterly, completely* (down from the summit) P. L. 909 b, ψῡχὴ κατὰ χθονὸς ᾤχετο *his soul went down under the earth* Ψ 100, μύρον κατὰ τῆς κεφαλῆς καταχέαντες *having poured myrrh (down) over their heads* P. R. 398 a; rarely of rest: ὁ κατὰ γῆς *the man under the earth* X. C. 4. 6. 5.

b. Temporal (very rare): κατὰ παντὸς τοῦ αἰῶνος *for all eternity* Lyc. 7.

c. Other relations: *against*, as κατ' ἐμαυτοῦ ἐρεῖν *to speak against myself* P. A. 37 b; rarely in a favourable or neutral sense, as οἱ κατὰ Δημοσθένους ἔπαινοι *the eulogies on Demosthenes* Aes. 3. 50, κατὰ πάντων λέγειν *to speak with regard to all* X. C. 1. 2. 16; *by* (with verbs of swearing), as ὀμνύντων τὸν ὅρκον κατὰ ἱερῶν τελείων *let them swear the oath by* (lit. down over) *full-grown victims* T. 5. 47.

2. **κατά** *with the Accusative*

a. Local: ἔπλεον κατὰ ποταμόν *they sailed down-stream* Hdt. 4. 44, κατὰ τὰς εἰσόδους ἑφεπόμενοι *following to the entrances* X. C. 3. 3. 64. Extension: καθ' ὅλην τὴν πόλιν *throughout the entire city* Lyc. 40, κατὰ γῆν *by land* L. 2. 32, διώκοντες τοὺς καθ' αὑτούς *pursuing those stationed opposite themselves* X. A. 1. 10. 4.

b. Temporal (post-Homeric): κατὰ πλοῦν *during the voyage* T. 3. 32, κατ' ἐκεῖνον τὸν χρόνον *at that time* 1. 139, οἱ καθ' ἑαυτόν *his contemporaries* D. 20. 73.

c. Other relations: Purpose: κατὰ θέᾱν ἧκεν *came for the purpose of seeing* T. 6. 31. Conformity: κατὰ τούτους ῥήτωρ *an orator after their style* P. A. 17 b, κατὰ τοὺς νόμους *according to the laws* D. 8. 2. Ground on which an act is based: κατὰ φιλίᾱν *owing to friendship* T. 1. 60. Comparisons: μείζω ἢ κατὰ δάκρυα πεπονθότες *having endured sufferings too great for* (than according to) *tears* 7. 75 (cp. *maior quam pro*). Manner: καθ' ἡσυχίᾱν *quietly* T. 6. 64. Distribution: κατ' ἔθνη *nation by nation* T. 1. 122, δέκα δραχμαὶ κατ' ἄνδρα *ten drachmae the man* Aes. 3. 187, κατὰ σφᾶς αὐτούς *per se* T. 1. 79. Approximate numbers: κατὰ πεντήκοντα *about fifty* Hdt. 6. 79.

3. **κατά** *in Composition*

Down from above (καταπίπτειν *fall down*), *back* (καταλείπειν *leave behind*), *against, adversely* (καταγιγνώσκειν *condemn, decide against*, καταφρονεῖν *despise*), *completely* (καταπετροῦν *stone to death*, κατεσθίειν *eat up*), often with an intensive force that cannot be translated. An intransitive verb when compounded with κατά may become transitive (1559).

1691. μετά: original meaning *amid, among* (cp. Germ. *mit*, Eng. *mid* in *midwife*). Hence properly only with plurals or collectives (so in Hom. with gen. and dat.). μετά denotes participation, community of action. πεδά (Lesb. and other dialects) agrees in meaning with μετά, but is of different origin.

1. **μετά** *with the Genitive*

Usually of persons and abstract nouns.

Local: *among, together with*, as *καθήμενος μετὰ τῶν ἄλλων sitting among the rest* P. R. 359 e, *θῦσαι μετ' ἐκείνων to sacrifice in company with them* X. C. 8. 3. 1; *on the side of*, as *οἱ μετὰ Κύρου βάρβαροι the barbarians in the army of Cyrus* X. A. 1. 7. 10, *μετὰ τῶν ἠδικημένων πολεμεῖν to wage war on the side of the wronged* D. 9. 24, *οὐ μετὰ τοῦ πλήθους without the consent of the people* T. 3. 66; *besides*: *γενόμενος μετὰ τοῦ ξυνετοῦ καὶ δυνατὸς showing himself powerful as well as sagacious* T. 2. 15. Accompanying circumstances (concurrent act or state): *μετὰ κινδύνων κτησάμενοι (τὴν τάξιν) having acquired their position amid dangers* D. 3. 36, *λύπη μετὰ φόβου grief and terror* T. 7. 75. Joint efficient cause: *μετὰ πόνων ἐλευθέρᾱν ἐποίησαν τὴν Ἑλλάδα by (amid) struggles they freed Greece* L. 2. 55. Conformity: *μετὰ τῶν νόμων in accordance with the laws* 3. 82.

2. **μετά** *with the Dative (Locative)*

Chiefly Epic (usually with the plural or with the collective singular of persons or things personified, or of the parts of living objects): *μετὰ μνηστῆρσιν ἔειπεν he spake amid the suitors* ρ 467, *μετὰ φρεσί in their hearts* Δ 245.

3. **μετά** *with the Accusative*

Local: *into the midst of*: *νεκροὺς ἔρυσαν μετὰ λᾱὸν Ἀχαιῶν they dragged the dead into the midst of the host of the Achaeans* E 573; with an idea of purpose: *ἰέναι μετὰ Νέστορα to go after* (in quest of) *Nestor* K 73. Extension over the midst of: *μετὰ πληθῦν throughout the multitude* B 143. Phrase: *μετὰ χεῖρας ἔχειν to have in hand* T. 1. 138.

N. — From the use in *μετ' ἴχνια βαῖνε θεοῖο he went after the steps of the goddess* γ 30 is derived the prose use: *after* (of *time* or *rank*), as *μετὰ τὰ Τρωϊκά after the Trojan war* T. 2. 68, *μετὰ θεοὺς ψῡχὴ θειότατον after the gods the soul is most divine* P. L. 726. The range of *μετά* with acc. in Attic prose is not wide.

4. **μετά** *in Composition*

Among (*μεταδιδόναι give a share*), *after, in quest of* (*μεταπέμπεσθαι send for*). When one thing is *among* other things, it may be said to *come after* another, to succeed or alternate with it; hence of succession (*μεθημερινός diurnus*; cp. *μεθ' ἡμέρᾱν after daybreak*), alteration or change (*μεταγράφειν rewrite*, *μεταμέλειν repent* i.e. *care for* something else).

When contrasted with *σύν*, *μετά* often denotes participation: *ὁ μέτοχος the partner*, *ὁ συνών the companion*. *σύν* often denotes something added. But *μετά* is usually the prose preposition for *σύν*, though it does not mean *inclusive of*.

1692. **παρά** (Hom. *παραί*, Lat. *por-* in *porrigere*) *alongside, by, near*. Except with the accusative *παρά* is commonly used of persons and personified things.

1. **παρά** *with the (Ablatival) Genitive*

Usually coming or proceeding *from* a person, in Hom. also of things; cp. *de chez*.

a. Local: οἱ αὐτομολοῦντες παρὰ βασιλέως *the deserters from the king* X. A. 2. 1. 6. In poetry, where we might expect the dat. (1659 a): ἔγρετο παρ' Ἥρης lit. *he awoke from the side of Hera* O 5. In standard Attic prose παρά with the gen. of a thing is excessively rare. When so used, the thing is personified, or the thing implies a person (as πόλις, ἀρχή, θέᾱτρον).

b. Author, Source (cp. 1410): with verbs of *receiving*, *taking*, *asking*, *learning*, *sending*, etc.: παρὰ Μήδων τὴν ἀρχὴν ἐλάμβανον Πέρσαι *the Persians wrested the empire from the Medes* X. A. 3. 4. 8, παρὰ σοῦ ἐμάθομεν *we learned from you* X. C. 2. 2. 6; ἡ παρὰ τῶν θεῶν εὔνοια *the good-will on the part of the gods* D. 2. 1 (less commonly ἀπό); with passives and intransitives (instead of ὑπό with the gen. of the agent): τὰ παρὰ τῆς τύχης δωρηθέντα *the gifts of Fortune* I. 4. 26, τοῦτο παρὰ πάντων ὁμολογεῖται *this is acknowledged on all sides (on the part of all)* L. 30. 12.

2. **παρά** *with the Dative*

Almost always of persons in standard Attic prose; cp. *chez*.

a. Local: οὐ παρὰ μητρὶ σῖτοῦνται οἱ παῖδες, ἀλλὰ παρὰ τῷ διδασκάλῳ *the boys do not eat with their mothers, but with their teachers* X. C. 1. 2. 8, παρ' ἐμοὶ σκηνοῦν *to mess with me* (as *chez moi*) 6. 1. 49; of things: τὰ παρὰ θαλάττῃ χωρία *the places along the sea* X. A. 7. 2. 25.

b. Other relations: Possessor: τὸ μὲν χρῡσίον παρὰ τούτῳ, οἱ δὲ κίνδῡνοι παρ' ὑμῖν *this man has the gold, you the dangers* Aes. 3. 240; of the superior in command: οἱ παρὰ βασιλεῖ ὄντες *those under the king* X. A. 1. 5. 16; of the person judging: ἀναίτιος παρὰ τοῖς στρατιώταις *blameless in the opinion of the troops* X. C. 1. 6. 10, ὁμολογεῖται παρὰ τῷ δήμῳ *it is agreed in the opinion of the people* Lyc. 54 (here παρά denotes the sphere of judgment); with the gen. after a passive (1692. 1. b) it denotes the source.

3. **παρά** *with the Accusative*

a. Local: of motion *to*, in prose only of persons: ἧκε παρ' ἐμέ *come to me* X. C. 4. 5. 25; motion *along*, *by*, *past* (a place): παρὰ γῆν πλεῖν *sail along shore* T. 6. 13; of parallel extent (*along*, *alongside*, *beside*) with verbs of motion and of rest (often the dat.), and often when no verb is used: ἥνπερ ἔλαβον ναῦν, ἀνέθεσαν παρὰ τὸ τροπαῖον *the ship they captured they set up alongside of the trophy* T. 2. 92, εἶπεν αὐτῷ μένειν παρ' ἑαυτόν *he told him to remain close by him* X. C. 1. 4. 18, τὸ πεδίον τὸ παρὰ τὸν ποταμόν *the plain extending along the river* X. A. 4. 3. 1, ἦν παρὰ τὴν ὁδὸν κρήνη *there was a spring by the road* 1. 2. 13. *Contrary to*: παρὰ τοὺς νόμους ἢ κατ' αὐτούς *contrary to* (*i.e.* going past) *the laws or in accordance with them* D. 23. 20; *in addition to* (along beside): ἔχω παρὰ ταῦτα ἄλλο τι λέγειν *besides this I have to say something else* P. Ph. 107 a. Phrase: παρ' ὀλίγον ἐποιοῦντο Κλέανδρον *they treated Cleander as of no account* (cp. 'next to nothing') X. A. 6. 6. 11.

b. Temporal: (duration) παρὰ πάντα τὸν χρόνον *throughout the whole time* D. 5. 2, (momentary) παρὰ τὰ δεινά *in the hour of danger* Aes. 3. 170, παρ' αὐτὰ τἀδικήματα *at the time of* (i.e. *immediately after*) *the offences themselves* D. 18. 13.

c. Other relations: Cause = διά: παρὰ τὴν ἡμετέρᾱν ἀμέλειαν *in consequence of our negligence* D. 4. 11, εἰ παρὰ τὸ προαισθέσθαι κεκώλῡται *if it was prevented by being perceived in advance* 19. 42. Dependence: παρὰ τοῦτο γέγονε τὰ τῶν Ἑλλήνων *the fortunes of the Greeks depend on this* D. 18. 232. Measure: παρὰ μῑκρὸν ἤλθομεν ἐξανδραποδισθῆναι *we had a narrow escape* (came by a little) *from being enslaved* I. 7. 6, παρὰ πολύ *by far* T. 2. 8. Comparison: ἐξέτασον παρ' ἄλληλα *contrast with each other* D. 18. 265, χειμὼν μείζων παρὰ τὴν καθεστηκυῖαν ὥρᾱν *stormy weather more severe than was to be expected at the season* then *present* T. 4. 6.

4. **παρά** *in Composition*

Alongside, by, beside (παριέναι *go alongside*), *beyond, past* (**παρελαύνειν** *drive past*), *over* (παρορᾶν *overlook*), *aside, amiss* (παρακούειν *misunderstand*).

1693. **περί** *around* (on all sides), *about;* cp. πέριξ *round about.* Lat. *per* in *permagnus.* περί is wider than ἀμφί: cp. X. Vect. 1. 7 οὐ περίρρυτος οὖσα ὥσπερ νῆσος . . . ἀμφιθάλαττος γάρ ἐστι *it* (Attica) *is not, like an island, surrounded by the sea . . . for it has the sea on two sides.* On περί post-positive, see 1665.

1. **περί** *with the Genitive*

a. Local (poetic): περὶ τρόπιος βεβαώς *riding on* (astride) *the keel* ε 130.

b. Other relations: *about, concerning* (Lat. *de*), the subject *about which* an act or thought centres: περὶ πατρίδος μαχούμενοι *fighting for their country* T. 6. 69 (cp. ὑπέρ), δείσᾱς περὶ τοῦ υἱοῦ *fearing for his son* X. C. 1. 4. 22, λέγειν περὶ τῆς εἰρήνης *to speak about peace* T. 5. 55; τὰ περί τινος instead of τὰ περί τινα is used in the neighbourhood of a verb of saying or thinking (which takes περί with gen.): τὰ περὶ τῆς ἀρετῆς *the relations of virtue* P. Pr. 360 e. Superiority (cp. 1402): περίεσσι γυναικῶν εἶδος *thou dost surpass women in beauty* σ 248, περὶ παντὸς ποιούμενοι *regarding as* (more than everything) *all-important* T. 2. 11 (cp. 1373).

2. **περί** *with the Dative*

a. Local: *about:* of arms, dress, etc., in prose: στρεπτοὶ περὶ τοῖς τραχήλοις *collars about their necks* X. A. 1. 5. 8, ἃ περὶ τοῖς σώμασιν ἔχουσιν *the clothes about their persons* I. ep. 9. 10 (only case in the orators), περὶ δουρί A 303.

b. Other relations (usually poetic): External cause: δείσαντες περὶ ταῖς ναυσίν *afraid for their ships* T. 7. 53 (with verbs of *fearing*, περί with the gen. is *fear of* or *fear for*). Inner impulse: περὶ τάρβει *from fear* A. Pers. 694.

3. **περί** *with the Accusative*

a. Local: of position: ἀπέστειλαν ναῦς περὶ Πελοπόννησον *they despatched ships round about Peloponnese* T. 2. 23, ᾤκουν περὶ πᾶσαν τὴν Σικελίᾱν *they settled all round Sicily* 6. 2; of persons: οἱ περὶ Ἡράκλειτον *the followers of Heraclitus* P. Crat. 440 c.

b. Indefinite statement of time and number: περὶ ὄρθρον *about dawn* T. 6. 101, περὶ ἑβδομήκοντα *about seventy* 1. 54.

c. Other relations: Occupation: οἱ περὶ τὴν μουσικὴν ὄντες *those who are engaged in liberal pursuits* I. 9. 4; *connected with,* of general relation (*with reference to*): οἱ νόμοι οἱ περὶ τοὺς γάμους *the laws about marriage* P. Cr. 50 d, περὶ θεοὺς ἀσεβέστατοι *most impious in regard to the gods* X. H. 2. 3. 53, τὰ περὶ τὰς ναῦς *naval affairs* T. 1. 13. Verbs of action (except verbs of *striving*) prefer περί with accus., verbs of perception, emotion, knowing, prefer περί with gen. But the cases often shift.

4. περί *in Composition*

Around, about (περιέχειν *surround*), *beyond, over* (περιεῖναι *excel;* and περιορᾶν *look beyond, overlook, suffer*), (remaining) *over* (περιγίγνεσθαι *remain over, result*, and *excel*), *exceedingly* (περιχαρής *very glad*).

1694. πρό (Lat. *pro*, for) *before.* Cp. ἀντί, which is narrower in meaning.

1. πρό *with the Genitive only*

a. Local: πρὸ τῶν ἁμαξῶν *in front of the wagons* X. C. 6. 2. 36.

b. Temporal: πρὸ τῆς μάχης *before the battle* X. A. 1. 7. 13.

c. Other relations: Defence or care (cp. ὑπέρ): διακινδῡνεύειν πρὸ βασιλέως *to incur danger in defence of* (prop. *in front of*) *the king* X. C. 8. 8. 4. Preference (cp. ἀντί): οἱ ἐπαινοῦντες πρὸ δικαιοσύνης ἀδικίᾱν *those who laud injustice in preference to justice* P. R. 361 e, πρὸ πολλοῦ ποιεῖσθαι *to esteem highly* (in preference to much) I. 5. 138, φωνεῖν πρὸ τῶνδε *to speak for them* (*as their spokesman*) S. O. T. 10 (ἀντὶ τῶνδε = *as their deputy*, ὑπὲρ τῶνδε *as their champion*).

2. πρό *in Composition*

Before, forward, forth (προβάλλειν *put forward*), *for, in behalf of, in defence of, in public* (προαγορεύειν *give public notice*), *beforehand* (πρόδηλος *manifest beforehand*), *in preference* (προαιρεῖσθαι *choose in preference*).

1695. πρός (Hom. also προτί), *at, by* (*fronting*). Of like meaning, but of different origin, is Hom. ποτί.

1. πρός *with the Genitive*

a. Local (not common in prose): τὸ πρὸς ἑσπέρᾱς τεῖχος *the wall facing the west* X. H. 4. 4. 18, τὰ ὑποζύγια ἔχοντες πρὸς τοῦ ποταμοῦ *having the pack-animals on the side toward the river* X. A. 2. 2. 4.

b. Other relations: Descent: πρὸς πατρός *on the father's side* Aes. 3. 169. Characteristic: οὐ γὰρ ἦν πρὸς τοῦ Κύρου τρόπου *for it was not the way of Cyrus* X. A. 1. 2. 11. Point of view of a person: πρὸς ἀνθρώπων αἰσχρός *base in the eyes of men* 2. 5. 20. Agent as the source, with passive verbs (instead of ὑπό): ὁμολογεῖται πρὸς πάντων *it is agreed by all* 1. 9. 20; *to the advantage of;* σπονδᾶς ποιησάμενος πρὸς Θηβαίων μᾶλλον ἢ πρὸς ἑαυτῶν *making a truce more to the advantage of the Thebans than of his own party* X. H. 7. 1. 17; in oaths and entreaties: πρὸς θεῶν *by the gods* X. H. 2. 4. 21.

2. πρός *with the Dative*

In a local sense, denoting proximity (generally, in prose, of towns or buildings, not of persons): πρὸς τῇ πόλει τὴν μάχην ποιεῖσθαι *to fight near the city* T. 6. 49; sometimes like ἐν, as πρὸς ἱεροῖς τοῖς κοινοῖς ἀνατεθῆναι *to be dedicated in the common shrines* T. 3. 57. Occupation: ἦν ὅλος πρὸς τῷ λήμματι *he was wholly intent upon his gain* D. 19. 127. *In addition to:* πρὸς αὐτοῖς *besides these* T. 7. 57. *In the presence of:* πρὸς τῷ διαιτητῇ λέγειν *to speak before the arbitrator* D. 39. 22.

3. **πρός** *with the Accusative*

a. Local (direction toward or to, strictly *fronting, facing*): ὑμᾶς ἄξομεν πρὸς αὐτούς *we will lead you to them* X. A. 7. 6. 6, πρὸς νότον (*toward the*) *south* T. 3. 6, ἰέναι πρὸς τοὺς πολεμίους *to go against the enemy* X. A. 2. 6. 10.

b. Temporal (rare): πρὸς ἡμέρᾱν *toward daybreak* X. H. 2. 4. 6.

c. Other relations: friendly or hostile relation: πρὸς ἐμὲ λέγετε *speak to me* X. C. 6. 4. 19, φιλίᾱ πρὸς ὑμᾶς *friendship with you* I. 5. 32, ἔχθρᾱ πρὸς τοὺς Ἀργείους *enmity to the Argives* T. 2. 68, but ἡ πρὸς ἡμᾶς ἔχθρᾱ *our enmity* 6. 80, ἡ ἀπέχθεια πρὸς τοὺς Θηβαίους *our enmity to the Thebans* and *the enmity of the Thebans to us* D. 18. 36. With words of *hating, accusing*, and their opposites, πρός is used either of the subject or of the object or of both parties involved. With words denoting *warfare* πρός indicates a double relation, and the context must determine which party is the aggressor or assailant: ναυμαχίᾱ Κορινθίων πρὸς Κερκῡραίους *a sea-fight between the Corinthians and the Corcyreans* T. 1. 13 (here καί often suffices, as ὁ Λακεδαιμονίων καὶ Ἠλείων πόλεμος X. H. 3. 2. 31). Relation in general: οὐδὲν αὐτῷ πρὸς τὴν πόλιν ἐστίν *he has nothing to do with the city* D. 21. 44, πρὸς τοὺς θεοὺς εὐσεβῶς ἔχειν *to be pious toward the gods* Lyc. 15. Purpose: πρὸς τί; *to what end?* X. C. 6. 3. 20, πρὸς χάριν λέγειν *to speak in order to court favour* D. 4. 51; *with a view to* (often nearly = διά): πρὸς ταῦτα βουλεύεσθε εὖ *wherefore be well advised* T. 4. 87, πρὸς τὰ παρόντα *in consequence of the present circumstances* 6. 41. Conformity: πρὸς τὴν ἀξίᾱν *according to merit* X. C. 8. 4. 29. Standard of judgment: οὐδὲ πρὸς ἀργύριον τὴν εὐδαιμονίᾱν ἔκρῑνον *nor did they estimate happiness by the money-standard* I. 4. 76, χώρᾱ ὡς πρὸς τὸ πλῆθος τῶν πολῑτῶν ἐλαχίστη *a territory very small in proportion to the number of its citizens* 4. 107; and hence of comparison: οἱ φαυλότεροι τῶν ἀνθρώπων πρὸς τοὺς ξυνετωτέρους . . . ἄμεινον οἰκοῦσι τὰς πόλεις *the simpler class of men, in comparison with the more astute, manage their public affairs better* T. 3. 37. Exchange: ἡδονὰς πρὸς ἡδονὰς καταλλάττεσθαι *to exchange pleasures for pleasures* P. Ph. 69 a.

4. **πρός** *in Composition*

To, toward (προσελαύνειν *drive to*, προστρέπειν *turn toward*), *in addition* (προσλαμβάνειν *take in addition*), *against* (προσκρούειν *strike against, be angry with*). Often in the general sense of *additionally*, qualifying the whole sentence rather than the verb.

1696. **σύν** (Older Attic ξύν; cp. Ion. ξῡνός from **κονιος = κοινός**, Lat. *cum*) *with*.

1. **σύν** *with the Instrumental Dative only.*

a. In standard (*i.e.* not Xenophontic) prose σύν has been almost driven out of use by μετά. It is used (1) in old formulas, as σὺν (τοῖς) θεοῖς *with the help of the gods*, σὺν (τοῖς) ὅπλοις *in arms*, etc. (of things attached to a person), σὺν νῷ *intelligently*; (2) of sum totals (*along with, including*), as σὺν τοῖς ἔργοις πλέον ἢ δέκα τάλαντα ἔχει *he has more than ten talents interest included* D. 28. 13.

b. σύν is usually poetic (rare in comedy) and Xenophontic; it is often used in the formulas of **a** (1) and of persons and things personified. Its older and poetic meaning is *along with* (of something secondary or added to the action) and *with the help of*. So in Xen.: *together with, along with*: σὺν τῇ γυναικὶ δειπνεῖν *to sup with your wife* X. C. 6. 1. 49; to reinforce the simple dative: ἀκολουθεῖν σύν τινι, πορεύεσθαι σύν τινι (1524); with the collateral notion of help: *with the aid of*, as σὺν ἐκείνῳ μάχεσθαι *to fight with his help* X. C. 5. 3. 5.

c. Means and Instrument (regarded as accompaniments of an action: the comitative instrumental): ἡ κτῆσις αὐτῶν ἔστιν οὐδαμῶς σὺν τῇ βίᾳ, ἀλλὰ μᾶλλον σὺν τῇ εὐεργεσίᾳ *they* (friends) *are acquired, not by forcible means, but by kindness* X. C. 8. 7. 13.

d. Manner: σὺν γέλωτι ἦλθον *they went laughing* X. A. 1. 2. 18. *In conformity with* (opp. to παρά): οὐκ ἐπέτρεψε τῷ δήμῳ παρὰ τοὺς νόμους ψηφίσασθαι, ἀλλὰ σὺν τοῖς νόμοις ἠναντιώθη κτλ. *he did not permit the people to vote contrary to the laws, but, in conformity with them, opposed himself*, etc. X. M. 4. 4. 2.

2. σύν *in Composition*

Together with (συμβιοῦν *live with*, συμπορεύεσθαι *march in company with*), *together* (συμβάλλειν *conicere*), *completely* (συμπληροῦν *fill up*), contraction in size (συντέμνειν *cut short*), and generally of union or connection. Standard prose uses συν- freely.

1697. ὑπέρ (Hom. also ὑπείρ) *over*, Lat. *super*. For the contrast with ἐπί, see 1689.

1. ὑπέρ *with the Genitive*

a. Local: *from over*: ὑπὲρ τῶν ἄκρων κατέβαινον *they came down over the heights* T. 4. 25; *over, above*: ὑπὲρ τῆς κώμης γήλοφος ἦν *above the village was a hill* X. A. 1. 10. 12.

b. Other relations: *in defence of, on behalf of*: μαχόμενος ὑπὲρ ὑμῶν *fighting for you* (standing *over* to protect) P. L. 642 c; *in place of, in the name of*: ἐγὼ λέξω καὶ ὑπὲρ σοῦ καὶ ὑπὲρ ἡμῶν *I will speak both for you and for ourselves* X. C. 3. 3. 14. Purpose: ὑπὲρ τοῦ ταῦτα λαβεῖν *in order to get this* D. 8. 44; *concerning, about* (often = περί in Demos. and the later orators; in inscr. after 300 B.C.): φόβος ὑπὲρ τοῦ μέλλοντος *fear for the future* T. 7. 71, μὴ περὶ τῶν δικαίων μηδ᾽ ὑπὲρ τῶν ἔξω πραγμάτων *not about your just claims nor about your foreign interests* D. 6. 35.

2. ὑπέρ *with the Accusative*

a. Local: ὑπὲρ οὐδὸν ἐβήσετο *he passed over the threshold* ν 63, οἱ ὑπὲρ Ἑλλήσποντον οἰκοῦντες *those who dwell beyond the Hellespont* X. A. 1. 1. 9.

b. Temporal (= πρό) rare: ὑπὲρ τὰ Μηδικά *before the Persian wars* T. 1. 41.

c. Measure: ὑπὲρ ἥμισυ *more than half* X. C. 3. 3. 47, ὑπὲρ ἄνθρωπον *beyond the power of man* P. L. 839 d.

3. **ὑπέρ** *in Composition*

Over, above (ὑπερβάλλειν *cross over*, ὑπερέχειν trans. *hold over*, intr. *be above*), *in behalf of, for* (ὑπερμαχεῖν poet. *fight for*), *exceedingly* (ὑπερφρονεῖν *be over-proud*).

1698. ὑπό (Hom. also ὑπαί, Lesbian ὔπα-), *under, by*, Lat. *sub.*

1. **ὑπό** *with the Genitive*

a. Local (rare in Attic prose): *out from under* (poet., cp. ὑπέκ): ῥέει κρήνη ὑπὸ σπείους *a spring flows out from a cave* ι 140, λαβὼν βοῦν ὑπὸ ἁμάξης *taking an ox from a wagon* X. A. 6. 4. 25; *under* (of rest): τὰ ὑπὸ γῆς (a fixed phrase) ἅπαντα *all things under the earth* P. A. 18 b.

b. Other relations (metaphorically *under the agency of*): Direct agent (with passives and with verbs having a passive force); contrast διά, 1685. 2. d: σωθέντες ὑπὸ σοῦ *saved by you* X. A. 2. 5. 14, αἰσθόμενος ὑπ' αὐτομόλων *informed by deserters* T. 5. 2, εὖ ἀκούειν ὑπὸ ἀνθρώπων *to be well spoken of by men* X. A. 7. 7. 23. With passive nouns: ἡ ὑπὸ Μελήτου γραφή *the indictment brought by Meletus* X. M. 4. 4. 4, κλῆσις ὑπὸ τῆς βουλῆς *invitation by the Senate* D. 19. 32. External cause: ἀπώλετο ὑπὸ λῑμοῦ *perished of hunger* X. A. 1. 5. 5, οὐκ ἐπὶ πολὺ ὑπὸ τῶν ἱππέων ἐξιόντες *not going out far because of the cavalry* T. 6. 37. Internal cause: ὑπὸ τῶν μεγίστων νῑκηθέντες, τῑμῆς καὶ δέους καὶ ὠφελίᾱς *constrained by the strongest motives, honour and fear and profit* T. 1. 76. External accompaniment, as pressure, in ἐτόξευον ὑπὸ μαστίγων *they shot under the lash* X. A. 3. 4. 25; sound, in ὑπὸ αὐλητῶν *to the accompaniment of flute-players* T. 5. 70; light, in ὑπὸ φᾱνοῦ πορεύεσθαι *to go with a torch* X. R. L. 5. 7. Manner: ὑπὸ σπουδῆς *hastily* T. 3. 33.

N. 1.—ὑπό with the genitive of a thing personifies the thing. The things so personified are (1) words implying a person, as λόγοι, (2) external circumstances, as συμφορά, κίνδῡνος, νόμος, (3) natural phenomena, as χειμών, (4) emotions, as φθόνος. The dative may also be employed. See 1493, 1494.

N. 2.—On ὑπό to express the personal agent with the perf. pass. see 1493.

2. **ὑπό** *with the Dative*

a. Local: *under* (of rest): ἑστάναι ὑπό τινι δένδρῳ *to stand under a tree* P. Phil. 38 c. ὑπό of place is more common with the dative than with the genitive.

b. Other relations: Agent (poetic, except with verbs signifying *to educate*): ὑπὸ παιδοτρίβῃ ἀγαθῷ πεπαιδευμένος *educated under* (the guidance of) *a good master* P. Lach. 184 e. Coöperative cause (poet.): βῆ ὑπ' ἀμύμονι πομπῇ *he went under a blameless convoy* Z 171. Subjection: οἱ ὑπὸ βασιλεῖ ὄντες *the subjects of* (*i.e.* those under) *the king* X. C. 8. 1. 6, ὑφ' αὑτῷ ποιήσασθαι *to bring under his own power* D. 18. 40.

3. **ὑπό** *with the Accusative*

a. Local: Motion under: ὑπ' αὐτὸν (τὸν λόφον) στήσᾱς τὸ στράτευμα *halting the army under the hill* X. A. 1. 10. 14. Motion down under (poet.): εἶμ' ὑπὸ γαῖαν *I shall go down under the earth* Σ 333. Extension or position: αἱ ὑπὸ τὸ ὄρος κῶμαι *the villages at the foot of the mountain* X. A. 7. 4. 5. Proximity: ὑποκειμένη ἡ Εὔβοια ὑπὸ τὴν Ἀττικήν *Euboea lying close by* (under) *Attica* I. 4. 108.

b. Temporal (of time impending or in progress): ὑπὸ νύκτα *at the approach of night* (*sub noctem*) T. 2. 92, ὑπὸ νύκτα *during the night* Hdt. 9. 58, ὑπὸ τὴν εἰρήνην *at the time of the peace* I. 4. 177.

c. Other relations. Subjection: ὑπὸ σφᾶς ποιεῖσθαι *to bring under their own sway* T. 4. 60.

4. **ὑπό** *in Composition*

Under (ὑποτιθέναι *place under*), *behind* (ὑπολείπειν *leave behind*), *secretly* (cp. *underhand;* ὑποπέμπειν *send as a spy*), *gradually* (ὑποκαταβαίνειν *descend by degrees*), *slightly* (ὑποφαίνειν *shine a little*); of accompaniment (ὑπᾴδειν *accompany with the voice*); of an action performed by another (ὑποκηρύττεσθαι *have oneself proclaimed by the herald*).

IMPROPER PREPOSITIONS

1699. Improper prepositions do not form compounds (1647).

1700. With the Genitive.

The list below contains some of the adverbial words used as prepositions.

[The more important words are printed in **fat** type. An asterisk denotes words used only in poetry.]

ἀγχοῦ *near*, poet. and Ionic (also with dat.). **ἄνευ** *without, except, besides, away from*, rarely after its case. ἀντία, ἀντίον *facing, against*, poet. and Ionic (also with dat.). ἄτερ *without, apart from, away from.* **ἄχρι** and **μέχρι** *as far as, until* (of place, time, and number). δίκην *after the manner of* (accus. of δίκη). δίχα* *apart from, unlike, except.* **ἐγγύς** *near* (with dat. poetical). **εἴσω** (ἔσω) *within.* ἑκάς *far from*, poetic and Ionic. ἑκατέρωθεν *on both sides of.* **ἐκτός** *without.* **ἔμπροσθεν** *before.* **ἐναντίον** *in the presence of* (poet. *against*, gen. or dat.). **ἕνεκα, ἕνεκεν** (Ion. εἵνεκα, εἵνεκεν) *on account of, for the sake of, with regard to*, usually postpositive. From such combinations as τούτου ἕνεκα arose, by fusion, the illegitimate preposition οὕνεκα (found chiefly in the texts of the dramatists). ἔνερθε* *beneath.* **ἐντός** *within.* **ἔξω** *out of, beyond* (of time), *except.* **εὐθύ** *straight to.* καταντικρύ *over against.* κρύφα, λάθρᾳ *unbeknown to.* **μεταξύ** *between.* **μέχρι** *as far as.* νόσφι* *apart from.* **ὄπισθεν** *behind.* πάρος* *before.* πέλας* *near* (also with dat.). πέρᾱ *beyond* (*ultra*). πέρᾱν *across* (*trans*). **πλήν** *except*, as πλὴν ἀνδραπόδων *except slaves* X. A. 2. 4. 27. Often an adverb or conjunction: παντὶ δῆλον πλὴν ἐμοί *it is clear to everybody except me* P. R. 529 a. **πλησίον** *near* (also with dat.). πόρρω, πρόσω *far from.* πρίν* *before* (Pindar). σχεδόν* *near.* τῆλε* *far from.* **χάριν** *for the sake of* (accus. of χάρις), usually after its case. **χωρίς** *without, separate from.*

1701. With the Dative.

ἅμα *together with, at the same time with.* **ὁμοῦ** *together with, close to.*

1702. With the Accusative.

ὡς *to*, of persons only, used after verbs expressing or implying motion. Probably used especially in the language of the people.

THE VERB: VOICES

ACTIVE VOICE

1703. The active voice represents the subject as performing the action of the verb: λούω *I wash.*

a. Under *action* is included *being*, as ἡ ὁδὸς μακρά ἐστι *the way is long.*

1704. Active verbs are *transitive* or *intransitive* (920).

1705. The action of a transitive verb is directed immediately upon an object, as τύπτω τὸν παῖδα *I strike the boy.*

1706. The object of a transitive verb is always put in the accusative (1553).

1707. The action of an intransitive verb is not directed immediately upon an object. The action may be restricted to the subject, as ἀλγῶ *I am in pain*, or it may be defined by an oblique case or by a preposition with its case, as ἀλγῶ τοὺς πόδας *I have a pain in my feet*, ἀφίκετο εἰς τὴν πόλιν *he arrived at the city.*

1708. Many verbs are used in the active voice both transitively and intransitively. So, in English, *turn*, *move*, *change*. Cp. 1557 ff.

a. The distinction between transitive and intransitive verbs is a grammatical convenience, and is not founded on an essential difference of nature.

1709. Active verbs ordinarily transitive are often used intransitively:

a. By the ellipsis of a definite external object, which in some cases may be employed, as ἄγειν (τὸ στράτευμα) *march*, αἴρειν (τὴν ἄγκῡραν) *hoist the anchor*, (τὰς ναῦς) *get under sail, start*, ἀπαίρειν (τὰς ναῦς, τὸν στρατόν) *sail away, march away*, διάγειν (τὸν βίον) *live*, ἐλαύνειν (τὸν ἵππον) *ride*, (τὸ ἅρμα) *drive*, (τὸν στρατόν) *march*, καταλύειν (τοὺς ἵππους, τὰ ὑποζύγια) *halt*, κατέχειν (τὴν ναῦν) *put in shore*, προσέχειν (τὸν νοῦν) *pay attention*, τελευτᾶν (τὸν βίον) *die.* The original sense has often been so completely forgotten that it becomes possible to say αἴρειν τῷ στρατῷ *set out with the army* T. 2. 12, ἐλαύνων ἱδροῦντι τῷ ἵππῳ *riding with his horse in a sweat* X. A. 1. 8. 1.

b. πράττειν, ἔχειν with adverbs often mean *to keep, to be:* εὖ πράττειν *fare well*, καλῶς ἔχειν *be well* (*bene se habere*), ἔχειν οὕτως *be so.* So when a reflexive pronoun is apparently omitted: ἔχ' αὐτοῦ *stop there!* D. 45. 26.

c. Many other transitive verbs may be used absolutely, *i.e.* with no definite object omitted, as νῑκᾶν *be a victor*, ἀδικεῖν *be guilty.* Cp. 'amare' *be in love*, 'drink' *be a drunkard.* This is especially the case in compounds, *e.g.* of ἀλλάττειν, ἀνύειν, διδόναι, κλῑ́νειν, λαμβάνειν, λείπειν, μειγνύναι.

d. In poetry many uncompounded transitive verbs are used intransitively. Many intransitive verbs become transitive when compounded with a prep., especially when the compound has a transferred sense, 1559. In some verbs 1st aorist and 1st perfect are transitive, 2d aorist and 2d perfect are intransitive. Cp. 819.

1710. Instead of the active, a periphrasis with γίγνεσθαι may be used, often to express solemnity. μηνῦταὶ γίγνονται *they turned informers* T. 3. 2, μὴ ὑβριστὴς γένῃ '*do not be guilty of outrage*' S. Aj. 1092.

1711. Causative Active. — The active may be used of an action performed at the bidding of the subject: Κῦρος τὰ βασίλεια κατέκαυσεν *Cyrus burnt down the palace* (i.e. had it burnt down) X. A. 1. 4. 10. So with ἀποκτείνειν *put to death*, θάπτειν *bury*, οἰκοδομεῖν *build*, παιδεύειν *instruct*, ἀνακηρῦττειν *publicly proclaim*.

1712. An infinitive limiting the meaning of an adjective is usually active where English employs the passive (cp. 2006).

MIDDLE VOICE

1713. The middle voice shows that the action is performed with special reference to the subject: λοῦμαι *I wash myself*.

1714. The middle represents the subject as doing something in which he is interested. He may do something *to himself*, *for himself*, or he may act with something *belonging to himself*.

1715. The future middle is often (807), the first aorist middle is almost never, used passively.

1716. The object of the middle (1) may belong in the sphere of the subject, as his property, etc.: λούομαι τὰς χεῖρας *I wash my hands*, or (2) it may be brought into the sphere of the subject: τοὺς ὁπλίτᾱς μετεπέμψαντο *they sent for the hoplites*, or (3) it may be removed from the sphere of the subject: ἀποδίδομαι τὴν οἰκίᾱν *I sell my house* (lit. *give away*). Here the object is also the property of the subject.

1717. The **Direct Reflexive Middle** represents the subject as acting directly *on himself*. *Self* is here the direct object. So with verbs expressing external and natural acts, as the verbs of the toilet: ἀλείφεσθαι *anoint oneself*, λοῦσθαι *wash oneself*; and κοσμεῖσθαι *adorn oneself*, στεφανοῦσθαι *crown oneself*; γυμνάζεσθαι *exercise oneself*.

a. The direct reflexive idea is far more frequently conveyed by the active and a reflexive pronoun, 1723.

b. The part affected may be added in the accusative: ἐπαίσατο τὸν μηρόν *he smote his thigh* X. C. 7. 3. 6.

1718. So with many other verbs, as ἵστασθαι *stand* (*place oneself*), τρέπεσθαι *turn* (lit. *turn oneself*), δηλοῦσθαι *show oneself*, τάττεσθαι *post oneself*, ἀπολογεῖσθαι *defend oneself* (*argue oneself off*), φαίνεσθαι *show oneself*, *appear*, παρασκευάζεσθαι *prepare oneself*, ἀπόλλυσθαι *destroy oneself*, *perish*.

1719. The **Indirect Reflexive Middle** represents the subject as acting *for himself*, *with reference to himself*, or *with something belonging to himself*. *Self* is often here the indirect object. So πορίζεσθαι *provide for oneself* (πορίζειν *provide*), φυλάττεσθαι *guard against* (φυλάττειν *keep guard*), αἱρεῖσθαι *choose* (*take for oneself*), παρέχεσθαι *furnish* (παρέχειν *offer, present*).

1720. Cases in which the object is to be removed from the sphere of the subject may be resolved into the dative *for oneself* (1483): τὴν ῥᾳθῡμίᾱν ἀποθέσθαι *to lay aside your indolence* D. 8. 46, ἐτρέψαντο τοὺς ἱππέᾱς *they routed the cavalry* T. 6. 98, τοὺς ἐχθροὺς ἀμύνεσθαι *to ward off the enemy for themselves*, i.e. *to defend themselves against the enemy* 1. 144.

1721. The middle often denotes that the subject acts with something belonging to himself (material objects, means, powers). It is often used of acts done willingly. Thus, παρέχεσθαι *furnish from one's own resources*, ἐπαγγέλλεσθαι *promise, make profession of*, τίθεσθαι τὴν ψῆφον *give one's vote*, τίθεσθαι τὰ ὅπλα *ground arms*, ἀποδείξασθαι γνώμην *set forth one's opinion*, λαμβάνεσθαί τινος *put one's hand on* (seize) *something*. Thus, ἐσπασμένοι τὰ ξίφη *having drawn their swords* X. A. 7. 4. 16, παῖδας ἐκκεκομισμένοι ἦσαν *they had removed their children* T. 2. 78, τροπαῖον στησάμενοι *having set up a trophy* X. H. 2. 4. 7, ὅπλα πορίσασθαι *to procure arms for themselves* T. 4. 9, ὁπλίτᾱς μετεπέμψατο *he sent for hoplites* 7. 31, γυναῖκα ἠγαγόμην *I married* L. 1. 6.

1722. Under the indirect middle belong the periphrases of ποιεῖσθαι with verbal nouns instead of the simple verb (cp. 1754). ποιεῖν with the same nouns means *to bring about, effect, fashion*, etc.

εἰρήνην ποιεῖσθαι *make peace* (of one nation at war with another).
εἰρήνην ποιεῖν *bring about a peace* (between opponents, nations at war: of an individual).
θήρᾱν ποιεῖσθαι (= θηρᾶν) *hunt*, θήρᾱν ποιεῖν *arrange a hunt*.
λόγον ποιεῖσθαι (= λέγειν) *deliver a speech*, λόγον ποιεῖν *compose a speech*.
ναυμαχίᾱν ποιεῖσθαι (= ναυμαχεῖν) *fight a naval battle*.
ναυμαχίᾱν ποιεῖν *bring on a naval battle* (of the commander).
ὁδὸν ποιεῖσθαι (= ὁδεύειν) *make a journey*, ὁδὸν ποιεῖν *build a road*.
πόλεμον ποιεῖσθαι *wage war*, πόλεμον ποιεῖν *bring about a war*.
σπονδᾱ̀ς ποιεῖσθαι *conclude* (*make*) *a treaty*, or *truce*.
σπονδᾱ̀ς ποιεῖν *bring about a treaty*, or *truce*.

1723. Active and Reflexive. — Instead of the direct middle the active voice with the reflexive pronoun is usually employed; often of difficult and unnatural actions (especially with αὐτὸς ἑαυτόν, etc.).

τὰ ὅπλα παρέδοσαν καὶ σφᾶς αὐτούς *they surrendered their arms and themselves* T. 4. 38, μισθώσᾱς αὑτόν *hiring himself out* D. 19. 29 (not μισθωσάμενος, which means *hiring for himself*), καταλέλυκε τὴν αὐτὸς αὑτοῦ δυναστείᾱν *he himself has put an end to his own sovereignty* Aes. 3. 233, ἠτίμωκεν ἑαυτόν *he has dishonoured himself* D. 21. 103. But regularly ἀπάγχεσθαι *hang oneself* (1717).

a. The active and a reflexive pronoun in the gen. or dat. may be used for the simple middle when the reflexive notion is emphatic: καταλείπειν συγγράμματα ἑαυτῶν *to leave behind them their written compositions* P. Phae. 257 d.

1724. Middle and Reflexive. — The reflexive pronoun may be used with the middle: ἑαυτὸν ἀποκρύπτεσθαι *to hide himself* P. R. 393 c; often for emphasis, as in contrasts: οἱ μὲν φᾱσι βασιλέᾱ κελεῦσαί τινα ἐπισφάξαι αὐτὸν Κύρῳ, οἱ δ' ἑαυτὸν ἐπισφάξασθαι *some say that the king issued orders for some one to slay him* (Artapates) *over* (the body of) *Cyrus, while others say that he slew himself with his own hand* X. A. 1. 8. 29, cp. also τί τὴν πόλιν προσῆκε ποιεῖν, ἀρχὴν καὶ τυραννίδα τῶν Ἑλλήνων ὁρῶσαν ἑαυτῷ κατασκευαζόμενον Φίλιππον; *what did it beseem the city to do when it saw Philip compassing for himself dominion and despotic sway over the Greeks?* D. 18. 66.

1725. The Causative Middle denotes that the subject has something done by another for himself: ἐγὼ γάρ σε ταῦτα ἐδιδαξάμην *for I had you taught this* X. C. 1. 6. 2, παρατίθεσθαι σῖτον *to have food served up* 8. 6. 12, ὅσοι ὅπλα ἀφῄρηνται, ταχὺ ἄλλα ποιήσονται *all who have had their arms taken from them will soon get others made* 6. 1. 12, ἑαυτῷ σκηνὴν κατεσκευάσατο *he had a tent prepared for himself* 2. 1. 30.

a. This force does not belong exclusively to the middle; cp. 1711.

1726. Reciprocal Middle. — With a dual or plural subject the middle may indicate a reciprocal relation. So with verbs of *contending, conversing* (*questioning, replying*), *greeting, embracing,* etc. The reciprocal middle is often found with compounds of διά.

οἱ ἀθληταὶ ἠγωνίζοντο *the athletes contended* T. 1. 6, καταστάντες ἐμάχοντο *when they had got into position they fought* 1. 49, ἀνὴρ ἀνδρὶ διελέγοντο *they conversed man with man* 8. 93, ἐπιμείγνυσθαι ἀλλήλοις *to have friendly intercourse with one another* X. C. 7. 4. 5, ταῦτα διανεμοῦνται *they will divide this up among themselves* L. 21. 14. So αἰτιᾶσθαι *accuse*, λῡμαίνεσθαι *maltreat*, μέμφεσθαι *blame*, ἁμιλλᾶσθαι *vie*, παρακελεύεσθαι *encourage one another*.

a. The active may also be employed, as πολεμεῖν *wage war*.

b. Some of these verbs have a passive aorist form, as διελέχθην (812).

1727. The reciprocal relation may also be expressed (1) by the use of the reflexive pronoun (cp. 1724) with the active: φθονοῦσιν ἑαυτοῖς *they are mutually envious* X. M. 3. 5. 16; (2) by the use of ἀλλήλων, etc., with the active: ἀμφισβητοῦμεν ἀλλήλοις *we are at variance with one another* P. Phae. 263 a; (3) by repetition of the noun: πτωχὸς πτωχῷ φθονέει = *beggars envy each other* Hesiod W. D. 26. The reflexive pronouns and ἀλλήλων, etc., may also be added to the middle.

1728. Differences between Active and Middle. — As contrasted with the active, the middle lays stress on the conscious activity, bodily or mental participation, of the agent.

In verbs that possess both active and middle: βουλεύεσθαι *deliberate*, βουλεύειν *plan*, σταθμᾶν *measure*, σταθμᾶσθαι *calculate*, σκοπεῖν *look at*, σκοπεῖσθαι *consider*, ἔχεσθαι *cling to*, παύεσθαι *cease* (1734. 14). The force of the middle often cannot be reproduced in translation (ἀκούεσθαι, τῑμᾶσθαι, ἀριθμεῖσθαι, ἀπορεῖσθαι), and in some other cases it may not have been felt, as in ὁρᾶσθαι in poetry (προορᾶσθαι occurs in prose).

a. Many such verbs form their futures from the middle: ἀκούσομαι, ᾄσομαι, ἁμαρτήσομαι. See 805.

b. In verbs in -ευω, the middle signifies that the subject is acting in a manner appropriate to his state or condition: πολῑτεύειν *be a citizen*, πολῑτεύεσθαι *act as a citizen, perform one's civic duties;* πρεσβεύειν *be an envoy,* πρεσβεύεσθαι *negotiate as envoy* or *send envoys* (of the State in its negotiations). But this force of the middle is not always apparent.

1729. Middle Deponents (810) often denote bodily or mental action (feeling and thinking): ἅλλεσθαι *jump,* πέτεσθαι *fly,* ὀρχεῖσθαι *dance,* οἴχεσθαι *be gone,* δέρκεσθαι *look;* βούλεσθαι *wish,* αἰσθάνεσθαι *perceive,* ἀκροᾶσθαι *listen,* μέμφεσθαι *blame,* οἴεσθαι *conjecture, think* (lit. *take omens for oneself,* from ὀϝις, Lat. *avis, auspicium*), ἡγεῖσθαι *consider;* ὀλοφύρεσθαι *lament.*

a. Some of the verbs denoting a functional state or process have the middle either in all forms or only in the future.

b. Verbs denoting bodily activity regularly have a middle future, 805–806.

1730. Deponent verbs are either direct or indirect middles; direct: ὑπισχνεῖσθαι *undertake, promise* (lit. *hold oneself under*); indirect: κτᾶσθαι *acquire for oneself,* ἀγωνίζεσθαι *contend* (with one's own powers).

1731. The middle may denote more vigorous participation on the part of the subject than the active: σεύεσθαι *dart,* but θέειν *run.*

1732. The active is often used for the middle when it is not of practical importance to mark the interest of the subject in the action. The active implies what the middle expresses. So with μεταπέμπειν *send for* T. 7. 15, δηλώσαντες τὴν γνώμην *setting forth their opinion* 3. 37, τροπαῖον στήσαντες *setting up a trophy* 7. 5.

1733. The passive form may have reflexive force, as κινηθῆναι *set oneself in motion,* ἀπαλλαγῆναι *remove oneself,* ἐναντιωθῆναι *oppose oneself,* σωθῆναι *save oneself* (σώθητι *save yourself* P. Cr. 44 b). Some of these middle passives may take the accusative, as αἰσχυνθῆναι *be ashamed before,* φοβηθῆναι *be afraid of,* καταπληγῆναί τινα *be amazed at some one.* See 814 ff.

1734. List of the chief verbs showing important differences of meaning between active and middle. It will be noted that the active is often transitive, the middle intransitive.

1. **αἱρεῖν** *take;* αἱρεῖσθαι *choose.*

2. **ἀμΰνειν** τί τινι *ward off something from some one,* ἀμύνειν τινί *help some one;* ἀμύνεσθαί τι *defend oneself against something,* ἀμύνεσθαί τινα *requite some one.*

3. **ἀποδοῦναι** *give back;* ἀποδόσθαι *sell* (give away for one's profit).

4. **ἅπτειν** *attach;* ἅπτεσθαί τινος *touch.*

5. **ἄρχειν** *begin,* contrasts one beginner of an action with another, as ἄρχειν πολέμου *take the aggressive, strike the first blow* (*bellum movere*), ἄρχειν λόγου *be the first to speak,* ἦρχε χειρῶν ἀδίκων *he began an unprovoked assault* L. 4. 11; ἄρχεσθαι make one's own beginning, as contrasted with the later stages, as ἄρχεσθαι πολέμου *begin warlike operations* (*bellum incipere*), ἄρχεσθαι τοῦ λόγου *begin one's speech.* πολέμου οὐκ ἄρξομεν, ἀρχομένους δὲ ἀμῡνούμεθα *we shall not take the initiative in the war, but upon those who take it up we shall retaliate* T. 1. 144.

6. **γαμεῖν** *marry* (of the man, *ducere*); γαμεῖσθαι *marry* (of the woman, *nubere*).

7. **γράφειν** νόμον *propose a law* (said of the maker of a law whether or not he is himself subject to it); γράφεσθαι γραφήν *draw up an indictment* for a public

offence, γράφεσθαί τινα *bring suit against some one* (have him written down in the magistrates' records).

8. **δανείζειν** (make of anything a δάνος *loan*) *i.e. put out at interest, lend;* δανείζεσθαι (have a δάνος *made to oneself*) *have lent to one, borrow at interest.*

9. **δικάζειν** *give judgment;* δικάζεσθαι (δίκην τινί) *go to law with a person, conduct a case* (properly *get some one to give judgment*).

10. **ἐπιψηφίζειν** *put to vote* (of the presiding officer); ἐπιψηφίζεσθαι *vote, decree* (of the people).

11. **ἔχειν** *hold;* ἔχεσθαί τινος *hold on to, be close to.*

12. **θύειν** *sacrifice;* θύεσθαι *take auspices* (of a general, etc.).

13. **μισθοῦν** (put a μισθός, *rent*, on anything) *i.e. let for hire* (*locare*); μισθοῦσθαι (lay a μισθός upon oneself) *i.e. hire* (*conducere*). Cp. 1723.

14. **παύειν** *make to cease, stop* (trans.); παύεσθαι *cease* (intr.). But **παῦε** λέγων *stop talking.*

15. **πείθειν** *persuade;* πείθεσθαι *obey* (*persuade oneself*); πέποιθα *I trust.*

16. **τιθέναι** νόμον *frame* or *propose a law* for others (said of the lawgiver, *legem ferre* or *rogare*) ; τίθεσθαι νόμον *make a law* for one's own interest, for one's own State (said of the State legislating, *legem sciscere* or *iubere*). **αὐτοὺς** (ἀγράφους νόμους) οἱ ἄνθρωποι ἔθεντο . . . θεοὺς οἶμαι τοὺς νόμους τούτους τοῖς ἀνθρώποις θεῖναι *men did not make the unwritten laws for themselves, but I think the gods made these laws for men* X. M. 4. 4. 19.

17. **τῑμωρεῖν** τινι *avenge some one,* τῑμωρεῖν τινά τινι *punish A for B's satisfaction;* τῑμωρεῖσθαί τινα *avenge oneself on* (punish) *some one.*

18. **τίνειν** δίκην *pay a penalty* (*poenas dare*); τίνεσθαι δίκην *exact a penalty* (*poenas sumere*).

19. **φυλάττειν** τινά *watch some one;* φυλάττεσθαί τινα *be on one's guard against some one.*

20. **χρᾶν** *give an oracle,* and *lend;* χρᾶσθαι *consult an oracle,* and *use.*

PASSIVE VOICE

1735. The passive voice represents the subject as acted on: ἐώθουν, ἐωθοῦντο, ἔπαιον, ἐπαίοντο *they pushed, were pushed, they struck, were struck* X. C. 7. 1. 38.

a. The passive has been developed from the middle. With the exception of some futures and the aorist, the middle forms do duty as passives: αἱρεῖται *takes for himself,* i.e. *chooses,* and *is chosen.* (For this development of the passive, cp. the reflexive use in *se trouver, sich finden.*) So κέχυται *has poured itself, has been poured.* In Homer there are more perfect middles used passively than any other middle tenses. Cp. 802.

b. Uncompounded ἐσχόμην sometimes retained its use as a passive. ἐσχέθην is late.

1736. The passive may have the sense *allow oneself to be, get oneself:* ἐξάγοντές τε καὶ ἐξαγόμενοι *carrying and allowing ourselves to be carried across the border* P. Cr. 48 d, ἀπεχθήσει Γοργίᾳ *you will incur the hatred of Gorgias* P. Phil. 58 c.

1737. Many future middle forms are used passively (807 ff.).

1738. The future middle forms in -σομαι are developed from the present stem, and express durative action; the (later) future passives in -ήσομαι, -θήσομαι are developed from the aorists in -ην and -θην, and are aoristic. This difference in kind of action is most marked when the future middle forms are used passively, but it is not always found. τοῖς ἄλλοις ξυμμάχοις παράδειγμα σαφὲς καταστήσατε, ὃς ἂν ἀφίστηται, θανάτῳ ζημιωσόμενον *give to the rest of the allies a plain example that whoever revolts shall be punished* (in each case) *with death* T. 3.40, ἐὰν ἁλῷ, θανάτῳ ζημιωθήσεται *if he is convicted, he will be punished* (a single occurrence) *with death* D. 23.80, ὁ δίκαιος μαστῑγώσεται, στρεβλώσεται, δεδήσεται, ἐκκαυθήσεται τὠφθαλμώ *the just man will be scourged, racked, fettered, will have his eyes burnt out* P. R. 361 e, τῑμήσομαι *I shall enjoy honour*, τῑμηθήσομαι *I shall be honoured* (on a definite occasion), ὠφελήσομαι *I shall receive lasting benefit*, ὠφεληθήσομαι *I shall be benefited* (on a definite occasion). Cp. 808, 809, 1911.

1739. The second aorist passive was originally a second aorist active (of the -μι form) that was used intransitively to distinguish it from the transitive first aorist, as ἔφηνα *showed*, ἐφάνην *appeared*; ἔφθειρα *destroyed*, ἐφθάρην *am destroyed*; ἐξέπληξα *was terrified*, ἐξεπλάγην *was alarmed*. So ἐδάην *learned*, ἐρρύην *flowed*. Cp. ἔστησα *placed*, ἔστην *stood* (819).

1740. In Hom. all the second aorist forms in -ην are intransitive except ἐπλήγην and ἐτύπην *was struck*. Most of the forms in -θην are likewise intransitive in Hom., as ἐφάνθην *appeared* (in Attic *was shown*).

1741. The perfect passive in the third singular with the dative of the agent (1488) is often preferred to the perfect active of the first person. Thus πέπρᾱκταί μοι *it has been done by me* is more common than πέπρᾱγα or πέπρᾱχα *I have done*.

1742. The passive may be passive of the middle as well as passive of the active: αἱρεῖται *is taken* or *is chosen*, βιάζεται *does violence* or *suffers violence* (*is forced*), ᾑρέθη *was taken* or *was chosen*, ἐγράφη *was written* or *was indicted* (γέγραμμαι is commonly middle). The use of the passive as passive of the middle is post-Homeric.

a. When deponent verbs have a passive force, the future and aorist have the passive form: ἐβιάσθην *I suffered violence* (*was forced*), but ἐβιασάμην *I did violence*. This holds when there was once an active form. Cp. also τῑμωρεῖσθαι, μεταπέμπεσθαι, ψηφίζεσθαι, κυκλεῖσθαι.

b. The aorist passive may have a middle sense (814).

1743. The direct object of an active verb becomes the subject of the passive: ἡ ἐπιστολὴ ὑπὸ τοῦ διδασκάλου γράφεται *the letter is written by the teacher* (active ὁ διδάσκαλος γράφει τὴν ἐπιστολήν).

1744. The cognate accusative may become the subject of the passive: πόλεμος ἐπολεμήθη *war was waged* P. Menex. 243 e (πόλεμον πολεμεῖν, 1564).

1745. Active or middle verbs governing the genitive or dative may form (unlike the Latin use) a personal passive, the genitive or dative (especially if either denotes a person) becoming the subject of the passive.

a. With the genitive: ἄρχειν, ἡγεμονεύειν, καταφρονεῖν, καταγελᾶν, καταψηφίζειν (καταψηφίζεσθαι), ἀμελεῖν.

b. With the dative: ἀπειλεῖν, ἀπιστεῖν, ἐγκαλεῖν, ἐπιβουλεύειν, ἐπιτῑμᾶν, ὀνειδίζειν, πιστεύειν, πολεμεῖν, φθονεῖν.

c. Examples: οὐκ ἠξίουν οὗτοι ἡγεμονεύεσθαι ὑφ' ἡμῶν *they did not think it right to be governed by us* T. 3. 61, ἐκεῖνος κατεψηφίσθη *he was condemned* X. H. 5. 2. 36, but θάνατος αὐτῶν κατεγνώσθη *the penalty of death was pronounced against them* L. 13. 39 (pass. of καταγνῶναι θάνατον αὐτῶν), ὥρᾱ ἡμῖν βουλεύεσθαι ὑπὲρ ἡμῶν αὐτῶν μὴ καταφρονηθῶμεν *it is time for us to take counsel for ourselves that we may not be brought into contempt* X. A. 5. 7. 12, πολεμοῦνται μὲν ὑπὸ τῶν τὴν χώρᾱν αὐτῶν περιοικούντων, ἀπιστοῦνται δ' ὑφ' ἁπάντων *they are warred against by those who dwell around their country, and are distrusted by all* I. 5. 49, πῶς ἂν ἐπεβούλευσά τι αὐτῷ, ὅ τι μὴ καὶ ἐπεβουλεύθην ὑπ' αὐτοῦ; *how could I have plotted against him, unless I had been plotted against by him?* Ant. 4. β. 5, φθονηθεὶς ὑπὸ τοῦ Ὀδυσσέως *envied by Odysseus* X. M. 4. 2. 33 (contrast Lat. *invidetur mihi ab aliquo*).

N. — The above principle does not hold when the accusative of an external object intervenes between the verb and the dative.

1746. A verb governing an oblique case rarely forms in Greek (unlike Latin) an impersonal passive: ἐμοὶ βεβοήθηται τῷ τε τεθνεῶτι καὶ τῷ νόμῳ *my aid has been given to the deceased and to the law* Ant. 1. 31. The tense used is one from the perfect stem.

1747. An active verb followed by two accusatives, one of a person, the other of a thing, retains, when transferred to the passive, the accusative of the thing, while the accusative of the person becomes the nominative subject of the passive. Examples 1621, 1625, 1627, 1632.

1748. An active verb followed by an accusative of the direct object (a thing) and an oblique case of a person, retains, when transferred to the passive, the accusative of the direct object, while the indirect object becomes the nominative subject of the passive. Cp. *I have been willed a large estate.*

a. With verbs signifying *to enjoin, entrust*: οἱ Βοιωτοὶ ταῦτα ἐπεσταλμένοι ἀνεχώρουν *the Boeotians having received these instructions withdrew* T. 5. 37 (pass. of ἐπιστέλλειν ταῦτα τοῖς Βοιωτοῖς), ἄλλο τι μεῖζον ἐπιταχθήσεσθε *you will have some greater command laid upon you* 1. 140 (pass. of ἐπιτάττειν ἄλλο τι μεῖζον ὑμῖν). Both accusatives are internal; and so, in οἱ τῶν Ἀθηναίων ἐπιτετραμμένοι τὴν φυλακήν *those of the Athenians who had been entrusted with the watch* T. 1. 126, φυλακήν is equivalent to an internal accusative. The nominative of the thing and the dative of the person sometimes occur (Ἴωνες, τοῖσι ἐπετέτραπτο ἡ φυλακή *the Ionians to whom the guard had been entrusted* Hdt. 7. 10). The dative is common when an inf. is used with the pass. verb: ἐπετέτακτο τοῖς σκευοφόροις ἰέναι *the baggage-carriers had been commanded to go* X. C. 6. 3. 3.

b. With other verbs: **ἀποτμηθέντες τὰς κεφαλάς** *having been decapitated* (had their heads cut off) X. A. 2. 6. 1 (pass. of ἀποτέμνειν τὰς κεφαλάς τισι or τινων).

1749. A passive may be formed in the case of verbs ordinarily intransitive but allowing a cognate accusative in the active: ἱκανὰ τοῖς πολεμίοις ηὐτύχηται *the enemy has had enough good fortune* T. 7. 77 (εὐτυχεῖν ἱκανά, 1573), κεκινδυνεύσεται *the risk will have been run* Ant. 5. 75. See 1746. This is common with neuter passive participles: τὰ ἠσεβημένα αὐτῷ *the impious acts committed by him* L. 6. 5, τὰ σοὶ κἀμοὶ βεβιωμένα *the life led by you and by me* D. 18. 265, τὰ πεπολῑτευμένα αὐτοῖς *their political acts* 1. 28, ἁμαρτηθέντα *errors committed* X. A. 5. 8. 20.

a. Some verbs describing the action of the weather may be used in the passive: νειφόμενοι ἀπῆλθον εἰς τὸ ἄστυ *they returned to the city covered with snow* X. H. 2. 4. 3.

1750. The cognate subject may be implied, as in the case of impersonal passives, in the perfect and tenses derived from the perfect. Thus, ἐπειδὴ αὐτοῖς παρεσκεύαστο *when their preparations were complete* T. 1. 46. λέγεται *it is said*, ἐδηλώθη *it was made known*, followed by the logical subject are not impersonal: ἐδηλώθη τῷ τρόπῳ ἀπωλώλει τὰ χρήματα *it was shown how the money had been lost* Ant. 5. 70. See 935.

1751. Greek uses impersonals from intransitives (corresponding to Lat. *ambulatur, itur, curritur*) only when the active is itself intransitive; as δέδοκται *it has seemed good* (cp. δοκεῖ).

1752. The active or the middle deponent of a transitive verb used transitively or of an intransitive verb may replace the passive of a transitive verb.

ἀκούειν (poet. κλύειν) *be called; be well* (εὖ, καλῶς) or *ill* (κακῶς) *spoken of*, = pass. of λέγειν: νῦν κόλακες ἀκούουσιν *now they are called flatterers* D. 18. 46, τίς ὑπ' ἐμοῦ κακῶς ἀκήκοεν ἢ πέπονθε; *who has been ill spoken of or suffered at my hands?* L. 8. 3. Cp. *bene, male audire;* Milton: "England hears ill abroad."

ἁλίσκεσθαι *be caught* = pass. of αἱρεῖν, as ἐὰν ἁλῷς τοῦτο πράττων *if you are caught doing this* P. A. 29 c.

ἀποθνῄσκειν (*die*) *be killed* = pass. of ἀποκτείνειν, as ἀπέθνῃσκον ὑπὸ ἱππέων *they were killed by the cavalry* X. C. 7. 1. 48. But not in the perfect, where the uncompounded τέθνηκα is used.

γίγνεσθαι *be born* = pass. of τίκτειν *beget, bring forth:* παῖδες αὐτῷ οὐκ ἐγίγνοντο ἐκ ταύτης *he had no children by her* X. H. 6. 4. 37.

δίκην δοῦναι *be punished* = pass. of ζημιοῦν, as ὑπ' αὐτῶν τούτων δίκην ἔδοσαν *they were punished by these very men* X. C. 1. 6. 45.

ἡττᾶσθαι *be defeated* = pass. of νῑκᾶν *conquer*, as ὑπὸ τῶν συμμάχων ἡττώμενοι *worsted by their allies* And. 4. 28.

κατιέναι (κατέρχεσθαι) *return from exile* = pass. of κατάγειν *restore from exile*, as ὑπ' ὀλιγαρχίᾱς κατελθεῖν *to be restored by an oligarchy* T. 8. 68.

κεῖσθαι (*lie*) *be placed* = pass. of the perfect of τιθέναι: πείθου τοῖς νόμοις τοῖς ὑπὸ τῶν βασιλέων κειμένοις *obey the laws established by kings* I. 1. 36.

λαγχάνειν (*obtain by lot*) *be drawn by lot* = pass. of κληροῦν: ἔλαχον ἱερεύς *I became priest by lot* D. 57. 47.

πάσχειν (*suffer*) *be treated well* (εὖ) or *ill* (κακῶς) = pass. of ποιεῖν (εὖ, κακῶς): εὖ παθόντες ὑπ' αὐτῶν *well treated by them* P. G. 519 c.

πίπτειν in ἐκπίπτειν (*fall out*) *be expelled* = pass. of ἐκβάλλειν: οἱ ἐκπεπτωκότες ὑπὸ τοῦ δήμου *those who had been expelled by the people* X. H. 4. 8. 20.

φεύγειν (*flee*) *be prosecuted* = pass. of διώκειν (*be indicted* = γράφεσθαι passive); *be exiled* = pass. of ἐκβάλλειν. So ἀποφεύγειν *be acquitted* = pass. of ἀπολύειν. Thus, ἀσεβείᾱς φεύγων ὑπὸ Μελήτου *prosecuted for impiety by Meletus* P. A. 35 d.

1753. Other equivalents of passive forms are ἔχειν, τυγχάνειν, λαμβάνειν, used with a substantive of like meaning with the active verb: ὄνομα ἔχειν = ὀνομάζεσθαι, συγγνώμην ἔχειν or συγγνώμης τυγχάνειν = συγγιγνώσκεσθαι, ἔπαινον λαμβάνειν or ἐπαίνου τυγχάνειν = ἐπαινεῖσθαι. So with middle deponents: αἰτίᾱν ἔχειν = αἰτιᾶσθαι.

1754. The passive of the periphrasis with ποιεῖσθαι (1722) is made with γίγνεσθαι: so εἰρήνη γίγνεται *peace is made*.

1755. The agent of the passive is regularly expressed by ὑπό and the genitive; sometimes by ἀπό, διά, ἐκ, παρά, πρός with the genitive, or by ὑπό with the dative (in poetry). See 1678.

1756. The instrument of an action, when regarded as the agent, is personified, and may be expressed by ὑπό with the genitive: ἁλίσκεται ὑπὸ τριήρους *he is captured by a trireme* D. 53. 6.

1757. The dative, or a prepositional phrase, is regularly used with the passive to denote the instrument, means, or cause (1506). The agent may be viewed as the instrument: in prose, when persons are regarded as instruments, the dative is usually that of military accompaniment (1526).

1758. The dative of the agent used with the perfect passive and verbal adjective is a dative of interest (1488); on ὑπό with the genitive used instead of the dative, see 1493, 1494.

THE MOODS

1759. Mood designates by the form of the verb the mode or manner (*modus*) in which the speaker conceives of an assertion concerning the subject.

1760. There are four moods proper in Greek: indicative, subjunctive, optative, and imperative. The infinitive (strictly a verbal noun) and the participle (strictly an adjective form of the verb) may be classed with the moods.

THE PARTICLE ἄν

1761. The particle ἄν (Hom. κέν, κέ) limits the meaning of the moods. It has two distinct uses:

a. In independent clauses: with the past tenses of the indicative and with the optative; also with the infinitive and participle representing the indicative or optative.

b. In dependent clauses: with the subjunctive.

1762. No separate word can be used to translate ἄν by itself; its force varies as it modifies the meaning of the moods. In general ἄν limits the force of the verb to particular conditions or circumstances ('under the circumstances,' 'in that case,' 'then').

1763. In Homer ἄν is preferred in negative, κέν, κέ in relative, sentences.

1764. Position of ἄν. — ἄν does not begin a sentence or a clause, except after a weak mark of punctuation, as τί οὖν, ἄν τις εἴποι, ταῦτα λέγεις ἡμῖν νῦν; *why then (some one might say) do you tell us this now?* D. 1. 14. In independent sentences with ἄν (indic. and opt.) the particle is often separated from its verb for emphasis, and is attached to negatives (οὐκ ἄν), interrogatives (τίς ἄν, πῶς ἄν), or to any emphatic modifier. It is commonly attached to verbs of *saying* or *thinking:* σὺν ὑμῖν μὲν ἂν οἶμαι εἶναι τίμιος if I should remain *with you, I think I should be esteemed* X. A. 1. 3. 6.

a. So with οὐκ οἶδ' ἂν εἰ (or οὐκ ἂν οἶδα εἰ) followed by a verb to which ἄν belongs: οὐκ οἶδ' ἂν εἰ πείσαιμι *I do not know whether I could persuade* E. Med. 941 (for πείσαιμι ἄν).

1765. Repetition of ἄν. — ἄν may be repeated once or twice in the same sentence.

a. ἄν is placed early in a sentence which contains a subordinate clause, in order to direct attention to the character of the construction: δοκοῦμεν δ' ἄν μοι ταύτῃ προσποιούμενοι προσβαλεῖν ἐρημοτέρῳ ἂν τῷ ὄρει χρῆσθαι *if we should make a feint attack here it seems to me we should find the mountain to have fewer defenders* X. A. 4. 6. 13.

b. For rhetorical emphasis ἄν is added to give prominence to particular words: τίς γὰρ τοιαῦτ' ἂν οὐκ ἂν ὀργίζοιτ' ἔπη κλύων; *and who would not be angered upon hearing such words?* S. O. T. 339, πῶς ἂν οὐκ ἂν ἐν δίκῃ θάνοιμ' ἄν; *how should I not justly die?* S. fr. 673.

1766. ἄν without a Verb. — ἄν sometimes stands without a verb, which is to be supplied from the context. So in the second member of a sentence with coördinate clauses: οἶδα ὅτι πολλοὺς μὲν ἡγεμόνας ἂν δοίη, πολλοὺς δ' ἂν (δοίη) ὁμήρους *I know that he would give many guides and many hostages* X. A. 3. 2. 24. Often with πῶς ἂν (εἴη); *how can (could) it be?* P. R. 353 c, τάχ' ἂν *perhaps* P. Soph. 255 c.

a. So with ὡς ἄν, ὥσπερ ἂν εἰ (2480): παρῆν ὁ Γαδάτᾱς δῶρα πολλὰ φέρων, ὡς ἂν (*scil.* φέροι τις) ἐξ οἴκου μεγάλου *Gadatas came with many gifts, such as one might offer from large means* X. C. 5. 4. 29, φοβούμενος ὥσπερ ἂν εἰ παῖς *fearing like a child* (ὥσπερ ἂν ἐφοβεῖτο, εἰ παῖς ἦν) P. G. 479 a.

b. κἂν εἰ is often used for the simple καὶ εἰ (2372) and without regard to the mood of the following verb; sometimes there is no verb in the apodosis to which the ἄν may be referred, as ἔστιν ἄρα τῇ ἀληθείᾳ, κἂν εἰ μή τῳ δοκεῖ, ὁ τῷ ὄντι τύραννος τῷ ὄντι δοῦλος *the very tyrant is then in truth a very slave even if he does not seem so to any one* P. R. 579 d (here καὶ εἰ μὴ δοκεῖ, εἴη ἂν is implied). κἂν εἰ may be also so used that ἄν belongs to the apodosis, while καί, though going with εἰ in translation (*even if*), affects the whole conditional sentence. Thus, νῦν δέ μοι δοκεῖ, κἂν ἀσέβειαν εἰ (τις) καταγιγνώσκοι, τὰ προσήκοντα ποιεῖν *but as it is, it seems to me that, even if any one should condemn his wanton assault, he would be acting properly*

D. 21. 51 (here ἄν goes with ποιεῖν, *i.e.* ποιοίη ἄν). κἄν *if only*, followed by a limiting expression, may generally be regarded as καὶ ἄν (= ἐάν) with a subjunctive understood; as ἀλλά μοι πάρες κἂν σμῑκρὸν εἰπεῖν *yet permit me to say but a word* (= καὶ ἐὰν παρῇς) S. El. 1482.

1767. Omission of ἄν. — ἄν is sometimes omitted when it may be supplied from the preceding sentence or clause. So often with the second of two verbs that are connected or opposed: τί ἐποίησεν ἄν; ἢ δῆλον ὅτι ὤμοσε (ἄν); *what would he have done? is it not clear that he would have taken an oath?* D. 31. 9, οὔτ' ἂν οὗτος ἔχοι λέγειν οὔθ' ὑμεῖς πεισθείητε *neither can he assert nor can you be made to believe* D. 22. 17. By retention of earlier usage the subjunctive is sometimes used without ἄν where it is commonly employed in the later language (2327, 2339, 2565 b, 2567 b). Here the difference is scarcely appreciable except that the omission gives an archaic tone.

DEPENDENT CLAUSES WITH ἄν

1768. Subjunctive with ἄν. — Conditional, relative, and temporal clauses requiring the subjunctive must have ἄν, which is more closely attached to the conditional, relative, and temporal words than it is to the subjunctive.

a. Hence the combinations ἐάν (ἤν, ἄν) on which cp. 2283; ὅταν, ὁπόταν, ἐπήν (ἐπάν), ἐπειδάν from εἰ, ὅτε, ὁπότε, ἐπεί, ἐπειδή + ἄν. When the particle does not thus coalesce, it is usually separated only by such words as μέν, δέ, τέ, γάρ.

b. The force of ἄν with the subjunctive cannot usually be expressed in English. For ἄν in final clauses with ὡς, ὅπως, and ὄφρα, see 2201. In Hom. ἄν (κέν) is found in dependent clauses, 2334 c.

THE MOODS IN SIMPLE SENTENCES

1769. §§ 1770–1849 treat of the use of the moods in independent sentences and principal clauses. The dependent construction of the moods was developed from their independent use. The use of the moods in subordinate clauses was not originally different from that in independent sentences and in the principal clauses of complex sentences. For the uses of the indicative, see also 1875–1958.

INDICATIVE WITHOUT ἄν

1770. The indicative mood makes a simple, direct assertion of fact; or asks a question anticipating such an assertion: ἦλθε *he came*, οὐκ ἦλθε *he did not come*, ἐλεύσεται *he will come*, πότε ταῦτα ποιήσει; *when will he do this?*

1771. The indicative states particular or general suppositions, makes affirmative or negative assertions, which may or may not be absolutely true. Thus, in assumptions, ἐξήμαρτέ τις ἄκων· συγγνώμη ἀντὶ τῑμωρίᾱς τούτῳ *suppose some one involuntarily committed an offence; for him there is pardon rather than punish-*

ment D. 18. 274, and often after καὶ δή, as καὶ δὴ τεθνᾶσι *and suppose they are dead* E. Med. 386.

1772. The indicative may be used to express a doubtful assertion about a present or past action (negative μή or μὴ οὐ): ἀλλ' ἄρα . . . μὴ ὁ Κτήσιππος ἦν ὁ ταῦτ' εἰπών *but* I suspect (*i.e.* perhaps) *after all it was Ctesippus who said this* P. Eu. 290 e, ἀλλὰ μὴ τοῦτο οὐ καλῶς ὡμολογήσαμεν *but perhaps we did not do well in agreeing to this* P. Men. 89 c. Such sentences are often regarded as questions with the effect of doubtful affirmation.

1773. The indicative may be used alone where in English we employ an auxiliary verb: πιστεύων δὲ θεοῖς πῶς οὐκ εἶναι θεοὺς ἐνόμιζεν; *since he trusted in the gods how could* (or *should*) *he believe there were no gods?* X. M. 1. 1. 5, ὀλίγου εἷλον τὴν πόλιν *a little more and they would have taken the city* T. 8. 35, ἀπωλλύμεθα *we might have perished* (*we were in danger of perishing*) X. A. 5. 8. 2. Cp. 2319.

1774. Unfulfilled Obligation (Propriety, Possibility). — With the imperfect indicative of impersonal expressions denoting obligation, propriety, necessity, or possibility, the action of a dependent infinitive is usually not realized. (Examples 1775–1776.)

Such expressions are ἔδει, χρῆν (or ἐχρῆν), προσῆκε, καιρὸς ἦν, ἄξιον ἦν, εἰκὸς ἦν, δίκαιον ἦν, αἰσχρὸν ἦν, ἐξῆν, καλῶς εἶχεν, verbals in -τόν or -τέον with ἦν, etc.

a. For the use of these expressions (also with ἄν) in the apodosis of unreal conditions, see 2313, 2315.

1775. Present. — Thus, ἔδει σε ταῦτα ποιεῖν *you ought to be doing this* (but are *not* doing it), τούσδε μὴ ζῆν ἔδει *these men ought not to be alive* S. Ph. 418, τί σῖγᾷς; οὐκ ἐχρῆν σῖγᾶν *why art thou silent? Thou shouldst not be silent* E. Hipp. 297, εἰκὸς ἦν ὑμᾶς . . . μὴ μαλακῶς, ὥσπερ νῦν, ξυμμαχεῖν *you should not be slack in your alliance, as you are at present* T. 6. 78.

1776. Past. — ἔδει σε ταῦτα ποιῆσαι (or ποιεῖν) *you ought to have done this* (but did *not* do it), ἐξῆν σοι ἐλθεῖν *you might have gone* (but did *not* go), ἐνῆν αὐτῷ ταῦτα ποιῆσαι *he could have done this* (almost equivalent to the potential indicative ταῦτα ἐποίησεν ἄν, 1784), ἔδει τὰ ἐνέχυρα τότε λαβεῖν *I ought to have taken the pledges then* X. A. 7. 6. 23, ἄξιον ἦν ἀκοῦσαι *it would have been worth hearing* P. Eu. 304 d, μένειν ἐξῆν *he might have remained* D. 3. 17.

1777. The Greek usage simply states the obligation (propriety, possibility) as a fact which existed in the past (and may continue to exist in the present). In English we usually express the non-fulfilment of the *action*.

1778. Present or past time is denoted when the present infinitive is used. When the reference is to present time, the action of the present infinitive is always denied. Past time is denoted when the aorist infinitive is used.

1779. The expressions in 1774 may also refer to simple past obligation (propriety, possibility) and have the ordinary force of past indicatives: ἔδει μένειν *he had to remain* (and did remain) D. 19. 124. The context determines the meaning; thus τί τὸν σύμβουλον ἐχρῆν ποιεῖν; (D. 18. 190) by itself might mean either *what was it the duty of the statesman to do* or *what was it the duty of the statesman to have done?*

1780. Unattainable Wish. — A wish, referring to the present or past, which cannot be realized, is expressed by a past tense of the indicative with εἴθε or with εἰ γάρ (negative μή). The imperfect refers to present time, the aorist to past time (cp. 2304, 2305).

εἴθ' εἶχες βελτίους φρένας *would that thou hadst* (now) *a better heart* E. El. 1061, εἴθε σοι τότε συνεγενόμην *would that I had then been with thee* X. M. 1. 2. 46.

1781. An unattainable wish may also be expressed by ὤφελον (*ought*) with the present or aorist infinitive: ὤφελε Κῦρος ζῆν *would that Cyrus were* (now) *alive* (Cyrus ought to be alive) X. A. 2. 1. 4 (1775). The negative is μή: μήποτ' ὤφελον λιπεῖν τὴν Σκῦρον *would that I had never left Scyros* S. Ph. 969. εἴθε or εἰ γάρ (poet. αἴθε, ὡς) may be used before ὤφελον: εἰ γὰρ ὤφελον οἷοί τε εἶναι οἱ πολλοὶ κακὰ ἐργάζεσθαι *would that the multitude were able to do evil* Pl. Cr. 44 d.

1782. ἐβουλόμην followed by an infinitive may express an unattainable wish: ἐβουλόμην μὲν οὐκ ἐρίζειν ἐνθάδε *I would that I were not contending here* (as I am) Ar. Ran. 866. (ἐβουλόμην ἄν *vellem*, 1789.)

1783. The indicative is also used in other than simple sentences: in final sentences (2203); in object sentences after verbs of *effort* (2211), of *caution* (2220 a), of *fearing* (2231, 2233); in consecutive sentences with ὥστε *so that* (2274), in conditional sentences (2300, 2303, 2323, 2326); in temporal sentences (2395); in object sentences after ὅτι and ὡς with a verb of *saying*, etc. (2577 ff.).

INDICATIVE WITH ἄν

1784. Past Potential. — The past tenses (usually the aorist, less commonly the imperfect) of the indicative with ἄν (κέν) denote past potentiality, probability (cautious statement), or necessity: ὃ οὐκ ἂν ᾤοντο *which they could not have expected* T. 7. 55, τίς γὰρ ἂν ᾠήθη ταῦτα γενέσθαι; *for who would have expected these things to happen?* D. 9. 68 (note that ἄν does not go with γενέσθαι by 1764), ἔγνω ἄν τις *one might* (*could, would*) *have known* X. C. 7. 1. 38, ὑπό κεν ταλασίφρονά περ δέος εἷλεν *fear might have seized even a man of stout heart* Δ 421.

a. This is especially frequent with τὶς and with the ideal second person (cp. *putares, crederes*): ἐπέγνως ἄν *you would* (*could, might*) *have observed* X. C. 8. 1. 33.

b. The potential optative (1829) in Homer refers also to the past.

1785. A protasis may often be extracted from a participle, or is intimated in some other word; but there is no reference to any definite condition, hence a definite ellipsis is not to be supplied.

1786. Unreal Indicative. — The indicative of the historical tenses with ἄν (κέν) may denote unreality: τότε δ' αὐτὸ τὸ πρᾶγμ' ἂν ἐκρίνετο ἐφ' αὑτοῦ *but the case would then have been decided on its own merits* D. 18. 224, καί κεν πολὺ κέρδιον ἦεν *and in that case it were far better* Γ 41.

1787. This use of the indicative with ἄν to denote unreality is not inherent in the meaning of the past tenses of that mood, but has been developed from the past potential with which the unreal indicative is closely connected. On the common use of this construction in the apodosis of unreal conditions see 2303. On ἔδει ἄν, etc., see 2315.

1788. The imperfect refers to the present or the past, the aorist to the past (rarely to the present), the pluperfect to the present (less commonly to the past).

1789. ἐβουλόμην ἄν (*vellem*) *I should like* or *should have liked* may express an unattainable wish: ἐβουλόμην ἂν Σίμωνα τὴν αὐτὴν γνώμην ἐμοὶ ἔχειν *I should have liked Simon to be* (or *I wish Simon were*) *of the same mind as myself* L. 3. 21. On ἐβουλόμην without ἄν, see 1782.

1790. Iterative Indicative (repeated action). — The imperfect and aorist with ἄν are used to express repeated or customary past action (post-Homeric): διηρώτων ἄν *I used to ask* P. A. 22 b, ἂν ἔλεξεν *he was wont to say* X. C. 7. 1. 10.

1791. This construction is connected with the past potential and denoted originally what *could* or *would* take place under certain past circumstances. Thus, ἀναλαμβάνων οὖν αὐτῶν τὰ ποιήματα . . . διηρώτων ἂν αὐτοὺς τί λέγοιεν *accordingly, taking up their poems, I used to* (*would*) *ask them* (as an opportunity presented itself) *what they meant* P. A. 22 b. In actual use, since the action of the verb *did* take place, this construction has become a statement of *fact*.

1792. In Herodotus this construction is used with the iterative forms: κλαίεσκε ἄν *she kept weeping* 3. 119, οἱ δὲ ἂν Πέρσαι λάβεσκον τὰ πρόβατα *the Persians were wont to seize the cattle* 4. 130.

1793. Homer and the early poets use ἄν (κέν) with the future indicative with a conditional or limiting force: καί κέ τις ὧδ' ἐρέει *and in such a case some one will* (*may*) *say thus* Δ 176. This use is found also in conditional relative sentences (2565 b). In Attic ἄν is found with the future in a few passages which have often been emended. In P. A. 29 c there is an anacoluthon.

1794. ἄν is not used with the present and perfect indicative.

SUBJUNCTIVE WITHOUT ἄν

1795. The chief uses of the independent subjunctive are the hortatory (1797), the prohibitive (1800), and the deliberative (1805).

a. The name *subjunctive* is due to the belief of the ancient grammarians that the mood was always subordinate. Thus, εἴπω *shall I speak?* (1805) was explained as due to the omission of a preceding βούλει, *i.e. do you wish that I speak?*

1796. The independent subjunctive refers to future time. It has three main uses: (1) the voluntative, expressing the *will* of the speaker. This is akin to the imperative. (2) The deliberative. This is possibly a form of the voluntative. (3) The anticipatory (or futural). This anticipates an action as an immediate future possibility. Whether the anticipatory is a form of the voluntative is uncertain (cp. *ich will sehen*, *je veux voir*, dialectal *il veut pleuvoir*).

1797. Hortatory Subjunctive. — The hortatory subjunctive (present or aorist) is used to express a request or a proposal (negative μή).

a. Usually in the first person plural: *νῦν ἴωμεν καὶ ἀκούσωμεν τοῦ ἀνδρός let us go now and hear the man* P. Prot. 314 b, *μήπω ἐκεῖσε ἴωμεν let's not go there yet* 311 a. ἄγε, φέρε (δή), in Hom. ἄγε (δή), sometimes precedes, as *ἄγε σκοπῶμεν come, let us consider* X. C. 5. 5. 15. ἴθι (δή) rarely precedes.

b. Less frequently in the first person singular, which is usually preceded (in affirmative sentences) by φέρε (δή), in Hom. by ἄγε (δή): *φέρε δὴ περὶ τοῦ ψηφίσματος εἴπω let me now speak about the bill* D. 19. 234.

1798. The first person singular in negative exhortations (rare and poetic) may convey a warning or a threat: *μή σε, γέρον, κοίλῃσιν παρὰ νηυσὶ κιχείω old man, let me not find thee by the hollow ships* A 26. This use is often regarded as prohibitive (1800).

1799. The hortatory use of the subjunctive compensates for the absence of an imperative of the first person.

1800. Prohibitive Subjunctive.—The subjunctive (in the second and third persons of the aorist) is often used to express prohibitions (negative μή).

a. Usually in the second person: *μηδὲν ἀθυμήσητε do not lose heart* X. A. 5. 4. 19. For the aorist subjunctive the present imperative may be employed (1840): μὴ ποιήσῃς (or μὴ ποίει) ταῦτα *do not do this* (*not* μὴ ποιῇς).

b. Less commonly in the third person, which usually represents the second: *ὑπολάβῃ δὲ μηδείς and let no one suppose* T. 6. 84 (= *μὴ ὑπολάβητε do not suppose*).

c. The third person of the present subjunctive is rare: μὴ τοίνυν τις οἴηται (= μὴ οἰώμεθα) *let not any one think* P. L. 861 E.

N.—οὐ μή with the subjunctive of the second person in the dramatic poets occasionally expresses a strong prohibition: *οὐ μὴ ληρήσῃς don't talk nonsense* Ar. Nub. 367.

1801. Doubtful Assertion.—The present subjunctive with μή may express a doubtful assertion, with μὴ οὐ a doubtful negation. The idea of apprehension or anxiety (real or assumed) is due to the situation. A touch of irony often marks this use, which is chiefly Platonic. With μή (of what may be true): μὴ ἀγροικότερον ᾖ τὸ ἀληθὲς εἰπεῖν *I suspect it's rather bad form* (lit. *too rude*) *to tell the truth* P. G. 462 e. With μὴ οὐ (of what may not be true): ἀλλὰ μὴ οὐχ οὕτως ἔχῃ *but I rather think this may not be so* P. Crat. 436 b, μὴ οὐκ ᾖ διδακτὸν ἀρετή *virtue is perhaps not a thing to be taught* P. Men. 94 e.

1802. In Hom. μή with the independent subjunctive is used to indicate fear and warning, or to suggest danger: μή τι χολωσάμενος ῥέξῃ κακὸν υἷας Ἀχαιῶν *may he not* (as I fear he may) *in his anger do aught to injure the sons of the Achaeans* B 195. Usually with the aorist, rarely with the present subjunctive (ο 19). The constructions of 1801, 1802 are used as object clauses after verbs of *fearing* (2221).

1803. ὅπως μή is occasionally so used with the aorist subjunctive, and with an idea of command: ὅπως μὴ φήσῃ τις *may no one say* (as I fear he may) X. S. 4. 8. See 1921.

1804. From the use in 1801 is probably developed the construction of οὐ μή with the aorist (less often the present) subjunctive to denote an emphatic denial; as οὐ μὴ παύσωμαι φιλοσοφῶν *I will not cease from searching for wisdom* P. A. 29 d, οὐκέτι μὴ δύνηται βασιλεὺς ἡμᾶς καταλαβεῖν *the king will no longer be able to overtake us* X. A. 2. 2. 12.

1805. Deliberative Subjunctive. — The deliberative subjunctive (present or aorist) is used in questions when the speaker asks *what he is to do* or *say* (negative μή).

a. Usually in the first person: εἴπωμεν ἢ σῑγῶμεν; *shall we speak or keep silence?* E. Ion 758, τί δράσω; ποῖ φύγω; *what am I to do? whither shall I fly?* E. Med. 1271, μὴ φῶμεν; *shall we not say?* P. R. 554 b.

b. The (rare) second person is used in repeating a question: A. τί σοι πιθώμεθα; B. ὅ τι πίθησθε; A. *In what shall we take your advice?* B. *In what shall you take my advice?* Ar. Av. 164.

c. The third person is generally used to represent the first person; commonly with τὶς, as τί τις εἶναι τοῦτο φῇ; *how shall anyone say this is so?* (= τί φῶμεν;) D. 19. 88.

N. — The subjunctive question does not refer to a future fact, but to what is, under the present circumstances, advantageous or proper to do or say.

1806. βούλει, βούλεσθε (poet. θέλεις, θέλετε) *do you wish* often precede the subjunctive: βούλει σοι εἴπω; *do you wish me to say to you?* P. G. 521 d. This is a fusion of two distinct questions: βούλει *do you wish?* and εἴπω *shall I say?*

1807. The deliberative subjunctive may be replaced by a periphrasis with δεῖ or χρή and the infinitive, or by the verbal adjective in -τέον ἐστί. Thus, ἡμεῖς δὲ προσμένωμεν; ἢ τί χρὴ ποιεῖν; *and shall we wait? or what must we do?* S. Tr. 390, τί ποιητέον; (= τί ποιῶμεν;) *what are we to do?* Ar. P. 922.

a. For the deliberative future see 1916.

1808. Deliberation in the past may be expressed by ἔδει, χρῆν (ἐχρῆν), ἔμελλον with the infinitive, and by -τέον (verbal adj.) ἦν.

1809. The Negative in Questions. — The use of μή (not οὐ) in questions is due to the fact that the construction of 1805 is simply the interrogative form of the hortatory subjunctive: φῶμεν *let us say*, μὴ φῶμεν; *are we not to say?* Distinguish πότερον βίᾱν φῶμεν ἢ μὴ φῶμεν εἶναι; *shall we say that it is force or that it is not?* X. M. 1. 2. 45, from φῶμεν ταῦτ' ὀρθῶς λέγεσθαι ἢ οὔ *shall we say that this is well said or not?* (οὔ = οὐκ ὀρθῶς λέγεσθαι) P. G. 514 c.

1810. Anticipatory Subjunctive (Homeric Subjunctive). — In Homer the subjunctive is often closely akin to the future indicative, and refers by anticipation to a future event (negative οὐ): οὐ γάρ πω τοίους ἴδον ἀνέρας, οὐδὲ ἴδωμαι *for never yet saw I such men, nor shall I see them* A 262, καί νύ τις ὧδ' εἴπῃσι *and one will say* ξ 275. ἄν (κέν) usually limits this subjunctive in Hom. (1813).

a. This futural subjunctive is retained in Attic only in subordinate clauses (2327), and in τί πάθω (1811).

1811. The subjunctive is used in τί πάθω; *what will become of me; what am I to do?* (lit. *what shall I undergo?*) as P. Eu. 302 d. So τί γένωμαι; *quid me fiet?* Thus, ὤ μοι ἐγώ, τί πάθω; τί νύ μοι μήκιστα γένηται; *ah, woe's me!*

what is to become of me? what will happen unto me at the last? ε 465. The subjunctive here is not deliberative, but refers to a future event.

1812. The subjunctive without ἄν is also used in dependent clauses of purpose (2196), after verbs of *fearing* (2225), in the protasis of conditional (2327, 2339) and conditional relative sentences (2567 b).

SUBJUNCTIVE WITH ἄν

1813. The subjunctive with ἄν (more commonly κέν) is used in Homer in independent sentences and clauses (negative οὐ). Cp. 1810. Thus, ἐγὼ δέ κ' ἄγω Βρῑσηΐδα *but in that case I will take Briseis* A 184, οὐκ ἄν τοι χραίσμῃ βιός *of no avail to thee shall be thy bow* Λ 387.

OPTATIVE WITHOUT ἄν

1814. Optative of Wish. — In independent sentences the optative without ἄν is used to express a wish referring to the future (negative μή): ὦ παῖ, γένοιο πατρὸς εὐτυχέστερος *ah, boy, mayest thou prove more fortunate than thy sire* S. Aj. 550. From this use is derived the name of the mood (Lat. opto *wish*).

a. So even in relative sentences: ἐάν ποτε, ὃ μὴ γένοιτο, λάβωσι τὴν πόλιν *if ever they capture the city, which Heaven forbid* L. 31. 14.

b. Under wishes are included execrations and protestations: ἐξολοίμην *may I perish* Ar. Ach. 324, καί σ' ἐπιδείξω, ἢ μὴ ζῴην, δωροδοκήσαντα *and I will prove that you took bribes, or may I not live* Ar. Eq. 833.

1815. The optative of wish is often introduced by εἰ γάρ, εἴθε (Hom. αἰ γάρ, αἴθε), or by εἰ, ὡς (both poetical): εἰ γὰρ γένοιτο *would that it might happen* X. C. 6. 1. 38, ὡς ὄλοιτο *may he perish* S. El. 126. (ὡς is properly an exclamation: *how.*)

1816. The optative introduced by εἰ γάρ, etc. is sometimes explained as a protasis with the conclusion omitted: εἴθε φίλος ἡμῖν γένοιο *oh, if you would become our friend* X. H. 4. 1. 38. Cp. 2352 e.

1817. An unattainable wish, referring to the present, may be expressed by the present optative in Homer: εἴθ' ἡβώοιμι *would that I were young again* H 157.

1818. Unattainable wishes, when they refer to the future, may be expressed by the optative: εἴ μοι γένοιτο φθόγγος ἐν βραχίοσι *would that I had a voice in my arms* E. Hec. 836. Wishes represented as hopeless are expressed in the post-Homeric language by the past tenses of the indicative (1780) or by ὤφελον (1781).

1819. Hom. often uses the optative with a concessive or permissive force: ἔπειτα δὲ καί τι πάθοιμι *after that I may* (lit. *may I*) *suffer come what will* Φ 274.

1820. Imperative Optative. — The optative may express a command or exhortation with a force nearly akin to the imperative: Χειρίσοφος ἡγοῖτο *let Chirisophus lead* X. A. 3. 2. 37.

1821. Potential Optative. — The potential optative, which in Attic regularly takes ἄν (1824), is occasionally found in Homer and later poetry in an earlier form, without that particle: ῥεῖα θεός γ' ἐθέλων καὶ τηλόθεν ἄνδρα σαώσαι *easily might a god, if he so willed, bring a man safe even from afar* γ 231, θᾶσσον ἢ λέγοι τις *quicker than a man could speak* E. Hipp. 1186. This construction is suspected in prose but cf. οὔτε γὰρ ὅπως ἀποκτείναιεν εἶχον *they knew not how they might cut* P.S. 190 c.

a. Usually in negative sentences or in questions expecting a negative answer (with οὐ): οὐ μὲν γάρ τι κακώτερον ἄλλο πάθοιμι *for I could not* (conceivably) *suffer anything worse* T 321, τεάν, Ζεῦ, δύνασιν τίς ἀνδρῶν ὑπερβασίᾱ κατάσχοι; *thy power, O Zeus, what trespass of man can check?* S. Ant. 604.

1822. The optative after οὐκ ἔστιν ὅστις (ὅπως, ὅποι) in the dramatists is probably potential: οὐκ ἔσθ' ὅπως λέξαιμι τὰ ψευδῆ καλά *I could not call false tidings fair* A. Ag. 620. ἄν is usually employed in this construction.

1823. The optative without ἄν (κέν) is also used elsewhere, as in purpose clauses (2196) and clauses of *fearing* (2225) after a secondary tense; in the apodosis of conditional sentences (2300 d, 2326 d, 2333), in relative sentences (2566, 2568); and as the representative of the indicative (2615) or subjunctive (2619) in indirect discourse after secondary tenses.

OPTATIVE WITH ἄν

1824. Potential Optative. — The potential optative with ἄν states a future possibility, propriety, or likelihood, as an *opinion* of the speaker; and may be translated by *may, might, can* (especially with a negative), *must, would, should* (rarely *will, shall*). So in Latin *velim, videas, cognoscas, credas.*

γνοίης δ' ἂν ὅτι τοῦθ' οὕτως ἔχει *you may see that this is so* X. C. 1. 6. 21, ἅπαντες ἂν ὁμολογήσειαν *all would agree* I. 11. 5, ἡδέως ἂν ἐροίμην *I* (would gladly ask) *should like to ask* D. 18. 64, οὐκ ἂν λάβοις *thou canst not take* S. Ph. 103, λέγοιμ' ἂν τάδε *I will tell this* A. Supp. 928. The second person singular is often indefinite (*one*), as γνοίης ἄν (*cognoscas*) = γνοίη τις ἄν.

a. The potential optative ranges from possibility to fixed resolve. The aorist optative with ἄν and a negative is very common.

b. When stress is laid on the idea of possibility and power, necessity and obligation, Greek uses δύναμαι, δεῖ or χρή with the infinitive (statement of *fact*).

c. The potential optative with ἄν is also used in dependent sentences; in purpose clauses (2202 b), in object clauses after verbs of *effort* (2216) and verbs of *fearing* (2232), in causal clauses (2243), in result clauses (2278), in the apodosis of conditional (see 2356) and conditional relative sentences (2566). In indirect discourse the infinitive with ἄν or the participle with ἄν may represent the optative with ἄν (1845 ff.).

1825. Usually these optatives are not limited by any definite condition present to the mind, and it is unnecessary to supply any protasis in thought. In some cases a protasis is dormant in a word of the sentence (such as δικαίως, εἰκότως). Thus, in οὓς ἀχαρίστους εἶναι δικαίως ἂν ὑπολαμβάνοιτε *whom you would justly consider to be ungrateful* Aes. 3. 196, δικαίως may stand for εἰ δικαίως ὑπολαμβάνοιτε: *if you should consider* the matter *justly*. So οὔτε ἐσθίουσι πλείω ἢ δύνανται φέρειν· διαρραγεῖεν γὰρ ἂν κτλ. *they neither eat more than they can bear, for* otherwise (*if they should eat more:* εἰ ἐσθίοιεν πλείω) *they would burst* X. C. 8. 2. 21. The potential optative is also used as the main clause of less vivid conditions (2329) in which the protasis has the optative by assimilation to the mood of the apodosis.

1826. The potential optative with ἄν is used to soften the statement of an opinion or fact, or to express irony: ἕτερόν τι τοῦτ' ἂν εἴη *this is* (would be) *another matter* D. 20. 116, νοσοῖμ' ἄν, εἰ νόσημα τοὺς ἐχθροὺς στυγεῖν *I must be mad, if it is madness to hate one's foes* A. Pr. 978. So often with ἴσως or τάχα *perhaps.*

a. With a negative, the potential optative may have the force of a strong assertion: οὐ γὰρ ἂν ἀπέλθοιμ', ἀλλὰ κόψω τὴν θύρᾱν *for I will not go away, but I will knock at the door* Ar. Ach. 236.

1827. βουλοίμην ἄν (*velim*) is often used as a softened optative of wish: βουλοίμην ἂν τοῦτο οὕτω γενέσθαι *I could wish that this might be the result* (οὕτω γένοιτο *may it result thus*) P. A. 19 a. For ἐβουλόμην ἄν see 1789.

1828. The present and aorist are used of what will be, or what will prove to be, true (future realization of a present fact): ἀρετὴ ἄρα, ὡς ἔοικεν, ὑγίειά τις ἂν εἴη *virtue then, it seems, will* (prove to) *be a kind of health* P. R. 444 d. The perfect is used of what will prove to be the case as regards a completed action: πῶς ἂν λελήθοι; *how can it have escaped my knowledge?* X. S. 3. 6. Usually the perfect is here equivalent to the present.

1829. The present and aorist are rarely used of the past: (a) in Hom. of past possibility: καί νύ κεν ἔνθ' ἀπόλοιτο *and now he might have perished* E 311 (Attic ἀπώλετο ἄν, 1784), ἀλλὰ τί κεν ῥέξαιμι; *but what could I do?* T 90. (b) in Hdt. of a mild assertion: ταῦτα μὲν καὶ φθόνῳ ἂν εἴποιεν *they may have said this out of envy* 9. 71, εἴησαν δ' ἂν οὗτοι Κρῆτες *these would prove to be* (might be, must have been) *Cretans* 1. 2. Both uses are doubtful in Attic prose.

1830. The potential optative with ἄν may be used, in a sense akin to that of the imperative, to express a command, exhortation, or request: λέγοις ἂν τὴν δέησιν *tell me* (you may tell) *your request* P. Par. 126 a, προάγοις ἂν *move on* P. Phae. 229 b. This courteous formula is used even where a harsh command might be expected: χωροῖς ἂν εἴσω σὺν τάχει *go within with all speed* S. El. 1491.

a. In ποῖ δῆτ' ἂν τραποίμην; *whither pray shall I turn?* Ar. Ran. 296 the use is akin to the deliberative subjunctive (1805) or deliberative future (1916).

1831. The potential optative with ἄν is used in questions: τίς οὐκ ἂν ὁμολογήσειεν; *who would not agree?* (οὐδείς: *scil.* οὐκ ἂν ὁμολογήσειε) X. M. 1. 1. 5. So even the optative of wish: τί δ' ὅρκῳ τῷδε μὴ 'μμένων πάθοις; *but if thou dost not abide by thy oath what dost thou invoke upon thyself?* E. Med. 754 (lit. *mayest thou suffer what?*).

1832. πῶς ἄν, τίς ἄν with the potential optative may be used to express a wish (especially in the tragic poets): πῶς ἂν ὀλοίμᾱν *oh, would that I might die* E. Med. 97, τίς ἂν ἐν τάχει μόλοι μοῖρα *oh, that some fate would speedily come* A. Ag. 1448. Properly this usage is not a wish, but is simply a question *how* the wish may be fulfilled.

1833. The potential optative with ἄν (especially with negatives) may exchange with the indicative: φημὶ καὶ οὐκ ἂν ἀρνηθείην *I assert and cannot deny* D. 21. 191. It is often stronger, though more courteous, than the future indicative: οὐκ ἂν πέρα φράσαιμι *I will speak no more* S. O. T. 343.

1834. The future optative with ἄν occurs only in a few suspected passages.

IMPERATIVE

1835. The imperative is used in commands and prohibitions (negative μή). All its tenses refer to the future.

a. Under commands are included requests, entreaties, summons, prescriptions, exhortations, etc.

b. For the tenses of the imperative, see 1840; for the infinitive used as an imperative, see 2013.

POSITIVE (COMMANDS)

1836. In exhortations ἄγε, φέρε, ἴθι (usually with δή, sometimes with νύν), often precede the imperative: ἄγε δὴ ἀκούσατε *come listen* X. Ap. 14, ἄγετε δειπνήσατε *go now, take your supper* X. H. 5. 1. 18, ἀλλ' ἴθι εἰπέ *but come, say* P. G. 489 e.

1837. πᾶς is sometimes used with the second person in poetry: ἄκουε πᾶς *hear, every one* Ar. Thesm. 372.

1838. The third person may be used in questions: οὐκοῦν κείσθω ταῦτα; *shall these points be established?* P. L. 820 e. Cp. 1842 a.

1839. The imperative may be used in assumptions (*hypothetical imperative*), to make a concession, or to grant permission: ἐμοῦ γ' ἕνεκ' ἔστω *let it be assumed as far as I am concerned* D. 20. 14, οὕτως ἐχέτω ὡς σὺ λέγεις *assume it to be as you say* P. S. 201 c. So even as a protasis: δειξάτω, κἀγὼ στέρξω *let him set it forth and I will be content* D. 18. 112.

NEGATIVE (PROHIBITIONS)

1840. Prohibitions are expressed by μή with the present or aorist subjunctive in the first person plural; by μή with the present imperative or the aorist subjunctive in the second and third person singular or plural (cp. 1800). The aorist imperative is rare in prohibitions.

A. 1 Person. — **μὴ γράφωμεν (μὴ γράψωμεν)**: μὴ μαινώμεθα μηδ' αἰσχρῶς ἀπολώμεθα *let us not act like madmen nor perish disgracefully* X. A. 7. 1. 29.

B. 2 Person. — **μὴ γράφε (μὴ γράφετε)**: μὴ θαύμαζε *don't be astonished* P. G. 482 a, μὴ θορυβεῖτε *don't raise a disturbance* P. A. 21 a, τὰ μὲν ποίει, τὰ δὲ μὴ ποίει *do this and refrain from doing that* P. Pr. 325 d, μὴ μέγα λέγε *don't boast so* P. Ph. 95 b. — **μὴ γράψῃς (μὴ γράψητε)**: μηδὲ θαυμάσῃς τόδε *and do not wonder at this* A. Ag. 879, μὴ θορυβήσητε *don't raise a disturbance* P. A. 20 e, μὴ ἄλλως ποιήσῃς *don't do otherwise* P. Lach. 201 b, μηδαμῶς ἄλλως ποιήσῃς Ar. Av. 133.

N. — The type **μὴ γράφῃς** is never used. **μὴ γράψον** occurs rarely in poetry (Δ 410, Σ 134. — ω 248, S. fr. 453 parodied in Ar. Thesm. 870).

C. 3 Person. — **μὴ γραφέτω (μὴ γραφόντων)**: *μηδεὶς διδασκέτω let no one tell me* T. 1. 86, *μηδεὶς τοῦτ' ἀγνοείτω let no one be ignorant of this fact* Aes. 3. 6. **μὴ γραψάτω (μὴ γραψάντων)**: *μηδεὶς νομισάτω let no one think* X. C. 7. 5. 73, *μήτ' ἀπογνώτω μηδὲν μήτε καταγνώτω let him neither acquit nor condemn in any way* Aes. 3. 60; and in five other passages giving the actual usage of the orators. In the third person the aorist imperative is much less common than the present imperative.

N. — The type **μὴ γράφῃ** is used only when the third person represents the first person (1800 c). **μὴ γράψῃ** is much more common than *μὴ γραψάτω* in the orators, *e.g.* *μηδεὶς θαυμάσῃ let no one be astonished* D. 18. 199, *μηδεὶς νομίσῃ let no one think* T. 3. 13, D. 23. 1.

D. The perfect imperative is rare in prohibitions (*μὴ πεφόβησθε* T 6. 17) and is usually poetical. Cp. 698, 712.

1841. a. *μὴ γράφε*, like *don't write*, is ambiguous and may mean, according to the situation, either *cease writing* or *abstain from writing*. Commonly *μὴ γράφε* means *do not go on writing, write no more*, and is an order to stop an action already begun. In many cases, however, *μή* with the present imperative does not refer to the interruption of an action already begun, but to an action still in the more or less distant future against which the speaker urges resistance. Sometimes the reference to the future is directly or indirectly indicated by the context.

b. *μὴ γράψῃς* usually has the force of (I beg that) *you will not write*, (take care that you) *don't write*, and is commonly a complete prohibition against doing something not already begun. Sometimes, and especially in expressions of a colloquial character, *μή* with the aorist subjunctive marks the speaker's interruption, by anticipation, of a mental (less often of a physical) action that is being done by the person he addresses; as *μὴ θαυμάσῃς* (P. L. 804 b) in reply to an exclamation of surprise. Here the type *μὴ γράψῃς* often expresses impatience.

c. If *μὴ γράφε* elicits a reply, it is (*ἀλλ'*) *οὐ γράφω*, while *μὴ γράψῃς* is answered by (*ἀλλ'*) *οὐ γράψω*. Thus, *μή μ' ἐκδίδασκε τοῖς φίλοις εἶναι κακήν. ἀλλ' οὐ διδάσκω do not teach me to be base to my friends. But I do not* S. El. 395, *εἰ οὖν ἔχεις ἐναργέστερον ἡμῖν ἐπιδεῖξαι ὡς διδακτόν ἐστιν ἡ ἀρετή, μὴ φθονήσῃς ἀλλ' ἐπίδειξον. ἀλλ' . . . οὐ φθονήσω now if you can show us more clearly that virtue is capable of being taught, don't refuse, but show us. Well, I will not refuse* P. Pr. 320 c. So *μὴ γράφε* commonly answers *γράφω*, as *θαυμάζω, ἦν δ' ἐγώ, καὶ αὐτός. ἀλλὰ μὴ θαύμαζ', ἔφη I myself am astonished, said I. Cease your astonishment, said she* P. S. 205 b, cp. S. El. 395. So *μὴ γράψῃς* answers *γράψω*, as in Hdt. 3. 140, Ar. Lys. 1036.

d. *μὴ γράφε* and *μὴ γράψῃς* are often found in closely connected clauses, as *μηδαμῶς θύμαινέ μοι, μηδέ μ' ἐπιτρίψῃς don't be angry with me at all, nor ruin me* Ar. Nub. 1478, *μήτ' ὀκνεῖτε μήτ' ἀφῆτ' ἔπος κακὸν do not shrink from me nor utter any harsh words* S. O. C. 731. The second prohibition may be more specific than the first, as *σιώπα· μηδὲν εἴπῃς νήπιον be silent, don't say anything childish* Ar. Nub. 105. Less often *μὴ γράψῃς* is followed by *μὴ γράφε*, as *μὴ βοηθήσατε τῷ πεπονθότι δεινά· μὴ εὐορκεῖτε* (they will say) '*do not come to the aid of one who has suffered grievously; have no regard for your oath*' D. 21. 211.

e. The difference between *μὴ γράφε* and *μὴ γράψῃς* is virtually a difference of tenses, the present denoting an action continuing, in process; the aorist, an action concluded, summarized. So μὴ φοβοῦ *don't be fearful*, μὴ φοβηθῇς *don't be frightened.* In maxims μή with the present imperative is preferred: μὴ κλέπτε *don't be a thief*, μὴ κλέψῃς *don't steal* this or that. μηκέτι may be used in either construction. The distinction is often immaterial, often a difference of tone rather than of meaning; sometimes too subtle for dogmatic statement.

1842. The imperative may be used in subordinate clauses: κρατῆρές εἰσιν . . . ὧν κρᾶτ' ἔρεψον *there are mixing-bowls, the brims of which thou must crown* S. O. C. 473.

a. Especially after οἶσθα interrogative in dramatic poetry: οἶσθ' ὃ δρᾶσον; *do you know what you are to do?* E. Hec. 225, οἶσθ' ὡς ποίησον; *do you know how I bid you act?* S. O. T. 543. οἶσθ' ὃ has become a partially fossilized expression, and can be used as subject or be governed by a verb: οἶσθά νυν ἅ μοι γενέσθω; *do you know what I must have done for me?* E. I. T. 1203.

1843. The use of the imperative is to be explained as equivalent to δεῖ or χρή with the infinitive.

1844. ἄν is not used with the imperative.

INFINITIVE AND PARTICIPLE WITH ἄν

1845. The infinitive or participle with ἄν represents either a past tense of the indicative with ἄν or the optative with ἄν. The context determines whether the indicative or the optative is meant. The participle with ἄν is post-Homeric.

1846. The present infinitive or participle with ἄν represents the imperfect indicative with ἄν or the present optative with ἄν.

a. (*inf.*) ἀκούω Λακεδαιμονίους ἂν ἀναχωρεῖν ἐπ' οἴκου *I hear the Lacedaemonians used to return home* (= ἂν ἀνεχώρουν, 1790) D. 9. 48, οἴεσθε γὰρ τὸν πατέρα οὐκ ἂν φυλάττειν; *for do you think my father would not have taken care?* (= οὐκ ἂν ἐφύλαττεν, 1786) D. 49. 35; νομίζοντες ἂν τῑμῆς τυγχάνειν *in the belief that they would obtain reward* (= ἂν τυγχάνοιμεν) X. A. 1. 9. 29.

b. (*part.*) ὅπερ ἔσχε μὴ κατὰ πόλεις αὐτὸν ἐπιπλέοντα τὴν Πελοπόννησον πορθεῖν, ἀδυνάτων ἂν ὄντων . . . ἀλλήλοις ἐπιβοηθεῖν *which prevented him from sailing against the Peloponnese and laying it waste city by city when* the Peloponnesians *would have been unable to come to the rescue of one another* (= ἀδύνατοι ἂν ἦσαν) T. 1. 73, πόλλ' ἂν ἔχων ἕτερ' εἰπεῖν, παραλείπω *though I might be able to say much else I pass it by* (= ἂν ἔχοιμι, 1824) D. 18. 258, σοφίᾱ λεγομένη δικαιότατ' ἂν *that might most justly be called wisdom* P. Phil. 30 c (= ἡ σοφίᾱ λέγοιτο ἄν).

1847. The future infinitive and participle with ἄν are rare and suspected.

1848. The aorist infinitive or participle with ἄν represents the aorist indicative with ἄν or the aorist optative with ἄν.

a. (*inf.*) Κῦρός γε, εἰ ἐβίωσεν, ἄριστος ἂν δοκεῖ ἄρχων γενέσθαι *it seems probable that Cyrus, if he had lived, would have proved himself a most excellent ruler* (= ἂν ἐγένετο) X. O. 4. 18, ὥστε καὶ ἰδιώτην ἂν γνῶναι *so that even a common man could have understood* (= ἂν ἔγνω) X. A. 6. 1. 31, τί ἂν οἰόμεθα παθεῖν; *what do we think our fate would be?* (= τί ἂν πάθοιμεν;) X. A. 3. 1. 17.

b. (*part.*) ὁρῶν τὸ παρατείχισμα ῥᾳδίως ἂν ληφθέν *seeing that the counter-wall could easily be captured* (= ἂν ληφθείη) T. 7. 42, Ποτείδαιαν ἑλὼν καὶ δυνηθεὶς ἂν αὐτὸς ἔχειν, εἰ ἐβουλήθη, παρέδωκεν *after he had seized Potidaea and would have been able to keep it himself, had he wished, he gave it up to them* (= ἐδυνήθη ἄν) D. 23. 107, οὔτε ὄντα οὔτε ἂν γενόμενα λογοποιοῦσιν *they fabricate stories which neither are, nor could be, true* T. 6. 38 (= ἃ οὔτε ἔστιν οὔτε ἂν γένοιτο).

1849. The perfect infinitive with ἄν represents the pluperfect indicative with ἄν or the perfect optative with ἄν: οἶδ' ὅτι (ἄν) φήσειεν πάντα ταῦθ' ὑπὸ τῶν βαρβάρων ἂν ἡλωκέναι *I know that he would say that all this would have been captured by the barbarians* (= ἂν ἡλώκεσαν) D. 19. 312, ἡγεῖτο τοὺς ἀγνοοῦντας ἀνδραποδώδεις ἂν δικαίως κεκλῆσθαι *he thought that those who did not know this might justly be deemed servile in nature* (= κεκλημένοι ἂν εἶεν) X. M. 1. 1. 16.

For the infinitive and participle without ἄν see 1865 ff., 1872 ff., and under Infinitive and Participle.

THE TENSES

1850. By the tenses ('tense' from *tempus*) are denoted:

1. The time of an action: present, past, future.
2. The stage of an action: action continued or repeated (in process of development), action simply brought to pass (simple occurrence), action completed with a permanent result.

a. The time of an action is either *absolute* or *relative*. Time that is absolutely present, past, or future is reckoned from the time of the speaker or writer. Time that is relatively present, past, or future in dependent clauses is reckoned from the time of some verb in the same sentence. In dependent clauses Greek has no special forms to denote the temporal relation of one action to another (antecedent, coincident, subsequent), but leaves the reader to infer whether one action happened *before*, *at the same time as*, or *after* another action. The aorist is thus often used where English has the pluperfect (1943). See 1888, 1944. Unless special reference is made to relative time, the expressions "kind of time," "time of an action," in this book are used of absolute time.

b. In independent clauses only the tenses of the indicative denote absolute time; in dependent clauses they express relative time. The tenses of the subjunctive, optative, imperative, infinitive and participle do not refer to the differences in kind of time. Thus γράφειν and γράψαι *to write*, γεγραφέναι *to finish writing*, may be used of the present, the past, or the future according to the context. On the tenses of the optative, infinitive, and participle in indirect discourse see 1862, 1866, 1874. The future infinitive may be used, outside of indirect discourse, to lay stress on the idea of futurity (1865 d).

c. Even in the indicative the actual time may be different from that which would seem to be denoted by the tense employed. Thus the speaker or writer may imagine the past as present, and use the present in setting forth an event that happened before his time (1883); or may use the aorist or perfect of an event that has not yet occurred (1934, 1950).

d. In the subjunctive, optative (except in indirect discourse), and imperative the kind of time is implied only by the mood-forms, not by the tenses. The relation of the time of one action to the time of another usually has to be inferred in all the moods.

e. The stage of an action is expressed by all the tenses of all the different moods (including the participle and infinitive).

f. The action of the verb of a subordinate clause may *overlap* with that of the verb of the main clause. See 2388.

KIND OF TIME

1851. Only in the indicative do the tenses show time absolutely present, past, or future.

a. Present time is denoted by

1. The Present: γράφω *I write, am writing.*
2. The Perfect: γέγραφα *I have written.*

b. Past time is denoted by

1. The Imperfect: ἔγραφον *I wrote, was writing.*
2. The Aorist: ἔγραψα *I wrote.*
3. The Pluperfect: ἐγεγράφη *I had written.*

N. — The only past tenses are the augmented tenses.

c. Future time is denoted by

1. The Future: γράψω *I shall write.*
2. The Future Perfect: γεγράψεται *it will have been written,* τεθνήξω *I shall be dead* (*shall have died*).

STAGE OF ACTION

1852. Every form of the verb denotes the stage of the action.

a. Continued action is denoted by the present stem:

1. Present: γράφω *I am writing,* πείθω *I am persuading* (*trying to persuade*), ἀνθεῖ *is in bloom.*
2. Imperfect: ἔγραφον *I was writing,* ἔπειθον *I was persuading* (*trying to persuade*), ἤνθει *was in bloom.*
3. Future: γράψω *I shall write* (*shall be writing*), βασιλεύσει *he will reign.*

N. — Continued action is incomplete: hence nothing is stated as to the conclusion. Thus φεύγει *he flees* does not state whether or not the subject succeeded in escaping.

b. Completed action with permanent result is denoted by the perfect stem:

1. Perfect: γέγραφα ἐπιστολήν *I have written a letter* (and it is *now* finished), ἤνθηκε *has bloomed* (and is in flower).
2. Pluperfect: ἐγεγράφη ἐπιστολήν *I had written a letter* (and it was *then* finished), ἠνθήκει *had bloomed* (and was in flower).

3. Future Perfect: γεγράψεται *it will have been written*, τεθνήξει *he will be dead.*

c. Action simply brought to pass (simple attainment) is denoted by the

1 Aorist: ἔγραψα *I wrote*, ἔπεισα *I persuaded (succeeded in persuading)*, ἐβασίλευσε *he became king* or *he was king*, ἤνθησε *burst into flower* or *was in flower.*

2. Future: γράψω *I shall write*, βασιλεύσει *he will become king.*

N. — The aorist tense (ἀόριστος χρόνος from ὁρίζω *define*; unlimited, indefinite, or undefined time) is so named because it does not show the limitation (ὅρος) of continuance (expressed by the imperfect) or of completion with permanent result (expressed by the perfect).

1853. The present stem may denote the simple action of the verb in present time without regard to its continuance; as θαυμάζω *I am seized with astonishment*, ἀστράπτει *it lightens* (once or continually), δίδωμι *I make a present.* This is called the *aoristic present.* On inceptive verbs, see 526.

1854. The future stem may denote either continued action (as in the present) or simple occurrence of the action of the verb (as in the aorist). Thus γράψω *I shall be writing* or *I shall write.* See 1910 b.

1855. Some verbs are, by their meaning, restricted to the tenses of continued action, as ὁρᾶν *behold*, φέρειν *carry*; others are exclusively aoristic, as ἰδεῖν properly *glance at*, ἐνεγκεῖν *bring.* Verbs expressing different kinds of action in their several tenses (as ὁρᾶν, ἰδεῖν) unite to form a verbal system.

1856. The difference between the present stem (present and imperfect) and the aorist stem may be compared to the difference between a *line* and a *point* (both starting point and end). Thus, ἔρχεσθαι *go*, ἐλθεῖν *come, arrive*; φέρειν *carry*, ἐνεγκεῖν *bring*; ἄγειν *accompany, lead*, ἀγαγεῖν *bring to a goal.*

1857. For the 'progressive' tenses of English (*is walking, has been giving,* etc.) Greek has no exact equivalent. The periphrasis of the present participle with ἐστί, etc. is employed to adjectivize the participle or to describe or characterize the subject like an adjective, *i.e.* the subject has a quality which it may display in action. Thus, ἀρέσκοντές ἐσμεν *we are acceptable* T. 1. 38, καὶ πάντ' ἀναδεχόμενος καὶ εἰς αὑτὸν ποιούμενος τὰ τούτων ἁμαρτήματ' ἐστίν *and he takes upon himself and adopts all their misdeeds* D. 19. 36. ἐστί may be emphatic: ἔστι που δίχα διαιρούμενον *there exists a twofold division* P. L. 895 d. Some participles have become completely adjectivized: συμφέρων *useful*, διαφέρων *superior.* Cp. 1961.

1858. Primary and Secondary Tenses. — The primary tenses refer to present and future time (present, future, perfect, and future perfect), the secondary or historical tenses refer to past time (imperfect, aorist, pluperfect).

a. The gnomic aorist (1931 b) is regarded as a primary tense, as is the aorist when used for the perfect (1940), and the imperfect indicative referring to present time (1788); the historical present (1883), as a secondary tense. The subjunctive, optative, and imperative moods in their independent uses point to the future, and all their tenses therefore count as primary.

THE TENSES OUTSIDE OF THE INDICATIVE

1859. The tenses of the moods except the indicative do not express time in independent sentences.

1860. Subjunctive. — The subjunctive mood as such refers to the future. The tenses do not refer to differences of time, and denote only the stage of the action (continuance, simple occurrence, completion with permanent result).

Present (continuance): τὰ αὑτῶν ἅμα ἐκποριζώμεθα *let us at the same time keep developing our resources* T. 1. 82; Aorist (simple occurrence): ποριζώμεθα οὖν πρῶτον τὴν δαπάνην *let us procure the money first* T. 1. 83; Perfect (completion with permanent result): ἵνα, ἢν μὴ ὑπακούωσι, τεθνήκωσιν *that, in case they do not submit, they may be put to death* (lit. *may be dead* at once) T. 8. 74. The aorist commonly replaces the more exact perfect because the perfect is rarely used.

a. The future time denoted by present or aorist (τί ποιῶμεν; or τί ποιήσωμεν; *what shall we do?*) may refer, according to the sense, either to the next moment or to some later time. Greek has no subjunctive form denoting an *intention* to do this or that. In dependent constructions (including general conditions) the action of the present is generally coincident (rarely subsequent), that of the aorist is generally anterior (rarely coincident), to the action of the leading verb: χαλεπαίνουσι, ἐπειδὰν αὐτοῖς παραγγέλλω πίνειν τὸ φάρμακον *they are angry whenever I bid them drink the poison* P. Ph. 116 c, ἐπειδὰν ἅπαντ' ἀκούσητε, κρίνατε *when you* (shall) *have heard everything, decide* D. 4. 14. The use of the aorist of time relatively anterior to the action of the leading verb (= Lat. future perfect) is, like its other references to relative time, only an inference from the connection of the thought (1850 a).

b. Present and aorist subjunctive are occasionally used in the same sentence without any great difference in sense (X. C. 1. 2. 6–7, 5. 5. 13).

c. An independent or dependent subjunctive may be ingressive (1924): ἢν γὰρ ὁ Πλοῦτος νυνὶ βλέψῃ *for if now Plutus recovers his sight* Ar. Pl. 494.

d. In general conditions (2336) the subjunctive refers to general time, denoting what holds true now and at all times.

1861. Optative (not in indirect discourse). — The reference is always to future time. The tenses do not refer to differences of time, and denote only the stage of the action.

Present (continuance): πλούσιον δὲ νομίζοιμι τὸν σοφὸν *may I* (always) *count the wise man wealthy* P. Phae. 279 b; Aorist (simple occurrence): εἰ γὰρ γένοιτο *would that it might happen* X. C. 6. 1. 38; Perfect (completion with permanent result): τεθναίης *die* (lit. *may you be dead*) Z 164.

a. In general conditions (2336) the optative is used of past time.

b. In dependent constructions (including general conditions) the action of the present is generally coincident (rarely anterior), that of the aorist generally anterior (rarely coincident), to the action of the leading verb: εἴ τις τάδε παραβαίνοι, ἐναγὴς ἔστω τοῦ Ἀπόλλωνος *if any one violates this, let him be accurst of*

Apollo Aes. 3. 110, *ἐπειδὴ δὲ ἀνοιχθείη (τὸ δεσμωτήριον), εἰσῇμεν παρὰ τὸν Σωκράτη whenever the prison was opened, we* (always) *went in to Socrates* P. Ph. 59 d. The aorist is often preferred to the more exact perfect because the perfect was rarely used.

c. An independent or dependent optative may be ingressive (1924): *εἰ πολεμήσαιμεν δι' Ὠρωπόν, οὐδὲν ἂν ἡμᾶς παθεῖν ἡγοῦμαι if we should enter upon a war on account of Oropus, I think we should suffer nothing* D. 5. 16.

1862. Optative (in indirect discourse).—When the optative in indirect discourse represents the indicative after a past tense of a verb of *saying* or *thinking*, each tense does denote time (as well as stage of action) relatively to that of the leading verb.

a. The present optative represents the imperfect as well as the present indicative.

b. The future optative (first in Pindar) occurs only in indirect discourse after verbs of *saying* and *thinking*, in object clauses after *ὅπως*, 2212, and in other indirect expressions of thought.

c. When the optative in indirect discourse represents the subjunctive (2619 b), its tenses denote only stage of action.

1863. a. Present opt. = present indic.: *ἀνηρώτᾱ τί βούλοιντο he demanded what they wanted* (= *τί βούλεσθε;*) X. A. 2. 3. 4.

b. Present opt. = imperf. indic.: *διηγοῦντο ὅτι ἐπὶ τοὺς πολεμίους πλέοιεν they explained that they kept sailing against the enemy* (= *ἐπλέομεν*) X. H. 1. 7. 5.

c. Future opt. = future indic.: *ὅ τι ποιήσοι οὐδὲ τούτοις εἶπε he did not tell even these what he would do* (= *ποιήσω*) X. A. 2. 2. 2.

d. Aorist opt. = aorist indic.: *ἠρώτᾱ τί πάθοιεν he asked what had happened to them* (= *τί ἐπάθετε;*) X. C. 2. 3. 19.

e. Perfect opt. = perfect indic.: *ἔλεγον ὅτι οἱ μετὰ Δημοσθένους παραδεδώκοιεν σφᾶς αὐτοὺς they said that the troops of Demosthenes had surrendered* (= *παραδεδώκᾱσι*) T. 7. 83.

1864. Imperative.—The imperative always implies future time. The tenses do not refer to differences of time, and denote only the stage of the action.

a. Present (continuance): *τοὺς γονεῖς τίμᾱ honour thy parents* I. 1. 16, *πάντα τἀληθῆ λέγε tell* (go on and tell in detail) *the whole truth* L. 1. 18, *τοὺς ἵππους ἐκείνοις δίδοτε offer the horses to them* X. C. 4. 5. 47.

b. Aorist (simple occurrence): *βλέψον πρὸς τὰ ὄρη look* (*cast a glance*) *toward the mountains* X. A. 4. 1. 20, *εἰπέ state* (in a word) P. A. 24 d, *ἡμῖν τοὺς ἵππους δότε give the horses to us* X. C. 4. 5. 47.

c. Perfect (completion with permanent result): *τετάχθω let him take his place* (and stay there) P. R. 562 a, *εἰρήσθω let it have been said* (once for all) 503 b.

N.—The perfect active and middle are generally used as presents (*τεθνάτω let him be put to death* P. L. 938 c, *μέμνησθε remember* D. 40. 30). The perfect passive (in the third person) is used of a fixed decision concerning what is to be done or has been done.

1865. Infinitive (not in indirect discourse). — The tenses of the infinitive (without ἄν) not in indirect discourse have no time of themselves and express only the stage of the action; their (relative) time depends on the context and is that of the leading verb (present, past, or future). The infinitive may have the article (2025 ff.).

a. Present (continuance): οὐδὲ βουλεύεσθαι ἔτι ὥρᾱ, ἀλλὰ βεβουλεῦσθαι *it is time no longer to be making up one's mind, but to have it made up* P. Cr. 46 a.

b. Aorist (simple occurrence): τοῦ πιεῖν ἐπιθῡμίᾱ *the desire of obtaining drink* T. 7. 84, ἤρξατο γενέσθαι *began to be* 1. 103, but ἤρχετο γίγνεσθαι 3. 18 (the tense of γίγνομαι depends on that of ἄρχομαι; *not* ἤρξατο γίγνεσθαι), δεῖ τοὺς ὑπὲρ αὐτοῦ λέγοντας μῑσῆσαι (ingressive) *one must conceive an aversion for those who speak in his behalf* D. 9. 53.

c. Perfect (completion with permanent result): see **a.** Often of certainty of action.

d. Future. — When the context shows that stress is laid on the idea of futurity, the future infinitive, referring to future time relative to the main verb, is sometimes used instead of the present or aorist: οὐκ ἀποκωλύσειν δυνατοὶ ὄντες *not being able to prevent* T. 3. 28, πολλοῦ δέω κατ' ἐμαυτοῦ ἐρεῖν *I am far from intending to speak to my own disadvantage* P. A. 37 b. On the future infinitive with μέλλω see 1959.

N. 1. — The action set forth by a dependent present or aorist infinitive (without ἄν) not in indirect discourse has no time except that which is implied by the context. With verbs signifying *to advise* or *to command*, and when the infinitive expresses purpose, the reference is to future time. Usually the action of the present and aorist is coincident with or antecedent to that of the main verb. The action of an aorist infinitive with the article and a subject is *not* always relatively past. The perfect (without ἄν) has no time apart from the context; its action is usually antecedent.

N. 2. — On the use of the present and aorist with verbs of *promising*, etc., see 1868; with μέλλω, see 1959.

N. 3. — Observe that verbs denoting continuance (as μένω *remain*) often appear in the aorist, while verbs of transitory action (as ἱέναι *send, hurl*) often appear in the present.

N. 4. — Present and aorist occasionally occur in close conjunction without any great difference in meaning, as προσήκει ὑμῖν τούτου καταψηφίζεσθαι . . ., δεῖ ὑμᾶς θάνατον αὐτοῦ καταψηφίσασθαι *it is fitting that you vote against him, it is necessary that you pass a vote of death against him* L. 13. 69; cp. ναυμαχῆσαι and ναυμαχεῖν T. 2. 83, βασανιστὴς γίγνεσθαι and γενέσθαι Ant. 1. 10, 1. 11.

1866. Infinitive (in indirect discourse). — The tenses of the infinitive in indirect discourse denote the same time relative to that of the leading verb (present, past, or future) as was denoted by the corresponding tenses of the indicative in direct discourse which they represent.

a. The present infinitive represents also the imperfect, the perfect infinitive represents also the pluperfect indicative.

b. The action of the present is usually coincident, that of the aorist anterior, to the action of the leading verb.

c. The future infinitive is found chiefly in indirect discourse and in analogous constructions. With μέλλω, see 1959. It may have the article (2026).

1867. **a.** Present = pres. indic.: *φημὶ ταῦτα μὲν φλυāρίᾱς εἶναι I say this is nonsense* (= ἐστί) X. A. 1. 3. 18.

b. Present = imperf. indic: *Κτησίᾱς ἰᾶσθαι αὐτὸς τὸ τραῦμά φησι Ktesias asserts that he himself cured the wound* (= ἰώμην) X. A. 1. 8. 26. With ἄν, 1846 a.

c. Future = fut. indic.: *ἔφη ἢ ἄξειν Λακεδαιμονίους ἢ αὐτοῦ ἀποκτενεῖν he said that he would either bring the Lacedaemonians or kill them on the spot* (= ἄξω, ἀποκτενῶ) T. 4. 28.

d. Aorist = aor. indic.: *ἐνταῦθα λέγεται Ἀπόλλων ἐκδεῖραι Μαρσύāν there Apollo is said to have flayed Marsyas* (= ἐξέδειρε) X. A. 1. 2. 8. With ἄν, 1848 a.

e. Perfect = perf. ind.: *φησὶ ἐγκώμιον γεγραφέναι he says that he has written an encomium* (= γέγραφα) I. 10. 14, *ἔφασαν τεθνάναι τὸν ἄνδρα they said the man was dead* (= τέθνηκε) Ant. 5. 29.

f. Perfect = pluperf. ind.: *λέγεται ἄνδρα τινὰ ἐκπεπλῆχθαι it is said that a certain man had been fascinated* (= ἐξεπέπληκτο) X. C. 1. 4. 27. With ἄν, 1849.

1868. **The construction of verbs of hoping, etc.** —Verbs signifying *to hope, expect, promise, threaten, swear*, with some others of like meaning, when they refer to a future event, take either the future infinitive (in indirect discourse), or the aorist, less often the present, infinitive (not in indirect discourse). The use of the aorist and present is due to the analogy of verbs of *will* or *desire* (1991) which take an object infinitive not in indirect discourse. The same analogy accounts for the use of μή instead of οὐ (2725). The present or aorist infinitive with ἄν, representing the potential optative with ἄν, occurs occasionally.

a. *ἐν ἐλπίδι ὢν τὰ τείχη τῶν Ἀθηναίων αἱρήσειν hoping that he would capture the walls of the Athenians* T. 7. 46, *ἐλπὶς . . . ἐκτραφῆναι hope of being brought up* L. 19. 8, *ἐλπίζει δυνατὸς εἶναι ἄρχειν he expects to be able to rule* P. R. 573 c, *ἔχεις τινὰ ἐλπίδα μὴ ἂν . . . τὴν ναῦν ἀπολέσαι; have you any expectation that you would not shipwreck the vessel?* X. M. 2. 6. 38. ἐλπίζω with the present infinitive may mean *I feel sure that I am*.

b. *τάχιστα οὐδένα εἰκὸς σὺν αὐτῷ βουλήσεσθαι εἶναι it is probable that very soon no one will wish to be with him* X. C. 5. 3. 30, *ἡμᾶς εἰκὸς ἐπικρατῆσαι it is likely that we shall succeed* T. 1. 121, *οὐκ εἰκὸς αὐτοὺς περιουσίᾱν νεῶν ἔχειν it is not likely that they will continue to have ships to spare* 3. 13. With εἰκός the aorist is preferred.

c. *ὑπέσχετο ταῦτα ποιήσειν he promised that he would do this* L. 12. 14, *ὑπέσχετο βουλεύσασθαι* (most Mss.) *he promised to deliberate* X. A. 2. 3. 20. The aorist infinitive is especially common with verbs of *promising* and must refer to the future. With the present infinitive ὑπισχνοῦμαι means *I assure, profess, pledge my word that I am*.

d. *ἀπείλει ἐκτρίψειν he threatened that he would destroy* them Hdt. 6. 37, *ἠπείλησαν ἀποκτεῖναι ἅπαντας they threatened to kill everybody* X. H. 5. 4. 7.

e. *δικάσειν ὀμωμόκατε you have sworn that you will give judgment* D. 39. 40, *ἀναγκάζει τὸν Κερσοβλέπτην ὀμόσαι . . . εἶναι μὲν τὴν ἀρχὴν κοινήν . . ., πάντας δ' ὑμῖν ἀποδοῦναι τὴν χώρāν he compelled Cersobleptes to swear that the kingdom* *should be in common and that they should all restore to you the territory* D. 23. 170.

f. With ὄμνῡμι a dependent infinitive may refer to the present, past, or future (e). Thus, ὀμνύντες βλέπειν . . . Ἀχιλλέᾱ πάλιν *swearing that they see Achilles again* S. Ph. 357, ὀμνύουσι μὴ 'κπιεῖν *they swear they did not drink* Pherecrates 143 (Com. fr. I. 187), ὤμνυε μηδὲν εἰρηκέναι *he swore that he had said nothing* (direct = οὐδὲν εἴρηκα) D. 21. 119.

1869. Verbs of *will* or *desire* (1991) regularly take the present or aorist infinitive not in indirect discourse; but in some cases we find the future infinitive by assimilation to indirect discourse through the analogy of verbs of *promising*, etc. (1868). So with βούλομαι, ἐθέλω *wish*, λέγω meaning *command*, δέομαι *ask*, ἐφίεμαι *desire* and some others (even δύναμαι *am able*) that have a future action as their object. Thus, ἐφῑέμενοι ἄρξειν *being desirous to gain control* T. 6. 6, ἀδύνατοι ἐπιμελεῖς ἔσεσθαι *unable to be careful* X. O. 12. 12. διανοοῦμαι may follow the analogy of μέλλω (1959): τὸν πόλεμον διενοοῦντο προθύμως οἴσειν *they intended to carry on the war with zeal* T. 4. 121. In these and similar cases the future is employed to stress the future character of the action. Some editors would emend many of these futures.

1870. Verbs signifying *to foretell by oracle* usually take the present or aorist infinitive like verbs signifying *to command.*

1871. A few cases stand in our texts of an aorist infinitive referring to the future after a verb of *saying* or *thinking*, *e.g.* ἐνόμισαν ῥᾳδίως κρατῆσαι *they thought they would easily master* them T. 2. 3. Many editors change to the future or insert ἄν.

1872. Participle (not in indirect discourse). — The participle, as a verbal adjective, is timeless. The tenses of the participle express only continuance, simple occurrence, and completion with permanent result. Whether the action expressed by the participle is antecedent, coincident, or subsequent to that of the leading verb (in any tense) depends on the context. The future participle has a temporal force only because its voluntative force points to the future.

a. **Present** (continuative). The action set forth by the present participle is generally coincident (rarely antecedent or subsequent) to that of the leading verb: ἐργαζόμεναι μὲν ἠρίστων, ἐργασάμεναι δὲ ἐδείπνουν *the women took their noonday meal while they continued their work, but took their supper when they had stopped work* X. M. 2. 7. 12.

1. Antecedent action (= imperf.): οἱ Κύρειοι πρόσθεν σὺν ἡμῖν ταττόμενοι νῦν ἀφεστήκᾱσιν *the forces of Cyrus that were formerly marshalled with us have now deserted* X. A. 3. 2. 17, τοὺς τότε παρόντας αἰτιάσονται συμβούλους *they will accuse those who were their counsellors at that time* P. G. 519 a, οἱ Κορίνθιοι μέχρι τούτου προθύμως πράσσοντες ἀνεῖσαν τῆς φιλονεικίᾱς *the Corinthians, who up to that time had been acting zealously, now slackened in their vehemence* T. 5. 32. An adverb (πρότερον, πρόσθεν, τότε, ποτέ) often accompanies the participle, which is sometimes called the *participle of the imperfect.*

2. Subsequent action (especially when the leading verb denotes motion): ἔπεμψαν πρέσβεις ἀγγέλλοντας τὴν τοῦ Πλημυρίου λῆψιν *they despatched messengers*

to announce the capture of Plemyrium T. 7. 25. An attributive present part. w. νῦν may refer to the absolute present, though the main verb is past: τὴν νῦν Βοιωτίᾱν καλουμένην ᾤκησαν *they settled in the country now called Boeotia* T. 1. 12.

3. The present participle denotes that an action is in process, is attempted, or is repeated.

b. Future (chiefly voluntative): οὐ συνήλθομεν ὡς βασιλεῖ πολεμήσοντες *we have not come together for the purpose of waging war with the king* X. A. 2. 3. 21.

c. Aorist (simple occurrence). The action set forth by the aorist participle is generally antecedent to that of the leading verb; but it is sometimes coincident or nearly so, when it defines, or is identical with, that of the leading verb, and the subordinate action is only a modification of the main action.

1. Antecedent: δειπνήσᾱς ἐχώρει *after supper he advanced* T. 3. 112, τοὺς ἐλευθέρους ἀποκτείναντες ἀνεχώρησαν *after killing the free men they withdrew* 5. 83. ἐπομόσᾱς ἔφη *he took an oath and said* X. C. 4. 1. 23, ἤδη δ' ἐπὶ ταῦτα πορεύσομαι τοσοῦτον αὐτὸν ἐρωτήσᾱς *I shall at once proceed to this matter after having put to him certain questions* D. 18. 124. The aorist participle is often thus used when it takes up the preceding verb: νῦν μὲν δειπνεῖτε· δειπνήσαντες δὲ ἀπελαύνετε *take your supper now, and when you have done so, depart* X. C. 3. 1. 37.

2. Coincident: μή τι ἐξαμάρτητε ἐμοῦ καταψηφισάμενοι *do not commit the error of condemning me* P. A. 30 d, εὖ γ' ἐποίησας ἀναμνήσᾱς με *you did well in reminding me* P. Ph. 60 c (= ἀνέμνησάς με εὖ ποιῶν). So also when an aorist participle is used with a future finite verb, as ἀπαλλαχθήσομαι βίου θανοῦσα *by dying I shall be delivered from life* E. Hipp. 356. See also 2103.

3. The action of an attributive aorist participle is rarely subsequent to that of the leading verb. When this is the case, the action of the participle is marked as past from the point of view of the present (like the aor. indic.): οἱ Ἕλληνες ὕστερον κληθέντες οὐδὲν πρὸ τῶν Τρωϊκῶν ἁθρόοι ἔπρᾱξαν *the people later called Hellenes carried out no joint enterprise prior to the Trojan war* T. 1. 3, Σάτυρος καὶ Χρέμων, οἱ τῶν τριάκοντα γενόμενοι, Κλεοφῶντος κατηγόρουν *Satyrus and Chremon, who* (afterwards) *became members of the Thirty, accused Cleophon* L. 30. 12; cp. γενόμενος T. 2. 49, 4. 81.

4. The aorist participle is often ingressive or complexive (1924, 1927).

d. Perfect (completion with permanent result): καταλαμβάνουσι Βρᾱσίδᾱν ἐπεληλυθότα *they found* (historical present) *that Brasidas had arrived* T. 3. 69. A perfect participle may have the force of a pluperfect if accompanied by an adverb like πρόσθεν (cp. 1872 a. 1): ὁ πρόσθε κεκτημένος *he who possessed it before* S. Ph. 778.

1873. Construction of λανθάνω, φθάνω, τυγχάνω. — A supplementary aorist participle with any tense, except the present or imperfect, of λανθάνω *escape the notice of*, φθάνω *anticipate*, τυγχάνω *happen* usually coincides in time with the leading verb: ἔλαθον ἐμαυτὸν οὐδὲν εἰπών *I was unconsciously talking nonsense* P. Ph. 76 d, λήσομεν ἐπιπεσόντες *we shall fall on them unawares* X. A. 7. 3. 43. But the action of an aorist participle with the present or imperfect is generally prior to that of the leading verb: ὅστις ἀντειπὼν γε ἐτύγχανε *who chanced to have spoken in opposition* L. 12. 27. See 2096.

1874. Participle (in indirect discourse). The tenses of the participle in indirect discourse after verbs of intellectual perception denote the same time relative to that of the leading verb (present, past, or future) as was denoted by the corresponding tenses of the indicative in direct discourse which they represent. See 2106, 2112 b.

a. Present = pres. indic.: the action is generally coincident: ἐπειδὰν γνῶσιν ἀπιστούμενοι *when they find out that they are distrusted* (= ὅτι ἀπιστούμεθα) X. C. 7. 2. 17; rarely antecedent (when the present = the imperf. ind.): οἶδά σε λέγοντα ἀεί *I know that you always used to say* (= ὅτι ἔλεγες) 1. 6. 6.

b. Future = fut. indic.: ἀγνοεῖ τὸν πόλεμον δεῦρ' ἥξοντα *he is ignorant that the war will come here* (= ὅτι ὁ πόλεμος ἥξει) D. 1. 15.

c. Aorist = aor. indic.: τὸν Μῆδον ἴσμεν ἐπὶ τὴν Πελοπόννησον ἐλθόντα *we know that the Mede came against the Peloponnese* (= ὅτι ὁ Μῆδος ἦλθε) T. 1. 69.

d. Perfect = perf. indic.: οὐ γὰρ ᾔδεσαν αὐτὸν τεθνηκότα *for they did not know that he was dead* (= ὅτι τέθνηκε) X. A. 1. 10. 16. The perfect may also represent the pluperfect (cp. 1872 d).

TENSES OF THE INDICATIVE

PRESENT INDICATIVE

1875. The present represents a present state, or an action going on at the present time: ἀληθῆ λέγω *I am telling the truth* L. 13. 72.

a. On the present without any idea of duration, see 1853.

1876. Present of Customary Action. — The present is used to express a customary or repeated action: οὗτος μὲν γὰρ ὕδωρ, ἐγὼ δ' οἶνον πίνω *for this man drinks water, whereas I drink wine* D. 19. 46.

1877. Present of General Truth. — The present is used to express an action that is true for all time: ἄγει δὲ πρὸς φῶς τὴν ἀλήθειαν χρόνος *time brings the truth to light* Men. Sent. 11.

a. The present is an *absolute* tense in such sentences. The future, aorist, and perfect may also express a general truth.

1878. Conative Present. — The present may express an action begun, attempted, or intended.

τὴν δόξαν ταύτην πείθουσιν ὑμᾶς ἀποβαλεῖν *they are trying to persuade you to throw away this renown* I. 6. 12, δίδωμί σοι αὐτὴν ταύτην γυναῖκα *I offer you this woman herself as a wife* X. C. 8. 5. 19, προδίδοτον τὴν Ἑλλάδα *they are trying to betray Greece* Ar. P. 408.

a. This use is found also in the infinitive and participle: Φιλίππου ἐπὶ Βυζάντιον παριόντος *when Philip is preparing to advance against Byzantium* D. 8. 66.

b. The idea of attempt or intention is an inference from the context and lies in the present only so far as the present does not denote completion.

1879. Present for the Future (Present of Anticipation). — The present is used instead of the future in statements of what is immediate, likely, certain, or threatening.

μεταξὺ τὸν λόγον καταλύομεν; *shall we break off in the middle?* P. G. 505 c, καὶ εἰ βούλει, παραχωρῶ σοι τοῦ βήματος, ἕως ἂν εἴπῃς *and if you wish, I will yield you the floor until you tell us* Aes. 3. 165, ἀπόλλυμαι *I am on the verge of ruin* Ant. 5. 35 (so ἀπώλλυτο 5. 37 of past time), εἰ αὕτη ἡ πόλις ληφθήσεται, ἔχεται καὶ ἡ πᾶσα Σικελίᾱ *if this city is taken, the whole of Sicily as well is in their power* T. 6. 91.

a. Sometimes in questions to indicate that the decision must be made on the spot: ἢ πῶς λέγομεν; *or how shall we say?* (what must we say?) P. G. 480 b.

1880. εἶμι is regularly future (*I shall go*) in the indicative present. In the subjunctive it is always future; in the optative, infinitive, and participle it may be either future or present. Cp. 774. In ἰὼν ταῦτα λέγε *go and say this* (X. C. 4. 5. 17) ἰών is used of time relatively past. In Hom. εἶμι means both *I go* and *I shall go*.

1881. ἔρχομαι, πορεύομαι, νέομαι (poet.) may be used in a future sense. χέω means either *I pour* or *I shall pour*. ἔδομαι *I shall eat*, πίομαι *I shall drink*, are present in form. Cp. 541.

1882. Oracular Present. — In prophecies a future event may be regarded as present: χρόνῳ ἀγρεῖ Πριάμου πόλιν ἅδε κέλευθος *in time this expedition will capture Priam's city* A. Ag. 126.

1883. Historical Present. — In lively or dramatic narration the present may be used to represent a past action as going on at the moment of speaking or writing. This use does not occur in Homer.

ὁ δὲ Θεμιστοκλῆς φεύγει ἐς Κέρκῡραν . . . διακομίζεται ἐς τὴν ἤπειρον *Themistocles fled (flees) to Corcyra . . . was (is) transported to the mainland* T. 1. 136.

a. The historical present may represent either the descriptive imperfect or the narrative aorist.

b. The historical present may be coördinated with past tenses, which may precede or follow it: ἅμα δὲ τῇ ἡμέρᾳ τῇ πόλει προσέκειτο καὶ αἱρεῖ *at daybreak he assaulted the town and took it* T. 7. 29, οὕτω δὴ ἀπογράφονται πάντες ἀνέλαβόν τε τὰ ὅπλα *accordingly they all enrolled themselves and took the arms* X. C. 2. 1. 19.

c. The historical present is less frequent in subordinate clauses (T. 2. 91. 3).

1884. Annalistic Present. — Closely connected with the historical present is the annalistic present, which is used to register historical facts or to note incidents.

Δᾱρείου καὶ Παρυσάτιδος γίγνονται παῖδες δύο *of Darius and Parysatis were (are) born two sons* X. A. 1. 1. 1, πρὸ Λευτυχίδεω γὰρ (Ζευξίδημος) τελευτᾷ . . . Λευτυχίδης γαμέει Εὐρυδάμην, ἐκ τῆς οἱ . . . γίνεται θυγάτηρ *for Zeuxidemus died before Leutychides . . . L. married Eurydame, from her was born to him a daughter* Hdt. 6. 71, καὶ ὁ ἐνιαυτὸς ἔληγεν, ἐν ᾧ Καρχηδόνιοι αἱροῦσι δύο πόλεις Ἑλληνίδας *and the year came to an end in which the Carthaginians captured two Greek cities* X. H. 1. 1. 37.

1885. Present of Past and Present Combined. — The present, when accompanied by a definite or indefinite expression of past time, is used to express an action begun in the past and continued in the present. The 'progressive perfect' is often used in translation.

Thus, πάλαι θαυμάζω *I have been long* (and am still) *wondering* P. Cr. 43 b. Cp. *iamdudum loquor.* So with πάρος, ποτέ. This use appears also in the other moods.

a. So with verbs of *hearing*, *saying*, *learning*, whose action commenced in the past, but whose effect continues into the present: ἐξ ὧν ἀκούω *from what I hear* (*have heard*) X. A. 1. 9. 28, ὅπερ λέγω *as I said* P. A. 21 a. So with αἰσθάνομαι, γιγνώσκω, μανθάνω, πυνθάνομαι. ἄρτι *just* is often found with these verbs.

b. The perfect is used instead of the present when the action is completed in the present.

1886. Present for Perfect. — ἥκω *I am come, I have arrived,* οἴχομαι *I am gone,* have a perfect sense; as also ἔρχομαι, ἀφικνοῦμαι. Thus, Θεμιστοκλῆς ἥκω παρὰ σέ *I Themistocles have come to you* T. 1. 137, οἶδα ὅπῃ οἴχονται *I know where they have gone* X. A. 1. 4. 8.

a. ἥκω may be used in connection with the gnomic aorist (P. S. **188 a**).

1887. The present of certain verbs often expresses an enduring result, and may be translated by the perfect: ἀδικῶ *I am guilty* (ἄδικός εἰμι), *I have done wrong*, νῑκῶ, κρατῶ, *I am victorious, I have conquered*, ἡττῶμαι *I am conquered*, φεύγω *I am the defendant* or *I am an exile* (οἱ φεύγοντες *the fugitives* and *the exiles*), προδίδωμι *I am a traitor*, ἁλίσκομαι *I am captured*, στέρομαι *I am deprived*, γίγνομαι *I am a descendant*.

ἥκω εἰς τὴν σὴν οἰκίᾱν, ἀδικῶ δ' οὐδέν *I am come to thy house, but have done no wrong* L. 12. 14, ἀπαγγέλλετε Ἀριαίῳ ὅτι ἡμεῖς γε νῑκῶμεν βασιλέᾱ *report to Ariaeus that we at least have conquered the king* X. A. 2. 1. 4.

a. So, in poetry, γεννῶ, φύω, τίκτω, θνῄσκω, ὄλλυμαι. Thus, ἥδε τίκτει σε *this woman* (*has born thee* =) *is thy mother* E. Ion 1560.

1888. In subordinate clauses, the action expressed by the present may be (a) contemporaneous, (b) antecedent, or (c) subsequent to that set forth by the main verb. The context alone decides in which sense the present is to be taken: (a) ἔλεγεν ὅτι ἕτοιμος εἴη ἡγεῖσθαι αὐτοῖς *he said that he was ready to lead them* X. A. 6. 1. 33; (b) when the present states an action begun in the past and continued in the present: ἐπείτε δὲ Πέρσαι ἔχουσι τὸ κράτος, (τὸ πεδίον) ἐστὶ τοῦ βασιλέος *from the time that the Persians began to hold sway, it belongs to the king* Hdt. 3. 117; and with the historical present: ὡς δὲ γίγνονται ἐπ' αὐτῷ, ἐσπίπτουσιν *when they came to it, they rushed in* T. 7. 84; (c) ἐγένετο ῥήτρᾱ . . . εἰ παρὰ ταῦτα ποιοῖεν, κολάζειν *an ordinance was passed . . . if they act contrary to this, to punish them* X. C. 1. 6. 33.

IMPERFECT

1889. The imperfect represents an action as still going on, or a state as still existing, in the past: Κῦρος οὔπω ἧκεν, ἀλλ' ἔτι προσήλαυνε *Cyrus had not yet arrived* (1886), *but was still marching on* X. A. 1. 5. 12, ἐβασίλευεν Ἀντίοχος *Antiochus was reigning* T. 2. 80. The conclusion of the action is usually to be inferred from the context.

1890. Imperfect of Continuance. — The imperfect thus represents an action as continuing in the past: διέφθειραν Ἀθηναίων πέντε καὶ εἴκοσι, οἳ ξυνεπολιορκοῦντο *they put to death twenty-five of the Athenians who were besieged* (*i.e.* from the beginning to the end of the siege) T. 3. 68.

1891. The imperfect of verbs of *sending*, *going*, *saying*, *exhorting*, etc., which imply continuous action, is often used where we might expect the aorist of concluded action. Thus, in ἔπεμπον, the action is regarded as unfinished since the goal is not reached: ἄγγελον ἔπεμπον καὶ τοὺς νεκροὺς ὑποσπόνδους ἀπέδοσαν *they sent a messenger and surrendered the dead under a truce* T. 2. 6. In ἐκέλευον *gave orders*, *urged*, *requested* the command, etc., is regarded as not yet executed. In ἔλεγεν αὐτοῖς τοιάδε *he spoke to them as follows* X. H. 1. 6. 4 (followed by the speech and ἐπεὶ δὲ ταῦτ' εἶπεν 1. 6. 12) the speech is not thought of as a finished whole, but as developed point by point, as in ἐπειδὴ δὲ οὗτος ταῦτα ἔλεγεν, ἔλεξα *but when he had said this, I said* Ant. 6. 21.

a. In messenger's speeches the speaker may go back to the time of receiving a command: ἰέναι σ' ἐκέλευον οἱ στρατηγοὶ τήμερον *the generals order you to depart to-day* Ar. Ach. 1073.

1892. The imperfect, when accompanied by an expression of past time, is used of actions which had been in progress for some time and were still in progress (cp. 1885): τὸ Ῥήγιον ἐπὶ πολὺν χρόνον ἐστασίαζε *Rhegium had been for a long time in a state of faction* T. 4. 1. If the action is regarded as completed the pluperfect is used.

1893. Imperfect of Customary Action. — The imperfect is used to express frequently repeated or customary past actions: ἐπεὶ εἶδον αὐτὸν οἵπερ πρόσθεν προσεκύνουν, καὶ τότε προσεκύνησαν *when they caught sight of him, the very men who before this were wont to prostrate themselves before him, prostrated themselves on this occasion also* X. A. 1. 6. 10, (Σωκράτης) τοὺς ἑαυτοῦ ἐπιθυμοῦντας οὐκ ἐπράττετο χρήματα Socrates *was not in the habit of demanding money from those who were passionately attached to him* X. M. 1. 2. 5. See also 2340.

a. The repetition of a simple act in the past is expressed by πολλάκις with the aorist (1930).

1894. Iterative Imperfect. — ἄν may be used with this imperfect (1790): ἐπεθύμει ἄν τις ἔτι πλείω αὐτοῦ ἀκούειν *people would* (*used to*) *desire to hear still more from him* X. C. 1. 4. 3.

1895. Conative Imperfect. — The imperfect may express an action attempted, intended, or expected, in the past.

ἔπειθον αὐτούς, καὶ οὓς ἔπεισα, τούτους ἔχων ἐπορευόμην *I tried to persuade them, and I marched away with those whom I succeeded in persuading* X. C. 5. 5. 22, Ἁλόννησον ἐδίδου· ὁ δ' ἀπηγόρευε μὴ λαμβάνειν Philip *offered* (proposed to give) *Halonnesus, but he* (Demosthenes) *dissuaded* them *from accepting it* Aes. 3. 83, Θηβαῖοι κατεδουλοῦντ' αὐτούς *the Thebans tried to enslave them* D. 8. 74, ἠπείγοντο ἐς τὴν Κέρκυραν *they were for pushing on to Corcyra* T. 4. 3.

a. Here may be placed the imperfect equivalent in sense to ἔμελλον with the infinitive. Thus, φονεὺς οὖν αὐτῶν ἐγιγνόμην ἐγὼ μὴ εἰπὼν ὑμῖν ἃ ἤκουσα. ἔτι δὲ τριᾱκοσίους Ἀθηναίων ἀπώλλυον *I was on the point of becoming their murderer* (*interfecturus eram*) *had I not told you what I heard. And besides I threatened three hundred Athenians with death* And. 1. 58. So ἀπωλλύμην *I was threatened with death.*

1896. Imperfect of Resistance or Refusal. — With a negative, the imperfect often denotes resistance or refusal (*would not* or *could not*). The aorist with a negative denotes unrestricted denial of a fact.

τὴν πρόκλησιν οὐκ ἐδέχεσθε *you would not accept the proposal* T. 3. 64 (τὴν ἱκετείᾱν οὐκ ἐδέξαντο *they did not receive the supplication* 1. 24), ὁ μὲν οὐκ ἐγάμει, ὁ δὲ ἔγημεν *the one would not marry, the other did* D. 44. 17, οὐδὲ φωνὴν ἤκουον, εἴ τις ἄλλο τι βούλοιτο λέγειν *they would not even listen to a syllable if ever any one wished to say anything to the contrary* D. 18. 43. So οὐκ εἴᾱ *he would not allow* (*he was not for allowing*).

1897. If simple positive and negative are contrasted, the aorist is preferred with the latter: τὰ ὑπάρχοντά τε σῴζειν (positive with present) καὶ ἐπιγνῶναι μηδέν (negative with aorist) *to preserve what you have, and to form no new plans* T. 1. 70. But where the verb itself contains or implies a negative idea, the present is used: παρεῖναι καὶ μὴ ἀποδημεῖν *to be present and not to be abroad* Aes. 2. 59.

1898. Imperfect of Description. — The imperfect describes manners and customs; the situation, circumstances, and details, of events; and the development of actions represented as continuing in past time.

ἐκεῖνός τε τοὺς ὑφ' ἑαυτῷ ὥσπερ ἑαυτοῦ παῖδας ἐτίμᾱ, οἵ τε ἀρχόμενοι Κῦρον ὡς πατέρα ἐσέβοντο *he* (Cyrus) *treated his subjects with honour as if they were his own children, and his subjects reverenced Cyrus like a father* X. C. 8. 8. 2, εὐθὺς ἀνεβόησάν τε πάντες καὶ προσπεσόντες ἐμάχοντο, ἐώθουν, ἐωθοῦντο, ἔπαιον, ἐπαίοντο *immediately all raised a shout and falling upon each other fought, pushed and were pushed, struck and were struck* 7. 1. 38, ἐπεὶ δὲ ταῦτα ἐρρήθη, ἐπορεύοντο· τῶν δὲ ἀπαντώντων οἱ μὲν ἀπέθνῃσκον, οἱ δὲ ἔφευγον πάλιν εἴσω, οἱ δὲ ἐβόων *and when these words had been spoken, they proceeded to advance; and of those who met them some were killed, others fled back indoors, and others shouted* 7. 5. 26, ἐστρατήγει δὲ αὐτῶν Ἀριστεύς *Aristeus was their commander* T. 1. 60; cp. X. C. 4. 2. 28, X. Ag. 2. 12, X. A. 4. 3. 8–25, Isocr. 1. 9, 7. 51–53, D. 18. 169 ff., Aes. 3. 192.

N. — The imperfect often has a dramatic or panoramic force: it enables the reader to follow the course of events as they occurred, as if he were a spectator of the scene depicted.

1899. The imperfect is thus often used to explain, illustrate, offer reasons for an action, and to set forth accompanying and subordinate circumstances that explain or show the result of the main action. Descriptive adverbs are often used with the imperfect.

ἐνταῦθα ἔμεινεν ἡμέρᾱς πέντε· καὶ τοῖς στρατιώταις ὠφείλετο μισθὸς πλέον ἢ τριῶν μηνῶν, καὶ πολλάκις ἰόντες ἐπὶ τὰς θύρᾱς ἀπῄτουν· ὁ δὲ ἐλπίδας λέγων διῆγε καὶ δῆλος ἦν ἀνιώμενος *there he remained for five days; and the soldiers whose pay was in arrears for more than three months kept going to headquarters and demanding their dues; but he kept expressing his expectation* (of making payment) *and was plainly annoyed* X. A. 1. 2. 11. See also 1907 a.

1900. Inchoative Imperfect. — The imperfect may denote the beginning of an action or of a series of actions: ἐπειδὴ δὲ καιρὸς ἦν, προσέβαλλον *but when the proper time arrived, they began an* (proceeded to) *attack* T. 7. 51.

1901. Imperfect for Present. — In descriptions of places and scenery and in other statements of existing facts the imperfect, instead of the present, is often used by assimilation to the time of the narrative (usually set forth in the main verb).

ἀφίκοντο ἐπὶ τὸν ποταμὸν ὃς ὥριζε τὴν τῶν Μακρώνων χώρᾱν καὶ τὴν τῶν Σκυθηνῶν *they came to the river which divided the country of the Macrones from that of the Scytheni* X. A. 4. 8. 1, ἐξελαύνει ἐπὶ ποταμὸν πλήρη ἰχθύων, οὓς οἱ Σύροι θεοὺς ἐνόμιζον *he marched to a river full of fish, which the Syrians regarded as gods* 1. 4. 9.

1902. — Imperfect of a Truth Just Recognized. — The imperfect, usually some form of εἶναι, with ἄρα, is often used to denote that a present fact or truth has just been recognized, although true before: οὐδὲν ἄρ' ἦν πρᾶγμα *it is, as it appears, no matter after all* P. S. 198 e, τοῦτ' ἄρ' ἦν ἀληθές *this is true after all* E. I. T. 351, ἄρα ἠπίστω *you know, sure enough* X. H. 3. 4. 9. ἄρα *sure enough, after all* appears with other tenses (P. Cr. 49 a, P. Ph. 61 a, D. 19. 160).

1903. The imperfect may refer to a topic previously discussed: ἦν ἡ μουσικὴ ἀντίστροφος τῆς γυμναστικῆς εἰ μέμνησαι *music is* (as we have seen) *the counterpart of gymnastics, if you remember the discussion* P. R. 522 a. This is called the *philosophical imperfect.*

1904. The epistolary imperfect is rare in Greek. See 1942 b.

1905. ἔδει, ἐχρῆν. — The imperfect of verbs expressing *obligation* or *duty* may refer to present time and imply that the obligation or duty is not fulfilled: σῑγήσᾱς ἡνίκ' ἔδει λέγειν *keeping silence when he ought to speak* D. 18. 189. So with ἐχρῆν *it were proper,* εἰκὸς ἦν *it were fitting* (1774). But the imperfect may also express past obligation without denying the action of the infinitive, as ἔδει μένειν *he was obliged to remain* (and did remain) D. 19. 124, ὅπερ ἔδει δεῖξαι *quod erat demonstrandum* Euclid 1. 5 (1779).

1906. Imperfect for Pluperfect. — The imperfect has the force of the pluperfect in the case of verbs whose present is used in the sense of the perfect (1886).

Thus, ἧκον *I had come* (rarely *I came*), ᾠχόμην *I had departed,* as ἐνίκων *I was victorious,* ἡττώμην *I was defeated* (1752). So (Ὀλύμπια) οἷς Ἀνδροσθένης παγκράτιον ἐνίκᾱ *the Olympic games, at which Androsthenes was the victor* (= *had won*) *in the pancratium* T. 5. 49.

1907. In subordinate clauses, the action expressed by the imperfect may be (a) contemporaneous with or (b) antecedent to that set forth by the main verb: (a) τοσοῦτοι ἦσαν οἱ ξύμπαντες ὅτε ἐς τὴν πολιορκίᾱν καθίσταντο *this was their total number when they began to be besieged* T. 2. 78; (b) τὸ πλοῖον ἧκεν, ἐν ᾧ ἐπλέομεν *the vessel arrived in which we* (*had*) *sailed* Ant. 5. 29. Greek has no special form to express time that is anterior to the past.

1908. Imperfect and Aorist.—The imperfect and aorist often occur in the same passage; and the choice of the one or the other often depends upon the manner in which the writer may view a given action. The imperfect may be represented by a line, along which an action progresses; the aorist denotes a point on the line (either starting point or end), or surveys the whole line from beginning to end.

a. The imperfect of 'continuance' or 'duration' implies nothing as to the absolute length of the action; cp. πάλιν κατὰ τάχος ἐκόμιζε τὴν στρατιάν *he took the army back as quickly as possible* T. 1. 114 with κατὰ τάχος ἀνεχώρησε *he retreated as quickly as possible* 1. 73. The imperfect does not indicate 'prolonged' action in contrast to 'momentary' action of the aorist.

b. The imperfect puts the reader in the midst of the events as they were taking place, the aorist simply reports that an event took place: ἔπειτα ψῑλοὶ δώδεκα ἀνέβαινον, ὧν ἡγεῖτο Ἀμμέᾱς, καὶ πρῶτος ἀνέβη *then twelve light-armed men proceeded to climb up under the leadership of Ammeas, who was the first to mount* T. 3. 22. Cp. T. 2. 49, 3. 15. 1–2, 4. 14, X. H. 4. 4. 1, I. 5. 53–54, 8. 99–100.

1909. The following statement presents the chief differences between imperfect and aorist as narrative tenses.

Imperfect	*Aorist*
circumstances, details, course of action	mere fact of occurrence, general statement
progress, enduring condition, continued activity	consummation (culmination, final issue, summary process)
general description	isolated points, characteristic examples
endeavour	attainment
actions subordinate to the main action	main actions, without reference to other actions

Cp. ξυνεστράτευον *they served with them in the war*, ξυνεστράτευσαν *they took the field with them* (both in T. 7. 57). ἔπειθον *I tried to persuade*, ἔπεισα *I succeeded in persuading* (both in X. C. 5. 5. 22).

FUTURE INDICATIVE

1910. The future denotes an action that will take place at some future time: λήψεται μισθὸν τάλαντον *he shall receive a talent as his reward* X. A. 2. 2. 20.

a. The action is future according to the opinion, expectation, hope, fear, or purpose of the speaker or the agent.

b. The action of the future is either continuative (like the present) or, like that of the aorist, expresses simple attainment. Thus πείσω means *I shall try to persuade*, or *I shall convince* (resultative), βασιλεύσω *I shall be king, shall reign* or *I shall become king* (ingressive).

1911. When a verb has two futures, that formed from the same stem as the present is properly continuative, that formed from the aorist stem marks simple attainment: thus, ἕξω *I shall have*, σχήσω *I shall get;* as καὶ ταῦτ' εἰκότως οὕτως ὑπελάμβανον ἕξειν *and I supposed with reason that this would continue so* D. 19. 153, Θηβαῖοι ἔχουσι μὲν ἀπεχθῶς, ἔτι δ' ἐχθροτέρως σχήσουσιν *the Thebans are hostile and will become still more so* 5. 18. (But ἕξω usually does duty for σχήσω.) So, ἀχθέσομαι *shall be angry*, ἀχθεσθήσομαι *shall get angry*, φοβήσομαι *shall continue fearful*, φοβηθήσομαι *shall be terrified*, αἰσχυνοῦμαι *shall feel* (continued) *shame*, αἰσχυνθήσομαι *shall be ashamed* (on a single occasion). Cp. 1738.

1912. The future represents both our *shall* and *will*. When voluntative (*will*), the action of the subject may be (1) the result of his own decision, as οὐ δὴ ποιήσω τοῦτο *that I never will do* D. 18. 11, or (2) dependent on the will of another, as ἡ βουλὴ μέλλει αἱρεῖσθαι ὅστις ἐρεῖ ἐπὶ τοῖς ἀποθανοῦσι *the Senate is about to choose some one to speak over the dead* P. Menex. 234 b. The use of the future is often similar to that of the subjunctive, especially in dependent clauses.

1913. Verbs of *wishing*, *asking*, and other voluntative verbs may appear in the future where English has the present: τοσοῦτον οὖν σου τυγχάνειν βουλήσομαι *I (shall) wish to obtain* only *so much at thy hands* E. Med. 259, παραιτήσομαι δ' ὑμᾶς μηδὲν ἀχθεσθῆναί μοι *I (shall) beg you not to take any offence at me* D. 21. 58. Cp. Lat. *censebo*.

a. In many cases the use of the future indicates that the wish remains unchanged; and there is no reference to a future *act*. Sometimes the future appears to be a more modest form of statement than the present.

1914. Gnomic Future. — The future may express a general truth: ἀνὴρ ἐπιεικὴς υἱὸν ἀπολέσᾱς ῥᾷστα οἴσει τῶν ἄλλων *a reasonable man, if he loses a son, will* (is expected to) *bear it more easily than other men* P. R. 603 e (cp. 1434).

a. Hdt. uses the future in descriptions of customs and in directions to travellers (1. 173, 2. 29).

1915. Future for Present. — The future may be used instead of the present of that which is possible at the moment of speaking: εὑρήσομεν τοὺς φιλοτίμους τῶν ἀνδρῶν . . . ἀντὶ τοῦ ζῆν ἀποθνῄσκειν εὐκλεῶς αἱρουμένους *we shall find that ambitious men choose a glorious death in preference to life* I. 9. 3.

a. The future may denote present intention: αἶρε πλῆκτρον, εἰ μαχεῖ *raise your spur if you mean to fight* Ar. Av. 759 (in this use μέλλω is more common (1959)). So in the tragic τί λέξεις; *what do you mean?* E. Med. 1310.

1916. Deliberative Future. — The future is often used in deliberative questions: τί ἐροῦμεν ἢ τί φήσομεν; *what shall we say or what shall we propose?* D. 8. 37.

a. The deliberative future may occur in connection with the deliberative subjunctive (1805): εἴπωμεν ἢ σῖγῶμεν; ἢ τί δράσομεν; *shall we speak or keep silent? or what shall we do?* E. Ion 758.

1917. Jussive Future. — The future may express a command, like the imperative; and, in the second person, may denote concession or permission. The negative is οὐ. The tone of the jussive future (which is post-Homeric) is generally familiar.

ὧς οὖν ποιήσετε *you will do thus* P. Pr. 338 a, ἀναγνώσεται τὸν νόμον — ἀναγίγνωσκε the clerk *will read the law — read* D. 24. 39, αὐτὸς γνώσει *you will judge for yourself* P. Phil. 12 a, σπουδὴ ἔσται τῆς ὁδοῦ *you will have to hurry on the march* T. 7. 77, ὑμεῖς οὖν, ἐὰν σωφρονῆτε, οὐ τούτου ἀλλ' ὑμῶν φείσεσθε *now, if you are wise, you will spare, not him, but yourselves* X. H. 2. 3. 34.

1918. The future with οὐ interrogative is used in questions in an imperative sense to express urgency, warning, or irony: οὐκ ἔξιμεν . . . οὐκ ἐπὶ τὴν ἐκείνου πλευσόμεθα; *shall we not go forth . . . shall we not set sail against his* country? D. 4. 44, οὐ φυλάξεσθε; *will you not be on your guard?* 6. 25. In exhortations addressed to oneself: οὐκ ἀπαλλαχθήσομαι θυμοῦ; *shall I not cease from my passion?* E. Med. 878.

a. μή with the future in a prohibitive sense is used in a few suspected passages (L. 29. 13, D. 23. 117).

1919. οὐ μή with the second person singular of the future in the dramatic poets denotes a strong prohibition; as οὐ μὴ διατρίψεις *don't dawdle* (you *shall* not dawdle) Ar. Ran. 462. οὐ μή with any person of the future indicative occasionally denotes an emphatic future denial; as τοὺς πονηροὺς οὐ μή ποτε βελτίους ποιήσετε *you will never make the bad better* Aes. 3. 177.

1920. ὅπως and ὅπως μή are used with the future in urgent exhortations and prohibitions: ὅπως οὖν ἔσεσθε ἄξιοι τῆς ἐλευθερίᾱς *prove yourselves then worthy of freedom* X. A. 1. 7. 3, ὅπως τοίνυν περὶ τοῦ πολέμου μηδὲν ἐρεῖς *say nothing therefore about the war* D. 19. 92. For the fuller form of this use after σκόπει, σκοπεῖτε, see 2213.

1921. ὅπως μή (negative ὅπως μὴ οὐ) may express the desire to avert something; as ὅπως μὴ αἰσχροὶ φαινούμεθα *mind we don't appear base* X. C. 4. 2. 39, ἀλλ' ὅπως μὴ οὐχ οἷός τ' ἔσομαι *but* (I fear that) *I shall not be able* P. R. 506 d. Cp. 1802, 1803, 2229.

1922. On ἄν (κέ) with the future indicative, see 1793. On the periphrastic future see 1959; on the future in dependent clauses, see 2203, 2211, 2220 a, 2229, 2231, 2328, 2549–2551, 2554, 2558, 2559, 2565 a, 2573 c.

AORIST INDICATIVE

1923. The aorist expresses the mere occurrence of an action in the past. The action is regarded as an event or single fact without reference to the length of time it occupied.

ἐνίκησαν οἱ Κερκῡραῖοι καὶ ναῦς πέντε καὶ δέκα διέφθειραν *the Corcyraeans were victorious and destroyed fifteen ships* T. 1. 29, Παιώνιος ἐποίησε *Paeonius fecit* I. G. A. 348, ἔδοξεν τῇ βουλῇ *it was voted by* (seemed good to) *the Senate* C. I. A. 1. 32.

a. The uses of the aorist may be explained by the figure of a point in time: 1. The starting point (ingressive aorist, 1924); 2. The end point (resultative aorist, 1926); 3. The whole action (beginning to end) concentrated to a point (complexive aorist, 1927).

1924. Ingressive Aorist. — The aorist of verbs whose present denotes a state or a continued action, expresses the entrance into that state or the beginning of that action.

a. This holds true of the other moods. Greek has no special form to denote entrance into a state in present time (1853).

1925. Most of the verbs in question are denominatives, and the forms are chiefly those of the first aorist: —

ἄρχω *rule*	ἦρξα *became ruler*
βασιλεύω *am king, rule*	ἐβασίλευσα *became king, ascended the throne*
βλέπω *look at*	ἔβλεψα *cast a glance*
δακρύω *weep*	ἐδάκρῡσα *burst into tears*
δουλεύω *am a slave*	ἐδούλευσα *became a slave*
ἐρῶ *love*	ἠράσθην *fell in love*
θαρρῶ *am courageous*	ἐθάρρησα *plucked up courage*
νοσῶ *am ill*	ἐνόσησα *fell ill*
πλουτῶ *am rich*	ἐπλούτησα *became rich*
πολεμῶ *make war*	ἐπολέμησα *began the war*
σῑγῶ *am silent*	ἐσίγησα *became silent*

a. Rarely with the second aorist: ἔσχον *took hold, took possession of, got*, as Πεισιστράτου τελευτήσαντος Ἱππίας ἔσχε τὴν ἀρχήν *when Peisistratus died Hippias succeeded to his power* T. 6. 54. So ᾐσθόμην *became aware*, ἔστην *took my stand* (perfect ἕστηκα *am standing*).

b. The aorist of these verbs denotes also a simple occurrence of the action as an historical fact: ἐβασίλευσα *was king, ruled*, ἐνόσησα *was ill*. Thus, ἐκεῖνοι πέντε καὶ τετταράκοντα ἔτη τῶν Ἑλλήνων ἦρξαν *they held the supremacy over Greece for forty-five years* D. 3. 24 (cp. 1927 b).

1926. Resultative Aorist. — In contrast to the imperfect (and present) the aorist denotes the result, end, or effect of an action. Thus, ἤγαγον *I brought*, ἐβούλευσα *I decided* (ἐβούλευον *I was deliberating*), ἔθηξα *I sharpened*, ἔπεσον *I struck in falling* (ἔπῑπτον *I was in the act of falling*), ἔπεισα *I succeeded in persuading* (1895).

a. The same verb may be a resultative aorist or an ingressive aorist. Thus, ἔβαλον *I let fly* a missile (ingressive), and *I hit* (resultative); κατέσχον *I got possession of* (ingressive), and *I kept back* (resultative).

b. ἔκτεινά σε E. Ion 1291 means *I tried to kill you*, since κτείνω denotes properly only the act of the agent, and does not, like *kill*, also connote the effect of the action upon another.

1927. Complexive Aorist. — The complexive aorist is used to survey at a glance the course of a past action from beginning to end: τούτῳ τῷ τρόπῳ τὴν πόλιν ἐτείχισαν *it was in this manner that they fortified the city* T. 1. 93. It may sum up the result of a preceding narrative (often containing imperfects, as T. 2. 47. 4; 3. 81). The complexive aorist appears also in other moods than the indicative.

a. This is often called the 'concentrative' aorist, because it concentrates the entire course of an action to a single point. When used of rapid or instantaneous action this aorist is often called 'momentary.'

b. The complexive aorist is used either of a long or of a short period of time: *τέσσαρα καὶ δέκα ἔτη ἐνέμειναν αἱ σπονδαί the peace lasted fourteen years* T. 2. 2, *ὀλίγον χρόνον ξυνέμεινεν ἡ ὁμαιχμίᾱ the league lasted a short time* 1. 18, *ἦλθον, εἶδον, ἐνίκησα veni, vidi, vici* ("Caesar's brag of came, and saw, and conquered") Plutarch, Caes. 50.

1928. The aorist is commonly used with definite numbers. The imperfect is, however, often employed when an action is represented as interrupted or as proceeding from one stage to another. Thus, *ἐνταῦθα ἔμεινε Κῦρος ἡμέρᾱς τριάκοντα Cyrus remained thirty days there* X. A. 1. 2. 9; *τέτταρας μῆνας ὅλους ἐσῴζοντο οἱ Φωκεῖς τοὺς ὕστερον, ἡ δὲ τούτου ψευδολογίᾱ μετὰ ταῦθ' ὕστερον αὐτοὺς ἀπώλεσεν for the four whole ensuing months the Phocians remained safe, but the falsehood of this man afterwards effected their ruin* D. 19. 78.

1929. The aorist enumerates and reports past events. It may be employed in brief continuous narration (X. A. 1. 9. 6). As a narrative tense it is often used to state the chief events and facts, while the other past tenses set forth subordinate actions and attendant circumstances.

1930. Empiric Aorist. — With adverbs signifying *often, always, sometimes, already, not yet, never*, etc., the aorist expressly denotes a fact of experience (*ἐμπειρίᾱ*).

πολλοὶ πολλάκις μειζόνων ἐπιθῡμοῦντες τὰ παρόντ' ἀπώλεσαν many men often lose what they have from a desire for greater possessions D. 23. 113, *ἀθῡμοῦντες ἄνδρες οὔπω τροπαῖον ἔστησαν faint heart never yet raised a trophy* P. Criti. 108 c. So with *πολύς*: *ἡ γλῶσσα πολλοὺς εἰς ὄλεθρον ἤγαγεν the tongue brings many a man to his ruin* Men. Sent. 205. From this use proceeds 1931.

a. The empiric aorist is commonly to be translated by the present or perfect. The statement in the aorist is often based upon a concrete historical fact set forth in the context, and the reader is left to infer that the thought holds good for all time.

1931. Gnomic Aorist (*γνώμη maxim, proverb*). — The aorist may express a general truth. The aorist simply states a past occurrence and leaves the reader to draw the inference from a concrete case that what has occurred once is typical of what often occurs: *παθὼν δέ τε νήπιος ἔγνω a fool learns by experience* Hesiod, Works and Days, 218, *κάλλος μὲν γὰρ ἢ χρόνος ἀνήλωσεν ἢ νόσος ἐμάρᾱνε for beauty is either wasted by time or withered by disease* I. 1. 6.

a. The gnomic aorist often alternates with the present of general truth (1877): *οὐ γὰρ ἡ πληγὴ παρέστησε τὴν ὀργήν, ἀλλ' ἡ ἀτῑμίᾱ· οὐδὲ τὸ τύπτεσθαι τοῖς ἐλευθέροις ἐστὶ δεινόν . . . ἀλλὰ τὸ ἐφ' ὕβρει for it is not the blow that causes anger, but the disgrace; nor is it the beating that is terrible to freemen, but the insult* D. 21. 72. Cp. P. R. 566 e.

b. The gnomic aorist is regarded as a primary tense (1858): *οἱ τύραννοι πλουσίους ὃν ἂν βούλωνται παραχρῆμ' ἐποίησαν tyrants make rich in a moment whomever they wish* D. 20. 15.

1932. Akin to the gnomic aorist is the aorist employed in general descriptions. So in imaginary scenes and in descriptions of manners and customs. Thus, ἐπειδὰν ἀφίκωνται οἱ τετελευτηκότες εἰς τὸν τόπον, οἷ ὁ δαίμων ἕκαστον κομίζει, πρῶτον μὲν διεδικάσαντο οἵ τε καλῶς καὶ ὁσίως βιώσαντες καὶ οἱ μή *when the dead reach the place whither each is severally conducted by his genius, first of all they have judgment pronounced upon them as they have lived well and devoutly or not* P. Ph. 113 d, φᾶρος δὲ αὐτημερὸν ἐξυφήναντες οἱ ἱρέες κατ' ὧν ἔδησαν ἑνὸς αὐτῶν μίτρῃ τοὺς ὀφθαλμούς *after having woven a mantle on the same day the priests bind the eyes of one of their number with a snood* Hdt. 2. 122.

1933. Iterative Aorist. — With ἄν the aorist may denote repetition (1790): εἶπεν ἄν *he used to say* X. C. 7. 1. 14. Distinguish 2303.

1934. Aorist for Future. — The aorist may be substituted for the future when a future event is vividly represented as having actually occurred: ἀπωλόμην ἄρ', εἴ με δὴ λείψεις *I am undone if thou dost leave me* E. Alc. 386.

1935. Aorist in Similes. — The aorist is used in similes in poetry, and usually contains the point of comparison. It may alternate with the present. Thus, ἤριπε δ' ὡς ὅτε τις δρῦς ἤριπεν *he fell as falls an oak* Π 482, οἷος δ' ἐκ νεφέων ἀναφαίνεται οὔλιος ἀστὴρ | παμφαίνων, τότε δ' αὖτις ἔδῡ νέφεα σκιόεντα, | ὣς Ἕκτωρ κτλ. *and as from out of the clouds all radiant appears a baneful star, and then again sinks within the shadowy clouds, so Hector*, etc. Λ 62.

a. The aorist in 1931, 1935 is used of time past (in 1934 of the future), from the point of view of an assumed or ideal present.

1936. Aorist for Present. — The aorist is used in questions with τί οὖν οὐ and τί οὐ to express surprise that something has not been done. The question is here equivalent to a command or proposal: τί οὖν οὐχὶ καὶ σὺ ὑπέμνησάς με; *why don't you recall it to my mind?* X. Hi. 1. 3. The (less lively) present, and the future, may also be used.

1937. Dramatic Aorist. — The first person singular of the aorist is used in the dialogue parts of tragedy and comedy to denote a state of mind or an act expressing a state of mind (especially approval or disapproval) occurring to the speaker in the moment just passed. This use is derived from familiar discourse, but is not found in good prose. In translation the present is employed. Thus, ἥσθην, ἐγέλασα *I am delighted, I can't help laughing* Ar. Eq. 696, ἐδεξάμην τὸ ῥηθέν *I welcome the omen* S. El. 668 (prose δέχομαι τὸν οἰωνόν). So ἐπῄνεσα *I approve*, ξυνῆκα *I understand.* Sometimes this use appears outside of dialogue (ἀπέπτυσα *I spurn* A. Pr. 1070, Ag. 1193).

1938. With verbs of *swearing*, *commanding*, *saying*, and *advising* the aorist may denote a resolution that has already been formed by the speaker and remains unalterable: σὲ . . . εἶπον τῆσδε γῆς ἔξω περᾶν *I command thee* (once and for all) *to depart from out this land* E. Med. 272, ἀπώμοσα *I swear 'nay'* S. Ph. 1289. This use is not confined to dialogue.

1939. So in other cases: πῶς τοῦτ' ἔλεξας; οὐ κάτοιδ' ὅπως λέγεις *how saidst thou (what dost thou mean)? I do not know how thou meanest* S. Aj. 270. Cp. νῦν with the aorist (Β 113, Γ 439).

1940. Aorist for Perfect. — In Greek the aorist, which simply states a past occurrence, is often employed where English uses the perfect denoting a present condition resulting from a past action. Thus, παρεκάλεσα ὑμᾶς, ἄνδρες φίλοι *I (have) summoned you, my friends* X. A. 1. 6. 6, ὁ μὲν τοίνυν πόλεμος ἁπάντων ἡμᾶς τῶν εἰρημένων ἀπεστέρηκεν· καὶ γὰρ πενεστέρους ἐποίησε καὶ πολλοὺς κινδύνους ὑπομένειν ἠνάγκασε καὶ πρὸς τοὺς Ἕλληνας διαβέβληκε καὶ πάντας τρόπους τεταλαιπώρηκεν ἡμᾶς *now the war has deprived us of all the blessings that have been mentioned; for it has made us poorer, compelled us to undergo many dangers, has brought us into reproach with the Greeks, and in every possible way has caused us suffering* I. 8. 19. Sometimes the aorist is chosen because of its affinity to the negative, as τῶν οἰκετῶν οὐδένα κατέλιπεν ἀλλ' ἅπαντας πέπρᾱκε *he* (has) *left not one of his servants, but has sold them all* Aes. 1. 99. This aorist is sometimes regarded as a primary tense.

a. Where an active transitive perfect is not formed from a particular verb, or is rarely used, the aorist takes its place: Φεραίων μὲν ἀφῄρηται τὴν πόλιν καὶ φρουρὰν ἐν τῇ ἀκροπόλει κατέστησεν *he has deprived the Pheraeans of their city and established a garrison in the acropolis* D. 7. 32 (καθέστᾰκε transitive is not classic). So ἤγαγον is used for ἦχα.

b. In Greek of the classical period the aorist and perfect are not confused though the difference between the two tenses is often subtle. Cp. D. 19. 72 with 19. 177.

1941. The aorist may be translated by the perfect when the perfect has the force of a present (1946, 1947): ἐκτησάμην *I have acquired* (κέκτημαι *I possess*), ἐθαύμασα *I have wondered* (τεθαύμακα *I admire*). Thus, ἔκτησο αὐτὸς τά περ αὐτὸς ἐκτήσαο *keep thyself what thyself hast gained* Hdt. 7. 29.

1942. Epistolary Tenses. — The writer of a letter or book, the dedicator of an offering, may put himself in the position of the reader or beholder who views the action as past: μετ' Ἀρταβάζου, ὃν σοι ἔπεμψα, πρᾶσσε *negotiate with Artabazus whom I send* (*sent*) *to you* T. 1. 129, Τροίᾱν ἑλόντες Ἀργείων στόλος λάφῡρα ταῦτα . . . ἐπασσάλευσαν *the Argive armament having captured Troy hang* (*hung*) *up these spoils* A. Ag. 577. Cp. 1923 (last two examples).

a. The perfect is also used: ἀπέσταλκά σοι τόνδε τὸν λόγον *I send* (*have sent*) *you this discourse* I. 1. 2.

b. The imperfect (common in Latin) occurs rarely: Μνησίεργος ἐπέστειλε τοῖς οἴκοι χαίρειν καὶ ὑγιαίνειν καὶ αὐτὸς οὕτως ἔφασκε [ἔχειν] *Mnesiergus sends greetings and wishes for good health to his friends at home and says that he himself is well* Jahresheft des oesterreichischen Archaeol. Inst. 7 (1904), p. 94, τῶν δὲ ταῦτα πρᾱξάντων ἄχρι οὗ ὅδε ὁ λόγος ἐγράφετο Τεισίφονος πρεσβύτατος ὢν τῶν ἀδελφῶν τὴν ἀρχὴν εἶχε *up to the date of this portion of my work, Tisiphonus, as the eldest of the brothers who wrought this deed, maintained control of the government* X. H. 6. 4. 37.

1943. Aorist for Pluperfect. — The aorist with many temporal and causal conjunctions, and in relative clauses, has the force of the Eng. pluperfect. So with ἐπεί, ἐπειδή *after that, since,* ὅτε, ὡς *when,* ὅτι *because;* regularly with πρίν *before,* ἕως, μέχρι *until:* ἐπεὶ ἐσάλπιγξε, ἐπῇσαν *after the trumpeter had given the signal, they advanced* X. A. 1. 2. 17, ἐπεὶ δὲ συνῆλθον, ἔλεξε τοιάδε *and when they had come together, he spoke as follows* X. C. 5. 1. 19, ἐκέλευσέ με τὴν ἐπιστολὴν ἣν ἔγραψα οἴκαδε δοῦναι *he requested me to give him the letter which I had written home* X. C. 2. 2. 9. So often in other moods than the indicative.

1944. In subordinate clauses the action expressed by the aorist may be (a) contemporaneous, (b) antecedent, or (c) subsequent to that set forth by the main verb. The context alone decides in which sense the aorist is to be taken. (a) ἐν τῷ χρόνῳ ὃν ἐπέσχε ὅσα ἐδύνατο κατενόησε *during the time he waited he learned all he could* T. 1. 138; (b) ἐτράποντο ἐς τὸν Πάνορμον, ὅθενπερ ἀνηγάγοντο *they turned toward Panormus, the very place from which they had put out* T. 2. 92 (see 1943); (c) ἐμάχοντο μέχρι οἱ Ἀθηναῖοι ἀπέπλευσαν *they kept fighting until the Athenians had sailed away* X. H. 1. 1. 3.

PERFECT INDICATIVE

1945. The perfect denotes a completed action the effects of which still continue in the present: τὰ οἰκήματα ᾠκοδόμηται *the rooms have been constructed* (their construction is finished) X. O. 9. 2, τὰς πόλεις αὐτῶν παρῄρηται *he has taken away* (and still holds) *their cities* D. 9. 26, ὑπείληφα *I have formed* (*hold*) *the opinion* 18. 123, βεβούλευμαι *I have* (*am*) *resolved* S. El. 947, τί βουλεύεσθον ποιεῖν; οὐδέν, ἔφη ὁ Χαρμίδης, ἀλλὰ βεβουλεύμεθα *what are you conspiring to do? Nothing, said Charmides; we have already conspired* P. Charm. 176 c.

a. The effects of a completed action are seen in the resulting present state. The state may be that of the subject or of the object: ἐφοβήθην, καὶ ἔτι καὶ νῦν τεθορύβημαι *I was struck with fear, and even at the present moment am still in a state of agitation* Aes. 2. 4, οἱ πολέμιοι τὰς σπονδὰς λελύκᾱσιν *the enemy have broken the truce* (which is now broken) X. A. 3. 2. 10.

1946. Perfect with Present Meaning. — When the perfect marks the enduring result rather than the completed act, it may often be translated by the present.

Thus, κέκλημαι (have received a name) *am called, my name is*, κέκτημαι (have acquired) *possess*, μέμνημαι (have recalled) *remember*, τέθνηκα (have passed away) *am dead*, εἴθισμαι (have accustomed myself) *am accustomed*, ἠμφίεσμαι (have clothed myself in) *have on*, πέποιθα (have put confidence) *trust*, ἕστηκα (have set myself) *stand*, βέβηκα (have stepped) *stand* and *am gone*, ἔγνωκα (have recognized) *know*, πέφῡκα (*natus sum*) *am by nature*, οἶδα (have found out) *know*.

a. These perfecta praesentia do not in nature differ from other perfects.

1947. 'Intensive' Perfect. — Many perfects seem to denote an action rather than a state resulting from an action, and to be equivalent to strengthened presents. These are often called *intensive* perfects.

Such are: verbs of the *senses* (δέδορκα *gaze*, πέφρῑκα *shudder*), of *sustained sound* (κέκρᾱγα *bawl*, λέληκα *shout*, βέβρῡχα *roar*), of *emotion* (πεφόβημαι *am filled with alarm*, γέγηθα *am glad*, μέμηλε *cares for*), of *gesture* (κέχηνα *keep the mouth agape*), and many others (σεσίγηκα *am still*, etc.).

a. But most if not all of the verbs in question may be regarded as true perfects, *i.e.* they denote a mental or physical state resulting from the accomplishment of the action; thus, πέφρῑκα *I have shuddered and am now in a state of shuddering.*

b. Certain verbs tend to appear in the perfect for emphasis: τέθνηκα *am dead,* ἀπόλωλα *perish,* πέπρᾱκα *sell* (*have sold*).

1948. Empiric Perfect.—The perfect may set forth a general truth expressly based on a fact of experience: ἡ ἀταξίᾱ πολλοὺς ἤδη ἀπολώλεκεν *lack of discipline ere now has been the ruin of many* X. A. 3. 1. 38. Cp. 1930.

1949. Perfect of Dated Past Action.—The perfect is sometimes used of a past action whose time is specifically stated: ὕβρισμαι τότε *I was insulted on that occasion* D. 21. 7. This use approaches that of the aorist.

1950. Perfect for Future Perfect.—The perfect may be used vividly for the future perfect to anticipate an action not yet done: κᾶν τοῦτο νῑκῶμεν, πάνθ' ἡμῖν πεποίηται *and if we conquer in that quarter, everything has been* (will have been) *accomplished by us* X. A. 1. 8. 12.

a. Especially with the phrase τὸ ἐπί τινι, the perfect anticipates the certain occurrence of an event: τὸ ἐπὶ τούτῳ ἀπολώλαμεν *for all he could do, we had perished* X. A. 6. 6. 23.

1951. In subordinate clauses, the action of the perfect is usually (a) contemporaneous, but may be (b) antecedent to that of the main verb. The context alone decides in which sense the perfect is to be taken. (a) οἱ δὲ θεράποντες, ἐπειδὴ ἐς ἀντίπαλα καθεστήκαμεν, αὐτομολοῦσι *while our attendants desert, now that we have been brought down to a level* with the Syracusans T. 7. 13. (b) ἃ σοι τύχη κέχρηκε, ταῦτ' ἀφείλετο *Fortune has taken back what she has lent you* Men. fr. 598.

On the epistolary perfect see 1942 a.

PLUPERFECT

1952. The pluperfect is the past of the perfect, hence it denotes a past fixed state resulting from a completed action: ἐβεβουλεύμην *I had* (*was*) *resolved.*

a. When the perfect is translated by the present, the pluperfect is rendered by the imperfect: ἐκεκτήμην *was in possession,* ἐτεθνήκει *he was dead,* ᾔδη *knew,* ἐμεμνήμην *remembered.* Cp. 1946.

1953. Pluperfect of Immediate Occurrence.—The pluperfect may denote that a past action occurred so immediately or suddenly that it was accomplished almost at the same moment as another action: ὡς δὲ ἐλήφθησαν, ἐλέλυντο αἱ σπονδαί *and when they were captured the truce was* (already) *at an end* T. 4. 47 (the fact of their capture was equivalent to the immediate rupture of the truce).

1954. In subordinate clauses the pluperfect is rarely used to mark an action as anterior to an action already past: ἦλθον οἱ Ἰνδοὶ ἐκ τῶν πολεμίων οὓς ἐπεπόμφει Κῦρος ἐπὶ κατασκοπήν *the Indians returned whom Cyrus had sent to get news of the enemy* X. C. 6. 2. 9. The aorist is usually employed (1943, 1944 b).

FUTURE PERFECT

1955. The future perfect denotes a future state resulting from a completed action: ἀναγεγράψομαι *I shall stand enrolled*, δεδήσεται *he shall be kept in prison*; ἡ θύρᾱ κεκλῄσεται *the door will be kept shut* Ar. Lys. 1071.

a. Most future perfects are middle in form, passive in meaning (581).

b. The active future perfect is usually periphrastic (600): τὰ δέοντ' ἐσόμεθα ἐγνωκότες *we shall have determined on our duty* D. 4. 50.

1956. When stress is laid upon complete fulfilment, the future perfect may *imply* rapidity, immediate consequence, or certainty, of action accomplished in the future: φράζε, καὶ πεπράξεται *speak, and it shall be done instanter* Ar. Pl. 1027, εὐθὺς Ἀριαῖος ἀφεστήξει· ὥστε φίλος ἡμῖν οὐδεὶς λελείψεται *Ariaeus will soon withdraw, so that we shall have no friend left* X. A. 2. 4. 5.

1957. The future perfect may have an imperative force (1917): εἰρήσεται γὰρ τἀληθές *for the truth shall* (let it) *be spoken* I. 7. 76.

1958. When the perfect has the force of a present, the future perfect is used like a simple future (1946): κεκλήσομαι *I shall bear the name*, μεμνήσομαι *shall remember*, κεκτήσομαι *shall possess*. So in the two active forms: τεθνήξω *I shall be dead*, ἑστήξω *I shall stand.*

a. The aorist subjunctive with ἄν (2324), not the future perfect, is used to denote a past action in relation to an action still in the future.

PERIPHRASTIC TENSES

On the periphrastic forms of perfect, pluperfect, and future perfect, see 599, 600.

1959. Periphrastic Future. — A periphrastic future is formed by μέλλω *I am about to*, *intend to*, *am* (*destined*) *to*, *am likely to* (strictly *think*) with the present or future (rarely the aorist) infinitive. Thus, ἃ μέλλω λέγειν σοὶ πάλαι δοκεῖ *what I am going to say has long been your opinion* X. C. 3. 3. 13 (cp. 1885), Κλέανδρος μέλλει ἥξειν *Cleander is on the point of coming* X. A. 6. 4. 18, θήσειν ἔμελλεν ἄλγεα *he purposed to inflict suffering* B 39, ἔμελλον ὄλβιος εἶναι *I was destined to be happy* σ 138, εἴ ποτε πορεύοιτο καὶ πλεῖστοι μέλλοιεν ὄψεσθαι, προσκαλῶν τοὺς φίλους ἐσπουδαιολογεῖτο *if ever* Cyrus *was on the march and many were likely to catch sight of him, he summoned his friends and engaged them in earnest talk* X. A. 1. 9. 28.

a. The present infinitive usually occurs with μέλλω as a verb of *will*, the future infinitive with μέλλω as a verb of *thinking*.

b. The aorist is used when it is important to mark the action as ingressive, resultative, or complexive: ὅπερ μέλλω παθεῖν *what I am doomed to suffer* A. Pr. 625.

c. μέλλω *I delay* usually takes the present, rarely the aorist, infinitive.

d. πῶς οὐ μέλλω and τί οὐ μέλλω mean *why should I not?* Thus, τί δ' οὐ μέλλει γελοῖον εἶναι; *how should it not be ridiculous?* P. R. 530 a.

1960. ἔμελλον is used of past intention in ἔμελλε καταλύειν *he was about to stop for the night* X. A. 1. 8. 1, τοὺς ἔσπλους κλῄσειν ἔμελλον *they intended to close the entrances* T. 4. 8. ἔμελλον with the infinitive denoting an unfulfilled past intention is a periphrasis for an aorist indicative with ἄν. Thus, οὐ συστρατεύειν ἔμελλον *they would not have joined forces* D. 19. 159 (= οὐκ ἂν συνεστράτευσαν). Cp. *recturus eram*, etc.

1961. With εἰμί. — The present and perfect participle are freely used with the forms of εἰμί to form a periphrasis, especially when the participle has an adjectival character (1857): ἡγεῖ διαφθειρομένους τινὰς εἶναι; *do you think that some are being ruined?* P. R. 492 a, αἱ τέχναι διεφθαρμέναι ἔσονται *the arts will be ruined* X. C. 7. 2. 13, ἦν τοῦτο συμφέρον *this was advantageous* Ant. 5. 18; ἦ θέλουσα is stronger than θέλῃ, S. O. T. 580.

1962. The aorist participle is rarely so used, since it denotes a single act, not a characteristic: ἦσαν δέ τινες καὶ γενόμενοι τῷ Νικίᾳ λόγοι πρότερον πρός τινας *and communications between Nicias and some persons had actually been held before* T. 4. 54.

a. With ἔσομαι the aorist participle equals the future perfect: οὐ σιωπήσᾱς ἔσῃ; *be silent, won't you, once and for all?* S. O. T. 1146.

1963. With ἔχω. — The periphrasis with ἔχω and the aorist participle is analogous to the perfect in meaning, and emphasizes the permanence of the result attained (chiefly in Hdt. and the drama): κηρύξᾱς ἔχω *I have proclaimed* S. Ant. 192.

a. In Attic prose ἔχω usu. has a separate force: Φερᾱ̀ς πρώην ἔχει καταλαβών *he lately seized and now occupies Pherae* D. 9. 12. So with the (rare) perfect: τὰ ἐπιτήδεια εἶχον ἀνακεκομισμένοι *they had carried up* to the forts *the provisions and kept them* there X. A. 4. 7. 1.

1964. With γίγνομαι. — The forms of γίγνομαι often combine with a participle to form periphrases. Thus, μὴ σαυτὸν . . . κτείνᾱς γένῃ *lest thou destroy thyself* S. Ph. 773; in prose this periphrasis has the tone of tragedy. On γίγνομαι with a substantive, see 1710, 1754.

1965. With φαίνομαι. — The aorist participle is used periphrastically with forms of φαίνομαι. Thus, οὐχ ὑπὲρ ὑμῶν οὐδὲ τῶν νόμων φροντίσᾱς οὐδ' ἀγανακτήσᾱς φανήσεται *it will appear that he took no heed, nor felt any resentment, concerning you or the laws* D. 21. 39.

VERBAL NOUNS

1. The Infinitive. 2. The Participle. 3. The Verbal Adjectives in -τός and -τέος.

THE INFINITIVE

1966. The infinitive is in part a verb, in part a substantive.

a. Many substantives are closely related to verbs, but not all verbs can form substantives. All verbs can, however, form infinitives.

b. The word *infinitive* denotes a verbal form without any limitations (*finis*) of number and person.

1967. The infinitive is like a verb herein:

a. It shows the distinctions of voice and tense (but not those of number and person). Having tenses, it can express different stages of action (action simply occurring, continuing, or finished); whereas the corresponding substantive sets forth the abstract idea without these distinctions. Contrast **ποιεῖν, ποιήσειν, ποιῆσαι, πεποιηκέναι** with **ποίησις** *making*.

b. It can have a subject before it and a predicate after it, and it can have an object in the genitive, dative, or accusative like the corresponding finite verb. Infinitives scarcely ever stand in the subjective genitive; and the object of an infinitive never stands in the objective genitive.

c. It is modified by adverbs, not by adjectives.

d. It may take **ἄν** and with that particle represent **ἄν** with the indicative (1784 ff.) or **ἄν** with the optative (1824).

e. It forms clauses of result with **ὥστε**, and temporal clauses with **πρίν**, etc.

1968. The infinitive is like a substantive herein:

a. It may be the subject or object of a verb.

b. With the (neuter) article it shows all the case forms (except the vocative): **τὸ (τοῦ, τῷ, τὸ) λύειν, λύσειν**, etc.

c. It may be governed by prepositions: **πρὸ τοῦ λύειν.**

1969. The infinitive was originally a verbal noun in the dative (in part possibly also in the locative) case. The use to express purpose (2008) is a survival of the primitive meaning, from which all the other widely diverging uses were developed in a manner no longer always clear to us. But the *to* or *for* meaning seen in **μανθάνειν ἥκομεν** *we have come to learn* (*for learning*) can also be discerned in **δύναμαι ἰδεῖν** *I have power for seeing*, then *I can see*. Cp. 2000, 2006 a. As early as Homer, when the datival meaning had been in part obscured, the infinitive was employed as nominative (as subject) and accusative (as object). After Homer, the infinitive came to be used with the neuter article, the substantive idea thus gaining in definiteness. The article must be used when the infinitive stands as an object in the genitive or dative, and when it depends on prepositions.

1970. The infinitive is used as subject, as predicate, and to supplement the meaning of words and clauses.

1971. The negative of the infinitive is **μή**; but **οὐ**, used with a finite mood in direct discourse, is retained when that mood becomes infinitive in indirect discourse. Sometimes, however, **μή** is used in place of this **οὐ** (2723 ff.).

SUBJECT AND PREDICATE NOUN WITH THE INFINITIVE

1972. In general the subject of the infinitive, if expressed at all, stands in the accusative; when the subject of the infinitive is the same as the subject or object of the governing verb, or when it has already been made known in the sentence, it is not repeated with the infinitive.

1973. When the subject of the infinitive is the same as that of the governing verb, it is omitted, and a predicate noun stands in the nominative case.

οἶμαι εἰδέναι *I think that I know* P. Pr. 312 e, Πέρσης ἔφη εἶναι *he said he was a Persian* X. A. 4. 4. 17, ἐγὼ οὐχ ὁμολογήσω ἄκλητος ἥκειν *I shall not admit that I have come uninvited* P. S. 174 d, ὁμολογεῖς περὶ ἐμὲ ἄδικος γεγενῆσθαι; *do you admit that you have been guilty as regards me?* X. A. 1. 6. 8 (cp. 4. 2. 27 in 2263).

a. The nominative is used when the infinitive, expressing some action or state of the subject of the main verb, has the article in an oblique case. Thus, τούτων ἀξιωθεὶς διὰ τὸ πατρικὸς αὐτῷ φίλος εἶναι *justifying these* requests *on the ground that he was his hereditary friend* Aes. 3. 52, τοῦτο δ' ἐποίει ἐκ τοῦ χαλεπὸς εἶναι *this he effected by reason of his being severe* X. A. 2. 6. 9, ἐπὶ τῷ ὁμοῖοι τοῖς λειπομένοις εἶναι ἐκπέμπονται (colonists) *are sent out to be the equals of those who stay at home* T. 1. 34.

b. The nominative stands usually in sentences with δεῖν, χρῆναι etc., dependent on a verb of *saying* or *thinking.* Thus, ἡγούμην . . . περιεῖναι δεῖν αὐτῶν καὶ μεγαλοψῡχότερος φαίνεσθαι *I thought I ought to surpass them and to show myself more magnificent* D. 19. 235. Here ἡγούμην δεῖν is equivalent to *I thought it proper.*

c. When the governing verb is a participle in an oblique case, a predicate noun usually agrees with the participle, and rarely stands in the nominative. Thus, ἀπαλλαγεὶς τούτων τῶν φασκόντων δικαστῶν εἶναι *being rid of those who profess to be judges* P. A. 41 a, τὰς ἀρχὰς δίδωσι . . . τοῖς ἀεὶ δόξᾱσιν ἀρίστοις εἶναι *it dispenses the offices to those who always seem to be the most deserving* P. Menex. 238 d.

1974. A pronoun subject of the infinitive, if (wholly or partially) identical with the subject of the main verb, is generally expressed when emphatic, and stands in the accusative (cases of the nominative are rare and suspected); but the indirect reflexive σφεῖς stands in the nominative or accusative.

οἶμαι ἐμὲ πλείω χρήματα εἰργάσθαι ἢ ἄλλους σύνδυο *I think I have made more money than any two others together* P. Hipp. M. 282 e, ἡγησάμενος ἐμαυτὸν ἐπιεικέστερον εἶναι (emphatic for ἡγησάμενος ἐπιεικέστερος εἶναι) *deeming myself to be too honest* P. A. 36 b, τοὺς δὲ Θηβαίους ἡγεῖτο . . . ἐάσειν ὅπως βούλεται πράττειν ἑαυτόν *he thought the Thebans would let him have his own way* D. 6. 9, οὐ σφεῖς ἀδικεῖσθαι, ἀλλ' ἐκείνους μᾶλλον he said *that not they* (the speaker and the other Lacedaemonians), *but they* (the Toroneans) *rather had been wronged* 4. 114 (but σφᾶς in 1228 b).

a. After a preceding accusative with the infinitive, a second pronoun referring to a different person, and also subject of an infinitive, must also stand in the accusative whether or not it denotes the same person as the subject of the governing verb. Thus, ἀλλὰ νομίζεις ἡμᾶς μὲν ἀνέξεσθαί σου, αὐτὸς (see below) δὲ τυπτήσειν; καὶ ἡμᾶς μὲν ἀποψηφιεῖσθαί σου, σὲ (*not* σύ) δ' οὐ παύσεσθαι *but do you think that we are going to put up with you, while you strike us yourself? and that we are going to acquit you, while you will not cease* your outrageous conduct? D. 21. 204. αὐτός, above and in Κλέων οὐκ ἔφη αὐτός, ἀλλ' ἐκεῖνον στρατηγεῖν *Cleon said that not he himself, but that* Nicias *was in command* T. 4. 28, is not the expressed subject of the infinitive, but αὐτός of direct discourse (αὐτὸς τυπτήσεις, αὐτὸς οὐ στρατηγῶ); hence αὐτός is *not* used here for σεαυτόν (ἑαυτόν).

1975. When the subject of the infinitive is different from that of the governing verb, it stands in the accusative; and a predicate noun stands also in the accusative.

νομίζω γὰρ ὑμᾶς ἐμοὶ εἶναι καὶ πατρίδα καὶ φίλους *for I think you are to me both fatherland and friends* X. A. 1. 3. 6, τὸν γὰρ καλὸν κἀγαθὸν ἄνδρα εὐδαίμονα εἶναί φημι *for I maintain that the noble and good man is happy* P. G. 470 e.

1976. A predicate noun takes the case of the subject of an infinitive itself dependent on a subjectless infinitive. Thus, ἡμῖν δὲ ποιοῦσι δοκεῖν σφᾶς παντοδαποὺς φαίνεσθαι *they manage it so that they seem to us to appear in various forms* P. R. 381 e.

1977. Several infinitives may be used in succession, one infinitive being the subject of another: περὶ πολλοῦ ποιούμενος μηδενὶ δόξαι ὑβρίζειν βούλεσθαι *regarding it of great importance not to seem to any one to wish to behave outrageously* L. 23. 5.

1978. When the subject of the infinitive is the same as the *object* (in the genitive or dative) of the governing verb, it is often omitted, and a predicate noun is either attracted into the genitive or dative, or stands in the accusative in agreement with the omitted subject of the infinitive. See 1060–1062.

ἔξεστιν ἡμῖν ἀγαθοῖς εἶναι or ἔξεστιν ἡμῖν ἀγαθοὺς εἶναι *it is in our power to be good* (lit. *to be good is possible for us*). Thus, δεόμεθ' οὖν ὑμῶν . . . ἀκροάσασθαι τῶν λεγομένων, ἐνθυμηθέντας ὅτι κτλ. *we ask you therefore to listen to what is said, considering that*, etc. 1. 14. 6. Cp. νῦν σοι ἔξεστιν ἀνδρὶ γενέσθαι quoted in 1062 with Λακεδαιμονίοις ἔξεστιν ὑμῖν φίλους γενέσθαι *it is in your power to become friends to the Lacedaemonians* T. 4. 29. The latter construction may be explained as abbreviated for ἔξεστιν ὑμῖν (ὑμᾶς) φίλους γενέσθαι.

1979. The subject of the infinitive is often retained when it is the same as the (omitted) oblique object of the governing verb. Thus, παρήγγειλε τὰ ὅπλα τίθεσθαι τοὺς Ἕλληνας *he issued orders that the Greeks should get under arms* X. A. 2. 2. 21.

1980. An indefinite or general subject of the infinitive (τινά, τινάς, ἀνθρώπους) is commonly omitted; and a predicate noun stands in the accusative. Thus, φιλάνθρωπον εἶναι δεῖ *one* (τινά) *must be humane* I. 2. 15 (cp. 1984), ῥᾷον παραινεῖν ἢ παθόντα καρτερεῖν *it is easier* for a man *to give advice than to endure suffering* Men. Sent. 471, δρῶντας γὰρ ἢ μὴ δρῶντας ἥδιον θανεῖν *for it is preferable to die in action rather than doing nothing* E. Hel. 814.

1981. The construction of the accusative with the infinitive seems to have originated from the employment of the infinitive to complement the meaning of transitive verbs; as in κελεύω σε ἀπελθεῖν *I command you to depart.* Here the accusative was separated from the transitive verb and felt to be the independent subject of the infinitive (*I command that you depart*). Gradually the accusative with the infinitive was used even after verbs incapable of taking an object-accusative.

PERSONAL AND IMPERSONAL CONSTRUCTION

1982. Instead of an impersonal passive verb with the accusative and infinitive as subject, Greek often uses the personal passive construction, the accusative becoming the nominative, subject to the leading verb.

Thus, Κῦρος ἠγγέλθη νικῆσαι *Cyrus was reported to have conquered* instead of ἠγγέλθη Κῦρον νικῆσαι *it was reported that Cyrus had conquered*, and δίκαιός εἰμι ἀπελθεῖν *I am justified in going away* instead of δίκαιόν ἐστιν ἐμὲ ἀπελθεῖν *it is right for me to go away.* English sometimes has to use the impersonal construction in place of the Greek personal construction (cp. 2107).

a. The personal construction is more common with λέγεται, ἀγγέλλεται, ὁμολογεῖται and other passive verbs of *saying* (regular with passive verbs of *thinking*); with συμβαίνει *it happens*; with ἀναγκαῖος *necessary*, ἄξιος *worthy*, δίκαιος *just*, δυνατός *possible*, ἐπιτήδειος *fit*, etc., followed by a form of εἶναι, instead of ἀναγκαῖον, ἄξιον, etc. Thus, ὁ Ἀσσύριος εἰς τὴν χώρᾱν αὐτοῦ ἐμβαλεῖν ἀγγέλλεται *the Assyrian is reported to be about to make an incursion into his country* X. C. 5. 3. 30, πολλή τις ἀλογίᾱ ξυμβαίνει γίγνεσθαι *much absurdity would result* P. Phil. 55 a, δίκαιος εἶ εἰπεῖν *it is right for you to speak* P. S. 214 c, τὴν αἰτίᾱν οὗτός ἐστι δίκαιος ἔχειν *it is right for him to bear the blame* D. 18. 4. Both constructions together: σοὶ γὰρ δὴ λέγεται πάνυ γε τεθεραπεῦσθαι ὁ Ἀπόλλων, καί σε πάντα ἐκείνῳ πειθόμενον πράττειν *for Apollo is said to have been greatly served by you, and* (it is said) *that you do everything in obedience to him* X. C. 7. 2. 15. Cp. 2104.

N.—δῆλός ἐστι and φανερός ἐστι take ὅτι or the participle (2107); δῆλόν ἐστι and φανερόν ἐστι take ὅτι, not the infinitive.

1983. The personal constructions δοκῶ, ἔοικα (2089 c), δέω are regular instead of δοκεῖ, ἔοικε *it seems*, δεῖ *it lacks* (much or little). So with φαίνομαι for φαίνεται.

δοκῶ γάρ μοι ἀδύνατος εἶναι *for I seem to be unable* P. R. 368 b, δοκοῦμέν μοι καθῆσθαι *it seems to me that we are encamped* X. A. 1. 3. 12, νῦν γε ἡμῶν ἔοικας βασιλεὺς εἶναι *now at least you seem to be our king* X. C. 1. 4. 6, πολλοῦ δέω ἐγὼ ὑπὲρ ἐμαυτοῦ ἀπολογεῖσθαι *I am far from speaking in my own defence* P. A. 30 d, μῑκροῦ ἐδέησεν Κύπρον ἅπᾱσαν κατασχεῖν *he almost* (lacked a little) *occupied the whole of Cyprus* I. 9. 62, εὖ σὺ λέγειν φαίνει *you seem to speak well* Ar. Nub. 403.

a. δοκεῖ μοί τινα ἐλθεῖν for δοκεῖ τίς μοι ἐλθεῖν *it seems to me that some one came* is very rare. δοκεῖ meaning *it seems good, it is decreed* always takes the infinitive (1984, 1991). δοκῶ *believe* has the construction of 1992 c. Cp. 1998.

THE INFINITIVE WITHOUT THE ARTICLE

AS SUBJECT, PREDICATE, AND APPOSITIVE

1984. As Subject.—The infinitive may be used as subject, especially with quasi-impersonal verbs and expressions (933 a).

γράμματα μαθεῖν δεῖ *to learn to read is necessary* Men. Sent. 96, τί χρὴ ποιεῖν; *what must be done?* X. A. 2. 1. 16, κόσμος (ἐστὶ) καλῶς τοῦτο δρᾶν *to perform this well is a credit* T. 1. 5, πᾶσιν ἁδεῖν χαλεπόν (ἐστι) *to please everybody is difficult* Solon 7, ἔδοξεν αὐτοῖς προϊέναι *it seemed best to them to proceed* X. A. 2. 1. 2, συμφέρει αὐτοῖς φίλους εἶναι *it is for their interest to be friends* X. O. 11. 23. Cp. 1062, 1978.

1985. Such quasi-impersonal verbs and expressions are δεῖ *it is necessary*, χρή (properly a substantive with ἐστί omitted, 793) *it is necessary*, δοκεῖ *it seems good*, ἔστι *it is possible*, ἔξεστι *it is in one's power*, οἷόν τέ ἐστι *it is possible*, πρέπει and προσήκει *it is fitting*, συμβαίνει *it happens*; and many expressions formed by ἐστί and a predicate noun, as ἄξιον *it is right*, δίκαιον *it is just*, ἀναγκαῖον *it is necessary*, δυνατόν *it is possible*, ἀδύνατον (or ἀδύνατα) *it is impossible*, αἰσχρόν *it is disgraceful*, καλόν *it is honourable*, ὥρᾱ and καιρός *it is time*. With the last two expressions the old dative use of the infinitive is clear: ὥρᾱ βουλεύεσθαι *it is time for considering* P. Soph. 241 b.

a. On the personal ἄξιός εἰμι, δίκαιός εἰμι, δοκῶ, see 1982. For δεῖ με τοῦτο λέγειν we find the personal δέομαι τοῦτο λέγειν. Note the attraction in τὸ πλῆθος τῶν ἐνόντων εἰπεῖν *the number of the things it is possible to mention* I. 5. 110 (for τούτων ἃ ἔνεστιν).

b. δεῖ and χρή regularly take the accusative and infinitive (cp. 1562); ἀνάγκη *it is necessary* takes the accusative or dative with the infinitive.

c. The subject of the infinitive is expressed or omitted according to the sense.

d. Homer shows only the beginnings of the use of the infinitive as a real subject, *i.e.* not a *grammatical* subject, as in 1984.

1986. **As Predicate.** — In definitions the infinitive may be used as a predicate noun with ἐστί.

τὸ γὰρ γνῶναι ἐπιστήμην λαβεῖν ἐστιν *for to learn is to get knowledge* P. Th. 209 e.

1987. **As an Appositive.** — The infinitive may stand in apposition to a preceding substantive, pronoun, or adverb.

εἷς οἰωνὸς ἄριστος, ἀμύνεσθαι περὶ πάτρης *one omen is best, to fight for our country* M 243, εἶπον . . . τοῦτο μόνον ὁρᾶν πάντας, τῷ πρόσθεν ἕπεσθαι *I told all to pay heed to this only*, viz., *to follow their leader* X. C. 2. 2. 8, καὶ ὑμᾶς δὲ οὕτως, ὦ παῖδες, . . . ἐπαίδευον, τοὺς μὲν γεραιτέρους προτῑμᾶν, τῶν δὲ νεωτέρων προτετῑμῆσθαι *and I have instructed you, too, my children (to this effect) to honour your elders in preference to yourselves and to receive honour from the younger in preference to them* X. C. 8. 7. 10.

1988. The infinitive not in indirect discourse, and in indirect discourse, is often used as the object of a verb.

THE INFINITIVE NOT IN INDIRECT DISCOURSE

1989. The infinitive as object not in indirect discourse is used after almost any verb that requires another verb to complete its meaning. The tenses of this infinitive are timeless, and denote only stage of action.

1990. The infinitive may be the only expressed object, or it may be one of two expressed objects, of the leading verb.

παίδευσις καλὴ διδάσκει χρῆσθαι νόμοις *a good education teaches obedience to the laws* X. Ven. 12. 14, διαγιγνώσκειν σε τοὺς ἀγαθοὺς καὶ τοὺς κακοὺς ἐδίδαξεν *he taught you to distinguish the good and the bad* X. M. 3. 1. 9.

a. Verbs signifying *to ask*, *bid*, *forbid*, *permit*, *teach*, etc., allow an infinitive as one of two objects.

b. Many verbal expressions, formed by a substantive and a verb, take the infinitive. Thus, τοὺς ἄλλους διδάσκειν τέχνην ἔχουσιν *they possess the skill to teach (the) others* I. 16. 11. Cp. 2000.

A. *Object Infinitive after Verbs of Will or Desire*

1991. Verbs of *will* or *desire* (and their opposites) are often followed by an infinitive. The infinitive with a subject accusative denotes that something *should* (*may*) *be* or *be done.* The negative is μή (see 2719–2721).

ἤθελον αὐτοῦ ἀκούειν *they were willing to listen to him* X. A. 2. 6. 11, ἐβουλεύοντο ἐκλιπεῖν τὴν πόλιν *they planned to leave the city* Hdt. 6. 100, τὰ ἥδιστα . . . ζητεῖ ποιεῖν *he seeks to do what he likes best* X. M. 4. 5. 11, βασιλεὺς ἀξιοῖ σὲ ἀποπλεῖν *the king asks that you sail away* X. H. 3. 4. 25, ἱκέτευε μὴ ἀποκτεῖναι *he entreated that* they *should not put* him (self) *to death* L. 1. 25, πέμπουσιν . . . στρατεύεσθαι ἐπὶ Κᾱρίᾱν *they send* orders *that he shall march upon Caria* X. H. 3. 1. 7, ἔδοξε πλεῖν τὸν Ἀλκιβιάδην *it was decided that Alcibiades should sail* T. 6. 29.

a. Verbs of *will* or *desire* with an accusative subject of the infinitive form one of the classes of substantive clauses introduced in English by *that*, though the infinitive in English is often more idiomatic.

1992. Of verbs of *will* or *desire* that take the infinitive some have an object

a. In the accusative (or are intransitive), *e.g.* : **αἱροῦμαι** *choose*, **αἰτῶ, αἰτοῦμαι** *ask*, **ἀξιῶ** *claim, ask*, **βουλεύομαι** *resolve*, **βούλομαι** *wish, will*, **δικαιῶ** *deem right*, **διανοοῦμαι** *intend*, **ἐθέλω** (poet. **θέλω**), *wish, will*, **εἴωθα** *am wont to*, **ἐπιχειρῶ** *attempt*, **ἐῶ** *permit*, **ζητῶ** *seek*, **κελεύω** *command, suggest, invite*, **μέλλω** *delay*, **πειρῶμαι** *try*, **πέμπω** *send*, **προθῡμοῦμαι** *am zealous*, **προκαλοῦμαι** *invite*, **προτρέπω** *urge*, **σπεύδω** *hasten, am eager*, **σπουδάζω** *am eager*, **τολμῶ** *dare*, **φιλῶ** *am wont to*, **ψηφίζομαι** *vote.*

b. In the genitive, *e.g.*: **δέομαι** *ask*, **ἐπιθῡμῶ** and **ὀρέγομαι** *desire.*

c. In the dative, *e.g.*: **εὔχομαι** *pray*, **παραγγέλλω** and **προστάττω** *command*, **ἐπιβουλεύω** *purpose*, **συμβουλεύω** *advise*, **ἐπιτρέπω** and **συγχωρῶ** *permit*, **παραινῶ** *exhort*, **δοκῶ μοι** *I have a mind to*; and **λέγω, εἶπον, φωνῶ, φράζω** *tell* (and **βοῶ** *shout*) in the sense of *command.*

N.—πείθω *urge* to a course of action, takes the infinitive, πείθω *convince* generally has ὡς, rarely the accusative with the infinitive. Thus, ἔπειθεν αὐτὸν καθ' αὑτὸν πορεύεσθαι *he urged him to go by himself* X. A. 6. 2. 13, οὐ γὰρ πείσονται οἱ πολλοί, ὡς σὺ αὐτὸς οὐκ ἠθέλησας ἀπιέναι *for most people will not be convinced that of your own free will you did not desire to go away* P. Cr. 44 c (infinitive X. M. 1. 1. 20).

1993. Verbs of will or desire *not to do anything* are *e.g.* : δέδοικα, φοβοῦμαι *fear*, φεύγω *avoid*, ὀκνῶ *scruple*, αἰσχύνομαι, αἰδοῦμαι (2126) *feel shame to*, ἀπαγορεύω *forbid*, κωλύω *hinder*, ἀπέχομαι *abstain from*, εὐλαβοῦμαι, φυλάττομαι *beware of.* Thus, φοβοῦμαι διελέγχειν σε *I fear to refute you* P. G. 457 e, αἰσχύνομαι ὑμῖν εἰπεῖν τἀληθῆ *I am ashamed to tell you the truth* P. A. 22 b.

1994. Under verbs of *will* or *desire* are included verbs expressing an activity to the end that something *shall* or *shall not be done.* Thus, δίδωμι *offer, give*, διαμάχομαι *struggle against*, ποιῶ, διαπράττομαι, κατεργάζομαι *manage, effect*, παρέχω *offer* (others in 1992, 1993).

1995. Several verbs of *will* or *desire* take ὅπως with the future or the subjunctive (verbs of *effort*, 2211, 2214); or μή with the subjunctive (verbs of *fear*, 2225); some take the participle (2123 ff.).

1996. The infinitive may be used with the

a. Genitive or dative when the expression of desire is addressed *to* a person and the genitive or dative depends on the leading verb. Here the sentence is simple. Thus, δέομαι ὑμῶν . . . τὰ δίκαια ψηφίσασθαι *I ask you to render a just verdict* I. 19. 51, τοῖς ἄλλοις πᾶσι παρήγγελλεν ἐξοπλίζεσθαι *he ordered all the rest to arm themselves* X. A. 1. 8. 3.

b. Accusative when the action *of* a person is desired (example in 1979). Such sentences are complex.

N. — Verbs of *commanding* allow either **a** or **b**; but only κελεύω with the accusative permits either meaning: κελεύω σὲ ταῦτα μὴ ποιεῖν *I tell you not to do this* and *I command that you shall not do this.* Cp. 1981.

1997. Several verbs signifying *to say* are also used as verbs of *will* and then mean *command.* The agent commanded usually stands in the accusative subject of the infinitive. So with λέγω, εἶπον, φράζω, φωνῶ. Thus λέγω σ' ἐγὼ δόλῳ Φιλοκτήτην λαβεῖν *I say that thou shalt take Philoctetes by craft* S. Ph. 101, τούτοις ἔλεγον πλεῖν *I told them that they should sail* D. 19. 150, πάντες ἔλεγον τοὺς τούτων ἄρξαντας δοῦναι δίκην *all said that the ringleaders should suffer punishment* X. A. 5. 7. 34, εἶπον τὴν θύρᾱν κεκλεῖσθαι *they commanded that the door should be shut* (and stay shut) X. H. 5. 4. 7, βασιλεὺς ἔγραψε πάσᾱς τὰς ἐν τῇ Ἑλλάδι πόλεις αὐτονόμους εἶναι *the king issued a written order that all the cities in Greece should be independent* (not: *wrote that they were independent*) X. H. 6. 3. 12.

a. The agent may stand in the dative as χαλᾶν λέγω σοι *I bid thee let go* S. O. C. 840.

1998. The present and aorist infinitive (both timeless) are the usual tenses of the infinitive after verbs of *will* or *desire* (see 1869). The perfect is rare; as εἶπον τὴν θύρᾱν κεκλεῖσθαι (1997). δοκῶ and δοκῶ μοι signifying *I have a mind to* or *I am determined to* take the present or aorist like δοκεῖ: τὸν ὄνον ἐξάγειν δοκῶ *I have a mind to bring out the ass* Ar. Vesp. 177, ἐγὼ οὖν μοι δοκῶ . . . ὑφηγήσασθαι κτλ. *now I have a mind to show*, etc. P. Eu. 288 c. Cp. 1983 **a.** When it is clearly denoted that the action resolved on is to follow without delay the future is used; as in ἀλλά μοι δοκῶ . . . οὐ πείσεσθαι αὐτῷ *but I am determined that I will not accept his opinion* P. Th. 183 d.

a. Some verbs, as κελεύω, which might be held to introduce indirect discourse, are classed under verbs of *will* or *desire*, because, like these verbs, they do not regularly take the future infinitive; and because, unlike verbs of *saying* and *thinking* (which admit *all* the tenses of the infinitive) they introduce infinitives which do not show differences of time. The future infinitive does not express a command. For a few cases of the future after verbs of *will* or *desire*, see 1869.

1999. Verbs signifying *to hope*, *expect*, *promise*, *threaten*, and *swear*, when followed by the aorist (less often the present) infinitive (1868), have the construction of verbs of *will* or *desire*. When such verbs take the future infinitive they have the construction of indirect discourse.

B. *Infinitive after Other Verbs*

2000. The infinitive follows many verbs, especially such as denote *ability, fitness, necessity*, etc. (and their opposites).

οὐκέτι ἐδύνατο . . . βιοτεύειν *he was no longer able to live* T. 1. 130, νεῖν ἐπιστάμενος *knowing how to swim* X. A. 5. 7. 25, πεφύκᾱσί τε ἅπαντες . . . ἁμαρτάνειν *and all men are by nature prone to err* T. 3. 45, μανθάνουσιν ἄρχειν τε καὶ ἄρχεσθαι *they learn how to govern and be governed* X. A. 1. 9. 4; also after the impersonals of 1985.

a. ἔχω *I can* is derived from the meaning *I have* especially with a verb of *saying*. Thus, Διὸς πλᾱγὰν ἔχουσιν εἰπεῖν *they can proclaim a stroke of Zeus* A. Ag. 367.

C. *Infinitive after Adjectives, Adverbs, and Substantives*

2001. The infinitive serves to define the meaning of adjectives, adverbs, and substantives, especially those denoting *ability, fitness, capacity*, etc. (and their opposites), and generally those analogous in meaning to verbs which take the infinitive (2000). Here the datival meaning (*purpose, destination*) is often apparent. Cp. 1969.

2002. Adjectives and Adverbs. — ἱκανοὶ ἡμᾶς ὠφελεῖν *able to assist us* X. A. 3. 3. 18, δεινὸς λέγειν, κακὸς βιῶναι *skilled in speaking, evil in life* Aes. 3. 174, οἷοι φιλεῖν *able to love* D. 25. 2, ἕτοιμοί εἰσι μάχεσθαι *they are ready to fight* X. C. 4. 1. 1, ἄρχειν ἀξιώτατος *most worthy to govern* X. A. 1. 9. 1, ὁδὸς . . . ἀμήχανος εἰσελθεῖν στρατεύματι *a road impracticable for an army to enter* 1. 2. 21, χαλεπὸν διαβαίνειν *hard to cross* 5. 6. 9, ἐπινοῆσαι ὀξεῖς *quick to conceive* T. 1. 70. So also after ῥᾴδιος *easy*, ἡδύς *pleasant*, δίκαιος *just*, ἀναγκαῖος *necessary*, ἐπιτήδειος *suitable*, ἀγαθός *good*, αἴτιος *responsible for*, μαλακός *incapable of*; cp. ὀλίγος 1063. After adverbs: κάλλιστα ἰδεῖν *most splendid to behold* X. C. 8. 3. 5.

a. Some of these adjectives take the infinitive by analogy to the related verbs, as πρόθυμος *zealous* (προθῡμοῦμαι), ἐπιστήμων *knowing how* (ἐπίσταμαι).

2003. οἷος *fit*, ὅσος *sufficient* take the infinitive like the fuller expressions τοιοῦτος οἷος, τοσοῦτος ὅσος. Thus, οὐ γὰρ ἦν ὥρᾱ οἵᾱ τὸ πεδίον ἄρδειν *for it was not the proper season to irrigate the plain* X. A. 2. 3. 13, ὅσον ἀποζῆν *sufficient to live off of* T. 1. 2, τοιοῦτος οἷος . . . πείθεσθαι *the kind of a man to be convinced* P. Cr. 46 b. On τοσοῦτος ὥστε (ὡς) see 2263. Hom. has the infinitive after τοῖος, τόσος, etc.

2004. Substantives. — As, οἱ παῖδες ὑμῖν ὀλίγου ἡλικίᾱν ἔχουσι παιδεύεσθαι *your children are almost of an age to be educated* P. Lach. 187 c. With ἐστί omitted: σχολή γε ἡμῖν μανθάνειν *we have leisure to learn* X. C. 4. 3. 12, ἀνάγκη πείθεσθαι *there is need to obey* X. H. 1. 6. 8, περαίνειν ἤδη ὥρᾱ *it is high time to finish* X. A. 3. 2. 32. Cp. 1985.

2005. The infinitive is added, like an accusative of respect (1601, 1602), to intransitive verbs (especially in poetry), to adjectives (more frequently in poetry), and to substantives (rarely). Thus, τοῖος ἰδεῖν *such in aspect* (lit. *to look on*) Theognis 216, ὁρᾶν στυγνός *of a repulsive expression* X. A. 2. 6. 9, ἀκοῦσαι παγκάλως ἔχει *it is very fine to hear* D. 19. 47, θαῦμα καὶ ἀκοῦσαι *a marvel even to hear of* P. L. 656 d.

2006. The infinitive limiting the meaning of an adjective is commonly active (or middle) in cases where the passive is more natural in English. Thus, λόγος δυνατὸς κατανοῆσαι *a speech capable of being understood* P. Ph. 90 c, ἄξιος θαυμάσαι *worthy to be admired* T. 1. 138 (but ἄξιος θαυμάζεσθαι X. C. 5. 1. 6).

a. The active use is due to the old datival function of the infinitive: δυνατὸς κατανοῆσαι *capable for understanding.*

2007. The infinitive, with or without ὥστε or ὡς, may be used with ἤ *than* after comparatives, depending on an (implied) idea of *ability* or *inability*. ἢ ὥστε is more common than ἤ or ἢ ὡς. Cp. 2264.

τὸ γὰρ νόσημα μεῖζον ἢ φέρειν *for the disease is too great to be borne* S. O. T. 1293, φοβοῦμαι μή τι μεῖζον ἢ ὥστε φέρειν δύνασθαι κακὸν τῇ πόλει συμβῇ *I fear lest some calamity befall the State greater than it can bear* X. M. 3. 5. 17, βραχύτερα ἢ ὡς ἐξικνεῖσθαι *too short to reach* X. A. 3. 3. 7.

a. The force of ἢ ὥστε may be expressed by the genitive; as, κρεῖσσον λόγου (T. 2. 50) = κρεῖσσον ἢ ὥστε λέγεσθαι. Cp. 1077.

b. Words implying a comparison may take the infinitive with ὥστε or ὡς (1063).

D. *Infinitive of Purpose and Result*

2008. Infinitive of Purpose.—The infinitive may express purpose (usually only with verbs taking the accusative).

ταύτην τὴν χώρᾱν ἐπέτρεψε διαρπάσαι τοῖς Ἕλλησιν *he gave this land over to the Greeks to plunder* X. A. 1. 2. 19, τὸ ἥμισυ (τοῦ στρατεύματος) κατέλιπε φυλάττειν τὸ στρατόπεδον *he left half* (*of the army*) *behind to guard the camp* 5. 2. 1, ἰέναι ἐπὶ βασιλέᾱ οὐκ ἐγίγνετο τὰ ἱερά *the sacrifices did not turn out* (favourable) *for going against the king* 2. 2. 3, Ἀριστάρχῳ . . . ἔδοτε ἡμέρᾱν ἀπολογήσασθαι *you granted a day to Aristarchus to make his defence* X. H. 1. 7. 28, ἡ θύρᾱ ἡ ἐμὴ ἀνέῳκτο . . . εἰσιέναι τῷ δεομένῳ τι ἐμοῦ *my door stood open for any petitioner of mine to enter* 5. 1. 14, παρέχω ἐμαυτὸν ἐρωτᾶν *I offer myself to be questioned* P. A. 33 b, τὰς γυναῖκας πιεῖν φερούσᾱς *the women bringing* (something) *to drink* X. H. 7. 2. 9. Cp. also 2032 e.

2009. The infinitive of purpose is used in prose especially after verbs meaning *to give, entrust, choose, appoint, take, receive.* Verbs signifying *to send, go, come* usually take the future active participle (2065); but T. 6. 50 has δέκα τῶν νεῶν προύπεμψαν ἐς τὸν μέγαν λιμένα πλεῦσαι *they sent ahead ten ships to sail into the great harbour;* and in poetry the infinitive often denotes purpose after these verbs, and after εἶναι in Homer (Α 20) and Hdt. (5. 25).

2010. After verbs meaning *to have* (or *be*) *at one's disposition:* οἱ στρατιῶται ἀργύριον οὐκ εἶχον ἐπισῑτίζεσθαι *the soldiers did not have money by means of which they could provision themselves* X. A. 7. 1. 7, ἐκεῖ σκιά τ᾽ ἐστὶ καὶ πόᾱ καθίζεσθαι *there is shade and grass to sit down in* P. Phae. 229 b.

2011. Infinitive of Result.—The infinitive may be used with ὥστε (sometimes with ὡς) to denote a result, often an intended result. See 2260 ff.

a. Several verbs, substantives, and adjectives usually taking the infinitive also admit ὥστε with the infinitive (2271); and the infinitive is found where ὥστε with the infinitive might be expected: μνημονεύουσιν ἀφεθέντα τοῦτον ἐλεύθερον εἶναι *they recall that he was emancipated* (lit. *released so as to be free*) D. 29. 25. Here the redundant infinitive expresses an intended result.

N. — This redundant use of εἶναι is common in Hom. and Hdt.

E. *Absolute Infinitive*

2012. Certain idiomatic infinitives are used absolutely in parenthetical phrases to limit the application of a single expression or of the entire sentence.

a. **Verbs of Saying.** — ὡς ἔπος εἰπεῖν, ὡς εἰπεῖν *so to speak, almost;* (ὡς) ἁπλῶς εἰπεῖν, ὡς συνελόντι (1497) εἰπεῖν, ὡς (ἐν βραχεῖ or) συντόμως εἰπεῖν *to speak briefly, concisely;* ὡς ἐπὶ πᾶν εἰπεῖν, τὸ σύμπαν εἰπεῖν *speaking generally;* σχεδὸν εἰπεῖν *so to say, almost* (*paene dixerim*); σὺν θεῷ εἰπεῖν *in God's name;* and so ὡς with λέγειν, φράζειν, εἰρῆσθαι, as ὡς ἐν τύπῳ εἰρῆσθαι *in general.* Examples: ἀληθές γε ὡς ἔπος εἰπεῖν οὐδὲν εἰρήκᾱσιν *not one word of truth, I may say, did they utter* P. A. 17 a, ἀγαθὸν μὲν ἁπλῶς εἰπεῖν οὐδὲν γέγονε τῇ πόλει *in a word the State gained no advantage* Dinarchus 1. 33.

b. ὡς (ἔπος) εἰπεῖν is often used to limit too strict an application of a general statement, especially πᾶς or οὐδείς. Thus, πάντες ὡς ἔπος εἰπεῖν *nearly every one,* οὐδεὶς ὡς ἔπος εἰπεῖν *almost no one.* It is thus used like *paene dixerim;* rarely, like *ut ita dicam,* to soften the strength of a metaphor.

c. Especially common is the absolute εἶναι in ἑκὼν εἶναι *willingly, intentionally, if you can help it,* usually in negative or quasi-negative statements (ἑκών may be inflected). Also in τὸ κατὰ τοῦτον (ἐπὶ τούτῳ) εἶναι *as far as he is concerned,* ὡς . . . εἶναι *as far as . . . is concerned,* τὸ νῦν εἶναι *at present.* Examples: οὐδὲ ξένοις ἑκὼν εἶναι γέλωτα παρέχεις *nor do you intentionally cause strangers to laugh* X. C. 2. 2. 15, ἑκοῦσα εἶναι οὐκ ἀπολείπεται *it is not willingly separated* P. Phae. 252 a, τό γε ἐπ' ἐκεῖνον εἶναι ἐσώθης (ἄν) *so far, at least, as it depended on him you would have been saved* L. 13. 58.

d. **Other expressions**: ἐμοὶ δοκεῖν, ὡς ἐμοὶ δοκεῖν, ὡς ἐμοὶ κρῖναι *as it seems to me, in my opinion,* (ὡς) εἰκάσαι *to make a guess,* (ὡς) συμβάλλειν *to compare,* (ὡς) ἀκοῦσαι *to the ear,* ὡς ὑπομνῆσαι *to recall the matter,* ὅσον γέ μ' εἰδέναι *as far as I know,* etc.; ὀλίγου δεῖν, μῑκροῦ δεῖν *almost, all but* (δεῖν may be omitted, 1399). Examples: ὁ γὰρ Κτήσιππος ἔτυχε πόρρω καθεζόμενος τοῦ Κλεινίου, ἐμοὶ δοκεῖν *for Ctesippus, it seems to me, happened to be sitting at a distance from Clinias* P. Eu. 274 b, μῑκροῦ δεῖν τρία τάλαντα *almost three talents* D. 27. 29.

e. Some of these absolute infinitives may be explained by reference to the idea of purpose (2008) or result. Thus, συνελόντι εἰπεῖν *for one compressing* the matter *to speak* (cp. *ut paucis dicam*), μῑκροῦ δεῖν *so as to lack little.* Others recall the adverbial accusative (1606); cp. ἐμοὶ δοκεῖν with γνώμην ἐμήν.

F. *Infinitive in Commands, Wishes, and Exclamations*

2013. Infinitive in Commands. — The infinitive may be used for the second person of the imperative. The person addressed is regarded as the subject. This infinitive is commoner in poetry than in prose (where it has a solemn or formal force).

θαρσῶν νῦν, Διόμηδες, ἐπὶ Τρώεσσι μάχεσθαι *with good courage now, Diomed, fight against the Trojans* E 124, σὺ δέ, Κλεαρίδᾱ . . . τᾱ̀ς πύλᾱς ἀνοίξᾱς ἐπεκθεῖν *but do you, Clearidas, open the gates and sally forth* T. 5. 9.

a. This infinitive may be used in conjunction with an imperative: ἀκούετε λεῴ· κατὰ τὰ πάτρια τοὺς χόας πίνειν *hear ye, good people! drink the Pitchers as our sires drank!* Ar. Ach. 1000.

b. The infinitive for the third person of the imperative often occurs in legal language (laws, treaties, etc.), and does not necessarily depend on the principal verb. Thus, ἔτη δὲ εἶναι τᾱ̀ς σπονδᾱ̀ς πεντήκοντα *and the treaty shall continue for fifty years* T. 5. 18. In this construction the infinitive has the force of an infinitive dependent on ἔδοξε (*it was voted that*) or the like. So in medical language, as πίνειν δὲ ὕδωρ it is well for the patient *to drink water* Hippocrates 1. 151.

c. The infinitive (with subject accusative) is rarely used for the third person of the imperative when there is an unconscious ellipsis of a word like δός *grant*, or εὔχομαι *I pray*. Thus, τεύχεα σῡλήσᾱς φερέτω κοίλᾱς ἐπὶ νῆας, σῶμα δὲ οἴκαδ' ἐμὸν δόμεναι πάλιν *let him strip off my arms and carry them to the hollow ships, but let him give back my body to my home* H 78.

d. In negative commands (prohibitions) μή with the infinitive is poetic and Ionic: οἷς μὴ πελάζειν *do not approach these* (=μὴ πέλαζε) A. Pr. 712, μηδὲ καλεῖν πω ὄλβιον *and do not call him happy yet* Hdt. 1. 32.

2014. Infinitive in Wishes. — The infinitive with a subject accusative may be used in the sense of the optative of wish, usually with the same ellipsis as in 2013 c.

θεοὶ πολῖται, μή με δουλείᾱς τυχεῖν *ye gods of my country, may bondage not be my lot!* A. Sept. 253, ὦ Ζεῦ, ἐκγενέσθαι μοι Ἀθηναίους τείσασθαι *oh Zeus, that it be granted to me to punish the Athenians!* Hdt. 5. 105 (cp. ὦ Ζεῦ, δός με τείσασθαι μόρον πατρός *oh Zeus, grant that I may avenge my father's murder!* A. Ch. 18). This construction is very rare in Attic prose: τὸν κυνηγέτην ἔχοντα ἐξιέναι . . . ἐλαφρᾱ̀ν ἐσθῆτα *the hunter should go forth in a light dress* X. Ven. 6. 11. Here no definite verb can be supplied.

a. The nominative with the infinitive (instead of the optative) after αἰ γάρ occurs in Homer (η 311, ω 376).

2015. Infinitive in Exclamations. — The infinitive is often used in exclamations of surprise or indignation. The subject stands in the accusative.

ἐμὲ παθεῖν τάδε *that I should suffer this!* A. Eum. 837, τοιουτονὶ τρέφειν κύνα *to keep a dog like that!* Ar. Vesp. 835.

On the infinitive with ἐφ' ᾧ (ἐφ' ᾧτε) see 2279; with πρίν, see 2453.

INFINITIVE AS OBJECT IN INDIRECT DISCOURSE

2016. The infinitive is used as the object of verbs of *saying* and *thinking*. Such infinitives denote both time and stage of action (cp. 1866).

a. The finite verb of a sentence placed in dependence on a verb of *saying* or *thinking* that requires the infinitive, becomes infinitive, which infinitive stands in the relation of a substantive as subject or object of the leading verb. Commonly as *object:* thus, Κῦρος νῑκᾷ *Cyrus is victorious*, when made the object of φησί *he says*, becomes a part of a new sentence φησὶ Κῦρον νῑκᾶν, in which Κῦρον νικᾶν is the object of φησί. As *subject*, when the verb of *saying* is passive: thus, in λέγεται Κῦρον νῑκᾶν, the last two words form the subject of λέγεται.

2017. Verbs of *saying* are *e.g.: say* φημί, φάσκω, λέγω; *confess* ὁμολογῶ; *promise* ὑπισχνοῦμαι, ὑποδέχομαι, ἐπαγγέλλομαι, ὑφίσταμαι; *pretend* προσποιοῦμαι; *swear* ὄμνῡμι; *deny* ἀπαρνοῦμαι; *gainsay* ἀντιλέγω; *dispute* ἀμφισβητῶ, etc.

Some verbs of *saying* admit other constructions than the infinitive, and especially ὅτι or ὡς (2579). λέγω, εἶπον, φράζω, φωνῶ with ὅτι or ὡς mean *say*, with the infinitive *command* (1997).

a. φημί *say, assert, express the opinion that* in classical Greek is almost always followed by the infinitive, but by ὅτι very often in the later language. φημὶ ὅτι occurs in X. A. 7. 1. 5 (φημὶ ὡς in L. 7. 19, X. H. 6. 3. 7; D. 4. 48, 27. 19 by anacoluthon).

b. λέγω *state* (impart a fact) takes either the infinitive or ὅτι or ὡς. The infinitive occurs usually with the passive (λέγεται, etc.) either in the personal or impersonal construction (1982 a). The active forms of λέγω with the infinitive mean *command* (1997).

c. εἶπον *said* usually takes ὅτι or ὡς; with the infinitive, it commonly means *commanded* (1997). Cp. the double use of *told*.

N. — εἶπον meaning *said* with the infinitive is rare, but occurs in good Attic prose: And. 1. 57, 80; Thuc. 7. 35; Lys. 10. 6, 10. 9, 10. 12; Xen. H. 1. 6. 7, 2. 2. 15, C. 5. 5. 24, S. 2. 13; Is. 2. 29; Lyc. 50; Aes. 3. 37, 3. 59; Dem. 15. 18; Plato, G. 473 a, 503 d, Lach. 192 b, Charm. 174 a, Hipp. Maj. 291 b, Pol. 263 c, 290 b, L. 654 a, Clitoph. 409 a, 410 b. In poetry this use is frequent.

2018. Verbs of *thinking* almost always take the infinitive. Such are: *think* ἡγοῦμαι, οἴομαι, δοκῶ, νομίζω; *hope* ἐλπίζω; *suppose* ὑπολαμβάνω; *suspect* ὑποπτεύω; *guess* εἰκάζω; *feel confident* πιστεύω; *disbelieve* ἀπιστῶ. The use of ὡς is rare, while ὅτι is very rare (2580).

a. Verbs of *perceiving* sometimes take the infinitive by analogy to verbs of *thinking;* as ἀκούω, αἰσθάνομαι, πυνθάνομαι (2144).

2019. Each tense of direct discourse is retained (with its proper meaning as regards stage of action) when it becomes infinitive in indirect discourse; but an imperfect is represented by the present infinitive; a pluperfect, by the perfect infinitive. See 1866, 1867.

2020. An original οὐ of direct discourse is generally, an original μή is always, retained in indirect discourse. But in some cases οὐ becomes μή (2723 ff.).

2021. The infinitive is the subject of the passive of verbs of *saying* and *thinking* (1982 a). So with δοκεῖ *it seems*, φαίνεται *it is plain*, etc.

2022. The infinitive represents a finite verb after verbs of *saying* and *thinking*.

a. εὖνοί φᾱσιν εἶναι *they assert that they are loyal* L. 12. 49, οὐδεὶς ἔφασκεν γιγνώσκειν αὐτόν *nobody said that he knew him* 23. 3, οἱ ἡγεμόνες οὔ φᾱσιν (2692) εἶναι ἄλλην ὁδόν *the guides say there is no other road* X. A. 4. 1. 21, πάντες ἐροῦσι τὸ λοιπὸν μηδὲν εἶναι κερδαλεώτερον τῆς ἀρετῆς *everybody in time to come will say that there is nothing more profitable than bravery* X. C. 7. 1. 18. Other examples 1867.

b. βασιλεὺς νῑκᾶν ἡγεῖται *the king thinks he is victorious* (= νῑκῶ, cp. 1887) X. A. 2. 1. 11, οἴομαι βέλτιστον εἶναι *I think it is best* 5. 1. 8, ὑπώπτευον ἐπὶ βασιλέᾱ ἰέναι *they suspected that they were to go against the king* 1. 3. 1, (Σωκράτης) τὸ ἀγνοεῖν ἑαυτὸν ἐγγυτάτω . . . μανίᾱς ἐλογίζετο εἶναι *Socrates was of the opinion that for a man not to know himself was very near to madness* X. M. 3. 9. 6.

c. When a word of *saying* is expressed or implied in what precedes, several infinitives may be used where the indicative is employed in translation. So in the narration in X. C. 1. 3. 5–6.

2023. The infinitive with ἄν represents an indicative with ἄν or a potential optative with ἄν. See 1846, 1848, 1849, 2270.

2024. Verbs signifying *to hope, expect, promise, threaten,* and *swear* take the future infinitive in indirect discourse, and the aorist (less often the present) infinitive not in indirect discourse (like verbs of *will* or *desire*, 1868, 1999). ἐλπίζω ταῦτα ποιήσειν *I hope that I shall do this*, ἐλπίζω ταῦτα ποιῆσαι or ποιεῖν *I hope to do this.*

THE INFINITIVE WITH THE ARTICLE (ARTICULAR INFINITIVE)

2025. The articular infinitive, while having the character of a substantive, retains the functions of a verb. In its older use the articular infinitive is a subject or object; the nearest approach to this use in Homer is ἀνίη καὶ τὸ φυλάσσειν *to watch is also trouble* υ 52. In the tragic poets the genitive and dative are rarely used; in the speeches in Thucydides and in Demosthenes all of its four cases appear with great frequency. The articular infinitive may take dependent clauses.

2026. The articular infinitive admits the constructions of an ordinary substantive.

Nom. **τὸ ποιεῖν** *making* or *to make*, **τὸ ποιήσειν, τὸ ποιῆσαι, τὸ πεποιηκέναι**
Gen. **τοῦ ποιεῖν** *of making*, **τοῦ ποιήσειν, τοῦ ποιῆσαι,** etc.
Dat. **τῷ ποιεῖν** *for making, by making*, **τῷ ποιήσειν, τῷ ποιῆσαι,** etc.
Acc. **τὸ ποιεῖν, τὸ ποιήσειν, τὸ ποιῆσαι,** etc.

2027. The articular infinitive is treated as subject, predicate noun, and object like the simple infinitive (1984–1986).

2028. The negative of the articular infinitive is μή.

2029. The articular infinitive may indicate time (after verbs of *saying* or *thinking*, 2034 g), or may be timeless.

2030. The articular infinitive is in general used like the infinitive without the article, and may take ἄν; as regards its constructions it has the value of a substantive. The article is regularly used when the connection uniting the infinitive to another word has to be expressed by the genitive, the dative, or a preposition.

a. The articular infinitive is rarely used, like a true substantive, with the subjective genitive: τό γ' εὖ φρονεῖν αὐτῶν μῑμεῖσθε *imitate at least their wisdom* D. 19. 269.

2031. NOMINATIVE OF THE ARTICULAR INFINITIVE

Subject (1984): νέοις τὸ σῑγᾶν κρεῖττόν ἐστι τοῦ λαλεῖν *in the young silence is better than speech* Men. Sent. 387, τὸ Πελοποννησίους αὐτοῖς μὴ βοηθῆσαι παρέσχεν ὑμῖν . . . Σαμίων κόλασιν *the fact that the Peloponnesians did not come to their assistance enabled you to punish the Samians* T. 1. 41.

2032. GENITIVE OF THE ARTICULAR INFINITIVE

a. The genitive of the articular infinitive is used to limit the meaning of substantives, adjectives, and verbs.

b. Adnominal (1290): τοῦ πιεῖν ἐπιθῡμίᾳ *from desire to drink* T. 7. 84, πρὸς τὴν πόλιν προσβαλόντες ἐς ἐλπίδα ἦλθον τοῦ ἑλεῖν *they attacked the city and entertained hopes of taking it* 2. 56.

c. Partitive (1306): τοῦ θαρσεῖν τὸ πλεῖστον εἰληφότες *having gained the greatest amount of courage* T. 4. 34. After comparatives (1431): τί οὖν ἐστιν . . . τοῦ τοῖς φίλοις ἀρήγειν κάλλῑον; *what then is nobler than to help one's friends?* X. C. 1. 5. 13.

d. After verbs: ἐπέσχομεν τοῦ δακρύειν *we desisted from weeping* P. Ph. 117 e (cp. 1392).

e. Purpose (cp. 1408), often a negative purpose: τοῦ μὴ τὰ δίκαια ποιεῖν *in order not to do what was just* D. 18. 107, ἐτειχίσθη Ἀταλάντη . . . τοῦ μὴ λῃστὰς . . . κακουργεῖν τὴν Εὔβοιαν *Atalante was fortified to prevent pirates from ravaging Euboea* T. 2. 32. More common is the use with ὑπέρ (2032 g) or ἕνεκα.

f. Genitive Absolute (2070): ἐπ' ἐκείνοις δὲ ὄντος αἰεὶ τοῦ ἐπιχειρεῖν καὶ ἐφ' ἡμῖν εἶναι δεῖ τὸ προαμύνασθαι *since* the power of *attack is always in their hands, so in our hands should lie* the power of *repelling it in advance* T. 3. 12.

g. After prepositions, *e.g.* ἀντὶ τοῦ ἐπὶ Κᾱρίᾱν ἰέναι . . . ἐπὶ Φρυγίᾱς ἐπορεύετο *instead of going against Caria, he marched toward Phrygia* X. H. 3. 4. 12, ἄνευ τοῦ σωφρονεῖν *without exercising self-control* X. M. 4. 3. 1. To express purpose the genitive with ὑπέρ is very common: ὑπὲρ τοῦ τούτων γενέσθαι κύριος . . . πάντα πρᾱγματεύεται *he devotes his every effort that he may become master of these* D. 8. 45, ὑπὲρ τοῦ μὴ τὸ κελευόμενον ποιῆσαι *in order not to do what was commanded* 18. 204. Furthermore, after ἀπό, πρό, διά, μετά, περί, ὑπό, ἕνεκα, χάριν, χωρίς, πλήν, μέχρι; and after adverbs. In Hdt. τοῦ may be omitted after ἀντί.

2033. DATIVE OF THE ARTICULAR INFINITIVE

a. With verbs, adjectives, and adverbs: thus, ἵνα . . . ἀπιστῶσι τῷ ἐμὲ τετῑμῆσθαι ὑπὸ δαιμόνων *that they may distrust my having been honoured by divine powers* X. Ap. 14, τῷ ζῆν ἐστί τι ἐναντίον, ὥσπερ τῷ ἐγρηγορέναι τὸ καθεύδειν; *is it something opposed to living, as sleeping to waking?* P. Ph. 71 c, οὐδενὶ τῶν πάντων πλέον κεκράτηκε Φίλιππος ἢ τῷ πρότερος πρὸς τοῖς πράγμασι γίγνεσθαι *Philip has conquered us by nothing so much as by being beforehand in his operations* D. 8. 11, ἅμα τῷ τῑμᾶν *at the same time that* we *honour* P. R. 468 e, ἴσον δὲ τῷ προστένειν *equal to sorrowing beforehand* A. Ag. 252.

b. After prepositions: *e.g.* οὐ γὰρ ἐπὶ τῷ δοῦλοι, ἀλλ' ἐπὶ τῷ ὁμοῖοι τοῖς λειπομένοις εἶναι ἐκπέμπονται (ἄποικοι) *for colonists are not sent out on the basis of being inferiors, but on the basis of being the equals of those who are left at home* T. 1. 34, ὁ μὲν πρὸς τῷ μηδὲν ἐκ τῆς πρεσβείᾱς λαβεῖν, τοὺς αἰχμαλώτους . . . ἐλύσατο *the one, in addition to gaining nothing from the embassy, ransomed the prisoners of war* D. 19. 229, ἐν τῷ φρονεῖν γὰρ μηδὲν ἥδιστος βίος *for life is sweetest in being conscious of nothing* S. Aj. 553.

2034. ACCUSATIVE OF THE ARTICULAR INFINITIVE

a. Object (cp. 1989): δείσᾱς τὸ ζῆν *fearing to live* P. A. 28 d, μεῖζον μέν φαμεν κακὸν τὸ ἀδικεῖν, ἔλᾱττον δὲ τὸ ἀδικεῖσθαι *we call doing wrong a greater evil, being wronged a lesser* P. G. 509 c.

b. After prepositions: *e.g.* μέγιστον ἀγαθὸν τὸ πειθαρχεῖν φαίνεται εἰς τὸ καταπράττειν τἀγαθά *obedience appears to be an advantage of the greatest importance with regard to the successful accomplishment of excellent objects* X. C. 8. 1. 3, τῶν ἁπάντων ἀπερίοπτοί εἰσι παρὰ τὸ νῑκᾶν *they are indifferent to everything in comparison with victory* T. 1. 41, πρὸς τὸ μετρίων δεῖσθαι πεπαιδευμένος *schooled to moderate needs* X. M. 1. 2. 1, πῶς ἔχεις πρὸς τὸ ἐθέλειν ἂν ἰέναι ἄκλητος ἐπὶ δεῖπνον; *how do you feel about being willing to go uninvited to supper?* P. S. 174 a (cp. ἐθέλοις ἂν ἰέναι). Furthermore, after διά, ἐπί, κατά, μετά, περί.

c. The accusative of the infinitive with τό appears after many verbs and verbal expressions which usually take only the simple infinitive. Such verbal expressions may be followed also by a genitive of a noun. Thus, τὸ σπεύδειν δέ σοι παραινῶ *I commend speed to thee* S. Ph. 620, καρδίᾱς δ' ἐξίσταμαι τὸ δρᾶν *I withdraw from my resolution so as to (= and) do this thing* S. Ant. 1105, μαθὼν γὰρ οὐκ ἂν ἀρνοίμην τὸ δρᾶν *when I am informed, I will not refuse the deed* S. Ph. 118, τὸ προθῡμεῖσθαι δὲ συναύξειν τὸν οἶκον ἐπαιδεύομεν αὐτήν *we trained her to show zeal in assisting to increase our estate* X. O. 9. 12 (cp. 1628), τὸ ἐρᾶν ἔξαρνος εἶ *you refuse to love* P. Lys. 205 a.

d. So after adjectives. Thus, μακρὸς τὸ κρῖναι ταῦτα χὠ λοιπὸς χρόνος *the future is long* (*i.e.* time enough) *to decide this* S. El. 1030

e. This object infinitive after verbs is often an internal accusative. The accusative after verbs and nouns is, in many cases, like an accusative of respect (1600); as τὸ δρᾶν οὐκ ἠθέλησαν *they refused to do it* S. O. C. 442, αἰσχύνονται τὸ τολμᾶν *they are ashamed to dare* P. Soph. 247 b, οὐδ' ἐμοί τοι τοὐξανιστάναι ἐστὶ θάρσος *nor have I courage to remove thee* S. O. C. 47, τὸ μὲν ἐς τὴν γῆν ἡμῶν ἐσβάλλειν . . . ἱκανοί εἰσι *they are able to make an inroad into our country* T. 6. 17. This infinitive after adjectives (and sometimes after verbs) occurs when the simple infinitive expresses purpose or result, as in τίς Μήδων . . . σοῦ ἀπελείφθη τὸ μή σοι ἀκολουθεῖν; *what one of the Medes remained away from you so as not to attend you?* X. C. 5. 1. 25.

f. Some verbs take the articular infinitive as an object when the simple infinitive could not be used: μόνον ὁρῶν τὸ παίειν τὸν ἁλισκόμενον *taking heed only to strike any one he caught* X. C. 1. 4. 21.

g. Verbs of *saying* and *thinking* rarely take the articular infinitive (also with ἄν): ἐξομεῖ τὸ μὴ εἰδέναι; *wilt thou swear thou didst not know?* S. Ant. 535, τῆς ἐλπίδος γὰρ ἔρχομαι δεδραγμένος, τὸ μὴ παθεῖν ἂν ἄλλο πλὴν τὸ μόρσιμον *for I come with good grip on the hope that I can suffer nothing save what is my fate* S. Ant. 235.

h. On the use of the object infinitive with τὸ μή and τὸ μὴ οὐ, see 2744 and 2749.

i. The accusative with the infinitive may stand in the absolute construction: ἐπεί γε τὸ ἐλθεῖν τοῦτον, οἶμαι θεόν τινα αὐτὸν ἐπ᾽ αὐτὴν ἀγαγεῖν τὴν τῑμωρίᾱν *as for his coming, I believe that some god brought him to his very punishment* Lyc. 91.

OTHER USES OF THE ARTICULAR INFINITIVE

2035. Apposition (cp. 1987). The articular infinitive, in any case, is often used in apposition to a preceding word, especially a demonstrative.

τοῦτό ἐστι τὸ ἀδικεῖν, τὸ πλέον τῶν ἄλλων ζητεῖν ἔχειν *injustice is this: to seek to have more than other people* P. G. 483 c, τί γὰρ τούτου μακαριώτερον, τοῦ γῇ μιχθῆναι κτλ. *for what is more blessed than this: to be commingled with the earth,* etc. X. C. 8. 7. 25, δοκεῖ τούτῳ διαφέρειν ἀνὴρ τῶν ἄλλων ζῴων, τῷ τῑμῆς ὀρέγεσθαι *man differs herein from other creatures that he aspires after honour* X. Hi. 7. 3.

2036. In Exclamation (cp. 2015). — Thus, τῆς τύχης· τὸ ἐμὲ νῦν κληθέντα δεῦρο τυχεῖν *my ill-luck! that I should happen now to have been summoned hither!* X. C. 2. 2. 3.

2037. With Adjuncts. — The articular infinitive may take various adjuncts including dependent clauses, the whole forming one large substantival idea.

τὸ μὲν γὰρ πόλλ᾽ ἀπολωλεκέναι κατὰ τὸν πόλεμον *the fact that we have lost much in the war* D. 1. 10, πέπεισμαι . . . τὰ πλείω τῶν πρᾱγμάτων ἡμᾶς ἐκπεφευγέναι τῷ μὴ βούλεσθαι τὰ δέοντα ποιεῖν, ἢ τῷ μὴ συνῑέναι *I am persuaded that more of your advantages have escaped you from your not being willing to do your duty than from your ignorance* 3. 3, καὶ γὰρ πάνυ μοι δοκεῖ ἄφρονος ἀνθρώπου εἶναι τὸ (μεγάλου ἔργου ὄντος τοῦ ἑαυτῷ τὰ δέοντα παρασκευάζειν) μὴ ἀρκεῖν τοῦτο, ἀλλὰ προσαναθέσθαι τὸ καὶ τοῖς ἄλλοις πολίταις ὧν δέονται πορίζειν *and in fact, since it is a serious business to provide for one's own necessities, it seems to me to be the part of an utter fool not to rest content with that, but in addition to take upon himself the burden of providing for the needs of the rest of the community* X. M. 2. 1. 8.

CONSTRUCTIONS OF THE INFINITIVE WITH VERBS OF *hindering*

2038. Verbs signifying (or suggesting) *to hinder* take both the simple infinitive and the articular infinitive. Such verbs may take the strengthening but redundant negative *μή* (2739); and some, when themselves negatived or appearing in a question expecting a negative answer, admit the addition of the sympathetic *οὐ* (2742). Hence we have a variety of constructions (described in 2744 ff.)

THE PARTICIPLE

2039. The participle (*μετοχή participation*) is a verbal adjective, in part a verb, in part an adjective.

2040. The participle is like a verb herein:

a. It shows the distinctions of voice and tense. Its tenses mark action simply occurring, continuing, and completed.

b. It can have an object in the same case (genitive, dative, accusative) as the finite forms.

c. It is modified by adverbs, not by adjectives.

d. It may take ἄν, and, with that particle, represents ἄν with the indicative or ἄν with the optative (1845 ff.).

2041. The participle shows its adjectival nature by being inflected and by admitting the article before it, both of which characteristics give it the character of a noun. It follows the rules of agreement like other adjectives (1020). Unlike the adjective, it represents a quality in action (cp. 1857).

2042. The participle is always used in connection with a substantive or a substantive pronoun, which may be contained in a verbal form, as διάγουσι μανθάνοντες *they spend their time in learning.*

2043. The tenses of the participle (except the future) not in indirect discourse are timeless, and denote only stage of action (1872). When they stand in indirect discourse and represent the indicative, they denote time relatively to that of the main verb.

2044. The future participle marks an action as in prospect at the time denoted by the leading verb. Since it expresses an idea of *will*, it shows that an action is purposed, intended, or expected. With the article it denotes the person or thing *likely* (or *able*) *to do* something (= μέλλων with inf. 1959). The nearest approach to mere futurity appears in general only after verbs of *knowing* and *perceiving* (2106, cp. 2112 b).

ὁ δ' ἀνὴρ αὐτῆς λαγὼς ᾤχετο θηράσων *but her husband had gone to hunt hares* X. A. 4. 5. 24, ὁ ἡγησόμενος οὐδεὶς ἔσται *there will be no one to guide* us 2. 4. 5, πολλὰ . . . δεῖ τὸν εὖ στρατηγήσοντα (= τὸν μέλλοντα εὖ στρατηγήσειν) ἔχειν *he who intends to be a good general must have many qualifications* X. M. 3. 1. 6, θανουμένη γὰρ ἐξῄδη *for I knew that I should* (or *must*) *die* S. Ant. 460 (cp. 2106).

2045. The negative of the participle is οὐ, except when the participle has a general or conditional force, or occurs in a sentence which requires μή. See 2728.

2046. The participle has three main uses.

A. Attributive: as an attributive to a substantive.

B. Circumstantial (or Adverbial): denoting some attendant circumstance and qualifying the main verb like an adverbial phrase or clause.

C. Supplementary: as a supplement to a verbal predicate, which, without such a supplement, would be incomplete.

2047. The circumstantial and supplementary participles are predicate participles.

2048. The attributive and circumstantial participles are commonly not necessary to the *construction;* but the removal of a supplementary participle may make the construction incomplete. The circumstantial participle is used by way of apposition to the subject of the verb and, though strictly predicative, may agree attributively with a noun or pronoun. An attributive participle may be circumstantial, as οἱ μὴ δυνάμενοι διατελέσαι τὴν ὁδὸν ἐνυκτέρευσαν ἄσῖτοι *those who* (i.e. *if any*) *were unable to complete the march passed the night without food* X. A. 4. 5. 11. A participle may be both circumstantial and supplementary, as ἀδικούμενοι ὀργίζονται (T. 1. 77) *they are enraged at being wronged* or *because* (*when, if*) *they are wronged.* Circumstantial and supplementary participles often cannot be sharply distinguished; as with verbs signifying *to be angry, ashamed, content, pleased* (2100), *inferior to, do wrong* (2101), *endure* (2098), *come* and *go* (2099). Thus, ἀδικῶ ταῦτα ποιῶν *I do wrong in doing this* or *I am guilty in doing this:* in the first case ταῦτα ποιῶν is appositive to the subject of the verb; in the second these words define the predicate adjective ἄδικος contained in ἀδικῶ (= ἄδικός εἰμι).

THE ATTRIBUTIVE PARTICIPLE

2049. The attributive participle (with any modifier), with or without the article, modifies a substantive like any other adjective.

ὁ ἐφεστηκὼς κίνδυνος τῇ πόλει *the danger impending over the State* D. 18. 176, οἱ ὄντες ἐχθροί *the existing enemies* 6. 15, ὁ παρὼν καιρός *the present crisis* 3. 3, τὸ Κοτύλαιον ὀνομαζόμενον ὄρος *the mountain called Cotylaeum* Aes. 3. 86, αἱ Αἰόλου νῆσοι καλούμεναι *the so-called islands of Aeolus* T. 3. 88 (cp. 1170). For the position of an attributive participle with its modifiers, see 1166.

2050. The substantive with which the attributive participle (with the article) agrees directly, may be omitted, the participle thus becoming a substantive (1153 b, and N. 1); as, ὁ οἴκαδε βουλόμενος ἀπιέναι *whoever wants to go home* X. A. 1. 7. 4. Neuter participles are often substantival, as τὰ δέοντα *duties.*

a. Substantives or relative clauses must often be used to translate such participles, as ὁ φεύγων *the exile* or *the defendant*, τὸ μέλλον *the future*, οἱ νῑκῶντες *the victors*, ὁ κλέπτων *the thief*, οἱ θανόντες *the dead*, ὁ σωθεὶς *the man who has been saved*, οἱ δεδιότες *those who are afraid*, οἱ ἀδικούμενοι *those who are* (*being*) *wronged*, ὁ τὴν γνώμην ταύτην εἰπών *the one who gave this opinion* T. 8. 68, ὁ ἐνταῦθ' ἑαυτὸν τάξᾱς τῆς πολῑτείᾱς εἴμ' ἐγώ *the man who took this position in the State was I* D. 18. 62. The participle with the article may represent a relative clause of purpose or result, as X. A. 2. 4. 5 cited in 2044.

2051. A participle may be modified by adjectives or take a genitive, when its verbal nature has ceased to be felt: τὰ μῑκρὰ συμφέροντα τῆς πόλεως *the petty interests of the State* D. 18. 28. Cp. συμφέρον ἦν τῇ πόλει *it was advantageous to the State* 19. 75 (here the participle is used like a predicate). Thucydides often uses in an abstract sense a substantival neuter participle where the infinitive would be more common, *e.g.*, τὸ δεδιός *fear*, τὸ θαρσοῦν *courage* (for τὸ δεδιέναι, τὸ θαρσεῖν) 1. 36. See 1153 b, N. 2. In poetry many participles are used substantively, as ὁ τεκών *father*, ἡ τεκοῦσα *mother*, οἱ τεκόντες *parents*.

2052. The article with the participle is either *generic* or *particular* (1124). Thus, ὁ λέγων *the* definite *speaker* on a particular occasion, or *orator* in general. So ὁ οὐ δράσᾱς the definite person who did not do something, ὁ μὴ δράσᾱς any one who did not do something (a supposed case), ὁ μὴ γαμῶν ἄνθρωπος οὐκ ἔχει κακά *the unmarried man has no troubles* Men. Sent. 437. Generic are ὁ τυχών, ὁ βουλόμενος, 2050 a.

a. Participles having an indefinite force may, especially in the plural number, be used without the article. Thus, κατασκεψομένους ἔπεμπε *he sent men to reconnoitre* X. C. 3. 1. 2, ἀδικοῦντα πειρᾱσόμεθα . . . ἀμύνασθαι *we shall endeavour to avenge ourselves on any one who injures us* X. A. 2. 3. 23.

2053. A participle and its substantive often correspond to a verbal noun with the genitive or to an articular infinitive. Cp. *post urbem conditam* and Milton's "Since created man."

τῷ σίτῳ ἐπιλείποντι ἐπιέζοντο *they suffered from the failure of the crops* (= τῇ τοῦ σίτου ἐπιλείψει) T. 3. 20, δι' ὑμᾶς μὴ ξυμμαχήσαντας *by reason of your not joining the alliance* (= διὰ τὸ ὑμᾶς μὴ ξυμμαχῆσαι) 6. 80, μετὰ Συρᾱκούσᾱς οἰκισθείσᾱς *after the foundation of Syracuse* 6. 3, ἐλύπει αὐτὸν ἡ χώρᾱ πορθουμένη *the ravaging of the country grieved him* X. A. 7. 7. 12, ἡ ὀργὴ σὺν τῷ φόβῳ λήγοντι ἄπεισι *his wrath will disappear with the cessation of his fear* X. C. 4. 5. 21.

a. Except in expressions of time, such as ἅμα ἦρι ἀρχομένῳ *at the beginning of spring* T. 2. 2, ἐπὶ Κόδρου βασιλεύοντος *in the reign of Codrus* Lyc. 84 (cp. 1689 b), this construction is in place only when the part. is necessary to the sense. In poetry: Ζεὺς γελοῖος ὀμνύμενος *swearing by Zeus is ridiculous* Ar. Nub. 1241; in Hom. A 601, I 682.

THE CIRCUMSTANTIAL PARTICIPLE

2054. The circumstantial participle is added, without the article, to a noun or pronoun to set forth some circumstance under which an action, generally the main action, takes place.

a. The circumstantial participle thus qualifies the principal verb of the sentence like an adverbial clause or supplementary predicate. Cp. μετὰ ταῦτα εἶπε *afterwards he said* with γελῶν εἶπε *he said laughingly.* Such participles usually have the force of subordinate clauses added to the main verb by conjunctions denoting *time, condition, cause,* etc.; but may often be rendered by adverbial phrases or even by a separate finite verb, which brings out distinctly the idea latent in the participle.

b. The circumstantial participle has no article. In agreement with a noun and its article, it stands before the article or after the noun (*i.e.* in the predicate position). By the agreement of the participle with a noun or pronoun, the predicate of the sentence is more exactly defined.

2055. The circumstantial participle has two main constructions each equivalent in meaning to a clause of *time, condition, cause,* etc.

2056. (I) The subject of the participle is identical with the noun or pronoun subject or object of the leading verb, and agrees with it in gender, number, and case.

(οἱ ἄνθρωποι) λιπόντες τὴν ὁδὸν φεύγοντες ὀλίγοι ἀπέθνῃσκον *by leaving the road and making off* only *a few were killed* X. A. 4. 2. 7, προπέμψαντες κήρῡκα πόλεμον προεροῦντα *having sent a herald in advance to proclaim war* T. 1. 29.

2057. (II) Absolute participial clauses, in which a participle, and not a finite verb, forms the predicate. These are of two kinds.

2058. A. **Genitive Absolute.**—A participle agreeing in the genitive with its own subject, which is not identical with the subject of the leading verb, is said to stand in the genitive absolute. Cp. 2070.

Κῦρος ἀνέβη ἐπὶ τὰ ὄρη οὐδενὸς κωλύοντος *Cyrus ascended the mountains without any one preventing him* X. A. 1. 2. 22.

N.—The English nominative absolute is represented by the Greek genitive absolute. Cp. Tennyson: "we sitting, as I said, the cock crew loud" = ἡμῶν καθημένων, ὅπερ ἔλεγον, μέγα ᾖσεν ὁ ἀλεκτρυών.

2059. B. **Accusative Absolute.**—When the participle has no definite subject (*i.e.* with impersonal verbs), the accusative absolute is used instead of the genitive absolute. Cp. 2076.

συνδόξαν τῷ πατρὶ καὶ τῇ μητρὶ γαμεῖ τὴν Κυαξάρου θυγατέρα *on the approval of* (lit. *it seeming good to*) *his father and mother he married the daughter of Cyaxares* X. C. 8. 5. 28.

2060. The circumstantial participle expresses simply circumstance or manner in general. It may imply various other relations, such as *time, manner, means, cause, purpose, concession, condition,* etc. But it is often impossible to assign a participle exclusively to any one of these relations (which are purely logical), nor can all the delicate relations of the participle be set forth in systematic form.

2061. Time.—The time denoted by the participle is only relative to that of the governing verb, and is to be inferred from the context. Each participial form in itself expresses only stage of action (1850).

ἀκούσᾱσι τοῖς στρατηγοῖς ταῦτα ἔδοξε τὸ στράτευμα συναγαγεῖν *on hearing this it seemed best to the generals to collect the troops* X. A. 4. 4. 19.

a. Several temporal participles have an adverbial force: **ἀρχόμενος** *in the beginning, at first,* **τελευτῶν** *at last, finally,* **διαλιπὼν** (or ἐπισχών) **χρόνον** *after a while,* **διαλείπων χρόνον** *at intervals,* **χρονίζων** *for a long time.* Thus, ἅπερ καὶ ἀρχόμενος εἶπον *as I said at the outset* T. 4. 64, τελευτῶν ἐχαλέπαινεν *at last he became angry* X. A. 4. 5. 16. Note **ἀρξάμενος ἀπό τινος** *beginning with* or *especially.*

2062. Manner. — παρήλαυνον τεταγμένοι *they marched past in order* X. A. 1. 2. 16, κραυγὴν πολλὴν ἐποίουν καλοῦντες ἀλλήλους *they made a loud noise by calling to each other* 2. 2. 17, προείλετο μᾶλλον τοῖς νόμοις ἐμμένων ἀποθανεῖν ἢ παρανομῶν ζῆν *he preferred rather to abide by the laws and die than to disobey them and live* X. M. 4. 4. 4, φατὲ μὲν εὐτυχεῖς εἶναι, ὡς καὶ ἐστὲ καλῶς ποιοῦντες *you claim to be favoured by fortune as happily you are in fact* Aes. 3. 232. To characterize a preceding statement with the participle in apposition to the subject of the preceding sentence; thus, ὀρθῶς γε ταῦτα λέγοντες *yes, and saying this correctly* X. O. 16. 2.

a. Several participles of manner have an idiomatic meaning, *e.g.* **ἀνύσᾱς** *quickly* (lit. *having accomplished*), **ἔχων** *continually, persistently* (lit. *holding on*), **λαθών** *secretly,* **κλαίων** *to one's sorrow* (lit. *weeping*), **χαίρων** *with impunity* (lit. *rejoicing*), **φέρων** *hastily* (lit. *carrying off*), **φθάσᾱς** *before* (lit. *anticipating*). Thus, ἄνοιγ' ἀνύσᾱς *hurry up and open* Ar. Nub. 181, ἔκπλουν ποιεῖται λαθὼν τὴν φυλακήν *he sailed out unobserved by the guard* T. 1. 65 (cp. 2096 f), φλυᾱρεῖς ἔχων *you keep trifling* P. G. 490 e, τοῦτον οὐδεὶς χαίρων ἀδικήσει *no one will wrong him with impunity* 510 d, ἀνέῳξάς με φθάσᾱς *you opened* the door *before* I could knock Ar. Plut. 1102 (cp. 2096 e).

2063. Means (often the present participle). — λῃζόμενοι ζῶσι *they live by pillaging* X. C. 3. 2. 25, μὴ κρῖν' ὁρῶν τὸ κάλλος, ἀλλὰ τὸν τρόπον *judge by regarding not beauty, but (by regarding) character* Men. Sent. 333.

2064. Cause. — Παρύσατις . . . ὑπῆρχε τῷ Κύρῳ, φιλοῦσα αὐτὸν μᾶλλον ἢ τὸν βασιλεύοντα Ἀρταξέρξην *Parysatis favoured Cyrus because she loved him more than she did Artaxerxes the king* X. A. 1. 1. 4, ἀπείχοντο κερδῶν αἰσχρὰ νομίζοντες εἶναι *they held aloof from gains because they thought them disgraceful* X. M. 1. 2. 22, τί γὰρ δεδιότες σφόδρα οὕτως ἐπείγεσθε; *for what are you afraid of, that you are so desperately in haste?* X. H. 1. 7. 26.

a. **τί μαθών** *what induced him to* (lit. *having learned what?*), **τί παθών** *what possessed him to* (lit. *having experienced what?*) are used with the general sense of *wherefore?* in direct (with ὅ τι in indirect) questions expressing surprise or disapprobation; as τί μαθόντες ἐμαρτυρεῖτε ὑμεῖς; *what put it into your heads to give evidence?* D. 45. 38, τί παθόντε λελάσμεθα; *what possessed us to forget?* Λ 313. Cp. τί βουλόμενος.

b. **τί ἔχων**; *what's the matter with you?* (lit. *having what?*)

2065. Purpose or Object. — The future (sometimes the present) participle is used to denote purpose, especially after verbs denoting *to come, go, send, summon,* etc. Thus, προπέμψαντες κήρῡκα πόλεμον προεροῦντα *having sent a herald in advance to proclaim war* T. 1. 29, ὁ βάρβαρος ἐπὶ τὴν Ἑλλάδα δουλωσόμενος ἦλθεν *the barbarians proceeded against Greece with the purpose of enslaving it* 1. 18, συνεκάλεσαν ἀπὸ τῶν πόλεων ἁπᾱσῶν ἀκουσομένους (2052 a) τῆς παρὰ βασιλέως ἐπιστολῆς *they summoned from all the cities men to listen to the letter from the king*

X. H. 7. 1. 39. Present: ἔπεμπον . . . λέγοντας ὅτι κτλ. *they sent men to say that,* etc. X. H. 2. 4. 37.

2066. Opposition or Concession. — οὐδὲν ἐρῶ πρὸς ταῦτα ἔχων εἰπεῖν *I will make no reply to this though I might* (speak) *do so* P. Lach. 197 c, πολλοὶ γὰρ ὄντες εὐγενεῖς εἰσιν κακοί *for many, albeit noble by birth, are ignoble* E. El. 551.

2067. Condition (negative always μή). — σὺ δὲ κλύων (= ἐὰν κλύῃς) εἴσει τάχα *but if you listen you shall soon know* Ar. Av. 1390, οὐκ ἂν δύναιο μὴ καμὼν (= εἰ μὴ κάμοις) εὐδαιμονεῖν *you cannot be happy unless you work* E. fr. 461.

2068. Any Attendant Circumstance. — συλλέξας στράτευμα ἐπολιόρκει Μίλητον *having collected an army he laid siege to Miletus* X. A. 1. 1. 7, παραγγέλλει τῷ Κλεάρχῳ λαβόντι ἥκειν ὅσον ἦν αὐτῷ στράτευμα *he gave orders to Clearchus to come with all the force he had* 1. 2. 1.

a. **ἔχων** *having*, **ἄγων** *leading*, **φέρων** *carrying* (mostly of inanimate objects), **χρώμενος** *using*, **λαβών** *taking* are used where English employs *with*. Thus, ἔχων στρατιὰν ἀφικνεῖται *he arrives with an army* T. 4. 30, βοῇ χρώμενοι *with a shout* 2. 84, ἐκέλευσε λαβόντα ἄνδρας ἐλθεῖν ὅτι πλείστους *he ordered him to come with all the men he could* (or to *take . . . and come*) X. A. 1. 1. 11.

b. In poetry participles (especially) of verbs denoting motion are often added to verbs of *giving*, *setting* to make the action more picturesque (H. 304, S. Aj. 854).

2069. The force of these circumstantial participles does not lie in the participle itself, but is derived from the context. Unless attended by some modifying adverb, the context often does not decide whether the participle has a temporal, a causal, a conditional, a concessive force, etc.; and some participles may be referred to more than one of the above classes. Thus, πατὴρ δ' ἀπειλῶν οὐκ ἔχει μέγαν φόβον (Men. fr. 454) may mean: *a father by threatening* (= *when* or *because* or *if* or *though, he threatens*) *does not excite much fear.*

GENITIVE ABSOLUTE. ACCUSATIVE ABSOLUTE

2070. Genitive Absolute. — A circumstantial participle agreeing with a genitive noun or pronoun which is not in the main construction of the sentence, stands in the genitive absolute. Like other circumstantial participles, the genitive absolute expresses time, cause, condition, concession, or simply any attendant circumstance.

a. Time: ταῦτ' ἐπράχθη Κόνωνος στρατηγοῦντος *these things were effected while Conon was in command* I. 9. 56, τούτων λεχθέντων ἀνέστησαν *this said, they rose* X. A. 3. 3. 1, Ἠϊόνα . . . Μήδων ἐχόντων πολιορκίᾳ εἷλον *they blockaded and captured Eïon which was held by the Medes* T. 1. 98.

b. Cause: τῶν σωμάτων θηλυνομένων καὶ αἱ ψυχαὶ ἀρρωστότεραι γίγνονται *by the enfeebling of the body, the spirit too is made weaker* X. O. 4. 2.

c. Opposition or Concession: καὶ μεταπεμπομένου αὐτοῦ οὐκ ἐθέλω ἐλθεῖν *even though he is sending for me, I am unwilling to go* X. A. 1. 3. 10. καίπερ is usually added (2083).

d. Condition: οἴομαι καὶ νῦν ἔτι ἐπανορθωθῆναι ἂν τὰ πράγματα τούτων γιγνομέ-

νων if these measures should be taken, I am of the opinion that even now our situation might be rectified D. 9. 76.

e. Attendant Circumstance: Κῦρος ἀνέβη ἐπὶ τὰ ὄρη οὐδενὸς κωλύοντος *Cyrus ascended the mountains without opposition* (lit. *no one hindering*) X. A. 1. 2. 22 (or *since* no one opposed him).

2071. ἑκών *willing*, ἄκων *unwilling* are properly participles and are treated as such (cp. 2117 c). Thus, ἐμοῦ οὐχ ἑκόντος *without my consent* S. Aj. 455.

a. ἄκων, ἀεκαζόμενος, ἀφρονέων, ἀελπτέων, ἀνάρμενος, ἀνομολογούμενος, ἀτίζων are the only cases in Greek showing the earlier method of negativing the participle with *alpha privative*. Elsewhere οὐ or μή is used.

2072. The genitive of the participle may stand without its noun or pronoun

a. When the noun or pronoun may easily be supplied from the context. Thus, οἱ δὲ πολέμιοι, προσιόντων (τῶν Ἑλλήνων, previously mentioned), τέως μὲν ἡσυχίαζον *the enemy, as they were approaching, for a while remained quiet* X. A. 5. 4. 16, ἐρώτᾱ, ἔφη, ὦ Κῦρε, . . . ὡς (ἐμοῦ) τἀληθῆ ἐροῦντος *put your question (said he), Cyrus, on the supposition that I will speak the truth* X. C. 3. 1. 9.

b. When the noun or pronoun may easily be supplied otherwise; here, *e.g.*, ἀνθρώπων or πρᾱγμάτων is said to be supplied grammatically. Thus, ἰόντων εἰς μάχην *when* (men) *are going into battle* X. C. 3. 3. 54, τοῦτον τὸν τρόπον πρᾱχθέντων τῆς πόλεως γίγνεται τὰ χρήματα *when* (things) *have happened in this way, the property belongs to the State* D. 24. 12; and in ὕοντος (Διός, 934 a) πολλῷ *when it was raining hard* X. H. 1. 1. 16. Quasi-impersonal verbs (933) thus take the genitive rather than the accusative absolute: οὕτως ἔχοντος *in this state of things* P. R. 381 c, influenced by οὕτως ἐχόντων X. A. 3. 1. 40.

c. When a subordinate clause with ὅτι follows upon the participle in the passive. Thus, ἐσαγγελθέντων ὅτι Φοίνισσαι νῆες ἐπ' αὐτοὺς πλέουσιν *it having been announced that Phoenician ships were sailing against them* T. 1. 116, δηλωθέντος ὅτι ἐν ταῖς ναυσὶ τῶν Ἑλλήνων τὰ πράγματα ἐγένετο *it having been shown that the salvation of the Greeks depended on their navy* 1. 74. The plural is used when the subject of the subordinate clause is plural, or when several circumstances are mentioned.

2073. Exceptionally, the subject of the genitive absolute is the same as that of the main clause. The effect of this irregular construction is to emphasize the idea contained in the genitive absolute. Thus, βοηθησάντων ὑμῶν προθύμως πόλιν προσλήψεσθε ναυτικὸν ἔχουσαν μέγα *if you assist us heartily, you will gain to your cause a State having a large navy* T. 3. 13. The genitive absolute usually precedes the main verb.

a. The genitive absolute may be used where the grammatical construction demands the dative. Thus, διαβεβηκότος Περικλέους . . . ἠγγέλθη αὐτῷ ὅτι Μέγαρα ἀφέστηκε *when Pericles had already crossed over, news was brought to him that Megara had revolted* T. 1. 114 (in Latin: *Pericli iam transgresso nuntiatum est*).

b. The subject of the genitive absolute may be identical with the object of the leading verb: ἦλθον ἐπὶ τὴν Ἐπίδαυρον ὡς ἐρήμου οὔσης . . . αἱρήσοντες *they came against Epidaurus expecting to capture it undefended* T. 5. 56.

2074. Observe that the genitive absolute differs from the Latin ablative absolute herein: 1. The subject need not be expressed (2072). 2. The subject *may* appear in the leading clause (2073 a). 3. With a substantive the participle ὤν is always added in prose, whereas Latin has to omit the participle. Thus, παίδων ὄντων ἡμῶν *nobis pueris* P. S. 173 a. On ἐμοῦ ἄκοντος *me invito*, see 2071. 4. Because it has a present participle passive and an aorist and perfect participle active, Greek can use the genitive absolute where Latin, through lack of a past participle active, has to use a clause with *dum*, *cum*, etc. Thus, ὅλης τῆς πόλεως ἐν τοῖς πολεμικοῖς κινδύνοις ἐπιτρεπομένης τῷ στρατηγῷ *cum bellicis in periculis universa respublica imperatori committatur* X. M. 3. 1. 3, τοῦ παιδὸς γελάσαντος *cum puer risisset*. Latin uses the absolute case more frequently than Greek because it employs the perfect participle passive where Greek uses the aorist participle active. Thus, Κῦρος συγκαλέσᾱς τοὺς στρατηγοὺς εἶπεν *Cyrus, convocatis ducibus, dixit* X. A. 1. 4. 8.

2075. The genitive absolute took its rise from such cases as Σαρπήδοντι δ' ἄχος γένετο Γλαύκου ἀπιόντος *but sorrow came on Sarpedon for Glaucus — departing* M 392. The genitive, here properly dependent on ἄχος γένετο, ceased to be felt as dependent on the governing expression, and was extended, as a distinct construction, to cases in which the governing expression did not take the genitive. Cp. the development of the accusative with the infinitive (1981).

2076. Accusative Absolute. — A participle stands in the accusative absolute, instead of the genitive, when it is impersonal, or has an infinitive as its subject (as under C). When impersonal, such participles have no apparent grammatical connection with the rest of the sentence. (Historically, these forms could also be nominative absolutes.)

A. Impersonal verbs: δέον, ἐξόν, μετόν, παρόν, προσῆκον, μέλον, μεταμέλον, παρέχον, παρασχόν, τυχόν, δοκοῦν, δόξαν, or δόξαντα (ταῦτα), γενόμενον ἐπ' ἐμοί *as it was in my power*.

οὐδεὶς τὸ μεῖζον κακὸν αἱρήσεται ἐξὸν τὸ ἔλᾱττον (αἱρεῖσθαι) *no one will choose the greater evil when it is possible to choose the less* P. Pr. 358 d, ἧς (βουλῆς) νῦν ἀξιοῖ τυχεῖν οὐ μετὸν αὐτῷ *to which he now claims admission though he has no right* L. 31. 32, δῆλον γὰρ ὅτι οἶσθα μέλον γέ σοι *for of course you know because it concerns you* P. A. 24 d, μετεμέλοντο ὅτι μετὰ τὰ ἐν Πύλῳ, καλῶς παρασχόν, οὐ ξυνέβησαν *they repented that after what had occurred at Pylos, although a favourable occasion had presented itself, they had not come to terms* T. 5. 14. Cp. 2086 d, 2087.

N. — Apart from δόξαν, τυχόν, the accusative absolute of the aorist participle of impersonal verbs is very rare.

B. Passive participles used impersonally: γεγραμμένον, δεδογμένον, εἰρημένον, προσταχθέν, προστεταγμένον. Cp. Eng. *granted this is so, this done, which said.*

εἰρημένον δ' αὐταῖς ἀπαντᾶν ἐνθάδε . . . εὕδουσι κοὐχ ἥκουσιν *though it was told them to meet here, they sleep and have not come* Ar. Lys. 13, προσταχθέν μοι ὑπὸ τοῦ δήμου Μένωνα ἄγειν εἰς Ἑλλήσποντον *a command having been given (it having been commanded) me by the people to convey Menon to the Hellespont* D. 50. 12.

N. — The aorist participle passive is rarely used absolutely: ἀμεληθέν, ἀπορρηθέν, καταχειροτονηθέν, κυρωθέν, ὁρισθέν, περανθέν, προσταχθέν, χρησθέν.

C. Adjectives with ὄν: ἄδηλον ὄν, δυνατὸν ὄν, ἀδύνατον ὄν, αἰσχρὸν ὄν, καλὸν ὄν, χρεών (χρεώ + ὄν), etc.

σὲ οὐχὶ ἐσώσαμεν . . . οἷόν τε ὂν καὶ δυνατόν *we did not rescue you although it was both feasible and possible* P. Cr. 46 a, ὡς οὐκ ἀναγκαῖον (ὂν) τὸ κλέπτειν, αἰτιᾷ τὸν κλέπτοντα *on the ground that stealing is not necessary you accuse the thief* X. C. 5. 1. 13.

2077. The impersonal character of the above expressions would not be shown by the genitive since the participle in that case marks a distinction between masculine (neuter) and feminine. The accusative absolute, which occurs first in Herodotus and the Attic prose writers of the fifth century, is probably in its origin an internal accusative, developed, at least in part, by way of apposition (991–994), the neuter of a participle or of an adjective standing in apposition to an idea in the leading clause. Thus, προσταχθὲν αὐτοῖς οὐκ ἐτόλμησαν εἰσαγαγεῖν (Is. 1. 22) *they did not dare to bring* him *in* — a duty *that was enjoined* (*although it was enjoined*) *upon them*. Cp. πείθει δ' Ὀρέστην μητέρα . . . κτεῖναι, πρὸς οὐχ ἅπαντας εὔκλειαν φέρον *he persuaded Orestes to slay his mother*, a deed *that brings not glory in the eyes of all* E. Or. 30.

2078. The participle of a *personal* verb may be used absolutely if it is preceded by ὡς or ὥσπερ. Thus, ηὔχετο πρὸς τοὺς θεοὺς τἀγαθὰ διδόναι, ὡς τοὺς θεοὺς κάλλιστα εἰδότας ὁποῖα ἀγαθά ἐστι (Socrates) *prayed to the gods that they would give him good things, in the belief that the gods know best what sort of things are good* X. M. 1. 3. 2, σιωπῇ ἐδείπνουν, ὥσπερ τοῦτο προστεταγμένον αὐτοῖς *they were supping in silence just as if this had been enjoined upon them* X. S. 1. 11.

a. Cases without ὡς or ὥσπερ are rare. Thus, δόξαντα ὑμῖν ταῦτα εἵλεσθε ἄνδρας εἴκοσι *on reaching this conclusion you chose twenty men* And. 1. 81; cp. δόξαν ταῦτα X. A. 4. 1. 13 (by analogy to ἔδοξε ταῦτα) and δοξάντων τούτων X. H. 1. 7. 30. Neuter participles so used come chiefly from impersonal verbs, but T. 4. 125 has κυρωθὲν οὐδὲν οἱ Μακεδόνες ἐχώρουν ἐπ' οἴκου *the Macedonians proceeded homewards, nothing having been accomplished.* The neuter subject is a pronoun, very rarely a substantive (I. 5. 12).

ADVERBS USED IN CONNECTION WITH CIRCUMSTANTIAL PARTICIPLES

2079. Adverbs are often used to set forth clearly the relations of time, manner, cause, concession, etc., that are implied in the participle. They occur also with the genitive and accusative absolute. These adverbs modify either the principal verb or the participle itself.

ADVERBIAL ADJUNCTS OF THE PRINCIPAL VERB

2080. The adverbs **ἔπειτα** *thereupon*, **τότε**, **εἶτα** (less often ἐνταῦθα) *then*, **ἤδη** *already*, **οὕτω** *so*, when used with the verb of the sentence which contains a temporal participle, emphasize the temporal relation: (ὑμῶν δέομαι) ἀκροᾱσαμένους διὰ τέλους τῆς ἀπολογίᾱς τότε ἤδη ψηφίζεσθαι κτλ. (*I beg you*) *when you have heard my defence to the end, then and not till then to vote*, etc. And. 1. 9, ὑπὲρ μεγίστων καὶ καλλίστων κινδῡνεύσαντες οὕτω τὸν βίον ἐτελεύτησαν *they incurred danger for a great and noble cause, and so ended their lives* L. 2. 79.

2081. **ἅμα** *at the same time*, **αὐτίκα** *immediately*, **εὐθύς** *straightway*, **μεταξύ** *between, in the midst*, though strictly modifying the main verb, are often placed close to a temporal participle which they modify *in sense*: ἅμα ταῦτ' εἰπὼν ἀνέστη *saying this, he rose* X. A. 3. 1. 47, τῷ δεξιῷ κέρᾳ τῶν Ἀθηναίων εὐθὺς ἀποβεβηκότι . . . ἐπέκειντο *they fell upon the right wing of the Athenians as soon as it had disembarked* (lit. *upon the right wing when it had disembarked*) T. 4. 43, ἐξαναστάντες μεταξὺ δειπνοῦντες *getting up in the middle of supper* D. 18. 169, πολλαχοῦ με ἐπέσχε λέγοντα μεταξύ *it often checked me when the words were on my lips* (in the very act of speaking) P. A. 40 b.

2082. A participle implying opposition or concession (2066) may have its meaning rendered explicit by **ὅμως** *yet, nevertheless* (with or without καίπερ, 2083), **εἶτα** *then* or **ἔπειτα** *afterwards* to express censure or surprise (*then, for all that*): σὺν σοὶ ὅμως καὶ ἐν τῇ πολεμίᾳ ὄντες θαρροῦμεν *with you, though we are in the enemies' country, nevertheless we have no fear* X. C. 5. 1. 26, ἔπειτ' ἀπολιπὼν τοὺς θεοὺς ἐνθάδε μενεῖς; *and then, though you desert the gods, will you remain here?* Ar. Pl. 1148. ὅμως may attach itself more closely to the participle, though belonging with the principal verb: πείθου γυναιξί, καίπερ οὐ στέργων ὅμως *take the advice of women none the less though thou likest it not* A. Sept. 712.

2083. With participles of opposition or concession (2066): **καίπερ** *although*, **καί** (infrequent), *although* **καὶ ταῦτα** (947) *and that too*. Thus, συμβουλεύω σοι καίπερ νεώτερος ὤν *I give you advice though I am your junior* X. C. 4. 5. 32, ἀποπλεῖ οἴκαδε καίπερ μέσου χειμῶνος ὄντος *he sailed off home though it was midwinter* X. Ag. 2. 31, Κλέωνος καίπερ μανιώδης οὖσα ἡ ὑπόσχεσις ἀπέβη *Cleon's promise, insane though it was, was fulfilled* T. 4. 39, καὶ δοῦλος ὢν γὰρ τίμιος πλουτῶν ἀνήρ *for, slave though he be, the man of wealth is held in esteem* E. fr. 142, ἀδικεῖς ὅτι ἄνδρα ἡμῖν τὸν σπουδαιότατον διαφθείρεις γελᾶν ἀναπείθων, καὶ ταῦτα οὕτω πολέμιον ὄντα τῷ γέλωτι *you do wrong in that you corrupt the most earnest man we have by tempting him to laugh, and that though he is such an enemy to laughter* X. C. 2. 2. 16. On καίτοι see 2893 b.

a. In Homer the parts of καίπερ are often separated by the participle or an emphatic word connected with it: καὶ ἀχνύμενοί περ *although distressed* M 178. πέρ may stand alone without καί: ἀνάσχεο κηδομένη περ *bear up, though vexed* A 586. Both uses occur in tragedy. The part. with πέρ is not always concessive.

b. In a negative sentence, **οὐδέ** (**μηδέ**), with or without πέρ, takes the place of καί; as γυναικὶ πείθου μηδὲ τἀληθῆ κλύων *listen to a woman, though thou hearest not the truth* E. fr. 440.

2084. With participles of cause (2064): **οὕτως, διὰ τοῦτο (ταῦτα), ἐκ τούτου.** Thus, ἀνελόμενοι τὰ ναυάγια . . . καὶ ὅτι αὐτοῖς . . . οὐκ ἀντεπέπλεον, διὰ ταῦτα τροπαῖον ἔστησαν *because they had picked up the wrecks and because they* (the enemy) *did not sail against them, (for this reason) they set up a trophy* T. 1. 54.

2085. With participles of cause (2064): **ἅτε** (ἅτε δή), **οἷα** or **οἷον** (οἷον δή) *inasmuch as*, state the cause as a fact on the authority of the speaker or writer. Thus, ὁ Κῦρος, ἅτε παῖς ὤν, . . . ἥδετο τῇ στολῇ *Cyrus, inasmuch as he was a child, was pleased with the robe* X. C. 1. 3. 3, ἥκομεν ἑσπέρᾱς ἀπὸ τοῦ στρατοπέδου, *οἷον δὲ διὰ χρόνου ἀφῖγμένος ᾖα ἐπὶ τὰς συνήθεις διατριβάς I returned in the evening from the camp, and, as I arrived after a long absence, I proceeded to my accustomed haunts* P. Charm. 153 a, *οἷα δὴ ἀπιόντων πρὸς δεῖπνον . . . τῶν πελταστῶν, . . . ἐπελαύνουσι inasmuch as the peltasts were going off to supper, they rode against them* X. H. 5. 4. 39. *ὥστε* has the same force in Hdt.

2086. With participles of cause or purpose, etc. (2064, 2065): **ὡς**. This particle sets forth the ground of belief on which the agent acts, and denotes the thought, assertion, real or presumed intention, in the mind of the subject of the principal verb or of some other person mentioned prominently in the sentence, without implicating the speaker or writer.

a. Thus, *ἀπῆλθον ὡς νῑκήσαντες* may mean either *they departed under the impression that they had been victorious* (though as a matter of fact they may have been defeated) or *pretending that they had been victorious* (when they knew they had been defeated). The use of *ὡς* implies nothing as to the opinion of the speaker or writer. On the other hand *ἀπῆλθον νῑκήσαντες* means that, as a matter of fact, and on the authority of the writer, they *had* been victorious.

b. *ὡς* may be rendered *as if* (though there is nothing conditional in the Greek use, as is shown by the negative *οὐ*, not *μή*), by *in the opinion (belief) that, on the ground that, under pretence of, under the impression that, because as he said* (or *thought*); *in the hope of, with the (avowed) intention of* (with the future participle).

c. *ἐνταῦθ' ἔμενον ὡς τὸ ἄκρον κατέχοντες· οἱ δ' οὐ κατεῖχον, ἀλλὰ μαστὸς ἦν ὑπὲρ αὐτῶν there they remained in the belief that they were occupying the summit; but in fact they were not occupying it, since there was a hill above them* X. A. 4. 2. 5, *ταύτην τὴν χώρᾱν ἐπέτρεψε διαρπάσαι τοῖς Ἕλλησιν ὡς πολεμίᾱν οὖσαν he turned this country over to the Greeks to ravage on the ground that it was hostile* 1. 2. 19, *τὴν πρόφασιν ἐποιεῖτο ὡς Πῑσίδᾱς βουλόμενος ἐκβαλεῖν he made his pretence as if he wished* (i.e. *he gave as his pretext his desire*) *to expel the Pisidians* 1. 2. 1, *παρεσκευάζοντο ὡς πολεμήσοντες they made preparations to go to war* (*with the avowed intention of going to war*) T. 2. 7, *συλλαμβάνει Κῦρον ὡς ἀποκτενῶν he seized Cyrus for the purpose* (*as he declared*) *of putting him to death* X. A. 1. 1. 3, and often with the future participle. After verbs of *motion* *ὡς* is rarely used.

d. *ὡς* with the absolute participle: *οὐ δεῖ ἀθῡμεῖν ὡς οὐκ εὐτάκτων ὄντων Ἀθηναίων we must not be discouraged on the ground that the Athenians are not well disciplined* X. M. 3. 5. 20, *ἔλεγε θαρρεῖν ὡς καταστησομένων τούτων ἐς τὸ δέον he bade him be of good cheer in the assurance that this would arrange itself in the right way* X. A. 1. 3. 8, *ὡς ἐξὸν ἤδη ποιεῖν αὐτοῖς ὅ τι βούλοιντο, πολλοὺς ἀπέκτεινον in the belief that it was already in their power to do what they pleased, they put many to death* X. H. 2. 3. 21. Cp. also 2078, and 2122.

2087. **ὥσπερ** *as, just as, as it were*, an adverb of comparison, denotes that the action of the main verb is compared with an assumed case. Thus, *κατακείμεθ' ὥσπερ ἐξὸν ἡσυχίᾱν ἄγειν we lie inactive just as if it were possible to take one's ease* X. A. 3. 1. 3, *ὠρχοῦντο . . . ὥσπερ ἐπιδεικνύμενοι they danced as it were making an exhibition* 5. 4. 34, *οἱ δὲ ὡς ἤκουσαν, ὥσπερ συὸς ἀγρίου φανέντος, ἵενται ἐπ' αὐτόν but when they heard him, just as though a wild boar had appeared, they rushed against him* 5. 7. 24. Cp. 2078.

a. Where a condition is meant, we have **ὥσπερ ἂν εἰ** (ὡσπερανεί). Cp. 2480 a.

b. Hom. uses ὥς τε, ὡς εἰ, ὡς εἴ τε like ὥσπερ or ὡς. ὡς εἰ, ὡς εἴ τε occur also in tragedy, and do not have a conditional force. Thus, ὀλοφῡρόμενοι ὡς εἰ θανατόνδε κιόντα *bewailing him as if he were going to death* Ω 328. Cp. 2481.

THE SUPPLEMENTARY PARTICIPLE

2088. The supplementary participle completes the idea of the verb by showing that to which its action relates.

2089. The supplementary participle agrees either with the subject or with the object of the main verb; with the subject when the verb is intransitive or passive, with the object when the verb is transitive.

οὔποτ' ἐπαυόμην ἡμᾶς οἰκτίρων *I never ceased pitying ourselves* X. A. 3. 1. 19, τοὺς πένητας ἔπαυσ' ἀδικουμένους *I put a stop to the poor being wronged* D. 18. 102, ἑώρων οὐ κατορθοῦντες καὶ τοὺς στρατιώτᾱς ἀχθομένους *they saw that they* (*themselves*) *were not succeeding and that the soldiers were indignant* T. 7. 47, ἀδικοῦντα Φίλιππον ἐξήλεγξα *I proved that Philip was acting unjustly* D. 18. 136, εὐθὺς ἐλεγχθήσεται γελοῖος ὤν *he will straightway be proved to be ridiculous* X. M. 1. 7. 2.

a. When the object is the same as the subject, it is commonly suppressed, and the participle agrees with the subject. Thus, ὁρῶ ἐξαμαρτάνων *I see that I err* E. Med. 350, ἴσθι ἀνόητος ὤν *know that you are a fool* X. A. 2. 1. 13, οὐκ αἰσθάνεσθε ἐξαπατώμενοι; *do you not perceive that you are being deceived?* X. H. 7. 1. 12, ἐδήλωσε τῶν νόμων καταφρονῶν *he showed that he despised the laws* And. 4. 14.

b. For the sake of emphasis or contrast (and to secure greater symmetry) the object may be expressed by the reflexive pronoun. Thus, οἶδα ἐμαυτὸν δικαίως κεχρημένον αὐτοῖς *I know that I have presented my case honestly* I. 15. 321, δεῖξον οὐ πεποιηκότα ταῦτα σαυτόν *show that you did not do this yourself* D. 22. 29, ἀμφότερ' οὖν οἶδε, καὶ αὐτὸν ὑμῖν ἐπιβουλεύοντα, καὶ ὑμᾶς αἰσθανομένους *now he knows both—that he is himself plotting against you and that you are aware of it* D. 6. 18. Observe ἐλάνθανον αὐτοὺς ἐπὶ τῷ λόφῳ γενόμενοι (agreeing with the subject) *without knowing it they found themselves on the hill* X. A. 6. 3. 22. On the use with σύνοιδα, see 2108.

c. **ἔοικα** (the personal use for the impersonal ἔοικε, 1983) usually takes the participle in the dative; as, ἔοικας ὀκνοῦντι λέγειν *you seem reluctant to speak* P. R. 414 c; but also in the nominative (see 2133).

2090. Many verbs supplementing their meaning by the participle admit of the construction with the infinitive (often with a difference of meaning; see 2123 ff.) or with a substantive clause with ὅτι or ὡς.

2091. The present or perfect participle is often used as a simple predicate adjective, especially with εἰμί and γίγνομαι. The aorist participle is chiefly poetic.

ἦσαν ἀπιστοῦντές τινες Φιλίππῳ *there were some who distrusted Philip* D. 19. 53, (Κλέαρχος) φιλοκίνδῡνός τ' ἦν καὶ ἡμέρᾱς καὶ νυκτὸς ἄγων ἐπὶ τοὺς πολεμίους Clearchus *was both fond of danger and by day and by night led* his men *against the enemy* X. A. 2. 6. 7, ἐγὼ τὸ πρᾶγμ' εἰμὶ τοῦθ' ὁ δεδρᾱκώς *I am the one who has done this deed* D. 21. 104, ἢ τοῦτο οὐκ ἔστι γιγνόμενον παρ' ἡμῖν; *or is not this something that takes place in us?* P. Phil. 39 c. So with adjectivized participles (1857), as συμφέρον ἦν τῇ πόλει *it was advantageous to the State* D. 19. 75. So with ὑπάρχω *am, am assumed* (D. 18. 228).

a. Here the participle has the article when it designates the subject itself (third example; cp. 1152). But the article is not used when the participle marks a class in which the subject is included.

2092. The supplementary participle after certain verbs represents a dependent statement.

In ἤκουσε Κῦρον ἐν Κιλικίᾳ ὄντα *he heard that Cyrus was in Cilicia* ὄντα stands for ἐστί, what was heard being "Κῦρος ἐν Κιλικίᾳ ἐστί." This is shown by the fact that the sentence might have been, according to the principles of *indirect discourse*, ἤκουσεν ὅτι Κῦρος ἐν Κιλικίᾳ εἴη (or ἐστί, 2615). With verbs not introducing indirect discourse, however, there is no such indirect statement; as in ἐπαύσαντο μαχόμενοι *they ceased fighting* L. 23. 9.

2093. Accordingly, from this point of view, the uses of the supplementary participle are two: (1) not in indirect discourse, and (2) in indirect discourse.

a. Some verbs take the participle *either* in indirect discourse *or* not in indirect discourse (2112). It is sometimes impossible to decide whether a participle stands in indirect discourse or not (2113); and the difference, especially after verbs of *perceiving* (2112 a, b), may be of no great importance to the sense.

THE SUPPLEMENTARY PARTICIPLE NOT IN INDIRECT DISCOURSE

2094. The supplementary participle not in indirect discourse is often like an object infinitive, the tenses denoting only stage of action and not difference of time (cp. 1850). Thus, compare παύομέν σε λέγοντα *we stop you from speaking* (of continued action) with κωλῡ́ομέν σε λέγειν *we prevent you from speaking* (also of continued action).

2095. With verbs denoting *being* in some modified way (2096–2097).

2096. **τυγχάνω** (poet. κυρῶ) *happen, am just now*, **λανθάνω** *escape the notice of, am secretly*, **φθάνω** *anticipate, am beforehand.*

a. With these verbs the participle contains the main idea, and is often represented in translation by the finite verb with an adverbial phrase; thus, παρὼν ἐτύγχανε *he happened to be there*, or *he was there by chance* X. A. 1. 1. 2.

b. The action of φθάνω and λανθάνω usually coincides with that of the supplementary participle (present with present, aorist with aorist). But the aorist of a finite verb is occasionally followed by the present participle when it is necessary to mark an action or a state as continuing. οὐκ ἔλαθον is like an imperfect and may take the present participle. The aorist of τυγχάνω very often takes the present participle. With a present or imperfect of τυγχάνω, λανθάνω, φθάνω, the (rare) aorist participle refers to an action or state anterior to that of the present or imperfect. Many of the cases of the present of τυγχάνω with the aorist participle are historical presents; and in some cases the aorist participle is used for the perfect. With other tenses than present or imperfect, an aorist participle with these verbs refers to an action or state coincident in time (cp. 1873).

c. τυγχάνω often loses the idea of *chance*, and denotes mere coincidence in time (*I am just now, I was just then*) or simply *I am* (*was*).

d. Examples. **τυγχάνω**: προξενῶν τυγχάνω *I happen to be proxenus* D. 52. 5, ἄριστα τυγχάνουσι πράξαντες *they happen to have fared the best* I. 4. 103, ἐτύγχανον λέγων *I was just saying* X. A. 3. 2. 10, ὅστις ἀντειπών γε ἐτύγχανε καὶ γνώμην ἀποδεδειγμένος *who happened to have spoken in opposition and to have declared his opinion* L. 12. 27, ἔτυχον καθήμενος ἐνταῦθα *I was, by chance, sitting there* P. Eu. 272 e. **λανθάνω**: φονέα τοῦ παιδὸς ἐλάνθανε βόσκων *he entertained the murderer of his son without knowing it* (*it escaped his notice that he was*, etc.) Hdt. 1. 44, ἔλαθον ἐσελθόντες *they got in secretly* T. 2. 2, οὐκ ἔλαθες ἀποδιδράσκων *you did not escape notice in attempting to escape* (*your attempt at escape did not escape notice*) P. R. 457 e, ἔλαθεν ἀποδρᾱ́ς *he escaped without being noticed* X. H. 1. 3. 22, λήσετε πάνθ' ὑπομείναντες *you will submit to every possible calamity ere you are aware* D. 6. 27. **φθάνω**: οὐ φθάνει ἐξαγόμενος ὁ ἵππος κτλ. *the horse is no sooner led out*, etc. X. Eq. 5. 10, φθάνουσιν (hist. pres.) ἐπὶ τῷ ἄκρῳ γενόμενοι τοὺς πολεμίους *they anticipated the enemy in getting upon the summit* (*they got to the summit before the enemy*) X. A. 3. 4. 49, οὐκ ἔφθασαν πυθόμενοι τὸν πόλεμον καὶ ἧκον *scarcely had they heard of the war when they came* I. 4. 86, ὁπότεροι φθήσονται τὴν πόλιν ἀγαθόν τι ποιήσαντες *which party shall anticipate* the other *in doing some service to the State* I. 4. 79. Without regard to its mood, the present and imperfect of φθάνω are followed by the present participle (rarely by the perfect); the future, aorist, and historical present are followed by the aorist participle.

e. οὐκ ἂν φθάνοις (φθάνοιτε) with the participle is used in urgent, but polite, exhortations, as οὐκ ἂν φθάνοις λέγων *the sooner you speak the better* (i.e. *speak at once*) X. M. 2. 3. 11. Strictly this is equivalent to *you would not be anticipating* (my wish or your duty), *if you should speak*. λέγε φθάσᾱς might be said according to 2061.

f. λανθάνω and φθάνω (rarely τυγχάνω) may appear in the participle, thus reversing the ordinary construction, as διαλαθὼν ἐσέρχεται ἐς τὴν Μῑτυλήνην *he entered Mitylene secretly* T. 3. 25, φθάνοντες ἤδη δῃοῦμεν τὴν ἐκείνων γῆν *we got the start of them by ravaging* t h e i r *territory* X. C. 3. 3. 18. Cp. also 2062 a. The present participle is rare.

2097. **διάγω, διαγίγνομαι, διατελῶ, διαμένω** *continue, keep on, am continually.*

διάγουσι μανθάνοντες *they are continually* (*they spend their time in*) *learning* X. C. 1. 2. 6, κρέᾱ ἐσθίοντες οἱ στρατιῶται διεγίγνοντο *the soldiers kept eating meat* X. A. 1. 5. 6, διατελεῖ μῑσῶν *he continues to hate* X. C. 5. 4. 35, θρηνοῦντες διετελοῦμεν *we lamented continually* I. 19. 27, ὁ ἥλιος λαμπρότατος ὢν διαμένει *the sun continues to be most brilliant* X. M. 4. 7. 7.

2098. With verbs signifying *to begin, cease, endure, grow weary of* an action.

ἄρχομαι *begin* (2128), **παύω** *cause to cease*, **παύομαι, λήγω** *cease*, **ἀπολείπω, διαλείπω, ἐπιλείπω** *leave off*, **ἐλλείπω** *fail*, **ἀνέχομαι** *support*, **καρτερῶ** *endure* (do something patiently), **κάμνω** *grow weary*, **ἀπαγορεύω** *give up*, etc.

ἄρξομαι ἀπὸ τῆς ἰατρικῆς λέγων *I will begin my speech with the healing art* P. S. 186 b, παύσω τοῦτο γιγνόμενον *I will put a stop to this happening* P. G. 523 c, παῦσαι λέγουσα lit. *stop talking* E. Hipp. 706, οὐπώποτε διέλειπον ζητῶν *I never left off seeking* X. Ap. 16, ἀνέχου πάσχων *support thy sufferings* E. fr. 1090, οὔτε τότ' ἐκαρτέρουν ἀκούων κτλ. *neither then did I listen patiently*, etc., Aes. 3. 118, μὴ κάμῃς φίλον ἄνδρα εὐεργετῶν *do not grow weary of doing good to your friend* P. G. 470 c, ἀπείρηκα . . . τὰ ὅπλα φέρων καὶ ἐν τάξει ἰὼν καὶ φυλακᾱ́ς φυλάττων καὶ μαχόμενος *I am tired of carrying my arms and going in the ranks and mounting guard and fighting* X. A. 5. 1. 2.

a. Verbs signifying *to support*, *endure* ordinarily take the present participle; but there are cases of the complexive aorist in reference to acts to which one must submit despite all resistance: so, with ἀνέχομαι, X. C. 6. 2. 18, D. 41. 1; cp. οὐκ ἠνέσχεσθε ἀκούσαντες L. 13. 8 (Hdt. 5. 89) with οὐκ ἠνείχοντο ἀκούοντες X. H. 6. 5. 49. The aorist participle seems not to be used with the object of ἀνέχομαι.

2099. With some verbs of *coming* and *going* the participle specifies the manner of coming and going, and contains the main idea.

βῆ φεύγων *he took to flight* (*went fleeing*) B 665, οἴχονται διώκοντες *they have gone in pursuit* X. A. 1. 10. 5, ᾠχόμην ἀναγόμενος *I put to sea* D. 50. 12, οἴχεται θανών *he is dead and gone* S. Ph. 414, οὐ τοῦτο λέξων ἔρχομαι *I am not going to say this* X. Ag. 2. 7.

2100. With verbs of emotion (*rejoicing* and *grieving*) the participle often denotes *cause* (cp. 2048).

χαίρω, ἥδομαι, τέρπομαι, γέγηθα (poet.) *am pleased, take pleasure*, **ἀγαπῶ, στέργω** *am content*, **ἀγανακτῶ, ἄχθομαι, χαλεπῶς φέρω** *am vexed, displeased*, **ῥᾳδίως φέρω** *make light of*, **λῡποῦμαι** *grieve*, **ὀργίζομαι** *am angry*, **αἰσχῡ́νομαι, αἰδοῦμαι** *am ashamed* (2126), **μεταμέλομαι, μεταμέλει μοι** *repent*. (Verbs of emotion also take ὅτι or ὡς, by which construction the object is simply stated; with the participle the connection is closer).

χαίρω διαλεγόμενος τοῖς σφόδρα πρεσβύταις *I like to converse with very old men* P. R. 328 d, ὅστις ἥδεται λέγων ἀεί, λέληθεν αὑτὸν τοῖς ξυνοῦσιν ὢν βαρύς *he who likes to be always talking is a bore to his companions without knowing it* S. fr. 99, οὐκ ἀγαπῶ ζῶν ἐπὶ τούτοις *I am not content to live on these conditions* I. 12. 8, οὐκ ἂν ἀχθοίμην μανθάνων *I should not be annoyed at learning* P. Lach. 189 a, χαλεπῶς ἔφερον οἰκίᾱς κατελείποντες *they took it hard at abandoning their homes* T. 2. 16, ἀδικούμενοι οἱ ἄνθρωποι μᾶλλον ὀργίζονται ἢ βιαζόμενοι *men are more angered at being the victims of injustice than of compulsion* 1. 77, οὐ γὰρ αἰσχύνομαι μανθάνων *for I am not ashamed to learn* P. Hipp. Min. 372 c, μετεμέλοντο τᾱ̀ς σπονδᾱ̀ς οὐ δεξάμενοι *they repented not having accepted the truce* T. 4. 27, οὔ μοι μεταμέλει οὕτως ἀπολογησαμένῳ *I do not repent having made such a defence* P. A. 38 e.

a. The participle agrees with the case of the person in regard to whom the emotion is manifested: ἀκούοντες χαίρουσιν ἐξεταζομένοις τοῖς οἰομένοις μὲν εἶναι σοφοῖς, οὖσι δ' οὔ *they like to hear the examination of those who pretend to be wise, but are not so in reality* P. A. 33 c. This construction must be distinguished from that occurring in *poetry*, whereby verbs like χαίρω and ἄχθομαι (which commonly take the dative) often admit the accusative and the participle: τοὺς γὰρ εὐσεβεῖς θεοὶ θνῄσκοντας οὐ χαίρουσι *for the gods do not rejoice at the death of the righteous* E. Hipp. 1339.

b. So with verbs meaning *to satiate oneself*: ὑπισχνούμενος οὐκ ἐνεπίμπλασο *you could not satiate yourself with promises* X. A. 7. 7. 46.

2101. With verbs signifying *to do well* or *ill, to surpass* or *be inferior*, the participle specifies the *manner* or *that in which the action of the verb consists* (cp. 2048, 2062). So with καλῶς (εὖ) ποιῶ, ἀδικῶ, ἁμαρτάνω; νῑκῶ, κρατῶ, περιγίγνομαι, ἡττῶμαι, λείπομαι.

εὖ γ' ἐποίησας ἀναμνήσᾱς με *you did well in reminding me* P. Ph. 60 c (cp. 1872 c. 2), καλῶς ἐποίησεν οὕτως τελευτήσᾱς τὸν βίον *he did well in ending his life thus* L. 28. 8, ὀνήσεσθε ἀκούοντες *you will profit by hearing* P. A. 30 c, ἀδικεῖτε πολέμου ἄρχοντες (1734. 5) *you do wrong in being the aggressors in the war* T. 1. 53, οὐχ ἡττησόμεθα εὖ ποιοῦντες *we shall not be outdone in well-doing* X. A. 2. 3. 23. Here belongs ἐμοὶ χαρίζου ἀποκρῑνάμενος *do me the favour to reply* (*gratify me by replying*) P. R. 338 a.

2102. With πειρῶμαι *try*, πολὺς ἔγκειμαι *am urgent*, πάντα ποιῶ *do everything*, the participle is rare in Attic; more common in Hdt. with πειρῶμαι, πολλὸς ἔγκειμαι, πολλός εἰμι *am urgent*, etc.

πειρᾱσόμεθα ἐλέγχοντες *I shall try to prove* Ant. 2. γ. 1; πολλὸς ἦν λισσόμενος *he begged often and urgently* Hdt. 9. 91.

2103. With περιορῶ (and sometimes with ἐφορῶ, εἰσορῶ, προΐεμαι), signifying *overlook, allow*. (But not with ἐῶ.) Cp. 2141.

μείζω γιγνόμενον τὸν ἄνθρωπον περιορῶμεν *we allow the man to grow greater* (*we look with indifference on his growing power*) D. 9. 29, οὐ περιεῖδον ἐμαυτὸν ἄδοξον γενόμενον *I did not suffer myself to become obscure* I. 12. 11, ἔτλησαν ἐπιδεῖν . . . ἐρήμην μὲν τὴν πόλιν γενομένην, τὴν δὲ χώρᾱν πορθουμένην *they had the courage to look calmly on their city made desolate and their country being ravaged* I. 4. 96. So even with the uncompounded ὁρῶ in poetry. (With the *infinitive* περιορῶ no longer connotes perception and simply equals ἐῶ *allow*.)

2104. With some impersonal expressions taking the dative, such as those signifying the advantage or consequence of an action (*it is fitting, profitable, good*, etc.), and those implying *confidence* or *fear*. (The personal construction is often preferred.)

ἐπηρώτων τὸν θεόν, εἰ (αὐτοῖς) πολεμοῦσιν ἄμεινον ἔσται *they asked the god whether it would be better for them to make war* T. 1. 118, εἰ τόδ' αὐτῷ φίλον (ἐστὶ) κεκλημένῳ *if it is pleasing to him to be called thus* A. Ag. 161. Personal: οἷς πολέμιον ἦν τὸ χωρίον κτιζόμενον *to whom the settlement of the place was a menace* T. 1. 100, οἴκοι μένων βελτίων (ἐστίν) *he is* all the *better by staying at home* D. 3. 34 (for μένειν αὐτὸν βέλτῑόν ἐστι).

2105. The participle occurs with various other verbs, such as θαμίζω *am* *wont;* συμπίπτω and συμβαίνω *happen;* ἀποδείκνῡμι, καθίζω, παρασκευάζω, meaning *render;* ἀρκῶ, ἱκανός εἰμι *am sufficient.*

On ἐμοὶ βουλομένῳ ἐστί, etc., see 1487. On ἔχω and the participle in periphrases, see 1963.

THE SUPPLEMENTARY PARTICIPLE IN INDIRECT DISCOURSE

2106. Verbs of Knowing and Showing.—After verbs signifying *to know, be ignorant of, learn* (not *learn of*), *remember, forget, show, appear, prove, acknowledge,* and *announce,* the participle represents a dependent statement, each tense having the same force as the corresponding tense of the indicative or optative with ὅτι or ὡς, the present including also the imperfect, the perfect including also the pluperfect.

Such verbs are: **οἶδα, γιγνώσκω, ἐπίσταμαι, ἐννοῶ, μανθάνω** (2136), **(οὐκ) ἀγνοῶ, μέμνημαι, ἐπιλανθάνομαι** (2134), **δηλῶ, (ἐπι) δείκνῡμι, φαίνω, ἀποφαίνω, φαίνομαι** (2143), **ἔοικα** (2089 c, 2133), **(ἐξ-)ἐλέγχω, ὁμολογῶ** (rarely), **ἀγγέλλω, ποιῶ** *represent* (2115).

οὐ γὰρ ᾔδεσαν αὐτὸν τεθνηκότα (= τέθνηκε) *for they did not know that he was dead* X. A. 1. 10. 16, ἔγνω τὴν ἐσβολὴν ἐσομένην (= ἔσται) *he knew that the invasion would take place* T. 2. 13, ὃν ὑμεῖς ἐπίστασθε ἡμᾶς προδόντα (= προὔδωκε) *you know that he betrayed us* X. A. 6. 6. 17, τίς οὕτως εὐήθης ἐστὶν ὑμῶν ὅστις ἀγνοεῖ τὸν ἐκεῖθεν πόλεμον δεῦρ' ἥξοντα (= ἥξει); *who of you is so simple-minded as not to know that the war will come hither from that quarter?* D. 1. 15, (Χερρόνησον) κατέμαθε πόλεις ἕνδεκα ἢ δώδεκα ἔχουσαν (= ἔχει) *he learned that Chersonesus contained eleven or twelve cities* X. H. 3. 2. 10, μέμνημαι ἀκούσᾱς (= ἤκουσα) *I remember to have heard* X. C. 1. 6. 6, μέμνημαι Κριτίᾳ τῷδε ξυνόντα σε (= ξυνῆσθα) *I remember that you were in company with Critias here* P. Charm. 156 a, ἐπιλελήσμεσθ' ἡδέως γέροντες ὄντες (= ἐσμέν) *we have gladly forgotten that we are old* E. Bacch. 188, δείξω (αὐτὸν) πολλῶν θανάτων ὄντ' (= ἐστί) ἄξιον *I will show that he deserves to die many times* D. 21. 21, δειχθήσεται τοῦτο πεποιηκώς (= πεποίηκε) *he will be shown to have done this* 21. 160, τοῦτο τὸ γράμμα δηλοῖ ψευδῆ τὴν διαθήκην οὖσαν (= ἐστί) *this clause shows that the will was forged* 45. 34, ἐὰν ἀποφαίνωσι τοὺς φεύγοντας παλαὶ πονηροὺς ὄντας (= εἰσί) *if they show that the exiles were inveterate rascals* L. 30. 1, ἡ ψῡχὴ ἀθάνατος φαίνεται οὖσα (= ἐστί) *it seems that the soul is immortal* P. Ph. 107 c, ἀδικοῦντα (= ἀδικεῖ) Φίλιππον ἐξήλεγξα *I convicted Philip of acting unjustly* D. 18. 136, ῥᾳδίως ἐλεγχθήσεται ψευδόμενος (= ψεύδεται) *he will easily be convicted of lying* 27. 19, ὁμολογούμεθα ἐλθόντες (= ἤλθομεν) *I acknowledge that I came* L. 4. 7, αὐτῷ Κῦρον ἐπιστρατεύοντα (= ἐπιστρατεύει) πρῶτος ἤγγειλα *I was the first to announce that Cyrus was taking the field against him* X. A. 2. 3. 19.

a. Except with ἀγγέλλω *announce* (*what is certain*), verbs of *saying* or *thinking* rarely take the participle in prose, *e.g.* πᾶσι ταῦτα δεδογμένα ἡμῖν νόμιζε (= εὖ ἴσθι) *think that this is our unanimous opinion* P. R. 450 a.

2107. The personal constructions **δῆλός εἰμι, φανερός εἰμι** *I am plainly* (impersonal δῆλόν and φανερόν ἐστιν ὅτι) are followed by a dependent statement in the participle. Thus, δῆλος ἦν οἰόμενος (= δῆλον ἦν ὅτι οἴοιτο) *it was clear that he thought* X. A. 2. 5. 27, θύων φανερὸς ἦν πολλάκις (= φανερὸν ἦν ὅτι θύοι) *it was* *evident that he often sacrificed* X. M. 1. 1. 2, ἀνιāθεὶς δῆλος ἦν (= δῆλον ἦν ὅτι ἀνιāθείη) *he showed his dissatisfaction* X. C. 2. 2. 3.

2108. The participle with **σύνοιδα** or **συγγιγνώσκω** *am conscious*, accompanied by the dative of the reflexive pronoun, may stand either in the nominative agreeing with the subject, or in the dative agreeing with the reflexive. Thus, συνειδὼς αὐτὸς αὑτῷ ἔργον εἰργασμένος *conscious* (to himself) *that he had done the deed* Ant. 6. 5, ἐμαυτῷ ξυνῄδη οὐδὲν ἐπισταμένῳ *I was conscious of knowing nothing* P. A. 22 c.

a. When the subject is not the same as the object, the latter, with the participle, may stand in the dative, or (rarely) in the accusative. Thus, ξυνίσᾱσι Μελήτῳ μὲν ψευδομένῳ, ἐμοὶ δὲ ἀληθεύοντι *they know as well as Meletus that he is lying, and* (as well as I do) *that I am speaking the truth* P. A. 34 b, συνειδὼς τῶν ἀθλημάτων δούλους μετέχοντας *knowing that slaves participate in the contests* D. 61. 23. (The force of σύν at times almost disappears.)

2109. The use of the participle to represent a dependent statement comes from its circumstantial use. Thus, in οὐ γὰρ ᾔδεσαν αὐτὸν τεθνηκότα (2106), τεθνηκότα agrees with the object of ᾔδεσαν; and from *they did not know him as dead* the thought passes into *they did not know* (the fact) *that he was dead.*

CONSTRUCTION OF VERBS OF PERCEIVING AND OF FINDING

2110. Verbs of Perception. — Verbs signifying *to see, perceive, hear, learn* (i.e. *learn by inquiry, hear of*), when they denote physical (actual) perception take the participle. When they denote intellectual perception they may take the participle or ὅτι or ὡς with a finite verb. (The Homeric usage is less strict.)

2111. Such verbs are, in Attic, **ὁρῶ** *see*, **αἰσθάνομαι** *perceive*, **ἀκούω** *hear*, **πυνθάνομαι** *learn*.

2112. The participle may stand either not in indirect discourse or in indirect discourse.

a. Not in Indirect Discourse. — Here verbs of *perceiving* denote *physical* perception — the act perceived or heard of. With ἀκούω and πυνθάνομαι the participle stands in the genitive; with αἰσθάνομαι it usually stands in the accusative (as with ὁρῶ), but sometimes in the genitive. (See 1361, 1367.)

εἶδε Κλέαρχον διελαύνοντα *he saw Clearchus riding through* X. A. 1. 5. 12; αἰσθόμενος Λαμπροκλέᾱ πρὸς τὴν μητέρα χαλεπαίνοντα *perceiving Lamprocles angry with his mother* X. M. 2. 2. 1, ᾔσθησαι πώποτέ μου ἢ ψευδομαρτυροῦντος ἢ σῡκοφαντοῦντος; *have you ever noticed me either bearing false witness or playing the part of an informer?* 4. 4. 11; ἤκουσαν αὐτοῦ φωνήσαντος *they heard him speaking* X. S. 3. 13; ὡς ἐπύθοντο τῆς Πύλου κατειλημμένης *when they learned of the capture of Pylos* T. 4. 6.

N. Verbs of physical perception, ὁρῶ (especially) and ἀκούω, regularly take the present participle in Attic prose, which usually refuses to distinguish between *I see a house burning* and *I see a house burn.* The complexive aorist, summing up the action, does however occur, as ὡς εἶδεν ἔλαφον ἐκπηδήσᾱσαν . . . ἐδίωκεν *when he saw a hind break cover he gave chase* X. C. 1. 4. 8. Cp. πεσόντα εἶδον Hdt. 9. 22.

b. In Indirect Discourse. — Here verbs of *perceiving* denote *intellectual* perception — the fact that something is perceived or heard of. With ἀκούω and πυνθάνομαι the participle stands in the accusative (as with ὁρῶ, αἰσθάνομαι). Cp. 1363, 1365, 2144, 2145.

ὁρῶμεν πάντα ἀληθῆ ὄντα ἃ λέγετε *we see that everything you say is true* X. A. 5. 5. 24, αἰσθάνομαι ταῦτα οὕτως ἔχοντα *I perceive that this is so* X. M. 3. 5. 5, ἤκουσε Κῦρον ἐν Κιλικίᾳ ὄντα *he heard that Cyrus was in Cilicia* X. A. 1. 4. 5, ὅταν κλύῃ τινὸς ἥξοντ' Ὀρέστην *when she hears from any one that Orestes will return* S. El. 293, πυθόμενοι Ἀρταξέρξην τεθνηκότα *having learned that Artaxerxes was dead* T. 4. 50.

2113. Verbs of Finding. — Verbs of *finding* and *detecting* (εὑρίσκω, (κατα)-λαμβάνω; pass. ἁλίσκομαι) in their capacity as verbs of *perceiving* take the participle (*a*) not in indirect discourse, of the act or state in which a person or thing is found; or (*b*) in indirect discourse, of the fact that a person or thing is found in an act or state.

a. κῆρυξ ἀφικόμενος ηὗρε τοὺς ἄνδρας διεφθαρμένους *the herald, on his arrival, found the men already put to death* T. 2. 6, εὕρηται πιστῶς πράττων *he has been found to have dealt faithfully* D. 19. 332, ἂν ἄρ' ἄλλον τινὰ λαμβάνῃ ψευδόμενον *if then he catch anybody else lying* P. R. 389 d, ἢν ἐπιβουλεύων ἁλίσκηται *if he be detected in plotting* X. Ag. 8. 3.

b. διὰ τὴν Ἰλίου ἅλωσιν εὑρίσκουσι σφίσι ἐοῦσαν τὴν ἀρχὴν τῆς ἔχθρης *they conclude that the beginning of their enmity was on account of the capture of Ilium* Hdt. 1. 5.

2114. It is often difficult to distinguish the two constructions of 2113. Thus, καταλαμβάνουσι νεωστὶ στάσει τοὺς τῶν Ἀθηναίων ἐναντίους ἐκπεπτωκότας (T. 7. 33) may mean *they found that the anti-Athenian party had been recently expelled by a revolution* (ind. disc.) or *them recently expelled* (not in ind. disc.). So καταλαμβάνουσι . . . τἆλλα ἀφεστηκότα *they found the other cities in a state of revolt* T. 1. 59 (*that they had revolted* would be possible). In the meaning *discover, find* καταλαμβάνω does not take the aorist participle.

2115. ποιῶ meaning *represent* has the construction of the verbs of 2113. Thus, πλησιάζοντας τοὺς θεοὺς τοῖς ἀνθρώποις οἷόν τ' αὐτοῖς ποιῆσαι *it is possible for them* (poets) *to represent the gods as drawing nigh to men* I. 9. 9. Cp. 2142.

OMISSION OF ὤν

2116. The participle ὤν is often omitted.

2117. After ἅτε, οἷα, ὡς, or καίπερ, ὤν is often omitted in prose with predicate adjectives: συνδείπνους ἔλαβεν ἀμφοτέρους πρὸς ἑαυτὸν ὡς φίλους ἤδη (ὄντας) *he took both to supper with him since they were now friends* X. C. 3. 2. 25. Such omission is rare in prose except after these particles: εἰ ἥττους (ὄντες) τῶν πολεμίων ληφθησόμεθα *if we shall be caught at the mercy of our enemies* X. A. 5. 6. 13. With predicate substantives, even after these particles, ὤν is very rarely omitted (P. R. 568 b).

a. In the genitive and accusative absolute the particles of 2117 usually precede when ὤν is omitted. With the genitive absolute the omission is very rare in prose: ὡς ἑτοίμων (ὄντων) χρημάτων *just as though the property was at their* *disposal* X. A. 7. 8. 11; but ἡμέρᾱς ἤδη (οὔσης) *it being already day* T. 5. 59. In poetry the substantive usually suggests the verb: ὑφηγητῆρος οὐδενὸς (ὄντος) φίλων *with no friend to guide* him S. O. C. 1588. Accusative absolute: ὡς καλὸν (ὂν) ἀγορεύεσθαι αὐτόν *on the ground that it is admirable for it* (the speech) *to be delivered* T. 2. 35. Without the particles of 2117, the omission of ὄν is poetical (S. Ant. 44). The omission of ὄν with adjectives ending in -ον aids euphony.

b. ἑκών *willing*, ἄκων *unwilling* are treated like participles (2071): ἐμοῦ μὲν οὐχ ἑκόντος *against my will* S. Aj. 455.

c. ὤν must be used when it has the force of *in the capacity of.*

2118. A predicate substantive or adjective, coördinated with a participle in the same construction, may omit ὤν; as οὐ ῥᾴδιον ἦν μὴ ἀθρόοις καὶ ἀλλήλους περιμείνᾱσι διελθεῖν τὴν πολεμίᾱν *it was not easy for them to pass through the enemy's country except in a body and after having waited for one another* T. 5. 64.

2119. ὤν may be omitted with verbs taking a supplementary participle; so with verbs meaning *to perceive* (2111 ff.), *know, show, announce, find, discover,* etc.; especially with φαίνομαι, τυγχάνω (poet. κυρῶ), διατελῶ, διαγίγνομαι, rarely with περιορῶ and συμβαίνω. Thus, ὁρῶ μέγαν (ὄντα) τὸν ἀγῶνα *I see that the contest is important* T. 2. 45, ἂν ἐν Χερρονήσῳ πύθησθε Φίλιππον (ὄντα) *if you learn that Philip is in Chersonesus* D. 4. 41, εἰ ψευδὴς φαίνοιτο (ὤν) ὁ Γωβρύᾱς *if Gobryas seem to be false* X. C 5. 2. 4, εἴ τις εὔνους (ὤν) τυγχάνει *if any one happens to be friendly* Ar. Eccl. 1141, ἀχίτων (ὤν) διατελεῖς *you are continually without a tunic* X. M. 1. 6. 2.

Ὡς WITH A PARTICIPLE IN INDIRECT DISCOURSE

2120. ὡς is often used with a participle in indirect discourse to mark the mental attitude of the subject of the main verb or of some other person mentioned prominently in the sentence (cp. 2086); sometimes, to denote emphasis, when that mental attitude is already clearly marked.

ὡς μηδὲν εἰδότ' ἴσθι με *be assured that I know nothing* (lit. *understand that you are to assume that I know nothing*) S. Ph. 253, δῆλος ἦν Κῦρος ὡς σπεύδων *Cyrus was plainly bent on haste* (Cyrus showed that it was his intention to make haste) X. A. 1. 5. 9.

2121. A participle with ὡς may follow a verb of *thinking* or *saying* though the verb in question does not take the participle in indirect discourse without ὡς. Thus, ὡς τὰ βέλτιστα βουλεύοντες ἰσχῡρίζοντο *they kept insisting in the belief that they were recommending the best course* T. 4. 68, ὡς στρατηγήσοντ' ἐμὲ ταύτην τὴν στρατηγίᾱν μηδεὶς ὑμῶν λεγέτω *let no one of you say* (i.e. *speak of me in the belief*) *that I will assume this command* X. A. 1. 3. 15.

2122. So after verbs admitting the supplementary participle in indirect discourse we may have the genitive or accusative absolute with ὡς instead of the participle or a clause with ὅτι or ὡς. Thus, ὡς πολέμου ὄντος παρ' ὑμῶν ἀπαγγελῶ; *shall I report from you (on the assumption) that there is war?* X. A. 2. 1. 21, ὡς ἐμοῦ οὖν ἰόντος, ὅπῃ καὶ ὑμεῖς, οὕτω τὴν γνώμην ἔχετε *make up your minds (on the assumption) that I am going wherever you go* (= *be sure that I am going,* etc.) 1. 3. 6 (here *τὴν γνώμην ἔχετε* could not take the participle without *ὡς*); *ὡς πάνυ μοι δοκοῦν, οὕτως ἴσθι rest assured that it is my decided opinion* (lit. *on the assumption that this seems so to me, understand accordingly*) X. M. 4. 2. 30. For *ὡς* with the absolute participle not in indirect discourse, see 2086 d.

VERBS TAKING EITHER THE PARTICIPLE OR THE INFINITIVE

2123. Some verbs admit either the supplementary participle or the infinitive, sometimes with only a slight difference in meaning. Cases where the difference is marked are given below. (Most of the verbs in question admit also a substantive clause with *ὅτι* or *ὡς*, 2577).

2124. Infinitive and participle here differ greatly when the infinitive expresses purpose or result. Where the infinitive shows only its abstract verbal meaning it differs but little from the participle (cp. 2144).

2125. A participle or infinitive standing in indirect discourse is indicated in 2126–2143 by O(ratio) O(bliqua); when not standing in O. O. this fact is ordinarily not indicated.

2126. αἰσχΰνομαι and **αἰδοῦμαι** with part. (2100) = *I am ashamed of* doing something which I do; with inf. = *I am ashamed to* do something which I have refrained from doing up to the present time and may never do. Thus, *τοῦτο μὲν οὐκ αἰσχΰνομαι λέγων· τὸ δὲ . . . αἰσχῡνοίμην ἂν λέγειν I am not ashamed of saying this; but the following I should be ashamed to say* X. C. 5. 1. 21, *αἰσχΰνομαι οὖν ὑμῖν εἰπεῖν τἀληθῆ, ὅμως δὲ ῥητέον I am ashamed to speak the truth to you; nevertheless it must be spoken* P. A. 22 b. With a negative the distinction may disappear: *οὐδ᾽ αἰσχΰνει φθόνου δίκην εἰσάγειν* (*v.l. εἰσάγων*), *οὐκ ἀδικήματος οὐδενός, καὶ νόμους μεταποιῶν; are you not ashamed to bring a cause into court out of envy—not for any offence—and to alter laws?* D. 18. 121.

2127. ἀνέχομαι (2098; rarely with the inf.), ***τλάω** and **τολμῶ** (both rarely with the part. in poetry), **ὑπομένω**: with part. = *endure, submit to* something that is present or past; with inf. *venture* or *have the courage to* do something in the future. Thus, *πάσχοντες ἠνείχοντο they submitted to suffer* T. 1. 77, *ἀνέσχοντο τὸν ἐπιόντα ἐπὶ τὴν χώρᾱν δέξασθαι they had the courage to receive the invader of their country* Hdt. 7. 139; *παῖδα . . . φᾱσὶν Ἀλκμήνης πρᾱθέντα τλῆναι they say that Alcmene's son bore up in bondage* (lit. *having been sold*) A. Ag. 1041; *ἐτόλμᾱ βαλλόμενος he submitted to be struck* ω 161, *τόλμησον ὀρθῶς φρονεῖν sapere aude* A. Pr. 1000; *οὐχ ὑπομένει ὠφελούμενος he cannot stand being improved* P. G. 505 c, *εἰ ὑπομενέουσι χεῖρας ἐμοὶ ἀνταειρόμενοι if they shall dare to raise their hands against me* Hdt. 7. 101.

2128. ἄρχομαι, cp. 1734 (Hom. *ἄρχω*) with part. (2098), *begin to do something* and continue with something else; with inf. (usually present, cp. 1865 b) *begin to do something* and continue with the same thing. Thus, *ἄρξομαι διδάσκων ἐκ τῶν θείων I will begin my instruction with things divine* (later the subject is the desire for wealth) X. C. 8. 8. 2, *πόθεν ἤρξατό σε διδάσκειν τὴν στρατηγίᾱν; at what point did he begin to teach you generalship?* X. M. 3. 1. 5. *ἄρχομαι* with the participle occurs only in Xenophon and Plato.

2129. γιγνώσκω with part. in O. O. (2106) = *recognize that something is;* with inf. in three uses: (1) in O. O. = *judge (decide) that something is* (a verb of *will*), as ἔγνωσαν κερδαλεώτερον εἶναι *they judged that it was more profitable* X. A. 1. 9. 17; (2) not in O. O. = *resolve, determine to do something*, as ἔγνω διώκειν τοὺς ἐκ τῶν εὐωνύμων προσκειμένους *he resolved to pursue those who were hanging on his left* X. H. 4. 6. 9; (3) not in O. O. = *learn how to do something* (rarely), as γίγνωσκε τῆς ὀργῆς κρατεῖν *learn to control thy temper* Men. Sent. 20.

2130. δείκνῡμι with part. in O. O. (2106) = *show that something is;* with inf. (ἀποδείκνῡμι) not in O. O. = *show how to do something, instruct.* Thus, ἀπέδειξαν οἱ ἡγεμόνες λαμβάνειν τὰ ἐπιτήδεια *the guides directed them to take provisions* X. A. 2. 3. 14.

2131. δηλῶ with part. (and inf.) in O. O. (2106) = *show that something is, indicate;* with inf. not in O. O. = *command, make known, signify;* as in κηρύγματι ἐδήλου τοὺς ἐλευθερίᾱς δεομένους ὡς πρὸς σύμμαχον αὐτὸν παρεῖναι *he made known by proclamation that those who wanted freedom should come to him as an ally* X. Ag. 1. 33.

2132. δοκιμάζω with part. in O. O. (2106) = *prove to be*, as ὁποῖοί τινες ὄντες αὐτοὶ περὶ τὴν πόλιν ἐδοκιμάσθητε *what sort of persons you proved yourselves to be in regard to the city* L. 31. 34; with inf. in O. O. = *pronounce an opinion to be correct.* Thus, ἐδοκιμάσαμεν ἀνδρὶ καλῷ τε κἀγαθῷ ἐργασίᾱν εἶναι . . . κρατίστην γεωργίᾱν *we approved the idea that tilling of the soil is the best occupation for a gentleman* X. O. 6. 8.

2133. ἔοικα (1983, 2089 c) with nom. part. = *appear*, oftener with dat. part. (strictly = *am like*), *appear;* with inf. = *seem.* Thus, ἐοίκατε τυραννίσι μᾶλλον ἢ πολῑτείαις ἡδόμενοι *you appear to take delight in despotisms rather than in constitutional governments* X. H. 6. 3. 8, ἔοικας δεδιότι τοὺς πολλούς strictly *you are like one who fears* (i.e. *you appear to fear*) *the multitude* P. R. 527 d, οὐκ ἔοικεν εἰδέναι *he seems not to know* X. Ap. 29, ἔοικα ἐποικτίρειν σε *methinks I pity thee* S. Ph. 317.

2134. ἐπιλανθάνομαι with part. in O. O. (2106) = *forget that something is;* with inf. not in O. O. = *forget (how) to do something.* Thus, ὀλίγου ἐπελαθόμεθ' εἰπεῖν *I have almost forgotten to mention* P. R. 563 b.

2135. εὑρίσκω with part. in O. O. = *judge* and not in O. O. (2113) = *find that something is;* less often with inf. in O. O. = *judge*, as εὕρισκε ταῦτα καιριώτατα εἶναι *he found (judged) that this was the most opportune way* Hdt. 1. 125. εὑρίσκομαι rarely with inf. = *find how to* (E. Med. 196), *procure* by asking (Hdt. 9. 28).

2136. μανθάνω with part. in O. O. (2106) = *learn that something is;* with inf. not in O. O. = *learn (how) to do something.* Thus, διαβεβλημένος οὐ μανθάνεις *you do not perceive that you have been calumniated* Hdt. 3. 1, ἂν ἅπαξ μάθωμεν ἀργοὶ ζῆν *if we once learn to live in idleness* X. A. 3. 2. 25.

2137. μεθίημι (*let go*), etc., with part. = *leave off;* with inf. = *neglect, permit.* Thus, οὐ γὰρ ἀνίει ἐπιών *for he did not stop coming after them* Hdt. 4. 125, μεθῑᾶσι τὰ δέοντα πράττειν *they neglect to perform their duties* X. M. 2. 1. 33, μεθεῖσά μοι λέγειν *allowing me to speak* S. El. 628.

2138. **μέμνημαι** with part. in O. O. (2106) = *remember that something is;* with inf. not in O. O. = *remember to do something.* Thus, *μεμνήσθω ἀνὴρ ἀγαθὸς εἶναι let him be mindful to be a brave man* X. A. 3. 2. 39.

2139. **οἶδα** and **ἐπίσταμαι** with part. in O. O. (2106) = *know that something is;* with inf. not in O. O. = *know how to do something.* Thus, *ἐπιστάμενος νεῖν knowing how to swim* X. A. 5. 7. 25. In poetry (very rarely in prose, except with *ἐπίσταμαι* in Hdt.) these verbs take also the inf. (in O. O.) in the meaning *know* or *believe: ἐπιστάμεθα μή πώ ποτ' αὐτὸν ψεῦδος λακεῖν we know that he has never yet spoken falsehood* S. Ant. 1094.

2140. **παύω** with part. (2098) = *stop* what is taking place; with inf. = *prevent* something from taking place. Thus, *ἔπαυσαν φοβουμένους πλῆθος νεῶν they stopped their terror at the number of ships* P. Menex. 241 b, *παύσαντες τὸ μὴ προσελθεῖν ἐγγὺς τὴν ὁλκάδα preventing the merchantman from drawing near* T. 7. 53.

2141. **περιορῶ**, etc. (2103) with pres. part. = *view with indifference*, with aor. part. = *shut one's eyes to;* with inf. = *let something happen through negligence*, or simply *permit* (*ἐᾶν*). Thus, *περιεῖδε τὸν αὑτοῦ πατέρα καὶ ζῶντα τῶν ἀναγκαίων σπανίζοντα καὶ τελευτήσαντ' οὐ τυχόντα τῶν νομίμων he looked on with indifference while his own father was in want of necessities when alive and* (shut his eyes) *to his failure to receive the customary rites after he had passed away* Dinarchus 2. 8, *οἱ Ἀχαρνῆς . . . οὐ περιόψεσθαι ἐδόκουν τὰ σφέτερα διαφθαρέντα it did not seem likely that the Acharnians would shut their eyes to the destruction of their property* T. 2. 20, *οὐδ' ἐσιέναι ἔφασαν περιόψεσθαι οὐδένα they refused to permit any one to enter* 4. 48.

2142. **ποιῶ** with part. (2115) = *represent;* with inf. not in O. O. = *cause, effect;* with inf. in O. O. = *assume.* Thus, *ἀνωνύμους τοὺς ἄλλους εἶναι ποιεῖ causes the others to lose their names* Hdt. 7. 129, *ποιώμεθα* (conj. *τί οἰώμεθα*) *τὸν φιλόσοφον νομίζειν κτλ. let us assume that the philosopher holds*, etc. P. R. 581 d.

2143. **φαίνομαι** with part in O. O. (2106) = *I am plainly;* with inf. in O. O. = *I seem* or *it appears* (but may not be true) *that I.* Thus, *φαίνεται τἀληθῆ λέγων he is evidently speaking the truth, φαίνεται τἀληθῆ λέγειν he appears to be speaking the truth* (but he may be lying). Cp. *τῇ φωνῇ . . . κλαίειν ἐφαίνετο* lit. *by his voice it appeared that he was weeping* (but he was *not* weeping) X. S. 1. 15. The above distinction is, however, not always maintained.

2144. The following verbs take either the participle or the infinitive (in O. O.) with no (or only slight) difference in meaning:

αἰσθάνομαι, ἀκούω, πυνθάνομαι (2112), *ἀγγέλλω* (2106), *καθίζω* (2105) and *καθίστημι, παρασκευάζομαι, ὁμολογῶ* (2106), *πειρῶμαι* (2102), *ἐπιτρέπω* and *νομίζω* (part. rare), *ἀποκάμνω* (inf. rare), *θαυμάζω wonder, τίθημι suppose*, the expressions of 2104, etc. Both infinitive and participle with *πυνθάνομαι* in Hdt. 5. 15, 8. 40.

2145. Verbs of intellectual perception (2112 b) take also **ὅτι** or **ὡς**. So with *ἀκούω, αἰσθάνομαι, πυνθάνομαι.* Cp.

ἀκούω with gen. part. = *I hear* (with my own ears).
ἀκούω with accus. part. = *I hear* (through others, *i.e. I am told*) *that.*
ἀκούω with inf. = *I hear* (of general, not certain knowledge, as *by report*) *that.*

THE PARTICIPLE WITH ἄν

2146. The participle with ἄν represents the indicative with ἄν (1784 ff.) or the potential optative with ἄν (1824). The present participle with ἄν thus represents either the imperfect indicative with ἄν or the present optative with ἄν; the aorist participle with ἄν represents either the aorist indicative with ἄν or the aorist optative with ἄν. Cp. 1845 ff.

REMARKS ON SOME USES OF PARTICIPLES

2147. The abundance of its participles is one of the characteristic features of Greek. Their use gives brevity to the sentence (cp. 2050), enabling the writer to set forth in a word modifications and amplifications of the main thought for which we require cumbersome relative clauses. But an excessive use of participles, especially in close conjunction, marked a careless style.

a. The participle may contain the leading thought, the finite verb the subordinate thought, of a sentence. Thus, τὸ ψήφισμα τοῦτο γράφω . . . τοὺς ὅρκους τὴν ταχίστην ἀπολαμβάνειν, ἵν' ἐχόντων τῶν Θρᾳκῶν . . . ταῦτα τὰ χωρία, ἃ νῦν οὗτος διέσυρε . . ., οὕτω γίγνοινθ' οἱ ὅρκοι *I moved this bill that* the envoys *should with all speed receive* Philip's *oaths in order that when the oaths were taken the Thracians might be in possession of the places which the plaintiff has just now been ridiculing* (lit. *while the Thracians were in possession*, etc. . . . *the oaths might under these circumstances be ratified*) D. 18. 27, βούλομαι ὀλίγα ἑκατέρους ἀναμνήσᾱς καταβαίνειν *I wish to recall a few things to the memory of each party and then sit down* (*descend* from the bema) L. 12. 92. Cp. also 2096, 2099.

b. The participle may repeat the stem and meaning of the finite verb. Thus, καὶ εὐχόμενος ἄν τις ταῦτα εὔξαιτο *and some one might (praying) utter this prayer* Ant. 6. 1.

c. A participial construction may pass over into a construction with a finite verb. Thus, μάρτυρα μὲν . . . οὐδένα παρασχόμενος . . . παρεκελεύετο δέ κτλ. lit. *producing on the one hand no witness . . . on the other hand he exhorted*, etc. D. 57. 11, προσέβαλον τῷ τειχίσματι, ἄλλῳ τε τρόπῳ πειράσαντες καὶ μηχανὴν προσήγαγον lit. *they attacked the rampart both making trial in other ways, and they brought up an engine* (i.e. *and after trying other devices brought up an engine*) T. 4. 100.

d. A participle may be used in close connection with a relative or interrogative pronoun. Thus, οὐδ' ὑπὲρ οἷα πεποιηκότων ἀνθρώπων κινδῡνεύσετε διαλογισάμενοι *not even calculating what had been the conduct of the men for whom you were going to risk your lives* D. 18. 98, ἐλαυνομένων καὶ ὑβριζομένων καὶ τί κακὸν οὐχὶ πασχόντων πᾶσ' ἡ οἰκουμένη μεστὴ γέγονε *the whole civilized world is filled with men who are harried to and fro and insulted, nay, what misery is there which they do not suffer?* 18. 48.

e. In contrasts, two subjects may, by anacoluthon, belong to one participle in the nominative, though the participle belongs to only one subject (T. 3. 34. 3).

f. Two or more participles may be coördinated without any connective.

This is common in Homer when one participle forms a contrast to, or intensifies, another participle. Cp. ἦ καὶ ἐπῶρτ' Ἀχιλῆι κυκώμενος ὑψόσε θύων, μορμύρων ἀφρῷ κτλ. *he spake, and swelling in tumult rushed upon Achilles, raging on high, roaring with foam*, etc. Φ 324. This is very rare in prose (Aes. 3. 94).

g. In prose such coördination without any connective is incomplete, one participle, *e.g.*, often defining another, as in ὁ Κῦρος ὑπολαβὼν τοὺς φεύγοντας συλλέξᾱς στράτευμα ἐπολιόρκει Μίλητον *taking the exiles under his protection, Cyrus collected an army, and laid siege to Miletus* X. A. 1. 1. 7. So even when the participles are connected, as ξηράνᾱς τὴν διώρυχα καὶ παρατρέψᾱς ἄλλῃ τὸ ὕδωρ *by draining the canal and* (*i.e.* in consequence of) *diverting the water elsewhere* T. 1. 109. One participle may be appositive to another. Thus, ἐξέτασιν ποιήσαντες ἐν τοῖς ἱππεῦσι, φάσκοντες εἰδέναι βούλεσθαι πόσοι εἶεν . . ., ἐκέλευον ἀπογράφεσθαι πάντας *by making a review in the presence of the cavalry, alleging that they wished to find out how many they were, they ordered all to inscribe themselves* X. H. 2. 4. 8.

h. A participle with case absolute may be coördinated with a participle not in an absolute case. Thus, οἱ δὲ ἀφικομένης τῆς νεὼς καὶ ἀνέλπιστον τὴν εὐτυχίᾱν ἀκούσαντες . . . πολὺ ἐπερρώσθησαν *they were much encouraged on the arrival of the ship and on hearing of the success which was unhoped for* T. 8. 106, μεταπεμφθέντες ἤλθομεν ἢ οὐδενὸς καλέσαντος *we came summoned or at no one's call* L. 4. 11.

i. A finite verb may have two or more participles attached to it in different relations. Thus, οἱ πελτασταὶ προδραμόντες . . . διαβάντες τὴν χαράδρᾱν, ὁρῶντες πρόβατα πολλὰ . . . προσέβαλλον πρὸς τὸ χωρίον *the light-armed troops after running forward and crossing the ravine, proceed to attack the stronghold on seeing quantities of sheep* X. A. 5. 2. 4. Of several aorist participles, one may be relatively earlier in time than another.

j. A participle may be added predicatively to another participle, and often follows the article belonging to the main participle. Thus, οἱ ζῶντες καταλειπόμενοι *those who were being left behind alive* T. 7. 75.

k. A participle is often omitted when it can be supplied from the context. Thus, ὡρμίσαντο καὶ αὐτοὶ . . . ἐπειδὴ καὶ τοὺς Ἀθηναίους (ὁρμισαμένους) εἶδον *they too came to anchor when they saw that the Athenians had done so* T. 2. 86.

2148. The participle often agrees with the logical, and not with the grammatical, subject. The participle thus often agrees with the subject of the finite verb which the writer had in mind when he began the sentence, but for which he later substitutes another verb; or the participle may later be used as if in agreement with the subject of another finite verb than the one actually employed.

a. A participle in the nominative may belong to a finite verb requiring an oblique case. Thus, ἀποβλέψᾱς πρὸς τοῦτον τὸν στόλον . . ., ἔδοξέ μοι πάγκαλος εἶναι (= ἡγησάμην πάγκαλον εἶναι) *on looking at this expedition, it seemed to me to be very admirable* P. L. 686 d, ἔχοντες . . . ἀρχὴν μεγίστην . . ., ὅμως οὐδὲν τούτων ἡμᾶς ἐπῆρε (= οὐδενὶ τούτων ἐπήρθημεν) ἐξαμαρτεῖν *although we possessed the greatest empire . . . nevertheless none of these reasons induced us to do wrong* I. 4. 108, ἔδοξεν αὐτοῖς (= ἐβουλεύσαντο) οὐ τοὺς παρόντας μόνον ἀποκτεῖναι ἀλλὰ καὶ τοὺς ἅπαντας Μυτιληναίους . . . ἐπικαλοῦντες τὴν ἀπόστασιν κτλ. *they decided* *to put to death not merely those who were there but also all the Mytilenaeans, urging against them their revolt*, etc. T. 3. 36.

b. Two or more substantives or pronouns with their participles may stand in partitive apposition (981) to the logical subject. Thus, τὰ περὶ Πύλον ὑπ' ἀμφοτέρων κατὰ κράτος ἐπολεμεῖτο (= ἀμφότεροι ἐπολέμουν), Ἀθηναῖοι μὲν . . . τὴν νῆσον περιπλέοντες . . ., Πελοποννήσιοι δὲ ἐν τῇ ἠπείρῳ στρατοπεδευόμενοι *the war at Pylus was vigorously waged by both sides, the Athenians on their part by sailing around the island . . . the Peloponnesians by encamping on the mainland* T. 4. 23. Cp. λόγοι δ' ἐν ἀλλήλοισιν ἐρρόθουν κακοί, φύλαξ ἐλέγχων φύλακα *bitter words flew loud from one to another, watchman accusing watchman* S. Ant. 259. As the sentence stands, we expect φύλακος ἐλέγχοντος φύλακα, but the first clause is equivalent to κακοὺς λόγους εἴπομεν ἀλλήλους. Cp. θαυμάζοντες ἄλλος ἄλλῳ ἔλεγεν *one spoke to the other in astonishment* P. S. 220 c. Cp. 982.

c. Without regard to the following construction, a participle may stand in the nominative. The use of the genitive absolute would here be proper, but would cause the main subject of the thought to occupy a subordinate position. Thus, ἐπιπεσὼν τῇ Φαρναβάζου στρατοπεδείᾳ, τῆς μὲν προφυλακῆς αὐτοῦ Μυσῶν ὄντων πολλοὶ ἔπεσον *attacking the camp of Pharnabazus, he slew a large number* (= πολλοὺς ἀπέκτεινε) *of Mysians who constituted his advance guard* X. H. 4. 1. 24.

N. The nominative participle is sometimes found in clauses without a finite verb, but only when some finite verb is to be supplied (cp. Ψ 546), as with εἰ, ἐάν, ὅταν (X. M. 2. 1. 23); with ὅσα μή *as far as is possible* (T. 1. 111); in replies in dialogue, where it stands in apposition to the subject of the preceding sentence (P. Ph. 74 b); or is interposed as a parenthesis (εὖ ποιοῦν in D. 23. 143).

d. Likewise a participle may stand in the accusative or (rarely) in the dative when the construction demands another case. Thus, σοὶ δὲ συγγνώμη (= συγγνώμη ἐστὶ σέ) λέγειν τάδ' ἐστί, μὴ πάσχουσαν ὡς ἐγὼ κακῶς *it is excusable for thee to speak thus, since thou dost not suffer cruelly as I do* E. Med. 814, ἦν ἡ γνώμη τοῦ Ἀριστέως (= ἔδοξε τῷ Ἀριστεῖ), τὸ μὲν μεθ' ἑαυτοῦ στρατόπεδον ἔχοντι ἐν τῷ ἰσθμῷ ἐπιτηρεῖν τοὺς Ἀθηναίους *Aristeus decided to keep his own forces at the Isthmus and watch for the Athenians* T. 1. 62.

VERBAL ADJECTIVES IN -τέος

On verbal adjectives in -τός, -τή, -τόν, see 425 c, 472, 473.

2149. Verbal adjectives in -τέος express necessity. They admit two constructions:

1. The personal construction (-τέος, -τέᾱ, -τέον), passive in meaning, and emphasizing the subject.

2. The (more common) impersonal construction (-τέον, -τέᾰ, 1052), practically active in meaning, and emphasizing the action.

Both constructions are used with the copula εἰμί, which may be omitted. The agent — the person on whom the necessity rests — is expressed, if at all, by the dative (never by ὑπό and the genitive).

2150. Verbal adjectives from transitive verbs take the personal construction when the subject is emphasized; but the impersonal construction, when the emphasis falls on the verbal adjective itself. Verbal adjectives from intransitive verbs (that is, such as are followed by the genitive or dative) take only the impersonal construction.

a. Oblique cases of verbal adjectives are rare. Thus, περὶ τῶν ὑμῖν πρᾱκτέων *concerning what need be done by us* D. 6. 28.

2151. The Personal (Passive) Construction. — The personal verbal in -τέος is used only when the verb from which it is derived takes the accusative. The verbal agrees with the subject in gender, number, and case. The agent, if expressed, must always stand in the dative.

ποταμός τις ἡμῖν ἐστι διαβατέος *a river must be crossed by us* X. A. 2. 4. 6, ὠφελητέᾱ σοι ἡ πόλις ἐστί *the State must be benefited by you* X. M. 3. 6. 3, ἐμοὶ τοῦτο οὐ ποιητέον *this must not be done by me* (*I must not do this*) X. A. 1. 3. 15, οἱ συμμαχεῖν ἐθέλοντες εὖ ποιητέοι *those who would be allies must be well treated* X. M. 2. 6. 27, οὐ . . . τοσαῦτα ὄρη ὁρᾶτε ὑμῖν ὄντα πορευτέα; *do you not see such high mountains that must be traversed by you?* X. A. 2. 5. 18.

2152. The Impersonal (Active) Construction. — The impersonal verbal stands in the neuter nominative, usually singular (-τέον), rarely plural (-τέᾰ). Its object stands in the case (genitive, dative, or accusative) required by the verb from which the verbal adjective is derived; verbs taking the genitive or dative have the impersonal construction only. The agent, if expressed, must always stand in the dative.

τῷ ἀδικοῦντι δοτέον δίκην *the wrong-doer must suffer punishment* P. Euth. 8 c, πιστὰ καὶ ὁμήρους δοτέον καὶ ληπτέον *we must give and receive pledges and hostages* X. H. 3. 2. 18, τὸν θάνατον ἡμῖν μετ' εὐδοξίᾱς αἱρετέον ἐστίν *we must prefer death with honour* I. 6. 91, πειστέον πατρὸς λόγοις *I must obey my father's commands* E. Hipp. 1182, πειστέον τάδε (σοί) *thou must obey in this* S. Ph. 994 (distinguish πειστέον ἐστί σε *one must persuade thee*), φημὶ δὴ βοηθητέον εἶναι τοῖς πράγμασιν ὑμῖν *I say that you must render assistance to the interests at stake* D. 1. 17, τοὺς φίλους εὐεργετητέον, τὴν πόλιν ὠφελητέον . . ., τῶν βοσκημάτων ἐπιμελητέον *you must do good to your friends, benefit your State, take care of your flocks* X. M. 2. 1. 28, ἡμῖν ξύμμαχοι ἀγαθοί, οὓς οὐ παραδοτέα τοῖς Ἀθηναίοις ἐστίν *we have serviceable allies, whom we must not abandon to the Athenians* T. 1. 86, ἐψηφίσαντο . . . πολεμητέα εἶναι *they voted that they must go to war* 1. 88.

a. Since the impersonal construction is virtually active, and hence equivalent to δεῖ with the accusative and infinitive (active or middle), the agent sometimes stands in the accusative, as if dependent on δεῖ. The copula is (perhaps) always omitted when the agent is expressed by the accusative. Thus, τὸν βουλόμενον εὐδαίμονα εἶναι σωφροσύνην διωκτέον καὶ ἀσκητέον (= δεῖ διώκειν καὶ ἀσκεῖν) *it is necessary that the man who desires to be happy should pursue and practice temperance* P. G. 507 c.

SUMMARY OF THE FORMS OF SIMPLE SENTENCES

§§ 906–2152 deal, in general, with the simple sentence. The following summary shows the chief forms of simple sentences (921) used in Attic.

2153. STATEMENTS

1. Statements of Fact (direct assertions) as to the present, past, or future are made in the indicative mood (negative οὐ), 1770.

A. Statements of fact include statements of present, past, or future possibility, likelihood, or necessity, which are expressed by the indicative of a verb denoting possibility, likelihood, or necessity, and an infinitive (1774–1779).

B. Statements of customary or repeated past action are made in the imperfect or aorist indicative with ἄν (negative οὐ), 1790.

2. Statement of Opinion (usually cautious, doubtful, or modest assertions) as to what *may be* (*might be*), *can be* (*could be*), *may* (*might, could, would*) *have been*, etc., are made:

A. In reference to the present or past: by ἐβουλόμην ἄν *I should like* or *I should have liked* (negative οὐ), 1789. (Rarely by the indicative without ἄν, negative μή or μὴ οὐ, 1772.)

B. In reference to the past: by the aorist or imperfect indicative with ἄν (negative οὐ), 1784, cp. 1786.

C. In reference to the present (statement of present opinion the verification of which is left to the future): by the optative with ἄν (negative οὐ), 1824.

D. In reference to the future: by the present subjunctive with μή or μὴ οὐ (1801); by οὐ μή with the aorist subjunctive to denote an emphatic denial (1804).

2154. ASSUMPTIONS

Assumptions, including concessions, are usually expressed by the imperative (negative μή), 1839. Other forms occur, as καὶ δή with the indicative (negative οὐ), 1771; a verb of *assuming* with the accusative and infinitive, etc.

2155. COMMANDS (INCLUDING EXHORTATIONS)

1. **Positive** Commands are expressed by the

A. Imperative, except in the first person (1835).
B. Subjunctive, in the first person (1797).
C. Future indicative (negative οὐ) 1917, 1918; with ὅπως (1920).

D. Optative without ἄν (1820); potential optative with ἄν (negative οὐ, 1830).

E. Infinitive used independently (2013).

2. **Negative** Commands (Prohibitions, 1840), including Exhortations, are expressed by μή with the

A. Present imperative (1840) or aorist subjunctive (second or third person), 1800.

B. Present or aorist subjunctive in the first person plural (1840).

C. Aorist imperative in the third person (rare), 1840.

D. Future indicative with ὅπως μή (1920); with οὐ μή (1919).

E. Aorist subjunctive with ὅπως μή (rare), 1803; with οὐ μή (rare), 1800, N.

F. Infinitive used independently (2013).

2156. WISHES

1. μή is the negative of a direct expression of a wish, and of all indirect expressions of wish except πῶς ἄν with the optative and a form of βούλομαι with the infinitive.

2. Wishes for the *future*, whether the object of the wish is reasonable or unreasonable, attainable or unattainable, are expressed by the optative with or without εἴθε or εἰ γάρ (1814, 1815). Indirect expressions are: πῶς ἄν with the optative (1832); βουλοίμην ἄν with the infinitive (1827).

3. Wishes for the *present:* that something might be otherwise than it now is, are expressed by the imperfect with εἴθε or εἰ γάρ (1780). Indirect expressions are: ὤφελον (with or without εἴθε or εἰ γάρ) and the present or aorist infinitive (1781); ἐβουλόμην (with or without ἄν) with the infinitive (1782, 1789).

4. Wishes for the *past:* that something might have been otherwise than it then was, are expressed by the aorist indicative with εἴθε or εἰ γάρ (1780). Indirect: ὤφελον (with or without εἴθε or εἰ γάρ) with the present or aorist infinitive (1781).

5. Unattainable wishes for the present or past may be entirely reasonable.

2157. QUESTIONS

A simple question results from making any form of statement interrogative. Direct and indirect questions are treated in 2636 ff. See also the Index.

2158. EXCLAMATIONS

Exclamations form complete or incomplete (904) sentences. Direct and indirect exclamatory sentences are treated in 2681 ff. See also the Index.

COMPOUND AND COMPLEX SENTENCES

COÖRDINATION AND SUBORDINATION

2159. All sentences other than simple sentences are formed by combining simple sentences either by coördination or subordination.

2160. Coördination produces compound sentences, subordination produces complex sentences. Complex sentences have been developed out of coördinate independent sentences, one of which has been subordinated in form, as in thought, to another.

2161. Comparative Grammar shows that, historically, coördination was preceded by simple juxtaposition and followed by subordination. Thus the simplest form of associating the two ideas *night fell* and *the enemy departed* was νὺξ ἐγένετο· οἱ πολέμιοι ἀπῆλθον (or in reverse order). From this was developed a closer connection by means of coördinating conjunctions, *e.g.* νὺξ (μὲν) ἐγένετο, οἱ δὲ πολέμιοι ἀπῆλθον or οἱ δὲ πολέμιοι ἀπῆλθον· νὺξ ἐγένετο (or νὺξ γὰρ ἐγένετο), or νὺξ ἐγένετο καὶ οἱ πολέμιοι ἀπῆλθον. Finally it was recognized that one of these ideas was a mere explanation, definition, or supplement of the other, and hence dependent or subordinate. This stage is represented by the *complex* sentence: ἐπεὶ (ὅτε) νὺξ ἐγένετο, οἱ πολέμιοι ἀπῆλθον or νὺξ ἐγένετο, ὥστε οἱ πολέμιοι ἀπῆλθον, and so on to express various other relations. Since Greek inherited from the parent Indo-European language both the subordinate and the coördinate sentence, it must be clearly understood that the above examples of the process of development of sentence-building, though taken from Greek, illustrate an earlier period of the history of language than Greek as we have it. Though it may be possible to reconstruct the form of the earlier, coördinate sentence out of the later, subordinate sentence, and though we have examples of parallel coördinate and subordinate sentences in Greek, the subordinate sentence did not *in Greek* regularly go through the previous stages of simple juxtaposition and coördination. A subordinate construction produced by analogy to another subordinate construction may not be resolved into the coördinate form.

SYNTAX OF THE COMPOUND SENTENCE

2162. A compound sentence consists of two or more simple sentences, grammatically independent of one another and generally united by a coördinating conjunction. Thus, τῇ δὲ ὑστεραίᾳ ἐπορεύοντο διὰ τοῦ πεδίου | καὶ | Τισσαφέρνης εἵπετο *but on the next day they proceeded through the plain and Tissaphernes kept following them* X. A. 3. 4. 18.

a. Abbreviated compound sentences, *i.e.* sentences containing a compound subject with a single verbal predicate or a single subject with a compound verbal predicate, are treated in this book as expanded simple sentences (923, 924).

2163. Greek has, among others, the following coördinating conjunctions, the uses of which in connecting sentences, clauses, phrases, and single words are described under Particles.

A. Copulative conjunctions: τέ (enclitic), καί *and*, τὲ . . . τέ, τὲ . .

καί, καὶ . . . καί *both . . . and*, οὐδέ (μηδέ) *and not, nor*, οὔτε . . . οὔτε (μήτε . . . μήτε) *neither . . . nor*.

B. Adversative conjunctions: ἀλλά *but*, δέ (postpositive, often with μέν in the preceding clause) *but, and*, ἀτάρ *but, yet, however*, μέντοι (postpositive) *however, yet*, καίτοι *and yet*.

C. Disjunctive conjunctions: ἤ *or*, ἤ . . . ἤ *either . . . or*, εἴτε . . . εἴτε (without a verb) *either . . . or*.

D. Inferential conjunctions: ἄρα *then, accordingly*, οὖν *therefore, then*, νῦν (in the poetic and enclitic forms νυν and νῦν) *then, therefore*, τοίνυν *now, then*, τοιγάρ (poetic), τοιγάρτοι, τοιγαροῦν *so then, therefore*.

E. Causal conjunction: γάρ *for*.

2164. Compound sentences are divided into Copulative, Adversative, Disjunctive, Inferential, and Causal sentences.

ASYNDETON

2165. Two or more sentences (or words) independent in form and thought, but juxtaposed, *i.e.* coördinated without any connective, are *asyndetic* (from ἀσύνδετον *not bound together*), and such absence of connectives is called *asyndeton*.

a. The absence of connectives in a language so rich in means of coördination as is Greek is more striking than in other languages. *Grammatical* asyndeton cannot always be separated from *rhetorical* asyndeton. Grammatical asyndeton is the absence of a conjunction where a connective might have been used without marked influence on the character of the thought; as especially in explanatory sentences (often after a preparatory word, usually a demonstrative) which take up the matter just introduced; also where, in place of a conjunction, a resumptive word, such as οὗτος, τοιοῦτος, τοσοῦτος, ἐνταῦθα, οὕτω, etc., is employed. Rhetorical asyndeton is the absence of a conjunction where the following sentence contains a distinct advance in the thought and not a mere formal explanation appended to the foregoing sentence. Rhetorical asyndeton generally expresses emotion of some sort, and is the mark of liveliness, rapidity, passion, or impressiveness, of thought, each idea being set forth separately and distinctly. Thus, οὐκ ἀσεβής; οὐκ ὠμός; οὐκ ἀκάθαρτος; οὐ συκοφάντης; *is he not impious? is he not brutal? is he not impure? is he not a pettifogger?* D. 25. 63.

2166. Asyndeton is frequent in rapid and lively descriptions.

συμβαλόντες τὰς ἀσπίδας ἐωθοῦντο, ἐμάχοντο, ἀπέκτεινον, ἀπέθνῃσκον *interlocking their shields, they shoved, they fought, they slew, they were slain* X. H. 4. 3. 19, προσπεσόντες ἐμάχοντο, ἐώθουν ἐωθοῦντο, ἔπαιον ἐπαίοντο *falling upon them, they fought; pushed* (and) *were pushed; struck* (and) *were struck* X. C. 7. 1. 38. Also with *anaphora* (2167 c), as in ἔχεις πόλιν, ἔχεις τριήρεις, ἔχεις χρήματα, ἔχεις ἄνδρας τοσούτους *you have a city, you have triremes, you have money, you have so many men* X. A. 7. 1. 21. Cp. T. 7. 71, D. 19. 76, 19. 215, P. S. 197 d.

2167. Asyndeton also appears when the unconnected sentence

a. Summarizes the main contents, or expresses the result, of the preceding.

Thus, πάντ' ἔχεις λόγον *you have the whole story* A. Ag. 582, ἀκηκόατε, ἑωράκατε, πεπόνθατε, ἔχετε· δικάζετε *you have heard, you have seen, you have suffered, you have the evidence; pronounce your judgment* L. 12. 100, φυλακῇ μέντοι πρὸ τῶν πυλῶν ἐντευξόμεθα· ἔστι γὰρ ἀεὶ τεταγμένη. οὐκ ἂν μέλλειν δέοι, ἔφη ὁ Κῦρος, ἀλλ' ἰέναι *however, we shall meet with a guard in front of the gates, for one is always stationed there. We must not delay, but advance, said Cyrus* X. C. 7. 5. 25. This is often the case when a demonstrative takes up the foregoing thought (as ἔδοξε ταῦτα X. A. 1. 3. 20) or continues the narrative, as in ἀκούσᾱσι τοῖς στρατηγοῖς ταῦτα ἔδοξε τὸ στράτευμα συναγαγεῖν 4. 4. 19 (cp. 2061).

b. Expresses a reason or explains the preceding. Thus, μῑκρὸν δ' ὕπνου λαχὼν εἶδεν ὄναρ· ἔδοξεν αὐτῷ . . . σκηπτὸς πεσεῖν κτλ. *when he had snatched a little sleep, he saw a vision; a bolt of lightning seemed to him to fall*, etc. X. A. 3. 1. 11, ἱκοῦ πρὸς οἴκους· πᾶς σε Καδμείων λεὼς καλεῖ *come home; all the Cadmean folk calls thee* S. O. C. 741. Here γάρ or ἄρα might have been used. So often after a preparatory word (often a demonstrative); as ταὐτὸν δή μοι δοκεῖ τοῦτ' ἄρα καὶ περὶ τὴν ψῡχὴν εἶναι· ἔνδηλα πάντα ἐστὶν ἐν τῇ ψῡχῇ ἐπειδὰν γυμνωθῇ τοῦ σώματος κτλ. *now it seems to me that this is the same with regard to the soul too; everything in the soul is open to view when a man is stripped of his body* P. G. 524 d, ἑνὶ μόνῳ προέχουσιν οἱ ἱππεῖς ἡμᾶς· φεύγειν αὐτοῖς ἀσφαλέστερόν ἐστιν ἢ ἡμῖν *in one point alone has the cavalry the advantage of us: it is safer for them to run away than for us* X. A. 3. 2. 19, and so when ὥσπερ is followed by οὕτω καί (P. R. 557 c). Also when μέν γε . . . δέ take up what precedes, as ὅμοιός γε Σόλων νομοθέτης καὶ Τῑμοκράτης· ὁ μέν γε . . . ὁ δέ D. 24. 106. Furthermore after τεκμήριον δέ (994), as T. 2. 50.

c. Repeats a significant word or phrase of the earlier sentence (*anaphora*). Thus, καὶ ὅτῳ δοκεῖ ταῦτα, ἀνατεινάτω τὴν χεῖρα· ἀνέτειναν ἅπαντες *and let him who approves this, hold up his hand; they all held up their hands* X. A. 3. 2. 33. In poetry a thought is often repeated in a different form by means of a juxtaposed sentence (S. Tr. 1082).

d. Sets forth a contrast in thought to the preceding. This is commoner in poetry than in prose. Thus, μέλλοντα ταῦτα· τῶν προκειμένων τι χρὴ πράσσειν *this lies in the future; the present must be thy care* S. Ant. 1334.

e. Introduces a new thought or indicates a change to a new form of expression. Thus, ἀλλ' ἰτέον, ἔφη. πρῶτόν με ὑπομνήσατε ἃ ἐλέγετε *but we must proceed, said he. First recall to my mind what you were saying* P. Ph. 91 c.

f. Is introduced by a word stressed by emotion, as ταῦτα D. 3. 32, ἐγώ 4. 29.

On juxtaposition of participles, see 2147.

COÖRDINATION IN PLACE OF SUBORDINATION — PARATAXIS

2168. The term *parataxis* (παράταξις *arranging side by side*), as here employed, is restricted to the arrangement of two independent sentences side by side, though one is *in thought* subordinate to the other.

a. In Greek, παράταξις means simply *coördination* in general, as ὑπόταξις means *subordination*.

2169. In many cases parataxis is a common form of expression not only in the earlier language of Homer, but also in Attic prose and poetry.

So frequently in Attic prose with καί, τὲ . . . καί, ἅμα . . . καί, εὐθὺς . . . καί, and with δέ meaning *for*. Thus, ἤδη δὲ ἦν ὀψὲ . . . καὶ οἱ Κορίνθιοι πρύμναν ἐκρούοντο *it was already late and* (for *when*) *the Corinthians started to row astern* T. 1. 50, καὶ ἤδη τε ἦν περὶ πλήθουσαν ἀγορὰν καὶ ἔρχονται . . . κήρῡκες *and it was already about the time when the market-place fills and* (= *when*) *heralds arrived* X. A. 2. 1. 7, καὶ ἅμα ταῦτ' ἔλεγε καὶ ἀπῄει *and as soon as he said this, he departed* X. H. 7. 1. 28, ἐπίστασθε μόνοι τῶν Ἑλλήνων τοὺς ἀγαθοὺς ἄνδρας τῑμᾶν· εὑρήσετε δὲ . . . παρ' ὑμῖν στρατηγοὺς ἀγαθοὺς (ἀνακειμένους) *you alone among the Greeks know how to honour men of merit; for you will find statues of brave generals set up among you* Lyc. 51. Cp. σκέψασθε δέ T. 1. 143.

a. Temporal conjunctions, as ἡνίκα, are rarely used to introduce such clauses, which often indicate a sudden or decisive occurrence or simultaneous action.

b. Thucydides is especially fond of καί or τέ to coördinate two ideas, one of which is subordinate to the other.

2170. Parataxis often occurs when a thought naturally subordinate is made independent for the sake of emphasis or liveliness. Such rhetorical parataxis occurs chiefly in the orators and in Pindar. So especially when μέν and δέ are used to coördinate two contrasted clauses, the former of which is logically subordinate and inserted to heighten the force of the latter. Here English uses *whereas, while*. Thus, αἰσχρόν ἐστι, εἰ ἐγὼ μὲν τὰ ἔργα τῶν ὑπὲρ ὑμῶν πόνων ὑπέμεινα, ὑμεῖς δὲ μηδὲ τοὺς λόγους αὐτῶν ἀνέξεσθε *it is a shame that, whereas I have undergone the toil of exertions in your cause, you will not endure even their recital* D. 18. 160.

2171. There exist many traces in Greek of the use of the older coördination in place of which some form of subordination was adopted, either entirely or in part, in the later language.

a. Thus several relative pronouns and adverbs were originally demonstrative, and as such pointed either to the earlier or the later clause. So ὁ, ἡ, τό (1105, cp. 1114): τεύχεα δ' ἐξενάριξε, τά οἱ πόρε χάλκεος Ἄρης (H 146) meant originally *he stripped him of his arms; these brazen Ares had given him.* τέως *so long* is properly demonstrative, but has acquired a relative function in καὶ τέως ἐστὶ καιρός, ἀντιλάβεσθε τῶν πρᾱγμάτων *and while there is time, take our policy in hand* D. 1. 20.

2172. Homer often places two thoughts in juxtaposition without any regard for logical connection. This is especially common with δέ, τέ, καί, αὐτάρ, ἀλλά. Thus, πολὺς δ' ὀρυμαγδὸς ἐπ' αὐτῷ ἀνδρῶν ἠδὲ κυνῶν, ἀπό τέ σφισιν (for οἷς) ὕπνος ὄλωλεν *and there is loud clamour around him of men and of dogs, and sleep is gone from them* K 185.

a. So also in clauses preceded by a relative word; as εἷος ὁ ταῦθ' ὥρμαινε . . ., ἐκ δ' Ἑλένη θαλάμοιο . . . ἤλυθεν *while he was pondering on this,* (but) *Helen came forth from her chamber* δ 120, ὅς κε θεοῖς ἐπιπείθηται, μάλα τ' ἔκλυον αὐτοῦ *whoever obeys the gods,* (and) *him they hear* A 218.

b. This use appears even in Attic prose; as οἰκοῦσι δ' ἐν μιᾷ τῶν νήσων οὐ μεγάλῃ, καλεῖται δὲ (for ἣ καλεῖται) Λιπάρᾱ *they dwell in one of the islands that is not large, and it* (which) *is called Lipara* T. 3.88. Cp. also 2837.

SYNTAX OF THE COMPLEX SENTENCE

2173. A complex sentence consists of a principal sentence and one or more subordinate, or dependent, sentences. The principal sentence, as each subordinate sentence, has its own subject and predicate. The principal sentence of a complex sentence is called the principal clause, the subordinate sentence is called the subordinate clause. The principal clause may precede or follow the subordinate clause.

2174. The principal clause may have any form of the simple sentence.

a. Parentheses belonging to the thought of the entire sentence, but standing in no close grammatical relation to it, count as principal clauses. So οἶμαι, δοκῶ, φημί, ὁρᾷς; οἶδα, οἶδ' ὅτι *certainly* (2585), εὖ ἴσθι *know well*, αἰτοῦμαί σε *I beseech thee*; πῶς (πόσον) δοκεῖς; and πῶς οἴει; in the comic poets and Euripides, etc. Some of these expressions are almost adverbial.

2175. The subordinate clause is always introduced by a subordinating conjunction, as εἰ *if*, ἐπεί *since* or *when*, ὅτι *that*, ἕως *until*, etc.

2176. A finite mood in a subordinate clause may be influenced by the tense of the principal clause. If the verb of the principal clause stands in a secondary tense, the verb of the subordinate clause is often optative instead of indicative or subjunctive, as it would have been after a primary tense. Dependence of mood after a secondary tense is never indicated by the subjunctive.

2177. Each tense in a subordinate clause denotes stage of action; the *time* is only relative to that of the leading verb. A subordinate clause may be marked by change of person in verb and pronoun.

2178. A subordinate clause in English may be expressed in Greek by a predicate adjective or substantive. Cp. 1169, 2647.

2179. A subordinate clause may be coördinate in structure.

ἐπεὶ δ' ἠσθένει Δᾱρεῖος καὶ ὑπώπτευε τελευτὴν τοῦ βίου, ἐβούλετό οἱ τὼ παῖδε παρεῖναι *but when Darius was ill and suspected that his end was near, he wished his two sons to be by him* X. A. 1. 1. 1.

a. So a relative clause, though properly subordinate, may be equivalent to a coördinating clause: εἰ δ' ὑμεῖς ἄλλο τι γνώσεσθε, ὃ μὴ γένοιτο, τίν' οἴεσθ' αὐτὴν ψῡχὴν ἕξειν; *but if you decide otherwise, — and may this never come to pass! — what do you think will be her feelings?* D. 28. 21. In such cases ὅς is equivalent to καὶ οὗτος, οὗτος δέ, οὗτος γάρ.

2180. A clause dependent upon the principal clause may itself be followed by a clause dependent upon itself (a sub-dependent clause).

οἱ δ' ἔλεγον (principal clause) ὅτι περὶ σπονδῶν ἥκοιεν ἄνδρες (dependent clause) οἵτινες ἱκανοὶ ἔσονται . . . ἀπαγγεῖλαι (sub-dependent clause) *and they said that they had come with regard to a truce and were men who were competent to . . . report* X. A. 2. 3. 4.

2181. A verb common to two clauses is generally placed in one clause and omitted from the other (so especially in comparative and relative clauses).

ἥπερ (τύχη) ἀεὶ βέλτιον (scil. ἐπιμελεῖται) ἢ ἡμεῖς ἡμῶν αὐτῶν ἐπιμελούμεθα *fortune, which always cares better for us than we for ourselves* D. 4. 12. Also as in English: ὅ τι δὲ μέλλετε (πράσσειν), . . . εὐθὺς . . . πράσσετε *but whatever you intend, do it at once* T. 7. 15. In comparative clauses with οὐχ ὥσπερ (or ὡς) the main and the subordinate clause are sometimes compressed, the predicate of the clause with οὐχ being supplied from the ὥσπερ clause, which is made independent; as οὐχ (οὐδὲν ἂν ἐγίγνετο) ὥσπερ νῦν τούτων οὐδὲν γίγνεται περὶ αὐτόν *it would not be as now, when none of these things is done for him* P. S. 189 c.

ANTICIPATION (OR PROLEPSIS)

2182. The subject of the dependent clause is often anticipated and made the object of the verb of the principal clause. This transference, which gives a more prominent place to the subject of the subordinate clause, is called *anticipation* or *prolepsis* (πρόληψις *taking before*).

δέδοικα δ' αὐτὴν μή τι βουλεύσῃ νέον *but I fear lest she may devise something untoward* E. Med. 37, ᾔδει αὐτὸν ὅτι μέσον ἔχοι τοῦ Περσικοῦ στρατεύματος *he knew that he held the centre of the Persian army* X. A. 1. 8. 21, ἐπεμέλετο αὐτῶν ὅπως ἀεὶ ἀνδράποδα διατελοῖεν *he took care that they should always continue to be slaves* X. C. 8. 1. 44. Note ὁρᾷς τὸν εὐτράπεζον ὡς ἡδὺς βίος *thou seest how sweet is the luxurious life* E. fr. 1052. 3.

a. Anticipation is especially common after verbs of *saying*, *seeing*, *hearing*, *knowing*, *fearing*, *effecting*.

b. When a subordinate clause defines a verbal idea consisting of a verb and a substantive, its subject may pass into the principal clause as a genitive depending on the substantive of that clause: ἦλθε δὲ καὶ τοῖς Ἀθηναίοις εὐθὺς ἡ ἀγγελίᾱ τῶν πόλεων ὅτι ἀφεστᾶσι *and there came straightway to the Athenians also the report that the cities had revolted* T. 1. 61 (= ὅτι αἱ πόλεις ἀφεστᾶσι).

c. The subject of the dependent clause may be put first in its own clause: ἐπιχειρήσωμεν εἰπεῖν, ἀνδρείᾱ τί ποτ' ἐστίν *let us try to say what courage is* P. Lach. 190 d.

d. The object of the subordinate clause may be anticipated and made the object of the principal clause. Thus, εἰρώτᾱ ὁ Δᾱρεῖος τὴν τέχνην εἰ ἐπίσταιτο *Darius asked if he understood the art* Hdt. 3. 130.

e. A still freer use is seen in ἐθαύμαζεν αὐτὸν ὁ Λύσανδρος ὡς καλὰ τὰ δένδρα εἴη *Lysander marvelled at the beauty of his trees* (for τὰ δένδρα αὐτοῦ ὡς κτλ.) X. O. 4. 21.

ASSIMILATION OF MOODS

2183. The mood of a subordinate clause which is intimately connected with the thought of the clause on which it depends, is often assimilated to the mood of that clause. Such subordinate clauses may be simply dependent or sub-dependent (2180).

a. This idiom is most marked in Unreal and Less Vivid Future conditions where the mood of the protasis is the same as that of the principal clause. It is also very common when a past indicative or an optative attracts the mood of a subordinate clause introduced by a relative word referring to indefinite persons or things or to an indefinite time or place. But subordinate clauses standing in a less close relation to the main clause, because they do not continue the same mental attitude but present a new shade of thought, retain their mood unassimilated; *e.g.* a relative clause, or a temporal clause expressing purpose, after an unreal condition may stand in the optative (Is. 4. 11, P. R. 600 e). On the other hand, there are many cases where the writer may, or may not, adopt modal assimilation without any great difference of meaning. The following sections give the chief occurrences of mood-assimilation apart from that found in Unreal and Less Vivid Future conditions (2302, 2329):

2184. An indicative referring simply to the present or past remains unassimilated.

ξυνενέγκοι μὲν ταῦτα ὡς βουλόμεθα *may this result as we desire* T. 6. 20, νῑκῴη δ' ὅ τι πᾶσιν μέλλει συνοίσειν *but may that prevail which is likely to be for the common weal* D. 4. 51, ἐπειδὰν διαπράξωμαι ἃ δέομαι, ἥξω *when I shall have transacted what I want, I will return* X. A. 2. 3. 29.

2185. Assimilation to the Indicative.—The subordinate clause takes a past tense of the indicative in dependence on a past tense of the indicative (or its equivalent) denoting unreality.

a. Conditional relative clauses: εἰ μὲν γὰρ ἦν μοι χρήματα, ἐτῑμησάμην ἂν χρημάτων ὅσα ἔμελλον ἐκτείσειν *for if I had money, I should have assessed my penalty at the full sum that I was likely to pay* P. A. 38 b, εἰ . . . κατεμαρτύρουν ἃ μὴ σαφῶς ᾔδη ἀκοῇ δὲ ἠπιστάμην, δεινὰ ἂν ἔφη πάσχειν ὑπ' ἐμοῦ *if I brought in as evidence against him matters which I did not know certainly but had learned by hearsay, he would have said that he was suffering a grave injustice at my hands* Ant. 5. 74.

b. Temporal clauses: οὐκ ἂν ἐπαυόμην . . ., ἕως ἀπεπειράθην τῆς σοφίᾱς ταυτησί *I would not have ceased until I had made trial of this wisdom* P. Crat. 396 c, ἐχρῆν . . . μὴ πρότερον περὶ τῶν ὁμολογουμένων συμβουλεύειν, πρὶν περὶ τῶν ἀμφισβητουμένων ἡμᾶς ἐδίδαξαν *they ought not to have given advice concerning the matters of common agreement before they instructed us on the matters in dispute* I. 4. 19.

c. Final clauses: here the principal clause is an unfulfilled wish, an unfulfilled apodosis, or a question with οὐ; and the indicative in the final clause denotes that the purpose *was not* or *cannot be* attained, and cannot be reached by the will of the speaker. Thus, εἰ γὰρ ὤφελον οἷοί τε εἶναι οἱ πολλοὶ τὰ μέγιστα κακὰ ἐργάζεσθαι, ἵνα οἷοί τε ἦσαν καὶ ἀγαθὰ τὰ μέγιστα *would that the many were able to work the greatest evil in order that they might be able* (as they are *not*) *to work also the greatest good* P. Cr. 44 d, ἐβουλόμην ἂν Σίμωνα τὴν αὐτὴν γνώμην ἐμοὶ ἔχειν ἵνα . . . ῥᾳδίως ἔγνωτε τὰ δίκαια *I should have liked Simon to be of the same opinion as myself in order that you might easily have rendered a just verdict* L. 3. 21, ἔδει τὰ ἐνέχυρα τότε λαβεῖν, ὡς μηδ' εἰ ἐβούλετο ἐδύνατο ἐξαπατᾶν *I ought to have taken security at the time in order that he could not have deceived us even if he wished* X. A. 7. 6. 23, τί δῆτ' οὐκ ἔρριψ' ἐμαυτὸν τῆσδ' ἀπὸ πέτρᾱς, ὅπως τῶν πάντων πόνων ἀπηλλάγην; *why indeed did I not hurl myself from this rock, that I might have been freed from all these toils?* A. Pr. 747.

N. 1. — In this (post-Homeric) construction, ἵνα is the regular conjunction in prose; ὡς and ὅπως are rare. ἄν is very rarely added and is suspected (Is. 11. 6, P. L. 959 e).

N. 2. — Assimilation does not take place when the final clause is the essential thing and sets forth a real future purpose of the agent of the leading verb, or does not show whether or not the purpose was realized. This occurs especially after ἵνα = *eo consilio ut*, rarely after ὅπως (X. A. 7. 6. 16); after ὡς only in poetry and Xenophon. The subjunctive or optative is used when the purpose of the agent, and not the non-fulfilment of the action, is emphasized. Thus, καίτοι χρῆν σε . . . ἢ τοῦτον μὴ γράφειν ἢ ἐκεῖνον λύειν, οὐχ, ἵν' ὃ βούλει σὺ γένηται, πάντα τὰ πράγματα συνταράξαι *you ought either not to have proposed this law or to have repealed the other; not to have thrown everything into confusion to accomplish your desire* D. 24. 44.

d. Causal clauses (rarely, as D. 50. 67). Modal assimilation never takes place in indirect questions or in clauses dependent on a verb of *fearing*.

2186. Assimilation to the Optative. — When an optative of the principal clause refers to *future* time (potential optative and optative of wish), the subordinate clause takes the optative by assimilation in the following cases.

a. Conditional relative clauses (regularly): πῶς γὰρ ἄν (1832) τις, ἅ γε μὴ ἐπίσταιτο, ταῦτα σοφὸς εἴη; *for how could any one be wise in that which he does not know?* X. M. 4. 6. 7, τίς μῑσεῖν δύναιτ' ἂν ὑφ' οὗ εἰδείη καλός τε καὶ ἀγαθὸς νομιζόμενος; *who could hate one by whom he knew that he was regarded as both beautiful and good?* X. S. 8. 17, ἔρδοι τις ἣν ἕκαστος εἰδείη τέχνην *would that every man would practise the craft that he understood* Ar. Vesp. 1431, τίς ἂν . . . μόλοι (1832), ὅστις διαγγείλειε τἄμ' εἴσω κακά *would that some one would come to report within my tale of woe* E. Hel. 435.

N. 1. — If the relative has a definite antecedent, assimilation does not take place; but not all relative clauses with an indefinite antecedent are assimilated. Cp. ὥσπερ ἂν ὑμῶν ἕκαστος αἰσχυνθείη τὴν τάξιν λιπεῖν ἣν ἂν ταχθῇ ἐν τῷ πολέμῳ *as each one of you would be ashamed to leave the post to which he may be appointed in war* Aes. 3. 7.

N. 2. — A relative clause depending on an infinitive rarely takes the optative: ἀλλὰ τοῦ μὲν αὐτὸν λέγειν ἃ μὴ σαφῶς εἰδείη εἴργεσθαι δεῖ *one should abstain from saying oneself what one does not know for certain* X. C. 1. 6. 19. (See 2573.)

b. Temporal clauses (regularly): τεθναίην, ὅτε μοι μηκέτι ταῦτα μέλοι *may I die when these things no longer delight me* Mimnermus 1.2, ὁ μὲν ἑκὼν πεινῶν φάγοι ἂν ὁπότε βούλοιτο *he who starves of his own free will can eat whenever he wishes* X. M. 2. 1. 18, εἰ δὲ πάνυ σπουδάζοι φαγεῖν, εἴποιμ' ἂν ὅτι παρὰ ταῖς γυναιξίν ἐστιν, ἕως παρατείναιμι τοῦτον κτλ. *but if he was very desirous of eating, I would tell him that "he was with the women" until I had tortured him*, etc. X. C. 1. 3. 11, ὄλοιο μήπω, πρὶν μάθοιμι *perish not yet . . . until I learn* S. Ph. 961. But οὐκ ἂν ἀπέλθοιμι πρὶν ἂν παντάπᾱσιν ἡ ἀγορᾱ̀ λυθῇ *I shall not be leaving until the gathering in the market-place is quite dispersed* X. O. 12. 1.

c. Final and object clauses (rarely in prose, but occasionally after an optative of wish in poetry): πειρῴμην (ἂν) μὴ πρόσω ὑμῶν εἶναι, ἵνα, εἴ που καιρὸς εἴη, ἐπιφανείην *I will try to keep not far away from you, in order that, if there should be any occasion, I may show myself* X. C. 2. 4. 17 (and five other cases in Xen.); ἔλθοι ὅπως γένοιτο τῶνδ' ἐμοὶ λυτήριος *may she come to prove my liberator from this affliction* A. Eum. 297. Ordinarily the subjunctive or future indicative is retained, as ὀκνοίην ἂν εἰς τὰ πλοῖα ἐμβαίνειν ἃ Κῦρος ἡμῖν δοίη μὴ ἡμᾶς . . . καταδύσῃ *I should hesitate to embark on the vessels which Cyrus might give us lest he sink us* X. A. 1. 3. 17, τεθναίην, δίκην ἐπιθεὶς τῷ ἀδικοῦντι, ἵνα μὴ ἐνθάδε μένω καταγέλαστος *let me die, when I have punished him who has done me wrong, that I may not remain here a laughing-stock* P. A. 28 d.

d. Indirect questions, when the direct question was a deliberative subjunctive: οὐκ ἂν ἔχοις ἐξελθὼν ὅ τι χρῷο σαυτῷ *if you should escape, you would not know what to do with yourself* P. Cr. 45 b (= τί χρῶμαι;). But when a direct question or a direct quotation stood in the indicative, that mood is retained, as εἰ ἀποδειχθείη τίνας χρὴ ἡγεῖσθαι τοῦ πλαισίου *if it should be settled who must lead the square* X. A. 3. 2. 36.

e. Very rarely in relative clauses of purpose (P. R. 578 e possibly); after ὥστε (X. C. 5. 5. 30), and in dependent statements with ὅτι or ὡς (X. C. 3. 1. 28).

f. Assimilation and non-assimilation may occur in the same sentence (E. Bacch. 1384 ff.)

2187. An optative referring to *general past* time in a general supposition usually assimilates the mood of a conditional relative or temporal clause depending on that optative.

ἔχαιρεν ὁπότε τάχιστα τυχόντας ὧν δέοιντο ἀποπέμποι *but he was wont to rejoice whenever he dismissed without delay his petitioners with their requests granted* (lit. *obtaining what they wanted*) X. Ag. 9. 2. But the indicative may remain unassimilated, as ἐκάλει δὲ καὶ ἐτίμᾱ ὁπότε τινὰς ἴδοι τοιοῦτόν τι ποιήσαντας ὃ αὐτὸς ἐβούλετο ποιεῖν *and he was wont to honour with an invitation any whom he saw practising anything that he himself wished them to do* X. C. 2. 1. 30.

So when the optative refers to past time through dependence on a verb of past time, as προσκαλῶν τοὺς φίλους ἐσπουδαιολογεῖτο ὡς δηλοίη οὓς τῑμᾷ *summoning his friends he used to carry on a serious conversation with them in order to show whom he honoured* X. A. 1. 9. 28 (here τῑμῴη would be possible).

2188. Assimilation to the Subjunctive. — Conditional relative clauses and temporal clauses referring to *future* or *general present* time, if dependent on a subjunctive, take the subjunctive.

a. In reference to future time: τῶν πρᾱγμάτων τοὺς βουλευομένους (ἡγεῖσθαι δεῖ), ἵν' ἃν ἐκείνοις δοκῇ, ταῦτα πράττηται *men of counsel must guide events in order that what they resolve shall be accomplished* D. 4. 39.

b. In reference to general present time: οὐδ', ἐπειδὰν ὧν ἂν πρίηται κύριος γένηται, τῷ προδότῃ συμβούλῳ περὶ τῶν λοιπῶν ἔτι χρῆται *nor when he has become master of what he purchases, does he any longer employ the traitor to advise him concerning his plans for the future* D. 18. 47. But the indicative may occur (D. 22. 22).

CLASSES OF SUBORDINATE CLAUSES

2189. Subordinate clauses are of three classes:

1. Substantival clauses: in which the subordinate clause plays the part of a substantive and is either the subject or the object: δῆλον ἦν | ὅτι ἐγγύς που βασιλεὺς ἦν *it was plain that the king was somewhere hard by* X. A. 2. 3. 6, οὐκ ἴστε | ὅ τι ποιεῖτε *you do not know what you are doing* 1. 5. 16.

2. Adjectival (attributive) clauses: in which the subordinate clause plays the part of an adjective, and contains a relative whose antecedent (expressed or implied) stands in the principal clause: λέγε δὴ τὴν ἐπιστολὴν | ἣν ἔπεμψε Φίλιππος *come read the letter which Philip sent* D. 18. 39 (= τὴν ὑπὸ Φιλίππου πεμφθεῖσαν).

3. Adverbial clauses: in which the subordinate clause plays the part of an adverb or adverbial expression modifying the principal clause in like manner as an adverb modifies a verb.

κραυγὴν πολλὴν ἐποίουν καλοῦντες ἀλλήλους, ὥστε καὶ τοὺς πολεμίους ἀκούειν *they made a loud noise by calling each other so that even the enemy heard them* X. A. 2. 2. 17 (here ὥστε . . . ἀκούειν may be regarded as having the force of an adverb: *and in a manner audible even to the enemy*); πῶς ἂν οὖν ὀρθῶς δικάσαιτε περὶ αὐτῶν; εἰ τούτους ἐάσετε τὸν νομιζόμενον ὅρκον διομοσαμένους κατηγορῆσαι κτλ. *how then would you judge correctly about them? if you permit* (*i.e.* by permitting) *them to make their accusations after having sworn the customary oath*, etc. Ant. 5. 90. Cp. 1095 end.

2190. Accordingly all complex sentences may be classified as Substantival sentences, Adjectival sentences, and Adverbial sentences. This division is, in general, the basis of the treatment of complex sentences in this book, except when, for convenience, closely connected constructions are treated together; as in the case of (adverbial) pure final clauses and (substantival) object clauses after verbs of *effort* and of *fearing*.

a. Some sentences may be classed both as substantival and adverbial, as clauses with ὥστε and ὅπως. An adverbial or adjectival clause may assume a substantival character (2247, 2488).

Complex sentences are considered in the following order: Adverbial, Adjectival, Substantival.

ADVERBIAL COMPLEX SENTENCES (2193–2487)

2191. In an adverbial complex sentence the subordinate clause denotes some one of the following adverbial relations: purpose (2193), cause (2240), result (2249), condition (2280), concession (2369), time (2383), comparison (2462).

2192. An adverbial sentence is introduced by a relative conjunction denoting *purpose, cause, result,* etc.

PURPOSE CLAUSES (FINAL CLAUSES)

2193. Final clauses denote purpose and are introduced by **ἵνα**, ὅπως, ὡς *in order that, that* (Lat. *ut*); negative ἵνα μή, ὅπως μή, ὡς μή, and μή alone, *lest* (Lat. *ne*).

a. Also by **ὄφρα**, strictly *while, until,* in Epic and Lyric; and **ἕως** in Epic (2418). **ἵνα** is the chief final conjunction in Aristophanes, Herodotus, Plato, and the orators. It is the only purely final conjunction in that it does not limit the idea of purpose by the idea of time (like ὄφρα and ἕως), or of manner (like ὅπως and ὡς); and therefore never takes ἄν (κέν), since the purpose is regarded as free from all conditions (2201 b). **ὅπως** is the chief final conjunction in Thucydides, and in Xenophon (slightly more common than ἵνα). **ὡς** often shows the original meaning *in which way, how, as* (cp. 2578, 2989). It is rare in prose, except in Xenophon, and does not occur on inscriptions; rare in Aristophanes, but common in tragedy, especially in Euripides. **μή** is very rare in prose, except in Xenophon and Plato (**μὴ οὐ** is very rare in Homer and in Attic: X. M. 2. 2. 14).

b. *In order that no one* is ἵνα (etc.) μηδείς or μή τις, *in order that . . . never* is ἵνα (etc.) μήποτε or μή ποτε, *and in order that . . . not* is μηδέ after μή.

2194. Final clauses were developed from original coördination.

θάπτε με ὅττι τάχιστα· πύλᾱς Ἀΐδᾱο περήσω *bury me with all speed; let me pass the gates of Hades* Ψ 71, where we have a sentence of will added without any connective; and (negative) ἀπόστιχε μή τι νοήσῃ Ἥρη *depart lest Hera observe aught* A 522 (originally *let Hera not observe anything*, 1802). Even in Attic, where subordination is regular, the original form of coördination can be (theoretically) restored, as in καί σε πρὸς . . . θεῶν ἱκνοῦμαι μὴ προδοὺς ἡμᾶς γένῃ *and I entreat thee by the gods | do not forsake us* S. Aj. 588. We can no longer trace the original coördination with ἵνα and ὡς.

2195. A final clause stands in apposition to τούτου ἕνεκα or διὰ τοῦτο expressed or understood. Thus, ἐκκλησίᾱν τούτου ἕνεκα ξυνήγαγον ὅπως ὑπομνήσω *I have convened an assembly for this reason that I may remind* you T. 2. 60. Here τούτου ἕνεκα might be omitted.

2196. The verb of a final clause stands in the subjunctive after an introductory primary tense, in the optative (sometimes in the subjunctive, 2197) after a secondary tense.

γράφω ἵνα ἐκμάθῃς *I write* (on this account) *that you may learn.*

γράφω ἵνα μὴ ἐκμάθῃς *I write* (on this account) *that you may not learn.*

ἔγραψα ἵνα ἐκμάθοις (or ἐκμάθῃς) *I wrote* (on this account) *that you might learn.*

ἔγραψα ἵνα μὴ ἐκμάθοις (or ἐκμάθῃς) *I wrote* (on this account) *that you might not learn.*

κατάμενε ἵνα καὶ περὶ σοῦ βουλευσώμεθα *remain behind that we may consider your case also* X. A. 6. 6. 28, βασιλεὺς αἱρεῖται οὐχ ἵνα ἑαυτοῦ καλῶς ἐπιμελῆται, ἀλλ' ἵνα καὶ οἱ ἑλόμενοι δι' αὐτὸν εὖ πράττωσι *a king is chosen, not that he may care for his own interest however nobly, but that those who choose him may prosper through him* X. M. 3. 2. 3, παρακαλεῖς ἰᾱτροὺς ὅπως μὴ ἀποθάνῃ *you call in physicians in order that he may not die* X. M. 2. 10. 2, φύλακας συμπέμπει (hist. pres., 1883) . . . ὅπως ἀπὸ τῶν δυσχωριῶν φυλάττοιεν αὐτόν *he sent guards along in order that they might guard him from the rough parts of the country* X. C. 1. 4. 7, καὶ ἅμα ταῦτ' εἰπὼν ἀνέστη ὡς μὴ μέλλοιτο ἀλλὰ περαίνοιτο τὰ δέοντα *and with these words on his lips he stood up in order that what was needful might not be delayed but be done at once* X. A. 3. 1. 47, μὴ σπεῦδε πλουτεῖν μὴ ταχὺς πένης γένῃ *haste not to be rich lest thou soon become poor* Men. Sent. 358. For the optative after an optative, see 2186 c.

2197. After a secondary tense, the subjunctive may be used in place of the optative.

a. In the narration of past events, the subjunctive sets forth a person's previous purpose in the form in which he conceived his purpose. Thus (τὰ πλοῖα) Ἀβροκόμᾱς . . . κατέκαυσεν ἵνα μὴ Κῦρος διαβῇ *Abrocomas burned the boats in order that Cyrus might* (may) *not cross* X. A. 1. 4. 18. Here the thought of A. was 'I will burn the boats that Cyrus may not cross' (ἵνα μὴ διαβῇ), and is given in a kind of quotation.

N.—Thucydides and Herodotus prefer this vivid subjunctive; the poets, Plato, and Xenophon, the optative. In Demosthenes, the subjunctive and optative are equally common.

b. When the purpose (or its effect) is represented as still continuing in the present. See the example in 2195. This use is closely connected with **a.**

c. After **τί οὐ, τί οὖν οὐ,** and the aorist indicative: τί οὖν οὐχὶ τὰ μὲν τείχη φυλακῇ ἐχυρὰ ἐποιήσαμεν ὅπως ἂν (2201) σοι σᾶ ᾖ κτλ.; *why then do we not make your walls strong by a garrison that they may be safe for you,* etc.? X. C. 5. 4. 37. Here the sentence with ἐποιήσαμεν is practically equivalent to one with ποιήσωμεν.

2198. The alternative construction of final clauses with subjunctive or optative is that of implicit indirect discourse (2622). The subjunctive is always possible instead of the optative. Observe that the subjunctive for the optative is relatively past, since the leading verb is past.

2199. After a secondary tense both subjunctive and optative may be used in the same sentence.

ναῦς οἱ Κορίνθιοι . . . ἐπλήρουν ὅπως ναυμαχίᾱς τε ἀποπειράσωσι . . ., καὶ τὰς ὁλκάδας αὐτῶν ἧσσον οἱ ἐν τῇ Ναυπάκτῳ Ἀθηναῖοι κωλύοιεν ἀπαίρειν *the Corinthians manned . . . ships both to try a naval battle and that the Athenians at Naupactus might be less able to prevent their transports from putting out to sea* T. 7. 17.

a. In some cases, especially when the subjunctive precedes, the subjunctive may express the immediate purpose, the realization of which is expected; while the optative expresses the less immediate purpose conceived as a consequence of the action of the subjunctive or as a mere possibility.

2200. The optative is very rare after a primary tense except when that tense implies a reference to the past as well as to the present.

οἴχονται ἵνα μὴ δοῖεν δίκην *they have gone away that they might not suffer punishment* L. 20. 21. Here οἴχονται is practically equivalent to ἔφυγον, and the optative δοῖεν shows that the purpose was conceived in the past. On the optative (without ἄν) by assimilation after an optative, see 2186 c.

2201. ὅπως with the subjunctive sometimes takes ἄν in positive clauses.

τοῦτ' αὐτὸ νῦν δίδασχ', ὅπως ἂν ἐκμάθω *tell me now this very thing, that I may learn* S. O. C. 575, ἄξεις ἡμᾶς ὅπως ἂν εἰδῶμεν *you will guide us in order that we may know* X. C. 5. 2. 21.

a. **ὡς** and **ὄφρα** with ἄν or κέ occur in poetry, especially in Homer. **ὡς ἄν** (first in Aeschylus) is very rare in Attic prose, but occurs eight times in Xenophon; as ὡς δ' ἂν μάθῃς . . ., ἀντάκουσον *but that you may learn, hear me in turn* X. A. 2. 5. 16. This use must not be confused with ὡς ἄν in conditional relative clauses (2565). — **ὅπως ἄν** is more common than simple ὅπως in Aristophanes and Plato, far less common in Xenophon. It is regular in official and legal language. — **ἵνα ἄν** is not final, but local (*wherever*, 2567). The original meaning of ἵνα was local and denoted the end to be reached.

b. ἄν (κέ) does not appreciably affect the meaning. Originally these particles seem to have had a limiting and conditional force (1762): ὡς ἄν *in whatever way, that so* (cp. *so* = *in order that so*) as in "Teach me to die that so I may Rise glorious at the awful day" (Bishop Ken), and cp. ὡς with ὅτῳ τρόπῳ in ἱκόμην τὸ Πυθικὸν μαντεῖον, ὡς μάθοιμ' ὅτῳ τρόπῳ πατρὶ δίκας ἀροίμην *I came to the Pythian shrine that I might learn in what way I might avenge my father* S. El. 33. With ὅπως ἄν cp. ἐάν πως. Both ὅπως and ὡς were originally relative adverbs denoting *manner* (*how*, cp. 2578), but when they became conjunctions (*in order that*), their limitation by ἄν ceased to be felt.

2202. ὡς ἄν and ὅπως ἄν with the optative occur very rarely in Attic prose (in Xenophon especially), and more frequently after secondary than after primary tenses.

ἔδωκε χρήματα Ἀνταλκίδᾳ ὅπως ἂν πληρωθέντος ναυτικοῦ . . . οἵ τε Ἀθηναῖοι . . . μᾶλλον τῆς εἰρήνης προσδέοιντο *he gave money to Antalcidas in order that, if a fleet were manned, the Athenians might be more disposed to peace* X. H. 4. 8. 16. ὡς ἄν final must be distinguished from ὡς ἄν consecutive (2278).

a. Homer has a few cases of ὡς ἄν (κέ) and ὄφρ' ἄν (κέ); ἵνα κεν once (μ 156). Hdt. has ὡς ἄν, ὅκως ἄν rarely.

b. After primary tenses the optative with ἄν is certainly, after secondary tenses probably, *potential.* Its combination with the final conjunction produces a conditional relative clause in which the relative and interrogative force of ὅπως and ὡς comes to light. With ὅπως ἄν the final force is stronger than with ὡς ἄν. In the example quoted above, πληρωθέντος ναυτικοῦ represents the protasis (εἰ ναυτικὸν πληρωθείη) to ἂν προσδέοιντο.

2203. The future indicative is used, especially in poetry, after ὅπως (rarely after ὡς, ὄφρα, and μή) in the same sense as the subjunctive.

οὐδὲ δι' ἓν ἄλλο τρέφονται ἢ ὅπως μαχοῦνται *nor are they maintained for any other single purpose than for fighting* (lit. *how they shall fight*) X. C. 2. 1. 21, σῖγᾶθ', ὅπως μὴ πεύσεταί (fut.) τις . . . γλώσσης χάριν δὲ πάντ' ἀπαγγείλῃ (subj.) τάδε *keep silence, lest some one hear and report all this for the sake of talk* A. Ch. 265. In prose the future occurs with ὅπως in Xenophon and Andocides. This usage is an extension of that after verbs of *effort* (2211).

2204. The principal clause is sometimes omitted.

ἵν' ἐκ τούτων ἄρξωμαι *to begin with this* D. 21. 43. ἵνα τί, originally *to what end* (cp. 946), and ὡς τί are also used colloquially: ἵνα τί ταῦτα λέγεις; *why do you say this?* P. A. 26 d.

2205. By assimilation of mood, final clauses may take a past tense of the indicative without ἄν (2185 c) or the optative without ἄν (2186 c.)

2206. Equivalents of a Final Clause. — The common methods of expressing purpose may be illustrated by the translations (in Attic) of *they sent a herald to announce:*

ἔπεμψαν κήρῡκα ἵνα (ὅπως) ἀπαγγέλλοιτο (2196).
ἔπεμψαν κήρῡκα ὅστις (ὅς) ἀπαγγελεῖται (2554).
ἔπεμψαν κήρῡκα ἀπαγγελοῦντα (2065), ἀπαγγέλλοντα (rare, 2065).
ἔπεμψαν κήρῡκα ὡς ἀπαγγελοῦντα (2086 c).
ἔπεμψαν κήρῡκα ἀπαγγέλλειν (rare in prose, 2009).
ἔπεμψαν κήρῡκα τοῦ ἀπαγγέλλειν (2032 e, often in Thucydides).
ἔπεμψαν κήρῡκα ὑπὲρ (ἕνεκα) τοῦ ἀπαγγέλλειν (2032 g).

For ὥστε denoting an intended result, see 2267.

OBJECT CLAUSES

2207. Two types of object (substantival) clauses are closely connected in construction with final clauses.

1. Object clauses after verbs of *effort.*
2. Object clauses after verbs of *fearing.*

Both stand in apposition to a demonstrative expressed or implied.

οὐδένα δεῖ τοῦτο μηχανᾶσθαι, ὅπως ἀποφεύξεται πᾶν ποιῶν θάνατον *no man ought to contrive (this) how he shall escape death at any cost* P. A. 39 a, μηχανᾶσθαι ὅκως τὸ σῶμα . . . κομιεῖ *to contrive how he might bring home the body* Hdt. 2. 121 γ, αὐτὸ τοῦτο φοβοῦμαι, μὴ . . . οὐ δυνηθῶ δηλῶσαι περὶ τῶν πρᾱγμάτων *I am afraid of this very thing, namely, that I may not be able to make the case plain* D. 41. 2, ἐφοβεῖτο . . . μὴ οὐ δύναιτο . . . ἐξελθεῖν *he was afraid that he could not escape* X. A. 3. 1. 12.

2208. Connection of Final with Object Clauses. — (1) Final clauses proper denote a purpose to accomplish or avert a result, which purpose is set forth in a definite action. (2) Object clauses after verbs of *effort* consider means to accomplish or avert a result; the action of the subordinate clause is the *object purposed.* Such clauses are *incomplete* final clauses, because, though the purpose is expressed, the action taken to effect the purpose is not expressed. (3) Object clauses after verbs of *fearing* deprecate an undesired result or express fear that a desired result may not be accomplished. According to the form of expression employed, the construction of these three kinds of clauses may differ in varying degree or be identical. Thus compare these usages of Attic prose:

(1) παρακαλεῖ ἰᾱτρὸν ὅπως μὴ ἀποθάνῃ (common)
παρακαλεῖ ἰᾱτρὸν ὅπως μὴ ἀποθανεῖται (occasionally)
παρακαλεῖ ἰᾱτρὸν μὴ ἀποθάνῃ (rare)
he summons a physician in order that he may not die.

(2) ἐπιμελεῖται ὅπως μὴ ἀποθανεῖται (common)
ἐπιμελεῖται ὅπως μὴ ἀποθάνῃ (occasionally)
he takes care that he shall not die.
ὅρᾱ μὴ ἀποθάνῃς (occasionally) *see to it that you do not die.*

(3) φοβεῖται μὴ ἀποθάνῃ (common)
φοβεῖται ὅπως μὴ ἀποθάνῃ (occasionally)
φοβεῖται ὅπως μὴ ἀποθανεῖται (occasionally)
he is afraid lest he die.

OBJECT CLAUSES AFTER VERBS OF EFFORT

2209. Object clauses after verbs of *effort* are introduced by ὅπως, rarely by ὡς (Herodotus, Xenophon), scarcely ever by ἵνα. The negative is μή.

2210. Verbs of *effort* include verbs denoting *to take care* or *pains, to strive.*

ἐπιμελοῦμαι, μέλει μοι, μελετῶ, φρουρῶ, πρόνοιαν ἔχω, βουλεύομαι, μηχανῶμαι, παρασκευάζομαι, προθῡμοῦμαι, πρᾱ́ττω, πάντα ποιῶ (ποιοῦμαι), σπουδάζω, etc.

a. The same construction follows certain verbs of will signifying *to ask, command, entreat, exhort,* and *forbid,* and which commonly take the infinitive (**αἰτῶ, δέομαι, παραγγέλλω, ἱκετεύω, δια-** or **παρακελεύομαι, ἀπαγορεύω,** etc.).

b. Some verbs take, by analogy, but in negative clauses only, the construction either of verbs of *effort* or of verbs of *fearing.* These verbs signify *to see to a thing:* **ὁρῶ, σκοπῶ (-οῦμαι), ἐσκεψάμην, σκεπτέον ἐστί, τηρῶ**; *to be on one's guard:* **εὐλαβοῦμαι, φροντίζω, φυλάττω (-ομαι).** See 2220.

These verbs may take μή with the infinitive. εὐλαβοῦμαι and φυλάττομαι take the infinitive when they mean *to guard against doing something.*

2211. Object clauses after verbs of *effort* take the future indicative with ὅπως after primary and secondary tenses (rarely the optative after secondary tenses, 2212).

ἐπιμελοῦμαι ὅπως ταῦτα ποιήσει *I take care that he shall do this.*
ἐπιμελοῦμαι ὅπως μὴ ταῦτα ποιήσει *I take care that he shall not do this.*
ἐπεμελούμην ὅπως ταῦτα ποιήσει (ποιήσοι) *I took care that he should do this.*
ἐπεμελούμην ὅπως μὴ ταῦτα ποιήσει (ποιήσοι) *I took care that he should not do this.*

εἰ ἀνάγκη ἐστὶ μάχεσθαι, τοῦτο δεῖ παρασκευάσασθαι ὅπως ὡς κράτιστα μαχούμεθα *if it is necessary to fight, we must prepare to fight bravely* X. A. 4. 6. 10, ἔπρᾱσσον ὅπως τις βοήθεια ἥξει *they were managing* (this, that) *how some reinforcements should come* T. 3. 4, σκοπεῖσθε τοῦτο, ὅπως μὴ λόγους ἐροῦσιν μόνον . . . ἀλλὰ καὶ ἔργον τι δεικνύειν ἕξουσιν *see to this, that they not only make speeches but also are able to show some proof* D. 2. 12, σκεπτέον μοι δοκεῖ εἶναι . . . ὅπως ὡς ἀσφαλέστατα ἄπιμεν (774) καὶ ὅπως τὰ ἐπιτήδεια ἕξομεν *it seems to me that we must consider how we shall depart in the greatest security and how we shall procure our provisions* X. A. 1. 3. 11. In δεῖ σε ὅπως δείξεις *it is needful that thou prove* S. Aj. 556 there is a confusion between δεῖ δεῖξαι and the construction of 2213.

2212 After secondary tenses the future optative occasionally occurs.

ἐπεμέλετο ὅπως μήτε ἄσῖτοι μήτε ἄποτοί ποτε ἔσοιντο *he took care that they should never be without food or drink* X. C. 8. 1. 43.

a. The future optative occurs especially in Xenophon, and represents a thought that was originally expressed by the future indicative. Here the indicative would present the thought vividly, *i.e.* as it was conceived in the mind of the subject.

2213. ὅπως and ὅπως μή with the future indicative may be used without any principal clause, to denote an urgent exhortation or a warning. Originally the ὅπως clause depended on σκόπει (σκοπεῖτε), ὅρᾱ (ὁρᾶτε) *see to it;* but the ellipsis was gradually forgotten and the construction used independently.

ὅπως οὖν ἔσεσθε ἄνδρες ἄξιοι τῆς ἐλευθερίᾱς ἧς κέκτησθε *be men worthy of the freedom which you possess* X. A. 1. 7. 3, ὅπως δὲ τοῦτο μὴ διδάξεις μηδένα *but don't tell anybody this* Ar. Nub. 824, and very often in Ar. This use is also preceded by ἄγε (X. S. 4. 20). The third person is very rare (L. 1. 21).

2214. Verbs of *effort* sometimes have the construction of final clauses, and take, though less often, ὅπως with the present or second aorist subjunctive or optative (cp. 2196). The subjunctive may be used after secondary tenses.

ἔπρᾱσσεν . . . ὅπως πόλεμος γένηται *he tried to bring it about that war should be occasioned* T. 1. 57, ὅρᾱ . . . ὅπως μὴ παρὰ δόξαν ὁμολογῇς *see to it that it does not prove that you acquiesce in what you do not really think* P. Cr. 49 c, οὐ φυλάξεσθ' ὅπως μὴ . . . δεσπότην εὕρητε; *will you not be on your guard lest you find a master?* D. 6. 25. Future and subjunctive occur together in X. A. 4. 6. 10. In Xenophon alone is the subjunctive (and optative) more common than the future.

a. The object desired by the subject of a verb of *effort* is here expressed by the same construction as is the purpose in the mind of the subject of a final clause.

2215. ἄν is sometimes added to ὅπως with the subjunctive to denote that the purpose is dependent on certain circumstances.

ὅπως ἂν . . . οἱ στρατιῶται περὶ τοῦ στρατεύεσθαι βουλεύωνται, τούτου πειράσομαι ἐπεμέλεσθαι *I will endeavour to make it my care that the soldiers deliberate about continuing the war* X. C. 5. 5. 48, μηχανητέον ὅπως ἂν διαφύγῃ *plans must be made for his escape* P. G. 481 a (the same passage has ὅπως with the subjunctive and the future). In Attic this use occurs in Aristophanes, Xenophon, and Plato.

2216. ὡς and ὡς ἄν with subjunctive and optative and ὅπως ἄν with the optative occur in Xenophon, ὡς ἄν and ὅπως ἄν with the optative being used after primary and secondary tenses. Hdt. has ὅκως ἄν after secondary tenses. The optative with ὡς ἄν and ὅπως ἄν is potential.

2217. After verbs meaning *to consider, plan,* and *try* ὅπως or ὡς with the subjunctive (with or without κέ) or optative is used by Homer, who does not employ the future indicative in object clauses denoting a purpose. Thus, φράζεσθαι . . . ὅππως κε μνηστῆρας . . . κτείνῃς *consider how thou mayest slay the suitors* α 295, πείρᾱ ὅπως κεν δὴ σὴν πατρίδα γαῖαν ἵκηαι *try that thou mayest come to thy native land* δ 545. Here ὅπως with the future indicative would be the normal Attic usage.

2218. Verbs of will or desire signifying *to ask, command, entreat, exhort,* and *forbid,* which usually have an infinitive as their object, may take ὅπως (ὅπως μή) with the future indicative (or optative) or the subjunctive (or optative). The ὅπως clause states both the *command,* etc. and the purpose in giving it. Between *take care to do this* and *I bid you take care to do this* the connection is close. Cp. *impero, postulo* with *ut* (*ne*).

διακελεύονται ὅπως τῑμωρήσεται *they urge him to take revenge* P. R. 549 e, δεήσεται δ' ὑμῶν ὅπως . . . δίκην μὴ δῷ *he will entreat you that he may not suffer punishment* Ant. 1. 23, παραγγέλλουσιν ὅπως ἂν (2215) τῇδε τῇ ἡμέρᾳ τελευτήσῃ *they give orders* (*to the end*) *that he die to-day* P. Ph. 59 e, Λακεδαιμονίων ἐδέοντο τὸ ψήφισμ' ὅπως μεταστραφείη *they begged the Lacedaemonians that the decree might be changed* Ar. Ach. 536, ἀπηγόρευες ὅπως μὴ τοῦτο ἀποκρινοίμην *you forbade me to give this answer* P. R. 339 a.

2219. Dawes' Canon. — The rule formulated by Dawes and afterwards extended (that the *first* aorist subjunctive active and middle after ὅπως, ὅπως μή, and οὐ μή is incorrect and should be emended) is applicable only in the case of verbs of *effort.* After these verbs the future is far more common than subjunctive or optative (except in Xenophon), and some scholars would emend the offending sigmatic subjunctives where they occur in the same sentence with second aorists (as And. 3. 14) or even where the future has a widely different form (as ἐκπλευσεῖται, subj. ἐκπλεύσῃ, cp. X. A. 5. 6. 21).

VERBS OF CAUTION

2220. Verbs of *caution* (2210 b, 2224 a) have, in *negative* clauses, the construction either of

a. Verbs of *effort*, and take ὅπως μή with the future indicative:

εὐλαβούμενοι ὅπως μὴ . . . οἰχήσομαι *taking care that I do not depart* P. Ph. 91 c, ὅρᾱ ὅκως μή σευ ἀποστήσονται *beware lest they revolt from thee* Hdt. 3. 36.

b. Verbs of *fearing*, and take μή (μὴ οὐ) or ὅπως μή (2230) with the subjunctive (or optative):

ὁρᾶτε μὴ πάθωμεν *take care lest we suffer* X. C. 4. 1. 15, φυλάττου ὅπως μὴ . . . εἰς τοὐναντίον ἔλθῃς *be on your guard lest you come to the opposite* X. M. 3. 6. 16, ὑποπτεύομεν . . . ὑμᾶς μὴ οὐ κοινοὶ ἀποβῆτε *we suspect that you will not prove impartial* T. 3. 53, ὑποπτεύσᾱς μὴ τὴν θυγατέρα λέγοι, ἤρετο κτλ. *suspecting that he meant his daughter, he asked*, etc. X. C. 5. 2. 9. So with a past indicative (2233).

OBJECT CLAUSES WITH VERBS OF FEARING

2221. Object clauses after verbs of *fear* and *caution* are introduced by μή *that, lest* (Lat. *ne*), μὴ οὐ *that . . . not, lest . . . not* (Lat. *ut = ne non*).

a. μή clauses denote a fear that something *may* or *might* happen; μὴ οὐ clauses denote a fear that something *may not* or *might not* happen. Observe that the verb is negatived by οὐ and not by μή, which expresses an apprehension that the result will take place. μή is sometimes, for convenience, translated by *whether;* but it is not an indirect interrogative in such cases.

2222. The construction of μή after verbs of *fearing* has been developed from an earlier coördinate construction in which μή was not a conjunction (*that, lest*) but a prohibitive particle. Thus, δείδω μή τι πάθῃσιν (Λ 470) *I fear lest he may suffer aught* was developed from *I fear + may he not suffer aught* (1802); φυλακὴ δέ τις . . . ἔστω, μὴ λόχος εἰσέλθῃσι πόλιν (Θ 521) *but let there be a guard, lest an ambush enter the city*, where the clause μὴ — εἰσέλθῃσι meant originally *may an ambush not enter.* Here μή expresses the desire to avert something (negative desire).

a. When μή had become a pure conjunction of subordination, it was used even with the indicative and with the optative with ἄν. Some scholars regard μή with the indicative as standing for ἆρα μή (hence an indirect interrogative). Observe that the character of μή after verbs of *fearing* is different from that in final clauses, though the construction is the same in both cases.

2223. For the use of the subjunctive, without a verb of fearing, with μή, see 1801, 1802; with μὴ οὐ see 1801, with οὐ μή see 1804.

2224. Verbs and expressions of *fear* are: **φοβοῦμαι**, **δέδοικα** or **δέδια**, **ταρβῶ**, **τρῶ** and **πέφρῑκα** (mostly poetical); **δεινός εἰμι**, **δεινόν ἐστι**, **δέος ἐστί**, **φοβερός εἰμι**, **φοβερόν ἐστι**, etc.

a. Sometimes it is not actual *fear* that is expressed but only *apprehension, anxiety, suspicion*, etc. These are the verbs and expressions of *caution:* **ὀκνῶ, ἀθῡμῶ, ἀπιστῶ, ἀπιστίᾱν ἔχω** (*παρέχω*), **ὑποπτεύω, ἐνθῡμοῦμαι, αἰσχῡ́νομαι** (rare), **κίνδῡνός ἐστι, προσδοκίᾱ ἐστί.** Here belong also, by analogy, **ὁρῶ, σκοπῶ, ἐννοῶ, εὐλαβοῦμαι, φροντίζω, φυλάττω** (-*ομαι*), which admit also the construction of verbs of *effort* (2210 b).

I. FEAR RELATING TO THE FUTURE

2225. Object clauses after verbs of *fear* and *caution* take the subjunctive after primary tenses, the optative (or subjunctive, 2226) after secondary tenses.

φοβοῦμαι μὴ γένηται *I fear it may happen.*
φοβοῦμαι μὴ οὐ γένηται *I fear it may not happen.*
ἐφοβούμην μὴ γένοιτο (or **γένηται**) *I feared it might happen.*
ἐφοβούμην μὴ οὐ γένοιτο (regularly **γένηται**) *I feared it might not happen.*

δέδοικα μὴ . . . ἐπιλαθώμεθα τῆς οἴκαδε ὁδοῦ *I am afraid lest we may forget the way home* X. A. 3. 2. 25, φοβεῖται μὴ . . . τὰ ἔσχατα πάθῃ *he is afraid lest he suffer the severest punishment* X. C. 3. 1. 22, φροντίζω μὴ κράτιστον ᾖ μοι σῑγᾶν *I am thinking that it may prove* (2228) *best for me to be silent* X. M. 4. 2. 39, ἔδεισαν οἱ Ἕλληνες μὴ προσάγοιεν πρὸς τὸ κέρας καὶ . . . αὐτοὺς κατακόψειαν *the Greeks were seized with fear lest they might advance against their flank and cut them down* X. A. 1. 10. 9, δέδιμεν μὴ οὐ βέβαιοι ἦτε *we fear you are not to be depended on* T. 3. 57, οὐ τοῦτο δέδοικα, μὴ οὐκ ἔχω ὅ τι δῶ ἑκάστῳ τῶν φίλων . . . ἀλλὰ μὴ οὐκ ἔχω ἱκανοὺς οἷς δῶ *I am afraid not that I may not have enough* (lit. *anything*) *to give to each of my friends, but that I may not have enough friends on whom to bestow my gifts* X. A. 1. 7. 7.

a. The aorist is very common after μή. After secondary tenses Hom. usually has the optative.

b. μὴ οὐ with the optative is rare and suspicious (X. A. 3. 5. 3).

2226. After secondary tenses, the subjunctive presents the fear vividly, *i.e.* as it was conceived by the subject. Cp. 2197.

ἐφοβοῦντο μή τι πάθῃ *they feared lest she might* (*may*) *meet with some accident* X. S. 2. 11, ἐφοβήθησαν μὴ καὶ ἐπὶ σφᾶς ὁ στρατὸς χωρήσῃ *they became fearful that the army might* (*may*) *advance against themselves too* T. 2. 101. So when the fear extends up to the present time: ἐφοβήθην . . . καὶ νῦν τεθορύβημαι μή τινες ὑμῶν ἀγνοήσωσί με *I was struck with fear and even now I am in a state of agitation lest some of you may disregard me* Aes. 2. 4. The vivid use of subjunctive is common in the historians, especially Thucydides.

2227. The optative after a primary tense is rare and suspected (I 245, Hdt. 7. 103, S. Aj. 279).

2228. The subjunctive and optative after μή (or ὅπως μή) may denote what *may prove to be* an object of fear (future ascertainment).

δέδοικα μὴ ἄριστον ᾖ *I am afraid lest it prove to be best* S. Ant. 1114, ἔδεισαν μὴ λύττα τις . . . ἡμῖν ἐμπεπτώκοι *they feared lest some madness might prove to have fallen upon us* X. A. 5. 7. 26. The aorist subjunctive refers to the past in δείδοικα . . . μή σε παρείπῃ *I fear it may prove that she beguiled thee* A 555; cp. K 99, ν 216, ω 491 (after ὁρῶ).

2229. The future is rare with verbs of *fearing* after μή.

φοβοῦμαι δὲ μή τινας ἡδονὰς ἡδοναῖς εὑρήσομεν ἐναντίας *and I apprehend that we shall find some pleasures opposite to* other *pleasures* P. Phil. 13 a. So with verbs of *caution:* ὅρα μὴ πολλῶν ἑκάστῳ ἡμῶν χειρῶν δεήσει *see to it lest each one of us may have need of many hands* X. C. 4. 1. 18.

a. The future optative seems not to occur except in X. H. 6. 4. 27, X. M. 1. 2. 7, P. Euth. 15 d.

2230. ὅπως μή with the subjunctive or optative is sometimes used instead of μή after verbs of *fear* and *caution* to imply fear that something *will* happen.

οὐ φοβεῖ . . . ὅπως μὴ ἀνόσιον πρᾶγμα τυγχάνῃς πράττων; *are you not afraid that you may chance to be doing an unholy deed?* P. Euth. 4 e, ἡδέως γ' ἂν (θρέψαιμι τὸν ἄνδρα), εἰ μὴ φοβοίμην ὅπως μὴ ἐπ' αὐτόν με τράποιτο *I should gladly keep the man if I did not fear lest he might turn against me* X. M. 2. 9. 3; see also 2220 b.

2231. ὅπως μή with the future indicative (as after verbs of *effort*) is sometimes used instead of μή with the subjunctive.

δέδοικα ὅπως μὴ . . . ἀνάγκη γενήσεται (*v. l.* γένηται) *I fear lest a necessity may arise* D. 9. 75. The future optative occurs once (I. 17. 22). On μή or ὅπως μή with verbs of *caution*, see 2220 a.

2232. The potential optative with ἄν is rarely used after μή.

δεδιότες μὴ καταλυθείη ἂν (Mss. καταλυθείησαν) ὁ δῆμος *fearful lest the people should be put down* L. 13. 51. The potential use is most evident when an optative occurs in the protasis: εἰ δέ τινες φοβοῦνται μὴ ματαία ἂν γένοιτο αὕτη ἡ κατασκευή, εἰ πόλεμος ἐγερθείη, ἐννοησάτω ὅτι κτλ. *if some are afraid that this condition of things may prove vain, if war should arise, let them (him) consider that,* etc. X. Vect. 4. 41.

II. FEAR RELATING TO THE PRESENT OR PAST

2233. Fear that something actually *is* or *was* is expressed by μή with the indicative (negative μὴ οὐ).

δέδοικα . . . μὴ πληγῶν δέει *I fear that you need a beating* Ar. Nub. 493, ἀλλ' ὅρα μὴ παίζων ἔλεγεν *but have a care that he was not speaking in jest* P. Th. 145 b, φοβούμεθα μὴ ἀμφοτέρων ἅμα ἡμαρτήκαμεν *we are afraid that we have failed of both objects at once* T. 3. 53, ὁρᾶτε μὴ οὐκ ἐμοὶ . . . προσήκει λόγον δοῦναι *have a care lest it does not rest with me to give an account* And. 1. 103.

a. Contrast φοβοῦμαι μὴ ἀληθές ἐστιν *I fear that it is true* with φοβοῦμαι μὴ ἀληθὲς ᾖ *I fear it may prove true* (2228).

b. The aorist occurs in Homer: δείδω μὴ δὴ πάντα θεὰ νημερτέα εἶπεν *I fear that all the goddess said was true* ε 300.

OTHER CONSTRUCTIONS WITH VERBS OF FEARING

2234. In Indirect Questions. — Here the ideas of fear and doubt are joined. Thus, φόβος εἰ πείσω δέσποιναν ἐμήν (direct πείσω; 1916) *I have my doubts whether I shall* (*can*) *persuade my mistress* E. Med. 184, τὴν θεὸν δ' ὅπως λάθω δέδοικα (direct πῶς λάθω; 1805) *I am fearful how I shall escape the notice of the goddess* E. I. T. 995, δέδοικα ὅ τι ἀποκρινοῦμαι *I am afraid what to answer* P. Th. 195 c.

2235. In Indirect Discourse with ὡς (rarely ὅπως) *that.* — Verbs of *fearing* may have the construction of verbs of *thinking* and be followed by a dependent statement. This occurs regularly only when the expression of fear is negatived. Thus, ἀνδρὸς δὲ τῇ θυγατρὶ μὴ φοβοῦ ὡς ἀπορήσεις *do not fear that you will be at a loss for a husband for your daughter* X. C. 5. 2. 12. Here μή or ὅπως μή would be regular. With ὡς the idea is *fear, thinking that.*

2236. With ὅτι (ὡς) Causal. — ἐφοβεῖτο ὅτι ἀπὸ Διὸς . . . τὸ ὄναρ ἐδόκει αὐτῷ εἶναι *he was afraid because the dream seemed to him to be from Zeus* X. A. 3. 1. 12.

2237. With a Causal Participle. — οὔτε τὴν ἀκρόπολιν . . . προδιδοὺς ἐφοβήθη *nor was he terrified at having betrayed the Acropolis* Lyc. 17.

2238. With the Infinitive. — Verbs of *fearing* often take an object infinitive (present, future or aorist) with or without the article; and with or without μή (2741). Thus, φοβήσεται ἀδικεῖν *he will be afraid to injure* X. C. 8. 7. 15, οὐ φοβούμεθα ἐλασσώσεσθαι *we are not afraid that we shall be beaten* T. 5. 105 (the future infinitive is less common than μή with the subjunctive), φυλαττόμενος τὸ λῡπῆσαί τινα (= μὴ λῡπήσω) *taking care to offend no one* D. 18. 258, ἐφυλάξατο μὴ ἄπιστος γενέσθαι *he took precautions not to become an object of distrust* X. Ag. 8. 5.

a. With the articular infinitive, φοβοῦμαι, etc. means simply *I fear;* with the infinitive without the article, φοβοῦμαι commonly has the force of *hesitate, feel repugnance,* etc. Cp. φοβοῦμαι ἀδικεῖν and φοβοῦμαι μὴ ἀδικεῖν; *I fear to do wrong* (and do not do it); φοβοῦμαι τὸ ἀδικεῖν *I fear wrong-doing* (in general, by myself or by another), like φοβοῦμαι τὴν ἀδικίᾱν.

2239. With ὥστε of Result (after a verb of *caution*). — ἢν οὖν ἔλθωμεν ἐπ' αὐτοὺς πρὶν φυλάξασθαι ὥστε μὴ ληφθῆναι *if then we move against them before they take precautions* (*so as*) *not to be caught* X. A. 7. 3. 35.

CAUSAL CLAUSES

2240. Causal clauses are introduced by ὅτι, διότι, διόπερ *because,* ἐπεί, ἐπειδή, ὅτε, ὁπότε *since,* ὡς *as, since, because.* The negative is οὐ.

a. Also by poetic **οὕνεκα** (= οὗ ἕνεκα) and **ὁθούνεκα** (= ὅτου ἕνεκα) *because,* **εὖτε** *since* (poetic and Ionic; also temporal), and by **ὅπου** *since* (Hdt. 1. 68, X. C. 8. 4. 31, I. 4. 186). Homer has **ὅ** or **ὅ τε** *because.*

b. ὡς frequently denotes a reason imagined to be true by the principal subject and treated by him as a fact (2241). **ὅτι** often follows διὰ τοῦτο, διὰ τόδε, ἐκ τούτου, τούτῳ. **διότι** stands for διὰ τοῦτο, ὅτι. **ὅτε** and **ὁπότε** usually mean *when* (cp. *cum*); as causal conjunctions they are rare, as ὅτε τοίνυν τοῦθ' *οὕτως ἔχει since then this is the case*, D. 1. 1, *χαλεπὰ . . . τὰ παρόντα ὁπότ' ἀνδρῶν στρατηγῶν τοιούτων στερόμεθα the present state of affairs is difficult since we are deprived of such generals* X. A. 3. 2. 2. Causal ὅτε, temporal ὅτε rarely, can begin a sentence. When they approach the meaning *if*, ὅτε and ὁπότε take μή. In Attic prose inscriptions ἐπεί is rare, διότι does not occur, and ὧν ἕνεκα is generally used for διόπερ.

2241. Causal clauses denoting a fact regularly take the indicative after primary and secondary tenses.

ἐπεὶ δὲ ὑμεῖς οὐ βούλεσθε συμπορεύεσθαι, ἀνάγκη δή μοι ἢ ὑμᾶς προδόντα τῇ Κύρου φιλίᾳ χρῆσθαι κτλ. but since you do not wish to continue the march with me, I must either retain the friendship of Cyrus by renouncing you, etc. X. A. 1. 3. 5, *ὃ δ' ἐζήλωσας ἡμᾶς ὡς τοὺς μὲν φίλους . . . εὖ ποιεῖν δυνάμεθα . . ., οὐδὲ ταῦθ' οὕτως ἔχει but as to that which has excited your envy of us, our supposed ability* (lit. *because, as you think, we are able*) *to benefit our friends, not even is this so* X. Hi. 6. 12, *ἐτύγχανε γὰρ ἐφ' ἁμάξης πορευόμενος διότι ἐτέτρωτο for he happened to be riding on a wagon from the fact that he had been wounded* X. A. 2. 2. 14.

2242. But causal clauses denoting an alleged or reported reason (implied indirect discourse, 2622) take the optative after secondary tenses.

(οἱ Ἀθηναῖοι) *τὸν Περικλέα ἐκάκιζον ὅτι στρατηγὸς ὢν οὐκ ἐπεξάγοι the Athenians reviled Pericles on the ground that, though he was general, he did not lead them out* T. 2. 21, *εἶχε λέγειν . . . ὡς Λακεδαιμόνιοι διὰ τοῦτο πολεμήσειαν αὐτοῖς ὅτι οὐκ ἐθελήσαιεν μετ' Ἀγησιλάου ἐλθεῖν ἐπ' αὐτόν* Pelopidas *was able to say that the Lacedaemonians had made war upon them* (the Thebans) *for the reason that they had not been willing to march against him* (the King of Persia) *with Agesilaus* X. H. 7. 1. 34.

2243. Cause may be expressed also by the unreal indicative with ἄν or the potential optative with ἄν.

ἐπεὶ διά γ' ὑμᾶς αὐτοὺς πάλαι ἂν ἀπολώλειτε since you would long ago have perished had it depended on yourselves D. 18. 49, *δέομαι οὖν σου παραμεῖναι ἡμῖν· ὡς ἐγὼ οὐδ' ἂν ἑνὸς ἥδιον ἀκούσαιμι ἢ σοῦ accordingly I beg you to stay with us; because there is no one (in my opinion) to whom I should more gladly listen than to you* P. Pr. 335 d.

2244. ἐπεί may introduce a coördinate *command* (imperative S. El. 352, potential optative, P. G. 474 b), *wish* (S. O. T. 661), or *question* (S. O. T. 390). Cp. the use of ὥστε, 2275. Sometimes, with the indicative, ἐπεί has the force of *although* (P. S. 187 a). — A causal clause may have the value of γάρ with a coördinate main clause. So often in tragedy with ὡς in *answers* (S. Aj. 39; cp. X. C. 4. 2. 25). — A clause with ὅτε, apparently introducing a consequence, may give the reason for a preceding question (Δ 32).

2245. Cause may also be expressed by a relative clause (2555), by a participle (2064, 2085, 2086), by τῷ or διὰ τὸ with the infinitive (2033, 2034 b).

2246. εἰ or εἴπερ, when it expresses the real opinion of the writer or speaker, may have a causal force, as ἐγὼ . . . ἥδομαι μὲν ὑφ' ὑμῶν τῑμώμενος, εἴπερ ἄνθρωπός εἰμι *I am pleased at being honoured by you, since* (lit. *if indeed*) *I am a man* X. A. 6. 1. 26.

2247. Many verbs of emotion state the cause more delicately with εἰ (ἐάν) *if* as a mere supposition than by ὅτι. The negative is μή or οὐ.

a. So with **ἀγανακτῶ** *am indignant*, **ἄγαμαι** *am content*, **αἰσχρόν ἐστι** *it is a shame*, **αἰσχῡ́νομαι** *am ashamed*, **ἄχθομαι** *take hard*, **δεινόν ἐστι** *it is a shame*, **δεινὸν ποιοῦμαι** *am indignant*, **θαυμάζω** *am astonished*, **μέμφομαι** *blame*, **φθονῶ** *am jealous*, etc. The *if* clause is usually indicative, sometimes an unreal indicative, a subjunctive, or a potential optative. Thus, θαυμάζω εἰ μὴ βοηθήσετε ὑμῖν αὐτοῖς *I am surprised if you will not help yourselves* X. H. 2. 3. 53, ἀγανακτῶ εἰ οὑτωσὶ ἃ νοῶ μὴ οἷός τ' εἰμὶ εἰπεῖν *I am grieved that I am thus unable to say what I mean* P. Lach. 194 a, δεινὸν ποιούμενοι εἰ τοὺς ἐπιβουλεύοντας σφῶν τῷ πλήθει μὴ εἴσονται *indignant that they could not discover those who were plotting against their commons* T. 6. 60, ἄτοπον ἂν εἴη, εἰ μηδὲν μὲν ἐμοῦ λέγοντος αὐτοὶ βοᾶτε τὴν ἐπωνυμίᾱν τῶν ἔργων . . . , ἐμοῦ δὲ λέγοντος ἐπιλέλησθε, καὶ μὴ γενομένης μὲν κρίσεως περὶ τοῦ πράγματος ἥλω ἄν, γεγονότος δὲ ἐλέγχου ἀποφεύξεται *it would be absurd if, when I say nothing, you shout out the name of what he has done, but when I do speak, you forget it; and* absurd *if, while he should have been condemned when no investigation was instituted concerning the matter, he should yet get off now when the proof has been given* Aes. 1. 85 (cp. 2904 b), μὴ θαυμάζετε δ' ἄν τι φαίνωμαι λέγων *do not be surprised if I seem to say something* I. Ep. 6. 7, τέρας λέγεις, εἰ . . . οὐκ ἂν δύναιντο λαθεῖν *it is a marvel you are telling if they could be undetected* P. Men. 91 d.

b. After a past tense we have either the form of direct discourse or the optative, as in indirect discourse. Thus, ἐθαύμαζον εἴ τι ἕξει τις χρήσασθαι τῷ λόγῳ αὐτοῦ *I kept wondering if any one could deal with his theory* P. Ph. 95 a, ἐπεῖπεν . . . ὡς δεινὸν εἴη εἰ ὁ μὲν . . . Ξανθίᾱς ὑποκρῑνόμενος οὕτως . . . μεγαλόψῡχος γένοιτο *he added that it was a shame if a man who played the rôle of Xanthias should prove himself so noble minded* Aes. 2. 157, ᾤκτῑρον εἰ ἁλώσοιντο *they pitied them in case they should be captured* X. A. 1. 4. 7 (cp. 2622 a). Sometimes the construction used after a primary tense is retained after a secondary tense (X. C. 4. 3. 3).

2248. These verbs admit also the construction with ὅτι.

μὴ θαυμάζετε ὅτι χαλεπῶς φέρω *do not be surprised that I take it hard* X. A. 1. 3. 3, ἐθαύμαζον ὅτι Κῦρος οὔτε ἄλλον πέμπει . . . οὔτε αὐτὸς φαίνοιτο (implied indirect discourse) *they were surprised that Cyrus neither sent some one else nor appeared himself* 2. 1. 2, ἥκομεν ἀγαπῶντες ὅτι τὰ σώματα διεσωσάμεθα *we have reached here, content that we have saved our lives* 5. 5. 13. The construction with ἐπὶ τῷ and the infinitive (2033 b) also occurs: (Σωκράτης) ἐθαυμάζετο ἐπὶ τῷ . . . εὐκόλως ζῆν *Socrates was admired because he lived contentedly* X. M. 4. 8. 2.

a. ὅτι after verbs of emotion really means *that*, not *because*.

RESULT CLAUSES (CONSECUTIVE CLAUSES)

2249. A clause of result denotes a consequence of what is stated in the principal clause.

2250. Result clauses are introduced by the relative word ὥστε (rarely by ὡς) *as, that, so that.* In the principal clause the demonstrative words οὕτως *thus,* τοιοῦτος *such,* τοσοῦτος *so great,* are often expressed. ὥστε is from ὡς and the connective τέ, which has lost its meaning.

a. To a clause with οὕτως, etc. Herodotus sometimes adds a clause either with τέ or without a connective, where Attic would employ ὥστε; cp. 3. 12.

2251. There are two main forms of result clauses: ὥστε with the infinitive and ὥστε with a finite verb. With the infinitive, the negative is generally μή; with a finite verb, οὐ. On the use in indirect discourse and on irregularities, see 2759.

2252. Consecutive ὡς occurs almost always with the infinitive (chiefly in Herodotus, Xenophon, Aeschylus, and Sophocles); with a finite verb occasionally in Herodotus and Xenophon. With the infinitive, the orators and Thucydides (except 7. 34) have ὥστε.

2253. Consecutive ὥστε (ὡς) with a finite verb does not occur in Homer, who uses coördination instead (cp. δέ in A 10). Two cases of ὥς τε occur with the infinitive (I 42; ζ 21 may mean *and so*), where the infinitive might stand alone, since Homer uses the infinitive to denote an intended or possible result.

2254. A clause with ὥστε and the infinitive is merely added to the clause containing the main thought in order to explain it. The consequence is stated without any distinction of time and only with difference of stage of action.

a. Since the infinitive expresses merely the abstract verbal idea, its use with ὥστε (as with πρίν) outside of indirect discourse cannot explicitly denote a *fact.* By its datival nature (1969), the infinitive is simply a complement to, or explanation of, the governing word. ὥστε is one of the means to reinforce this explanatory office of the infinitive. The origin of its use is suggested by the comparison with ὅσος *sufficient for,* οἷος *capable of* (2003) and the infinitive, which was not *originally* dependent on these words.

2255. A clause with ὥστε and a finite verb contains the main thought, and is often so loosely connected with the leading verb as to be practically independent and coördinate. ὥστε may thus be simply introductory and take any construction found in an independent sentence. The consequence expresses distinctions of time and stage of action.

2256. Result may also be expressed by relative clauses (2556).

DIFFERENCE BETWEEN ὥστε WITH THE INDICATIVE AND ὥστε WITH THE INFINITIVE

2257. A clause of result with ὥστε stating that something actually occurred *as a fact* must be expressed by the indicative.

2258. A clause of result with ὥστε stating that something may occur in consequence of an *intention, tendency, capacity,* and in general in consequence of the *nature* of an object or action, is regularly expressed by the infinitive. When a consequence is stated without affirming or denying its actual occurrence, the infinitive is in place. The infinitive *may* therefore denote a fact, but does not explicitly state this to be the case; and is, in general, permissible in all cases where the attainment of the result is expected, natural, or possible, and its actual occurrence is not emphasized; as it is emphasized by the indicative.

a. ὥστε with the infinitive does not state a particular fact. The infinitive is preferred in clauses containing or implying a negative. ὥστε with the indicative is preferred after εἰς τοῦτο ἥκει and like phrases when affirmative (cp. 2265, 2266, 2274).

2259. This difference may be illustrated by examples.

ἔχω τριήρεις ὥστε ἑλεῖν τὸ ἐκείνων πλοῖον *I have triremes (so as) to catch their vessel* X. A. 1. 4. 8 (ὥστε εἷλον would mean *so that I caught* with an essentially different meaning), πάντας οὕτω διατιθεὶς ὥστε αὐτῷ εἶναι φίλους *treating all in such a manner that they should be his friends* X. A. 1. 1. 5 (an intended result, 2267), οὕτω διάκειμαι ὑφ' ὑμῶν ὡς οὐδὲ δεῖπνον ἔχω ἐν τῇ ἐμαυτοῦ χώρᾳ *I am treated by you in such a manner that I cannot even sup in my own country* X. H. 4. 1. 33 (a fact), ὥστε πάροδον μὴ εἶναι παρὰ πύργον, ἀλλὰ δι' αὐτῶν μέσων διῇσαν *so that it was impossible to pass by the side of a tower, but* the guards *went through the middle of them* T. 3. 21, κραυγὴν πολλὴν ἐποίουν καλοῦντες ἀλλήλους ὥστε καὶ τοὺς πολεμίους ἀκούειν· ὥστε οἱ μὲν ἐγγύτατα τῶν πολεμίων καὶ ἔφυγον *they made a loud noise by calling each other so that even the enemy could hear; consequently those of the enemy who were nearest actually fled* X. A. 2. 2. 17. Here the fact that some of the enemy fled is proof that they *actually* heard the cries; but the Greek states merely that the noise was loud enough to be heard. Had the clause ὥστε . . . ἔφυγον not been added, we could only have *inferred* that the noise was heard.

ὥστε (RARELY ὡς) WITH THE INFINITIVE

2260. The infinitive with ὥστε denotes an anticipated or possible result; but the actual occurrence of the result is not stated, and is to be inferred only. The negative is μή, but οὐ is used when the ὥστε clause depends on a clause itself subordinate to a verb of *saying* or *thinking* (2269). Cp. 2759.

a. ὥστε with the infinitive means *as to, so as to;* but with a subject necessary in English it must often be translated by *so that.*

2261. The infinitive with ὥστε is usually present or aorist, rarely perfect (*e.g.* D. 18. 257). The future is common only in indirect discourse (D. 19. 72).

2262. ὥστε (ὡς) with the infinitive is used when its clause serves only to explain the principal clause. Thus,

2263. (I) After expressions denoting *ability, capacity,* or *to effect something.*

πολλὰ πράγματα παρεῖχον οἱ βάρβαροι . . . ἐλαφροὶ γὰρ ἦσαν, ὥστε καὶ ἐγγύθεν φεύγοντες ἀποφεύγειν *the barbarians caused great annoyance; for they were so nimble that they could escape even though they made off after they had approached quite near* X. A. 4. 2. 27, ὁ ποταμὸς τοσοῦτος βάθος ὡς μηδὲ τὰ δόρατα ὑπερέχειν *the river of such a depth that the spears could not even project above the surface* 3. 5. 7 (on τοσοῦτος ὅσος etc. see 2003), τοσαύτην κραυγὴν . . . ἐποίησαν ὥστε . . . τοὺς ταξιάρχους ἐλθεῖν *they made such an uproar as to bring the taxiarchs* D. 54. 5.

a. The idea of *effecting* may be unexpressed: (Κλέαρχος) ἤλαυνεν ἐπὶ τοὺς Μένωνος ὥστ' ἐκείνους ἐκπεπλῆχθαι *Clearchus advanced against the soldiers of Menon so* (*i.e.* by so doing he brought it about) *that they were thoroughly frightened* X. A. 1. 5. 13; cp. 2267. Several verbs of *effecting* take ὥστε when the result is intended and where the simple infinitive is common (2267 b).

2264. (II) After a comparative with ἤ *than.*

ᾔσθοντο αὐτὸν ἐλάττω ἔχοντα δύναμιν ἢ ὥστε τοὺς φίλους ὠφελεῖν *they perceived that he possessed too little power to benefit his friends* X. H. 4. 8. 23, οἱ ἀκοντισταὶ βραχύτερα ἠκόντιζον ἢ ὡς ἐξικνεῖσθαι τῶν σφενδονητῶν *the javelin throwers hurled their javelins too short a distance to reach the slingers* X. A. 3. 3. 7. After a comparative, ὡς is as common as ὥστε.

a. ὥστε may here be omitted: κρείσσον' ἢ φέρειν κακά *evils too great to be endured* E. Hec. 1107.

b. On positive adjectives with a comparative force, see 1063.

2265. (III) After a principal clause that is negatived.

οὐκ ἔχομεν ἀργύριον ὥστε ἀγοράζειν τὰ ἐπιτήδεια *we have no money (so as) to buy provisions* X. A. 7. 3. 5, οὐδεὶς πώποτ' εἰς τοσοῦτ' ἀναιδείᾱς ἀφίκετο ὥστε τοιοῦτόν τι τολμῆσαι ποιεῖν *no one ever reached such a degree of shamelessness as to dare to do anything of the sort* D. 21. 62 (cp. 2258 a). Here are included questions expecting the answer *no:* τίς οὕτως ἐστὶ δεινὸς λέγειν ὥστε σε πεῖσαι; *who is so eloquent as to persuade you?* X. A. 2. 5. 15. After negative (as after comparative, 2264) clauses, the infinitive is used, since there would be no reason for the ὥστε clause if the action of the principal clause did not take place. But the indicative occurs occasionally (L. 13. 18, Ant. 5. 43).

2266. (IV) After a principal clause that expresses a condition.

εἰ μὴ εἰς τοῦτο μανίᾱς ἀφῑκόμην ὥστε ἐπιθῡμεῖν . . . πολλοῖς μάχεσθαι *if I had not reached such a degree of madness as to desire to contend with many* L. 3. 29 (cp. 2258 a).

2267. (V) To express an intended result, especially after a verb of *effecting*, as ποιῶ, διαπρᾱ́ττομαι, etc.

πᾶν ποιοῦσιν ὥστε δίκην μὴ διδόναι *they use every effort (so as) to avoid being punished* P. G. 479 c, διφθέρᾱς . . . συνέσπων ὡς μὴ ἅπτεσθαι τῆς κάρφης τὸ ὕδωρ *they stitched the skins so that the water should not touch the hay* X. A. 1. 5. 10.

a. The infinitive here expresses only the result, while the idea of purpose comes only from the general sense and especially from the meaning of the leading verb. ἵνα μή in the above examples would express only purpose.

b. A clause of intended result is often used where ὅπως might occur in an object clause after a verb of *effort* (2211); as μηχανᾱ̀ς εὑρήσομεν ὥστ᾽ ἐς τὸ πᾶν σε τῶνδ᾽ ἀπαλλάξαι πόνων *we will find means (so as) to free thee entirely from these troubles* A. Eum. 82. The infinitive alone, denoting purpose, is here more usual.

2268. (VI) To state a condition or a proviso (*on condition that, provided that*).

πολλὰ μὲν ἂν χρήματ᾽ ἔδωκε Φιλιστίδης ὥστ᾽ ἔχειν Ὠρεόν *Philistides would have given a large sum on condition of his holding Oreus* D. 18. 81, ὑπῑσχνοῦντο ὥστε ἐκπλεῖν *they gave their promise on the condition that they should sail out* X. A. 5. 6. 26. *On condition that* is commonly expressed by ἐφ᾽ ᾧ or ἐφ᾽ ᾧτε (2279) with or without a preceding ἐπὶ τούτῳ.

2269. A result clause with ὥστε and the indicative, dependent on an infinitive in indirect discourse, and itself quoted, takes the infinitive, and usually retains the negative of the direct form.

ἔφασαν τοὺς στρατιώτᾱς εἰς τοῦτο τρυφῆς ἐλθεῖν ὥστ᾽ οὐκ ἐθέλειν πίνειν, εἰ μὴ ἀνθοσμίᾱς εἴη *they said that the soldiers reached such a degree of daintiness as to be unwilling to drink wine unless it had a strong bouquet* X. H. 6. 2. 6 (direct: ὥστε οὐκ ἤθελον πίνειν, with οὐ retained in indirect discourse). See also 2270 b.

So even when the principal verb takes ὅτι, as ἐννοησάτω ὅτι οὕτως ἤδη τότε πόρρω τῆς ἡλικίᾱς ἦν ὥστ᾽ . . . οὐκ ἂν πολλῷ ὕστερον τελευτῆσαι τὸν βίον *let him consider that he was then so far advanced in years that he would have died soon afterwards* X. M. 4. 8. 1.

a. The future infinitive here represents the future indicative: οἴεται ὑμᾶς εἰς τοσοῦτον εὐηθείᾱς ἤδη προβεβηκέναι ὥστε καὶ ταῦτα ἀναπεισθήσεσθαι *he thinks that you have already reached such a degree of simplicity as to allow yourselves to be persuaded even of this* Aes. 3. 256. Outside of indirect discourse, the future infinitive with ὥστε is rare (γενήσεσθαι D. 16. 4, εἴσεσθαι D. 29. 5).

b. ὥστε with the optative in indirect discourse is very rare (X. H. 3. 5. 23, I. 17. 11).

2270. ἄν with the infinitive expressing *possibility*, and representing either a potential indicative or a potential optative, occasionally follows ὥστε (ὡς).

a. Not in indirect discourse: καί μοι οἱ θεοὶ οὕτως ἐν τοῖς ἱεροῖς ἐσήμηναν ὥστε καὶ ἰδιώτην ἂν γνῶναι (= ἰδιώτης ἔγνω ἄν or γνοίη ἄν) ὅτι τῆς μοναρχίᾱς ἀπέχεσθαί με δεῖ *and the gods declared to me* so clearly *in the sacrifices that even a common man could understand that I must keep aloof from sovereignty* X. A. 6. 1. 31, ἐν τῷ ἀσφαλεῖ ἤδη ἔσομαι ὡς μηδὲν ἂν ἔτι κακὸν παθεῖν (= οὐδὲν ἂν ἔτι πάθοιμι) *I shall soon be safe from suffering any further evil* X. C. 8. 7. 27. The difference in meaning is very slight between the construction with the potential optative and that with the infinitive with ἄν representing the potential optative.

N. — Rarely in other cases. Thus, τὰ δὲ ἐντὸς οὕτως ἐκαίετο ὥστε . . . ἥδιστα ἂν ἐς ὕδωρ ψῦχρὸν σφᾶς αὐτοὺς ῥίπτειν (= ἔρρῖπτον, 2304) *but their internal parts were inflamed to such a degree that they would have been most glad to throw themselves into cold water (had they been permitted)* T. 2. 49.

b. In indirect discourse: ἆρ' οὖν δοκεῖ τῳ ὑμῶν ὀλιγώρως οὕτως ἔχειν χρημάτων Νῑκόδημος ὥστε παραλιπεῖν (= παρέλιπεν) ἄν τι τῶν τοιούτων; *does it seem to any one of you that Nicodemus so despised money that he would have neglected any agreement of the sort?* Is. 3. 37.

2271. ὥστε is often used with the infinitive when the infinitive without ὥστε is regular or more common.

a. So with many verbs, especially of *will* or *desire*. Thus, ἔπεισαν τοὺς Ἀθηναίους ὥστε ἐξαγαγεῖν ἐκ Πύλου Μεσσηνίους *they prevailed upon the Athenians (so as) to withdraw the Messenians from Pylus* T. 5. 35, δεηθέντες . . . ἑκάστων ἰδίᾳ ὥστε ψηφίσασθαι τὸν πόλεμον *having begged each privately (so as) to vote for the war* 1. 119, ἐποίησα ὥστε δόξαι τούτῳ τοῦ πρὸς ἐμὲ πολέμου παύσασθαι *I brought it about so that it seemed best to him to desist from warring against me* X. A. 1. 6. 6.

N. — Such verbs are: ἀπέχομαι, δέομαι *ask*, διαπράττομαι, διδάσκω, δικαιῶ, δύναμαι, ἐθέλω, εἴργω, ἐλπίδα τινὰ ἔχω, ἐπαγγέλλομαι, ἐπαίρω, ἔχω *am able*, θέσφατόν τί τινι ἱκνεῖται, a phrase with καθίσταμαι, ξυγχωρῶ, παραδίδωμι, πείθω (and παρασκευάζω = πείθω), πέφῡκα, ποιῶ, προθῡμοῦμαι, προτρέπομαι, φυλάττομαι (2239), ψηφίζομαι.

b. When the infinitive is the subject: πάνυ γάρ μοι ἐμέλησεν ὥστε εἰδέναι *for it concerned me exceedingly to know* X. C. 6. 3. 19.

N. — So with ἔστι, γίγνεται, etc., δόξαν *when it was decreed*, συνέβη (Thuc.), συνέπῖπτε, συνήνεικε (Hdt.), προσήκει. Cp. 1985.

c. With adjectives, especially such as are positive in form but have a comparative force and denote a deficiency or the like (1063); as ἡμεῖς γὰρ ἔτι νέοι ὥστε τοσοῦτον πρᾶγμα διελέσθαι *for we are still too young to decide so important a matter* P. Pr. 314 b. So with ἰδιώτης, ὀλίγος, ψῡχρός, γέρων; and with ἱκανός, ἀδύνατος (and with δύνασθαι).

2272. On the absolute infinitive with ὡς (less often with ὥστε) see 2012.

ὥστε (ὡς) WITH A FINITE VERB

2273. Any form used in simple sentences may follow ὥστε (rarely ὡς) with a finite verb. ὥστε has no effect on the mood of a finite verb.

a. ὡς is found especially in Xenophon.

2274. ὥστε *so that* with the indicative states the *actual* result of the action of the leading verb. This is especially common in narrative statements with the aorist tense. The negative is οὐ.

ἐπιπίπτει χιὼν ἄπλετος ὥστε ἀπέκρυψε καὶ τὰ ὅπλα καὶ τοὺς ἀνθρώπους *an immense amount of snow fell so that it buried both the arms and the men* X. A. 4. 4. 11, εἰς τοσοῦτον ὕβρεως ἦλθον ὥστ' ἔπεισαν ὑμᾶς ἐλαύνειν αὐτόν *they reached such a pitch of insolence that they persuaded you to expel him* I. 16. 9 (cp. 2258 a), οὕτω σκαιὸς εἶ . . . ὥστ' οὐ δύνασαι κτλ. *are you so stupid that you are not able,* etc. D. 18. 120 (of a definite fact; with μὴ δύνασθαι the meaning would be *so stupid as not to be able*, expressing a characteristic). So after the locution τοσούτου δέω, as τοσούτου δέω περὶ τῶν μὴ προσηκόντων ἱκανὸς εἶναι λέγειν, ὥστε δέδοικα κτλ. *I am so far from able to speak about that which does not refer to my case that I fear,* etc. L. 17. 1. ὡς is very rare: νομίζω οὕτως ἔχειν ὡς ἀποστήσονται αὐτοῦ αἱ πόλεις *I consider that it is the case that the cities will revolt from him* X. H. 6. 1. 14.

a. So when ὥστε introducing an independent sentence practically has the force of οὖν, τοίνυν, τοιγαροῦν *and so therefore, consequently.* Thus καὶ εἷς μὲν τὴν ὑστεραίᾱν οὐχ ἧκεν· ὥσθ' οἱ Ἕλληνες ἐφρόντιζον *and on the next day he did not come; consequently the Greeks were anxious* X. A. 2. 3. 25. Cp. 2275. This use appears sometimes with the infinitive: ὥστ' ἐμὲ ἐμαυτὸν ἀνερωτᾶν *and so I kept asking myself* P. A. 22 e.

2275. With an imperative, a hortatory or prohibitory subjunctive, or an interrogative verb, a clause with ὥστε is coördinate rather than subordinate, and ὥστε has the force of καὶ οὕτως.

ὥστε θάρρει *and so be not afraid* X. C. 1. 3. 18, ὥστε . . . μὴ θαυμάσῃς *and so do not wonder* P. Phae. 274 a, ὥστε πόθεν ἴσᾱσιν; *and so how do they know?* D. 29. 47.

2276. ὥστε (ὡς) occurs rarely with the participle (instead of the infinitive) by attraction to a preceding participle (And. 4. 20, X. C. 7. 5. 46, D. 10. 40, 58. 23).

2277. ὥστε (ὡς) may be used with a past tense of the indicative with ἄν (potential indicative and unreal indicative).

τοιοῦτόν τι ἐποίησεν ὡς πᾶς ἂν ἔγνω ὅτι ἀσμένη ἤκουσε *she made a movement so that every one could recognize that she heard* the music *with pleasure* X. S. 9. 3, κατεφαίνετο πάντα αὐτόθεν ὥστε οὐκ ἂν ἔλαθεν αὐτὸν ὁρμώμενος ὁ Κλέων τῷ στρατῷ *everything was clearly visible from it, so that Cleon could not have escaped his notice in setting out with his force* T. 5. 6.

2278. ὥστε (ὡς) is used rarely with the optative without ἄν (by assimilation to a preceding optative) and with the potential optative with ἄν.

εἴ τις τὴν γυναῖκα τὴν σὴν οὕτω θεραπεύσειεν ὥστε φιλεῖν αὐτὴν μᾶλλον ποιήσειεν ἑαυτὸν ἢ σέ κτλ. *if some one should pay such attention to your wife as to make her love him better than yourself* X. C. 5. 5. 30 (cp. 2266), τοσούτου δεῖς ἐλέου τινὸς ἄξιος εἶναι ὥστε μῑσηθείης ἂν δικαιότατ' ἀνθρώπων *you are so far unworthy of compassion that you would be detested most justly of all men* D. 37. 49, ὡς ἄν X. Ag. 6. 7, X. C. 7. 5. 37, 7. 5. 81.

CLAUSES WITH ἐφ' ᾧ AND ἐφ' ᾧτε INTRODUCING A PROVISO

2279. ἐφ' ᾧ and ἐφ' ᾧτε *on condition that, for the purpose of* take the infinitive or (less often) the future indicative, and may be introduced, in the principal clause, by the demonstrative ἐπὶ τούτῳ. Negative μή.

αἱρεθέντες ἐφ' ᾧτε συγγράψαι νόμους *having been chosen for the purpose of compiling laws* X. H. 2. 3. 11, ἔφασαν ἀποδώσειν (τοὺς νεκροὺς) ἐφ' ᾧ μὴ καίειν τὰς οἰκίᾱς the barbarians *said they would surrender* the dead *on condition that he would not burn their houses* X. A. 4. 2. 19, ἀφίεμέν σε, ἐπὶ τούτῳ μέντοι, ἐφ' ᾧτε μηκέτι . . . φιλοσοφεῖν *we release you, on this condition however, that you no longer search after wisdom* P. A. 29 c. Future indicative: ξυνέβησαν ἐφ' ᾧτε ἐξίᾱσιν ἐκ Πελοποννήσου ὑπόσπονδοι καὶ μηδέποτε ἐπιβήσονται αὐτῆς *they made an agreement on condition that they should depart from the Peloponnesus under a truce and never set foot on it again* T. 1. 103.

a. These constructions do not occur in Homer. The future indicative is used by Herodotus and Thucydides on the analogy of relative clauses equivalent to consecutive clauses. These authors also use ἐπὶ τοῖσδε for ἐπὶ τούτῳ.

CONDITIONAL CLAUSES

2280. A condition is a supposition on which a statement is based. A conditional sentence commonly consists of two clauses:

The protasis: the conditional, or subordinate, clause, expressing a supposed or assumed case (*if*).

The apodosis: the conclusion, or principal clause, expressing what follows if the condition is realized. The truth or fulfilment of the conclusion depends on the truth or fulfilment of the conditional clause.

a. The protasis has its name from πρότασις, lit. *stretching forward, that which is put forward* (in logic, a premiss); the apodosis, from ἀπόδοσις, lit. *giving back, return; i.e.* the *resuming* or *answering* clause.

2281. The protasis usually precedes, but may follow, the apodosis.

2282. The protasis is introduced by εἰ *if.*

a. Homer has also αἰ, which is an Aeolic (and Doric) form.

2283. With the subjunctive mood, εἰ commonly takes ἄν (Epic εἴ κε or εἴ κεν, not ἐάν).

a. There are three forms, ἐάν, ἤν, ἄν. ἐάν is the ordinary form in Attic prose and inscriptions; ἤν appears in Ionic and in the older Attic writers (the tragic poets and Thucydides); ἄν, generally in the later writers (sometimes together with ἐάν), very rarely in Attic inscriptions. In Plato ἄν is commoner than ἐάν. Xenophon has all three forms.

b. ἤν is from εἰ + ἄν, ἄν from ἤ (another form of εἰ) + ἄν. The etymology of ἐάν is uncertain: either from ἤ + ἄν or from εἰ + ἄν.

2284. The particle ἄν is used in the apodosis: (1) with the optative, to denote possibility (cp. 1824); (2) with the past tenses of the indicative, to denote either the non-fulfilment of the condition (1786) or, occasionally, repetition (1790).

2285. The apodosis may be introduced by δέ or ἀλλά, less often by αὐτάρ. See under Particles. νῦν δέ *as it is, as it was* corrects a supposition contrary to fact. The apodosis sometimes has τότε, τότε δή, οὕτως (Hom. τῷ) comparable to Eng. *then, in that case* in the conclusion of conditional sentences.

2286. The negative of the protasis is μή because the subordinate clause expresses something that is *conceived* or *imagined.* μή negatives the conditional clause *as a whole.* On οὐ adherescent in protasis, see 2698.

The negative of the apodosis is οὐ, in case the principal clause states the conclusion as a *fact* on the supposition that the protasis is true; μή, when the construction requires that negative (2689).

2287. The indicative, subjunctive, and optative moods, and the participle may stand in protasis and apodosis. The imperative and infinitive may be used in the apodosis. The future optative is not used in conditional sentences except in indirect discourse. The tenses in conditional sentences, except unreal conditions, have the same force as in simple sentences.

2288. Instead of a formal conditional sentence the two members may be simply coördinated, the protasis having the form of an independent clause.

σμῑκρὸν λαβὲ παράδειγμα, καὶ πάντα εἴσει ἃ βούλομαι *take an insignificant example, and you will know what I mean* P. Th. 154 c, πράττεταί τι τῶν ὑμῖν δοκούντων συμφέρειν· ἄφωνος Αἰσχίνης *something is going on (of a kind) that seems to be to your advantage. Aeschines is dumb.* D. 18. 198. Cp. "Take with you this great truth, and you have the key to Paul's writings" (Channing); "Petition me, perhaps I may forgive" (Dryden). Cp. 1839.

CLASSIFICATION OF CONDITIONAL SENTENCES

A. CLASSIFICATION ACCORDING TO FORM

2289. Conditional sentences may be classified according to *form* or *function* (*i.e.* with reference to their meaning). Classified according to form, all conditional sentences may be arranged with regard to the form of the protasis or of the apodosis.

Protasis: εἰ with the indicative.
ἐάν (rarely εἰ) with the subjunctive.
εἰ with the optative.

Apodosis: with ἄν, denoting what *would (should) be* or *have been.*
without ἄν, not denoting what *would (should) be* or *have been.*

B. CLASSIFICATION ACCORDING TO FUNCTION

2290. Greek possesses a great variety of ways to join protasis and apodosis, but certain types, as in English, are more common than others and have clear and distinct meanings. In the case of some of the less usual types the exact shade of difference cannot be accurately known to us; as indeed to the Greeks themselves they were often used with no essential difference from the conventional types. In the following classification only the ordinary forms are given.

ACCORDING TO TIME

2291. This is the only functional distinction that characterizes *all* conditional sentences. Here are included also 2292, 2295, 2296.

1. *Present*

Protasis: a primary tense of the indicative.
Apodosis: any form of the simple sentence.
εἰ ταῦτα ποιεῖς, καλῶς ποιεῖς *if you do this, you do well.*

2. *Past*

Protasis: a secondary tense of the indicative.
Apodosis: any form of the simple sentence.
εἰ ταῦτα ἐποίεις, καλῶς ἐποίεις *if you were doing this, you were doing well,* εἰ ταῦτα ἐποίησας, καλῶς ἐποίησας *if you did this, you did well.*

3. *Future*

a. Protasis: ἐάν with the subjunctive.
Apodosis: any form expressing future time.
ἐὰν ταῦτα ποιῇς (ποιήσῃς), καλῶς ποιήσεις *if you do this, you will do well.*

b. Protasis: εἰ with the future indicative.
Apodosis: any form expressing future time.
εἰ ταῦτα ποιήσεις, πείσει *if you do this, you will suffer for it.*

c. Protasis: εἰ with the optative.
Apodosis: ἄν with the optative.
εἰ ταῦτα ποιοίης (ποιήσειας), καλῶς ἂν ποιοίης (ποιήσειας) *if you should (were to) do this, you would do well.*

According to Fulfilment or Non-fulfilment

2292. Only one class of conditional sentences distinctly expresses non-fulfilment of the action.

1. *Present or Past*

Protasis: εἰ with the imperfect indicative.
Apodosis: ἄν with the imperfect indicative.

εἰ ταῦτα ἐποίεις, καλῶς ἂν ἐποίεις if you were (now) *doing this, you would be doing well; if you had been doing this, you would have been doing well.*

2. *Past*

Protasis: εἰ with the aorist indicative.
Apodosis: ἄν with the aorist indicative.

εἰ ταῦτα ἐποίησας, καλῶς ἂν ἐποίησας if you had done this, you would have done well.

N. — Greek has no special forms to show that an action *is* or *was* fulfilled, however clearly this may be implied by the context. Any form of conditional sentence in which the apodosis does not express a rule of action may refer to an impossibility.

According to Particular or General Conditions

2293. A particular condition refers to a definite act or to several definite acts occurring at a definite time or at definite times.

2294. A general condition refers to any one of a series of acts that may occur or may have occurred at any time.

2295. General conditions are distinguished from particular conditions only in present and past time, and then only when there is no implication as to the fulfilment of the action. General conditions have no obligatory form, as any form of condition may refer to a rule of action or to a particular act; but there are two common types of construction:

1. *Present*

Protasis: ἐάν with the subjunctive.
Apodosis: present indicative.

ἐὰν ταῦτα ποιῇς (ποιήσῃς), σὲ ἐπαινῶ if ever *you do this, I* always *praise you.*

2. *Past*

Protasis: εἰ with the optative.
Apodosis: imperfect indicative.

εἰ ταῦτα ποιοίης (ποιήσειας), σὲ ἐπῄνουν if ever *you did this, I* always *praised you.*

2296. But equally possible, though less common, are:
εἰ ταῦτα ποιεῖς, σὲ ἐπαινῶ and *εἰ ταῦτα ἐποίεις, σὲ ἐπῄνουν.*

TABLE OF CONDITIONAL FORMS

2297. In this Grammar the ordinary types of conditional sentences are classified primarily according to *time*. The Homeric and other more usual variations from the ordinary forms are mentioned under each class, the less usual Attic variations are mentioned in 2355 ff. The following table shows the common usage:

Time	Form	Protasis	Apodosis
Present	Simple	εἰ with present or perfect indicative	present or perfect indicative or equivalent
	Unreal	εἰ with imperfect indicative	imperfect indicative with ἄν
	General	ἐάν with subjunctive	present indicative or equivalent
Past	Simple	εἰ with imperfect, aorist, or pluperfect indicative	imperfect, aorist, or pluperfect indicative
	Unreal	εἰ with aorist or imperfect indicative	aorist or imperfect indicative with ἄν
	General	εἰ with optative	imperfect indicative or equivalent
Future	More Vivid	ἐάν with subjunctive	fut. indic. or equivalent
	Emotional	εἰ with future indicative	fut. indic. or equivalent
	Less Vivid	εἰ with optative	ἄν with optative

PRESENT AND PAST CONDITIONS

First Form of Conditions

SIMPLE PRESENT AND PAST CONDITIONS

2298. Simple present or past conditions simply *state* a supposition with no implication as to its reality or probability. The protasis has the indicative, the apodosis has commonly the indicative, but also any other form of the simple sentence appropriate to the thought.

εἰ ταῦτα ποιεῖς, καλῶς ποιεῖς *if you do this, you do well.*

εἰ ταῦτα ἐποίησας, καλῶς ἐποίησας *if you did this, you did well.*

a. This form of condition corresponds to the logical formula *if this is so, then that is so; if this is not so, then that is not so; if A = B, then C = D.* The truth of the conclusion depends solely on the truth of the condition, which is not implied in any way. In these conditions something is supposed to be true only in order to draw the consequence that something else is true.

b. The conditional clause may express what the writer knows is physically impossible. Even when the supposition *is* true according to the real opinion of the writer, this form of condition is employed. In such cases εἴπερ is often used for εἰ. Both εἰ and εἴπερ sometimes have a causal force (2246); cp. *si quidem* and *quia*.

c. The simple condition is particular or general. When the protasis has εἴ τις and the apodosis a present indicative, the simple condition has a double meaning referring both to an individual case and to a rule of action. When a present general condition is distinctly expressed, ἐάν with the subjunctive is used (2337.)

2299. There are many possible combinations of present and past conditions with different forms of the protasis and apodosis. Protasis and apodosis may be in different tenses, and present and future may be combined.

2300. The apodosis may be the simple indicative or any other form of the simple sentence appropriate to the thought.

a. **Simple Indicative:** εἰ τοῦτ᾽ ἔχει καλῶς, ἐκεῖνο αἰσχρῶς *if this is excellent, that is disgraceful* Aes. 3. 188, εἰ μὲν (Ἀσκληπιὸς) θεοῦ ἦν, οὐκ ἦν αἰσχροκερδής· εἰ δ᾽ αἰσχροκερδής, οὐκ ἦν θεοῦ *if Asclepius was the son of a god, he was not covetous; if he was covetous, he was not the son of a god* P. R. 408 c, εἴ τέ τι ἄλλο . . . ἐγένετο ἐπικίνδυνον τοῖς Ἕλλησι, πάντων . . . μετέσχομεν *and if any other danger befell the Greeks, we took our share in all* T. 3. 54, ἦ καλὸν . . . τέχνημα ἄρα κέκτησαι, εἴπερ κέκτησαι *in truth you do possess a noble art, if indeed you do possess it* P. Pr. 319 a, εἴπερ γε Δαρείου . . . ἐστι παῖς . . . , οὐκ ἀμαχεὶ ταῦτ᾽ ἐγὼ λήψομαι *if indeed he is a son of Darius, I shall not gain this without a battle* X. A. 1. 7. 9, Κλέαρχος εἰ παρὰ τοὺς ὅρκους ἔλυε τὰς σπονδάς, τὴν δίκην ἔχει *assuming that Clearchus broke the truce contrary to his oath, he has his deserts* 2. 5. 41, εἰ δὲ δύο ἐξ ἑνὸς ἀγῶνος γεγένησθον, οὐκ ἐγὼ αἴτιος *but if two trials have been made out of one, I am not responsible* Ant. 5. 85.

b. **Indicative with ἄν** (unreal indicative, 1786): καίτοι τότε . . . τὸν Ὑπερείδην, εἴπερ ἀληθῆ μου νῦν κατηγορεῖ, μᾶλλον ἂν εἰκότως ἢ τόνδ᾽ ἐδίωκεν *and yet, if indeed his present charge against me is true, he would have had more reason for prosecuting Hyperides than he now has for prosecuting my client* D. 18. 223 (here ἂν ἐδίωκεν implies εἰ ἐδίωκεν, 2303). So also an unreal indicative without ἄν, 1774: τοῦτο, εἰ καὶ τἆλλα πάντ᾽ ἀποστεροῦσιν . . . ἀποδοῦναι προσῆκεν *even if they steal everything else, they should have restored this* D. 27. 37. In the above examples each clause has its proper force.

c. **Subjunctive** of exhortation or prohibition (cp. the indicative δεῖ or χρή with the infinitive, 1807): ὅθεν δὲ ἀπελίπομεν ἐπανέλθωμεν, εἴ σοι ἡδομένῳ ἐστίν *but let us return to the point whence we digressed, if it is agreeable to you* P. Ph. 78 b, εἰ μὲν ἴστε με τοιοῦτον . . . μηδὲ φωνὴν ἀνάσχησθε *if you know that I am such a man . . . do not even endure* the sound of *my voice* D. 18. 10.

d. **Optative of wish** (cp. the indicative ἐλπίζω): κάκιστ᾽ ἀπολοίμην, Ξανθίαν εἰ μὴ φιλῶ *may I perish most vilely, if I do not love Xanthias* Ar. Ran. 579.

e. **Potential optative:** θαυμάζοιμ᾽ ἂν εἰ οἶσθα *I should be surprised if you* *know* P. Pr. 312 c. The potential optative (or indicative with ἄν, above b) sometimes suggests an inference (cp. the indicative δοκεῖ and inf. with ἄν). Thus, εἰ μὲν γὰρ τοῦτο λέγουσιν, ὁμολογοίην ἂν ἔγωγε οὐ κατὰ τούτους εἶναι ῥήτωρ *for if they mean this, I must admit* (it seems to me that I must admit) *that I am an orator, but not after their style* P. A. 17 b (cp. τοῦτό γέ μοι δοκεῖ καλὸν εἶναι, εἴ τις οἷός τ' εἴη παιδεύειν ἀνθρώπους *this seems to me a fine thing, if any one should be able to train men* 19 e), εἰ γὰρ οὗτοι ὀρθῶς ἀπέστησαν, ὑμεῖς ἂν οὐ χρεὼν ἄρχοιτε *for if they were right in revolting, you must be wrong in holding your empire* T. 3. 40 (cp. οὐκ ἄρα χρὴ ὑμᾶς ἄρχειν).

f. **Imperative** (cp. the indicative κελεύω *order*, ἀπαγορεύω *forbid*): εἴ τις ἀντιλέγει, λεγέτω *if any one objects, let him speak* X. A. 7. 3. 14.

2301. If the protasis expresses a *present intention* or *necessity*, the future indicative may be used.

εἰ δὲ καὶ τῷ ἡγεμόνι πιστεύσομεν ὃν ἂν Κῦρος διδῷ, τί κωλύει καὶ τὰ ἄκρα ἡμῖν κελεύειν Κῦρον προκαταλαβεῖν; *but if we are going to trust any guide that Cyrus may give us, what hinders our also ordering Cyrus to occupy the heights in advance in our behalf?* X. A. 1. 3. 16, αἶρε πλῆκτρον, εἰ μαχεῖ *raise your spur if you mean (are going) to fight* Ar. Av. 759. The future here has a modal force and expresses something besides futurity; hence it is equivalent to μέλλεις μαχεῖσθαι (1959), but not to ἐὰν μάχῃ (2323) or to εἰ μαχεῖ (a threat, 2328), both of which refer to future time. The periphrasis with μέλλω and the present or future infinitive is more common in prose.

Second Form of Conditions

PRESENT AND PAST UNREAL CONDITIONS

2302. In present and past unreal conditions the protasis implies that the supposition cannot or could not be realized because contrary to a known fact. The apodosis states what *would be* or *would have been* the result if the condition *were* or *had been* realized.

2303. The protasis has εἰ with the imperfect, aorist, or pluperfect indicative; the apodosis has ἄν with these past tenses. The protasis and apodosis may have different tenses. Unreal conditions are either particular or general.

2304. The **imperfect** refers to present time or (sometimes) to a continued or habitual past act or state. The imperfect may be conative.

εἰ ταῦτα ἐποίεις, καλῶς ἂν ἐποίεις *if you were* (now) *doing this, you would be doing well*, or *if you had been doing this, you would have been doing well.*

The implied opposite is a present (ἀλλ' οὐ ποιεῖς *but you are* **not** *doing this*) or an imperfect (ἀλλ' οὐκ ἐποίεις *but you were* **not** *doing this*).

The imperfect of past time emphasizes the continuance of the action.

2305. The **aorist** refers to a simple occurrence in the past.

εἰ ταῦτα ἐποίησας, καλῶς ἂν ἐποίησας *if you had done this, you would have done well.*

The implied opposite is an aorist (ἀλλ' οὐκ ἐποίησας *but you did* **not** *do this*).

2306. The (rare) **pluperfect** refers to an act completed in past or present time or to the state following on such completion.

εἰ ταῦτα ἐπεποιήκης, καλῶς ἂν ἐπεποιήκης *if you had finished doing this* (now or on any past occasion), *you would have done well.*

The implied opposite is a perfect (ἀλλ' οὐ πεποίηκας *but you have* **not** *done this*) or a pluperfect (ἀλλ' οὐκ ἐπεποιήκης *but you had* **not** *done this*).

a. The pluperfect is used only when stress is laid on the completion of the act or on the continuance of the result of the act, and generally refers to present time. In reference to past time, the aorist is generally used instead of the pluperfect.

2307. In reference to *past* time, the imperfect or aorist is used according as either tense would be used in an affirmative sentence not conditional. The pluperfect is commonly used when the perfect would have been used of present time.

2308. In the *form* of the protasis and the apodosis of unreal conditions there is nothing that denotes unreality, but, in the combination, the unreality of the protasis is always, and that of the apodosis generally, implied. The past tenses of the indicative are used in unreal conditions referring to present time, because the speaker's thought goes back to the past, when the realization of the condition was still possible, though at the time of speaking that realization is impossible.

2309. Same Tenses in Protasis and Apodosis. — **a. Imperfect** of present time: ταῦτα δὲ οὐκ ἂν ἐδύναντο ποιεῖν, εἰ μὴ καὶ διαίτῃ μετρίᾳ ἐχρῶντο *but they would not be able to do this, if they were not also following a temperate diet* X. C. 1. 2. 16.

b. Imperfect of past time: οὐκ ἂν οὖν νήσων . . . ἐκράτει, εἰ μή τι καὶ ναυτικὸν εἶχεν *accordingly he would not have ruled over islands, if he had not possessed also some naval force* T. 1. 9. Present and past combined: εἰ μὴ τότ' ἐπόνουν, νῦν ἂν οὐκ εὐφραινόμην *if I had not toiled then, I should not be rejoicing now* Philemon 153.

c. Aorist of past time: οὐκ ἂν ἐποίησεν Ἀγασίας ταῦτα, εἰ μὴ ἐγὼ αὐτὸν ἐκέλευσα *Agasias would not have done this, if I had not ordered him* X. A. 6. 6. 15.

2310. Different Tenses in Protasis and Apodosis. — **a. Imperfect and Aorist:** εἰ μὲν πρόσθεν ἠπιστάμην, οὐδ' ἂν συνηκολούθησά σοι *if I had known this before, I would not even have accompanied you* X. A. 7. 7. 11.

N. — With an imperfect of present time in the protasis, εἶπον ἄν, ἀπεκρινάμην ἄν and like verbs, denote an act in present time (*I should at once say*). Thus, εἰ μὴ πατὴρ ἦσθ', εἶπον ἄν σ' οὐκ εὖ φρονεῖν *if thou wert not my father, I would say* (would have said) *thou wast unwise* S. Ant. 755. Often in Plato, as εἰ μὲν οὐ, σύ με ἠρώτᾱς τι τῶν νῦν δή, εἶπον ἂν κτλ. *if now you were asking me any one of the questions with which we are now dealing, I should say* etc., P. Euth. 12 d, cp. P. G. 514 d, X. A. 7. 6. 23.

b. Imperfect and Pluperfect: καὶ τἄλλ' ἂν ἅπαντ' ἀκολούθως τούτοις ἐπέπρᾱκτο, εἴ τις ἐπείθετό μοι *and everything else would have been effected consistently with what I have said, if my advice had been followed* D. 19. 173.

c. Aorist and Imperfect: εἰ μὴ ὑμεῖς ἤλθετε, ἐπορευόμεθα ἂν ἐπὶ βασιλέᾱ *if you had not come, we should* now *be marching against the king* X. A. 2. 1. 4.

d. Aorist and Pluperfect: εἰ ἐγὼ πάλαι ἐπεχείρησα πράττειν τὰ πολῑτικὰ πράγματα, πάλαι ἂν ἀπολώλη *if I had long ago essayed to meddle with politics, I should long ago have perished* P. A. 31 d, εἰ μία ψῆφος μετέπεσεν, ὑπερώριστ' ἂν *if one vote had been transferred to the other side, he would have been transported across the borders* (and *now* be in exile) Aes. 3. 252.

e. Pluperfect and Imperfect: ἡ πόλις ἐλάμβανεν ἂν δίκην, εἴ τι ἠδίκητο *the State would inflict punishment, if it had been wronged* Ant. 6. 10.

f. Pluperfect and Aorist: οὐκ ἂν παρέμεινα, εἰ ἐλελύμην *I should not have stayed, if I had been free* Ant. 5. 13.

2311. Homeric Constructions.—In Homer the imperfect in unreal conditions refers only to past time. The apodosis may have κέ or ἄν with the optative.

a. The present unreal condition with εἰ with the optative in the protasis and ἄν with the optative in the apodosis (in *form* like a less vivid future condition in Attic) is very rare (Ψ 274). In B 80, Ω 220 we have a combination of a past protasis (imperfect or aorist indicative) with present apodosis (with κέν and the optative).

b. Past unreal conditions have, in the protasis, the imperfect or aorist indicative; in the apodosis, either the imperfect or aorist indicative with ἄν or κέ or the aorist or present optative with κέ. Thus, καί νύ κεν ἔνθ' ἀπόλοιτο . . . Αἰνείᾱς, εἰ μὴ ἄρ' ὀξὺ νόησε . . . Ἀφροδίτη *and here Aeneas had perished, if Aphrodite had not quickly observed him* E 311.

2312. Unreal conditions with ἄν and the optative in apodosis (cp. 2311) in Attic are rare and some are suspected. Either the common reading is at fault (X. M. 3. 5. 8), or we have a simple condition with a potential optative (2300 e), as in And. 1. 57, L. 6. 39, I. 4. 102. In εἰ μὲν τοίνυν τοῦτ' ἐπεχείρουν λέγειν . . ., οὐκ ἔσθ' ὅστις οὐκ ἂν εἰκότως ἐπιτῑμήσειέ μοι *if now I were attempting to say this, there would be no one who would not censure me with good reason* (D. 18. 206) the implied conclusion is οὐκ ἂν ἦν ὅστις κτλ.

a. The optative in protasis and apodosis occur in E. Med. 568 (present unreal). Hdt. uses the potential optative occasionally (*e.g.* 7. 214) where English uses a past expression.

UNREAL CONDITIONS—APODOSIS WITHOUT ἄν

2313. ἄν may be omitted in the apodosis of an unreal condition when the apodosis consists of an imperfect indicative denoting unfulfilled obligation, possibility, or propriety. Such are the impersonal expressions ἔδει, χρῆν, ἐξῆν, εἰκὸς ἦν, καλὸν ἦν, etc., with the infinitive, the action of which is (usually) not realized.

εἰ ταῦτα ἐποίει, ἔδει (ἐξῆν) αἰτιᾶσθαι αὐτόν if he were doing this (as he is not), *one ought to (might) blame him.*

εἰ ταῦτα ἐποίησε, ἔδει (ἐξῆν) αἰτιάσασθαι (or *αἰτιᾶσθαι*) *αὐτόν if he had done this* (as he did not), *one ought to (might) have blamed him.*

a. Here ἔδει and ἐξῆν are auxiliaries and the emphasis falls on the infinitive. The impersonal verb has the effect of a modifying adverb denoting obligation, possibility, or propriety: thus ἔδει αἰτιᾶσθαι αὐτόν is virtually equivalent to δικαίως ἂν ᾐτιᾶτο, and εἰκὸς ἦν αἰτιάσασθαι αὐτόν to εἰκότως ἂν ᾐτιάθη *he would properly have been blamed.*

b. ἔδει, χρῆν, etc., may be used in simple sentences (1774 ff.) without any protasis either expressed or implied. But a protasis may often be supplied in thought.

2314. The present infinitive generally expresses what *would necessarily, possibly,* or *properly be done* now. The aorist, and sometimes the present, infinitive expresses what *would necessarily, possibly,* or *properly have been done* in the past.

a. Present infinitive of present time: χρῆν δήπου, εἴτε τινὲς αὐτῶν πρεσβύτεροι γενόμενοι ἔγνωσαν ὅτι νέοις οὖσιν αὐτοῖς ἐγὼ κακὸν πώποτέ τι ξυνεβούλευσα, νυνὶ αὐτοὺς ἀναβαίνοντας ἐμοῦ κατηγορεῖν *if some of them on growing older had perceived that I ever gave them any bad counsel when they were young, they ought of course now to rise up in person and accuse me* P. A. 33 d.

b. Present infinitive of past time: εἴ τινα (προῖκα) ἐδίδου, εἰκὸς ἦν καὶ τὴν δοθεῖσαν ὑπὸ τῶν παραγενέσθαι φασκόντων μαρτυρεῖσθαι *if he had given any* dowry, *that which was actually delivered would naturally have been attested by those who claimed to have been present* Is. 3. 28.

c. Aorist infinitive of past time: εἰ ἐβούλετο δίκαιος εἶναι περὶ τοὺς παῖδας, ἐξῆν αὐτῷ . . . μισθῶσαι τὸν οἶκον *if he had wished to be just in regard to the children, he might properly have let the house* L. 32. 23.

2315. With the same impersonal expressions, ἄν is regularly used when the obligation, possibility, or propriety, and not the action of the verb dependent on ἔδει, etc., is denied. Here the main force of the apodosis falls on the necessity, possibility, or propriety of the act.

εἰ ταῦτα ἐποίει, ἔδει (ἐξῆν) ἂν αἰτιᾶσθαι αὐτόν *if he were doing this* (as he is not), *it would be necessary (possible) to blame him;* but, as the case now stands, it is not necessary (possible). Thus, εἰ μὲν ἠπιστάμεθα σαφῶς ὅτι ἥξει πλοῖα . . . ἄγων ἱκανά, οὐδὲν ἂν ἔδει ὧν μέλλω λέγειν *if we knew for certain that he would return with a sufficient number of vessels, there would be no need to say what I am going to say* (but there is *need*) X. A. 5. 1. 10, ταῦτα εἰ μὲν δι' ἀσθένειαν ἐπάσχομεν, στέργειν ἂν ἦν ἀνάγκη τὴν τύχην *if we had suffered this because of our weakness, we should have* (necessity would compel us) *to rest content with our lot* L. 33. 4.

2316. With ἄν, it is implied that the obligation does (or did) not exist; without ἄν, it is implied that the action of the dependent infinitive is (or was) not realized. Thus the first sentence in 2315, without ἄν, would mean: *if he were doing this* (as he is not), *one ought to blame him;* but, as the case now stands, one does not blame him.

2317. ἐβουλόμην, or ἐβουλόμην ἄν, with the infinitive may stand in the apodosis. Cp. 1782, 1789.

2318. ἄν is regularly omitted in an apodosis formed by the imperfect of μέλλω and the infinitive (usually future) to denote an unfulfilled past intention or expectation (cp. the Lat. future participle with *eram* or *fui*). Cp. 1895 a, 1960.

ἦ μάλα δὴ Ἀγαμέμνονος . . . φθίσεσθαι κακὸν οἶτον ἐνὶ μεγάροισιν ἔμελλον, εἰ μὴ . . . ἔειπες *in sooth I was like to have perished in my halls by the evil fate of Agamemnon, hadst thou not spoken* ν 383 (*periturus eram, nisi dixisses*).

2319. ἄν may be omitted with the aorist of κινδῡνεύω *run a risk* when the emphasis falls on the dependent infinitive.

εἰ μὴ δρόμῳ μόλις ἐξεφύγομεν εἰς Δελφούς, ἐκινδῡνεύσαμεν ἀπολέσθαι *if we had not escaped with difficulty to Delphi by taking to our heels, we ran the risk of perishing* (= *we should* probably *have perished:* ἂν ἀπωλόμεθα) Aes. 3. 123. Contrast εἰ μέντοι τότε πλείους συνελέγησαν, ἐκινδύνευσεν ἂν διαφθαρῆναι πολὺ τοῦ στρατεύματος *if they had mustered in larger force at this time, a large part of the troops would have been in danger of being destroyed* X. A. 4. 1. 11.

2320. Some expressions containing a secondary tense of the indicative without ἄν, and not followed by a dependent infinitive, are virtually equivalent to the apodosis of an unreal condition.

τούτῳ δ' εἰ μὴ ὡμολόγουν ἃ οὗτος ἐβούλετο, οὐδεμιᾷ ζημίᾳ ἔνοχος ἦν *but if they had not acknowledged to him what he wished, he would have been* (lit. *was*) *liable to no penalty* L. 7. 37.

a. Imperfects (not impersonal) without ἄν are often emended, as ᾐσχῡνόμην μέντοι (some editors μέντἄν), εἰ ὑπὸ πολεμίου γε ὄντος ἐξηπατήθην *I should, however, be ashamed, if I had been deceived by any one who was an enemy* X. A. 7. 6. 21. Cp. "Tybalt's death was woe enough, if it had ended there" (Shakesp.). Cases like 1895 a do not belong here.

FUTURE CONDITIONS

2321. Future conditions set forth suppositions the fulfilment of which is still undecided. There are two main forms of future conditions:

More Vivid Future conditions.

Less Vivid Future conditions.

A variety of the first class is the Emotional Future (2328).

Future conditions may be particular or general (2293, 2294).

2322. The difference between the More Vivid Future and the Less Vivid Future, like the difference between *if I (shall) do this* and *if I should do this,* depends on the mental attitude of the speaker. With the Vivid Future the speaker sets forth a thought as prominent and distinct in his mind; and for any one or more of various reasons. Thus, he may (and generally does) regard the conclusion as more likely to be realized; but even an impossible (2322 c) or dreaded result may be expressed by this form if the speaker chooses to picture the result vividly and distinctly. The More Vivid Future is thus used whenever the speaker clearly desires to be graphic, impressive, emphatic, and to anticipate a future result with the distinctness of the present.

The Less Vivid Future deals with suppositions less distinctly conceived and of less immediate concern to the speaker, mere assumed or imaginary cases. This is a favourite construction in Greek, and is often used in stating suppositions that are merely possible and often impossible; but the form of the condition itself does not imply an expectation of the speaker that the conclusion may *possibly* be realized. The difference between the two forms, therefore, is not an inherent difference between *probable* realization in the one case and *possible* realization in the other. The same thought may often be expressed in either form without any essential difference in meaning. The only difference is, therefore, often that of temperament, tone, or style.

a. ἐάν with the subjunctive and εἰ with the optative are rarely used in successive sentences. In most such cases the difference lies merely in the degree of distinctness and emphasis of the expression used; but where the speaker wishes to show that the conclusion is expected or desired, he uses ἐάν with the subjunctive rather than the other form. Thus, εἰ οὖν ἴδοιεν καὶ νῷ καθάπερ τοὺς πολλοὺς ἐν μεσημβρίᾳ μὴ διαλεγομένους, ἀλλὰ νυστάζοντας καὶ κηλουμένους ὑφ᾽ αὑτῶν δι᾽ ἀργίᾱν τῆς διανοίᾱς, δικαίως ἂν καταγελῷεν· . . . ἐὰν δ᾽ ὁρῶσι διαλεγομένους . . ., τάχ᾽ ἂν δοῖεν ἀγασθέντες *if now they should see that we, like the many, are not conversing at noon-day but slumbering and charmed by them because of the indolence of our thoughts, they would rightly laugh at us; but if they see us conversing, they will, perhaps, out of admiration make us gifts* P. Phae. 259 a.

b. Cases of both forms in successive sentences are I 135, Hdt. 8. 21, 9. 48; P. Cr. 51 d, Ph. 105 b, Phae. 259 a, Pr. 330 c–331 a, D. 4. 11, 18. 147–148. In D. 18. 178 both the desired and the undesired alternative have ἐάν with the subjunctive.

c. Impossibilities may be expressed by ἐάν with the subjunctive. Thus, τί οὖν, ἂν εἴπωσιν οἱ νόμοι; *what, then, if the laws say?* P. Cr. 50 c; cp. P. Eu. 299 b, R. 610 a, 612 b (opt. in 359 c, 360 b), Ar. Aves 1642, E. Or. 1593, Phoen. 1216. Cp. 2329 a.

Third Form of Conditions

MORE VIVID FUTURE CONDITIONS

2323. More vivid future conditions have in the protasis ἐάν (ἤν, ἄν) with the subjunctive; in the apodosis, the future indicative or any other form referring to future time.

ἐὰν ταῦτα ποιῇς (ποιήσῃς), καλῶς ποιήσεις *if you do this, you will do well.*

2324. This form of condition corresponds to the use of *shall* and *will* in conditional sentences in older English ("if ye shall ask . . . I will do it": St. John).

Modern English substitutes the present for the more exact future in ordinary future conditions of this class; and often uses *shall* in the protasis with an emotional force. The English present subjunctive, although somewhat rarely used in the modern language, corresponds more nearly to the Greek subjunctive ("if she be there, he shall not need": Beaumont and Fletcher).—Since *if you do this* may be expressed in Greek by ἐὰν ταῦτα ποιῇς or εἰ ταῦτα ποιήσεις (2328), and by εἰ ταῦτα ποιεῖς (2298), the difference in meaning is made clear only by the apodosis. The form ἐὰν ταῦτα ποιῇς in vivid future conditions must be distinguished from the same form in present general conditions (*if ever you do this*, 2337). ἐὰν ταῦτά σοι δοκῇ, ποίει may be particular or general: *if* (or *if ever*) *this seems good to you, do it.*

2325. The present subjunctive views an act as continuing (not completed); the aorist subjunctive as simply occurring (completed). Neither tense has any time of itself. The aorist subjunctive may mark the action of the protasis as completed before the action of the principal clause (cp. the Lat. future perfect). Ingressive aorists (1924) retain their force in the subjunctive.

2326. The apodosis of the more vivid future condition is the future indicative or any other form of the simple sentence that refers to future time.

a. Future Indicative: ἐὰν ζητῇς καλῶς, εὑρήσεις *if you seek well, you shall find* P. G. 503 d, ἐὰν δ' ἔχωμεν χρήμαθ', ἕξομεν φίλους *if we have money, we shall have friends* Men. Sent. 165, χάριν γε εἴσομαι, ἐὰν ἀκούητε *I shall be grateful, if you listen* P. Pr. 310 a, ἂν αὐτῷ διδῷς ἀργύριον καὶ πείθῃς αὐτόν, ποιήσει καὶ σὲ σοφόν *if you give him money and persuade him, he will make you too wise* 310 d, ἢν γὰρ τοῦτο λάβωμεν, οὐ δυνήσονται μένειν *for if we take this, they will not be able to remain* X. A. 3. 4. 41, ἐὰν κύκλου ἐπὶ τῆς περιφερείας ληφθῇ δύο τυχόντα σημεῖα, ἡ ἐπὶ τὰ σημεῖα ἐπιζευγνυμένη εὐθεῖα ἐντὸς πεσεῖται τοῦ κύκλου *if any two points be taken in the circumference of a circle, the straight line which joins them shall fall within the circle* Euclid 3. 2.

b. Primary Tenses of the indicative other than the future. **Present** (1879): ἢν θάνῃς σύ, παῖς ὅδ' ἐκφεύγει μόρον *if thou art slain, yon boy escapes death* E. And. 381, δίδωσ' ἑκὼν κτείνειν ἑαυτόν, ἢν τάδε ψευσθῇ λέγων *freely he offers himself to death, if he lies in speaking thus* (δίδωσι = he says that he is ready) S. Phil. 1342. **Aorist**: see 1934, and cp. εἰ μέν κ' αὖθι μένων Τρώων πόλιν ἀμφιμάχωμαι, ὤλετο μέν μοι νόστος *if I tarry here and wage war about the city of the Trojans, my return home is lost for me* I 413. **Perfect**: see 1950. Cp. "if I shall have an answer no directlier, I am gone": Beaumont and Fletcher.

c. Subjunctive of exhortation, prohibition, or deliberation, and with μή (μὴ οὐ) of doubtful assertion (1801). Thus, μηδ' ἄν τι ὠνῶμαι, ἔφη, ἢν πωλῇ νεώτερος τριάκοντα ἐτῶν, ἔρωμαι, ὁπόσου πωλεῖ; *even if I am buying something, said he, am I not to ask 'what do you sell it for?' if the seller is under thirty years of age?* X. M. 1. 2. 36, κἂν φαινώμεθα ἄδικα αὐτὰ ἐργαζόμενοι, μὴ οὐ δέῃ ὑπολογίζεσθαι κτλ. *and if we appear to do this unjustly, I rather think it may not be necessary to take notice, etc.* P. Cr. 48 d.

d. Optative of wish, or potential optative with ἄν ('something *may* happen' instead of 'something *will* happen'). Thus, ἤν σε τοῦ λοιποῦ ποτ' ἀφέλωμαι χρόνου,

. . . κάκιστ' ἀπολοίμην *if ever in the future I take them away from you, may I perish most vilely!* Ar. Ran. 586, ἐὰν κατὰ μέρος φυλάττωμεν . . ., ἧττον ἂν δύναιντο ἡμᾶς θηρᾶν οἱ πολέμιοι *if we keep guard by turns, the enemy will (would) be less able to harry us* X. A. 5. 1. 9. See also 2356 a.

e. Imperative, or infinitive for the imperative (2013): ἢν πόλεμον αἱρῆσθε, μηκέτι ἥκετε δεῦρο ἄνευ ὅπλων *if you choose war, do not come here again without your arms* X. C. 3. 2. 13, σὺ δ', ἄν τι ἔχῃς βέλτῖόν ποθεν λαβεῖν, πειρᾶσθαι καὶ ἐμοὶ μεταδιδόναι *but if you can find anything better from any quarter, try to communicate it to me too* P. Crat. 426 b.

2327. Homeric Constructions.—a. εἰ alone without κέ or ἄν with the subjunctive with no appreciable difference from εἴ κε (ἄν): εἴ περ γάρ σε κατακτάνῃ, οὔ σ' . . . κλαύσομαι *for if he slay thee, I shall not bewail thee* X 86. This construction occurs in lyric and dramatic poetry, and in Hdt., as δυστάλαινα τἆρ' ἐγώ, εἴ σου στερηθῶ *wretched indeed shall I be, if I am deprived of thee* S. O. C. 1443. In Attic prose it is very rare and suspected (T. 6. 21).

b. Subjunctive with κέ in both protasis and apodosis (the anticipatory subjunctive, 1810): εἰ δέ κε μὴ δώῃσιν, ἐγὼ δέ κεν αὐτὸς ἕλωμαι *and if he do not give her up, then will I seize her myself* A 324.

c. εἴ (αἴ) κε with the future in protasis (rare): σοὶ . . . ὄνειδος ἔσσεται, εἴ κ' Ἀχιλῆος . . . ἑταῖρον . . . κύνες ἑλκήσουσιν *it will be a reproach unto thee, if the dogs drag the companion of Achilles* P 557. Some read here the subjunctive.

2328. Emotional Future Conditions.—When the protasis expresses strong feeling, the future indicative with εἰ is commonly used instead of ἐάν with the subjunctive, and may often be rendered by *hall.* The protasis commonly suggests something undesired, or feared, or intended independently of the speaker's will; the apodosis commonly conveys a threat, a warning, or an earnest appeal to the feelings. The apodosis is generally expressed by the future indicative, but other forms of 2326 are possible.

εἰ ταῦτα λέξεις, ἐχθαρεῖ μὲν ἐξ ἐμοῦ *if thou speakest thus, thou wilt be hated by me* S. Ant. 93, εἰ μὴ καθέξεις γλῶσσαν, ἔσται σοι κακά *if you won't hold your tongue, there's trouble in store for you* E. frag. 5, ἀποκτενεῖς γάρ, εἴ με γῆς ἔξω βαλεῖς *for thou wilt slay me if thou shalt thrust me out of the land* E. Phoen. 1621, εἰ ὧδε στρατευσόμεθα, οὐ δυνησόμεθα μάχεσθαι *if we keep the field thus, we shall not be able to fight* X. C. 6. 1. 13, ἀθλιώτατος ἂν γενοίμην (potential optative), εἰ φυγὰς ἀδίκως καταστήσομαι *I should become most wretched, were I to be driven unjustly into exile* L. 7. 41.

a. When εἰ with the future indicative is directly contrasted with ἐάν with the subjunctive, the former usually presents the unfavourable, the latter the favourable, alternative. Thus,

ἢν μὲν γὰρ ἐθέλωμεν ἀποθνῄσκειν ὑπὲρ τῶν δικαίων, εὐδοκιμήσομεν . . ., εἰ δὲ φοβησόμεθα τοὺς κινδύνους, εἰς πολλὰς ταραχὰς καταστήσομεν ἡμᾶς αὐτούς *if we are (shall be) willing to die for the sake of justice, we shall gain renown; but if we are going to fear dangers, we shall bring ourselves into great confusion* I. 6. 107. Cp. X. C. 4. 1. 15, Ar. Nub. 586–591, L. 27. 7, I. 12. 237, 15. 130, 17. 9, D. 8. 17, 18. 176, 27. 20–22. Both constructions are rarely used in successive clauses without any essential difference (X. Ap. 6). ἐάν with the subjunctive, when used in threats or warnings, is a milder form of statement than εἰ with the future (Hdt. 1. 71). An unfavourable alternative *may* thus be expressed by ἐάν with the subjunctive (A 135–137, Hdt. 3. 36, Aes. 3. 254).

b. εἰ with the future indicative may have a modal force like that of δεῖ or μέλλω (*am to, must*) with the infinitive: βαρεῖα (κήρ), εἰ τέκνον δαΐξω *hard is fate, if I must slay my child* A. Ag. 208. The future of present intention (2301) is different.

Fourth Form of Conditions

LESS VIVID FUTURE CONDITIONS

2329. Less vivid future conditions (*should . . . would* conditions) have in the protasis εἰ with the optative, in the apodosis ἄν with the optative.

εἰ ταῦτα ποιοίης, καλῶς ἂν ποιοίης or εἰ ταῦτα ποιήσειας, καλῶς ἂν ποιήσειας *if you should do this, you would do well.*

εἴης φορητὸς οὐκ ἄν, εἰ πράσσοις καλῶς *thou wouldst be unendurable shouldst thou be prosperous* A. Pr. 979, εἰ δ' ἀναγκαῖον εἴη ἀδικεῖν ἢ ἀδικεῖσθαι, ἑλοίμην ἂν μᾶλλον ἀδικεῖσθαι ἢ ἀδικεῖν *but if it should be necessary to do wrong or be wronged, I should prefer to be wronged than to do wrong* P. G. 469 c, δεινὰ ἂν εἴην εἰργασμένος, . . . εἰ λίποιμι τὴν τάξιν *I should be in the state of having committed a dreadful deed, if I were to desert my post* P. A. 28 d.

a. Anything physically impossible may be represented as supposable, hence this construction may be used of what is contrary to fact. Thus, φαίη δ' ἂν ἡ θανοῦσά γ' εἰ φωνὴν λάβοι *the dead would speak if gifted with a voice* S. El. 548. Cp. A. Ag. 37, P. Pr. 361 a, Eu. 299 d, and see 2311 a, 2322 c.

2330. Conditional sentences of this class arose partly from optatives of wish (1814, 1815), partly from potential optatives (1824). Cp. εἴθ' ὣς ἡβώοιμι . . . τῷ κε τάχ' ἀντήσειε μάχης . . . Ἕκτωρ *would that I were thus young . . . in that case Hector would soon find his combat* H 157; see also ξ 193.

2331. The present optative views an action as continuing (not completed); the aorist optative, as simply occurring (completed). (The future optative is never used except to represent a future indicative in indirect discourse.) The perfect (rare) denotes completion with resulting state. In Hdt. 7. 214 it is used vaguely of the *past:* εἰδείη μὲν γὰρ ἂν . . . ταύτην τὴν ἀτραπὸν Ὀνήτης, εἰ τῇ χώρᾳ πολλὰ ὡμῑληκὼς εἴη *for Onetes might know of this path . . . if he had been well acquainted with the country.*

2332. English *would* is equivocal, being used either in the translation of ἄν with the optative or of ἄν with the past indicative (2302). Thus, cp. εἴ τίς σε ἤρετο . . ., τί ἂν ἀπεκρίνω; *if any one had asked you . . ., what would you have replied?* with εἰ οὖν τις ἡμᾶς . . . ἔροιτο . . ., τί ἂν αὐτῷ ἀποκρῑναίμεθα; *if then some one should (were to) ask us . . ., what would (should) we reply to him?* P. Pr. 311 b, d. *If I were* may be used to translate both εἰ with the optative and εἰ with the past indicative. English shows examples of *were* in the protasis followed by *would*, *shall*, *will*, *is* (*was*, etc.). *Were* occurs also in apodosis ("should he be roused out of sleep to-night, it were not well": Shelley).

2333. The apodosis has the optative without ἄν in *wishes.*

εἰ μὲν συμβουλεύοιμι ἃ βέλτιστά μοι δοκεῖ, πολλά μοι καὶ ἀγαθὰ γένοιτο *if I should give the advice that seems best to me, may many blessings fall to my lot* X. A. 5. 6. 4.

On the optative with εἰ followed by other forms of the apodosis, see 2359.

2334. Homeric Constructions.—**a.** In the protasis, εἴ κε (εἰ ἄν) with the optative with the same force as εἰ alone. This use is exclusively Homeric. Thus, οὐ μὲν γάρ τι κακώτερον ἄλλο πάθοιμι, οὐδ' εἴ κεν τοῦ πατρὸς ἀποφθιμένοιο πυθοίμην *for I could not suffer anything worse, not even if I should learn of my father's death* T 321. On εἰ ἄν in Attic, see 2353.

b. In the apodosis, a primary tense of the indicative: the present (η 52), the future (I 388), the future with κέ (μ 345: but this may be the aorist subjunctive).

c. In the apodosis, the hortatory subjunctive (Ψ 893), the subjunctive with ἄν or κέ (Λ 386).

d. In the apodosis, the optative without ἄν not in a wish, but with the same force as the optative with ἄν. See T 321 in a.

e. For κέ with the optative in the apodosis where we should expect, in Homeric and Attic Greek, a past indicative with ἄν (κέ) in an unreal condition, see 2311 b.

GENERAL CONDITIONS

2335. General conditions refer indefinitely to any act or series of acts that are supposed to occur or to have occurred at any time; and without any implication as to fulfilment.

The *if* clause has the force of *if ever* (*whenever*), the conclusion expresses a repeated or habitual action or a general truth.

2336. Any simple or unreal condition of present or past time, or any future condition, may refer to a customary or frequently repeated act or to a general truth. But for the present and past only (when nothing is implied as to fulfilment) there are two forms of expression: either a *special* kind of conditional sentence or (less frequently) the *simple* condition, as regularly in English and in Latin:

Present. Protasis: ἐάν (= ἐάν ποτε) with the subjunctive; apodosis: the present indicative (2337).

Protasis: εἰ (= εἴ ποτε) with the present indicative; apodosis: the present indicative (2298 c, 2342).

Past. Protasis: εἰ with the optative; apodosis: the imperfect indicative (2340).

Protasis: εἰ with the imperfect; apodosis: the imperfect (2298 c, 2342).

a. By reason of the past apodosis, the optative in the protasis refers to the past. Only in this use (and when the optative in indirect discourse represents a past indicative) does the optative refer distinctly to the past.

b. The present subjunctive and optative view the action as continuing (not completed); the aorist subjunctive and optative, as simply occurring (completed). The tenses of the protasis have no time of themselves, but usually the action of the present is relatively contemporaneous with, the action of the aorist relatively antecedent to, the action of the main verb.

c. The indicative forms in the protasis are more common in temporal and relative sentences. Observe that it is the character of the *apodosis* alone which distinguishes the special kind of general condition from the two forms of future conditions.

Fifth Form of Conditions

PRESENT GENERAL CONDITIONS

2337. Present general conditions have, in the protasis, ἐάν (ἤν, ἄν) with the subjunctive; in the apodosis, the present indicative or an equivalent. ἐὰν ταῦτα ποιῇς (ποιήσῃς), σὲ ἐπαινῶ *if* ever *you do this, I* always *praise you.* The conclusion holds true of any time or of all time.

ἢν δ' ἐγγὺς ἔλθῃ θάνατος, οὐδεὶς βούλεται θνῄσκειν *but if death draws near, no one wishes to die* E. Alc. 671, γελᾷ δ' ὁ μῶρος, κἄν τι μὴ γελοῖον ᾖ *the fool laughs even if there is nothing to laugh at* Men. Sent. 108, ἐὰν ἴσοις ἴσα προστεθῇ, τὰ ὅλα ἐστὶν ἴσα *if equals be added to equals, the wholes are equal* Euclid, Ax. 2.

2338. The gnomic aorist is equivalent to the present indicative in apodosis. ἢν δέ τις τούτων τι παραβαίνῃ, ζημίᾱν αὐτοῖς ἐπέθεσαν *but if any one* ever *transgresses any one of these regulations, they* always *impose punishment upon them* (*him*) X. C. 1. 2. 2.

2339. Homer and Pindar prefer εἰ to ἐάν or εἴ κε (A 81); and this εἰ is sometimes found in Attic poetry (S. Ant. 710). ἄν is more often absent in general conditions than in vivid future conditions.

Sixth Form of Conditions

PAST GENERAL CONDITIONS

2340. Past general conditions have, in the protasis, εἰ with the optative; in the apodosis, the imperfect indicative or an equivalent. εἰ ταῦτα ποιοίης (ποιήσειας), σὲ ἐπῄνουν *if* ever *you did this, I* always *praised you.*

εἴ πού τι ὁρῴη βρωτόν, διεδίδου *if* ever *he saw anything to eat anywhere, he* always *distributed it* X. A. 4. 5. 8, εἰ δέ τις καὶ ἀντείποι, εὐθὺς . . . ἐτεθνήκει *but if any one even made an objection, he was promptly put to death* T. 8. 66, εἰ μὲν ἐπίοιεν οἱ Ἀθηναῖοι, ὑπεχώρουν, εἰ δ' ἀναχωροῖεν, ἐπέκειντο *if the Athenians advanced, they retreated; if they retired, they fell upon them* 7. 79, ἐτίμᾱ δ' εἴ τι καλὸν πράττοιεν, παρίστατο δ' εἴ τις συμφορᾱ̀ συμβαίνοι *he honoured* them *if* ever *they performed some noble action, and stood by* them *in times of misfortune* (lit. *if any misfortune befell*) X. Ag. 7. 3.

a. The optative is here sometimes called the *iterative* optative. This mood has however no iterative force in itself, the idea of repetition being derived solely from the context. In Homer the iterative optative after εἰ (found only Ω 768) is an extension of the iterative optative in temporal clauses where this use originated.

2341. The **iterative imperfect** or **aorist** with ἄν (1894, 1933): εἰ δέ τις αὐτῷ περί του ἀντιλέγοι . . ., ἐπὶ τὴν ὑπόθεσιν ἐπανῆγεν ἂν πάντα τὸν λόγον *if* ever *any one opposed him on any matter, he would* always *bring the entire discussion back to the main point* X. M. 4. 6. 13, εἴ τις αὐτῷ δοκοίη . . . βλᾱκεύειν, ἐκλεγόμενος τὸν ἐπιτήδειον ἔπαισεν ἄν *if* ever *any one seemed to be lagging, he would* always *pick out the likely man and strike him* X. A. 2. 3. 11. These cases are not to be confused with the apodoses of unreal conditions.

INDICATIVE FORM OF GENERAL CONDITIONS

2342. Present: protasis, εἰ with the present; apodosis, the present. Past: protasis, εἰ with the imperfect; apodosis, the imperfect.

The protasis usually has εἴ τις, εἴ τι (cp. ὅστις, ὅ τι) with the indicative, as εἴ τις δύο ἢ καί τι πλείους ἡμέρᾱς λογίζεται, μάταιός ἐστιν *if* ever *any one counts upon two or even perchance on more days, he is rash* S. Tr. 944, ἐλευθέρως δὲ . . . πολῑτεύομεν . . ., οὐ δι' ὀργῆς τὸν πέλας, εἰ καθ' ἡδονήν τι δρᾷ, ἔχοντες *we are tolerant in our public life, not being angry at our neighbour if he acts as he likes* T. 2. 37, τὰ μὲν ἀγώγιμα, εἴ τι ἦγον, ἐξαιρούμενοι φύλακας καθίστασαν *taking out the cargoes, if* the vessels *carried anything, they appointed guards* X. A. 5. 1. 16, εἴ τίς τι ἐπηρώτᾱ, ἀπεκρίνοντο *if* ever *anybody asked any questions (for additional information) they answered* T. 7. 10, ἐμίσει οὐκ εἴ τις κακῶς πάσχων ἠμύνετο, ἀλλ' εἴ τις εὐεργετούμενος ἀχάριστος φαίνοιτο (2340) *he hated not the man who, on suffering ill, retaliated, but him who seemed ungrateful though he had received kindness* X. Ag. 11. 3.

DIFFERENT FORMS OF CONDITIONAL SENTENCES IN THE SAME SENTENCE

2343. The same period may show different forms of conditional sentences according to the exigency of the thought.

ταὐτὸ τοίνυν τοῦτ' ἂν ἐποίησε Φίλιππος, εἴ τινα τούτων εἶδε δίκην δόντα, καὶ νῦν, ἂν ἴδῃ, ποιήσει *this very same thing then Philip would have done, if he had seen any one of these men being punished; and will do so now, if he sees it* D. 19. 138, εἰ οὖν ἐπιθῡμεῖς εὐδοκιμεῖν . . ., πειρῶ κατεργάσασθαι ὡς μάλιστα τὸ εἰδέναι ἃ βούλει πράττειν· ἐὰν γὰρ τούτῳ διενέγκᾱς τῶν ἄλλων ἐπιχειρῇς τὰ τῆς πόλεως πράττειν, οὐκ ἂν θαυμάσαιμι εἰ πάνυ ῥᾳδίως τύχοις ὧν ἐπιθῡμεῖς *if then you desire to enjoy an honourable fame . . ., try to acquire as far as possible the knowledge of what you wish to do; for if, differing in this regard from other men, you attempt to deal with affairs of state, I should not be surprised if you were to attain the object of your ambition with great ease* X. M. 3. 6. 18.

VARIATIONS FROM THE ORDINARY FORMS AND MEANINGS OF CONDITIONAL SENTENCES

MODIFICATIONS OF THE PROTASIS

2344. Substitutions for the Protasis. — For the protasis with εἰ there may be substituted a participle, often in the genitive absolute (2067, 2070), an adverb, a prepositional phrase, a relative clause (2560), or some other single word or phrase. The present participle represents the imperfect, as the perfect represents the pluperfect.

πῶς δῆτα δίκης οὔσης (= εἰ δίκη ἐστίν) ὁ Ζεὺς οὐκ ἀπόλωλεν τὸν πατέρ' αὑτοῦ δήσᾱς; *how, pray, if there is* any *justice, has Zeus not perished since he bound his own father?* Ar. Nub. 904, οὐ γὰρ ἦν μοι δήπου βιωτὸν τοῦτο ποιήσαντα (= εἰ ἐποίησα) *for of course life had not been worth living if I had done this* D. 21. 120, οὐ γὰρ ἂν ἐβλήθη ἀτρεμίζων καὶ μὴ διατρέχων (= εἰ ἠτρέμιζε καὶ μὴ διέτρεχε) *for he would not have been hit if he had been keeping quiet and not running across* Ant. 3. β. 5, δικαίως ἂν ἀπέθανον *I should justly* (*i.e.* if I had met with my deserts) *have been put to death* D. 18. 209, ἐμοὶ δὲ ἀρκοῦν ἂν ἐδόκει εἶναι *for myself* (*i.e.* if I had to decide) *it would seem to be sufficient* T. 2. 35, διά γε ὑμᾶς αὐτοὺς (= εἰ ὑμεῖς αὐτοὶ μόνοι ἦτε) πάλαι ἂν ἀπολώλειτε *if you had been left to yourselves, you would have perished long ago* D. 18. 49, ὀλοῦμαι μὴ μαθών (= ἐὰν μὴ μάθω) *I shall be undone if I don't learn* Ar. Nub. 792, νῑκῶντες (= εἰ νῑκῷεν) μὲν οὐδένα ἂν κατακάνοιεν, ἡττηθέντων (= εἰ ἡττηθεῖεν) οὐδεὶς ἂν λειφθείη *should they be victorious they would kill no one, but if defeated no one would be left* X. A. 3. 1. 2, οὕτω (= εἰ οὕτως ἔχοιεν) γὰρ πρὸς τὸ ἐπιέναι τοῖς ἐναντίοις εὐψῡχότατοι ἂν εἶεν *for thus they would be most courageous in regard to attacking the enemy* T. 2. 11, οὐδ' ἂν δικαίως ἐς κακὸν πέσοιμί τι *nor should I justly come to any trouble* S. Ant. 240.

a. Sometimes the protasis has to be supplied from what precedes (example in 1825); or from a main clause with ἀλλά, which follows: οὐδέ κεν αὐτὸς ὑπέκφυγε κῆρα μέλαιναν· ἀλλ' Ἥφαιστος ἔρυτο (= εἰ μὴ ἔρυτο) *nor would he himself have escaped black fate; but Hephaestus guarded him* E 23 (cp. X. A. 3. 2. 24–25).

2345. Verb of the Protasis Omitted. — The verb of the protasis is usually omitted when the apodosis has the same verb. The protasis is often introduced by εἴ τις, εἴ ποτε, εἴπερ (ποτέ).

εἴ τις καὶ ἄλλος ἀνήρ, καὶ Κῦρος ἄξιός ἐστι θαυμάζεσθαι *if any other man* (is worthy to be admired), *Cyrus, too, is worthy to be admired* X. C. 5. 1. 6, φημὶ δεῖν . . . τῷ πολέμῳ προσέχειν, εἴπερ ποτέ (ἔδει), καὶ νῦν *I say that we must now, if ever, apply ourselves to the war* D. 1. 6.

2346. So with certain special phrases:

a. εἰ μή (*if not*) *except*: οὐ γὰρ . . . ὁρῶμεν εἰ μὴ ὀλίγους τούτους ἀνθρώπους *for we do not see* any *except a few men yonder* X. A. 4. 7. 5, οὐ γὰρ ἄν ποτε ἐξηῦρον ὀρθῶς τὰ μετέωρα πράγματα, εἰ μὴ κρεμάσᾱς τὸ νόημα *for I could never have discovered aright things celestial, except by suspending the intellect* Ar. Nub. 229. So ἐὰν μή D. 24. 45 (in a decree).

b. εἰ μὴ εἰ (*if not if, unless if*) *except if*: ἐπράχθη τε οὐδὲν ἀπ' αὐτῶν ἔργον ἀξιόλογον, εἰ μὴ εἴ τι πρὸς τοὺς περιοίκους τοὺς αὐτῶν ἑκάστοις *and nothing noteworthy* *was done on their part except it might be* (lit. *except if* there was done) *something between each of them and his neighbours* T. 1. 17. Here εἰ μή is adverbial.

c. εἰ μὴ διά (*if not on account of*) *except for*: (οὐ) Μιλτιάδην . . . εἰς τὸ βάραθρον ἐμβαλεῖν ἐψηφίσαντο, καὶ εἰ μὴ διὰ τὸν πρύτανιν, ἐνέπεσεν ἄν; *did they not vote to throw Miltiades into the pit, and except for the prytan would he not have been thrown there?* P. G. 516 e. With εἰ μὴ διά the ellipsis (which was not conscious to the Greeks) is to be supplied by the negatived predicate of the main clause (here οὐκ ἐνέπεσεν).

d. εἰ δὲ μή (*but if not* = *si minus, sin aliter*) *otherwise*, in alternatives, introduces a supposition opposed to something just said: ἀπῄτει τὰ τῶν Καλχηδονίων χρήματα· εἰ δὲ μή, πολεμήσειν ἔφη αὐτοῖς *he demanded back the property of the Calchedonians; otherwise* (*i.e.* if they should not restore it: εἰ μὴ ἀποδοῖεν) *he said that he should make war upon them* X. H. 1. 3. 3.

N. 1.—εἰ δὲ μή often occurs even where the preceding clause is negative and we expect εἰ δέ, as μὴ ποιήσῃς ταῦτα· εἰ δὲ μὴ . . . αἰτίαν ἕξεις *do not do this; but if you do, you will have the blame* X. A. 7. 1. 8. Conversely εἰ δέ, where we expect εἰ δὲ μή, as εἰ μὲν βούλεται, ἑψέτω· εἰ δ', ὅ τι βούλεται, τοῦτο ποιείτω *if he wishes, let him boil me; otherwise, let him do whatever he wishes* P. Eu. 285 c.

N. 2.—εἰ δὲ μή is used where (after a preceding ἐάν) we expect ἐὰν δὲ μή, as ἐὰν μέν τι ὑμῖν δοκῶ ἀληθὲς λέγειν, ξυνομολογήσατε· εἰ δὲ μή, ἀντιτείνετε *if I seem to you to speak the truth, agree with me; otherwise, oppose me* P. Ph. 91 c.

N. 3.—The verb of the apodosis of the first of the alternatives is often omitted: ἐὰν μὲν ἑκὼν πείθηται (scil. καλῶς ἕξει)· εἰ δὲ μὴ . . . εὐθύνουσιν ἀπειλαῖς *if he willingly obeys* (*it will be well*); *otherwise they straighten him by threats* P. Pr. 325 d.

2347. On ὡς εἰ in comparative conditional clauses see 2484.

2348. In the Homeric εἰ δ' ἄγε *come now, well!* εἰ probably has the force of an interjectional or demonstrative adverb (cp. Lat. *eia age*). Thus, εἰ δ' ἄγε τοι κεφαλῇ κατανεύσομαι *come now! I will nod assent to thee with my head* A 524.

2349. Omission of the Protasis.—The potential optative, and the indicative, with ἄν stand in independent sentences; in many cases a protasis may be supplied either from the context or generally; in other cases there was probably no conscious ellipsis at all; and in others there was certainly no ellipsis. Cp. 1785, 1825.

ποῦ δῆτ' ἂν εἶεν οἱ ξένοι; *where, pray* (should I inquire) *would the strangers be found to be?* S. El. 1450, ἀριθμὸν δὲ γράψαι . . . οὐκ ἂν ἐδυναίμην ἀκριβῶς *but to give the number accurately I should not be able* (if I were trying) T. 5. 68, δεινὸν οὖν ἦν ψεύσασθαι *it had been terrible to break my word* (if it had been possible) D. 19. 172.

MODIFICATIONS OF THE APODOSIS

2350. The apodosis may be expressed in a participle or infinitive with or without ἄν as the construction may require; cp. 1846, 1848.

αἰτεῖ αὐτὸν εἰς δισχιλίους ξένους καὶ τριῶν μηνῶν μισθόν, ὡς οὕτως περιγενόμενος (= περιγενοίμην) ἂν τῶν ἀντιστασιωτῶν *he asked him for pay for two thousand mercenaries and for three months, stating that thus he would get the better of his adversaries* X. A. 1. 1. 10. (Here οὕτως represents the protasis, 2344.) οὐδενὸς ἀντειπόντος διὰ τὸ μὴ ἀνασχέσθαι ἂν τὴν ἐκκλησίᾱν *no one spoke in opposition because the assembly would not have suffered it* (= εἰ ἀντεῖπε, οὐκ ἂν ἠνέσχετο ἡ ἐκκλησίᾱ) X. H. 1. 4. 20, εἰ (Τεγέᾱ) σφίσι προσγένοιτο, νομίζοντες ἅπᾱσαν ἂν ἔχειν Πελοπόννησον *they thought that, if Tegea too should come over to them, they would have the whole of the Peloponnese* T. 5. 32. (See 2616). The future is rare (1847).

2351. Verb of the Apodosis Omitted.—The verb of the apodosis is often omitted, and especially when the protasis has the same verb (cp. 2345). Here a potential optative with ἄν is represented by ἄν alone (1764 a, 1766 a). Thus, εἰ δή τῳ σοφώτερός του φαίην εἶναι, τούτῳ ἂν (φαίην εἶναι) *if I should say that in any respect I am wiser than any one, (I should say) in this* P. A. 29 b. Also in other cases, as τί δῆτ' ἂν (λέγοις), ἕτερον εἰ πύθοιο Σωκράτους φρόντισμα; *what then would (you say), if you should hear another excogitation of Socrates?* Ar. Nub. 154. On ὥσπερ εἰ, ὥσπερ ἂν εἰ, ὡς εἰ, see 1766 a, 2478, 2484.

2352. Omission of the Apodosis.—**a.** When the conclusion is *it is well* (καλῶς ἔχει) or the like, it is often omitted. So often when the second of alternative opposing suppositions is expressed by εἰ δὲ μή (2346 d, N. 3). Cp. "yet now, if thou wilt forgive this sin, —: and if not, blot me . . . out of thy book" (Exodus 32. 32).

b. When we should introduce the conclusion by *know that* or *I tell you*: εἰ καὶ οἴει με ἀδικοῦντά τι ἄγεσθαι, οὔτε ἔπαιον οὐδένα οὔτε ἔβαλλον *if you possibly think that I was taken for some wrong-doing*, know that *I neither struck nor hit any one* X. A. 6. 6. 27. Here the apodosis might be introduced by σκέψασθε, ἐνθῡμήθητε, etc.

c. Sometimes when the protasis is merely parenthetical: ὁ χρῡσός, εἰ βούλοιο τἀληθῆ λέγειν, ἔκτεινε τὸν ἐμὸν παῖδα *it was the gold—wouldst thou only tell the truth—that slew my child* E. Hec. 1206.

d. In passionate speech for rhetorical effect (aposiopēsis, 3015): εἴ περ γάρ κ' ἐθέλησιν Ὀλύμπιος ἀστεροπητὴς ἐξ ἑδέων στυφελίξαι· ὁ γὰρ πολὺ φέρτατός ἐστιν *for if indeed the Olympian lord of the lightning will to thrust us out from our habitations*, thrust us he will; *for he is by far the most powerful* A 581.

e. There is properly no omission of an apodosis after clauses with εἰ, εἰ γάρ, εἴθε, etc., in *wishes* (see 1816). In such clauses it is often *possible* to find an apodosis in an appended final clause: ποτανὰν εἴ μέ τις θεῶν κτίσαι, διπόταμον ἵνα πόλιν μόλω *if only some one of the gods were to make me winged so that I might come to the city of twin rivers!* E. Supp. 621.

PROTASIS AND APODOSIS COMBINED

2353. εἰ and ἄν both in Protasis.—The potential optative with ἄν or the unreal indicative with ἄν, standing as the apodosis in the conditional clause with εἰ, is the apodosis of another protasis expressed or understood.

a. Potential Optative.—ἀλλὰ μὴν εἴ γε μηδὲ δοῦλον ἀκρατῆ δεξαίμεθ' ἄν, πῶς οὐκ ἄξιον αὐτόν γε φυλάξασθαι τοιοῦτον γενέσθαι; *and yet indeed if we would not accept even a slave who was intemperate, how is it not right for a man* (the master) *to guard against becoming so himself?* X. M. 1. 5. 3. Here δεξαίμεθα is the protasis with εἰ; and also, with ἄν, the apodosis to an understood protasis (*e.g.* if we should think of so doing). The verb of the protasis may be contained in a participle, as εἰ δὲ μηδεὶς ἂν ὑμῶν ἀξιώσειε ζῆν ἀποστερούμενος τῆς πατρίδος, προσήκει κτλ. *but if no one of you should think life worth having if he were to be deprived of his country, it is right*, etc. I. 6. 25. Such clauses form simple present conditions (*if it is true that we would accept*, etc.). The verb following the compressed condition stands usually in the present, at times in the future, indicative. X. C. 3. 3. 55: θαυμάζοιμι ἂν . . . εἰ ἂν ὠφελήσειε is an exception.

b. Unreal Indicative. — εἰ τοίνυν τοῦτο ἰσχῡρὸν ἦν ἂν τούτῳ τεκμήριον . . ., κἀμοὶ γενέσθω τεκμήριον *if then this would have been strong evidence for him* (*if he had been able to bring it forward*), *let it be evidence for me too* D. 49. 58. This is a present condition (*if it is true that this would*, etc.) except in so far as the unexpressed protasis refers to the past. Such conditions may also be past.

N. 1. — The real protasis is: *if it is* (or *was*) *the case that something could now* (or *hereafter*) *be* (or *could have been*), *it follows that.*

N. 2. — In some of these cases, εἰ has almost the force of ἐπεί *since* (D. 49. 58).

2354. εἰ, ἐάν, on the chance that. — εἰ or ἐάν may set forth the motive for the action or feeling expressed by the apodosis, and with the force of *on the chance that, in case that, in the hope that, if haply.*

After primary tenses in the apodosis, we have εἰ with the indicative or ἐάν (πως) with the subjunctive; after secondary tenses, εἰ with the optative or, occasionally, ἐάν (πως) with the subjunctive. Homer has sometimes the optative after primary tenses. The reference is to the future as in final clauses.

The protasis here depends, not on the apodosis proper, but on the idea of purpose or desire suggested by the thought. The accomplishment of the purpose may be desired or not desired, and by the subject either of the apodosis or of the protasis.

νῦν αὖτ' ἐγχείῃ πειρήσομαι, αἴ κε τύχωμι *but now I will make trial with my spear on the chance* (*in the hope*) *that I may hit thee* E 279, ἄκουσον καὶ ἐμοῦ, ἐάν σοι ἔτι ταὐτὰ δοκῇ *listen to me too on the chance* (*in the hope*) *that you may still have the same opinion* P. R. 358 b, πορευόμενοι ἐς τὴν Ἀσίᾱν ὡς βασιλέᾱ, εἴ πως πείσειαν αὐτὸν *going into Asia to the king in the hope that somehow they might persuade him* T. 2. 67, πρὸς τὴν πόλιν, εἰ ἐπιβοηθοῖεν, ἐχώρουν *they advanced toward the city on the chance that they* (the citizens) *should make a sally* 6. 100.

N. — This use is to be distinguished from that of εἰ ἄρα *if perchance*, εἰ μὴ ἄρα *unless perchance* (often ironical).

a. This construction should be distinguished from cases like ἐπιβουλεύουσιν . . . ἐξελθεῖν . . ., ἢν δύνωνται βιάσασθαι *they planned to get out, if they might make their way by force* T. 3. 20, where we have implied indirect discourse (ἐξέλθωμεν, ἢν δυνώμεθα βιάσασθαι).

b. Homer uses this construction as an object clause in dependence on οἶδα, εἶδον, or on a verb of *saying*. Thus τίς δ' οἶδ', εἴ κέν οἱ σὺν δαίμονι θῡμὸν ὀρίνω παρειπών; *who knows if, perchance, with God's help I may rouse his spirit by persuasion?* O 403 (*i.e.* the chances of rousing his spirit, if haply I may), ἐνίσπες, εἴ πως . . . ὑπεκπροφύγοιμι Χάρυβδιν *tell me if haply I shall* (*might*) *escape Charybdis* μ 112. Here the apodosis is entirely suppressed. Observe that this construction is *not* an indirect question.

LESS USUAL COMBINATIONS OF COMPLETE PROTASIS AND APODOSIS

2355. In addition to the ordinary forms of correspondence between protasis and apodosis (2297), Greek shows many other combinations expressing distinct shades of feeling. Most of these combinations, though less frequent than the ordinary forms, are no less "regular." Shift of mental attitude is a known fact of all speech, though the relation of cause to effect must not be obscured. A speaker or writer, having begun his sentence with a protasis of one type, may alter the course of his thought: with the result that he may conclude with an apodosis of another form, in some cases even with an apodosis "unsymmetrical" with the protasis and logically dependent upon a protasis that is only suggested by the form actually adopted. Since either protasis or apodosis may choose the form of expression best suited to the meaning, the student should beware of thinking that conditional sentences invariably follow a conventional pattern, departure from which is to be counted as violation of rule. Some combinations are less usual than others: most of the more common variations from the ordinary type have been mentioned under the appropriate sections, and are here summarized (2356–2358). Special cases are considered in 2359–2365.

2356. The optative with ἄν (the potential optative) may be used as the apodosis of

εἰ with the indicative in Simple Present and Past conditions (2300 e),

εἰ with the past indicative in Unreal conditions in Homer (rarely in Attic, 2312),

εἰ with the future indicative in Emotional Future conditions (2328),

εἰ with the optative in Less Vivid Future conditions (2329). In Present conditions (2353): εἰ λέγοιμ᾽ ἄν *supposing I would say*, whereas εἰ λέγοιμι means *supposing I should say*.

ἐάν with the subjunctive in More Vivid Future conditions (2326 d).

a. When the protasis is a future indicative or a subjunctive, the optative with ἄν sometimes seems to be merely a mild future and to have no potential force. Thus, ἢν οὖν μάθῃς μοι τὸν ἄδικον τοῦτον λόγον, οὐκ ἂν ἀποδοίην οὐδ᾽ ἂν ὀβολὸν οὐδενί *if then you learn this unjust reason for me, I will not pay even an obol to anybody* Ar. Nub. 116.

2357. The subjunctive of exhortation, prohibition, or deliberation, the optative of wish, and the imperative, may be used as the apodosis of

εἰ with the indicative in Simple Present and Past conditions (2300 c, d, f),

εἰ with the future indicative in Emotional Future conditions (2328),

ἐάν with the subjunctive in More Vivid Future conditions (2326 c–e).

2358. The unreal indicative with or without ἄν may be used as the apodosis of

a. εἰ with the indicative in Simple Present and Past conditions (2300 b). So after εἰ with the future denoting present intention or necessity that something shall be done (2301), as εἰ γὰρ γυναῖκες εἰς τόδ᾽ ἥξουσιν θράσους . . ., παρ᾽ οὐδὲν αὐταῖς ἦν ἂν ὀλλύναι πόσεις *for if women are to reach this height of boldness, it would be as nothing for them to destroy their husbands* E. Or. 566.

b. εἰ with the past indicative in Present and Past Unreal conditions (2302).

εἰ with the Optative, Apodosis a primary tense of the Indicative, etc.

2359. εἰ with the optative (instead of ἐάν with the subjunctive) is not infrequent in the protasis with a primary tense of the indicative, a subjunctive, or an imperative, in the apodosis. The reference is usually either to general present time (with the present indicative), or to future time. When the apodosis contains a present indicative it frequently precedes the protasis.

a. Compare the analogous usage in English commonly with *should, would:* "There is some soul of goodness in things evil, would men observingly distil it" (Shakespeare). "If you should die, my death shall follow yours" (Dryden). "I shall scarcely figure in history, if under my guidance such visitations should accrue" (Disraeli). "If he should kill thee . . ., he has nothing to lose" (Sedley). "But if an happy soil should be withheld . . . think it not beneath thy toil" (Philips).

2360. Present Indicative.—a. In general statements and maxims. The apodosis is sometimes introduced by a verb requiring the infinitive.

ἀνδρῶν γὰρ σωφρόνων μέν ἐστιν, εἰ μὴ ἀδικοῖντο, ἡσυχάζειν *for it is the part of prudent men to remain quiet if they should not be wronged* T. 1. 120, εἴ τι τυγχάνοι κακόν, εἰς ὄμματ' εὔνου φωτὸς ἐμβλέψαι γλυκύ (ἐστιν) *if any ill betide, 'tis sweet to look into the face of a loyal friend* E. Ion 731, τί δεῖ καλῆς γυναικός, εἰ μὴ τὰς φρένας χρηστὰς ἔχοι; *what boots the beauty of a woman if she have not a mind that is chaste?* E. fr. 212.

b. The present indicative sometimes has the force of an emphatic future. Thus, πάντ' ἔχεις, εἴ σε τούτων μοῖρ' ἐφίκοιτο καλῶν *thou hast all things, should the portion of these honours come to thee* Pindar, Isthm. 4 (5). 14. Present and future occur together in Ant. 4. α. 4.

c. Other examples of the present: Hom. I 318, α 414, ε 484, η 51, θ 138, ξ 56; Hesiod Op. 692 (εἴ κε); Pind. Pyth. 1. 81, 8. 13, Isthm. 2. 33; Bacchylides 5. 187; Hdt. 1. 32; S. Ant. 1032, O. T. 249; E. Hec. 786, fr. 212, 253 (v. l.); T. 2. 39, 3. 9, 4. 59, 6. 86; X. C. 1. 6. 43, H. 6. 3. 5, 6. 5. 52, O. 1. 4, 1. 5; P. A. 19 e, Cr. 46 b, Pr. 316 c, 329 a, b, L. 927 c; Isocr. 14. 39; D. 18. 21, 20. 54, 20. 154, 24. 35; Antiphanes fr. 324.

2361. Future Indicative.—εἰ σώσαιμί σ', εἴσῃ μοι χάριν; *should I save thee, wilt thou be grateful to me?* E. frag. 129, τί τῷ πλήθει περιγενήσεται εἰ ποιήσαιμεν ἃ ἐκεῖνοι προστάττουσιν; *what profit will there be for the people, if we should do what they enjoin?* L. 34. 6.

a. Other examples: Hom. I 388, K 222, Υ 100 (B 488, ρ 539, ἄν (κέ) with fut. or subj.); Pind. Ol. 13. 105; S. O. T. 851; Ant. 4. α. 4; T. 1. 121; P. Meno 80 d, Ph. 91 a, L. 658 c; Isocr. 2. 45, 9. 66; Aristotle, Nic. Eth. 1095 b. 6, 1100 b. 4; Lucian, Timon 15.

2362. Perfect Indicative (very rare).—εἰ . . . διδάξειεν ὡς οἱ θεοὶ ἅπαντες τὸν τοιοῦτον θάνατον ἡγοῦνται ἄδικον εἶναι, τί μᾶλλον ἐγὼ μεμάθηκα . . . τί ποτ' ἐστὶν τὸ ὅσιον; *if he should prove that all the gods consider such a death unjust, how have I learned anything more of the nature of piety?* P. Euth. 9 c.

2363. **Subjunctive** (very rare). — εἰ δὲ βούλοιό γε, καὶ τὴν μαντικὴν εἶναι συγχωρήσωμεν ἐπιστήμην τοῦ μέλλοντος ἔσεσθαι *but if you will, let us agree that mantic too is a knowledge of the future* P. Charm. 173 c. Cp. X. O. 8. 10; Λ 386 (ἄν with subj.), Ψ 893, δ 388 (?).

2364. **Imperative.** — εἴ τις τάδε παραβαίνοι . . ., ἐναγὴς ἔστω *if any one transgresses these injunctions, let him be accursed* Aes. 3. 110 (quoted from an ancient imprecation), τὸ μὲν δὴ ἀργύριον, εἰ μή τις ἐπίσταιτο αὐτῷ χρῆσθαι, οὕτω πόρρω ἀπωθείσθω ὥστε μηδὲ χρήματα εἶναι *but as regards money then, if a man does not know how to use it, let him remove it so far from his consideration as not to be regarded even as property* X. O. 1. 14. Cp. P. Hipp. M. 297 e, L. 642 a.

2365. An unreal indicative in conjunction with εἰ and the optative is very rare.

εἰ μὲν γὰρ εἰς γυναῖκα σωφρονεστέρᾱν ξίφος μεθεῖμεν, δυσκλεὴς ἂν ἦν φόνος (for ἂν εἴη) *for if we should draw the sword upon a purer woman, foul were the murder* E. Or. 1132. Cp. L. 10. 8, X. C. 2. 1. 9 (text doubtful) and X. Ven. 12. 22, P. Alc. 1, 111 e, Lyc. 66.

TWO OR MORE PROTASES OR APODOSES IN ONE SENTENCE

2366. A conditional sentence may have several protases and one apodosis or one protasis and several apodoses. Two such protases or apodoses are coördinate or one of the two is subordinate to the other.

2367. Two coördinated protases with a single apodosis, or two coördinated apodoses with a single protasis, may refer to the same time or to different times.

εἰ δὲ μήτ' ἔστι (τι βέλτῑον) μήτ' ἦν μήτ' ἂν εἰπεῖν ἔχοι μηδεὶς μηδέπω καὶ τήμερον, τί τὸν σύμβουλον ἐχρῆν ποιεῖν; *but if there neither is nor was any better plan, and if yet even to-day no one can suggest any, what was it the duty of the statesman to do?* D. 18. 190, καὶ γὰρ ἂν καὶ ὑπερφυὲς εἴη, εἰ κατὰ μὲν τῶν Ὀλυνθίους προδόντων πολλὰ καὶ δεινʼ ἐψηφίσασθε, τοὺς δὲ παρ' ῡ̔μῖν αὐτοῖς ἀδικοῦντας μὴ κολάζοντες φαίνοισθε *and in fact it would be actually monstrous if, whereas you have passed many severe votes against the betrayers of the Olynthians, you appear not to punish the wrongdoers in your midst* D. 19. 267, εἰ ἐγὼ ἐπεχείρησα πράττειν τὰ πολῑτικὰ πράγματα, πάλαι ἂν ἀπολώλη καὶ οὔτ' ἂν ῡ̔μᾶς ὠφελήκη οὐδὲν οὔτ' ἂν ἐμαυτόν *if I had tried to engage in politics, I should have long ago perished and benefited neither you nor myself at all* P. A. 31 d.

2368. When two or more protases are not coördinated in the same sentence, one is of chief importance and any other protasis is subordinate to it. Such protases may follow each other or one may be added after the apodosis; and may show the same or a different modal form.

ἀξιοῦμεν, εἰ μέν τινα ὁρᾶτε σωτηρίᾱν ἡμῖν (ἐσομένην), ἐὰν διακαρτερῶμεν πολεμοῦντες, διδάξαι καὶ ἡμᾶς κτλ. *if you see any safety for us if we persist in making war, we beg that you will inform us too* what it is X. H. 7. 4. 8 (here ἐὰν διακαρτερῶμεν depends on εἰ ὁρᾶτε); ἐὰν δὲ ἡδέα πρὸς λῡπηρά (ἱστῇς), ἐὰν μὲν τὰ ἀνιᾱρὰ ὑπερβάλληται ὑπὸ τῶν ἡδέων, ἐάν τε τὰ ἐγγὺς ὑπὸ τῶν πόρρω ἐάν τε τὰ πόρρω ὑπὸ τῶν ἐγγύς, ταύτην τὴν πρᾶξιν πρᾱκτέον ἐν ᾗ ἂν ταῦτ' ἐνῇ· ἐὰν δὲ τὰ ἡδέα ὑπὸ τῶν ἀνιᾱρῶν, οὐ πρᾱκτέα *but if you weigh pleasures against pains, if on the one hand what is painful is exceeded by what is pleasurable (whether the near by the distant or the distant by the near), you must adopt that course of action in which this is the case; if on the other hand the pleasurable (is exceeded) by the painful, the former must not be adopted* P. Pr. 356 b (here to ἐὰν ἡδέα ἱστῇς are subordinated ἐὰν μέν and ἐὰν δέ, and to ἐὰν μέν are subordinated ἐάν τε . . . ἐάν τε); εἰ δέ σε ἠρόμην ἐξ ἀρχῆς τί ἐστι καλόν τε καὶ αἰσχρόν, εἴ μοι ἅπερ νῦν ἀπεκρῑνω, ἆρ' οὐκ ἂν ὀρθῶς ἀπεκέκρισο; *but if I had asked you at the start what beauty and ugliness is—if you had answered me as you have now done, would you not have answered me rightly?* P. Hipp. M. 289 c; ἢν μὲν πόλεμον αἱρῆσθε, μηκέτι ἥκετε δεῦρο ἄνευ ὅπλων, εἰ σωφρονεῖτε *if you choose war, come no more hither without arms if you are wise* X. C. 3. 2. 13, εἰ μετὰ Θηβαίων ἡμῖν ἀγωνιζομένοις οὕτως εἵμαρτο πρᾶξαι, τί χρῆν προσδοκᾶν εἰ μηδὲ τούτους ἔσχομεν συμμάχους ἀλλὰ Φιλίππῳ προσέθεντο; *if it was decreed by fate that we should fare thus with the Thebans fighting on our side, what ought we to have expected if we had not even secured them as allies but they had joined Philip?* D. 18. 195.

a. A second protasis may be added to the first protasis to explain or define it. Thus, καὶ οὐ τοῦτο λέξων ἔρχομαι ὡς πολὺ μὲν ἐλάττους πολὺ δὲ χείρονας ἔχων ὅμως συνέβαλεν· εἰ γὰρ ταῦτα λέγοιμι, Ἀγησίλᾱόν τ' ἄν μοι δοκῶ ἄφρονα ἀποφαίνειν καὶ ἐμαυτὸν μῶρον, εἰ ἐπαινοίην τὸν περὶ τῶν μεγίστων εἰκῇ κινδῡνεύοντα *and I am not going to say that he made the engagement in spite of having much fewer and inferior troops; for if I should maintain this, I think that I should be proving Agesilaus senseless and myself a fool, if I should praise the man who rashly incurs danger when the greatest interests are at stake* X. Ag. 2. 7.

CONCESSIVE CLAUSES

2369. Concessive clauses are commonly formed by καί in conjunction with the εἰ or ἐάν of conditional clauses: καὶ εἰ (κεἰ), καὶ ἐάν (κἄν) *even if*, εἰ καί, ἐὰν καί *although*.

2370. Such concessive clauses are conditional, but indicate that the condition which they introduce may be granted without destroying the conclusion. The apodosis of concessive clauses thus has an adversative meaning, *i.e.* it states what is regarded as true *notwithstanding* (ὅμως) what is assumed in the protasis.

2371. Concessive clauses have the construction of conditional clauses. The protasis, if negative, takes μή.

2372. καὶ εἰ (*even if*) **clauses.**—καὶ εἰ commonly implies that the conclusion must be true or must take place even in the extreme, scarcely conceivable, case which these words introduce (*even supposing that, even in the case that*). In such cases the speaker does not grant that the alleged condition really exists. On κἂν εἰ see 1766 b.

κεἰ μὴ πέποιθα, τοὔργον ἔστ' ἐργαστέον *even if I have no confidence*, yet *the deed must be done* A. Ch. 296, καὶ ἐὰν μὴ ἡμεῖς παρακελευώμεθα, (ἡ πόλις) ἱκανῶς ἐπιμελήσεται *and even if we do not use exhortations*, the city *will take sufficient care* P. Menex. 248 d, γελᾷ δ' ὁ μῶρος, κἄν τι μὴ γελοῖον ᾖ *the fool laughs even if there is nothing to laugh at* Men. Sent. 108, Μυσοῖς βασιλεὺς πολλοὺς μὲν ἡγεμόνας ἂν δοίη . . ., καὶ εἰ σὺν τεθρίπποις βούλοιντο ἀπιέναι *the king would give many guides to the Mysians even supposing they should want to depart with four-horse chariots* X. A. 3. 2. 24.

2373. The καί of καὶ εἰ may mean simply *and*, as κεἰ τάδ' εἴσεται Κρέων *and if Creon learns this* S. Ant. 229.

2374. Some scholars hold that the difference between καὶ εἰ and εἰ καί is that καὶ εἰ concedes a supposition and is used of an assumed fact, while εἰ καί concedes a fact and is used of an actual fact. But this distinction cannot be supported. καὶ εἰ sometimes differs from εἰ καί only in being more emphatic. When an actual fact is referred to, we expect εἰ καί; but καὶ εἰ sometimes occurs, as ἴσως τοι, κεἰ βλέποντα μὴ 'πόθουν, θανόντ' ἂν οἰμώξειαν *perhaps, though they did not miss him when alive, they will lament him now that he is dead* S. Aj. 962, cp. πειστέον, κεἰ μηδὲν ἡδύ *although it is in no wise sweet, I must obey* S. O. T. 1516.

2375. εἰ καί (*although*) **clauses.**—εἰ καί commonly admits that a condition exists (*granting that*), but does not regard it as a hindrance. The condition, though it exists, is a matter of no moment so far as the statement in the principal clause is concerned.

εἰ καὶ τυραννεῖς *king though thou art* S. O. T. 408, πόλιν μέν, εἰ καὶ μὴ βλέπεις, φρονεῖς δ' ὅμως οἵᾳ νόσῳ σύνεστιν *though thou canst not see, thou yet dost feel with what a plague our city is afflicted* S. O. T. 302, εἰ καὶ τῳ σμικρότερον δοκεῖ εἶναι *although it seems too unimportant to some* P. Lach. 182 c.

2376. The verb is omitted in εἰ καὶ γελοιότερον εἰπεῖν *though the expression be ridiculous* P. A. 30 c (cp. 944).

2377. The καί of εἰ καί may go closely with a following word. Here the meaning is either *also* or *indeed*; as εἰ καὶ δυνήσει γε *if thou shalt also be able* (besides having the will) S. Ant. 90, δεινόν γ' εἶπας, εἰ καὶ ζῇς θανών *a strange thing truly hast thou uttered, if, though slain, thou indeed livest* S. Aj. 1127. Where trajection is assumed (εἰ μὴ καί for εἰ καὶ μή) the καί is intensive, as εἰ μὴ καὶ νῦν . . . ἀλλά *if not* already . . . *at least* T. 2. 11. 6, εἰ μὴ καὶ δέδρᾱκεν *unless he has actually done it* 6. 60. 3.

2378. εἰ (ἐὰν) καί not infrequently means *even if* in prose as well as poetry.

εἵλετο μᾶλλον συνειδέναι ὑμᾶς, ἵν', εἰ καὶ βούλοιτο κακὸς εἶναι, μὴ ἐξείη αὐτῷ *he preferred rather that you should know of it, in order that, even if he should wish to be base, it might not be possible* L. 20. 23, ἀλλ' εἰ καὶ μηδὲν τούτων ὑπῆρχεν ἡμῖν, οὐδ' ὡς χαλεπόν ἐστι γνῶναι περὶ αὐτῶν ὁπότεροι τἀληθῆ λέγουσιν *but even if I had none of these points to rely on, even so it is not difficult to find out which tells the truth* D. 41. 15. Cp. also Ant. 5. 27, And. 1. 21, L. 31. 20; Is. 11. 23, D. 16. 24, Aes. 3. 211. εἰ καί for καὶ εἰ is especially common in Isocrates, who does not use καὶ εἰ or κεἰ except in 21. 11. Demosthenes is not fond of καὶ εἰ, and often substitutes κἂν εἰ for it (19. 282, 24. 109, 45. 12). Cp. 1766 b.

2379. εἰ (ἐάν) sometimes has a concessive force (X. Eq. 1. 17). εἴπερ (ἐάνπερ) has, rarely in Attic, a sort of concessive meaning (P. Euth. 4 b), and especially when the truth of a statement is implicitly denied or doubted. Cp. L. 16. 8.

2380. ἐπεί, usually with a following γέ, is sometimes translated *although*, where a speaker is strictly giving the reason for his statement of a fact (or for something in that statement) and *not* for the fact itself. Here there is a thought in the speaker's mind which is suppressed. Thus, αἰσχυνοίμην ἂν ἔγωγε τοῦτο ὁμολογεῖν, ἐπεὶ πολλοί γέ φᾶσι τῶν ἀνθρώπων *for my part I should be ashamed to acknowledge this* (and I say this for myself) *since there are many men who do assert it* P. Pr. 333 c.

2381. Negative concessive clauses have οὐδ' (μηδ') εἰ or ἐάν *not even if*. Here *not* (οὐ-, μη-) belongs to the leading clause, while *even* (-δέ, cp. καί) belongs to the dependent clause. The negative is frequently repeated in the leading clause.

οὐδ' εἰ πάντες ἔλθοιεν Πέρσαι, πλήθει οὐχ ὑπερβαλοίμεθ' ἂν τοὺς πολεμίους *even if all the Persians should come, we should not exceed the enemy in numbers* X. C. 2. 1. 8, μὴ θορυβήσητε, μηδ' ἐὰν δόξω τι ὑμῖν μέγα λέγειν *do not raise a disturbance, even if I seem to you to be speaking presumptuously* P. A. 20 e. Cp. 2382.

2382. The idea of concession or opposition is often expressed by the participle alone (2066) or by the participle with καίπερ or καὶ ταῦτα (2083). The negative is οὐ. In negative concessive sentences we find also the participle with οὐδέ (μηδέ), οὐδέ (μηδέ) περ.

οὐδὲ πεπονθὼς κακῶς ἐχθρὸν εἶναί μοι τοῦτον ὁμολογῶ *not even though I have been ill-treated do I admit that he is my enemy* D. 21. 205, γυναικὶ πείθου μηδὲ τἀληθῆ κλύων *listen to a woman, even if thou dost not hear the truth* E. fr. 440.

TEMPORAL CLAUSES

2383. Temporal clauses are introduced by conjunctions or relative expressions having the force of conjunctions

A. Denoting time usually *the same* as that of the principal verb: ὅτε, ὁπότε, ἡνίκα, ὁπηνίκα *when*; ὁσάκις *as often as*; ἕως, μέχρι (rarely ἄχρι), ὅσον χρόνον *so long as*; ἕως, ἐν ᾧ (rarely ἐν ὅσῳ and ἔστε) *while*.

N. 1.—**ἕως** means *so long as* in reference to actions that are coëxtensive; *while*, in reference to actions not coëxtensive.

N. 2.—**ἡνίκα, ὁπηνίκα** have the force of *what time, at the moment when, when,* (rarely *while*), and are more precise than ὅτε.

N. 3.—Poetic or Ionic are **εὖτε** (= ὅτε) *when*, **ἦμος** (only with the indicative) *when*, **ὅπως** *when* (ὅκως in Hdt. of antecedent action), **ὄφρα** *so long as*. Hom. has **εἷος** (*i.e.* ἧος) or εἵως for ἕως.

N. 4.—**ἔστε** is used (rarely) in lyric, Sophocles, Euripides, Herodotus, Xenophon.

B. Denoting time usually *prior* to that of the principal verb: ἐπεί, ἐπειδή *after, after that* (less exactly *when*); ἐπεὶ πρῶτον, ὡς (or ἐπεὶ) τάχιστα, ἐπειδὴ τάχιστα (rarely ὅπως τάχιστα) *as soon as*; ἐξ οὗ (rarely ἐξ ὧν), ἐξ ὅτου, ἀφ' οὗ *since, ever since*; ὡς *when, as soon as, since*.

N.—**ἐπείτε** *after* is very common in Herodotus.

C. Denoting time *subsequent* to that of the principal verb:
ἕως, ἔστε, μέχρι, μέχρι οὗ (rarely ἄχρι), ἄχρι οὗ *until:* followed by a finite verb.
πρίν, πρότερον ἤ *before, until:* followed by a finite verb or by an infinitive.

N. — Homer has also **ὄφρα** (also final), **εἰς ὅτε** (κε), **εἰς ὅ** (κε). Herodotus has **ἐς ὅ, ἕως οὗ, ἐς οὗ** *until.* **ὁππότε** with the optative in Homer after a past tense of a verb of *waiting* or *expecting* means *for the time when* (H 414). **ἔστε** (first in Hesiod) is rare in lyric, tragedy, Herodotus, and Plato, very common in Xenophon. — **μέχρι** is avoided by the orators. — μέχρι and ἄχρι take the articular infinitive in Demosthenes. — **τέως** for ἕως is rare (2171).

2384. Demonstrative adverbs in the principal clause often correspond to the relative conjunctions, as ὅτε . . . τότε, ἐν ᾧ . . . ἐν τούτῳ, ἕως . . . τέως (μέχρι τούτου). So also ἐπεὶ . . . τότε, ὡς (ὅτε) . . . ἐνταῦθα, etc.

2385. Some temporal conjunctions also denote *cause:*
ὅτε, ὁπότε, ἐπεί, εὖτε (poet.), ἐπειδή *since, whereas,* ὡς *because.* ὡς means also *as, as to,* rarely, in prose, *in order that.* ἕως in Homer has in part become a final conjunction (2419); for the Attic use, see 2420.

2386. A temporal sentence and a conditional sentence may occur in close conjunction without marked difference of signification.

ὅταν δὲ νοσήσωσιν, ὑγιεῖς γενόμενοι σῴζονται· ἐάν τέ τις ἄλλη συμφορὰ καταλαμβάνῃ αὐτούς, τὰ ἐναντία ἐπιγιγνόμενα ὀνίνησιν *whenever they fall ill, they are saved by regaining their health; and if ever any other calamity overtakes them, the reversal* to prosperity *that follows is to their benefit* Ant. 2. β. 1.

2387. A temporal conjunction is often used in Greek where English employs a conditional or a concessive conjunction.

οὐκ ἂν ἔγωγε Κρονίονος ἆσσον ἱκοίμην, . . . ὅτε μὴ αὐτός γε κελεύοι *I would not draw nearer to Cronus' son unless* (lit. *when not*) *he should himself bid me* Ξ 248.

2388. The time denoted by a temporal clause is not always solely contemporaneous, antecedent, or subsequent to that of the principal clause, but may overlap with the time of the principal clause (before and at the same time, at the same time and after, until and after).

ἐπεὶ δὲ ἠσθένει Δᾱρεῖος καὶ ὑπώπτευε τελευτὴν τοῦ βίου, ἐβούλετο τὼ παῖδε παρεῖναι *when Darius was ill and suspected that his life was coming to an end, he wished his two sons to be with him* X. A. 1. 1. 1 (here the situation set forth by ἠσθένει and ὑπώπτευε occurred both before and after the time indicated in ἐβούλετο), τοιαῦτα ἐποίει ἕως διεδίδου πάντα ἃ ἔλαβε κρέᾱ *he kept doing thus until he saw that* (and *so long as*) *he was distributing all the meat he had received* X. C. 1. 3. 7 (the imperfect is rare with ἕως or πρὶν *until*), ὁ δ' ἔν τε τῷ παρόντι πρὸς τὰ μηνύματα ἀπελογεῖτο καὶ ἑτοῖμος ἦν πρὶν ἐκπλεῖν κρίνεσθαι *he both defended himself then and there against the charges and offered to be tried before he sailed* T. 6. 29.

a. Conjunctions of antecedent action usually take the aorist, rarely the imperfect except when that tense represents overlapping action, as in T. 5. 72. 3. Cp. T. 1. 13. 5 with 1. 5. 1.

b. A verb of aoristic action is used: in the temporal clause when complete priority, in the main clause when complete subsequence, is to be clearly marked.

2389. Clauses introduced by relative adverbs (or conjunctions) of time, have, in general, the same constructions as clauses introduced by relative pronouns (340, 2493 ff.) and by relative adverbs of place and manner. Temporal clauses are treated separately for the sake of clearness.

a. Temporal clauses introduced by a word meaning *until* differ from ordinary conditional relatives in some respects, as in the use of the optative in implied indirect discourse (2408, 2420); and in the frequency of the absence of ἄν (2402).

b. Strictly ὅτε, ἔνθα, ὡς, etc., are *subordinating conjunctions* when the clause introduced by them fixes the time, place, or manner of the main clause; but are *relative adverbs* when they serve only to define the antecedent and introduce a clause merely supplementary to the main clause.

2390. Temporal clauses are either *definite* or *indefinite.*

2391. A temporal clause is definite when the action occurs at a definite point of time (negative οὐ, except when the special construction requires μή). Definite temporal clauses usually refer to the present or to the past.

2392. A temporal clause is indefinite when the action (1) occurs in the indefinite future, (2) recurs an indefinite number of times, (3) continues for an indefinite period. The same clause may have more than one of these meanings. (3) is rare. The negative is μή. Indefinite temporal clauses refer either to the future or to general present or past time.

2393. The same temporal conjunction may refer either to definite or to indefinite time; sometimes with a difference of meaning.

2394. When the time is definite, the indicative is used; when indefinite, the subjunctive with ἄν, the optative, or (rarely) the indicative.

Temporal conjunctions with the subjunctive take ἄν. (For exceptions, see 2402, 2412, 2444 b.) ἄν is not used with the optative except when the optative is potential, 2406, 2421 (cp. 2452).

INDICATIVE TEMPORAL CLAUSES REFERRING TO PRESENT OR PAST TIME

2395. Present or past temporal clauses take the indicative when the action is marked as a *fact* and refers to a definite occasion (negative οὐ). The principal clause commonly has the indicative, but may take any form of the simple sentence.

A. Temporal clauses denoting the *same* time as that of the principal verb (2383 A).

ὅτε ταῦτα ἦν, σχεδὸν μέσαι ἦσαν νύκτες *it was about midnight when this was taking place* X. A. 3. 1. 33, cp. 1. 1. 1, cited in 2388, ἡνίκα δὲ δείλη ἐγίγνετο, ἐφάνη κονιορτός *but when it was getting to be afternoon, a cloud of dust appeared* 1. 8. 8, μέχρι ἀπὸ τοῦ ἴσου ἡγοῦντο, προθύμως εἱπόμεθα *as long as they led on equal terms we followed willingly* T. 3. 10, ὅσον χρόνον ἐκαθέζετο . . . ἀμφὶ τὴν περὶ τὸ φρούριον οἰκονομίᾱν, . . . ἀπῆγον ἵππους *as long as he was employed with regulations about the fortress, they kept bringing horses* X. C. 5. 3. 25, ἐν ᾧ ὡπλίζοντο, ἧκον . . . οἱ σκοποί *while they were arming, the scouts came* X. A. 2. 2. 15, ἕως ἐστὶ καιρός, ἀντιλάβεσθε τῶν πρᾱγμάτων '*while there is opportunity, take our public policy in hand*' D. 1. 20.

N. μέμνημαι, οἶδα, ἀκούω often take ὅτε *when* instead of ὅτι *that.* Thus, μέμνημαι ὅτε ἐγὼ πρὸς σὲ ἦλθον *I remember when* (*that*) *I came to you* X. C. 1. 6. 12. ἡνίκα (and ἦμος in poetry) has a similar use. οἶδα ὅτε, ἀκούω ὅτε are probably due to the analogy of μέμνημαι ὅτε, originally *I remember* (the moment) *when.*

B. Temporal clauses denoting time *prior* to that of the principal verb (2383 B).

ἐπεὶ δ' ἐξῆλθεν, ἐξήγγειλε τοῖς φίλοις τὴν κρίσιν τοῦ Ὀρόντᾱ ὡς ἐγένετο *but after he came out, he announced to his friends how the trial of Orontas had resulted* X. A. 1. 6. 5 (observe that the aorist, and not the pluperfect, is commonly used to denote time previous to that of the main verb; cp. 1943), ἐπειδὴ δὲ ἐτελεύτησε Δᾱρεῖος . . ., Τισσαφέρνης διαβάλλει τὸν Κῦρον *after Darius died Tissaphernes calumniated Cyrus* 1. 1. 3, ὡς τάχιστα ἕως ὑπέφαινεν, ἐθύοντο *as soon as daylight indistinctly appeared, they sacrificed* 4. 3. 9, ἐξ οὗ φίλος εἶναι προσποιεῖται, ἐκ τούτου ὑμᾶς ἐξηπάτηκεν *ever since* Philip *pretended to be friendly, from that time on he had deceived you* D. 23. 193. (On *ever since* expressed by the dative of the participle, see 1498.)

C. Temporal clauses denoting time *subsequent* to that of the principal verb (2383 C).

ἔμειναν ἕως ἀφίκοντο οἱ στρατηγοί *they waited until the generals arrived* X. H. 1. 1. 29, λοιδοροῦσι τὸν Σωτηρίδᾱν ἔστε ἠνάγκασαν . . . πορεύεσθαι *they kept reviling Soteridas until they forced him to march on* X. A. 3. 4. 49, καὶ ταῦτα ἐποίουν μέχρι σκότος ἐγένετο *and they kept doing this until darkness came on* 4. 2. 4, τοὺς Ἕλληνας ἀπελύσατο δουλείᾱς ὥστ' ἐλευθέρους εἶναι μέχρι οὗ πάλιν αὐτοὶ αὑτοὺς κατεδουλώσαντο *she released the Greeks from slavery so as to be free until they enslaved themselves* P. Menex. 245 a.

2396. When the principal verb is a past indicative with ἄν and denotes non-fulfilment, a temporal clause has, by assimilation of mood, a past tense of the indicative denoting non-fulfilment.

ὁπηνίκ' ἐφαίνετο ταῦτα πεποιηκὼς . . ., ὡμολογεῖτ' ἂν ἡ κατηγορίᾱ τοῖς ἔργοις αὐτοῦ *if it appeared that he had ever done this, his form of accusation would tally with his acts* D. 18. 14 (here *whenever* would make the condition ambiguous), ἐβασάνιζον ἂν μέχρι οὗ αὐτοῖς ἐδόκει *they would have kept questioning them under torture as long as they pleased* 53. 25, οὐκ ἂν ἐπαυόμην . . . ἕως ἀπεπειράθην τῆς σοφίᾱς ταυτησί *I would not cease until I had made trial of this wisdom* P. Crat. 396 c. See 2185 b.

2397. The negative is μή only when the temporal relation is regarded as conditional.

ὁπότε τὸ δίκαιον μὴ οἶδα, ὃ ἐστι, σχολῇ εἴσομαι εἴτε ἀρετή τις οὖσα τυγχάνει εἴτε καὶ οὔ *when (if) I do not know what justice is, I am scarcely likely to know whether it is or is not a virtue* P. R. 354 c.

TEMPORAL CLAUSES REFERRING TO THE FUTURE

2398. The future indicative is rarely used in temporal clauses; and when used refers to definite time.

τηνικαῦτα . . . ὅτε οὐδ' ὅ τι χρὴ ποιεῖν ἕξετε *at that time, when you will not be able to do even what is necessary* D. 19. 262.

a. The future is rare because that tense does not usually make clear the difference between action continuing and action simply occurring in the future. ὅτε with the future indicative has thus been almost entirely displaced by ὅταν with the subjunctive.

b. For the future with κέ in θ 318 the subjunctive is probably correct.

2399. Temporal clauses referring indefinitely to the future take either the subjunctive with ἄν or the optative without ἄν.

a. The addition of ἄν produces the forms **ὅταν, ὁπόταν; ἐπάν, ἐπήν** (both rare in Attic), **ἐπειδάν. ἕως ἄν, μέχρι ἄν, ἔστ' ἄν** mean *as long as* or *until.* **ὡς** *when* scarcely ever takes ἄν (for ὡς ἄν *while* ἕως ἄν is read in S. Aj. 1117, Ph. 1330).

b. The temporal conjunctions have here, in general, the same constructions as conditional ἐάν or εἰ. Thus ὁπόταν = ἐάν ποτε, ὁπότε = εἴ ποτε.

2400. The present marks the action as continuing (not completed), the aorist marks the action as simply occurring (completed). The present usually sets forth an action contemporaneous with that of the leading verb; the aorist, an action antecedent to that of the leading verb.

a. The present may denote time antecedent when the verb has no aorist, and in the case of some other verbs: Thus, (ὁ πόλεμος) ὃς λυπήσει ἕκαστον, ἐπειδὰν παρῇ the war *which will afflict every one when it comes* D. 6. 35, ἐπειδὰν ἀκούῃ . . . ἑτέρους κρίνοντας, τί καὶ ποιήσῃ; *when he hears that they are prosecuting other men, what should he then do?* 19. 138.

FUTURE TEMPORAL CLAUSES WITH THE SUBJUNCTIVE

2401. Temporal clauses referring to the future take the subjunctive with ἄν in sentences corresponding to more vivid future conditions. The principal clause has the future indicative or any form of the verb referring to the future except the simple optative. The negative is μή.

ἡνίκα δ' ἄν τις ὑμᾶς ἀδικῇ, ἡμεῖς ὑπὲρ ὑμῶν μαχούμεθα *but when any one wrongs you, we will fight in your defence* X. C. 4. 4. 11, ὅταν μὴ σθένω, πεπαύσομαι *when my strength fails, I shall cease* S. Ant. 91, ἐπειδὰν ἅπαντ' ἀκούσητε, κρίνατε *when you have heard everything, decide* D. 4. 14, ἐμοὶ . . . δοκεῖ, ἐπὰν τάχιστα ἀριστήσωμεν, ἰέναι *in my judgment we must go as soon as we have breakfasted* X. A. 4.

6. 9, *μέχρι δ' ἂν ἐγὼ ἥκω, αἱ σπονδαὶ μενόντων but until I return, let the armistice continue* 2. 3. 24, *λέξω . . . ἕως ἂν ἀκούειν βούλησθε I will speak so long as you wish to listen* D. 21. 130, *περιμένετε ἔστ' ἂν ἐγὼ ἔλθω wait until I come* X. A. 5. 1. 4, *μὴ ἀναμείνωμεν ἕως ἂν πλείους ἡμῶν γένωνται let us not wait until* the enemy *outnumbers us* X. C. 3. 3. 46, *οὐκ ἀναμένομεν* (present as emphatic future) *ἕως ἂν ἡ ἡμετέρᾱ χώρᾱ κακῶται we do not wait until our land shall be ravaged* 3. 3. 18. The present subjunctive is rare with *ἕως until*, and marks overlapping action (here = *ἕως ἂν ἴδωμεν κακουμένην*).

2402. The subjunctive without *ἄν* (*κέ*) is sometimes found in poetry and in Herodotus; in Attic prose only with *μέχρι*, *μέχρι οὗ until* (and *πρίν*, 2444 b). Thus, *ἐβούλευσαν δεσμοῖς αὐτοὺς φυλάσσειν μέχρι οὗ τι ξυμβῶσιν they decided to guard them in fetters until they should reach some agreement* T. 4. 41. The omission of *ἄν* is more common after temporal conjunctions than after *εἰ* (2327 a) and in writers later than Homer lends an archaic colouring to the style.

2403. The principal clause may be a potential optative, which is at times nearly equivalent to the future: *ἐγὼ δὲ ταύτην μὲν τὴν εἰρήνην, ἕως ἂν εἷς Ἀθηναίων λείπηται, οὐδέποτ' ἂν συμβουλεύσαιμι ποιήσασθαι τῇ πόλει so long as a single Athenian is left, I never would recommend the city to make peace* D. 19. 14.

FUTURE TEMPORAL CLAUSES WITH THE OPTATIVE

2404. Temporal clauses referring to the future in sentences corresponding to less vivid future conditions usually take the optative without *ἄν*. An optative referring to the future stands in the principal clause (2186 b). The negative is *μή*.

τεθναίην, ὅτε μοι μηκέτι ταῦτα μέλοι may I die, when I shall no longer care for these delights Mimnermus 1. 2, *πεινῶν φάγοι ἂν ὁπότε βούλοιτο when hungry he would eat whenever he wished* X. M. 2. 1. 18, *εἰ δὲ βούλοιο τῶν φίλων τινὰ προτρέψασθαι, ὁπότε ἀποδημοίης, ἐπιμελεῖσθαι τῶν σῶν, τί ἂν ποιοίης; should you desire to induce one of your friends to care for your interests when you were away from home, what would you do?* 2. 3. 12, *δέοιτό γ' ἂν αὐτοῦ μένειν, ἕως ἀπέλθοις he would beg him to remain until you should depart* X. C. 5. 3. 13 (here the temporal clause depends on *μένειν*, itself dependent on *δέοιτο ἄν*).

2405. The optative with *ἄν* (*κέ*) in Homer, where Attic would have the simple optative, is potential or virtually equivalent to a future. Thus, *αὐτίκα γάρ με κατακτείνειεν Ἀχιλλεὺς . . ., ἐπὴν γόου ἐξ ἔρον εἴην for let Achilles slay me forthwith, when I have satisfied my desire for lamentation* Ω 227. Cp. I 304, δ 222, *ἕως κε* β 78 (potential), *εἰς ὅ κε* Ο 70 (elsewhere this expression always takes the subjunctive in Homer).

2406. The potential optative or indicative (with *ἄν*) having its proper force may appear in temporal clauses (cp. 2353).

φυλάξᾱς . . . τὸν χειμῶν' ἐπιχειρεῖ, ἡνίκ' ἂν ἡμεῖς μὴ δυναίμεθ' ἐκεῖσ' ἀφικέσθαι by watching for winter to set in *he begins his operations when we are unable* (he thinks) *to reach the spot* D. 4. 31. Cp. 2405.

2407. The principal clause rarely has the present or future indicative, when the temporal clause has the optative without ἄν (cp. 2360, 2361, 2573 b, c).

φρονήσεως δεῖ πολλῆς πρὸς τοὺς πολὺ πλείους . . ., ὁπότε καιρὸς παραπέσοι *when the critical moment arrives, he must have great judgment to cope with forces much more numerous* than his own X. Hipp. 7. 4, αἰπύ οἱ ἐσσεῖται . . . νῆας ἐνιπρῆσαι, ὅτε μὴ αὐτός γε Κρονίων ἐμβάλοι αἰθόμενον δᾶλὸν νήεσσι *hard will it be for him to fire the ships unless* (when . . . not) *Kronion himself hurl upon the ships a blazing brand* N 317.

a. Homer has ἄν (κέ) with the subjunctive; as οὐκ ἄν τοι χραίσμῃ κίθαρις . . ., ὅτ' ἐν κονίῃσι μιγείης *thy cithern will not avail thee when thou grovellest in the dust* Γ 55.

2408. After a secondary tense introducing indirect discourse (real or implied) the optative may represent the subjunctive with ἄν as the form in which the thought was conceived.

παρήγγειλαν, ἐπειδὴ δειπνήσαιεν . . . πάντας ἀναπαύεσθαι καὶ ἕπεσθαι ἡνίκ' ἄν τις παραγγέλλῃ *they issued orders that, when they had supped, all should rest and follow when any one should give the command* (= ἐπειδὰν δειπνήσητε . . . ἀναπαύεσθε) X. A. 3. 5. 18, ἐπιμεῖναι κελεύσαντες ἔστε βουλεύσαιντο, ἐθύοντο *ordering them to wait until they had taken counsel, they proceeded to sacrifice* (= ἐπιμείνατε ἔστ' ἂν βουλευσώμεθα) 5. 5. 2, ἔδοξεν αὐτοῖς . . . προϊέναι . . ., ἕως Κύρῳ συμμείξειαν *they resolved to keep advancing until they should join Cyrus* (= προΐωμεν ἕως ἂν συμμείξωμεν) 2. 1. 2.

TEMPORAL CLAUSES IN GENERIC SENTENCES

2409. If the leading verb denotes a repeated or customary action or a general truth, a temporal clause takes the subjunctive with ἄν after primary tenses, the optative after secondary tenses. The negative is μή. Cp. 2336.

a. A present tense denotes action continuing (not completed) and is of the same time as that of the leading verb; an aorist tense denotes action simply occurring (completed) and time usually antecedent to that of the leading verb when the action of the dependent clause takes place before the action of the main clause. In clauses of contemporaneous action the aorist denotes the same time as that of the main verb; in clauses of subsequent action, time later than that of the main verb.

b. ὡς is rare in these temporal clauses (Hdt. 1. 17, 4. 172; ὅκως with the optative occurs in 1. 17, 1. 68).

c. On Homeric similes with ὡς ὅτε, ὡς ὁπότε, see 2486.

2410. In temporal sentences of indefinite frequency the temporal clause has the subjunctive with ἄν when the principal clause has the present indicative, or any other tense denoting a present customary or repeated action or a general truth. Cp. 2337.

μαινόμεθα πάντες ὁπόταν ὀργιζώμεθα *we are all mad whenever we are angry* Philemon 184, φωνή τις, ἥ, ὅταν γένηται, ἀεὶ ἀποτρέπει με *a kind of voice which, whenever it comes, always deters me* P. A. 31 d, ὅταν σπεύδῃ τις αὐτός, χὡ θεὸς συνάπτεται *whenever a man is eager himself, God too works with him* A. Pers. 742, ἕως ἂν σῴζηται τὸ σκάφος . . ., χρὴ καὶ ναύτην καὶ κυβερνήτην . . . προθύμους εἶναι . . ., ἐπειδὰν δ' ἡ θάλαττα ὑπέρσχῃ, μάταιος ἡ σπουδή *as long as the vessel remains in safety, both sailor and pilot should exert themselves; but when the sea has overwhelmed it, their efforts are fruitless* D. 9. 69, ποιοῦμεν ταῦθ' ἑκάστοθ' . . . ἕως ἂν αὐτὸν ἐμβάλωμεν ἐς κακόν *we do this on each occasion until we plunge him into misfortune* Ar. Nub. 1458.

2411. The verb of the main clause may stand in the participle, or in other tenses than the present indicative: καίπερ τῶν ἀνθρώπων, ἐν ᾧ μὲν ἂν πολεμῶσι, τὸν παρόντα (πόλεμον) ἀεὶ μέγιστον κρῑνόντων *although men always consider the present war the greatest so long as they are engaged in it* T. 1. 21, ὅταν δ' ἑτέρῳ ταῦτα παραδῷ, καταλέλυκε τὴν αὐτὸς αὑτοῦ δυναστείᾱν *but whenever he surrenders these* rights *to another, he destroys once and for all his own sovereignty* Aes. 3. 233, πολέμιοι . . . ἤδη ὅταν . . . καταδουλώσωνταί τινας, πολλοὺς δὴ βελτίους ἠνάγκασαν εἶναι *enemies ere now have forced improvement upon those whom they have enslaved* X. O. 1. 23 (cp. 2338), πολλάκις ἐθαύμασα τῆς τόλμης τῶν λεγόντων ὑπὲρ αὐτοῦ, πλὴν ὅταν ἐνθῡμηθῶ κτλ. *I have often marvelled at the effrontery of the speakers in his behalf, except when(ever) I consider,* etc. L. 12. 41.

2412. ἄν (κέ) is frequently omitted in Homer, and occasionally in lyric and dramatic poetry and in Herodotus, *e.g.* ἐπεὶ δ' ἁμάρτῃ, κεῖνος οὐκέτ' ἔστ' ἀνὴρ ἄβουλος *but whenever a man commits an error, that man is no longer heedless* S. Ant. 1025.

2413. The present indicative is very rarely used instead of the subjunctive with ἄν in temporal clauses of indefinite frequency. Thus, περὶ τῶν ἄλλων τῶν ἀδικούντων, ὅτε (ὅτου conj.) δικάζονται, δεῖ παρὰ τῶν κατηγόρων πυθέσθαι *with regard to other malefactors, one has to learn during their trial* (lit. *when they are tried*) *from the accusers* L. 22. 22. Cp. 2342.

2414. In temporal sentences of indefinite frequency the temporal clause has the optative when the principal clause has the imperfect or any other tense denoting a past customary or repeated action.

ἐθήρευεν ἀπὸ ἵππου ὁπότε γυμνάσαι βούλοιτο ἑαυτόν *he was wont to hunt on horseback, whenever he wanted to exercise himself* X. A. 1. 2. 7, ὁπότε ὥρᾱ εἴη ἀρίστου, ἀνέμενεν αὐτοὺς ἔστε ἐμφάγοιέν τι *whenever it was breakfast time, he used to wait until they had eaten something* X. C. 8. 1. 44, περιεμένομεν ἑκάστοτε ἕως ἀνοιχθείη τὸ δεσμωτήριον· ἐπειδὴ δὲ ἀνοιχθείη, εἰσῇμεν *we used to wait about on each occasion until the prison was opened; but when(ever) it was opened, we used to go in* P. Ph. 59 d. Observe that ἀνοιχθείη marks a repeated past action (*until it was regularly opened*) and represents the thought of the subject (*until it should be opened,* cf. 2420; *i.e.* direct = ἕως ἂν ἀνοιχθῇ).

2415. The optative is rare after a primary tense, and occurs only when that tense includes a reference to the past (ω 254; cp. 2573). — ὅτε κεν with the optative occurs once (I 525).

2416. Other tenses than the imperfect in the principal clause: ἀλλ' ὅτε δὴ . . .

ἀνᾱΐξειεν Ὀδυσσεύς, στάσκεν, ὑπαὶ δὲ ἴδεσκε κτλ. (cp. 495) *but whenever Odysseus arose, he* always *kept his position and looked down* Γ 215, ὁπότε προσβλέψειέ τινας τῶν ἐν ταῖς τάξεσιν, εἶπεν ἄν κτλ. *whenever he looked toward any of the men in the ranks, he would say*, etc. X. C. 7. 1. 10. Cp. 2341.

2417. The indicative (cp. 2342) is rare in temporal clauses of past indefinite frequency, as καὶ ᾖδον καὶ ἐχόρευον ὁπότε οἱ πολέμιοι αὐτοὺς ὄψεσθαι ἔμελλον *they both sang and danced whenever the enemy were likely to look at them* X. A. 4. 7. 16. So with ὁσάκις referring to particular events of repeated occurrence, as ὁσάκις κεχορήγηκε . . . νενίκηκε *as often as he has been choregus, he has gained a victory* X. M. 3. 4. 3.

TEMPORAL CLAUSES DENOTING PURPOSE

2418. Temporal conjunctions denoting limit as to duration (*so long as, while*) or limit as to termination (*until, till*) may imply purpose.

a. So ἕως *till, against the time when, in order that*, πρίν *before, in order that not*. ὄφρα (poet.) is usually final (*in order that*) rather than temporal (*so long as, while, till, up to the time that*). Sometimes in post-Homeric Greek ἕως and the subjunctive (with or without ἄν) has a touch of purpose.

2419. In the *Odyssey* ἕως, usually with the aorist optative after a secondary tense, is almost a final conjunction. Thus, δῶκεν . . . ἔλαιον εἵως χυτλώσαιτο *she gave olive oil that (against the time when) she might anoint herself* ζ 79. So δ 799, ε 385, τ 367. In ι 375 the present optative expresses durative action (θερμαίνοιτο *gradually get hot*).

2420. After a secondary tense ἕως with the aorist optative sometimes in Attic prose implies an *expectation, hope*, or *purpose* on the part of the subject of the main verb that the action of the temporal clause may be attained. Since such optatives are due to the principle of indirect discourse, the subjunctive with ἄν, denoting mere futurity, might have been used instead.

σπονδὰς ἐποιήσαντο ἕως ἀπαγγελθείη τὰ λεχθέντα *they made a truce* (which they hoped would last) *until the terms should be announced* X. H. 3. 2. 20 (here we might have had ἕως ἂν ἀπαγγελθῇ), τὰ ἄλλα χωρία εἶχον μένοντες ἕως σφίσι κἀκεῖνοι ποιήσειαν (= ἂν ποιήσωσι) τὰ εἰρημένα *they retained the other places, waiting until they* (the Lacedaemonians) *on their part should have performed for them* (the Athenians) *what had been agreed on* T. 5. 35. Compare ἕως ἂν ταῦτα διαπράξωνται φυλακὴν . . . κατέλιπε *he left a garrison* (to remain there) *until they should settle these matters* X. H. 5. 3. 25 (here ἕως διαπράξαιντο might have been used). Other examples are L. 13. 25, Is. 1. 10, 7. 8 (ἕως οὗ ?), X. H. 4. 4. 9, D. 27. 5, 29. 43 (τέως), 33. 8 ; cp. also Ar. Eq. 133. Present optative in T. 3. 102, X. H. 5. 4. 37.

2421. ἕως ἄν with the optative occurs rarely where it might be thought that the simple optative or ἄν with the subjunctive should be used. Many editors emend, but ἄν may generally be defended as potential, expressing the conviction of the agent. Thus, εἵλεσθε ἄνδρας εἴκοσι· τούτους δὲ ἐπιμελεῖσθαι τῆς πόλεως, ἕως ἂν οἱ νόμοι τεθεῖεν *you elected twenty men* whose duty it should be *to care for the State until such a time as* in all probability *the laws would be made* And. 1. 81. Cp. S. Tr. 687, I. 17, 15, P. Ph. 101 d. So ὅταν A. Pers. 450, πρὶν ἄν X. H. 2. 3. 48, 2. 4. 18.

SUMMARY OF THE CONSTRUCTIONS OF ἕως AND OF OTHER WORDS MEANING BOTH *SO LONG AS* AND *UNTIL*

ἕως *so long as, while*

Temporal Limit as to Duration (*during the time when*)

2422. **Indicative,** when the action of the temporal clause denotes definite duration in the present or past. The present often connotes cause (*while, now that, because*). The imperfect is used of past action: the main clause has the imperfect usually, but the aorist occurs (T. 5. 60).

2423. **Subjunctive** (present) with ἄν, when the action lies in the

a. Future, and the verb of the main clause is future indicative or an equivalent form.

b. Present, and the verb of the main clause states a present customary or repeated action or a general truth.

2424. The present optative (of future time) is very rare: in dependence on a past tense (X. H. 5. 4. 37, Aristotle, Athen. Pol. 28 end); by regular assimilation (2186 b) in a less vivid condition (P. Th. 155 a).

ἕως *until, till*

Temporal Limit as to Termination (*up to the time when*)

2425. **Indicative,** of a definite present or past action. The present connotes cause. The aorist is normally used of past action: the main verb is usually imperfect, but the aorist occurs (I. 17. 12).

a. Of a future action the future is very rare: X. C. 7. 5. 39 (ἐς ὅ Hdt. 9. 58).

2426. **Subjunctive** with ἄν, when the action lies in the

a. Future, and the main clause contains a verb referring to the future (except the optative without ἄν). The tense is usually the aorist: the present marks overlapping.

b. Present, and the verb of the main clause states a present customary or repeated action or a general truth.

2427. **Optative** (usually aorist), when the action lies in the

a. Future, and depends on an optative with ἄν.

b. Past, and depends on a secondary tense expressing or implying indirect discourse. Here the optative represents ἄν with the subjunctive after a primary tense.

c. Past, and the verb of the main clause states a past customary or repeated action.

N. — The present optative in b is rare; the future optative occurs only in X. H. 4. 4. 9, where some read the aorist.

2428. Conjunctions meaning *until* may have, as an implied or expressed antecedent, *μέχρι τούτου up to the time.* Thus, *μέχρι τούτου Λᾱσθένης φίλος ὠνομάζετο, ἕως προὔδωκεν Ὄλυνθον Lasthenes was called a friend (up to the time when) until he betrayed Olynthus* D. 18. 48.

2429. With conjunctions meaning *until*, when the principal clause is *affirmative*, it is implied that the action of the verb of the principal clause continues only up to the time when the action of the verb of the *until* clause takes place. Thus, in the passage cited in 2428, it is implied that Lasthenes ceased to be called a friend after he had betrayed Olynthus.

a. When the principal clause is *negative*, it is implied that the action of the verb of the principal clause does not take place until the action of the *until* clause takes place; as in *οὐ πρότερον ἐπαύσαντο ἕως τὴν πόλιν εἰς στάσεις κατέστησαν they did not stop until they divided the city into factions* L. 25. 26. In sentences like *δεῖ μὴ περιμένειν ἕως ἂν ἐπιστῶσιν we must not wait until they are upon us* (I. 4. 165), by reason of the meaning of *περιμένειν* the action of the principal clause ceases before the action of the *until* clause takes place.

GENERAL RULE FOR πρίν BEFORE, UNTIL

2430. *πρίν* is construed like other conjunctions meaning *until* except that it takes the infinitive as well as the indicative, subjunctive, and optative.

2431. After an *affirmative* clause *πρίν* usually takes the infinitive and means *before.*

2432. After a *negative* clause *πρίν* means *until,* and usually takes the indicative (of definite time), the subjunctive or optative (of indefinite time). Cf. 2455.

a. The subjunctive or optative is never used with *πρίν* unless the principal clause is negative.

b. When the principal clause is negative, *πρίν* is construed like *ἕως* and other words for *until* (*οὐ πρίν* = *ἕως*).

2433. When the principal clause is affirmative, the clause with *πρίν* simply adds a closer definition of the time. When the principal clause is negative, *πρίν* defines the time as before, but the closer definition serves also as a *condition* that must be realized before the action of the principal clause can be realized. Thus, *μὴ ἀπέλθητε πρὶν ἂν ἀκούσητε do not go away until you hear* X. A. 5. 7. 12 (*i.e. without hearing* = *ἐὰν μὴ ἀκούσητε*). Cp. *οὔτε γὰρ εἰρήνην οἷόν τε βεβαίᾱν ἀγαγεῖν, ἢν μὴ κοινῇ τοῖς βαρβάροις πολεμήσωμεν, οὔθ' ὁμονοῆσαι τοὺς Ἕλληνας, π ρ ὶ ν ἂν . . . τοὺς κινδύνους πρὸς τοὺς αὐτοὺς ποιησώμεθα neither is it possible to make a lasting peace unless we war in common against the barbarians, nor can the Greeks attain unanimity of sentiment until we encounter our perils in the front of the same enemies* I. 4. 173.

2434. *πρίν* is used with the aorist or (less often) with the imperfect indicative only when *πρίν* is equivalent to *ἕως until*; but, when the verb of the main clause is negatived, *πρίν may* be translated by *before* or *until.* When *πρίν must* be rendered by *before*, it takes the infinitive.

ταῦτα ἐποίουν πρὶν Σωκράτης ἀφίκετο *I was doing this until Socrates arrived* (rare even in poetry; cp. 2441 c).

οὐ ταῦτα ἐποίουν πρὶν Σωκράτης ἀφίκετο *I was not doing this until* (or *before*) *Socrates arrived.*

ταῦτα ἐποίουν πρὶν Σωκράτην ἀφικέσθαι (not Σωκράτης ἀφίκετο) *I was doing this before Socrates arrived.*

2435. It is correct to say οὐ ποιήσω τοῦτο πρὶν ἂν κελεύσῃς, ποιήσω (or οὐ ποιήσω) τοῦτο πρὶν κελεῦσαι, but incorrect to say ποιήσω τοῦτο πρὶν ἂν κελεύσῃς.

2436. The action of an infinitive introduced by πρίν *before* may or may not (according to the sense) actually take place at some time later than the action of the leading verb. The clause with πρίν signifies merely that the action of the infinitive had not taken place at the time of the leading verb.

2437. The clause with πρίν may precede or follow the correlated clause. Cp. 2455.

2438. πρίν is originally a comparative adverb meaning *before*, i.e. *sooner* or *formerly;* and seems to be connected with πρό, πρότερον *before.* The adverbial force survives in Attic only after the article, as ἐν τοῖς πρὶν λόγοις *in the foregoing statements* T. 2. 62. The adverbial and original use appears also in Homer wherever πρίν occurs with the indicative, the anticipatory (futural) subjunctive (1810), or the optative with κέ. Thus, τὴν δ' ἐγὼ οὐ λύσω· πρίν μιν καὶ γῆρας ἔπεισιν *but her I will not release; sooner shall old age come upon her* A 29, οὐδέ μιν ἀνστήσεις· πρὶν καὶ κακὸν ἄλλο πάθησθα *nor shalt thou recall him to life; sooner* (*before this*) *thou wilt suffer yet another affliction* Ω 551.—From this early coördination was developed the construction of the *conjunction* πρίν with the finite moods; but in general only after Homer, who never uses the indicative, and the optative only once (Φ 580), with πρίν. The required sense was given by ἕως or πρίν γ' ὅτε δή. A finite mood was first used of the future, and after negative clauses (οὐ πρότερον πρίν like οὐ πρότερον ἕως).— Homer commonly uses the infinitive with πρίν meaning *before* and *until.* Here the infinitive (as with ὥστε) simply states the abstract verbal notion, and thus has no reference to differences of time or mood; πρίν being used almost like πρό *before* as πρὶν ἰδεῖν = πρὸ τοῦ ἰδεῖν *before seeing* (first in Xenophon). This early use with the infinitive was, with some restrictions, retained in Attic, where the infinitive *may* sometimes be used instead of the finite verb. πρίν came more and more to take the subjunctive with ἄν and to assume conditional relations (cp. 2433); while the use with the infinitive was more and more confined to cases where the leading verb was affirmative.

2439. The comparative idea in πρίν explains its negative force: an event A happened before another event B, *i.e.* A occurred when B had *not yet* (οὔπω) occurred. Because of its negative force πρίν commonly takes the aorist in all the moods. The aorist has an affinity for the negative because it marks simple and total negation of an action regarded in its mere occurrence; whereas the imperfect with a negative denotes resistance or refusal (1896) in respect of an action regarded as continuing. When πρίν takes the present in any mood the actions of the correlated clauses usually overlap. The present occurs chiefly in the prose writers of the fourth century.

2440. πρότερον or πρόσθεν may be used in the principal clause as a forerunner of πρίν. Examples in 2441, 2444, 2445.

a. Homer has πρὶν . . . πρίν B 348. Attic has also φθάνω . . . πρίν, as φθήσονται πλεύσαντες πρὶν τὴν ξυμφορὰν Χίους αἰσθέσθαι *they will succeed in making their voyage before the Chians hear of the disaster* T. 8. 12.

πρίν WITH THE INDICATIVE

2441. πρίν in Attic prose takes the indicative of a definite past action when the verb of the principal clause is negative or implies a negative, rarely when it is affirmative.

οὔτε τότε Κύρῳ ἰέναι ἤθελε πρὶν ἡ γυνὴ αὐτὸν ἔπεισε *nor was he willing then to enter into relations with Cyrus until his wife persuaded him* X. A. 1. 2. 26, οὐ πρότερον ἐπαύσαντο πρὶν τόν τε πατέρ' ἐκ τοῦ στρατοπέδου μετεπέμψαντο καὶ τῶν φίλων αὐτοῦ τοὺς μὲν ἀπέκτειναν, τοὺς δ' ἐκ τῆς πόλεως ἐξέβαλον *they did not stop until they sent for his father from the camp, put some of his friends to death and expelled others from the city* I. 16. 8, οὐ πρόσθεν ἐπαύσαντο πρὶν ἐξεπολιόρκησαν τὸν Ὄλουρον *they did not cease from hostilities until they had captured Olurus by siege* X. H. 7. 4. 18, οὐδ' ὥς . . . ἠξίωσαν νεώτερόν τι ποιεῖν ἐς αὐτόν . . . πρίν γε δὴ . . . ἀνὴρ Ἀργίλιος μηνυτὴς γίγνεται (historical present = aorist) *not even under these circumstances did they think it right to take any severe measures against him, until finally a man of Argilus turned informer* T. 1. 132.

a. The tense in the πρίν clause is usually the aorist (the tense of negation, 2439, and of prior action); rarely the imperfect (of contemporaneous, overlapping action), as D. 9. 61. The historical present is also used as an equivalent of the aorist. The principal clause usually has a secondary tense of the indicative. πρίν with the indicative is not common until Herodotus and the Attic writers.

b. The verb of the principal clause may be *virtually* negative, as τοὺς . . . Ἀθηναίους λανθάνουσι πρὶν δὴ τῇ Δήλῳ ἔσχον *they escaped the notice of the Athenians* (*i.e.* οὐχ ὁρῶνται) *until they reached Delos* T. 3. 29. Cp. T. 3. 104, X. A. 2. 5. 33. Observe that οὐ παύομαι (2441) is not regarded as virtually affirmative.

c. The verb of the principal clause is affirmative in prose only in T. 7. 39, 7. 71, Aes. 1. 64. In all of these cases the leading verb is an imperfect, which emphasizes the continuation of the action up to the point of time expressed by the πρίν clause.

d. The use in Herodotus is the same as in Attic prose. Homer has the indicative (after affirmative or negative clauses) only with πρίν γ' ὅτε *until*. In the drama πρίν with the indicative is rare. Euripides uses it only after affirmative clauses. When πρίν is = ἕως it often takes δή.

2442. A πρίν clause, depending on a past tense denoting non-fulfilment, itself denotes non-fulfilment and takes a past indicative by assimilation (2185 b).

χρῆν τοίνυν Λεπτίνην μὴ πρότερον τιθέναι τὸν ἑαυτοῦ νόμον πρὶν τοῦτον ἔλυσε *Leptines ought not then to have proposed his own law until (before) he had repealed this* D. 20. 96. Cp. 2455 b.

πρίν WITH THE SUBJUNCTIVE

2443. πρίν with the subjunctive and ἄν refers to the future or to general present time.

2444. (I) πρίν takes the subjunctive with ἄν to denote a future action anticipated by the subject of the leading verb. The principal clause is negative, and contains any verb referring to the future except the simple optative.

οὐ πρότερον κακῶν παύσονται αἱ πόλεις πρὶν ἂν ἐν αὐταῖς οἱ φιλόσοφοι ἄρξωσιν *States will not cease from evil until philosophers become rulers in them* P. R. 487 e, μὴ ἀπέλθητε πρὶν ἂν ἀκούσητε *do not go away until you hear (shall have heard)* X. A. 5. 7. 12, οὐ χρή μ' ἐνθένδε ἀπελθεῖν πρὶν ἂν δῶ δίκην *I must not depart hence until I have suffered punishment* 5. 7. 5, μηδένα φίλον ποιοῦ πρὶν ἂν ἐξετάσῃς πῶς κέχρηται τοῖς πρότερον φίλοις *make no one your friend until you have inquired how he has treated his former friends* I. 1. 24, μή ποτ' ἐπαινήσῃς πρὶν ἂν εἰδῇς ἄνδρα σαφηνέως *never praise a man until you have come to know him well* Theognis 963. Observe that the last two examples contain a general truth.

a. The aorist subjunctive is usual (the tense of negation, 2439, and of action prior to that of the principal clause); much less common is the present subjunctive (usually of contemporaneous, overlapping action) as X. C. 2. 2. 8 (2446).

b. Homer does not use κέ or ἄν in this construction since πρίν is here adverbial and its clause is simply coördinated. But Hom. has πρίν γ' ὅτ' ἄν. The subjunctive without ἄν occurs occasionally as an archaism in Hdt. and the dramatic poets. In Attic prose especially in Thuc. (*e.g.* 6. 10, 29, 38); but ἄν is often inserted by editors.

c. The leading verb is rarely the optative with ἄν (as a form of future expression): οὐκ ἂν ἀπέλθοιμι πρὶν παντάπᾱσιν ἡ ἀγορᾱ̀ λυθῇ (cp. b) *I will not go away until the market is entirely over* X. O. 12. 1.

2445. (II) After a negative clause of present time that expresses a customary or repeated action or a general truth, πρίν takes the subjunctive with ἄν.

οὐ πρότερον παύονται πρὶν ἂν πείσωσιν οὓς ἠδίκησαν *they do not cease* to endure *until they have won over those whom they have wronged* P. Ph. 114 b.

a. The leading verb may stand in another tense than the present indicative, as οὐδεὶς πώποτε ἐπέθετο (empiric aorist, 1930) πρότερον δήμου καταλύσει πρὶν ἂν μεῖζον τῶν δικαστηρίων ἰσχύσῃ *no one has ever attempted the subversion of the people until he became superior to the courts of justice* Aes. 3. 235.

2446. After a secondary tense in actual or implied indirect discourse, πρίν with the subjunctive and ἄν is common instead of the optative without ἄν (2449).

εἶπον μηδένα τῶν ὄπισθεν κῑνεῖσθαι πρὶν ἂν ὁ πρόσθεν ἡγῆται *I ordered that none in the rear should move until the one before him led the way* X. C. 2. 2. 8 (here πρὶν ἡγοῖτο is possible).

2447. The principal clause may be affirmative in form, but virtually negative.

αἰσχρὸν (= οὐ καλὸν or οὐ δεῖν) δ' ἡγοῦμαι πρότερον παύσασθαι πρὶν ἂν ὑμεῖς περὶ αὐτῶν ὅ τι ἂν βούλησθε ψηφίσησθε *I consider it base* (*i.e.* I do not consider it to be honourable) *to stop until you have voted what you wish* L. 22. 4. Cf. Thuc. 6. 38, D. 38. 24, E. Heracl. 179.

πρίν WITH THE OPTATIVE

2448. πρίν with the optative is used only in indirect discourse or by assimilation to another optative.

2449. (I) The optative without ἄν follows πρίν to denote an action anticipated in the past when the principal clause is negative and its verb is in a secondary tense. The optative is here in indirect discourse (actual or implied) and represents ἄν with the subjunctive, which is often retained (2446). Cp. 2420.

ἀπηγόρευε μηδένα βάλλειν πρὶν Κῦρος ἐμπλησθείη θηρῶν *he forbade any one to shoot until Cyrus should have had his fill of hunting* X. C. 1. 4. 14 (= μηδεὶς βαλλέτω πρὶν ἂν Κῦρος ἐμπλησθῇ), οἱ Ἠλεῖοι . . . ἔπειθον (αὐτοὺς) μὴ ποιεῖσθαι μάχην πρὶν οἱ Θηβαῖοι παραγένοιντο *the Eleans persuaded them not to engage in battle until the Thebans should have come up* X. H. 6. 5. 19 (= μὴ ποιεῖτε μάχην πρὶν ἂν παραγένωνται).

a. In indirect discourse the infinitive is preferred (2455 d).

2450. (II) By assimilation of mood, πρίν may take the optative when the negative principal clause has the optative. Cp. 2186 b.

εἰ ἕλκοι τις αὐτόν . . . καὶ μὴ ἀνείη πρὶν ἐξελκύσειεν ἐς τὸ τοῦ ἡλίου φῶς κτλ. *if one should drag him and not let him go until he had dragged him out into the sunlight*, etc. P. R. 515 e.

2451. The optative with πρίν in clauses of customary or repeated action seems not to be used.

2452. πρὶν ἄν with the optative is rare and suspected (cp. 2421).

πρίν WITH THE INFINITIVE

2453. πρίν takes the infinitive in Attic especially when the principal clause is affirmative. The infinitive must be used, even with negative clauses, when πρίν must mean only *before* (and not *until*).

a. The infinitive is obligatory in Attic when the action of the πρίν clause *does not take place* or *is not to take place* (cp. ὥστε μή with the infinitive).

b. The infinitive takes the accusative when its subject is different from that of the principal clause.

c. The usual tense is the aorist, the tense of negation (2439) and of the simple occurrence of the action. Less frequent is the present (chiefly in Xenophon), of action continuing, repeated, or attempted (*before undertaking to*, *before proceeding to*). The perfect, of action completed with permanent result, is rare.

οἱ καὶ πρὶν ἐμὲ εἰπεῖν ὁτιοῦν εἰδότες *who know even before I say anything at all* D. 18. 50, σύνιστε μὲν καὶ πρὶν ἐμὲ λέγειν *you know as well as I do even before I proceed to set forth in detail the matter of my speech* Aes. 1. 116, ἀπετράποντο ἐς τὴν πόλιν πρὶν ὑπερβαίνειν *they turned back to the city before they attempted to scale* the wall T. 3. 24.

2454. When the principal clause is affirmative, πρίν *before* regularly takes the infinitive.

ἐπὶ τὸ ἄκρον ἀναβαίνει Χειρίσοφος πρὶν τινας αἰσθέσθαι τῶν πολεμίων *Chirisophus ascended the height before any of the enemy perceived him* X. A. 4. 1. 7, πρὶν καταλῦσαι τὸ στράτευμα πρὸς ἄριστον βασιλεὺς ἐφάνη *before the army halted for breakfast, the king appeared* 1. 10. 19, πέμψᾱς, πρὶν ἐν Τεγέᾳ αὐτὸς εἶναι, πρὸς τὸν ἄρχοντα τῶν ξένων, ἐκέλευε κτλ. lit. *before he himself arrived at Tegea, sending to the commander of the mercenaries, he gave orders*, etc. X. H. 5. 4. 37 (αὐτός, by attraction to the subject of πέμψᾱς).

2455. When the main clause is negative, πρίν sometimes takes the infinitive in Attic, and generally means *before*, rarely *until*. When *before* and *after* are contrasted, *until* is out of place, and the πρίν clause often precedes.

a. In reference to present or past time: πρὶν ὡς Ἄφοβον ἐλθεῖν μίαν ἡμέρᾱν οὐκ ἐχήρευσεν *before she came to Aphobus she was not a widow a single day* D. 30. 33, πρὶν μὲν τοῦτο πρᾶξαι Λεωκράτην ἄδηλον ἦν ὁποῖοί τινες ἐτύγχανον, νῦν δέ κτλ. *before Leocrates did this, it was uncertain what sort of men they were; but now*, etc. Lyc. 135, πρὶν ἀνάγεσθαί με εἰς τὴν Αἶνον . . . οὐδεὶς ᾐτιάσατό με *before I proceeded to set sail for Aenus no one accused me* Ant. 5. 25.

b. In reference to action unfulfilled: οὓς (λόγους) εἴ τις ἐπέδειξεν αὐτοῖς πρὶν ἐμὲ διαλεχθῆναι περὶ αὐτῶν, οὐκ ἔστιν ὅπως οὐκ ἂν . . . δυσκόλως πρὸς σὲ διετέθησαν *and if any one had shown these words to them before I discussed them, it is inevitable that they would have been discontented with you* I. 12. 250.

c. In reference to future time: οὐχ οἷόν τ' ἐστὶν αἰσθέσθαι πρὶν κακῶς τινας παθεῖν ὑπ' αὐτῶν *it is not possible to perceive this before some suffer injury at their hands* I. 20. 14, καί μοι μὴ θορυβήσῃ μηδεὶς πρὶν ἀκοῦσαι *and let no one raise a disturbance before he hears* D. 5. 15 (cp. ὅπως μὴ θορυβήσει μηδεὶς πρὶν ἂν ἅπαντα εἴπω D. 13, 14).

N.—With verbs of *fearing*, the positive being the thing dreaded; as δέδοικα μὴ πρὶν πόνοις ὑπερβάλῃ με γῆρας πρὶν σὰν χαρίεσσαν προσιδεῖν ὤρᾱν *I fear lest old age overcome me with its troubles before I live to behold thy gracious beauty* E. fr. 453.

d. Infinitive instead of the optative after a leading verb in a secondary tense: ἱκέτευον μηδαμῶς ἀποτρέπεσθαι πρὶν ἐμβαλεῖν εἰς τὴν τῶν Λακεδαιμονίων χώρᾱν *they entreated them by no means to turn aside until they should invade the territory of the Lacedaemonians* X. H. 6. 5. 23 (here the optative might stand in indirect discourse to represent the subjunctive with ἄν), οὔτ' αὐτός ποτε πρὶν ἱδρῶσαι δεῖπνον ᾑρεῖτο *neither was he ever accustomed to take his supper until he got into a sweat* by exercise X. C. 8. 1. 38 (for ἱδρώσειε, see 2451).

e. Infinitive after an optative with ἄν in a principal clause: εἴ τίς τινα μηχανὴν ἔχοι πρὸς τοῦτο . . ., οὐκ ἄν ποτε λέγων ἀπείποι τὸ τοιοῦτον πρὶν ἐπὶ τέλος ἐλθεῖν; *if ever any* lawgiver *should have any plan for this, would he ever be weary of discussing such a scheme until he reached the end?* P. L. 769 e. Here the subjunctive with ἄν is permitted.

2456. The lyric poets and Herodotus use πρίν with the infinitive as it is used in Attic prose and poetry. Homer has the infinitive after affirmative or negative clauses alike (*before* and *until*), and often where a finite verb would be used in Attic; as ναῖε δὲ Πήδαιον πρὶν ἐλθεῖν υἷας Ἀχαιῶν *he dwelt in Pedaeon before the sons of the Achaeans came* N 172, οὔ μ' ἀποτρέψεις πρὶν χαλκῷ μαχέσασθαι (= Attic ἂν μαχέσῃ) *thou shalt not dissuade me until thou hast fought with the spear* Υ 257; often in correspondence with the adverbial πρίν, as οὐδέ τις ἔτλη πρὶν πιέειν, πρὶν λεῖψαι *nor durst any man (sooner) drink before he had offered a libation* H 480.

2457. ἢ πρίν *than before*, with a past tense suppressed after ἤ, occurs first in Xenophon (C. 5. 2. 36, 7. 5. 77).

πρότερον ἤ, πρόσθεν ἤ, πρὶν ἤ, πάρος

2458. **πρότερον ἤ** *sooner than, before* is used especially in Herodotus and Thucydides. (a) With the indicative: οὐ πρότερον ἐνέδοσαν ἢ αὐτοὶ ἐν σφίσιν αὐτοῖς . . . ἐσφάλησαν *they did not succumb before they were overthrown by themselves* T. 2. 65. (b) With the infinitive: τὰς δ' ἄλλας πόλεις ἔφη ἀδικεῖν, αἳ ἐς Ἀθηναίους πρότερον ἢ ἀποστῆναι ἀνήλουν *he said the other States were wrong, which, before they revolted, used to pay money into the treasury of the Athenians* T. 8. 45. (c) With the subjunctive (without ἄν) rarely (T. 7. 63). Chiefly in Hdt.

2459. So **πρόσθεν ἤ** *sooner than, before*: ἀπεκρίνατο . . . ὅτι πρόσθεν ἂν ἀποθάνοιεν ἢ τὰ ὅπλα παραδοίησαν *he answered that they would die before (sooner than that) they would surrender their arms* X. A. 2. 1. 10. **ὕστερον ἤ** *later than* takes, by analogy, the infinitive once in Thuc. (6. 4). For **ὕστερον ἤ** with finite form cf. T. 1. 60. 3.

2460. **πρὶν ἤ** *sooner than, before* with the infinitive occurs in Homer (only E 288, X 266) and Hdt. (2. 2); and in Hdt. also with the indicative (6. 45) and subjunctive (7. 10 η, without ἄν). πρὶν ἤ is rare and suspected in Attic (X. C. 1. 4. 23); but is common in late Greek.

2461. **πάρος** *before* in Homer takes the infinitive (Z 348).

CLAUSES OF COMPARISON

2462. Clauses of comparison (*as* clauses) measure an act or state qualitatively or quantitatively with reference to an act or state in the leading clause.

a. Comparative clauses with ἤ *than* are used in disjunctive coördinated sentences. See under Particles (2863).

2463. Comparative clauses of quality or manner are introduced by **ὡς** *as*, ὥσπερ, καθάπερ *just as*, ὅπως, ᾗ, ὅπῃ, ᾗπερ *as*. The principal clause may contain a demonstrative adverb (**οὕτως, ὧδε** *so*). ὥσπερ may be correlated with **ὁ αὐτός**.

ὡς, etc., are here properly conjunctive relative adverbs of manner, some uses of which fall under conditional relative clauses.

a. Other comparative conjunctive adverbs are ὥστε *as* (poetic and Ionic), ἠΰτε, εὖτε *as, like as* (Epic). Demonstrative adverbs in Epic are ὥς, τώς, τοίως, αὕτως, ὡσαύτως.

b. On other uses of ὡς, etc., see under Particles (2990 ff.). On ὡς, ὥσπερ with a participle, see 2086, 2087.

2464. The verb of the comparative clause is commonly omitted if it is the same as the verb of the leading clause. Thus, ἐὰν σοὶ ξυνδοκῇ ὥσπερ ἐμοί *if it seems good also to you as (it seems) to me* P. Ph. 100 c.

2465. The subject of a comparative clause with ὡς or ὥσπερ, the verb of which is omitted, is often attracted into the case (usually the accusative) of the other member of the comparison. Thus, οὐδαμοῦ γὰρ ἔστιν Ἀγόρατον Ἀθηναῖον εἶναι ὥσπερ Θρασύβουλον *it is in no wise possible for Agoratus to be an Athenian as Thrasybulus* is (= Θρασύβουλος Ἀθηναῖός ἐστι) L. 13. 72. Attraction into the dative is less common: Κύρῳ ἥδετο . . . ὥσπερ σκύλακι γενναίῳ ἀνακλάζοντι *he was delighted with Cyrus, who set up a cry like a young and noble dog* (= σκύλαξ γενναῖος ἀνακλάζει) X. C. 1. 4. 15.

a. Usually, however, we have the nominative with the verb omitted: πέπεισμαί σε μᾶλλον ἀποθανεῖν ἂν ἑλέσθαι ἢ ζῆν ὥσπερ ἐγώ *I am persuaded that you would prefer to die rather than live as I* live X. M. 1. 6. 4.

2466. Comparative clauses of quality are often fused with the leading clause by the omission of the preposition in the correlated member of the comparison, but only when ὡς precedes. Cp. 1673.

2467. The antecedent clause may contain a wish: οὕτω (ὥς) . . . ὡς (which may be omitted); as οὕτω νικήσαιμί τ' ἐγὼ καὶ νομιζοίμην σοφός, ὡς ὑμᾶς ἡγούμενος εἶναι θεατὰς δεξιοὺς . . . πρώτους ἠξίωσ' ἀναγεῦσ' ὑμᾶς *as surely as I thought it proper to let you first taste this comedy because I thought you were clever spectators, so* surely *may I win and be accounted a master* Ar. Nub. 520. Cp. N 825, Ar. Thesm. 469.

2468. Comparative clauses of quantity or degree are introduced by ὅσῳ, ὅσον *in proportion as.* The principal clause usually contains the corresponding demonstratives τοσούτῳ, τοσοῦτον (τόσῳ, τόσον are usually poetic).

a. Greek, like Latin, uses the adjective relative pronoun ὅσος (*quantus*) in the subordinate clause in correlation to τοσοῦτος agreeing with a substantive. Here English uses the conjunctive adverb *as.* So with τοιοῦτος . . . οἷος. — τοσούτῳ, τοσοῦτον may be followed by ὡς, ὥστε.

2469. τοσοῦτον . . . ὅσον or ὅσον . . . τοσοῦτον denotes that the action of the main clause takes place in the same degree as the action of the subordinate clause. ὅσῳ . . . τοσούτῳ with a comparative or superlative adjective or adverb is equivalent to *the more . . . the more, the less . . . the less.*

2470. The demonstrative antecedent may be omitted, especially when its clause precedes: καὶ χαλεπώτεροι ἔσονται ὅσῳ νεώτεροί εἰσιν *and they will be the more severe the younger they are* P. A. 39 d.

2471. One member may contain a comparative, the other a superlative; as ὅσῳ γὰρ ἑτοιμότατ' αὐτῷ (τῷ λόγῳ) δοκοῦμεν χρῆσθαι, τοσούτῳ μᾶλλον ἀπιστοῦσι πάντες αὐτῷ *for the more we are thought to excel all others in ability to speak, so much the more do all distrust it* D. 2. 12.

2472. ὅσῳ (ὅσον) may be used without a comparative or superlative when the correlative clause has a comparative or superlative with or without τοσούτῳ (τοσοῦτον). Thus, ὥσπερ ἐν ἵπποις, οὕτω καὶ ἐν ἀνθρώποις τισὶν ἐγγίγνεται, ὅσῳ ἂν ἔκπλεα τὰ δέοντα ἔχωσι, τοσούτῳ ὑβριστέροις εἶναι *as it is in the nature of horses, so it is in the case of certain men: in so far as they have their wants satisfied, the more they are wanton* X. Hi. 10. 2. ὅσῳ may stand for the logical ὅτι in τοσούτῳ Σύρων κακίων ἐγένετο, ὅσῳ Σύροι ἔφυγον *he proved himself a greater coward than the Syrians all the more because they fled* X. C. 6. 2. 19.

2473. The correlated clauses may be fused when both ὅσῳ (ὅσον) and τοσούτῳ (τοσοῦτον) are omitted and the predicate of the subordinate clause is a comparative or superlative with a form of εἶναι. Thus, ἐνδεεστέροις γὰρ οὖσι ταπεινοτέροις αὐτοῖς οἴονται χρῆσθαι *for the more indigent they are so much the more submissive do they expect to find them* X. Hi. 5. 4 (= ὅσῳ ἐνδεέστεροί εἰσι, τοσούτῳ ταπεινοτέροις).

EXAMPLES OF COMPARATIVE CLAUSES

2474. The moods in comparative clauses are used with the same meaning as in conditional clauses or other conditional relative clauses.

2475. **Indicative**: in assertions and statements of fact: ἔρξον ὅπως ἐθέλεις *do as thou wilt* Δ 37, ὡς δὲ πρὸς τὴν οὐσίᾱν ἥρμοττεν, οὕτως ἑκάστοις προσέταττον *but as was suitable to their property, so they gave directions to each* I. 7. 44, ἔστιν γὰρ οὕτως ὥσπερ οὗτος ἐννέπει *for it is so even as he says* S. Tr. 475, ὅσον αἱ κατὰ τὸ σῶμα ἡδοναὶ ἀπομαραίνονται, τοσοῦτον αὔξονται αἱ περὶ τοὺς λόγους ἐπιθῡμίαι *in proportion as the pleasures of the body wane the appetite for philosophical conversation increases* P. R. 328 d, ἧκεν ἄγων στρατιὰν ὅσην πλείστην ἐδύνατο *he came with an army as large as possible* T. 7. 21 (cp. 1087).

a. With ἄν and the potential or unreal indicative: εἰσπηδήσαντες . . . θᾶττον ἢ ὡς τις ἂν ᾤετο *jumping in quicker than (as) one could think* X. A. 1. 5. 8, ὥσπερ οὖν, εἰ ἀληθῆ ἦν ταῦτα ἅ μου κατηγόρησαν, ἐμοὶ ἂν ὠργίζεσθε . . ., οὕτως ἀξιῶ κτλ. *for just as you would be angry with me if their accusations against me were true, so I beg*, etc. And. 1. 24.

2476. **Subjunctive with ἄν.** — **a.** Of future time, as ἀλλ' ἄγεθ', ὡς ἂν ἐγὼ εἴπω, πειθώμεθα *but come, as I shall direct, let us obey* B 139, ὅπως γὰρ ἂν τοὺς ἄλλους πρὸς σαυτὸν διαθῇς, οὕτω καὶ σὺ πρὸς ἐκείνους ἕξεις *for as you dispose others towards yourself, so you too will feel towards them* I. 2. 23, τοῖς αὐτοῖς ἐνεχέσθω καθάπερ ἂν τὸν Ἀθηναῖον ἀποκτείνῃ *let him be subject to the same penalties just as if he kills the Athenian* D. 23. 41, ἐν τοῖς ἀργυρείοις ὅσῳπερ ἂν πλείους ἐργάζωνται, τόσῳ πλείονα τἀγαθὰ εὑρήσουσι *in silver mines the larger the number who coöperate, so much the more abundant will be the riches they find* X. Vect. 4. 32, οὐκοῦν ὅσῳ ἄν τις μείζω ἀγαθὰ παθὼν μὴ ἀποδιδῷ χάριν, τοσούτῳ ἀδικώτερος ἂν εἴη; *then will he be the more unjust in proportion to the greatness of the benefits he* *has received and for which he does not return proper gratitude?* X. M. 2. 2. 3 (cp. 2326 d).

b. Of present time, as in general conditions: τὸ μὲν γὰρ πέρας, ὡς ἂν ὁ δαίμων βουληθῇ, πάντων γίγνεται *for the end of all events happens as God wills* D. 18. 92, τοσούτῳ χαλεπώτερον ἀκούειν τῶν λεγομένων, ὅσῳ περ ἂν αὐτῶν τις ἀκριβέστερον ἐξετάζῃ τὰς ἁμαρτίᾱς *it is the more difficult* for them *to pay heed to what is said in proportion to the precision with which their errors are scrutinized* I. 11. 3.

2477. Optative.—**a.** With ἄν (potential): ἔστι μείζω τἀκείνων ἔργα ἢ ὡς τῷ λόγῳ τις ἂν εἴποι *their deeds are too great for any one to tell in words* D. 6. 11, ὥσπερ αὐτοὶ οὐκ ἂν ἀξιώσαιτε κακῶς ἀκούειν ὑπὸ τῶν ὑμετέρων παίδων, οὕτω μηδὲ τούτῳ ἐπίτρεπε περὶ τοῦ πατρὸς βλασφημεῖν *just as you yourselves would not think it right to be ill spoken of by your children, even so do not permit him either to utter slanders about his father* D. 40. 45.

b. With ἄν, as in less vivid future conditions: ὅσῳ δὲ πρεσβύτερος γίγνοιτο, μᾶλλον ἀεὶ ἀσπάζοιτο ἂν (χρήματα) *the older he grows, the more he would always respect wealth* P. R. 549 b.

c. The optative without ἄν in indirect discourse may represent ἄν with the subjunctive of direct discourse; as νομίζων, ὅσῳ μὲν θᾶττον ἔλθοι, τοσούτῳ ἀπαρασκευαστοτέρῳ βασιλεῖ μαχεῖσθαι, ὅσῳ δὲ σχολαιότερον, τοσούτῳ πλέον συναγείρεσθαι βασιλεῖ στράτευμα *in the belief that, the more quickly he advanced, the more unprepared for battle would the king be, while the slower* he advanced, *the greater would be the army that was collecting for the king* X. A. 1. 5. 9 (direct = ὅσῳ ἂν θᾶττον ἔλθω . . . μαχοῦμαι, ὅσῳ ἂν σχολ. ἔλθω τοσούτῳ πλέον συναγείρεται).

d. Without ἄν, of past time, as in general conditions. Thus, ξυνετίθεσαν ὡς ἕκαστόν τι ξυμβαίνοι *they put* the stones *together as each happened to fit* T. 4. 4.—Also after a present tense: εἰκῇ κράτιστον ζῆν, ὅπως δύναιτό τις *'tis best to live at hazard, as one may* S. O. T. 979 (cp. 2573).

2478. ὥσπερ εἰ (ὡσπερεί), **ὥσπερ ἂν εἰ** (ὡσπερανεί) *just as if* (= *just as would be the case, if*) form a combination of a comparison and a condition, and are used with the indicative imperfect (of past time) or aorist or with the optative (commonly when τὶς is the subject). ὥσπερ (ἄν) here represents the suppressed apodosis to the condition with εἰ. In some cases the ellipsis may easily be supplied, but it was usually unconscious.

a. When ὥσπερ ἄν has its own verb it is used like *for instance*, as ὥσπερ ἄν (1766 a), εἴ τίς με ἔροιτο . . ., εἴποιμ' ἂν *for instance, if any one were to ask me, I should say* P. G. 451 a.

b. With ὥσπερ εἰ, ὥσπερ ἂν εἰ cp. καθάπερ εἰ, καθάπερ ἂν εἰ.

2479. ὥσπερ εἰ: θαυμάζω δέ σε . . . ἀλλόθρουν πόλιν κυρεῖν λέγουσαν, ὥσπερ εἰ παρεστάτεις *but I marvel that of a city speaking another tongue thou dost as truly tell as* (*thou wouldst tell*) *if thou hadst always been dwelling therein* A. Ag. 1201.

2480. ὥσπερ ἂν εἰ is more common than ὥσπερ εἰ. Thus, πρὸς μόνους τοὺς προγόνους τοὺς ἡμετέρους συμβαλόντες ὁμοίως διεφθάρησαν, ὥσπερ ἂν (διεφθάρησαν) εἰ πρὸς ἅπαντας ἀνθρώπους ἐπολέμησαν *in contending against our ancestors alone they were destroyed as* completely *as if they had waged war against all mankind*

I. 4. 69, ὅμοια γάρ μοι δοκοῦσι πάσχειν ὥσπερ (ἂν τις πάσχοι) εἴ τις πολλὰ ἐσθίων μηδέποτε ἐμπίπλαιτο *for they seem to me to be in the same condition as if any one for all his eating were never to be filled* X. S. 4. 37, ἠσπάζετο αὐτὸν ὥσπερ ἂν (ἀσπάζοιτο) εἴ τις . . . πάλαι φιλῶν ἀσπάζοιτο *he greeted him as one would do who had long loved him* X. C. 1. 3. 2.

a. With a participle ὥσπερ ἂν εἰ is sometimes used with much the same force as ὥσπερ, the εἰ being added by a confusion of constructions. Thus, ὥσπερ ἂν εἰ καὶ κατακλυσμὸν γεγενῆσθαι τῶν πρāγμάτων ἡγούμενοι *as if you believed that there had been also a revolution in politics* D. 18. 214: lit. *as* (you would think) *if you believed* (for ὥσπερ ἂν ἡγούμενοι or ὥσπερ ἂν εἰ ἡγεῖσθε). Cp. 1766 a. Similarly ὥσπερ εἰ has virtually the force of ὥσπερ alone (2087).

SIMILES AND COMPARISONS

2481. ὡς, ὡς εἰ, ὡς εἴ τε *as if*, ὡς ὅτε, ὡς ὁπότε *as when* are often used in poetry in similes and comparisons.

a. The present and aorist indicative and subjunctive (usually without ἄν) are regularly used. The optative occurs only with ὡς εἰ or ὡς εἴ τε. The verb of the apodosis may sometimes be supplied from the main clause, and the sense may be satisfied in other cases by supplying *as happens, as is the case;* but as early as Homer the ellipsis was probably unconscious, as it is in English *as if, as when.* Hence ὡς εἰ, ὡς ὅτε are scarcely to be distinguished from ὡς.

b. The tense of the main clause may be primary or secondary without influence on the construction. Cp. 1935 and 1935 a.

2482. ὡς (ὥς τε) is followed by the indicative present (less often aorist) or by the subjunctive. Thus, ὡς δὲ πατὴρ οὗ παιδὸς ὀδύρεται ὀστέα καίων . . . , ὣς Ἀχιλεὺς ἑτάροιο ὀδύρετο ὀστέα καίων *and as a father waileth when he burneth the bones of his son, so Achilles wailed as he burned the bones of his comrade* Ψ 222.

2483. ὡς is common in Homer with the subjunctive (without ἄν) depending on the verb of the introductory clause, which is usually past. The simile may begin with ὡς or with a demonstrative (οἱ or τούς) after which ὥς τε is placed. Thus, ὡς δὲ λέων μήλοισιν ἀσημάντοισιν ἐπελθὼν . . . κακὰ φρονέων ἐνορούσῃ, ὣς μὲν Θρήικας ἄνδρας ἐπῴχετο Τῡδέος υἱός *and as a lion, coming on flocks without a shepherd, with evil purpose leaps upon them, so the son of Tydeus attacked the men of Thrace* K 485, οἱ δ', ὥς τ' αἰγυπιοὶ . . . πέτρῃ ἐφ' ὑψηλῇ μεγάλα κλάζοντε μάχωνται, ὣς οἱ κεκλήγοντες ἐπ' ἀλλήλοισιν ὄρουσαν *and they, like vultures who contend with loud screams on a lofty cliff, even so they rushed screaming against each other* Π 429. After the subjunctive with ὡς or ὡς ὅτε an independent indicative may follow (M 167, Π 296).

2484. ὡς εἰ, commonly ὡς εἴ τε, in Homer is used rarely with the indicative and subjunctive, more frequently with the optative; but usually without any finite verb. Thus, λᾱοὶ ἕπονθ' ὡς εἴ τε μετὰ κτίλον ἕσπετο μῆλα *the soldiers followed as sheep follow after the ram* N 492 (the only occurrence in Homer of the indicative), καί με φίλησ' ὡς εἴ τε πατὴρ ὃν παῖδα φιλήσῃ *and he loved me as a father loveth his son* I 481 (the only occurrence in Homer of the subjunctive), δόκησε δ' ἄρα σφίσι θῡμὸς ὣς ἔμεν, ὡς εἰ πατρίδ' ἱκοίατο *and their feeling seemed to be as* (it would be) *if they had come to their own country* κ 416 (the optative occurs only after a past tense, except Λ 389, a negative present); τὼ δέ οἱ ὄσσε λαμπέσθην ὡς εἴ τε πυρὸς σέλας *and his eyes flashed like gleaming fire* Τ 366.

2485. Attic poetry does not use the Epic and Lyric ὡς εἴ τε for ὡς εἰ. In Attic ὡς εἰ (ὡσεί) is practically equivalent to ὡς *as, like;* thus, ἀλλ' οὖν εὐνοίᾳ γ' αὐδῶ, μάτηρ ὡσεί τις πιστά *but at any rate I speak in good-will at least as some faithful mother* S. El. 234.

2486. ὡς ὅτε, ὡς ὁπότε are used with the indicative (present or aorist) or the subjunctive (as in general conditions). With the subjunctive ἄν is generally absent in Homer; but ὡς δ' ὅτ' ἄν (never κέν) occurs. The clause with ὡς ὅτε, ὡς ὁπότε generally precedes the main clause. ὡς ὅτε without appreciable difference from ὡς in 'Εριφύλᾱν, ὅρκιον ὡς ὅτε πιστόν, δόντες Οἰκλείδᾳ γυναῖκα *having given to the son of Oecles Eriphyle to wife, as a sure pledge* Pind. Nem. 9. 16.

2487. A relative pronoun referring to a substantive accompanied by ὡς, ὥστε *as* often takes the subjunctive (without ἄν). Thus, ὁ δ' ἐν κονίῃσι χαμαὶ πέσεν αἴγειρος ὥς, ἥ ῥά τ' ἐν εἱαμενῇ ἕλεος μεγάλοιο πεφύκῃ λείη *and he fell to the ground amid the dust like a poplar that has grown up smooth in the lowland of a great marsh* Δ 483.

ADJECTIVE CLAUSES (RELATIVE CLAUSES: 2488–2573)

2488. Relative clauses correspond to attributive adjectives (or participles), since like adjectives they serve to define substantives. Like adjectives, too, they often have the value of substantives and stand in any case.

ὃν γὰρ θεοὶ φιλοῦσιν (= ὁ θεοφιλής), ἀποθνήσκει νέος *for whom the gods love, dies young* Men. Sent. 425, ἦ θίγω δῆθ' οἵ μ' ἔφῡσαν; (= τῶν με φῡσάντων) *am I to embrace him who begat me?* E. Ion 560, σὺν τοῖς θησαυροῖς οἷς ὁ πατὴρ κατέλιπεν (= τοῖς ὑπὸ τοῦ πατρὸς καταλειφθεῖσι) *with the treasures which my father left* X. C. 3. 1. 33, ἐν αὐτοῖς οἷς ἐτῑμᾶσθε (= ἐν αὐταῖς ταῖς τῑμαῖς) *in the very honours which you received* D. 19. 238, ὧν ἔλαβεν ἅπᾱσι μετέδωκεν *it shared with all what it received* I. 4. 29.

2489. Relative clauses are introduced by relative pronouns or by relative adverbs of *time, place,* or *manner* (cp. 340, 346), and refer to an antecedent expressed or implied in the main clause.

a. Temporal clauses, which are like relative clauses in many respects, have been treated in 2389 ff. On relatives used as indirect interrogatives and as exclamations, see 2668 ff., 2685 ff.

2490. Many relative clauses are equivalent to coördinate clauses (*e.g.* 2553). In such cases the relative has the force of a demonstrative or personal pronoun with a connective (καί, ἀλλά, δέ, γάρ, οὖν, ἄρα, etc.). Thus, πῶς οὖν ἂν ἔνοχος εἴη τῇ γραφῇ; ὃς (= οὗτος γὰρ) . . . φανερὸς ἦν θεραπεύων τοὺς θεοὺς *how then could he be subject to the indictment? For he manifestly worshipped the gods* X. M. 1. 2. 64. Greek often uses here the demonstrative (contrast ταῦτα δὲ εἰπών with *quae cum dixisset*).

2491. A relative must often be resolved into a conjunction and a pronoun (2555).

2492. A truly subordinate relative clause may precede the main clause or be incorporated into it (2536). The relative clause is often made emphatic by placing after it the main clause with the demonstrative antecedent. Thus, ὅ τι βούλεται, τοῦτο ποιείτω *whatever he wants, that let him do* P. Eu. 285 e.

2493. **ὅς** *who* and the other simple relatives (*e.g.* οἷος, ὅσος) refer to a particular and individual person or thing.

ἦν τις ἐν τῇ στρατιᾷ Ξενοφῶν Ἀθηναῖος, ὃς οὔτε στρατηγὸς οὔτε στρατιώτης ὢν συνηκολούθει *there was in the army one Xenophon, an Athenian, who accompanied it though he was neither general nor soldier* X. A. 3. 1. 4.

a. On the relation of the relative ὅς to the demonstrative ὅς, see 1113, 1114.

b. ὅς is often used instead of ὅστις (or οἷος) especially with ἄν or μή. Cp. 2508. ὅς *whoever* with the indicative generally adds (in prose) δή ποτε, δή ποτ' οὖν (339 e).

2494. **ὅ** (sometimes ἅ) at the beginning of a sentence may have the force of *as to what* (cp. *quod*), suggesting the matter to which it pertains.

ὃ δ' ἐζήλωσας ἡμᾶς, ὡς τοὺς μὲν φίλους . . . εὖ ποιεῖν δυνάμεθα . . ., οὐδὲ ταῦθ' οὕτως ἔχει *as to what excited your envy of us—that we are able to benefit our friends—not even is this as you suppose* X. Hi. 6. 12. The postponed antecedent may be omitted (X. A. 6. 1. 29).

a. An introductory relative clause with ὅ may stand in apposition to an entire clause that follows. Thus, ὃ πάντων θαυμαστότατον, Σωκράτη μεθύοντα οὐδεὶς πώποτε ἑώρᾱκεν ἀνθρώπων *what is most wonderful, no one whatsoever ever saw Socrates drunk* P. S. 220 a. (So with an infinitive, I. 14. 18.) The main clause, following such a relative clause, may be introduced by ὅτι or γάρ. Thus, ὃ μὲν πάντων θαυμαστότατον ἀκοῦσαι, ὅτι ἓν ἕκαστον ὧν ἐπηνέσαμεν ἀπόλλῡσι τὴν ψῡχήν *what is most wonderful of all to hear,* (that) *each one of the things we approved ruins the soul* P. R. 491 b. Cp. 994, 995.

2495. **ὅσπερ** *the same as* (*qui quidem*) is especially definite and denotes identity (338 c). **ὅς γε** (*quippe qui*) is causal (2555 a).

2496. **ὅστις** *whoever* and the other compound relatives (*e.g.* ὁποῖος, ὁπόσος) denote a person or thing in general, or mark the *class, character, quality,* or *capacity* of a person (less often of a thing).

μακάριος ὅστις οὐσίᾱν καὶ νοῦν ἔχει *happy is the man who possesses property and sense* Men. Sent. 340.

a. After a negative expressed or implied, ὅστις (not ὅς) is used because of its general meaning. So οὐκ ἔστιν ὅστις, τίς ἐστιν ὅστις; οὐδείς ἐστιν ὅστις (rarely οὔτις ἐστὶν ὅς), πᾶς ὅστις (plural usually πάντες ὅσοι). Cp. 2557.

b. ἐξ ὅτου is common for ἐξ οὗ *since*. In Ionic (and Thuc. 6. 3) ὅστις is used of a definite object. Cp. Hdt. 1. 7, 2. 99.

2497. **οἷος** *of such sort as to, proper for,* and **ὅσος** *of such amount as* *to, enough for,* denote result and commonly take the infinitive (negative μή).

καλόν τε (δοκεῖ) εἶναι ἡ ἐπιστήμη καὶ οἷον ἄρχειν τοῦ ἀνθρώπου *knowledge seems to be both a noble thing and able to command man* P. Prot. 352 c, ὅσον μόνον γεύσασθαι ἑαυτῷ καταλιπών *leaving himself only enough to taste* X. A. 7. 3. 22. So οἷός τε *able to* (for τοιοῦτος οἷός τε); thus, συμβουλεύειν οἷοί τ' ἐσόμεθα *we shall be able to give counsel* P. G. 455 d.

a. On clauses with οἷος or ὅσος following a main clause after which we supply a verb of *reflection*, see 2687.

b. ὅσος is used elliptically in ὅσαι ἡμέραι (ὁσημέραι) *daily,* ὅσα ἔτη *yearly.*

2498. Local clauses are introduced by the relative adverbs οὗ, ὅπου, ἔνθα, ἵνα (usually poetic, but sometimes in Plato) *where,* οἷ, ὅποι, ἔνθα *whither,* ὅθεν, ὁπόθεν, ἔνθεν *whence,* ᾗ, ὅπῃ *which way, where, whither.* ὅθι and ὁπόθι *where* are Epic and Lyric, ἧχι *where* is Epic. ἔνθα and ἔνθεν are also demonstratives (*there, thence*).

2499. With names of things the relative adverbs **ἔνθα, ᾗ, ὅθεν, οἷ, οὗ** are often used instead of the relative pronouns preceded by ἐν, εἰς, ἐξ. Thus, πλησίον ἦν ὁ σταθμὸς ἔνθα (= εἰς ὅν) ἔμελλε καταλύειν *the stopping-place was near where he intended to make a halt* X. A. 1. 8. 1, ἐν τῷ σταθμῷ . . . ὅθεν (= ἐξ οὗ) ὡρμῶντο *at the stopping-place whence they set out* 2. 1. 3. A relative adverb may also refer to a personal antecedent, as καταβαίνειν πρὸς τοὺς ἄλλους ἔνθα τὰ ὅπλα ἔκειντο *to descend to the others where the armed force was stationed* X. A. 4. 2. 20.

2500. On comparative clauses of manner introduced by **ὡς, ὥσπερ** etc., see 2463 ff.

CONCORD OF RELATIVE PRONOUNS

2501. A relative pronoun agrees with its antecedent in gender, number, and person; its case is determined by the construction of the clause in which it stands.

οὗτός ἐστιν ὁ ἀνὴρ ὃς ἦλθε *this is the man who came,* αὕτη ἐστὶν ἡ γυνὴ ἣν ἐζητοῦμεν *this is the woman whom we were looking for,* λαβὼν τοὺς ἱππέας οἳ ἦσαν αὐτῷ *taking the cavalry which he had,* ἔχων τοὺς ὁπλίτας ὧν ἐστρατήγει *having the hoplites which he commanded,* τριῶν θυρῶν οὐσῶν, ἃς ἔδει με διελθεῖν *there being three doors through which I had to go.*

a. If the main clause as a whole is regarded as the antecedent, the relative stands in the neuter singular with or without a demonstrative. Thus, πλεῖν ἐπὶ Σελῑνοῦντα πάσῃ τῇ στρατιᾷ, ἐφ' ὅπερ μάλιστα ἐπέμφθησαν *to sail for Selinus with all their force, for which purpose especially they had been sent* T. 6. 47.

b. The person of the verb in a relative clause, in which the relative pronoun is the subject, is regularly determined by the person of the antecedent pronoun expressed or implied. Thus, οὐκ οἶδ' ὅστις ἄνθρωπος γεγένημαι *I do not know what sort of a person I have become* X. C. 1. 4. 12, καὶ οἰκίᾱ γε πολὺ μείζων ἡ ὑμετέρᾱ τῆς ἐμῆς, οἵ γε οἰκίᾳ χρῆσθε γῇ τε καὶ οὐρανῷ *and your habitation is much larger than mine since you occupy both heaven and earth as a habitation* 5. 2. 15. The third person rarely follows a vocative (P 248).

2502. Variations from the law of agreement are, in general, the same as in the case of other pronouns (926).

a. The construction according to sense (950, 1013) often occurs, as φίλον θάλος, ὃν τέκον αὐτή *my dear child, whom I myself bore* X 87; so with collective nouns, as τὰ δόξαντα πλήθει, οἵπερ δικάσουσι *what is approved by the multitude, who will judge* P. Phae. 260 a.

b. A relative in the plural may follow a singular antecedent denoting a whole class: θησαυροποιὸς ἀνήρ, οὓς . . . ἐπαινεῖ τὸ πλῆθος *a man who lays up a store*, the class of men *which the multitude approves* P. R. 554 a. This construction is less common in prose than in poetry; as ἦ μάλα τις θεὸς ἔνδον, οἳ οὐρανὸν εὐρὺν ἔχουσιν *in truth there is within some one of the gods who occupy the wide heaven* r 40.

c. A relative in the singular having a collective force may have its antecedent in the plural; as τούτους ἐπαινεῖν, ὃς ἂν ἑκὼν μηδὲν κακὸν ποιῇ *to commend those who voluntarily do nothing evil* P. Pr. 345 d, ᾧτινι ἐντυγχάνοιεν . . . πάντας ἔκτεινον *they slew all whom they met* X. A. 2. 5. 32. Here ὅς with the indicative is rare.

d. The relative may stand in the neuter, in agreement with the notion implied in the antecedent rather than with the antecedent itself; as διὰ τὴν πλεονεξίᾱν, ὃ πᾶσα φύσις διώκειν πέφῡκεν ὡς ἀγαθόν *for the sake of profit*, a thing *which every nature is inclined to pursue as a good* P. R. 359 c.

e. The relative may agree in gender and number, not with the antecedent but with a following predicate noun. This is common with verbs of *naming;* as λόγοι μήν εἰσιν ἐν ἑκάστοις ἡμῶν, ἃς ἐλπίδας ὀνομάζομεν; *assuredly there are propositions in each of us which we call hopes?* P. Phil. 40 a, εἶπεν ὅτι . . . διαγεγένηται πράττων τὰ δίκαια καὶ τῶν ἀδίκων ἀπεχόμενος, ἥνπερ νομίζοι καλλίστην μελέτην ἀπολογίᾱς εἶναι *he said that he had continued to do what was just and to refrain from what was unjust, which he thought was the best practice for his defence* X. M. 4. 8. 4.

f. A relative may agree with a predicate noun when it follows that noun immediately and not its own substantive: καὶ δίκη ἐν ἀνθρώποις πῶς οὐ καλόν, ὃ πάντα ἡμέρωκε τὰ ἀνθρώπινα; *and justice among men, how is not that something beautiful, which civilizes all human things?* P. L. 937 d.

THE ANTECEDENT OF RELATIVE CLAUSES

2503. The demonstrative antecedents of the relative pronouns are commonly: οὗτος . . . ὅς, τοιοῦτος . . . οἷος, τοσοῦτος . . . ὅσος, τηλικοῦτος . . . ἡλίκος, etc.

a. The antecedent of ὅς is often τοιοῦτος (1249). The antecedent of ὅς, ὅσπερ, οἷος, may be ὅμοιος, παραπλήσιος, ἴσος.

2504. On comparative clauses of degree with τοσούτῳ . . . ὅσῳ, etc., see 2468 ff.

2505. Definite and Indefinite Antecedent. — The antecedent of a relative pronoun or adverb may be definite or indefinite.

a. A *definite* antecedent refers to a definite or particular person, thing, time, place, or manner. When the antecedent is definite, the relative clause takes any form that occurs in an independent sentence (921); with οὐ as the negative, unless the particular construction requires μή.

b. An *indefinite* antecedent refers to an indefinite person, thing, time, place, or manner. When the antecedent is indefinite, the relative clause commonly has a conditional force, and, if negative, takes μή like the protasis of a conditional sentence.

2506. In general when the relative clause has the indicative, the antecedent is either definite (negative οὐ) or indefinite (negative μή). When the relative clause has the subjunctive with ἄν or the optative (not in a wish), the antecedent is indefinite (negative μή).

DEFINITE: ταῦτα ἃ βούλεται πράττει *he does what he wants* (*i.e.* the particular thing he wants to do). Negative ταῦτα ἃ οὐ βούλεται πράττει.

INDEFINITE: ταῦτα ἅτινα βούλεται πράττει *he does whatever he wants* (*i.e.* if he wants to do anything, he does it); negative ταῦτα ἅτινα μὴ βούλεται πράττει. So ταῦτα ἅτινα ἂν βούληται πράττει *whatever he wants to do, that he* always *does*, ταῦτα ἅτινα βούλοιτο ἔπραττε *whatever he wanted to do, that he* always *did*, ταῦτα ἅτινα ἂν βούληται πράξει *whatever he wants to do, that he will do*, ταῦτα ἅτινα βούλοιτο, πράττοι ἂν *whatever he might want to do, that he would* (*will*) *do*. In the last four sentences the negative of the relative clause is μή.

2507. When the verb of the relative clause stands in the indicative, the distinction between a definite and indefinite antecedent is commonly clear only in negative sentences.

ἃ μὴ οἶδα οὐδὲ οἴομαι εἰδέναι *whatever I do not know* (= εἴ τινα μὴ οἶδα) *I do not even think I know* P. A. 21 d. Here ἃ οὐκ οἶδα would mean *the particular things I am ignorant of*, and would have no conditional force whatever. So in οὐκ οἶδ'· ἐφ' οἷς γὰρ μὴ φρονῶ σῑγᾶν φιλῶ *I do not know; for I am wont to be silent in matters which I do not understand* S. O. T. 569.

2508. When the antecedent is definite, the simple relatives (ὅς, οἷος, ὅσος, etc.) are used; when indefinite, the compound relatives (ὅστις, ὁποῖος, ὁπόσος, etc.) are used, but the simple relatives are often employed instead. When the antecedent is indefinite, ὅς usually has the subjunctive with ἄν or the optative; while ὅστις is preferred to ὅς if the verb is indicative (2569).

2509. Omission of the Antecedent to a Relative.—The demonstrative pronoun antecedent to a relative is often omitted: either when it is in the same case as the relative, or in a different case from the relative. The omission occurs when the antecedent expresses the general idea of person or thing, and often when the relative clause precedes.

ἐγὼ δὲ καὶ (οὗτοι) ὧν κρατῶ μενοῦμεν *but I and* those *whom I command will remain* X. C. 5. 1. 26, καλὸν τὸ θνῄσκειν οἷς (for τούτοις οἷς) ὕβριν τὸ ζῆν φέρει *death is sweet* to those *to whom life brings contumely* Men. Sent. 291, λέγω πάντας εἰσφέρειν ἀφ' ὅσων (for ἀπὸ τοσούτων ὅσα) ἕκαστος ἔχει *I say that all must contribute according to the ability of each (from such means as each man has)* D. 2. 31.

2510. In general statements in the subjunctive with ἄν or the indicative, the relative, referring to a person, is often without an antecedent and has the force of εἴ τις. In such cases the main clause contains a substantive or a neuter adjective with ἐστί (which is commonly omitted), and the relative is the subject of the sentence or in apposition to it.

συμφορᾶ δ', ὃς ἂν τύχῃ κακῆς γυναικός *it* is *a calamity if a man gets a bad wife* E. fr. 1056, καὶ τοῦτο μεῖζον τῆς ἀληθείᾱς κακόν, ὅστις τὰ μὴ προσόντα κέκτηται κακά *and this* is *a misfortune exceeding the reality, if a man incurs* the blame for *evils that are not his doing* E. Hel. 271, ὅστις . . . πρὸς θεῶν κακοῦται, βαρύ *if a man suffers ill-usage from the gods, it* is *grievous* E. Hel. 267.

a. The antecedent may be a genitive of quality (1320). Thus, ἀπόρων ἐστὶ . . ., οἵτινες ἐθέλουσι δι' ἐπιορκίᾱς . . . πράττειν τι *it is the characteristic of men without resources to wish* (lit. *who wish*) *to accomplish their purposes by perjury* X. A. 2. 5. 21 (here ἐθέλειν alone might be expected, but οἵτινες ἐθέλουσι follows as if ἄποροί εἰσιν had preceded), τοῦτο ἡγοῦμαι μέγα τεκμήριον ἄρχοντος ἀρετῆς εἶναι ᾧ ἂν (= ἐάν τινι or αὐτῷ) ἑκόντες ἕπωνται *I regard this as striking testimony to the merit of a ruler if men follow one* (*him*) *of their own free will* X. O. 4. 19.

2511. The antecedent of a neuter relative is often omitted, leaving the relative with the force of a conjunction. So ἐξ οὗ and ἀφ' οὗ *since*, ἐν ᾧ *while*, εἰς ὅ *till*, μέχρι (ἄχρι) οὗ *until*. ἀνθ' ὧν and ἐξ ὧν *because* (cp. οὕνεκα, ὁθούνεκα), ἐφ' ᾧτε *on condition that* (2279).

2512. A demonstrative adverb may be suppressed: ἄξω ὑμᾶς ἔνθα (for ἐκεῖσε ἔνθα) τὸ πρᾶγμα ἐγένετο *I will bring you* to the spot *where the affair took place* X. C. 5. 4. 21, ἀποκλείοντες ὅθεν (for ἐκεῖθεν ὅθεν) ἄν τι λαβεῖν ᾖ *shutting them out* from places *whence it may be possible to take anything* X. M. 2. 1. 16.

2513. ἔστιν ὅστις, εἰσὶν οἵ.—The antecedent is omitted in the phrases ἔστιν ὅστις (rarely ὅς) *there is some one who, somebody,* plural εἰσὶν οἵ *some* (less often ἔστιν οἵ), ἦσαν οἵ (of the past).

ἔστιν οὖν ὅστις βούλεται ὑπὸ τῶν συνόντων βλάπτεσθαι; *is there then any one who wishes to be harmed by his companions?* P. A. 25 d, οὔτε . . ἔστιν οὔτ' ἔσται ὅτῳ ἐγὼ καταλείψω τὸν ἐμὸν οἶκον *there neither is nor will there be any one to whom I may leave my property* X. C. 5. 4. 30, εἰσὶ δὲ καὶ οἳ . . . φεύγουσιν *some* horses *too run away* X. Eq. 3. 4, εἰσὶ δ' αὐτῶν οὓς οὐδ' ἂν παντάπᾱσι διαβαίητε *and some of them you would not be able even to cross at all* X. A. 2. 5. 18, ἦσαν δὲ οἳ καὶ πῦρ προσέφερον *and some brought firebrands too* 5. 2. 14, ἔστιν ὅτῳ . . . πλείω ἐπιτρέπεις ἢ τῇ γυναικί; *is there any one to whom you entrust more than to your wife?* X. O. 3. 12, ἔστιν οἳ καὶ ἐτύγχανον καὶ θωράκων καὶ γέρρων *some hit both the cuirasses and wicker-shields* X. C. 2. 3. 18. ἔστιν οἵ is not an example of 961, but due to the analogy of ἔστιν ὅτε (ἐνίοτε), ἔστιν οὗ, etc.

2514. The oblique cases of εἰσὶν οἵ *there are those who* = *some* (ἔνιοι) are regularly formed by ἔστιν ὧν, ἔστιν οἷς, ἔστιν οὕς (or οὕστινας), which are used also of the past and future.

πλὴν Ἰώνων . . . καὶ ἔστιν ὧν ἄλλων ἐθνῶν *except the Ionians and some other nations* T. 3. 92, αὐχμοὶ ἔστι παρ' οἷς μεγάλοι *great droughts among some* 1. 23, ἔστι μὲν οὓς αὐτῶν κατέβαλον *some of them they struck down* X. H. 2. 4. 6, ἔστιν ἃ καὶ πολίσματα εἷλεν *he captured also some towns* T. 1. 65.

a. Xenophon also uses ἦν οἵ; thus, τῶν δὲ πολεμίων ἦν οὓς ὑποσπόνδους ἀπέδοσαν *there were some of the enemy whom they restored under a truce* X. H. 7. 5. 17.

2515. Here belong certain idiomatic phrases due to the omission of the antecedent: **ἔστιν οὗ** (**ὅπου**) *somewhere, sometimes,* **ἔστιν ᾗ** *in some way,* **ἔστιν ὅτε** and ἐνίοτε (= ἔνι ὅτε, cp. 175 b) *sometimes,* **ἔστιν ὅπως** *somehow* (in questions = *is it possible that?*), **οὐκ ἔστιν ὅπως** *in no way, it is not possible that* (lit. *there is not how*).

ἔστι δ' οὗ σιγὴ λόγου κρείσσων γένοιτ' ἂν *but sometimes silence may prove better than speech* E. Or. 638, ἔστιν ὅτε καὶ οἷς (2514) βέλτιον τεθνάναι ἢ ζῆν *sometimes and for some people it is better to die than to live* P. Ph. 62 a, οὐκ ἔσθ' ὅπως . . . ἂν ἡμᾶς ἔτι λάθοι *it is not possible that he should elude us again* A. Vesp. 212, οὐκ ἔστιν ὅπως οὐκ ἐπιθήσεται ἡμῖν *it is not possible that he will not attack us* X. A. 2. 4. 3.

2516. **οὐδὲν οἷον** (with the inf.) *there is nothing like* stands for οὐδέν ἐστι τοιοῦτον, οἷόν ἐστι. Thus, οὐδὲν οἷον τὸ αὐτὸν ἐρωτᾶν *there is nothing like questioning him* P. G. 447 c.

2517. Relative not repeated. — If two or more relative clauses referring to the same antecedent are connected by a copulative conjunction and the second relative would have to stand in a different case from the first, it is either omitted or its place is taken by αὐτός (less frequently by οὗτος or ἐκεῖνος) or a personal pronoun. Here, instead of a repeated relative, we have an independent sentence coördinated with the relative clause.

Ἀριαῖος, ὃν ἡμεῖς ἠθέλομεν βασιλέᾱ καθιστάναι, καὶ (ᾧ) ἐδώκαμεν καὶ (παρ' οὗ) ἐλάβομεν πιστὰ . . . ἡμᾶς κακῶς ποιεῖν πειρᾶται *Ariaeus, whom we wished to set up as king, and to whom we gave, and from whom we received pledges, is attempting to injure us* X. A. 3. 2. 5, ποῦ δὴ ἐκεῖνός ἐστιν ὁ ἀνὴρ ὃς συνεθήρᾱ ἡμῖν καὶ σύ μοι μάλα ἐδόκεις θαυμάζειν αὐτόν; *where, pray, is that man who used to hunt with us and whom you seemed to me to admire greatly?* X. C. 3. 1. 38, καὶ νῦν τί χρὴ δρᾶν; ὅστις ἐμφανῶς θεοῖς ἐχθαίρομαι, μῑσεῖ δέ μ' Ἑλλήνων στρατὸς *and now what must I do? Since I* (lit. *I who*) *am manifestly hateful to the gods, and the army of the Greeks hates me* S. Aj. 457. Cp. "Whose fan is in His hand, and He shall thoroughly purge His floor."

a. The relative is sometimes repeated as in English (X. A. 1. 7. 3, T. 2. 43. 2, 44. 1).

2518. If the demonstrative would have to stand in the nominative, it is commonly omitted unless the demands of emphasis require its presence: (τέχναις) ἃς ἐπιστήμᾱς μὲν πολλάκις προσείπομεν διὰ τὸ ἔθος, δέονται δὲ ὀνόματος ἄλλου arts *which we have often called sciences because it is usual to do so, but* they *require another name* P. R. 533 d (here αὗται, not αἵ, is the subject).

2519. Preposition not repeated. — A preposition governing a relative pronoun is usually omitted if it stands in the same case as the preceding noun or pronoun before which the preposition has already been used. See 1671.

2520. Verb omitted. — The verb of a relative clause is often omitted when it belongs also to the main clause.

φίλους νομίζουσ' οὕσπερ ἂν πόσις σέθεν (νομίζῃ φίλους) *regarding as friends those whom thy husband* so regards E. Med. 1153. Or the verb of the main clause may be omitted: τὰ γὰρ ἄλλα (ἐποίει) ὅσαπερ καὶ ὑμεῖς ἐποιεῖτε *for the rest* he did *just what you too were doing* X. C. 4. 1. 3.

2521. Transition from a relative to an independent clause sometimes occurs.

(ἰχθύων) οὓς οἱ Σύροι θεοὺς ἐνόμιζον καὶ ἀδικεῖν οὐκ εἴων, οὐδὲ τὰς περιστεράς fish *which the Syrians regard as gods and* which *they will not permit to be injured, nor* do they permit *the doves* to be injured X. A. 1. 4. 9.

2522. Attraction. — A relative pronoun is often attracted from its proper case into the case of its antecedent, especially from the accusative into the genitive or dative. A demonstrative pronoun to whose case the relative is attracted, is usually omitted if unemphatic. Cp. "Vengeance is his, or whose he sole appoints:" Milton.

a. **Genitive.** — ἄξιοι τῆς ἐλευθερίας ἧς (for ἣν) κέκτησθε *worthy of the freedom which you possess* X. A. 1. 7. 3, πρὸ τῶν κακῶν ὧν (for ἃ) οἶδα *instead of the evils which I know* P. A. 29 b, ἀφ' ὧν (for τούτων ἃ) ἴστε *from what you know* D. 19. 216, Μήδων ὅσων (for ὅσους) ἑώρακα . . . ὁ ἐμὸς πάππος κάλλιστος *my grandfather is the handsomest of* all *the Medes I have seen* X. C. 1. 3. 2, μὴ ὑποκειμένων οἵων δεῖ θεμελίων (for τοιούτων οἷα δεῖ ὑποκεῖσθαι) *if the foundations were not as they ought to be* X. Eq. 1. 2.

b. **Dative.** — φοβοίμην ἂν τῷ ἡγεμόνι ᾧ (for ὃν) δοίη ἕπεσθαι *I should fear to follow the leader whom he might give* X. A. 1. 3. 17, ἐπαινῶ σε ἐφ' οἷς (for ἐπὶ τούτοις ἃ) λέγεις *I commend you for what you say* 3. 1. 45, οἷς (for τούτοις ἃ) ηὐτυχήκεσαν ἐν Λεύκτροις οὐ μετρίως ἐκέχρηντο *they had not used with moderation the success they gained at Leuctra* D. 18. 18.

2523. A relative in the nominative or dative is very rarely attracted. Thus, βλάπτεσθαι ἀφ' ὧν (for ἀπὸ ἐκείνων ἃ) ἡμῖν παρεσκεύασται *to be harmed by what has been prepared by us* T. 7. 67, ὀλίγοι ὧν (for τούτων οἷς) ἐγὼ ἐντετύχηκα *a few of those whom I have met with* P. R. 531 e.

2524. The pronouns subject to attraction are ὅς, οἷος, ὅσος, but not ὅστις (except in 2534). Attraction is not *necessary*, and takes place only (but not always) when the relative clause is essential to complete the meaning of the antecedent. When the relative clause is added merely as a remark, attraction does not take place. An attracted relative clause virtually has the force of an attributive adjective.

2525. Predicate nouns follow the case of the relative attracted to an antecedent expressed or omitted (2531 b).

2526. An omitted antecedent to which the relative has been attracted may afterward be supplied in the main clause. Thus, ἀφ' ὧν (for ἀπὸ τούτων ἃ) . . . προσαιτεῖ καὶ δανείζεται, ἀπὸ τούτων διάγει *from what he begs and borrows, from that he lives* D. 8. 26.

2527. Before βούλει, which with the relative is treated almost like one word (cp. *quivis*), attraction to various cases from the accusative is rare. Thus, οἷα τούτων ὃς (for ὃν) βούλει εἴργασται *such deeds as any one you please of these has done* P. G. 517 a; cp. P. Crat. 432 a, Phil. 43 d.

2528. Attraction takes place also in the case of relative adverbs; as διεκομίζοντο ὅθεν (for ἐκεῖθεν οἷ) ὑπεξέθεντο παῖδας *they conveyed their children from the places where (whither) they had deposited them* T. 1. 89.

2529. Case of the Relative with Omitted Antecedent. — When the antecedent is omitted the relative either retains its own case or is attracted.

2530. When the omitted antecedent is nominative or accusative, the relative retains its own case. Thus, οἷς μάλιστα τὰ παρόντα ἀρκεῖ (οὗτοι) ἥκιστα τῶν ἀλλοτρίων ὀρέγονται *those who are best satisfied with what they have, covet least what is their neighbour's* X. S. 4. 42, στυγῶν μὲν ἥ (= ἐκείνην ἥ) μ' ἔτικτεν *hating* her *who bore me* E. Alc. 338.

2531. When the omitted antecedent is genitive or dative, the relative (if standing in a different case) is usually attracted into the genitive or dative. But a relative in the nominative masculine or feminine (sometimes in the neuter), or a relative depending on a preposition, retains its own case.

a. **Genitive**: ὧν (for τούτων οἷς) ἐντυγχάνω πολὺ μάλιστα ἄγαμαι σέ *of those whom I meet with, I admire you by far the most* P. Pr. 361 e, δηλοῖς δὲ καὶ ἐξ ὧν (for ἐκ τούτων ἃ) ζῇς *you show it also by the life you lead* D. 18. 198. But εἰδέναι τὴν δύναμιν (τούτων) ἐφ' οὓς ἂν ἴωσιν *to discover the strength* of those *against whom they are to proceed* X. A. 5. 1. 8. Cp. E. Ion 560 (in 2488) where οἷ = τούτων οἷ.

b. **Dative**: τοῦτο δ' ὅμοιόν ἐστιν ᾧ (for τούτῳ ὃ) νῦν δὴ ἐλέγετο *this is like that which was said just now* P. Ph. 69 a, ἐμμένομεν οἷς (for τούτοις ἃ) ὡμολογήσαμεν δικαίοις οὖσιν ἢ οὔ; *do we abide by what we agreed was just, or not?* P. Cr. 50 a. But διὰ τὸ ἀναγκαῖον αὐτοῖς εἶναι διαλέγεσθαι (τούτοις) παρ' ὧν λάβοιεν τὸν μισθὸν *because it is necessary for them to give lessons* to those *from whom they expect to receive their fee* X. M. 1. 2. 6.

2532. The relatives οἷος, ὅσος, ἡλίκος, ὅστις δή, ὁστισοῦν (and some others) and a following nominative with the copula may be attracted to the case of the antecedent. Thus, χαριζόμενος τοιούτῳ ἀνδρὶ οἷος σὺ εἶ *showing favour to such a man as you are* is commonly condensed to χαριζόμενος οἵῳ σοι ἀνδρί (X. M. 2. 9. 3). Here the whole relative clause (with copula omitted) is attracted. The antecedent, if expressed, is often incorporated (2536) in the relative clause.

πρὸς ἄνδρας τολμηροὺς οἵους καὶ Ἀθηναίους (for οἷοι καὶ Ἀθηναῖοί εἰσι) *to bold men such as the Athenians* T. 7. 21, ἀνίστη Ἀγριᾶνας . . . καὶ ἄλλα ὅσα ἔθνη Παιονικά *he called out the Agrianes and all the other Paeonian tribes* 2. 96, χειμῶνος ὄντος οἵου λέγεις *when the weather is such as you describe* X. A. 5. 8. 3, ἀνέλαμψεν οἰκίᾱ . . . ὅτου δὴ ἐνάψαντος (for ἐνάψαντός τινος ὅστις δὴ ἦν) *the house burst into flames, some one or other having set it on fire* 5. 2. 24.

a. οἷος is often attracted with superlatives: ὄντος πάγου οἵου δεινοτάτου (for τοιούτου οἷός ἐστι δεινότατος) *when the frost was tremendous* P. S. 220 b. Cp. 1087.

b. The article may appear in this construction with οἷος and ἡλίκος, the relative clause being treated like a substantive: τοῖς οἵοις ἡμῖν *to such as we are* X. H. 2. 3. 25.

c. The subject of the relative clause rarely stands in the nominative, not being attracted along with οἷος. Thus, κιναίδους οἵουσπερ σύ *rascals just like you* Aes. 2. 151. This occurs only when the number of the subject is different from that of the attracted relative. When the article precedes, as in Σόλων ἐμίσει τοὺς οἷος οὗτος ἀνθρώπους *Solon detested men like him* (D. 19. 254), editors generally read τοὺς οἵους οὗτος.

2533. Inverse Attraction. — An antecedent nominative or (oftener) accusative may be attracted to the case of the relative. The attracted antecedent is often prefixed for emphasis to the relative clause, which thus separates it from the verb it governs or by which it is governed. Cp. *urbem quam statuo vestra est*, and "Him (= he whom) I accuse, By this, the city ports hath enter'd" (Shakespeare), where the antecedent is attracted into the case of the (omitted) relative.

τάσδε (for αἵδε) δ' ἅσπερ εἰσορᾷς . . . χωροῦσι *but the women whom thou seest are coming* S. Tr. 283, πολῑτείᾱν (for πολῑτείᾱ) οἵᾱν εἶναι χρὴ παρὰ μόνοις ἡμῖν ἐστιν *we alone have an ideal constitution* (lit. *such as ought to be*) I. 6. 48, ἔλεγον ὅτι Λακεδαιμόνιοι ὧν δέονται πάντων (for πάντα) πεπρᾱγότες εἶεν *they said that the Lacedaemonians had gained all they asked for* X. H. 1. 4. 2.

a. The main clause may contain a resumptive demonstrative pronoun; as τὸν ἄνδρα τοῦτον, ὃν πάλαι ζητεῖς . . ., οὗτός ἐστιν ἐνθάδε *this man whom you have long been searching for, this man is here* S. O. T. 449.

b. The rare cases of the inverse attraction of the dative are suspected or admit another explanation (E. Med. 12, S. El. 653, X. Hi. 7. 2).

c. So with adverbs: καὶ ἄλλοσε (for ἄλλοθι) ὅποι ἂν ἀφίκῃ ἀγαπήσουσί σε *and elsewhere, wherever you go, they will love you* P. Cr. 45 c.

2534. οὐδεὶς ὅστις οὐ *every one* (lit. *nobody who not*) for οὐδείς ἐστιν ὅστις οὐ, commonly shows inverse attraction, is treated like a single pronoun, and inflected οὐδενὸς ὅτου οὐ, οὐδενὶ ὅτῳ οὐ, οὐδένα ὅντινα οὐ.

οὐδενὸς ὅτου οὐχὶ ἀλογώτερον *than which there is nothing more irrational* P. Charm. 175 c, οὐδενὶ ὅτῳ οὐκ ἀποκρῑνόμενος *replying to every one* P. Men. 70 c, περὶ ὧν οὐδένα κίνδῡνον ὅντιν' οὐχ ὑπέμειναν οἱ πρόγονοι *for which our ancestors underwent every danger* D. 18. 200.

a. Cp. οὐδαμῶν Ἑλληνικῶν τῶν οὐ πολλὸν μέζω his power *was much greater than any Hellenic power* Hdt. 7. 145 (= οὐδαμά ἐστι τῶν), οὐδαμῶς ὡς οὐ φήσομεν *it can in no wise be that we should say no* P. Pol. 308 b.

2535. ὅσος preceded by an Adjective. — Here the subject of the relative clause is identical with that of the main clause, and is omitted together with the copula: χρήματα ἔλαβε θαυμαστὰ ὅσα (for θαυμαστόν ἐστιν ὅσα) *he received a wonderful amount of money* P. Hipp. M. 282 c, μετὰ ἱδρῶτος θαυμαστοῦ ὅσου (for θαυμαστόν ἐστιν μεθ' ὅσου) *with an astonishing amount of sweat* P. R. 350 d. So θαυμασίως ὡς (for θαυμαστόν ἐστιν ὡς) P. Ph. 92 a.

2536. Incorporation. — The antecedent taken up into the relative clause is said to be incorporated. The relative and antecedent then stand in the same case, the relative agreeing adjectively with its antecedent. If the antecedent is a substantive, it often stands at the end of the relative clause, and commonly has no article. An antecedent in the nominative or accusative is more frequently incorporated than one in the genitive or dative.

2537. A nominative, accusative, or vocative antecedent, when incorporated, usually conforms to the case of the relative.

εἰ ἔστιν, ἣν σὺ πρότερον ἔλεγες ἀρετήν, ἀληθής (for ἔστιν ἡ ἀρετὴ ἀληθής, ἥν) *if the virtue which you were speaking of before, is real* P. G. 503 c, εἰς δὲ ἣν ἀφίκοντο κώμην μεγάλη ἦν (for ἡ κώμη εἰς ἥν) *the village at which they arrived was large* X. A. 4. 4. 2, κλῦθί μευ, ὃ χθιζὸς θεὸς ἤλυθες (for θεὸς ὁ or ὦ θεός) *hear me thou that camest yesterday in thy godhead* β 262.

a. An accusative antecedent is incorporated in the accusative when the verb of the relative clause takes the accusative. Thus, οὐκ ἀπεκρύπτετο ἣν εἶχε γνώμην (for τὴν γνώμην ἥν) *he did not conceal the opinion he had* X. M. 4. 4. 1, μηδ' . . . ἀφέλησθε ὑμῶν αὐτῶν ἣν διὰ παντὸς ἀεὶ τοῦ χρόνου δόξαν κέκτησθε καλήν (for τὴν καλὴν δόξαν ἥν) *do not deprive yourselves of the fair fame which you have enjoyed throughout all time* D. 20. 142.

b. An accusative antecedent may be incorporated as nominative, genitive, or dative, *e.g.* εἴ τινα ὁρῴη . . . κατασκευάζοντα ἧς ἄρχοι χώρᾱς (for τὴν χώρᾱν ἧς ἄρχοι) *if ever he saw any one improving the district which he governed* X. A. 1. 9. 19.

2538. A genitive or dative antecedent, when incorporated, usually attracts the relative to its own case.

περὶ δ' οὗ πρότερον . . . ἔθηκε νόμου διελθών (for τοῦ νόμου ὅν) *dealing in detail with the law which he formerly passed* D. 24. 61, ἐπορεύετο σὺν ᾗ εἶχε δυνάμει (for σὺν τῇ δυνάμει ἥν) *he advanced with what force he had* X. H. 4. 1. 23. Even when the antecedent is omitted, the attraction takes place: πρὸς ᾧ εἶχε συνέλεγε . . . στράτευμα (for πρὸς τούτῳ τῷ στρατεύματι ὅ) *he was collecting an army in addition to that which he had* X. H. 4. 1. 41.

a. But a genitive or dative antecedent, when incorporated, is attracted into the case of a *nominative* relative. Thus, ἐν δικαστηρίοις καὶ ὅσοι ἄλλοι δημόσιοι σύλλογοι (sc. εἰσί) *in courts and all the other public assemblies* P. Phae. 261 a (for τοσούτοις ἄλλοις συλλόγοις, ὅσοι δημόσιοί εἰσι).

b. When an antecedent in the genitive or dative is incorporated, the place of the antecedent is usually taken by a demonstrative pronoun in the genitive or dative. Thus, οὐδέ νυ τῶν περ μέμνηαι, ὅσα δὴ πάθομεν κακά *nor do you remember all the evils we suffered* Φ 441.

OTHER PECULIARITIES OF RELATIVE CLAUSES

2539. Appositives to the antecedent may be drawn into the relative clause as the nearest construction or for the sake of emphasis. Thus, εὑρήσει τοὺς . . . δικαστάς, οἵπερ καὶ λέγονται ἐκεῖ δικάζειν, Μίνως τε καὶ Ῥαδάμανθυς κτλ. *he will find the judges, who are said to pronounce judgment there, Minos and Rhadamanthys*, etc. P. A. 41 a.

2540. A substantive, usually with the article, is often taken over into the relative clause, to explain, by a necessary addition, the idea conveyed by that clause; and stands in the same case as the relative. Thus, εἰ μανθάνεις ὃ βούλομαι λέγειν τὸ εἶδος *if you understand the class I wish to describe* P. R. 477 c, οὔτε αὐτοὶ οὔτε οὓς φαμεν ἡμῖν παιδευτέον εἶναι τοὺς φύλακας *neither ourselves nor the guardians whom we say we must instruct* 402 c.

2541. The antecedent may be reserved for the main clause, which follows the relative clause. Thus, καθ' οὓς μὲν ἀπήχθην, οὐκ ἔνοχός εἰμι τοῖς νόμοις *I am not subject to the laws in virtue of which I was arrested* Ant. 5. 85.

2542. An attributive adjective, or an attributive genitive belonging to a substantive standing in the main clause, may be placed either in the relative clause (if either is emphatic) or in the main clause. Two adjectives may be divided between the two clauses. The substantives may remain in the main clause or be transferred to the relative clause. Thus, τὸ τείχισμα ὃ ἦν αὐτόθι τῶν Συρᾱκοσίων αἱροῦσι *they captured the fort of the Syracusans which was there* T. 7. 43, ὧν ἐγὼ ἤθελον τούτῳ ταύτην ἥτις εἴη μεγίστη πίστις δοῦναι *of which I was willing to offer to the plaintiff the assurance that was most solemn* D. 52. 12, ἐπιδεῖξαι . . . τὴν δικαίᾱν ἥτις ἐστὶν ἀπολογίᾱ *to show what the fair line of defence is* 19. 203, ἔφρῖξεν δὲ μάχη . . . ἐγχείῃσιν μακρῇς, ᾶς εἶχον ταμεσίχροας *and the battle bristled with the long spears, the flesh-piercing spears, which they grasped* N 339.

a. From the transference of superlatives to the relative clause arise such expressions as ἤγαγον συμμάχους ὁπόσους πλείστους ἐδυνάμην (1087). Similarly ὡς τάχιστα (scil. δύνασαι or the like) *as soon as, as soon as possible*, ἐπεὶ (ὅτε) τάχιστα *as soon as*.

2543. A participial or subordinate clause depending on a following main clause may be joined to a preceding clause containing the antecedent of the relative. Thus, ἔφη εἶναι ἄκρον ὃ εἰ μή τις προκαταλήψοιτο, ἀδύνατον ἔσεσθαι παρελθεῖν *he said that there was a height which would be impossible to pass, unless it was seized in advance* X. A. 4. 1. 25. The case of the relative may be not that required by its own verb, but that of an omitted pronoun dependent on a participle or a subordinate verb inserted in the relative clause. Thus, καταλαμβάνουσι τεῖχος . . . ὅ ποτε Ἀκαρνᾶνες τειχισάμενοι κοινῷ δικαστηρίῳ ἐχρῶντο (for ᾧ ἐχρῶντο τειχισάμενοι αὐτό) *they seized a fortress which the Acarnanians once built and used as a common place of judgment* T. 3. 105.

2544. When the relative clause contains a verb of *naming*, the main clause is fused with the relative clause. Thus, ἔνθα καλεῖται Ἀρτέμιδος τέμενος (for ἔνθα τέμενός ἐστι, ὃ καλεῖται Ἀρτέμιδος) *where there is a precinct of Artemis* Simonides 107.

USE OF THE MOODS IN RELATIVE CLAUSES

2545. The ordinary uses of the moods in relative clauses are as follows:

a. The present and past tenses of the indicative without ἄν express a fact or the assumption of a fact. The future indicative is used to denote purpose, present intention, or an intended result.

b. The indicative with ἄν denotes unreality.

c. The subjunctive with ἄν expresses a possible or supposed fact in future time or a generality in present time. The subjunctive without ἄν is used in indirect questions (1805 b).

d. The optative without ἄν expresses a wish, a possibility less distinctly conceived, or a generality in past time.

e. The optative with ἄν is potential, and is used either in conditional relative clauses with an optative in the main clause, or alone, as μί' ἔστιν ἐλπίς, ᾗ μόνῃ σωθεῖμεν ἄν *there is one hope by which alone we may be saved* E. Hel. 815.

f. The imperative occurs in relative clauses (1842, 2553).

g. The infinitive occurs in relative clauses in indirect discourse (2631).

THE USE OF THE MOODS IN CERTAIN RELATIVE CLAUSES

2546. An extension of the deliberative subjunctive not infrequently occurs in relative clauses after such expressions as οὐκ ἔχω, οὐκ ἔστι, etc., which usually denote baffled will, the existence of an obstacle to carrying out an act desired by the speaker or some one else. The subjunctive is much less common after the positive ἔχω *I have the means.* The pronoun or adverb introducing such clause is an interrogative that has taken on the function of a relative.

2547. The subjunctive here follows primary tenses; the optative follows secondary tenses.

a. οὐ τοῦτο δέδοικα μὴ οὐκ ἔχω ὅ τι δῶ ἑκάστῳ τῶν φίλων . . ., ἀλλὰ μὴ οὐκ ἔχω ἱκανοὺς οἷς δῶ *I do not fear that I shall not have something to give to each of my friends, but that I shall not have enough friends to give to* X. A. 1. 7. 7, οὐχ ἕξουσιν ἐκεῖνοι ὅποι φύγωσιν *they will not have* any place *whither to escape* 2. 4. 20, οὐκέτ' εἰσὶν ἐλπίδες ὅποι τραπόμενος θάνατον . . . φύγω *I have no longer any hopes to which I may turn and escape death* E. Or. 722, ἕξει ὅ τι λέγῃ *he will be able to say something* L. 6. 42.

b. οὐδένα γὰρ εἶχον ὅστις . . . τὰς ἐμὰς ἐπιστολὰς πέμψειε *for I had no one to bring my letter* E. I. T. 588.

c. Attic never, or rarely, has the *positive* forms ἔχω ὅ τι ἄν, ἔστιν ὅς ἄν (K 170), πέμπω ὅστις ἄν, with the potential optative.

2548. The subjunctive *with* κέ in Homer does not involve *will* in οὐκ ἔσθ' οὗτος ἀνὴρ . . . οὐδὲ γένηται, ὅς κεν Φαιήκων . . . ἐς γαῖαν ἵκηται *that man lives not nor will ever be born who shall come to the land of the Phaeacians* ζ 202; cp. δ 756, Ψ 345. Φ 103 involves a different aspect of *will* from that in 2547 a.

2549. The deliberative future (1916) occurs in relative clauses; as ὅπως μολούμεθ' ἐς δόμους οὐκ ἔχω *I do not know how we are to go home* S. O. C. 1742.

The deliberative subjunctive is more common; as *οὐκ ἔχω ὅ τι χρήσωμαι τοῖς λόγοις I am not able to deal with your argument* P. Eu. 287 c.

2550. In a few cases the future is used like the subjunctives of 2547 a; and may be explained as a dependent deliberative future. Thus, *οὐ γάρ τις ὅρμος ἔστιν, οὐδ' ὅποι πλέων ἐξεμπολήσει κέρδος for there is no harbour, nor is there* any place *to which a man may voyage and sell his wares at a profit* S. Ph. 303, *αὐτὸν γάρ σε δεῖ προμηθέως ὅτῳ τρόπῳ τῆσδ' ἐκκυκλισθήσει τύχης for thou thyself hast need of forethought whereby thou shalt extricate thyself from this trouble* A. Pr. 86.

2551. οὐκ ἔστιν ὅς (ὅπως, ὅπου, ὡς) are used with the future indicative to introduce *statements* as regards the future. Thus, *οὐ γάρ τις ἔστιν ὃς πάροιθ' αἱρήσεται τὴν σὴν ἀχρεῖον δύναμιν ἀντ' Εὐρυσθέως there is no one who will prefer thy feeble power rather than Eurystheus* E. Heracl. 57, *οὐκ ἔσθ' ὅπως ὄψει σὺ δεῦρ' ἐλθόντα με thou wilt in no wise* (lit. *it is not possible how thou shalt*) *see me coming here* S. Ant. 329. The indicative present or aorist is also used in statements as regards the present or past. All these indicatives may be dependent deliberatives. Cp. 2557.

2552. The optative without *ἄν* (probably potential) occurs in Attic poetry after *οὐκ ἔστιν ὅστις* (*ὅπως, ὅποι*) and the interrogative *τίς ἐστὶν ὅς* (*ὅστις*) and *ἔσθ' ὅπως*. Thus, *οὐκ ἔστιν ὅστις πλὴν ἐμοῦ κείραιτό νιν there is no one except myself who could cut it* A. Ch. 172, *οὐκ ἔσθ' ὅπως λέξαιμι τὰ ψευδῆ καλά I could not* (lit. *there is no way how I could*) *call false tidings fair* A. Ag. 620, *τίς τῶνδ' . . . δωμάτων ἔχει κράτος, ὅστις ξένους δέξαιτο; who has authority in this house that might receive guests?* Ar. Thesm. 871, *ἔστ' οὖν ὅπως Ἄλκηστις ἐς γῆρας μόλοι; is there a way by which Alcestis might reach old age?* E. Alc. 52. The potential optative *with ἄν* occurs after these expressions (E. Alc. 80, S. O. C. 1168, P. Lach. 184 c). Attic does not use the optative with *ἄν* after the positive form *ἔστιν ὅπως* (*ὅστις*).

CLASSES OF RELATIVE CLAUSES

2553. Ordinary Relative Clauses define more exactly a definite antecedent, and show the mood and the negative of simple sentences.

Indicative: *ταῦτ' ἐστὶν ἃ ἐγὼ δέομαι this is what I want* X. A. 7. 2. 34, *ὦ δύστᾱνα γένη βροτῶν, οἷς μὴ μέτριος αἰών alas, ill-starred races of men, whose destiny is beyond due measure* S. Ph. 179, *ὅθεν οὖν ῥᾷστα μαθήσεσθε περὶ αὐτῶν, ἐντεῦθεν ὑμᾶς καὶ ἐγὼ πρῶτον πειράσομαι διδάσκειν I will first try to inform you* (lit.) *from the source from which you will most easily learn about them* D. 27. 3, *παρ' ἐμὲ ἀφικόμενος οὐ πείσεται ἅπερ ἂν ἔπαθεν ἄλλῳ τῳ συγγενόμενος τῶν σοφιστῶν in coming to me he will not meet with the treatment he would have suffered had he consorted with any other of the sophists* P. Pr. 318 d.

Subjunctive: *Ἄνυτος ὅδε παρεκαθέζετο, ᾧ μεταδῶμεν τῆς ζητήσεως Anytus has taken his seat here* (lit.) *to whom let us give a share in the investigation* P. Men. 89 e, *κλύων ὁθούνεκα . . . μήτηρ δ' ἐν οἴκοις· ἣν σὺ μὴ δείσῃς hearing that our mother is in the house,* (lit.) *of whom have thou no fear* S. El. 1309.

Optative: οἴομαι ἂν ἡμᾶς τοιαῦτα παθεῖν, οἷα τοὺς ἐχθροὺς οἱ θεοὶ ποιήσειαν *I think we should endure such things as* I pray *the gods may inflict upon our enemies* X. A. 3. 2. 3, δόρατα ἔχοντες . . . ὅσα ἀνὴρ ἂν φέροι μόλις *having spears, such as a man could carry with difficulty* 5. 4. 25, ἄρξομαι δ' ἐντεῦθεν ὅθεν . . . ἐγὼ τάχιστ' ἂν διδάξαιμι *I will begin at (from) that point where I can most quickly inform* you D. 29. 5. The potential optative without ἄν is very rare (2552).

Imperative: πλάνην φράσω, ἣν ἐγγράφου σὺ μνήμοσιν δέλτοις φρενῶν *I will tell thy wandering, which do thou inscribe in the tablets of thy memory* A. Pr. 788. On οἶσθ' ὃ δρᾶσον, see 1842 a.

a. Ordinary relative clauses are explanatory, and (in sense) are equivalent to independent coördinated clauses. See 2490.

b. Homer has κέ or ἄν with the future: παρ' ἐμοί γε καὶ ἄλλοι, οἵ κέ με τῑμήσουσι *I have others by my side who will honour me* A 175.

2554. Relative Clauses of Purpose (Final Relative Clauses) regularly take the future indicative, even after past tenses (negative μή). The antecedent of final relative clauses is usually indefinite. ὅς is commoner than ὅστις. (The construction with the future participle is more frequent: 2065).

φημὶ δὴ δεῖν ἡμᾶς . . . πρεσβείᾱν πέμπειν, ἣ τοὺς μὲν διδάξει ταῦτα, τοὺς δὲ παροξυνεῖ *I say that we must send an embassy, which will inform some of this and incite others* D. 2. 11, πέμψον τιν' ὅστις σημανεῖ *send some one who will announce* E. I. T. 1209, ἔδοξε τῷ δήμῳ τριάκοντα ἄνδρας ἑλέσθαι, οἳ τοὺς πατρίους νόμους συγγράψουσι, καθ' οὓς πολῑτεύσουσι *the people voted to choose thirty men who should codify the ancestral laws by which they were to conduct the government* X. H. 2. 3. 2. So in local clauses: κρύψω τόδ' ἔγχος . . . ἔνθα μή τις ὄψεται *I will hide this sword where no one shall see it* S. Aj. 659.

a. After a secondary tense the future optative occurs rarely: οἱ δὲ τριάκοντα ᾑρέθησαν μὲν ἐπεὶ τάχιστα τὰ μακρὰ τείχη . . . καθῃρέθη· αἱρεθέντες δ' ἐφ' ᾧτε ξυγγράψαι νόμους, καθ' οὕστινας πολῑτεύσοιντο κτλ. *the thirty were chosen as soon as the long walls were destroyed; and having been chosen for the purpose of codifying the laws, according to which they were to conduct the government*, etc. X. H. 2. 3. 11. In local clauses: S. O. T. 796.

b. A past purpose may be expressed by ἔμελλον and the infinitive. Thus, ναύαρχον προσέταξαν Ἀλκίδᾱν, ὃς ἔμελλεν ἐπιπλεύσεσθαι *they appointed Alcidas as admiral who was to sail in command* T. 3. 16.

c. Homer uses the subjunctive (with κέ, except Γ 287) after primary tenses, the optative after secondary tenses. Thus, μάντις ἐλεύσεται, ὅς κέν τοι εἴπῃσιν ὁδόν *a seer will come to tell thee the way* κ 538, ἄγγελον ἧκαν ὃς ἀγγείλειε γυναικί *they sent a messenger to tell the woman* ο 458. The future also occurs (ξ 332). The present or aorist optative is rare in Attic (S. Tr. 903, Ph. 281).

2555. Relative Clauses of Cause take the indicative (negative οὐ). ὅς is more common than ὅστις.

θαυμαστὸν ποιεῖς, ὃς (= ὅτι σὺ) ἡμῖν . . . οὐδὲν δίδως *you do a strange thing in giving us nothing* X. M. 2. 7. 13, Λοξίᾳ δὲ μέμφομαι, ὅστις μ' ἐπάρᾱς ἔργον ἀνοσιώτατον τοῖς μὲν λόγοις ηὔφρᾱνε κτλ. *I blame Loxias, who after inciting me to a deed most unhallowed, cheered me with words*, etc. E. Or. 285. So when the relative is a dependent exclamation (οἷος = ὅτι τοιοῦτος, etc., 2687).

a. γε is often added to ὅς or ὅστις.

b. μή is used when there is also an idea of characteristic (*of such a sort*) or condition (perhaps to avoid a harsher form of statement). Cp. 2705 g.

2556. Relative Clauses of Result (Consecutive Relative Clauses) usually take the indicative (for οἷος, ὅσος with the infinitive see 2497). The negative is οὐ when the relative clause approximates ὥστε (οὐ) with the indicative, as is generally the case when the main clause is negative, expressed or implied. Here ὅστις is commoner than ὅς. The negative is μή when the relative clause expresses an intended (2557) or anticipated (2558) result, where ὥστε μή with the infinitive would be less precise.

τίς οὕτω μαίνεται ὅστις οὐ βούλεταί σοι φίλος εἶναι; *who is so mad that he does not wish to be a friend to you?* X. A. 2. 5. 12, οὐδὲν γὰρ οὕτω βραχὺ ὅπλον ἑκάτεροι εἶχον ᾧ οὐκ ἐξικνοῦντο ἀλλήλων *for each side did not have weapons so short that they could not reach each other* X. H. 7. 5. 17.

a. The indicative with ἄν and the optative with ἄν are rare. Thus, τίς δ' ἦν οὕτως . . . μισαθήναιος, ὅστις ἐδυνήθη ἂν ἄτακτον αὑτὸν ὑπομεῖναι ἰδεῖν; *who was such a hater of Athens that he could endure to see himself not at his post?* Lyc. 39, τίς οὕτως ἰσχυρός, ὃς . . . ῥίγει δύναιτ' ἂν μαχόμενος στρατεύεσθαι *who is so vigorous that he could carry on war while battling with cold?* X. C. 6. 1. 15. A potential optative with ὅς follows a potential optative in P. R. 360 b.

2557. The indicative is normal in consecutive relative clauses introduced by οὐκ ἔστιν ὅστις (οὐ), οὐδείς ἐστιν ὅστις (οὐ), οὐκ ἔστιν ὅπως (οὐ), εἰσὶν οἵ, ἔστιν οἷς, etc.

οὐκ ἔστιν οὐδεὶς ὅστις οὐχ αὑτὸν φιλεῖ *there is no one who does not love himself* Men. Sent. 407, οὐκ ἔστιν ὅπως ἥβην κτήσῃ πάλιν αὖθις *in no way canst thou regain thy youth* E. Heracl. 707. See 2551.

a. The indicative with ἄν and the optative with ἄν also occur. Thus, οὐ γὰρ ἦν ὅ τι ἂν ἐποιεῖτε *for there was nothing that you could have done* D. 18. 43, ὧν οὐκ ἔστιν ὅστις οὐκ ἂν καταφρονήσειεν *whom every one would despise* I. 8. 52.

b. On the subjunctive and optative without ἄν, see 2546, 2547, 2552.

2558. The future indicative is often used to express an *intended* result (negative μή).

ἀνόητον ἐπὶ τοιούτους ἰέναι ὧν κρατήσᾱς μὴ κατασχήσει τις *it is senseless to attack men of such a kind that we shall not hold them in subjection if we conquer them* T. 6. 11, οὗτοι δὲ τοιαῦτ' . . . ὑποσχήσονται, ἐξ ὧν μηδ' ἂν ὁτιοῦν ᾖ κῑνηθήσονται *these men shall make promises in consequence of which* the Athenians *will not better themselves under any circumstances* (lit. *even if anything occurs*) D. 19. 324.

2559. The future indicative is especially common when the main clause contains an idea of *ability, capacity,* or *characteristic,* and the relative clause denotes what is to be expected of the subject.

ἱκανοί ἐσμεν . . . ὑμῖν πέμψαι ναῦς τε καὶ ἄνδρας οἵτινες συμμαχοῦνταί τε καὶ τὴν ὁδὸν ἡγήσονται (cp. *ὥστε συμμάχεσθαι*) *we are able to send you ships and men who will fight with you and direct your journey* X. A. 5. 4. 10, *οὔτε πλοῖα ἔστι τὰ ἀπάξοντα οὔτε σῖτος ᾧ θρεψόμεθα μένοντες we have neither ships to convey us away nor provisions to feed us while we remain* 6. 5. 20, *δεῖταί τινος ὅστις αὐτὸν ὀνήσει he needs some one to improve him* P. Eu. 306 d, (*ἔδει*) *ψήφισμα νικῆσαι τοιοῦτο δι' οὗ Φωκεῖς ἀπολοῦνται a bill had to be passed of such a character as to destroy the Phocians* D. 19. 43.

2560. Conditional Relative Clauses may be resolved into *if* clauses, *ὅς* (*ὅστις*) corresponding to *εἴ τις* and *ὅς* (*ὅστις*) *ἄν* to *ἐάν τις*. The negative is *μή*.

a. The antecedent of conditional relative clauses is indefinite (2505 b).

b. Such relative clauses, like temporal clauses, correspond in form to the protases of ordinary conditional sentences. Conditional relative sentences show, in general, the same substitutions permitted in the corresponding conditional sentences. *ὃς ἄν* is always generic, *ἐάν* may be particular in prose.

2561. The correspondence in construction between the common forms of conditional, temporal, and conditional relative, sentences is shown by the following table:

		Present	
Simple:	εἴ (ὅτε, ὅ) τι	ἔχει	δίδωσι
Unreal:	εἴ (ὅτε, ὅ) τι	εἶχεν	ἐδίδου ἄν
General:	ἐάν τι (ὅταν τι, ὅ τι)	ἔχῃ	δίδωσι
		Past	
Simple:	εἴ (ὅτε, ὅ) τι	εἶχεν (ἔσχεν)	ἐδίδου (ἔδωκε)
Unreal:	εἴ (ὅτε, ὅ) τι	ἔσχεν (εἶχεν)	ἔδωκεν (ἐδίδου) ἄν
General:	εἴ (ὅτε, ὅ) τι	ἔχοι	ἐδίδου
		Future	
More Vivid:	ἐάν τι (ὅταν τι, ὅ τι ἄν)	ἔχῃ	δώσει
Less Vivid:	εἴ (ὅτε, ὅ) τι	ἔχοι	διδοίη (δοίη) ἄν

N. — English cannot always, without obscurity, use a relative to translate *ὅτε* or *ὅ τι* with an unreal indicative; in such cases *when(ever)* or *whatever* are best rendered by *if ever*. Cp. 2396.

PRESENT AND PAST CONDITIONAL RELATIVE CLAUSES

First Form

SIMPLE PRESENT AND PAST CONDITIONAL RELATIVES

2562. Simple present and past conditional relative clauses have the present or past indicative. The main clause has the indicative or any other form of the simple sentence (cp. 2298, 2300).

οὐ γὰρ ἃ πράττουσιν οἱ δίκαιοι, ἀλλ' ἃ (= *εἴ τινα*) *μὴ πράττουσι, ταῦτα λέγεις for it is not what the just do, but what they do not do, that you keep telling* us

X. M. 4. 4. 11, τῶν Ἑλλήνων οἳ (= εἴ τινες) μὴ ἔτυχον ἐν ταῖς τάξεσιν ὄντες εἰς τὰς τάξεις ἔθεον *those of the Greeks who happened not to be in rank ran into their ranks* X. A. 2. 2. 14, διέβαλλεν αὐτὸν ὅ τι ἐδύνατο *he slandered him all he could* 6. 1. 32, ἄνδρας τῶν Ἀθηναίων ἀπέκτειναν ὅσοι μὴ ἐξένευσαν *they killed* all *of the Athenians who had not escaped by swimming* T. 2. 90, ὃ δέ γε μηδὲν κακὸν ποιεῖ οὐδ' ἄν τινος εἴη κακοῦ αἴτιον; *and that which produces no evil cannot be the cause of any evil either?* P. R. 379 b, ἃ μὴ προσήκει μήτ' ἄκουε μήθ' ὅρα *neither hear nor behold that which beseems thee not* Men. Sent. 39, ὅστις ζῆν ἐπιθυμεῖ, πειράσθω νικᾶν *whoever longs to live, let him strive to conquer* X. A. 3. 2. 39.

a. Since the antecedent of these clauses is indefinite, simple present conditional relative clauses with the present indicative in the main clause often have the value of *general* conditions. But general clauses with ὅς (μή) usually take the subjunctive or optative (2567, 2568), and those with ὅστις (μή) the indicative (2569).

2563. If the relative clause expresses a *present intention* or *necessity*, the future indicative may be used.

ἐν τούτῳ κεκωλῦσθαι (1950) ἐδόκει ἑκάστῳ τὰ πράγματα ᾧ μή τις αὐτὸς παρέσται *each thought that progress was surely impeded in any undertaking in which he was not going to take part in person* (= ἐν τούτῳ κεκώλῡται ᾧ μὴ παρέσομαι) T. 2. 8. Cp. P. Th. 186 c. More common is μέλλω with the present or future infinitive: ἕλοισθ' ὅ τι . . . ἅπᾱσι συνοίσειν ὑμῖν μέλλει *may you adopt whatever course is likely to be of advantage to you all* D. 3. 36.

a. Elsewhere the future indicative is not regular in conditional relative sentences.

Second Form

PRESENT AND PAST UNREAL CONDITIONAL RELATIVES

2564. Present and past unreal conditional relative clauses have a secondary tense of the indicative. The main clause has a secondary tense with ἄν (cp. 2303).

οὔτε γὰρ ἂν αὐτοὶ ἐπεχειροῦμεν πράττειν ἃ (= εἴ τινα) μὴ ἠπιστάμεθα κτλ. *for* (if that were so) *neither should we ourselves be undertaking* (as we are) *to do what we did not understand*, etc. P. Charm. 171 e, οἱ παῖδες ὑμῶν, ὅσοι (= εἴ τινες) ἐνθάδε ἦσαν, ὑπὸ τούτων ἂν ὑβρίζοντο (if that were so) *your children, as many of them as were present* (but none were present), *would be insulted by these men* L. 12. 98, ὁπότερα τούτων ἐποίησεν, οὐδενὸς ἂν ἧττον πλούσιοι ἦσαν *whichever of these things he had done, they would be no less rich than any one* 32. 23.

FUTURE CONDITIONAL RELATIVE CLAUSES

Third Form

MORE VIVID FUTURE CONDITIONAL RELATIVES

2565. Conditional relative clauses that vividly anticipate the realization of a future event take the subjunctive with ἄν. The main clause has the future indicative or any other form referring to the future.

τῷ ἀνδρὶ ὃν ἂν (= ἐάν τινα) ἕλησθε πείσομαι *I will obey whatever man you may choose* X. A. 1. 3. 15, οἷς (for ἃ) ἂν οἱ ἄλλοι ἐργάζωνται, τούτοις σὺ χρήσῃ *whatever others acquire by labour, that you shall enjoy* X. M. 2. 1. 25, πειράσομαι ὅ τι ἂν δύνωμαι ὑμᾶς ἀγαθὸν ποιεῖν *I will try to do you all the good I can* X. A. 6. 1. 33, ὅποι ἂν ἔλθω, λέγοντος ἐμοῦ ἀκροάσονται οἱ νέοι *wherever I go the young men will listen to my speaking* P. A. 37 d, ἀπόκρῖναι ὅ τι ἄν σε ἐρωτῶ *answer whatever I ask you* L. 12. 24, ἕπεσθε ὅπῃ ἄν τις ἡγῆται *follow where any one may lead you* T. 2. 11, ὡς ἂν (= ἐάν πως) ἐγὼ εἴπω, πειθώμεθα *let us all obey as I shall bid* B 139. Potential optative: ὥστ' ἀποφύγοις ἂν ἥντιν' ἂν βούλῃ δίκην *so that you can get off in any suit you please* Ar. Nub. 1151.

a. The future indicative is scarcely ever used in a conditional relative clause of this sort (T. 1. 22 ὅσοι βουλήσονται; cp. 1913).

b. Homer has some cases of the subjunctive without κέ or ἄν (*e.g.* N 234). Homer sometimes uses the future with κέ or ἄν in the main clause: ὁ δέ κεν κεχολώσεται, ὅν κεν ἵκωμαι *and he will be wroth to whom I shall come* A 139.

Fourth Form

LESS VIVID FUTURE CONDITIONAL RELATIVES

2566. Conditional relative clauses that set forth less vividly the realization of a future event take the optative. The main clause has the optative with ἄν.

ὀκνοίην ἂν εἰς τὰ πλοῖα ἐμβαίνειν ἃ (= εἴ τινα) ἡμῖν Κῦρος δοίη *I should hesitate to embark in the vessels that Cyrus might give us* X. A. 1. 3. 17, ὃ δὲ μὴ ἀγαπῴη, οὐδ' ἂν φιλοῖ *nor could he love what he does not desire* P. Lys. 215 b.

a. The main clause has the optative without ἄν in *wishes*: δῶρα θεῶν ἔχοι, ὅττι διδοῖεν *may he keep the gifts of the gods whatever they may give* σ 142.

b. Homer sometimes uses κέ or ἄν in the relative clause (φ 161).

GENERAL CONDITIONAL RELATIVE CLAUSES

Fifth Form

PRESENT GENERAL CONDITIONAL RELATIVES

2567. Present general conditional relative clauses have ἄν with the subjunctive. The main clause has the present indicative or an equivalent.

νέος δ' ἀπόλλυθ' ὅντιν' (= εἴ τινα) ἂν φιλῇ θεός '*he dieth young, whome'er a god doth love*' Stob. Flor. 120. 13, οὓς (= εἴ τινας) ἂν ὁρᾷ φιλοκινδύνως ἔχοντας πρὸς τοὺς πολεμίους, τῑμᾷ *whomever he sees zealous of danger in the face of the enemy, these he honours* X. H. 6. 1. 6, γαμοῦσί τε ὁπόθεν ἂν βούλωνται, ἐκδιδόασί τε εἰς οὓς ἂν ἐθέλωσι *they both get a wife from whatever family they please and give their daughters in marriage to whomsoever they choose* P. R. 613 d, πατρὶς γάρ ἐστι πᾶσ' ἵν' ἂν πράττῃ τις εὖ *for every land is a man's own country wheresoever he fares well* Ar. Plut. 1151.

a. Gnomic aorist in the main clause: ὅς κε θεοῖς ἐπιπείθηται, μάλα τ' ἔκλυον αὐτοῦ *whoever obeys the gods, him they most do hear* A 218.

b. The subjunctive without ἄν (κέ) is usual in Homer and occurs occasionally in Attic and lyric poetry. Thus, ἀνθρώπους ἐφορᾷ καὶ τίνυται ὅς τις ἁμάρτῃ *he watches over men and punishes whoever transgresses* ν 214, τῶν δὲ πημονῶν μάλιστα λῦποῦσ' αἳ φανῶσ' αὐθαίρετοι *but those griefs pain the most which are seen to be self-sought* S. O. T. 1231. Cases of the sort appear in Hdt., but are very rare in Attic prose, *e.g.* T. 4. 18. The subjunctive without ἄν (κέ) is much commoner in Homer than in the corresponding clauses with εἰ (2339).

c. The apodosis here usually expresses a general truth, less often iterative action. In 2568 the apodosis refers to iterative action, usually on the part of designated individuals.

Sixth Form

PAST GENERAL CONDITIONAL RELATIVES

2568. Past general conditional relative clauses have the optative. The main clause has the imperfect or an equivalent.

ἀεὶ πρὸς ᾧ (= εἰ πρός τινι) εἴη ἔργῳ, τοῦτο ἔπρᾱττεν *whatever work he was engaged in, that he always performed* X. H. 4. 8. 22, ἔπρᾱττεν ἃ δόξειεν αὐτῷ *he always did whatever he pleased* D. 18. 235, πάντας . . . ὅσους λάβοιεν διέφθειρον *they used to destroy as many as they captured* T. 2. 67, ἐθήρᾱ ὅπου περ ἐπιτυγχάνοιεν θηρίοις *he used to hunt wherever they fell in with large game* X. C. 3. 3. 5, ἀνέκραγον . . . ἱκετεύουσαι πάντας ὅτῳ ἐντυγχάνοιεν μὴ φεύγειν *they screamed out, entreating all they met not to flee* X. C. 3. 3. 67.

a. An iterative tense with ἄν in the main clause: ὅπῃ μέλλοι ἀριστοποιεῖσθαι τὸ στράτευμα . . ., ἐπανήγαγεν ἂν τὸ κέρας, *when the squadron was about to take breakfast, he would draw back the wing* X. H. 6. 2. 28.

INDICATIVE FORM OF GENERAL CONDITIONAL RELATIVE CLAUSES

2569. The present indicative instead of the subjunctive with ἄν occurs in general conditional relative clauses (cp. 2342). This occurs chiefly after ὅστις, which is itself sufficiently general in meaning.

οἵτινες πρὸς τὰς ξυμφορὰς γνώμῃ ἥκιστα λῡποῦνται, ἔργῳ δὲ μάλιστα ἀντέχουσιν *those who in feeling are least depressed at misfortunes, in action resist them most* T. 2. 64, ὅστις δ' ἐπὶ μεγίστοις τὸ ἐπίφθονον λαμβάνει, ὀρθῶς βουλεύεται *he counsels wisely who incurs envy in a great cause* 2. 64, ὅστις δὲ πλοῦτον ἢ εὐγένειαν εἰσιδὼν γαμεῖ πονηράν, μῶρός ἐστιν *whoever fixes his gaze on wealth or noble lineage and weds a wicked woman, is a fool* E. El. 1097, ὅ τι καλὸν φίλον ἀεί *whatsoever is fair is dear forever* E. Bacch. 881.

a. Cases of the imperfect instead of the optative are rare and generally ill supported: ὅπου ᾤετο τὴν πατρίδα τι ὠφελήσειν, οὐ πόνων ὑφίετο *whenever he thought that he could benefit his country in any respect, he did not shrink from toil* X. Ag. 7. 1. Cp. X. A. 1. 1. 5, 1. 9. 27.

2570. The indicative is generally used in parenthetical or appended relative clauses with ὅστις (ὅστις ποτέ). Thus, δουλεύομεν θεοῖς, ὅ τι ποτ' εἰσὶν οἱ θεοί *we serve the gods, whatever those gods are* E. Or. 418.

a. The subjunctive with ἄν is also used when the reference is to future time or to general present time. Cp. Aes. 1. 127, D. 4. 27.

LESS USUAL FORMS OF CONDITIONAL RELATIVE SENTENCES

2571. The potential optative with ἄν in the main clause with the indicative (2562) or subjunctive (2565) in the relative clause.

2572. Indicative with ἄν or potential optative with ἄν in the relative clause.

ὅντιν' ἂν ὑμεῖς εἰς ταύτην τὴν τάξιν κατεστήσατε . . ., οὗτος . . . τῶν ἴσων ἂν αἴτιος ἦν κακῶν ὅσωνπερ καὶ οὗτος *whomsoever you might have appointed to this post, such a one would have been the cause of as many evils as this man has been* D. 19. 29, τὰς δ' ἐπ' Ἰλλυρίους . . . καὶ ὅποι τις ἂν εἴποι παραλείπω στρατείᾱς *I omit his expeditions against the Illyrians and many others* (lit. *whithersoever*) *one might speak of* D. 1. 13. Cp. X. Ag. 2. 24.

2573. The optative in the relative clause with the present or future indicative or the imperative in the main clause (cp. 2359). With the present this occurs especially in general statements and maxims. The main clause is often introduced by a verb requiring the infinitive.

ἀλλ' ὃν πόλις στήσειε, τοῦδε χρὴ κλύειν *but whomever the State might appoint, him we must obey* S. Ant. 666, τοῦ μὲν αὐτὸν λέγειν, ἃ μὴ σαφῶς εἰδείη, εἴργεσθαι δεῖ *one should refrain from saying oneself what one does not know for certain* X. C. 1. 6. 19.

a. The present indicative sometimes may have the force of an emphatic future (ζ 286). Sometimes the optative indicates a case that is not likely to occur; as ἄλλῳ νεμεσᾶτον, ὅτις τοιαῦτά γε ῥέζοι *you are ready to be wroth with another, supposing any one do such things* Ψ 494.

b. Other examples of the present: Homer P 631 (doubtful); Theognis 689; Aes. Pr. 638; Soph. O. T. 315, 979; Lys. 12. 84; Xen. C. 2. 4. 10, 7. 5. 56, H. 3. 4. 18, 7. 3. 7; Plato Charm. 164 a, Eu. 292 e (doubtful), L. 927 c. Temporal: S. Tr. 92, P. R. 332 a.

c. The future indicative occurs in τ 510 (temporal N 317); the perfect indicative in Δ 262 and ω 254 (temporal); the aorist imperative in X. C. 1. 4. 14.

DEPENDENT SUBSTANTIVE CLAUSES (2574–2635)

2574. A subordinate clause may play the part of a substantive in relation to the main clause. Such clauses are generally the object, sometimes the subject, of the verb of the main clause.

εἶπεν ὅτι οὐ πόλεμον ποιησόμενοι ἥκοιεν *he said that they had not come to wage war* X. A. 5. 5. 24, ἔπρᾱσσον ὅπως τις βοήθεια ἥξει *they were managing how some reinforcements should come* T. 3. 4, δέδοικα μὴ . . . ἐπιλαθώμεθα τῆς οἴκαδε ὁδοῦ *I am afraid lest we may forget the way home* X. A. 3. 2. 25; ἐλέγετο ὅτι . . . Πῶλος ὅσον οὐ παρείη *it was said that Polus had all but arrived* 7. 2. 5.

2575. There are four main divisions of substantive clauses.

1. **Dependent Statements**: subordinate clauses stating that something *is*; as λέγει ὡς οὐδέν ἐστιν ἀδικώτερον φήμης *he says that nothing is more unjust than talk about a man's character* Aes. 1. 125.

2. **Dependent Clauses of *will* or *desire*:** subordinate clauses denoting that something *should be* or *should be done.* These clauses have been treated under the following divisions:

a. Dependent clauses after verbs of *effort* (2209).

b. Dependent clauses after verbs of *fearing* (2221).

N.—On dependent voluntative clauses with the accusative and infinitive (indirect petition), see 1991 ff.

3. **Dependent Questions**: subordinate clauses asking a question; both parts of the sentence together forming a *statement;* as ἠρώτων ὅ τι ἐστὶ τὸ πρᾶγμα *I asked what the matter was* X. A. 5. 7. 23.

4. **Dependent Exclamations**: subordinate clauses setting forth an exclamation; both parts of the sentence together forming a *statement;* as διαθεώμενος αὐτῶν ὅσην μὲν χώρᾱν καὶ οἵᾱν ἔχοιεν *observing how great the extent of their territory was and how excellent its quality* X. A. 3. 1. 19.

DEPENDENT STATEMENTS

2576. Dependent statements, or subordinate clauses stating *that* something *is*, are expressed in various ways:

1. By an infinitive, with or without an accusative (explained in 1972 ff., 2016 ff.). Thus, νομίζω γὰρ ὑμᾶς ἐμοὶ εἶναι καὶ πατρίδα καὶ φίλους *for I think that you are both fatherland and friends to me* X. C. 1. 3. 6, οἶμαι εἰδέναι *I think that I know* P. Pr. 312 c.

2. By a participle, with or without an accusative (explained in 2106 ff.). Thus, οὐ γὰρ ᾔδεσαν αὐτὸν τεθνηκότα *for they did not know that he was dead* X. A. 1. 10. 16, μέμνημαι ἀκούσᾱς *I remember that I heard* X. C. 1. 6. 6.

3. By ὅτι or ὡς (and some other conjunctions) with the indicative or optative. On this form of dependent statement see 2577 ff., and under Indirect Discourse.

a. In any form of substantive clause the subject of the subordinate verb may be made the object of the principal verb (2182).

b. A clause with ὅτι (ὡς) may precede the principal clause. Cp. 2586.

DEPENDENT STATEMENTS INTRODUCED BY ὅτι OR ὡς

2577. The conjunctions ὅτι or ὡς *that* introduce dependent statements in the indicative and optative

After verbs of *saying, knowing, perceiving, showing,* etc.

After verbs of *emotion* (*rejoicing, grieving, wondering*), etc.

Or such dependent statements contain an explanation of the main clause or of a word in that clause, no special verb introducing the conjunction.

τοῦτο ἄξιον ἐπαινεῖν τῶν ἀνδρῶν τῶν τότε ναυμαχησάντων, ὅτι τὸν . . . φόβον διέλῡσαν τῶν Ἑλλήνων *it is right to praise this in the men who engaged in the sea-fight of those days,* (namely) *that they dispelled the fear felt by the Greeks* P. Menex. 241 b.

2578. The conjunctions introducing dependent statements are ὅτι (Homeric also ὅττι, ὅ and ὅτε), ὡς, διότι, ὅπως (rarely), οὕνεκα and ὁθούνεκα (both poetic).

a. **ὅτι** meaning *that* was originally, like Hom. ὅ, perhaps an accusative of the inner object (cognate): ὁρῶ ὃ νοσεῖς lit. *I see what* sickness *you are sick* (= ἣν νόσον νοσεῖς). But by the time of Homer both ὅ and ὅτι had become mere formal conjunctions. Hom. ὅτε *that* seems to be a weakened ὅτε *when;* but this is disputed.

b. **διότι** originally = διὰ τοῦτο, ὅτι *on account of this, that* = *because* (as T. 1. 52); then = ὅτι *that* in Hdt. and in Attic after Isocrates, who uses διότι for ὅτι to avoid hiatus.

c. **ὡς** strictly an old ablative of ὅς (2989) meaning *how, in what way,* as in exclamatory clauses and indirect questions. The meaning *how* (cp. *how that*) may be seen in οἶδα γὰρ ὥς μοι ὀδώδυσται κλυτὸς ἐννοσίγαιος *for I know how (that) the famed earth-shaker has been wroth against me* ε 423, and also in Attic (And. 2. 14; I. 2. 3, 3. 10, 16. 11, 16. 15; Aes. 2. 35; D. 24. 139). The development of ὡς *how* to ὡς *that* followed from the use of ὡς after verbs signifying *to see, perceive, know,* and the like. Cp. "he sayed how there was a knight."

d. **ὅπως** (2929) *that* is common in Herodotus (ὅκως), rare in Attic, most used in poetry and Xenophon. From its original use in indirect questions ὅπως *how* gradually acquired the meaning *that.* Thus, ἀλλ' ὅπως μὲν . . . ἐγὼ ἄχθομαι ὑμᾶς τρέφων, μηδ' ὑπονοεῖτε *do not even entertain the thought that I am annoyed at maintaining you* X. C. 3. 3. 20.

e. **οὕνεκα** = οὗ ἕνεκα, for τούτου ἕνεκα, ὅ, properly causal: *on account of (as regards) this, that,* and then = *that,* even in Homer (*Odyssey* and Λ 21) and later in poetry. Thus, ἐξάγγελλε . . . οὕνεκ' Οἰδίπους τοιαῦτ' ἔνειμε παισὶ τοῖς αὑτοῦ γέρᾱ *announce that Oedipus has distributed such honours to his sons* S. O. C. 1393.

f. **ὁθούνεκα** = ὅτου ἕνεκα, for τούτου ἕνεκα, ὅτι; and then = *that.* It is found only in tragedy, as ἄγγελλε . . . ὁθούνεκα τέθνηκ' Ὀρέστης *report that Orestes is dead* S. El. 47.

2579. Some verbs of *saying* are followed either by ὅτι or ὡς or by an infinitive (2017). In most cases the choice is optional with the writer. Affirmative clauses usually take the infinitive or ὅτι; but ὡς is apparently preferred to ὅτι when a writer wishes to mark a statement as an opinion, a pretext, as untrue, and so when the main clause is negative, or when the subordinate clause is negative (or both are negative). Thus, νομίζουσιν οἱ ἐκείνῃ ἄνθρωποι . . . ὡς ὁ Ἥφαιστος χαλκεύει *the local belief is that Hephaestus is working at his forge* T. 3. 88, διαβαλὼν αὐτοὺς ὡς οὐδὲν ἀληθὲς ἐν νῷ ἔχουσιν *slanderously attacking them on the score that their intentions were not sincere* 5. 45, πολλάκις ἐθαύμασα τίσι ποτὲ λόγοις Ἀθηναίους ἔπεισαν οἱ γραψάμενοι Σωκράτην ὡς ἄξιος εἴη θανάτου *I have often wondered with what possible arguments the accusers of Socrates succeeded in convincing the Athenians that he deserved death* X. M. 1. 1. 1, οὐ τοῦτο λέγω ὡς οὐ δεῖ ποτε καὶ ἐλάττονι ἔτι μορίῳ ἰέναι *I do not say (this) that it is not ever necessary to attack* the enemy *with a still smaller detachment* X. C. 5. 4. 20. ὅτι may be used of an untrue statement designed to create belief (S. El. 43).

a. Dependent statements in the optative in indirect discourse after verbs of *saying* are chiefly post-Homeric.

2580. Verbs of *thinking* almost always take the infinitive (2018) but ὡς occurs; as once with νομίζω T. 3. 88 (2579), ἐλπίζω 5. 9, οἴομαι X. H. 6. 3. 12, ὑπολαμβάνω X. C. 8. 3. 40. ὅτι is very rare (with οἴομαι in P. Ph. 87 c). λογίζομαι (ὅτι) is a verb of *saying*.

a. μαρτυρῶ with ὅτι (ὡς) expresses reality; with the infinitive it denotes uncertainty.

2581. Verbs of intellectual perception usually take ὅτι (ὡς); less often the participle, which is normal after verbs of physical perception. A verb of physical perception, if followed by ὅτι (ὡς), virtually becomes a verb of intellectual perception.

2582. Many verbs take ὅτι (ὡς) or the participle either in indirect discourse or not in indirect discourse (2106–2115). Here the construction with the finite verb is less dependent than that with the participle; but the meaning is essentially the same in Attic. Many verbs take ὅτι (ὡς), the infinitive, or the participle, often without great difference in meaning in Attic (2123–2145).

2583. ὅτι (ὡς), when separated from its clause by another clause, may be repeated. Thus, ἔλεγεν ὅτι, εἰ μὴ καταβήσονται . . . , ὅτι κατακαύσει . . . τᾶς κώμᾱς *he said that, if they did not descend, he would burn their villages to the ground* X. A. 7. 4. 5.

2584. The personal **δῆλός εἰμι ὅτι, λανθάνω ὅτι**, etc. are often used instead of the impersonal δῆλόν ἐστιν ὅτι, λανθάνει ὅτι, etc. Thus, ὅτι πονηρότατοί εἰσιν οὐδὲ σὲ λανθάνουσιν *not even you fail to perceive that they are the very worst* X. O. 1. 19.

2585. **δῆλον ὅτι** (δηλονότι) *evidently*, **οἶδ' ὅτι** (**εὖ οἶδ' ὅτι**) *surely*, **εὖ ἴσθι ὅτι** *be assured* are so often used parenthetically and elliptically as to become mere formal expressions requiring no verb. ὅτι here loses all conjunctive force. Thus, ἔχει δὴ οὑτωσὶ δῆλον ὅτι τούτων πέρι *the case then stands clearly thus about these matters* P. G. 487 d, οὔτ' ἂν ὑμεῖς οἶδ' ὅτι ἐπαύσασθε *nor assuredly would you have ceased* D. 6. 29, καὶ πάντων οἶδ' ὅτι φησάντων γ' ἄν (for καὶ οἶδ' ὅτι πάντες φήσαιέν γ' ἄν) *and all assuredly would say* 9. 1.

a. Plato (*Sophistes* and *Leges*) uses δῆλον (ἐστίν) ὡς for δῆλον ὅτι.

2586. ὅτι (and by analogy ὡς) are often attached loosely to the main clause with the meaning *as a proof (in support) of the fact that*. Thus, ὅτι δ' οὕτω ταῦτ' ἔχει, λέγε μοι τὸ τοῦ Καλλισθένους ψήφισμα *as a proof of the fact that this is so, read me the bill of Callisthenes* D. 18. 37.

2587. Verbs of *emotion* (*to rejoice, grieve, be angry, wonder*, etc.) take ὅτι (ὡς) with a finite verb (negative οὐ), but more commonly the participle (2100) when the subject is not changed.

a. Hom. prefers ὅτι, ὡς to the participle or infinitive.

b. The accusative and infinitive with verbs of *emotion* are rare; as with θαυμάζω E. Alc. 1130. (θαυμάζω may be followed by a dependent question: D. 37. 44).

c. On verbs of *emotion* with εἰ instead of ὅτι, ὡς (negative, generally μή), see 2247. On the use in dependent exclamations, see 2687.

2588. **μέμνημαι, οἶδα, ἀκούω** and like verbs, may take ὅτε instead of ὅτι (2395 A. N.). Cp., in Homer, Φ 396, π 424.

INDIRECT DISCOURSE

2589. The words or thoughts of a person may be quoted in direct or indirect form after verbs, or other expressions, of *saying* or *thinking*.

a. In reporting a speech, in making a quotation, or in dialogue, a verb of *saying* is often repeated (P. Pr. 310 b, 345 c, X. A. 7. 6. 5–6). So also in such cases as Πάνθεια εἶπεν, ἀλλὰ θάρρει, ἔφη, ὦ Κῦρε X. C. 7. 3. 13.

2590. (I) **Direct Discourse (Oratio Recta).** — In a *direct* quotation the words or thoughts quoted are given at first hand in the exact form used by the original speaker or thinker.

Μεγαρέες ἔπεμπον ἐπὶ τοὺς στρατηγοὺς τῶν Ἑλλήνων κήρυκα, ἀπικόμενος δὲ ὁ κῆρυξ πρὸς αὐτοὺς ἔλεγε τάδε· "Μεγαρέες λέγουσι· 'ἡμεῖς, ἄνδρες σύμμαχοι, οὐ δυνατοί εἰμεν τὴν Περσέων ἵππον δέκεσθαι μοῦνοι'" *the Megarians sent a herald to the generals of the Greeks, and on his arrival the herald spoke as follows: "The Megarians say: 'we, oh allies, are not able to sustain the attack of the Persian cavalry by ourselves'"* Hdt. 9. 21; and often in Hdt. (cp. 3. 40, 3. 122, 5. 24, 7. 150, 8. 140).

a. Direct quotation may, in prose, be introduced by ὅτι, which has the value of quotation marks. Thus, οἱ δὲ εἶπον ὅτι ἱκανοί ἐσμεν *but they said (that) "we are ready"* X. A. 5. 4. 10. So usually when the finite verb is omitted; as ἀπεκρίνατο ὅτι οὔ *he answered (that) "no"* 1. 6. 7. The use of direct speech introduced by ὅτι is, in general, that of familiar style. The first example is Hdt. 2. 115. ὡς for ὅτι is very rare (Dinarchus 1. 12, 1. 102). Cp. "the emperor sends thee this word *that*, if thou love thy sons, let Marcus . . ., or any one of you, chop off your hand" Shakesp. *Tit. Andr.* 3. 1. 151.

2591. (II) **Indirect Discourse (Oratio Obliqua).** In an *indirect* quotation the words or thoughts are given at second hand with certain modifications to indicate that the words or thoughts are reported.

a. The original form may be preserved except that there is a change from the first or second person to the third person: so πάντ' ἐθέλει δόμεναι H 391 reporting πάντ' ἐθέλω δόμεναι H 364. In such cases there is no grammatical dependence.

b. The narrator may report in dependent form the words or thoughts of a person from the point of view of that person. This is the common form of indirect discourse.

c. The narrator may report in dependent form the words or thoughts of a person from his own point of view. See 2624.

2592. The constructions of indirect discourse are regulated by the character of the leading verb or expression.

a. Verbs of *saying* take either ὅτι or ὡς and a finite verb or the infinitive (2017, 2579).

b. Most verbs of *thinking* and *believing* take the infinitive (2018, cp. 2580).

c. Most verbs of *knowing*, *perceiving*, *hearing*, *showing* take the participle (2106, 2110), but admit the construction with ὅτι or ὡς. Some are followed by the infinitive (2123 ff.).

d. **On the construction of verbs of *hoping*, *promising*, and *swearing*, see 1868, 1999, 2024.**

2593. Indirect discourse is said to be *implied* in subordinate clauses dependent on verbs which involve an idea of *saying* or *thinking* (2622).

2594. A speaker may state his own words or thoughts in the form of indirect discourse. Cp. 2614, 2615, etc.

2595. Clauses standing in indirect discourse are substantive clauses, and usually *object* of the leading verb; its *subject*, when that verb is passive or intransitive. The infinitive in substantive clauses after verbs of *saying* and *thinking* retains the *time* of the corresponding finite verb of direct discourse.

2596. Indirect questions (2677) have the constructions of indirect discourse.

GENERAL PRINCIPLES OF INDIRECT DISCOURSE

2597. Simple and compound sentences, and **principal** clauses of complex sentences, introduced by ὅτι or ὡς are treated as follows:

2598. (I) After *primary* tenses, the original mood and tense are retained, except that the person of the verb may be changed.

2599. (II) After *secondary* tenses, primary tenses of the indicative and all subjunctives *may* be changed to the same tense of the optative; but an indicative denoting unreality (with or without ἄν) is retained. Imperfects and pluperfects are generally retained (2623 b).

2600. The verb of simple and compound sentences, and of principal clauses of complex sentences, when introduced by a verb taking the infinitive or participle, passes into the infinitive or participle in the corresponding tense. ἄν is kept, if it was used in the direct form. But note 1847.

2601. **Subordinate** clauses of complex sentences introduced by ὅτι or ὡς are treated as follows:

2602. (I) Subordinate clauses of a sentence introduced by a leading verb in a *primary* tense, *must* remain unchanged in mood and tense.

2603. (II) If subordinate clauses are introduced by a leading verb in a *secondary* tense, all primary tenses of the indicative and all subjunctives (with or without ἄν) *may* be changed to the corresponding tenses of the optative without ἄν. All secondary tenses of the indicative (with or without ἄν) remain unchanged.

2604. Verbs standing in subordinate clauses of sentences introduced by a leading verb requiring the participle or the infinitive, follow the rules of 2602, 2603.

2605. The principal and subordinate clauses of the direct form retain the names *principal* and *subordinate* in indirect discourse though the whole clause in which they stand itself depends on the verb introducing the indirect discourse (the *leading* verb).

2606. The change from direct to indirect discourse is almost always a change of *mood*, not of *tense*. The time of a participle introducing indirect discourse is determined by that of the leading verb. The *person* of the verb is often changed.

2607. ἄν of the direct form is retained in indirect discourse except when a dependent subjunctive with ἄν becomes optative after a secondary tense. Here ἐάν, ὅταν, ἐπειδάν, ἕως ἄν, etc., become εἰ, ὅτε, ἐπειδή, ἕως, etc.

2608. The same negative (οὐ or μή) used in the direct discourse is commonly kept in the indirect form. But in some cases with the infinitive and participle μή takes the place of οὐ (2723 ff., 2730, 2737).

2609. No verb ever *becomes* subjunctive by reason of indirect discourse. The subjunctive (with or without ἄν) may, after a secondary tense, become optative without ἄν.

2610. No verb can be changed to the optative in indirect discourse except after a secondary tense, and since, even after a secondary tense, indicatives or subjunctives may be retained for vividness, no verb *must* become optative by reason of indirect discourse.

2611. All optatives with or without ἄν in the direct form are retained (with or without ἄν) in indirect discourse introduced by ὅτι or ὡς. After verbs requiring the participle or infinitive, such optatives in principal clauses become participles or infinitives (with or without ἄν), but remain unchanged in subordinate clauses.

a. The optative in indirect discourse may represent either the indicative or the subjunctive after a secondary tense.

b. A present optative in indirect discourse may represent (1) the present indicative; (2) the imperfect (2623 b) indicative; (3) the present subjunctive with or without ἄν; (4) the present optative.

2612. The imperative is commonly replaced in indirect discourse by a periphrasis with χρῆναι. Cp. 2633 b.

2613. The retention of the mood of direct discourse, where either the direct or indirect form is possible, lies solely in the option of the writer or speaker. The vivid form reproduces the time and situation in which the quoted words were used. The vivid form is preferred by some writers, as Thucydides; the indirect form by others, as the orators, Plato, and Xenophon.

SIMPLE SENTENCES IN INDIRECT DISCOURSE

1. *Indicative and Optative after* ὅτι *or* ὡς

2614. After primary tenses, the verb of the direct form remains unchanged in mood and tense.

λέγει δ' ὡς ὑβριστής εἰμι *he says that I am an insolent person* L. 24. 15 (= ὑβριστὴς εἶ), ἀλλ' ἐννοεῖν χρὴ τοῦτο μέν, γυναῖχ' ὅτι ἔφῡμεν *but we must remember on the one hand that we were born women* S. Ant. 61, οἶδ' ὅτι οὐδ' ἂν τοῦτό μοι ἐμέμφου *I know that you would not blame me even for this* X. O. 2. 15, ἀπεκρίνατο ὅτι οὐδὲν ἂν τούτων εἴποι *he replied that he would say nothing of this* X. A. 5. 6. 37 (= ἂν εἴποιμι).

2615. After secondary tenses, an indicative without ἄν usually becomes optative, but may be retained unchanged. An indicative with ἄν and an optative with ἄν are retained.

a. Optative for Indicative. — ἔγνωσαν ὅτι κενὸς ὁ φόβος εἴη *they recognized that their fear was groundless* X. A. 2. 2. 21 (= ἐστί), ἔλεξαν ὅτι πέμψειε σφᾶς ὁ Ἰνδῶν βασιλεύς *they said that the king of the Indians had sent them* X. C. 2. 4. 7 (= ἔπεμψεν ἡμᾶς), ἠγγέλθη ὅτι ἡττημένοι εἶεν οἱ Λακεδαιμόνιοι . . . καὶ Πείσανδρος τεθναίη *it was reported that the Lacedaemonians had been defeated and that Peisander was dead* X. H. 4. 3. 10 (= ἡττημένοι εἰσί and τέθνηκε).

N. — The first example of the optative in indirect discourse is later than Homer (*Hymn to Aphrodite* 214). Aeschylus has four cases. See 2624 c.

b. Direct Form Retained. — διῆλθε λόγος ὅτι διώκει αὐτοὺς Κῦρος *a report spread that Cyrus was pursuing them* X. A. 1. 4. 7, ἀποκρῑνάμενοι ὅτι πέμψουσι πρέσβεις, εὐθὺς ἀπήλλαξαν *they withdrew immediately on answering that they would send envoys* T. 1. 90 (= πέμψομεν). See also 2623, 2625.

2. *Infinitive and Participle*

2616. The infinitive and participle are used in indirect discourse to represent the finite verb of direct discourse.

ὑπώπτευον ἐπὶ βασιλέᾱ ἰέναι *they suspected that they were to go against the king* X. A. 5. 1. 8 (= ἴμεν), ἔφη ἢ ἄξειν Λακεδαιμονίους ἢ αὐτοῦ ἀποκτενεῖν *he said that he would either bring the Lacedaemonians or kill them on the spot* T. 4. 28 (= ἄξω, ἀποκτενῶ), οὐ γὰρ ᾔδεσαν αὐτὸν τεθνηκότα *for they did not know that he was dead* X. A. 1. 10. 16 (= ὅτι τέθνηκε).

For examples of the infinitive, see 1846, 1848, 1849, 1867, 2022; for examples of the participle, see 1846, 1848, 1874, 2106, 2112 b.

COMPLEX SENTENCES IN INDIRECT DISCOURSE

2617. When a complex sentence passes into indirect discourse, its principal verb is treated like the verb of a simple sentence and stands either in a finite mood (after ὅτι or ὡς) or in the infinitive or in the participle.

2618. After primary tenses, all subordinate verbs retain the original mood and tense.

λέγουσιν ὡς, ἐπειδάν τις ἀγαθὸς ὢν τελευτήσῃ, μεγάλην μοῖραν καὶ τῑμὴν ἔχει *they say that, when a good man dies, he enjoys great esteem and honour* P. Crat. 398 b, προλέγω ὅτι, ὁπότερ' ἂν ἀποκρίνηται, ἐξελεγχθήσεται *I tell you in advance that, whichever answer he makes, he will be confuted* P. Eu. 275 e, παράδειγμα σαφὲς καταστήσατε, ὃς ἂν ἀφιστῆται θανάτῳ ζημιωσόμενον *give plain warning that whoever revolts shall be punished with death* T. 3. 40 (= ὅτι ζημιώσεται).

2619. After secondary tenses, all subordinate verbs in the present, future, or perfect indicative, and all subjunctives, are usually changed to the corresponding tenses of the optative, or they are retained. Subjunctives with ἄν lose ἄν on passing into the optative.

a. **Optative for Indicative and Indicative Retained.** — εἶπε . . . ὅτι ἄνδρα ἄγοι . . . ὃν εἶρξαι δέοι *he said that he was bringing a man whom it was necessary to lock up* X. H. 5. 4. 8 (= ἄγω, δεῖ), Κῦρος . . . τῷ Κλεάρχῳ ἐβόᾱ ἄγειν τὸ στράτευμα κατὰ μέσον τὸ τῶν πολεμίων, ὅτι ἐκεῖ βασιλεὺς εἴη *Cyrus shouted to Clearchus to lead his troops against the enemy's centre because the king was there* X. A. 1. 8. 12 (= ἐστί), εὖ δὲ εἰδέναι ἔφασαν ὅτι παρέσοιντο *for they said that they knew well that they would come* X. H. 6. 5. 19 (= ἴσμεν ὅτι παρέσονται), ἔλεγεν ὅτι ἕτοιμος εἴη ἡγεῖσθαι αὐτοῖς . . . εἰς τὸ Δέλτα . . ., ἔνθα πολλὰ κἀγαθὰ λήψοιντο *he said that he was ready to be their leader to the Delta, where they would obtain an abundance of good things* X. A. 7. 1. 33 (= ἕτοιμός εἰμι, λήψεσθε), ἔλεγον ὅτι . . . ἥκοιεν ἡγεμόνας ἔχοντες, οἳ αὐτούς, ἐὰν σπονδαὶ γένωνται, ἄξουσιν ἔνθεν ἕξουσι τὰ ἐπιτήδεια *they said that they had come with guides who would lead them, should a truce be made*, to a place *where they would get their supplies* 2. 3. 6 (= ἥκομεν, ὑμᾶς, ἕξετε), ἀγαπήσειν με ἔφασκεν, εἰ τὸ σῶμα σώσω *he said I might think myself well off if I saved my life* L. 12. 11 (= ἀγαπήσεις, εἰ σώσεις).

N. — Except in the future the change to the optative of the indicative after εἰ is rare: as προσῆλθον λέγων ὅτι . . . ἕτοιμός εἰμι, εἴ τινα βούλοιτο (= βούλει), παραδοῦναι βασανίζειν *I went and said that I was ready to give up* the slaves *to be tortured, if he wished any one of them* L. 7. 34, εἶπεν ὅτι Δέξιππον μὲν οὐκ ἐπαινοίη, εἰ ταῦτα πεποιηκὼς εἴη *he said that he did not commend Dexippus, if he had done this* X. A. 6. 6. 25 (= ἐπαινῶ, εἰ πεποίηκε).

b. **Optative for Subjunctive and Subjunctive Retained.** — εἶπεν ὅτι οἰμώξοιτο, εἰ μὴ σιωπήσειεν *he said that he would smart for it unless he kept quiet* X. H. 2. 3. 56 (= οἰμώξει, ἐὰν μὴ σιωπήσῃς), οὐκ ἔφασαν ἰέναι, ἐὰν μή τις αὐτοῖς χρήματα διδῷ *they refused to go unless a largess were given them* X. A. 1. 4. 12 (= οὐκ ἴμεν), εἶπεν ὅτι ἐπιτίθεσθαι μέλλοιεν αὐτῷ, ὁπότε ἀπάγοι τὸ στράτευμα *he said that they intended to attack him when he led his forces away* X. C. 7. 5. 2 (= μέλλουσι, σοί, ὁπόταν ἀπάγῃς), τοὺς ἵππους ἐκέλευε φυλάττειν μένοντας τοὺς ἀγαγόντας ἕως ἄν τις σημαίνῃ *he ordered that those who brought the horses should guard them and wait until orders were given* 4. 5. 36, ὤμοσεν Ἀγησιλάῳ, εἰ σπείσαιτο ἕως ἔλθοιεν οὓς πέμψειε πρὸς βασιλέᾱ ἀγγέλους, διαπράξεσθαι κτλ. *he swore to Agesilaus that, if he would make a truce until the messengers whom he would send to the king should arrive, he would bring it about that*, etc. X. Ages. 1. 10 (= ἐὰν σπείσῃς ἕως ἂν ἔλθωσιν οὓς ἂν πέμψω, διαπράξομαι).

2620. Subordinate verbs in the imperfect, aorist (but see 2623 c, N. 3), or pluperfect indicative, and all optatives, remain unchanged.

ἐπιστεῖλαι δὲ σφίσιν αὐτοῖς τοὺς ἐφόρους . . . εἰπεῖν ὡς ὧν μὲν πρόσθεν ἐποίουν μέμφοιντο αὐτοῖς κτλ. they reported *that the ephors enjoined them to say that they blamed them for what they had done before* X. H. 3. 2. 6 (= ἐποιεῖτε, μεμφόμεθα ὑμῖν), ἤλπιζον τοὺς Σικελοὺς ταύτῃ, οὓς μετέπεμψαν, ἀπαντήσεσθαι *they expected that the Sicels whom they had sent for would meet them here* T. 7. 80, εἶπεν ὅτι ἔλθοι ἂν εἰς λόγους, εἰ ὁμήρους λάβοι *he said that he would enter into negotiations if he should receive hostages* X. H. 3. 1. 20 (ἔλθοιμ' ἄν, εἰ λάβοιμι). See 2623 a, 2625.

2621. The following table shows where, after εἶπεν ὅτι or ἔφη, the optative (and infinitive after ἔφη) may be substituted for the indicative or subjunctive in conditional sentences in indirect discourse.

Direct	Indirect: εἶπεν ὅτι	Indirect: ἔφη
εἴ τι ἔχω, δίδωμι	εἴ τι ἔχοι, διδοίη	(διδόναι)
εἴ τι εἶχεν, ἐδίδουν	εἴ τι εἶχεν, ἐδίδου	(διδόναι)
εἴ τι ἔσχον, ἔδωκα	εἴ τι ἔσχεν, δοίη *	(δοῦναι)
ἐάν τι ἔχω, δώσω	εἴ τι ἔχοι, δώσοι	(δώσειν)
εἴ τι ἕξω, δώσω	εἴ τι ἕξοι, δώσοι	(δώσειν)
ἐάν τι ἔχω, δίδωμι	εἴ τι ἔχοι, διδοίη	(διδόναι)

* The combination of aorist indicative and aorist optative is unusual.

In the following sentences there is no change of mood after ὅτι:

εἴ τι εἶχον, ἐδίδουν ἄν	εἴ τι εἶχεν, ἐδίδου ἄν	(διδόναι ἄν)
εἴ τι ἔσχον, ἔδωκα ἄν	εἴ τι ἔσχεν, ἔδωκεν ἄν	(δοῦναι ἄν)
εἴ τι ἔχοιμι, διδοίην ἄν	εἴ τι ἔχοι, διδοίη ἄν	(διδόναι ἄν)

Temporal and relative sentences (cp. 2561) are converted in the same way. For an infinitive representing an imperative in the apodosis, see 2633 c.

IMPLIED INDIRECT DISCOURSE

2622. Indirect discourse is *implied* in the case of any subordinate clause, which, though not depending formally on a verb of *saying* or *thinking*, contains the *past thought of another person* and not a statement of the writer or speaker. Implied indirect discourse appears only after secondary tenses, and in various kinds of dependent clauses.

a. Conditional clauses, the conclusion being implied in the leading verb. Thus, after a verb of *emotion*, οἱ δ' ᾤκτιρον εἰ ἁλώσοιντο *others pitied them if they should be captured* X. A. 1. 4. 7. The original form was 'we pity them thinking what they will suffer εἰ ἁλώσονται *if they shall be captured*.' In other εἰ clauses, as τὰ χρήματα τῷ δήμῳ ἔδωκεν, εἴ πως τελευτήσειεν ἄπαις *he gave his property to the people in case he died childless* And. 4. 15 (*i.e.* that the people might have it, in case he should die: direct ἐὰν τελευτήσω, and here ἐὰν τελευτήσῃ might have been used).

b. Temporal clauses implying purpose, expectation, or the like (cp. 2420). Thus, σπονδὰς ἐποιήσαντο, ἕως ἀπαγγελθείη τὰ λεχθέντα *they made a truce* (which they agreed should continue) *until what had been said should have been reported* X. H. 3. 2. 20 (ἕως ἂν ἀπαγγελθῇ would be the direct form). Cp. ἕως δ' ἂν ταῦτα διαπράξωνται, φυλακὴν . . . κατέλιπε *he left behind a guard* (which he intended should remain) *until they should settle these matters* 5. 3. 25.

c. Causal clauses. See 2242.

d. Ordinary relative clauses. Thus, εἴρετο παῖδα, τὸν Εὐάδνᾱ τέκοι *he asked for the child which Evadna had borne* Pindar, Ol. 6. 49. Here relative and interrogative are not sharply distinguished.

e. Clauses depending on an infinitive especially when introduced by a verb of *will* or *desire*, e.g. *command*, *advise*, *plan*, *ask*, *wish* (1991, 1992). Here the infinitive expressing command, warning, wish, is not itself in indirect discourse. The negative is μή. Thus, ἀφικνοῦνται (historical present) ὡς Σιτάλκην . . . βουλόμενοι πεῖσαι αὐτόν, εἰ δύναιντο, . . . στρατεῦσαι ἐπὶ τὴν Ποτείδαιαν *they came to Sitalces with the desire of persuading him* (*if they could*) *to make an expedition against Potidaea* T. 2. 67 (= ἐὰν δυνώμεθα), cp. 2633 a.

f. Clauses of purpose and object clauses after verbs of *effort* admit the alternative constructions of indirect discourse.

REMARKS ON THE CONSTRUCTIONS OF INDIRECT DISCOURSE

2623. Past Tenses in Indirect Discourse. — The following rules govern *past tenses* in indirect discourse.

a. The potential indicative with ἄν, the indicative in a condition denoting unreality with ἄν or without ἄν (as ἐχρῆν, ἔδει, etc.), always remain unchanged in order to prevent confusion with the optative of the direct form.

ἀπελογοῦντο ὡς οὐκ ἄν ποτε οὕτω μῶροι ἦσαν . . . εἰ ᾔδεσαν *they pleaded that they never would have been so foolish, if they had known* X. H. 5. 4. 22 (= οὐκ ἂν ἦμεν, εἰ ᾔσμεν), (ἔλεγεν) ὅτι κρεῖττον ἦν αὐτῷ τότε ἀποθανεῖν *he said that it would have been better for him to die then* L. 10. 25 (= κρεῖττον ἦν μοι).

b. The imperfect and pluperfect in simple sentences usually remain unchanged after secondary tenses to prevent ambiguity; but when there is no doubt that a past tense stood in the direct form, the imperfect passes into the present optative, the pluperfect into the perfect optative. In subordinate clauses both tenses are retained unaltered.

ἤκουσεν ὅτι πολλάκις πρὸς τὸν Ἰνδὸν οἱ Χαλδαῖοι ἐπορεύοντο *he heard that the Chaldaeans often went to the Indian king* X. C. 3. 2. 27, εἶχε γὰρ λέγειν καὶ ὅτι μόνοι τῶν Ἑλλήνων βασιλεῖ συνεμάχοντο ἐν Πλαταιαῖς, καὶ ὅτι ὕστερον οὐδεπώποτε στρατεύσαιντο (cp. c) ἐπὶ βασιλέᾱ *for he was able to say both that alone of the Greeks they had fought on the side of the king at Plataea and that later they had never at any time taken the field against the king* X. H. 7. 1. 34 (= συνεμαχόμεθα, ἐστρατευσάμεθα), τὰ πεπρᾱγμένα διηγοῦντο, ὅτι αὐτοὶ μὲν . . . πλέοιεν, τὴν δὲ ἀναίρεσιν τῶν ναυᾱγῶν προστάξαιεν *they related what had occurred to the effect that they were themselves sailing* against the enemy *and that they had given orders for the rescue of the men on the wrecks* X. H. 1. 7. 5 (= ἐπλέομεν, προσετάξαμεν).

N. — The change to the optative is not made when the time of the action of imperfect (and pluperfect) is earlier than that of a coördinated verb in the same quoted sentence; as ἔλεγέν τ' ὡς φιλαθήναιος ἦν καὶ τἀν Σάμῳ πρῶτος κατείποι *he said that he both had been a lover of Athens and that* (afterwards) *he was the first to tell what had happened at Samos* Ar. Vesp. 282.

c. The aorist indicative without ἄν in a simple sentence or in a principal clause may be changed to the aorist optative after a secondary tense; but in subordinate clauses (except those denoting cause, N. 3) it remains unchanged to avoid ambiguity with the aorist optative, which usually represents the aorist subjunctive.

ἀπεκρῑνάμην αὐτῷ ὅτι . . . οὐ λάβοιμι *I answered him that I did not take* D. 50. 36 (= οὐκ ἔλαβον), τοῖς ἰδίοις χρήσεσθαι ἔφη, ἃ ὁ πατὴρ αὐτῷ ἔδωκεν *he said that he would use his own money that his father had given him* X. H. 1. 5. 3 (= χρήσομαι, ἔδωκεν).

N. 1. — The retention of the aorist indicative is here the essential point of difference between subordinate clauses and principal clauses or simple sentences.

N. 2. — In a subordinate clause the time of the aorist usually expresses an action prior to that of the leading verb.

N. 3. — In causal clauses with ὅτι or ὡς a dependent aorist indicative may become aorist optative; as εἶχε γὰρ λέγειν . . . ὡς Λακεδαιμόνιοι διὰ τοῦτο πολεμήσειαν αὐτοῖς, ὅτι οὐκ ἐθελήσαιεν μετ' Ἀγησιλάου ἐλθεῖν ἐπ' αὐτόν *for he was able to say that the Lacedaemonians had gone to war with them* (the Thebans) *for the reason that they* (the Thebans) *had not been willing to attack him* (the Persian king) *in company with Agesilaus* X. H. 7. 1. 34 (direct ἐπολέμησαν ἡμῖν, ὅτι οὐκ ἠθελήσαμεν). Rarely in temporal clauses with ἐπεί (X. C. 5. 3. 26).

2624. Inserted Statement of Fact. — When the present or perfect indicative would have stood in the direct discourse, a past tense of historical narration is often used as a *statement of fact* by the writer from his own point of view, though the rest of the sentence may be given in indirect discourse after a secondary tense from the point of view of the subject of the leading verb.

ᾔδει ὅτι οὐχ οἷόν τ' ἦν αὐτῇ σωθῆναι *she knew that it was not possible for her to be saved* Ant. 1. 8 (= οὐχ οἷόν τ' ἐστὶ ἐμοὶ σωθῆναι. With ἦν the sentence virtually has the force of οὐχ οἷόν τ' ἦν σωθῆναι καὶ ᾔδει *she could not be saved and she knew it*). So ἔλεγον οὐ καλῶς τὴν Ἑλλάδα ἐλευθεροῦν αὐτόν, εἰ ἄνδρας διέφθειρεν *they said that he was not freeing Greece in the right way if he put men to death* T. 3. 32 (= ἐλευθεροῖς, διαφθείρεις), τοὺς φυγάδας ἐκέλευσε σὺν αὐτῷ στρατεύεσθαι, ὑποσχόμενος αὐτοῖς, εἰ καλῶς καταπράξειεν ἐφ' ἃ ἐστρατεύετο, μὴ πρόσθεν παύσεσθαι πρὶν αὐτοὺς καταγάγοι οἴκαδε *he urged the exiles to make the expedition with him, promising them that, if he should succeed in accomplishing the purposes of his campaign, he would not cease until he had brought them back to their homes* X. A. 1. 2. 2 (= ἢν καταπράξω ἐφ' ἃ στρατεύομαι, οὐ παύσομαι πρὶν ἂν καταγάγω), ἀποθανὼν ἐδήλωσεν ὅτι οὐκ ἀληθῆ ταῦτα ἦν *he showed by his death that this was not true* L. 19. 52 (= ἐστί), ἔφη εἶναι παρ' ἑαυτῷ ὅσον μὴ ἦν ἀνηλωμένον *he said that he had in his possession all that had not been expended* D. 48. 16 (= παρ' ἐμοί ἐστιν ὅσον μὴ ἔστιν ἀνηλωμένον), ἐν πολλῇ δὴ ἀπορίᾳ ἦσαν οἱ Ἕλληνες, ἐννοούμενοι μὲν ὅτι ἐπὶ ταῖς βασιλέως θύραις ἦσαν *the Greeks were accordingly in great perplexity on reflecting that they were at the king's gates* X. A. 3. 1. 2 (*i.e.* they were there in fact and they knew it).

a. The use of past tenses of historical narration instead of present tenses of direct discourse occurs, in simple sentences, especially after verbs of *knowing*, *perceiving*, *showing*, and verbs of *emotion* (rarely after verbs of *saying* w. ὅτι).

b. Such inserted statements of fact are often difficult to distinguish from indicatives in indirect discourse; and the two forms of expression may occur in the same sentence (X. C. 4. 2. 35–36). The common explanation of the use of the imperfect and pluperfect for the present and perfect is that Greek had the same assimilation of tense as English.

c. Except in indirect questions, the optative of indirect discourse is unknown to Homer. (εἰπεῖν ὡς ἔλθοι ω 237 may be considered as interrogative.) After primary or secondary tenses Homer employs, in the dependent clause, the same past tense that would have been used in an independent clause, from the point of view of the speaker, and not the tense which would have been used in direct discourse from the point of view of the subject of the main clause. Thus, γίγνωσκον ὃ (= ὅτι) δὴ κακὰ μήδετο *I knew that he was planning evil* γ 166 (*i.e* κακὰ ἐμήδετο καὶ ἐγίγνωσκον *he was planning evil and I knew it*). In Attic we should commonly have μήδεται or μήδοιτο. After secondary tenses the future is usually expressed in Homer by ἔμελλον and the infinitive, as οὐδὲ τὸ ᾔδη, ὃ οὐ πείσεσθαι ἔμελλεν *nor did he know this, that she had no thought to comply* γ 146.

d. That this use of statements of fact standing outside indirect discourse is optional only, is seen from a comparison of the first example in 2624 with καλῶς γὰρ ᾔδειν ὡς ἐγὼ ταύτῃ κράτιστός εἰμι *for he knew full well that I am first-rate in this line* Ar. Vesp. 635 and with ᾔδει αὐτὸν ὅτι μέσον ἔχοι τοῦ Περσικοῦ στρατεύματος *he knew that he held the centre of the Persian army* X. A. 1. 8. 21.

2625. An optative with or without ἄν is regularly retained after ὅτι (ὡς).

ἐδίδασκον ὡς . . . συνεστρατεύοντο ὅποι ἡγοῖντο *they showed that they always followed them in their campaigns wherever they led* X. H. 5. 2. 8 (= συνεστρατευόμεθα, ὅποι ἡγοῖσθε, cp. 2568), ἀπεκρίνατο . . . ὅτι πρόσθεν ἂν ἀποθάνοιεν ἢ τὰ ὅπλα παραδοίησαν *he replied that they would sooner die than surrender their arms* X. A. 2. 1. 10 (= ἂν ἀποθάνοιμεν, παραδοῖμεν).

2626. In some cases the optative *with* ἄν in temporal and relative sentences is used to represent the subjunctive with ἄν; but many scholars expel ἄν.

παρήγγειλαν αὐτοῖς μὴ πρότερον ἐπιτίθεσθαι πρὶν ἂν τῶν σφετέρων ἢ πέσοι τις ἢ τρωθείη *they gave orders to them that they should not attack before some one of their number had either fallen or been wounded* X. H. 2. 4. 18. Cp. 2421.

2627. An optative occasioned by indirect discourse may stand after a *primary* tense when it is implied that the thought quoted has been expressed in the past.

λέγει ὁ λόγος ὅτι Νεοπτόλεμος Νέστορα ἔροιτο *the story goes that Neoptolemus asked Nestor* P. Hipp. M. 286 b. This may be expressed by λέγεται εἰπεῖν ὅτι. Cp. λέγεται εἰπεῖν ὅτι βούλοιτο *it is reported that he said that he wished* X. C. 1. 4. 25.

a. The historical present is a secondary tense: οἱ δὲ πεμφθέντες λέγουσι Κύρῳ ὅτι μῑσοῖεν τοὺς Ἀσσυρίους *and those who had been sent told Cyrus that they hated the Assyrians* X. C. 4. 2. 4.

2628. Indirect discourse may be introduced by ὅτι (ὡς) and then pass into the infinitive as if the introductory verb had required the infinitive.

ἡ δὲ ἀπεκρίνατο ὅτι βούλοιτο μὲν ἅπαντα τῷ πατρὶ χαρίζεσθαι, ἄκοντα μέντοι τὸν παῖδα χαλεπὸν εἶναι νομίζειν (= νομίζοι) καταλιπεῖν *she answered that she wished to do everything to oblige her father, but that she considered it unkind to leave the child behind against his inclination* X. C. 1. 3. 13.

a. It is unusual to have the infinitive first, and then ὅτι (T. 5. 65).

b. One and the same clause may even begin with ὅτι (ὡς) and then (sometimes after a parenthesis) be continued by an infinitive, less often by a participle. Thus, ἀκούω ὅτι (omitted in one Ms.) καὶ συνθηρευτάς τινας τῶν παίδων σοι γενέσθαι αὐτοῦ *I hear too that some of his sons became your companions in the chase* X. C. 2. 4. 15. Continuation with a participle in T. 4. 37.

2629. An optative dependent on ὅτι (ὡς) may be followed, in a parenthetical or appended clause (often introduced by γάρ or οὖν), by an *independent* optative, which is used as if it itself directly depended on ὅτι (ὡς).

ἔλεγον πολλοὶ . . . ὅτι παντὸς ἄξια λέγοι Σεύθης· χειμὼν γὰρ εἴη καὶ οὔτε οἴκαδε ἀποπλεῖν τῷ ταῦτα βουλομένῳ δυνατὸν εἴη κτλ. *many said that what Seuthes said was of much value; for it was winter and neither was it possible for any one who so desired to sail home*, etc. X. A. 7. 3. 13 (here we might have had χειμῶνα γὰρ εἶναι by 2628).

a. Such an independent optative may also follow an infinitive in indirect discourse (L. 13. 78), an indicative after ὅτι (Is. 8. 22), or a participle (Is. 9. 5). After an optative in indirect discourse the appended clause may contain an indicative (X. A. 6. 2. 10, I. 17. 21).

2630. An infinitive in indirect discourse may follow a sentence which merely *involves* the idea of indirect statement.

ὁ δὲ αὐτοὺς εἰς Λακεδαίμονα ἐκέλευεν ἰέναι· οὐ γὰρ εἶναι κύριος αὐτὸς *he recommended them to go to Lacedaemon; for* (he said that) *he was not himself empowered to act* X. H. 2. 2. 12.

2631. In subordinate temporal and relative clauses the infinitive is often used for the indicative or optative by attraction to an infinitive standing in the principal clause after a verb of *saying*. In some cases ἔφη may be mentally inserted.

ἔφη . . . ἐπειδὴ δὲ γενέσθαι ἐπὶ τῇ οἰκίᾳ τῇ Ἀγάθωνος, ἀνεῳγμένην καταλαμβάνειν τὴν θύραν *he said that, when he arrived at the house of Agathon, he found the door open* P. S. 174 d (= ἐπειδὴ ἐγενόμην, καταλαμβάνω). See also the sentence quoted in 1228 b, end. So οὗτοι δὲ ἔλεγον ὅτι πολλοὺς φαίη Ἀριαῖος εἶναι Πέρσᾱς ἑαυτοῦ βελτίους, οὓς οὐκ ἂν ἀνασχέσθαι αὐτοῦ βασιλεύοντος *and they said that Ariaeus said that there were many Persians better than himself, who would not endure his being king* X. A. 2. 2. 1 (= πολλοί εἰσι ἐμαυτοῦ βελτίους, οἳ οὐκ ἂν ἀνάσχοιντο ἐμοῦ β.). Here the relative is equivalent, in sense, to καὶ τούτους. The infinitive occurs even in clauses with εἰ (T. 4. 98, and often in Hdt.), and with διότι (Hdt. 3. 55).

a. The infinitive is rare in such relative clauses as διορίζουσι σαφῶς ἐν οἷς ἐξεῖναι ἀποκτιννύναι *they make a clear distinction in cases where it is permitted to kill* D. 23. 74.

2632. For the sake of variation, a mood of the direct form may be used in the same sentence with a mood of the indirect. The main verb may be kept in the direct form, while the subordinate verb becomes optative, or, less often, the subordinate verb may be retained in the direct form though the main verb becomes optative.

οὗτοι ἔλεγον ὅτι Κῦρος μὲν τέθνηκεν, Ἀριαῖος δὲ πεφευγὼς . . . εἴη *these said that Cyrus was dead but that Ariaeus had fled* X. A. 2. 1. 3 (here we might have had τεθνήκοι or πέφευγε), αἱ δὲ ἀπεκρίναντο ὅτι οὐκ ἐνταῦθα εἴη, ἀλλ' ἀπέχει ὅσον παρασάγγην *and they replied that he was not there but was a parasang distant* 4. 5. 10 (here we might have ἐστί or ἀπέχοι), ἐδόκει δῆλον εἶναι ὅτι αἱρήσονται αὐτὸν εἴ τις ἐπιψηφίζοι *it seemed to be clear that they would elect him if any one should put it to vote* X. A. 6. 1. 25 (here we might have αἱρήσοιντο or ἐᾱ̀ν ἐπιψηφίζῃ), ἔλεξας . . . ὅτι μέγιστον εἴη μαθεῖν ὅπως δεῖ ἐξεργάζεσθαι ἕκαστα *you said that it was essential to learn how it is necessary to conduct each process* X. O. 15. 2 (here ἐστί or δέοι might have been used), παρήγγειλαν, ἐπειδὴ δειπνήσαιεν, . . . ἀναπαύεσθαι καὶ ἕπεσθαι, ἡνίκ' ἄν τις παραγγέλλῃ *they gave orders that, when they had supped, they should rest and follow when any one gave the command* X. A. 3. 5. 18 (here we might have had ἐπειδὰν δειπνήσωσι or ἡνίκα παραγγέλλοι). Other examples 2619. Subjunctive (in some Mss.), then optative: X. A. 7. 7. 57.

2633. The idea conveyed by an imperative or a hortatory (or even deliberative) subjunctive of direct discourse may be set forth in the infinitive by a *statement* as to what *ought to be.*

a. In an infinitive dependent on a verb of *will* or *desire* (such as *ask, command, advise, forbid,* etc. 1992) which does not properly take the construction of indirect discourse.

εἷς δὲ δὴ εἶπε (1997) . . . στρατηγοὺς μὲν ἑλέσθαι ἄλλους *and some one urged that they choose other generals* X. A. 1. 3. 14 (cp. ἕλεσθε or ἕλωμεν), ἀπηγόρευε μηδένα βάλλειν *he forbade any one to shoot* X. C. 1. 4. 14 (cp. μηδεὶς βαλλέτω).

N. — Here may be placed the infinitive after ἡγοῦμαι, νομίζω, οἴομαι in the sense of δοκῶ *I think it proper* (or *necessary*); as ᾤοντο ἀπιέναι *they thought that they should retire* X. H. 4. 7. 4 (cp. ἀπίωμεν).

b. In an infinitive dependent on ἔφη χρῆναι (δεῖν), as ἔφη . . . χρῆναι πλεῖν ἐπὶ Συρᾱκούσᾱς *he said that they ought to sail to Syracuse* T. 4. 69.

c. In the simple infinitive, as τὰς μὲν ἐπιστολὰς . . . ἀνέγνωσαν, ἐν αἷς πολλῶν ἄλλων γεγραμμένων κεφάλαιον ἦν πρὸς Λακεδαιμονίους οὐ γιγνώσκειν ὅ τι βούλονται . . . εἰ οὖν τι βούλονται σαφὲς λέγειν, πέμψαι μετὰ τοῦ Πέρσου ἄνδρας ὡς αὐτόν *they read the dispatches, in which of much besides therein written to the Lacedaemonians the substance was that* the king *did not understand what they wanted; if therefore* *they wished to make explicit statements, let them send men to him in company with the Persian* T. 4. 50. Cp. T. 1. 27. 1 μένειν = μενέτω.

2634. Long sentences (and even some short complex sentences), or a series of sentences, in indirect discourse depending on a single verb of *saying* or *thinking*, are uncongenial to the animated character of Greek, which resists the formal regularity of Latin. Some long speeches in indirect discourse do, however, appear, *e.g.* Andoc. 1. 38–42, Thuc. 6. 49, Xen. C. 8. 1. 10–11, Plato R. 614 b (the entire *Symposium* is given in reported form). To effect variety and to ensure clearness by relieving the strain on the leading verb, Greek has various devices.

a. ἔφη (ἔλεξε, εἶπεν, ἤρετο) is repeated, *e.g.* T. 7. 48.

b. The indirect form is abandoned for the direct form, *e.g.* X. A. 1. 3. 14, 1. 9. 25, 4. 8. 10; often with a change, or repetition, of the verb of *saying* (X. A. 5. 6. 37, X. H. 2. 1. 25).

c. ἔφη χρῆναι (δεῖν) or ἐκέλευσε is inserted or repeated (T. 6. 49. 4).

N. 1. — Transition from direct to indirect discourse is rare (X. A. 7. 1. 39, cp. X. C. 3. 2. 25).

N. 2. — An interrogative clause always depends immediately on the introductory verb, hence such clauses do not occur in the course of a long sentence in indirect discourse.

2635. EXAMPLES OF INDIRECT DISCOURSE

ἔφη γὰρ εἶναι μὲν ἀνδράποδόν οἱ ἐπὶ Λαυρίῳ, δεῖν δὲ κομίσασθαι ἀποφοράν. ἀναστὰς δὲ πρῴ ψευσθεὶς τῆς ὥρᾱς βαδίζειν· εἶναι δὲ πανσέληνον. ἐπεὶ δὲ παρὰ τὸ προπύλαιον τοῦ Διονύσου ἦν, ὁρᾶν ἀνθρώπους πολλοὺς ἀπὸ τοῦ Ὠιδείου καταβαίνοντας εἰς τὴν ὀρχήστρᾱν· δείσᾱς δὲ αὐτούς, εἰσελθὼν ὑπὸ τὴν σκιᾶν καθέζεσθαι μεταξὺ τοῦ κίονος καὶ τῆς στήλης ἐφ' ᾗ ὁ στρατηγός ἐστιν ὁ χαλκοῦς. ὁρᾶν δὲ ἀνθρώπους τὸν μὲν ἀριθμὸν μάλιστα τριᾱκοσίους, ἑστάναι δὲ κύκλῳ ἀνὰ πέντε καὶ δέκα ἄνδρας, τοὺς δὲ ἀνὰ εἴκοσιν· ὁρῶν δὲ αὐτῶν πρὸς τὴν σελήνην τὰ πρόσωπα τῶν πλείστων γιγνώσκειν. καὶ πρῶτον μέν, ὦ ἄνδρες, τοῦθ' ὑπέθετο δεινότατον πρᾶγμα, οἶμαι, ὅπως ἐν ἐκείνῳ εἴη ὅντινα βούλοιτο Ἀθηναίων φάναι τῶν ἀνδρῶν τούτων εἶναι, ὅντινα δὲ μὴ βούλοιτο, λέγειν ὅτι οὐκ ἦν. ἰδὼν δὲ ταῦτ' ἔφη ἐπὶ Λαύριον ἰέναι, καὶ τῇ ὑστεραίᾳ ἀκούειν ὅτι οἱ Ἑρμαῖ εἶεν περικεκομμένοι· γνῶναι οὖν

For Dioclides *said that he had a slave at Laurium, and that he had to fetch a payment due him. Rising early he mistook the time and set out, and there was a full moon. When he was by the gateway of the sanctuary of Dionysus, he saw a body of men coming down from the Odeum into the orchestra, and through fear of them he betook himself into the shade and sat down between the column and the block on which the Bronze General stands. He saw about three hundred men, some standing round about in groups of fifteen, others in groups of twenty. On seeing them in the moonlight he recognized the faces of most. In the first place, gentlemen, he has concocted this most extraordinary tale, in order, as I believe, that it might be in his power to include among these men any Athenian he wished, or to*

εὐθὺς ὅτι τούτων εἴη τῶν ἀνδρῶν τὸ ἔργον. ἥκων δὲ εἰς ἄστυ ζητητάς τε ἤδη ᾑρημένους καταλαμβάνειν καὶ μήνῦτρα κεκηρῦγμένα ἑκατὸν μνᾶς. — Andocides 1. 38.

exclude any he did not wish. On seeing this he said he went to Laurium, and on the day after heard that the statues of Hermes had been mutilated. So he knew forthwith that it was the work of these men. On his return to the city he found that commissioners of inquiry had already been appointed and that a hundred minae had been offered as a reward.

INTERROGATIVE SENTENCES (QUESTIONS)

2636. Questions are either direct (independent) or indirect (dependent). Thus, τίς ἔλεξε ταῦτα; *who said this?* ἐρωτῶ ὅστις ἔλεξε ταῦτα *I ask who said this.*

2637. Questions may have the assertive form with the interrogation expressed simply by the tone of the voice, or may be introduced by an interrogative pronoun, adjective, adverb, or particle.

a. A question gains in animation and has its emphatic part clearly marked if the interrogative word is placed late in the sentence. Thus, ἡδέα δὲ καλεῖς οὐ τὰ ἡδονῆς μετέχοντα; *you call pleasant, do you not, that which participates in pleasure?* P. Pr. 351 d, τὸ πεινῆν ἔλεγες πότερον ἡδὺ ἢ ἀνιᾱρὸν εἶναι; *did you say that to be hungry was pleasant or painful?* P. G. 496 c.

2638. ***Yes* and *No* Questions** (or sentence-questions) are asked by the verb (whether a given thing *is* or *is done*). Such questions are commonly introduced by an interrogative particle. **Pronoun-questions** (or word-questions) are asked by an interrogative pronoun, adjective, or adverb (*who, what, where, when, how*).

a. A sentence-question may follow a word-question; as τί δοκοῦσιν ὑμῖν, ὦ ἄνδρες; ἆρά γε ὁμοίως ὑμῖν περὶ τῶν ἀδικούντων γιγνώσκειν κτλ.; *what do you think of* your ancestors, *gentlemen of the jury? Do they seem to entertain the same sentiments with yourselves about wrong-doers?* Lyc. 119.

2639. Deliberative Questions ask what *is to be done* or what *was to be done.* Questions asking what *is to be done* in the present or future are expressed by the deliberative subjunctive (negative μή, 1805), by δεῖ or χρή and the infinitive, by the verbal in -τέον with ἐστί (1808) or by the deliberative future (1916). Questions asking what *was to be done* are expressed by χρῆν (ἐχρῆν) or ἔδει with the infinitive, or by the verbal in -τέον with ἦν. In *direct* questions the optative is not used to denote what *was to be done.*

2640. **Rhetorical Questions** are questions asked for effect and not for information, since the speaker knows the answer in advance and either does not wait for, or himself gives, the answer. Thus, ἀλλ' οὐκ ἔστι ταῦτα· πόθεν; *but this is not so. How can it be?* D. 18. 47, τί οὖν αἴτιον εἶναι ὑπολαμβάνω; ἐγὼ ὑμῖν ἐρῶ *what then do I regard as the explanation? I will tell you* P. A. 40 b. Such questions are often introduced by μή (2651 b). Other examples 2638 a, 2641.

a. Rhetorical questions awaken attention and express various shades of emotion; and are often used in passing to a new subject. Such questions are very rare in Lysias, somewhat frequent in Plato, common in Isaeus, highly developed in Demosthenes. The rhetorical question is much more favoured in Greek than in English.

DIRECT (INDEPENDENT) QUESTIONS

2641. Any form of statement (2153) may be used as a direct question. The interrogative meaning may be indicated only by the context, or it may be expressed by placing an emphatic word first or by the use of certain particles (2650, 2651).

ἐγὼ οὔ φημι; *I say no?* P. G. 446 e, οὐ γὰρ ἀπεκρῑνάμην ὅτι εἴη ἡ καλλίστη; *for did I not answer that it was the noblest* art? 448 e, Ἕλληνες ὄντες βαρβάροις δουλεύσομεν; *shall we, who are Greeks, be subject to barbarians?* E. fr. 719, ἡγούμεθά τι τὸν θάνατον εἶναι; *do we regard death as anything?* P. Ph. 64 c. Cp. 1831, 1832.

2642. Questions which cannot be answered by *yes* or *no* are introduced by interrogative pronouns, adjectives or adverbs (340, 346), usually without any interrogative particle, and may have any form of the simple sentence.

τί οὖν κελεύω ποιῆσαι; *what then do I urge* you *to do?* X. A. 1. 4. 14, πόσον . . . ἄπεστιν ἐνθένδε τὸ στράτευμα; *how far distant from here is the army?* X. C. 6. 3. 10, πῶς εἶπας; *what* (lit. *how*) *did you say?* P. G. 447 d, τί ἂν αὐτῷ εἶπες; *what would you have said to him?* P. R. 337 c.

2643. An interrogative pronoun or adverb often depends on a participle and not on the main verb of the sentence. Thus, τί οὖν ποιήσαντος κατεχειροτονήσατε τοῦ Εὐάνδρου; *for what act then did you condemn Evander?* D. 21. 176, (Ὀλύνθιοι) οἷ τί πεποιηκότος αὐτοῖς Φιλίππου πῶς αὐτῷ χρῶνται; *for whom what has Philip done and how do they treat him?* 23. 107. Cp. 2147 d. On τί παθών see 2064 a.

2644. A subordinate clause introduced by a conjunction or a relative pronoun may suddenly change into a direct pronoun-question, though the construction of the clause remains unaltered. Thus, ἐπειδὴ περὶ τίνος Ἀθηναῖοι διανοοῦνται βουλεύεσθαι, ἀνίστασαι συμβουλεύων; *when the Athenians are intending to deliberate* (lit. *about what?*) *do you get up to give them advice?* P. Alc. I. 106 c, πόθ' ἃ χρὴ πράξετε; ἐπειδὰν τί γένηται; *when will you do what you ought to do? in what event?* (lit. *when what shall have happened?*) D. 4. 10.

a. Here belong the elliptical phrases **ἵνα τί, ὡς τί** (*scil.* γένηται, 946), **ὅτι τί** (*scil.* γίγνεται). Thus, ἵνα τί ταῦτα λέγεις; *why* (lit. *that what* shall happen?) *do you say this?* P. A. 26 d, ἔτι καὶ τοῦτ' αὐτῷ προσθήσετε; ὅτι τί; *will you give him this* distinction *too in addition? for what reason?* D. 23. 214.

2645. Two questions may be condensed into one in an interrogative sentence by placing an interrogative between the article and its noun. Thus, ἐγὼ οὖν τὸν ἐκ ποίᾱς πόλεως στρατηγὸν προσδοκῶ ταῦτα πράξειν; *am I waiting for a general to do this? From what city?* X. A. 3. 1. 14.

2646. Two or more interrogative pronouns, without a connective, may occur in the same sentence (question within a question). Thus, ἀπὸ τούτων τίς τίνος αἴτιός ἐστι γενήσεται φανερὸν *from this it will become clear who is chargeable with* *what* D. 18. 73, ἐπειδάν τις τινα φιλῇ, πότερος ποτέρου φίλος γίγνεται; *whenever one person loves another, which one is the lover of which?* P. Lys. 212 a.

2647. With a substantive and the article or with a demonstrative pronoun an interrogative pronoun may be used as a predicate adjective. Here the interrogative sentence is equivalent to an interrogative clause with a dependent (relative) clause (cp. 1169).

ποῖον τὸν μῦθον ἔειπες; *what is the word that thou hast uttered?* A 552 (lit. *the word* being *what?* In fuller form = ποῖός ἐστιν ὁ μῦθος ὃν ἔειπες;), τίς ὁ πόθος αὐτοὺς ἵκετο; *what is this longing that has come upon them?* S. Ph. 601, οὗτος δὲ τίς . . . κρατεῖ; *who is this man who holds sway?* S. O. C. 68, τίνας τούσδ' εἰσορῶ; *who are these I see?* E. Or. 1347, διὰ σοφίᾱν τινὰ τοῦτο τὸ ὄνομα ἔσχηκα. ποίᾱν δὴ σοφίᾱν ταύτην; *thanks to a kind of wisdom I obtained this name.* (*Thanks to*) *this wisdom being what?* (that is, *what is this wisdom?*) P. A. 20 d.

2648. τίς, τί, ποῖος referring to something mentioned before may take the article; as A. πάσχει δὲ θαυμαστόν. B. τὸ τί; A. *A strange thing is happening to him.* B. (*The*) *what?* Ar. Pax 696, A. νῦν δὴ ἐκεῖνα ἤδη . . . δυνάμεθα κρίνειν. B. τὰ ποῖα; A. *Now at last we are able to decide those matters.* B. (*The*) *what matters?* P. Phae. 277 a.

2649. τίς, ποῖος as adjective pronouns, and πῶς etc., when followed by οὐ, have the force of an affirmative assertion. Thus, ποίους λόγους οὐκ ἀνηλώσαμεν; *what arguments did we not expend?* I. 8. 67 (= πάντας), τί κακὸν οὐχί; = πᾶν κακόν in 2147 d.

QUESTIONS INTRODUCED BY INTERROGATIVE PARTICLES

2650. ἦ and ἆρα introduce questions asking merely for information and imply nothing as to the answer expected (neither *yes* nor *no*).

ἦ τέθνηκεν Οἰδίπου πατήρ; *is Oedipus' father* really *dead?* S. O. T. 943, ἦ λέγω (delib. subj.); *shall I tell you?* X. C. 8. 4. 10, ἦ καὶ οἴκοι τῶν πλουσίων ἦσθα; *were you* really *one of the rich men when you were at home?* 8. 3. 36.

ἆρ' εἰμὶ μάντις; *am I a prophet?* S. Ant. 1212, ἆρ' Ὀδυσσέως κλύω; *can it be that I am listening to Odysseus?* S. Ph. 976, ἆρα ἐθελήσειεν ἂν ἡμῖν διαλεχθῆναι; *will he* really *be willing to talk with us?* P. G. 447 b.

a. ἆρα is from ἦ + ἄρα. ἦ is chiefly poetic. Homer uses ἦ, not ἆρα. Both particles denote interest on the part of the questioner (often = *really? surely?*).

2651. οὐ, ἆρ' οὐ, οὐκοῦν expect the answer *yes* (*nonne*), μή, ἆρα μή, μῶν (= μὴ οὖν) expect the answer *no* (*num*).

a. οὐχ οὕτως ἔλεγες; *did you not say so?* P. R. 334 b (*i.e.* 'I think you did, did you not?'), ἆρ' οὐχ ὕβρις τάδε; *is not this insolence?* S. O. C. 883, οὐκοῦν . . . εὖ σοι δοκοῦσι βουλεύεσθαι; *do they not then seem to you to plan well?* X. C. 7. 1. 8. οὐκοῦν οὐ expects the answer *no.*

b. μή τι νεώτερον ἀγγέλλεις; *no bad news, I hope?* P. Pr. 310 b, ἆρα μὴ αἰσχυνθῶμεν; *surely we are not ashamed, are we?* (or *can it be that we should be ashamed?*) X. O. 4. 4, μὴ ἀποκρίνωμαι; *am I not to answer?* P. R. 337 b, μῶν τί σε ἀδικεῖ; *surely he has not wronged you, has he?* (or *can it be that*, etc.) P. Pr. 310 d. μῶν οὐ expects the answer *yes.*

c. μῶν is confined to Attic. Since the fact of its composition was lost, we find μῶν οὖν (A. Ch. 177) and μῶν μή (P. Lys. 208 e).

d. οὐ after μή or ἆρα μή belongs to a single word, not to the sentence (P. Men. 89 c, Lys. 213 d). On μή or μὴ οὐ with the subjunctive in half-questions, see 1801.

e. ἆρα placed before οὐ or μή gives greater distinctness to the question. οὐ questions ask concerning facts; μή questions imply uncertainty or even apprehension, but sometimes are asked merely for effect.

f. οὔ που; οὔ τί που; οὐ δή; οὐ δή που mean *surely it is not so?* Here the negative belongs to the sentence.

2652. **ἄλλο τι ἤ**; *is it anything else than?* and **ἄλλο τι**; *is it not?* are used as direct interrogatives. Thus, ἄλλο τι ἢ οὐδὲν κωλύει παρεῖναι; *there's nothing to hinder our passing, is there?* (lit. *is there anything else* the case *than* this that *nothing prevents*, etc.) X. A. 4. 7. 5, ἄλλο τι φιλεῖται ὑπὸ θεῶν; *is it not loved by the gods?* P. Euth. 10 d. Cp. τί γὰρ ἄλλο ἢ κινδῡνεύσεις ἐπιδεῖξαι κτλ.; *for what other risk will you run than that of showing*, etc.? (= *for what else will* you do *than that you will very likely show?*) X. M. 2. 3. 17.

2653. **εἶτα** and **ἔπειτα** (more emphatic κᾆτα, κἄπειτα) introduce questions expressing surprise, indignation, irony, etc.; and often indicate a contrast between what a person has or has not done and what is or was to be expected of him. Thus, εἶτα πῶς οὐκ εὐθὺς ἐπήγειράς με; *then why did you not rouse me at once?* P. Cr. 43 b.

2654. **ἀλλά** (**ἀλλ' ἦ**) introduces a question opposed to an expressed or implied thought of the speaker (especially an objection). Thus, ᾔτουν τί σε καὶ ἐπεί μοι οὐκ ἐδίδους ἔπαιον; ἀλλ' ἀπῄτουν; ἀλλὰ περὶ παιδικῶν μαχόμενος; ἀλλὰ μεθύων ἐπαρῴνησα; *did I ask anything of you and strike you when you would not give it to me? Or did I demand anything back? Or was I quarreling about an object of affection? Or was I the worse for liquor and did I treat you with drunken violence?* X. A. 5. 8. 4, ἀλλ' ἦ, τὸ λεγόμενον, κατόπιν ἑορτῆς ἥκομεν; *but have we arrived, as the proverb says, late for a feast?* P. G. 447 a. Cp. 2785.

2655. **δέ** sometimes introduces a suppressed thought, as an objection. Thus, εἰπέ μοι, σὺ δὲ δὴ τί τὴν πόλιν ἡμῖν ἀγαθὸν πεποίηκας; *tell me, (but) what good, pray, have you done the State?* D. 8. 70.

DIRECT ALTERNATIVE QUESTIONS

2656. Direct alternative questions are usually introduced by πότερον (πότερα) . . . ἤ *whether . . . or* (Lat. *utrum . . . an*).

πότερον δέδρᾱκεν ἢ οὔ; *has he done it or not?* D. 23. 79. πότερόν σέ τις, Αἰσχίνη, τῆς πόλεως ἐχθρὸν ἢ ἐμὸν εἶναι φῇ; *shall I say, Aeschines, that you are the enemy of the State or mine?* 18. 124 (τις φῇ = φῶ, 1805 c), πότερα δ' ἡγεῖ . . . ἄμεινον εἶναι σὺν τῷ σῷ ἀγαθῷ τὰς τῑμωρίᾱς ποιεῖσθαι ἢ σὺν τῇ σῇ ζημίᾳ; *do you think that it is better to inflict the* proper *punishments in your own interest or to your own loss?* X. C. 3. 1. 15.

2657. ἤ often stands alone without πότερον (as *an* without *utrum*). Thus, ἔλῡε τὴν εἰρήνην ἢ οὔ; *did he break the peace or not?* D. 18. 71, ἣν χρήματα πολλὰ ἔχῃ, ἐᾷς πλουτεῖν ἢ πένητα ποιεῖς; *if he has great wealth, do you let him keep on being rich or do you make him poor?* X. C. 3. 1. 12. So when the first question expresses uncertainty on the part of the questioner; as ἀλλὰ τίς σοι διηγεῖτο; ἢ αὐτὸς Σωκράτης; *but who told you the story?* (was it some one else) *or was it Socrates himself?* P. S. 173 a. Cp. 2860.

2658. An alternative question may follow upon a simple direct (or indirect) question. Thus, πόθεν πλεῖθ' ὑγρὰ κέλευθα; ἤ τι κατὰ πρῆξιν ἢ μαψιδίως ἀλάλησθε; *whence do ye sail over the watery ways? Or is it perchance on some enterprise or by way of rash adventure that ye rove?* ι 252. Cp. E 85 (cited in 2660).

2659. πότερον (πότερα) may stand alone when the second member of the question is implicit in another sentence. Thus, ἐννοήσατε δὲ κἀκεῖνο, τίνα πρόφασιν ἔχοντες ἂν προσιοίμεθα κακίονες ἢ πρόσθεν γενέσθαι. πότερον ὅτι ἄρχομεν; . . . ἀλλ' ὅτι εὐδαιμονέστεροι δοκοῦμεν νῦν ἢ πρότερον εἶναι; *and consider this too: what pretence should we have for allowing ourselves to become less deserving than heretofore? Is it because we are rulers? Or is it because we seem to be more prosperous than before?* X. C. 7. 5. 83.

2660. πότερον (πότερα) was originally the neuter of πότερος *which of the two?* placed in front of a double question and later made a part of the first question. Thus, ἐρωτῶ πότερον φιλεῖ ἢ μισεῖ σε *I ask which of the two* (is true): *does he love or does he hate you?* Cp. Τυδεΐδην δ' οὐκ ἂν γνοίης ποτέροισι μετείη, ἠὲ μετὰ Τρώεσσιν ὁμιλέοι ἢ μετ' Ἀχαιοῖς *you could not tell on which side Tydides was, whether he consorted with Trojans or with Achaeans* E 85, τίνες κατῆρξαν, πότερον Ἕλληνες, μάχης, ἢ παῖς ἐμός; *who began the battle—was it the Greeks or my son?* A. Pers. 351, cp. X. C. 1. 3. 2.

2661. ἤ (ἠέ) . . . ἦ (ἦε), or ἦ (ἦε) alone, occurs in Homer, who does not use πότερον. Thus, ἤ ῥά τι ἴδμεν ἐνὶ φρεσίν, ἦε καὶ οὐκί; *do we know aught in heart, or do we not?* δ 632, ψεύσομαι ἢ ἔτυμον ἐρέω; *shall I speak falsehood or the truth?* K 534.

a. All the ancient grammarians attest the accentuation of these particles as given above. Modern editors often adopt other accents. ἠέ and ἦε are derived from ἠ-ϝέ and ἦ-ϝε (whence ἤ and ἦ). With this enclitic ϝέ, cp. Lat. *-ve.*

MOODS IN DIRECT QUESTIONS

2662. The moods used in direct questions are the same as those used in statements.

a. *Indicative* (examples in 2642): sometimes in a past tense with ἄν, as πῶς δὲ πάντες ἐζήλουν ἂν τοὺς τυράννους; *but why should all men envy despotic rulers?* X. Hi. 1. 9, εἴ τις ἕνα νόμον . . . ἐξαλείψειεν . . . , ἆρ' οὐκ ἂν ἀπεκτείνατ' αὐτόν; *if any one should cancel a single law . . ., would you not have put him to death?* Lyc. 66. On τί οὐ or τί οὖν οὐ with the aorist, see 1936.

b. *Subjunctive:* in deliberative questions (2639). On the anticipatory subjunctive in τί πάθω, see 1811.

c. *Optative* (potential), as τίς φράσειεν ἄν; *who can tell?* E. I. T. 577. Without ἄν this optative is rare, as τίς λέγοι; *who can tell?* A. Ch. 595. Cp. 1821 a.

INDIRECT (DEPENDENT) QUESTIONS

2663. Indirect questions are introduced by interrogative pronouns, adjectives, and adverbs, indefinite relative pronouns and adverbs (340, 346), or by certain interrogative particles (2671, 2675).

2664. The interrogatives of the direct question may be retained in an indirect question. But it is more common to use the indefinite relatives which (in interrogative sentences) are employed only in indirect questions.

ἠρώτων αὐτοὺς τίνες εἶεν *they asked them who they were* X. A. 4. 5. 10 (= τίνες ἐστέ;), ἠρώτων ὅ τι ἐστὶ τὸ πρᾶγμα *I asked what the matter was* 5. 7. 23 (= τί ἐστι;), ἠρώτᾱ αὐτὸν πόσον χρῡσίον ἔχοι *he asked him how much money he had* 7. 8. 1 (= πόσον ἔχεις;), ἠρώτων αὐτὸν τὸ στράτευμα ὁπόσον εἴη *they asked him how large the army was* 4. 4. 17 (= πόσον ἐστί;), ἀπορῶν ποῖ τράποιτο ἐπὶ λόφον τινὰ καταφεύγει *being in doubt whither he should turn, he fled to a hill* X. C. 3. 1. 4 (= ποῖ τράπωμαι;), ᾔδει δὲ οὐδεὶς ὅποι στρατεύουσιν *but no one knew where they were going to march* T. 5. 54 (= ποῖ στρατεύομεν;).

2665. The use of the direct interrogatives is a relic of original juxtaposition, *e.g.* εἰπέ μοι, ποῖόν τι νομίζεις εὐσέβειαν εἶναι; *tell me, what sort of a thing do you think holiness is?* X. M. 4. 6. 2. The interrogative force of the indefinite relatives is derived, not from any interrogative idea in these words, but from the connection in which they stand.

2666. An indirect interrogative is often used in the same sentence after a direct interrogative. Thus, οὐκ οἶδα οὔτ' ἀπὸ ποίου ἂν τάχους οὔτε ὅποι ἄν τις φεύγων ἀποφύγοι οὔτ' εἰς ποῖον ἂν σκότος ἀποδραίη οὔθ' ὅπως ἂν εἰς ἐχυρὸν χωρίον ἀποσταίη *I do not know with what swiftness of foot nor by fleeing to what quarter a man might escape nor into what darkness he might run away nor how he could withdraw into any stronghold* X. A. 2. 5. 7. The indirect form precedes less often, as οὐ γὰρ αἰσθάνομαί σου ὁποῖον νόμιμον ἢ ποῖον δίκαιον λέγεις *for I do not perceive what you mean by 'conformable to law' or what you mean by 'just'* X. M. 4. 4. 13.

2667. Two interrogatives may occur in the same sentence without a connective; as πῶς οἶδεν ὁποῖα ὁποίοις δυνατὰ κοινωνεῖν; *how does he know what* letters *are able to unite with what?* P. Soph. 253 a. Cp. 2646.

2668. After verbs of *saying, knowing, seeing, making known, perceiving*, etc. (but not after verbs of *asking*) the simple relatives are found where the indefinite relatives (or the interrogatives) might stand in an indirect question. Where ὅς is so used, it has the force of οἷος (cp. *qualis* in such questions); and rarely follows a negative clause, because verbs denoting lack of knowledge are allied in meaning to verbs of *asking*. The usual forms are *e.g.* οἶδά σε ὃς εἶ and οὐκ οἶδά σε ὅστις εἶ. But we find οἶδά σε ὅστις εἶ and οὐκ οἶδά σε ὃς εἶ. Thus, πέμπει . . . εἰπὼν ὃς ἦν *he sends . . . telling who he was* X. C. 6. 1. 46 (here ἦν represents the point of view of the *writer*), ἐκέλευσε . . . δεῖξαι ὃς εἴη *he ordered him to explain who he was* D. 52. 7, μήποτε γνοίης ὃς εἶ *mayest thou never come to know who thou* *art* S. O. T. 1068, ὁρᾷς ἡμᾶς, ὅσοι ἐσμέν; *do you see how many there are of us?* P. R. 327 c. So with the adverbs ἔνθα, οὗ, ᾗ, ὡς, ὅθεν; as τὴν ὁδὸν ἔφραζεν ᾗ εἴη *he told where the road was* X. A. 4. 5. 34. In some cases these sentences may be exclamatory (2685).

a. That the simple relatives are never thus used after verbs of *asking* indicates that such clauses are not true indirect questions (as in Latin), and that the pronouns have their value as *relatives*. But some scholars allow an indirect question after all these words except ὅς; and others admit no such limitation.

b. Only in late Greek are the pronouns or adverbs of the indirect form used in direct questions.

c. ὅπως is used occasionally (often in poetry) in the sense of ὡς. Thus, μή μοι φράζ' ὅπως οὐκ εἶ κακός *tell me not that* (lit. *how*) *thou art not vile* S. O. T. 548.

d. The context must sometimes determine whether a sentence is an indirect question or a relative clause. Thus, without the context, οὐκ εἶχον ὅποι ἀποσταῖεν (X. H. 3. 5. 10) might mean *they did not know to whom* (= ἠγνόουν πρὸς τίνας) *to revolt* or *they had no* allies *to whom* (= πρὸς οὓς) *to revolt.* But the present or aorist optative in relative final clauses is rare; cp. 2554 c.

2669. An indirect question may depend (especially in poetry) on an idea involved in the principal verb; or may depend on a verb to be supplied. Thus, ὥστε μ' ὠδίνειν τί φῄς *so that I am in travail to know thy meaning* S. Aj. 794, ὁποτέρως οὖν σοι . . . ἀρέσκει *in whatever way it pleases you* (*scil.* ἡδέως ἂν ἀκούσαιμι) P. R. 348 b.

2670. The indefinite relative is commonly used when a question is repeated by the respondent before his reply. Here *you ask?* is supplied in thought. Thus, A. ἀλλὰ τίς γὰρ εἶ; B. ὅστις; πολίτης χρηστός A. *But who are you, pray?* B. *Who am I? an honest burgher* Ar. Ach. 594, πῶς δή; φήσω ἐγώ. ὅπως; φήσει *how are you? I will say; How am I? he will say* Hippocrates 1. 292 c.

2671. Simple indirect questions are introduced by εἰ *whether,* less often by ἆρα.

ἐρωτῶντες εἰ λῃσταί εἰσιν *asking whether they are pirates* T. 1. 5, τοῦτον οἶσθ' εἰ ζῶν κυρεῖ; *dost thou know whether he is alive?* S. Ph. 444, ἤρετο αὐτὸν εἰ βληθείη *he asked him whether he had been struck* X. C. 8. 3. 30 (= ἐβλήθης;), φόβος εἰ πείσω δέσποιναν ἐμήν *I am afraid* (about the question) *whether I can persuade my mistress* E. Med. 184 (2234), ἴδωμεν ἆρ' οὑτωσὶ γίγνεται πάντα *let us see whether everything is thus produced* P. Ph. 70 d. With the deliberative subjunctive: ἐπανερομένου Κτησιφῶντος εἰ καλέσῃ Δημοσθένην *when Ctesiphon was asking if he was to call Demosthenes* Aes. 3. 202 (= καλέσω;).

a. εἰ has an affirmative force (*whether*) or a negative force (*whether . . . not*). The latter is seen *e.g.* after verbs expressing uncertainty or doubt, as after οὐκ οἶδα. Thus, εἰ μὲν δὴ δίκαια ποιήσω, οὐκ οἶδα *I don't know whether I shall do what is right* X. A. 1. 3. 5 (*i.e.* I may possibly not do what is right). The assumption is affirmative in τὰ ἐκπώματα . . . οὐκ οἶδ' εἰ Χρυσάντᾳ τουτῳὶ δῶ *I don't know whether I must not give the cups to Chrysantas here* X. C. 8. 4. 16 (*i.e.* I think I shall give them).

b. The interrogative use of εἰ is derived from the conditional meaning *if,* as in σὺ δὲ φράσαι εἴ με σαώσεις *but do thou tell me whether thou wilt save me* A 83 (*i.e.* 'if thou wilt save me, tell me so').

2672. ἐάν rarely, if ever, means *whether*, even after verbs of *examining, considering* (σκοπῶ ἐσκεψάμην, καθορῶ), where its use is best explained by 2354. In form such conditional sentences often approach closely to indirect questions. Thus, cp. σκέψαι . . . ἐὰν ἄρα καὶ σοὶ συνδοκῇ ἅπερ ἐμοί *consider if* (in case that, on the chance that) *you too agree with me* (P. Ph. 64 c) with σκέψασθε εἰ ἄρα τοῦτο . . . πεποιήκᾱσιν οἱ βάρβαροι *consider whether the barbarians have* (not) *done this* X. A. 3. 2. 22. Cp. ἀναμιμνήσκεσθαι ἐὰν ἀληθῆ λέγω *to recall to your recollection if I speak the truth* And. 1. 37.

a. Some scholars maintain that, in Greek, *if* was at an early period confused with *whether* in such sentences as εἶμι γὰρ ἐς Σπάρτην . . . νόστον πευσόμενος πατρὸς φίλου, ἤν που ἀκούσω strictly *for I will go to Sparta to inquire about the return of my dear father, in the hope that I may hear of it* β 359. When the conditional clause was attached to πευσόμενος, ἤν acquired (it is claimed) the force of *whether*. Cp. ᾤχετο πευσόμενος . . . εἴ (*v.l.* ἤ) που ἔτ' εἴης *he had gone to inquire whether you were still living* ν 415. Cp. German *ob*, once meaning *if*, now *whether*.

2673. Homer has ἤν, εἴ κε, αἴ κε with the subjunctive after verbs of *knowing, seeing, saying* (but not after verbs of *asking*). Such cases belong under 2354 b.

2674. μή is sometimes translated by *whether* after verbs of *fear* and *caution*; but such dependent clauses with μή are not indirect questions (2221 a). After verbs of *seeing, considering* and the like (ὁρῶ, ἐννοοῦμαι, ἐνθῡμοῦμαι, σκοπῶ) μή is properly a conjunction and not the interrogative particle. In such clauses there is an idea of purpose or desire to *prevent* something or a notion of fear that something *is* or *may be done*. Thus, φροντίζω μὴ κράτιστον ᾖ μοι σῑγᾶν *I am considering whether it is not best for me to be silent* X. M. 4. 2. 39, ὁρῶμεν μὴ Νῑκίᾱς οἴεταί τι λέγειν *let us see whether Nicias is of the opinion that he is saying something important* P. Lach. 196 c. That μή does not properly mean *whether not* (indirect question) is clear from the fact that, in these clauses, it is not used of something that is *hoped for*. Cp. 2676 b.

INDIRECT ALTERNATIVE QUESTIONS

2675. Indirect alternative questions are introduced by the particles signifying *whether . . . or:* πότερον (πότερα) . . . ἤ, εἴτε . . . εἴτε, εἰ . . . ἤ, εἰ . . . εἴτε. See also under Particles.

a. πότερον (πότερα) . . . ἤ: Thus, διηρώτᾱ τὸν Κῦρον πότερον βούλοιτο μένειν ἢ ἀπιέναι *she asked Cyrus whether he wanted to stay or go away* X. C. 1. 3. 15, θαυμάζω πότερα ὡς κρατῶν βασιλεὺς αἰτεῖ τὰ ὅπλα ἢ ὡς διὰ φιλίᾱν δῶρα *I wonder whether the king asks for our arms as a conqueror or as gifts on the plea of friendship* X. A. 2. 1. 10.

N. — πότερον . . . ἤ may denote that the second alternative is more important than the first. πότερον is omitted when the introductory clause contains the adjective πότερος (X. C. 1. 3. 2).

b. εἴτε . . . εἴτε gives equal value to each alternative. Thus, τὴν σκέψιν ποιώμεθα εἴτε ὠφελίᾱν εἴτε βλάβην παρέχει *let us make the inquiry whether it produces benefit or injury* P. Phae. 237 d.

N. 1. — In Homer εἴτε . . . εἴτε (εἴ τε . . . εἴ τε) almost always retains the meaning *either . . . or* (A 65).

N. 2. — The first εἴτε is rarely omitted in prose, as πόλις εἴτε ἰδιῶταί τινες *a State or certain individuals* P. L. 864 a; more often in poetry, as λόγοισιν εἴτ' ἔργοισιν *by words or deeds* S. O. T. 517.

c. εἰ . . . ἤ indicates that the second alternative is preferable or more probable. Thus, ἠρώτᾱ εἰ αὐτοῖς τοῖς ἀνδράσι σπένδοιτο τοῖς ἰοῦσι καὶ ἀπιοῦσιν, ἢ καὶ τοῖς ἄλλοις ἔσοιντο σπονδαί *he asked whether he was making a truce merely with the individual men who were coming and going or* whether *the truce would be with the rest as well* X. A. 2. 3. 7.

d. εἰ . . . εἴτε is like εἴτε . . . εἴτε. Thus, εἰ δ' ἔτ' ἐστὶν ἔμψῡχος γυνὴ εἴτ' οὖν ὄλωλεν, εἰδέναι βουλοίμεθ' ἄν *we should like to know whether the lady is still alive or dead* E. Alc. 140.

e. ἤ (ἠὲ) . . . ἤ (ἦε) occurs in Homer, as ὄφρ' εὖ εἰδῶ ἠὲ νέον μεθέπεις ἦ καὶ πατρώϊός ἐσσι ξεῖνος *that I may know well whether thou art newly a visitor or art actually an ancestral guest-friend* α 175. Cp. 2661. ἤ . . . ἤ is doubtful in Attic.

THE NEGATIVES IN INDIRECT QUESTIONS

2676. The negative of the direct form is usually preserved in indirect questions.

εἴσομαι . . . πότερον ὁ ἔχων αὐτὸ οὐκ εὐδαίμων ἐστὶν ἢ εὐδαίμων *I shall know whether its possessor is happy or not* P. R. 354 c, οὐκ οἶδ' ὅπως φῶ τοῦτο καὶ μὴ φῶ *I know not how I am to say this and not to say it* E. I. A. 643 (= πῶς μὴ φῶ;).

a. Indirect single questions introduced by interrogative pronouns, adjectives, and adverbs, usually have οὐ.

b. μή appears after verbs of *seeing, considering* and the like (σκοπῶ, ὁρῶ, ἐννοοῦμαι, ἐνθῡμοῦμαι) when there is an idea of purpose or desire to prevent something. Thus, ὁρᾶτε . . . ὅτῳ τρόπῳ κάλλιστα ἀμυνεῖσθε αὐτοὺς καὶ μήτε καταφρονήσαντες ἄφαρκτοι ληφθήσεσθε κτλ. *consider how you may best defend yourselves and may neither be caught off your guard through contempt*, etc. T. 6. 33. So also with the potential optative with ἄν; as τί οὖν οὐ σκοποῦμεν πῶς ἂν αὐτῶν μὴ διαμαρτάνοιμεν; *why then do we not consider how we may avoid mistaking them?* X. M. 3. 1. 10. Indirect questions with μή thus belong under μή with verbs of fear and apprehension, where μή is the negative of the *will*. Cp. 2674.

c. Indirect questions introduced by εἰ have οὐ or μή. Thus, ἤρετο τὸν δῆμον εἰ οὐκ αἰσχύνοιντο *he asked the people whether they were not ashamed* Aes. 1. 84, ἤρετό με . . . εἰ μὴ μέμνημαι *he asked me whether I did not remember* 2. 36.

d. In relative clauses joined by καί and standing in an indirect question (*what . . . and what not*), μή must be used when the verb is to be supplied with the second clause; but when the verb is repeated, either μή, or οὐ if the antecedent is definite, may be used. Thus, διαγιγνώσκουσιν ἅ τε δύνανται καὶ ἃ μή *they distinguish between what they can do and what they cannot* X. M. 4. 2. 26, οἶσθα . . . ὁπόσοι τε φρουροὶ ἱκανοί εἰσι καὶ ὁπόσοι μή εἰσιν *you know how many garrisons are advantageously situated and how many are not* 3. 6. 10. The antecedent is definite in ἀπέδειξεν οὓς χρὴ δημηγορεῖν καὶ οὓς οὐ δεῖ λέγειν ἐν τῷ δήμῳ *he showed who must speak in the assembly and who must not speak before the people* Aes. 1. 27.

e. As the second member of an alternative question introduced by εἰ, *or not* is either ἢ οὐ or ἢ μή. Thus, σκοπῶμεν εἰ ἡμῖν πρέπει ἢ οὔ *let us consider whether it is proper for us or not* P. R. 451 d, νῦν ἔμαθον ὃ λέγεις· εἰ δὲ ἀληθὲς ἢ μή, πειράσομαι μαθεῖν *now I have made out what you mean; and I will try to make out whether it is true or not* 339 a.

f. A shift from μή to οὐ in sequent alternative indirect questions appears to be due to the desire to attain variety. Thus, οὐ δεῖ ὑμᾶς ἐκ τῶν τοῦ κατηγόρου λόγων τοὺς νόμους καταμανθάνειν, εἰ καλῶς ὑμῖν κεῖνται ἢ μή, ἀλλ' ἐκ τῶν νόμων τοὺς τοῦ κατηγόρου λόγους, εἰ ὀρθῶς καὶ νομίμως ὑμᾶς διδάσκουσι τὸ πρᾶγμα ἢ οὔ *you must not start from the pleas of the accuser to learn whether your laws have been established well or not, but you must start from the laws to learn whether his pleas set forth the case fairly and legally or not* Ant. 5. 14. Cp. Ant. 6. 2, Is. 8. 9, D. 20. 83. Some scholars hold that οὐ here lays stress on a negative fact or on something conceived as a negative fact, and that μή puts the question abstractly as a mere conception.

MOODS IN INDIRECT QUESTIONS

2677. The moods and tenses of indirect questions follow the same rules as govern clauses in indirect discourse. The person may be changed.

After primary tenses, the mood and tense of the direct question are retained (indicative, past indicative with ἄν, deliberative subjunctive, potential optative with ἄν).

After secondary tenses, the mood and tense of the direct form may be retained or the optative may be used instead. The latter is more common. But a past indicative with ἄν always remains unchanged.

a. Direct Form Retained. — πολλάκις ἐσκόπει τί διαφέρει μανίᾱς ἀμαθίᾱ *he often considered in what respect ignorance differed from madness* X. M. 1. 2. 50, ἠπορεῖτο τι ποιήσει *he was uncertain what to do* X. A. 7. 3. 29 (= τί ποιήσω, deliberative future, 1916), ἐβουλεύοντο εἴτε κατακαύσωσιν . . . εἴτε τι ἄλλο χρήσωνται *they deliberated whether they should burn them or dispose of them in some other manner* T. 2. 4 (= κατακαύσωμεν, χρησώμεθα;), ἠρώτησε . . . ποῦ ἂν ἴδοι Πρόξενον *he asked where he could see Proxenus* X. A. 2. 4. 15 (= ποῦ ἂν ἴδοιμι;).

b. Optative: ἤρετο εἴ τις ἐμοῦ εἴη σοφώτερος *he asked whether any one was wiser than I* P. A. 21 a (= ἐστί;), ὅ τι δὲ ποιήσοι οὐ διεσήμηνε *he did not announce publicly what he was going to do* X. A. 2. 1. 23 (= τί ποιήσω;), τὸν θεὸν ἐπηρώτων εἰ παραδοῖεν Κορινθίοις τὴν πόλιν *they questioned the god whether they should surrender the city to the Corinthians* T. 1. 25 (= παραδῶμεν;). Here παραδοῖεν might represent the aorist indicative, but that tense is usually retained to avoid confusion (exceptionally ἠρώτᾱ τι πάθοιεν X. C. 2. 3. 19; cp. X. A. 6. 3. 25, D. 50. 55). An imperfect relatively anterior to the time of the main verb is retained in D. 30. 19.

c. A dubitative subjunctive in an indirect question, when dependent on an optative, may be attracted into the optative; as ἔλεγες . . . ὅτι οὐκ ἂν ἔχοις ἐξελθὼν ὅ τι χρῷο σαυτῷ *you were saying that if you went out you would not know what to do with yourself* P. Cr. 45 b (= τί χρῶμαι ἐμαυτῷ;).

d. Homer has the optative for the indicative due to indirect discourse only in indirect questions; as εἴροντο τίς εἴη καὶ πόθεν ἔλθοι *they asked who he was and whence he had come* ρ 368. See 2624 c.

2678. After a secondary tense the mood of a direct question may be retained (usually for vividness) in the same sentence with the mood of an indirect question (cp. 2632). Thus, ὁμοῖοι ἦσαν θαυμάζειν ὅποι ποτὲ τρέψονται οἱ Ἕλληνες καὶ τί ἐν νῷ ἔχοιεν *they seemed to be wondering to what direction the Greeks would turn and what they had in mind* X. A. 3. 5. 13, ἤρετο ὅ τι θαυμάζοι καὶ ὁπόσοι αὐτῶν τεθνᾶσιν *he asked what it was that he was astonished at and how many of them were dead* T. 3. 113 (= τί θαυμάζεις, πόσοι τεθνᾶσιν;).

a. In some cases there is no apparent reason (apart from desire for variety) for this use of the indicative and optative in the same sentence. Sometimes the indicative may ask for a statement of *fact*, the optative request an *opinion* of the person questioned.

2679. Parallel to 2624 are cases like ᾔδει ὅπου ἔκειτο ἡ ἐπιστολή *he knew where the letter had been put* X. C. 2. 2. 9.

ANSWERS TO *YES* AND *NO* QUESTIONS

2680. *Yes* and *No* questions may be answered in various ways, *e.g.*:

a. By repeating the verb or another emphatic word with or without one or more confirmative adverbs. Thus, φῂς σὺ ἀμείνω πολίτην εἶναι, ὃν σὺ ἐπαινεῖς, ἢ ὃν ἐγώ; φημὶ γὰρ οὖν *do you assert that the citizen whom you approve is better than the one I approve? I do say so* X. M. 4. 6. 14, οἶσθ' οὖν ἃ λέξαι σοι . . . θέλω; οὐκ οἶδα *dost thou know what I fain would tell thee? No.* E. Hec. 999.

b. By ἐγώ, ἔγωγε, οὐκ ἐγώ, οὐκ ἔγωγε, sometimes with νὴ Δία or μὰ Δία.

c. *Yes* may be expressed by ναί, ναὶ μὰ τὸν Δία, μάλιστα, φημί, πάνυ γε, πάνυ μὲν οὖν, εὖ γε, ἔστι ταῦτα, ἔστιν οὕτως, ἀληθῆ λέγεις, ἀληθέστατα, ὀρθῶς γε, κομιδῇ, etc.

No may be expressed by οὔ, οὐκ ἔστιν, οὐ δῆτα, οὐ μὰ Δία, οὐδαμῶς, οὔ φημι, μὴ γάρ, ἥκιστα, ἥκιστά γε, etc.

d. In the form of a question: τί μήν; τί γάρ; ἀλλὰ τί; πῶς; πόθεν; πῶς γὰρ οὔ;

EXCLAMATORY SENTENCES

2681. Direct (independent) exclamatory sentences with a verb expressed (or easily supplied) are formed

2682. (I) By the relative pronouns οἷος, ὅσος, or by the relative adverb ὡς in exclamations of wonder. The sentences introduced by these words are commonly associated with vocatives or interjections. Cp. 340.

οἷα ποιεῖς, ὦ ἑταῖρε *what are you about, my friend!* P. Euth. 15 c, ὦ φίλοι . . ., οἵην τερπωλὴν θεοὶ ἤγαγον ἐς τόδε δῶμα *friends, such sport the gods have brought into this house!* σ 37, ὅσην ἔχεις τὴν δύναμιν *how great your power is!* Ar. Pl. 748, ὦ πάππε, ὅσα πράγματα ἔχεις *oh grandfather, how much trouble you have!* X. C. 1. 3. 4, ὦ φίλταθ' Αἷμον, ὥς σ' ἀτιμάζει πατήρ, *oh dearest Haemon, how thy father insults thee!* S. Ant. 572, ὡς ἀστεῖος ὁ ἄνθρωπος *how charming the man is!* P. Ph. 116 d.

a. Exclamatory ὡς may be the relative ὡς; but if it is the demonstrative ὥς, it means properly not *how* but *so*. Cp. 2998.

b. Double **οἷος** (exclamation within an exclamation) marks a strong contrast (cp. 2646) in direct and indirect exclamations. Thus, οἷα πρὸς οἵων ἀνδρῶν πάσχω *what I suffer and at the hands of what men!* S. Ant. 942, ἀπὸ οἵας . . . αὐχήματος τοῦ πρώτου ἐς οἵᾱν τελευτὴν καὶ ταπεινότητα ἀφῖκατο *from what boasting at first they had come to what a humiliating end* T. 7. 75. Triple οἷος in Gorgias, Helen 10.

c. Cp. 2647 for such sentences as οἵᾱν ἔχιδναν τήνδ' ἔφῡσας *what a viper is this woman whom thou hast begotten!* E. Ion 1262.

d. **οἴμ' ὡς** is common in expressions of impatience, anger, pity, grief, or fear; as οἴμ' ὡς καταγελᾷς *ah me, how you mock me!* Ar. Nub. 1238, οἴμ' ὡς ἔοικας ὀψὲ τὴν δίκην ἰδεῖν *ah me, how thou seemest all too late to see the right!* S. Ant. 1270, οἴμ' ὡς δέδοικα *ah me, how I fear!* Ar. Pax 173.

2683. (II) By the infinitive (2015, 2036).

2684. Direct exclamations without a verb may be expressed by the vocative or nominative (1288) or by the genitive of cause (1407).

2685. **Indirect** (dependent) exclamations form subordinate clauses in sentences which, taken as a whole, are *statements* (2575. 4). They are introduced by οἷος, ὅσος, οἵως, ὡς, οἷ, ἵνα. The negative is οὐ. It is often difficult to distinguish between indirect exclamations and indirect questions introduced by οἷος or ὅσος. But observe that dependent exclamations are not introduced by the direct interrogatives ποῖος, πόσος, πῶς, etc., nor by the indefinite relatives ὁποῖος, ὁπόσος, ὅπως, etc., both of which classes of words may stand in indirect questions.

a. ὁποῖος in L. 30. 4 and ὁπόσος in P. G. 522 a are suspected.

b. The introductory verb is sometimes omitted; as ὦ μιαρώτατος, ἵν' ὑποδέδῡκεν *oh the rascal!* (to think) *where he crept in!* Ar. Vesp. 188.

2686. Dependent exclamatory clauses follow, as regards mood and tense, the same rules as govern indirect questions (2677). An original indicative remains unchanged after primary tenses of verbs followed by a finite mood, but may become optative after secondary tenses on the principle of indirect discourse.

a. Indicative: οἷον ἄνδρα λέγεις ἐν κινδύνῳ εἶναι *what a noble man you say is in danger!* P. Th. 142 b, σκόπει . . . ἵν' ἥκει τοῦ θεοῦ μαντεύματα *judge to what the oracles of the god have come* S. O. T. 953 (cp. ὦ θεῶν μαντεύματα, ἵν' ἐστέ 946), τίς οὐκ οἶδεν ἐξ οἵων συμφορῶν εἰς ὅσην εὐδαιμονίᾱν κατέστησαν; *who does not know into what good fortune they came and after what sufferings?* I. 6. 42, ἐνθῡμούμενοι ὅσον πλοῦν . . . ἀπεστέλλοντο *reflecting on how long a voyage they were on the point of being sent* T. 6. 30, ἐννοηθέντες οἷά τε πάσχουσιν ὑπὸ τῶν Ἀσσυρίων καὶ ὅτι νῦν τεθναίη ὁ ἄρχων αὐτῶν *reflecting what they were suffering at the hands of the Assyrians and that their ruler was now dead* X. C. 4. 2. 3.

b. Optative: διαθεώμενος αὐτῶν ὅσην μὲν χώρᾱν καὶ οἵᾱν ἔχοιεν *observing how great the extent of their country was and how excellent its quality* X. A. 3. 1. 19, ἐπιδεικνύντες οἷα εἴη ἡ ἀπορία *pointing out what their difficulty was* 1. 3. 13. See also 2687.

2687. Verbs and other words of *emotion* (praise, blame, wonder, etc.) and the expression of its results are often followed by a dependent exclamatory clause with οἷος, ὅσος, ὡς, etc. Here a causal sentence would have ὅτι τοιοῦτος, ὅτι τοσοῦτος, ὅτι οὕτως. English generally introduces such clauses by *considering, thinking, upon the reflection how*, etc. Thus, τῷ σ' αὖ νῦν ὀίω ἀποτεισέμεν, ὅσσα μ' ἔοργας *therefore I think now thou shalt in turn atone for all thou hast done unto me* Φ 399, ἀπέκλᾱον . . . τὴν ἐμαυτοῦ τύχην, οἵου ἀνδρὸς ἑταίρου ἐστερημένος εἴην *I bewailed my fate considering what a companion I had lost* (direct = οἵου ἀνδρὸς ἑταίρου (ὄντος) ἐστέρημαι) P. Ph. 117 c, μάκαρ ὦ Στρεψίαδες, αὐτός τ' ἔφῡς ὡς σοφὸς χοἷον τὸν υἱὸν τρέφεις *oh happy Strepsiades, how wise you are yourself and what a son you have!* Ar. Nub. 1206, τὸ γῆρας ὑμνοῦσιν ὅσων κακῶν σφίσιν αἴτιον *they rehearse how many evils old age occasions them* P. R. 329 b, εὐδαίμων μοι ἀνὴρ ἐφαίνετο . . . ὡς ἀδεῶς καὶ γενναίως ἐτελεύτᾱ *the man seemed to me to be happy so fearlessly and nobly did he die* P. Ph. 58 e, ζηλῶ γε τῆς εὐτυχίᾱς τὸν πρέσβυν, οἷ μετέστη ξηρῶν τρόπων *I envy the old fellow his fortune, how* (lit. *whither*) *he has changed his arid ways* Ar. Vesp. 1451.

NEGATIVE SENTENCES

2688. The simple negative particles are οὐ and μή. οὐ is the negative of fact and statement, and *contradicts* or *denies*; μή is the negative of the will and thought, and *rejects* or *deprecates*. The difference between the simple negatives holds true also of their compounds οὔτε μήτε, οὐδέ μηδέ, οὐδείς μηδείς, etc.

a. τὰ οὐκ ὄντα is *that which does not exist* independently of any opinion of the writer: τὰ οὐκ ὄντα λογοποιεῖν *to fabricate what does not* actually *exist* And. 3. 35. τὰ μὴ ὄντα is *that which is* regarded as *not existing*, that which is dependent on the opinion of the writer, the whole sum of things that are outside of actual knowledge: τὰ μὴ ἐόντα οὔτε ὁρᾶται οὔτε γῑνώσκεται *that which does not exist is neither seen nor known* Hippocrates, de arte § 2; cp. τὸ μὴ ὄν P. R. 478 b.

b. The rarer **οὐχί** (οὐ-χί) denies with greater emphasis than οὐ. The form **μηκέτι** *no longer* is due to the analogy of οὐκ-έτι.

2689. μή as the negative of will and thought is used in various expressions involving emotion, as commands, prohibitions, wishes, hopes, prayers, petitions, promises, oaths, asseverations, and the like; in expressions marking condition, purpose, effort, apprehension, cautious assertion, surmise, and fear; in setting forth ideality, mere conceptions, abstractions as opposed to reality or to definite facts; in marking ideas as general and typical; when a person or thing is to be characterized as conceived of rather than real. — μή is used not merely when the above notions are apparent but also when they are latent. Greek often conceives of a situation as marked by feeling where English regards it as one of fact; and hence uses μή where we should expect οὐ.

a. μή corresponds to the Sanskrit prohibitive particle *mā́*, which in the Rig Veda is used with the independent indicative of an augmentless aorist or imperfect which has the force of the subjunctive; rarely with the optative. In later Sanskrit *mā́* was used with the subjunctive, optative, and imperative.

b. μή was originally used only in independent clauses; but later was employed in subordinate clauses, and with dependent infinitives and participles. On the origin of μή as a conjunction, see 2222. In Homer μή is used especially with the subjunctive, optative, and imperative (*i.e.* in commands and wishes); rarely with the indicative (in μὴ ὤφελλον, in oaths, in questions, after verbs of *fearing* referring to a past event); with the infinitive when used for the imperative after a verb of *saying*, etc. when the infinitive expresses a command or a wish, and when a dependent infinitive is used in an oath; with the participle only in connection with a command (Ξ 48) or a wish (δ 684).

c. In later Greek (Polybius, Lucian, Dio Chrysostomus, etc.) μή has encroached on οὐ, generally by extension of usages occurring rarely in the classical language. Thus Lucian has μή after causal ὡς, ὅτι, διότι, ἐπεί; in relative clauses (sometimes οὐδέν ἐστιν ὅτι μή); with participles of cause (even ἅτε μή) or of concession; with participles without the article following an adjective; with the infinitive after verbs of *saying* and *thinking*. ὅτι μή appears in indirect discourse (complete or partial) where the classical language would use the infinitive or ὅτι with the optative or ὡς with the participle; so after verbs of *saying* and *thinking*, after verbs of *emotion*, and even after verbs of *knowing*.

POSITION OF οὐ AND μή

2690. οὐ and μή are generally placed before the word they negative; but may follow, when emphasis is laid on a particular word, as in contrasts.

ὑπολάβῃ δὲ μηδείς *but let no one suppose* T. 6. 84, οἱ δὲ στρατηγοὶ ἐξῆγον μὲν οὔ, συνεκάλεσαν δέ *and the generals did not lead them out, but called them together* X. A. 6. 4. 20, ξύμμαχοι ἐγενόμεθα οὐκ ἐπὶ καταδουλώσει τῶν Ἑλλήνων Ἀθηναίοις, ἀλλ' ἐπ' ἐλευθερώσει ἀπὸ τοῦ Μήδου τοῖς Ἕλλησιν *we became allies, not to the Athenians, for the purpose of enslaving the Greeks, but to the Greeks for the purpose of freeing them from the Mede* T. 3. 10, ἀπόλοιτο μὲν μή *perish indeed — may he not* E. Med. 83.

a. A contrast must be supplied in thought when the negative precedes the article, a relative, a conjunction, or a preposition. Thus, εἰ δὲ περὶ ἡμῶν γνώσεσθε μὴ τὰ εἰκότα *but if you pass upon us a sentence that is unjust* T. 3. 57, πολεμεῖν δὲ μὴ πρὸς ὁμοίαν ἀντιπαρασκευὴν ἀδύνατοι *unable to carry on a war against a power dissimilar in character to their own* 1. 141, ἀμυνούμεθα τοὺς πολεμίους οὐκ εἰς μακρὰν *we shall shortly* (lit. *in no long time*) *punish the enemy* X. C. 5. 4. 21, οὐ κατὰ κόσμον *disorderly* B 214.

b. The order of the parts of a negative compound may be reversed for strong emphasis; as ἔτ' οὐκ ὤν (= οὐκέτι ὤν) S. Tr. 161, μίαν οὐκ (= οὐδεμίαν) Hdt. 8. 119.

c. The negative may be placed in front of an infinitive when English transfers it to another verb in the sentence; as εἰ βουλόμεθ' ἡμεῖς μὴ προσποιεῖσθαι πολεμεῖν αὐτὸν ἡμῖν *if we wish to assume that he is not waging war with us* D. 8. 58, ἡμᾶς οὐδ' ἐναυλισθῆναι ἐπιτρέπεις *you do not permit us even to take up our quarters* X. A. 7. 7. 8 (= οὐκ ἐπιτρέπεις = κωλύεις).

οὐ ADHERESCENT

2691. οὐ adherescent (or privative) placed before a verb (or other single word) not merely negatives the meaning of the simple verb but gives it an *opposite* meaning, the two expressing a single negative idea; as οὔ φημι *I deny, I refuse* (not *I say not*). οὔ φημι is preferred to φημὶ οὐ as *nego* is preferred to *aio non.*

2692. Adherescent οὐ is especially common with verbs of *saying* or *thinking,* but occurs also with many verbs of *will* or *desire.* In such cases οὐ goes closely with the leading verb, forming a *quasi-*compound; whereas it belongs in sense to a following infinitive if an infinitive depends on the leading verb. In Latin actual composition has taken place in *nego, nescio, nequeo, nolo.*

οὐκ ἔφη ἰέναι *he refused to go* X. A. 1. 3. 8, οὔ φᾱσιν εἶναι ἄλλην ὁδόν *they say that there is no other road* 4. 1. 21 (cp. φῄς ἢ οὔ; *yes or no?* P. A. 27 d), τίνας δ' οὐκ ᾤετο δεῖν λέγειν; *who were those whom he thought ought not to speak?* Aes. 1. 28, ἃ οὐκ ἐᾶτε ἡμᾶς . . . ποιεῖν *what you forbid us to do* X. C. 1. 3. 10, οὐκ ἀξιοῖ . . . φεύγοντα τῑμωρεῖσθαι *he said that it was not right to avenge himself on an exile* T. 1. 136.

a. So with οὔ φημι and οὐ φάσκω *deny, refuse* (= ἀπαρνοῦμαι), οὐκ οἴομαι, οὐ νομίζω, οὐ δοκῶ, οὐκ ἐῶ and οὐ κελεύω *forbid* (*veto*), οὐκ ἀξιῶ *regard as unworthy, do not expect that, refuse,* οὐχ ὑπισχνοῦμαι *refuse,* οὐ προσποιοῦμαι *dissimulo,* οὐ συμβουλεύω *dissuade, advise not to,* οὐκ ἐθέλω *am unwilling,* οὐκ ἐπαινῶ *disapprove.* This association often persists in participles, as οὐκ ἐῶν, οὐκ ἐθέλων. Homer has οὔ φημι, φημὶ οὐ, and οὔ φημι οὐ.

2693. οὐ with the principal verb may be equivalent in sense to μή with a dependent infinitive; as οὐ συμβουλεύων Ξέρξῃ στρατεύεσθαι ἐπὶ τὴν Ἑλλάδα *advising Xerxes not to march against Greece* (= συμβουλεύων μὴ στρατεύεσθαι) Hdt. 7. 46.

2694. Analogous to this use with verbs is the use of οὐ with adjectives and adverbs.

οὐκ ὀλίγοι = πολλοί, οὐκ ἐλάχιστος = μέγιστος, οὐχ ἧττον = μᾶλλον, οὐχ ἥκιστα = μάλιστα, οὐ καλῶς *basely,* οὐκ ἀφανής *famous,* οὐκ εἰκότως *unreasonably,* οὐ περὶ βραχέων *on important matters* (cp. 2690 a), regularly οὐ πάνυ *not at all,* as οὐ πάνυ χαλεπόν *easy.*

2695. The origin of adherescent οὐ is to be found partly in the unwillingness of the early language to use the negative particle with the infinitive, partly in the preference for a negative rather than a positive assertion, and to the disinclination to make a strong positive statement (*litotes,* as in some of the cases of 2694), and partly in the absence of negative compounds, the development of which in adjectives and participles (2071 a) was in turn restricted by the use of adherescent οὐ.

2696. Adherescent οὐ is often found in a protasis with εἰ and in other constructions where we expect μή.

εἰ δ' ἀποστῆναι Ἀθηναίων οὐκ ἠθελήσαμεν . . ., οὐκ ἠδικοῦμεν *but if we refused to revolt from the Athenians, we were not doing wrong* T. 3. 55, εἰ οὐκ ἐᾷς *if thou forbiddest* S. Aj. 1131 (= εἰ κωλύεις), εἰ μὴ Πρόξενον οὐχ ὑπεδέξαντο, ἐσώθησαν ἄν *if it had not been that they did not receive Proxenus, they would have been saved* D. 19. 74, εἰ μὲν οὐ πολλοὶ ἦσαν *if they were few* L. 13. 62 (emended by some to οὖν μή). **ἐὰν οὐ** is rare, as ἐάν τε οὐ φῆτε ἐάν τε φῆτε *both if you deny it and if you admit it* P. A. 25 b (cp. L. 13. 76, D. 26. 24).

2697. But μή often does not yield to οὐ, as ἄν τ' ἐγὼ φῶ ἄν τε μὴ φῶ *both if I assent and if I do not* D. 21. 205, οὐκ οἶδ' ὅπως φῶ τοῦτο καὶ μὴ φῶ *I know not how I shall say this and not say it* E. I. A. 643, ἐὰν μὴ . . . ἐᾶτε D. 16. 12, and in many cases where μή goes closely with the following word, as εἰ ἐδίδου κρίσιν καὶ μὴ ἀφῃρεῖτο *if he were granting a trial and not taking it away* D. 23. 91.

οὐ AFTER εἰ (ἐάν)

2698. οὐ is sometimes found in clauses introduced by εἰ (ἐάν).

a. When οὐ is adherescent (2696).

b. When there is an emphatic assertion of fact or probability, as where a direct statement is quoted. Thus, εἰ δὲ οὐδὲν ἡμάρτηταί μοι *if* (as I have shown) *no error has been committed by me* And. 1. 33, εἰ, ὡς νῦν φήσει, οὐ παρεσκεύαστο *if, as he will presently assert, he had not made preparations* D. 54. 29. Cp. X. A. 1. 7. 18, quoted in 2790.

c. When εἰ (ἐάν) is used instead of ὅτι *that* (*because*) after verbs of *emotion* (2247). Thus, μὴ θαυμάσῃς εἰ πολλὰ τῶν εἰρημένων οὐ πρέπει σοι *do not be surprised if much of what has been said does not apply to you* I. 1. 44. Here μή is possible.

d. When εἰ (ἐάν) approaches the idea of ἐπεί *since* (cp. 2246, 2298 b). So εἰ τούσδε . . . οὐ στέργει πατήρ *if* (*since*) *their father has ceased to love these* children E. Med. 88 (often explained as οὐ adherescent). Here μή is possible.

e. When a single εἰ introduces a bimembered protasis *as a whole*, the μέν clause and the δέ clause of that protasis may have οὐ. Such bimembered protases often depend on a preceding apodosis introduced by αἰσχρόν, ἄτοπον, δεινόν, θαυμαστόν ἐστι (ἂν εἴη) and like expressions of emotion (c). Thus, εἶτ' οὐκ αἰσχρὸν . . . εἰ τὸ μὲν Ἀργείων πλῆθος οὐκ ἐφοβήθη τὴν Λακεδαιμονίων ἀρχὴν . . ., ὑμεῖς δὲ ὄντες Ἀθηναῖοι βάρβαρον ἄνθρωπον φοβήσεσθε; *is it not then disgraceful, if* it is true that *whereas the Argive commons did not fear the empire of the Lacedaemonians, you, who are Athenians, are going to be afraid of a barbarian?* D. 15. 23, αἰσχρὸν γάρ, εἰ πατὴρ μὲν ἐξεῖλεν Φρύγας, ὁ δ' ἄνδρ' ἕν' οὐ δυνήσεται κτανεῖν *for it is disgraceful that, whereas the father destroyed the Phrygians, the other* (the son) *is not going to be able to destroy one* foe E. El. 336, δεινὸν ἂν εἴη, εἰ οἱ μὲν ἐκείνων ξύμμαχοι ἐπὶ δουλείᾳ τῇ αὑτῶν (χρήματα) φέροντες οὐκ ἀπεροῦσιν, ἡμεῖς δὲ ἐπὶ τῷ . . . αὐτοὶ σῴζεσθαι οὐκ ἄρα δαπανήσομεν *it would be strange if, whereas their allies will not fail to pay tribute for their own enslavement, we on the other hand will not expend it for the purpose of saving ourselves* T. 1. 121.

N. 1. — The second member of such protases has οὐ if the verb stands in the indicative, but μή (in classical Greek) if the verb is in the optative. In Aes. 2. 157 οὐ κατάσχοιμι is due to indirect discourse.

N. 2. — In such sentences εἰ may (1) have a conditional force in both clauses, as L. 30. 16, 31. 24; (2) have a conditional force in the second member, but the force of ἐπεί in the first member, as L. 20. 36, Is. 14. 52; (3) have the force of ἐπεί in the first member, and that of ὅτι in the second member, as D. 8. 55, Aes. 3. 242; (4) have the force of ὅτι in both members, as T. 1. 35, 1. 121, X. C. 7. 5. 84.

f. A bimembered clause introduced by εἰ may contain a negative clause with οὐ directly opposed to a positive clause; as εἰ δὲ τῷ μέν, τοῖς δ' οὔ D. 23. 123.

g. εἰ *whether* in simple and alternative indirect questions takes either οὐ or μή (2676 c, e).

2699. Homer has εἰ and the indicative with οὐ (12 times) when the subordinate clause precedes the main clause; but usually εἰ μή, when the subordinate clause follows. Thus, εἰ δέ μοι οὐ τείσουσι βοῶν ἐπιεικέ' ἀμοιβήν, δύσομαι εἰς 'Αΐδαο *but if they will not pay a fitting compensation for the cattle, I will go down to Hades* μ 382, ἔνθα κεν 'Αργείοισιν ὑπέρμορα νόστος ἐτύχθη, εἰ μὴ 'Αθηναίην Ἥρη πρὸς μῦθον ἔειπεν *then in that case the return of the Argives had been accomplished against fate, if Hera had not spoken a word to Athena* B 155.

a. The Homeric εἰ οὐ with the indicative has been explained either as a retention of the original use, μή with that mood being an extension through the analogy of the subjunctive and optative; or because οὐ went with the predicate, whereas μή was closely attached to εἰ.

2700. Homer has εἰ οὐ (adherescent) with the subjunctive in εἰ δ' ἂν . . . οὐκ ἐθέλωσιν Γ 289, εἰ δέ κ' . . . οὐκ εἰῶσιν Υ 139.

2701. Herodotus has a few cases of εἰ οὐ with the indicative, as 6. 9; ἢν οὐ with the subjunctive is doubtful (6. 133).

GENERAL RULE FOR μή

2702. μή stands

1. With the imperative.
2. In clauses with εἰ, ἐάν (exceptions, 2698).
3. With the subjunctive, except after μή *lest*, when οὐ is used.
4. With the optative, except after μή *lest*, or when the optative has ἄν or is in indirect discourse.
5. With the infinitive, except in indirect discourse.
6. With participles when they have a conditional or general force.

οὐ AND μή WITH THE INDICATIVE AND OPTATIVE

SIMPLE SENTENCES AND INDEPENDENT CLAUSES

2703. Statements (2153) expressed by simple sentences and independent clauses take οὐ. Direct questions take either οὐ or μή (2651). The independent future indicative has μή only in questions.

2704. In *wishes* μή is used with the indicative (1780–1781) or the optative (1814, cp. 2156).

εἴθε σε μήποτ' εἰδόμᾱν *would that I had never seen thee* S. O. T. 1218, μήποτ' ὤφελον λιπεῖν τὴν Σκῦρον *would that I had never left Scyrus* S. Ph 969.

μὴ ζῴην *may I not live* Ar. Eq. 833, ἀναιδὴς οὔτ' εἰμὶ μήτε γενοίμην *I neither am nor may I become shameless* D. 8. 68, οὔτ' ἂν δυναίμην μήτ' ἐπισταίμην λέγειν *neither could I tell nor may I be capable of telling* S. Ant. 686.

a. That ὤφελον takes μή, not οὐ, shows that it has lost to a certain extent its verbal nature. In late Greek it even became a particle like εἴθε.

b. Indirect expressions of wishing with πῶς ἄν and the optative (1832), βουλοίμην ἄν (1827), ἐβουλόμην (ἄν) with the infinitive, take οὐ (1782, 1789).

c. The use is the same in dependent clauses; as ἐπειδὴ δ' ἃ μήποτ' ὤφελε (συμβῆναι) συνέβη *but when that happened which I would had never happened* D. 18. 320.

SUBORDINATE CLAUSES IN THE INDICATIVE OR OPTATIVE

2705. In subordinate clauses μή or οὐ is used.

a. Final clauses have μή, as φίλος ἐβούλετο εἶναι τοῖς μέγιστα δυναμένοις, ἵνα ἀδικῶν μὴ διδοίη δίκην *he wished to be on friendly terms with men in power in order that he might not pay the penalty for his wrong-doing* X. A. 2. 6. 21, ἔδει τὰ ἐνέχυρα τότε λαβεῖν, ὡς μηδ' εἰ ἐβούλετο ἐδύνατο ἐξαπατᾶν quoted in 2185 c.

b. Object clauses with ὅπως after verbs of *effort* have μή, as φρόντιζ' ὅπως μηδὲν ἀνάξιον τῆς τῑμῆς ταύτης πράξεις *see to it that you do nothing unworthy of this honour* I. 2. 37, ἐπεμέλετο ὅπως μήτε ἄσῖτοι μήτε ἄποτοί ποτε ἔσοιντο *he took care that they should never be without food or drink* X. C. 8. 1. 43.

c. Conditional clauses regularly have μή. Thus, εἰ μὴ ὑμεῖς ἤλθετε, ἐπορευόμεθα ἂν ἐπὶ βασιλέᾱ *if you had not come, we should be marching against the king* X. A. 2. 1. 4, οὐκ ἀπελείπετο αὐτοῦ, εἰ μή τι ἀναγκαῖον εἴη *he never left him unless there was some necessity for it* X. M. 4. 2. 40. So in concessive clauses (2369). On οὐ adherescent in conditional clauses see 2696.

d. Relative Clauses, if conditional, have οὐ with a definite antecedent, μή with an indefinite antecedent (2505). μή is thus used when the case in question is typical of a class (μή 'generic'). Thus, προσημαίνουσιν ἅ τε χρὴ ποιεῖν καὶ ἃ οὐ χρή *they signify beforehand what one must do and what not* X. C. 1. 6. 46, ἃ μὴ οἶδα οὐδὲ οἴομαι εἰδέναι *what I do not know, I do not even think I know* P. A. 21 d.

N. 1. — Homer has ὅς (ὅσος) οὐ with the indicative (μή B 301).

N. 2. — οὐ is regular in relative clauses when an opposition is expressed (T. 1. 11. 2), and when a negative clause precedes; as οὐκ ἔστιν ὅστις (ὅπως) οὐ, οὐδεὶς ὅστις οὐ, etc. (X. C. 1. 4. 25, X. A. 2. 4. 3).

e. The expression **τοιοῦτος, ὅς (ὅστις,** etc.), when preceded by a negative, takes οὐ; as ταμιεῖον μηδενὶ εἶναι μηδὲν τοιοῦτον, εἰς ὃ οὐ πᾶς ὁ βουλόμενος εἴσεισι it is necessary that *no one shall have (such) a storehouse that anybody who pleases may not enter it* P. R. 416 d. But even when no negative precedes, we have οὐ, when the relative clause makes an assertion or defines attributively; as συγγραφεὺς τῶν λόγων . . . τοιοῦτος, οἷος οὐδεὶς ἄλλος γέγονε *such a writer of speeches as no one had been* I. 15. 35. When the antecedent is general or is thought of in respect of its *character* we have μή; as βουληθεὶς τοιοῦτον μνημεῖον καταλιπεῖν, ὃ μὴ τῆς ἀνθρωπίνης φύσεώς ἐστιν *wishing to leave behind him such a memorial as would surpass human nature* **I. 4. 89; cp. 2705 g.**

f. Relative clauses of purpose take μή, as θαλάσσιον ἐκρίψατ', ἔνθα μήποτ' εἰσόψεσθ' ἔτι *cast me out into the sea where ye may never see me more* S. O.T. 1411, κρύψᾱσ' ἑαυτήν, ἔνθα μή τις εἰσίδοι *hiding herself where no one might see her* S. Tr. 903.

g. Clauses with a relative pronoun referring to an antecedent thought of in respect of its *character* (*of such a sort*) take μή. The use of μή characteristic comes from the generic meaning of μή, *i.e.* the antecedent is not regarded simply as a person *who* does something but as a person *of such a nature as, one who typifies a class.* In such cases ὅς μή may refer to a definite person or thing. So especially in relative clauses of cause and result, which ordinarily take οὐ. Thus, ταλαίπωρος ἄρα τις σύ γε ἄνθρωπος εἶ . . . , ᾧ μήτε θεοὶ πατρῷοί εἰσι μήτε ἱερά *a wretched being art thou then, who hast neither ancestral gods nor shrines* P. Eu. 302 b, ψηφίσασθε τοιαῦτα ἐξ ὧν μηδέποτε ὑμῖν μεταμελήσει *pass such a vote that you will never repent of it* And. 3. 41, τοιαῦτα λέγειν . . . , οἷς μηδεὶς ἂν νεμεσῆσαι *to use language at which no one could feel just resentment* D. 21. 161, ὁ . . . μηδὲν ἂν ὀμόσᾱς *the man who would not take an oath* 54. 40. Sophocles is especially fond of the generic μή.

h. Consecutive clauses (and consecutive relative clauses) with ὥστε take οὐ with the indicative and optative. Thus, (Λακεδαιμόνιοι) εἰς τοῦτ' ἀπληστίᾱς ἦλθον ὥστ' οὐκ ἐξήρκεσεν αὐτοῖς ἔχειν τὴν κατὰ γῆν ἀρχήν the Lacedaemonians *became so insatiate in their desires that they were not satisfied with their empire on the land* I. 12. 103, ὥστ' οὐκ ἂν αὐτὸν γνωρίσαιμ' ἂν εἰσιδών *so that I should not recognize him, if I were to see him* E. Or. 379. On τοιοῦτος ὅς οὐ see 2705 e.

i. *Oaths* and *protestations* in the indicative with μή express a solemn denial or refusal, or repudiate a charge. Thus, ἴστω νῦν Ζεὺς . . . μὴ μὲν τοῖς ἵπποισιν ἀνὴρ ἐποχήσεται ἄλλος *let Zeus now know* (*i.e.* I swear by Zeus) *that no other man shall mount these horses* K 329, μὰ τὴν Ἀφροδίτην . . . μὴ 'γώ σ' ἀφήσω *by Aphrodite*, far be it from me *that I should release you* Ar. Eccl. 999. Cp. 2716.

μή WITH THE SUBJUNCTIVE AND IMPERATIVE

2706. The subjunctive is a mood of *will*, and therefore takes μή.

2707. Independent clauses take μή : the hortatory subjunctive (1797), the prohibitive subjunctive (1800), the deliberative subjunctive (1805), the subjunctive of doubtful assertion (1801).

a. The anticipatory subjunctive in Homer takes οὐ (1810, cp. 1813).

2708. Dependent clauses take μή : final clauses, as δοκεῖ μοι κατακαῦσαι τὰς ἁμάξᾱς . . . ἵνα μὴ τὰ ζεύγη ἡμῶν στρατηγῇ *it seems to me advisable to burn the wagons that our baggage-train may not be our general* X. A. 3. 2. 27. Object clauses after verbs of *effort*, as οὐ φυλάξεσθ' ὅπως μὴ . . . δεσπότην εὕρητε; *will you not be on your guard lest you find a master?* D. 6. 25. So in conditional clauses with ἐάν, in conditional relative clauses and in relative clauses referring to indefinite time, place, and manner.

a. After μή *lest*, οὐ is used (2221).

2709. The imperative is a mood of *will* and therefore takes μή in prohibitions (1840).

a. The future indicative after interrogative οὐ has an imperative sense (1918).

NEGATIVES OF INDIRECT DISCOURSE

2710. The negatives of direct discourse are retained in indirect discourse introduced by ὅτι or ὡς.

ἐνθῡμηθῆναι χρὴ ὅτι οὐδείς ἐστιν ἀνθρώπων φύσει οὔτε ὀλιγαρχικὸς οὔτε δημοκρατικός *it must be borne in mind that no man by nature is disposed either to oligarchy or to democracy* L. 25. 8.

εἶπε . . . ὅτι οὐ περὶ πολῑτείᾱς ὑμῖν ἔσται ἀλλὰ περὶ σωτηρίᾱς, εἰ μὴ ποιήσαιθ' ἃ Θηρᾱμένης κελεύοι *he said that the question would not be about your constitution but about your safety, if you did not accept the propositions of Theramenes* L. 12. 74.

a. In προεῖπεν ὡς μηδεὶς κῑνήσοιτο ἐκ τῆς τάξεως *he gave orders that no one should move from his position* X. H. 2. 1. 22 μηδείς is due to the fact that the main verb denotes a command.

On the negative in indirect discourse with the infinitive see 2722, 2737, 2738; with the participle, 2729, 2737, 2738; and in indirect questions, 2676.

οὐ AND μή WITH THE INFINITIVE

2711. The infinitive not in indirect discourse has μή; the infinitive in indirect discourse has οὐ, but sometimes μή. The articular infinitive has μή. On the use with μὴ οὐ see 2742 ff.

a. The ordinary negative of the infinitive is μή, which could be so used since the infinitive was employed as early as Homer in an imperative sense. οὐ with the infinitive in indirect discourse is probably due to the analogy of οὐ with the indicative and optative in clauses of indirect discourse introduced by ὅτι (ὡς). οὐ became the natural negative of indirect discourse as soon as the infinitive came to represent the indicative or optative.

2712. μή is used with the articular infinitive.

παράδειγμα τοῦ μὴ ὑμᾶς ἀδικεῖν *a warning not to injure you* L. 27. 5, ὑπὲρ τοῦ μὴ τὸ κελευόμενον ποιῆσαι *in order to avoid doing what was commanded* D. 18. 204. On τὸ (τοῦ) μὴ οὐ, see 2744. 9. 10, 2749 b, d.

οὐ AND μή WITH THE INFINITIVE NOT IN INDIRECT DISCOURSE

2713. μή is the regular negative after all verbs, adjectives, adverbs, and substantives, which take an infinitive not in indirect discourse. Thus, after verbs and other words denoting *ability*, *fitness*, *necessity* (and their opposites). Cp. 2000–2007.

εἰκὸς σοφὸν ἄνδρα μὴ ληρεῖν *it is proper for a wise man not to talk idly* P. Th. 152 b, τᾱ̀ς ὁμοίᾱς χάριτας μὴ ἀντιδιδόναι αἰσχρόν *it is disgraceful not to repay like services* T. 3. 63.

2714. **χρή** (χρῆν, ἐχρῆν) takes either μή or οὐ.

χρὴ μὴ καταφρονεῖν τοῦ πλήθους *one must not despise the multitude* I. 5. 79, χρῆν οὔ σ' ἁμαρτάνειν *thou oughtst not to do wrong* E. Hipp. 507, χρῆ δ' οὔποτ' *εἰπεῖν οὐδέν' ὄλβιον βροτῶν it is not right ever to call any son of man happy* E. And. 100.

a. For original οὐ χρή was substituted (for emphasis) χρὴ οὐ, where the οὐ was still taken with χρή; ultimately οὐ was felt to belong with the infinitive and hence came to be separated from χρή.

b. δεῖ takes μή, as μὴ ὀκνεῖν δεῖ αὐτούς *they must not fear* T. 1. 120. οὐ δεῖ may be used for δεῖ μή (2693). In δεῖ οὐχ ἁπλῶς εἰπεῖν *one must not speak in a general way* I. 15. 117 οὐχ is adherescent. Note οἶμαι δεῖν οὐ, φημὶ χρῆναι οὐ, οἶμαι χρῆναι μή.

2715. μή is used with the infinitive in wishes and prohibitions. Thus, θεοὶ πολῖται, μή με δουλείᾱς τυχεῖν *ye gods of my country, may bondage not be my lot* A. Sept. 253, οἷς μὴ πελάζειν *do not approach these* A. Pr. 712.

2716. μή is used with the infinitive in oaths and protestations. Thus, ἴστω νῦν τόδε γαῖα . . . μή τί τοι αὐτῷ πῆμα κακὸν βουλευσέμεν ἄλλο *let earth now know this* (*i.e.* I swear by earth) *that I will not devise any harmful mischief to thine own hurt* ε 187. Cp. 2705 i.

2717. μή is used with the infinitive of purpose (cp. 2719) or result (2260). Cp. 2759. On ἐφ' ᾧ μή see 2279; on ὥστε οὐ see 2269.

2718. μή is used when the infinitive stands in *apposition* (1987), and hence is like τὸ μή with the infinitive. Thus, τοῦτο ἕν ἐστιν ὧν φημι, μηδένα ἂν ἐν βραχυτέροις ἐμοῦ τὰ αὐτὰ εἰπεῖν *this is one of the things I maintain — that no one can say the same things in fewer words than I can* P. G. 449 c. Cp. A. Pr. 173, 431, 435, P. R. 497 b. Such cases are not to be confused with μή after verbs of *asseveration* or *belief* (2725).

2719. μή is used with the infinitive introduced by verbs of *will* or *desire* (1991) or by verbs expressing activity to the end that something *shall* or *shall not be done*; as τὴν Κέρκῡραν ἐβούλοντο μὴ προέσθαι *they wished not to give up Corcyra* T. 1. 44, φυλακὴν εἶχε μήτ' ἐκπλεῖν . . . μηδένα μήτ' ἐσπλεῖν *he kept guard against any one either sailing out or in* T. 2. 69.

2720. Verbs of *commanding* and *exhorting* (κελεύω, λέγω, βοῶ), *asking* (αἰτῶ, ἀξιῶ), *advising* (συμβουλεύω), and other verbs of *will* or *desire* of like meaning, take μή.

ἐκέλευε . . . μὴ ἐρεθίζειν *he ordered* him *not to provoke his wrath* P. R. 393 e, ἔλεγον αὐτοῖς μὴ ἀδικεῖν *they told them not to commit injustice* T. 2. 5, ἐβόων ἀλλήλοις μὴ θεῖν *they shouted to each other not to run* X. A. 1. 8. 19, ἱκέτευε μὴ κτεῖναι *he besought* them *not to kill* him L. 1. 25, συμβουλεύω σοι . . . μὴ ἀφαιρεῖσθαι ἃ ἂν δῷς *I advise you not to take away what you may have given* X. C. 4. 5. 32.

2721. οὐ is used after verbs of *will* or *desire* only when it is attached to the leading verb or to some particular word; when it marks a contrast inserted parenthetically; where a compound negative takes up οὐ used with the leading verb; and when οὐδείς may be resolved into οὐ and τίς, οὐ going with the leading verb. Examples in 2738.

οὐ AND μή WITH THE INFINITIVE IN INDIRECT DISCOURSE

2722. Verbs of *saying* and *thinking* take οὐ with the infinitive in indirect discourse. Here οὐ is retained from the direct discourse.

ᾗ (ἀνάγκῃ) φαμὲν οὐδένα θεῶν οὔτε μάχεσθαι τὰ νῦν οὔτε μαχεῖσθαί ποτε *we declare that no one of the gods either now contends with necessity, or ever will* P. L. 818 e (= οὐδεὶς . . . μάχεται . . . μαχεῖται), λέγοντες οὐκ εἶναι αὐτόνομοι *saying that they were not independent* T. 1. 67, (= οὐκ ἐσμεν), οἶμαι γὰρ ἂν οὐκ ἀχαρίστως μοι ἔχειν *for I think it would not be unattended with gratitude to me* X. A. 2. 3. 18 (= οὐκ ἂν ἔχοι), ἡγήσαντο ἡμᾶς οὐ περιόψεσθαι *they thought that we should not view it with indifference* T. 1. 39 (= οὐ περιόψονται), ἐμοὶ δὲ δοκοῦσιν οὗτοι οὐ τὸ αἴτιον αἰτιᾶσθαι *but these persons seem to me not to blame the real cause* P. R. 329 b, ἐνόμισεν οὐκ ἂν δύνασθαι μένειν τοὺς πολιορκοῦντας *he thought the besiegers would not be able to hold their position* X. A. 7. 4. 22 (= οὐκ ἂν δύναιντο).

2723. Verbs of *saying* and *thinking* take μή in emphatic declarations and expressions of thought which involve a wish that the utterance may hold good. So with φημί, λέγω, ἡγοῦμαι, νομίζω, οἶμαι. Cp. 2725.

φαίην δ' ἂν ἔγωγε μηδενὶ μηδεμίαν εἶναι παίδευσιν παρὰ τοῦ μὴ ἀρέσκοντος *but for my part I would maintain that no one gets any education from a teacher who is not pleasing* X. M. 1. 2. 39, πάντες ἐροῦσι . . . μηδὲν εἶναι κερδαλεώτερον ἀρετῆς *all will say that nothing is more profitable than bravery* X. C. 7. 1. 18, τίς δ' ἂν ἀνθρώπων θεῶν μὲν παῖδας ἡγοῖτο εἶναι, θεοὺς δὲ μή; *who in the world would think that they were the sons of gods and not gods?* P. A. 27 d, ἀπῆσαν . . . νομίσαντες μὴ ἂν ἔτι . . . ἱκανοὶ γενέσθαι κωλῦσαι τὸν ἐπὶ τὴν θάλασσαν τειχισμόν *they departed in the belief that they would no longer prove able to prevent the building of the wall to the sea* T. 6. 102.

a. Cp. P. Th. 155 a (φημί), T. 1. 139, 6. 49, P. R. 346 e (λέγω), X. M. 1. 2. 41, D. 54. 44 (οἶμαι), X. C. 7. 5. 59 (νομίζω), P. Soph. 230 c (διανοοῦμαι).

b. Cases where the infinitive is in apposition, or depends on an imperative, or occurs after a condition, do not belong here.

2724. μή with the infinitive is often found after verbs denoting an oracular response or a judicial decision actual or implied. Cp. 2725. Thus, ἀνεῖλεν ἡ Πῡθίᾱ μηδένα σοφώτερον εἶναι *the Pythian prophetess made answer that no one was wiser* P. A. 21 a (in direct discourse οὐδεὶς σοφώτερός ἐστι). So after κρίνω, as ἔκρῑνε μὴ Ἀρίστωνος εἶναι Δημάρητον παῖδα the Pythian prophetess *gave decision that Demaretus was not the son of Ariston* Hdt. 6. 66, κέκρισθε . . . μόνοι τῶν πάντων μηδενὸς ἂν κέρδους τὰ κοινὰ δίκαια τῶν Ἑλλήνων προέσθαι *you are adjudged to be the only people who would not betray for lucre the common rights of the Greeks* D. 6. 10. So καταγιγνώσκω μή T. 7. 51, X. C. 6. 1. 36.

2725. μή is often used with verbs and other expressions of *asseveration* and *belief*, after which we might expect οὐ with the infinitive in indirect discourse. Such verbs are those signifying *to hope, expect, promise, put trust in, be persuaded, agree, testify, swear,* etc.

The use of μή indicates strong assurance, confidence, and resolve; and generally in regard to the *future*. Cp. 2723.

ἐλπὶς ὑμᾶς μὴ ὀφθῆναι there is *hope that you will not be seen* X. C. 2. 4. 23, ὑπισχνοῦντο μηδὲν χαλεπὸν αὐτοὺς πείσεσθαι *they promised that they should suffer no harm* X. H. 4. 4. 5, πιστεύω . . . μὴ ψεύσειν με ταύτᾱς τὰς ἀγαθὰς ἐλπίδας *I trust that these good hopes will not deceive me* X. C. 1. 5. 13, θαυμάζω ὅπως ἐπείσθησαν Ἀθηναῖοι Σωκράτην περὶ θεοὺς μὴ σωφρονεῖν *I wonder how the Athenians were persuaded that Socrates did not hold temperate opinions regarding the gods* X. M. 1. 1. 20, ὁμολογεῖ μὴ μετεῖναί οἱ μακρολογίᾱς *he acknowledges that he cannot make a long speech* P. Pr. 336 b, αὐτὸς ἑαυτοῦ καταμαρτυρεῖ μὴ ἐξ ἐκείνου γεγενῆσθαι *he proves by his own testimony that he is not his son* D. 40. 47, ὤμοσεν ἦ μὴν μὴ εἶναί οἱ υἱὸν ἄλλον μηδὲ γενέσθαι πώποτε *he swore that he had no other son and that none other had ever been born to him* And. 1. 126, ὤμνυε . . . μηδὲν εἰρηκέναι *he swore that he had said nothing* D. 21. 119, ὀμοῦμαι μήποτ᾽. . . ἀλεξήσειν κακὸν ἦμαρ *I will swear that I will never ward off the evil day* Φ 373. Cp. Ar. Vesp. 1047, 1281, And. 1. 90, Lyc. 76. With ὄμνῡμι the infinitive may refer to the present, past, or future.

2726. Such verbs are *hope* **ἐλπίζω**; *expect* **ἐλπίζω, προσδοκῶ, δοκῶ, οἴομαι, εἰκός ἐστι**; *promise* **ὑπισχνοῦμαι, ἐπαγγέλλομαι**; *swear* **ὄμνῡμι**; *agree* **ὁμολογῶ, συγχωρῶ**; *pledge* **ἐγγυῶμαι**; *put trust in* **πιστεύω**; *am persuaded* **πέπεισμαι**; *testify* **μαρτυρῶ**; *repudiate* **ἀναίνομαι**; *threaten* **ἀπειλῶ**, etc.

a. μή is regular after verbs of *promising*; common after verbs of *hoping* and *swearing*. With ὄμνῡμι, πιστεύω, πείθομαι, μαρτυρῶ, etc. there is an idea of *deprecation.*

2727. **ἐπίσταμαι** and **οἶδα** usually take μή when they denote confident belief (= *I warrant* from what I know; cp. πιστεύω μή, ὄμνῡμι μή). Thus, ἐξίσταμαι μή του τόδ᾽ ἀγλάϊσμα πλὴν κείνου μολεῖν *I assure you this fair offering has not come from any one save from him* S. El. 908 (cp. Ant. 1092). In τοσοῦτόν γ᾽ οἶδα μήτε μ᾽ ἂν νόσον μήτ᾽ ἄλλο πέρσαι μηδέν *so much at least I know—that neither sickness nor aught else can undo me* (S. O. T. 1455) the infinitive may be appositional (2718). Cases of ἴσθι μή (*be assured* = *I assure you*) may have μή by reason of the imperative (2737 a). So S. Ph. 1329.

οὐ AND μή WITH THE PARTICIPLE

2728. The participle has οὐ when it states a fact, μή when it states a condition. On μή due to the force of the leading verb, see 2737.

οὐ πιστεύων *since* (*as, when*, etc.) *he does not believe*, μὴ πιστεύων *if he does not believe*, ἀνέβη ἐπὶ τὰ ὄρη οὐδενὸς κωλύοντος *he went up on the mountains since no one hindered him* X. A. 1. 2. 22, οὐκ ἂν δύναιο μὴ καμὼν εὐδαιμονεῖν *thou canst not be happy if thou hast not toiled* E. fr. 461, ὡς ἡδὺ τὸ ζῆν μὴ φθονούσης τῆς τύχης *how sweet* is *life if fortune is not envious* Men. Sent. 563.

a. μή with the articular participle is the abridged equivalent of a conditional relative sentence. Thus, in ὁ μὴ ταῦτα ποιῶν ἄδικός ἐστι, ὁ μὴ ποιῶν is virtually the generic ὃς ἂν μὴ ποιῇ or ὅστις μὴ ποιεῖ compressed into a noun.

2729. οὐ is used with a supplementary participle (in indirect discourse) in agreement with a noun (or pronoun, expressed or unexpressed) depending on a verb of *knowing, showing, seeing, perceiving*, etc. (2106–2115); and also with such supplementary participles (not in indirect discourse) after verbs of *emotion* (2100), etc. In most such cases ὅτι οὐ might have been used.

οὐδένα γὰρ οἶδα μῑσοῦντα τοὺς ἐπαινοῦντας *for I know of no one who dislikes his admirers* X. M. 2. 6. 33, φανερὸν πᾶσιν ἐποίησαν οὐκ ἰδίᾳ πολεμοῦντες *they made it clear to all that they were not waging war for their own interests* Lyc. 50, ὁρῶσι τοὺς πρεσβυτέρους οὐ . . . ἀπιόντας *they see that their elders do not depart* X. C. 1. 2. 8, οὐδεὶς μήποθ' εὕρῃ . . . οὐδὲν ἐλλειφθὲν *no one will ever find that anything has been left undone* D. 18. 246; Κύρῳ ἥδετο οὐ δυναμένῳ σῑγᾶν *he rejoiced that Cyrus was unable to remain silent* X. C. 1. 4. 15.

2730. **ἐπίσταμαι** and **οἶδα** denoting confident belief may take μή for οὐ. Thus, ἔξοιδα φύσει σε μὴ πεφῡκότα τοιαῦτα φωνεῖν κακά *well do I know that by nature thou art not adapted to utter such guile* S. Ph. 79; cp. S. O. C. 656, T. 1. 76, 2. 17. This use of μή is analogous to that with the infinitive (2727).

2731. μή is used when the reason for an action is regarded as the condition under which it takes place; as οὐ τοῦ πλέονος μὴ στερισκόμενοι χάριν ἔχουσιν *they are not grateful at not being deprived of the greater part* of their rights T. 1. 77 (= εἰ μὴ στερίσκοντο).

2732. The participle with **ὡς, ὥσπερ, ἅτε, οἷον, οἷα** (2085–2087) has οὐ; as ἐθορυβεῖτε ὡς οὐ ποιήσοντες ταῦτα *you made a disturbance by way of declaring that you did not intend to do this* L. 12. 73. The use of οὐ shows that there is nothing conditional in the use of ὡς though it is often translated by *as if*. μή occurs only after an imperative or a conditional word (2737).

2733. Participles of opposition or concession (2083) take οὐ; as πείθου γυναιξὶ καίπερ οὐ στέργων ὅμως *hearken to women albeit thou likest it not* A. Sept. 712.

2734. The participle with the article has οὐ when a definite person or thing is meant, but μή when the idea is indefinite and virtually conditional (*whoever, whatever*); and when a person or thing is to be characterized (*of such a sort, one who*; 2705 g). Cp. 2052.

οἱ οὐκ ὄντες *the dead* T. 2. 44, οἱ οὐκ ἐθέλοντες the particular *persons* (or *party*) *who are unwilling* Ant. 6. 26, οἱ οὐ βουλόμενοι ταῦτα οὕτως ἔχειν *the party of opposition* And. 1. 9; οἱ μὴ δυνάμενοι *any who are unable* X. A. 4. 5. 11 (= οἵτινες μὴ δύνανται or ὅσοι ἂν μὴ δύνωνται), ὁ μὴ δαρεὶς ἄνθρωπος οὐ παιδεύεται *he who gets no flogging gets no training* Men. Sent. 422, ὁ μὴ λέγων ἃ φρονεῖ *the man who does not say what he thinks* D. 18. 282, ὁ μηδὲν ἀδικῶν οὐδενὸς δεῖται νόμου *he who does no wrong needs no law* Antiph. 288.

οὐ AND μή WITH SUBSTANTIVES AND ADJECTIVES USED SUBSTANTIVELY

2735. οὐ and μή are used with substantives and substantivized adjectives with the same difference as with participles. Here the generic μή is much more common than οὐ.

ἡ τῶν γεφῡρῶν . . . οὐ διάλυσις *the non-destruction of the bridges* T. 1. 137, *κατὰ τὴν τῶν χωρίων ἀλλήλοις οὐκ ἀπόδοσιν because of their non-surrender of the places to each other* 5. 35 (= *ὅτι οὐκ ἀπέδοσαν*), *διὰ τὴν τῶν Κορινθίων οὐκέτι ἐπαναγωγήν because the Corinthians no longer sailed out against them* 7. 36. Cp. *non-regardance* (Shakesp.), *nonresidences* (Milton). So even with concrete nouns: *οἱ οὐχὶ δοῦλοι* E. fr. 831.

ἡ μὴ ἐμπειρία lack of experience Ar. Eccl. 115, *ὁ μὴ ἰατρός he who is not a physician (the non-physician)* P. G. 459 b, *οἱ μὴ πλούσιοι whoever are not rich (the non-rich)* P. R. 330 a, *οὐκ ἔστιν ἐν τοῖς μὴ καλοῖς βουλεύμασιν οὐδ' ἐλπίς in schemes that are unwise there is no place even for hope* S. Tr. 725.

a. The use of the negative here compensates for the absence of negative compounds. Cp. *αἱ οὐκ ἀναγκαῖαι πόσεις unnecessary potations* X. R. L. 5. 4.

οὐδείς, μηδείς

2736. *οὐδείς, οὐδέν* denote that which is actually non-existent or of no account; *μηδείς, μηδέν* denote that which is merely thought of as non-existent or of no account. Both are used as the opposite of *τὶς* or *τὶ* (*εἶναι*) *to be somebody* (*something*, cp. 1269). The neuter forms are often used of persons; *τὸ μηδέν* (indeclinable) is used of persons and things.

ὦ νῦν μὲν οὐδείς, αὔριον δ' ὑπέρμεγας oh thou who art now a nobody (an actual fact), *but to-morrow exceeding great* Ar. Eq. 158, *ὄντες οὐδένες being nobodies* E. And. 700, *οὐ γὰρ ἠξίου τοὺς μηδένας for he was not wont to esteem* (those whom he regarded as) *nobodies* S. Aj. 1114, *τὸ μηδὲν εἰς οὐδὲν ῥέπει what was thought to be nothing* now *inclines* (shows itself) to be *actually nothing* E. fr. 532, *ὅτ' οὐδὲν ὢν τοῦ μηδὲν ἀνέστης ὕπερ when though naught thyself* (a fact) *thou hast stood up for him who is as naught* S. Aj. 1231. So *τὸ οὐδέν zero*, actually nothing, *τὸ μηδέν* abstract nonentity.

a. The construction may influence the choice between *οὐδείς* and *μηδείς*; as *ἐὰν δοκῶσί τι εἶναι μηδὲν ὄντες, ὀνειδίζετε αὐτοῖς rebuke them if they think they are something when* in reality *they are nothing* P. A. 41 e. Cp. 2737 b.

APPARENT EXCHANGE OF οὐ AND μή

2737. Where *μή* is used when we expect *οὐ* the negative expression usually depends on a verb that either has *μή* or would have it, if negatived.

a. After imperatives. Thus, *σάφ' ἴσθι μή με θωπεύσοντά σε know well that I shall not fawn upon thee* E. Heracl. 983, *νόμιζε μηδὲν εἶναι τῶν ἀνθρωπίνων βέβαιον εἶναι consider nothing in human life to be secure* I. 1. 42 (= *μὴ νόμιζέ τι κτλ.*), *ὡς οὖν μὴ μόνον κρίνοντες, ἀλλὰ καὶ θεωρούμενοι, οὕτω τὴν ψῆφον φέρετε cast your ballots then in the belief not only that you are passing judgment but also that the eyes of the world are upon you* Aes. 3. 247 (cp. 2732). See also 2086 b.

b. After conditional expressions. Thus, *εἰ δέ τις . . . νομίζει τι μὴ ἱκανῶς εἰρῆσθαι but if any one thinks some point has not been sufficiently mentioned* And. 1. 70, *λύσετε δὲ οὐδὲ τὰς Λακεδαιμονίων σπονδὰς δεχόμενοι* (= *ἐὰν δέχησθε*) *ἡμᾶς μηδετέρων ὄντας ξυμμάχους and by receiving us, who are allies of neither,* *you will not be violating the treaty with the Lacedaemonians either* T. 1. 35. Cp. 2736 a.

c. Other cases: κελεύει μεῖναι ἐπὶ τοῦ ποταμοῦ μὴ διαβάντας *he ordered them to remain by the river without crossing* X. A. 4. 3. 28 (here μεῖναι, if negatived, would take μή, 2720), ὑπέσχετο εἰρήνην ποιήσειν μήτε ὅμηρα δοὺς μήτε τὰ τείχη καθελών *he promised that he would bring peace about without giving hostages or destroying the walls* L. 12. 68 (here ποιήσειν, if negatived, would take μή, 2725).

N. — But οὐ may assert itself even under the above circumstances; as μὴ ὅ γε οὐ χρὴ ποίει *don't do what is* really *wrong* P. Eu. 307 b, ἢ ἀφίετέ με ἢ μὴ ἀφίετε ὡς ἐμοῦ οὐκ ἂν ποιήσαντος ἄλλα *either acquit me or do not acquit me in the knowledge that I should not act otherwise* P. A. 30 b (cp. 2732), εἰ νομίζεις οὐχ ὑφέξειν τὴν δίκην *if thou thinkest not to suffer the penalty* S. O. T. 551 (= οὐχ ὑφέξω), εἰ γνωσθησόμεθα ξυνελθόντες μέν, ἀμύνεσθαι δὲ οὐ (some Mss.) τολμῶντες *if we shall be known to have come together, and yet not to have the courage to avenge ourselves* T. 1. 124 (it would be said of them: ξυνῆλθον μέν, ἀμύνεσθαι δὲ οὐκ ἐτόλμων, a contrast, cp. 2690).

d. On μή in questions where we might expect οὐ, see 2676 b.

2738. οὐ is sometimes used where we expect μή.

a. Where οὐ stands in a clause introduced by εἰ or other words after which μή might be expected (2698). Thus, ὄφρα καὶ οὐκ ἐθέλων τις ἀναγκαίῃ πολεμίζοι *that every one must of necessity fight even though he would not* Δ 300 (cp. 2692 a).

b. Where οὐ goes strictly with the leading verb though it stands with the infinitive. Thus, βουλοίμην δ' ἂν οὐκ εἶναι τόδε *I would fain it were not so* (*I should not wish that this were so*) E. Med. 73, ὀμώμοκεν οὐ χαριεῖσθαι . . . ἀλλὰ δικάσειν κατὰ τοὺς νόμους *he has sworn, not that he will show favour, but that he will judge according to the laws* P. A. 35 c (some explain this as the οὐ of direct discourse).

c. Where οὐ in a contrast goes closely with a following word or words, or stands in a partial parenthesis. Thus, κελεύων οὐκ ἐν τῇ ἐκκλησίᾳ ἀλλ' ἐν τῷ θεάτρῳ τὴν ἀνάρρησιν γίγνεσθαι (he has violated the law) *in demanding that the proclamation be made not in the Assembly but in the theatre* Aes. 3. 204, ὁμολογοίην ἂν ἔγωγε οὐ κατὰ τούτους εἶναι ῥήτωρ *I should acknowledge that I am an orator, but not after their style* P. A. 17 b, ὑμᾶς νῦν ἀξιοῦντες οὐ ξυμμαχεῖν, ἀλλὰ ξυναδικεῖν *demanding that you should be, not their allies, but their partners in wrong-doing* T. 1. 39.

d. When a compound negative with the infinitive repeats οὐ used with the leading verb. Thus, (ὁ νόμος) οὐκ ἐᾷ εἰσιέναι, οὗ ἂν ᾖ ὁ τετελευτηκώς, οὐδεμίαν γυναῖκα *the law does not permit any women to enter where the dead may be* D. 43. 63.

e. When οὐδείς may be resolved into οὐ and τίς, οὐ going with the leading verb. Thus, οὐδενὸς (= οὔ τινος) ἁμαρτεῖν . . . δίκαιός ἐστιν *there is nothing he deserves to miss* Ant. 4. α. 6 (= he does not deserve to miss anything), ἀξιῶ ἐγὼ ὧν ὀμωμόκατε παραβῆναι οὐδέν *I ask that you do not break any of the conditions to which you have sworn* X. H. 2. 4. 42 (= οὐκ ἀξιῶ . . . παραβῆναι τι). Cp. S. Ph. 88.

μή AND μὴ οὐ WITH THE INFINITIVE

REDUNDANT OR SYMPATHETIC NEGATIVE

I. With the Infinitive depending on Verbs of Negative Meaning

2739. Verbs and expressions of negative meaning, such as *deny, refuse, hinder, forbid, avoid,* often take the infinitive with a redundant μή to confirm the negative idea of the leading verb.

With this compare: "First he denied you had in him no right" (Shakesp., Com. of Er. 4. 2. 7); and "La pluie . . . empêche qu'on ne se promène" (Racine); "Verbot ihnen Jesus, dass sie Niemand sagen sollten" (St. Mark 9. 9).

καταρνῇ μὴ δεδρᾱκέναι τάδε; *dost thou deny that thou hast done this?* S. Ant. 442, ἀποκωλῦσαι τοὺς Ἕλληνας μὴ ἐλθεῖν *to hinder the Greeks from coming* X. A. 6. 4. 24, κήρῡκα προέπεμψεν αὐτοῖς . . . ἀπεροῦντα μὴ πλεῖν *they sent a herald to forbid them to sail* T. 1. 29, εὐλαβήσεσθε μὴ πολλῶν ἐναντίον λέγειν *you will beware of speaking in public* P. Eu. 304 a, ἀπέσχοντο μὴ ἐπὶ τὴν ἑκατέρων γῆν στρατεῦσαι *they abstained from marching upon each other's territory* T. 5. 25.

2740. The redundant μή is used after **ἀμφιλέγω** and **ἀμφισβητῶ** *dispute,* **ἀνατίθεμαι** *retract an opinion,* **ἀντιλέγω** *speak against,* **ἀπαγορεύω** and **ἀπειπεῖν** *forbid,* **ἀπιστῶ** *doubt,* **ἀπογιγνώσκω** *abandon an intention,* **ἀποκρύπτομαι** *conceal,* **ἀπολῡ́ω** *acquit,* **ἀποστερῶ** *deprive,* **ἀποστρέφω** *divert,* **ἀποχειροτονῶ** and **ἀποψηφίζομαι** *vote against,* **ἀρνοῦμαι** (and compounds, and **ἄπαρνός εἰμι, ἔξαρνός εἰμι**) *deny,* **διαμάχομαι** *refuse,* **εἴργω** and **ἐμποδών εἰμι** *prevent,* **ἐναντιοῦμαι** *oppose,* **εὐλαβοῦμαι** *beware of,* **ἔχω** and **ἀπέχω** *prevent,* **ἀντέχω, ἀπέχομαι, ἐπέχω, κατέχω** *abstain from,* **κωλῡ́ω** (and compounds) *hinder,* **μεταβουλεύομαι** *alter one's plans,* **μεταγιγνώσκω** *change one's mind,* **ὄκνον παρέχω** *make hesitate,* **φεύγω** (and compounds) *escape, avoid, disclaim,* **φυλάττομαι** *guard against,* etc.

2741. Also after the following verbs: **ἀπαυδῶ** *forbid,* **ἀπεύχομαι** *deprecor,* **ἀποδοκεῖ** *resolve not,* **ἀπροσδόκητός εἰμι** *do not expect,* **ἀφαιροῦμαι** *prevent,* **ἀφίημι** *acquit,* **δέδοικα** and **φοβοῦμαι** *fear,* **ἐρῡ́κω** *hinder,* **καταδεῖ** *lack,* **μεταδοκεῖ μοι** *change one's mind,* **παύω** *put an end to,* **ῥύομαι** and **σῴζω** *save from,* **ὑπεκτρέχω** *escape from,* **ὑφίεμαι** *give up,* etc.

2742. When a verb of *denying, refusing, hindering, forbidding,* etc., is itself negatived, either directly or by appearing in a question expecting a negative answer, the infinitive has μὴ οὐ. Here both the introductory clause and the dependent clause have virtually an affirmative sense.

οὐδεὶς πώποτ' ἀντεῖπεν μὴ οὐ καλῶς ἔχειν αὐτούς (τοὺς νόμους) *no one ever denied that they* (the laws) *were excellent* D. 24. 24, τίνα οἴει ἀπαρνήσεσθαι μὴ οὐχὶ καὶ αὐτὸν ἐπίστασθαι τὰ δίκαια; *who, think you, will deny that he too understands what is just?* P. G. 461 c (= οὐδεὶς ἀπαρνήσεται). But μὴ οὐ is not used after οὔ φημι, οὐκ ἐῶ, οὐκ ἐθέλω (2692 a).

a. μὴ οὐ with the infinitive here, and elsewhere, is used only when the introductory word or words has an actual or a virtual negative. Since, in ἀρνοῦμαι μὴ ταῦτα δρᾶσαι *I deny that I did this,* μή confirms the negative idea in ἀρνοῦμαι, so in οὐκ ἀρνοῦμαι μὴ οὐ ταῦτα δρᾶσαι *I do not deny that I did this*, οὐ after the strengthening μή confirms the οὐ prefixed to the leading verb. Cp. "Je ne nie pas que je ne sois infiniment flatté" (Voltaire). In the first sentence μή repeats the 'negative result' of ἀρνοῦμαι (single sympathetic negative, untranslatable); in the second sentence οὐ is repeated with the infinitive to sum up the effect of οὐκ ἀρνοῦμαι (double sympathetic negative; both untranslatable). After verbs negative in meaning (*deny*, etc.) μή and μὴ οὐ cannot be translated in modern English (see 2739). After verbs not negative in character but preceded by a negative, and after virtually negative expressions, μή or μὴ οὐ has a negative force (2745, 2746).

b. μὴ οὐ with the infinitive regularly indicates a certain pressure of interest on the part of the person involved.

2743. After *deny, speak against, doubt*, etc., followed by ὡς or ὅτι, a redundant οὐ is often inserted. Thus, ὡς μὲν οὐκ ἀληθῆ ταῦτ' ἐστίν, οὐχ ἕξετ' ἀντιλέγειν *that this is true you will not be able to deny* D. 8. 31.

a. Here the ὡς clause is an internal accusative (accusative of content) after ἀντιλέγειν. Originally the meaning seems to have been 'you will not be able to deny in this way — this is not true' where οὐ is not redundant.

2744. *Summary of Constructions after Verbs of Hindering, etc.*

After verbs signifying (or suggesting) *to hinder* and the like, the infinitive admits the article τό or τοῦ (the ablatival genitive, 1392). Hence we have a variety of constructions, which are here classed under formal types. The simple infinitive is more closely connected with the leading verb than the infinitive with τὸ μή or τὸ μὴ οὐ, which often denotes the result (cp. ὥστε μή) of the action of the leading verb and is either an accusative of respect or a simple object infinitive. The genitive of the infinitive is very rare with κωλύω and its compounds.

a. Some scholars regard the infinitive with the negative as an internal accusative, not as a simple object infinitive; and the infinitive without the negative as an external accusative.

1. **εἴργει με μὴ γράφειν** (the usual construction: examples 2739).

2. **εἴργει με γράφειν** (less common). Since the redundant μή is not obligatory, we have the simple infinitive as object (1989), as εἰ τοῦτό τις εἴργει δρᾶν ὄκνος *if some scruple prevents* us *from doing this* P. Soph. 242 a, ὃν θανεῖν ἐρρυσάμην *whom I saved from death* E. Alc. 11, οἱ θεῶν ἡμᾶς ὅρκοι κωλύουσι πολεμίους εἶναι ἀλλήλοις *the oaths sworn in the name of the gods prevent our being enemies to each other* X. A. 2. 5. 7, and so usually with κωλύω (cp. 2744. 7).

3. **εἴργει με τὸ μὴ γράφειν** (rather common; cp. 1): εἶργον τὸ μὴ . . . κακουργεῖν *they prevented* them *from doing damage* T. 3. 1, οἷοί τε ἦσαν κατέχειν τὸ μὴ δακρύειν *they were able to restrain their weeping* P. Ph. 117 c.

4. **εἴργει με τὸ γράφειν** (not uncommon; cp. 2): ἐπέσχον τὸ εὐθέως τοῖς Ἀθηναίοις ἐπιχειρεῖν *they refrained from immediately attacking the Athenians* T. 7. 33, ἔστιν τις, ὃς σε κωλύσει τὸ δρᾶν *there is some one who will prevent thee from the deed* S. Ph. 1241.

5. **εἴργει με τοῦ μὴ γράφειν**, with the ablatival genitive, 1392 (not so common as 3): πᾶς γὰρ ἀσκὸς δύο ἄνδρας ἕξει τοῦ μὴ καταδῦναι *for each skin-bag will pre-*

vent two men from sinking X. A. 3. 5. 11. Other cases are: Hdt. 1. 86, T. 1. 76, X. C. 2. 4. 13, 2. 4. 23, 3. 3. 31, I. 7. 17, 12. 80, 15. 122, P. L. 637 c, 832 b, D. 23. 149, 33. 25. Observe that this idiom does not have the logical meaning 'from *not*,' which we should expect. Some write τὸ μή or μή alone.

6. **εἴργει με τοῦ γράφειν** (not common, and very rare with κωλύω, as X. A. 1. 6. 2): τοῦ δὲ δραπετεύειν δεσμοῖς ἀπείργουσι; *do they prevent* their slaves *from running away by fetters?* X. M. 2. 1. 16, ἐπέσχομεν τοῦ δακρύειν *we desisted from weeping* P. Ph. 117 e (cp. 3).

7. **οὐκ εἴργει με γράφειν** (not very common, but more often with οὐ κωλύω; cp. 2): οὐδὲ διακωλύουσι ποιεῖν ὧν ἂν ἐπιθυμῇς; *nor will they prevent you from doing what you desire?* P. Lys. 207 e, τί κωλύει (= οὐδὲν κ.) καὶ τὰ ἄκρα ἡμῖν κελεύειν Κῦρον προκαταλαβεῖν; *what hinders our ordering Cyrus to take also the heights in advance for us?* X. A. 1. 3. 16, ταῦτά τινες οὐκ ἐξαρνοῦνται πράττειν *certain people do not deny that they are doing these things* Aes. 3. 250.

8. **οὐκ εἴργει με μὴ οὐ γράφειν** (the regular construction): οὐκ ἀμφισβητῶ μὴ οὐχὶ σὲ σοφώτερον ἢ ἐμέ *I do not dispute that you are wiser than I* P. Hipp. Minor 369 d, οὐδὲν ἐδύνατο ἀντέχειν μὴ οὐ χαρίζεσθαι *he was not able to resist granting the favour* X. C. 1. 4. 2, τί ἐμποδὼν (= οὐδὲν ἐμποδών) μὴ οὐχὶ . . . ὑβριζομένους ἀποθανεῖν; *what hinders our being put to death ignominiously?* X. A. 3. 1. 13, τί δῆτα μέλλεις μὴ οὐ γεγωνίσκειν τὸ πᾶν; *why pray dost thou hesitate to declare the whole?* A. Pr. 627.

9. **οὐκ εἴργει με τὸ μὴ γράφειν** (since occasionally the sympathetic οὐ is not added; cp. 3): καὶ φημὶ δρᾶσαι κοὐκ ἀπαρνοῦμαι τὸ μή (δρᾶσαι) *I both assent that I did the deed and do not deny that I did it* S. Ant. 443, τίς . . . σοῦ ἀπελείφθη τὸ μή σοι ἀκολουθεῖν; *who failed to follow you?* X. C. 5. 1. 25.

10. **οὐκ εἴργει με τὸ μὴ οὐ γράφειν** (very common; cp. 8): οὐκ ἐναντιώσομαι τὸ μὴ οὐ γεγωνεῖν πᾶν *I will not refuse to declare all* A. Pr. 786, τὸ μὲν οὖν μὴ οὐχὶ ἡδέα εἶναι τὰ ἡδέα λόγος οὐδεὶς ἀμφισβητεῖ *no argument disputes that sweet things are sweet* P. Phil. 13 a.

Very unusual constructions are

11. **οὐκ εἴργει τὸ γράφειν** (οὐκ ἂν ἀρνοίμην τὸ δρᾶν *I will not refuse the deed* S. Ph. 118).

12. **οὐκ εἴργει μὴ γράφειν** (οὔτ' ἠμφεσβήτησε μὴ σχεῖν *neither did he deny that he had* the money D. 27. 15).

13. **οὐκ εἴργει τοῦ μὴ οὐ γράφειν** (once only: E. Hipp. 48, where τὸ μὴ οὐ is read by some).

On the negative after ὥστε, see 2759.

II. μὴ οὐ with the Infinitive depending on Negatived Verbs

2745. Any infinitive that would take μή, takes μὴ οὐ (with a negative force), if dependent on a negatived verb. Here οὐ is the sympathetic negative and is untranslatable.

οὐκ ἂν πιθοίμην μὴ οὐ τάδ' ἐκμαθεῖν σαφῶς *I cannot consent not to learn this exactly as it is* S. O. T. 1065.

2746. μὴ οὐ with the infinitive thus often follows verbs and other expressions formed by οὐ (or α-*privative*) with a positive word and denoting what is *impossible, improbable, wrong, senseless*, and the like.

οὐδεὶς οἷός τ' ἐστὶν ἄλλως λέγων μὴ οὐ καταγέλαστος εἶναι *no one by speaking otherwise can avoid being ridiculous* P. G. 509 a, ὑπέσχου ζητήσειν ὡς οὐχ ὅσιόν σοι ὂν μὴ οὐ βοηθεῖν δικαιοσύνῃ *you promised to make the inquiry on the ground that it would not be right for you not to assist justice* P. R. 427 e, πάνυ ἀνόητον ἡγοῦμαι εἶναί σοι μὴ οὐ καὶ τοῦτο χαρίζεσθαι *I think it is utterly senseless for me not to grant you this favour also* P. S. 218 c.

2747. Such expressions are, *e.g.* οὐχ ὅσιός τ' εἰμί, οὐχ οἷόν τ' ἐστί, οὐχ ἱκανός εἰμι, οὐκ ἔστι, ἀδύνατός εἰμι, οὐ δίκαιόν ἐστι, οὐχ ὅσιόν ἐστι, οὐ προσδοκίᾱ ἐστί, ἄλογόν ἐστι, οὐκ ἀνεκτόν ἐστι, ἄνοιά ἐστι, and many others.

2748. Some expressions denoting repugnance to the moral sense involve a negative idea, and may have the same construction. Thus, ὥστε πᾶσιν αἰσχύνην εἶναι μὴ οὐ συσπουδάζειν *so that all were ashamed not* (*i.e.* felt it was *not* right) *to coöperate zealously* X. A. 2. 3. 11. So with αἰσχρόν ἐστι (= οὐ καλόν ἐστι), δεινόν ἐστι.

2749. Instead of μὴ οὐ we find also μή, τὸ μή, τοῦ μή, τὸ μὴ οὐ (but not τοῦ μὴ οὐ).

a. μή (rarely; cp. 2744. 1): ἔλεγον ὅτι . . . οὐ δυνήσοιντο μὴ πείθεσθαι τοῖς Θηβαίοις *they said that they could not help submitting to the Thebans* X. H. 6. 1. 1, αἰσχρὸν . . . γίγνεται ἐμέ γε μὴ ἐθέλειν *it is disgraceful for me at least not to be willing* P. G. 458 d.

b. τὸ μή (cp. 2744. 3): ἔφη . . . οὐχ οἷόν τ' εἶναι τὸ μὴ ἀποκτεῖναί με *he said it was not possible not to condemn me to death* P. A. 29 c.

c. τοῦ μή (cp. 2744. 5): ἡ ἀπορίᾱ τοῦ μὴ ἡσυχάζειν *the inability to rest* T. 2. 49.

d. τὸ μὴ οὐ (cp. 2744. 10): οὐ μέντοι ἔπειθέ γε τὸ μὴ οὐ μεγαλοπράγμων . . . εἶναι *he could not, however, persuade them that he was not a man who entertained grand designs* X. H. 5. 2. 36, ἄλογον τὸ μὴ οὐ τέμνειν διχῇ *it is irrational not to make a two-fold division* P. Soph. 219 e.

μὴ οὐ WITH THE PARTICIPLE DEPENDING ON NEGATIVED VERBS

2750. μὴ οὐ, instead of μή, is sometimes found with the participle after expressions preceded by οὐ or involving a negative, and usually when such expressions denote impossibility or moral repugnance. μὴ οὐ here denotes an exception, and has the force of *except, unless* (cp. εἰ μή, 2346 a).

οὐκ ἄρα ἐστὶν φίλον τῷ φιλοῦντι οὐδὲν μὴ οὐκ ἀντιφιλοῦν *nothing then is beloved by a lover except it love in return* P. Lys. 212 d, δυσάλγητος γὰρ ἂν εἴην τοιάνδε μὴ οὐ κατοικτίρων ἕδρᾱν *for I should prove hard of heart, did I not pity such a supplication as this* S. O. T. 11 (δυσάλγητος = οὐκ οἰκτίρμων, μὴ οὐ κατοικτίρων = εἰ μὴ κατοικτίροιμι).

μή AND μὴ οὐ WITH THE SUBJUNCTIVE AND INDICATIVE

2751. The use of μή and μὴ οὐ with the subjunctive is different from that with the infinitive.

a. In doubtful assertions (1801–1802) expressing *anxiety*, *suspicion*, *surmise*, μή is used of that which may be true, μὴ οὐ of that which may not be true.

b. After verbs of *fear* and *caution*, where μή means *lest*, μὴ οὐ means *lest not*, *that not* (2221, 2225).

2752. μή and μὴ οὐ are used with the indicative in doubtful assertions (1772). In questions with μὴ οὐ the οὐ belongs to a single word (2651 d).

On ὅπως μή, ὅπως μὴ οὐ with the future, see 1920, 1921, 2203.

REDUNDANT οὐ WITH πλήν, ETC.

2753. Redundant οὐ appears after the negative words πλήν, χωρίς, ἐκτός, ἄνευ *except*, *without*, and after πρίν (and μᾶλλον ἤ usually) preceded by a negative, which may be involved in a question.

νῦν δὲ φαίνεται (ἡ ναῦς) . . . πλέουσα πανταχόσε πλὴν οὐκ εἰς Ἀθήνᾱς *but now it seems that the ship is sailing everywhere except to Athens* D. 56. 23, πρὶν δ' οὐδὲν ὀρθῶς εἰδέναι, τί σοι πλέον λῡπουμένῃ γένοιτ' ἄν; *before thou knowest the facts, what can sorrow avail thee?* E. Hel. 322, εὖ δ' ἴστε ὅτι οὐ περὶ τῶν ἐμῶν ἰδίων μᾶλλον τῑμωρήσεσθε Πολυκλέᾱ ἢ οὐχ ὑπὲρ ὑμῶν αὐτῶν *but be assured that you will punish Polycles rather for your own good than for my private interests* D. 50. 66. Cp. "j'irai vous voir avant que vous *ne* preniez aucune résolution," "le bon Dieu est cent fois meilleur qu'on *ne* le dit."

οὐ μή

2754. οὐ μή, and the compounds of each, are used in emphatic negative predictions and prohibitions.

a. οὐ μή marks strong personal interest on the part of the speaker. In its original use it may have belonged to colloquial speech and as such we find it in comedy; but in tragedy it is often used in stately language. οὐ μή is rare in the orators.

2755. (I) In negative predictions to denote a strong denial.

a. With the (first or second) aorist subjunctive, less often with the present subjunctive (1804). Thus, ἢν νῑκήσωμεν, οὐ μή ποτε ὑμῖν Πελοποννήσιοι ἐσβάλωσιν ἐς τὴν χώρᾱν *if we are victorious, the Peloponnesians will never invade your territory* T. 4. 95, οὐδεὶς μηκέτι μείνῃ τῶν πολεμίων *not one of the enemy will stand his ground any longer* X. A. 4. 8. 13, οὔτι μὴ φύγητε *you shall not escape* (a threat) E. Hec. 1039, οὐ μή σοι δύνωνται ἀντέχειν οἱ πολέμιοι *your enemies will not be able to withstand you* X. Hi. 11. 15.

b. With the future indicative (first and third person). Thus, οὔ σοι μὴ μεθέψομαί ποτε *never will I follow thee* S. El. 1052, οὐ μὴ δυνήσεται Κῦρος εὑρεῖν *Cyrus* *will not be able to find* X. C. 8. 1. 5. In indirect discourse, the future optative or infinitive; as ἐθέσπισεν . . . ὡς οὐ μή ποτε πέρσοιεν *he prophesied that they never would destroy* S. Ph. 611, εἶπεν . . . οὐ μή ποτε εὖ πράξειν πόλιν *he declared that the city would never prosper* E. Phoen. 1590.

2756. (II) In strong prohibitions (cp. 1919).

a. With the future indicative (second person singular). Thus, οὐ μὴ καταβήσει *don't come down* Ar. Vesp. 397.

b. With the aorist subjunctive rarely (1800 N.). Thus οὐ μὴ ληρήσῃς *don't talk twaddle* Ar. Nub. 367. Many editors change the aorist subjunctive to the future indicative.

2757. There are two cases in which οὐ μή is not used in conjunction, but where each negative has its own verb.

a. A positive command in the future indicative (second person) may be joined by ἀλλά or δέ to a prohibition introduced by οὐ μή. Thus, οὐ μὴ λαλήσεις ἀλλ' ἀκολουθήσεις ἐμοί *don't prattle but follow me* Ar. Nub. 505, οὐ μὴ δυσμενὴς ἔσει τοῖς φίλοις, παύσει δὲ θυμοῦ *do not be angry with thy friends, but cease thy wrath* E. Med. 1151. (In E. Bacch. 343 δέ with the future is followed by μηδέ with the future.) In such sentences the force of οὐ continues into the ἀλλά or δέ clause. Such sentences are generally printed as questions.

b. A positive command with οὐ and the future indicative (second person) may be followed by the future in a prohibition introduced by μηδέ or καὶ μή. Here the clause with οὐ has the form of a question expecting the answer *yes*, while the whole sentence has the form of a question expecting the answer *no*. Thus, οὐ σῖγ' ἀνέξει μηδὲ δειλίᾱν ἀρεῖ; *wilt thou not keep silence and not win for thyself the reputation of cowardice?* (= *keep silence and do not get the reputation of being a coward*) S. Aj. 75, οὐκοῦν καλεῖς αὐτὸν καὶ μὴ ἀφήσεις; *will you not call him and (will you not) send him away?* (= *call him and don't send him away*) P. S. 175 a. Here οὐ is to be taken also with the following clause. Some scholars make the question in the second clause independent of οὐ.

2758. The origin of the use of οὐ μή is obscure and disputed. See Kvičala *Zeitschrift für österreichische Gymnasien* 1856, p. 755; Goodwin *Moods and Tenses* 389; Gildersleeve *American Journal of Philology* 3. 202, 23. 137; Jebb on Sophocles *Ajax* 75 (appendix); Chambers *Classical Review* 10. 150, 11. 109; Wharton *o.c.* 10. 239; Whitelaw *o.c.* 10. 239, 16. 277; Sonnenschein *o.c.* 16. 165; Kühner-Gerth *Grammatik der griechischen Sprache* 2. § 514. 8.

NEGATIVES WITH ὥστε AND THE INFINITIVE

2759. ὥστε with the infinitive shows the following uses of the negatives.

a. μή in ordinary result clauses including such as express an intended result; as πᾶν ποιοῦσιν ὥστε δίκην μὴ διδόναι μηδ' ἀπαλλάττεσθαι τοῦ μεγίστου κακοῦ *they use every effort* (*so as*) *to avoid being punished and released from the greatest of evils* P. G. 479 c.

b. μή *sympathetic*, after verbs of *hindering*; as ἀπεχόμενοι ὥστε μὴ ἐμβάλλειν *refraining from attacking* T. 1. 49 (cp. 2744. 1).

N. — After verbs of *hindering* ὥστε is rarely used for ὥστε μή (cp. 2744. 2); as ὥστε γὰρ τὴν σύντομον πρὸς τοὺς Πελληνέᾱς ἀφικέσθαι ἡ πρὸ τοῦ τείχους φάραγξ εἶργε *the ravine in front of the walls prevented them from reaching the short cut to the Pellenians* X. H. 7. 2. 13. Cp. P. Eu. 305 d.

c. **οὐ**, when the ὥστε clause depends on a clause itself subordinate to a verb of *saying* or *thinking* (2269).

d. **μὴ οὐ** after a negatived verb of *hindering* (cp. 2744. 8); as οὔτε σφέας Εὐρυβιάδης κατέχειν δυνήσεται . . . ὥστε μὴ οὐ διασκεδασθῆναι τὴν στρατιήν *neither will Eurybiades be able to prevent the fleet from being scattered* Hdt. 8. 57. Also when the ὥστε clause depends on a negatived verb (2745); as πείσομαι γὰρ οὐ τοσοῦτον οὐδὲν ὥστε μὴ οὐ καλῶς θανεῖν *for I will suffer nothing so much as not to die nobly* S. Ant. 97.

e. **οὐ μή** (cp. 2754 a); as οὕτως ἐπιτεθύμηκα ἀκοῦσαι ὥστε . . . οὐ μή σου ἀπολειφθῶ *I have conceived such a desire to hear that I shall not fall behind you* P. Phae. 227 d.

ACCUMULATION OF NEGATIVES

2760. If in the same clause a *simple* negative (οὐ or μή) with a verb follows a negative, each of the two negatives keeps its own force if they belong to different words or expressions. If they belong to the same word or expression, they make an affirmative.

οὐ διὰ τὸ μὴ ἀκοντίζειν οὐκ ἔβαλον αὐτόν *it was not because they did not throw that they did not hit him* Ant. 3. δ. 6, οὔ τοι μὰ τὴν Δήμητρα δύναμαι μὴ γελᾶν *by Demeter I am not able to help laughing* Ar. Ran. 42, οὐδεὶς οὐκ ἔπασχέ τι *no one was not suffering something* (*i.e.* everybody suffered) X. S. 1. 9 (οὐδεὶς ὅστις οὐ = *everybody* is commonly used for οὐδεὶς οὐ), οὐδὲ τὸν Φορμίων' ἐκεῖνος οὐχ ὁρᾷ *nor does he not see Phormio* (*i.e.* he sees him very well) D. 36. 46, οὐδ' εἴ τις ἄλλος σοφός (ἐστιν) οὐ φιλοσοφεῖ *nor if there is any other man who is wise, does he love wisdom* P. S. 204 a, οὐδέ γε ὁ ἰδίᾳ πονηρὸς οὐκ ἂν γένοιτο δημοσίᾳ χρηστός *nor can the man who is base in private prove himself noble in a public capacity* Aes. 3. 78.

2761. If in the same clause one or more *compound* negatives follow a negative with the same verb, the compound negative simply confirms the first negative.

οὐδεὶς οὐδὲν πενίᾳ δράσει *no one will do anything because of want* Ar. Eccl. 605, μὴ θορυβήσῃ μηδείς *let no one raise an uproar* D. 5. 15, καὶ οὔτε ἐπέθετο οὐδεὶς οὐδαμόθεν οὔτε πρὸς τὴν γέφῡραν οὐδεὶς ἦλθε *and neither did any one make an attack from any quarter nor did any one come to the bridge* X. A. 2. 4. 23, τούτους φοβούμενοι μήποτε ἀσεβὲς μηδὲν μηδὲ ἀνόσιον μήτε ποιήσητε μήτε βουλεύσητε *holding them* (the gods) *in fear never do or intend anything either impious or unholy* X. C. 8. 7. 22. So οὐ . . . οὐδέ *non . . . ne . . quidem*, οὐ μὴν οὐδέ (2768). οὐδὲ πολλοῦ δεῖ, after a negative, means *far from it.* Cp. "no sonne, were he never so old of years, might not marry" (Ascham's Scholemaster), "We may not, nor will we not suffer this" (Marlowe).

a. In **οὐδὲ γὰρ οὐδέ** the first negative belongs to the whole sentence, while the second limits a particular part. Thus, *οὐδὲ γὰρ οὐδὲ τοῦτο ἐψεύσατο* *for he did not deceive me even in this* X. C. 7. 2. 20 (cp. *neque enim . . . ne . . quidem*). Cp. E 22, θ 32. So *οὐδὲ μὲν οὐδέ* B 703, κ 551.

2762. The negative of one clause is often repeated in the same or in another clause either for emphasis or because of lax structure.

ὃς οὐκ, ἐπειδὴ τῷδε ἐβούλευσας μόρον, δρᾶσαι τόδ' ἔργον οὐκ ἔτλης *who did not, after you had planned his death, dare to do this deed* A. Ag. 1634. The repetition is rhetorical when the negative is repeated directly, as *οὐ σμῑκρός, οὔχ, ἁγὼν ὅδε* *not trifling, is this struggle, no in truth* S. O. C. 587.

SOME NEGATIVE PHRASES

2763. **μὴ ὅτι, οὐχ ὅπως,** rarely **οὐχ ὅτι** and **μὴ ὅπως,** *not to speak of, to say nothing of, not only, not only not, so far from* (Lat. *tantum aberat ut*) are idiomatic phrases probably due to an (early, and later often unconscious) ellipsis of a verb of *saying*. Thus, *οὐ λέγω* (or *οὐκ ἐρῶ*) *ὅπως, μὴ εἴπω* (*λέγε* or *εἴπῃς*) *ὅτι* *I do* (*will*) *not say that, let me not say that, do not say that.* *μὴ ὅτι*, etc. are often used where these verbal forms cannot be supplied by reason of the form of the sentence.

a. **οὐχ ὅτι** (**οὐχ ὅπως, μὴ ὅτι**) . . . **ἀλλὰ** (**καί**) *not only . . . but* (*also*). Thus, *οὐχ ὅτι μόνος ὁ Κρίτων ἐν ἡσυχίᾳ ἦν, ἀλλὰ καὶ οἱ φίλοι αὐτοῦ* *not only was Crito in peace, but his friends also* X. M. 2. 9. 8, *οἶμαι ἂν μὴ ὅτι ἰδιώτην τινά, ἀλλὰ τὸν μέγαν βασιλέᾱ εὑρεῖν κτλ.* *I think that not merely any private person but the Great King would find*, etc. P. A. 40 d.

b. **οὐχ ὅπως** (rarely **οὐχ ὅτι**) or **μὴ ὅτι . . . ἀλλὰ** (**καί**) is shown by the context to mean *not only not* (*so far from*) . . . *but* (*also*). Thus, *οὐχ ὅπως χάριν αὐτοῖς ἔχεις, ἀλλὰ μισθώσᾱς σαυτὸν κατὰ τουτωνὶ πολῑτεύει* *not only are you not grateful to them, but you let yourself out for hire as a public man to their prejudice* D. 18. 131; *μὴ ὅτι* P. R. 581 e.

c. **οὐχ ὅπως** (rarely **οὐχ ὅτι**) or **μὴ ὅτι** (**μὴ ὅπως**) . . . **ἀλλ' οὐδέ** (**μηδέ**) or **ἀλλ' οὐ** (**μή**) is shown by the context to mean *not only not* (*so far from*) . . . *but not even*. Thus, *οὐχ ὅπως τῆς κοινῆς ἐλευθερίᾱς μετέχομεν, ἀλλ' οὐδὲ δουλείᾱς μετρίᾱς τυχεῖν ἠξιώθημεν* *not only do we not share in the general freedom, but we were not thought worthy of obtaining even a moderate servitude* I. 14. 5, *νομίζει ἑαυτὸν μὴ ὅτι Πλαταιέᾱ εἶναι, ἀλλ' οὐδ' ἐλεύθερον* *he considers himself not only not a Plataean but not even a free man* L. 23. 12.

N. When a negative precedes, the meaning may be *not only . . . but not even*; as *τὴν οἰκίᾱν . . . οὐδενὶ ἂν μὴ ὅτι προῖκα δοίης, ἀλλ' οὐδ' ἔλᾱττον τῆς ἀξίᾱς λαβών* *you would offer your house to no one not only gratis, but not even for a lower price than it is worth* X. M. 1. 6. 11.

d. **μὴ ὅτι** (less often **οὐχ ὅπως**) in the second of two balanced clauses, after an expressed or implied negative in the first clause, means *much less* (Lat. *nedum*); as *οὐδὲ πλεῖν, μὴ ὅτι ἀναιρεῖσθαι τοὺς ἄνδρας δυνατὸν ἦν* *it was not possible even to sail, much less to rescue the man* (i.e. *to say nothing of rescuing*) X. H. 2. 3. 35. The preceding negative may be contained in a question or be otherwise implicit. Thus, *δοκεῖ σοι ῥᾴδιον εἶναι οὕτω ταχὺ μαθεῖν . . . ὁτιοῦν πρᾶγμα, μὴ ὅτι τοσοῦτον κτλ.*; *does it appear to you to be easy to learn so quickly any subject whatever, much less a subject of so great importance?* P. Crat. 427 e; cp. D. 54. 17.

The rare **οὐχ ὅτι** in the second member means *though* (P. Pr. 336 d).

e. **μή τί γε**, in the orators instead of μὴ ὅτι, after a negative means *much less*, after a positive *much more*. Cp. D. 19. 137, 8. 27.

2764. οὐ μόνον . . . ἀλλὰ καί (negative ἀλλ' οὐδέ) *not only . . . but also* (Lat. *non solum . . . sed etiam*). καί may be omitted: usually when the ἀλλά clause either includes the first clause or is strongly contrasted with it. Thus, ἱμάτιον ἠμφίεσαι οὐ μόνον φαῦλον, ἀλλά τὸ αὐτὸ θέρους τε καὶ χειμῶνος *you put on a cloak that is not merely wretched but is the same both summer and winter alike* X. M. 1. 6. 2; cp. D. 18. 26.

2765. ὅ τι μή, ὅσον μή *except, unless.* ὅ τι (sometimes written ὅτι) μή, and ὅσον μή, ὅσα μή are used, without any verb, to limit a preceding assertion (cp. εἰ μή 2346 a).

οὐ γὰρ ἦν κρήνη, ὅ τι μὴ μία ἐν αὐτῇ τῇ ἀκροπόλει *for there was no spring, except one on the acropolis itself* T. 4. 26, πείθουσα δὲ ἐκ τούτων μὲν ἀναχωρεῖν, ὅσον μὴ ἀνάγκη αὐτοῖς χρῆσθαι philosophy *persuading* the soul *to withdraw from them, except so far as she has to make use of them* P. Ph. 83 a, τῆς γῆς ἐκράτουν ὅσα μὴ προϊόντες πολὺ ἐκ τῶν ὅπλων *they were masters of the country, so far as they could be without advancing far from their camp* T. 1. 111 (ὅσα κρατεῖν ἐδύναντο).

2766. μόνον οὐ (lit. *only not*), **ὅσον οὐ** (of time) *almost, all but* (Lat. *tantum non*). Thus, μόνον οὐ διεσπάσθην *I was almost torn in pieces* D. 5. 5, ἐνόμιζε . . . ὅσον οὐκ ἤδη ἔχειν τὴν πόλιν *he thought that he already was all but in possession of the city* X. H. 6. 2. 16.

2767. οὐ μὴν ἀλλά, οὐ μέντοι ἀλλά *nevertheless, notwithstanding*, cp. Lat. *uerum tamen*; the colloquial **οὐ γὰρ ἀλλά** has about the force of *nay, for indeed*, cp. Lat. *non enim . . . sed.* These elliptical phrases require a verb or some other word to be supplied from the context or general run of the thought; but they often resist strict analysis since the contrasted idea is too vague to be supplied. Thus, ὁ ἵππος . . . μῑκροῦ κἀκεῖνον ἐξετραχήλισεν· οὐ μὴν (ἐξετραχήλισεν) ἀλλὰ ἐπέμεινεν ὁ Κῦρος *the horse was within a little of throwing him also over its head; (not* that it did throw him *however, but* =) *nevertheless Cyrus kept his seat* X. C. 1. 4. 8, ἀεὶ μὲν οὖν οἵ θ' ἡμέτεροι πρόγονοι καὶ Λακεδαιμόνιοι φιλοτίμως πρὸς ἀλλήλους εἶχον, οὐ μὴν (*scil.* περὶ κακῶν) ἀλλὰ περὶ καλλίστων . . . ἐφιλονίκησαν *while our ancestors and the Lacedaemonians were continually jealous of each other* (*not indeed* about base objects *but* =) *nevertheless they were rivals about the noblest objects* I. 4. 85, καὶ γὰρ ἂν δόξειεν οὕτω γ' εἶναι ἄλογον· οὐ μέντοι (*scil.* ἄλογόν ἐστιν) ἀλλ' ἴσως ἔχει τινὰ λόγον *and in fact put thus it would seem to be unreasonable;* (it is *not however* unreasonable *but* =) *nevertheless perhaps it has some sense* P. Ph. 62 b, μὴ σκῶπτέ μ', ὦδελφ', οὐ γὰρ ἀλλ' ἔχω κακῶς *don't mock me, brother; nay, for really I am in a bad way* Ar. Ran. 58 (lit. *for* it is *not* so *but*, *i.e.* it is *not* a case for mocking, *but*). In these phrases ἀλλά seems to show traces of its original force of *otherwise* (2775).

2768. οὐ μὴν οὐδέ *nor (yet) again, not however that* corresponds to the positive οὐ μὴν (μέντοι) ἀλλά. Thus, οὐ μὴν οὐδὲ βαρβάρους εἴρηκε *nor again has he spoken of barbarians* T. 1. 3, οὐ μὰν οὐδ' Ἀχιλεύς *no, nor even Achilles* B 703, οὐ μὴν οὐδὲ ἀναισθήτως αὐτοὺς κελεύω τοὺς . . . ξυμμάχους ἡμῶν ἐᾶν βλάπτειν *not however that I bid you tamely permit them to injure our allies* T. 1. 82.

PARTICLES

2769. Under the head of particles are included sentence adverbs (1094) and conjunctions. Many sentence adverbs remained such, some sank to mere enclitics, others became pure conjunctions, while still others fluctuated in function, being now adverbial, now conjunctional, as καί *even* and *and*, οὐδέ *not even* and *nor*, γάρ *in fact* and *for*, πρίν *sooner* and *until* or *before*.

2770. Conjunctions are either coördinating or subordinating. The coördinating conjunctions with their several varieties are given in 2163. The subordinating conjunctions are

Causal: ὅτι, διότι, διόπερ, ἐπεί, ἐπειδή, ὅτε, ὁπότε, ὡς (2240).
Comparative: ὡς, ὥσπερ, καθάπερ, ὅπως, ᾗ, ὅπῃ, ᾗπερ (2463; cp. 2481).
Concessive: καὶ εἰ (κεἰ), καὶ ἐάν (κἄν), εἰ καί, ἐὰν καί (2369).
Conditional: εἰ, ἐάν, ἤν, ἄν (2283).
Consecutive: ὥστε, ὡς (2250).
Declarative: ὅτι, διότι, οὕνεκα, ὁθούνεκα, ὡς (2578).
Final: ἵνα, ὅπως, ὡς, μή, etc. (2193; cp. 2209, 2221).
Local: οὗ, ὅπου, οἷ, ὅποι, ἔνθα, ὅθεν, ὁπόθεν, ᾗ, ὅπῃ, etc (2498).
Temporal: ὅτε, ὁπότε, ἡνίκα, ἐπεί, ἐπειδή, ὡς, μέχρι, ἔστε, ἕως, πρίν, etc. (2383).

Some conjunctions belong to more than one class.

2771. Greek has an extraordinary number of sentence adverbs (or particles in the narrow sense) having a logical or emotional (rhetorical) value. Either alone or in combination these sentence adverbs give a distinctness to the relations between ideas which is foreign to other languages, and often resist translation by separate words, which in English are frequently over emphatic and cumbersome in comparison to the light and delicate nature of the Greek originals (*e.g.* ἄρα, γέ, τοί). The force of such words is frequently best rendered by pause, stress, or alterations of pitch. To catch the subtle and elusive meaning of these often apparently insignificant elements of speech challenges the utmost vigilance and skill of the student.

2772. The particles show different degrees of independence as regards their position. Many are completely independent and may occupy any place in the sentence; some may occur only at the beginning (*prepositive* particles, as ἀτάρ); others find their place only after one or more words at the beginning (*postpositive* particles, as γάρ, δέ); and some are attached closely to a preceding word or even form compounds with that word wherever it may occur (γέ, τέ).

2773. Some verbal forms have virtually become particles, *e.g.* ἄγε used with the second person plural, ὁρᾷς used of several persons, parenthetic οἶμαι, δῆλοι ὅτι, εὖ οἶδ' ὅτι, εὖ ἴσθ' ὅτι (2585).

2774. As regards their *meaning*, particles may be arranged in classes, *e.g* *adversative*, *affirmative*, *asseverative*, *concessive*, *confirmative*, *conjunctive*, *infer*

ential, *intensive*, *interrogative*, *limitative*, *negative*, etc. These classes cannot always be sharply distinguished: some particles fall under two or more classes. Many particles, which serve to set forth the logical relation between clauses, had originally only an intensive or confirmatory force that was confined to their own clause. The following sections deal only with the commoner uses of the most noteworthy particles.

ἀλλά

2775. **ἀλλά**, a strongly adversative conjunction (stronger than δέ), connects sentences and clauses, and corresponds pretty closely to *but;* at times ἀλλά need not or cannot be translated (2781 b). In form (but with changed accent) ἀλλά was originally the same word as the accusative neuter plural ἄλλα *other things* used adverbially = *on the other hand.* ἀλλά marks opposition, contrast, protest, difference, objection, or limitation; and is thus used both where one notion entirely excludes another and where two notions are not mutually exclusive. ἀλλά is often freely repeated in successive clauses.

2776. The Antecedent Statement is Negative.—In its simplest use ἀλλά introduces a positive statement after a negative clause. Thus, οὐκ ἀνδρὸς ὅρκοι πίστις, ἀλλ' ὅρκων ἀνήρ *his oath is not the warrant of a man, but the man is warrant of his oath* A. fr. 394, οὐ γὰρ κραυγῇ ἀλλὰ σιγῇ ὡς ἀνυστὸν . . . προσῇσαν *for they came on, not with shouts, but with as little noise as possible* X. A. 1. 8. 11.

a. After a question implying a negative answer or a question to be refuted ἀλλά may have the force of (*nay*) *rather*, *on the contrary*. Thus, τί δεῖ σε ἰέναι . . . ; ἀλλὰ ἄλλους πέμψον *what's the need of your going? Nay rather send others* X. A. 4. 6. 19. Here ἀλλ' οὐ (μή) has the force of *and not rather* (2781 b); as τί δεῖ ἐμβαλεῖν λόγον περὶ τούτου, ἀλλ' οὐχὶ προειπεῖν ὅτι οὕτω ποιήσεις; *why is it necessary to propose a discussion about this and not rather announce that you will have it so?* X. C. 2. 2. 19.

2777. After a negative clause, or a question implying a negative answer, ἀλλά, or more commonly the colloquial ἀλλ' ἤ, may mean *except*, the combination being equivalent either to ἀλλά or to ἤ. In the preceding clause a form of ἄλλος or ἕτερος is often expressed. Thus, ἔπαισε . . . νιν οὔτις ἀλλ' ἐγώ *no one smote him except myself* S. O. T. 1331, οὐδὲν ἐθέλοντες ἐπαινεῖν ἀλλ' ἢ τὸν πλοῦτον *wishing to praise nothing except wealth* P. R. 330 c (here ἀλλ' ἤ is detached from οὐδέν), τίνα ἄλλον ἔχουσι λόγον βοηθοῦντες ἐμοὶ ἀλλ' ἢ τὸν ὀρθὸν κτλ.; *what other reason have they for supporting me except the true reason*, etc.? P. A. 34 b.

a. Distinguish the use of ἀλλ' ἤ *except* (= εἰ μή) in τὸ γοῦν σημεῖον ἕτερον φαίνεται, ἀλλ' ἢ οὐ καθορῶ *the device at any rate appears different, unless I can't see* Ar. Eq. 953.

2778. **οὐδὲν ἀλλ' ἤ** *nothing but* is also used elliptically, apparently by an original suppression of a form of ποιῶ or γίγνομαι; in effect, however, the phrase has acquired a purely adverbial sense (*merely*). Thus, διεφθάρμεθα . . . ὑπ' ἀνδρῶν οὐδὲν ἀλλ' ἢ φενᾱκίζειν δυναμένων *we have been ruined by men who are able* (to do) *nothing except deceive* (i.e. *able merely to deceive*) I. 8. 36.

a. With the above use compare **οὐδὲν ἄλλο ἤ** *nothing else than*, used without, and with, ellipse; as οἱ μύριοι ἱππεῖς οὐδὲν ἄλλο ἢ μύριοί εἰσιν ἄνθρωποι *your ten thousand horse are nothing more* (*else*) *than ten thousand men* X. A. 3. 2. 18, οὐδὲν ἄλλο ἢ πόλιν τὴν ἑαυτοῦ ἀπολείπων ἕκαστος doing *nothing else than each abandoning his own city* T. 2. 16. So also οὐδὲν ἄλλο . . . ἤ D. 8. 27. Cp. **ἄλλο οὐδὲν ἤ**, as in ἄλλο οὐδὲν ἢ ἐκ γῆς ἐναυμάχουν *they* did *nothing else than conduct* (= *they practically conducted*) *a sea-fight from the land* T. 4. 14. Cp. 946, 2652.

2779. The origin of ἀλλ' ἤ is disputed, some scholars regarding ἀλλ' as ἀλλά (originally ἄλλα, 2775), while others derive ἀλλ' directly from ἄλλο, which is thought to have lost its force and consequently its accent. In some passages the Mss. do not distinguish between ἀλλ' and ἄλλ'; and ἀλλ' ἤ and ἄλλο ἤ differ only slightly in meaning. In some of the above cases ἀλλ' has an adjectival force, in some it hovers between an adjective and a conjunction, and in others it clearly has become a conjunction.

2780. After a comparative (μᾶλλον, τὸ πλέον) in a negative clause ἀλλά has the force of *as*. Thus, καὶ ἔστιν ὁ πόλεμος οὐχ ὅπλων τὸ πλέον ἀλλὰ δαπάνης *and war is not so much* (lit. *more*) *a matter of arms as* (*but rather*) *of money* T. 1. 83. Here the clause with ἀλλά is more emphatic than if ἤ had been used. Cp. "there needed no more but to advance one step": Steele.

2781. The Antecedent Statement is Affirmative. — ἀλλά is sometimes found after an affirmative statement.

a. The antecedent clause often has a concessive force, and frequently takes μέν (2900). Thus, τὰ μὲν καθ' ἡμᾶς ἔμοιγε δοκεῖ καλῶς ἔχειν· ἀλλὰ τὰ πλάγια λυπεῖ με *the part where we are seems to me to be well disposed, but the wings cause me uneasiness* X. C. 7. 1. 16.

b. ἀλλ' οὐ (μή) after an affirmative statement often has the force of *and not, and not rather, instead of* (sometimes with a touch of irony). Thus, ἐκεῖθεν ἀλλ' οὐκ ἐνθένδε ἡρπάσθη *she was carried off from there and not* (or simply *not*) *from here* P. Phae. 229 d, ἐμοὶ ὀργίζονται ἀλλ' οὐχ αὑτοῖς *they are angry with me instead of* (or *and not rather with*) *themselves* P. A. 23 c. In such cases καὶ οὐ (μή) would not repudiate the opposition.

2782. ἀλλά in Apodosis. — After a concession or a condition expressed or implied, the apodosis may be emphatically introduced by **ἀλλά, ἀλλὰ . . . γε, ἀλλ' οὖν γε** *still, yet, at least*. Thus, εἰ σῶμα δοῦλον, ἀλλ' ὁ νοῦς ἐλεύθερος *if the body is enslaved, the mind at least is free* A. fr. 854, εἰ δ' ἐν πᾶσι τούτοις ἡττῴμεθα, ἀλλὰ τό γέ τοι πῦρ κρεῖττον καρποῦ ἐστιν *but if we should be baffled in all these points, still, as they say, fire is stronger than the fruit of* the field X. A. 2. 5. 19. So also in clauses other than conditional; as ἀλλ' ἐπεὶ . . . πατέρα τόνδ' ἐμὸν οὐκ ἀνέτλᾱτ', . . . ἀλλ' ἐμὲ . . . οἰκτίρατε *but since ye did not bear with my father, pity me at least* S. O. C. 241.

2783. ἀλλά attached to Single Words. — ἀλλά, attached to a single word in an adverbial sense, may stand in the interior of the sentence (not in Hom.). Thus, **ἀλλὰ νῦν** *now at least*, as in τί δῆτ' ἂν ἀλλὰ νῦν σ' ἔτ' ὠφελοῖμ' ἐγώ; *how pray, can I serve thee even now?* S. Ant. 552. So with **γέ**, as ἐὰν οὖν ἀλλὰ νῦν γ' ἔτι . . . ἐθελήσητε *if therefore you still desire even now* D. 3. 33 (and often in D.). Here ἀλλὰ νῦν implies εἰ μὴ πρότερον. ἀλλά sometimes apparently implies εἰ μή τι ἄλλο or εἰ μὴ ἄλλοις, etc., as λέγ' ἀλλὰ τοῦτο *say this at least* (*say but this*) S. El. 415.

2784. ἀλλά opposing Whole Sentences. — ἀλλά *well*, *well but*, *nay but*, *however* is often used, especially at the beginning of a speech, in opposition either to something said (or supposed to be meant) by another, or to a latent feeling in the mind of the writer or speaker himself. Thus, ἀλλὰ πρῶτον μὲν μνησθήσομαι . . . ὃ τελευταῖον κατ' ἐμοῦ εἶπε *well, I will first allude to the charge against me which he mentioned last* X. H. 2. 3. 35, ἀλλ' ὤφελε μὲν Κῦρος ζῆν· ἐπεὶ δὲ τετελεύτηκεν κτλ. *well, I would that Cyrus were alive; but since he is dead*, etc. X. A. 2. 1. 4. Often of remonstrance or protest, as ἀλλ' ἀμήχανον *nay, it is impossible* E. El. 529. ἀλλά is also especially common when a previous train of thought or remark is impatiently interrupted, as ἀλλὰ ταῦτα μὲν τί δεῖ λέγειν; *but what is the need of recounting this?* S. Ph. 11. Similarly in

a. Replies (often in quick, abrupt, or decisive answers): ἤρετο ὅ τι εἴη τὸ σύνθημα· ὁ δ' ἀπεκρίνατο· Ζεὺς σωτὴρ καὶ νίκη· ὁ δὲ Κῦρος ἀκούσᾱς Ἀλλὰ δέχομαί τε, ἔφη, καὶ τοῦτο ἔστω *he asked what the watchword was; and he replied: "Zeus the saviour and Victory;" and Cyrus, on hearing this, said, "Well, I accept it and so let it be"* X. A. 1. 8. 17.

b. Assent, with an adversative sense implied (cp. *oh, well*): ἀλλ' εἰ δοκεῖ, χωρῶμεν *well, if it pleases thee, let us be going* S. Ph. 645.

c. Appeals, exhortations, proposals, and commands: ἀλλ' ἴωμεν *but let us go* P. Pr. 311 a, ἀλλ' ἐμοὶ πείθου καὶ μὴ ἄλλως ποίει *nay, take my advice and don't refuse* P. Cr. 45 a. The tone here is often impatient.

d. Wishes and imprecations: ἀλλ' εὐτυχοίης *well, my blessings on thee!* S. O. T. 1478.

e. Questions, to mark surprise: πῶς εἶπας; ἀλλ' ἦ καὶ σοφὸς λέληθας ὤν; *what dost thou mean? can it really be that thou art subtle too and without my knowing it?* E. Alc. 58.

2785. ἀλλά is often used when a speaker introduces a supposed objection (either in his own name or in that of his opponent), and immediately answers it; as ἀλλὰ νὴ τὸν Δία ἐκεῖν' ἂν ἴσως εἴποι πρὸς ταῦτα κτλ. *but, by Zeus, he might perhaps say in reply to this*, etc. D. 20. 3. ἀλλά may here put the supposed objection and also give the answer. Thus, τί γὰρ καὶ βουλόμενοι μετεπέμπεσθ' ἂν αὐτοὺς ἐν τούτῳ τῷ καιρῷ; ἐπὶ τὴν εἰρήνην; ἀλλ' ὑπῆρχεν ἅπᾶσιν· ἀλλ' ἐπὶ τὸν πόλεμον; ἀλλ' αὐτοὶ περὶ τῆς εἰρήνης ἐβουλεύεσθε *for with what possible desire would you have been sending them at that juncture? With a view to peace? Why (but) peace was open to all. With a view to war? Why (but) you were yourselves deliberating about peace* D. 18. 24. Cp. French *mais* introducing a reply to a question.

a. So in rapid dialogue objections may take the form of questions, in which each ἀλλά after the first may be rendered by *or*. Cp. 2654.

2786. ἀλλά with other Particles. — For example:

ἀλλὰ γάρ 2816; on **οὐ γὰρ ἀλλά**, see 2767.
ἀλλὰ . . . γε *but at any rate.*
ἀλλά γέ τοι (τοί γε) *yet at least, yet be sure.*
ἀλλὰ δή *well then.*

ἀλλ' ἦ; *why how? can it really be that? what, can it be true?* Here ἀλλά marks surprise, while ἦ asks the question.

ἀλλὰ μέντοι *nay, but; well, however; yet truly.* On **οὐ μέντοι ἀλλά**, see 2767.

ἀλλὰ μήν *nay, but; but then; but surely.* Often to introduce an objection, to reject an alternative, often merely to introduce a new idea or to resume an interrupted thought. On **οὐ μὴν ἀλλά**, see 2767.

ἀλλ' ὅμως *but still.* Often without a verb, to introduce the reply to an objection.

ἀλλ' οὐδέ is sometimes used elliptically, as in ὑπὲρ . . . ὧν οὗτος ἀπήγγειλε πρὸς ὑμᾶς ἀλλ' οὐδὲ μῑκρόν *nay, there is not even ever so little* (not only not a great deal *but not even a little*) *concerning which he reported to you* D. 19. 37. **ἀλλ' οὐδὲ μὲν δή** is often used to reject an alternative.

ἀλλ' οὖν (γε) *but then, well then, well at any rate;* stronger than δ' οὖν.

ἄρα

2787. ἄρα (Epic ἄρα and enclitic ἄρ before a consonant, ῥά usually after monosyllables; all postpositive), a connective, confirmatory, and inferential particle marking the immediate connection and succession of events and thoughts; the natural, direct, and expected consequence of a previous statement of the existing situation, or of the realization of experience of some sort; and agreement of various kinds, as between assertion and reality, cause and result, premise and conclusion, explanation and what was to be explained.

a. ἄρα marks a consequence drawn from the connection of thought, and expresses impression or feeling; the stronger οὖν marks a consequence drawn from facts (a positive conclusion).

2788. The etymology of ἄρα, and hence its original meaning, is obscure. Some derive it from the root ἀρ, seen in ἀρ-αρ-ίσκω *fit, join,* ἄρτι *just;* and thus regard the proper sense as *fittingly, accordingly.* Others think the earliest meaning was *truly, forsooth* and connect ἄρα with a lost adj. ἀρίς, surviving in ἄρι-στος, ἀρί-γνωτος. On this interpretation ἄρα would originally assert the truth of its *own* clause. ἄρα is found also in ἆρα and γάρ.

2789. ἄρα is used in Homer much more freely than in Attic, and often so as to defy exact translation. In general ἄρα in Epic marks immediate connection and succession, a natural consequence of something already said or done; gives an explanation of an antecedent statement; or is used in recapitulations and transitions. Thus, αὐτὰρ ἐπεὶ ῥ' ἤγερθεν . . . , βῆ ῥ' ἴμεν εἰς ἀγορήν *but when they were collected, then he started to go to the assembly* β 9, ὣς ἔφαθ', οἱ δ' ἄρα πάντες ἀκὴν ἐγένοντο σιωπῇ *thus he spake, and all accordingly became hushed in silence* H 92, σῖτον δέ σφιν ἔνειμε Μεσαύλιος, ὅν ῥα συβώτης αὐτὸς ἐκτήσατο *and Mesaulius distributed food to them,* a slave *whom* (and this was the reason for his so doing) *the swineherd had acquired* ξ 449, ὣς ἄρ' ἐφώνησεν καὶ ἀπὸ ἕο τόξον ἔθηκεν *thus then he spake and put the bow from him* φ 163. So also in the later language; as ἐρωτήσης δὲ αὐτὸν τῆς μητρὸς . . . ἀπεκρίνατο ἄρα ὁ Κῦρος *on his mother's questioning him Cyrus naturally replied* X. C. 1. 3. 2.

2790. In Attic, and in part also in Homer, ἄρα marks an inference (*conse-*

quently, *so then*, *therefore*, *it seems*, *after all*, *of course*, etc.). Thus, εἶπεν αὐτῷ ὅτι βασιλεὺς οὐ μαχεῖται δέκα ἡμερῶν· Κῦρος δ' εἶπεν· οὐκ ἄρα ἔτι μαχεῖται, εἰ ἐν ταύταις οὐ μαχεῖται ταῖς ἡμέραις the seer *said to him that the king would not fight within ten days. And Cyrus answered: "Well then if he does not fight within that time he will not fight at all"* X. A. 1. 7. 18, οὐδεὶς ποτοῦ ἐπιθυμεῖ, ἀλλὰ χρηστοῦ ποτοῦ . . . , πάντες γὰρ ἄρα τῶν ἀγαθῶν ἐπιθυμοῦσιν *no one desires drink* merely, *but good drink, since of course everybody desires good things* P. R. 438 a.

2791. ἄρα is often used of direct logical conclusions in conducting an argument (especially in Plato); as τί οὖν περὶ ψυχῆς λέγομεν; ὁρᾱτὸν ἢ ἀόρᾱτον εἶναι; οὐχ ὁρᾱτόν. ἀιδὲς ἄρα; ναί. ὁμοιότερον ἄρα ψυχὴ σώματός ἐστιν τῷ ἀιδεῖ, τὸ δὲ τῷ ὁρᾱτῷ *what then do we say about the soul? That it is visible or invisible? Not visible. Then it is invisible? Yes. Consequently soul has a closer resemblance to the invisible than the body, and the latter to the visible* P. Ph. 79 b.

2792. In the argument *ex contrario* set forth in clauses with μέν and δέ, ἄρα, usually meaning *in sooth*, is commonly placed with the second clause (P. Ph. 80 d, R. 445 b), occasionally with the first (P. Cr. 46 d, L. 840 b), or with both (P. Ph. 97 a, R. 600 c).

2793. In direct questions ἄρα adds liveliness, while at the same time it marks connection or consequence. So τίς ἄρα *who then?* πῶς ἄρα *how then?* In questions of anxiety ἄρα marks increase of feeling. Thus, τί μ' ἄρα τί μ' ὀλέκεις; *why then, why dost thou destroy me?* S. Ant. 1285.

2794. ἄρα occurs in questions in which the admissibility of one opinion is inferred from the rejection of another. Thus, εἰπέ μοι, ἔφη, ὦ Θεοδότη, ἔστι σοι ἀγρός; οὐκ ἔμοιγ', ἔφη. ἀλλ' ἄρα οἰκίᾱ προσόδους ἔχουσα; *'tell me,' said he, 'Theodote, have you an estate?' 'Not I indeed,' said she. 'But perhaps then you have a house that brings in an income?'* X. M. 3. 11. 4. Such questions are often ironical (P. A. 25 a).

2795. ἄρα is often used to indicate new perception, or surprise genuine or affected; as when the truth is just realized after a previous erroneous opinion and one finds oneself undeceived either agreeably or disagreeably. So, especially with the imperfect of εἶναι, ἄρα means *after all*, *it seems*, *why then*, *so then*, *sure enough*. See 1902.

2796. **εἰ ἄρα, ἐὰν ἄρα** *if really*, *if after all*, *if indeed*, are commonly used of that which is improbable or undesirable; **εἰ (ἐὰν) μὴ ἄρα** *unless perhaps* (*nisi forte*, *nisi vero*) is often ironical. Thus, εἰ ἄρα γέγονεν ὡς οὗτοι ἔλεγον *if indeed it did take place as they said* D. 56. 28, καὶ μὴν εἰ καὶ τοῦτ' ἄρα δεῖ μ' εἰπεῖν *and yet if I must after all say this too* 18. 317, πολλάκις τοῖς Ἀθηναίοις παρῄνει, ἢν ἄρα ποτὲ κατὰ γῆν βιασθῶσι . . . ταῖς ναυσὶ πρὸς ἅπαντας ἀνθίστασθαι *he often counselled the Athenians, if after all they should ever be hard pressed on the land side, to fight the world with their fleet* T. 1. 93, πῶς ἂν οὖν ὁ τοιοῦτος ἀνὴρ διαφθείροι τοὺς νέους; εἰ μὴ ἄρα ἡ τῆς ἀρετῆς ἐπιμέλεια διαφθορά ἐστιν *how then could such a man corrupt the young? unless perchance the study of virtue is corruption* X. M. 1. 2. 8.

2797. εἰ (ἐάν) ἄρα is common after σκοπῶ, etc. See 2672.

2798. ἄρα is often used, especially with ὡς, to introduce the statement of others which, in the view of the speaker, is (usually) to be rejected. Thus, ἀκούω αὐτὸν ἐρεῖν ὡς ἄρ' ἐγὼ πάντων ὧν κατηγορῶ κοινωνὸς γέγονα *I hear that he is going to say that I forsooth* (or *if you please*) *have been a partner in all that I denounced* D. 19. 202.

2799 Attic has, in bimembral clauses, **εἴτε ἄρα . . . εἴτε** or **εἴτε . . . εἴτε ἄρα**, as εἴτ' ἀληθὲς εἴτ' ἄρ' οὖν μάτην *whether truly or after all, it may be, falsely* S. Ph. 345. Hom. has also a similar use with οὔτε . . . οὔτε, and ἤ . . . ἤ. Hom. has ἄρα . . . ἄρα (Ψ 887).

ἆρα

2800. **ἆρα**, a confirmative particle from ἦ + ἄρα, is used in lyric and dramatic poetry in the sense of ἄρα. ἆρα is postpositive, except in New Comedy.

σὸν ἆρα τοὔργον, οὐκ ἐμὸν κεκλήσεται *it shall then be called thy work, not mine* S. Aj. 1368. Often with τίς, as τίς ἆρ' ἐμοῦ γένοιτ' ἂν ἀθλιώτερος; *who then could be more wretched than I am?* Trag. fr. 280. On interrogative ἆρα, see 2650, 2651. Epic **ἦ ῥα** is both confirmatory and interrogative.

ἀτάρ

2801. **ἀτάρ** (prepositive; Hom. also αὐτάρ from αὖτε + ἄρ) usually poetical, but found in Xenophon and Plato, is an adversative conjunction commonly used to introduce a strong or surprising contrast (*but, but yet, however*); sometimes to introduce a slight contrast (*and, and then*), but one stronger than that marked by δέ. ἀτάρ is common as a correlative to μέν. It is often found in lively questions to introduce an objection; in rapid transitions; and sometimes it serves to introduce the apodosis of a conditional sentence. ἀτάρ was largely displaced by the stronger ἀλλά.

αὖ

2802. **αὖ** (postpositive), an adversative particle meaning *on the other hand, on the contrary* (properly *again*). In Hom. it serves as a correlative to μέν or ἤ τοι, and to introduce the apodosis of conditional or relative clauses.

αὖ is often used with personal pronouns, as ἀλλὰ σὺ αὖ . . . λέγε *but do you in turn tell us* X. S. 3. 5; and is often added to δέ, as οἱ Ἕλληνες ἐπῇσαν . . . οἱ δ' αὖ βάρβαροι οὐκ ἐδέχοντο *the Greeks came on, but the barbarians on their part did not wait to receive them* X. A. 1. 10. 11. Connected in meaning are the derivatives **αὖτε** (poetic) and **αὖθις**.

γάρ

2803. **γάρ** (postpositive) *in fact, indeed,* and *for*, a confirmatory adverb and a causal conjunction. As a conjunction, γάρ usually stands after the first word in its clause; as an adverb, its position is freer. γάρ is especially common in sentences which offer a reason for, or an explanation of, a preceding or following statement. It may be used in successive clauses.

a. γάρ is from γέ + ἄρ (= ἄρα), γέ originally giving prominence either to the word it followed or to the whole clause, while ἄρα marked this prominence as due to something previously expressed or latent in the context. The compound γάρ originally emphasized a thought either as the result of existing circumstances or as a patent and well known fact. In most uses of the word, however, the force of its component parts cannot be distinguished; nor is it clear in many cases whether γάρ is a conjunction or an adverb marking assurance.

2804. Adverbial γάρ appears in questions, answers, and wishes; and in many other cases where recourse is had to conscious or unconscious ellipse by those scholars who hold that γάρ is always a conjunction. Ellipse is sometimes natural and easy, but often clumsy and artificial. Though we find in parallel use both incomplete and complete clauses with γάρ, it is improbable that the Greeks were conscious of the need of any supplement to explain the thought. In many uses γάρ has become formulaic, serving only to show the natural agreement with the existing situation.

2805. In questions, γάρ asks for confirmation of a preceding statement, or expresses assent or dissent; asks whether an act before mentioned was not reasonable; asks a question prompted by some form of emotion; and serves to indicate transition, etc.

a. In questions γάρ often marks surprise or indignation, and may frequently be translated by *what, why, then, really, surely.* Thus, ταυτὶ λέγεις σὺ στρατηγὸν πτωχὸς ὤν; ἐγὼ γάρ εἰμι πτωχός; *do you, beggar that you are, address your general thus? what! I a beggar?* Ar. Ach. 593, ἦ ζῇ γὰρ ἀνήρ; *is the man really alive?* S. El. 1221, οἴει γάρ σοι μαχεῖσθαι . . . τὸν ἀδελφόν; *do you really think that your brother is going to fight?* X. A. 1. 7. 9. So τίς γάρ; *who then, why who?*

b. Brief interrogative formulae asking for confirmation of a preceding statement are:

τί γάρ; *what then, how then, how else?* τί γάρ also serves as a formula of transition (*now, well then, now what . . ., furthermore*).

ἦ γάρ; *is it not so? surely this is so?* (cp. *n'est ce pas*). Often of surprise.

οὐ γάρ; *is it not so?* often in indignant questions; when not standing alone, *why not?*

πῶς γάρ; πόθεν γάρ; imply that something is impossible (often of surprise). Cp. πῶς γὰρ οὔ; in negative rhetorical questions.

2806. In answers γάρ marks assent, assurance, sometimes dissent. Thus, δεινόν γε τοὐπίσαγμα τοῦ νοσήματος. δεινὸν γὰρ οὐδὲ ῥητόν *dread indeed is the burden of the disease. Aye dread indeed and beyond all words* S. Ph. 755, ὁμολογεῖς οὖν περὶ ἐμὲ ἄδικος γεγενῆσθαι; ἦ γὰρ ἀνάγκη *do you then confess that you have proved yourself unjust toward me? In truth I must indeed* X. A. 1. 6. 8, μηδ' αἱ μητέρες τὰ παιδία ἐκδειματούντων . . . μὴ γάρ, ἔφη *nor let mothers frighten their children. No indeed, said he* P. R. 381 e, φῄς τάδ' οὖν; ἃ μὴ φρονῶ γὰρ οὐ φιλῶ λέγειν *dost thou then consent to this? No, for I am not wont to utter words I do not mean* S. O. T. 1520.

a. γάρ is common in brief answers, as after οὐ, δεῖ, ἔοικε, εἰκός, λέγω, ὡμολόγηται. So in the rhetorical questions πῶς γάρ; πῶς γὰρ οὔ; used as answers.

2807. In **wishes**: εἰ γὰρ . . . ἐν τούτῳ εἴη *would that it depended on that* P. Pr. 310 d, κακῶς γὰρ ἐξόλοιο *oh that you might perish wretchedly* E. Cyc. 261. Here γάρ marks the agreement of the wish with the existing situation.

2808. **Explanatory** (or **prefatory**) **γάρ** has the force of *now, namely, that is, for example;* but usually is not to be translated, and especially when the preceding sentence contains a verb of *saying, showing,* etc. It usually introduces, as an explanation, the details of that which was promised in an incomplete or general statement; sometimes, without any such statement, it introduces a new fact. Whether this γάρ is an adverb or a conjunction is uncertain. Thus, δοκεῖ τοίνυν μοι χαριέστερον εἶναι μῦθον ὑμῖν λέγειν. ἦν γάρ ποτε κτλ. *I think it will be more interesting to tell you a myth. Once upon a time there was*, etc. P. Pr. 320 c, οὕτω γὰρ σκοπεῖτε *look at it in this light* L. 19. 34 (at the beginning of a new point in the discussion).

2809. Explanatory γάρ often introduces a clause in apposition to a preceding demonstrative, to such expressions as τεκμήριον δέ or μαρτύριον δέ *now the proof is this*, δῆλον δέ (ἐστιν) *it is clear*, τὸ δὲ μέγιστον *but, what is of the greatest importance*, or to relative clauses (995). Thus, ὡς δ' ἔτι μᾶλλον θαρρῇς, καὶ τόδε κατανόησον· οἱ μὲν γὰρ (explaining τόδε) πολέμιοι πολὺ μὲν ἐλάττονές εἰσι νῦν ἢ πρὶν ἡττηθῆναι ὑφ' ἡμῶν *and that you may be still more encouraged, consider this fact too. The enemy (namely) are much fewer now than they were before they were beaten by us* X. C. 5. 2. 36, ἐννοήσωμεν δὲ καὶ τῇδε, ὡς πολλὴ ἐλπίς ἐστιν ἀγαθὸν αὐτὸ εἶναι. δυοῖν γὰρ θάτερόν ἐστιν τὸ τεθνάναι κτλ. *let us consider the matter also in this way* and we shall see *that there is abundant reason to hope that it is a good: now death must be one of two things*, etc. P. A. 40 c, μαρτύριον δέ· Δήλου γὰρ καθαιρομένης κτλ. *and this is a proof of it: now when Delos was being purified*, etc. T. 1. 8, ὃ δὲ πάντων σχετλιώτατον· οὓς γὰρ ὁμολογήσαιμεν ἂν πονηροτάτους εἶναι τῶν πολῑτῶν, τούτους πιστοτάτους φύλακας ἡγούμεθα τῆς πολῑτείᾱς εἶναι *but the most abominable of all is this: we consider the most trustworthy guardians of the State to be those men whom we should agree were the worst citizens* I. 8. 53.

2810. **Causal γάρ** is a conjunction: *for* (*nam, enim*). It serves to introduce a cause of, or a reason for, an action before mentioned; to justify a preceding utterance; to confirm the truth of a previous statement. Causal γάρ often refers to a thought *implied* in what has preceded. Thus, λεκτέα ἃ γιγνώσκω· ἔμπειρος γάρ (causal) εἰμι καὶ τῆς χώρᾱς τῶν Παφλαγόνων καὶ τῆς δυνάμεως. ἔχει γὰρ (explanatory) ἀμφότερα, καὶ πεδία κάλλιστα καὶ ὄρη ὑψηλότατα *I must tell what I know, for I am acquainted with the country of the Paphlagonians and its resources; now the country has very fertile plains and very lofty mountains* X. A. 5. 6. 6, ἰού, δύστηνε· τοῦτο γάρ σ' ἔχω μόνον προσειπεῖν *alas, ill-fated one! for by this name alone can I address thee* S. O. T. 1071, ἐπιστευόμην δὲ ὑπὸ τῶν Λακεδαιμονίων· οὐ γὰρ ἄν με ἔπεμπον πάλιν πρὸς ὑμᾶς *but I was trusted by the Lacedaemonians; for* (otherwise, *i.e.* εἰ μὴ ἐπίστευον) *they would not have sent me back to you* P. A. 30 c.

2811. **Anticipatory γάρ** states the cause, justifies the utterance, or gives the explanation, of something set forth in the main clause which *follows*. The main clause usually contains an inferential word, a demonstrative pointing backward, or καί, δέ, ἀλλά; or stands without a connective. Anticipatory γάρ may often be rendered by *since*, but is often omitted in translation. Thus, ἔτι τοίνυν ἀκούσατε καὶ τάδε. ἐπὶ λείᾱν γὰρ ὑμῶν ἐκπορεύσονταί τινες. οἶμαι νῦν βέλτιστον εἶναι κτλ. *listen therefore to this proposal also. Some of you will be going out to plunder. Now it is my opinion that it is best*, etc. X. A. 5. 1. 8, ἐσελθὼν δὲ τὴν ταχίστην, ἦν γάρ οἱ παῖς εἷς μοῦνος . . ., τοῦτον ἐκπέμπει *and when he had come in straightway, he sent out his son, for he had one only son* Hdt. 1. 119, ὦ φίλοι, οὐ γάρ τ' ἴδμεν ὅπῃ ζόφος οὐδ' ὅπῃ ἠώς . . . ἀλλὰ φραζώμεθα κτλ. *friends, since we do not know where is the place of darkness nor of the dawn, let us consider*, etc. κ 190, ὦ φίλτατε, σπονδαὶ γάρ εἰσί σοι μόνῳ, μέτρησον εἰρήνης τί μοι *my dear fellow, since you alone have got a truce, measure me out a bit of peace* Ar. Ach. 102.

a. In this construction γάρ may be an adverb, not a conjunction. Cases of explanatory γάρ (2808) and of parenthetical γάρ (2812), especially after vocatives, may fall under 2811.

2812. The clause with γάρ *since* is often inserted parenthetically in the clause which it is intended to explain; as ὁ δὲ (κρίνουσι γὰρ βοῇ καὶ οὐ ψήφῳ) οὐκ ἔφη διαγιγνώσκειν τὴν βοὴν ποτέρᾱ μείζων *but, since they decide by shouts and not by ballot, he said he could not decide which side shouted the louder* T. 1. 87.

2813. καὶ γάρ has in general two distinct meanings according as γάρ is an adverb or a conjunction. As καὶ γάρ has become a formula, it is often uncertain which of the two words is the adverb, which the conjunction.

2814. (I) **καὶ γάρ** *and in fact, and indeed*, καί being a conjunction, and γάρ an adverb. Here the clause in which καὶ γάρ stands is added as a new and important thought; where γάρ alone would state the reason or the explanation with less independence and with slighter emphasis. The negative is οὐδὲ γάρ. Thus Κῦρος δ' ὁρῶν τοὺς Ἕλληνας νῑκῶντας τὸ καθ' αὑτοὺς . . . ἐπεμελεῖτο ὅ τι ποιήσει βασιλεύς. καὶ γὰρ ᾔδει αὐτὸν ὅτι μέσον ἔχοι τοῦ Περσικοῦ στρατεύματος *on seeing the Greeks victorious over the troops opposed to them, Cyrus watched to see what the king would do; and in fact he knew that he commanded the centre of the Persian force* X. A. 1. 8. 21 (cp. 1. 1. 6, 2. 5. 5, 2. 6. 2). So often in affirmative responses: ἢ οὐκ ἀγαπήσεις τούτων τυγχάνων; ἐγὼ μὲν γὰρ ἂν ἀγαπῴην. καὶ γὰρ ἐγώ, ἔφη *or will you not be content if you obtain this? For my part I shall be. And so shall I, he said* P. R. 473 b.

a. καὶ γὰρ καί *and even* is καὶ γάρ *and in fact* reënforced by καί. Thus, καὶ γὰρ καὶ ἄδεια ἐφαίνετο αὐτοῖς *and in fact it looked to them as if there was perfect safety* in so doing T. 4. 108. The negative is οὐδὲ γὰρ οὐδέ (2938).

2815. (II) **καὶ γάρ** *for even, for also.* Here καί is an adverb affecting a single word, several words, or the whole sentence, and γάρ is a conjunction. The negative is οὐδὲ γάρ. Thus, καὶ γὰρ οὗτοι *for these too* P. A. 22 c, καὶ γὰρ ἠδικημένοι σῑγησόμεσθα *for even wronged as I am I'll keep silent* E. Med. 314, καὶ γὰρ μόνος ἡγοῖτ' ἂν δύνασθαι πείθειν *for, though quite unaided, he would think that he was able to persuade* X. M. 1. 2. 11.

a. καὶ γὰρ . . . καί *for both . . . and*: here καί is correlated with a second καί; as καὶ γὰρ ὑγιαίνουσιν οἱ τὰ σώματα εὖ ἔχοντες καὶ ἰσχύουσι *for those who keep their bodies in good condition are both healthy and strong* X. M. 3. 12. 4.

2816. **ἀλλὰ γάρ** occurs both in conjunction and separated by one or several words, which are generally emphatic.

2817. First Form (often *but since, since however*): here there are two predicates. In prose separation is the rule. Thus, ἀλλ', οὐ γὰρ ἔπειθε, διδοῖ τὸ φᾶρος *but since he could not persuade her, he gave her the mantle* Hdt. 9. 109, ἀλλ' ἴσως γὰρ καὶ ἄλλοι ταὐτὰ ἐνθῡμοῦνται, . . . μὴ ἀναμένωμεν ἄλλους ἐφ' ἡμᾶς ἐλθεῖν κτλ. *since however others too perhaps entertain the same opinion, let us not wait for others to come to us*, etc. X. A. 3. 1. 24. In poetry the words are generally not separated. Thus, ἀλλὰ γὰρ Κρέοντα λεύσσω τόνδε . . . πρὸς δόμους στείχοντα, παύσω τοὺς . . . γόους *since however I see Creon yonder coming to the palace, I will cease my lamentations* E. Phoen. 1307. Here the clause coördinated by the conjunction γάρ is parenthetical and gives, by anticipation, the reason for the ἀλλά clause. Cp. ἀλλ' ἐπεί ε 137, and Shakesp. *Sonnet* 54: "but, for their virtue only is their show, They live unwoo'd." — The first form is found chiefly in Homer, Pindar, Herodotus, and in the drama.

2818. Second Form (usually *but indeed, but in fact, but the truth is, but be that as it may*). Here there is a single predicate. Thus, καὶ οὐχ ὡς ἀτῑμάζων λέγω . . . ἀλλὰ γὰρ ἐμοὶ τούτων . . . οὐδὲν μέτεστι *and I do not speak in disparagement; but the truth is I have nothing to do with these matters* P. A. 19 c, ἀλλὰ γιγνώσκω γὰρ . . . ὅτι κτλ. *but indeed I know that*, etc. X. C. 2. 1. 13, ἀλλ' εἰσορῶ γὰρ τόνδε . . . Πυλάδην δρόμῳ στείχοντα *but indeed I see Pylades yonder coming at full speed* E. Or. 725, ἀλλ' οὐ γὰρ ἔστι τἀμφανῆ κρύπτειν *but indeed it is impossible to hide what lies open* S. O. C. 755.

a. In this use γάρ may have preserved, or regained, its primitive adverbial (confirmatory) force. Many scholars, however, claim that there was a conscious or unconscious ellipse, after ἀλλά, of an idea pertinent to the situation; and thus regard this form as logically equivalent to the form in which γάρ is a causal conjunction. In actual use ἀλλὰ γάρ was clearly a formula used without any consciousness of an omitted idea.

2819. ἀλλὰ γάρ has a great variety of uses, most of which may be classed as follows:

a. In statements of direct opposition: καὶ ταῦτά σε πολλοῦ δεῖ λεληθέναι, ἀλλὰ γὰρ οἶμαι ὃ ἄρτι οὐκ ἔφησθα ποιεῖν, τοῦτο ποιεῖς *and you are far from forgetting this, but in fact I think you are doing that which you just denied you were doing* P. Charm. 166 c.

N. This use is post-Homeric, rare in the drama, common in the orators and Plato. It is especially frequent in putting and setting aside an objection supposed to be raised by an opponent (*hypophora*). Cp. **b**.

b. In real and assumed objections (cp. *at enim*): καὶ ἀληθῆ γε ἔλεγον, ὦ Σώκρατες. ἴσως. ἀλλὰ γάρ, ὦ Εὐθύφρων, καὶ ἄλλα πολλὰ φῄς εἶναι ὅσια *yes, and I said what was true, Socrates. Perhaps, but in fact, Euthyphron, you say that many other things too are holy* P. Euth. 6 d, ἀλλὰ γάρ, φήσει τις, οὐ ῥᾴδιον ἀεὶ λανθάνειν κακὸν ὄντα *yes, but some one will say that it is not easy always to conceal the fact that one is wicked* P. R. 365 c.

c. In transitions. — (1) At the close of the discussion of an argument, where the force of ἀλλά is like that of *and yet* or emphatic *but*. Thus, ἀλλὰ γάρ, ὦ *βουλή, ταῦτα μὲν ἐνθάδε οὐκ οἶδ' ὅ τι δεῖ λέγειν but, Senators, I do not know why I should discuss these matters here* L. 7. 42, *ἀλλὰ γὰρ ἤδη ὥρᾱ ἀπιέναι but it is already time to depart* P. A. 42 a.

(2) To restrain the expression of emotion; as *ἀλλ' ἄναξ γάρ ἐστ' ἐμός, σῑγῶ but no, I am silent for he is my king* E. El. 1245.

(3) When the approach of a new actor is announced. Cp. 2817, 2818.

2820. Other Combinations. — **γὰρ ἄρα** *for sure enough.*

γὰρ δή *for of course, for indeed, for you must know,* as *φαμὲν γὰρ δή for of course we say so.*

γὰρ δή που *for I presume, for doubtless.*

γὰρ οὖν often of frank assent, as *οὐ γὰρ οὖν certainly not, λέγω γὰρ οὖν certainly, I do say so;* less often to explain (*for certainly*); *καὶ γὰρ οὖν* (not very common) is stronger than *καὶ γάρ.*

γάρ που *for I suppose.*

γάρ τοι *for surely, for mark you;* sometimes *καὶ γάρ τοι.*

γέ

2821. **γέ** (postpositive and enclitic) is an intensive and restrictive particle with the force of *at least, at any rate, even, certainly, indeed;* but often to be rendered by intonation. γέ may indicate assent, concession, banter, scorn, deprecation, irony, etc. γέ emphasizes single words or whole phrases or clauses.

a. Single words. So often with pronouns, as *ἔγωγε I at least* (excluding others), *ἐμέ γε* cp. *mi-ch, ὅ γε even he* (Hom.), *οὗτός γε,* and with a repeated pronoun (S. Ph. 117). Other words, as *ὅ τι βούλει γε whatever you like* Ar. Ran. 3, *πλήθει γε οὐχ ὑπερβαλοίμεθ' ἂν τοὺς πολεμίους in numbers at least we should not surpass the enemy* X. C. 2. 1. 8.

b. With phrases or clauses. Thus, *ὡς μή μ' ἄτῑμον, τοῦ θεοῦ γε προστάτην, οὕτως ἀφῇ με that he may not thus send me away in dishonour — who am the suppliant of the god* S. O. C. 1278, *ἀνθρώπους τίνυσθον, ὅτις γ' ἐπίορκον ὀμόσσῃ* ye who *punish men who swear falsely* Γ 279.

2822. *γέ* may be used twice in the same sentence. Thus, *ἐπεί γ' ἀρκοῦνθ' ἱκανὰ τοῖς γε σώφροσιν since indeed that which suffices their wants is enough for the wise* E. Phoen. 545. Cp. Hdt. 1. 187, Ar. Vesp. 1507.

2823. *γέ* stands between article and noun, as *οἵ γ' ἄνθρωποι* (after a preposition, as *ἔν γε τῷ φανερῷ*); between noun and adjective, or after the adjective, as *ἀνήρ γε σοφός,* or *ἀνὴρ σοφός γε;* after a possessive pronoun, as *ἐμός γε θῡμός;* after *μέν, δέ, τέ,* as *ὅτι δέ γε ἀληθῆ λέγω.* When *γέ* influences a whole clause it stands as near as possible to the introductory conjunction; as *εἴ γε, ἆρά γε.*

2824. *γέ* in contrasts and alternatives; as *σὺ δ' οὐ λέγεις γε (αἰσχρά), δρᾷς δέ με thou dost not indeed say, but do shameful things to me* E. And. 239, *ἤτοι κρύφα γε ἢ φανερῶς either secretly or openly* T. 6. 34, *ἢ σοφοὶ ἢ τίμιοι ἢ γέροντές γε or wise or held in honour aye or old* P. Hipp. M. 301 a (here *γέ* indicates a change in an alternative series; cp. *οὔτε . . . οὔτε . . οὐδέ γε* and *καὶ . . . γε* 2829).

2825. γέ in replies and comments (*yes, well*). Thus, δοκεῖ παρεικαθεῖν; ὅσον γ', ἄναξ, τάχιστα *does it seem best* to you *that I should give way? Aye, my lord, and with all speed* S. Ant. 1102. Here καὶ . . . γε is common, as καὶ οὐδέν γε ἀτόπως *yes, and no wonder* P. Th. 142 b.

2826. **ὅς γε** (rarely **ὅστις γε**) has a causal force, much like *qui quidem, quippe qui*. Thus, ἄτοπα λέγεις . . . ὅς γε κελεύεις ἐμὲ νεώτερον ὄντα καθηγεῖσθαι *you are talking absurdly in bidding me who am the younger take precedence* X. M. 2. 3. 15. So with other relatives, as οἷος, ὅσος, ὥσπερ.

2827. γέ sometimes marks an ellipse (S. Ph. 1409). When the verb of the apodosis is omitted, the protasis often has γέ (so usually in Aristophanes, *e.g* Nub. 267).

2828. When γέ is followed by other particles, it belongs with the emphasized word, and the other particles retain their original force; as τούς γε μέντοι ἀγαθούς *yet the brave at least* X. A. 1. 9. 14. So γε δή, γε μὲν δή, γέ τοι (often used like γοῦν in giving a reason for a belief), γέ τοι δή. With the imperative, γέ is rare except when it is followed by another particle, as ὅρᾱ γε μήν S. O. C. 587.

2829. After other Particles. — For example:

δέ γε: here γέ usually does not emphasize δέ but either a single word or the whole clause; as ἡμῖν δέ γε οἶμαι πάντα ποιητέα *but we at least, in my opinion, should adopt every means* X. A. 3. 1. 35. δὲ . . . γε is often used when two things are compared, in order to show that one is more important than the other.

καὶ . . . γε sometimes means *yes, and* and sometimes γέ emphasizes the intervening word. Thus, κοὐδέν γε θαῦμα *yes, and no wonder* S. O. T. 1132, καὶ στίβου γε οὐδεὶς κτύπος *and of footsteps there is no sound* S. Ph. 29. καὶ . . . γε often emphasizes one item in a series, and especially the last item. Here καὶ . . . γέ προς (καὶ πρός γε) *and besides* is common. Cp. P. G. 450 d, 469 b.

μέν γε lends force to a contrast (P. S. 180 d); sometimes it has the force of *that is to say, for example* (T. 6. 86).

Frequent combinations are **ἀλλ' οὖν . . . γε, μέντοι . . . γε, μὴν . . . γε, οὐκοῦν . . . γε.**

γοῦν

2830. **γοῦν** (postpositive; first in Aeschylus) is a restrictive particle from γέ + οὖν. Its meaning varies according to the prominence of the γέ or οὖν; often *certainly, at any rate* (*at all events, at least*). γοῦν commonly confirms a previous general assertion by giving a special instance of its truth (the special instance may be a seeming exception). γοῦν is thus used in bringing forward a reason, which, while not absolutely conclusive, is the most probable explanation of a previous statement.

ἔτι γὰρ οὗτοι κακίονές εἰσι τῶν ὑφ' ἡμῶν ἡττημένων· ἔφευγον γοῦν πρὸς ἐκείνους καταλιπόντες ἡμᾶς *for they are even more cowardly than those who were beaten by us. At any rate they deserted us and sought refuge with them* X. A. 3. 2. 17.

2831. γοῦν may emphasize a pronoun; as πρὸς γοῦν ἐμοῦ S. Aj. 527, τὰ γοῦν σά S. El. 1499.

2832. In answers γοῦν means *well, at least; yes certainly;* as εἰκὸς γοῦν X. C. 5. 3. 14.

2833. γοῦν finds the proof of an assertion in *one* of several possible facts or occurrences; γάρ gives the reason in general, but gives no particular instance; δ' οὖν has an adversative force: 'be that as it may, *yet at any rate.*'

δέ

2834. δέ (postpositive) was originally an adverb with a force not unlike that of *on the other hand, on the contrary;* later it became a conjunction commonly represented by *but* or *and,* which are, however, mere makeshifts of translation. δέ serves to mark that something is different from what precedes, but only to offset it, not to exclude or contradict it; it denotes only a slight contrast, and is therefore weaker than ἀλλά, but stronger than καί. δέ is adversative and copulative; but the two uses are not always clearly to be distinguished.

2835. Adversative δέ often marks a silent contrast, as at the beginning of speeches (ἐγὼ δὲ οὕτω γιγνώσκω X. A. 4. 6. 10); in questions which imply opposition to something just said (S. O. C. 57); in answers (S. O. T. 379); in objections or corrections (S. Ant. 517); in τὸ δέ, τὰ δέ *on the contrary, whereas really,* where a true opinion is opposed to a false one; similarly in νῦν δέ *but in fact, but as the case stands.* When δέ is balanced by μέν (2904) it is antithetical rather than adversative.

a. δέ after a pronoun following a vocative produces a pause; as Νιόβā σὲ δ' ἔγωγε νέμω θεόν *ah Niobe, thee I regard as divine* S. El. 150.

b. δέ instead of ἀλλά is rare except in the poets and Thucydides. Thus, προμηνύσῃς γε τοῦτο μηδενὶ τοὔργον, κρυφῇ δὲ κεῦθε *make known this plan to no one, but hide it in secret* S. Ant. 85, οὐκ ἐπὶ κακῷ, ἐπ' ἐλευθερώσει δὲ τῶν Ἑλλήνων παρελήλυθα *I have come, not to harm, but to liberate, the Greeks* T. 4. 86. Sometimes οὐ μέν precedes when δέ is used like ἀλλά (T. 1. 50).

c. *But not* is ἀλλ' οὐ or οὐ μέντοι, not οὐ δέ, in order to avoid confusion with οὐδέ *nor, not even.* But οὐ and δέ may be separated, as οὐ βουλομένων δέ . . . προσχωρεῖν *but since they did not wish to surrender* X. H. 1. 6. 13.

2836. Copulative δέ marks transition, and is the ordinary particle used in connecting successive clauses or sentences which add something new or different, but not opposed, to what precedes, and are not joined by other particles, such as γάρ or οὖν.

Copulative δέ is common in marking *continuation,* especially when something subordinate is added. Thus, when a new phase of a narrative is developed (X. A. 1. 2. 7–8); where attention is called to a new point or person (as in τί δ' ἔστιν;); when an interrupted speech or narrative is resumed (X. C. 1. 6. 41, S. Tr. 281); where a second relationship is added (μήτηρ βασιλέως, βασίλεια δ' ἐμή *the mother of the King, and my Queen* A. Pers. 151, Ἠιόνα . . . Μενδαίων ἀποικίāν, πολεμίāν δὲ οὖσαν he seized *Eïon, a colony of Mende, and which had been hostile* T. 4. 7):

when δέ has a force like that of γάρ (X. C. 6. 3. 16); and in καὶ . . . δέ *and also* (Epic καὶ δέ), 2891.

2837. Apodotic δέ. — The beginning of the principal clause (apodosis) of conditional and concessive sentences is often marked by δέ. Apodotic δέ is found also in the principal clause of causal, temporal, comparative, and relative sentences; and regularly gives greater emphasis to the main clause, which is thus distinctly set off against the subordinate clause. Apodotic δέ is very common in Homer and Herodotus, not rare in Attic poetry, but infrequent in Attic prose, where it is used especially after an emphatic personal or demonstrative pronoun or when a participle represents the antecedent clause. Thus, εἷος ὁ ταῦθ' ὥρμαινε . . ., ἦλθε δ' Ἀθήνη *while he was revolving these things, then came Athene* A 193, εἰ οὖν ἐγὼ μὴ γιγνώσκω μήτε τὰ ὅσια μήτε τὰ δίκαια, ὑμεῖς δὲ διδάξετέ με *accordingly if I have no knowledge either of what is holy or what is just, do you then instruct me* X. H. 4. 1. 33, ἐπεὶ τοίνυν οὐ δύναμαί σε πείθειν μὴ ἐκθεῖναι, σὺ δὲ ὧδε ποίησον *since therefore I am not able to persuade you not to expose it, do you then do as follows* Hdt. 1. 112, ἐκάθευδον . . . ὥσπερ οἱ ὁπλῖται οὕτω δὲ καὶ οἱ πελτασταί *as the hoplites so also the peltasts sleep* X. C. 8. 5. 12, ἐπειδὴ δὲ ἀφικόμενοι μάχῃ ἐκράτησαν . . ., φαίνονται δ' οὐδ' ἐνταῦθα πάσῃ τῇ δυνάμει χρησάμενοι *but when on their arrival they had conquered in battle, not even then did they appear to have made use of their entire force* T. 1. 11, καί ποτε ὄντος πάγου . . . οὗτος δ' ἐν τούτοις ἐξῄει *and once when there was a frost he went out in the midst of this* P. S. 220 b.

a. Apodotic δέ often resumes a δέ in the subordinate clause and carries on the opposition expressed by that clause; as εἰ δὲ βούλεσθε . . . ἐκλεξάμενοι ὅποι ἂν βούλησθε κατασχεῖν . . ., πλοῖα δ' ὑμῖν πάρεστιν *but if you wish to select* some place *wherever you please and take possession of it, you have ships at command* X. A. 5. 6. 20, ἃ δ' αἰσχύνην ἡμῖν φέρει . . ., ταῦτα δὲ κατὰ χώρᾱν μένει *but* the terms *which cause us shame, these remain in force* I. 4. 176.

b. The use of apodotic δέ should not be regarded as a survival of original *coördination.*

2838. δέ without μέν. — A clause with δέ often has no correlative particle in the clause with which it is contrasted. Here μέν is not used because the opposition in the first clause was too weak, or because the speaker did not intend to announce a following contrast or did not think he was going to use a contrasted δέ clause. Sometimes the entire first clause may have to be supplied in thought from the general connection or from what has gone before. δέ without μέν in such cases is common in poetry, but not rare in prose, even in brief antitheses, as ἃ πάντες ἀεὶ γλίχονται λέγειν, ἀξίως δ' οὐδεὶς εἰπεῖν δεδύνηται exploits *which everybody continually desires to recount, but which no one has been able to set forth adequately* D. 6. 11. See also 2835.

a. When a relative construction passes over into a construction with a personal or demonstrative pronoun, the relative clause usually has no μέν. Cp. Soph. Aj. 457, quoted in 2517.

b. οἱ δέ, when opposed to a larger number of persons or things, is often used without οἱ μέν, as προεληλυθότες ἐπὶ χιλόν, οἱ δ' ἐπὶ ξύλα *having gone for fodder, and some for fuel* X. C. 6. 3. 9.

2839. Δέ with other Particles.—For example:

δ' ἄρα, which sometimes follows *μέν*.

δ' αὖ and **ὅμως δέ** mark stronger opposition than *δέ* alone.

δὲ δή *but then, but now, well but* is often used in passing to a new point. In Aristophanes this collocation is used almost always in questions.

δή

2840. δή (postpositive except in Hom. δὴ γάρ and poetic δὴ τότε) marks something as immediately present and clear to the mind, and gives greater precision, positiveness, and exactness. It sets forth what is obvious, acknowledged, and natural, and often corresponds to *voilà*. δή is used with single words (especially adjectives, adverbs, pronouns, and conjunctions) or, as a sentence adverb, with whole clauses. δή usually stands after the word it emphasizes, though it may be separated from it by one or more other words.

2841. δή of what is Obvious and Natural.—Thus, *ἴστε δή you know of course, δεῖ δή it is manifestly necessary.* So *οὐχ οὕτως ἔχει; ἔχει δή is not this so? Of course it is* P. A. 27 c, *νῦν δ' ὁρᾶτε δή but now you certainly see* X. C. 3. 2. 12, *Παρύσατις μὲν δὴ ἡ μήτηρ ὑπῆρχε τῷ* Κύρῳ *Parysatis, his mother, naturally supported Cyrus* X. A. 1. 1. 4.

2842. Ironical δή.—Thus, *Σωκράτης ὁ σοφὸς δή Socrates the wise forsooth* P. A. 27 a; often **ὡς δή**, as *ὡς δὴ σύ μοι τύραννος Ἀργείων ἔσῃ that you forsooth should be the lord and master of the Argives!* A. Ag. 1633.

2843. Intensive δή emphasizes, and makes definite, adjectives, adverbs, pronouns, and other words. Thus, *ἅπαντες δή absolutely all, κράτιστοι δή the very best, μόνος δή quite alone, ὀλίγοι δή very few; οὕτω δή just so, ὥσπερ δή exactly as, πολλάκις δή very often, δῆλα δή quite plain, νῦν δή just now, now at once; ἐκεῖνος δή this* (*and no other*), *ὅς δή who indeed.* With indefinite pronouns *δή* increases the indefiniteness (339 e); as *ὅστις δή whoever at all.* With other words: *εἰ δή if indeed, οὐ δή no indeed, ἵνα δή that in truth.*

a. With imperatives and in questions *δή* adds urgency; as *ἄκουε δή pray listen! τί δή; why, pray?*

2844. *δή* may introduce emphatically the conclusion of a temporal sentence or of a narrative on passing to a new topic; as *ἐνταῦθα δή, τότε δή then indeed, then and not till then then it was that.* Cp. X. A. 1. 10. 1.

2845. Temporal δή often, especially with *καί*, approximates in meaning to *ἤδη already.* Thus, *ὁ δὲ θανὼν κεύθει κάτω δὴ γῆς but he is dead and already is hidden beneath the earth* S. O. T. 967, *ὁπότε . . . θηρῴης καὶ δὴ δύο ἡμέρᾱς when you have hunted* (*already*) *for two days* X. C. 2. 4. 17, *καὶ δὴ λέγω σοι well I will tell thee* (without further ado) S. Ant. 245. So also in *τέλος δή, νῦν δή.*—Of succession, *δή* means *next.*—Poetic **δαὖτε** (*δὴ αὖτε*) means *now again.*

2846. Consecutive and Resumptive δή is used to set forth an inference, draw a conclusion, denote a consequence, and mark a transition (*μὲν δή . . . δέ*). Here *δή* is a sentence adverb: *accordingly, then, of course, clearly, you* *see, I say*. Thus, ἔλεγον ὅτι κατίδοιεν νύκτωρ πολλὰ πυρὰ φαίνοντα. ἐδόκει δὴ τοῖς στρατηγοῖς οὐκ ἀσφαλὲς εἶναι διασκηνοῦν *they said that they had seen many fires visible in the night; accordingly it seemed to the generals to be unsafe to encamp apart* X. A. 4. 4. 10, Φεραύλᾱς μὲν δὴ οὕτως εἶπεν· ἀνίσταντο δὲ καὶ ἄλλοι πολλοί *Pheraulas then spake thus; and many others also rose to speak* X. C. 2. 3. 16.

2847. **καὶ δή**: (a) Introduces a climax, as καὶ δὴ τὸ μέγιστον *and above all, what is the main thing* P. A. 41 b. (b) In replies = *well*; as βλέψον κάτω· καὶ δὴ βλέπω *look down! Well, I am looking* Ar. Av. 175. This is akin to the temporal use. (c) In assumptions = *suppose* (1771). On καὶ δὴ καί see 2890.

δαί, δῆθεν, δήπου, δῆτα

2848. **δαί** is used in colloquial Attic after interrogative words to express wonder, indignation, etc. Thus, τί δαί; πῶς δαί; *what then? how so?*

2849. **δῆθεν** *truly*, *forsooth*, is commonly used of apparent or pretended truth, and mostly with an ironical tone. Thus, ἐκερτόμησας δῆθεν ὡς παῖδ' ὄντα με *thou hast mocked me forsooth as though I were a child* A. Pr. 986.

2850. **δήπου** *probably*, *I presume*, *I should hope*, *doubtless*, *you will admit*, is stronger than πού *perhaps*, *I suppose*. δήπου often has a touch of irony or doubt in stating a case that would seem to be certain; as ἴστε δήπου ὅθεν ἥλιος ἀνίσχει *you know, I presume, where the sun rises* X. A. 5. 7. 6. In questions δήπου expects the answer *yes*. οὐ δήπου *certainly not* and *is it not so?* (with irony).

2851. **δῆτα** *assuredly*, *really*, *in truth*, is rare outside of Attic. It occurs: (a) In answers, often when a word is repeated with assent; as γιγνώσκεθ' ὑμεῖς ἥτις ἔσθ' ἥδ' ἡ γυνή; γιγνώσκομεν δῆτα *do you know who this woman is? Yes indeed we do* Ar. Thesm. 606; οὐ δῆτα *surely not*, in strong or indignant denial. (b) In questions, to mark an inference or consequence, as πῶς δῆτα; *how in truth?* τί δῆτα; *what then?* καὶ δῆτα ἐτόλμας; *and didst thou really dare?* S. Ant. 449. (c) In wishes and deprecations (stronger than δή), as σκόπει δῆτα *only look* P. G. 452 b, μὴ δῆτα, θυμέ, μή σύ γ' ἐργάσῃ τάδε *no indeed, my heart, do not this deed* E. Med. 1056.

εἴτε

2852. **εἴτε** (from εἰ + τέ), a disjunctive particle, generally doubled: εἴτε . . . εἴτε *whether . . . or* (2675), *if . . . or* (*siue . . . siue*), giving equal value to each supposition.

a. With the subjunctive we find ἐάν τε (ἤν τε, ἄν τε). Hom. has εἴτε . . . εἴτε, but not ἤν τε . . . ἤν τε, with the subjunctive. In the same sense Hom. has ἤ . . . ἤ and ἤτε . . . ἤτε with the subjunctive.

2853. There are various forms of εἴτε clauses:

a. Both εἴτε clauses may have the same finite verb in common, which verb is used only once; as εἴτε βούλεσθε πολεμεῖν ἡμῖν εἴτε φίλοι εἶναι *whether you wish to wage war upon us or to be our friends* X. C. 3. 2. 13.

b. Each εἴτε clause has its own verb and its own main clause; as ἐκέλευσέ σε, εἴτε πάντας αἰτιᾷ, κρίναντα σὲ αὐτὸν χρῆσθαι ὅ τι ἂν βούλῃ, εἴτε ἕνα τινὰ ἢ δύο . . . αἰτιᾷ, τούτους ἀξιοῦσι παρασχεῖν σοι ἑαυτοὺς εἰς κρίσιν the army *requests that, if you accuse all, you pass sentence on them and treat them as you may think best; or, if you accuse one or two, they think it right that these men should surrender themselves to you for judgment* X. A. 6. 6. 20.

c. One main clause refers to both εἴτε clauses; as ὁ ἀγαθὸς ἀνὴρ . . . εὐδαίμων ἐστὶ . . . ἐάν τε μέγας καὶ ἰσχῡρός, ἐάν τε σμῑκρὸς καὶ ἀσθενὴς ᾖ *the good man is happy whether he is large and strong or small and weak* P. L. 660 e.

d. Neither εἴτε clause has a verb, which is to be supplied from the main clause; as λέγοντες, εἴτ' ἀληθὲς εἴτ' ἄρ' οὖν μάτην (ἔλεγον) *saying, whether truly or after all, it may be, falsely* S. Ph. 345.

e. One εἴτε clause has its own verb, while the other gets its verb from the main clause (rare); as ἐμοὶ σὺ . . . φαίνῃ . . . χρησμῳδεῖν, εἴτε παρ' Εὐθύφρονος ἐπίπνους γενόμενος (χρησμῳδεῖς), εἴτε καὶ ἄλλη τις μοῦσα πάλαι σε ἐνοῦσα ἐλελήθει *you seem to me to utter prophecies, whether you were inspired by Euthyphron or whether some other muse has long been present in you without your knowing it* P. Crat. 428 c.

2854. **Variations**: **εἴτε . . . ἤ** (common): εἴτε Λῡσίᾱς ἤ τις ἄλλος πώποτε ἔγραψεν ἢ γράψει κτλ. *whether Lysias or anybody else whoever wrote or will write*, etc. P. Phae. 277 d. **ἤ . . . εἴτε**: only in poetry (S. Aj. 175). **εἴτε . . . εἰ δέ**: when the second member is more important (P. L. 952 c). On **εἰ . . . εἴτε** see 2675 d. On **εἴτε** for εἴτε . . . εἴτε see 2675 b, N. 2.

2855. εἴτε may be strengthened by ἄρα, δή, καί, or οὖν. οὖν is usually placed after the first εἴτε; like καί, it may stand after the second also. When καί stands only after the second εἴτε, its clause is weaker than the first (D. 18. 57).

ἤ

2856. **Disjunctive ἤ** (Epic ἠέ) *or* (*uel, aut*); and repeated: ἢ . . . ἤ *either . . . or* (*uel . . . uel, aut . . . aut*) to connect the two members more closely.

ἀγαθὸν ἢ κακόν *good or bad* X. A. 1. 9. 11, ἤ τι ἢ οὐδέν *little or nothing* P. A. 17 b. ἤ with the subjunctive is often used when a speaker corrects himself; as νῦν δ' αὖ τρίτος ἦλθέ ποθεν σωτήρ, ἢ μόρον εἴπω; *and now, again, the third has come, the deliverer — or shall I call it* a deed of *death?* A. Ch. 1074. On ἤ in questions, see 2657, 2675.

2857. Between ascending numbers ἤ has the force of Eng. *to*, as ἐν ἓξ ἢ ἑπτὰ ἡμέραις *in six to seven days* X. C. 5. 3. 28.

2858. **ἤτοι** may be used instead of the first ἤ when the first member, as is commonly the case, contains the more probable choice. In English the order is often inverted. Thus, ἤτοι κλύουσα παιδὸς ἢ τύχῃ πάρα *she comes either by chance or because she has heard about her son* S. Ant. 1182. ἤτοι may be followed by ἤ several times. **ἤτοι . . . γε** is more emphatic, as ἤτοι κρύφα γε ἢ φανερῶς *either secretly or openly* T. 6. 34.

2859. ἤ often indicates that a given result will follow in case the action of the previous clause is not realized: *or else* (cp. εἰ δὲ μή, 2346 d). Thus, ὅπως . . . ὑμεῖς ἐμὲ ἐπαινέσετε, ἐμοὶ μελήσει· ἢ μηκέτι με Κῦρον νομίζετε *it shall be my concern that you commend me; or else my name is no longer Cyrus* X. A. 1. 4. 16.

2860. ἤ often does not introduce an alternative to a previous question, but substitutes instead another question which is more specific and intended to anticipate the answer to the first (*or rather, or precisely*). Thus, λέγε ἡμῖν πῶς με φῂς διαφθείρειν τοὺς νεωτέρους; ἢ δῆλον δὴ ὅτι . . . θεοὺς διδάσκειν μὴ νομίζειν οὓς ἡ πόλις νομίζει; *tell us how you mean that I corrupt the young? Or rather clearly you mean that* (*I corrupt them*) *by teaching them not to acknowledge the gods which the State acknowledges?* P. A. 26 b.

2861. ἤ often introduces an argument *ex contrario* (D. 31. 14).

2862. ἢ καί is often used where ἤ would suffice (cp. 2888 a); as ἢ ξένος ἢ καί τις πολίτης *either an alien or a citizen if you will* (or *as well*) D. 20. 123.

2863. Comparative ἤ *than* is used to mark difference. It stands after comparatives where the genitive or a preposition (1069 ff.) is not used, and after words indicating difference or diversity or having a comparative force, *e.g.*, ἄλλος or ἕτερος *other*, ἄλλως *otherwise*, διάφορος *different*, διαφέρειν *to be different*, ἐναντίος *contrary*, διπλάσιος *twice as much*, πρίν *sooner*.

ἄλλα ἢ τὰ γενόμενα *things different from what occurred* X. C. 3. 1. 9, ἄλλο οὐδὲν ἢ ἐκ γῆς ἐναυμάχουν T. 4. 14 (2778 a), τῇ ὑστεραίᾳ δεῖ με ἀποθνῄσκειν ἢ ᾗ ἂν ἔλθῃ τὸ πλοῖον *I must die the day after* (*that on which*) *the ship arrives* P. Cr. 44 a (here ἤ or ᾗ might be omitted), τἀναντία . . . ἢ τοὺς κύνας ποιοῦσι *differently from* the way *they treat dogs* X. A. 5. 8. 24, τὸν ἥμισυν σῖτον ἢ πρόσθεν *half as much corn as before* X. H. 5. 3. 21.

a. After τί or a negative, ἤ may be used without ἄλλος, as τί ποιῶν ἢ εὐωχούμενος; *doing what* else *except feasting?* P. Cr. 53 e, εἶπε μηδένα παριέναι ἢ τοὺς φίλους *he said that they should let no one pass except his friends* X. C. 7. 5. 41.

b. Often after verbs of *willing, choosing*, etc.; as θάνατον μετ' ἐλευθερίας αἱρούμενοι ἢ βίον μετὰ δουλείας *preferring death with freedom rather than life with servitude* L. 2. 62. Here we might have μᾶλλον ἤ, which is usually not separated, and especially when μᾶλλον belongs to the whole sentence.

c. If two clauses connected by ἤ have the same verb it may be omitted in the clause following ἤ; as ἔπραττες ἀλλοῖον ἢ οἱ πολλοί (πράττουσι) *you behaved differently from the rest* P. A. 20 c.

d. On ἢ ὥστε (ὡς), or ἤ alone, *than so as to*, see 2264.

ἦ

2864. Asseverative ἦ (prepositive) *in truth, in sooth, verily, upon my honour*, etc.; as ἦ καλῶς λέγεις P. G. 447 c.

2865. ἦ is usually associated with other particles.

ἦ γάρ when used alone in dialogue = *is it not so?* Cp. *n'est ce pas, nicht wahr?* Elsewhere it often has the force of *am I to understand that* asked with surprise. Thus, ἦ γὰρ νοεῖς θάπτειν σφ', ἀπόρρητον πόλει; *what, dost* *thou in truth intend to bury him, when it is forbidden to the citizens?* S. Ant. 44.

ἦ δή expresses lively surprise.

ἦ καί is found in animated questions. Here καί goes closely with ἦ.

ἦ μήν (Hom. ἦ μέν, ἦ μάν) prefaces strong asseverations, threats, and oaths, in direct and indirect discourse. Thus, ἦ μὴν ἐγὼ ἔπαθόν τι τοιοῦτον *in truth this was my experience* P. A. 22 a, ὄμνυμι θεοὺς . . . ἦ μὴν μήτε με Ξενοφῶντα κελεῦσαι ἀφελέσθαι τὸν ἄνδρα μήτε ἄλλον ὑμῶν μηδένα *I swear by the gods upon my honour neither did Xenophon nor any one else among you bid me rescue the man* X. A. 6. 6. 17.

ἦ που *indeed, methinks*, in poetry *I ween*. Here the shade of doubt indicated by πού is not real.

2866. Interrogative ἦ (2650) is probably the same as asseverative ἦ.

ἠδέ (AND ἰδέ)

2867. **ἠδέ** *and* (Epic, lyric, tragic); also in conjunction with τε καί, or δέ. ἠμέν . . . ἠδέ (Epic) is used like τὲ . . . τέ, καὶ . . . καί.

ἰδέ *and* (Epic, rare in tragedy) is used where ἠδέ does not suit the metre.

καί

2868. **καί** is both a copulative conjunction (*and*) connecting words, clauses, or sentences; and an adverb meaning *also, even.*

Conjunctional καί

2869. Copulative καί often has an intensive or heightening force; as where it joins a part and the whole, the universal and the particular. Thus, ἐν Ἀθηναίοις καὶ τοῖς Ἕλλησι Ar. Nub. 413, ὦ Ζεῦ καὶ θεοί Ar. Pl. 1 (θεοὶ καὶ Ζεύς *the gods and above all Zeus*), ἐνταῦθα ἔμειναν ἡμέρᾱς τρεῖς καὶ ἧκε Μένων X. A. 1. 2. 6. On **καὶ ταῦτα**, see 947, 2083.

a. Here καί often = *namely, for example, and so* where an antecedent statement is explained either by another word or by an example. Cp. X. A. 1. 9. 14, 4. 1. 19, 5. 2. 9, 5. 6. 8.

2870. The heightening force is also seen where καί with corrective force may be rendered by *or;* often to set forth a climax and not an alternative. Thus, σοφίᾱ ὀλίγου τινὸς ἀξίᾱ καὶ οὐδενός *wisdom worth little or nothing* P. A. 23 a, μαχαιροποιοὶ . . . ἀνὰ πέντε μνᾶς καὶ ἕξ *sword-cutlers worth five or six minas each* D. 27. 9, προιοῦσι δὲ καὶ ἀπιοῦσι πόλεμος *but war if we advance or retire* X. A. 2. 1. 21, καὶ δίκαια κἄδικα *right or wrong* Ar. Nub. 99, σὸς (γόνος), κεἰ μὴ σός *thy son, or if not thine* S. O. C. 1323.

2871. καί often has an adversative force; as where it joins a negative to an affirmative clause. Here καὶ οὐ (μή) is almost = *but not*, as in ἐμ' ἐχειροτόνησαν καὶ οὐχ ὑμᾶς *they elected me and* (= *but*) *not you* D. 18. 288. So also where καί is like *καίτοι* *and yet;* as *χαίρων ἄπιθι· καί σ' ἄκων ἐγὼ λείπω* *fare thee well; and yet I leave thee unwillingly* Ar. Eq. 1250. To connect *negative* clauses *οὐδέ* is used.

2872. In questions, *καί before* an interrogative expression marks an objection occasioned by surprise or indignation; as *καὶ τίς θανόντων ἦλθεν ἐξ Ἅιδου πάλιν;* *and, pray, who of the dead has come back from Hades?* E. H. F. 297. So *καὶ πῶς;* *pray, how comes it that?* Cp. Eng. *and* when a speaker is stopped by an abrupt question.

a. *After* an interrogative expression adverbial *καί* asks for further information concerning a statement assumed to be true. Thus, *ποίου χρόνου δὲ καὶ πεπόρθηται πόλις;* *but when* was *the city captured?* A. Ag. 278. Cp. 2884.

2873. In imperative sentences *καί* often means *and now, just.* Thus, *καί μοι ἀνάγνωθι τὸ ψήφισμα* *and now read me the bill* L. 13. 35, *καί μοι ἀπόκρῖναι* *just answer me* P. A. 25 a.

2874. *καί* may mark a result (P. Th. 154 c, quoted in 2288).

2875. After expressions of *sameness* and *likeness* *καί* has the force of *as* (Lat. *ac*). Thus, *ὁ αὐτὸς ὑμῖν στόλος ἐστὶ καὶ ἡμῖν* *your expedition is the same as ours* X. A. 2. 2. 10, *οὐχ ὁμοίως καὶ πρίν* *not the same as before* T. 7. 28, *ἴσα καὶ ἱκέται* *the same as suppliants* 3. 14, *ταὐτὰ καί* *the same as* X. C. 1. 3. 18. This use is commoner in prose than poetry.

2876. In expressions denoting coincidence of time *καί* often has the force of *when.* So **ἅμα . . . καί** (2169), **ἤδη . . . καί** X. A. 2. 1. 7, **οὔπω . . . καί** P. Eu. 277 b, **οὐκ ἔφθην . . . καί** (**εὐθύς**) *I had not got the start . . . when* I. 19. 22, D. 43. 69. Cp. **καὶ . . . καί** in *καὶ ἥκομεν καὶ ἡμῖν ἐξελθὼν ὁ θυρωρὸς . . . εἶπεν περιμένειν* *as soon as we arrived the doorkeeper came out and told us to wait* P. Ph. 59 e.

2877. **καὶ . . . καί** *both . . . and, not only . . . but also, as . . . so, as well as . . . as also,* sometimes *whether . . . or,* emphasizes each member separately, and forms a less close combination than *τὲ καί.* Thus, *καὶ τότε καὶ νῦν* *not only then but also now.* So *τῑμὰς δοτέον καὶ ζῶντι καὶ τελευτήσαντι* *honours must be paid him both when living and after death* P. R. 414 a, *σὺ καὶ δέδορκας κοὐ βλέπεις* *thou both hast sight and* (yet) *dost not see* S. O. T. 413, *κἀπεμπόμην πρὸς ταῦτα καὶ τὸ πᾶν φράσω* *as I was sent for this purpose so I will tell thee all* S. El. 680, *τολμᾶν ἀνάγκη, κἂν τύχω κἂν μὴ τύχω* *I must dare whether I succeed or fail* E. Hec. 751.

2878. In a series of more than two ideas *καί* is used before each, where English would use *and* only before the last. Thus, *συντυγχάνουσιν αὐτῷ καὶ λαμβάνουσιν αὐτὸν καὶ γυναῖκα καὶ παῖδας καὶ τοὺς ἵππους καὶ πάντα τὰ ὄντα* *they fell upon him and seized him, his wife, his children, his horses, and all his possessions* X. A. 7. 8. 22.

2879. Adjectives of quantity, as **πολύς** and **ὀλίγος** in the plural, are usually joined to an adjective in the same construction by *καί* or *τὲ καί* (also by *τέ* or *τὲ . . . τέ* in poetry). Thus, *πολλὰ καὶ δεινά* D. 37. 57 (*δεινὰ καὶ πολλά* 37. 57), *πολλά τε καὶ δεινά* X. A. 5. 5. 8. In *πολλὰ καὶ μεγάλα ἀγαθά* (X. C. 1. 5. 9), the substantive is qualified by two adjectives; whereas in English the second adjective is taken with the substantive and treated as a *unit* modified by the first adjective (*many good-things*).

a. **πολλοὶ καὶ ἄλλοι** means *many others also* (with καί adverbial). For *many others* we find ἄλλοι πολλοί (very common) or πολλοὶ ἄλλοι.

2880. Some combinations of conjunctional καί are:

καὶ . . . μέντοι *and however*, *and of course* (in καὶ μέντοι καί the first καί may be adverbial: *yes indeed and*).

καὶ . . . τοίνυν *and . . . further*, in connecting a thought with the preceding.

Adverbial καί

2881. Adverbial καί *also*, *even* (Lat. *etiam*) influences single words or whole clauses. Adverbial καί stresses an important idea; usually the idea set forth in the word that follows, but sometimes also a preceding word when that word stands first in its clause. καί often serves to increase or diminish the force of particular words; sometimes it gives a tone of modesty.

2882. With single words: **a.** κᾆτα *then too*, καὶ ἐγώ *I on my part*, σὸν ἢ κἀμὸν γένος *offspring from thee or me either* S. El. 965, βουλόμενος δὲ καὶ αὐτὸς λαμπρόν τι ποιῆσαι *desirous of himself too doing something illustrious* X. C. 5. 4. 15.

b. καὶ πρίν *even before*, καὶ ὀψέ *late though it be*, καὶ οὕτως *even so*, καὶ ἔτι καὶ νῦν *and now too*, *and still even now*, ὀκνῶ καὶ λέγειν *I fear even to say it*, πολλὴ μωρίᾱ καὶ τοῦ ἐπιχειρήματος *the very attempt is utter folly* P. Pr. 317 a. On καί *though* with a participle, see 2083.

c. Often with adverbs of intensity, as καὶ μάλα *exceedingly*, *certainly*, καὶ κάρτα *very greatly*, καὶ πάνυ *absolutely*. With comparatives and superlatives: καὶ μᾶλλον *yet more*, καὶ μωρότατον *altogether the most foolish thing* X. A. 3. 2. 22.

2883. With a whole phrase or clause; as ἄμφω γὰρ αὐτὼ καὶ κατακτανεῖν νοεῖς; *what, dost thou indeed intend to put them both to death?* S. Ant. 770. Other examples in 2885–2887.

2884. When καί stresses a verb in interrogative and conditional sentences it is often to be rendered by an emphatic auxiliary, often by *at all*. Thus, πολλάκις ἐσκεψάμην τί καὶ βούλεσθε *I have often asked myself the question what you* **can** *want* T. 6. 38, τί καὶ χρὴ προσδοκᾶν; *what on earth* **is** *one to expect?* D. 4. 46, τί γὰρ ἄν τις καὶ ποιοῖ ἄλλο; *for what else* **could** *one do?* P. Ph. 61 e, εἰ δεῖ καὶ μῦθον λέγειν καλόν *if it is well to tell a fable at all* P. Ph. 110 b. Cp. 2872 a.

a. In affirmative independent clauses or sentences καί often has an emphasis which is difficult to render; as ὁ κίνδῡνος νῦν δὴ καὶ δόξειεν ἂν δεινὸς εἶναι *the danger must now indeed seem to be dreadful* P. Ph. 107 c.

2885. Καί of Balanced Contrast. — In order to mark the connection of thought between antecedent and consequent, καί *also*, *too*, is often placed in the subordinate clause or in the main clause or in both.

a. Greek has thus the following modes of expression where a comparison is instituted between the parts of such bimembral sentences: "What *I* do, that you *also* do" (as in English) or "What I *also* (= I on my part) do, that you do" or "What I *also* do, that you *also* do." In the subordinate clause καί seems superfluous to English idiom.

2886. Καί of balanced contrast occurs frequently when the subordinate clause sets forth something corresponding to, or deducible from, the main clause; and when an antithesis is to be emphasized. It is found especially in relative, causal, and final clauses, and has the effect of putting such subordinate clauses on a plane with the main clause. A relative word often adds -περ or is followed by δή. Thus, τὰ δὲ τῆς πόλεως ἔπρᾱττον, ὧνπερ ἕνεκεν καὶ Σωκράτει προσῆλθον *they devoted themselves to those affairs of state on account of which they had in fact associated with Socrates* X. M. 1. 2. 47, καὶ ἡμῖν ταὐτὰ δοκεῖ ἅπερ καὶ βασιλεῖ *we hold exactly the same views as the king* X. A. 2. 1. 22, ἐπειδὴ καὶ ἡ πόλις ἐσώθη . . . ἀξιῶ κἀμοὶ σωτηρίᾱν γενέσθαι *since the city has been saved I beg that safety be granted to me as well* And. 1. 143, ἔμαθον καὶ ἐγὼ ὥσπερ καὶ οἱ ἄλλοι *I* (on my part) *learned just as the rest did too* P. Alc. 110 d, τῑμωρίᾱ γὰρ οὐκ εὐτυχεῖ δικαίως ὅτι καὶ ἀδικεῖται *for vengeance is not successful in accordance with justice, because it is taken upon a wrong* T. 4. 62.

2887. In final clauses ἵνα καί is common, and sometimes, like Eng. *just*, serves to show that the fact answers to the expectation, or the effect to the cause (or *vice versa*). Thus, βούλει οὖν ἕπεσθαι ἵνα καὶ ἴδῃς τοὺς ὄντας αὐτόθι; *do you wish to go along then just to see those who are there?* P. Lys. 204 a, ἄρξομαι δὲ ἀπὸ τῆς ἰᾱτρικῆς λέγων ἵνα καὶ πρεσβεύωμεν τὴν τέχνην *I will begin my speech with medicine in order that we may do honour to our art* P. S. 186 b.

2888. Καί of balanced contrast appears also in coördinate clauses; as ἤδη γὰρ ἔγωγε καὶ Φιλολάου ἤκουσα . . . ἤδη δὲ καὶ ἄλλων τινῶν *for I have ere now heard Philolaus . . . and ere now certain others besides him* P. Ph. 61 e, κατὰ πολλὰ μὲν καὶ ἄλλα, οὐχ ἥκιστα δὲ καὶ κατὰ ταῦτα *as in many other respects also and not least (too) in this* Aes. 1. 108, ὑπὸ τῶν τἀνταῦθα διοικήσειν . . . καὶ πρὶν ὑπεσχημένων καὶ νῦν δὲ πρᾱττόντων *by those who had promised to manage things there before and are now also doing them* D. 7. 5. The negative of καί . . . καί . . . δέ is οὐδὲ . . . οὐδὲ . . . δέ.

a. So in disjunctive phrases or clauses. Thus, εἴτε διὰ τὸ ἐπιβόημα εἴτε καὶ αὐτῷ ἄλλο τι . . . δόξαν *either because of the exclamation or also because some other thought occurred to him* T. 5. 65; and so ἢ καί 2862. Cp. ἐζητεῖτο οὐδέν τι μᾶλλον ὑπὸ τῶν ἄλλων ἢ καὶ ὑπ' ἐμοῦ *he was not searched for by the others more than he was by me (on my part)* Ant. 5. 23.

2889. Similarly the καί of **εἴ τις καὶ ἄλλος** is superfluous; as εἴπερ τι καὶ ἄλλο καὶ τοῦτο μαθητόν *if any other thing is learnable, this is too* X. S. 2. 6. But καί is usually omitted in the main clause; as ἐπίσταται δ' εἴ τις καὶ ἄλλος *he knows as well as anybody else* X. A. 1. 4. 15. So ὥς τις καὶ ἄλλος *as also any other* X. A. 2. 6. 8.

2890. **καὶ δὴ καί** *and especially, and in particular, and what is more*, lays stress on a particular instance or application of a general statement. Here the second καί emphasizes the following word. καὶ δὴ καί is usually attached to a preceding τέ or καί. Thus, καὶ δὴ καὶ τότε πρῳαίτερον συνελέγημεν *and on that especial occasion we came together somewhat earlier* than usual P. Ph. 59 d, ἐν ἄλλοις τε πολλοῖς καὶ δὴ καὶ ἐν τοῖς κάμνουσιν *in the case of many others and particularly in that of the sick* X. C. 1. 6. 21.

2891. **καὶ . . . δέ** *and . . . also, and . . . moreover*. Here καί emphasizes the important intervening word or words, while δέ connects. Thus, καὶ σὲ δ' ἐν τούτοις λέγω *and I count thee also among these* A. Pr. 973. *And also not* is οὐδὲ . . . δέ. Hom. has καὶ δέ *and further, and even* (H 113), not καί . . . δέ. καί . . . δέ (for τέ) is different (S. Ant. 432).

καίπερ

2892. καίπερ *although* is common with participles (2083). As a conjunction (cp. *quanquam*) without a main clause it is very rare (P. S. 219 c).

καίτοι

2893. καίτοι (καί + τοί), not in Homer, means *and yet, although,* rarely *and so then.* Here τοί marks something worthy of note, which is commonly opposed to what precedes. καίτοι is used in making a correction (sometimes in the form of a question), in passing to a new idea, and in the statement of a conclusion. The common καίτοι . . . γε is stronger than καίτοι.

καίτοι οὐδὲν ὅτι οὐκ ἀληθὲς εἴρηκα ὧν προεῖπον *and yet there is nothing untrue in what I said before* P. Euth. 3 c.

a. A sentence preceding καίτοι is often *restated* by a clause introduced by ἀλλά (ἀλλ' ὅμως), δέ, or νῦν δέ. Cp. P. Ph. 77 a, Charm. 175 c, A. 40 b, G. 499 c.

b. καίτοι is rarely, if ever, used with the participle in classical Greek. It is best attested in P. R. 511 d; emendation is resorted to in L. 31. 34, Ar. Eccl. 159.

μά

2894. μά asseverative (cp. μήν, μέν asseverative) with the accusative of the divinity or thing by which one swears. In negative sentences we have οὐ μά or μά alone with the accusative; in affirmative sentences, ναὶ μά, but more commonly νή. The omission of the accusative may sometimes be due to indecision or to indifference and not always to scrupulousness (1596 c). μά means properly *in truth, verily;* but apparently governs the accusative after the ellipse of such verbs as *I call to witness.*

μέν

2895. μέν was originally an asseverative, emphatic particle (*surely, certainly, indeed*) and a weaker form of μήν. Cp. Epic ἦ μέν, καὶ μέν, οὐ μέν in asseverations and protestations. Asseverative μέν survived as μέν *solitarium* and in combination with other particles. Antithetical (concessive) μέν owes its origin to the fact that, as emphasis may indicate a contrast, the clause in which μέν stood was felt as preliminary to an adversative member of the sentence. Through association with this adversative member μέν gradually lost its primitive asseverative force.

2896. *μέν solitarium* occurs when a clause with μέν is not followed by a clause with δέ. This is especially common when the antithetical clause is to be supplied in thought, as when μέν emphasizes a statement made by a person with reference to himself as opposed to others (often with a tone of arrogance or of credulity). Here any possible opposition or difference of opinion, however justifiable, is left unexpressed. Thus, ἐγὼ μὲν οὐκ οἶδα *I for my part do not know* (though others *may*) X. C. 1. 4. 12, ἀπέπλευσαν, ὡς μὲν τοῖς πλείστοις ἐδόκουν, φιλοτιμηθέντες *they sailed away since they were jealous as it seemed to the majority at least* X. A. 1. 4. 7. So in such phrases as δοκῶ μέν, ἡγοῦμαι μέν, οἶμαι μέν.

2897. Sometimes *μέν solitarium* merely emphasizes a word in its clause and does not imply a contrast. Thus, ἐμοὶ μὲν οἰστέα τάδε *this must be borne by me on my part* S. O. C. 1360.

2898. *μέν solitarium* is commonest after personal pronouns; but occurs also after demonstrative pronouns (L. 25. 16), after relatives (Aes. 3. 209), after substantives without the article (D. 9. 15), or after the article and before its substantive (L. 29. 1), after adjectives (L. 1. 27), after adverbs (L. 12. 91), after verbs (D. 19. 231). In questions μέν alone is rare (P. Men. 82 b).

2899. In combination with other particles, especially δή and οὖν, asseverative μέν either has a simple confirmatory force or is used adversatively. The following cases must be distinguished from those in which μέν is correlative to δέ.

2900. **μὲν δή** expresses positive certainty, especially in conclusions. It is common in summing up and in transitions, and is used either alone or with other particles (sometimes it is followed by ἀλλά or δέ). Thus, ταῦτα μὲν δὴ τοιαῦτα *so much for that* A. Pr. 500. So also, *e.g.* **ἀλλὰ μὲν δή** *but certainly in fact* (ἀλλ' οὐδὲ μὲν δή in rejecting an alternative); **εἰ μὲν δή** *if indeed in truth;* **καὶ μὲν δή** *and in truth, and in fact* (often in transitions); **οὐ μὲν δή** *certainly not at all, nor yet, in truth* (often used adversatively).

2901. **μὲν οὖν** lit. *certainly in fact*, μέν being a weaker form of μήν. μὲν οὖν has two common uses, according as the particles have a compound force, or each has its own force.

a. The **compound** force of μὲν οὖν is seen in affirmations; as in replies: πάνυ (μάλιστα) μὲν οὖν *yes, by all means; certainly, by all means; aye truly,* εὖ μὲν οὖν οἶδα *nay, I am sure of it,* οὐ μὲν οὖν *indeed not,* ἆρ' οὐ τόδε ἦν τὸ δένδρον ἐφ' ὅπερ ἦγες ἡμᾶς; τοῦτο μὲν οὖν αὐτό *isn't this the tree to which you were bringing us? To be sure this is it* P. Phae. 230 a.

b. The compound force appears also when μὲν οὖν indicates a correction; *nay rather* (*imo vero*); as λέγε σύ· σὺ μὲν οὖν μοι λέγε *do you say. Nay, rather* you Ar. Eq. 13, ἄτοπον τὸ ἐνύπνιον, ὦ Σώκρατες. ἐναργὲς μὲν οὖν *the dream is strange, Socrates. Nay rather, it was distinct* P. Cr. 44 b.

c. **Each particle has its own force** especially where μὲν οὖν indicates a transition to a new subject. Here μέν points forward to an antithesis to follow and indicated by δέ, ἀλλά, μέντοι, while οὖν (inferential) connects with what precedes. Here *so then, therefore* may be used in translation. Thus, Κλέαρχος μὲν οὖν τοσαῦτα εἶπε. Τισσαφέρνης δὲ ὧδε ἀπημείφθη *such then were the words of Clearthus; and on the other hand Tissaphernes answered as follows* X. A. 2. 5. 15

Sometimes μὲν οὖν (like *igitur*) shows that a subject announced in general terms is now to be treated in detail (P. Ph. 70 c).

2902. Common collocations are **ἀλλὰ μέν** (ἀλλὰ . . . μέν) *but for a fact*, **γὲ μέν, ἦ μέν, καὶ μέν.**

2903. Antithetical (concessive) μέν distinguishes the word or clause in which it stands from a following word or clause marked usually by δέ or by other particles denoting contrast, such as ἀλλά, ἀτάρ, μέντοι, μήν; and even by copulative τέ, καί (Hom. ἠδέ). μέν never connects words, clauses, or sentences.

2904. **μὲν . . . δέ** serves to mark stronger or weaker contrasts of various kinds, and is sometimes to be rendered by *on the one hand . . . on the other hand, indeed . . . but;* but is often to be left untranslated. The μέν clause has a concessive force when it is logically subordinate (*while, though, whereas*, cp. 2170). Thus, ἡ μὲν ψῡχὴ πολυχρόνιόν ἐστι, τὸ δὲ σῶμα ἀσθενέστερον καὶ ὀλιγοχρονιώτερον *the soul lasts for a long time, the body is weaker and lasts for a shorter time* P. Ph. 87 d, καὶ πρόσθεν μὲν δὴ πολλοὶ ἡμῶν ἦρχον μὲν οὐδενός, ἤρχοντο δέ· νῦν δὲ κατεσκεύασθε οὕτω πάντες οἱ παρόντες ὥστε ἄρχετε οἱ μὲν πλειόνων, οἱ δὲ μειόνων *and whereas in fact many of us hitherto commanded no one, but were subject to the command of others, now however all of you who are present are so placed that you have command, some over more, others over fewer* X. C. 8. 1. 4.

a. So **ἄλλοτε μὲν . . . ἄλλοτε δέ, ἅμα μὲν . . . ἅμα δέ** *at once . . . and, partly . . . partly*, **ἔνθα μὲν . . . ἔνθα δέ, ἐνταῦθα μὲν . . . ἐκεῖ δέ, πρῶτον μὲν . . . ἔπειτα δέ** (or **ἔπειτα** alone). On **ὁ μὲν . . . ὁ δέ** see 1107. Instead of ὁ (οἱ) δέ we find *e.g.* ἄλλος δέ, ἔνιοι δέ, ἔστι δ' οἵ. So τοῦτο μὲν . . . τοῦτ' ἄλλο (or αὖθις).—μέν may stand with a participle, δέ with a finite verb, in an antithetical sentence. Example in 2147 c.

b. εἰ, οὐ (μή) standing before μὲν . . . δέ exercise their force on *both* opposed clauses.

2905. When several verbs referring to the same person or thing are contrasted, or when several attributes are contrasted, the first has μέν, the others δέ. Cp. Lyc. 5, X. A. 3. 1. 19. But μέν is sometimes omitted.

2906. μέν . . . δέ is used in successive clauses which contain either the same word (*anaphora*) or a synonymous word; as ἐγὼ δὲ σύνειμι μὲν θεοῖς, σύνειμι δὲ ἀνθρώποις τοῖς ἀγαθοῖς quoted in 1159, ἦλθε μὲν καὶ ἀπὸ τῆς Ἐρυθραίᾱς ἀγγελίᾱ, ἀφῑκνεῖτο δὲ καὶ πανταχόθεν *news came from the district of Erythrae itself and arrived also from all quarters* T. 3. 33. But μέν is sometimes omitted, as στήσω σ' ἄγων, στήσω δ' ἐμαυτόν *I will bring thee and stablish thee, and I will stablish myself* S. O. C. 1342.

2907. If more than two clauses are contrasted, only the first clause has μέν, while each of the following clauses has δέ (X. A. 1. 3. 14, X. C. 4. 2. 28).

2908. A contrast indicated by μέν and δέ may stand inside another contrast indicated in the same manner, as ὁ μὲν ἀνὴρ τοιαῦτα μὲν πεποίηκε, τοιαῦτα δὲ λέγει· ὑμῶν δὲ σὺ πρῶτος, ὦ Κλέαρχε, ἀπόφηναι γνώμην ὅ τι σοι δοκεῖ *the man has acted thus, and speaks thus; but do you, Clearchus, be the first to make known what you think best* X. A. 1. 6. 9.

2909. Two relative (or conditional) clauses each with μέν may be followed by two demonstrative clauses each with δέ; but the second δέ is usually omitted, and there are other variations. Thus, ὁπόσοι μὲν . . . οὗτοι μὲν . . . ὁπόσοι δὲ . . . τούτους ὁρῶ X. A. 3. 1. 43, cp. X. O. 4. 7, P. A. 28 e.

2910. A clause with μέν is often followed by a contrasted clause without δέ but with a particle containing an element of opposition, as πρῶτον μὲν . . . ἔπειτα . . . εἶτα.

2911. A shift in the construction may cause δέ to be omitted (S. Ant. 1199).

2912. μέν after an emphatic demonstrative may resume μέν of the antecedent clause (D. 2. 18).

2913. **μὲν . . . τε** (and even καί) is used where the second clause is merely *added* instead of being coördinated by means of δέ. Thus, ταχὺ μὲν ὅποι ἔδει περιγιγνόμεθα ἀθρόοι τε τῷ ἄρχοντι ἑπόμενοι ἀνυπόστατοι ἦμεν *we have quickly reached the places to which we had to go, and by following our leader in a compact body we have been invincible* X. C. 8. 1. 3.

2914. Position of μέν (and δέ). — μέν and δέ are commonly placed next to the words they contrast, and take precedence over other postpositive particles. But when two words belong closely together, μέν and δέ are placed between. Thus, when nouns with the article are contrasted, μέν and δέ stand after the article; if the nouns depend on prepositions μέν and δέ stand after the preposition and before the article.

a. But this rule may be neglected in order to emphasize the preceding word, as τὰ μὲν ἀνθρώπινα παρέντες, τὰ δαιμόνια δὲ σκοποῦντες *neglecting human affairs, but speculating on things divine* X. M. 1. 1. 12, ἀνὰ τὸ σκοτεινὸν μέν *in the darkness* T. 3. 22.

b. If the noun has no article and is governed by a preposition, δέ usually takes the third place.

c. Postponement of δέ (and some other postpositive particles) to the fourth place is only *apparent* after an introductory vocative, which is not regarded as forming an integral part of the sentence.

2915. μέν and δέ are sometimes referred to the entire clause or to the predicate and not to the words that are opposed to each other. This arrangement is often adopted to preserve the symmetry of the juxtaposed clause. μέν and δέ are thus often placed after personal or demonstrative pronouns. Thus, ἔλεγε μὲν ὡς τὸ πολύ, τοῖς δὲ βουλομένοις ἐξῆν ἀκούειν Socrates *for the most part was wont to talk, while any who chose could listen* X. M. 1. 1. 10, πῶς ἂν πολλοὶ μὲν ἐπεθύμουν τυραννεῖν . . . ; πῶς δὲ πάντες ἐζήλουν ἂν τοὺς τυράννους; *why should many desire to possess despotic power? why should everybody envy despotic rulers?* X. Hi. 1. 9 (for πάντες δὲ πῶς ἐζήλουν ἄν). Cp. ἐν μὲν τούτοις . . . ἐν ἐκείνοις δέ Lyc. 140, περὶ αὐτῶν μὲν . . . περὶ δὲ τῶν δεσποτῶν L. 7. 35, etc.

a. The transposition is often designed to produce a chiastic (3020) order, as ἔπαθε μὲν οὐδέν, πολλὰ δὲ κακὰ ἐνόμιζε ποιῆσαι *he suffered no loss, but thought that he had done a great deal of damage* X. A. 3. 4. 2 (here οὐδέν and πολλά are brought close together).

2916. In poetry μέν and δέ often have a freer position than in prose. δέ may often come *third* when an emphatic word is placed before it, and even *fourth*.

μέντοι

2917. **μέντοι** (postpositive) from *μέν* (= *μήν*, 2895) + *τοί*, is an asseverative and adversative particle.

2918. Asseverative *μέντοι* *certainly, surely, of course, in truth* is very common in replies, where it expresses positive, eager, or reflective assent. Often with *νὴ* (*μὰ*) *Δία*. Thus, *ἐγώ; σὺ μέντοι I? certainly, you* Ar. Eq. 168, *τί γάρ, ἔφη, . . . μέμνησαι ἐκεῖνα . . .; ναὶ μὰ Δία . . . μέμνημαι μέντοι τοιαῦτα ἀκούσᾱς σου* *well then, said he, do you recall those matters; Yes, by Zeus, certainly I do recall that I heard things to that effect from you* X. C. 1. 6. 6, *ἀληθέστατα μέντοι λέγεις* *well, certainly you say what is very true* P. Soph. 245 b.

μέντοι may strengthen asseverations or emphasize questions; as *οὕτω μέντοι χρὴ λέγειν* *in truth we must speak thus* P. Th. 187 b; often with demonstrative pronouns, as *ὦ τοῦτο μέντοι νὴ Δία αὐτοῖσιν πιθοῦ* *oh, by Zeus do oblige them in* **this** Ar. Aves 661.

a. Asseverative *μέντοι* in combinations, *e.g.*:

ἀλλὰ μέντοι *but surely, but in fact* (in *ἀλλὰ . . . μέντοι*, *μέντοι* refers to the preceding word).

καὶ . . . μέντοι *and . . . indeed, and . . . in fact, and . . . moreover*, as *φιλοθηρότατος ἦν καὶ πρὸς τὰ θηρία μέντοι φιλοκινδῡνότατος* *he was very fond of hunting and moreover exceedingly fond of danger* X. A. 1. 9. 6.

οὐ μέντοι *no indeed* (also adversative: *yet not*).

2919. Adversative *μέντοι* *however, yet* often marks a contrast or a transition; as *ἀφίεμέν σε, ἐπὶ τούτῳ μέντοι* *we let you go, on this condition however* P. A. 29 c. *μέντοι γε* is stronger. **μὲν . . . μέντοι** is much stronger than *μὲν . . . δέ*, as *φιλοσόφῳ μὲν ἔοικας . . . ἴσθι μέντοι ἀνόητος ὢν* *you resemble a philosopher—know however that you are a fool* X. A. 2. 1. 13. On **οὐ μέντοι ἀλλά (γε)** see 2767.

μήν

2920. **μήν** (postpositive): (1) asseverative, *in truth, surely*; (2) adversative, especially after a negative, *yet, however*. The forms *μήν* (Hom., Att.), *μᾱ́ν* (Hom., Lesb., Dor., lyric parts of tragedy), *μέν* *truly* (Hom., Att.) and *μά* in oaths are all connected. *μήν* emphasizes either a whole statement or a single word.

ὧδε γὰρ ἐξερέω, καὶ μὴν τετελεσμένον ἔσται *for thus I will declare, and verily it shall be accomplished* Ψ 410; *καλὸν μὲν ἡ ἀλήθεια . . ., ἔοικε μὴν οὐ ῥᾴδιον πείθειν* *truth is a fine thing, yet it does not seem an easy thing to persuade* P. L. 663 e, *εἰ δ' ἄγε μήν* *come now, on then* A 302, *οὐδὲν μὴν κωλύει* *but nothing hinders* P. Phae. 268 e.

2921. Combinations of μήν:

ἀλλὰ μήν (. . . γε) *but surely; but yet; nay, indeed; well, in truth.* Often used to add something of greater importance, or in transitions when a new idea is opposed to the foregoing. *ἀλλὰ μήν* is often separated by a negative.

ἦ μήν *verily, verily.* Often to introduce an oath or a threat.

καὶ μήν *and verily* or *and yet* according to the context. καὶ μήν frequently introduces a new fact or thought and hence often denotes transition, sometimes opposition (*further, however, and yet*). In tragedy this formula is used to mark the beginning of a new scene, as when the arrival of a newcomer is thus signalized (*but here comes*); as καὶ μὴν ἄναξ ὅδε *and lo! here is the king* S. O. C. 549. In *replies*, καὶ μήν usually confirms the last remark, accedes to a request, or denotes hearty assent; sometimes there is an adversative sense (*and yet; and (yet) surely; oh, but*). In *enumerations*, καὶ μήν adds a new fact (*and besides*).

καὶ μὴν . . . γε in transitions or enumerations marks something of still greater importance; but it is not so strong as καὶ μὲν δή. Here γέ emphasizes the word or words with which it is immediately connected. In replies, *and indeed, and yet* or *oh, but;* as καὶ μὴν ποιήσω γε *and yet I will do it* S. El. 1045.

καὶ μὴν καί (neg. καὶ μὴν οὐδέ) *and in truth also.*

οὐ μήν *surely not,* **οὐ μὴν ἀλλά** *nevertheless* (2767), **οὐ μὴν οὐδέ** *nor again* (2768), **οὐδὲ μήν** *and certainly not.*

τί μήν; lit. *what indeed* (*quid uero*), as ἀλλὰ τί μὴν δοκεῖς; *but what in truth is your opinion?* P. Th. 162 b. τί μήν; standing alone, has the force of *naturally, of course.* Thus, λέγουσιν ἡμᾶς ὡς ὀλωλότας, τί μήν; *they speak of us as dead, and why should they not?* A. Ag. 672. Often in Plato to indicate assent. **τί μὴν οὔ;** (*why indeed not* =) *of course I do.*

ναί, νή

2922. **ναί** (cp. Lat. *nae*) asseverative (*truly, yea*), with the accusative in oaths where it is usually followed by μά (1596 b). ναί *yes*, in answers, is found only in Attic.

2923. **νή** (cp. Lat. *nē*) asseverative (*truly, yea*), with the accusative in oaths, and only in an affirmative sense. νή is found only in Attic. See 1596 b.

νῦν, νυνί, νῦν, νύν, νύ

2924. νῦν *now, at present* often has a causal sense, as νῦν δέ *but as the case stands, as it is;* often to mark reality in contrast to an assumed case.

2925. νυνί (νῦν + deictic ῑ, 333 g) is stronger than νῦν: *even now, at this moment;* rarely in a causal sense.

2926. **νῦν** (enclitic; lyric, tragic, Herodotus, rare and suspected in Homer), a weakened form of νῦν, is rarely temporal, usually inferential, as *now* is used for *then, therefore.* νύν thus marks the connection of the speaker's thought with the situation in which he is placed. It is commonly used after imperatives, prohibitive and hortatory subjunctives. Thus, κάθιζέ νύν με *seat me, then* S. O. C. 21. In Xenophon and Plato νυν is written by some editors, where the Mss. have νῦν (X. C. 4. 2. 37, H. 4. 1. 39).

2927. **νῦν** (enclitic) is adopted by some scholars in Attic tragedy where a long syllable is required (S. O. T. 644). Others write νῦν (with the *force* of νῦν).

2928. **νύ** (enclitic; Epic and Cyprian), a still weaker form of νῦν, and less emphatic than δή. It is common in questions and appeals; less frequent in statements; as τίς νυ; *who now?* Also after other particles, as καί νύ κε, ἦ ῥά νυ.

ὅπως

2929. **ὅπως**, originally a relative adverb meaning *how*, is derived from the relative particle σϝοδ (with which Eng. *so* is connected), to which the indefinite πώς has been added. Hom. ὅππως from σϝοδ-πως, as ὅττι from σϝοδ-τι (81 D 2).

a. The adverbial meaning of ὅπως is still seen in its use as an indefinite relative and as an indirect interrogative; and by the fact that in its place ὅπῃ, ὅτῳ τρόπῳ, ἐξ ὅτου τρόπου are sometimes used. By association with the subjunctive ὅπως became a conjunction (cp. μή πως) used with or without ἄν in final clauses (see 2196, 2201). On the use as a conjunction in object clauses after verbs of *effort* and of *fear*, see 2211, 2228. So in dependent statements ὅπως passed from *how* into *that* (2578 d).

οὐδέ, οὔτε (μηδέ, μήτε)

2930. **οὐδέ** (**μηδέ**) is an adverb and a conjunction, and is to be broken up into the negative οὐ (μή) and δέ meaning *and, even, also,* or *but.*

οὐδέ (μηδέ) *as an Adverb*

2931. Adverbial οὐδέ (μηδέ) *not even, not . . . either, also . . . not, nor yet* (*ne . . quidem*). Cp. the use of καί *even, also* in affirmative sentences; as οὐδ᾽ ὥς *not even in that case* (καὶ ὥς *even in that case*).

ἀλλ᾽ οὐδὲ τούτων στερήσονται *but not even of these shall they be deprived* X. A. 1. 4. 8, ὅτ᾽ οὐδ᾽ οὕτω ῥᾴδιον ἦν *when besides it was not so easy* I. 18. 65 (= καὶ οὐ *also not*). With οὐδ᾽ εἰ (ἐάν) *not even if* οὐ belongs with the main clause, while δέ *even* goes with the dependent clause. Thus, οὐδ᾽ ἂν εἰ βούλοιντο, ῥᾳδίως πονηροὶ γένοιντο *even if they wished, they could not easily become wicked* X. C. 7. 5. 86 (= καὶ εἰ βούλοιντο, οὐκ ἂν γένοιντο). Similarly with a participle: οὐδὲ πεπονθὼς κακῶς ἐχθρὸν εἶναί μοι τοῦτον ὁμολογῶ *I do not admit that this man is my enemy even though I have been ill-used* D. 21. 205.

οὐδέ (μηδέ) *as a Conjunction*

2932. οὐδέ (μηδέ) as a conjunction (*and not, nor*) connects two or more whole clauses.

2933. In Attic prose οὐδέ is used only to join a negative clause to another clause itself negative; as οὐδεμία ἐλπὶς ἦν τῑμωρίᾱς οὐδὲ ἄλλη σωτηρίᾱ ἐφαίνετο *there was no hope of assistance nor did any chance of safety appear* T. 3. 20.

a. A negative clause is joined to an affirmative clause by καὶ οὐ (μή). Thus, ἐμμενῶ τῇ ξυμμαχίᾳ . . . καὶ οὐ παραβήσομαι *I will abide by the alliance and I will not violate it* T. 5. 47. καὶ οὐ (μή) may have an adversative force (*but not*).

N.—But in poetry and Ionic prose οὐδέ may continue an affirmative clause; as δεινὸν γὰρ οὐδὲ ῥητόν *dread indeed and not to be uttered* S. Ph. 756.

2934. οὐδέ is used by the poets for *but not*, where Attic prose writers have ἀλλ᾽ οὐ or καὶ οὐ. Thus, ἔνθ᾽ ἄλλοις μὲν πᾶσιν ἐήνδανεν, οὐδέ ποθ᾽ Ἥρῃ οὐδὲ Ποσειδάωνι *then it was pleasing to all the others, but not to Hera or to Poseidon* Ω 25, ἐμαῖσι οὐδὲ σαῖσι δυσβουλίαις *by my folly but not by thine* S. Ant. 1269 (cp. the *negative* form οὐκ ἐμὸν τόδ' ἀλλὰ σόν *this is not my part, but thine* S. El. 1470). Cp. σοῦ τάδε κινδυνεύεις, ἀλλ' οὐκ ἐμοῦ ἀκηκοέναι *you probably heard this from yourself and not from me* P. Alc. 113 c.

2935. οὐδέ may stand in an apodosis corresponding to apodotic δέ (2837). Cp. S. O. C. 590.

2936. οὐδέ may negative a preceding word also; as αἱ Φοίνισσαι νῆες οὐδὲ ὁ Τισσαφέρνης . . . ἧκον *the Phoenician ships had not arrived nor had Tissaphernes* T. 8. 99. Cp. 2943. In such cases we usually find another negative, which goes with the verb; as ἁπλοῦν μὲν οὐδὲ δίκαιον οὐδὲν ἂν εἰπεῖν ἔχοι *he could say nothing straightforward nor just* D. 22. 4.

οὐδέ (μηδέ) *with other Negatives*

2937. **οὐδὲ . . . οὐδέ** commonly means *not even . . . nor yet* (or *no, nor*), the first οὐδέ being adverbial, the second conjunctive. οὐδὲ . . . οὐδέ is not correlative, like οὔτε . . . οὔτε, and hence never means *neither . . . nor*. Thus, οὐδὲ ἥλιον οὐδὲ σελήνην ἄρα νομίζω θεοὺς εἶναι; *do I then hold that not even the sun nor yet the moon are gods?* P. A. 26 c, σύ γε οὐδὲ ὁρῶν γιγνώσκεις οὐδὲ ἀκούων μέμνησαι *you do not even understand though you see, nor yet do you remember though you hear* X. A. 3. 1. 27. οὐδὲ . . . οὐδέ both copulative (*and not . . nor yet*) in X. C. 3. 3. 50. **οὐδὲ . . . οὐδὲ . . . δέ** is the negative of καὶ . . . καὶ . . . δέ in X. A. 1. 8. 20.

a. So in both members of comparative sentences (cp. καί 2885); as ὥσπερ οὐδὲ γεωργοῦ ἀργοῦ οὐδὲν ὄφελος, οὕτως οὐδὲ στρατηγοῦ ἀργοῦντος οὐδὲν ὄφελος *as there is no good in an idle tiller of the soil, so there is no good in an idle general* X. C. 1. 3. 18.

2938. **οὐδὲ γὰρ οὐδέ** (negative of καὶ γὰρ καί); as οὐδὲ γὰρ οὐδὲ τοῦτο ἐψεύσατο *for neither did he deceive me even in this* X. C. 7. 2. 20. Here the first οὐδέ negatives the whole sentence, the second οὐδέ negatives τοῦτο.

2939. **οὐ . . . οὐδέ**: οὐδέ *not even* as well as *nor* (2933) may resume a preceding οὐ. Thus, ὕβριν γὰρ οὐ στέργουσιν οὐδὲ δαίμονες lit. *not even the gods do not love insolence* S. Tr. 280, οὐ μέντοι ἔφη νομίζειν οὐδ' εἰ παμπόνηρος ἦν Δέξιππος βίᾳ χρῆναι πάσχειν αὐτόν *he said however that he did not think that, even if Dexippus was a downright rascal, he ought to suffer by an act of violence* X. A. 6. 6. 25, οὐ δεῖ δὴ τοιοῦτον . . . καιρὸν ἀφεῖναι οὐδὲ παθεῖν ταὐτὸν ὅπερ . . . πεπόνθατε *we must not let such an opportunity go by nor suffer the same as you have suffered* D. 1. 8.

οὐ μέντοι οὐδέ *not by any means however*. On **οὐ μὴν οὐδέ** see 2768.

2940. **οὐδὲ . . . οὐ**: οὐδέ may be resumed by οὐ; as οὐδέ γε ὁ ἰδίᾳ πονηρὸς οὐκ ἂν γένοιτο δημοσίᾳ χρηστός *nor can the man who is bad in his private life prove himself good in a public capacity* Aes. 3. 78.

2941. **οὐδὲ . . . οὔτε** is rare (P. Charm. 171 b).

οὔτε (μήτε)

2942. **οὔτε (μήτε)** is usually repeated: **οὔτε . . . οὔτε (μήτε . . . μήτε)** *neither . . . nor* (*nec . . . nec*). οὔτε . . . οὔτε is the negative of τὲ . . . τέ, and unites single words or clauses.

οὔτε ἔστιν οὔτε ποτὲ ἔσται *neither is nor ever shall be* P. Phae. 241 c, οὔτε Χειρίσοφος ἧκεν οὔτε πλοῖα ἱκανὰ ἦν οὔτε τὰ ἐπιτήδεια ἦν λαμβάνειν ἔτι *neither had Chirisophus come nor were there enough boats nor was it possible any longer to secure provisions* X. A. 5. 3. 1.

After a negative clause: οὐκ ἔπειθεν οὔτε τοὺς στρατηγοὺς οὔτε τοὺς στρατιώτᾱς *he could not persuade either the generals or the soldiers* T. 4. 4.

a. **οὔτε . . . μήτε** is found when each negative is determined by a different construction, as ἀναιδὴς οὔτ' εἰμὶ μήτε γενοίμην *neither am I nor may I become shameless* D. 8. 68.

b. When οὔτε . . . οὔτε stands between οὐδὲ . . . οὐδέ the members thus correlated are subordinate to those expressed by οὐδὲ . . . οὐδέ. Cp. Aes. 1. 19.

2943. Sometimes the first οὔτε is omitted in poetry: νόσοι δ' οὔτε γῆρας *disease nor old age* Pindar, Pyth. 10. 41, ἑκόντα μήτ' ἄκοντα *willingly nor unwillingly* S. Ph. 771. Cp. "my five wits nor my five senses" (Shakesp.).

2944. For the first οὔτε the poets sometimes have οὐ, as οὐ νιφετὸς οὔτ' ἂρ χειμών *not snow nor storm* δ 566.

2945. **οὔτε . . . τέ** *on the one hand not . . . but, not only not . . . but* (cp. *neque . . . et*). The τέ clause often denotes the contrary of that set forth in the οὔτε clause (*so far from*). Thus, οὔτε διενοήθην πώποτε ἀποστερῆσαι ἀποδώσω τε *so far from ever thinking to deprive* them of their pay *I will give* it to them X. A. 7. 7. 48, ὤμοσαν . . . μήτε προδώσειν ἀλλήλους σύμμαχοί τε ἔσεσθαι *they swore that they would not betray one another and that they would be allies* 2. 2. 8. So **οὔτε . . . οὔτε . . . τέ. τὲ . . . οὔτε** is not used.

a. Sometimes the negative may be added in the τέ clause: οὔτε ἐκεῖνος ἔτι κατενόησε τό τε μαντεῖον οὐκ ἐδήλου *neither did he stop to consider and the oracle would not make it plain* T. 1. 126.

2946. **οὔτε . . . τε οὐ** S. Ant. 763. **οὔτε . . . τε . . . οὔτε** E. H. F. 1341.

2947. **οὔτε . . . δέ** is used when the second clause is opposed to the first; as οὔτε πλοῖά ἐστιν οἷς ἀποπλευσόμεθα, μένουσι δὲ αὐτοῦ οὐδὲ μιᾶς ἡμέρᾱς ἔστι τὰ ἐπιτήδεια *we have no vessels by which we can sail away; on the other hand, if we stay here, we haven't provisions even for a single day* X. A. 6. 3. 16. Cp. E. Supp. 223, P. R. 388 e, 389 a.

2948. **οὔτε . . . οὐ** is rare in prose; as οὔτε νιφετός, οὐκ ὄμβρος *neither rain nor snow* Hdt. 8. 98. Cp. S. Ant. 249. **οὔτε . . . οὐ . . . οὔτε** A. Pr. 479. **οὐ . . . οὔτε** is generally changed to οὐ . . . οὐδέ in Attic prose.

2949. **οὔτε . . . οὐδέ** corresponds to the sequence of τὲ . . . δέ in affirmative clauses. The emphatic οὐδέ here adds a new negative idea as after any other preceding negative; and is most common after οὔτε . . . οὔτε: *neither . . . nor . . . no, nor yet* (*nor . . . either*). οὐδέ is often followed by an emphasizing particle, as αὖ, γέ, μήν. Thus, οὔτε πόλις οὔτε πολῑτείᾱ οὐδέ γ' ἀνήρ *neither a State nor a constitution nor yet an individual* P. R. 499 b, μήτε παιδείᾱ . . . μήτε δικαστήρια μήτε νόμοι μηδὲ ἀνάγκη μηδεμία *neither education nor courts of justice nor laws, no nor yet restraint* P. Pr. 327 d.

2950. A subordinate clause with οὐδέ may come between οὔτε . . . οὔτε. Thus, οὔτε γὰρ ὡς ὀφείλοντά με κατέλειπεν ὁ πατὴρ . . . ἀπέφηνεν οὐδὲ . . . παρέσχηται μάρτυρας οὔτ' αὖ τὸν ἀριθμὸν . . . ἐπανέφερεν *for neither did he show that my father left me in debt, nor yet has he adduced witnesses, nor did he put into the account the sum* D. 27. 49.

οὐκοῦν, οὔκουν

2951. οὐκοῦν interrogative: *not therefore? not then?* (*nonne, igitur? nonne ergo?*). Here the stress lies on the inferential οὖν and an affirmative answer is expected as a matter of course. οὐκοῦν stands at the beginning of its clause.

οὐκοῦν . . . εὖ σοι δοκοῦσι βουλεύεσθαι; πρός γε ἃ ὁρῶσι *do you not then think that they lay their plans well? Yes, with regard to what they see* X. C. 7. 1. 8.

a. When a negative answer is expected we have οὐκοῦν οὐ (P. Phil. 43 d).

b. οὐκοῦν and οὖν stand in parallel questions in X. A. 1. 6. 7–8.

c. Some scholars write οὔκουν or οὐκ οὖν for οὐκοῦν interrogative (and inferential).

2952. οὐκοῦν inferential: *then, well then, therefore, accordingly* (*ergo, igitur*). Inferential οὐκοῦν was developed, probably in colloquial speech, from the interrogative use, the speaker anticipating the affirmative answer to his question and emphasizing only the inference. From the negative question all that was left was an expression of his own opinion on the part of the speaker. οὐκοῦν has become so completely equivalent to οὖν that a negative has to be added if one is required.

οὐκοῦν, ὅταν δὴ μὴ σθένω, πεπαύσομαι *well then, when my strength fails, I shall cease* S. Ant. 91, ἢ . . . τοὺς ἀμύνεσθαι κελεύοντας πόλεμον ποιεῖν φήσομεν; οὐκοῦν ὑπόλοιπον δουλεύειν *or shall we say that those who bid us defend ourselves make war? Then it is left for us to be slaves* D. 8. 59. οὐκοῦν is used even with imperatives; as οὐκοῦν . . . ἱκανῶς ἐχέτω *accordingly let it suffice* P. Phae. 274 b.

a. Editors often differ whether, in certain cases, οὐκοῦν is interrogative or inferential.

2953. οὔκουν *not then, therefore not, so not, at any rate . . . not, surely not* (*non igitur, non ergo*). Here οὐ is strongly emphasized, and οὖν is either confirmative or inferential. οὔκουν is usually placed at the beginning of its clause.

a. In emphatic negative answers; as οὔκουν ἔμοιγε δοκεῖ *certainly not, in my opinion at least* X. O. 1. 9.

b. In continuous discourse (P. L. 807 a).

c. οὔκουν . . . γε returns a negative answer with qualified acquiescence in a preceding statement. Thus, τούτων ἄρα Ζεύς ἐστιν ἀσθενέστερος; οὔκουν ἂν ἐκφύγοι γε τὴν πεπρωμένην *is Zeus then weaker than these? Fate at least he surely cannot escape* A. Pr. 517.

d. In impatient or excited questions (*non? non igitur?*). Thus, οὔκουν ἐρεῖς ποτ', εἶτ' ἀπαλλαχθεὶς ἄπει; *wilt thou not speak and so depart and be gone?* S. Ant. 244.

2954. **οὐκ (μὴ) οὖν** is to be distinguished from οὐκοῦν or οὔκουν. Thus, ὁπότε καὶ πείρᾳ του σφαλεῖεν, οὐκ οὖν καὶ τὴν πόλιν γε τῆς σφετέρᾱς ἀρετῆς ἀξιοῦντες στερίσκειν *whenever they were foiled in any attempt they did not for this reason think it right to deprive their city of their valour* T. 2. 43 (μὴ οὖν 8. 91).

a. Hdt. has **οὐκ ὦν** (sometimes written οὔκων) to emphasize an idea opposed to what goes before (*non tamen*). Thus, ταῦτα λέγοντες τοὺς Κροτωνιήτᾱς οὐκ ὦν ἔπειθον *by these words they did not however persuade the men of Croton* 3. 137.

οὖν

2955. **οὖν** (Ionic, Lesbic, Doric ὦν), a postpositive particle, is either confirmatory or inferential. οὖν points to something already mentioned or known or to the present situation.

2956. Confirmatory οὖν *in fact, at all events, in truth* belongs properly to the entire clause, but usually, for purposes of emphasis, attaches itself to some other particle, to a relative pronoun, or at times to other words (P. A. 22 b). On γοῦν, see 2830; on μὲν οὖν, 2901; on τοιγαροῦν, 2987. In some of its combinations with other particles οὖν may be inferential or transitional.

2957. **ἀλλ' οὖν** or **ἀλλ' οὖν . . . γε** (stronger than δ' οὖν) *well, at all events; well, certainly, for that matter*; as ἀλλ' οὖν πονηροί γε φαινόμενοι *well, at all events they look like sorry fellows, that they are* X. C. 1. 4. 19, ἀλλ' οὖν τοσοῦτόν γ' ἴσθι *well, at any rate you know this at least* S. Ph. 1305. ἀλλ' οὖν may stand in the apodosis to an hypothetical proposition (P. Ph. 91 b).

2958. **γὰρ οὖν** (and **καὶ γὰρ οὖν**) *for in fact (indeed, in any case)*; as εὖ γὰρ οὖν λέγεις *for indeed thou sayest well* S. Ant. 1255, ὀνήσεσθε ἀκούοντες· μέλλω γὰρ οὖν ἄττα ὑμῖν ἐρεῖν καὶ ἄλλα *you will profit by listening; for I am certainly going to tell you some other things* P. A. 30 c.

Also to mark a consequence (X. A. 1. 9. 11), and in replies, as οὐ γὰρ οὖν P. Phae. 277 e, and also when the speaker repeats an important word of his interlocutor, as φημὶ γὰρ οὖν P. G. 466 e.

2959. **δ' οὖν** *but certainly, at all events, anyhow, be that as it may* with or without μέν in the preceding clause. Here οὖν shows that an unquestionable fact is to be set forth in its own clause; while the adversative δέ marks opposition to what has preceded and implies that the foregoing statement is uncertain and liable to dispute: 'be that true or not, *at any rate* what follows is certainly true.' δ' οὖν is used (**a**) to set aside conjecture, surmise, or hearsay; (**b**) to resume the main argument after long digression, and to cut short further discussion and come to the point; (**c**), with imperatives, to denote assent marked by unwillingness, impatience, or indifference. Thus, (**a**) εἰ μὲν δὴ δίκαια ποιήσω, οὐκ οἶδα· αἱρήσομαι δ' οὖν ὑμᾶς *whether I shall do what is right (or not), I do not know; be that as it may, I will choose you* X. A. 1. 3. 5, καὶ ἐλέγετο Κύρῳ δοῦναι πολλὰ χρήματα. τῇ δ' οὖν στρατιᾷ τότε ἀπέδωκε Κῦρος μισθὸν τεττάρων μηνῶν *and she is said to have given Cyrus a large sum; at any rate Cyrus then gave the army four months' pay* 1. 2. 12; (b) cp. T. 1. 3, 6. 15, 8. 81. Resumptive δ' οὖν may also set aside doubtful statements. (c) σὺ δ' οὖν λέγε, εἴ σοι τῷ λόγῳ τις ἡδονή *well speak on then, if thou hast delight in speaking* S. El. 891, ἔστω δ' οὖν ὅπως ὑμῖν φίλον *however, be it as you wish* S. O. C. 1205.

εἰ δ' οὖν = *but if indeed, but if in point of fact*; as εἰ δ' οὖν τι κἀκτρέποιτο τοῦ πρόσθεν λόγου *but if he should deviate at all from his former statement* S. O. T. 851.

2960. **δὴ οὖν** *certainly then*; cp. **οὖν δή**. Thus, τί δὴ οὖν; or τί οὖν δή; *well then pray?* πῶς δὴ οὖν; *how then pray?* **οὖν δῆτα** *really then.*

2961. **εἴτε οὖν, οὔτε οὖν**: in alternative clauses οὖν (*indeed*) is added to one or both clauses as emphasis may be desired: **εἴτε οὖν . . . εἴτε** *whether indeed . . . or*, **εἴτε . . . εἴτε οὖν** *whether . . . or indeed*, or **εἴτε οὖν . . . εἴτε οὖν** *whether indeed . . . or indeed.* So also in exclusive clauses: **οὔτε (μήτε) . . . οὔτε (μήτε) οὖν** *neither . . . nor yet*, **οὔτε (μήτε) οὖν . . . οὔτε (μήτε)** *neither indeed . . . nor.*

2962. οὖν often follows interrogative pronouns and adverbs (in dialogue); as **τίς οὖν**; *who pray?* **τί οὖν**, generally with the aorist, in impatient questions asks why that which is desired has not been done (2197 c).

2963. οὖν affixed to a relative pronoun has a generalizing force and makes it indefinite (339 e). Such indefinite relative pronouns are construed like the indefinite τὶς or demonstratives; and do not introduce relative clauses (unlike *whosoever*, etc., which are both indefinite and relative).

So with adverbs (346 c), as ὁπωσοῦν *in any way, no matter how* (= *utique* not = *utcunque*). Thus, οὐδ' ὁπωσοῦν *not even in the slightest degree.*

a. Simply placed *after* relatives οὖν has a strengthening force; as ὥσπερ οὖν *as in fact* (often in parentheses), οἷός περ οὖν *just as in fact.*

2964. **Inferential οὖν** *therefore, accordingly* (*igitur, ergo*), usually classed as a conjunction, signifies that something *follows* from what precedes. Inferential οὖν marks a transition to a new thought and continues a narrative (often after ἐπεί, ἐπειδή, ὅτε), resumes an interrupted narration (T. 3. 42, X. C. 3. 3. 9), and in general states a conclusion or inference. It stands alone or in conjunction with other particles. Thus, ἀναρχίᾳ ἂν καὶ ἀταξίᾳ ἐνόμιζον ἡμᾶς ἀπολέσθαι. δεῖ οὖν πολὺ μὲν τοὺς ἄρχοντας ἐπιμελεστέρους γενέσθαι τοὺς νῦν τῶν πρόσθεν *they were of the opinion that we would be overcome through our lack of leaders and discipline. It is imperative therefore that the leaders we have now should be much more watchful than those we had before* X. A. 3. 2. 29.

a. The inferential and transitional use is derived from the confirmative meaning, and is scarcely marked until Herodotus and the Attic poets. Cp. μὲν οὖν. ἐπεὶ οὖν in Hom. is sometimes used in transitions.

πέρ

2965. **πέρ** (postpositive and enclitic) *very, just, even.* Cp. Epic πέρι *very much*, and περί in composition. In Attic prose πέρ is common only with relatives (338 c) and conjunctions.

ὅσπερ the very one who (i.e. *none other*), *οἷός περ just such*, *ἔνθα περ just where*, *ὥσπερ just as, in the very way in which*, (sometimes not very different from ὡς, to which it is related as ὅσπερ to ὅς), *εἴπερ if really*. καίπερ (Hom. καὶ . . . περ) *however much, though*, Epic *ἠΰτε περ just as*.

a. After other words especially in Epic and Lyric and in Aeschylus; as *μένει τὸ θεῖον δουλίᾳ περ ἐν φρενί the divine power remains in the mind though it be enslaved* A. Ag. 1084, *μάχετ', ἀχνύμενός περ ἑταίρου he fought, (though) sore grieving for his comrade* P 459, *ὀψέ περ howbeit late* Pind. Nem. 3. 80.

πλήν

2966. **πλήν** an adverb, is used (*a*) as a preposition with the genitive (1700) meaning *except, save,* when that which is excepted is a single substantival idea; (*b*) as a conjunction, *except, except that, save that, unless, only, but* (often almost = ἀλλά).

ἀφειστήκεσαν . . . πᾶσαι πλὴν Μιλήτου *all* the Ionic cities *had revolted except Miletus* X. A. 1. 1. 6; οὐδεὶς ἀπῄει πρὸς βασιλέα, πλὴν Ὀρόντᾱς ἐπεχείρησε *no one went off to the king save that Orontas made the attempt* 1. 9. 29, πλὴν ἓν μόνον δέδοικα *but there is one thing and only one that I fear* Ar. Plut. 199. A substantive-equivalent may follow πλήν, not in the genitive, but in the case required by the verb of the sentence, as συνῆλθον πάντες πλὴν οἱ Νέωνος *all assembled except the men under Neon* X. A. 7. 3. 2.

a. **πλὴν οὐ** *only not, except* (2753); **πλὴν ἤ** *except*, as οὐ γὰρ ἄλλῳ γ' ὑπακούσαιμεν . . . πλὴν ἢ Προδίκῳ *we would not listen to any one (else) except Prodicus* Ar. Nub. 361; **πλὴν ὅτι** *except that;* **πλὴν εἰ** *except if*, cp. εἰ μή (*nisi si*), after a negative πλὴν εἰ μή; often with the verb omitted, as οὐδεὶς οἶδεν . . . πλὴν εἴ τις ἄρ' ὄρνις *no one knows except perhaps some bird* Ar. Av. 601.

b. πλήν may be followed by the infinitive, as τί σοι πέπρᾱκται πρᾶγμα πλὴν τεύχειν κακά; *what hast thou accomplished save to work mischief?* A. Eum. 125.

τέ

2967. **τέ** *and* (postpositive, and enclitic as *-que*) is generally used with a correlative conjunction.

2968. τέ alone sometimes in prose links whole clauses or sentences which serve to explain, amplify, supplement, or to denote a consequence of, what precedes (*and thus, and therefore, and as a result*). Thus, ὁ δ' ἐχαλέπαινεν . . ., ἐκέλευσέ τ' αὐτὸν ἐκ τοῦ μέσου ἐξίστασθαι *but he was angry and (therefore) ordered him to get out of the way* X. A. 1. 5. 14. Cp. 2978.

a. This use of τέ (*τέ consequential*) is quite common in Herodotus and Thucydides, rather rare in Xenophon, and infrequent in other prose writers. It occurs also in poetry.

N. — In poetry τέ alone (cp. *-que*) often connects single parallel nouns and pronouns so that the two connected ideas form a whole; as σκῆπτρον τῑμάς τε *sceptre and prerogatives* A. Pr. 171. In prose, participles and infinitives are occasionally linked by τέ; as καθαρωτέρᾱ οὖσα πρεπόντως τε μᾶλλον ἠμφιεσμένη *being fairer and dressed more becomingly* X. O. 10. 12.

2969. *τέ* (or *καί*) meaning *both* may be followed by asyndeton (S. Ant. 296).

2970. Homer often, and Herodotus sometimes, adds *τέ* to relative pronouns and conjunctions introducing subordinate clauses, which are usually postpositive. So after ὅς, ὅσος, οἷος, ὡς, ὅτε, ἐπεί, ἔνθα, ὅθι, etc. Thus, φίληθεν ἐκ Διός, ὅς τε θεοῖσι . . . ἀνάσσει *they were loved by Zeus, who rules over the gods* B 669. This untranslatable *τέ* is probably connective (not indefinite), and belongs to the whole clause. It has the effect of showing that its clause corresponds in some way to the preceding clause. ὅς τε is found in lyric poetry and in the lyric parts of tragedy (rarely in dialogue parts). ὥστε, οἷός τε became common.

2971. This connective force is also seen when *τέ* stands in the principal clause, sometimes both in the principal and in the subordinate clause, *e.g.* ὅς κε θεοῖς ἐπιπείθηται, μάλα τ' ἔκλυον αὐτοῦ *whosoever obeys the gods, him especially they hear* A 218, ὅππῃ τ' ἰθύσῃ, τῇ τ' εἴκουσι στίχες ἀνδρῶν *wheresoever he rushes, there the ranks of men give way* M 48.

2972. Homer has *τέ* after the coördinating conjunctions *καί, δέ, οὐδέ, ἀλλά, ἤ*; after ἦ, μέν, πέρ, γάρ, and before ἄρα in questions.

2973. **τὲ . . . τέ** usually serves to connect clauses, less frequently single words. In English *and* often suffices, but *as . . . so* is often in place. *τὲ . . . τέ* is more common in poetry than in prose, but in prose more common than *τέ* standing alone. Thus, πατὴρ ἀνδρῶν τε θεῶν τε *father of men and gods* A 544, ἐμοί τε γὰρ πολέμιοι Ἀσσύριοι, σοί τε νῦν ἐχθίονές εἰσιν ἢ ἐμοί *for the Assyrians are enemies to me, and they are now more hostile to you than to me* X. C. 4. 5. 23, περὶ ὧν εἰδέναι τε κάλλιστον μὴ εἰδέναι τε αἴσχιστον *knowledge of which is most excellent and ignorance most disgraceful* P. G. 472 c.

a. One clause may be negative, the other affirmative (T. 2. 22); but we usually have *οὔτε* instead of *τὲ οὐ*.

2974. **τὲ καί** or **τὲ . . . καί** often serves to unite complements, both similars and opposites. *τὲ . . . καί* is not used when one clause is subordinate to another. The two words or clauses thus united may show a contrast, or the second may be stronger than the first. *τέ* is commonly separated from *καί* by one or more words. *τὲ . . . καί* is weaker than *καὶ . . . καί*, and will not easily bear the translation *both . . . and*. It is rare in colloquial Attic. Thus, ἄρχειν τε καὶ ἄρχεσθαι *to rule and be ruled* X. A. 1. 9. 4, κάλλιστόν τε καὶ ἄριστον *fairest and best* 2. 1. 9, τό τ' ἄρχειν καὶ τὸ δουλεύειν *to rule and to be a slave* A. Pr. 927, βίᾳ τε κοὐχ ἑκών *by force and not willingly* S. O. C. 935, γυμνάσαι . . . ἑαυτόν τε καὶ τοὺς ἵππους *to exercise himself and his horses* X. A. 1. 2. 7. Clauses dissimilar in form may be linked by *τὲ . . . καί*; as ἀπεκρίνατο διὰ βραχέων τε καὶ αὐτὰ τὰ ἐρωτώμενα *he answered briefly and only the questions put to him* P. Pr. 336 a.

2975. *τὲ . . . καί* is often used of actions coincident in time, or of actions standing in a causal relation to each other; as ἡμέρᾱ τε σχεδὸν ὑπέφαινε καὶ εἰς τὸ μέσον ἧκον οἱ ἄρχοντες *day was just breaking and (= when) the officers came into the centre* of the camp X. A. 3. 3. 1 (temporal parataxis; cp. 2169).

2976. *τὲ . . . καί* is sometimes used of alternatives (for *εἴτε . . . εἴτε*). Thus, θεοῦ τε γὰρ θέλοντος . . . καὶ μὴ θέλοντος *whether God wills or not* A. Sept. 427. Here *καὶ . . . καί* is more common (2877).

2977. We find **τὲ . . . καὶ . . . τέ, τὲ . . . καὶ . . . τὲ . . . τέ . . . (τέ), τὲ . . . τὲ . . . καί, τὲ . . . τὲ . . . καὶ . . . τέ, τὲ . . . καὶ . . . καὶ . . . τέ.** But in prose *τέ* before and after *καί* is rare.

2978. When *τέ* follows *τὲ . . . καί*, *τέ* does not point back to *καί*, but denotes an addition to the preceding member (*and besides*). Thus, *τείχη τε περιελόντες καὶ ναῦς παραδόντες φόρον τε ταξάμενοι both destroying their walls and surrendering their ships and besides assessing tribute on themselves* T. 1. 108. Cp. 2968.

2979. **καί τε** is Epic; elsewhere the *καί* of *καὶ . . . τε* belongs to the whole clause (A. Ch. 252).

2980. **ἄλλως τε καί** *both in other ways and especially*, *on other grounds and particularly*, or simply *especially*. This combination usually stands before conditional clauses (or clauses with a conditional participle), causal, and temporal clauses. Thus, *χαλεπὸν οἶμαι διαβαίνειν ἄλλως τε καὶ πολεμίων πολλῶν ἔμπροσθεν ὄντων I think it hard to cross, especially when the enemy faces us in full force* X. A. 5. 6. 9, *πάντων . . . ἀποστερεῖσθαι λυπηρόν ἐστι . . ., ἄλλως τε κἂν ὑπ' ἐχθροῦ τῳ τοῦτο συμβαίνῃ it is grievous to be deprived of anything, especially if this happens to any one at the hands of a personal enemy* D. 18. 5. Cp. *τά τ' ἄλλα ἐτίμησε καὶ μυρίους ἔδωκε δαρεικούς he both honoured me in other ways and gave me ten thousand darics* X. A. 1. 3. 3.

2981. **τὲ . . . δέ** is used when a writer begins as if he were going simply to *add* the second member (*both . . . and*), but instead *contrasts* it with the first. This combination of copulative and adversative particles is often rendered less harsh by the form of the *δέ* clause and by other reasons. **(a)** The *δέ* clause contains a *καί*; as *ἅμα* (*ἔπειτα, ἔτι, πολλαχοῦ, ὡσαύτως*) *δὲ καί*; *e.g. ἔν τε τῇ τῶν ἐπῶν ποιήσει πολλαχοῦ δὲ καὶ ἄλλοθι*, lit. *both in the construction of epic poetry but also in many other cases* P. R. 394 c. **(b)** The second clause contains a formula with *δέ* but not with *καί*; as *ἔτι δέ, τί δέ, τὸ δὲ κεφάλαιον, μετὰ δὲ ταῦτα.* Thus, *πρότερόν τε . . . νῦν δέ* (*both*) *formerly . . . but now* X. H. 7. 1. 24. Cp. P. L. 664 b, 947 a, 967 d. **(c)** After a considerable interval occasioned by the extension of the *τέ* clause, it is natural to resume with *δέ*. So T. 6. 83. 1, X. A. 7. 8. 11, X. C. 2. 1. 22, L. 2. 17.

2982. Rare combinations are, *e.g.:*

ἤ . . . τέ instead of *ἤ . . . ἤ*. Thus, *ἠ παῖδες νεαροὶ χῆραί τε γυναῖκες either young children and* (= *or*) *widowed women* B 289. **τὲ . . . ἤ** is often emended in X. O. 20. 12, P. Men. 95 b.

τὲ . . . οὐδέ (**μηδέ**) with *τέ* instead of *οὔτε* (*μήτε*); as E. I. T. 697, P. Pol. 271 e. *τέ* is not followed by *οὔτε* (*μήτε*).

2983. Position of τέ. — *τέ* usually follows the word with which the sentence or sentence-part to be connected is most concerned. Apart from many irregularities there are certain exceptions to this rule which are commonly observed.

a. *τέ* may come between two words which go closely together, as between article (preposition, attributive genitive) and its noun. Thus, *τό τε βαρβαρικὸν καὶ τὸ Ἑλληνικόν the barbarian and the Greek force* X. A. 1. 2. 1, *εἶμι πρός τε λουτρὰ καὶ λειμῶνας I will go to the bathing places and the meadows* S. Aj. 654 (for *πρὸς λουτρά τε*). But *ἡ πόλις τε καὶ ἡμεῖς οἱ νόμοι the State and we the laws* P. Cr. 53 a.

b. τέ connecting an entire clause stands as near as possible to the beginning. Cp. X. A. 1. 8. 3.

c. τέ may stand after a word or expression which, though common to two members of a clause, is placed either at the beginning (especially after a preposition) or in the second member. Thus, ἅ τε δεῖ φίλια καὶ (ἃ δεῖ) πολέμια ἡμᾶς νομίζειν *what we must consider as belonging to our friends and what to our enemies* X. C. 5. 2. 21, ἔν τε τῷ θερμοτέρῳ καὶ ψῡχροτέρῳ *in the hotter and colder* P. Phil. 24 b, ἅπᾱσι φίλον ἄνδρα τε σοφώτατον *a man dear to all and most wise* Ar. Vesp. 1277.

d. The freer position of τέ is often due to the fact that several words are taken as forming a single notion. Thus, ἡ καλλίστη δὴ πολῑτείᾱ τε καὶ ὁ κάλλιστος ἀνήρ *the very noblest constitution and the noblest man* P. R. 562 a.

τοί

2984. **τοί** (postpositive and enclitic) *in truth, surely, doubtless, mark you, be assured, you (must) know,* was originally the dative of feeling (1486) of σύ.

a. This τοί (Sanskrit *tē*), found in all dialects, is to be distinguished from Doric τοί (= σοί) from τϝοι (Skt. *tvē*). τοί may thus occur in the same sentence with σοί; as τοιαῦτά τοί σοι . . . λέγω S. fr. 25.

2985. τοί is often used in statements of a general truth and in expressions of personal conviction (sometimes with a tone of hesitation); in remarks of a confidential nature; to introduce an explanation; and in general where the special attention of the person addressed is desired. τοί often gives an easy and familiar tone to a reply. Thus, τῶν τοι ματαίων ἀνδράσιν φρονημάτων ἡ γλῶσσ' ἀληθὴς γίγνεται κατήγορος *true it is that of men's vain conceits their tongue is the true accuser* A. Sept. 438, ἀεί τοι ὁ Κέβης λόγους τινὰς ἀνερευνᾷ *for Cebes, you know, is always investigating some speculation or other* P. Ph. 63 a.

a. τοί may emphasize particular words, as ἐγώ τοι, ἐμοί τοι, σέ τοι; and other words not pronouns.

2986. τοί is frequently used after other particles, as ἀλλά, γάρ, γέ, δή (and γέ τοι δή, cp. δή τοι . . . γε), ἐπεί *because*, μή, οὐ (οὔτοι). On ἤτοι, see 2858; on καίτοι, 2893; on μέντοι, 2917.

2987. The inferential conjunctions **τοιγάρ, τοιγαροῦν, τοιγάρτοι, τοίνυν** contain τοί, the locative of the demonstrative τό, which case had the meaning of τῷ (τῶ) *therefore, on this account, so* lit. *by that, therein.* (This τῷ is chiefly Epic, and stands at the beginning of the verse. Cp. τό *therefore* Γ 176, S. Ph. 142.)

τοιγάρ (prepositive; Ionic and poetic) *therefore, wherefore, so then, that is surely the reason why* (often to announce a purpose).

τοιγαροῦν, τοιγάρτοι (both prepositive) are more emphatic than τοιγάρ. The final syllable of τοιγάρτοι is the τοί of 2984.

τοίνυν (postpositive and post-Homeric; -νυν 2927) is transitional (*now then, further*) or inferential (*therefore, accordingly;* less emphatic than τοιγάρ). τοίνυν is common when a speaker refers to something present in his mind, when he continues or resumes what he has been saying, and when he passes to a new aspect of a subject. It is often found with imperatives (*σκόπει τοίνυν* P. Cr. 51 c).

ὧς, ὡς

2988. Demonstrative ὧς (also accented ὥς, ὣς) *thus, so* is originally an ablative from the demonstrative stem ὁ- (from σο-), from which come the article and ὅς *he* in καὶ ὅς, ἦ δ' ὅς (1113). For the -ς, see 341. Cp. also ὧ-δε *thus*.

So καὶ ὧς *even so, nevertheless*, οὐδ' (μηδ') ὧς *not even thus, in no wise*, ὡς αὔτως (ὡσαύτως) *in the same way, just so* (ablative of ὁ αὐτός). ὡς ἑτέρως (lit. *thus otherwise, in that other way*) *quite otherwise* and ὡς ἀληθῶς (lit. *thus truly*) *in very truth* also probably belong here.

a. In some cases it is uncertain whether ὡς is demonstrative or relative; *e.g.* ὡς in exclamatory clauses. Cp. 2998, 3001.

2989. Relative ὡς *as, how* is originally an ablative (*in which way*) from the relative stem ι̯ο-, whence come also ὅς, ἥ, ὅ. For the -ς, see 341. Relative ὡς has various uses as an adverb or a conjunction, all of which represent the primitive meaning.

Relative ὡς as an Adverb

2990. In comparative clauses, often correlated with οὕτως. Thus, πιστὸς ἦν, ὡς ὑμεῖς ἐπίστασθε *I was faithful, as you know* X. A. 3. 3. 2, ἐκέλευσε τοὺς Ἕλληνας, ὡς νόμος αὐτοῖς εἰς μάχην, οὕτω ταχθῆναι *he ordered the Greeks (thus) to be stationed as was their custom for battle* 1. 2. 15. Cp. 2462 ff. In similes and comparisons, 2481 ff.

2991. ὡς is rarely used for ἤ after comparatives; as μή μου προκήδου μᾶσσον ὡς ἐμοὶ γλυκύ *care not for me further than I wish* A. Pr. 629. Cp. 1071.

2992. In adverbial clauses ὡς is often used parenthetically; as ὡς ἐμοὶ δοκεῖ *as it seems to me*. Instead of ὡς δοκεῖ, ὡς ἔοικε the personal construction is often preferred; as ἀπέπλευσαν, ὡς μὲν τοῖς πλείστοις ἐδόκουν, φιλοτῑμηθέντες *they sailed away out of jealousy, as it seemed to most people* X. A. 1. 4. 7.

2993. ὡς **restrictive** *for* (cp. *ut*), involving the judgment of the observer, occurs often in elliptical phrases; as (Βρᾱσίδᾱς) ἦν οὐδὲ ἀδύνατος, ὡς Λακεδαιμόνιος, εἰπεῖν *Brasidas was, for a Lacedaemonian, not a bad speaker either* T. 4. 84, ταῦτα ἀκούσᾱς Ξέρξης ὡς ἐκ κακῶν ἐχάρη *on hearing this Xerxes rejoiced* as much as could be expected *considering his misfortunes* Hdt. 8. 101. On ὡς restrictive with the dative, cp. 1495 a, 1497; with the absolute infinitive, 2012.

2994. ὡς is often used to heighten a superlative (1086).

2995. With numerals and words indicating degree ὡς means *about, nearly, not far from*; as ὁπλῑ́τᾱς ἔχων ὡς πεντακοσίους *having about five hundred hoplites* X. A. 1. 2. 3, ὡς ἐπὶ πολύ *for the most part* P. R. 377 b (lit. *about over the great(er) part*).

2996. ὡς often indicates the thought or the assertion of the subject of the principal verb or of some other person prominent in the sentence. Here ὡς expresses a real intention or an avowed plea. So often with participles (2086); and also with the prepositions εἰς, ἐπί, πρός; as ἀπέπλεον . . . ἐκ τῆς Σικελίᾱς ὡς ἐς τᾱ̀ς Ἀθήνᾱς *they sailed away from Sicily as though bound for Athens* T. 6. 61.

2997. ὡς ἕκαστος means *each for himself;* as ἀπέπλευσαν ἐξ Ἑλλησπόντου ὡς ἕκαστοι (ἀπέπλευσαν) κατὰ πόλεις *they sailed away from the Hellespont each to his own State* T. 1. 89.

2998. ὡς *exclamatory* (2682) may be the relative adverb ὡς *how*, the relative clause originally being used in explanation of an exclamation. Exclamatory ὡς has also been explained as ὡς demonstrative (*so*).

2999. On ὡς in wishes, see 1815.

Relative ὡς *as a Conjunction*

3000. ὡς conjunctive is found in dependent clauses.

Declarative: *that*, like ὅτι. Cp. 2577 ff., 2614 ff.

Final: *that, in order that;* like ἵνα, but not used in standard Attic prose. Cp. 2193.

Object clauses after verbs of *effort: that*, like ὅπως; cp. 2209. Rarely after verbs of *fearing: that.* Cp. 2235.

Causal: *as, inasmuch as, since, seeing that*, like ὅτι, ἐπεί, etc. Cp. 2240.

Consecutive: *so that*, like ὥστε. Usually with the infinitive, sometimes with the indicative. Cp. 2260.

Temporal: *after*, like ἐπεί; sometimes *when, whenever.* Cp. 2383.

3001. ὡς is often found before sentences apparently independent, where it is sometimes explained as a conjunction with the verb suppressed. Thus, ὡς τῆσδ' ἑκοῦσα παιδὸς οὐ μεθήσομαι (*know*) *that of my own accord I will not relinquish my child* E. Hec. 400, ὡς δὴ σύ μοι τύραννος Ἀργείων ἔσει (*do you mean*) *that you forsooth shall be lord and master of Argives* A. Ag. 1633. Some scholars regard this ὡς as causal, others regard it as demonstrative, others as comparative.

ὧς *as, like*

3002. ὧς *as, like* (postpositive) in Hom., as ὄρνῑθες ὧς Γ 2, stands for ϝως, which is of uncertain origin.

ὡς *to*

3003. ὡς *to*, a preposition with persons (once in Hom., ρ 218) is obscure in origin.

SOME GRAMMATICAL AND RHETORICAL FIGURES

3004. **Anacolūthon** (ἀνακόλουθον *inconsequent*), or grammatical inconsistency, is inadvertent or purposed deviation in the structure of a sentence by which a construction started at the beginning is not followed out consistently Anacoluthon is sometimes real, sometimes only slight or apparent. It is natural to Greek by reason of the mobility and elasticity of that language; but in English it could not be tolerated to an equal extent because our tongue — a speech of few inflected forms — is much more rigid than Greek.

3005. Anacoluthon is, in general, caused either (a) by the choice of some form of expression more convenient or more effective than that for which the sentence was grammatically planned; at times, too, the disturbing influence is the insertion of a brief expression of an additional thought not foreseen at the start. Or (b) by the intrusion of some explanation requiring a parenthesis of such an extent that the connection is obscured or the continuation of the original structure made difficult. In this case the beginning may be repeated, or what has already been said may be summed up in a different grammatical form and sometimes with the addition of a resumptive particle, such as δή, οὖν *well then, then, as I was saying* (X. A. 1. 8. 13, 3. 1. 20, X. C. 3. 3. 9). So with δέ (T. 8. 29. 2).

3006. Anacoluthon usually produces the effect of naturalness and liveliness, sometimes of greater clearness (as after long parentheses), or of brevity, force, or concentration.

3007. Anacoluthon is either natural or artificial. Natural anacoluthon is seen in the loose and discursive style of Herodotus; in the closely packed sentences of Thucydides, who hurries from one thought to another with the least expenditure of words; and in the slovenliness of Andocides. Artificial or rhetorical anacoluthon is the result of a deliberate purpose to give to written language the vividness, naturalness, and unaffected freedom of the easy flow of conversation, and is best seen in the dialogues of Plato. Such anacoluthon is usually graceful and free from obscurity.

3008. There are very many forms of anacoluthon, *e.g.*

a. Many cases are due to the fact that a writer conforms his construction, not to the words which he has just used, but to another way in which the antecedent thought might have been expressed: the construction πρὸς τὸ νοούμενον (or σημαινόμενον) *according to what is thought.* Cp. 2148 and X. H. 2. 2. 3, S. O. T. 353, E. Hec. 970.

b. Some cases are due to changes in the subject, as T. 1. 18. 2.

c. Many cases occur in connection with the use of a participle (2147, 2148).

d. Coördinate clauses connected by τὲ . . . καί, καὶ . . . καί, οὔτε . . . οὔτε, ἢ . . . ἤ often show anacoluthon, especially when a finite verb takes the place of a participle. Cp. 2147 c, and T. 5. 61. 4, 6. 32. 3, 7. 47. 1–2.

e. The nominative "in suspense" may stand at the head of a sentence instead of another case required by the following construction. This involves a redundant pronoun. Thus, Πρόξενος δὲ καὶ Μένων, ἐπείπερ εἰσὶν ὑμέτεροι εὐεργέται . . . πέμψατε αὐτοὺς δεῦρο (for Πρόξενον καὶ Μένωνα . . . πέμψατε δεῦρο) X. A. 2. 5. 41. Cp. "The prince that feeds great natures, they will slay him:" Ben Jonson.

f. The accusative often stands absolutely when at the head of a sentence. Thus, ἀλλὰ μὴν καὶ τῑμάς γε . . ., τῶν μὲν μεθέξει καὶ γεύσεται ἑκών, ἃς ἂν ἡγῆται ἀμείνω αὐτὸν ποιήσειν, ἃς δ' . . . φεύξεται *but furthermore as regards honours, those he will partake of and be glad to taste which he thinks will make him a* *better man, but others he will shun* P. R. 591 e, Ἕλληνας τοὺς ἐν τῇ Ἀσίᾳ οἰκοῦντας οὐδέν πω σαφὲς λέγεται εἰ ἕπονται (for λέγουσιν εἰ ἕπονται or λέγεται ἕπεσθαι) *as to the Greeks who dwell in Asia there is as yet no certain intelligence whether they are to accompany* the expedition X. C. 2. 1. 5.

g. A main clause may take the construction of a parenthetical clause (T. 4. 93. 2). Here belongs the attraction into the relative clause of a verb that should have been principal. So after ὡς ἤκουσα, ὡς οἶμαι, ὡς λέγουσι, etc. Thus, τόδε γε μήν, ὡς οἶμαι, περὶ αὐτοῦ ἀναγκαιότατον εἶναι (for ἐστί) λέγειν *this indeed is, as I think, most necessary to state about it* P. Phil. 20 d. Often in Hdt., as ὡς δ' ἐγὼ ἤκουσα . . . εἶναι αὐτὸν Ἰδανθύρσου . . . πάτρων *but as I have heard he was the uncle of Idanthyrsus on the father's side* 4. 76. A construction may be introduced by ὅτι or ὡς and then pass to the infinitive, or the infinitive may precede and a finite verb follow (2628).

h. After a subordinate clause with parentheses the main clause sometimes follows in the form of an independent sentence (P. A. 28 c, cp. 36 a).

i. An infinitive may resume the idea set forth by the principal verb; as τοῦ δὲ θεοῦ τάττοντος, ὡς ἐγὼ ᾠήθην τε καὶ ὑπέλαβον, φιλοσοφοῦντά με δεῖν ζῆν κτλ. *whereas when God orders me, as I think and believe, to pass my life in the pursuit of wisdom,* etc. P. A. 28 e. Cp. X. H. 7. 4. 35.

j. Anacoluthon is sometimes due to the desire to maintain similarity of form between contrasted expressions; as τοὺς μὲν γὰρ ἱπποκενταύρους οἶμαι ἔγωγε πολλοῖς μὲν ἀπορεῖν τῶν ἀνθρώποις ηὑρημένων ἀγαθῶν ὅπως δεῖ χρῆσθαι, πολλοῖς δὲ τῶν ἵπποις πεφῡκότων ἡδέων πῶς αὐτῶν χρὴ ἀπολαύειν *for I think that the horse-centaurs were at a loss how to make use of many conveniences devised for men and how to enjoy many of the pleasures natural to horses* X. C. 4. 3. 19. Here πολλοῖς δέ is used as if it were to be governed by χρῆσθαι, instead of which αὐτῶν ἀπολαύειν is substituted.

3009. Anadiplōsis (ἀναδίπλωσις *doubling*) is the rhetorical repetition of one or several words. Cp. "The Isles of Greece, the Isles of Greece, where burning Sappho loved and sung:" Byron.

Θῆβαι δέ, Θῆβαι πόλις ἀστυγείτων, μεθ' ἡμέρᾱν μίαν ἐκ μέσης τῆς Ἑλλάδος ἀνήρπασται *Thebes, Thebes, a neighbouring city, in the course of one day has been extirpated from the midst of Greece* Aes. 3. 133.

3010. Anaphora (ἀναφορά *carrying back*) is the repetition, with emphasis, of the same word or phrase at the beginning of several successive clauses. This figure is also called *epanaphora* or *epanalepsis.* Cp. "Strike as I would Have struck those tyrants! Strike deep as my curse! Strike! and but once:" Byron.

οὗτοι γὰρ πολλοὺς μὲν τῶν πολῑτῶν εἰς τοὺς πολεμίους ἐξήλασαν, πολλοὺς δ' ἀδίκως ἀποκτείναντες ἀτάφους ἐποίησαν, πολλοὺς δ' ἐπιτίμους ὄντας ἀτίμους κατέστησαν *many of the citizens they drove out to the enemy; many they slew unjustly and left unburied; many who were in possession of their civic rights they deprived of them* L. 12. 21. Cp. D. 18. 48, 75, 121, 310.

3011. Anastrophe (ἀναστροφή *return*) is the use, at the beginning of one clause, of the same word that concluded the preceding clause.

Also called *epanastrophe*. Cp. "Has he a gust for blood? Blood shall fill his cup."

οὐ δήπου Κτησιφῶντα δύναται διώκειν δι' ἐμέ, ἐμὲ δ' εἴπερ ἐξελέγξειν ἐνόμιζεν, αὐτὸν οὐκ ἂν ἐγράψατο *for surely it cannot be that he is prosecuting Ctesiphon on my account, and yet would not have indicted me myself, if he had thought that he could convict me* D. 18. 13.

3012. Antistrophe (ἀντιστροφή *turning about*) is the repetition of the same word or phrase at the end of successive clauses.

ὅστις δ' ἐν τῷ πρώτῳ λόγῳ τὴν ψῆφον αἰτεῖ ὅρκον αἰτεῖ, νόμον αἰτεῖ, δημοκρατίᾱν αἰτεῖ *whoever in his first speech asks for your vote* as a favour, *asks the surrender of your oath, asks the surrender of the law, asks the surrender of the democratic constitution* Aes. 3. 198.

3013. Antithesis (ἀντίθεσις *opposition*) is the contrast of ideas expressed by words which are the opposite of, or are closely contrasted with, each other. Cp. "Wit is negative, analytical, destructive; Humor is creative:" Whipple.

δι' ὧν ἐκ χρηστῶν φαῦλα τὰ πράγματα τῆς πόλεως γέγονε, διὰ τούτων ἐλπίζετε τῶν αὐτῶν πράξεων ἐκ φαύλων αὐτὰ χρηστὰ γενήσεσθαι; *do you expect that the affairs of state will become prosperous instead of bad by the same measures by which they have become bad instead of prosperous?* D. 2. 26.

a. Antithesis is sometimes extended to a parallelism in sense effected (1) by the use of two words of opposite meaning in the expression of one idea, (2) by the opposition of ideas which are not specifically contrasted in words.

3014. Aporia (ἀπορίᾱ *doubt*) is an artifice by which a speaker feigns doubt as to where he shall begin or end or what he shall do or say, etc. Cp. "Then the steward said within himself, What shall I do?" St. Luke 16. 3.

ἀπορῶ τοῦ πρώτου μνησθῶ *I am uncertain what I shall recall first* D. 18. 129. When the doubt is between *two* courses it is often called *diaporēsis.*

3015. Aposiopēsis (ἀποσιώπησις *becoming silent*) is a form of ellipse by which, under the influence of passionate feeling or of modesty, a speaker comes to an abrupt halt. Examples 2352 d, D. 18. 3, 22, 195, S. O. T. 1289, Ar. Vesp. 1178. Cp. "Massachusetts and her people . . . hold him, and his love . . . and his principles, and his standard of truth in utter — what shall I say? — anything but respect:" Webster.

3016. Asyndeton (ἀσύνδετον *not bound together*) is the absence of conjunctions in a series of coördinate words or phrases. See 2165 ff.

a. Here is sometimes placed the omission of the verb after μή (μὴ σύ γε, μὴ γάρ, etc.); as μὴ τριβὰς ἔτι (ποιεῖσθε) *no more delays!* S. Ant. 577, τίς οὐχὶ κατέπτυσεν ἂν σοῦ; μὴ γὰρ (εἰπὲ) τῆς πόλεως γε, μηδ' ἐμοῦ *who would not have reviled* **you**? *Do not say the State, nor me* D. 18. 200. Cp. 946, 1599.

3017. Brachylogy (βραχυλογίᾱ *brevity of diction, abbreviated expression* or *construction*) is a concise form of expression by which an element is not repeated or is omitted when its repetition or use would make the thought or the grammatical construction complete. The suppressed element must be supplied from some corresponding word in the context, in which case it often appears with some change of form or construction; or it must be taken from the connection of the thought.

a. *Brachylogy* and *ellipse* cannot always be distinguished sharply. In ellipse the suppressed word is not to be supplied from a corresponding word in the context; and, in general, ellipse is less artificial and less dependent on the momentary and arbitrary will of the speaker or writer. Compendious Comparison (1501), Praegnans Constructio (3044), and Zeugma (3048) are forms of brachylogy.

3018. There are many forms of brachylogy; for example:

a. One verbal form must often be supplied from another; *e.g.* a passive from an active, an infinitive from a finite verb, a participle from an infinitive. Thus, τὴν τῶν πέλας δῃοῦν μᾶλλον ἢ τὴν ἑαυτῶν ὁρᾶν (δῃουμένην) *rather to ravage the territory of their neighbours than to see their own* (*being ravaged*) T. 2. 11, ταῦτα ἐγώ σοι οὐ πείθομαι . . ., οἶμαι δὲ οὐδὲ ἄλλον ἀνθρώπων οὐδένα (πείθεσθαί σοι) *of this I am not persuaded by you and I do not believe that any other human being is either* P. A. 25 e, οὔτε πάσχοντες κακὸν οὐδὲν οὔτε μέλλοντες (πάσχειν) *neither suffering, nor being likely* (*to suffer*), *any evil* I. 12. 103, ἀνεχώρησαν δὲ καὶ οἱ Ἀθηναῖοι . . ., ἐπειδὴ καὶ ἐκείνους εἶδον (ἀναχωρήσαντας) *and the Athenians too withdrew when they saw that they* (the Lacedaemonians) *had done so* T. 3. 16.

b. A verb must often be supplied from a coördinate or subordinate clause either preceding or following. Thus, ἔγειρε καὶ σὺ τήνδ᾽, ἐγὼ δὲ σέ *do you wake her, as I* (*wake*) *you* A. Eum. 140, ἐὰν δὲ αὐτόχειρ μὲν μή (ᾖ), βουλεύσῃ δὲ θάνατόν τις ἄλλος ἑτέρῳ *if a person shall not kill with his own hand, but if some one shall suggest murder to another* P. L. 872 a; φίλους νομίζουσ᾽ οὕσπερ ἂν πόσις σέθεν (νομίζῃ) *regarding as friends even those whom thy husband* (*so regards*) E. Med. 1153. A verb is rarely supplied from the subordinate to the main construction.

c. In clauses with δεῖ, χρή etc.: ἵνα φαίνησθε ἀμύνοντες οἷς δεῖ (ἀμύνειν) *that you may seem to assist those you ought* (*to assist*) T. 3. 13. When a form of τυγχάνω stands in the subordinate clause; ἀπέπλευσαν ὡς ἕκαστοι ἔτυχον (ἀποπλέοντες) *they sailed away as each best could* T. 4. 25. In conditional clauses when the protasis indicates that the assertion made in the apodosis holds true of a person or a thing more than of any other person or thing (εἴπερ τις καὶ ἄλλος, εἴπερ που, εἴπερ ποτέ, ὥς τις καὶ ἄλλος, etc.); as συμφέρει δ᾽ ὑμῖν, εἴπερ τῳ καὶ ἄλλῳ, τὸ νῑκᾶν *victory is of advantage to you, if it* (*is of advantage*) *to any* X. C. 3. 3. 42. Hence εἴ τις (που, ποθεν) is almost = τὶς, etc. (T. 7. 21. 5).

d. Compound verbs (especially those compounded with μετά and ἐξ) are often so used that the force both of the compound and of the simple verb is requisite to the meaning. Thus, (οἱ Ἀθηναῖοι) μετέγνωσαν Κερκῡραίοις ξυμμαχίᾱν μὴ ποιήσασθαι *the Athenians changed their minds* and decided *not to make an alliance with the Corcyraeans* T. 1. 44.

e. A compound verb on its second occurrence often omits the preposition (rarely *vice versa*); as ἀπεργάζηται . . . εἰργάζετο P. Ph. 104 d. **Euripides is** fond of such collocations as ὑπάκουσον ἄκουσον Alc. 400. Cp. the difference in metrical value of repeated words in Shakespeare, as "These víolént desires have víolent ends."

N. — In καὶ ξυμμετίσχω καὶ φέρω τῆς αἰτίᾱς *I share and bear alike the guilt* (S. Ant. 537) φέρω, though capable of taking the partitive genitive, is influenced by ξυμμετίσχω and has the force of ξυμφέρω.

f. From a following verb of special meaning a verb of more general meaning, such as ποιεῖν, γίγνεσθαι, εἶναι, must be supplied with the phrases οὐδὲν ἄλλο ἤ, ἄλλο τι ἤ, τί ἄλλο ἤ. Examples in 946, 2652, 2778.

g. A verb of *saying* or *thinking* must often be supplied from a foregoing verb of *exhorting*, *commanding*, *announcing*, or from any other verb that implies *saying* or *thinking*. Thus, Κριτόβουλος καὶ Ἀπολλόδωρος κελεύουσί με τριᾱ́κοντα μνῶν τῑμήσασθαι, αὐτοὶ δὲ ἐγγυᾶσθαι *Critobulus and Apollodorus urge me to set a penalty of thirty minae, and (say) that they themselves are sureties* P. A. 38 b.

h. When two verbs taking the same or different cases have an object in common, that object is expressed only once, and usually is dependent on the nearer verb. See 1634, 1635.

i. A substantive or a verb is often to be supplied from a substantive or a verb related in meaning: ναυμαχήσαντας μίαν (ναυμαχίᾱν) *having fought one (sea-fight)* Ar. Ran. 693, ἡ μὲν ἔπειτα εἰς ἅλα ἆλτο . . ., Ζεὺς δὲ ἑὸν πρὸς δῶμα (ἔβη) *she then sprang into the sea, but Zeus (went) to his abode* A 532.

j. The subject of a sentence is often taken from a preceding object or from some other preceding noun in an oblique case without a pronoun of reference to aid the transition. Thus, ἐξεφόβησαν μὲν τοὺς πολλοὺς οὐκ εἰδότας τὰ πρᾱσσόμενα, καὶ ἔφευγον (οἱ πολλοί) *they frightened away most* of the citizens, *who were in ignorance of the plot and began to fly* T. 8. 44. Cp. 943.

k. In general an object is frequently omitted when it can readily be supplied from the context. Thus, ἐγχεῖν (τὸν οἶνον) ἐκέλευε *he gave orders to pour in (the wine)* X. A. 4. 3. 13. An unemphatic pronoun in an oblique case is often omitted when it can be supplied from a preceding noun. Cp. 1214.

l. A dependent noun must often be supplied, in a different construction, from one coördinate clause to another. Thus, ὅρκους ἔλαβον καὶ ἔδοσαν παρὰ Φαρναβάζου *they received oaths from Pharnabazus and gave* him theirs X. H. 1. 3. 9. So in contrasts where one member is to be supplied from the other, as οὐκ ἐκεῖνος (ἐκείνην), ἀλλ' ἐκείνη κεῖνον ἐνθάδ' ἤγαγεν *he did not bring (her) here, but she brought him* E. Or. 742.

m. From a preceding word its opposite must often be supplied, especially an affirmative after a negative. Thus, ἀμελήσᾱς ὧνπερ οἱ πολλοί (ἐπιμελοῦνται) *neglecting the very things which most people (care for)* P. A. 36 b. This laxity of expression is especially frequent in the case of ἕκαστος, τίς, or πάντες, to be supplied after οὐδείς (μηδείς), as μηδεὶς τὴν ὑπερβολὴν θαυμάσῃ, ἀλλὰ μετ' εὐνοίᾱς ὃ λέγω θεωρησάτω *let no one wonder at the extravagance of my statement, but let (every one) consider kindly what I say* D. 18. 199. Cp. "No person held to service or labor in one state . . ., escaping into another, shall . . . be discharged from said service or labor, but shall be delivered up, etc.": U. S. Constitution.

n. The same word though placed only once may stand in two different constructions; as αἰνέω δὲ καὶ τόνδε (νόμον) . . . μήτε τῶν ἄλλων Περσέων μηδένα τῶν ἑωυτοῦ οἰκετέων . . . ἀνήκεστον πάθος ἔρδειν *and I approve also this custom that no one of the other Persians shall do irremediable hurt to any one of his own servants* Hdt. 1. 137. Here μηδένα is both subject and object of ἔρδειν.

o. An assertion may be made concerning an action or a thing when the absence of that action or thing is meant (*res pro rei defectu*). Thus, εἴ τ' ἄρ' ὅγ' εὐχωλῆς ἐπιμέμφεται *whether then he blames us on account of an (unfulfilled) vow* A 65, ἐν ᾗ καὶ περὶ χρημάτων καὶ περὶ ἀτῑμίᾱς ἄνθρωποι κινδῡνεύουσιν *on which* charge *men run the risk both of (loss of) money and civil degradation* D. 29. 16. So δύναμις *powerlessness*, φυλακή *neglect of the watch*, μελέτημα *lack of liberal exercise.*

3019. Catachrēsis (κατάχρησις *misuse of a word*) is the extension of the meaning of a word beyond its proper sphere; especially a violent metaphor. In English: "a palatable tone," "to take arms against a sea of troubles."

δαιμόνιος *extraordinary*, θαυμάσιος *decided, strange, capital*, ἀμηχάνως and ὑπερφυῶς *decidedly*, ὑποπτεύω *expect*, ναυστολεῖν χθόνα E. Med. 682. Such usages are less often occasioned by the poverty of the language than by the caprice of the writer.

3020. Chiasmus (χῑασμός *marking with diagonal lines like a* X) is the crosswise arrangement of contrasted pairs to give alternate stress. By this figure both the extremes and the means are correlated. Cp. "Sweet is the breath of morn, her rising sweet": Milton.

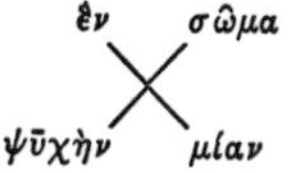

ἓν σῶμ' ἔχων καὶ ψῡχὴν μίαν *having one body and one soul* D. 19. 227.

So τοσοῦτον σὺ ἐμοῦ σοφώτερος εἶ τηλικούτου ὄντος τηλικόσδ' ὤν; *are you at your age so much wiser than I at mine?* P. A. 25 d, πᾶν μὲν ἔργον πᾶν δ' ἔπος λέγοντάς τε καὶ πράττοντας lit. *doing every deed and uttering every word* P. R. 494 e, δουλεύειν καὶ ἄρχεσθαι . . . ἄρχειν καὶ δεσπόζειν *to be a slave and be ruled . . . to rule and be a master* P. Ph. 80 a.

3021. Climax (κλῖμαξ *ladder*) is an arrangement of clauses in succession whereby the last important word of one is repeated as the first important word of the next, each clause in turn surpassing its predecessor in the importance of the thought. Cp. "But we glory in tribulations also: knowing that tribulation worketh patience . . . and experience, hope; and hope maketh not ashamed": Romans v. 3–5.

οὐκ εἶπον μὲν ταῦτα, οὐκ ἔγραψα δέ, οὐδ' ἔγραψα μέν, οὐκ ἐπρέσβευσα δέ, οὐδ' ἐπρέσβευσα μέν, οὐκ ἔπεισα δὲ Θηβαίους *I did not utter these words without proposing a motion; nor did I propose a motion without becoming ambassador; nor did I become ambassador without convincing the Thebans* D. 18. 179; cp. 4. 19. This figure is very rare in Greek.

3022. Ellipse (ἔλλειψις *leaving out, defect*) is the suppression of a word or of several words of minor importance to the logical expression of the thought, but necessary to the construction. Ellipse gives brevity, force, and liveliness; it is usually readily to be supplied, often unconscious, and appears especially in common phrases, constructions, and expressions of popular speech (such as ἐξ ὀνύχων λέοντα to judge *a lion from his claws*).

a. Ellipse occurs in the case of substantives and pronouns, subject, object, finite verbs, main clauses, and (less often) subordinate clauses. See the Index under *Ellipse*.

3023. Enallage (ἐναλλαγή *interchange*) is the substitution of one grammatical form for another, as plural for singular (1006–1008). Thus: "They fall successive, and successive rise": Pope.

3024. Euphemism (εὐφημισμός lit. *speaking favourably*) is the substitution of a less direct expression in place of one whose plainer meaning might be unpleasant or offensive. Thus: "The merchant prince had stopped payment" (for "became bankrupt").

συμφορά *occurrence* for ἀτύχημα *misfortune*, ἑτέρως *otherwise* = *not well*, εὐφρόνη 'the kindly time' for νύξ *night*, εὐώνυμος *left* (lit. *of good omen*, whereas the left was the unlucky side), εἴ τι πάθοι *if anything should happen to him* = *if he should die*.

3025. Hendiadys (ἓν διὰ δυοῖν *one by two*) is the use of two words connected by a copulative conjunction to express a single complex idea; especially two substantives instead of one substantive and an adjective or attributive genitive.

χρόνῳ καὶ πολιορκίᾳ *by length of time and siege* = *by a long siege* D. 19. 123, ἐν ἁλὶ κύμασί τε *in the waves of the sea* E. Hel. 226, ἀσπίδων τε καὶ στρατοῦ = ὡπλισμένου στρατοῦ *armed force* S. El. 36.

3026. Homoioteleuton (ὁμοιοτέλευτος *ending alike*) is end-rhyme in clauses or verses.

τὴν μὲν ἀρχὴν εἰς τὸν πόλεμον κατέστησαν ὡς ἐλευθερώσοντες τοὺς Ἕλληνας, ἐπὶ δὲ τελευτῆς οὕτω πολλοὺς αὐτῶν ἐκδότους ἐποίησαν, καὶ τῆς μὲν ἡμετέρᾱς πόλεως τοὺς Ἴωνας ἀπέστησαν, ἐξ ἧς ἀπῴκησαν καὶ δι' ἣν πολλάκις ἐσώθησαν *in the beginning they entered upon the war with the avowed object of liberating the Greeks, at the end they have betrayed so many of them, and have caused the Ionians to revolt from our State, from which they emigrated and thanks to which they were often saved* I. 4. 122. Cp. S. Aj. 62–65. *Homoioteleuton* is most marked in *paromoiosis*.

3027. Hypallage (ὑπαλλαγή *exchange*) is a change in the relation of words by which a word, instead of agreeing with the case it logically qualifies, is made to agree grammatically with another case. Hypallage is almost always confined to poetry.

ἐμὰ κήδεα θῡμοῦ *the troubles of my spirit* ξ 197, νεῖκος ἀνδρῶν ξύναιμον *kindred strife of men* for *strife of kindred men* S. Ant. 794. Here the adjective virtually agrees with the rest of the phrase taken as a compound.

3028. Hyperbaton (*ὑπέρβατον transposition*) is the separation of words naturally belonging together. Such displacement usually gives prominence to the first of two words thus separated, but sometimes to the second also. In prose hyperbaton is less common than in poetry, but even in prose it is frequent, especially when it secures emphasis on an important idea by placing it at the beginning or end of a sentence. At times hyperbaton may mark passionate excitement. Sometimes it was adopted to gain rhythmical effect. Thus: "Such resting found the sole of unblest feet": Milton.

σὺ δὲ αὐτός, ὦ πρὸς θεῶν, Μένων, τί φῄς ἀρετὴν εἶναι; *but what do you yourself, in heaven's name, Meno, say virtue is?* P. Men. 71 d, ὦ πρός σε γονάτων (946) *by thy knees* (*I entreat*) *thee* E. Med. 324, ὑφ' ἑνὸς τοιαῦτα πέπονθεν ἡ Ἑλλὰς ἀνθρώπου *from one man Greece endured such sufferings* D. 18. 158, κρατῶν τοὺς ὁποιουσδήποθ' ὑμεῖς ἐξεπέμπετε στρατηγούς *conquering the generals you kept sending out—such as they were* 18. 146.

a. The displacement is often caused by the intrusion of a clause of contrast or explanation. Thus τοὺς περὶ Ἀρχίαν . . . οὐ ψῆφον ἀνεμείνατε ἀλλ' . . . ἐτιμωρήσασθε *you did not postpone your vote but took vengeance upon Archias and his company* X. H. 7. 3. 7.

b. Adverbs and particles may be displaced. Thus, οὕτω τις ἔρως δεινός *a passion so terrible* P. Th. 169 c, πολὺ γὰρ τῶν ἵππων ἔτρεχον θᾶττον *for they ran much faster than the horses* X. A. 1. 5. 2; so εὖ, μάλα; on ἄν see 1764.

c. Prepositions often cause the displacement (1663, 2690). On displacement in connection with participles see 1166, 1167; with the negatives, see 2690 ff.

d. Similar or contrasted words are often brought into juxtaposition. Here a nominative precedes an oblique case. Thus, ἀπὸ τῶν ὑμετέρων ὑμῖν πολεμεῖ συμμάχων *he wages war on you from* the resources of *your allies* D. 4. 34, οὐ γάρ τίς με βίῃ γε ἑκὼν ἀέκοντα δίηται *for no one shall chase me by force, he willing me unwilling* H 197. Note ἄλλος ἄλλο (ἄλλοθεν, ἄλλοτε, etc.), αὐτὸς αὐτοῦ.

e. **Construction ἀπὸ κοινοῦ.**—In poetry an attributive genitive or an object, common to two coördinate words, is often placed with the second only, as φράζων ἅλωσιν Ἰλίου τ' ἀνάστασιν *telling of the capture and overthrow of Ilium* A. Ag. 587.

3029. Hypophora (*ὑποφορά putting under*) is the statement of an objection (together with its refutation) which a speaker supposes to be made by an opponent or makes himself. Both objection and reply often take the form of questions (2654, 2785, 2819). Cp. "But I hear it continually rung in my ears . . . 'what will become of the preamble, if you repeal this tax?'": Burke.

τί οὖν, ἄν τις εἴποι, ταῦτα λέγεις ἡμῖν νῦν; ἵνα γνῶτ' κτλ. *why then, some one will say, do you tell us this now? In order that you may know*, etc. D. 1. 14.

3030. Hysteron Proteron (*ὕστερον πρότερον later earlier*) is an arrangement reversing the natural order of time in which events occur. It is used when an event, later in time, is regarded as more important than one earlier in time.

τράφεν ἠδὲ γένοντο were bred and born A 251 (so τροφὴ καὶ γένεσις X. M. 3. 5. 10; cp. "for I was bred and born": Shakespeare), εἵματά τ' ἀμφιέσᾶσα θυώδεα καὶ λούσᾶσα *having put on fragrant robes and washed* ε 264.

3031. Isocōlon (ἰσόκωλον *having equal members*) is the use of two or more sequent cola (clauses) containing an equal number of syllables.

τοῦ μὲν ἐπίπονον καὶ φιλοκίνδῡνον τὸν βίον κατέστησεν, τῆς δὲ περίβλεπτον καὶ περιμάχητον τὴν φύσιν ἐποίησεν *the life of the one he rendered full of toil and peril, the beauty of the other he made the object of universal admiration and of universal contention* I. 10. 16.

3032. Litotes (λῑτότης *plainness, simplicity*) is understatement so as to intensify, affirmation expressed by the negative of the contrary. Cp. 2694. *Meiōsis* (μείωσις *lessening*) is ordinarily the same as *litotes.* Thus: "One of the few immortal names That were not born to die": Halleck.

3033. Metonymy (μετωνυμίᾱ *change of name*) is the substitution of one word for another to which it stands in some close relation. Thus: "We wish that infancy may learn the purpose of its creation from maternal lips": Webster.

μῖσος *loathed object*, ὦ κάθαρμα *you scum!* συμμαχίᾱ *allies*, ἐν Βοιωτοῖς *in Boeotia*, θέᾱτρον *spectators*, μάχη *battlefield*, ἵππος *cavalry*, ἰχθύες *fish-market.*

3034. Onomatopoeia (ὀνοματοποιίᾱ *making of a name* or *word*) is the formation of names to express natural sounds.

βληχῶμαι *bleat*, βομβῶ *buzz*, βρῡχῶμαι *roar*, κοάξ *quack*, κακκαβίζω *cackle*, κόκκυξ *cuckoo*, κράζω *croak*, τῑτίζω *cheep*, πιππίζω *chirp*. Sometimes the sound of a whole verse imitates an action; as αὖτις ἔπειτα πέδονδε κυλίνδετο λᾶας ἀναιδής *down again to the plain rolled the shameless stone* λ 598 (of the stone of Sisyphus).

3035. Oxymōron (ὀξύμωρον *pointedly* or *cleverly foolish*) is the juxtaposition of words apparently contradictory of each other.

νόμος ἄνομος *a law that is no law* A. Ag. 1142, ἄχαρις χάρις *a graceless grace* A. Pr. 545, πίστις ἀπιστοτάτη *most faithless faith* And. 1. 67, αὐτοὶ φεύγοντας φεύγουσι *they themselves are flying from those who fly* T. 7. 70.

3036. Paraleipsis (παράλειψις *passing over*) is pretended omission for rhetorical effect.

τὰς δ' ἐπ' Ἰλλυρίους καὶ Παίονας αὐτοῦ καὶ πρὸς Ἀρύββᾱν καὶ ὅποι τις ἂν εἴποι παραλείπω στρατείᾱς *I omit his expeditions to Illyria and Paeonia and against Arybbas and many others that one might mention* (lit. *whithersoever one might speak of*) D. 1. 13.

3037. Parechēsis (παρήχησις *likeness of sound*) is the repetition of the same sound in words in close or immediate succession. *Alliteration* is initial rhyme.

ἄγαμος, ἄτεκνος, ἄπολις, ἄφιλος E. I. T. 220 (cp. "unwept, unhonoured, and unsung"), πόνος πόνῳ πόνον φέρει *toil upon toil brings* only *toil* S. Aj. 866, τυφλὸς *τά τ' ὦτα τόν τε νοῦν τά τ' ὄμματ' εἶ blind art thou in thy ears, thy reason, and thy eyes* S. O. T. 371, οἱ οὐδὲ . . . δὶς ἀποθανόντες δίκην δοῦναι δύναιντ' ἂν *who would not be able to give satisfaction even by dying twice* L. 12. 37, ἔσωσά σ'· ὡς ἴσᾱσιν Ἑλλήνων ὅσοι κτλ. *I saved thee; as all of the Greeks know who*, etc. E. Med. 476, θανάτου θᾶττον θεῖ wickedness '*fleeth faster than fate*' P. A. 39 a.

3038. **Parisōsis** (παρίσωσις *almost equal*) is approximate equality of clauses as measured by syllables. *Parisōsis* is sometimes regarded as synonymous with *isocōlon.*

3039. **Paromoiōsis** (παρομοίωσις *assimilation*) is parallelism of sound between the words of two clauses either approximately or exactly equal in size. This similarity in sound may appear at the beginning, at the end (*homoioteleuton*), in the interior, or it may pervade the whole.

μαχομένους μὲν κρείττους εἶναι τῶν πολεμίων, ψηφιζομένους δὲ ἥττους τῶν ἐχθρῶν *by fighting to be superior to our public enemies, and by voting to be weaker than our private enemies* L. 12. 79.

3040. **Paronomasia** (παρονομασίᾱ) is play upon words.

οὐ γὰρ τὸν τρόπον ἀλλὰ τὸν τόπον μετήλλαξεν *for he changed not his disposition but his position* Aes. 3. 78. Often in etymological word-play; as Πρόθοος θοός B 758, Μέλητος . . . ἐμέλησεν P. A. 26 a, Παυσανίου παυσαμένου P. S. 185 c, εἰς . . . τόπον . . . ἀειδῆ, εἰς Αἴδου *to an invisible place, to Hades* P. Ph. 80 d. Cp. "Old Gaunt indeed, and gaunt in being old": Shakespeare. Sometimes this figure deals with the same word taken in different senses (*homonyms*): ἅμα γὰρ ἡμεῖς τε τῆς ἀρχῆς ἀπεστερούμεθα καὶ τοῖς Ἕλλησιν ἀρχὴ τῶν κακῶν ἐγίγνετο '*no sooner were we deprived of the first place than the first disaster came upon the Greeks*' I. 4. 119.

3041. **Periphrasis** (περίφρασις *circumlocution*) is the use of more words than are necessary to express an idea.

θρέμματα Νείλου *nurslings of the Nile = the Egyptians* P. L. 953 e, Οἰδίπου κάρᾱ *Oedipus* S. O. T. 40 (κάρᾱ expresses reverence or affection). The substantive on which another substantive depends often stands for an adjective, as ἶς Τηλεμάχοιο = *mighty Telemach* (cp. 1014). For various other periphrases, see the Index.

3042. **Pleonasm** (πλεονασμός *excess*), or redundancy, is the admission of a word or words which are not necessary to the complete logical expression of the thought. Such words, though logically superfluous, enrich the thought by adding greater definiteness and precision, picturesqueness, vigour and emphasis; and by expressing subtle shadings of feeling otherwise impossible. Cp. "All ye inhabitants of the world, and dwellers on the earth."

a. Adverbs or adverbial expressions combined: of *time*, as πάλιν αὖ, αὖθις αὖ πάλιν, πάλιν μετὰ ταῦτα ὕστερον, ἔπειτα μετὰ ταῦτα, διὰ τέλους τὸν πάντα χρόνον; of *manner*, as κατὰ ταὐτὰ ὡσαύτως, μάτην ἄλλως, εἰς δυνατὸν ὅτι μάλιστα; of *infer-*

ence, as τοιγάρτοι διὰ ταῦτα, ἐκ τούτου . . . διὰ ταῦτα; of *verification*, as ἀληθῶς τῷ ὄντι; and various other expressions, as ἴσως τάχ' ἄν, λόγῳ εἰπεῖν.

b. Adverb and adjective combined (usually poetical): κεῖτο μέγας μεγαλωστί *huge he lay with his huge length* Π 776.

c. Adjective and verb: ὡς δὲ μὴ μακροὺς τείνω λόγους *but not to speak at length* E. Hec. 1177.

d. Adjective and substantive in the dative: νῆσος μεγάθει μὲν οὐ μεγάλη *an island not large in size* Hdt. 5. 31.

e. Verb with an abstract substantive in the dative or accusative (1516, 1564): βασιλεὺς . . . φύσει πεφῡκέναι *to be a true-born king* X. C. 5. 1. 24.

f. Compound verb or substantives with substantives: οἶκον καλῶς οἰκονομεῖν *to build a house well* X. M. 4. 5. 10, ἡ τῶν νεογνῶν τέκνων παιδοτροφίᾱ *the rearing of young children* X. O. 7. 21. Here the force of the first member of the compound is quiescent.

g. Compound verb and adverb: προὔγραψα πρῶτον *I wrote first* T. 1. 23, ἀπαγαγὼν δ' ὑμᾶς ἄπωθεν ἀπὸ τοῦ κλέμματος *having diverted your attention away from the fraud* Aes. 3. 100.

h. Verb and participle (2147 b): τί δὴ λέγοντες διέβαλλον οἱ διαβάλλοντες; *in what words then did my calumniators calumniate me?* P. A. 19 b.

i. Amplification by synonymous doublets (especially common in Demosthenes): ἀξιῶ καὶ δέομαι *I beg and beseech* D. 18. 6, ἐναργὲς καὶ σαφές *visible and clear* 14. 4.

j. Parallelism of positive and negative: ὡς ἔχω περὶ τούτων, λέξω πρὸς ὑμᾶς καὶ οὐκ ἀποκρύψομαι *I will tell you and I will not conceal my opinion on these matters* D. 8. 73, οὐκ ἄκλητοι, παρακληθέντες δέ *not unbidden but invited* T. 6. 87.

k. A person and a characteristic or quality connected by καί or τέ; as καταδείσαντες τοῦτον καὶ τὸ τούτου θράσος *fearing him and his audacity* D. 21. 20.

l. A relative clause takes up a preceding expression: καὶ εὐχὴν δέ τινες αὐτοῦ ἐξέφερον ὡς εὔχοιτο κτλ. *and some reported also a prayer he made*, etc. (lit. *how he prayed*) X. A. 1. 9. 11.

m. 'Polar' expressions may be placed here. These are opposites placed in pairs so as to intensify such ideas as *all*, *no one*, *at all times*, *everywhere*, *everything possible*. Thus, καὶ ἐν θεοῖς καὶ ἐν ἀνθρώποις *both among the gods and among men* P. G. 508 a, οὐδὲν οὔτε μέγα οὔτε μῑκρόν *nothing either great or small = absolutely nothing* P. A. 19 c, ἐν γῇ καὶ θαλάττῃ *on land and sea* D. 18. 324, οὔτε δοῦλος οὔτ' ἐλεύθερος *nor bond nor free* T. 2. 78, ῥητὰ καὶ ἄρρητα *fanda nefanda* D. 18. 122. For other cases of pleonasm, see the Index.

3043. Polysyndeton (cp. *Asyndeton*) is the repetition of conjunctions in a series of coördinate words or phrases.

καὶ τοσούτων καὶ ἑτέρων κακῶν καὶ αἰσχρῶν καὶ πάλαι καὶ νεωστὶ καὶ μῑκρῶν καὶ μεγάλων αἰτίου γεγενημένου *who has shown himself the guilty cause of so many other base and disgraceful acts, both long ago and lately, both small and great* L. 12. 78. Cp. D. 4. 36.

3044. Praegnans Constructio is a form of brachylogy by which two expressions or clauses are condensed into one.

Here belong, apart from 1659 ff., such cases as εἰς τὸ βαλανεῖον βούλομαι *I want* to go *to the bath* Ar. Ran. 1279 (cp. "he will directly to the lords": Milton, Samson Agon. 1250) and φανερὸς ἦν οἴκαδε παρασκευαζόμενος *he was evidently preparing* to go *home* X. A. 7. 7. 57. In παραγγέλλει ἐπὶ τὰ ὅπλα *he ordered them to get under arms* X. A. 1. 5. 13 the command was ἐπὶ τὰ ὅπλα *to arms!*

3045. Prolēpsis (πρόληψις *taking before*) in the case of objective predicate adjectives or nouns is the anticipation of the result of the action of a verb. Examples in 1579.

On the prolepsis of the subject of dependent clauses which is put into the main clause, see 2182. So in "Consider the lilies of the field how they grow." Prolepsis is also used to designate the anticipation of an opponent's arguments and objections. One variety is *prodiorthōsis* or preparatory apology (P. A. 20 e, D. 18. 199, 256).

3046. Symploce (συμπλοκή *interweaving*) is the repetition, in one or more successive clauses, of the first and last words of the preceding clause.

ἐπὶ σαυτὸν καλεῖς, ἐπὶ τοὺς νόμους καλεῖς, ἐπὶ τὴν δημοκρατίᾱν καλεῖς *it is against yourself that you are summoning him, it is against the laws that you are summoning him, it is against the democratic constitution that you are summoning him* Aes. 3. 202.

3047. Synecdoche (συνεκδοχή *understanding one thing with another*) is the use of the part for the whole, or the whole for the part. The name of an animal is often used for that which comes from, or is made from, the animal. Cp. "they sought his blood"; "Belinda smiled, and all the world was gay": Pope.

δόρυ *ship* for *plank, beam*, ἀλώπηξ *fox-skin* for *fox*, χελώνη *tortoise-shell* for *tortoise*, πορφύρᾱ *purple dye* for *purple-fish*, ἐλέφᾱς *ivory* for *elephant*, μέλιττα *honey* for *bee*.

3048. Zeugma (ζεῦγμα *junction, band*) is a form of brachylogy by which two connected substantives are used jointly with the same verb (or adjective) though this is strictly appropriate to only one of them. Such a verb expresses an idea that may be taken in a wider, as well as in a narrower, sense, and therefore suggests the verb suitable to the other substantive. Cp. "Nor Mars his sword, nor war's quick fire shall burn The living record of your memory."

οὔτε φωνὴν οὔτε του μορφὴν βροτῶν ὄψει *thou shalt know neither voice nor form of mortal man* A. Pr. 21, ἀλλ' ἢ πνοαῖσιν ἢ βαθυσκαφεῖ κόνει κρύψον νιν *no, either* give them *to the winds or in the deep-dug soil bury them* S. El. 435, ἔδουσί τε πίονα μῆλα οἶνόν τ' ἔξαιτον *they eat fat sheep* and drink *choice wine* M 319.

a. Different from zeugma is *syllēpsis* (σύλληψις *taking together*), by which the same verb, though governing two different objects, is taken both in its literal and its metaphorical sense; but does not properly change its meaning. Thus, χρήματα τελοῦντες τούτοις . . . καὶ χάριτας *paying money and rendering thanks to them* P. Cr. 48 c.

APPENDIX: LIST OF VERBS

This List in general includes the common verbs showing any formal peculiarity of tense. The forms printed in heavy-faced type belong to standard Attic, that is, to the language used in common speech and in ordinary prose; others are poetical, doubtful, dialectal or late. Many regular forms are omitted because they do not appear in the classical writers; though their non-appearance in the extant texts may often be accidental. Later forms are usually excluded, but reference is made to Aristotle, and to Hippocrates, though many works ascribed to him are of later date. The determination of the forms of Attic prose as distinguished from those of poetry is often difficult because of insufficient evidence, and in many cases certainty is not to be attained. The tenses employed in the dialogue parts of Aristophanes and other early writers of Attic comedy are usually to be regarded as existing in the spoken language except when the character of the verb in question is such as to indicate borrowing from Epic or tragedy. Sometimes a tense attested only in tragedy and in Attic prose of the latter part of the fourth century may have been used in the best Attic prose. The expression *in prose* means *in Attic prose*.

A prefixed hyphen indicates that a form used in prose is attested generally, or only, in composition; and that a poetical form occurs only in composition. Rigid consistency would have led to too great detail; besides, many tenses cited as existing only in composition may have occurred also in the simple form. For the details of usage on this and other points the student is referred to Veitch, *Greek Verbs, Irregular and Defective*, and to Kühner-Blass, *Griechische Grammatik*.

The tenses cited are those of the *principal parts* (369). Tenses inferred from these are omitted, but mention is made of the future perfect, future passive, and of the future middle when it shows a passive sense.

An assumed form is marked by * or has no accent; the abbreviations *aor.* and *perf.* denote *first aorist* and *first perfect*; of alternative forms in ττ or σσ (78), that in ττ is given when the verb in question belongs to the classical spoken language. In the citation of Epic forms, futures and aorists with σσ, and several other Epic peculiarities, are usually not mentioned.

The appended Roman numerals indicate the class (497–529) to which the present system of each verb belongs; all verbs not so designated belong to the *first* class (498–504).

***ἀάω** (ἀϝα-ω), ἀάζω *harm, infatuate:* pres. only in mid. ἀᾶται; aor. ἄασα (ἄᾱσα or ἄασσα), ἆσα, ἀασάμην (and ἀᾱσάμην or ἀασσάμην) *erred;* aor. pass. ἀάσθην; v. a. in ἀ-άατος, ἀ-ᾱ́ατος, ἄν-ᾱτος. Chiefly Epic.

ἀγάλλω (ἀγαλ-) *adorn, honour* (act. in Com. poets): **ἀγαλῶ, ἤγηλα**; mid. **ἀγάλλομαι** *glory in*, only pres. and imperf. (III.)

ἄγα-μαι *admire* (725): aor. **ἠγάσθην** (489 e), rarely **ἠγασάμην**, v. a. **ἀγαστός.** Epic fut. ἀγάσ(σ)ομαι, Epic aor. ἠγασ(σ)άμην. Hom. has also ἀγάομαι *admire* and ἀγαίομαι (ἀγα- for ἀγασ-) *envy, am indignant at* or *with.*

ἀγγέλλω (ἀγγελ-) *announce:* **ἀγγελῶ, ἤγγειλα, ἤγγελκα, ἤγγελμαι, ἠγγέλθην, ἀγγελθήσομαι, ἀγγελτός.** 2 aor. pass. ἠγγέλην rarely on Att. inscr. (III.)

ἀγείρω (ἀγερ-) *collect:* **ἤγειρα.** Epic are aor. mid. ξυν-ηγειράμην; 2 aor. mid. ἀγέροντο *assembled*, ἤγρετο (mss. ἔγρετο), ἀγερέσθαι, 425 a, D. (some read with mss. ἀγέρεσθαι), ἀγρόμενος; plup. 3 pl. ἀγηγέρατο; aor. pass. ἠγέρθην. Epic by-form ἠγερέθομαι. (III.)

ἀγῑνέω Epic and Ion. = **ἄγω.** Inf. ἀγῑνέμεναι Epic.

ἀγνοέω *not to know:* regular, but **ἀγνοήσομαι** as pass. (808). Hom. ἀγνοιέω.

ἄγ-νῡμι (ἀγ- for ϝαγ-, 733) *break*, in prose generally **κατᾱ́γνῡμι, κατᾱγνύω** in all tenses: **-άξω**, **-έαξα** (431), 2 perf. **-έαγα** (443), 2 aor. pass. **-εάγην** (434), **-ακτός**. Epic aor. *ἦξα*, and 2 aor. pass. *ἐάγην* and *ἄγην*; Ion. 2 perf. *ἔηγα*. (IV.)

ἄγω *lead:* **ἄξω**, 2 aor. **ἤγαγον**, **ἦχα**, **ἦγμαι**, **ἤχθην**, **ἀχθήσομαι**, **ἀκτέος**. Fut. mid. **ἄξομαι**, also = fut. pass. (809). Aor. *ἦξα* suspected in Att., Hom. *ἀξάμην*: Hom. has mixed aor. *ἄξετε*, *ἀξέμεναι*, *ἀξέμεν* (542 D.).

ἀδε- or *ἀδε-* *be sated* in Epic aor. opt. *ἀδήσειεν* and perf. *ἀδηκότες*.

ᾄδω *sing:* **ᾄσομαι** (806), **ᾖσα**, **ᾖσμαι**, **ᾔσθην**, **ᾀστέος**. Uncontracted forms in Epic and Ion. are *ἀείδω*, *ἀείσω* and *ἀείσομαι*, *ἤεισα*.

ἀε- *rest, sleep:* Epic aor. *ἄεσα*, *ἆσα*.

ἀείρω: see **αἴρω**.

ἀέξω: Hom. for **αὔξω** (**αὐξάνω**).

ἄημι (*ἀη-*, *ἀε-*, 724, 741) *blow:* 3 s. *ἄησι*, 3 du. *ἄητον*, 3 pl. *ἀεῖσι*, inf. *ἀήμεναι*, *ἀῆναι*, part. *ἀείς*, imperf. 3 s. *ἄη*; mid. pres. *ἄηται*, part. *ἀήμενος*, imperf. *ἄητο*. Poetic, chiefly Epic.

αἰδέομαι (*αἰδε-* for *αἰδεσ-*) *respect, feel shame:* **αἰδέσομαι** (488 a), **ᾔδεσμαι** (489 c), **ᾐδέσθην**, **αἰδεσθήσομαι** rare (812), **ᾐδεσάμην** *pardon a criminal* in prose, otherwise Tragic. Imper. *αἰδεῖο* Hom. (650). Poetic *αἴδομαι*.

αἰκίζομαι *outrage:* **αἰκιοῦμαι**, **ᾐκισάμην**, **ᾔκισμαι**, **ᾐκίσθην** *was outraged*. *αἰκίζω* act. *plague* poetic. Epic *ἀεικίζω*. 512. (III.)

αἰνέω *praise*, usu. comp. w. *ἐπί*, *παρά*, etc., in prose: *-αινέσω* (in prose usu. **-αινέσομαι**, 488 b, 806), **-ῄνεσα**, **-ῄνεκα**, **-ῄνημαι**, *-ῃνέθην*, **-αινεσθήσομαι**, **-αινετέος**, *-τός* Aristotle. Epic and Lyric are *αἰνήσω*, *ᾔνησα*.

αἴ-νυμαι *take:* only pres. and imperf. (*αἰνύμην*). Epic. (IV.)

αἱρέω (*αἱρε-*, *ἑλ-*) *take*, mid. *choose:* **αἱρήσω**, 2 aor. **εἷλον** (431), **ᾕρηκα**, **ᾕρημαι** (mid. or pass.), **ᾑρέθην** (usu. *was chosen*), **αἱρεθήσομαι**, **αἱρετός**, **-τέος**. Fut. perf. **ᾑρήσομαι** rare. Hdt. perf. *ἀραίρηκα*, *ἀραίρημαι*; Hom. v. a. *ἑλετός*. (VI.)

αἴρω (544 c) *raise:* **ἀρῶ**, **ἦρα** (**ἄρω**, **ἄραιμι**, **ἆρον**, **ἆραι**, **ἄρᾱς**), **ἦρκα**, **ἦρμαι**, **ἤρθην**, **ἀρθήσομαι**, *ἀρτέος*. Ionic and poetic *ἀείρω* (*ἀϝερ-*): *ἀερῶ*, *ἤειρα*, *ἠέρθην*, Hom. plup. *ἄωρτο* (from *ἤορτο*) for *ἤερτο*. Fut. *ἀροῦμαι* and aor. *ἠρόμην* belong to *ἄρνυμαι* (*ἀρ-*) *win*. (III.)

αἰσθ-άνομαι (*αἰσθ-*, *αἰσθε-*) *perceive:* **αἰσθήσομαι**, 2 aor. **ᾐσθόμην**, **ᾔσθημαι**, **αἰσθητός**. The by-form *αἴσθομαι* is doubtful. (IV.)

ἀΐσσω *rush:* see **ᾄττω**.

αἰσχ-ύνω (*αἰσχυν-*) *disgrace*, mid. *feel ashamed:* **αἰσχυνῶ**, **ᾔσχῡνα**, **ᾐσχύνθην** *felt ashamed*, **αἰσχυντέος**. On fut. mid. **αἰσχυνοῦμαι** and fut. pass. **αἰσχυνθήσομαι**, see 1911. Hom. perf. pass. part. *ᾐσχυμμένος*. (III.)

ἀΐω *hear*, with ᾱ usu. in Att. poets, ᾰ in Epic, Lyric, and in some Att. poets: imperf. Hom. *ἤϊον*, *ἄϊον* and *ἄϊον*, aor. *ἐπ-ῇσε* Hdt. (MSS. *ἐπῄισε*), v. a. *ἐπ-αΐστος* Hdt. Poetic and Ion. Hom. has also *ἀείω*, of which *ἀϊών* (MSS. *ἀΐων*) may be the 2 aor.

ἀΐω *breathe out:* imperf. *ἄϊον* Epic.

ἀκ-αχ-ίζω (*ἀκαχιδ-*, *ἀκαχ-*, *ἀκαχε-*, from *ἀχ-* redupl.) *afflict, grieve:* *ἀκαχήσω*, *ἀκάχησα* (rare), 2 aor. *ἤκαχον*, *ἀκάχημαι* *am grieved* (3 pl. *ἀκηχέδαται*), inf. *ἀκάχησθαι* (425 a, D.), part. *ἀκαχήμενος* and *ἀκηχέμενος* (425 b, (2) D.) Cp. *ἀχέω*, *ἀχεύω*, *ἄχνυμαι*. Epic. 512. (III.)

ἀκ-αχ-μένος (*ἀκ-*; cp. *ἄκ-ρον* *peak*) *sharpened;* Epic redupl. perf. part., with no present in use.

ἀκέομαι (ἀκε- for ἀκεσ-; cp. τὸ ἄκος *cure*) *heal*: **ἠκεσάμην, ἀκεστός.** Hom. has also ἀκείω.

ἀκηδέω (ἀκηδε- for ἀκηδεσ-, 488 D.; cp. ἀκηδής *uncared for*) *neglect*: ἀκήδεσα Epic. Epic and poetic.

ἀκούω (ἀκου-, ἀκοϝ-, 43) *hear*: **ἀκούσομαι** (806), **ἤκουσα,** 2 perf. **ἀκήκοα** (562 a), 2 plup. **ἠκηκόη** or **ἀκηκόη, ἠκούσθην** (489 e), **ἀκουσθήσομαι, ἀκουστός, -τέος.**

ἀλαλάζω (ἀλαλαγ-) *raise the war-cry*, usu. poetic or late prose: ἀλαλάξομαι (806), **ἠλάλαξα.** (III.)

ἀλάομαι *wander*, rare in prose: pres. Epic imper. ἀλάου (MSS. ἀλόω, 643), perf. Epic ἀλάλημαι as pres. (ἀλάλησο, ἀλάλησθαι, ἀλαλήμενος), aor. Epic ἀλήθην.

ἀλαπάζω (ἀλαπαγ-) *destroy, plunder*: Epic are ἀλαπάξω, ἀλάπαξα. By-forms λαπάζω, λαπάσσω. (III.)

ἀλδαίνω (ἀλδαν-) with the by-forms ἀλδάνω, ἀλδήσκω, *nourish*: Epic 2 aor. (or imperf.) ἤλδανον, v. a. Epic ἄν-αλτος *insatiate*. Poetic. (IV.)

ἀλείφω (ἀλειφ-, ἀλιφ-) *anoint*: **ἀλείψω, ἤλειψα, ἀπ-αλήλιφα** (477 a), **ἀλήλιμμαι, ἠλείφθην, ἀλειφθήσομαι, ἐξ-αλειπτέος.** 2 aor. pass. ἠλίφην, ἠλείφην are doubtful.

ἀλέξω and ἀλέκω (ἀλεξ-, ἀλεξε-, ἀλεκ-, ἀλκ-) *ward off*: fut. ἀλέξω poetic (rare), ἀλέξομαι Xen., Soph., ἀλεξήσω Hom., ἀλεξήσομαι Hdt.; aor. ἤλεξα Aesch., ἠλέξησα Epic, ἠλεξάμην Ion., Xen., ἠλεξησάμην (?) Xen., 2 aor. ἄλαλκον poetic (549). By-form ἀλκάθω poetic (490 D.).

ἀλέομαι *avoid*: aor. ἠλεάμην (43, 607). Cp. ἀλεύω. Poetic.

ἀλεύω *avert*: ἤλευσα. Usu. in mid. ἀλεύομαι *avoid*, aor. ἠλευάμην, subj. ἐξ-αλεύ-σωμαι (ἐξ-αλύξωμαι ?). Poetic. Other forms with like meaning are ἀλεείνω, ἀλύσκω, ἀλυσκάζω, ἀλυσκαίνω.

ἀλέω *grind*: **ἀλῶ** (539), **ἤλεσα, ἀλήλεμαι** (ἀλήλεσμαι, 489 b). By-form ἀλήθω.

ἀλῆναι: see εἴλω.

ἄλθομαι (ἀλθ-, ἀλθε-) *am healed*: Epic ἄλθετο and ἐπ-αλθήσομαι. Hippocr. has aor. -ηλθέσθην.

ἀλίνδω *cause to roll* (also ἀλινδέω, ἀλίω), usu. comp. with ἐξ: **-ἤλῖσα, -ἤλῖκα, ἠλίνδημαι.** ἀλίω is a pres. derived from ἤλῖσα (= ἤλινδσα).

ἁλ-ίσκομαι (ἁλ- for ϝαλ-, ἁλο-, 486) *am captured* (used as pass. of αἱρῶ): **ἁλώσομαι,** 2 aor. **ἑάλων** or **ἥλων** (**ἁλῶ, ἁλοίην, ἁλῶναι, ἁλούς,** 687), **ἑάλωκα** (443) or **ἥλωκα, ἁλωτός.** Epic 2 aor. subj. ἁλώω. Act. ἁλίσκω is not used, but see ἀνᾱλίσκω *expend*. (V.)

ἀλιταίνομαι (ἀλιτ-, ἀλιταν-) *sin*: Epic are aor. ἤλιτον (-όμην), perf. part. ἀλιτήμενος *sinning*. Mostly Epic. Epic by-form ἀλιτραίνω. (III. IV.)

ἀλλάττω (ἀλλαγ-) *change*, often comp. w. ἀπό, διά, μετά: **ἀλλάξω, ἤλλαξα, -ἤλλαχα, ἤλλαγμαι, ἠλλάχθην** (usu. in tragedy) and **ἠλλάγην** (both usu. in comp.), fut. pass. **ἀπ-αλλαχθήσομαι** (so in tragedy) and **ἀπ-αλλαγήσομαι,** fut. mid. **-αλλάξομαι,** fut. perf. **ἀπ-ηλλάξομαι,** v. a. **ἀπ-αλλακτέος.** (III.)

ἅλλομαι (ἁλ-) *leap*: **ἁλοῦμαι, ἡλάμην.** 2 aor. ἡλόμην rare and uncertain in Att. Epic 2 aor. ἆλσο, ἆλτο, ἅλμενος (688). (III.)

ἀλυκτάζω *am distressed* Ion., ἀλυκτέω *am anxious* late Ion.: Epic ἀλαλύκτημαι w. reduplication. 512. (III.)

ἀλύσκω (ἀλυκ-, 526 d) *avoid*: ἀλύξω, ἤλυξα. Hom. has also ἀλυσκάζω and ἀλυσκάνω. Poetic. (V.)

ἀλφ-άνω (ἀλφ-) *find, acquire*: Epic 2 aor. ἦλφον. (IV.)

ἁμαρτ-άνω (ἁμαρτ-, ἁμαρτε-) *err*: **ἁμαρτήσομαι** (806), 2 aor. **ἥμαρτον**, **ἡμάρτηκα**, **ἡμάρτημαι**, **ἡμαρτήθην**, **ἀν-αμάρτητος**, **ἐπεξ-αμαρτητέος**. Epic 2 aor. ἤμβροτον (for β, see 130). (IV.)

ἀμβλ-ίσκω (ἀμβλ-) and **ἀμβλόω** *miscarry*; reg. in comp. w. ἐξ: **-ήμβλωσα**, **-ήμβλωκα**, **-ήμβλωμαι**. Other forms are late. (V.)

ἀμείβω *change*, rare in Att. prose: **ἀμείψω**, **ἤμειψα**. Mid. **ἀμείβομαι** *make return*, rare in prose and comedy: **ἀμείψομαι**, **ἠμειψάμην**. In the meaning *answer* ἠμειψάμην and ἠμείφθην are poetic.

ἀμείρω (ἀμερ-) *deprive*, only in pres. Poetic. (III.)

ἀμέρδω *deprive*: ἤμερσα, ἠμέρθην. Poetic.

ἀμπ-έχω and rare ἀμπ-ίσχω (ἀμφί + ἔχω, 125 d) *put about, clothe*: imperf. **ἀμπ-εῖχον** (Hom. ἄμπ-εχον), ἀμφ-έξω, 2 aor. ἤμπ-ισχον. Mid. **ἀμπ-έχομαι** (ἀμπ-ίσχομαι and ἀμφ-ισκνέομαι) *wear*: imperf. **ἠμπ-ειχόμην** (451), fut. **ἀμφ-έξομαι**, 2 aor. **ἠμπ-εσχόμην** and **ἠμπ-ισχόμην**. See **ἔχω** and **ἴσχω**.

ἀμπλακ-ίσκω (ἀμπλακ-, ἀμπλακε-) *err, miss*: 2 aor. ἤμπλακον and ἤμβλακον (part. ἀμπλακών and ἀπλακών), ἠμπλάκημαι, ἀν-αμπλάκητος. Poetic. (V.)

ἄμπνυε, ἀμπνύνθην, ἄμπνῦτο (Epic): see **πνέω**.

ἀμῦνω (ἀμυν-) *ward off*: **ἀμυνῶ**, **ἤμῦνα**. Mid. **ἀμῦνομαι** *defend myself*: **ἀμυνοῦμαι**, **ἠμῦνάμην**, v. a. **ἀμυντέος**. By-form ἀμῡνάθω, 490 D. (III.)

ἀμύττω (ἀμυχ-) *scratch*: ἀμύξω, ἤμυξα. Poetic and Ion. (III.)

ἀμφι-γνοέω *doubt*: imperf. **ἠμφ-εγνόουν** (**ἠμφι-γνόουν** ?), aor. **ἠμφ-εγνόησα**. 451.

ἀμφι-έννῡμι (late ἀμφιεννύω) *clothe*: **ἀμφι-ῶ** (539 c), **ἠμφί-εσα** (450), **ἠμφί-εσμαι**. Mid. fut. **ἀμφι-έσομαι**, aor. ἀμφι-εσάμην poetic. (IV.)

ἀμφισβητέω *dispute*: the augmented (451) **ἠμφεσβήτουν**, **ἠμφεσβήτησα** (inscr.) are better than ἠμφι- (MSS.). Fut. mid. **ἀμφισβητήσομαι** as pass. (808).

ἀναίνομαι (ἀναν-) *refuse*, only pres. and imperf. in prose; aor. ἠνανάμην poetic. (III.)

ἀν-ᾱλ-ίσκω (ἀλ-, ἀλο-, 486) and **ἀνᾱλόω** *expend* (from ἀνα-ϝαλ-): imperf. **ἀνήλισκον** (**ἀνήλουν**, rare), **ἀνᾱλώσω**, **ἀνήλωσα**, **ἀνήλωκα**, **ἀνήλωμαι**, **ἀνηλώθην**, fut. pass. **ἀνᾱλωθήσομαι**, **ἀνᾱλωτέος**. Att. inscr. prove the MSS. forms ἀνάλωσα, ἀνάλωκα, ἀνάλωμαι, ἀνᾱλώθην to be late. κατ-ηνάλωσα, -ηνάλωμαι, -ηνᾱλώθην are also late. See **ἁλίσκομαι**. (V.)

ἁνδάνω (ἁδ- for σϝαδ-, 123, and ἁδε-) usu. Epic and Ion., but the pres. occurs in Att. poetry: imperf. Hom. probably ἑάνδανον and ἅνδανον (MSS. ἑήνδανον and ἥνδανον), Hdt. ἥνδανον (some write ἑάνδανον); fut. Hdt. ἁδήσω; 2 aor. Hdt. ἕαδον, Hom. εὔαδον (for ἐϝϝαδον from ἐσϝαδον) and ἅδον; 2 perf. Hom. ἕᾱδα (443). Adj. **ἄσμενος** *pleased*, in common use. Chiefly Epic and Ion. (IV.)

ἀν-έχω *hold up*, poetic and New Ion.: ἀν-εῖχον, ἀν-έξω and ἀνα-σχήσω, ἀν-έσχον. **ἀν-έχομαι** *endure*: **ἠν-ειχόμην** (451), **ἀν-έξομαι** and **ἀνα-σχήσομαι**, 2 aor. **ἠν-εσχόμην**, **ἀν-εκτός**, **-τέος**.

ἀνήνοθε (ἀνεθ-, ἀνοθ-) *mounts up* ρ 270, *sprang forth* Λ 266. ἀν- is probably the prep. Cp. -ενήνοθε.

ἀν-οίγ-νῡμι and **ἀν-οίγω** *open*: imperf. **ἀν-έῳγον** (431), **ἀν-οίξω**, **ἀν-έῳξα**, 1 perf. **ἀν-έῳχα**, 2 perf. **ἀν-έῳγα** (rare, 443) *have opened*, **ἀν-έῳγμαι** *stand open*, **ἀν-εῴχθην**, fut. perf. **ἀν-εῴξομαι**, **ἀν-οικτέος**. Cp. 808. οἴγνῡμι and οἴγω (*q.v.*) poetic. Imperf. ἀνῷγον Ξ 168 may be written ἀνέῳγον w. synizesis. ἤνοιγον and ἤνοιξα in Xen. are probably wrong; Hom. has ᾦξα (οἶξα ?), and ὤειξα (MSS. ὤϊξα) from ὀείγω (Lesb.); Hdt. ἄνοιξα and ἀνῷξα (MSS.). (IV.)

ἀν-ορθόω *set upright* has the regular augment (**ἀν-ώρθωσα**); but **ἐπ-ανορθόω** has double augment: **ἐπ-ην-ώρθουν, ἐπ-ην-ώρθωσα, ἐπ-ην-ώρθωμαι** (451).

ἀντιβολέω *meet, beseech* often has two augments: **ἠντ-εβόλουν, ἠντ-εβόλησα** (451).

ἀντιδικέω *am defendant* may have double augment: **ἠντ-εδίκουν, ἠντ-εδίκησα** (451).

ἀνύω and (rarer) **ἀνύτω** (531) (often written ἀνύω, ἀνύτω) *accomplish:* **ἀνύσω, ἤνυσα, ἤνυκα, δι-ήνυσμαι** (?) Xen., **ἀνυστός**, ἀν-ήνυ(σ)τος poetic. Hom. fut. -ανύω. Poetic forms are ἄνω, ἄνω (pres. and imperf.), and ἄνυμι (ἤνυτο ε 243), ἐπ-ηνύσθην Epic.

ἄνωγα (439 D.) Epic 2 perf. as pres. *command* (1 pl. ἄνωγμεν, imper. ἄνωχθι, ἀνώχθω, ἄνωχθε), 2 plup. as imperf. ἠνώγεα, 3 s. ἠνώγει and ἀνώγει. To ἀνώγω, a pres. developed from the perf., many forms may be referred, as pres. ἀνώγει, subj. ἀνώγω, opt. ἀνώγοιμι, imper. ἄνωγε, inf. ἀνωγέμεν, part. ἀνώγων, imperf. ἤνωγον, fut. ἀνώξω, aor. ἤνωξα. Poetic and Ion.

ἀπ-αντάω *meet:* **ἀπ-αντήσομαι** (806), **ἀπ-ήντησα, ἀπ-ήντηκα, ἀπ-αντητέος.**

ἀπατάω *deceive:* regular, but as fut. pass. **ἀπατήσομαι** and **ἐξ-απατηθήσομαι** (809). Cp. 454 a.

ἀπ-αυράω *take away*, found in the imperf. ἀπηύρων (with aoristic force), fut. ἀπουρήσω, aor. part. ἀπούρᾱς (as if from ἀπούρημι), ἀπουράμενος. The root is probably ϝρᾱ, ἀπηύρων representing ἀπ-ευρων for ἀπ-εϝρων (with η for ε by mistake), as ἀπούρᾱς represents ἀπο-ϝρᾱς. Poetic and Epic.

ἀπ-αφ-ίσκω (ἀπ-αφ-, ἀπ-αφε-) *deceive*, comp. w. ἐξ: -απαφήσω rare, -απάφησα rare, 2 aor. -ήπαφον, mid. opt. -απαφοίμην. Poetic. (V.)

ἀπ-εχθ-άνομαι (ἐχθ-, ἐχθε-) *am hated:* **ἀπ-εχθήσομαι,** 2 aor. **ἀπ-ηχθόμην, ἀπ-ήχθημαι.** Simple forms are ἔχθω, ἔχθομαι. (IV.)

ἀπό-(ϝ)ερσε *swept off:* ἀπο-έρσῃ, ἀπο-έρσειε. Epic.

ἀπο-λαύω *enjoy* (the simple λαύω is unused): **ἀπο-λαύσομαι** (806), **ἀπ-έλαυσα, ἀπο-λέλαυκα** (450).

ἅπ-τω (ἁφ-) *fasten, kindle*, mid. *touch:* **ἅψω, ἧψα, ἧμμαι, ἥφθην, ἁπτός, -τέος.** (II.)

ἀράομαι *pray* (Epic ἀράομαι), often comp. w. ἐπί or κατά: **ἀρᾱ́σομαι, ἠρᾱσάμην, -ήρᾱμαι,** ἀρᾱτός poetic. Epic act. inf. ἀρήμεναι. Ion. ἀρέομαι.

ἀρ-αρ-ίσκω (ἀρ-) *fit, join* trans.: ἦρσα, 2 aor. ἤραρον trans. and intrans. (448 D.), 2 perf. ἄρᾱρα intrans., aor. pass. ἤρθην. Ion. and Epic 2 perf. ἄρηρα, plup. ἀρήρεα and ἠρήρεα. 2 aor. part. mid. ἄρμενος, as adj., *fitting*. Poetic. (V.)

ἀράττω (ἀραγ-) *strike*, comp. in prose w. ἀπό, ἐξ, ἐπί, κατά, σύν; **-αράξω, -ήραξα, -ηράχθην.** Cp. ῥάττω. (III.)

ἀρέ-σκω (ἀρε- for ἀρεσ-; cp. τὸ ἄρος *help*) *please:* **ἀρέσω, ἤρεσα**; mid. **ἀρέσκομαι** *appease:* **ἀρέσομαι, ἠρεσάμην, ἠρέσθην** (?), **ἀρεστός** *pleasing.* (V.)

ἀρημένος *oppressed.* Epic perf. mid. of uncertain derivation.

ἀρκέω (ἀρκε- for ἀρκεσ-; cp. τὸ ἄρκος *defence*) *assist, suffice:* **ἀρκέσω, ἤρκεσα.**

ἁρμόττω and poetic ἁρμόζω (ἁρμοδ-) *fit:* **ἁρμόσω, ἥρμοσα, ἥρμοσμαι, ἡρμόσθην.** Aor. συνάρμοξα Pind., perf. ἥρμοκα Aristotle. 516. (III.)

ἄρ-νυμαι (ἀρ-) *win:* ἀροῦμαι, 2 aor. ἠρόμην (inf. ἀρέσθαι). Chiefly poetic. Cp. αἴρω. (IV.)

ἀρόω *plough:* aor. act. ἤροσα and aor. pass. ἠρόθην are, in Attic, attested only in poetry; perf. mid. ἀρήρομαι Epic and Ion.

ἁρπάζω (ἁρπαγ-) *seize, snatch:* **ἁρπάσομαι** (806), less often **ἁρπάσω, ἥρπασα,**

ἥρπακα, ἥρπασμαι, ἡρπάσθην, ἁρπασθήσομαι. Fut. ἁρπάξω Epic, aor. ἥρπαξα poetic, aor. pass. ἡρπάχθην Hdt., v. a. ἁρπακτός Hesiod. 516. (III.)

ἀρτύω (Hom. ἀρτύω) *prepare:* in prose often comp. w. ἐξ or κατά: **ἀρτύσω, ἤρτυσα, -ήρτυκα, -ήρτυμαι, -ηρτύθην.** Cp. Epic ἀρτύνω (ἀρτυν-): ἀρτυνέω, ἤρτυνα, ἠρτύθην.

ἀρύω (**ἀρύτω**) *draw water:* **ἤρυσα, ἐπ-ηρύθην, ἀπ-αρυστέος**; ἠρύσθην Hippocr. 531.

ἄρχω *begin, rule,* mid. *begin;* **ἄρξω, ἦρξα,** ἦρχα late, **ἦργμαι** mid., **ἤρχθην, ἀρκτέος,** fut. mid. **ἄρξομαι** sometimes as pass. (808), ἀρχθήσομαι Aristotle.

ἀστράπ-τω (ἀστραπ-) *lighten, flash:* ἀστράψω, **ἤστραψα.** (II.)

ἀτιτάλλω (ἀτιταλ-) *rear,* Epic and Lyric: ἀτίτηλα. (III.)

ᾄττω (ᾄσσω; from ϝαι-ϝικ-ιω) *rush,* rare in prose: **ᾄξω, ᾖξα.** From Ion. and poetic ἀΐσσω (Hom. ἀΐσσω) come ἀΐξω, ἤϊξα (-άμην), ἠΐχθην (with act. meaning). (III.)

αὑαίνω and αὐαίνω (αὑαν-) *dry:* αὑανῶ Soph., ηὕηνα or αὕηνα Hdt., ηὑάνθην or αὑάνθην Aristoph., fut. pass. αὑανθήσομαι Aristoph., fut. mid. αὑανοῦμαι as pass. Soph. Mainly poetic and Ion., rare in Att. prose. (III.)

αὐξ-άνω and (less often) **αὔξω** (αὐξ-, αὐξε-) *make increase, grow:* imperf. **ηὔξανον** or **ηὖξον** (**ηὐξανόμην** or **ηὐξόμην**), **αὐξήσω, ηὔξησα, ηὔξηκα, ηὔξημαι, ηὐξήθην, αὐξηθήσομαι** (fut. pass. also **αὐξήσομαι,** 809), αὐξητέος Aristotle. Cp. Epic and Ion. ἀέξω (-ομαι), imperf. ἄεξον. (IV.)

ἀφάσσω (515 a) *feel, handle* (Hdt.): ἤφασα. Cp. Ion. and Epic ἀφάω or ἀφάω *handle* (rare in Att.); Hom. ἀφόων, Ion. ἐπ-αφήσω, ἐπ-ήφησα. (III.)

ἀφίημι *let go:* in the imperf. **ἠφ-ίην** or **ἀφ-ίην.** See 450.

ἀφύσσω (ἀφυγ-) *dip up:* ἀφύξω. Poetic, chiefly Epic. (III.)

ἀφύω *dip up:* ἤφυσα (-άμην). Poetic, chiefly Epic.

ἄχθομαι *am vexed;* as if from *ἀχθέομαι (ἀχθε- for ἀχθεσ-; cp. τὸ ἄχθος *distress*) come **ἀχθέσομαι, ἠχθέσθην** (489 e), fut. pass. as mid. **ἀχθεσθήσομαι** (812).

ἄχ-νυμαι (ἀχ-) *am troubled,* imperf. ἄχνυτο Ξ 38. Poetic. (IV.)

ἄχομαι (ἀχ-) *am troubled.* Epic present.

*ἄω *satiate* (cp. ἄ-δην *sufficiently,* Lat. *sa-tis*): ἄσω, ἆσα, 2 aor. *satiate myself* (subj. ἔωμεν or ἑῶμεν, from ἥομεν, inf. ἄμεναι). Mid. ἄαται (better ἄεται), ἄσομαι, ἀσάμην, ἆτος (ἄ-ατος?). Epic.

ἄωρτο: see **αἴρω.**

βαδίζω *go:* **βαδιοῦμαι** (806), βεβάδικα Aristotle, **βαδιστέος.** 512. (III.)

βάζω (βακ-) *speak, utter:* βάξω, βέβακται. Poetic. (III.)

βαίνω (βα-, βαν-, 523 h) *go:* **-βήσομαι** (806), 2 aor. **-ἔβην** (551, 682 a, 687), **βέβηκα,** 2 perf. **βεβᾶσι** (subj. **-βεβῶσι,** 704 a), **-βέβαμαι** rare, **-εβάθην** rare, **βατός, δια-βατέος.** The *simple* verb appears in Att. prose only in the pres. and perf. act. Epic aor. mid. ἐβησάμην (rare) and ἐβησόμην (542 D.). Causative (*make go*) are βήσω poetic, ἔβησα poetic and Ion. prose. Cp. also βάσκω, βιβάω, βίβημι. 530. (III. IV.)

βάλλω (βαλ-, βλη-, 128 a, βαλλε-) *throw:* **βαλῶ** in good prose in comp. (**βαλλήσω** Aristoph. of continued action), 2 aor. **ἔβαλον** (-όμην usu. in comp.), **βέβληκα, βέβλημαι** (opt. δια-βεβλῆσθε, 711 d), **ἐβλήθην,** fut. pass. **βληθήσομαι,** fut. perf. **βεβλήσομαι** usu. in comp., **ἀπο-βλητέος.** Epic forms of the fut. are ξυμ-βλήσεαι; of the 2 aor. act. ξυμ-βλήτην (688), ξυμ-βλήμεναι; of the 2 aor-mid. as pass. ἐβλήμην (subj. βλήεται, opt. βλῇο or βλεῖο, inf. βλῆσθαι, part. βλήμενος); of the perf. 2 s. βέβληαι and 1 s. βεβόλημαι. (III.)

βάπ-τω (βαφ-) *dip:* **ἐμ-βάψω, ἔβαψα, βέβαμμαι,** 2 aor. pass. **ἐβάφην** (1 aor. pass. ἐβάφθην Aristoph.), **βαπτός.** (II.)

βαρύνω (βαρυν-) *load, annoy:* **βαρυνῶ, ἐβαρύνθην.** (III.)

βάσκω (βα-) *go:* poetic form of **βαίνω.** ἐπιβασκέμεν B 234 *cause to go.* (V.)

βαστάζω (βασταδ-) *carry:* βαστάσω, ἐβάστασα. Poetic. Late forms are from βασταγ-. (III.)

βήττω (βηχ-) *cough.* Ion. are βήξω, ἔβηξα.

βιβάζω (βα-) *make go:* usu. comp. w. ἀνά, διά, etc. in prose: **-βιβάσω** (**-ομαι**) and **-βιβῶ** (539 d), **-εβίβασα,** ἐβιβάσθην Aristotle, **-βιβαστέος.** 447 a, 512. (III.)

βιβάω (βα-) *step:* part. βιβῶν. Epic.

βίβημι (βα-) *go:* part. βιβάς. Epic.

βι-βρώ-σκω (βρω-) *eat:* **βέβρωκα** (2 perf. part. βεβρώς poetic), **βέβρωμαι,** ἐβρώθην Hdt., fut. perf. βεβρώσομαι Hom., βρωτός Eur. Epic 2 aor. ἔβρων (688). In Att. other tenses than perf. act. and pass. are supplied from **ἐσθίω.** (V.)

βιόω *live* (for pres. and imperf. **ζάω** and **βιοτεύω** were preferred): **βιώσομαι** (806), **ἐβίωσα** rare, 2 aor. **ἐβίων** (687), **βεβίωκα, βεβίωται** (with the dat. of a pronoun), **βιωτός, -τέος.**

(βιώσκομαι) usu. **ἀνα-βιώσκομαι** *reanimate, revive* intrans.: ἀν-εβίωσα late Att., intrans., **ἀν-εβιωσάμην** *reanimated,* 2 aor. **ἀν-εβίων** intrans. (V.)

βλάπ-τω (βλαβ-) *hurt, injure:* **βλάψω, ἔβλαψα, βέβλαφα, βέβλαμμαι, ἐβλάφθην** and 2 aor. **ἐβλάβην,** fut. mid. **βλάψομαι** (also as pass., 809), 2 fut. pass. **βλαβήσομαι,** fut. perf. βεβλάψομαι Ion. Cp. βλάβομαι *am injured* T 82. (II.)

βλαστ-άνω (βλαστ-, βλαστε-) *sprout:* 2 aor. **ἔβλαστον, βεβλάστηκα** (less often **ἐβλάστηκα,** 440 a). ἐβλάστησα Ion. and poetic. (IV.)

βλέπω *see:* **βλέψομαι** (806), **ἔβλεψα, βλεπτέος,** -τός poetic. Hdt. has fut. ἀναβλέψω. βλέπομαι is rare in pass. sense.

βλίττω for μ(β)λιτ-ι̯ω (from μλιτ-, cp. μέλι, μέλιτ-ος *honey,* 130) *take honey:* **ἔβλισα.** (III.)

βλώ-σκω for μ(β)λω-σκω from μολ-, μλω- (130 D.) *go:* fut. μολοῦμαι (806), 2 aor. ἔμολον, perf. μέμβλωκα. Poetic. (V.)

βοάω *shout:* **βοήσομαι** (806), **ἐβόησα.** Ion. are βώσομαι, ἔβωσα, βέβωμαι, ἐβώσθην. Cp. 59 D. 1, 489 g.

βό-σκω (βο-, βοσκ-, βοσκε-) *feed:* **βοσκήσω** and **βοσκητέος** Aristoph. **βόσκομαι** *eat.* (V.)

βούλομαι (βουλ-, βουλε-) w. augment ἐβουλ- or ἠβουλ- (430) *will, wish:* **βουλήσομαι, βεβούλημαι, ἐβουλήθην, βουλητός,** -τέος Aristotle. Epic 2 perf. προβέβουλα *prefer.* Hom. has also βόλομαι.

βραχ-: 2 aor. (ἔ)βραχε, βραχεῖν *resound.* Epic.

βρέχω *wet:* **ἔβρεξα, βέβρεγμαι, ἐβρέχθην.**

βρίζω *slumber, am drowsy:* ἔβριξα. Poetic. 512. (III.)

βρίθω *am heavy:* βρίσω, ἔβρῑσα, βέβρῑθα. Mainly poetic.

βροχ- *swallow,* often w. ἀνά, κατά: -έβροξε, 2 perf. -βέβροχε, 2 aor. pass. part. -βροχείς. The common verb is **κατα-βροχθίζω** (Aristoph.). Epic.

βρύκω *bite, grind the teeth:* βρύξω (147 c), ἔβρυξα, 2 aor. ἔβρυχον. Chiefly Ion.

βρῡχάομαι (βρῡχ-, 486) *roar:* βέβρῡχα as pres. (poetic), **ἀν-εβρῡχησάμην** Plato, βρῡχηθείς Soph.

βρώ-θω eat: 2 perf. opt. βεβρώθοις Δ 35. Cp. βιβρώσκω.

βῡνέω (βῡ- for βυσ-) *stop up*, often w. ἐπί, πρό: **-βύσω, -έβῡσα, βέβυσμαι, παρά-βυστος.** Hdt. has δια-βύνεται. Comic and Ion. (IV.)

γαμέω (γαμ-, γαμε-, 485) *marry* (of the man): fut. **γαμῶ, ἔγημα, γεγάμηκα.** Mid. **γαμέομαι** (of the woman): fut. **γαμοῦμαι, ἐγημάμην, γεγάμημαι,** v. a. **γαμετός** (**γαμετή** *wife*), **-τέος.**

γά-νυμαι (γα-) *rejoice*: Epic fut. γανύσσομαι (w. νυ of the pres. stem). Chiefly poetic. (IV.)

γέγωνα (γων-, γωνε-) 2 perf. as pres. *shout*: part. γεγωνώς Epic. Other forms may be referred to γεγώνω or γεγωνέω; as subj. γεγώνω, imper. γέγωνε, inf. γεγωνέμεν (Epic) and γεγωνεῖν, imperf. ἐγεγώνει and ἐγέγωνε, 1 pl. ἐγεγώνευν, fut. γεγωνήσω, aor. ἐγεγώνησα, v. a. γεγωνητέος. Poetic, occasionally in prose. By-form **γεγωνίσκω.**

γείνομαι (γεν-) *am born* Epic; aor. ἐγεινάμην *begat* (poetic) yields in Hdt., Xen. γεινάμενος, γειναμένη *parent.* (III.)

γελάω (γελα- for γελασ-) *laugh*: **γελάσομαι** (806), **ἐγέλασα, ἐγελάσθην** (489 e), **κατα-γέλαστος.** 488.

γέντο seized, Epic 2 aor. Σ 476. Also = **ἐγένετο** (**γίγνομαι**).

γηθέω (γηθ-, γηθε-, 485) *rejoice*: **γέγηθα** as pres.; γηθήσω and ἐγήθησα poetic.

γηρά-σκω and less com. **γηράω** (γηρα-) *grow old*: **γηράσομαι** (806), less often **γηράσω, ἐγήρᾱσα, γεγήρᾱκα** *am old.* 2 aor. ἐγήρᾱ Epic and Ion., inf. γηρᾶναι poetic, part. γηράς Hom. (687). (V.)

γηρύω (500. 1. a) *speak out*: γηρύσομαι (806), ἐγήρῡσα, ἐγηρύθην. Poetic.

γίγνομαι (γεν-, γενε-, γον-, 478) *become, am*: **γενήσομαι,** 2 aor. **ἐγενόμην,** 2 perf. **γέγονα** *am, have been,* **γεγένημαι, γενηθήσομαι** rare. γίνομαι Doric and New Ion. (89). 2 aor. 3 s. γέντο Epic; aor. pass. ἐγενήθην Doric, Ion., late Att. comedy; 2 perf. part. **γεγώς** (other -μι forms w. γα- for γν̥- 479, 482, 573, 704 b).

γι-γνώ-σκω (γνω-, γνο-) *know*: **γνώσομαι** (806), 2 aor. **ἔγνων** (687) *perceived,* **ἔγνωκα, ἔγνωσμαι** (489 c), **ἐγνώσθην, γνωσθήσομαι, γνωστός** (γνωτός poetic), **-στέος.** 1 aor. ἀν-έγνωσα *persuaded* Hdt. Doric, New Ion. γῑνώσκω (89). (V.)

γλύφω *carve*: **γέγλυμμαι** and **ἔγλυμμαι** (440 a). Hdt. has ἐνέγλυψα. Other forms are late.

γνάμπ-τω (γναμπ-) *bend*: γνάμψω, ἔγναμψα, ἀν-εγνάμφθην. Poetic for **κάμπτω.** (II.)

γοάω bewail: inf. γοήμεναι Hom., 2 aor. γόον (γο-) Epic. Mid. γοάομαι poetic: γοήσομαι Hom.

γράφω *write*: **γράψω, ἔγραψα, γέγραφα, γέγραμμαι,** 2 aor. pass. **ἐγράφην,** 2 fut. pass. **γραφήσομαι,** fut. perf. pass. **γεγράψομαι, γραπτός, -τέος.** γεγράφηκα, ἔγραμμαι, and ἐγράφθην are late.

γρύζω (γρυγ-) *grunt*: **γρύξομαι** (806, late γρύξω); **ἔγρυξα, γρυκτός.** Mostly in Att. comedy. (III.)

δα- teach, learn, no pres.: 2 aor. ἔδαον *learned*, redupl. δέδαον *taught*, 2 aor. mid. δεδαέσθαι (δεδάασθαι MSS.), 1 perf. δεδάηκα (δαε-) *have learned*, 2 perf. part. δεδαώς *having learned*, perf. mid. δεδάημαι *have learned*, 2 aor. pass. as intrans. ἐδάην *learned*, 2 fut. pass. as intrans. δαήσομαι *shall learn*; ἀ-δάητος. Cp. Hom. δήω *shall find* and **διδάσκω.** Poetic, mainly Epic.

δαι-δάλλω (δαιδαλ-, δαιδαλο-) *deck out*: Pind. has perf. part. δεδαιδαλμένος, aor. part. δαιδαλθείς, and fut. inf. δαιδαλωσέμεν. Epic and Lyric. (III.)

δαΐζω (*δαϊγ-*) *rend:* *δαΐξω*, *ἐδάϊξα*, *δεδάϊγμαι*, *ἐδαΐχθην*. Epic, Lyric, Tragic. (III.)

δαί-νῡμι (*δαι-*) *entertain:* *δαίνῡ* Epic imperf. and pres. imper., *δαίσω*, *ἔδαισα*. Mid. *δαίνυμαι* *feast* (opt. *δαινῦτο* Ω 665, cp. 750 D.), *ἐδαισάμην*, aor. pass. part. *δαισθείς*, *ἄ-δαιτος*. Poetic, rare in Ion. prose. (IV.)

δαίομαι *divide:* perf. 3 pl. *δεδαίαται* α 23; subj. *δάηται* Υ 316 (for *δαίηται*) from *δαίομαι* or *δαίω*? Cp. *δατέομαι*. Poetic.

δαίω (*δαϝ-ι̯ω*) *kindle:* 2 perf. *δέδηα* *burn* intrans., plup. *δεδήει*. Mid. *δαίομαι* *burn* intrans. Mainly poetic. (III.)

δάκ-νω (*δακ-*, *δηκ-*) *bite:* **δήξομαι** (806), 2 aor. **ἔδακον**, **δέδηγμαι**, **ἐδήχθην**, **δαχθήσομαι**. (IV.)

δαμ-άζω *tame, subdue:* fut. *δαμάσω*, *δαμάω*, *δαμῶ* (Hom. 3 s. *δαμᾷ* and *δαμάᾳ*, 3 pl. *δαμόωσι*, 645), aor. *ἐδάμασα*. Att. prose has only **δαμάζω**, **κατ-εδαμασάμην**, **ἐδαμάσθην**. Mostly poetic, rare in prose. 512. (III.)

δάμ-νη-μι (and *δαμ-νά-ω*?) (*δαμ-*, *δμη-*) *tame, subdue:* perf. mid. *δέδμημαι*, pass. 1 aor. *ἐδμήθην* and (more commonly) 2 aor. *ἐδάμην*, fut. perf. *δεδμήσομαι*. Poetic. 737. (IV.)

δαρθ-άνω (*δαρθ-*, *δαρθε-*) *sleep*, usu. in comp., espec. w. *κατά*: 2 aor. **-έδαρθον** (Hom. *ἔδραθον*), perf. **-δεδάρθηκα**. (IV.)

δατέομαι (*δατ-*, *δατε-*) *divide:* *δάσ(σ)ομαι*, **ἀν-εδασάμην** rare in prose (*ἐδασ(σ)άμην* Epic), *δέδασμαι*, *ἀνά-δαστος*. *δατέασθαι* in Hesiod should be *δατέεσθαι*. Cp. *δαίομαι* *divide*. Mainly poetic and New Ion.

δέαμαι *appear*, only imperf. *δέατο* ζ 242. From a kindred root aor. *δοάσσατο* N 458.

δέδια, **δέδοικα**, *δείδω* (703) *fear:* see **δι-**.

δεδίττομαι *frighten* (rare in Att. prose): **ἐδεδιξάμην** rare. Poetic, mainly Epic, are *δεδίσσομαι*, *δεδίσκομαι*, *δειδίσσομαι*: fut. *δειδίξομαι*, aor. *ἐδειδιξάμην*. Derived from **δέδια** (*δι-*). (III.)

δείδεκτο *greeted* I 224, *δειδέχαται* η 72 (*-ατο* Δ 4) are referred by some to the mid. of *δείκνῡμι*. Others read *δηκ-* from another root. Cp. *δεικανόωντο* *welcomed* O 86.

δειδίσκομαι *greet*, only pres. and imperf., to be read *δηδίσκομαι* (445 D., 527 b). Epic. (V.)

δείκ-νῡμι and **δεικ-νύ-ω** (*δεικ-*) *show* (418): **δείξω**, **ἔδειξα**, **δέδειχα**, **δέδειγμαι**, **ἐδείχθην**, **δειχθήσομαι**, **δεικτέος**. Hdt. has forms from *δεκ-*: *-δέξω*, *-έδεξα* (*-άμην*), *-δέδεγμαι*, *-εδέχθην*. (IV.)

δέμω (*δεμ-*, *δμη-*) *build:* *ἔδειμα*, *δέδμημαι*. Poetic and Ion.

δέρκομαι (*δερκ-*, *δορκ-*, *δρακ-*) *see:* 2 aor. *ἔδρακον*, perf. *δέδορκα* as pres., pass. 1 aor. *ἐδέρχθην* (in tragedy) *saw* and 2 aor. *ἐδράκην* *saw*, *μονό-δερκτος*. Poetic.

δέρω (*δερ-*, *δαρ-*) *flay:* **δερῶ**, **ἔδειρα**, **δέδαρμαι**, 2 aor. pass. **ἐδάρην**, *δρατός* Hom. Pres. *δείρω* (*δερ-ι̯ω*) Hdt., Aristoph.

δέχομαι *receive, await:* **δέξομαι**, **ἐδεξάμην**, **δέδεγμαι**, **εἰσ-εδέχθην**, **ἀπο-δεκτέος**. *δέκομαι* New Ion., Pindaric, and Aeolic. Fut. perf. as act. *δεδέξομαι* poetic. On Epic *ἐδέγμην*, *δέξαι*, *δέχθαι*, *δέγμενος*, Hom. *δέχαται* (3 pl.), see 634, 688.

δέω *bind* (397 a): **δήσω**, **ἔδησα**, **δέδεκα** (*δέδηκα* doubtful), **δέδεμαι**, **ἐδέθην**, fut. pass. **δεθήσομαι**, fut. perf. **δεδήσομαι**, **σύν-δετος**, **ἀν-υπό-δητος**, **συν-δετέος** Aristoph. Mid. in prose only in comp., as **περιδήσομαι**.

δέω (*δεϝω*; *δε-*, *δεε-*) *need, lack* (397 a): **δεήσω**, **ἐδέησα**, **δεδέηκα**, **δεδέημαι**, **ἐδεήθην**. Epic aor. *δῆσεν* Σ 100, *ἐδεύησεν* ι 540. Mid. **δέομαι** *want, ask* (Epic *δεύομαι*): **δεήσομαι** (Epic *δευήσομαι*). Impers. **δεῖ** *it is necessary:* **ἔδει**, **δεήσει**, **ἐδέησε** (397 a).

δηριάω and δηρίω *contend*: ἐδήρῖσα Theocr. Mid. δηριάομαι and δηρίομαι as act.: δηρίσομαι Theocr., ἐδηρῖσάμην θ 76, ἐδηρίνθην Π 756 *contended* (as if from δηρίνω), ἀμφι-δήρῖτος Thuc. Epic and Lyric.

δήω *shall find*, Epic pres. w. fut. meaning. Cp. δα-.

δι- (δϝι-, δϝει-, δϝοι-) *fear* (477 a): **ἔδεισα, δέδοικα** as pres., 2 perf. **δέδια** as pres. (rare in the sing.; inflection, 703). Epic forms: δείδω (from δεδϝοια, 445 D.) as pres., δείσομαι (806), ἔδδεισα (= ἐδϝεισα), δείδοικα, δείδια (703 D.). Hom. has imperf. δίον *feared, fled* from an assumed pres. δίω.

διαιτάω *arbitrate* (from δίαιτα, but augmented as if a comp. w. double augment in perf., plup., and in comps.; cp. 451): **διαιτήσω, διῄτησα** (but **ἀπ-εδιῄτησα**), **δεδιῄτηκα** (plup. **κατ-εδεδιῃτήκη**), **δεδιῄτημαι** (plup. **ἐξ-εδεδιῄτητο**), **διῃτήθην**. Mid. *pass one's life*: **διαιτήσομαι, κατ-εδιῃτησάμην** *effected arbitration*.

διᾱκονέω *minister* (from διάκονος): **ἐδιᾱκόνουν, διᾱκονήσω, δεδιᾱκόνηκα, δεδιᾱκόνημαι, ἐδιᾱκονήθην**. Forms in δεδιη- are wrong, forms in διη- are Ion. and late (uncertain in classical poetry).

δι-δά-σκω (for διδαχ-σκω, 97 a) *teach*, mid. *cause to teach, learn*: **διδάξω, ἐδίδαξα, δεδίδαχα, δεδίδαγμαι, ἐδιδάχθην, διδάξομαι** (808), **διδακτός, -τέος**. Epic aor. ἐδιδάσκησα (διδασκε-) 447 a. (V.)

δί-δη-μι (δη-, δε-) *bind*, pres. and imperf. Poetic for **δέω**. Xen. has διδέᾱσι.

-δι-δρᾱ́-σκω (δρᾱ-) *run away*, only in comp. w. ἀπό, ἐξ: **-δρᾱ́σομαι** (806), 2 aor. **-ἔδρᾱν** (**-δρῶ, -δραίην**, -δρᾶθι late, **-δρᾶναι, -δρᾱ́ς**, 687), **-δέδρᾱκα**. Hdt. has -διδρήσκω, -δρήσομαι, -ἔδρην (but -δρᾱ́ς), -δέδρηκα. (V.)

δί-δω-μι (δω-, δο-) *give*: see 416, 421. Fut. **δώσω**, 1 aor. **ἔδωκα** in s., 2 aor. **ἔδοτον** dual, **ἔδομεν** pl. (756), **δέδωκα, δέδομαι, ἐδόθην, δοθήσομαι, δοτός, -τέος**. See 747 ff. for pres. in Hom. and Hdt. Fut. διδώσω Epic, 2 aor. iter. δόσκον (492 a).

δί-ζη-μαι (from δι-διη-) *seek* (cp. ζητέω) keeps η throughout in the pres. (imperf. ἐδιζήμην), διζήσομαι, ἐδιζησάμην. Poetic and Ion. 726 a, 741.

δίη-μι *cause to flee*, only in imperf. ἐν-δίεσαν *set on* Σ 584. Mid. δίεμαι *flee, cause to flee*, subj. δίωμαι (accent 424 c, N. 2), opt. διοίμην (accent 424 c, N. 2), inf. δίεσθαι referred by some to the middle of δίω. Epic.

δικ- only in 2 aor. ἔδικον *threw*. In Pindar and the tragic poets.

διψάω (διψα-, διψη-) *thirst*: pres. see 394, 641: **διψήσω, ἐδίψησα**.

δίω: see δι-.

διώκω *pursue*: **διώξομαι** (806) and (less well supported) **διώξω, ἐδίωξα, δεδίωχα, ἐδιώχθην, διωκτέος**. For ἐδιώκαθον see 490 D.

δοκέω (δοκ-, δοκε-, 485) *seem, think*: **δόξω, ἔδοξα, δέδογμαι, κατ-εδόχθην, ἀ-δόκητος**. Poetic forms are δοκήσω, ἐδόκησα, δεδόκημαι, ἐδοκήθην. In trimeter Aristoph. uses only the shorter forms.

δουπέω (δουπ-, δουπε-) *sound heavily*: ἐδούπησα, 2 perf. δέδουπα *fell*. Epic aor. ἐγδούπησα. Poetic.

δράττομαι (δραγ-) *seize*: ἐδραξάμην, δέδραγμαι. (III.)

δράω *do*: **δρᾱ́σω, ἔδρᾱσα, δέδρᾱκα, δέδρᾱμαι** (δέδρασμαι, 489 e, doubtful), **ἐδρᾱ́σθην, δρᾱστέος**.

δρέπω *pluck*: **ἔδρεψα**, 2 aor. ἔδραπον Pind., ἄ-δρεπτος Aesch. Cp. δρέπ-τω poetic.

δύναμαι *am able, can* (augment usually ἐδυν-, but also ἠδυν-, 430): **δυνήσομαι, δεδύνημαι, ἐδυνήθην, δυνατός**. Pres. 2 s. **δύνασαι**, δύνᾳ poetic, δύνῃ Ion. (465 a, N. 2), imperf. **ἐδύνω** (ἐδύνασο late), aor. pass. ἐδυνάσθην Epic, New Ion., Pind. (489 g).

δύω *enter, go down, sink, cause to enter* (trans. generally in comp. w. ἀπό or κατά (819): also δύ-νω (Ion., poetic, rare in Xen.) *enter*: **-δύσω** trans., **-έδυσα** trans., 2 aor. **ἔδυν** intrans. (p. 140), **δέδυκα** intrans., **-δέδυκα** trans., **-δέδυμαι**, **-εδύθην**, **-δυθήσομαι** Aristoph., **-δυτέος**. Fut. mid. **δύσομαι**, aor. mid. **-εδυσάμην** (Epic also ἐδυσόμην, 542 D.). Hom. 2 aor. opt. δύη and ἐκδῦμεν (758 D).

ἐάφθη N 543, aor. pass., *was hurled* (?), possibly from ϝαπ- (ἰάπτω); sometimes referred to ἅπτω or to ἕπομαι.

ἐάω *permit, let alone*: **ἐάσω**, **εἴασα** (431), **εἴακα** (443), **εἴαμαι**, **εἰάθην**, **ἐάσομαι** pass. (808), **ἐατέος**. Epic pres. also εἰάω, imperf. ἔα E 517, aor. ἔασα; Hdt. does not augment.

ἐγγυάω *pledge*: the forms in ἠγγυ- are better than those in ἐνεγυ- or ἐγγεγυ-; see 453 a.

ἐγείρω (ἐγερ-, ἐγορ-, ἐγρ-, 36) *wake, rouse*: **ἐγερῶ**, **ἤγειρα**, 2 perf. **ἐγρήγορα** 478, 705 *am awake* (for ἐγ-ηγορα, but ρ is also redupl.), **ἐγήγερμαι**, **ἠγέρθην**, 2 aor. mid. **ἠγρόμην** *awoke*, **ἐγερτέος**, ἐγερτός Aristotle. Hom. 2 perf. 3 pl. ἐγρηγόρθᾱσι, imper. ἐγρήγορθε (for -γορσθε), inf. ἐγρήγορθαι or ἐγρηγόρθαι (for -γορσθαι). (III.)

ἐγκωμιάζω *praise*: **ἐγκωμιάσω** and **ἐγκωμιάσομαι** (806), **ἐνεκωμίασα**, **ἐγκεκωμίακα**, **ἐγκεκωμίασμαι**, ἐνεκωμιάσθην Hdt. 512. (III.)

ἔδω *eat*: poetic for **ἐσθίω**.

ἕζομαι (ἑδ- for σεδ-, cp. *sedeo*) *sit*, usu. **καθ-έζομαι** (which is less common than **καθ-ίζομαι**): **ἐκαθ-εζόμην** (450), **καθ-εδοῦμαι** (539 b), **εἱσάμην** rare in prose, **καθ-εστέος**. Fut. ἐφ-έσσομαι trans. ι 455, aor. ἑσσάμην and ἐεσσάμην Epic. Act. aor. Epic εἷσα (imper. ἕσσον or εἷσον, inf. ἕσσαι, part. ἕσᾱς). See ἵζω. (III.)

ἐθέλω (ἐθελ-, ἐθελε-) and **θέλω** *wish*: imperf. always **ἤθελον** in Att.; **ἐθελήσω**, or **θελήσω** (rare); **ἠθέλησα** (subj. **ἐθελήσω** or **θελήσω**, opt. **ἐθελήσαιμι** or **θελήσαιμι**), **ἠθέληκα**. The commoner Att. form is **ἐθέλω** except in the iambic trimeter of tragedy, and in formulas as ἂν θεὸς θέλῃ.

ἐθίζω (for σϝεθ-ιδ̯ω, 123) *accustom*: **ἐθιῶ** (539 e), **εἴθισα** (431), **εἴθικα** (443), **εἴθισμαι** (1946), **εἰθίσθην**, **ἐθιστέος**, -τός Aristotle. 512. (III.)

ἔθω (for σϝεθω, 123) *am accustomed*: pres. part. ἔθων *being accustomed* only in Hom., 2 perf. **εἴωθα** (443, 563 a) *am accustomed*, 2 plup. **εἰώθη** (perf. ἔωθα, plup. ἐώθεα Hdt.). See **ἐθίζω**.

εἶδον *saw*: see ἰδ- and **ὁράω**.

εἰκάζω (εἰκαδ-) *liken, conjecture* augments to ᾐκ- rather than to εἰκ- in Att. prose (437): **ᾔκαζον**, **εἰκάσω**, **ᾔκασα**, **ᾔκασμαι** (εἴκασμαι?), **ᾐκάσθην**, **εἰκασθήσομαι**, **εἰκαστός**, **ἀπ-εικαστέος**. Fut. mid. **-εικάσομαι** sometimes as act.

εἴκω *yield*: **εἴξω**, **εἶξα**, **ὑπ-εικτέος**. On εἴκαθον see 490.

εἴκω (εἰκ-, οἰκ-, ἰκ-; for ϝεικ-, etc.) *resemble, appear* (no pres. in use): **εἴξω** rare, 2 perf. **ἔοικα** as pres. 443, 502 a (impers. **ἔοικε** *it seems*): **ἐοίκω**, **ἐοίκοιμι**, **ἐοικέναι** (poet. εἰκέναι), **ἐοικώς**, neut. **εἰκός** *fitting* (εἰκώς chiefly poetic; also Platonic); 2 plup. **ἐῴκη** and **ᾔκη**. εἶκε *seemed likely* (Σ 520) may be imperf.; some regard it as perf. or plup. For ἔοικα, ἐοίκω, ἐοικώς Hdt. has οἶκα, οἴκω, οἰκώς. Forms of the μι-conjugation are ἔϊκτον, ἐΐκτην Hom., ἔοιγμεν Att. poets, εἴξᾱσι mainly in Att. poets (704 d.). Cp. ἐΐσκω.

εἰλέω or εἱλέω *roll up, pack close*, mostly Epic. εἴλεομαι Hdt., συν-ειλέομαι Xen.: ἀπ-είλημαι Hdt., **ἀν-ειλήθην** Thuc.

εἴλλω *roll* pres. act. and pass. in Att. (rare). Cp. ἴλλω.

εἰλύω (ϝειλυ- for ἐ-ϝλυ-) *roll, cover, gather up*: εἰλύσω, εἴλῡμαι. Cp. ἐλύω. Poetic and Ion.

εἴλω (ἐλ- for ϝελ-, cp. *volvere*) *roll up, drive together*: no pres. act. (εἴλομαι Hom.), ἔλσα and ἔελσα, ἔελμαι, 2 aor. pass. ἐάλην and ἄλην (3 pl. ἄλεν, inf. ἀλῆναι, ἀλήμεναι, part. ἀλείς). Homeric.

εἵμαρται *it is fated*: see μείρομαι.

εἰμί *am*: fut. **ἔσομαι** (806). See p. 211.

εἶμι *go*: see p. 212.

εἶπον (ἐπ- for ϝεπ-,) *said*, 2 aor. (**εἴπω, εἴποιμι, εἰπέ, εἰπεῖν, εἰπών**), Epic ἔειπον and εἴπεσκον. First aor. **εἶπα** rare in Att. (**εἴπαιμι**, imper. **εἶπον**, inf. εἶπαι Hdt., part. εἴπᾱς Hdt. and late Att.), ἔειπα poetic; 1 aor. mid. ἀπ-ειπάμην New Ion. Other tenses are supplied from εἴρω. 529. (VI.)

εἴργω *shut in* or *out*, also **εἴργνῡμι** and (rarely) **εἰργνύω** (with ει- from εε-, cp. Hom. ἐ(ϝ)έργω): **εἴρξω, εἶρξα, εἶργμαι, εἴρχθην, εἰρκτός, -τέος**. Fut. mid. **εἴρξομαι** is pass. or reflex. (808). The distinction that the forms with the smooth breathing mean *shut out*, those with the rough breathing mean *shut in*, is late and not always observed in classical Att. Hom. has ἐέργω (in pres.) and ἔργω *shut in* or *out*: ἔρξα, 2 aor. ἔργαθον and ἐέργαθον, ἔργμαι and ἔεργμαι (3 pl. ἔρχαται, 439 D., plup. ἔρχατο, ἐέρχατο), ἔρχθην. Hom. has ἐέργνῡ K 238. Hdt. usu. has ἔργω (in comp.), with some forms from -έργνῡμι and ἐργνύω. Old Att. forms in ἐργ-, ἑργ- are doubtful: Soph. has -έρξω, ἕρξεται; Plato -έρξᾱς.

εἴρομαι (εἰρ-, εἰρε-) *ask*: εἰρήσομαι Hom. and New Ion. Hom. has also (rarely) ἐρέ(ϝ)ω, subj. ἐρείομεν (= ἐρεύομεν) A 62; and ἐρέ(ϝ)ομαι, imper. ἔρειο or ἐρεῖο Λ 611 (650). Att. fut. **ἐρήσομαι** and 2 aor. **ἠρόμην** presuppose a pres. ἔρομαι, which is supplied by **ἐρωτάω**.

εἴρω (ἐρ- for σερ-, cp. Lat. *sero*) *join*: rare except in comp. w. **ἀπό, διά, σύν**, etc.: aor. -εῖρα (Ion. -ερσα), perf. -εῖρκα, perf. mid. ἔερμαι Epic.

εἴρω Hom. *say* (ἐρ-, ῥη- for ϝερ-, ϝρη-, cp. Lat. *verbum*), for which pres. Att. uses **λέγω, φημί** and (esp. in comp.) **ἀγορεύω**: fut. **ἐρῶ**, aor. supplied by **εἶπον**, perf. **εἴρηκα** (= ϝε-ϝρη-κα), perf. pass. **εἴρημαι**, aor. pass. **ἐρρήθην**, fut. pass. **ῥηθήσομαι**, fut. perf. **εἰρήσομαι**, v. a. **ῥητός, -τέος**. Ion. are ἐρέω fut., εἰρέθην (but ῥηθῆναι) aor. pass.

εἷσα *seated*: see ἵζω.

ἐΐσκω (= ϝε-ϝικ-σκω, from redupl. ϝικ-) *liken* (also ἴσκω): imperf. Hom. ἤϊσκον and ἔϊσκον; perf. mid. προσῄξαι *art like* Eur., plup. Hom. ᾔκτο and ἔϊκτο have been referred by some to εἴκω. Poetic, chiefly Epic. (V.)

εἴωθα: see ἔθω.

ἐκκλησιάζω *call an assembly*: augments **ἐξ-εκλησίαζον** or **ἠκ-κλησίαζον**, etc. (453 a).

ἐλαύνω (from ἐλα-νυ-ω, 523 e) *drive, march*: **ἐλῶ** (539 b), **ἤλασα, -ελήλακα** (w. ἀπό, ἐξ), **ἐλήλαμαι, ἠλάθην, ἐλατέος**, ἐξ-ήλατος Hom., ἐλατός Aristotle. Aor. mid. **ἠλασάμην** rare. Fut. ἐλάσσω ψ 427, ἐλόωσι Hom. (645), ἐλάσω rarely in MSS. of Xen., perf. ἐλήλασμαι Ion. and late, plup. ἠληλάμην (Hom. 3 pl. ἐληλάδατο or ἐληλέατο or ἐληλέδατο), ἠλάσθην Hdt., Aristotle (489 g). ἐλάω is rare and poetic. (IV.)

ἐλέγχω *examine, confute*: **ἐλέγξω, ἤλεγξα, ἐλήλεγμαι** (407), **ἠλέγχθην, ἐλεγχθήσομαι, ἐλεγκτέος**.

ἐλελίζω *raise the war-cry, shout:* ἠλέλιξα Xen. 512. (III.)

ἐλελίζω *whirl, turn round:* ἐλέλιξα, ἐλελίχθην. Poetic. 512. (III.)

ἑλίττω (ἑλικ- for ϝελικ-) *roll* (rarely **εἱλίττω**); sometimes written ἐλ-: **ἑλίξω**, **εἵλιξα** (431), **εἵλιγμαι** (443), **εἱλίχθην**, ἐξ-ελιχθήσομαι Aristotle, **εἱλικτός**. Epic aor. mid. ἑλιξάμην. Epic ἐλέλικτο, ἐλελίχθησαν should be ἐελ-. εἱλίσσω is the usual form in Hdt. (III.)

ἕλκω *draw* (ἑλκ- for σελκ-; most tenses from ἑλκυ-; ἑλκύω late), often w. ἀνά, ἐξ, κατά, σύν: **-ἕλξω**, **εἵλκυσα** (431), **καθ-είλκυκα** (443), **-είλκυσμαι** (489 c), **-ειλκύσθην**, **-ελκυσθήσομαι**, **ἑλκτέος**, **συν-ελκυστέος**. Fut. ἑλκύσω Ion. and late. By-form ἑλκέω Epic.

ἔλπω (ϝελπ-) *cause to hope*, mid. (also ἐέλπομαι) *hope* like **ἐλπίζω**: 2 perf. as pres. ἔολπα (= ϝεϝολπα), 2 plup. ἐώλπεα, v. a. ἄ-ελπτος. Mainly Epic.

ἐλύω *roll:* ἐλύσθην Hom. (= ἐ-ϝλυ-σθην), 489 e. Cp. εἰλύω.

ἐμέω *vomit:* **ἐμοῦμαι** (806), **ἤμεσα**.

ἐναίρω (ἐναρ-) *kill:* 2 aor. ἤναρον. 1 aor. mid. ἐνηράμην as act. Poetic. (III.)

ἐναρίζω *slay, spoil:* ἐναρίξω, ἐνάριξα, κατ-ηνάρισμαι, κατ-ηναρίσθην. Poetic. 512. (III.)

ἐν-εδρεύω *waylay, lie in ambush* regular: fut. mid. as pass. (808).

ἐν-έπω and ἐννέπω (ἐν + σεπ-, σπ-, σπε-) *say, tell:* ἐνι-σπήσω and ἐνίψω (ἐνί-σπω?), 2 aor. ἔνι-σπον (ἐνί-σπω, ἐνί-σποιμι, imper. ἐνί-σπες or ἔνι-σπε, 2 pl. ἔσπετε for ἐν-σπετε, inf. ἐνι-σπεῖν and ἐνι-σπέμεν). Poetic.

ἐνήνοθε defect., w. pres. and imperf. meaning: *sit on, be on, grow on, lie on.* In comp. w. ἐπί in Hom. Epic. Connected by some w. ἀνήνοθε.

ἐνίπ-τω (ἐν-ιπ) *chide:* 2 aor. ἐνένῑπον and ἠν-ίπ-απον (448 D.). Epic also ἐνίσσω. Poetic, chiefly Epic. (II.)

ἕν-νῡμι (ἑ- for ϝεσ-, cp. *ves-tio*) *clothe*, pres. act. only in comp., in prose **ἀμφι-έννῡμι**: **ἀμφι-ῶ** (539 c), **ἠμφί-εσα** (450), **ἠμφί-εσμαι** (489 d). Epic forms: imperf. κατα-είνυον, fut. ἕσσω and -έσω, aor. ἕσσα and -εσα, mid. pres. inf. ἐπ-είνυσθαι Hdt., fut. -έσσομαι, aor. ἑσ(σ)άμην and ἐεσσάμην for ἐ-ϝεσσαμην, perf. ἕσμαι and εἷμαι (part. εἱμένος in tragedy). Cp. 439 D. The simple verb is poetic, mainly Epic. (IV.)

ἐν-οχλέω *harass* has double augment (451): **ἠν-ώχλουν** (ἐν-ώχλουν Aristotle), **ἐν-οχλήσω**, **ἠν-ώχλησα**, **ἠν-ώχλημαι**.

ἐξετάζω *investigate:* **ἐξετάσω** (rarely **ἐξετῶ**, 539 d), **ἐξήτασα**, **ἐξήτακα**, **ἐξήτασμαι**, **ἐξητάσθην**, **ἐξετασθήσομαι**, **ἐξεταστέος**. 512. (III.)

ἔοικα *seem, resemble:* see εἴκω.

ἑορτάζω *keep festival:* ἑώρτασα (for ἡορ-, 34). Ion. ὀρτάζω.

ἐπ-αυρέω and ἐπ-αυρίσκω (αὐρ-, αὐρε-) *enjoy* (Epic and Lyric) are both rare: 2 aor. ἐπαῦρον. Mid. ἐπαυρίσκομαι Ion., poetic, rare in Att. prose: ἐπαυρήσομαι, ἐπηυράμην rare, 2 aor. ἐπηυρόμην. (V.)

ἐπενήνοθε: see ἐνήνοθε.

ἐπιβουλεύω *plot against:* regular, but fut. mid. as pass. (808).

ἐπίσταμαι *understand* (725): 2 s. **ἐπίστασαι**, ἐπίστᾳ and ἐπίστῃ poetic (465 a, N. 2), -επίστεαι Hdt.; subj. **ἐπίστωμαι** (accent, 424 c, N. 2), opt. **ἐπισταίμην**, **ἐπίσταιο** (accent, 424 c, N. 2), imper. **ἐπίστω** (ἐπίστασο poetic and New Ion.), imperf. **ἠπιστάμην**, **ἠπίστασο** and **ἠπίστω** (450, 465 b, N. 1), fut. **ἐπιστήσομαι**, aor. **ἠπιστήθην**, v. a. **ἐπιστητός**. Distinguish ἐφ-ίσταμαι from ἐφ-ίστημι.

ἕπω (σεπ-, σπ-) *am busy about*, usu. w. ἀμφί, διά, ἐπί, μετά, περί (simple only in part.): imperf. -εἶπον (Epic also -ἑπον w. no augm.), fut. -ἕψω, 2 aor. -έσπον for ἕ-σ(ε)πον (-σπῶ, -σποῖμι, -σπών, -σπεῖν), aor. pass. περι-έφθην Hdt. The act. forms are poetic, Ion. (imperf. and fut. also Xenophontic). Mid. **ἕπομαι** *follow:* **εἱπόμην** (431), **ἕψομαι**, 2 aor. **ἑσπόμην** (**σπῶμαι, σποίμην, σποῦ, σπέσθαι, σπόμενος**). Hom. has σπεῖο for σποῦ. For ἕσπωμαι, ἑσποίμην, ἑσπέσθω, etc., following an elided vowel in the MSS. of Hom. we probably have, not a redupl. aor. without augment (ἑσπ- for σε-σπ-), but wrong readings for σπῶμαι etc. with the vowel of the preceding word unelided.

ἐπριάμην *bought:* see πρια- (416).

ἔραμαι (poetic) deponent pass., pres. in prose supplied by **ἐράω** (ἐρα- for ἐρασ-): imperf. **ἤρων** (ἠράμην poetic); aor. **ἠράσθην** *fell in love*, 489 e (ἠρασ(σ)άμην poetic), fut. ἐρασθήσομαι poetic, **ἐραστός**, ἐρατός poetic.

ἐργάζομαι (ϝεργ-) *work*, augments to ἠ- and εἰ- (431, 432), redupl. to εἰ- (443): **ἠργαζόμην, ἐργάσομαι, ἠργασάμην, εἴργασμαι, ἠργάσθην, ἐργασθήσομαι, ἐργαστέος**. In Hdt. without augment and reduplication. 512. (III.)

ἔργω: see **εἴργω**.

ἔρδω (from ϝερζω = ϝεργ-ιω, 511) *work, do* (also ἕρδω): ἔρξω, ἔρξα, 2 perf. ἔοργα (= ϝεϝοργα), 2 plup. ἐώργεα (= ἐϝεϝοργεα) Epic, ἐόργεα Hdt. Ion. and poetic; cp. ῥέζω. (III.)

ἐρείδω *prop:* **ἤρεισα**, ἐρήρεισμαι Hdt. (for Hom. ἐρηρέδαται, -ατο some read ἐρηρίδαται, -ατο), plup. ἠρήρειστο, ἠρείσθην, ἐρείσομαι Aristotle, ἐρεισάμην Hom. Hippocr. has -ήρεικα, -ήρεισμαι, ἐρηρείσεται. Mainly poetic.

ἐρείκω (ἐρεικ-, ἐρικ-) *tear, burst:* ἤρειξα, 2 aor. ἤρικον trans. and intrans., ἐρήριγμαι. Poetic and New Ion.

ἐρείπω (ἐρειπ-, ἐριπ-) *throw down:* ἐρείψω, ἤρειψα, 2 aor. ἤριπον, 2 perf. -ερήριπα *have fallen* Epic (plup. ἐρέριπτο Ξ 15), ἠρείφθην, 2 aor. pass. ἐρίπην. Ion. and poetic.

ἐρέσσω (ἐρετ-) *row:* δι-ήρεσ(σ)α Hom. Late prose has ἐρέσσω and ἐρέττω. (III.)

ἐρέω *ask* Epic: see εἴρομαι.

ἐριδαίνω (ἐριδαν-) *contend* Epic (III. IV.). ἐρῑδήσασθαι Ψ 792 (v. l. ἐριζήσασθαι) as if from ἐρῑδέομαι. By-form ἐριδμαίνω Epic.

ἐρίζω (ἐριδ-) *contend:* ἤρισ(σ)α, ἐρήρισμαι, ἐριστός. Poetic. (III.)

ἔρομαι *ask:* see εἴρομαι.

ἕρπω (σερπ-) and ἑρπύζω *creep* augment to εἰ- (431): **εἷρπον, ἐφ-έρψω, εἵρπυσα**, ἑρπετόν *a beast*.

ἔρρω (ἐρρ-, ἐρρε-) *go away, go (to destruction), perish:* **ἐρρήσω, ἤρρησα, εἰσ-ήρρηκα.**

ἐρυγγ-άνω *cast forth, eruct:* pres. Att., poetic, New Ion., 2 aor. **ἤρυγον.** Cp. ἐρεύγομαι Epic, New Ion.: ἐρεύξομαι Hippocr. (806). (IV.)

ἐρύκω *hold back:* ἐρύξω, ἤρυξα (also Xen.), 2 aor. ἠρύκακον (448 D.). Epic, poetic, New Ion. Hom. has also ἐρῡκάνω, ἐρῡκανάω.

ἔρῡμαι (for ϝερῡμαι) and εἴρυμαι (for ἐϝρῡμαι) *protect* Epic: pres. 3 pl. εἰρύαται and εἰρύαται (for εἴρυνται), inf. ε(ἴ)ρυσθαι; imperf. ε(ἴ)ρῦτο, εἰρύατο (for εἴρυντο); fut. ε(ἰ)ρύσ(σ)ομαι; aor. ε(ἰ)ρυσ(σ)άμην, perf. ἔρῦτο Hesiod. The pres. and imperf. are often taken as μι-forms of ἐρύομαι. By-form ῥύομαι, *q. v.*

ἐρύω (ϝερυ-, ϝρῡ-) *draw:* augments to εἰ- (431 D): fut. ἐρύω Hom.; aor. ε(ἴ)ρυσ(σ)α Hom. Mid. ἐρύομαι *draw to one's self:* ἐρύσσομαι, ε(ἰ)ρυσ(σ)άμην, εἴρῦμαι and εἴρυσμαι 489 d (3 pl. εἰρύαται and εἰρύαται), plup. εἰρύμην (3 pl. εἰρύατο), ε(ἰ)ρύσθην Hippocr., ἐρυστός Soph. Epic and Ion. εἰρύω is poetic (esp. Epic) and New Ion. Late fut. ἐρύσ(σ)ω.

ἔρχομαι (ἐρχ-, ἐλθ-, ἐλευθ-, ἐλυθ-) *go, come:* ἐλεύσομαι, 2 aor. **ἦλθον**, 2 perf. **ἐλήλυθα.** In Att. ἔρχομαι is common only in indic.; subj. Epic and Ion.; opt. (in comp.) Xen.; imper. Epic; inf. Epic, Tragic, Ion., in comp. in Att. prose rarely; part. poetic, in comp. in Att. prose. Imperf. ἠρχόμην uncomp. is rare. For the above tenses Att. prose uses **ἴω, ἴοιμι, ἴθι, ἰέναι, ἰών, ᾖα** simple and in comp. (but not ὑπιέναι for ὑπέρχεσθαι *flatter*). Fut.: Att. prose uses **εἶμι** (774), **ἀφίξομαι** or **ἥξω** for ἐλεύσομαι (which is Epic, Ion., Tragic); 2 aor. ἤλυθον poetic; 2 perf. ἐλήλουθα or εἰλήλουθα Epic, **ἐλήλυμεν, -υτε** in Comic and Tragic fragments; 2 plup. ἐληλύθει Epic. (VI.)

ἐσ-θίω (for ἐδ-θι-ω) *eat:* imperf. **ἤσθιον**, fut. **ἔδομαι** (541, 806), 2 aor. **ἔφαγον**, perf. **ἐδήδοκα, κατ-εδήδεσμαι, ἐδεστός, -τέος.** Epic are ἔδμεναι pres., ἐδηδώς 2 perf. part., ἐδήδομαι (?) perf. pass.; ἠδέσθην Comic, Hippocr., Aristotle. (VI.) ἔσθω Epic and poetic, ἔδω Epic, poetic, and Ion.

ἑστιάω *entertain* augments and reduplicates to εἱ- (431, 443).

εὕδω *sleep*, rare in prose, which usually has **καθ-εύδω**: imperf. **ἐκάθ-ευδον** and **καθ-ηῦδον** (450), fut. **καθ-ευδήσω**, v. a. **καθ-ευδητέος.** εὕδω is chiefly poetic and Ion. (imperf. εὗδον and ηὗδον).

εὐεργετέω *do good.* The augmented form εὐηρ- is to be rejected (452).

εὑρ-ίσκω (εὑρ-, εὑρε-) *find:* **εὑρήσω**, 2 aor. **ηὗρον** or **εὗρον** (imper. **εὑρέ**, 424 b), **ηὕρηκα** or **εὕρηκα, εὕρημαι, εὑρέθην, εὑρεθήσομαι, εὑρετός, -τέος**; εὑράμην Hesiod. The augment is ηὑ- or εὑ- (437). (V.)

εὐφραίνω (εὐφραν-) *cheer:* **εὐφρανῶ, ηὔφρᾱνα.** Mid. *rejoice:* **εὐφρανοῦμαι** and **εὐφρανθήσομαι, ηὐφράνθην.** The augment is also εὐ- (437). (III.)

εὔχομαι *pray, boast:* **εὔξομαι, ηὐξάμην, ηὖγμαι, εὐκτός**, -τέος Hippocr., ἀπ-εύχετος Aesch. The augment is also εὐ- (437).

ἐχθαίρω (ἐχθαρ-) *hate:* ἐχθαρῶ, ἐχθαροῦμαι (808), ἤχθηρα, ἐχθαρτέος. Epic and poetic. (III.)

ἔχθω *hate*, ἔχθομαι: only pres. and imperf. Poetic for **ἀπ-εχθάνομαι.**

ἔχω (ἐχ-, for σεχ-, and σχ-, σχε-) *have, hold:* imperf. **εἶχον** (431), **ἕξω** or **σχήσω** (1911), 2 aor. **ἔσχον** for ἐ-σ(ε)χ-ον (**σχῶ, σχοίην** or **-σχοιμι, σχές, σχεῖν, σχών**), **ἔσχηκα, παρ-έσχημαι, ἑκτέος, ἀνα-σχετός, -τέος.** Mid. **ἔχομαι** *hold by, am near:* **ἕξομαι** (sometimes pass., 808), and **σχήσομαι** (often in comp.), 2 aor. **ἐσχόμην** usu. in comp. (**σχῶμαι, σχοίμην, σχοῦ, σχέσθαι, σχόμενος**), used as pass. for ἐσχέθην (late). Epic forms are perf. συν-όχωκα (for -οκ-οχ-α) B 218, plup. pass. ἐπ-ώχατο *were shut* M 340. Poetic is 2 aor. ἔσχεθον (490 D.). See **ἀμπέχω**, ἀνέχω, **ὑπισχνέομαι.** By-form **ἴσχω** for σι-σ(ε)χ-ω.

ἕψω (ἑψ-, ἑψε-) *cook, boil:* **ἑψήσομαι** (ἑψήσω Comic), **ἥψησα, ἑφθός** (for ἑψθος), **ἑψητός**, ἥψημαι Hippocr., ἡψήθην Hdt. The pres. ἑψέω is not Att.

*ζάω (**ζῶ**) *live* (ζα-, ζη-, 395): (**ζῇς, ζῇ**): imperf. **ἔζων**, fut. **ζήσω** and **ζήσομαι.** For late ἔζησα, ἔζηκα Att. has **ἐβίων, βεβίωκα. βιώσομαι** is commoner than **ζήσομαι.** ζώω Epic, New Ion., dramatic. See 522 b, 641 and D.

ζεύγ-νῡμι (ζευγ-, ζυγ-, cp. Lat. *jugum*) *yoke:* **ζεύξω, ἔζευξα, ἔζευγμαι, ἐζεύχθην** rare, 2 aor. pass. **ἐζύγην.** (IV.)

ζέω (ζε- for ζεσ-) *boil* (intrans. in prose): **ἐξανα-ζέσω, ἔζεσα**, ἀπ-έζεσμαι Hippocr.

ζώννῡμι (ζω-, 731) *gird:* **ἔζωσα, ἔζωμαι** (Att. inscr.) and **ἔζωσμαι** (preferred in MSS.). (IV.)

ἡβά-σκω *come to manhood,* **ἡβάω** *am at manhood:* **ἐφ-ηβήσω, ἥβησα, παρ-ήβηκα.** Epic ἡβώοντα, etc. (643). (V.)

ἠγερέθομαι *am collected:* see **ἀγείρω.**

ἥδομαι *am pleased:* **ἡσθήσομαι** (812), **ἥσθην,** aor. mid. ἡσάμην ι 353. ἥδω (ἧσα) is very rare.

ἡδύνω (ἡδυν-) *sweeten:* **ἥδῡνα, ἥδυσμαι, ἡδύνθην, ἡδυντέος.** (III.)

ἠερέθομαι *am raised:* see **αἴρω.**

ἧμαι *sit:* see 789.

ἠμί *say:* see 792.

ἠμύω *sink, bow:* ἤμῡσα, ὑπ-εμν-ήμῡκε X 491 from ἐμ-ημῡκε with ν inserted. Poetic, mostly Epic.

ἡττῶμαι from ἡττάομαι (Ion. ἑσσοῦμαι from ἑσσόομαι) *am vanquished:* regular, but fut. **ἡττήσομαι** and **ἡττηθήσομαι** (812).

θάλλω (θαλ-) *bloom,* rare in prose: ἔθαλλε *made grow* Pind., 2 perf. τέθηλα (as pres.) is poetic. By-form θαλέθω (490). (III.)

θάπ-τω (θαφ-, 125 g) *bury:* **θάψω, ἔθαψα, τέθαμμαι,** 2 aor. pass. **ἐτάφην,** 2 fut. pass. **ταφήσομαι,** fut. perf. **τεθάψομαι, θαπτέος**; 1 aor. pass. ἐθάφθην Ion. (rare). (II.)

θαυμάζω (θαυμ-αδ-) *wonder, admire:* fut. **θαυμάσομαι** (806), otherwise regular. 512. (III.)

θείνω (θεν-) *smite:* θενῶ, ἔθεινα Epic, 2 aor. ἔθενον. Poetic (and in Att. comedy). (III.)

θέλω *wish:* see **ἐθέλω.**

θεραπεύω *serve, heal:* regular, but fut. mid. **θεραπεύσομαι** is usu. pass. (808).

θέρομαι *warm myself* (in prose only pres. and imperf.), fut. θέρσομαι τ 23 (536), 2 aor. pass. as intrans. ἐθέρην (only in the subj. θερέω ρ 23).

θέω (θευ-, θεϝ-, θυ-, 503) *run:* **θεύσομαι** (806). Other forms supplied by other verbs (see **τρέχω**).

θη- in θῆσθαι *milk,* ἐθησάμην *sucked.* Epic.

θηπ-: see ταφ-.

θι-γ-γ-άνω (θιγ-) *touch:* θίξομαι (806), 2 aor. ἔθιγον, ἄ-θικτος. Poetic, rare in prose (Xen.). (IV.)

θλάω *bruise, break:* θλάσω, ἔθλασα, τέθλασμαι (489 c) Theocr., ἐθλάσθην Hippocr., θλαστός. Ion. and poetic. See φλάω.

θλίβω (θλῑβ-, θλἴβ-, 501) *press:* **ἔθλῑψα, τέθλῑφα, ἐθλίφθην,** τέθλιμμαι and ἐθλίβην Aristotle. Fut. mid. θλίψομαι Hom.

θνῄ-σκω, older **θνή-σκω** (θαν-, θνη-, 492, 526 b) *die:* **ἀπο-θανοῦμαι** (806), 2 aor. **ἀπ-έθανον, τέθνηκα** *am dead,* 2 perf. **τέθνατον** (704 c), fut. perf. **τεθνήξω** (659 a, 1958), **θνητός.** In prose regularly **ἀπο-θνῄσκω** in fut. and 2 aor., but always **τέθνηκα.** (V.)

θρᾱ́ττω (θρᾱχ-, τρᾱχ-) *disturb:* **ἔθρᾱξα,** ἐθράχθην Soph. See **ταράττω.** Mostly poetic. (III.)

θραύω *break, bruise:* **θραύσω, ἔθραυσα, τέθραυμαι** and **τέθραυσμαι** (489 c), **ἐθραύσθην.**

θρύπ-τω (θρυφ-, 125 g and N.) *crush, weaken:* **τέθρυμμαι,** ἐθρύφθην Aristotle, 2 aor. pass. ἐτρύφην Hom., **ἔν-θρυπτος. θρύπτομαι** *put on airs.* (II.)

θρῴ-σκω and *θρώ-σκω* (*θρω-*, *θορ-*, 492) *leap*: *-θοροῦμαι* (806; w. *ὑπέρ*) poetic, 2 aor. **ἔθορον**. Mainly poetic. By-form *θορνύομαι* Hdt. (V.)

θύω (*θυ-*, *θῡ-*, 500. 1 a) *sacrifice*: **θύσω, ἔθῡσα, τέθυκα, τέθυμαι, ἐτύθην, θυτέος.**

θύω and *θύνω* *rush* poetic: in the classical language only pres. and imperf. *θῡνέω* Hesiod.

ἰαίνω (*ἰαν-*) *warm*: *ἴηνα*, *ἰάνθην* without augm. Epic and Lyric. (III.)

ἰάλλω (*ἰαλ-*) and *ἰάλλω* *send*: *-ιαλῶ*, *ἴηλα* without augm. Epic. Poetic (comp. with *ἐπί* in Aristoph.). (III.)

ἰαχέω and *ἰάχω* (for *ϝιϝαχω*) *sound, shout*: *ἰαχήσω*, *ἰάχησα*, 2 perf. part. *ἀμφιαχυῖα*. Hom. has both *ἴαχον* and *ἴαχον*. For *ἰᾱχ-* in tragedy *ἰακχ-* is commonly written. Poetic, mainly Epic. 485 d.

ἰδ-, *εἰδ-*, *οἰδ-* (for *ϝιδ-*, etc.) in **εἶδον** *saw* from *ἐ-ϝιδον* 431 (**ἴδω, ἴδοιμι, ἰδέ, ἰδεῖν, ἰδών**), fut. **εἴσομαι** *shall know* (Epic *εἰδήσω*), plup. **ᾔδη** or **ᾔδειν** *knew* (794 ff.), **ἰστέος**. Mid. *εἴδομαι* *seem, resemble* Epic, poetic, New Ion.: *εἰσάμην* and *ἐεισάμην*, 2 aor. *εἰδόμην* *saw* Epic, poetic, Hdt., **προ-ιδέσθαι** Thuc. *οἰδ-* in **οἶδα**, 794 ff.

ἰδρόω *sweat*: *ἰδρώσω*, *ἵδρωσα*. For the contraction to *ω* instead of *ου* (*ἰδρῶσι*, etc.) see 398. Epic *ἰδρώω*, *ἰδρώουσα*, etc.

ἱδρύω *place* (Epic *ἱδρύω*): often comp. w. *κατά*: **-ιδρύσω, -ἵδρῡσα, -ἵδρῡκα, ἵδρῡμαι, ἱδρύθην** (*ἱδρύνθην* Epic), **ἱδρῡτέος.**

ἵε-μαι (*ϝῑε-*, cp. Lat. *in-vi-tus*) *strive*: usu. in comp., as *παρ-ίεμαι* *beg*. The forms are like those from the mid. of *ἵημι* *send* (cp. 778). Epic aor. *ἐεισάμην* and *εἰσάμην*.

ἵζω (for *σι-σ(ε)δ-ω*, cp. *sedeo*) *seat*, usu. *sit*, mid. *ἵζομαι* *sit*, classic only in pres. and imperf. Mainly Ionic and poetic. See **καθίζω, καθίζομαι**, the usual forms in prose. See also **ἕζομαι, κάθημαι** *sit*. By-form *ἱζάνω* *seat, place*. (III.)

ἵημι (*σι-ση-μι*) *send*: **ἥσω, ἧκα**, 2 aor. **εἶτον**, etc., **εἷκα, εἷμαι, εἵθην, ἑθήσομαι, ἑτός, ἑτέος** (except pres. all forms in comp. in prose). For inflection and synopsis, see 777 ff.

ἱκνέομαι (*ἱκ-*) *come*, in prose usu. **ἀφ-ικνέομαι**: **ἀφ-ίξομαι**, 2 aor. **ἀφ-ῑκόμην, ἀφ-ῖγμαι**. Uncomp. **ἱκνούμενος** *suitable* (rare). The simple forms *ἱκνέομαι*, *ἵξομαι*, *ἱκόμην* are poetic. Connected forms are poetic *ἵκω* (imperf. *ἷκον*, aor. *ἷξον*) and *ἱκάνω*, only pres. and imperf. (Epic and Tragic). (IV.)

ἱλά-σκο-μαι (*ἱλα-*) *propitiate*: **ἱλάσομαι, ἱλασάμην, ἱλάσθην** (489 e). Epic aor. *ἱλασσάμην*, Epic pres. also *ἱλάομαι*. (V.)

ἵλημι (*ἱλη-*, *ἱλα-* for *σι-σλη-*, *σι-σλα-*) *am propitious*: pres. imper. *ἵληθι* or *ἵλαθι*, perf. *ἵληκα*. Mid. *ἵλαμαι* *propitiate*. Epic.

ἴλλω (*ἴλλομαι*) *roll*: *ἶλα*. See *εἰλέω* and *εἴλω*. (III or IV.)

ἱμάσσω (*ἱμαντ-*) *lash*: *ἵμασ(σ)α* Epic. (III.)

ἱμείρω (*ἱμερ-*) and *ἱμείρομαι* *desire*: *ἱμειράμην* Epic, *ἱμέρθην* Hdt., *ἱμερτός*. Poetic and Ion. (III.)

ἵπταμαι *fly*: (725, 726 a): see **πέτομαι**.

ἴσᾱμι: Doric for **οἶδα** *know*: *ἴσᾳς* (or *ἴσαις*), *ἴσᾱτι*, *ἴσαμεν*, *ἴσατε*, *ἴσαντι*, part. *ἰσᾱς*.

ἴσκω *liken* (= *ϝικ-σκω*): see *ἐΐσκω*.

ἵστημι (*στη-*, *στα-*) *set, place*: **στήσω** *shall set*, **ἔστησα** *set, caused to stand*, 2 aor. **ἔστην** *stood*, 1 perf. **ἕστηκα** *stand* (= *σε-στηκα*), plup. **εἱστήκη** *stood* (**ἑστήκη**, rare, 444 b), 2 perf. **ἕστατον** *stand* (417), perf. mid. **ἕσταμαι** rare, fut. perf. **ἑστήξω** *shall stand* (754 a, 1958), aor. pass. **ἐστάθην** *was set*, v. a. **στατός, -τέος.** For the inflection see 416, for dialectal forms of present see 747 D. ff. Epic 1 aor. 3 pl. ἔστασαν and ἔστησαν, 2 aor. 3 pl. ἔσταν (inf. στήμεναι), 2 perf. inf. ἑστάμεν and ἑστάμεναι, part. ἑσταώς and ἑστεώς. Iterat. imperf. ἵστασκε, 2 aor. στάσκε (495 a). 819.

ἰσχναίνω (ἰσχναν-) *make dry* or *lean*: -ισχνανῶ (-οῦμαι), ἴσχνᾱνα Aesch. (544 a, ἴσχνηνα Ion., also Att. ?), ἰσχνάνθην Hippocr., -ισχαντέος Aristotle. (III.)

ἴσχω (for σι-σ(ε)χ-ω), *have, hold*: see **ἔχω.**

καδ- (καδε-) in Hom. κεκαδών *depriving*, κεκαδήσω *shall deprive*. Not the same as καδ-(κήδω). κεκαδόμην *withdrew* may be from χάζω.

καθαίρω (καθαρ-) *purify*: **καθαρῶ, ἐκάθηρα** (and ἐκάθᾱρα ?), **κεκάθαρμαι, ἐκαθάρθην,** καθαρτέος Hippocr. (III.)

καθέζομαι: see **ἕζομαι.**

καθεύδω *sleep*: see εὕδω.

κάθημαι: see 790.

καθίζω *set, sit*: imperf. **ἐκάθιζον** (450), fut. **καθιῶ** (539), aor. **ἐκάθισα** or **καθῖσα.** Mid. **καθίζομαι** *sit*: **ἐκαθιζόμην, καθιζήσομαι** (521), **ἐκαθισάμην.** Hom. has imperf. κάθιζον or καθῖζον, aor. καθεῖσα and κάθισα, Hdt. κατεῖσα. See ἵζω, **ἕζομαι.** (IV.)

καί-νυμαι *excel*: perf. κέκασμαι (κεκαδμένος Pind.). Poetic. (IV.)

καίνω (καν-, κον-) *kill*: κανῶ, 2 aor. ἔκανον, 2 perf. κέκονα (κατα-κεκονότες Xen.). Poetic. (III.)

καίω (for καιϝω from καϝ-ι̯ω ; καυ-, καϝ-, και-) and **κᾱ́ω** (uncontracted, 396) *burn*, often w. ἐν, κατά: **καύσω, ἔκαυσα, -κέκαυκα, κέκαυμαι, ἐκαύθην, -καυθήσομαι, -καυτός.** 2 aor. ἔκηα Epic, poetic (part. κήᾱς Epic, **κέᾱς** Att.), 2 aor. pass. ἐκάην *burned* (intrans.) Epic and Ion. The MSS. show καίω in tragedy, Thuc., and in Xen. usu., κάω in Aristoph., Isocr., Plato. 520. (III.)

καλέω (καλε-, κλη-) *call*: **καλῶ** (539 a), **ἐκάλεσα, κέκληκα, κέκλημαι** *am called* (opt. 711 c), **ἐκλήθην,** fut. pass. **κληθήσομαι** (**καλοῦμαι** S. El. 971), fut. perf. **κεκλήσομαι** *shall bear the name*, **κλητός, -τέος.** Aeolic pres. κάλημι, Epic inf. καλήμεναι; fut. καλέω Hom., καλέσω Aristotle, aor. ἐκάλεσσα Hom. Iterative καλέεσκον, καλέσκετο. Epic pres. κι-κλή-σκω.

καλύπ-τω (καλυβ-) *cover* (in prose usu. in comp. w. ἀπό, ἐν, etc.): **καλύψω, ἐκάλυψα, κεκάλυμμαι, ἐκαλύφθην, καλυπτός,** συγ-καλυπτέος poetic. (II.)

κάμ-νω (καμ-, κμη-) *labor, am weary* or *sick*: **καμοῦμαι** (806), 2 aor. **ἔκαμον, κέκμηκα, ἀπο-κμητέος.** Epic 2 aor. subj. also κεκάμω, 2 aor. mid. ἐκαμόμην, 2 perf. part. κεκμηώς. (IV.)

κάμπ-τω (καμπ-) *bend*: **κάμψω, ἔκαμψα, κέκαμμαι, ἐκάμφθην, καμπτός.** (II.)

κατηγορέω *accuse*: regular. For augment, see 453.

καφ-ε- *pant*, in Epic 2 perf. part. κεκαφηώς.

κεδάν-νῡμι: see **σκεδάννῡμι.**

κεῖ-μαι *lie*: **κείσομαι.** See 791.

κείρω (κερ-, καρ-) *shear*: **κερῶ, ἔκειρα, κέκαρμαι, ἀπο-καρτέος** Comic. Epic aor. ἔκερσα (544 b), aor. pass. ἐκέρθην Pind., 2 aor. pass. ἐκάρην (Hdt.) prob. Att. (III.)

κείω *split*: Epic κείων ξ 425.

κείω and κέω *wish to lie down*. Epic. Cp. **κεῖμαι.**

κελαδέω *roar*: κελαδήσω, κελάδησα. By-form Hom. κελάδω in pres. part. Epic and Lyric.

κελεύω *command:* **κελεύσω, ἐκέλευσα, κεκέλευκα, κεκέλευσμαι** (489 c), **ἐκελεύσθην, παρα-κελευστός, δια-κελευστέος.**

κέλλω (κελ-) *land:* κέλσω (536), ἔκελσα. Poetic = Att. **ὀκέλλω.** (III.)

κέλομαι (κελ-, κελε-, κλ-) *command:* κελήσομαι, ἐκελησάμην, 2 aor. ἐκεκλόμην (448 D., 549 D.). Poetic = Att. **κελεύω.**

κεντέω (κεντ-, κεντε-, 485) *goad:* κεντήσω, ἐκέντησα, κεκέντημαι Hippocr., ἐκεντήθην late Att., συγ-κεντηθήσομαι Hdt., κεστός Hom., aor. inf. κένσαι Hom. for κεντσαι. Poetic and New Ion.

κεράν-νῡμι and κεραν-νύω (κερα-, κρᾱ-) *mix:* **ἐκέρασα, κέκρᾱμαι, ἐκρᾱ́θην** and **ἐκεράσθην** (489 g), **κρᾱτέος.** Ion. are ἔκρησα (ἐκέρασσα poetic), κέκρημαι, ἐκρήθην. By-forms κεράω and κεραίω, and κίρνημι and κιρνάω. (IV.)

κερδαίνω (κερδ-, κερδε-, κερδαν-) *gain:* **κερδανῶ, ἐκέρδᾱνα** (544 a), **προσ-κεκέρδηκα.** Hdt. has fut. κερδήσομαι, aor. ἐκέρδηνα and ἐκέρδησα (523 h). (III. IV.)

κεύθω (κευθ-, κυθ-) *hide:* κεύσω, ἔκευσα, Epic 2 aor. ἔκυθον and redupl. 2 aor. in subj. κεκύθω, 2 perf. κέκευθα as pres. (in Trag. also *am hidden*, and so κεύθω in trag.). Epic by-form κευθάνω. Poetic.

κήδω (κηδ-, κηδε-, καδ-) *distress:* κηδήσω, ἐκήδησα, 2 perf. κέκηδα as pres., *sorrow.* Poetic. Mid. **κήδομαι** *am concerned:* κεκαδήσομαι Hom., ἐκηδεσάμην Aesch.

κηρῡ́ττω (κηρῡκ-) *proclaim:* **κηρύξω** (147 c), **ἐκήρυξα, ἐπι-κεκήρῡχα, κεκήρῡγμαι, ἐκηρῡ́χθην,** fut. pass. **κηρῡχθήσομαι** and (Eur.) κηρύξομαι (809). (III.)

κι-γ-χ-άνω (κιχ-, κιχε-), Epic κιχάνω, *come upon, reach, find:* κιχήσομαι (806), 2 aor. ἔκιχον, Epic ἐκιχησάμην, ἀ-κίχητος. Hom. has 2 aor. pass. ἐκίχην as intrans.: κιχήω (MSS. -είω), κιχείην, κιχῆναι and κιχήμεναι, κιχείς and (mid.) κιχήμενος. These forms may come from a pres. κίχημι (688), but they all have aoristic force. Poetic. (IV.)

κίδ-νημι: see **σκεδάννῡμι.** (IV.)

κί-νυμαι *move myself.* Pres. and imperf. Epic. Att. **κῑνέω.** (IV.)

κίρ-νημι and κιρνάω Epic: see **κεράννῡμι.**

κί-χρη-μι (χρη-, χρα-) *lend:* **ἔχρησα, κέχρηκα, κέχρημαι.** Fut. χρήσω Hdt., probably also Att. Mid. *borrow:* **ἐχρησάμην.**

κλάζω (κλαγγ-, κλαγ-, 510) *resound, clang:* κλάγξω, ἔκλαγξα, 2 aor. ἔκλαγον, 2 perf. **κέκλαγγα** as pres., fut. perf. **κεκλάγξομαι** as fut. *shall scream* (581, 806). Epic 2 perf. κεκλήγοντες (557 D. 2, 700 D.). By-form κλαγγάνω. Mainly poetic. (III.)

κλαίω *weep* (for κλαιϝω from κλαϝ-ιω: κλαυ-, κλαϝ-, κλαι-, κλαιε-), **κλᾱ́ω** in prose (not contracted, 520): **κλαιήσω** or **κλᾱήσω** (**κλαύσομαι** *shall suffer for it*), **ἔκλαυσα.** Poetic are κλαυσοῦμαι (540), κέκλαυμαι, κέκλαυσμαι, κλαυτός, κλαυστός (?). The MSS. have κλαίω in Xen. usu., κλάω in Aristoph. (III.)

κλάω *break*, in prose w. ἀνά, ἀπό, ἐπί, κατά, πρός, σύν: **-ἔκλασα** (488 a), **-κέκλασμαι** (489 c), **-εκλάσθην,** ἀνα-κλασθήσομαι Aristotle.

κλείω *shut* (Older Att. **κλῄω**): **κλείσω** and **κλῄσω, ἔκλεισα** and **ἔκλῃσα, ἀπο-κέκλῃκα, κέκλειμαι** and **κέκλῃμαι** (**κέκλεισμαι** has some support), **ἐκλείσθην** and **ἐκλῄσθην** (489 e), **κλειστός** and **κλῃστός.** κληΐω is Ion.

κλέπ-τω (κλεπ-, κλοπ-) *steal:* **κλέψω** (less often **κλέψομαι**), **ἔκλεψα, κέκλοφα, κέκλεμμαι,** 2 aor. pass. **ἐκλάπην, κλεπτός, -τέος.** 1 aor. pass. ἐκλέφθην Ion. and poetic. (II.)

κλῄζω *celebrate in song:* κλῄσω, ἔκλῃσα (Dor. **ἐκλέϊξα** from **κλεΐζω**). Poetic. 512. (III.)

κλίνω (κλι-ν-) *bend*, usu. comp. w. κατά: **-κλινῶ, ἔκλῑνα,** κέκλικα late, **κέκλιμαι** (491), 2 aor. pass. **-εκλίνην**, 2 fut. pass. **-κλινήσομαι**, 1 aor. pass. ἐκλίθην poetic, ἐκλίνθην Epic, poetic, ἀπο-κλιτέος Aristotle. (III.)

κλύω *hear*: imperf. ἔκλυον is an old 2 aor. from an assumed pres. κλεύω; 2 aor. imper., without thematic vowel, κλῦθι and (Epic) κέκλυθι; perf. κέκλυκα rare; part. κλύμενος as adj. *famous* = κλυτός. Poetic.

κναίω *scratch*, usu. comp. w. διά: -κναίσω Eur., **-έκναισα, -κέκναικα, -κέκναισμαι** (489 c), **-εκναίσθην, -κναισθήσομαι.**

*κνάω (**κνῶ**) *scrape* (κνα-, κνη-) (on pres. contraction **κνῇς, κνῇ**, etc. see 394, 641) often comp. w. κατά: κνήσω Hippocr., **ἔκνησα, -κέκνησμαι** (489 c), **-εκνήσθην.** Cp. **κναίω.**

κοιλαίνω (κοιλ-αν-) *hollow*: **κοιλανῶ, ἐκοίλᾱνα** (544 a), κεκοίλασμαι (489 h) and ἐκοιλάνθην Hippocr. (III. IV.)

κομίζω (κομιδ-) *care for*: **κομιῶ, ἐκόμισα, κεκόμικα, κεκόμισμαι** (usu. mid.), **ἐκομίσθην, κομισθήσομαι, κομιστέος.** (III.)

κόπ-τω (κοπ-) *cut*, usu. in comp. in prose: **κόψω, ἔκοψα, -κέκοφα** (διά, ἐξ, σύν, etc.), **κέκομμαι**, 2 aor. pass. **-εκόπην** (ἀπό, περί), 2 fut. pass. **-κοπήσομαι**, fut. perf. **-κεκόψομαι, κοπτός.** Hom. has 2 perf. part. κεκοπώς. (II.)

κορέν-νῡμι (κορε- for κορεσ-) *satiate*: fut. κορέω Hom., κορέσω Hdt., aor. ἐκόρεσα poetic, 2 perf. part. κεκορηώς *satisfied* Epic, perf. mid. κεκόρεσμαι (489 c) Xen., κεκόρημαι Ion., poetic, aor. pass. ἐκορέσθην poetic (489 g) ἀ-κόρητος and ἀ-κόρε(σ)τος *insatiate*, both poetic. Ion. and poetic, rare in prose. (IV.)

κορύσσω (κορυθ-) *arm with the helmet, arm*: act. only pres. and imperf. Hom. aor. part. κορυσσάμενος, perf. part. κεκορυθμένος. Poetic, mostly Epic. (III.)

κοτέω *am angry*: ἐκότεσα (-άμην) and κεκοτηώς Epic.

κρᾱ́ζω (κρᾱγ-, κραγ-) *cry out*: 2 aor. **ἔκραγον**, 2 perf. **κέκρᾱγα** as pres. (imper. 698, 704 e), fut. perf. as fut. **κεκρᾱ́ξομαι** *shall cry out* (581, 806). By-form **κραυγάζω.** (III.)

κραίνω (κραν-) *accomplish*: κρανῶ, ἔκρᾱνα, perf. 3 s. and pl. κέκρανται, ἐκράνθην, κρανθήσομαι, ἄ-κραντος. Epic by-form κραιαίνω (κρᾱαίνω?): ἐκρήηνα (ἐκράηνα?), perf. 3 s. κεκράανται, plup. κεκράαντο, aor. pass. ἐκράανθεν Theocr., ἀ-κράαντος. Poetic. (III.)

κρέμα-μαι (κρεμα-) *hang*, intrans., used as pass. of **κρεμάννῡμι.** Pres. inflected as ἵσταμαι (subj. **κρέμωμαι**, opt. **κρεμαίμην**, 749 b, 750 b), **κρεμήσομαι.** Cp. κρίμνημι and **κρεμάννῡμι.**

κρεμάν-νῡμι (κρεμα-, 729) *hang*, trans.: **κρεμῶ, ἐκρέμασα, ἐκρεμάσθην, κρεμαστός.** Mid. intrans. see **κρέμαμαι.** Fut. κρεμάσω Comic poets, κρεμόω Epic. (IV.)

κρίζω (κρικ- or κριγ-) *creak*: 2 aor. Epic κρίκε (v. l. κρίγε), 2 perf. **κέκρῑγα** Aristoph. (III.)

κρίμ-νημι (κριμ-νη-, κριμ-να-) often miswritten κρήμνημι, *hang*, trans., rare in act. Mid. κρίμναμαι *am suspended* = **κρέμαμαι.** Poetic. (IV.)

κρίνω (κρι-ν-) *judge*: **κρινῶ, ἔκρῑνα, κέκρικα** (491), **κέκριμαι, ἐκρίθην** (ἐκρίνθην Epic, 491), **κριθήσομαι** (**κρινοῦμαι** rarely pass., 809), **κριτέος**, κριτός poetic. (III.)

κρούω *beat*: **κρούσω, ἔκρουσα, -κέκρουκα, -κέκρουμαι** and **-κέκρουσμαι** (489 g), **-εκρούσθην, κρουστέος.**

κρύπ-τω (κρυφ-) *hide*: **κρύψω** (prose w. ἀπό, κατά), **ἔκρυψα, κέκρυμμαι** (prose w. ἀπό), **ἐκρύφθην, κρυπτός,** κρυπτέος poetic. Poetic 2 aor. pass. ἐκρύφην is rare (Soph.), κεκρύψομαι Hippocr. (II.)

κτάομαι *acquire:* **κτήσομαι, ἐκτησάμην, κέκτημαι** (442 N.) *possess* (subj. **κεκτῶμαι, -ῇ, -ῆται,** 709; opt. **κεκτῄμην, -ῇο, -ῇτο,** 711; doubtful are **κεκτῴμην, -ῷο, -ῷτο**); fut. perf. **κεκτήσομαι** *shall possess* (581); **ἐκτήθην** pass.; **κτητός, -τέος.** Aor. mid. **ἐκτησάμην** usu. = *have possessed.* Ion. perf. mid. *ἔκτημαι* (442 D.) and fut. perf. *ἐκτήσομαι shall possess* (both in Plato).

κτείνω (*κτεν-, κτον-, κτα-ν-*, 478, 480) *kill*, in prose usually comp. w. *ἀπό*, in poetry w. *κατά*; **ἀπο-κτείνω**: **κτενῶ, ἔκτεινα,** 2 perf. **ἀπ-έκτονα.** Ion. fut. *κτενέω* (*κτανέω* from *καίνω*). Poetic 2 aor. *ἔκτανον* and *ἔκταν* (551 D.); subj. *κτέωμεν* MSS. χ 216, inf. *κτάμεναι*, part. *κτάς*; mid. *ἐκτάμην was killed* (687). Epic aor. pass. *ἐκτάθην.* In Att. prose **ἀπο-θνῄσκω** is generally used as the pass. of **ἀπο-κτείνω.** By-forms **ἀπο-κτείνῡμι** and **ἀπο-κτεινύω** (sometimes written *κτείννῡμι, -ύω, κτίννῡμι, -ύω*, 733). (III.)

κτίζω *found:* **κτίσω, ἔκτισα,** *ἔκτισμαι* Pind., **ἐκτίσθην,** *ἐΰ-κτιτος* poetic. Epic 2 aor. mid. part. *κτίμενος* (*κτι-*) as pass., *founded.* 512. (III.)

κτυπέω (*κτυπ-, κτυπε-*, 485) *sound: ἐκτύπησα*, 2 aor. *ἔκτυπον* Hom. (546 D). Poetic.

κῡδαίνω (*κῡδ-αν-*) *honor: ἐκύδηνα* Epic. Hom. has also *κῡδάνω* and *κῡδιάω.* 523 h. (III. IV.)

κυέω (*κυ-, κυε-*, 485) *am pregnant:* **ἐκύησα** *conceived*, **κεκύηκα.** Fut. *κυήσω* Hippocr., aor. pass. *ἐπ-εκυήθην* Aristotle. Mid. *bring forth.* Connected forms are *κύω* (usu. poetic): *ἔκῡσα impregnated* Aesch. (*κῡσαμένη being pregnant*), caus. *κυΐσκω impregnate* and *conceive*, **κυΐσκομαι** *conceive.*

κυλίνδω and **κυλινδέω,** later **κυλΐω,** *roll:* **ἐκύλῑσα, κατα-κεκύλῑσμαι** (489 c), **ἐκυλΐσθην, ἐκ-κυλῑσθήσομαι, κυλῑστός.** From *ἐκύλῑσα* (= *ἐκυλινδσα*) the pres. *κυλΐω* was formed. Connected is *καλινδέομαι.*

κυ-νέ-ω (*κυ-*) *kiss: κυνήσομαι* (?), *ἔκυσα.* Poetic. **προσ-κυνέω** *render homage to:* **προσ-κυνήσω, προσ-εκύνησα** (*προσ-έκυσα* poetic). (IV.)

κύπ-τω (*κυφ-*, cp. *κύβδα*; or *κῡφ-*, cp. *κῡφός*) *stoop:* **ἀνα-κύψομαι** (806), **ἔκυψα, κέκῡφα.** If the verb-stem is *κῡφ-* the *υ* is long in all forms. (II.)

κυρέω (*κυρ-, κυρε-*, 485) *meet, happen* is regular (poetic and Ion.). *κύρω* (*κυρ-*) = *κυρέω* is mainly poetic: *κύρσω* (536), *ἔκυρσα.* (III.)

κωκύω (500, 1. a) *lament: κωκύσω* Aesch., *κωκύσομαι* (806) Aristoph., *ἐκώκῡσα* poetic.

κωλῡ́ω *hinder:* regular, but (rare) fut. mid. **κωλῡ́σομαι** as pass. (808) T. 1. 142.

λα-γ-χ-άνω (λαχ-, ληχ-) *obtain by lot:* **λήξομαι** (806), 2 aor. **ἔλαχον,** 2 perf. **εἴληχα** (445), **εἴληγμαι, ἐλήχθην, ληκτέος.** Ion. fut. *λάξομαι*, Ion. 2 perf. *λέλογχα* (also poetic). Hom. 2 aor. *ἔλλαχον* (redupl. *λέλαχον made partaker*). (IV.)

λάζομαι and *λάζυμαι* (Epic and Ion.) = **λαμβάνω.**

λα-μ-β-άνω (λαβ-, ληβ-) *take:* **λήψομαι** (806), 2 aor. **ἔλαβον, εἴληφα** (445), **εἴλημμαι, ἐλήφθην, ληφθήσομαι, ληπτός, -τέος.** Fut. *λάμψομαι* (better *λάψομαι*) Ion., *λᾱψοῦμαι* Doric; 2 aor. inf. *λελαβέσθαι* Hom.; perf. *λελάβηκα* (*λαβε-*) Ion. and Doric; perf. mid. *λέλημμαι* poetic, *λέλαμμαι* Ion.; aor. pass. *ἐλάμφθην* Ion., *ἐλάφθην* Doric; v. a. *κατα-λαμπτέος* Hdt. (IV.)

λάμπω *shine:* **λάμψω, ἔλαμψα,** 2 perf. *λέλαμπα* poetic.

λα-ν-θ-άνω (λαθ-, ληθ-) *escape the notice of, lie hid:* **λήσω,** 2 aor. **ἔλαθον,** 2 perf. **λέληθα** as pres., v. a. *ἄ-λαστος* poetic. Mid. in prose usu. **ἐπι-λανθάνομαι** *forget* (*λανθάνομαι* poetic, rare in prose; *λήθομαι* poetic): **ἐπι-λήσομαι,** 2 aor.

ἐπ-ελαθόμην, perf. mid. ἐπι-λέλησμαι. Hom. has 2 aor. λέλαθον *caused to forget* and λελαθόμην *forgot* (448 D.), perf. mid. λέλασμαι. λελήσομαι is poetic. By-forms are λήθω, -ομαι, chiefly poetic: ἔλησα poetic; and ληθάνω *cause to forget* Epic, poetic. (IV.)

λάπ-τω (λαβ- or λαφ-) *lap, lick*: pres. late: ἐκ-λάψομαι Aristoph., ἐξ-έλαψα Aristoph., λέλαφα Aristoph. Fut. λάψω Hom. (II.)

λάσκω, for λακ-σκω, 526 d (λακ-, λακε-) *speak*: λακήσομαι (806), 2 aor. ἔλακον (ἐλάκησα rare), 2 perf. as pres. λέληκα Epic = λέλᾱκα Tragic (part. λελᾰκυῖα Epic), 2 aor. mid. λελακόμην Epic. Poetic verb. By-forms ἐπι-ληκέω Epic, λακάζω Tragic. (V.)

λάω *see*: only part. λάων and imperf. λάε. Epic.

*λάω (λῶ) *wish* (λα-, λη-): contr. λῇς, λῇ, inf. λῆν. Doric verb. Also λείω. Cp. 394.

λέγω *say*: λέξω, ἔλεξα, perf. εἴρηκα (see under εἴρω), λέλεγμαι, ἐλέχθην, fut. pass. λεχθήσομαι, fut. perf. λελέξομαι, λεκτέος, -τός poetic. Fut. mid. λέξομαι as pass. is poetic (809). δια-λέγομαι *discuss*: δια-λέξομαι and δια-λεχθήσομαι (812), δι-είλεγμαι, δι-ελέχθην (δι-ελέγην Aristotle), δια-λεκτέος.

λέγω *collect, count*, usu. in comp. w. ἐξ or σύν: -λέξω, -έλεξα, 2 perf. -είλοχα (445), -είλεγμαι and -λέλεγμαι, 2 aor. pass. -ελέγην (-ελέχθην rare in Att.), fut. perf. -λεγήσομαι, -λεκτέος, λεκτός poetic. 2 aor. mid. ἐλέγμην ι 335.

λείπω (λειπ-, λοιπ-, λιπ-, 477 a) *leave*, often in comp. w. ἀπό, κατά, ὑπό, etc.: λείψω, 2 aor. ἔλιπον, 2 perf. λέλοιπα *have left, have failed*. λείπομαι mid. *remain*, pass. *am left, am inferior*: λέλειμμαι, ἐλείφθην, fut. pass. λειφθήσομαι, fut. perf. λελείψομαι, λειπτέος. Fut. mid. λείψομαι is rarely pass. (809). 2 aor. mid. ἐλιπόμην in prose only in comp. (as pass. Α 693). By-form κατα-λιμπάνω. On the inflection of the 2 aor. see 384.

λεπτύνω (λεπτυν-) *thin*: ἐλέπτῡνα, λελέπτυσμαι (489 h), ἐλεπτύνθην. (III.)

λέπω (λεπ-, λαπ-) *peel*, usu. comp. w. ἀπό, ἐκ: -λέψω, -έλεψα, λέλαμμαι (inscr.), -ελάπην.

λεύω *stone to death*, usu. comp. w. κατά in prose: -λεύσω, -έλευσα, -ελεύσθην (489 e), -λευσθήσομαι.

λεχ- *lay to rest* (cp. λέχ-ος *bed*): λέξομαι, ἔλεξα (ἐλεξάμην *went to rest*, imper. λέξεο, 542 D.), 2 aor. athematic forms (688) ἔλεκτο *went to rest*, imper. λέξο for λεχ-σο, inf. κατα-λέχθαι for -λεχσθαι, part. κατα-λέγμενος. Epic.

λήθω: see λανθάνω.

λι-λαίομαι (λα- for λασ-, 624 a) *desire eagerly* only pres. and imperf.; with perf. λελίημαι (λια-). Epic. Cp. λάω. (III.)

λίσσομαι rarely λίτομαι (λιτ-) *supplicate*: ἐλλισάμην Epic, 2 aor. ἐλιτόμην Epic, πολύ-λλιστος. Poetic, rare in prose. (III.)

λιχμάω (and λιχμάζω) *lick*: perf. part. λελιχμότες Hesiod. Usually poetic.

λοέω (= λοϝεω) *wash*: λοέσσομαι, ἐλόε(σ)σα, -άμην. Epic. See λούω.

λούω *wash* loses υ before a short vowel and then contracts (398 a): λούω, λούεις, λούει, λοῦμεν, λοῦτε, λοῦσι, ἔλουν, λούσομαι (λούσω late), ἔλουσα, λέλουμαι, ἄ-λουτος. Hom. has λόω, λοέω: λοέσσομαι, λοῦσα ζ 217, λόεσσα (-ατο), Hippocr. ἐλούθην.

λῡμαίνω (λῡμαν-) *abuse*: usu. λῡμαίνομαι as act.: λῡμανοῦμαι, ἐλῡμηνάμην, λελῡ́μασμαι (usu. mid. 489 h), ἐλῡμάνθην Tragic. (III.)

λύω (λυ-, λῡ-) *loose*. λύσω, ἔλῡσα, λέλυκα, λέλυμαι, ἐλύθην, λυθήσομαι, λελῡ́σομαι,

λυτός, -τέος. Inflection p. 114. On 2 aor. mid. Epic ἐλύμην as pass., see 688. On perf. opt. λελῦτο, see 711 D.

μαίνω (μαν-, μην-) *madden*, act. usu. poetic: **ἔμηνα, μέμηνα** *am mad.* Mid. **μαίνομαι** *rage:* μανοῦμαι Hdt., 2 aor. pass. **ἐμάνην.** (III.)

μαίομαι (for μα(σ)-ιομαι, 624 a) *desire, strive:* μάσσομαι, ἐμα(σ)σάμην, ἐπί-μαστος. Epic. Connected are Aeol. μάομαι (μῶται, opt. μῷτο, imper. μῶσο) and μαιμάω, Epic, poetic. (III.)

μα-ν-θ-άνω (μαθ-, μαθε-) *learn:* **μαθήσομαι** (806), 2 aor. **ἔμαθον, μεμάθηκα, μαθητός, -τέος.** Hom. has 2 aor. ἔμμαθον (429 a, D.). (IV.)

μαραίνω (μαραν-) *cause to wither:* **ἐμάρᾱνα,** ἐμαράνθην Hom. (III.)

μάρ-ναμαι (μαρ-να-) *fight:* only in pres. and imperf., subj. μάρνωμαι (749 b), imper. μάρναο. Poetic. (IV.)

μάρπ-τω (μαρπ-) *seize:* μάρψω, ἔμαρψα, 2 aor. ἔμαρπον (?) and redupl. μέμαρπον (?) Epic, 2 perf. μέμαρπα Epic. Poetic. (II.)

μάττω (μαγ-) *knead:* **μάξω, ἔμαξα, μέμαχα, μέμαγμαι,** 2 aor. pass. **ἐμάγην** (προσεμάχθην Soph.). (III.)

μάχομαι (μαχ-, μαχε-) *fight:* **μαχοῦμαι** (539 b), **ἐμαχεσάμην, μεμάχημαι, μαχετέος.** Pres. Hom. μαχέομαι (part. μαχεούμενος and μαχειόμενος, fut. Hom. μαχήσομαι (-έσσομαι ?) and μαχέομαι, Hdt μαχήσομαι; aor. Epic ἐμαχεσ(σ)άμην (v. l. -ησάμην), Hdt. ἐμαχεσάμην; v. a. μαχητός Hom., ἀ-μάχετος Aesch.

μέδω and μεδέω *rule* (485 d). Epic and poetic. μέδομαι *am concerned about.*

μεθύ-σκω *make drunk:* **ἐμέθυσα. μεθύσκομαι** *get drunk,* **ἐμεθύσθην** *got drunk* (489 e). (V.)

μεθύω *am drunk:* only pres. and imperf.; other tenses from the pass. of **μεθύσκω.**

μείγ-νῡμι (μειγ-, μιγ-) *mix* (often written μίγνῡμι), also **μειγνύω,** and less com. **μίσγω** (526 c): **μείξω, ἔμειξα, μέμειγμαι, ἐμείχθην, ἀνα-μειχθήσομαι** rare, 2 aor. pass. **ἐμίγην, μεικτός, -τέος.** The forms with ει are restored on the authority of inscr. Epic 2 fut. pass. μιγήσομαι, Epic 2 aor. mid. ἔμικτο (ἔμεικτο ?), poetic fut. perf. μεμείξομαι. (IV.)

μείρομαι (μερ-, for σμερ-, μορ-, μαρ-) *obtain part in:* 2 perf. ἔμμορε (442 D.) *has a share in.* Epic. **εἵμαρται** *it is fated* (from σε-σμαρ-ται, 445 a). (III.)

μέλλω (μελλ-, μελλε-) *intend,* augments w. ε, rarely w. η (430): **μελλήσω, ἐμέλλησα, μελλητέος.**

μέλω (μελ-, μελε-) *care for, concern* poetic: μελήσω poetic, μελήσομαι Epic, 2 perf. μέμηλα Epic, μεμέλημαι as pres. poetic (Epic μέμ-β-λεται, 130 D.), ἐμελήθην poetic. Impersonal: **μέλει** *it is a care,* **μελήσει, ἐμέλησε, μεμέληκε, μελητέος.** Prose **ἐπι-μέλομαι** or **ἐπι-μελέομαι** *care for* (the latter form is far more com. on Att. inscr. after 380 B.C.): **ἐπι-μελήσομαι, ἐπι-μεμέλημαι, ἐπ-εμελήθην, ἐπι-μελητέος.**

μέμονα (μεν-, μον-, μα-) *desire:* 2 perf. as pres.; sing. μέμονας, -ονε; otherwise μι-forms (705), as μέματον (573), μέμαμεν, -ατε, -ᾱ́ᾱσι, imper. μεμάτω, part. μεμᾱώς and μεμᾱώς, μεμαυῖα, inf. μεμονέναι Hdt. Epic, poetic.

μέμφομαι *blame:* **μέμψομαι, ἐμεμψάμην, ἐμέμφθην** rare in prose, **μεμπτός.**

μένω (μεν-, μενε-) *remain:* **μενῶ, ἔμεινα, μεμένηκα** (485 c), **μενετός, μενετέος.** By-form μί-μν-ω Epic and poetic.

μερ-μηρίζω *ponder, devise:* ἀπ-εμερμήρισα Aristoph., μερμήριξα Epic. Poetic. 512. (III.)

μήδομαι *devise:* *μήσομαι, ἐμησάμην.* Poetic.

μηκάομαι (*μηκ-, μακ-*, 486 D.) *bleat:* pres. and imperf. not used; Hom. 2 aor. part. *μακών*, 2 perf. part. *μεμηκώς, μεμακυῖα*, 2 plup. *ἐμέμηκον* (557 D. 3).

μητιάω (*μητι-*, 486 D., cp. *μῆτις*) *plan:* also *μητιάομαι* and (Pind.) *μητίομαι:* *-ίσομαι, -ῑσάμην.* Epic and Lyric.

μιαίνω (*μιαν-*) *stain:* **μιανῶ, ἐμίᾱνα, μεμίασμαι** (489 h), **ἐμιάνθην, μιανθήσομαι,** *ἀ-μίαντος* poetic. (III.)

μι-μνῄ-σκω and **μι-μνή-σκω** (*μνα-*, 526 b) *remind*, mid. *remember*. Act. usu. **ἀνα-** or **ὑπο-μιμνῄσκω** (the simple is poetic except in pass.): **-μνήσω, -ἔμνησα,** perf. **μέμνημαι** = pres. (442 N.) *remember*, **ἐμνήσθην** (489 e) as mid. *remembered, mentioned*, fut. pass. = mid. **μνησθήσομαι** *shall remember*, fut. perf. **μεμνήσομαι** *shall bear in mind* (581), v. a. **ἐπι-μνηστέος,** *ἄ-μναστος* Theocr. **μέμνημαι** has subj. **μεμνῶμαι** (709), opt. **μεμνῄμην** (**μεμνῴμην** doubtful, 711 b), imper. **μέμνησο** (Hdt. *μέμνεο*), inf. **μεμνῆσθαι,** part. **μεμνημένος.** Fut. *μνήσω* (*-ομαι*), aor. *ἔμνησα* (*-άμην*) are poetic. Epic *μνάομαι* in Hom. *ἐμνώοντο, μνωόμενος* (643). (V.)

μίμνω *remain:* poetic for **μένω.**

μίσγω (for *μι-(μ)σγω*, 526 c) *mix*, pres. and imperf. See **μείγνῡμι.**

μύζω *suck*, Ion. *μυζέω*, late *ἐκ-μυζάω.* Hom. *ἐκ-μυζήσᾱς* *squeezing out.*

μύζω (*μυγ-*) *grumble:* **ἔμυξα.** (III.)

μῡκάομαι (*μῠκ-, μῡκ-, μῡκα-*, 486) *bellow:* **ἐμῡκησάμην,** Epic 2 aor. *μύκον* (546 D.), Epic 2 perf. *μέμῡκα* as pres.

μύττω (*μυκ-*) *wipe* usu. comp. w. *ἀπό:* **-έμυξα, -εμεμύγμην.** (III.)

μύω *shut* the lips or eyes (*ῡ* late, uncertain in Att.): **ἔμυσα, μέμῡκα.**

ναίω (*νασ-ι̯ω*, 624 a) *dwell:* *ἔνασσα* *caused to dwell*, *ἐνασσάμην* *took up my abode* and *caused to dwell*, *ἐνάσθην* *was settled* or *dwelt*. Poetic. (III.)

ναίω (*ναϝ-ι̯ω*, 624 b) *swim:* *ναῖον* ι 222 (*v. l.* *νᾶον*). (III.)

νάττω (*ναδ-, ναγ-*, 514 a, 515 b) *compress:* *ἔναξα* Epic and Ion., **νένασμαι** Aristoph. (*νέναγμαι* Hippocr.), **ναστός** Aristoph. Mostly Ion. and poetic. (III.)

νάω (*ναϝ-ω*) *flow* only in pres. Epic. Cp. *ναίω* *swim.*

νάω* (νῶ**) *spin* (*να-, νη-*, 394): pres. **νῇς, νῇ, νῶσι,** inf. **νῆν,** part. **νῶν,** fut. **νήσω,** aor. **ἔνησα,** aor. pass. **ἐνήθην.**

νεικέω (*νεικε-* for *νεικεσ-*; cp. *τὸ νεῖκος* *strife*) *chide*, usu. *νεικείω* in Hom.: *νεικέσω, ἐνείκεσ(σ)α.* Epic (also Hdt.). (III.)

νείφει (*νειφ-, νιφ-*, 477; better form than *νίφει*) *snows, covers with snow:* **κατ-ένειψε.** Pass. **νείφεται.**

νέμω (*νεμ-, νεμε-*) *distribute*, mid. also *go to pasture:* **νεμῶ, ἔνειμα, δια-νενέμηκα, νενέμημαι, ἐνεμήθην, δια-νεμητέος.**

νέομαι (*νεσ-*) *go, come*, only in pres. and imperf.: usu. in fut. sense. Mainly poetic. Cp. *νίσομαι.* 541.

νεύω *nod:* **-νεύσομαι** w. *ἀνά* or *κατά* (806), **ἔνευσα, νένευκα.** Hom. has fut. *νεύσω* and *κατα-νεύσομαι.*

νέω (*νευ-, νεϝ-, νυ-*, originally *σνευ-*, etc.) *swim*, often comp. w. *διά, ἐξ:* **νευσοῦμαι** Xen. (540, 806), **-ἔνευσα, -νένευκα, νευστέος.** Cp. *νήχομαι.*

νέω *heap up*, pres. in comp. and only in Hdt. (Att. usu. has **χόω**): **ἔνησα, νένημαι** (*νένησμαι?* 489 g), *νητός* Hom. Epic *νηέω.*

νίζω (*νιβ-, νιγ-*, 509 a) *wash*, in Att. usu. comp. w. *ἀπό, ἐξ:* **-νίψομαι** (*νίψω* poetic).

-ένιψα, -νένιμμαι, *-ενίφθην* Hippocr., *ἄ-νιπτος* Hom. = **ἀν-από-νιπτος.** *νίπτω* is late, *νίπτομαι* Hom. (III.)

νίσομαι go or *will go:* from *νι-ν(ε)σ-ι̯ομαι*, cp. *νόσ-τος return.* Often printed *νίσσομαι* (MSS. often have *νείσομαι*). Poetic. (III.)

νοέω *think, perceive*, regular in Att. Mid. **νοοῦμαι** usu. in comp., fut. **δια-νοήσομαι** (rare) and **δια-νοηθήσομαι** (812). Ion. contracts *οη* to *ω* in *ἔνωσα, νένωκα, νένωμαι.*

νομίζω *believe:* **νομιῶ** (539 e), **ἐνόμισα, νενόμικα, νενόμισμαι, ἐνομίσθην, νομισθήσομαι, νομιστέος.** 512. (III.)

ξαίνω (*ξαν-*) *scratch:* **ξανῶ, ἔξηνα,** *ἔξαμμαι* late Att., *ἔξασμαι* Hippocr. (III.)

ξέω (*ξε-* for *ξεσ-*) *scrape:* **ἔξεσμαι** (489 d). Epic are *ἔξεσα* and *ξέσσα, ξεστός.*

ξηραίνω (*ξηραν-*) *dry:* **ξηρανῶ, ἐξήρᾱνα, ἐξήρασμαι** (489 h), **ἐξηράνθην.** Ion. *ἐξήρηνα*, late *ἐξήραμμαι.* (IV.)

ξύω polish: **ἔξῡσα, ἐξύσθην** (489 c), *ἔξυσμαι* Aristotle, *ξυστός* Hdt.

ὁδοιπορέω *travel:* regular, but observe *ὁδοιπεπόρηκα* for *ὡδοιπόρηκα.* See 453.

ὁδοποιέω *make a way:* regular, but *ὡδοπεποιημένος* in Xen. for *ὡδοποιημένος.* 453.

ὀδυ- am angry: in Hom. aor. *ὠδυσ(σ)άμην*, perf. *ὀδώδυσται* as pres. (489 d).

ὄζω (*ὀδ-, ὀζε-*) *smell:* **ὀζήσω, ὤζησα.** Hippocr. *ὀζέσω* and *ὤζεσα*, Epic plup. *ὀδώδει* as imperf., Aeolic *ὄσδω.* (III.)

οἴγω open: οἴξω, ᾦξα, οἰχθείς Pind. Poetic, as is also *οἴγνῡμι.* In prose **ἀν-οίγω** and **ἀν-οίγνῡμι,** *q.v.* The older form is *ὀείγω*, found in Hom. aor. *ὤειξα* (MSS. *ὤϊξα*). Hom. has also *ὠϊγνύμην* (*ὠειγ-*?).

οἶδα (*οἰδ-*) : see *ἰδ-* and 794.

οἰδέω *swell:* **ᾤδησα, ᾤδηκα.** By-form *οἰδάνω* poetic.

οἰκτίρω (*οἰκτιρ-*, 620. iii) *pity:* **ᾤκτῑρα.** *οἰκτείρω* is a late spelling. (III.)

οἰμώζω *lament:* **οἰμώξομαι** (806), **ᾤμωξα,** *οἴμωγμαι* (?) Eur., *ᾠμώχθην* poetic. 512. (III.)

οἰνοχοέω and *-χοεύω* Hom. *pour wine:* imperf. *οἰνοχόει, ᾠνοχόει* (*ἐῳνοχόει*, Δ 3, is incorrect for *ἐϝοιν-*), **οἰνοχοήσω,** *οἰνοχοῆσαι.* Epic and Lyric, and in Xen.

οἴομαι (*οἰ-, οἰε-*) *think:* 1 pers. in prose usu. **οἶμαι**: imperf. **ᾤμην** (rarely **ᾠόμην**), **οἰήσομαι, ᾠήθην, οἰητέος.** Epic *ὀΐω, ὀΐω*, and *οἴω, ὀΐομαι* (500. 2. D.), *ὀϊσάμην, ὠΐσθην* (489 e). **οἶμαι** is probably a perfect (634).

οἴσω: *shall bear.* See **φέρω.**

οἴχομαι (*οἰχ-, οἰχε-, οἰχο-*, 486) *am gone* as perf. (1886) : **οἰχήσομαι,** *οἴχωκα* poetic and Ion. (some MSS. *ᾤχωκα*), *παρ-ῴχηκα* (?) K 252. *οἴχωκα* is probably due to Att. redupl. Ion. *-οἴχημαι* is doubtful.

ὀκέλλω (*ὀκελ-*) *run ashore:* **ὤκειλα.** Cp. *κέλλω.* (III.)

ὀλισθ-άνω (*ὀλισθ-*) *slip*, also **δι-ολισθαίνω**: 2 aor. *ὤλισθον* Ion., poetic; *δι-ωλίσθησα* and *ὠλίσθηκα* Hippocr. (*ὀλισθε-*). (IV.)

ὄλ-λῡμι destroy, ruin, lose, for *ὀλ-νῡ-μι* (*ὀλ-, ὀλε-, ὀλο-*) also *-ολλύω*, in prose usu. comp. w. *ἀπό*, also w. *διά* or *ἐξ*: **-ολῶ** (539 b), **-ώλεσα, -ολώλεκα** *have ruined*, 2 perf. **-όλωλα** *am ruined.* Fut. *ὀλέσ(σ)ω* Epic, *ὀλέσω* rare in comedy, *ὀλέω* Hdt. Mid. **ὄλλυμαι** *perish:* **-ολοῦμαι,** 2 aor. **-ωλόμην,** part. *ὀλόμενος ruinous* (*οὐλ-* Epic). By-form *ὀλέκω* Epic, poetic. (IV.)

ὀλ-ολύζω (*ὀλολυγ-*) *shout*, rare in prose: **ὀλολύξομαι** (806), **ὠλόλυξα.** (III.)

ὀλοφῡ́ρομαι (*ὀλοφυρ-*) *bewail:* **ὀλοφυροῦμαι, ὠλοφῡράμην, ὠλοφύρθην** *made to lament* Thuc. 3. 78. (III.)

ὄμ-νῡμι (*ὀμ-*, *ὀμο-*, 486) and **ὀμνύω** *swear:* **ὀμοῦμαι** (806) for *ὀμοσομαι*, **ὤμοσα**, **ὀμώμοκα**, **ὀμώμομαι** and **ὀμώμοσμαι** (489 g), **ὠμόθην** and **ὠμόσθην**, **ὀμοσθήσομαι**, **ἀπ-ώμοτος**. (IV.)

ὀμόργ-νῡμι (*ὀμοργ-*) *wipe*, usu. comp. w. *ἐξ* in poetry: *-ομόρξω*, *ὤμορξα*. **ἐξ-ομόργνυμαι**: **-ομόρξομαι**, **-ωμορξάμην**, **-ωμόρχθην**. (IV.)

ὀνί-νη-μι (*ὀνη-*, *ὀνα-*; for *ὀν-ονη-μι*, but the redupl. has no regard for the *ο*) *benefit:* **ὀνήσω**, **ὤνησα**, 2 aor. mid. **ὠνήμην** *received benefit* (opt. **ὀναίμην**), **ὠνήθην**, **ἀν-όνητος**. 2 aor. mid. imper. *ὄνησο* Hom., w. part. *ὀνήμενος* Hom.; 1 aor. mid. *ὠνάμην* is late.

ὄνο-μαι (*ὀνο-*, 725) *insult:* pres. and imperf. like *δίδομαι*, opt. *ὄνοιτο* Hom.; *ὀνόσσομαι*, *ὠνοσ(σ)άμην*, aor. pass. subj. *κατ-ονοσθῇς* Hdt. (489 e), *ὀνοτός* Pind., *ὀνοστός* Hom. *ὤνατο* P 25 may be imperf. of a by-form *ὄναμαι*.

ὀξῡ́νω (*ὀξυν-*) *sharpen*, in prose **παρ-οξῡ́νω** *provoke:* **-οξυνῶ**, **ὤξῡνα**, **-ώξυμμαι**, **-ωξύνθην**. (III.)

ὀπ- in fut. **ὄψομαι**, perf. mid. **ὦμμαι**, aor. pass. **ὤφθην**, **περι-οπτέος**. See **ὁράω**.

ὀπυίω (*ὀπυ-*) *take to wife* (later *ὀπύω*): *ὀπύσω* Aristoph. Epic, poetic. (III.)

ὁράω (*ὁρα-* for *ϝορα-*) *see:* imperf. **ἑώρων** (434), fut. **ὄψομαι** 806 (**ὄψει** 2 s.), 2 aor. **εἶδον** (*ἰδ-* for *ϝιδ-*), 1 perf. **ἑόρᾱκα** (443) and **ἑώρᾱκα** (plup. **ἑωρᾱ́κη**), **ἑώρᾱμαι** and **ὦμμαι**, **ὤφθην**, **ὀφθήσομαι**, **ὁρᾱτός**, **περι-οπτέος**. Aeolic *ὄρημι*, Epic *ὁρόω* (643), New Ion. *ὁρέω*. Imperf. *ὥρων* Hdt., fut. *ἐπ-όψομαι* in Hom. = *shall look on*, *ἐπι-όψομαι shall choose*, aor. mid. *ἐπ-ωψάμην saw* Pind., *ἐπι-ωψάμην chose* Plato, 2 perf. *ὄπωπα* poetic, Ion. See *ἰδ-* and *ὀπ-*. (VI.)

ὀργαίνω (*ὀργαν-*) *am angry:* *ὤργᾱνα* (544 a) *made angry*. Tragic. 523 h. (III.)

ὀργίζω *enrage:* **ἐξ-οργιῶ**, **ὤργισα**, **ὤργισμαι**, **ὠργίσθην**, **ὀργισθήσομαι**, **ὀργιστέος**. 512, 815. (III.)

ὀρέγω reach Epic, poetic, *ὀρέγ-νῡμι* Epic (only part. *ὀρεγνύς*): *ὀρέξω*, **ὤρεξα** rare in prose. **ὀρέγομαι** *stretch myself, desire:* **ὀρέξομαι** rare in prose, **ὠρεξάμην** but usu. **ὠρέχθην** as mid., *ὀρεκτός* Hom. Perf. *ὤρεγμαι* Hippocr., *ὀρώρεγμαι* (3 pl. *ὀρωρέχαται* Π 834, plup. *ὀρωρέχατο* Λ 26). By-form *ὀριγνάομαι*: **ὠριγνήθην**.

ὄρ-νῡμι (*ὀρ-*) *raise, rouse:* *ὄρσω* (536), *ὦρσα*, 2 aor. trans. and intrans. *ὤρορον* Epic (448 D.), 2 perf. *ὄρωρα* as mid. *have roused myself, am roused*. Mid. *ὄρνυμαι rise, rush:* fut. *ὀροῦμαι* Hom., 2 aor. *ὠρόμην* (Epic are *ὦρτο*, imper. *ὄρσο*, *ὄρσεο* (542 D.) and *ὄρσευ*, inf. *ὄρθαι*, part. *ὄρμενος*), perf. *ὀρώρεμαι* Hom. Poetic. (IV.)

ὀρύττω (*ὀρυχ-*) *dig*, often comp. w. *διά*, *κατά*: **-ορύξω**, **ὤρυξα**, **-ορώρυχα**, **ὀρώρυγμαι** (**ὤρυγμαι**?), **ὠρύχθην**, **-ορυχθήσομαι**, 2 fut. pass. **-ορυχήσομαι** Aristoph., **ὀρυκτός**. Mid. aor. *ὠρυξάμην caused to dig* Hdt. (III.)

ὀσφραίνομαι (*ὀσφραν-*, *ὀσφρε-*) *smell:* **ὀσφρήσομαι**, 2 aor. **ὠσφρόμην**, *ὠσφράνθην* late Com. and Hippocr. Hdt. has *ὠσφράμην*. 530. (III. IV.)

ὀτοτύζω lament: *ὀτοτύξομαι* (806), *ὠτότυξα*. 512. (III.)

οὐρέω make water: **ἐούρουν**, **οὐρήσομαι** (806), **ἐν-εούρησα**, **ἐν-εούρηκα**. New Ion. has *οὐρ-* for Att. *ἐουρ-* (as *οὐρήθην* Hippocr.).

οὐτάζω wound: *οὐτάσω*, *οὔτασα*, *οὔτασμαι*. Epic and Tragic. 512. (III.)

οὐτάω wound: *οὔτησα*, 2 aor. (*μι*-form) 3 s. *οὗτα* 551 D., 634, 688 (inf. *οὐτάμεναι* and *οὐτάμεν*), 2 aor. mid. *οὐτάμενος* as pass., *ἀν-ούτατος*. Epic and Tragic.

ὀφείλω (*ὀφελ-*, *ὀφειλε-*) *owe:* **ὀφειλήσω**, **ὠφείλησα**, 2 aor. **ὤφελον** in wishes, *would that!* **ὠφείληκα**, aor. pass. part. **ὀφειληθείς**. Hom. usu. has *ὀφέλλω*, the Aeolic form. (III.)

ὀφέλλω (ὀφελ- 519 a) *increase:* aor. opt. ὀφέλλειε Hom. Poetic, mainly Epic. (III.)

ὀφλ-ισκ-άνω (ὀφλ-, ὀφλε-, ὀφλ-ισκ-, 530): *owe, am guilty, incur a penalty:* **ὀφλήσω, ὤφλησα** (rare and suspected), 2 aor. **ὦφλον, ὤφληκα, ὤφλημαι.** For 2 aor. ὀφλεῖν, ὀφλών MSS often have ὄφλειν and ὄφλων, as if from ὄφλω, a late present. (IV. V.)

παίζω (παιδ-, παιγ-) *sport:* **ἔπαισα, πέπαικα, πέπαισμαι, παιστέος.** Att. fut. prob. παίσομαι (806). παιξοῦμαι in Xen. S. 9. 2 is used by a Syracusan.

παίω (παι-, παιε-) *strike:* **παίσω** and **παιήσω** Aristoph., **ἔπαισα, ὑπερ-πέπαικα;** for ἐπαίσθην Aesch. (489 e), Att. usu. has **ἐπλήγην,** as **πέπληγμαι** for πέπαικα.

παλαίω *wrestle:* **ἐπάλαισα,** ἐπαλαίσθην Eur. (489 e), παλαίσω Epic, δυσ-πάλαιστος Aesch.

πάλλω (παλ-) *shake, brandish:* ἔπηλα, πέπαλμαι. Hom. has 2 aor. redupl. ἀμ-πεπαλών and 2 aor. mid. (ἔ)παλτο. Epic and poetic. (III.)

πάομαι (πα-) *acquire, become master* = **κτάομαι**; pres. not used: πᾶσομαι, ἐπᾱσάμην, πέπᾱμαι. Doric verb, used in poetry and in Xen. Distinguish πᾰ̆σομαι, ἐπᾰσάμην from πατέομαι *eat.*

παρα-νομέω *transgress the law* augments **παρ-ενομ-** rather than παρ-ηνομ- though the latter has support (T. 3. 67. 5), perf. **παρα-νενόμηκα.** See 454.

παρ-οινέω *insult (as a drunken man):* **ἐπαρ-ῴνουν, ἐπαρ-ῴνησα, πεπαρ-ῴνηκα, ἐπαρ-ῳνήθην** (best MS. παρῳνήθην D. 22. 63). See 454.

πάσχω *suffer* (πενθ-, πονθ-, παθ-) for π(ε)ν̥θ-σκω (36 b, 526 d): **πείσομαι** (806) for πενθ-σομαι, 2 aor. **ἔπαθον,** 2 perf. **πέπονθα** (Hom. πέποσθε or πέπασθε 573, 705 and fem. part. πεπαθυῖα); Doric πέποσχα. (V. VI.)

πατάσσω *strike:* pres. and imperf. Epic (for which Att. has **τύπτω** and **παίω**), **πατάξω, ἐπάταξα,** ἐκ-πεπάταγμαι Hom. (Att. **πέπληγμαι**), ἐπατάχθην late (Att. **ἐπλήγην**). (III.)

πατέομαι (πατ-, πατε-) *eat, taste:* πᾰ̆σομαι (?) Aesch., ἐπᾰσ(σ)άμην Hom., plup. πεπάσμην Hom., ἄ-παστος Hom. Mainly Epic, also New Ion.

πάττω (πατ-, 515 a) *sprinkle:* usu. in comp. w. ἐν, ἐπί, κατά: **πάσω, -έπασα, -επάσθην, παστέος.** Hom. has only pres. and imperf. Often in comedy. (III.)

παύω *stop, cause to cease:* **παύσω, ἔπαυσα, πέπαυκα, πέπαυμαι, ἐπαύθην, παυθήσομαι,** fut. perf. **πεπαύσομαι** (581), **ἄ-παυστος, παυστέος.** Mid. **παύομαι** *cease:* **παύσομαι, ἐπαυσάμην.** In Hdt. MSS. have ἐπαύθην and ἐπαύσθην.

πείθω (πειθ-, ποιθ-, πιθ-) *persuade:* **πείσω, ἔπεισα, πέπεικα,** 2 perf. **πέποιθα** *trust,* **πέπεισμαι, ἐπείσθην, πεισθήσομαι, πιστός, πειστέος.** Mid. **πείθομαι** *believe, obey:* **πείσομαι.** 2 aor. ἔπιθον and ἐπιθόμην poetic; redupl. 2 aor. πέπιθον Epic, 448 D. (πεπίθω, -οιμι); 2 plup. 1 pl. ἐπέπιθμεν (573) for ἐπεποίθαμεν; 2 perf. imper. πέπεισθι Aesch. Eum. 599 (πέπισθι ?). From πιθε- come Hom. πιθήσω *shall obey,* πεπιθήσω *shall persuade,* πιθήσᾱς *trusting.*

πεινάω (πεινα-, πεινη-) *hunger* (for contraction in pres. see 394, 641): **πεινήσω, ἐπείνησα, πεπαίνηκα.** Inf. pres. πεινήμεναι Hom.

πείρω (περ-, παρ-) *pierce,* Epic in pres.: ἔπειρα, πέπαρμαι, 2 aor. pass. **ἀν-επάρην** Hdt. Ion. and poetic. (III.)

πεκτ-έ-ω (πεκ-, πεκτ-ε-, 485) *comb, shear* = Epic pres. πείκω: ἔπεξα Theocr., ἐπεξάμην Hom., ἐπέχθην Aristoph. For *comb* Att. usu. has **κτενίζω, ξαίνω;** for *shear* **κείρω.**

πελάζω (πέλας *near*) *bring near, approach:* πελάσω and Att. πελῶ (538), ἐπέλασα (Epic also ἐπέλασσα, and mid. ἐπελασάμην), πέπλημαι Epic, ἐπελάσθην Epic (ἐπλάθην in tragedy), 2 aor. mid. ἐπλήμην *approached* Epic (688), v. a. πλαστός. Poetic and Ion. Kindred are πελάω (πελα-, πλα-) poetic, πελάθω and πλάθω dramatic, πίλναμαι and πιλνάω Epic. Prose **πλησιάζω** (cp. πλησίον). 512. (III.)

πέλω and πέλομαι (πελ-, πλ-) *am* (orig. *turn, move myself*) : ἔπελον and ἐπελόμην, 2 aor. ἔπλε, ἔπλετο, -πλόμενος. Poetic.

πέμπω (πεμπ-, πομπ-) *send:* **πέμψω, ἔπεμψα,** 2 perf. **πέπομφα, πέπεμμαι, ἐπέμφθην, πεμφθήσομαι, πεμπτός, πεμπτέος.**

πεπαίνω (πεπαν-) *make soft* or *ripe:* **ἐπέπᾱνα** (544 a), **ἐπεπάνθην, πεπανθήσομαι;** perf. inf. πεπάνθαι Aristotle. (III.)

πεπορεῖν or πεπαρεῖν *show:* see πορ-.

πέπρωται *it is fated:* see πορ-.

περαίνω (περαν-, cp. πέρας *end*) *accomplish:* **περανῶ, ἐπέρᾱνα, πεπέρασμαι** (489 h), **ἐπεράνθην, ἀ-πέραντος, δια-περαντέος.** (III.)

πέρδομαι (περδ-, πορδ-, παρδ-) = Lat. *pedo:* **ἀπο-παρδήσομαι,** 2 aor. **ἀπ-έπαρδον,** 2 perf. **πέπορδα.**

πέρθω (περθ-, πραθ-) *sack, destroy:* πέρσω, ἔπερσα, 2 aor. ἔπραθον, and ἐπραθόμην (as pass.). Inf. πέρθαι for περθ-σθαι (688). πέρσομαι is pass. in Hom. Poetic for prose **πορθέω.**

πέρ-νημι *sell,* mid. πέρναμαι: fut. περάω, aor. ἐπεράσ(σ)α, perf. mid. part. πεπερημένος. Poetic, mainly Epic, for **πωλέω** or **ἀποδίδομαι.** Akin to περάω (cp. πέρᾱν) *go over, cross* (περάσω, etc.) ; cp. πιπράσκω. (IV.)

πέταμαι *fly:* see **πέτομαι.**

πετάν-νῡμι (πετα-, πτα-, 729) and **πεταννύω** (rare) *expand,* in prose usu. comp. w. ἀνά: **-πετῶ** (539), **-επέτασα, -πέπταμαι.** Fut. ἐκ-πετάσω Eur., perf. mid. πεπέτασμαι poetic (489 g), aor. pass. πετάσθην Hom. (489 e). By-forms: poetic πίτνημι and πιτνάω (only pres. and imperf.). (IV.)

πέτομαι (πετ-, πετε-, πτ-) *fly,* in prose usu. comp. w. ἀνά, ἐξ: **-πτήσομαι** (Aristoph. also πετήσομαι), 2 aor. **-επτόμην.** Kindred is poetic πέταμαι: 2 aor. ἔπτην (poetic) and **ἐπτάμην,** inflected like ἐπριάμην (ἐπτάμην is often changed to ἐπτόμην), 687. Poetic forms are ποτάομαι and ποτέομαι (πεπότημαι, ἐποτήθην, ποτητός) ; πωτάομαι is Epic. ἵπταμαι is late.

πέττω (πεκ-, πεπ-, 513 a) *cook:* **πέψω, ἔπεψα, πέπεμμαι, ἐπέφθην, πεπτός.** (III.)

πεύθομαι (πευθ-, πυθ-) *learn,* poetic for **πυνθάνομαι.**

πέφνον *slew:* see φεν-.

πήγ-νῡμι (πηγ-, παγ-) *fix, make fast:* **πήξω, ἔπηξα,** 2 perf. **πέπηγα** *am fixed,* 2 aor. pass. **ἐπάγην** intrans., 2 fut. pass. **παγήσομαι.** Epic 2 aor. 3 s. κατέπηκτο *stuck* (athematic, 736 D.), ἐπηξάμην poetic and Ion., ἐπήχθην and πηκτός poetic. πηγνύω rare (Hdt., Xen.). πηγνῦτο (Plato, Ph. 118 a) pres. opt. for πηγνυ-ι-το (some MSS. πηγνύοιτο) ; cp. 819. (IV.)

πηδάω *leap,* often comp. w. ἀνά, εἰς, ἐξ, ἐπί: **-πηδήσομαι** (806), -επήδησα, -πεπήδηκα.

πῑαίνω (πῑαν-) *fatten:* πῑανῶ, ἐπίᾱνα, **κατα-πεπίασμαι** (489 h). Mostly poetic and Ion. (IV.)

πίλ-νημι, πίλ-ναμαι, πιλ-νάω, *approach:* see πελάζω.

πί-μ-πλη-μι (πλη-, πλα-, 741 ; w. μ inserted) *fill.* In prose comp. w. ἐν (727) : **ἐμ-πλήσω, ἐν-έπλησα, ἐμ-πέπληκα, ἐμ-πέπλησμαι** (489 c), **ἐν-επλήσθην, ἐμ-πλησθήσομαι, ἐμ-πληστέος.** 2 aor. mid. athematic ἐπλήμην (poetic) :

πλῆτο and πλῆντο Epic, ἐν-έπλητο Aristoph., opt. ἐμ-πλήμην Aristoph., imper. ἔμπλησο Aristoph. By-forms: πιμπλάνομαι Hom., πλήθω *am full* poetic (2 perf. πέπληθα) except in πλήθουσα ἀγορά, πληθύω *abound*, πληθύνομαι Aesch., πληρόω.

πί-μ-πρη-μι (πρη-, πρα-, w. μ inserted) *burn*. In prose usu. comp. w. ἐν (cp. 727): -πρήσω, -έπρησα, -πέπρημαι, -επρήσθην (489 e). Hdt. has ἐμ-πέπρησμαι, and ἐμ-πρήσομαι (as pass.) or ἐμ-πεπρήσομαι (6. 9). πέπρησμαι Hdt., Aristotle. By-form ἐμ-πρήθω Hom.

πινύ-σκω (πινυ-) *make wise:* ἐπίνυσσα. Poetic. (V.)

πίνω (πι-, πο-, πω-) *drink* often comp. w. ἐξ or κατά: fut. **πίομαι** 806 (usu. ῑ after Hom., 541) and (rarely) **πιοῦμαι**, 2 aor. **ἔπιον** 548 a (imper. πῖθι, 687), **πέπωκα**, **-πέπομαι**, **-επόθην**, **-ποθήσομαι**, **ποτός**, **ποτέος**, πιστός poetic. Aeolic πώνω. 529. (IV. VI.)

πι-πί-σκω (πῑ-) *give to drink:* πίσω, ἔπῖσα. Poetic and New Ion. Cp. **πίνω**. 819. (V.)

πι-πρά-σκω (πρᾱ-) *sell*, pres. rare = Att. **πωλέω, ἀποδίδομαι**: **πέπρᾱκα, πέπρᾱμαι, ἐπράθην**, fut. perf. **πεπρᾱ́σομαι, πρᾱτός, -τέος**. In Att. **πωλήσω, ἀποδώσομαι, ἀπεδόμην** are used for fut. and aor. (V.)

πί-πτω (πετ-, πτ-, 36, πτω-) *fall* for πι-π(ε)τ-ω: **πεσοῦμαι** (540 c, 806), 2 aor. **ἔπεσον** (540 c), **πέπτωκα**. Fut. πεσέομαι Ion., 2 aor. ἔπετον Doric and Aeolic, 2 perf. part. πεπτώς Soph., πεπτηώς and πεπτεώς Hom.

πίτ-νημι and πιτ-νάω *spread out:* poetic for **πετάννῡμι**. (IV.)

πίτ-νω *fall:* poetic for **πίπτω**. (IV.)

πλάζω (πλαγγ-, 510) *cause to wander:* ἔπλαγξα. Mid. πλάζομαι *wander:* πλάγξομαι, ἐπλάγχθην *wandered*, πλαγκτός. Poetic. (III.)

πλάθω: dramatic for πελάζω, **πλησιάζω**.

πλάττω (πλατ-, 515 a) *mould, form:* **ἔπλασα, πέπλασμαι, ἐπλάσθην, πλαστός**. Fut. ἀνα-πλάσω Ion. (III.)

πλέκω (πλεκ-, πλοκ-, πλακ-) *weave, braid:* **ἔπλεξα, πέπλεγμαι, ἐπλέχθην** rare, 2 aor. pass. **-επλάκην** (ἐν, σύν), 2 perf. ἐμ-πέπλοχα Hippocr., probably Att., and ἐμ-πέπλεχα Hippocr., fut. pass. ἐμ-πλεχθήσομαι Aesch., πλεκτός Aesch.

πλέω (πλευ-, πλεϝ-, πλυ-, 503, 607) *sail* (on the contraction see 397): **πλεύσομαι** or **πλευσοῦμαι** (540, 806), **ἔπλευσα, πέπλευκα, πέπλευσμαι** (489 d), **πλευστέος**. ἐπλεύσθην is late. Epic is also πλείω, Ion. and poetic πλώω: πλώσομαι, ἔπλωσα, 2 aor. ἔπλων (Epic, 688), πέπλωκα, πλωτός. Att. by-form πλῴζω.

πλήττω (πληγ-, πλαγ-) *strike*, in prose often comp. w. ἐξ, ἐπί, κατά: **-πλήξω, -έπληξα**, 2 perf. **πέπληγα, πέπληγμαι**, 2 aor. pass. **ἐπλήγην**, but in comp. always **-επλάγην** (ἐξ, κατά), 2 fut. pass. **πληγήσομαι** and **ἐκ-πλαγήσομαι**, fut. perf. **πεπλήξομαι, κατα-πληκτέος**. 2 aor. redupl. (ἐ)πέπληγον Hom., mid. πεπλήγετο Hom., ἐπλήχθην poetic and rare, -επλήγην Hom. Thuc. 4. 125 has ἐκ-πλήγνυσθαι (πλήγνῡμι). In pres., imperf., fut., and aor. act. Att. uses **τύπτω, παίω** for the *simple* verb, but allows the *compounds* ἐκπλήττω, ἐπιπλήττω. In the perf. and pass. the *simple* verb is used. (III.)

πλῡ́νω (πλυν-) *wash:* **πλυνῶ, ἔπλῡνα, πέπλυμαι** (491), ἐπλύθην Ion. (prob. also Att.), **πλυτέος**, πλυτός Ion. Fut. mid. **ἐκ-πλυνοῦμαι** as pass. (808). (III.)

πλώω *sail:* see **πλέω**.

πνέω(πνευ-, πνεϝ-, πνυ-, 503, 607) *breathe, blow*, often comp. w. ἀνά, ἐν, ἐξ, ἐπί, σύν:

πνευσοῦμαι (540) and **-πνεύσομαι** (806), **ἔπνευσα**, **-πέπνευκα**. Epic also πνείω. From ἀνα-πνέω *take breath*: 2 aor. imper. ἄμ-πνυε X 222. See πνῡ-.

πνίγω (πνῑγ-, πνιγ-) *choke*, usu. comp. w. ἀπό: **-πνίξω** (147 c), **-ἔπνιξα**, **πέπνῑγμαι**, **-επνίγην**, **-πνιγήσομαι**.

πνῡ- *to be vigorous* in mind or in body: Epic forms ἄμ-πνῡτο, ἀμ-πνύθην (v. l. -πνύνθην), πέπνῡμαι *am wise*, πεπνῡμένος *wise*, plup. πέπνῡσο. Often referred to πνέω or πινύσκω.

ποθέω *desire, miss*: **ποθήσω** or **ποθέσομαι** (806), **ἐπόθησα** or **ἐπόθεσα** (488 b). All other forms are late.

πονέω *labour*, in early Greek πονέομαι: regular, but πονέσω and ἐπόνεσα in MSS. of Hippocr.; Doric πονάω.

πορ- (and πρω-) *give, allot*: 2 aor. ἔπορον poetic, 2 aor. inf. πεπορεῖν (in some MSS. πεπαρεῖν) Pind. *to show*, perf. pass. πέπρωται *it is fated*, ἡ πεπρωμένη (αἶσα) *fate*. Poetic.

πρᾱ́ττω (πρᾱγ-) *do*: **πρᾱ́ξω**, **ἔπρᾱξα**, 2 perf. **πέπρᾱχα** (prob. late) *have done*, **πέπρᾱγα** *have fared* (*well* or *ill*) and also *have done*, **πέπρᾱγμαι**, **ἐπρᾱ́χθην**, fut. pass. **πρᾱχθήσομαι**, fut. perf. **πεπρᾱ́ξομαι**, **πρᾱκτέος**. Fut. mid. **πρᾱ́ξομαι** is rarely pass. (809). Ion. πρήσσω, πρήξω, etc. (III.)

πρᾱΰνω (πρᾱϋν-) *soothe*: **ἐπρᾱ́ϋνα**, **ἐπρᾱΰνθην**. (III.)

πρέπω *am conspicuous*: πρέψω poetic. Impersonal **πρέπει**, **πρέψει**, **ἔπρεψε**.

πρια- *buy*, only 2 aor. mid. **ἐπριάμην** (p. 138). Other tenses from **ὠνέομαι**.

πρίω *saw*: **ἔπρῑσα**, **πέπρῑσμαι** (489 c), **ἐπρίσθην**.

προΐσσομαι (προϊκ-, cp. προΐξ *gift*): pres. in *simple* only in Archilochus: fut. κατα-προΐξομαι Aristoph. (Ion. καταπροΐξομαι). (III.)

πταίω *stumble*: **πταίσω**, **ἔπταισα**, **ἔπταικα**, **ἄ-πταιστος**.

πτάρ-νυμαι (πταρ-) *sneeze*: 2 aor. **ἔπταρον**; 1 aor. ἔπταρα and 2 aor. pass. ἐπτάρην Aristotle. (IV.)

πτήσσω (πτηκ-, πτακ-) *cower*: **ἔπτηξα**, **ἔπτηχα**; 2 aor. part. κατα-πτακών Aesch. From πτα- Hom. has 2 aor. dual κατα-πτήτην (688) and 2 perf. part. πεπτηώς. Ion. and poetic also πτώσσω (πτωκ-). (III.)

πτίττω (πτισ-) *pound*: ἔπτισα Hdt., **περι-έπτισμαι** Aristoph., περι-επτίσθην late Att. (489 c). Not found in classic prose. (III.)

πτύσσω (πτυχ-) *fold* usu. comp. in prose w. ἀνά, περί: **-πτύξω**, **-ἔπτυξα**, **-έπτυγμαι**, **-επτύχθην**, 2 aor. pass. -επτύγην Hippocr., πτυκτός Ion. (III.)

πτύω (πτυ-, πτῡ-) *spit*: **κατ-έπτυσα**, **κατά-πτυστος**. Hippocr. has πτύσω, ἐπτύσθην.

πυ-ν-θ-άνομαι (πευθ-, πυθ-) *learn, inquire*: **πεύσομαι** (for πευθσομαι), πευσοῦμαι A. Prom. 990, 2 aor. **ἐπυθόμην**, **πέπυσμαι**, **πευστέος**, ἀνά-πυστος Hom. Hom. has 2 aor. opt. redupl. πεπύθοιτο. πεύθομαι is poetic. (IV.)

ῥαίνω (ῥα-, ῥαν-, 523 h, perhaps for ῥαδ-νιω) *sprinkle*: ῥανῶ, ἔρρᾱνα, ἔρρασμαι, (489 h), ἐρράνθην. Apparently from ῥαδ- come Epic aor. ἔρασσα, Epic perf. ἐρράδαται and plup. ἐρράδατο. Perf. ἔρρανται Aesch. Ion., poetic. (III. IV.)

ῥαίω *strike*: ῥαίσω, ἔρραισα, ἐρραίσθην (489 e). Fut. mid. as pass. δια-ρραίσεσθαι Ω 355. Poetic, mainly Epic.

ῥάπ-τω (ῥαφ-) *stitch*: **ἀπο-ρράψω**, **ἔρραψα**, **ἔρραμμαι**, 2 aor. pass. **ἐρράφην**, **ῥαπτός**. (II.)

ῥάττω (ῥαγ-) *throw down* (late pres. for **ἀράττω**): **ξυρ-ράξω**, **ἔρραξα**. (III.)

ῥέζω (ϝρεγ-ιω, 511) *do*: ῥέξω, ἔρεξα (less often ἔρρεξα), aor. pass. part. ῥεχθείς, ἄ-ρεκτος. Poetic. Cp. ἔρδω. (III.)

ῥέω (ῥευ-, ῥεϝ-, ῥυ-, and ῥυε-) *flow* (on the contraction in Att. see 397): **ῥυήσομαι** 806 (2 fut. pass. as act.; ῥεύσομαι rare in Att.), **ἐρρύην** (2 aor.; pass. as act.; ἔρρευσα rare in Att.), **ἐρρύηκα**, ῥυτός and ῥευστέος poetic. ῥευσοῦμαι Aristotle.

ῥη- stem of **εἴρηκα, εἴρημαι, ἐρρήθην, ῥηθήσομαι, εἰρήσομαι.** See εἴρω.

ῥήγ-νῡμι (ῥηγ-, for ϝρηγ-, ῥωγ-, ῥαγ-) *break*, in prose mostly in comp. w. ἀνά, διά: **-ῥήξω, ἔρρηξα**, 2 perf. **-ἔρρωγα** *am broken*, 2 aor. pass. **ἐρράγην**, 2 fut. pass. **-ραγήσομαι**; -έρρηγμαι and -ερρήχθην Ion., ῥηκτός Hom. (IV.)

ῥῑγέω (ῥῑγ-, ῥῑγε-, 485) *shudder*: ῥῑγήσω, ἐρρίγησα and ῥίγησα, 2 perf. **ἔρρῑγα** as pres. Chiefly poetic.

ῥῑγόω *shiver*. On the contraction in the pres. see 398: ῥῑγώσω, ἐρρίγωσα.

ῥίπτω (ῥῑπ-, ῥιπ-) and **ῥῑπ-τ-έω** (485 d) *throw*: **ῥίψω, ἔρρῑψα**, 2 perf. **ἔρρῑφα, ἔρρῑμμαι, ἐρρίφθην**, 2 aor. pass. ἐρρίφην, fut. pass. **ἀπο-ρρῑφθήσομαι**, ῥῑπτός Soph. (II.)

ῥοφέω *sup up*: **ῥοφήσω** and **ῥοφήσομαι** (806), **ἐρρόφησα.**

ῥύομαι (Epic also ῥύομαι, rare in Att.) for ϝρῡομαι, *defend*: ῥύσομαι, ἐρρῡσάμην, and ῥυσάμην O 29, ῥῡτός. Athematic forms are **ἔρ(ρ)ῡτο**, 3 pl. ῥύατο, ῥῦσθαι. See **ἔρῡμαι.** Chiefly poetic.

ῥυπόω *soil*: Epic perf. part. ῥερυπωμένος (442 b. D.). Cp. ῥυπάω *am dirty*.

ῥών-νῡμι (ῥω-) *strengthen*: **ἐπ-έρρωσα, ἔρρωμαι** (imper. **ἔρρωσο** *farewell*, part. **ἐρρωμένος** *strong*), **ἐρρώσθην** (489 e), **ἄ-ρρωστος.** (IV.)

σαίνω (σαν-) *fawn upon*: ἔσηνα. Poetic, prob. also in prose. (III.)

σαίρω (σηρ-, σαρ-) *sweep*: 2 perf. **σέσηρα** *grin*: ἔσηρα Soph. (III.)

σαλπίζω (σαλπιγγ-) *sound the trumpet*: **ἐσάλπιγξα** (also **ἐσάλπιξα** ?). (III.)

σαόω (cp. σαϝος *safe*) *save*: σαώσω, ἐσάωσα, ἐσαώθην. Epic and poetic (but not Att.). Epic pres. subj. σόῃς, σόῃ, σόωσι, which editors change to σαῷς (σάῳς, σαοῖς, σοῷς), σαῷ (σάῳ, σαοῖ, σοῷ), σαῶσι (σάωσι, σόωσι). For σάω pres. imper. and 3 s. imperf. editors usu. read σάου (= σαο-ε), but some derive the form from Aeolic σάωμι. Cp. **σῴζω.**

σάττω (σαγ-) *pack, load*: **ἔσαξα, σέσαγμαι.** (III.)

σάω *sift*: ἔσησα, σέσησμαι. New Ion. Here belong perf. ἔττημαι and **διαττάω** Att. for δια-σσάω.

σβέν-νῡμι (σβε- for σβεσ-, 523 f. N. 1) *extinguish*, usu. comp. w. ἀπό or κατά: **σβέσω, ἔσβεσα, ἔσβηκα** intrans. *have gone out*, **ἐσβέσθην** (489 c), 2 aor. pass. **ἔσβην** intrans. *went out* (415, 756 a), **σβήσομαι**, ἔσβεσμαι Aristotle. 819. (IV.)

σέβω *revere*, usu. **σέβομαι**: aor. pass. as act. **ἐσέφθην**, σεπτός Aesch.

σείω *shake*: **σείσω, ἔσεισα, σέσεικα, σέσεισμαι** (489 c), **ἐσείσθην, σειστός.**

σεύω (σευ-, συ-) *urge, drive on*, mid. *rush*: ἔσσευα (543 a. D.) and σεῦα, ἔσσυμαι as pres. *hasten*, ἐσ(σ)ύθην *rushed*, 2 aor. mid. ἐσ(σ)ύμην *rushed* (ἔσσυο, ἔσσυτο or σύτο, σύμενος, 688), ἐπί-σσυτος Aesch. Mostly poetic, esp. tragic. Here belongs ἀπ-εσσύᾱ (or ἀπ-έσσουα) *he is gone* in Xen. Probably from σοέομαι (σόος, σοῦς *motion*), or from σόομαι, come dramatic σοῦμαι (Doric σῶμαι), σοῦσθε (ind. and imper.), σοῦνται, σοῦ, σούσθω. For σεῦται (S. Trach. 645), often regarded as from a form σεῦμαι, σοῦται may be read.

σημαίνω (σημαν-, cp. σῆμα *sign*) *show*: **σημανῶ, ἐσήμηνα** (ἐσήμᾱνα not good Att though in MSS. of Xen.), **σεσήμασμαι** (489 h), **ἐσημάνθην, ἐπι-σημανθήσομαι**, ἀ-σήμαντος Hom., ἐπι-σημαντέος Aristotle. (III.)

σήπω (σηπ-, σαπ-) *cause to rot*: 2 perf. **σέσηπα** *am rotten*, 2 aor. pass. **ἐσάπην**

rotted as intrans., 2 fut. pass. **κατα-σαπήσομαι**. *σήψω* Aesch., *σέσημμαι* Aristotle, *σηπτός* Aristotle. 819.

σῑγάω *am silent*: **σῑγήσομαι** (806), **ἐσίγησα, σεσίγηκα, σεσίγημαι, ἐσῑγήθην, σῑγηθήσομαι**, fut. perf. **σεσῑγήσομαι**, *σῑγητέος* poetic.

σίνομαι (*σιν-*) *injure*, very rare in Att. prose: *σῑνήσομαι* (?) Hippocr., *ἐσῑνάμην* Hdt. (III.)

σιωπάω *am silent*: **σιωπήσομαι** (806), **ἐσιώπησα, σεσιώπηκα, ἐσιωπήθην, σιωπηθήσομαι, σιωπητέος.**

σκάπ-τω (*σκαφ-*) *dig*, often comp. w. *κατά*: **σκάψω, -έσκαψα**, 2 perf. **-έσκαφα, ἔσκαμμαι**, 2 aor. pass. **-εσκάφην**. (II.)

σκεδάν-νῡμι (*σκεδα-*), rarely **σκεδαννύω**, *scatter*, often comp. w. *ἀπό, διά, κατά*: **-σκεδῶ** (539 c), **-εσκέδασα, ἐσκέδασμαι** (489 c), **ἐσκεδάσθην, σκεδαστός**. Fut. *σκεδάσω* poetic. By-forms: Epic *κεδάννῡμι*: *ἐκέδασσα, ἐκεδάσθην*; mainly poetic and Ion. *σκίδ-νημι* and *σκίδ-ναμαι*; poetic and Ion. *κίδ-νημι* and *κίδ-ναμαι*. (IV.)

σκέλλω (*σκελ-, σκλη-*) *dry up*: pres. late, Epic aor. *ἔσκηλα* (*σκαλ-*; as if from *σκάλλω*) *made dry*, 2 aor. intrans. *ἀπ-έσκλην* (687) Aristoph., *ἔσκληκα am dried up* Ion. and Doric. (III.)

σκέπ-τομαι (*σκεπ-*) *view*: **σκέψομαι, ἐσκεψάμην, ἔσκεμμαι** (sometimes pass.), fut. perf. **ἐσκέψομαι**, pass. **σκεπτέος**. For pres. and imperf. (Epic, poetic, and New Ion.) Att. gen. uses **σκοπῶ, ἐσκόπουν, σκοποῦμαι, ἐσκοπούμην**. Aor. pass. *ἐσκέφθην* Hippocr. (II.)

σκήπ-τω (*σκηπ-*) *prop*, gen. comp. w. *ἐπί* in prose: **-σκήψω, -έσκηψα, -έσκημμαι, -εσκήφθην**. By-form *σκίμπτω* Pind., Hippocr. (II.)

σκίδ-νημι (*σκιδ-νη-, σκιδ-να-*) *σκίδ-ναμαι scatter*: mainly poetic for **σκεδάννῡμι**. (IV.)

σκοπέω *view*: good Att. uses only pres. and imperf. act. and mid., other tenses are supplied from **σκέπτομαι**. *σκοπήσω*, etc., are post-classical.

σκώπ-τω (*σκωπ-*) *jeer*: **σκώψομαι** (806), **ἔσκωψα, ἐσκώφθην**. (II.)

σμάω* (σμῶ**) *smear* (*σμα-, σμη-*, 394, 641) Ion., Comic: pres. **σμῇς, σμῇ, σμῆται**, etc., **ἔσμησα**, *ἐσμησάμην* Hdt. By-form *σμήχω* chiefly Ion.: *ἔσμηξα, δι-εσμήχθην* (?) Aristoph., *νεό-σμηκτος* Hom.

σοῦμαι hasten: see *σεύω*.

σπάω (*σπα-* for *σπασ-*) *draw*, often w. *ἀνά, ἀπό, διά, κατά*: **-σπάσω** (488 a), **ἔσπασα, ἀν-έσπακα, ἔσπασμαι, -εσπάσθην, δια-σπαθήσομαι**, *ἀντί-σπαστος* Soph., *ἀντι-σπαστέος* Hippocr.

σπείρω (*σπερ-, σπαρ-*) *sow*: **σπερῶ, ἔσπειρα, ἔσπαρμαι**, 2 aor. pass. **ἐσπάρην**, *σπαρτός* Soph. (III.)

σπένδω *pour libation*, **σπένδομαι** *make a treaty*: **κατα-σπείσω** (for *σπενδ-σω* 100), **ἔσπεισα, ἔσπεισμαι.**

σπουδάζω *am eager*: **σπουδάσομαι** (806), **ἐσπούδασα, ἐσπούδακα, ἐσπούδασμαι, σπουδαστός, -τέος**. 512. (III.)

στάζω (*σταγ-*) *drop*: *ἔσταξα, ἐν-έσταγμαι, ἐπ-εστάχθην*, **στακτός**. Fut. *στάσω* late, *σταξεῦμαι* Theocr. Ion. and poetic, rare in prose. (III.)

στείβω (*στειβ-*) *tread*, usu. only pres. and imperf.: *κατ-έστειψα, στειπτός*. Poetic. From *στιβε-*, or from a by-form *στιβέω*, comes *ἐστίβημαι* Soph.

στείχω (*στειχ-, στιχ-*) *go*: *περι-έστειξα*, 2 aor. *ἔστιχον*. Poetic, Ion.

στέλλω (*στελ-, σταλ-*) *send*, in prose often comp. w. *ἀπό* or *ἐπί*: *στελῶ* poetic, **ἔστειλα, -έσταλκα, ἔσταλμαι**, 2 aor. pass. **ἐστάλην, -σταλήσομαι**. (III.)

στενάζω (*στεναγ-*) *groan*, often comp. w. *ἀνά*: *-στενάξω* poetic, **ἐστέναξα**, *στενα-*

κτός and -τέος poetic. By-forms: Epic and poetic στενάχω, Epic στεναχίζω, poetic στοναχέω, mainly Epic and poetic στένω.

στέργω (στεργ-, στοργ-) *love*: **στέρξω, ἔστερξα**, 2 perf. ἔστοργα Hdt., **στερκτέος**, στερκτός Soph.

στερέω (usu. **ἀπο-στερέω** in prose) *deprive*: **στερήσω, ἐστέρησα, -εστέρηκα, ἐστέρημαι, ἐστερήθην**. Aor. ἐστέρεσα Epic, 2 aor. pass. ἐστέρην poetic. Pres. mid. **ἀπο-στεροῦμαι** sometimes = *am deprived of*; **στερήσομαι** may be fut. mid. or pass. (809). Connected forms: **στερίσκω** *deprive* (rare in pres. except in mid.) and **στέρομαι** *have been deprived of, am without* w. perf. force, 528, 1887.

στευ- in στεῦται, στεῦνται, στεῦτο *affirm, pledge one's self, threaten*. Poetic, mainly Epic.

στίζω (στιγ-) *prick*: **στίξω, ἔστιγμαι**. ἔστιξα Hdt., στικτός Soph. (III.)

στόρ-νῡμι (στορ-, στορε-) *spread out*, in prose often w. κατά, παρά, σύν, ὑπό (in prose usu. **στρώννῡμι**): **παρα-στορῶ** Aristoph., **ἐστόρεσα**, κατ-εστορέσθην Hippocr. (489 e). Fut. στορέσω in late poetry (στορεσῶ Theocr.). (IV.)

στρέφω (στρεφ-, στροφ-, στραφ-) *turn*, often in comp. in prose w. ἀνά, ἀπό, διά, etc.: **-στρέψω, ἔστρεψα, ἔστραμμαι, ἐστρέφθην** (in prose only **στρεφθῶ, στρεφθείς**), usu. 2 aor. pass. as intrans. **ἐστράφην, ἀνα-στραφήσομαι, στρεπτός**. Prose has **κατ-εστρεψάμην**. 2 perf. ἀν-έστροφα trans. is doubtful (Comic), aor. pass. ἐστράφθην Doric, Ion.

στρώννῡμι (στρω-) *spread out*: **ὑπο-στρώσω**, ἔστρωσα Tragic, Hdt., **ἔστρωμαι**, στρωτός poetic. Cp. **στόρνῡμι**. (IV.)

στυγέω (στυγ-, στυγε-, 485) *hate*: ἐστύγησα (ἔστυξα Hom. *made hateful*), 2 aor. κατ-έστυγον Epic (546 D.), ἀπ-εστύγηκα Hdt., ἐστυγήθην, fut. mid. στυγήσομαι as pass. (808), στυγητός. Ion. and poetic.

στυφελίζω (στυφελιγ-) *dash*: ἐστυφέλιξα. Mostly Epic and Hippocr. (III.)

σῡρίττω (σῡριγγ-) *pipe, whistle*: **ἐσύριξα**. By-form σῡρίζω. (III.)

σύρω (συρ-) *draw*, in comp. in prose esp. w. ἀπό, διά, ἐπί: **-έσῡρα, -σέσυρκα**, -σέσυρμαι and -συρτέος Aristotle. (III.)

σφάλλω (σφαλ-) *trip up, deceive*: **σφαλῶ, ἔσφηλα, ἔσφαλμαι**, 2 aor. pass. **ἐσφάλην, σφαλήσομαι**. (III.)

σφάττω (σφαγ-) *slay*, often in comp. w. ἀπό, κατά: **σφάξω, ἔσφαξα, ἔσφαγμαι**, 2 aor. pass. **-εσφάγην, -σφαγήσομαι**, ἐσφάχθην Ion., poetic, σφακτός poetic. By-form σφάζω (so always in Trag.). 516. (III.)

σχάζω *cut open, let go*: **ἀπο-σχάσω, ἔσχασα** Trag. (**ἐσχασάμην** Comic), ἐσχάσθην Hippocr. From **σχάω** comes imperf. **ἔσχων** Aristoph. 512. (III.)

σχεθεῖν: see **ἔχω**.

σῴζω (σω- and σωι-, σῶς *safe*), later **σώζω**, *save*; many forms come from σαόω: **σώσω** (from σαώσω) and **σωῶ** (Att. inscr.), **ἔσωσα** (from ἐσάωσα w. recessive acc.) and **ἔσῳσα** (Att. inscr.), **σέσωκα** (from *σεσάωκα) and **σέσῳκα** (?), **σέσωμαι** rare (from *σεσάωμαι) and **σέσῳσμαι** (MSS. σέσωσμαι), **ἐσώθην** (from ἐσαώθην), **σωθήσομαι, σῳστέος** (MSS. σωστέος). By-forms: Epic σώω (cp. σῶς) and σαόω (cp. σάος), *q.v.* 512. (III.)

ταγ- *seize*: 2 aor. part. τεταγών Hom. Cp. Lat. *tango*.

τα-νύω (for τṇ-νυω, 35 b; cp. **τείνω** from τεν-) *stretch*, mid. τά-νυμαι (734): τανύω (539 D.) and -τανύσω (?), ἐτάνυσ(σ)α, τετάνυσμαι, (489 c), ἐτανύσθην; fut. pass. τανύσσομαι Lyric. Poetic, rare in New Ion. (IV.)

ταράττω (ταραχ-) *disturb*: **ταράξω, ἐτάραξα, τετάραγμαι, ἐταράχθην, ταράξομαι** as pass. (808). Epic 2 perf. intrans. τέτρηχα *am disturbed*. Cp. **θράττω**. (III.)

τάττω (ταγ-) *arrange*: **τάξω, ἔταξα**, 2 perf. **τέταχα, τέταγμαι, ἐτάχθην, ἐπι-ταχθήσομαι**, fut. perf. **τετάξομαι**, 2 aor. pass. ἐτάγην (?) Eur., **τακτός, -τέος**. (III.)

ταφ- (for θαφ-, 125 g; cp. τάφος and θάμβος) *astonish*: 2 aor. ἔταφον poetic, 2 perf. τέθηπα *am astonished* Epic, Ion., plup. ἐτεθήπεα.

τέγγω *wet*: τέγξω, ἔτεγξα, ἐτέγχθην. Rare in prose.

τείνω (τεν-, τα- from τ̥ν-, 35 b) *stretch*, in prose usu. comp. w. ἀνά, ἀπό, διά, ἐξ, παρά, πρό, etc.; **τενῶ, -έτεινα, -τέτακα, τέταμαι, -ετάθην, -ταθήσομαι, -τατέος**, τατός Aristotle. Cp. τανύω and τιταίνω. (III.)

τεκμαίρομαι (τεκμαρ-) *judge, infer*: **τεκμαροῦμαι, ἐτεκμηράμην, τεκμαρτός** Comic, τεκμαρτέος Hippocr. Poetic τεκμαίρω *limit, show*: ἐτέκμηρα. (III.)

τελέω (τελε- for τελεσ-; cp. τὸ τέλος *end*) *finish*: **τελῶ, ἐτέλεσα, τετέλεκα, τετέλεσμαι** (489 c), **ἐτελέσθην, ἐπι-τελεστέος**. Fut. τελέσω rare in prose, ἀπο-τελεσθήσομαι Aristotle. Epic also τελείω.

τέλλω (τελ-, ταλ-) *accomplish*: ἔτειλα Pind. **ἀνα-τέλλω** *cause to rise, rise*: **ἀν-έτειλα**; **ἐν-τέλλομαι** (ἐν-τέλλω poetic) *command*: **ἐν-ετειλάμην, ἐν-τέταλμαι**; ἐπι-τέλλω *enjoin, rise* poetic: ἐπ-έτειλα; ἐπ-ανα-τέλλω usu. *rise*, poetic and Ion. (III.)

τεμ- (in τμ-) *find*: Epic redupl. 2 aor. ἔτετμον and τέτμον.

τέμ-νω (τεμ-, ταμ-, τμη-) *cut*: **τεμῶ**, 2 aor. **ἔτεμον, -τέτμηκα** (ἀνά, ἀπό), **τέτμημαι, ἐτμήθην**, fut. perf. **-τετμήσομαι** (ἀπό, ἐξ), **τμητέος**. τάμνω Doric and Epic. τέμω Epic, 2 aor. ἔταμον, Doric, Ion., and poetic, τμηθήσομαι Aristotle, τμητός poetic, Aristotle. Cp. also τμήγω. (IV.)

τέρπω (τερπ-, ταρπ-, τραπ-) *amuse*: **τέρψω, ἔτερψα, ἐτέρφθην** (rare in prose) *amused myself*. Hom. 2 aor. mid. ἐταρπόμην and redupl. τεταρπόμην, Hom. aor. pass. ἐτάρφθην and 2 aor. pass. ἐτάρπην (subj. τραπήομεν; MSS. ταρπείομεν). All aor. forms in Hom. with α have the older meaning *satisfy, satiate*.

τερσαίνω (τερσ-αν-, cp. *torreo* from *torseo*) *dry*: τέρσηνα trans. Epic. (III. IV.)

τέρσομαι *become dry*. Mainly Epic. 2 aor. pass. ἐτέρσην as intrans. *became dry*.

τεταγών: see ταγ-.

τετίημαι Hom. perf.: see τιε-.

τέτμον: see τεμ-.

τε-τραίν-ω (τετραν-, and τερ-, τρη-) *bore*: **ἐτέτρᾱνα** and **ἔτρησα, τέτρημαι**. Fut. δια-τετρανέω Hdt., aor. ἐτέτρηνα Epic. By-form τορέω, *q.v.* Late presents τί-τρη-μι, τι-τρά-ω. (III. IV.)

τεύχω (τευχ-, τυχ-, τυκ-) *prepare, make* (poetic): τεύξω, ἔτευξα, 2 aor. τέτυκον Hom., 2 aor. mid. τετυκόμην Hom. (as if from *τεύκω), 2 perf. τέτευχα as pass. in τετευχώς *made* M 423, τέτυγμαι often in Hom. = *am* (3 pl. τετεύχαται and plup. ἐτετεύχατο Hom.), fut. perf. τετεύξομαι Hom., aor. pass. ἐτύχθην Hom. (ἐτεύχθην Hippocr.), v. a. τυκτός Hom. Hom. τέτυγμαι and ἐτύχθην often mean *happen, hit* (cp. τετύχηκα, ἔτυχον from **τυγχάνω**). By-form τι-τύσκομαι Epic.

τῆ *here! take!* in Hom., often referred to τα- (cp. τείνω, *teneo*), is prob. the instrumental case of the demonstr. stem το-. It was however regarded as a verb, and the pl. τῆτε formed by Sophron.

τήκω (τηκ-, τακ-) *melt*: **τήξω, ἔτηξα**, 2 perf. **τέτηκα** *am melted*, 2 aor. pass. as intrans. **ἐτάκην** *melted*, **τηκτός**. Aor. pass. **ἐτήχθην** *was melted* rare.

τιε-, in Hom. 2 perf. *τετιηώς* *troubled*, dual mid. *τετίησθον* *are troubled*, mid. part. *τετιημένος*.

τί-θη-μι (*θη-*, *θε-*) *place, put*: **θήσω, ἔθηκα** (inflection 755), 2 aor. **ἔθετον**, etc. (756), **τέθηκα** (762), **τέθειμαι** (but usu. instead **κεῖμαι**, 767), **ἐτέθην, τεθήσομαι, θετός, -τέος**. For inflection see 416, for synopsis 419, for dialectal forms 747 ff.

τίκτω (for *τι-τεκ-ω*; *τεκ-*, *τοκ-*) *beget, bring forth*: **τέξομαι** (806), 2 aor. **ἔτεκον**, 2 perf. **τέτοκα**. Fut. *τέξω* poetic, *τεκοῦμαι* rare and poetic, aor. pass. *ἐτέχθην* poetic (late).

τίλλω (*τιλ-*) *pluck*: *τιλῶ, ἔτῖλα, τέτιλμαι, ἐτίλθην*. Mostly poetic. (III.)

τινάσσω *swing*: often w. *διά*: *τινάξω* (*-τινάξομαι* reflex. or pass.), *ἐτίναξα, τετίναγμαι, ἐτινάχθην*. Mostly poetic. (III.)

τίνω (*τει-*, *τι-*) *pay, expiate*, often comp. w. *ἀπό, ἐξ*: mid. (poetic) *take payment, avenge*: **τείσω, ἔτεισα, τέτεικα, -τέτεισμαι** (489 c), **-ετείσθην, ἀπο-τειστέος** (Hom. *ἄ-τῖτος* *unpaid*). The spelling with *ει* is introduced on the authority of inscriptions; the MSS. have *τίσω*, etc. Hom. has *τίνω* from **τινϝω*, also *τίω*. Poetic and Ion. Connected is *τεί-νυμαι* (MSS. *τι-*) *avenge myself*: *τείσομαι, ἐτεισάμην* (rare in Att. prose). Cp. *τίω*. (IV.)

τι-ταίνω (*τιταν-*, *i.e.* *ταν-* redupl.) *stretch*: *ἐτίτηνα* Hom. Cp. **τείνω**. (III.)

τι-τρώ-σκω (*τρω-*) *wound*: **τρώσω** (w. *κατά* in prose), **ἔτρωσα, τέτρωμαι, ἐτρώθην, τρωθήσομαι** (*τρώσομαι* as pass. M 66), *τρωτός* Hom. Epic *τρώω* is rare. (V.)

τίω and *τίω* (*τειω* ?) *honour*: *τίσω, ἔτῖσα* (*προ-τίσᾱς* S. Ant. 22), *τέτῖμαι, ἄ-τιτος*. Mainly Epic. In the pres. Att. has *ῐ*, Hom. *ῑ* or *ῐ*. Cp. **τίνω**.

τλα-, τλη-, ταλα- *endure*: *τλήσομαι* (806), *ἐτάλασσα* Epic, 2 aor. *ἔτλην* (687), *τέτληκα* usu. as pres., 2 perf. (athematic) *τέτλαμεν*, etc. (705), *τλητός*. Poetic, rare in prose, which uses **τολμάω**.

τμήγω (*τμηγ-*, *τμαγ-*) *cut*: *τμήξω, ἔτμηξα*, 2 aor. *δι-έτμαγον*, 2 aor. pass. *ἐτμάγην*. Poetic for **τέμνω**.

τορέω (*τορ-*, *τορε-*, 485) *pierce*: *τορήσω*, and (redupl.) *τετορήσω* *utter in a piercing tone* Aristoph., *ἐτόρησα*, 2 aor. *ἔτορον*. Cp. **τετραίνω**. Mainly Epic.

τοτ- *hit, find* in *ἐπ-έτοσσε* Pind.

τρέπω (*τρεπ-*, *τροπ-*, *τραπ-*), *turn*, mid. *flee*: **τρέψω, ἔτρεψα**, mid. **ἐτρεψάμην** usu. *put to flight*, 2 aor. mid. **ἐτραπόμην** *turned* or *fled* (intrans. or reflex.; rarely pass.), 2 perf. **τέτροφα** (and **τέτραφα** ?, rare), **τέτραμμαι, ἐτρέφθην** *fled* or *was turned* (rare in Att.), 2 aor. pass. **ἐτράπην** usu. intrans., **τρεπτέος**, *τρεπτός* Aristotle. In Att. **ἐτραπόμην** was gen. displaced by **ἐτράπην**. *τράπω* New Ion., Doric, 2 aor. *ἔτραπον* Epic and poetic, aor. pass. *ἐτράφθην* Hom., Hdt. *τρέπω* has six aorists. Cp. 554 c, 595, 596. Hom. has also *τραπέω* and *τροπέω*.

τρέφω (*τρεφ-*, *τροφ-*, *τραφ-*; for *θρεφ-*, etc., 125 g) *support, nourish*: **θρέψω, ἔθρεψα**, 2 perf. **τέτροφα, τέθραμμαι, ἐθρέφθην** very rare in Att. prose, usu. 2 aor. pass. **ἐτράφην, τραφήσομαι, θρεπτέος**. Fut. mid. **θρέψομαι** often pass. (808). *τράφω* Doric, 2 aor. Epic *ἔτραφον* *grew up, was nourished*. Cp. 595.

τρέχω (*τρεχ-* from *θρεχ-*, 125 g, and *δραμ-*) *run*: **δραμοῦμαι** (806), 2 aor. **ἔδραμον, -δεδράμηκα** (*κατά, περί, σύν*), **ἐπι-δεδράμημαι, περι-θρεκτέος**. *τράχω* Doric, **ἀπο-θρέξομαι** Aristoph., *ἔθρεξα* rare and poetic, 2 perf. *-δέδρομα* (*ἀνά, ἐπί*) poetic. Poetic *δραμάω*. (VI.)

τρέω (*τρε-* for *τρεσ-*; cp. Lat. *terreo* for *terseo*) *tremble*: **ἔτρεσα** (488 a), *ἄ-τρεστος* poetic. Rare in prose.

τρίβω (*τρῑβ-*, *τριβ-*) *rub*: **τρίψω, ἔτρῖψα**, 2 perf. **τέτριφα, τέτρῖμμαι, ἐτρίφθην**, but usu. 2 aor. pass. **ἐτρίβην**, **-τριβήσομαι** (*ἐξ, κατά*), fut. perf. **ἐπι-τετρίψομαι**, *ἄ-τριπτος* Hom. Fut. mid. **τρίψομαι** also as pass. (808).

τρίζω (*τριγ-, τρῑγ-*) *squeak, chirp:* 2 perf. *τέτρῑγα* as pres. (part. *τετρῑγῶτες, τετρῑγυῖα*, Hom.). Ion. and poetic. (III.)

τρῡχόω *exhaust, waste:* pres. poet. and rare, usu. comp. w. *ἐξ*: **-τρῡχώσω**, **-ετρῡ́χωσα**, **τετρῡ́χωμαι**, *ἐτρῡχώθην* Hippocr. Also *τρύχω*: *τρύξω* (147 c) Hom.; and *τρύω*: *τρῡ́σω* Aesch., **τέτρῡμαι**, *ἄ-τρῡτος* poetic and Ion.

τρώγω (*τρωγ-, τραγ-*) *gnaw:* **τρώξομαι** (806), 2 aor. **ἔτραγον**, **δια-τέτρωγμαι**, **τρωκτός**, *κατ-έτρωξα* Hippocr.

τυ-γ-χ-άνω (*τευχ-, τυχ-, τυχε-*) *hit, happen, obtain:* **τεύξομαι** (806), 2 aor. **ἔτυχον**, **τετύχηκα**. Epic also *ἐτύχησα*, 2 perf. *τέτευχα* Ion. (the same form as from *τεύχω*). *τέτυγμαι* and *ἐτύχθην* (from *τεύχω*) often have almost the sense of **τετύχηκα** and **ἔτυχον**. (IV.)

τύπ-τω (*τυπ-, τυπτε-*) *strike:* **τυπτήσω**, **τυπτητέος**; other tenses supplied: aor. **ἐπάταξα** or **ἔπαισα**, perf. **πέπληγα**, **πέπληγμαι**, aor. pass. **ἐπλήγην**. *ἔτυψα* Epic, Ion. and Lyric, *ἐτύπτησα* Aristotle, 2 aor. *ἔτυπον* poetic, *τέτυμμαι* poetic and Ion., 2 aor. pass. *ἐτύπην* poetic, fut. mid. as pass. *τυπτήσομαι*, or 2 fut. pass. *τυπήσομαι*, Aristoph. Nub. 1379. (II.)

τῡ́φω (*τῡφ-, τυφ-*, for *θῡφ-, θυφ-*, 125 g) *raise smoke, smoke:* **τέθῡμμαι**, 2 aor. pass. as intrans. **ἐπ-ετύφην**, **ἐκ-τυφήσομαι** Com.

τωθάζω *taunt:* **τωθάσομαι** (806), **ἐτώθασα**. 512. (III.)

ὑγιαίνω (*ὑγιαν-*) *am in health, recover health:* **ὑγιανῶ**, **ὑγίᾱνα**, *ὑγιάνθην* Hippocr. (III.)

ὑπ-ισχ-νέομαι (*ἰσχ-*, a by-form of *ἐχ-*; *σχ-, σχε-*) *promise:* **ὑπο-σχήσομαι**, 2 aor. **ὑπ-εσχόμην**, **ὑπ-έσχημαι**. Ion. and poetic usu. *ὑπ-ίσχομαι*. Cp. **ἔχω** and **ἴσχω**. (IV.)

ὑφαίνω (*ὑφαν-*) *weave:* **ὑφανῶ**, **ὕφηνα**, **ὕφασμαι** (489 h), **ὑφάνθην**, **ὑφαντός**. Hom. also *ὑφάω*. (III.)

ὕω *rain:* **ὕσω**, *ὗσα* Pind., Hdt., Aristotle, **ἐφ-ῦσμαι** (489 c), *ὕσθην* Hdt., *ὕσομαι* as pass. (808) Hdt.

φαείνω (*φαεν-*) *appear, show:* aor. pass. *ἐφαάνθην* (w. *αα* for *αε*, 643) *appeared*. Epic. (III.)

φαίνω (*φαν-*) *show:* **φανῶ**, **ἔφηνα**, perf. **πέφαγκα** (rare in good Att.) *have shown*, 2 perf. **πέφηνα** *have appeared*, **πέφασμαι** (489 h), **ἐφάνθην** (rare in prose) *was shown*, 2 aor. pass. **ἐφάνην** as intrans. *appeared*, 2 fut. pass. **φανήσομαι** *shall appear;* fut. mid. **φανοῦμαι** *shall show* and *shall appear*. On the trans. and intrans. use see 819; for the inflection of certain tenses see 401 ff. Hom. has 2 aor. iter. *φάνεσκε* *appeared*, v. a. *ἄ-φαντος*; and, from root *φα-*: *φάε* *appeared* and fut. perf. *πεφήσεται* *shall appear*. Connected forms *πι-φαύσκω, φαείνω, φαντάζομαι*. (III.)

φά-σκω (*φα-*) *say:* only pres. and imperf.: see **φημί**. (V.)

φείδομαι (*φειδ-, φιδ-*) *spare:* **φείσομαι**, **ἐφεισάμην**, **φειστέος**. Epic 2 aor. mid. redupl. *πεφιδόμην* (448 D.). Epic fut. *πεφιδήσομαι* (*φιδε-*).

φεν-, φν-, φα- (for *φν̥-*, 35 b) *kill:* 2 aor. *ἔπεφνον* and *πέφνον* (part. *κατα-πεφνών*, also accented *-πέφνων*), perf. mid. *πέφαμαι*, fut. perf. *πεφήσομαι*. Epic. Cp *φόνος* *murder* and *θείνω*(*θεν-*) *smite*.

φέρω (*φερ-, οἰ-, ἐνεκ-, ἐνεγκ-* for *ἐν-ενεκ*, 529) *bear, carry:* fut. **οἴσω**, 1 aor. **ἤνεγκα**,

2 aor. **ἤνεγκον**, 2 perf. **ἐνήνοχα**, perf. mid. **ἐνήνεγμαι** (3 s. -γκται inscr.), aor. pass. **ἠνέχθην** also intrans., fut. pass. **κατ-ενεχθήσομαι** and **οἰσθήσομαι**, v. a. **οἰστός**, **-τέος**. Other Att. forms are: **οἴσομαι** fut. mid. and pass. (809), **ἠνεγκάμην** 1 aor. mid., **ἠνεγκόμην** 2 aor. mid. (rare: S. O. C. 470). Poetic and dial. forms are: 2 pl. pres. imper. *φέρτε* (for *φέρετε*) Epic, 1 aor. imper. *οἶσε* for *οἶσον* Epic (and Aristoph.), 1 aor. inf. *ἀν-οῖσαι* or *ἀν-ῷσαι* (once in Hdt.), fut. inf. *οἰσέιν* Pind., *οἰσέμεν(αι)* Hom., 1 aor. *ἤνεικα*, *-άμην* Hom., Hdt., *ἤνικα* Aeol., Dor., etc., 2 aor. *ἤνεικον* rare in Hom., perf. mid. *ἐνήνειγμαι* Hdt., aor. pass. *ἠνείχθην* Hdt., v. a. *φερτός* Hom., Eur., *ἀν-ώιστος* Hdt. (*ἄνοιστος*?). (VI.)

φεύγω (*φευγ-*, *φυγ-*) *flee:* **φεύξομαι** 806 (**φευξοῦμαι**, 540, rare in prose), 2 aor. **ἔφυγον**, 2 perf. **πέφευγα**, **φευκτός**, **-τέος**. Hom. has perf. act. part. *πεφυζότες* as if from a verb *φύζω* (cp. *φύζα flight*), perf. mid. part. *πεφυγμένος*, v. a. *φυκτός*. By-form *φυγ-γάνω*, New Ion. and Att. poetry, in comp. in prose.

φη-μί (*φη-*, *φα-*) *say*, inflected 783: **φήσω**, **ἔφησα**, **φατός**, **-τέος**. Poetical and dial. forms 783 D. ff.

φθά-νω (*φθη-*, *φθα-*) *anticipate:* **φθήσομαι** (806), **ἔφθασα**, 2 aor. **ἔφθην** (like *ἔστην*). Fut. *φθάσω* doubtful in Att., 2 aor. mid. part. *φθάμενος* Epic. Hom. *φθᾶνω* = **φθάνϝω*. (IV.)

φθείρω (*φθερ-*, *φθορ-*, *φθαρ-*) *corrupt:* **φθερῶ**, **ἔφθειρα**, **ἔφθαρκα**, but usu. 2 perf. **δι-έφθορα** *am ruined* (*have corrupted* in Att. poetry), **ἔφθαρμαι**, 2 aor. pass. **ἐφθάρην**, **δια-φθαρήσομαι**, *φθαρτός* Aristotle. Fut. *δια-φθέρσω* N 625, *δια-φθερέω* Hdt. (III.)

φθίνω (*φθι-*) *waste, perish*, mostly poetical and usu. intrans., Epic *φθίνω* (= *φθινϝω*): fut. *φθίσω* poetic (Hom. *φθίσω*) trans., aor. *ἔφθισα* poetic (Hom. *ἔφθῖσα*) trans., 2 aor. mid. athematic *ἐφθίμην perished* poetic (*φθίωμαι*, *φθίμην* for *φθι-ῑμην*, *φθίσθω*, *φθίσθαι*, *φθίμενος*), *ἔφθιμαι* poetic (plup. 3 pl. *ἐφθίατο*), *ἐφθίθην* Hom., *φθιτός* Tragic. The form *φθίω* in Hom. is assumed on the basis of *φθίῃς* and *ἔφθιεν*, for which *φθίεαι*, *ἔφθιτο* (or *ἔσθιεν*) have been conjectured. Hom. *φθίσω*, *ἔφθῖσα* are also read *φθείσω*, etc. By-form *φθινύθω*. (IV.)

φιλέω *love:* regular (cp. 385); fut. mid. **φιλήσομαι** may be pass. (808). Hom. has *φιλήμεναι* pres. inf. and *ἐφῑλάμην* (*φιλ-*) aor. mid. Aeolic *φίλημι*.

φλάω *bruise* (cp. *θλάω*): *φλασσῶ*, for *φλάσω*, Theocr., *ἔφλα(σ)σα*, *πέφλασμαι* (489 c) and *ἐφλάσθην* Hippocr. *φλάω eat greedily, swallow:* only pres. and imperf., and only in Comedy.

φλέγω *burn*, trans. and intrans: **ἐξ-έφλεξα** Aristoph., **κατ-εφλέχθην**, *ἄ-φλεκτος* Eur. Very rare in prose. By-form *φλεγέθω* poetic.

φράγ-νῡμι (*φραγ-*) and **φάργνῡμι** *fence*, mid. **φράγνυμαι**; only in pres. and imperf. Cp. **φράττω**. (IV.)

φράζω (*φραδ-*) *tell, point out, declare*, mid. *consider, devise:* **φράσω**, **ἔφρασα**, **πέφρακα**, **πέφρασμαι** rarely mid., **ἐφράσθην** as mid., **φραστέος**. Epic 2 aor. (*ἐ*)*πέφραδον* 448 D. (part. *πεφραδμένος*). Mid. fut. *φράσ(σ)ομαι* Epic, *ἐφρασ(σ)άμην* poetic and Ion. (III.)

φράττω (*φραγ-*) *fence:* **ἔφραξα** (and **ἔφαρξα** Att. inscr.), **πέφραγμαι** and **πέφαργμαι**, **ἐφράχθην**, **ἄ-φρακτος**. The forms with **αρ** for **ρα** are common and are Old Att. See **φράγνῡμι**. (III.)

φρίττω (φρῑκ-) *shudder:* **ἔφριξα** (147 c), **πέφρῑκα** *am in a shudder* (part. πεφρίκοντας Pind.). (III.)

φρύγω (φρυγ-, φρῡγ-) *roast:* **ἔφρυξα** (147 c), **πέφρῡγμαι**, **φρῡκτός**, 2 aor. pass. ἐφρύγην Hippocr.

φυλάττω (φυλακ-) *guard:* **φυλάξω, ἐφύλαξα**, 2 perf. **πεφύλαχα, πεφύλαγμαι** *am on my guard*, **ἐφυλάχθην, φυλακτέος.** Fut. mid. **φυλάξομαι** also as pass. in Soph. (808). (III.)

φύρω (φυρ-) *mix, knead:* ἔφυρσα Hom., **πέφυρμαι**, ἐφύρθην Aesch., fut. perf. πεφύρσομαι Pind., σύμ-φυρτος Eur. **φῡράω** *mix* is regular. (III.)

φύω (φυ-, φῡ-; Hom. φύω, rare in Att.) *produce:* **φύσω, ἔφῡσα**, 2 aor. **ἔφῡν** *grew, was* (687), **πέφῡκα** *am by nature, am* (693), **φυτόν** *plant.* 2 aor. pass. ἐφύην late (doubtful in Att.). 2 perf. Epic forms: πεφύᾱσι, ἐμ-πεφύῃ Theognis, πεφυώς, ἐμ-πεφυυῖα; 1 plup. with thematic vowel ἐπέφῡκον Hesiod.

χάζω (χαδ-) *force back*, usu. χάζομαι *give way.* Pres. act. in prose only ἀνα-χάζω Xen., χάσσομαι, ἀν-έχασσα Pind., δι-εχασάμην Xen. See also καδ-. Poetic, chiefly Epic. (III.)

χαίρω (χαρ-, χαρε-, χαιρε-) *rejoice:* **χαιρήσω, κεχάρηκα**, κεχάρημαι and κέχαρμαι Att. poetry, 2 aor. pass. **ἐχάρην** intrans. *rejoiced*, **χαρτός.** Hom. has 2 perf. act. part. κεχαρηώς, 1 aor. mid. χηράμην, 2 aor. mid. κεχαρόμην, fut. perf. κεχαρήσω and κεχαρήσομαι. (III.)

χαλάω *loosen:* **ἐχάλασα, ἐχαλάσθην** (489 e). Fut. χαλάσω Hippocr., aor. ἐχάλαξα Pind., perf. κεχάλακα Hippocr.

χαλεπαίνω (χαλεπαν-) *am offended:* **χαλεπανῶ, ἐχαλέπηνα, ἐχαλεπάνθην.** (III.)

χα-ν-δ-άνω (χενδ-, χονδ-, χαδ- for χ̥δ-, 35 b) *contain:* χείσομαι for χενδσεται, 2 aor. ἔχαδον, 2 perf. κέχανδα as pres. (κέχονδα ? cp. v. l. Ω 192). Poetic (mostly Epic) and Ion. (IV.)

χάσκω (χην-, χαν-; χάσκω for χ̥-σκω ? 35 b) *gape:* **ἐγ-χανοῦμαι** (806), 2 aor. **ἔχανον**, 2 perf. **κέχηνα** *am agape* (698). Ion., Epic, and in Aristoph. (V.)

χέζω (χεδ-, χοδ-), = Lat. *caco:* **χεσοῦμαι** (540, 806), rarely **χέσομαι, ἔχεσα**, 2 aor. **ἔχεσον** rare, 2 perf. **κέχοδα, κέχεσμαι.** (III.)

χέω (χευ-, χεϝ-, χυ-) *pour;* on the contraction see 397. In prose usu. in comp. (ἐξ, ἐν, κατά, σύν, etc.): fut. **χέω** (541, 1881), aor. **ἔχεα** (543 a), **κέχυκα, κέχυμαι, ἐχύθην, χυθήσομαι, χυτός.** Mid. **χέομαι** pres. and fut., **ἐχεάμην** aor. Epic forms: pres. (rarely) χείω (Aeolic χεύω), fut. χεύω (?) β 222, aor. also **ἔχευα** (543 a), 1 aor. mid. ἐχευάμην = Att. **ἐχεάμην**, 2 aor. mid. athematic ἐχύμην as pass.

χλαδ- in 2 perf. part. κεχλᾱδώς *swelling*, pl. κεχλάδοντας, inf. κεχλάδειν. Pind.

χόω (= χοϝω) *heap up:* **χώσω, ἔχωσα, ἀνα-κέχωκα, κέχωσμαι, ἐχώσθην, χωσθήσομαι, χωστός.** Cp. 489 a, c.

χραισμέω (χραισμε-, χραισμ-) *profit*, pres. late: χραισμήσω, ἐχραίσμησα, 2 aor. ἔχραισμον. Hom.

*χράομαι (**χρῶμαι**) *use* (χρα-, χρη-): pres. **χρῇ, χρῆται**, etc. 395, **χρήσομαι, ἐχρησάμην, κέχρημαι** *have in use* (poetic also *have necessary*), **ἐχρήσθην** (489 e), **χρηστός** *good*, **χρηστέος.** Hdt. has χρᾶται, 3 pl. χρέωνται (from χρήονται), subj. χρέωμαι, imper. χρέω, inf. χρᾶσθαι (Ion. inscr. χρῆσθαι), part. χρεώμενος. Cp. 641 D. Fut. perf. κεχρήσομαι Theocr.

*χράω (**χρῶ**) *utter an oracle* (χρα-, χρη-): pres. **χρῇς, χρῇ**, 394 (sometimes in the meaning of **χρῄζεις, χρῄζει**), **χρήσω, ἔχρησα, κέχρηκα,** *κέχρησμαι* Hdt., **ἐχρήσθην** (489 e). Mid. *χράομαι* (**χρῶμαι**) *consult an oracle: χρήσομαι* Ion., *ἐχρησάμην* Hdt. Cp. **χρῄζω**. 522 b, 641 D. Hdt. has *χρέων*.

χρή *it is necessary*, **ἀπό-χρη** *it suffices:* see 793.

χρῄζω *want, ask,* Att. chiefly pres. and imperf.: *χρῄσω*. Epic and Ion. *χρηΐζω* (later *χρείζω*): *χρηΐσω, ἐχρήϊσα*. 512. (III.)

χρίω (*χρῑ-* for *χρῑσ-*) *anoint, sting:* **χρίσω, ἔχρῑσα, κέχρῑμαι** (and **κέχρῑσμαι** ?) 489 b), *ἐχρίσθην* (489 e) Tragic, *χρῑστός* Tragic.

χρῴζω (for *χρω-ίζω*; cp. *χρώ-ς complexion*) *colour, stain:* **κέχρωσμαι** (489 c; (better **κέχρῳσμαι** ?), **ἐχρώσθην** (**ἐχρῴσθην** ?). Poetic *χροΐζω*. 512. (III.)

χωρέω *give place, go:* regular. Fut. **χωρήσω** and **χωρήσομαι** 806 a.

ψάω* (ψῶ**) *rub* (*ψα-, ψη-*): pres **ψῇς, ψῇ**, etc., 394; **ἀπο-ψήσω, ἔψησα**, perf. **κατ-έψηγμαι** from the by-form **ψήχω**.

ψέγω *blame:* **ψέξω, ἔψεξα,** *ἔψεγμαι* Hippocr., **ψεκτός**.

ψεύδω *deceive,* mid. *lie:* **ψεύσω, ἔψευσα, ἔψευσμαι** usu. *have deceived* or *lied,* but also *have been deceived,* **ἐψεύσθην, ψευσθήσομαι.**

ψῡ́χω (*ψυχ-, ψῡχ-*) *cool:* **ψύξω** (147 c), **ἔψυξα, ἔψῡγμαι, ἐψῡ́χθην,** *ψῡχθήσομαι* (?) Hippocr., 2 aor. pass. **ἀπ-εψύχην** as intrans. *cooled, ψῡκτέος* Hippocr.

ὠθέω (*ὠθ-* for *ϝωθ-, ὠθε-,* 485 a) *push:* imperf. **ἐώθουν** (431), **ὤσω, ἔωσα** (431), **ἔωσμαι** (443), **ἐώσθην, ὠσθήσομαι.** Fut. *ὠθήσω* only in Att. poetry, aor. *ὦσα* and perf. *ὦσμαι* Ion., *ἀπ-ωστός* Ion., poetic, *ἀπ-ωστέος* poetic.

ὠνέομαι (*ϝωνε-*; cp. Lat. *ve-num*) *buy:* imperf. **ἐωνούμην** (431), **ὠνήσομαι, ἐώνημαι** (443) *have bought* or *been bought,* **ἐωνήθην** *was bought,* **ὠνητός, -τέος.** For *ἐωνησάμην* (late), Att. has **ἐπριάμην** (p. 138). Imperf. *ὠνεόμην* Hdt., *ὠνούμην* **Att. in comp.** (*ἀντί, ἐξ*). **(VI.)**

NOTE (see page 105, paragraph 350d)

The successive days of the Athenian civil month were referred to in official documents as follows:

νουμηνία (the first)	*ἑβδόμη ἱσταμένου*	*τετρὰς ἐπὶ δέκα*
δευτέρα ἱσταμένου	*ὀγδόη ἱσταμένου*	*πέμπτη ἐπὶ δέκα*
τρίτη ἱσταμένου	*ἐνάτη ἱσταμένου*	*ἕκτη ἐπὶ δέκα*
τετρὰς (*not τετάρτη*) *ἱσταμένου*	*δεκάτη ἱσταμένου*	*ἑβδόμη ἐπὶ δέκα*
πέμπτη ἱσταμένου	*ἑνδεκάτη*	*ὀγδόη ἐπὶ δέκα*
ἕκτη ἱσταμένου	*δωδεκάτη*	*ἐνάτη ἐπὶ δέκα*
εἰκοστή or *δεκάτη προτέρα*	*τρίτη ἐπὶ δέκα*	

δεκάτη φθίνοντος or *δεκάτη ὑστέρα* **(the twenty-first)**
ἐνάτη φθίνοντος or *ἐνάτη μετ' εἰκάδας* **(22nd)**
ὀγδόη φθίνοντος or *ὀγδόη μετ' εἰκάδας* **(23rd)**
ἑβδόμη φθίνοντος or *ἑβδόμη μετ' εἰκάδας* **(24th)**
ἕκτη φθίνοντος or *ἕκτη μετ' εἰκάδας* **(25th)**
πέμπτη φθίνοντος or *πέμπτη μετ' εἰκάδας* **(26th)**
τετρὰς φθίνοντος or *τετρὰς μετ' εἰκάδας* **(27th)**
τρίτη φθίνοντος or *τρίτη μετ' εἰκάδας* **(28th)**
δευτέρα φθίνοντος or *δευτέρα μετ' εἰκάδας* **(29th in a "full" i.e. 30-day month)**
ἕνη καὶ νέα **(29th in a "hollow" i.e. 29-day month)**
ἕνη καὶ νέα **(30th: full month)**

ENGLISH INDEX

GREEK INDEX

The references are to the sections. Verbs included in the List of Verbs are, in general, not cited except when a special form has been referred to in the Grammar.